Dictionary of the Middle Ages

AMERICAN COUNCIL OF LEARNED SOCIETIES

The American Council of Learned Societies, organized in 1919 for the purpose of advancing the study of the humanities and of the humanistic aspects of the social sciences, is a nonprofit federation comprising forty-five national scholarly groups. The Council represents the humanities in the United States in the International Union of Academies, provides fellowships and grants-in-aid, supports research-and-planning conferences and symposia, and sponsors special projects and scholarly publications.

MEMBER ORGANIZATIONS

AMERICAN PHILOSOPHICAL SOCIETY, 1743
AMERICAN ACADEMY OF ARTS AND SCIENCES, 1780
AMERICAN ANTIQUARIAN SOCIETY, 1812
AMERICAN ORIENTAL SOCIETY, 1842
AMERICAN NUMISMATIC SOCIETY, 1858
AMERICAN PHILOLOGICAL ASSOCIATION, 1869
ARCHAEOLOGICAL INSTITUTE OF AMERICA, 1879
SOCIETY OF BIBLICAL LITERATURE, 1880
MODERN LANGUAGE ASSOCIATION OF AMERICA, 1883
AMERICAN HISTORICAL ASSOCIATION, 1884
AMERICAN ECONOMIC ASSOCIATION, 1885
AMERICAN FOLKLORE SOCIETY, 1888
AMERICAN DIALECT SOCIETY, 1889
AMERICAN PSYCHOLOGICAL ASSOCIATION, 1892
ASSOCIATION OF AMERICAN LAW SCHOOLS, 1900
AMERICAN PHILOSOPHICAL ASSOCIATION, 1901
AMERICAN ANTHROPOLOGICAL ASSOCIATION, 1902
AMERICAN POLITICAL SCIENCE ASSOCIATION, 1903
BIBLIOGRAPHICAL SOCIETY OF AMERICA, 1904
ASSOCIATION OF AMERICAN GEOGRAPHERS, 1904
HISPANIC SOCIETY OF AMERICA, 1904
AMERICAN SOCIOLOGICAL ASSOCIATION, 1905
AMERICAN SOCIETY OF INTERNATIONAL LAW, 1906
ORGANIZATION OF AMERICAN HISTORIANS, 1907
AMERICAN ACADEMY OF RELIGION, 1909
COLLEGE ART ASSOCIATION OF AMERICA, 1912
HISTORY OF SCIENCE SOCIETY, 1924
LINGUISTIC SOCIETY OF AMERICA, 1924
MEDIAEVAL ACADEMY OF AMERICA, 1925
AMERICAN MUSICOLOGICAL SOCIETY, 1934
SOCIETY OF ARCHITECTURAL HISTORIANS, 1940
ECONOMIC HISTORY ASSOCIATION, 1940
ASSOCIATION FOR ASIAN STUDIES, 1941
AMERICAN SOCIETY FOR AESTHETICS, 1942
AMERICAN ASSOCIATION FOR THE ADVANCEMENT OF SLAVIC STUDIES, 1948
METAPHYSICAL SOCIETY OF AMERICA, 1950
AMERICAN STUDIES ASSOCIATION, 1950
RENAISSANCE SOCIETY OF AMERICA, 1954
SOCIETY FOR ETHNOMUSICOLOGY, 1955
AMERICAN SOCIETY FOR LEGAL HISTORY, 1956
AMERICAN SOCIETY FOR THEATRE RESEARCH, 1956
SOCIETY FOR THE HISTORY OF TECHNOLOGY, 1958
AMERICAN COMPARATIVE LITERATURE ASSOCIATION, 1960
AMERICAN SOCIETY FOR EIGHTEENTH-CENTURY STUDIES, 1969
ASSOCIATION FOR JEWISH STUDIES, 1969

Monastic kitchen (octagonal) of Fontevrault Abbey. Twelfth century (restored). J. FEUILLIE. ©ARCH. PHOTO./ S.P.A.D.E.M., PARIS/V.A.G.A., NEW YORK, 1985

Dictionary of the Middle Ages

JOSEPH R. STRAYER, *EDITOR IN CHIEF*

Volume 8

MACBETH—MYSTERY PLAYS

CHARLES SCRIBNER'S SONS • NEW YORK

Copyright © 1987 American Council of Learned Societies

Library of Congress Cataloging in Publication Data
Main entry under title:

Dictionary of the Middle Ages.

Includes bibliographies and index.
1. Middle Ages-—Dictionaries.   I. Strayer,
Joseph Reese, 1904–1987

D114.D5   1982   909.07   82-5904
ISBN 0-684-16760-3 (v. 1)   ISBN 0-684-18169-X (v. 7)
ISBN 0-684-17022-1 (v. 2)   ISBN 0-684-18274-2 (v. 8)
ISBN 0-684-17023-X (v. 3)   ISBN 0-684-18275-0 (v. 9)
ISBN 0-684-17024-8 (v. 4)   ISBN 0-684-18276-9 (v. 10)
ISBN 0-684-18161-4 (v. 5)   ISBN 0-684-18277-7 (v. 11)
ISBN 0-684-18168-1 (v. 6)   ISBN 0-684-18278-5 (v. 12)

Published simultaneously in Canada
by Collier Macmillan Canada, Inc.
Copyright under the Berne convention.

5 7 9 11 13 15 17 19   Q/C   20 18 16 14 12 10 8 6

PRINTED IN THE UNITED STATES OF AMERICA.

The *Dictionary of the Middle Ages* has been produced with
support from the National Endowment for the Humanities.

The paper in this book meets the guidelines for
permanence and durability of the Committee on
Production Guidelines for Book Longevity of the
Council on Library Resources.

Maps prepared by Sylvia Lehrman.

$990.00/set

Editorial Board

Advisory Committee

GUSTAVE ALEF, *University of Oregon*

JEANETTE M. A. BEER, *Purdue University*

THOMAS N. BISSON, *University of California, Berkeley*

JEAN BONY, *University of California, Berkeley*

JAMES F. BURKE, *University of Toronto*

ANGUS F. CAMERON, *University of Toronto*

MARK COHEN, *Princeton University*

E. TALBOT DONALDSON, *Indiana University*

ANN DOOLEY, *University of Toronto*

D. J. GEANAKOPLOS, *Yale University*

KEVIN J. HARTY, *Temple University*

ANDREW HUGHES, *University of Toronto*

W. T. H. JACKSON, *Columbia University*

ROBERT E. LERNER, *Northwestern University*

R. M. LUMIANSKY, *American Council of Learned Societies*

THOMAS F. MATHEWS, *New York University*

BRIAN S. MERRILEES, *University of Toronto*

HELMUT NICKEL, *Metropolitan Museum of Art*

KENNETH D. OSTRAND, *University of New Orleans*

ROGER E. REYNOLDS, *University of Toronto*

TIMOTHY R. ROBERTS, *Jefferson City (Mo.) High School*

FRANZ ROSENTHAL, *Yale University*

KENNETH M. SETTON, *Institute for Advanced Study, Princeton*

ECKEHARD SIMON, *Harvard University*

PRISCILLA P. SOUCEK, *New York University*

E. A. SYNAN, *University of Toronto*

BRIAN TIERNEY, *Cornell University*

KARL DAVID UITTI, *Princeton University*

CRAIG B. VITTETOE, *Palo Alto (Calif.) City Schools*

LYNN WHITE, Jr., *University of California, Los Angeles*

Editorial Staff

JOHN F. FITZPATRICK, *MANAGING EDITOR*

JONATHAN G. ARETAKIS, *Assistant Editor*

NORMA FRANKEL, *Associate Editor*

LAURA D. GROSS, *Senior Editorial Assistant*

SANDRA D. KNIGHT, *Administrative Assistant*

ANJU MAKHIJANI, *Production Manager*

BETH ANN McCABE, *Editorial Assistant*

W. KIRK REYNOLDS, *Associate Editor*

DAVID J. BABIN, *Assistant Photo Editor*

JEFFREY L. BENEKE, *Associate Editor*

LESLEY ANN BENEKE, *Assistant Editor*

ILENE COHEN, *Associate Editor*

EDWARD FERRARO, *Associate Editor*

EMILY GARLIN, *Proofreader*

GEOFFREY B. GNEUHS, *Assistant Editor*

ROBERT HALASZ, *Associate Editor*

ROBERT K. HAYCRAFT, *Associate Editor*

JOEL HONIG, *Associate Editor*

JACK RUMMEL, *Proofreader*

IRINA RYBACEK, *Associate Editor*

SAM TANENHAUS, *Proofreader*

DEBBIE TAYLOR, *Photo Editor*

MIMI THOMPSON, *Photo Editor*

TERENCE WALZ, *Associate Editor*

WILLIAM K. WEST, *Associate Editor*

ELIZABETH I. WILSON, *Associate Editor*

G. MICHAEL McGINLEY, *DIRECTOR, REFERENCE BOOKS DIVISION*

Contributors to Volume 8

DOROTHY ABRAHAMSE
California State University, Long Beach
Magic and Folklore, Byzantine

ROBERT W. ACKERMAN
Stanford University
Malory, Sir Thomas

DOROTHY AFRICA
Martyrology, Irish

MANSOUR J. AJAMI
Princeton University
Masʿūdī, al-

GUSTAVE ALEF
University of Oregon
Muscovy, Rise of

ROBERT AMIET
Facultés Catholiques, Lyon
Masses, Votive

RHIAN M. ANDREWS
Queen's University of Belfast
Meilyr Brydydd

MARY-JO ARN
English Institute, Groningen
Map, Walter

ŞAHAN ARZRUNI
Music, Armenian

ESIN ATIL
Freer Gallery of Art
Mamluk Art

TERENCE BAILEY
University of Western Ontario
Mediatio; Mode

JÁNOS M. BAK
University of British Columbia
Magyars

JOHN W. BARKER
University of Wisconsin
Mistra

CARL F. BARNES, JR.
Mathieu d'Arras; Misericord; Moissac, St. Pierre; Molding; Mouchette; Muldenfaltenstil; Mullion

MICHAEL L. BATES
American Numismatic Society
Mints and Money, Islamic

RICHARD BEADLE
Cambridge University
Mystery Plays

PAUL Z. BEDOUKIAN
Mints and Money, Armenian

CAROLINE J. BEESON
Mashhad

MALACHI BEIT-ARIÉ
The Jewish National and University Library
Manuscripts and Books: Hebrew

LUIS BELTRÁN
Indiana University
Mena, Juan de

CAROL MANSON BIER
The Textile Museum, Washington, D.C.
Mulḥam

GHAZI I. BISHEH
Jordan Archaeological Museum
Miḥrab; Minbar

BRADFORD B. BLAINE
Scripps College
Mills

JONATHAN M. BLOOM
Harvard University
Mashra Biya; Mosque; Muṣalla

IMRE BOBA
University of Washington
Moravia

PERE BOHIGAS
March, Ausiàs

JANE CUYLER BORGERHOFF
Mayor

EDMUND A. BOWLES
Minstrels; Music in Medieval Society; Musical Instruments, European

CHARLES M. BRAND
Bryn Mawr College
Manuel I Komnenos

MICHAEL BRETT
University of London
Maghrib, al-; Marinids; Marrakech

LESLIE BRUBAKER
Wheaton College, Norton, Massachusetts
Macedonian Renaissance; Martyrium; Menologion; Michael Astrapas; Missal

RICHARD W. BULLIET
Columbia University
Muʿāwiya; Muḥtasib; Muqaffaʿ, ʿAbd Allāh ibn al-; Muqtadir, al-; Mustanṣir, al-; Mustaʿṣim, al-; Muʿtaṣim, al-; Mutawakkil, al-

VINCENT BURANELLI
Manṣūr, Ibn Abī ʿĀmir al-; Marseilles; Mirror of Justices

GLYN S. BURGESS
University of Liverpool
Marie de Champagne

ROBERT G. CALKINS
Cornell University
Malouel, Jean

DANIEL CALLAM
St. Thomas More College
Martyrdom, Christian

AVERIL CAMERON
King's College, University of London
Malalas, John

CONTRIBUTORS TO VOLUME 8

GRETEL CHAPMAN
Mosan Art

PETER CHARANIS
Rutgers University
Monasticism, Byzantine; Monemvasia

YVES CHARTIER
University of Ottawa
Musical Treatises

COLIN CHASE
University of Toronto, Centre for Medieval Studies
Modoin

LAWRENCE I. CONRAD
The Wellcome Institute for the History of Medicine
Marj Dābiq; Marj Rāhiṭ; Marwān I ibn al-Ḥakam; Marwān II ibn Muḥammad; Marwān, ᶜAbd al-Malik ibn

DEMETRIOS J. CONSTANTELOS
Stockton State College
Medicine, Byzantine

BERNARD CULLEN
Queen's University of Belfast
Malachy, St.; Marsilius of Padua; Mendicant Orders

MICHAEL CURSCHMANN
Princeton University
Middle High German Literature

MICHAEL T. DAVIS
Mount Holyoke College
Mandorla; Mappa Mundi

LUKE DEMAITRE
Pace University
Medicine, Schools of

PETER F. DEMBOWSKI
University of Chicago
Marie de France

DON DENNY
University of Maryland
Moulins, Master of

LUCY DER MANUELIAN
Mastara; Mren, Church of

ALAN DEYERMOND
Westfield College, University of London
Mocedades de Rodrigo

WACHTANG DJOBADZE
California State University, Los Angeles
Mcᶜxetᶜa; Meteḥi

JERRILYNN D. DODDS
Columbia University
Mozarabic Art; Mudéjar Art

FRED M. DONNER
University of Chicago
Muezzin

ANN DOOLEY
St. Michael's College, University of Toronto
Maelgwn; Munster

AARON DOTAN
Tel-Aviv University
Masoretes

DIANE L. DROSTE
University of Toronto, Centre for Medieval Studies
Mass Cycles, Plainsong; Monophony; Musical Notation, Alphabetic, Daseian, Hufnagel

A. A. M. DUNCAN
University of Glasgow
Macbeth; Malcolm I of Alba; Malcolm II, III, IV of Scotland

CHARLES W. DUNN
Harvard University
Middle English Literature: Prosody and Versification

PETER N. DUNN
Wesleyan University
Manuel, Don Juan

MANUEL DURAN
Yale University
Misa de Amor, La

BRUCE STANSFIELD EASTWOOD
University of Kentucky
Martianus Capella

PATRICIA J. EBERLE
University of Toronto
Mirror of Princes

MARCIA J. EPSTEIN
University of Calgary
Madrigal; Marcabru

JOHN H. ERICKSON
St. Vladimir's Seminary
Mark Eugenikos

ROBERT FALCK
University of Toronto
Musical Notation, Bilingual, Western

T. S. FAUNCE
Princeton University
Mercadé, Eustache

PAULA SUTTER FICHTNER
Brooklyn College, City University of New York
Maximilian I, Emperor

JOHN V. A. FINE, JR.
University of Michigan
Marko

JOHN H. FISHER
University of Tennessee
Middle English Literature

CLIVE FOSS
University of Massachusetts, Harbor Campus, Boston
Melitene

ROBERTA FRANK
University of Toronto, Centre for Medieval Studies
Málsháttakvæði; Merlínússpá

JOHN B. FREED
Illinois State University, Normal
Ministerials

EDWARD FRUEH
Columbia University
Micon of St. Riquier; Manfred of Magdeburg

GEDEON GÁL, O.F.M.
Franciscan Institute, St. Bonaventure University
Matthew of Aquasparta

AUBREY E. GALYON
Iowa State University
Matthew of Vendôme

STEPHEN GARDNER
Fogg Art Museum, Harvard University
Michael of Canterbury

NINA G. GARSOÏAN
Columbia University
Mamikonean; Manazkert; Marzpanate; Mātakdān i Hazār Dātastān

CONTRIBUTORS TO VOLUME 8

ADELHEID M. GEALT
Indiana University
MAITANI, AMBROGIO; MARIOTTO DI NARDO; MASO DI BANCO; MASOLINO; MASACCIO, TOMMASO CASSAI; MICHELOZZO DI BARTOLOMEO

DENO J. GEANAKOPLOS
Yale University
MANUEL CHRYSOLORAS; MICHAEL VIII PALAIOLOGOS

PATRICK GEARY
University of Florida
MEROVINGIANS; MAYOR OF THE PALACE; MISSI DOMINICI

E. MICHAEL GERLI
Georgetown University
MARTÍNEZ DE TOLEDO, ALFONSO

INGEBORG GLIER
Yale University
MINNEREDEN

PETER B. GOLDEN
Rutgers University
MALIKSHĀH; MEHMED (MUḤAMMAD) I; MEHMED (MUḤAMMAD) II; MURAD I; MURAD II

RAMÓN GONZÁLVEZ
MOZARABIC RITE

ANTHONY GRAFTON
Princeton University
MIDDLE AGES

JAMES A. GRAHAM-CAMPBELL
University College, London
MAMMEN STYLE

GORDON K. GREENE
Wilfrid Laurier University
MASS CYCLES, EARLY POLYPHONIC

MARY GRIZZARD
University of New Mexico
MAJOLICA; MARTORELL, BERNARDO; MARQUETRY; MARZAL DE SAX, ANDRÉS

JACQUES GUILMAIN
State University of New York at Stony Brook
MANUSCRIPT ILLUMINATION, EUROPEAN

JOSEPH GUTMANN
MENORAH

RICHARD GYUG
University of Toronto
MILANESE RITE

ANDRAS HAMORI
Princeton University
MUTANABBĪ, AL-

NATHALIE HANLET
MEGINHART OF FULDA; MILO OF ST. AMAND

BERT HANSEN
New York University
MAGIC, BOOKISH (WESTERN EUROPEAN)

CONRAD HARKINS, O.F.M.
Franciscan Institute, St. Bonaventure University
MARSH, ADAM

HUBERT HEINEN
University of Texas
MEINLOH VON SEVELINGEN

JOHN BELL HENNEMAN
Princeton University Library
MALTOLTE; MARMOUSETS

P. L. HEYWORTH
University of Toronto
MIDDLE ENGLISH LITERATURE: ALLITERATIVE VERSE

BENNETT D. HILL
St. Anselm's Abbey
MISSIONS AND MISSIONARIES, CHRISTIAN

ROBERT HILLENBRAND
University of Edinburgh
MADRASA; MALWIYA; MANUSCRIPT BOOKS, BINDING OF: ISLAMIC; MINARET

ANDREW HUGHES
University of Toronto
MELODY; MUSIC, POPULAR; MUSIC, WESTERN EUROPEAN; MUSICA FICTA

R. STEPHEN HUMPHREYS
University of Wisconsin—Madison
MAMLŪK; MAMLUK DYNASTY

MOSHE IDEL
Hebrew University of Jerusalem
MOSES BEN SHEM TOV DE LEON

ALFRED L. IVRY
Brandeis University
MAIMONIDES, ABRAHAM BEN MOSES

W. T. H. JACKSON
Columbia University
MARBOD OF RENNES; MEINZO OF CONSTANCE

PETER JEFFERY
University of Delaware
MUSIC, JEWISH

D. W. JOHNSON
Catholic University of America
MANICHAEANS; MONOPHYSITISM; MELCHITES

JENNIFER E. JONES
MAJESTAS DOMINI; MISSION OF THE APOSTLES

WILLIAM CHESTER JORDAN
Princeton University
MAINMORT; MARGRAVE, MARQUIS; MARSHAL; MORTMAIN

MARIANNE E. KALINKE
University of Illinois
MÁGUS SAGA JARLS; MÍRMANNS SAGA; MÖTTULS SAGA

ALEXANDER P. KAZHDAN
Dumbarton Oaks Research Center
MENANDER PROTECTOR

HERBERT L. KESSLER
The Johns Hopkins University
MANUALS, ARTISTIC

MAJID KHADDURI
School of Advanced International Studies, The Johns Hopkins University
MOSUL

DALE KINNEY
Bryn Mawr College
MILAN CATHEDRAL

STEVEN D. KIRBY
Niagara University
MESTER DE CLERECÍA

JULIUS KIRSCHNER
University of Chicago
MEDICI

CONTRIBUTORS TO VOLUME 8

DAVID N. KLAUSNER
University of Toronto, Centre for Medieval Studies
Music, Celtic

ALAN E. KNIGHT
Pennsylvania State University
Miracle Plays

MARYANNE KOWALESKI
Fordham University
Markets, European; Mead

BARIŠA KREKIĆ
University of California, Los Angeles
Marica River

ANGELIKI LAIOU
Harvard University
Manuel II Palaiologos

JACOB LASSNER
Wayne State University
Mahdī, al-; Maʾmūn, al-; Manṣūr, Abū Jaʿfar al-

R. WILLIAM LECKIE, JR.
University of Toronto, Centre for Medieval Studies
Minneburg

ROBERT E. LERNER
Northwestern University
Millennialism, Christian

ARTHUR LEVINE
University of Toronto
Musica Ficta; Mutation

KENNETH LEVY
Princeton University
Music, Byzantine

KEITH LEWINSTEIN
Princeton University
Muqaddasī, al-

ARCHIBALD R. LEWIS
University of Massachusetts, Amherst
Montpellier

JOHN LINDOW
University of California, Berkeley
Midgard Serpent; Mímir

MICHAEL P. LONG
Columbia University
Marchettus of Padua

R. M. LUMIANSKY
American Council of Learned Societies
Malory, Sir Thomas

MAXWELL LURIA
Middle English Literature: Lyric

MICHAEL McCORMICK
Dumbarton Oaks Research Center
Manuscript Books, Binding of: European

JOHN M. McCULLOH
Kansas State University
Martyrology

WILLIAM C. McDONALD
University of Virginia
Michel Beheim

JAMES T. McDONOUGH, JR.
St. Joseph's College, Philadelphia, Pennsylvania
Macrobius; Martin of Braga

TIMOTHY J. McGEE
University of Toronto
Musical Ornamentation; Musical Performance

D. R. McLINTOCK
University of London
Merigarto; Muspilli

MICHAEL McVAUGH
University of North Carolina
Medicine, History of

W. MADELUNG
The Oriental Institute, Oxford
Millennialism, Islamic

MICHAEL S. MAHONEY
Princeton University
Mathematics

KRIKOR H. MAKSOUDIAN
Manazkert, Council of; Maštocʿ, St.; Matthew of Edessa; Michael the Syrian; Movsēs Dasxurancʿi; Mxitʿar Goš

MICHAEL E. MARMURA
University of Toronto
Muʿtazila, al-

RICHARD C. MARTIN
Arizona State University
Mecca; Medina

H. SALVADOR MARTÍNEZ
New York University
Mester de Juglaría

RALPH WHITNEY MATHISEN
University of South Carolina
Merobaudes

BRIAN MERRILEES
University of Toronto
Manière de Langage; Matthew Paris

RENÉ METZ
Monasticism, Origins

JOHN MEYENDORFF
Fordham University
Maximus the Confessor, St.; Metropolitan; Michael Keroularios

ANNE M. MORGANSTERN
Ohio State University
Morel, Pierre

MICHAEL MORONY
University of California, Los Angeles
Muʿāwiya

BEZALEL NARKISS
Hebrew University of Jerusalem
Manuscript Illumination: Hebrew

ALAN H. NELSON
University of California, Berkeley
Medwall, Henry; Morality Play

JOHN W. NESBITT
Dumbarton Oaks Research Center
Mints and Money, Byzantine

HELAINE NEWSTEAD
City University of New York
Mannyng, Robert; Matter of Britain, France, Rome

DONALD M. NICOL
King's College, University of London
Meteora; Michael I of Epiros; Michael II of Epiros

CONTRIBUTORS TO VOLUME 8

THOMAS S. NOONAN
University of Minnesota
MINTS AND MONEY, RUSSIAN

VIVIAN NUTTON
The Wellcome Institute for the History of Medicine
MONDINO DEI LUZZI

DONNCHADH Ó CORRÁIN
University College, Cork
MAC LONÁIN, FLANN

W. A. ODDY
Research Laboratory, The British Museum
METALSMITHS, GOLD AND SILVER; METALWORKERS

BARBARA OEHLSCHLAEGER-GARVEY
University of Illinois at Urbana-Champaign
MANDYLION; MANIERA GRECA; MANUEL EUGENIKOS; MANUEL PANSELINOS; MAPHORION; MICHAEL ATTALEIATES; MISSORIUM

NICOLAS OIKONOMIDES
Université de Montreal
MAGISTROS

PATRICK P. O'NEILL
University of North Carolina
MANUSCRIPTS, CELTIC LITURGICAL

DUANE J. OSHEIM
University of Virginia
MATILDA OF TUSCANY

ANGELO PAREDI
Biblioteca Ambrosiana
MILAN

IVANA PELNAR-ZAIKO
MINNESINGERS

KENNETH PENNINGTON
Syracuse University
MAXIMS, LEGAL

RICHARD W. PFAFF
University of North Carolina
MARIAN FEASTS

CHRISTOPHER PINET
Montana State University
MAISTRE PIERRE PATHELIN

JAMES F. POAG
Washington University
MAI UND BEAFLOR

NORMAN J. G. POUNDS
MINING

JAMES M. POWELL
Syracuse University
MELFI, CONSTITUTIONS OF

MARY LYNN RAMPOLLA
MARIANUS SCOTUS

ROGER E. REYNOLDS
Pontifical Institute of Mediaeval Studies, Toronto
MASS, LITURGY OF THE; METZ, USE OF; MISSAL

ELIAS L. RIVERS
State University of New York at Stony Brook
MANRIQUE, JORGE

ELAINE GOLDEN ROBISON
MICHAEL SCOT

EDWARD H. ROESNER
New York University
MAGNUS LIBER ORGANI; MONTPELLIER MS H 196; MOTET MANUSCRIPTS

LINDA C. ROSE
MAGISTER MILITUM; MAGISTER OFFICIORUM; MICHAEL III; MARIA LEKAPENA; MAURICE, EMPEROR; MESEMBRIA; MONOTHELITISM; MYRIOKEPHALON

RICHARD H. ROUSE
University of California, Los Angeles
MANUSCRIPT BOOKS, PRODUCTION OF

TEOFILO F. RUIZ
Brooklyn College, City University of New York
MESTA

JAMES R. RUSSELL
Columbia University
MAGIC AND FOLKLORE: ARMENIAN; MAZDAKITES; MŌBADĀN MŌBAD

WILLIAM SAMOLIN
MONGOL EMPIRE

ERNEST H. SANDERS
Columbia University
MOTET; MUSICAL NOTATION, MODAL

PAULA SANDERS
Harvard University
MU^{c}IZZ AL-DAWLA

MARC SAPERSTEIN
Washington University
MAIMONIDEAN CONTROVERSY

GEORGE DIMITRI SAWA
MAQĀM; MUSIC, ISLAMIC; MUSIC, ISLAMIC INFLUENCE ON NON-WESTERN; MUSIC, ISLAMIC INFLUENCE ON WESTERN; MUSIC, MIDDLE EASTERN; MUSICAL INSTRUMENTS, MIDDLE EASTERN

NICOLAS SCHIDLOVSKY
Smithsonian Institution
MUSIC, SLAVIC; MUSIC, SYRIAN

JEAN-CLAUDE SCHMITT
École des Hautes Études en Sciences Sociales
MAGIC AND FOLKLORE: WESTERN EUROPEAN

HAIM SCHWARZBAUM
Hebrew University of Jerusalem
MAGIC AND FOLKLORE, JEWISH

IRFAN SHAHÎD
Georgetown University
NAJRĀN

LON R. SHELBY
Southern Illinois University at Carbondale
MASONS AND BUILDERS

GIULIO SILANO
Pontifical Institute of Mediaeval Studies, Toronto
MARTINUS GOSIA

LARRY SILVER
Northwestern University
MEIT, CONRAD; MOSER, LUCAS; MULTSCHER, HANS

MARIANNA S. SIMPSON
National Gallery of Art
MANUSCRIPT ILLUMINATION, ISLAMIC

BARRIE SINGLETON
Courtauld Institute, University of London
MASSINGHAM, JOHN

JAMES SNYDER
Bryn Mawr College
MEMLING, HANS

CONTRIBUTORS TO VOLUME 8

HAYM SOLOVEITCHIK
Yeshiva University, Bernard Revel Graduate School
MARTYRDOM, JEWISH

ERNST H. SOUDEK
University of Virginia
MECHTHILD VON MAGDEBURG

SUSAN SPECTORSKY
Queens College, City University of New York
MĀLIK IBN ANAS

ALAN M. STAHL
American Numismatic Society
MINTS AND MONEY, WESTERN EUROPEAN

NORMAN A. STILLMAN
YEDIDA K. STILLMAN
State University of New York at Binghamton
MAGIC AND FOLKLORE, ISLAMIC

ALAIN J. STOCLET
MONTE CASSINO

JOSEPH R. STRAYER
Princeton University
MARIGNY, ENGUERRAN DE; MARONITE CHURCH; MOAT

JAMES H. STUBBLEBINE
Rutgers University
MAESTÀ

JOSEPH SZÖVÉRFFY
Wissenschaftskolleg zu Berlin
METELLUS OF TEGERNSEE

JOHN TAYLOR
University of Leeds
MODUS TENENDI PARLIAMENTUM

MICHAEL D. TAYLOR
University of Houston
MAITANI, LORENZO

J. WESLEY THOMAS
University of Kentucky
MARNER, DER; MORIZ VON CRAÛN

ROBERT W. THOMSON
Harvard University
MOVSĒS XORENAC^{c}I

PETER TOPPING
Dumbarton Oaks Research Center
MOREA; MOREA, CHRONICLE OF; MOREA, DESPOTATE OF

ANTONIO TORRES-ALCALÁ
University of Texas
MOZARABIC LITERATURE

IRINA ANDREESCU TREADGOLD
MOSAICS AND MOSAIC MAKING

WARREN T. TREADGOLD
Hillsdale College
MACEDONIANS

LEO TREITLER
State University of New York at Stony Brook
MELISMA; MUSIC, ORAL TRADITION IN

RALPH V. TURNER
Florida State University
MAGNA CARTA

ISADORE TWERSKY
Harvard University
MAIMONIDES

ANNE HAGOPIAN VAN BUREN
Tufts University
MARMION, SIMON; MARY OF BURGUNDY, MASTER OF

ARJO VANDERJAGT
Filosofisch Instituut, Groningen
MANEGOLD OF LAUTENBACH

MILOŠ VELIMIROVIĆ
University of Virginia
MUSICAL NOTATION, BYZANTINE; MUSICAL NOTATION, EKPHONETIC

PHILIPPE VERDIER
METALLURGY

CHARLES VERLINDEN
MADEIRA ISLANDS

STEPHEN L. WAILES
Indiana University
MÄREN

SETH WARD
University of Haifa
MALI

W. MONTGOMERY WATT
University of Edinburgh
MUḤAMMAD

J. R. WEBSTER
St. Michael's College, University of Toronto
METGE, BERNAT

ELLEN T. WEHNER
University of Toronto
MANUEL DES PÉCHÉS; MELIOR ET YDOINE; MERURE DE SEINTE ÉGLISE

MARTIN WERNER
Temple University
MIGRATION AND HIBERNO-SAXON ART

ESTELLE WHELAN
MUQARNAS

MARINA D. WHITMAN
MINAI WARE

GREGORY WHITTINGTON
Institute of Fine Arts, New York University
MACHICOLATION; MODILLION; MONASTERY

J. WILLIAMS
University of Pittsburgh
MAIUS

SARAH JANE WILLIAMS
MACHAUT, GUILLAUME DE

JAMES L. YARRISON
MALTA; MEKNES

DAVID YERKES
Columbia University
MIDDLE ENGLISH LANGUAGE

CHRISTIAN K. ZACHER
Ohio State University
MANDEVILLE'S TRAVELS

RONALD EDWARD ZUPKO
Marquette University
MARC; MILE; MUID

Dictionary of the Middle Ages

Dictionary of the Middle Ages

MACBETH—MYSTERY PLAYS

MACBETH (*d.* 1057), king of Scotland (1040–1057). He was of the family of mormaers (provincial rulers) of Moray for which a claim has been made that they represent a northern "kingdom." Macbeth killed Duncan I, probably at Elgin, in 1040. In 1045 Crinan, abbot of Dunkeld and father of Duncan I, was killed in civil strife. In 1046 Siward, earl of Northumbria, invaded Scotland and appointed "another" from whom Macbeth recovered the kingdom. It is possible that these dates should be reversed and that Crinan was the "another."

By 1050, when he was in Rome as a pilgrim, Macbeth fully controlled Scotland, perhaps by reason of an agreement with Edward the Confessor, for in 1052 Macbeth received two Norman retainers expelled from Edward's court in a reaction against his Normanizing tendency. In 1054, however, Earl Siward invaded Scotland by land and sea, defeating Macbeth decisively. He may have installed Malcolm (III), son of Duncan I, as king in southern Scotland. In 1057 Malcolm defeated and killed Macbeth at Lumphanan.

The Macbeth of Shakespeare's play may be traced back to the fictional history of Scotland written by Hector Boece (1526). Almost nothing of the play is true except that there may have been a Macduff mormaer in Fife expelled by Macbeth.

BIBLIOGRAPHY

A. A. M. Duncan, *Scotland: The Making of the Kingdom* (1975); William E. Kapelle, *The Norman Conquest of the North* (1980).

A. A. M. DUNCAN

[See also **Duncan I of Scotland; Edward the Confessor, St.; Malcolm III of Scotland; Scotland: History.**]

MACEDONIAN RENAISSANCE, a label sometimes applied to the period of the Macedonian dynasty in Byzantium (867–1056), and particularly to the tenth century, which some scholars have seen as a time of increased interest in classical art and scholarship, expressed either by overt emulation or by assimilating classical motifs into a Christian context. Because the term "renaissance" was coined in the fifteenth century by Italian humanists to describe the peculiarities of their own period, its use in any other context is problematic. Certainly, however, the immediate posticonoclastic period in Byzantium was an innovative one, saw itself as a new era, and produced texts and works of art that to some extent reflect a conscious reassessment of classical ideas.

In art, this assimilation of classical ideas is best seen in the Paris Psalter (Bibliothèque Nationale, cod. gr. 139), the Joshua Roll (Vatican, Biblioteca, Cod. Pal. gr. 431), and on a glass bowl with mythological medallions in Venice. Here, respectively, pagan compositions are transformed into Christian scenes (David as Orpheus), ancient formats are revived (the scroll used for the Joshua Roll), and pre-Christian gems and coins are copied directly. The influence of the classical style has also been seen in tenth-century Byzantine monuments, notably the Paris Psalter and a gospelbook at Mount Athos (Stavronikita cod. 43).

The classicizing tendency assumed by the label "Macedonian renaissance" is not ubiquitous. Neither architecture nor sculpture seem to have been affected, and many paintings of the period fail to show any impact of antiquity. Further, the Byzantine attitude toward the pre-Christian era was ambivalent at best, at least until the late eleventh century. Hence, the concept of a Macedonian renaissance must be treated cautiously. It is of limited value except in relation to a small group of works created for a distinct and elite body of patrons.

BIBLIOGRAPHY

Hans Belting, "Problemi vecchi e nuovi sull'arte della cosiddetta 'rinascenza macedone' a bisanzio," in *XXIX Corso di cultura sull'arte ravennate e bizantine* (1982);

Hugo Buchtal, *The Miniatures of the Paris Psalter: A Study in Middle Byzantine Painting* (1938); Anthony Cutler, "The Mythological Bowl in the Treasury of San Marco at Venice," in *Near Eastern Numismatics, Iconography, Epigraphy, and History: Studies in Honor of George C. Miles,* Dickran K. Kouymjian, ed. (1974); Cyril Mango, "The Date of Cod. Vat. Regin. Gr. 1 and the 'Macedonian Renaissance,' " in *Acta ad archaeologiam et artium historiam pertinentia,* 4 (1969), 121–126; Kurt Weitzmann, "The Character and Intellectual Origins of the Macedonian Renaissance," in *Studies in Classical and Byzantine Manuscript Illumination,* Herbert L. Kessler, ed. (1971), 176–223, and *The Joshua Roll: A Work of the Macedonian Renaissance* (1948).

LESLIE BRUBAKER

[See also **Byzantine Art; Joshua Roll; Paris Psalter.**]

MACEDONIANS, a Byzantine dynasty. Although the emperors and empresses of the dynasty reigned from 867 to 1056, during almost half that time real power was in the hands of other rulers who associated themselves with the Macedonians, usually by marriage. The dynasty was called Macedonian because its founder, Basil I (867–886), came from the theme of Macedonia, although his birthplace was in Thrace. He was of a peasant family that may have been Armenian.

Basil was succeeded by his supposed son, Leo, and his real son, Alexander. As senior emperor, Leo exercised full power until his death. He became involved in a major conflict with the church over the validity of his fourth marriage and the consequent legitimacy of his son and heir, Constantine VII Porphyrogenitos, which remained in dispute. Leo died in 912, and Alexander, after ruling briefly, in 913. Constantine then succeeded at the age of seven, having first the patriarch Nikolaos Mystikos and then his mother, Zoë Karbonopsina, as regent. In 920 the general Romanos I Lekapenos took power as senior emperor, associating himself with the dynasty by marrying his daughter Helena to Constantine VII. In 944 Romanos was overthrown by his sons, and the following year Constantine took advantage of legitimist sentiment to seize power, which he passed on to his son Romanos II in 959.

Romanos died young in 963, leaving his sons Basil II and Constantine VIII, aged five and three, in the care of his widow, Theophano. She protected her position by marrying the general Nikephoros II Phokas, making him senior emperor. In 969, after assassinating Nikephoros in a plot with Theophano, another general, John I Tzimiskes, became senior emperor. Forced to exile Theophano, he married Theodora, daughter of Constantine VII. After John's death in 976, Basil II virtually reigned alone, but he had full authority only from 985, when he exiled the powerful eunuch Basil the Parakoimomenos, an illegitimate son of Romanos I. Constantine took little interest in ruling. To stay in power, Basil had to defeat a rebellion of the generals Bardas Skleros and Bardas Phokas between 987 and 989. He died childless in 1025. His brother Constantine ruled until his death in 1028, leaving only daughters past childbearing age as heirs.

Constantine's daughter Zoë married the senator Romanos III Argyros, who became emperor. He was murdered in 1034 with the complicity of Zoë and the eunuch John the Orphanotrophos, whose brother, Michael IV the Paphlagonian, married Zoë and became emperor. At Michael's death in 1041, Zoë adopted John's cousin Michael V Calaphates, making him emperor; but when Michael tried to exile her, he was overthrown by a popular revolt in favor of the legitimate dynasty. For two months in 1044, Zoë and her sister Theodora reigned. Finally Zoë married Constantine IX Monomachos, who continued to reign after her death in 1050. When he died in 1055, Theodora took power. With her death in 1056, the Macedonians died out, having reigned during the height of middle Byzantine power and the "Macedonian Renaissance" of art and learning.

BIBLIOGRAPHY

George Ostrogorsky, *History of the Byzantine State,* Joan Hussey, trans. (1957, rev. ed. 1969).

WARREN T. TREADGOLD

[See also **Bardas Phokas; Bardas Skleros; Basil I the Macedonian, Emperor; Basil II the "Killer of the Bulgars," Emperor; Byzantine Church; Byzantine Empire; Constantine VII Porphyrogenitos; Constantine IX Monomachos; John I Tzimiskes; Macedonian Renaissance; Romanos I Lekapenos; Romanos II; Theodora II, Empress; Theophano, Empress; Zoë the Macedonian.**]

MACHAUT, GUILLAUME DE (*ca.* 1300–1377). Like the trouvères of an earlier century, Guillaume de Machaut was both a poet and a composer. In France he was the most influential of his time in both spheres. A highly self-conscious creator, he was aware of the value of his works and of his role as a

MACHAUT, GUILLAUME DE

formal innovator. He systematically cultivated a remarkable variety of forms and styles in his works and supervised their collection and preservation as well. Machaut's poetry influenced Froissart, Deschamps, Christine de Pizan, Martin le Franc, Oton de Granson, and Charles of Orléans, among later French poets. In England his younger contemporary, Chaucer, read and imitated his works.

The details of Machaut's life are sketchy. His biography can be filled in with information supplied in part by recollections furnished in his longer poems. Little is known of his education, though he is given the title of master in a number of documents. The first of his powerful patrons was John of Luxemburg, king of Bohemia, at whose request Machaut was granted various ecclesiastical offices. In a late poem Machaut says that he served the king for more than thirty years, but a more accurate indication seems to be provided in a papal document of 1335, in which Guillaume de Machaut is said to have been in the king's service for twelve years. A member of the king's household, serving him as almoner, notary, and secretary, the poet shared the European travels and campaigns of the adventurous monarch. Machaut was evidently traveling with the king when he took possession of his canonry at the cathedral of Rheims by procuration in 1337 but was no longer with him when the valiant king met his death in 1346 at the Battle of Crécy. Having settled in Rheims, Guillaume is listed among the auditors of a sermon at the cathedral in April 1340.

Machaut later recalled his service to John's daughter, the queen of France, Bonne of Luxemburg, wife of John II of France. In 1349 he dedicated a poem to another king, Charles II of Navarre, who also became the recipient of the *Confort d'ami* in 1357. Despite Charles's enmity with Machaut's patrons in the house of France, he presented the poet, as late as 1361, with the gift of a horse. In the same year the dauphin, Charles of Normandy, the future Charles V, directed officials of Rheims to visit him at the house of Machaut, where he was staying. The *Fonteinne amoureuse* was written around 1360 for Jean, duke of Berry, the famous bibliophile and collector and younger brother of Charles V. One of the surviving Machaut manuscripts once belonged to the duke's library.

A third royal brother, Philip the Bold of Burgundy, may have been another of Machaut's patrons, and in 1371 the poet is listed among the creditors of Count Amadeus of Savoy. His last long poem was written in praise of the martyred king of Cyprus, Pierre de Lusignan, whose name has also been found in one of the *complaintes.* Machaut died in April 1377 and was buried in the cathedral of Rheims, where he had served as a canon. Eustache Deschamps, his follower and fellow Champenois, wrote a pair of ballades calling on "ladies, knighthood, clerks, musicians," musical instruments, and woodland nymphs, to mourn the death of "Machaut le noble rethorique." They were set to music by the composer F. Andrieu as a double ballade with two texted voices, following the example of the master.

Some half dozen manuscripts contain the complete works of Machaut at various stages of his career, a few of them dating from his lifetime, including several apparently prepared under his supervision. There are others, less complete, which include Machaut's works along with those of other composers and poets. Most of them are richly illuminated, with miniatures that include some of the masterpieces of fourteenth-century French art. An index with the heading, "Vesci l'ordenance que .G. de Machau vuet qu'il ait en son livre" (This is the order .G. de Machau wishes his book to have), precedes one of the most complete manuscripts.

In the manuscripts Guillaume de Machaut's works are set out in well-defined sections. However, although he groups his pieces according to genre, he also has a sense of the unity of his complete works, as expressed in a *Prologue* that sets out his artistic aims and ambitions. The three speakers of the *Prologue* are Nature, Love, and Machaut himself. Addressing the poet by name in a ballade, Nature commands him to compose "nouviaus dis amoureus plaisans" (pleasant new amorous tales), and presents him with her three children, Reason, Rhetoric, and Music. Guillaume answers Nature, whereupon Love, who has overheard the exchange, presents the poet with his three children, Sweet Thinking, Pleasure, and Hope, and is thanked. After the opening ballades, a section in octosyllabic couplets enumerates some of the forms in which Machaut will compose, elaborates a moral and psychological theory of art, and discusses the power of music. Thus the creator's powers are boldly and proudly compared to those of Nature herself, and his works, large and small, to a created world, while Love is to be his chief inspiration and subject.

Following the *Prologue* in the most complete manuscripts come the longer poems, called dits. The first, and probably the earliest, is the *Dit dou vergier* (The orchard poem), in which the poet-lover tells of his encounter in the garden with the god of Love, who reveals his powers and his allegorical friends and enemies and gives advice on the conduct proper to a lover. It draws heavily on the *Romance of the Rose,* a strong influence in all of Machaut's works.

It is the second of the longer poems, the *Jugement dou Roy de Behaigne* (Judgment of the king of Bohemia), which seems to have established Machaut's literary reputation. Written in an unusual stanzaic form, it concerns a debate between a knight whose lady has been unfaithful to him and a lady whose lover is dead over who is more unhappy. Invited to settle the quarrel, the king of Bohemia, on advice from his allegorical court, pronounces in favor of the knight and then offers his guests entertainment. Machaut gives his name in an anagram in the last line of the *Jugement.* Only the *Dit dou vergier* fails to identify its author.

This problem of love casuistry and the *Jugement*'s solution apparently aroused so much discussion that Machaut was moved to reopen the question in the *Jugement dou Roy de Navarre,* "contre le Jugement dou Roy de Behaigne." Its opening is in sharp contrast to the earlier *Jugement.* Instead of the usual springtime setting, it is autumn (Machaut gives the specific date, 9 November 1349); the poet's mood is autumnal and somber as he sits alone in his room, overwhelmed by melancholy reflections on the state of the world. He meditates on the ravages of the war, the persecution of the Jews, the religious mania of the flagellants, and the terrors of the plague. But finally the epidemic runs its course, and the poet rides out to hunt on his palfrey, Grisart. No anagram is needed, although one is later provided, to identify the author-narrator of this *Jugement,* since he is recognized by the company he encounters: "There is Guillaume de Machaut." He is accused of maligning ladies in his earlier dit, and brought before the king of Navarre. Although Guillaume defends his earlier position vigorously he is attacked even more vigorously by the allegorical figures of the court. The judgment goes against him, and he is sentenced to make poetic amends by composing a lai, a virelai, and a ballade.

The *Remède de Fortune,* which follows the two *Jugements* in the manuscripts, is notable for its inclusion within the narrative structure of lyrics set to music. These are presented in a systematic way, for each of the seven musical compositions of the *Remède* is in a different form: a lai, a *complainte,* a chanson royal, a "baladelle," a ballade, a virelai, and a rondeau. Machaut evidently wished to provide a model of each of the musical-poetic genres of the period, genres whose contemporary forms were largely his own creation. The lover of the *Remède* becomes a victim of Fortune by reason of a lai he composed to honor his beloved. The lai somehow falls into her hands; she makes the lover read it to her and wants to know who wrote it. This presents a dilemma, since to admit writing it would be to risk disapproval and rejection, and to deny it would be to lie. The helpless lover leaves in tears, retires to the park of Hesdin, and utters a long *complainte* against Fortune. This provokes the appearance of Hope, whose Boethian discussions with the lover constitute the allegorical core of the poem. Hope is the "remedy to Fortune." The lover is reunited with his lady and her friends as Machaut paints a picture of a morning's activities in polite society.

The adventure of the *Dit dou lyon* is said to take place 2 April 1342. (The paired nature of the two *Jugements* dictates the manuscripts' unchronological arrangement.) It draws on the motifs of courtly romance, as a magic boat carries the lover to a marvelous country, guarded by a faithful lion, to which only loyal lovers are admitted. The allegorical methods of the *Dit de l'alerion* (Tale of the eaglet), which compares hunting birds to various ladies, are related to those of the bestiaries.

The *Confort d'ami* was written to console Charles II of Navarre for his imprisonment. Yet Machaut includes praise of his captor, the "good king of France." As well as offering consolation through biblical examples of the workings of a benevolent providence, he proffers much advice on matters ranging from food and dress to elements of statecraft.

A different sort of consolation is offered in the *Fonteinne amoureuse* to Jean, duke of Berry, who is about to leave for England as a hostage, leaving behind a young bride. The poem, which celebrates Morpheus, the god of dreams, includes lyrics: a *complainte,* a *confort de l'amant,* and a rondeau, which the lover sings. But although Machaut has rhymed them most carefully, even pointing out that the *complainte* contains one hundred rhymes, without any repetition, he has not provided music for them.

Longest of Machaut's poems is the *Livre dou voir dit* (True story) of about 1364, which tells of a love affair between the aging poet and a young lady who falls in love with him through reading his works and initiates a poetic correspondence. The poem includes the prose letters they exchanged and many lyrics, eight of them with music. An anagram gives the real name of the lady, usually called "Toute Belle" by the

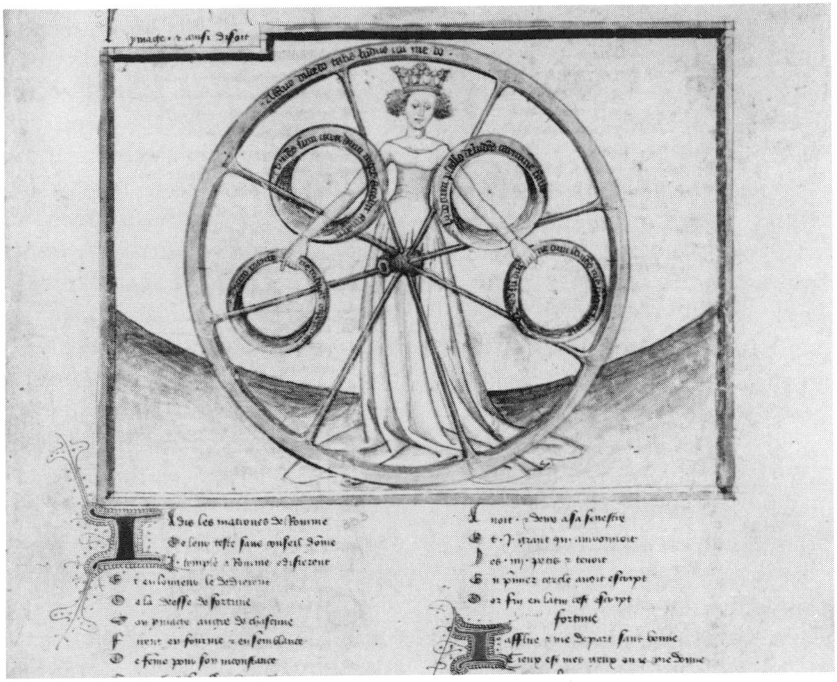

Fortune and her wheel. Lightly washed drawing from MS of Machaut's *Livre dou voir dit, ca.* 1364. NEW YORK, PIERPONT MORGAN LIBRARY, MS 396, f. 175

poet, as Péronne d'Armentières. Machaut tells of reports of her infidelity that reach him and of the doubts that torment him, doubts that are not wholly resolved by the ending, which again glorifies "Toute Belle" to the skies.

Machaut's last long poem, the *Prise d'Alexandrie* (Taking of Alexandria), is a verse chronicle of the life of Pierre de Lusignan, king of Cyprus, assassinated 17 January 1369. (The horror that regicide inspired is typified in the *Dit de l'alerion* by the story of the prize hunting bird who is decapitated for killing an eagle.) The poem is curiously like the *Voir dit* in offering a double perspective on its protagonist. Pierre is seen as a cruel and arbitrary tyrant as well as a valiant knight and martyr.

There are several shorter dits, the *Dit de la rose,* the *Dit de la harpe* (whose anagram is still to be solved), the *Dit de la marguerite* (Tale of the daisy), the *Dit de la fleur de lis et de la marguerite* (Tale of the lily and the daisy), as well as *Vesci les biens que ma dame me fait* (These are the gifts my lady makes me), a poem of sixty-four lines rhymed entirely on *our.*

The practice of the *Remède* suggests that ideally all lyrics are meant to be set to music. But though other texts may speak of "chanson," "chant," or "en chantant," the *complainte* and chant royal of the *Remède* are the only ones of their kind to be provided with music. The collection of several hundred literary lyrics, known as the *Louange des dames,* contains mainly ballades, along with dozens of rondeaux, ten *complaintes,* seven *chants royaux,* and a single virelai. Some of these texts can also be found in musical settings. Sung or not, Machaut's poetry, both narrative and lyric, was meant for oral presentation, to be read aloud, and is written with great attention to sound and rhyme patterns.

In the *Prologue* that introduces his complete works Machaut plans to put the gifts of Nature and Love to work in making "tales and little songs," "double hoquets and pleasant lais, motets, rondeaux, and virelais," "complaintes and ballads," a list including every genre cultivated by Machaut except for his Mass. In the manuscripts, the music sections, arranged by genres, follow the dits and the lyrics without music.

Machaut's music takes full advantage of fourteenth-century theoretical and notational changes. The full equality for the first time of triple and duple division of all note values makes possible extensive syncopation. The use of accidentals and chromatic alteration, musica ficta, colors the melodic lines with intervals of augmented seconds or augmented fourths; it gives to cadences the distinctive character of the so-called double leading tone cadence, in which both the octave and the fifth of the final accord are approached by raised tones.

The music sections begin with the monophonic lais. Though a pioneer of polyphonic style, Guillaume de Machaut was the last composer to write secular monophonic music, and his lais were the last to have musical settings. The lais are the most traditional of the musical forms and, from a poetic point of view, are esteemed the most difficult. Most of the lais follow the pattern of the one from the *Remède.* It has twelve stanzas, each of which is divided in two parts with identical rhyme schemes. The half stanzas contain a varying number of rhymes and employ both long and short verses. The rhyme scheme is different for each stanza except the last, which is identical with the first in form. The musical form of the lai, as of all medieval song forms, corresponds closely to that of the poetry. The first and last stanzas are musically identical, and the parallelism of half stanzas demands exact musical parallelism as well. The half stanzas are often further subdivided into two sections, musically identical, but with open and closed endings.

The union of poetry and music is especially strong in the lais. The declamation is predominantly syllabic, and the lengths of the verse lines, the alternation of long with short verses, are reflected in the musical phrases. There is much melodic variety, from stanzas using simple repeated notes to those using syncopation and chromatic alterations. The repetition of the last stanza is usually made a fifth higher, as the last half of the lai shifts to a higher register, giving the lai an extremely wide range. A few of the twenty-five lais differ in one or more respects from this pattern. Six have no music. The first lai, of twenty-four stanzas, with repeated music for each, is more like the thirty-six-stanza *complainte* or the five-stanza *chanson royal* of the *Remède.* The second lai has only seven instead of twelve stanzas, and like several others, keeps its musical repetition for the last stanza at the same pitch. Two lais are canonic, one of them carrying out the musical symbolism of the Trinity, the three in one, through alternating stanzas of one voice, and of three-voice canon. "Hidden polyphony" has been discovered in the two lais that are found only in Jean, duke of Berry's, manuscript.

When Machaut began composing, the motet was the leading form of polyphonic composition. His motets carry the technique of rhythmic repetition known as isorhythm further than his predecessors'. In keeping with his overall emphasis, most of his twenty-three motets have French texts that treat of love and three are even written on secular tenors, a practice rare in the fourteenth century. (Six motets have Latin texts, and two, mixed French and Latin texts.) His earliest datable work is the Latin motet, probably written for the installation of the archbishop of Rheims, Guillaume de Trie, in 1324. The foundation of the usual motet is its lowest voice, the tenor, a preexisting melody drawn from the chant repertory. It is organized into repeated rhythmic patterns, independent of melodic repetition, and even in conflict with it. The tenor moves much more slowly than the two texted voices above it—the faster motetus, and the even faster triplum. In Machaut's practice the upper voices too fall into isorhythmic patterns, which even govern the rhyme schemes of the verses. Half of the time the tenor pattern is diminished in the second section, with quicker note values. The upper parts then also become more lively, in hocket rhythms, where the musical lines are interspersed with rests, and short verses are tossed back and forth between triplum and motetus. Five motets are for four voices, adding above the tenor a contratenor, creating new subtleties of rhythmic patterns.

The legend that Machaut's celebrated polyphonic Mass was composed for the coronation of Charles V at Rheims is no longer accepted. The *Messe de nostre dame,* as it is called in one manuscript, is a setting of the six movements of the ordinary, Kyrie, Gloria, Credo, Sanctus, Agnus, and Ite missa est, for four voices. The movements with lengthy texts, the Gloria and Credo, are in a syllabic, note against note style, except for their elaborate Amens, with tenors that seem to be newly composed, while the movements with short texts are isorhythmic, over liturgical tenors. The style of the Mass, in contrast to much of Machaut's other polyphonic writing, is one of severity and strength. The most florid passages in the upper voices or its extensive passages in syncopation are never allowed to obscure the rhythmic skeleton, the basic motion of the longer note values.

Another work unique to Machaut's repertory is the textless hocket for two voices over the tenor melody, *David.*

The ballades, rondeaux, and (to a lesser extent) the virelais are the forms that embody Machaut's greatest innovations of musical style. They constitute the so-called *formes fixes,* forms with a dual literary and musical basis. Descendants of thirteenth-century dance songs, they are characterized by their use of refrains. The ballade, as standardized by Machaut, is

MACHAUT, GUILLAUME DE

a poem of three stanzas, the last line of each stanza being repeated as a refrain and the same rhymes maintained in each stanza. The first half of the stanza is always symmetrical and almost always consists of four lines with alternate rhymes. Two stanza forms account for over four-fifths of the ballades: *ab, ab, bcC* for the seven-line stanza and *ab, ab, ccdD* for the eight-line stanza, where capital letters indicate the refrain. Most of Machaut's rondeaux are in the eight-line form inherited from the thirteenth century, rhyming *A B a A a b A B.* The virelai is like the ballade in having three stanzas and like the rondeau in being surrounded by its refrain. It begins with a refrain of several verses, followed by a symmetrical section, a cauda based on the same rhymes as the refrain, and the refrain again.

The general outlines of the musical settings are governed by the poetic forms. Thus each stanza of the usual ballade has a tripartite form, with open and closed endings for the repetition of the first section, although there are a few symmetrical forms, like the "baladelle" of the *Remède* in which both sections are repeated. In the rondeau the first section is repeated five times, and the second three times, in the exact pattern of the rhyme scheme. The virelai, like the ballade, has repeated sections for the first part of the stanza that follows the opening refrain but uses the music of the refrain for the last part, in accordance with the rhyme pattern.

With the exception of a single monophonic ballade, the forty-two ballades and twenty-one rondeaux set to music are for various arrangements of two to four voices. To a two-voice core of cantus and textless tenor, a triplum may be added above the cantus, or a contratenor below, or both, with the combination of cantus, tenor, contratenor the most common one. The setting of the vocal lines dissolves the traditional unity of word and tone characteristic of the monophonic works. Machaut makes extensive use of melisma, long musical phrases set to a single syllable and contrasting with syllabic passages. Lively rhythms, syncopation, dissonance (including passages of parallel seconds and sevenths), contrast between individual voices, between phrases of different lengths, and between rapid motion and points of rest are characteristic of the style. There are two triple ballades, with three texts of identical form and refrain set simultaneously (one of the ballades as a canon), and a double ballade whose texts are the result of a poetic contest described in the *Voir dit.* The rondeau form, with its refrain constantly circling back on itself, lends itself to Machaut's fondness for playful, punning rhymes and for puzzles. Three rondeaux conceal the names of Jehanne, Péronne, and Isabel. The quintessence of the form is expressed in another riddle, the retrograde rondeau, *Ma fin est mon commencement* (My end is my beginning), whose music is the same, read forward or backward. Of the *formes fixes* only the virelai still keeps its connection with the dance. The virelai of the *Remède* is introduced specifically as a song to be danced to. Most of the thirty-three virelais set to music are for one voice, in a tuneful and rhythmic style simpler than and different from that of the ballades and rondeaux.

Descriptions in the *Remède* of an outdoor concert and in the *Prise* of the festivities accompanying the entrance of the king of Cyprus into Prague contain long lists of musical instruments. The dancing in the *Remède,* on the other hand, is said to occur without any instruments, but only with songs. Yet the lively rhythms of the virelais lend themselves well to added percussion and instrumental ornamentation. In the *Confort* Machaut tells us that Orpheus tuned his harp and played and sung his lai, and in the *Voir dit* he suggests that a ballade could be performed by instruments. But it is not clear whether untexted lines are meant to be performed as an instrumental accompaniment or vocalized. The possibilities for performance are flexible rather than fixed, with varying choices for pitch range, instruments, and even the number of voices.

International celebrations in 1977 marked the six-hundredth anniversary of the death of Guillaume de Machaut, the master who celebrated ideal beauty and sought to perfect many intricate forms. While scholars continue to study aspects of his poetic and musical styles, of chronological problems, and of manuscript structure, increasing numbers of musical performances and recordings are bringing his music to an enthusiastic and ever-widening public.

BIBLIOGRAPHY

Sources. Vladimir Chichmaref, ed., *Guillaume de Machaut: Poésies lyriques,* 2 vols. (1909), the only source for *Vesci les biens;* Ernest Hoepffner, ed., *Oeuvres de Guillaume de Machaut,* 3 vols. (1908–1921), the major narrative poems except for the last two; Friedrich Ludwig, ed., *Guillaume de Machaut: Musikalische Werke,* 4 vols. (1926–1929, 1954), the most detailed description of the manuscripts; Louis de Mas-Latrie, ed., *La prise d'Alexandrie; ou, Chronique du roi Pierre Ier de Lusignan, par Guillaume de Machaut* (1877); Paulin Paris, ed., *Le Livre du voir-dit de Guillaume de Machaut* (1875); Leo Schrade, ed., *Polyphonic Music of the Fourteenth Century,* II and III, and *Commentary to Volumes II and III* (1956), with transcriptions in modern clefs; Prosper Tarbé, *Les oeuvres de Guillaume de Machault* (1849), the only source for editions of the *Dit de la rose* and the *Dit de la marguerite;* Nigel Wilkins, ed., *La louange des dames* (1972), a new edition of the collection of lyric poetry with an extensive bibliography.

Studies. François Avril, *Manuscript Painting at the Court of France* (1978), 84–98; Kevin Brownlee, *Poetic Identity in Guillaume de Machaut* (1984); William Calin, *A Poet at the Fountain* (1974); Jacqueline Cerquiglini, *"Un engin si soutil": Guillaume de Machaut et l'écriture au XIVe siècle* (1985); Jacques Chailley, "Du Cheval de Guillaume de Machaut à Charles II de Navarre," in *Romania,* **94** (1973); Madeleine Pelner Cosman and Bruce Chandler, eds., *Machaut's World* (1978), a volume of papers presented at a conference of the New York Academy of Sciences; Eustache Deschamps, *Oeuvres complètes,* Le Marquis de Queux de Saint-Hilaire and Gaston Raynaud, eds., 11 vols. (1878–1903). Deschamps's ballades CXXII, CXXIV, CXXVII (vol. I), and CCCCXLVII (vol. III) are about Machaut, and his *Art de Dictier* (vol. VII, 266–292) quotes his works.

Early Music, **5,** no. 4 (1977), is a special issue devoted to Machaut; *Guillaume de Machaut: Poète et compositeur* (Colloque—*Table ronde, Reims* [*19–22 avril, 1978*]) (1982); Margaret Hasselman and Thomas Walker, "More Hidden Polyphony in a Machaut Manuscript," in *Musica disciplina,* **24** (1970); Richard H. Hoppin, "An Unrecognized Polyphonic Lai of Machaut," in *Musica disciplina,* **12** (1958), and *Medieval Music* (1978), 353–432; Elizabeth Keitel, "The So-called Cyclic Mass of Guillaume de Machaut: New Evidence for an Old Debate," in *Musical Quarterly,* **68** (1982); Armand Machabey, *Guillaume de Machault 130?–1377,* 2 vols. (1955), the standard biography; Daniel Poirion, *Le poète et le prince* (1965), a masterly treatment of the lyric poetry; Gilbert Reaney, *Guillaume de Machaut* (1971), a brief but excellent survey of the music; James I. Wimsatt, ed., *The Marguerite Poetry of Guillaume de Machaut* (1970); Karl Young, ed., "The Dit de la Harpe of Guillaume de Machaut," in *Essays in Honor of Albert Feuillerat* (1943), 1–20.

SARAH JANE WILLIAMS

[See also **Ars Nova; Ballade; Cauda; Chant Royal; Charles of Orléans; Christine de Pizan; Complainte; Deschamps, Eustache; Dit; Duplum; French Literature; Froissart, Jehan; Hocket; Isorhythm; Jean, Duke of Berry; Lai, Lay; Ma Fin Est Mon Commencement; Mass; Melisma; Motet; Music, Western European; Musica Ficta; Romance of the Rose; Rondeau; Virelai.**]

MACHICOLATION, an opening in the floor, a projecting parapet, or the gallery atop a fortified building—between the corbels that support it or in the vault of a portal—through which molten lead, stones, and other missiles could be dropped on assailants. Machicolated battlements became common in European fortifications after the late twelfth century.

Machicolation over doorway, castle of Almodóvar del Rio, Spain. PHOTO: WIM SWAAN

GREGORY WHITTINGTON

[See also **Castles and Fortifications; Corbel.**]

MAC LONÂIN, FLANN (*d.* 896), Connacht poet. He is described in an annalistic entry (which was certainly retouched) as "the Vergil of the Scotic race, the leading poet of all the Irish, and the best poet in the Ireland of his time." His death (at the hands of the Déisi of Munster) is also entered wrongly under the year 918 [=920] in the Annals of the Four Masters, and this has caused great confusion among scholars. The genealogists state that Flann was seventh in descent from Guaire Aidne (*d.* 663), king of Connacht and a paragon of hospitality in Irish tradition.

Though only a few possible fragments of his compositions survive, Flann became the very model of the poet in the bardic tradition of the tenth century and later. His poems (or what were thought to be such) are cited as examples in a poet's manual, compiled perhaps in the tenth century and expanded in the eleventh. A number of demonstrably late poems (especially on place-name lore) are fathered on Flann, and he is credited with at least two posthumous poems, a poem of repentance and a poem on the antiquities of Slieve Aughty, which he recited when he was summoned back from the dead. These pieces form part of the legendary persona of the poet elaborated in the bardic schools in later centuries. That persona has many of the characteristics of the poets themselves and, to a degree, is normative in that it warns the poets against their professional vices.

According to a late medieval tale, Flann "was called the son of the demon, for his covetousness and surliness: for he never entered a house without causing loss therein." His poem of repentance, understandably, has him speak from hell. He is the central character in an allegory on the poet's calling in which Óengus in Mac Óc (in his aspect of god of poetry) appears to him in disguise and reaffirms the enduring value of the craft of poetry. Tradition represents Flann as the son of an aristocratic poetess, Laitheog of the northern Uí Néill, who is said to have advised her son to be fair and honorable as a poet and to be as generous in giving as he was greedy in taking. The same tradition asserts that Flann and his father, mother, and son are buried at the monastery of Terryglas in Ormond.

BIBLIOGRAPHY

Osborn J. Bergin, ed., "A Story of Flann mac Lonáin," in *Anecdota from Irish Manuscripts,* I (1907); Robin Flower, *The Irish Tradition* (1947), 67–72; Edward J. Gwynn, *The Metrical Lindsenchas,* III (1913), 304–313, 531–535; J. G. O'Keeffe, "Flann mac Lonáin in Repentant Mood," in J. Fraser, P. Grosjean, and J. G. O'Keeffe, eds., *Irish Texts,* I (1931), 22–24; R. Thurneysen, "Mittelirische Verslehren," in Whitley Stokes and Ernst Windisch, eds., *Irische Texte,* 3rd ser., I (1891).

DONNCHADH Ó CORRÁIN

[See also **Bard; Irish Literature.**]

MACROBIUS (Macrobius Ambrosius Theodosius) (*ca.* 360–*ca.* 435) is the name traditionally assigned to the author of three Late Latin works. Nothing is known with certainty about his life, but almost everything is known about his intense, idealistic, mystical view of life, for he reveals his personal vision of humanity throughout his writings. His "afterlife"—his influence on the Middle Ages—was immense; from 500 to 1500 he was more widely copied and studied than such giants as Homer and Plato. Contrary to his wishes, he was often read instead of Homer and Plato, his discussions of the classics used the same way plot summaries have been used by twentieth-century students.

He was probably named Macrobius Ambrosius Theodosius and was born on a fringe of the Roman Empire. Perhaps it was a Greek-speaking community in Egypt where those who tried to write Latin felt uneasy about their prose style, for in the preface to his *Saturnalia* he apologizes (needlessly—his is a superbly clear Latin) for his possible imprudence in daring to write Latin despite being born "under a different sky" and without the "native elegance of a Roman mouth."

Macrobius' were troubled times that allowed few men the luxury of a literary education. During his youth Emperor Valens died fighting the Goths; in his prime Alaric sacked Rome; in his old age Attila ravaged Italy; about the time of his death the Vandals sacked Rome. Yet, somehow—he hints that it was a result of his father's loving concern—he managed to obtain a remarkable education in the pagan rhetorical tradition, which stressed Cicero and Vergil.

Macrobius read widely, referring in his surviving works to about 90 Greek authors (especially Homer and Plato) and to about 115 Latin ones (especially Cicero, Ennius, Lucretius, Varro, and Vergil). His occasional blunders show that he sometimes relied too heavily on summaries, digests, commentaries, and other reference works of his own day. The many more times that his literary references are precisely on target, however, show that he must have frequently pored over the original sources, wisely and well.

In the 380's Macrobius probably had a son, Eustachius, for whom during the next two decades he wrote the grammar school textbook *On the Differences and Similarities Between Greek and Latin Verbs* (only a summary exists); the high school compendium of miscellaneous antiquarian information, chiefly literary criticism of Vergil, set in the form of a dialogue among twelve learned men at Rome during three days of the feast of Saturn and hence called the *Saturnalia* (most of this work is extant); and the college-level outline of Neoplatonic philosophy called *Commentary on the Dream of Scipio,* based on a work of that title by Cicero. This commentary exists in its entirety.

While writing these three works Macrobius was apparently pursuing one of the most successful political careers of his day, serving as vicar of Spain (399–400), proconsul of Africa (410), and finally grand chamberlain of the empire (422).

The above is a synthesis of recent scholarly conjectures—each reasonable, but each also open to reasonable doubt. For example, recent research has suggested placing his writing about half a century later than the 380's.

Despite such doubts, his place as schoolmaster at large to Western Europe, the author of three books that changed the mental world of the Middle Ages, remains unquestioned.

BIBLIOGRAPHY

Macrobius, *Opera,* J. Willis, ed., 2 vols. (1963, 2nd ed. 1970). Also: A. Cameron, "The Date and Identity of Macrobius," in *Journal of Roman Studies,* **56** (1966); William H. Stahl, "Macrobius, Ambrosius Theodosius," in *Dictionary of Scientific Biography,* IX (1974), 1–2; E. Tuerk, "À propos de la bibliothèque de Macrobe," in *Latomus,* **27** (1968), 433–435.

JAMES T. MCDONOUGH, JR.

[See also **Allegory; Classical Literary Studies; Latin Literature.**]

MADAᶜĪN, AL-. See **Ctesiphon.**

MADEIRA ISLANDS, a group of islands in the Atlantic, southwest of Portugal. They appear for the first time in the Medici Atlas of 1351 (Biblioteca Laurenziana, Florence), with Italian names. Thus, the largest island is called Legname (Italian for timber); the Portuguese later named it Madeira (which has the same meaning). Both names refer to the heavy forest then covering the island. Madeira was discovered shortly before 1351 by Genoese sailors in the service of Portugal under the command of the admirals Carlo and Bartolomeo Pessagno. The islands were not inhabited at that time. Settlement began in 1425 under the leadership of João Gonçalves Zarco and Tristão Vaz Teixeira, both nobles in the retinue of Prince Henry the Navigator. Henry the Navigator held Madeira in fief from the king of Portugal and in 1439 was given an exemption from the tithe and from paying duties on products shipped from the islands to Lisbon. The following year the Prince subinfeudated part of the main island to Tristão, who acquired the monopoly for licensing grain mills. All grants of land were made on the condition that the land be cleared and put under cultivation within five years. There were similar conditions for the grant of grazing land.

In 1446 Prince Henry gave the island of Porto Santo as a fief to Bartolomeo Perestrello, the son of an Italian immigrant, who was later the father-in-law of Christopher Columbus. Conduits were built on the island to irrigate the crops and to furnish water power for the mills. Salt was produced on the island, as well as a little iron. There was also some raising of livestock and production of resin, beeswax, and honey.

In 1452 sugar production began on Madeira. Diogo de Teive, a squire of Prince Henry, was given the right to build an *engenho,* a mill, for which the prince provided a press. Diogo was to give his lord one-third of the yield.

At about the same time foreign settlers appeared on Madeira. In 1457 a German was producing sugar and wine. In 1461, under Prince Ferdinand, the successor of Henry the Navigator, the island was exporting wine, sugar, lumber, grain, and flour. There was free trade with the areas under Portuguese sovereignty, but the settlers were forbidden to trade with other countries. Jews and Genoese, however, could export anything they bought and could lease agricultural lands. Exports at first were rather disorganized, especially in dealings with Flanders after 1468. The result was a fall in prices, which the prince remedied by giving an export monopoly to a group of Italian-Portuguese traders in 1470.

Bruges was the principal market for Madeira sugar. The accounts of the Bruges firm of Jacques Despars (1478–1499) describe this trade. At times agents of the company went directly to Madeira to buy sugar, shipping it to Lisbon and then to Bruges. An associate of Despars, Henri Nieulant (Portuguese: Henrique de Terra Nova), was the largest sugar grower on the island of Madeira after a Picard whose Portuguese name was Esmaraldo. The latter produced more than 15,000 arrobas (1 arroba = about 13 kilograms or 28.6 pounds) per year of sugar early in the sixteenth century. The total export quota was fixed at 120,000 arrobas by a royal ordinance in

1498. About this time the principal market for sugar moved from Bruges to Antwerp. Soon afterward Madeira lost its preeminence as a sugar producer, first to the Canary Islands, then to São Tomé and Brazil.

BIBLIOGRAPHY

O. Mus, "Du Brugse compagnie Despars op het einde van de 15e eeuw," in *Annales de la société d'émulation de Bruges pour l'étude de l'histoire et des antiquités de la Flandre,* **101** (1964); Virgínia Rau and Jorge de Macedo, *O açúcar da Madeira nos fins do século XV: Problemas de produção e comercio* (1962); Charles Verlinden, "Formes féodales et domaniales de la colonisation portugaise dans la zone atlantique aux XIVe et XVe siècles et spécialement sous Henri le Navigateur," in *Revista portuguesa de história,* **9** (1960), "Les débuts de la production et de l'exportation du sucre à Madère: Quel rôle y jouèrent les Italiens?" in *Studi in memoria di Luigi dal Pane* (1982), and "Madère et la Flandre à la fin du XVème et au début du XVIème siècle," in *Euripedes Simões de Paula: In Memoriam* (1983).

CHARLES VERLINDEN

[See also **Exploration by Western Europeans; Portugal; Trade, European; Trade, Regulation of.**]

MADRASA. Commonly translated as "theological college," the word madrasa (Turkish: *medrese;* Maghribi: *medersa*) derives from the Arabic verb *darasa,* meaning "to study." It denotes an Islamic building, usually erected under state patronage but often by private benefactors, which housed students of the orthodox Islamic sciences, principally law and theology, and the salaried staff that taught them there. Earlier, such religious instruction was given in the great mosques (such as al-Azhar in Cairo or al-Qarawiyyīn in Fēs), which always remained centers of intellectual life and were the medieval Islamic equivalent of universities. Ample literary evidence, however, also proves that the institution of the madrasa took shape in ninth- and tenth-century Khorāsān, with classes meeting in the houses of the most sought-after teachers. In the eastern Islamic world this movement prepared the ground for a chain of custom-built madrasas erected during the later eleventh century in the major cities of the Seljuk empire by the celebrated Iranian vizier Niẓām al-Mulk (*fl.* 1063–1092), and named *Niẓāmiyas* in his honor. The greatest of them was founded in 1065–1067 in Baghdad, a city that for over half a century had spearheaded an orthodox Sunni revival of which the madrasa was an expression. None of these *Niẓāmiyas* can now be identified with certainty, though two much-ruined structures at Rayy and Khargird have been claimed as Seljuk madrasas. Nevertheless, the cumulative evidence that the madrasa, both as an institution and as a building type, first reached full maturity in the Iranian world is overwhelming. Local domestic architecture and the Buddhist *vihara* have both been proposed as its architectural model; to judge by later Iranian examples (Madrasa-yi Imāmī, Iṣfahān; Ghiyyāthiya madrasa, Khargird), its basic form featured a central courtyard surrounded by four *īwāns* in cruciform disposition, a formula also used for contemporary mosques and caravansaries. Smaller madrasas were sometimes incorporated into major mosques (the Isfahan Jāmiᶜ, 1368).

This architectural schema accompanied the institution itself to the western territories of the Seljuk empire, though the *īwāns* were sometimes reduced to one or two and the courtyard roofed over (Bosra, Syria, 1136). In addition to lecture halls and cells for the students, Syrian madrasas of the twelfth and thirteenth centuries, of which almost 200 are recorded in the medieval sources, often had an oratory and an attached mausoleum for the founder. From Syria the fashion quickly spread to Egypt, encouraged by Saladin after 1171, following his victory over the heterodox Fatimids. In the following 150 years Cairo was embellished with a succession of the most ingeniously designed and most varied madrasas in the Islamic world. These included the earliest surviving (if irregular) four-*īwān* madrasa, the Ṣāliḥiya (1242), built on either side of a street; the first surviving cruciform four-*īwān* madrasa, the Ẓāhiriya (1262–1263); and large complexes including the founder's tomb, a mosque, minaret, and hospital, as well as a madrasa (complex of Qalāᵓūn, 1281). Sometimes lengthy endowment *(waqf)* inscriptions would spell out the source of the revenues which financed the madrasa (Mirjāniya, Baghdad, 1356).

Islamic law was early codified into four distinct systems, and at first it was customary for the precepts of only one such school *(madhhab)* to be taught at a given madrasa. By the thirteenth century, however, madrasas which catered for all four orthodox schools were being built (Mustanṣiriya, Baghdad, 1233–1234), and it was a natural corollary that four-*īwān* madrasas should allot an *īwān* to each *madhhab* for its own teaching and for prayer (Nāṣiriya, Cairo, 1303–1304). Cairene architects, grappling with a chronic shortage of space, proved adept at accommodating madrasas to unpromising and irregular sites, often emphasizing height rather than breadth, creating imposing, lavishly ornamented street facades for these buildings. Many Cairene madrasas are scarcely distinguishable from four-*īwān* mosques except by their smaller size and the student cells disposed in two tiers around the courtyard. These courtyards are not used for prayer and are thus typically much smaller than mosque courtyards.

No area of the Islamic world is more richly endowed in madrasas than Anatolia, with some 200 surviving examples datable before 1500. The thirteenth century was the golden age. Numerous types are known. Some comprise a single dome chamber or a single *īwān,* with rooms for study in the corners, but cramped four-*īwān* madrasas also occur. Especially diagnostic of this area and period is the two-minaret facade (several examples at Sivas and Erzurum). Anatolia, too, favored multiple foundations of which madrasas were simply one part; indeed, in the postmedieval period these became the rule there. After 1400 the Iranian world (which included Afghanistan and central Asia) lagged behind Anatolia in that its madrasas were simply much larger versions of their predecessors, though sometimes enlivened by large domed oratories.

Maghribi madrasas are best studied in the many examples erected during the fourteenth century by the Marinid dynasty in Fēs, Salé, and Marrakech. These dictated the subsequent development of the genre for the rest of the medieval period. Their dimensions are smaller than those of madrasas elsewhere. Their ground floor features a central courtyard, often marked by a pool and a fountain, with mosque, lecture halls, and an entrance vestibule grouped around it. Carved wooden panels, glazed tilework, and densely worked stucco decorate these facades; there are no *īwān*s. A narrow gallery on the first floor overlooks the courtyard and gives access to the cells. Some later madrasas boast up to a hundred rooms and rise to three stories in height.

ROBERT HILLENBRAND

[See also **Alp Arslan; Isfahan; Islamic Art and Architecture; Nizām al-Mulk; Philosophy and Theology, Islamic.**]

MADRIGAL, a poetic and musical form first employed in fourteenth-century Italy. The fourteenth-century madrigal (or *madrigale*) is not to be confused with the madrigal of the sixteenth and seventeenth centuries, with which it has no apparent connection. The musical texture is always polyphonic; usually for two voices, sometimes for three.

The earliest known madrigals come from northern Italian sources, probably in the 1320's. Texts may be pastoral, panegyric, amorous, satirical, contemplative, or moralistic. The form reached its maturity in the 1340's, when it typically appeared with two or three verses *(stanze)* of three lines, and a concluding *ritornello* of one or two lines. The musical structure is similar to that of other song forms of the time (for example, the *ballata* or *caccia*): a florid texted upper voice predominates, harmonized by a simpler lower voice, which may be texted or instrumental. The *stanze,* which usually reiterate the same musical material, are often in duple meter, while the *ritornello* is in triple.

Trecento madrigals appeared among the works of the Florentine composers Gherardello da Firenze, Lorenzo da Firenze, and Francesco Landini, and the northern Italians Bartolino da Padova, Jacopo da Bologna, and Ciconia, among others. The form declined in popularity after the 1360's, when it was largely superseded by the *ballata.* The last such madrigals appeared early in the fifteenth century.

BIBLIOGRAPHY

A. von Königslöw, *Die italienischen Madrigalisten des Trecento* (1940); Ettore Li Gotti, *La poesia musicale italiana del secolo XIV* (1944); W. Thomas Marrocco, "The Fourteenth-century Madrigal," in *Speculum,* **26** (1951).

MARCIA J. EPSTEIN

[See also **Ars Nova; Ballata; Caccia; Landini, Francesco; Music, Western European.**]

MÂEL SECHNAILL. See **Uí Néill.**

MAELGWN (Maglocunus) (*fl.* second quarter of the sixth century), king of Gwynedd, in northwest Wales, and a descendant of Cunedda—who is credited by Welsh tradition as the destroyer of Irish power in northwest Wales and as the founder of several dynastic lines, including the dynasty of Gwynedd. (That Cunedda was ruler of Gwynedd, which in the sixth century seems to have been accorded a primacy among the Welsh kingdoms, rests on reliable historical tradition.)

If Cunedda is seen as having a significant part in the establishment of the immediate post-Roman political framework, then Maelgwn's own career as described by Gildas seems to represent a re-Celticization of these models of power. As the fifth *tyrannus* of Gildas' list, he is accorded Gildas' particular attention. Educated by the church and having committed himself to Christianity, Maelgwn is portrayed as lapsing back into native barbarity, wresting and maintaining power by bloody dynastic struggle, extravagant gift-giving and feasting, and the patronage of native poets. His seat, by tradition, was Degannwy—a sea defense site—and this may imply the continued activity of Irish piracy and attempted settlement. Later hagiographical tradition remembers him in the same unfavorable light as King Arthur, but his hostile encounters with saints may be a fictional device to represent the lands and privileges given by the dynasty of Gwynedd to various monastic centers. He died in 547 according to the *Annales cambriae,* but an earlier date has also been suggested. In any event, Maelgwn seems to have left behind a strong kingdom and a stable dynasty capable of maintaining primacy for Gwynedd during the following centuries.

BIBLIOGRAPHY

Gildas, *De exidio Britonum,* in Michael Winterbottom, ed. and trans., *The Ruins of Britain and Other Works.* For most recent bibliographical information on Welsh history of this early period, see Wendy Davies, *Wales in the Early Middle Ages* (1982).

ANN DOOLEY

[See also **Cunedda Wledig; Wales: History.**]

MAESTÀ, a term derived from the Latin *majestas Mariae,* refers to a representation of the Virgin with saints and angels around her throne in majesty. Although occasionally applied to images with only a few figures, it is more often reserved for more elaborate presentations, such as Duccio di Buoninsegna's *Maestà* for the Siena cathedral (1308–1311); the 1315 fresco by Simone Martini in the Sala del Mappamondo (council chamber) of the Palazzo Pubblico, Siena; and the painting by his brother-in-law, Lippo Memmi (*fl.* 1317–1357), in the Palazzo del Popolo, San Gimignano (1317).

BIBLIOGRAPHY

Cesare Brandi, *Il restauro della "Maestà" di Duccio* (1959); E. T. de Wald, "Observations on Duccio's Maestà," in *Late Classical and Mediaeval Studies in Honour of Albert Mathias Friend, Jr.* (1955), 362–386; James H. Stubblebine, *Duccio di Buoninsegna and His School,* 2 vols. (1979); John White, *Art and Architecture in Italy: 1250–1400* (1966), 149–155.

JAMES H. STUBBLEBINE

[See also **Duccio di Buoninsegna (with illustration); Lippo Memmi; Simone Martini.**]

MAGHRIB, AL- (Arabic, "the West"), a term employed from the ninth century by the earliest extant Arabic authors to designate North Africa to the west of Egypt, together with al-Andalus or Muslim Spain. It is synonymous with Gharb, a term now applied to the region of the lower Sebou in Morocco and surviving in the name of the Portuguese province of the Algarve. Al-Maghrib, however, established itself as the principal geographical term for the area without ever losing its general application entirely.

In the tenth century al-Iṣṭakhrī distinguished between al-Maghrib al-Sharqī, or "eastern Maghrib," comprising North Africa west of Alexandria, and al-Maghrib al-Gharbī or "western Maghrib," meaning Muslim Spain. Ibn Ḥawqal, however, reserved al-Maghrib for North Africa to the west of Ifrīqiya, that is, for western Algeria and Morocco. In the twelfth century, al-Zuhrī described this region as al-Maghrib al-Awsaṭ, or "middle Maghrib," lying between Ifrīqiya and al-Sūs al-Aqṣā, "the furthest Sūs" on the edge of the ocean, a region of which the present valley of the Sous in southern Morocco is a truncated remnant. Early in the fourteenth century, Ibn ᶜIdhārī employed al-Maghrib for North Africa as distinct from al-Andalus, and al-Maghrib al-Aqṣā, "the furthest Maghrib," for the region beyond Ifrīqiya, essentially Morocco. This usage became normal. Al-Maghrib al-Awsaṭ, "the middle Maghrib," became a less common term for the region of modern Algeria north of the Sahara.

Al-Maghrib figured in medieval Arabic legend as the tail of the bird in whose likeness the inhabited world was formed after the Flood; as a land of marvels at the edge of the earth visited by Dhūᵓl-Qar-

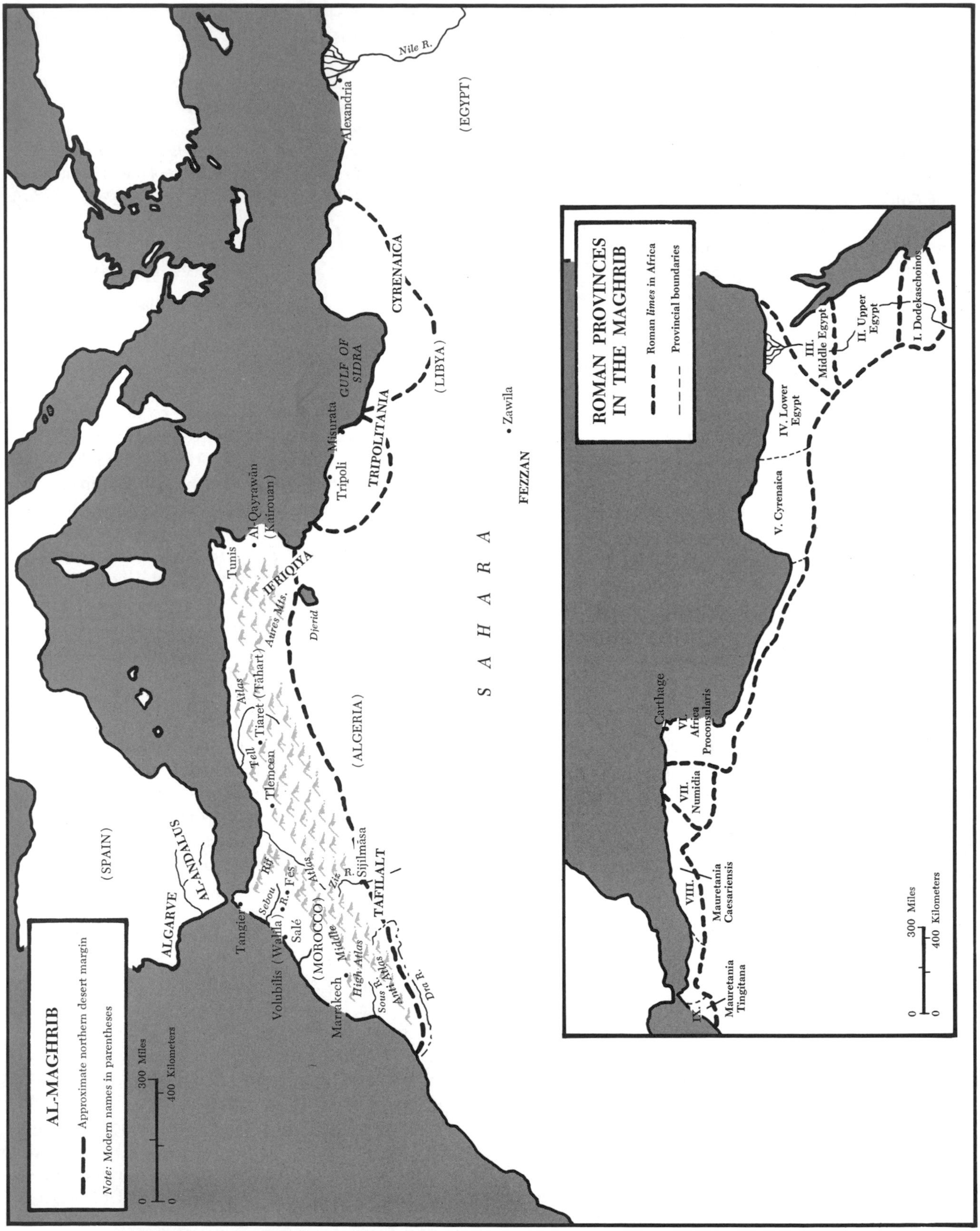
AL-MAGHRIB
Approximate northern desert margin
Note: Modern names in parentheses
0 300 Miles
0 400 Kilometers
ALGARVE
AL-ANDALUS
(SPAIN)
Tangier
Volubilis (Walila)
Salé
Marrakech
Fes
Sebou R.
Rif
Middle Atlas
(MOROCCO)
High Atlas
Anti Atlas
Sous R.
Dra R.
Ziz R.
Sijilmāsa
TAFILALT
Tlemcen
Tell
Tiaret (Tāhart)
Atlas
(ALGERIA)
Aures Mts.
Djerid
IFRIQIYA
Tunis
Al-Qayrawān (Kairouan)
Tripoli
Misurata
TRIPOLITANIA
GULF OF SIDRA
CYRENAICA
(LIBYA)
Alexandria
Nile R.
(EGYPT)
S A H A R A
FEZZAN
Zawila
ROMAN PROVINCES IN THE MAGHRIB
Roman limes in Africa
Provincial boundaries
I. Dodekaschoinos
II. Upper Egypt
III. Middle Egypt
IV. Lower Egypt
V. Cyrenaica
VI. Africa Proconsularis
Carthage
VII. Numidia
VIII. Mauretania Caesariensis
IX. Mauretania Tingitana
0 300 Miles
0 400 Kilometers

nayn, the Arabic name for Alexander the Great; and as the country of al-Khaḍir, the mysterious prophet sent by God to bring his word to fabulous nations. Geographical descriptions grew in length and accuracy with the arrival of travelers from the East, such as al-Ya^{c}qūbī in the ninth century and Ibn Ḥawqal in the tenth, and the appearance of Maghribi writers such as al-Bakrī in the eleventh century and al-Idrīsī in the twelfth. Uncertainty, however, persisted; Jabal Daran, the High Atlas, tended to be considered as the extremity of a Saharan range that terminated in Egypt, a notion perpetuated by early European maps.

Roman North Africa stretched along the Mediterranean coastal belt from Tangier to Misurata, east of which the Sahara comes to the sea around the Gulf of Sidra to form a natural frontier with Cyrenaica and Egypt. Running eastward from Salé on the Atlantic coast, the Roman *limes* (boundaries) excluded the Atlantic plains of Morocco, the Moroccan Atlas, and the steppes of western Algeria, but followed the edge of the desert in eastern Algeria and southern Tunisia to include the Aurès mountains and the oases of the Djerid. This easterly region, comprising the provinces of Numidia and Africa Proconsularis, was sparsely occupied by the Vandals from their base at Carthage after their conquest of North Africa in the fifth century, while the western provinces of Mauretania Tingitana and Mauretania Caesariensis were abandoned to their citizens and to Berber tribal chiefs. In the sixth century, the Byzantine reconquest converted the same region into the province of Africa. In turn, it passed into Arab hands (670–700) as the province of Ifrīqiya.

Tunis replaced Carthage, while the capital was transferred to Qayrawān (Kairouan), a newly founded inland city. From there the Arabs advanced westward through the former Mauretanian provinces to conquer Spain in 711. The whole of the Maghrib, "the West," was then ruled from Qayrawān until the rebellions surrounding the fall of the Umayyads in 750 left Muslim Spain independent and only Ifrīqiya remaining within the Abbasid empire. Western Algeria was dominated by Kharijite principalities at Tlemcen and Tāhart (Tiaret), while northern Morocco fell to the Idrisids, refugees from Arabia who moved from the Roman Volubilis (Walīla) to the new city of Fēs. Despite changes of dynasty, this political pattern, continuing that of the late classical period, prevailed until the mid eleventh century.

From Tripoli, however, the Arabs had advanced to Zawīla in the Fezzan, and from Tlemcen to the Tafilelt (Sijilmāsa, founded *ca.* 755), the Dra, and the Sous. As raiding gave way to trading, the Berbers of the northern Sahara opened routes across the desert for slaves, ivory, and gold, feeding these into the traffic by land and sea along the coastal route between Egypt and Spain which the Arab conquests had established. In the eleventh century this novel development led to the appearance of the Almoravids, Saharan Berbers who created a North African empire based in Marrakech. For the first time the Atlantic plains and the Moroccan Atlas were fully incorporated into the state system of North Africa. The empire of the Almoravids, indeed, transformed Morocco from a frontier region into the center of power in the Muslim West. Under the Almohads, Berbers of the High Atlas who succeeded the Almoravids in the twelfth century, this position was confirmed as the empire extended to embrace the whole of the Maghrib, including Muslim Spain. Although the empire disintegrated in the thirteenth century, the new political pattern it imposed upon North Africa survived until the end of the Middle Ages under the Marinids of Fēs, the Ziyanids of Tlemcen, and the Hafsids of Tunis.

The Saharan trade was only one aspect of a market economy in North Africa whose growth was stimulated by the concentrations of population and long-distance communications developing from the Arab conquests. Silver, copper, and iron were mined; new fruits and vegetables were introduced from the East; and a wide range of manufactures, especially textiles, was produced in both town and country. From the eleventh century, however, the requirement of Christian Europe for the products of the pastoral economy, wool and leather, brought a partial return to the conditions of the classical period, when North Africa supplied the primary products of the agricultural economy—grain, oil, and wine—to Rome. Tunis, which replaced Qayrawān as the capital of Ifrīqiya, resumed the role of Carthage as a great Mediterranean port.

MICHAEL BRETT

[See also **Almoravids; Atlas Mountains; Berbers; Geography, Islamic; Hafsids; Idrisids; Ifrīqiya; Marinids; Qayrawān, Al-; Tunis.**]

MAGIC AND FOLKLORE, ARMENIAN. In his *History of the Armenians,* Movsēs Xorenac^{c}i (late Sasanian period) portrays Semiramis, the Mother

 MAGIC AND FOLKLORE, ARMENIAN

Goddess, as a Medea-like witch who attempts unsuccessfully to revive Ara the Beautiful (equivalent to the dying and rising Attis) through spells; later, she casts her talismanic beads into the sea to escape capture. These references to the earliest magic in Armenia may be unreliable, but the discovery of magical implements at sites such as Hattushash, the capital of the Hittite empire, and the abundance of magical texts in Mesopotamia to the south, indicate that the earliest Armenians lived in a milieu where magic was common.

From the sixth century B.C. to the seventh century A.D., Armenia flourished in the Iranian political and cultural world. The Zoroastrian vision of a cosmic struggle between divine and demonic forces deeply impressed the Armenian view of the supernatural, and Iranian terms are common in the Armenian magical vocabulary.

From the fourth century A.D., when the Armenian Arsacid dynasty converted to Christianity, the texts of the new faith came to be adapted to magical purposes. Saints battled old demons, and connections with Anatolian Greek beliefs are apparent.

Later still, Armenian spells are seen to include Muslim phrases in Persian and Arabic. Magic squares, arcane symbols (usually Arabic numbers and sticklike figures terminating in tiny loops), and certain terms such as "talisman" *(t^{c}əlsəmen),* Greek in origin, are introduced through the intermediary of Muslim magic.

Magical texts were used until modern times to gain esoteric wisdom or to achieve practical, desired ends. They were to be studied with single-minded concentration, accompanied by prayers to certain angels on certain days and the mystical chanting of sets of letters, especially vowels (as in Greco-Roman magic).

The most common text (found in manuscripts with very considerable variations) goes under a variety of names, the most common being "The Book of the 6,000-Year Cycle" *(Vec^{c} hazareak)* and "The Seven Letters" *(Eōt^{c}nagreank^{c}).* The latter refers to the vowels used in magical chants, the former to the 12,000-year cosmological theory of the Zoroastrians, which is broken in half by the incursion of the Destructive Spirit, Ahriman, into the world. Christians apparently substituted the birth of Christ for this climactic event.

The manuscripts of this text contain information on such topics as the Armenian alphabet, music, mathematics, astronomy, medicine, and the calendar. Often a chain of authors and transmitters is given, starting in biblical antiquity (Abraham, Solomon) and proceeding through a list of Armenian scholars (the philosopher David the Invincible, the scientist Anania Širakac^{c}i).

Other magical texts are talismanic and apotropaic in nature. A number are directed against Al, the demon of puerperal fever, who is overcome by St. Sisianos or St. Cyprian. Such texts, with invocations and prayers framing a *historiola,* or short tale of magical potency (drawn, often, from hagiographical literature), are often written on a scroll and illustrated: The resplendent saint, looking like a young Roman soldier, confronts the black, bloblike demon, which holds a human windpipe or entrails in its primitive claw.

Another manuscript, abundantly if primitively illustrated, gives in question-and-answer form a catalog of demons together with spells (in Arabic and gibberish) against their particular diseases.

The earliest Armenian printed book, *Urbat^{c}agirk^{c}* (Venice, 1512), contains prayers to cure the "serpent-afflicted" *(awjahar).* Such affliction was apparently considered a supernatural calamity. Ethnographers working in the nineteenth and twentieth centuries recorded a number of spells for "wolf-binding" *(gaylakap).* These spells are closely similar to the Zoroastrian prayers or spells against the wolf *(nīrang).* The Iranians regarded the wolf as a demonic creature.

Traces of the *gaylakap* have been seen in the *Book of Lamentation* of the tenth-century Armenian poet Grigor Narekac^{c}i; Grigor's own compositions are used as talismans against diverse evils. The writer Simeon of Ałjnik^{c} mentions among magical acts the interpretation of dreams *(erazahan).* This practice may go back to the cult of the Zoroastrian god Tir in Armenia, whose temple was called "dream-interpreting" *(Erazamoyn).*

The methods *(dromena)* of Armenian magic include hydromancy and lecanomancy, the preparation and consumption of various vile mixtures, and the weaving of stitches in the clothes of one against whom a spell is directed. Other acts are less precisely known: "divination with hops" *(garənkec^{c}ut^{c}iwn),* "extinguishing [?] a lamp" (*čragamah*[*r*?]), "burying leaven" *(xmorat^{c}ał).* "And Satan gives yet other, innumerable evils to do," notes one text.

As for Armenian folklore, the motifs conform generally to the recorded range of Indo-European themes. Although Armenian folktales have only been written down in modern times, many motifs and characters are clearly of great antiquity. A good example is the young hero Mher in the epic of Sasun, who is the ancient god Mithra.

The "mighty ones" *(kʿajkʿ),* mentioned by Movsēs Xorenacʿi, are still believed by some to feast immortally in their mountain halls, while nymphs *(yaweržaharsunkʿ)* bathe and dragons *(višap)* emerge from rivers to kidnap maidens or devour animals. (The great stone steles found near rivers and elsewhere in Armenia are called *višap* by the Armenians and *aždahā* "[evil] dragon" by the Kurds.) Medieval Armenians believed supernatural winged dogs called *yaralēzkʿ* descended to the battlefield to revive fallen heroes by licking their wounds; those less fortunate knew their lives were over when the "Inscriber" *(Groł)* came to take their souls away. Wicked *ayskʿ* and *hnarkʿ* wait to blow or snatch the unwary traveler off a bridge and drag him into the depths; demons called *dew* deviously substitute their own spawn as changelings for human children.

The ancient *genius loci* of classical Armenian texts, the *šahapet,* reappears in modern Armenian as the *švod,* who lives in the walls of houses and complains when housewives send it out for the warm months with the bang of a broom and the words *Švod durs, Adar ners!* ("Out with the *švod,* in with March!").

BIBLIOGRAPHY

Mardiros H. Ananikian, "Armenian Mythology," in John A. MacCulloch, ed., *The Mythology of All Races,* VII (1925); J. A. Boyle, "Mher in the Carved Rock," in *Journal of Mithraic Studies,* **1** (1976); Moses Khorenatsʿi, *History of the Armenians,* Robert W. Thomson, trans. (1978); Jean-Pierre Mahé, "Échos mythologiques et poésie orale dans l'oeuvre de Grigor Narekacʿi," in *Revue des études arméniennes,* n.s. **17** (1983); J. R. Russell, *Zoroastrianism in Armenia* (in press), chaps. 8 and 14; Artin K. Shalian, trans., *David of Sassoun: The Armenian Folk Epic in Four Cycles* (1964); Leon Surmelian, *Apples of Immortality: Folktales of Armenia* (1968); J. S. Wingate, "The Scroll of Cyprian: An Armenian Family Amulet," in *Folk-Lore,* **41** (1930).

JAMES R. RUSSELL

[See also **Anania Širakacʿi; Armenia: History of; Armenian Literature; Armenian Saints; David of Sasun; David the Invincible; Grigor Narekacʿi, St.; Movsēs Xorenacʿi; Zoroastrianism.**]

MAGIC AND FOLKLORE, BYZANTINE. The study of Byzantine folklore presents modern scholars with particularly difficult problems. More than any other medieval civilization, Byzantium was dominated by conservative and rhetorical literary traditions. Its surviving sources reflect learned court conventions to an unparalleled degree and mirror a society bound up in the preservation of antiquarian ceremonial and custom. The body of extant folk literature is small, and many sources available to the student of Western medieval folklore, such as law codes, penitentials, and church records, either do not exist or do not reflect popular customs. Much of the surviving vernacular literature is learned satire or recasting of ancient works.

In consequence, studies of Byzantine folk traditions have generally been restricted to a few approaches. The Byzantine role in the transmission of ancient and Oriental motifs to the West has been investigated, and the poetry (which appears to derive from an oral epic tradition) has been extensively studied. A fruitful new methodology has been the study of Byzantine ritual in the context of modern survivals; however, such studies have argued for the development of literary forms and analytical models rather than the preservation of historical information. Much of the evidence for Byzantine folklore survives in hagiography, hymns, and scattered texts and has yet to be systematically studied. Byzantine magic beliefs present similar problems: copyists transmitted ancient treatises on various kinds of sorcery and divinations, and chroniclers ascribed the appellation of magician to controversial figures. But this evidence for "learned magic" must be treated carefully and distinguished from scattered sources suggesting the survival of popular beliefs in magic.

MAGIC

The Byzantine world inherited from antiquity a pervasive complex of magic beliefs and practices ranging from Neoplatonic astrological speculations to the popular use of amulets and charms. Although most varieties of magic and sorcery were condemned in ecclesiastical and imperial legislation, ample evidence documents the survival of interest in magic throughout Byzantine history. The tradition of learned magic centered on astrology and various kinds of divination preserved in technical treatises. The extent of Byzantine interest is evidenced in the large number of extant manuscripts of Greek astrological works. In the early Byzantine period Julianos of Laodicea, Hephaestion of Thebes, and Paul of Alexandria summarized Roman astrology; an astrological school still existed in Alexandria in 564. John Lydus (sixth century) excerpted their works and in-

 MAGIC AND FOLKLORE, BYZANTINE

cluded material from the *Tetrabiblos* of Ptolemy in his treatise *Peri Diosemeion.* The manuscripts of the ninth-century patriarch Leo the Mathematician included a codex of Paul of Alexandria, and the emperors Leo VI and Constantine VII incorporated astrology into their encyclopedic works. Compilations based on earlier writings were made in the eleventh and twelfth centuries by Eleutherios Zebalenos, Joannes Katameros, and Constantine Manasses, and a defense of astrology survives in a letter of Emperor Manuel I Komnenos. Although some late Byzantine astronomers condemned astrology (for example, Theodoros Meliteniotes, *ca.* 1310–*ca.* 1388), manuscript evidence documents the existence of a fourteenth-century school of astrologers under Joannes Abramios.

Other traditions of ancient prophecy retained their popularity throughout Byzantine history. Copyists preserved treatises on divination by mirrors (catoptromancy), water (hydromancy), divining dishes (lekanomancy), sand (geomancy), and dream interpretation *(oneirokritika).* Leo VI commented on oracles, and Constantine VII's encyclopedic work contained material from an anonymous compendium of prophetic and magic learning of the seventh or eighth century. Twelfth-century chroniclers noted the political importance of such oracles and of numerological and alphabetic predictions. Late ancient compendiums of astrology, medicine, and magic (which also included treatises on plants and stones) were Christianized in the early Byzantine period, and although most manuscripts are post-Byzantine, scattered references indicate that some (*Hermippas,* the *Koiranides*) circulated in the middle and late Byzantine periods.

At a popular level, belief in herbs, charms, and spells seems to have been widely accepted throughout the empire. Magic amulets, identified by their reference to Medusa and the inclusion of the word *hystera* (womb) in their formulas, and typical of a popular fertility spell of late antiquity, have been found from as late as the twelfth century. Theodore of Studios praised his mother for not making use of standard female charms and spells in the eighth century. Hagiographical texts of the middle Byzantine period refer to herbal magic *(pharmaka)* in popular use; and magicians *(magoi),* major rivals to saints in early Byzantine texts, continue to be mentioned as efficacious manipulators of spells. Papyri document the everyday use of magic only for early Byzantine Egypt, but it is probable that, as in the West, recourse to folk magic was constant but undocumented.

Modern scholars have frequently condemned Byzantine society as superstitious and preoccupied with magic, but Byzantine scholarly interest in astrology and divination must be seen as part of an attempt to preserve late ancient secular learning. Although church and imperial legislation frequently condemned all such study as demonology, even opponents of astrology and oracles considered them theurgy rather than sorcery and drew distinctions between different aspects of the tradition. Thus Michael Psellos expressed doubt in the eleventh century about the predictive powers of astrology, but wrote a treatise on the symbolic properties of stones. Anna Komnena, explaining her father's opposition to the astrologer Symeon Seth, was careful to distinguish his predictions from magic and did not doubt their efficacy, though she thought them too dangerous for the ignorant public (*Alexiad* 6.7).

Accusations of actual magic practice were relatively rare and (as in the West) tied to political and religious crises. The ninth-century iconoclast patriarch John the Grammarian was accused of sorcery, in part because of his secular learning, and a tenth-century abbot (Santabarenos) was called a magician by his monastic enemies. The only sustained campaign against magic was carried out by the partriarchate in the fourteenth century, during the civil wars and the disintegration of the empire. The reputation of the Byzantine empire as a superstitious society derived from its preservation of ancient astrology and divination and from the ambivalence of chroniclers and scholars who were unsure whether it represented science or demonology. We have no concrete evidence for excessive fear or practice of what contemporaries considered to be magic arts.

FOLKLORE

Byzantium's most important contribution to Western folklore was probably the transmission of popular classical and Oriental literary motifs, often reshaped by Byzantine copyists. The *Physiologus,* a late ancient fable collection that formed the basis for medieval bestiaries, was translated to Western literature from early Byzantine manuscripts (fourth–sixth century) in its original form, but the life and fables of Aesop were developed into a highly diversified tradition in Greek and Syriac before they were passed on to the West. A version of the Indian Bodisattva legend that reached Byzantium in the early

 MAGIC AND FOLKLORE, BYZANTINE

Middle Ages was narrated as the lives of Sts. Barlaam and Josaphat by an author with a recognizable interest in theology and the defense of icons, traditionally identified as John of Damascus (eighth century). This version was widely circulated in the West, as were the Sanskrit *Panchatantra* (reworked as the story of Stephanites and Ichnelates and attributed to the eleventh-century author Symeon Seth) and *Syntipas* (the Sindbād legend), which also was transmitted to the West through Hebrew versions. The Faust theme appeared first in Byzantine texts of the seventh century, and apocalyptic writers of the same period were responsible for the translation into Greek of the Syriac apocalypse of Pseudo-Methodius and the composition of the Vision of Daniel. In these forms apocalyptic visions were spread throughout the medieval world. Finally, some of the most popular saints' legends in the medieval West had Byzantine origins. The cults of Sts. Nicholas, George, and Theodore were especially popular, and Greek hagiographical literature was widely diffused from the early Middle Ages, when the Greek communities in Rome and Italy served as important centers of transmission.

The most important survivals of Byzantine folk literature lie in the remnants of its heroic cycles and epics. Some modern scholars, notably Henri Grégoire, have argued that the ninth and tenth centuries were a "heroic age" in Byzantium, when warfare against the Arabs provided the setting for an oral epic tradition. Heroic songs surviving from later periods (the Armouris song, with a manuscript tradition from the fifteenth century, and the songs of the sons of Andronikos, dating to the seventeenth century) are believed by these scholars to have their genesis in the fall of Amorion (838) and in the deeds of the tenth-century general Andronikos Doukas.

The most important work is the poem *Digenis Akritas,* often designated the "Byzantine national epic." *Digenis Akritas* epitomizes the heroic legends of the Byzantine-Arab border in the birth and exploits of its central character, Basilios Digenis ("Double race") Akritas ("Border warrior"). Modern research has shown that the extant poem, in diverse versions dating as early as the fourteenth century, is a fusion of two earlier works. The first part ("The Song of the Emir") is an independent epic, the background of which may be located in events of the ninth- or tenth-century Cappadocian border. It narrates the kidnapping of a Byzantine general's daughter by an Arab emir, rescue attempts by her brothers, the eventual conversion of the emir to Christianity, his marriage, his emigration to Cappadocia, and the birth of Digenis. A second part, a more episodic and romantic description of the exploits of the adult Digenis, probably took shape in the eleventh century, whereas the present composite poem may have been compiled in the twelfth century. Most scholars believe that *Digenis Akritas* derives from an oral epic tradition and that the author of the final composition wrote in a literary style. The history and dates of characters and events, the relation of popular and literary traditions in the poem, and the relation of the extant versions of the epic are still debated.

The vernacular songs *(tragoudia)* of the late Byzantine period include a group of "Akritic" ballads celebrating further deeds of Digenis, early love songs, political songs, and laments *(threnoi)* over Byzantine losses, especially of Constantinople. Although the extant works were generally composed using vernacular forms and language, they were based on traditional material that often remained unrecorded until the transcriptions of nineteenth-century ballad collectors. Recent scholarship has demonstrated a high degree of continuity between some Byzantine genres and modern survivals, and has shown the extent to which literary sources may be inseparable from popular folklore. Thus the ritual lament *(threnos)* has remained a part of Greek funerary practices from ancient times to the present, and its oral tradition is reflected in the works of Byzantine hymn writers as well as in modern ballads. Special laments for the loss of cities and the lament of the Virgin (embodied in the liturgy for Good Friday, the *epitaphios threnos*) also derive from Byzantine ritual, and scholars have argued for the antiquity of political songs and a ritual children's song, the *Chelidonismata.* The evidence for a Byzantine tradition of folk poetry is, however, too sparse for any conclusions to be drawn about its specific contents, performance, or transmission before the late Byzantine period.

Broadly defined, Byzantine folklore may be found in religious tradition. The cult of the Virgin developed especially in Byzantium in the late sixth century, when, as the *Theotokos,* she was adopted as the symbol of the city of Constantinople. Western Mariology drew from this devotion, and an extensive literature records Byzantine veneration. In the middle Byzantine period the Virgin was especially identified with the church at Blachernae, where she was believed to make a miraculous appearance each Friday evening. A second focus of special devotion was the relic of the True Cross, discovered by Constantine's empress Helena and recovered from Persian captivity by the seventh-century emperor Heraklios. Apocalyptic literature reflects a recurring millennialism and anticipation of the antichrist in Byzantium: a particular feature of this genre was the development of a legend of the last Roman emperor and the circumstances in which he would hand over his crown. A large corpus of saints' lives provides evidence for popular belief in the devil, in varieties of demonic possession, and in the miraculous properties of icons and relics of holy men and women, including Christ and the Virgin.

Imperial legends and prophecies were especially common in Byzantine folklore. As founder of its capital, Constantine was a natural focus, but later rulers, especially the seventh-century Heraklios, the iconoclasts Leo III and Constantine V, and the ninth-century rulers Basil I and Michael III inspired recurring legends emphasizing their antecedents, prophesying their rise to the throne, and on occasion predicting their return. Here too, recent scholarship has argued for a continuum between literary sources and popular belief, and modern folklore suggests the longevity of Byzantine traditions.

BIBLIOGRAPHY

Folklore. Hans-Georg Beck, *Geschichte der byzantinischen Volksliteratur* (1971), and *Kirche und theologische Literatur im byzantinischen Reich* (1959) (reference works with full bibliographies).

Studies. Margaret Alexiou, *The Ritual Lament in Greek Tradition* (1974); Roderick Beaton, *Folk Poetry of Modern Greece* (1980); Averil Cameron, "The Theotokos in Sixth Century Constantinople: A City Finds Its Symbol," in *Journal of Theological Studies,* **29** (1978); Michael Jeffreys, "The Nature and Origins of the Political Verse," in *Dumbarton Oaks Papers,* **28** (1974).

Magic. Peter Brown, "Sorcery, Demons, and the Rise of Christianity: From Late Antiquity into the Middle Ages," in his *Religion and Society in the Age of St. Augustine* (1972); Herbert Hunger, *Die hochsprachliche profane Literatur der Byzantiner* II (1970), 221–284 (with bibliography); J. Grosdidier de Matons, "Psellos et le monde de l'irrationel," in *Travaux et Mémoires* (Centre de Recherche d'Histoire et Civilisation Byzantine), **6** (1976); David Pingree, "The Astrological School of John Abramius," in *Dumbarton Oaks Papers,* **25** (1971).

DOROTHY ABRAHAMSE

[See also **Alchemy; Angel/Angelology; Astrology/Astronomy; Byzantine Literature; Digenis Akritas; Fables; Hagiography, Byzantine; Magic, Bookish; Mysticism, Byzantine; Translation and Translators, Byzantine; Witchcraft, European.**]

MAGIC AND FOLKLORE, ISLAMIC. Early Islam inherited a considerable corpus of folklore and magic from the pagan Arabian environment in which it was born. The pre-Islamic Arabs believed the world to be inhabited by beings known as jinn (sing., *jinnī,* perhaps related to the Latin *genius*). The jinn and related beings, such as *ghīlān* (sing., *ghūl*) and *ᶜafārīt* (sing., *ᶜifrīt*), were thought to live within natural objects, such as dunes, rocks, pools, trees, and caves, and were comparable with the nymphs, fairies, and satyrs of Europe. These creatures, whose basic substance was fire rather than clay (as in the case of humans) or light (as in the case of angels), were normally imperceptible to the senses but could appear in a variety of forms. Like the Greek daemon, the jinn were believed to inspire poets. They were sometimes venerated as demigods.

The principal intermediaries between ordinary mortals and the jinn in pre-Islamic Arabia were the *kahana* (sing., *kāhin*) or *kuhhān* (diviners; compare the Hebrew *kohen,* priest). A person possessed by the jinn was referred to as *majnūn,* which also meant "mad." The *kahana* spoke in rhymed prose (Arabic: *sajᶜ*) and swore strange oaths. One of the accusations Muḥammad most bitterly resented was that he was a poet or *kāhin* possessed by jinn—or worse, that he was a magician *(sāḥir)* or one under a magic spell *(masḥūr).* Although the Prophet rejected being identified with any of these, he accepted the existence of magic *(siḥr)* and of jinn—some of whom were thought to be believing Muslims.

According to the Koran (2:102), magic was introduced to humanity by devils at the time of King Solomon and (in Babylon) by the angels Hārūt and Mārūt, who clearly specified to all whom they taught that they were offering a temptation. The connection between magic and Babylon is very ancient and is expressed in the Bible (see Isaiah 47). In the koranic account the occult knowledge taught by Hārūt and Mārūt allows practitioners to "cause division between man and wife." However, those who practice such arts "injure thereby no one except by Allah's permission." The verse goes on to deny magicians a portion in the world to come and warns that "surely evil is the price for which they sell their souls." In the koranic view, magic does only harm.

The Koran alludes to a variety of magical practices. In the next-to-last sura, the believer seeks refuge "from the evil of the female blowers upon knots," a reference to a form of witchcraft whereby curses were muttered over magical knots onto which the witch spat. According to Muslim tradition, Mu-

MAGIC AND FOLKLORE, ISLAMIC

ḥammad became ill when a spell of this sort was cast upon him by one of his Jewish enemies in Medina.

The Koran (Suras 2:219 and 5:90) also castigates divination by the casting of magical arrows as lots, a practice known as *maysir.* Such divining arrows are condemned as "Satan's handiwork." Later Islam did, however, permit certain types of divination that sought help from Allah in choosing the best course *(istikhāra),* either through dream incubation *(ruʾyā),* whereby one goes to sleep seeking a dream that will reveal a sign, which some traditions attribute to the authority of the Prophet, or through drawing lots *(qurʿa).*

Because of the overwhelmingly negative depiction of magic in the Koran, official Islam tended to forbid it outright, under penalty of death. The great jurist Mālik ibn Anas (*d.* 795) was of the opinion that a person convicted of practicing black magic should not be given the chance to repent (as he also held in cases of heresy). Nevertheless, there were countertraditions on the permissibility of magic in some forms. Muḥammad is reported to have permitted the use of spells (*ruqan;* sing., *ruqya*) for treating certain diseases and as an antidote to poison and the evil eye. Although the Prophet did not employ amulets as such, his use of religious formulas from the Koran paved the way for their use. Certain koranic passages were particularly popular for charms, including Sura 2:255 (the "Throne Verse"), Suras 113 and 114 ("The Two Preservers"), and Sura 36 *(Sura yā sīn).* Amulets have been so popular in the Muslim world since medieval times that they constitute perhaps the most ubiquitous class of Middle Eastern jewelry.

At a fairly early stage of medieval Islamic civilization there developed a concept of authorized and unauthorized (that is, white and black) magic. Ibn al-Nadīm's tenth-century bibliographical encyclopedia, the *Fihrist,* devotes an entire chapter to magic and the very extensive current literature on the subject. In the *Fihrist* authorized magic is characterized as "the praiseworthy system" *(al-ṭarīqa al-maḥmūda),* while unauthorized magic is called "the blameworthy system" *(al-ṭarīqa al-madhmūma).* Citing practitioners of both types, the *Fihrist* explains magic as the harnessing of devils, jinn, and spirits to do a person's bidding. Seventy spirits who attended Solomon are mentioned by name; he is said to have adjured them and imposed a covenant upon them.

The great philosopher of history Ibn Khaldūn (*d.* 1406) devotes a lengthy chapter to the subject of magic in his *Muqaddima* (Prolegomenon [to the study of history]). Following the philosophers, he tries to offer a rationalistic explanation of magic. He makes the distinction between true magic and that performed with talismans (*ṭilasmāt;* sing., *ṭilasm*). In the former the magician needs no aids, for the magical powers emanate from the soul. The other sort of magic employs talismans that seek the aid of the spirituality of the stars, the temper of the spheres, and the properties of numbers. Ibn Khaldūn also recognizes a form of magic that consists of the power of suggestion. In this type of magic, which he calls *shaʿwadha* (or *shaʿbadha*), observers are made to perceive things that are not really there.

Ibn Khaldūn provides a great deal of information on types of magic practiced in his day. Among these is "letter magic" *(sīmiyāʾ),* which was very popular among the Sufis. This form of magic employs the supposed mystical properties inherent in words and letters and resembles the cabalists' manipulation of letters and numbers. One branch of letter magic that became very well developed in the later Middle Ages was *zāʾiraja* (perhaps derived from the Persian *zāycha,* "horoscope"), a form of divination employing tables to carry out magical calculations. The *zāʾiraja* came to be regarded as a science and was the subject of several well-known books, the most famous of which was a treatise by the North African mystic al-Sabtī (*fl.* twelfth or thirteenth century).

The magical sciences par excellence, of course, were alchemy *(al-kīmīyāʾ)* and astrology *(aḥkām al-nujūm),* both of which appeared in Islam very early, probably in Umayyad times. Of the two, alchemy enjoyed the more scientific reputation and was considered to be less at odds with Islamic religious tenets. The intellectual preeminence accorded to alchemy is clear from its popular designation *al-ṣināʿa* (the Art).

Magic and supernatural spirits occupy a prominent place in medieval Muslim folklore. The *Thousand and One Nights (Alf layla wa-layla)* is replete with tales involving spirits of all sorts: jinn, *ghīlān, ʿafārīt,* and *shayāṭīn.* In it some of these creatures have developed aspects that go beyond the simple nature spirits of ancient Arabian legend. The *ʿifrīt* often appears as a giant ogre, and the *ghūl* as a vampirelike creature that feeds upon the dead (whence the French *goule* and English "ghoul").

Magical accoutrements such as wonder-working rings, lamps, and stones, magic mirrors in which can be seen things that are far off, and flying carpets and other marvelous vehicles are all regular features in the *Nights.* The magical elements in this popular cycle of tales, which in its earliest form was current in the Muslim world by the late ninth century, have a variety of sources, both indigenous and non-Arab. As a general rule, in those stories where the supernatural beings act of their own accord, an Iranian origin may be assumed. In the Arab tales, particularly those from Egypt of the High and later Middle Ages, the spirits are usually subject to a charm or some magic object, acting only at the will of its possessor. Another magical element that seems to be genuinely Arab—although it exists throughout world folklore—is that of metamorphosis of humans into animals *(maskh)*. The Koran contains an allusion to Jews who desecrated the Sabbath and were transformed into apes (Sura 2:65). There were also traditions attributed to the Prophet about people who had been transformed into riding animals, pigs, and even mice. Metamorphosis was a common motif in Sufi legends from North Africa in the later Middle Ages. In the Sufi tales holy men changed either themselves or others into animals.

Some of the magic elements in Islamic lore go back ultimately to Greek sources. A number of the Sinbad stories in the *Thousand and One Nights,* for example, can be traced directly to Pseudo-Callisthenes. Indeed, the Alexander romance attributed to Callisthenes was available in the medieval Arab world in several different recensions.

Most of the magical elements found in the *Nights* are also found to a greater or lesser degree in other works of popular literature from the medieval Muslim world, such as the romances of ᶜAntar (*Sīrat ᶜAntar,* Life of ᶜAntar) and Dhu'l-Himma *(Sīrat al-amīra Dhāt al-Himma wa-waladihā ᶜAbd al-Wahhāb,* Life of Princess Dhāt al-Himma and her son ᶜAbd al-Wahhāb), and the *Aḥādīth al-Baṭṭāl* (Tales of al-Baṭṭāl).

Because of the highly traditional nature of Islamic society, which was less immediately penetrated by the Renaissance and the Industrial Revolution, these magical and folkloric beliefs remained essentially intact in many sectors until modern times.

BIBLIOGRAPHY

Nikita Elisséeff, *Themes et motifs des Mille et une nuits* (1949); Toufic Fahd, *La divination arabe* (1966); Mia Gerhardt, *The Art of Story-telling* (1963); Ibn Khaldūn, *The Muqaddimah,* Franz Rosenthal, trans., 3 vols. (1958, 2nd ed. 1967), III, 156–280; Ibn al-Nadīm, *The Fihrist,* Bayard Dodge, trans. (1970), II, 725–733; Edward W. Lane, *The Manners and Customs of the Modern Egyptians* (1923), 228–234, 270–282; Duncan B. Macdonald, *The Religious Attitude and Life in Islam* (1965), 95–156; H. Ritter, "Picatrix, ein arabisches Handbuch hellenistischer Magie," in *Vorträge, Bibliothek Warburg* (1921–1922), 94–124; Manfred Ullmann, *Die Natur- und Geheimwissenschaften im Islam* (1972); Edvard A. Westermarck, *Ritual and Belief in Morocco,* 2 vols. (1926, repr. 1968).

NORMAN A. STILLMAN
YEDIDA K. STILLMAN

[See also **Alchemy; Astrology/Astronomy, Islamic; Jinn; Khaldūn, Ibn; Thousand and One Nights; Witchcraft, Islamic.**]

MAGIC AND FOLKLORE, JEWISH. The efflorescence of medieval Jewish folklore and magic constitutes one of the most remarkable phenomena in the cultural history of the Jews. The close of the fifth century coincided with the final redaction of the Talmud, which is not only a vast commentary on the Old Testament but also a magnum opus presenting the folklore, wit, wisdom, and scholarship of the Jews accumulated over many generations. The talmudic-midrashic literature consists of two main disciplines: the halakhah, or Jewish law, and the Haggadah, or narrative sections (in Hebrew or frequently in the Aramaic folk vernacular). The latter embraces a wide range of folklore genres, such as myths, legends, fables, hagiographic exempla, folktales, historical anecdotes, jests and drolleries, proverbs, riddles, various aspects of folk religion, magic, popular astrology, angelology, demonology, amulets, incantations, interpretation of dreams, theurgy, folk medicine, and folk customs associated with the ceremonial year and life cycle.

Jewish folklore in the Middle Ages initially derived much sustenance from this vast talmudic heritage, but the numerous midrashim of the seventh through twelfth centuries show basic departures from talmudic-midrashic sources. As a matter of fact, the latter underwent radical transformation, expansion, and embellishment in the process of adapting to changing life conditions. For example, the medieval *Midrash eleh ezkerah,* also known as *Maᶜaseh ᶜasevet ha-rugei malkhut* (Story of the ten martyrs), while graphically elaborating talmudic-midrashic legends of the tragic death of such historical luminaries as Rabbi Akiva (*d.* 135), also echoes the contemporary persecution of medieval Jewry.

Whereas talmudic-midrashic patterns usually are ancillary to some didactic, homiletic, or exegetical context, the medieval midrashim often attain the standard of independent creations, freed from non-

MAGIC AND FOLKLORE, JEWISH

folkloristic ingredients and suffused with artistic consciousness. Thus the ninth-century *Midrash va-Yissa*ᶜ*u,* describing the legendary wars waged by Jacob and his sons, is rooted in the *Testaments of the Twelve Patriarchs* and the *Book of Jubilees,* but it nevertheless pictures these pseudobiblical battles in terms of medieval warfare. The *Decalogue Midrash (Midrash aseret ha-dibberot)* is based on the Ten Commandments, but it is also an exquisite collection of legends and folktales, some of which belong to internationally attested narrative types and motifs.

Some medieval midrashim reflect the impact of Islamic folklore. *Pirkei de-Rabbi Eliezer* (eighth century) presents a continuous series of biblical legends modeled on Islamic collections of the *qiṣaṣ al-anbiyā*ᵓ (prophetic tales) genre. Curiously enough, these Arabic biblical legends were themselves deeply influenced by the old classical talmudic-midrashic prototypes. Thus the early midrashic account of Abraham's gradual adoption of monotheism influenced Muḥammad's retelling of that story as well as the many post-Koranic collections of biblical legends in Islamic garb. The latter, in turn, exercised their influence on such medieval midrashim as *Ba-Midbar Rabbah* (Numbers), that on the Book of Proverbs, and particularly the vast *Midrash ha-gadol* (thirteenth century) of Yemenite derivation.

The most important collection of medieval Hebrew legends and folktales are the *Alphabet of Ben Sira* (late ninth century), the Arabic *Elegant Composition Concerning Relief After Distress*—being the original of the Hebrew *Ḥibbur yafeh me-ha-Yeshu*ᶜ*ah,* an admirable synthesis of talmudic-midrashic and Islamic folklore by the eleventh-century rabbi Nissim ben Jacob—and the Hebrew *Sefer ha-sha*ᶜ*ashu*ᶜ*im* (Book of delight) by Joseph Ibn Zabara of Barcelona (*b. ca.* 1140). Ibn Zabara was well versed not only in biblical and talmudic-midrashic literature but also in Arabic *adab*, consisting of fanciful, witty, and facetious stories, anecdotes and proverbs, and aphorisms of poignant satire. He was one of the first medieval Hebrew writers to adopt a remarkable form of rhetorical rhymed prose interspersed with verse, full of humor and sparkling wit—an admirable imitation of the classical Arab *maqāmāt* style displayed by such masters as al-Hamadhānī (968–1008) and al-Ḥarīrī (1054–1122). As a matter of fact, a great deal of medieval European folklore should be studied against the background of Ibn Zabara's work.

During the Middle Ages the Jews were the inheritors and disseminators not only of their own culture but of the Greek and Arab civilizations as well. The work of medieval Jewish translators was one of the most important links in the long chain of translations that transmitted the great creations of Oriental folklore to medieval Europe. The *Kalīla wa-Dimna,* an eighth-century Arabic version of the Indian *Pañchatantra,* was translated into Hebrew by Rabbi Joel (twelfth century). In turn, the baptized Jew John of Capua (thirteenth century) rendered the Hebrew version into Latin as *Directorium vitae humanae,* which became the fountainhead of all European versions of this storybook. The Spanish rabbi Moshe Sefardi, alias Petrus Alfonsi (*fl.* early twelfth century), produced a collection of stories and exempla, *Disciplina clericalis,* which occupies a prominent place in the history of the transplantation of Oriental folklore to Europe. Jewish merchants of the Middle Ages, traversing many Eastern and Western countries, carried with them not only merchandise but Jewish and Oriental legends as well. Of particular interest are the Jewish versions of the Alexander romances, the Barlaam and Josaphat storybook (*Ben hamelekh ve-ha-nazir),* the Arthurian romances, and the *Seven Sages* cycle (*Mishlei Sendebar,* or the Sindbād legend).

There were also Jewish tales of the supernatural, such as the well-known *Story of a Jerusalemite,* who, after many adventures, is carried to a land of demons, where he marries their king's daughter. The remarkable legends narrated with much gusto by the ninth-century traveler Eldad ha-Dani describe the Ten Lost Tribes of Israel living in a wonderland beyond the banks of the magical river Sambatyon. These fabulous stories are extremely interesting from the point of view of comparative folklore. They raised expectations of a miraculous gathering together of all the scattered remnants of Israel in preparation for the ultimate redemption by the Messiah. Not surprisingly, messianic legends were very popular in medieval Jewish folklore.

Medieval Jewish historiography was also rich in legendary material. The *Yosippon,* the *Sefer ha-yashar,* the *Yeraḥme'el Chronicles,* the *Sefer ha-qabbalah* (Book of tradition) by Abraham Ibn Dā'ūd, and other pseudohistorical books should really be read as historical fiction: the folkloristic and mythical elements far outweigh the sober historical core. The most conspicuous example of a pseudohistorical work pregnant with magic and folklore is the *Me-*

MAGIC AND FOLKLORE, JEWISH

gillat Aḥima'aẓ, a remarkable family chronicle in exquisite Hebrew rhymed prose completed in 1054 by Aḥima'aẓ of Oria. It affords us a firsthand glimpse of politics, society, culture, and Jewish folkways and magic in ninth-century southern Italy.

Aḥima'aẓ conjures up a fantastic world of miraculous feats performed by saints, such as Abū Aaron of Baghdad (or Babylonia), "the Father of Mysteries" (ninth century). According to legend, Abū Aaron's father owned a mill driven by a mule. When a lion devoured the mule, Abū Aaron seized the animal, gave him a nice thrashing, and forced him to drive the mill and grind the wheat. His father rebuked him, saying, "How do you dare bring under bondage a creature chosen by the Almighty as king of all animals?" and exiled his son for three years. A boy transformed by a witch into an ass was restored to human shape by Abū Aaron, who also detected a ghost passing for a cantor in a synagogue. The Saracen king of Bari, Saudan, sumptuously entertained Abū Aaron and learned much from his wisdom. The king insisted that Abū Aaron should stay in his palace, but the sage sailed away to Egypt. Saudan sent ships to capture Abū Aaron, who promptly invoked the Divine Name and paralyzed the king's fleet. Ultimately Saudan implored the saint to tell him whether he would succeed in entering and capturing the city of Benevento. Abū Aaron correctly predicted that he would enter it under compulsion, as a prisoner.

Other legends concern the saintly Rabbi Sheftiah, who saves a neighbor's child from witches, cures King Basil, and predicts the exact hour of his death, and exorcises the devil from the body of Basil's daughter. He even imprisons the devil in a lead utensil, seals it with the Divine Name, and then casts it into the sea. In another story he writes the sacred letters of the Ineffable Name on the hooves of his horse and is transported home at magical speed before the holy sabbath, when traveling is forbidden. Another saint of legend was Rabbi Paltiel, whose patron, Caliph al-Muʿizz, once looked at the sky and saw his own star devouring three other stars. Rabbi Paltiel predicted that al-Muʿizz would soon become the ruler of three other countries, and when the prophecy came true he was rewarded by the caliph. Yet another myth tells of a pestilence that broke out when the sanctity of the occult *Sefer ha-merkavah* (Book of the divine chariot) was once profaned by a certain woman. A clever saint put the holy book into a lead container and was about to cast it into the sea, but the water "fled backwards" about a mile. Nevertheless the saint threw the book into the ocean, which returned to its former position, and the plague ceased at once.

The legends, according to Joshua Trachtenberg, show that "the primary principle of medieval Jewish magic was an implicit reliance upon the Powers of Good, which were invoked by calling upon their names, the holy Names of God and His angels. This simple dependence upon names for every variety of effect obviated resort to all the other magical acts with which the non-Jewish tradition has familiarized us." In fact, the famous *Sefer Ḥasidim,* which is extremely rich in all kinds of weird legends and folktales, reveals that the Jews shared almost all the superstitions, folk beliefs, and magical practices prevailing in medieval Germany. Yet despite all these non-Jewish influences, the medieval hasidim were intimately rooted in Jewish folkways. The *Sefer Ḥasidim* is a moral, didactic guide to worship and prayer, sin and repentance, sabbath observance, Torah study, the conduct of Jews in relation to God and men, rules and regulations in all matters of daily life, and the sacred relations of love and marriage. But it also deals with demons and evil spirits who prowl about at night, with sorcerers and witches who prey on innocent people. It tells how a mortal should defend himself against these powers of evil, drawing on numerous legends, folktales, exempla, and anecdotes, some of which belong to the international repertoire of folklore. This literature was culled not only from the vast storehouse of talmudic-midrashic folklore but also from the treasure trove of medieval German legends. It was precisely this exuberant folk element permeating a religious fabric that gave the *Sefer Ḥasidim* the popularity it has enjoyed throughout the centuries.

BIBLIOGRAPHY

Moses Gaster, ed., *The Exempla of the Rabbis* (1924, repr. 1968); Louis Ginzberg, *The Legends of the Jews* (1925–1947); Gershom Scholem, *Major Trends in Jewish Mysticism,* 3rd rev. ed. (1954), *Jewish Mysticism in the Middle Ages* (1964), and *Kabbalah* (1974); Haim Schwarzbaum, *Studies in Jewish and World Folklore* (1968); Frank Talmage, ed., *Studies in Jewish Folklore* (1980); Joshua Trachtenberg, *Jewish Magic and Superstition* (1939, repr. 1970); Isadore Twersky, *Studies in Medieval Jewish History and Literature* (1979).

HAIM SCHWARZBAUM

[See also **Angel/Angelology; Apocalyptic Literature and Movements, Jewish; Astrology; Cabala; Disciplina Clericalis; Fables; Judeo-Arabic Literature; Magic, Bookish;**

MAGIC AND FOLKLORE, WESTERN

Talmud, Jewish Study and Exegesis of; Translations and Translators, Jewish; Yiddish.]

MAGIC AND FOLKLORE, WESTERN EUROPEAN. Up to about the year 1000, the authority of the church in Western Europe was still quite limited in comparison to what it would later become. Although its desire was always to extirpate any survivals of paganism—or to christianize pagan practices by adapting them to the uses of the new religion—in many cases church officials found it the course of wisdom simply to look the other way.

An example is the church's attitude toward funeral rituals. Sulpicius Severus tells us that St. Martin of Tours (fourth century) stopped a procession one day, believing it to be some pagan rite. However, once he learned that it was a funeral procession, he let it proceed. The first explicit regulations concerning burial practices do not come until 785/786, and even then they were a special case, because they were directed at the Saxons, who were accused of practicing cremation and of building tumuli according to pagan custom.

Such pieces of evidence must be opposed to the more familiar success stories, in which an urban Latin church moved out into the countryside from its centers of influence in the episcopal cities, transforming pagan sanctuaries into churches and co-opting pagan feasts for the Christian calendar.

We have ample evidence that throughout the Middle Ages there was a vibrant "unofficial" culture that coexisted with official church practice and doctrine. Recent research in this area has greatly aided our understanding of this evidence and has thrown considerable light on the ways of life and structures of belief of the lower social classes. However, the difficulties associated with this research have also fueled a number of debates, which may, if nothing else, remind us that the evidence does have its limitations.

Among these limitations, the most important is that practically every extant document comes from people who were trying to stamp out the very practices under review in this essay. Although inquisitors certainly learned a great deal about the way sorcerers thought, we must always remember that they were biased, hostile witnesses who thought like inquisitors, and not like sorcerers, and who usually wrote in a language—Latin—that was alien to the popular culture. In short, we are dealing with a very thick filter.

Another limitation is our frequent inability to document change over the course of time—the historian's stock in trade. And there has often been a tendency to view popular culture as static and unchanging. However, although it is certainly true that some folktales, for instance, are very old and that in the whole area of premodern popular culture the pace of change is slow, change there is, and also innovation. Although many folk traditions, such as the funeral procession witnessed by St. Martin, may have been survivals of a pagan past, others, such as the shivaree and the pre-Lenten carnival, are pretty clearly innovations of the later medieval period. Concerning other practices, we may never know. But we may say that popular culture is not outside of time; it is a historical phenomenon.

Finally, we must admit limits to our ability to understand the medieval mind, for medieval society, after all, accepted the power of the supernatural in everyday life. "Superstition" is, in fact, difficult to define in medieval terms. The church itself, as Keith Thomas notes in his study of late medieval and early modern England, may be seen as a "magical agency." Thomas goes on to suggest that, in general, "the ceremonics of which it disapproved were 'superstitious'; those which it accepted were not."

The church's many compromises with the pagan past certainly give this statement a veneer of truth. And yet the compromises were always calculated to advance the cause of Christianity. It is in this context, perhaps, that the cult of the saints is best understood. Historians have often expressed the view that, through the cult of saints, pagan practices contaminated the "original" Christianity. Yet the saints effectively replaced ancestor worship, displaced local deities from their shrines, and reinforced the great liturgical feasts in the campaign to christianize the calendar.

All this the saints did after their deaths. But what functions, in life, earned them their later canonization? After the era of the martyrs was over, the task par excellence of the saint was to gain new converts for the church. Frequently the saint did this by performing miracles; indeed he had to perform miracles to become a saint. Always, however, it is the progress of Christianity that validates these marvels.

On the other hand, the church very early focused on three types of practices that it considered particularly dangerous. First of all was behavior that appeared to deny the one true God—in particular, the worshiping of springs, trees, stones, or graven images. Second was behavior that sought to subvert

MAGIC AND FOLKLORE, WESTERN

God's ownership of time. The church controlled the calendar, and although it took over pagan feasts and adapted them to its own use, it was not prepared to tolerate observances that were not in the Christian calendar. Even more importantly, only God could know the future, and so augury, astrology, and the other kinds of fortune-telling were prohibited by St. Augustine, Isidore of Seville, Hrabanus Maurus, Burchard of Worms, Ivo of Chartres, John of Salisbury, and Gratian. The third area of particular concern was health. The church condemned the use of spells to harm people or cattle, and it also tried to exert a monopoly on spells that sought to heal the sick.

The tug-of-war in the medical field was actually a three-way contest. Christian practices of healing by liturgical means (benedictions, rogation processions, sprinkling of holy and salt water, exorcisms) competed with ancient medical knowledge as well as folk healing practices. The church finally dealt with the body of medical knowledge by adopting it in the main as its own. It dealt with folk medicine by condemning treatments that had not been prescribed by a doctor or a churchman. It is clear that the church was less concerned with the actual means of treatment than it was with the formal recognition of its own authority. Thus, at the end of the eighth century, Bishop Halitgarius of Cambrai wrote in his *Liber poenitentialis* that it was not proper to pronounce certain incantations when gathering medicinal herbs unless one also honored the Lord by, for instance, reciting the Lord's Prayer. This formula was so successful that we find Thomas Aquinas using it five centuries later.

It is important to note that the church did not deny the effectiveness of folk remedies. St. Augustine, in a passage of the *City of God* that is echoed in the writings of Hrabanus Maurus, Burchard of Worms, and Gratian, affirms that magi and *sortilegi* seemed effective in curing the sick and harming the healthy. Augustine feels that God allows this in order to test the faith of those who see it.

Individual churchmen were also far from denying the value of fortune-telling. Throughout the Middle Ages it was, in fact, common to use the Scriptures as a kind of fortune-telling device, despite the regular condemnations that the church issued against these *sortes sanctorum.* Before the election of a bishop, for instance, it was a common practice to open the Psalter at random, seeking inspiration or more probably confirmation of the election in the first verse on the open page. This happened at the election of St. Martin of Tours and also St. Aignan of Orléans.

Throughout much of the Middle Ages this must have been a game for churchmen only, since only they had sufficient access to the books. But in the course of time it definitely reached the laity as well. We have from the thirteenth or fourteenth century a manuscript in Provençal called the *Oracles of the Apostles.* It was found in the wall of a house at Cordes, France, and consists of fifty-seven biblical verses to which yellow and blue strings are attached. One simply pulled a string to get an answer to one's question about a proposed course of action.

Although superstition clearly permeated medieval society, its home was the countryside. The roots of this are very deep. A country-dweller is, etymologically, a pagan (*paganus* in Latin or *paysan* in French), whatever the quality of his belief. The church clearly felt that its problems in this area were in the country, as the title of a work written by Martin of Braga in 580 indicates—*De correctione rusticorum.*

The ability to objectify superstition, to create discontinuity where the historian sees a continuum, was aided by the thought that superstition was a rural, and also a lay, phenomenon. In addition, practices the church called superstitious very early began to coalesce around the concept of the devil, who, in the form we know him, is a medieval invention.

The medieval devil is a synthesis of the biblical Satan, the fallen angels myth, and the *daimones* of Hellenistic paganism. We owe him primarily to the labors of Tertullian, Augustine, and John Cassian between the third and the fifth century. Instigator of vice and sin and, in particular, of superstitious practices, the devil was above all the Deceiver. As St. Paul wrote, Satan could transform himself into "an angel of light" (2 Cor. 11:14); he could assume false appearances and disturb the spirits of men, making them believe in the reality of vain illusions—*fantasmata.* Above all the dreams of men were the prey of the devil, who filled them with false and tempting images. "True" dreams came from God, but only churchmen could tell the difference between true and false dreams, and even the saints were assailed by the illusions of the devil, as was St. Anthony in the desert.

Throughout the early Middle Ages, however, the domain of the devil remained quite limited, especially if we compare it to the powers attributed to him later on. Much behavior that, in the later Middle Ages, would arouse charges of a pact with the devil, in the early Middle Ages is denounced only for its ill effects on men, cattle, or harvest without any

MAGIC AND FOLKLORE, WESTERN

further charge of devil worship. The church did not doubt that the devil was behind these evil deeds, but it held that the devil had deceived the evildoers, not that he had enlisted them openly in his cause.

In the early Middle Ages, the devil's field of action was the imagination. He worked by summoning illusions into the minds of men, and although these were perfectly "real," they had no materiality; as we shall see, in the later Middle Ages, the church reversed its position, and the devil's *fantasmata* were seen as having corporeal reality.

The famous canon *Episcopi* sums up several beliefs about the devil's ways. (Although this canon was attributed during the Middle Ages to the Council of Ancyra of 314, its first documentary appearance was actually around 916 in the work of Regino of Prüm.) The canon attacked those who believed the statements of "certain wicked women, instruments of Satan who were themselves deceived by diabolical apparitions." These women asserted that they rode by night on herds of animals, following the "sorceress Holda" or the pagan goddess Diana, whom they called their mistress. These names probably conceal those of a Germanic deity linked to the world of the dead, Holla or Holda-Perchta. In French-speaking areas, later documents (for instance, the *De universo* of William of Auvergne, bishop of Paris) called her *Abundia* or *Satia,* recognizing a favorable role in agricultural or domestic prosperity.

Nonetheless, until the later Middle Ages these beliefs were only "illusions of the devil" that "led the soul astray." In these alleged nocturnal voyages only the soul participates, and not the body, "but the human mind believes that all these phantasms have material reality and that they are not imaginary."

Although the church regularly denounced such beliefs, its punitive actions remained quite limited. Without trying to penetrate the mind of the sinner (unlike later inquisitors, who were fascinated by motive), the church simply imposed penance for the confessed misdeeds of the faithful, and this was normally light except for cases of idolatry, the abuse of corpses, or spells resulting in death or impotence.

With the revival of the eleventh century, there was a burst of creativity in the area of folk culture, as there was in so many areas of Western society. Although there is certainly no radical break between the early and the later Middle Ages, the development was such that by the beginning of the fourteenth century European popular culture had assumed the form it would retain until the Industrial Revolution. In this process, four elements are of particular note: the transformation of rural space; the emergence of a lay aristocracy in need of a culture that would legitimate its power; the growth of the towns; and the continuing central, if ambiguous, role of the church.

The High Middle Ages witnessed the transformation of rural space in Europe. Until this time, European settlement had been a matrix of isolated communities. During the High Middle Ages a rapidly growing population, largely directed by local seigneurial power, cleared the forests and drained the swamps, until one community touched another, and wasteland largely disappeared. Indeed, before the Black Death of the fourteenth century dramatically reduced the population, land was put to the plough that has not been cultivated since.

With the wasteland, of course, went much mystery. Yet certain spots of this tamed land retained their power. At the center of the community there was the village cemetery, where young people, braving divine wrath and the interdicts of the clergy, performed masked dances that were condemned as demoniac but that may also be viewed as practices parallel to, and competitive with, those of the church. At the borders between communities, at crossroads or in the remaining forests, lay other grounds marked in the collective memory for certain practices. In a woods near the Ain River, equidistant from several villages, archaeologists have confirmed a legend reported by the inquisitor Étienne de Bourbon in the thirteenth century. A slightly fortified settlement, built around 1000 but quickly abandoned, became a spot where sick children could be cured. These borderlands are also the places where people saw the noctural rides of the "army of the dead"—Hellequin and his troop of ghosts.

The second fundamental element is the emergence of a lay aristocracy whose internal divisions were a powerful stimulus to cultural innovation. Newly arrived seigneurs lacked the forebears of older aristocratic families, so they drew on folklore to produce legendary origins for their houses in an attempt to justify their positions. Such is the role played by the legend of the fairy-serpent Mélusine. Several families tried to appropriate this well-known story, the most successful being the Lusignans of Poitou, who used it to explain their remarkable climb up the social ladder, which culminated in the kingdom of Cyprus.

On a broader level, the aristocracy as a whole was developing for the first time a culture that gave it some intellectual independence from the church. In this process, the growth of a vernacular literature

MAGIC AND FOLKLORE, WESTERN

was central, and the writers did not fail to turn to all the motifs of Celtic mythology—fairies and enchanted lakes, dwarfs and giants, magical objects and formulas.

The third element was the growth of the towns, which drew people and folklore from the countryside and urbanized them both. Towns offered a novel organization of social space (urban parishes, neighborhoods, a network of fraternal organizations) and a firmer and more detailed structure of time. It was in the towns that the carnival was born, as a crystallization into the three days preceding Lent of festivities that had previously extended over a longer period. The carnival is first mentioned at Rome in 1142, in the *De mirabilibus urbis Romae;* its real growth as an institution, however, seems to have come in the fourteenth century.

Such rituals allowed towns and the various groups in them to assert their identity. In Paris the very old legend of the dragon subdued by St. Marcel gave birth to a ritual procession: at Rogation Days a wicker dragon was paraded, and children threw delicacies into its mouth. The Paris dragon was not unique, since Tarascon had, as early as the twelfth century, its procession of the Tarasque, an aquatic monster tamed by St. Martha. Other dragons and processional giants appeared in other cities. They were expressions of the collective identity of the people, linked by ritual to the legendary origins of the city.

The fourth element in the evolution of folk culture was the church. Although it clearly saw itself threatened by the loss of its cultural monopoly, its role remained central, and it participated actively, probably more than at any other period, in this folk culture. The church may have disapproved of the Paris dragon, but a sculpture of the same dragon appeared on the cathedral of Notre Dame. Many churchmen undertook the systematic collection of folktales, which preachers used in their sermons, adapting as usual the ideological meaning to the needs of the church. Still they returned these stories to the lay audiences from which they came, keeping them on people's tongues. Preachers also carried stories from place to place, contributing very likely to the unification of themes and narrative motifs that is a dominant trait of European folklore.

From the thirteenth century, however, the church's role began to stiffen. The development of scholastic thinking led to criticism of the marvelous both within the church and outside it. Miracles, the cult of relics, legal practices (such as the ordeal) that relied on divine intervention—all the Christian marvels so characteristic of the early Middle Ages—suffered from the rationalizing scrutiny of the schoolmen long before the Reformation.

The late Middle Ages was a time of great social stress, and this stress had a strong impact on popular culture, leading finally to the organized persecution of alleged sorcerers by inquisitors whose original task had been the pursuit of heretics. This is also the period in which the towns came finally to dominate the countryside, both economically and culturally. The more highly structured urban environment led in turn to the development of a minutely detailed organization of individual and collective life, which we may discern in the documents for the first time in the fourteenth and fifteenth centuries, and which remained a characteristic of European society until the nineteenth century.

Among the most characteristic social institutions of this period were the fraternal organizations of young men, which served an important role in integrating young rural immigrants into the urban social milieu and also marked out in an institutional way the period between childhood and parenthood. (Normally marriage or the birth of the first child signaled a man's retirement from his fraternal organization.)

These youth groups were remarkably given to satire. In this they must have received some inspiration from the church, which as early as the twelfth century celebrated the Feast of Fools just after Christmas. The canons and choirboys attached to a cathedral would indulge in dances and a parody of episcopal authority. Such relatively tame entertainments were, however, only a starting point for the lay fraternal organizations, which were soon calling themselves "societies of fools."

One of the most remarkable activities of these groups was the shivaree, a noisy mock serenade (*charivari* means "rough music" in French) with which the youth groups mocked marriages of which they disapproved. Normally the disapproval stemmed from an excessive age difference in the couple, a mismatch common enough if one of them had been previously married. Other events could easily provoke a shivaree. Wife-beating, or husband-beating, were fair game. Adultery would provoke a parade in which a donkey carried a mannequin, riding backwards, to represent the cuckold.

Some historians view the shivaree as a "consecrating" event: the ceremonial uproar may be seen as a ritual aimed at overcoming the discontinuity

MAGIC AND FOLKLORE, WESTERN

caused by any marriage, but particularly by a remarriage—the forced rearrangement that the marriage brings to a whole constellation of social relationships in the community. A remarriage in particular carried with it overtones of transgression—bigamy or adultery—and the shivaree may be seen as an attempt to induce the deceased spouse to recognize the new union. By extension permission is also asked of other deceased members of the family and the community. From this line of reasoning we may perceive the link between the shivaree and Hellequin's army of the dead.

Such a folkloric consecration was all the more necessary because the church refused to bless second marriages, even though it tolerated and even encouraged them in the case of the death of one of the partners—whence the idea that a second marriage did not have the same validity as a first marriage and that it was fitting to provide the union with ritual confirmation outside the church.

However, most historians tend to emphasize the "judicial" rather than the "consecrating" function of the shivaree. In this view, the young men of the community collectively sanction a marriage that reduces by one the number of young women in the community that they may themselves hope to marry. Marriage to a widower, presumably older and wealthier, or even to a stranger from outside the community, harms the young men by reducing their options. Through the shivaree the young men assert their control over such alliances, and the new couple recognize their power and gain their permission by paying a fee.

Finally, through the shivaree, the young men of the community may be seen demonstrating their concern for the heirs of the first marriage, who might well be the same age as those participating in the shivaree, and whose inheritance rights might well suffer as a result of the new union.

Beginning with the Council of Compiègne in 1329–1330 and the synod of Avignon in 1337, the church violently condemned shivarees for three reasons. First, with their abusive language and obscene gestures, shivarees seemed to be one of those "dishonest games" *(ludos inhonnestos)* that the church had consistently condemned throughout the centuries. Other such games were New Year celebrations and the masquerades held in cemeteries. Second, shivarees appeared to be a mockery of the sacrament of matrimony, and in some cases shivarees actually succeeded in preventing weddings. Third, shivarees often ended in brawling or even murder. The church threatened to excommunicate the organizers of shivarees and was concerned above all that churchmen did not participate in them.

The civil authorities were much slower to act. Throughout the fourteenth and fifteenth centuries they generally deferred to custom and even benefited from the shivaree by levying a fee on it or the second marriage that caused it. In the sixteenth and seventeenth centuries shivarees were finally prohibited as menaces to public safety. By this time the shivaree had evolved to a point where the municipal authorities might more clearly perceive a threat to their own authority. Shivarees had moved well beyond their original domain of marriage and sexual relations to address any number of communal issues—usurpation of the common land, conflicts with gamekeepers, the defense of customs. They had in fact become politicized, so it is not surprising that the political authorities moved against them at this time.

The carnival was to the cycle of the year what the shivaree was to the cycle of life. With a very rich symbolism, these two rituals summarized and focused the community's complex feelings about two fundamental issues—sex, on the one hand, and time, on the other. The reaction of municipal authorities, however, was different. Rather than tolerating the carnival, or trying to suppress it, the authorities took it over. Thus, little by little, the lower classes of the towns were deprived of their active role in the carnival and became mere spectators at festivities organized by and for the magistrates and the merchant class. A festival in which the people had expressed their identity became instead an expression of the power and wealth of the ruling classes. Neighboring cities often sent envoys to view these displays, and in fact the dates of local carnivals were often arranged to avoid conflicts in ambassadorial schedules. In the end, the expense of these ostentatious entertainments grew so great that we find the magistrates of Lille, for instance, appealing to their duke for financial assistance—an indication of how far away from the people the carnival had grown.

The co-optation of the carnival is only one sign of the growth of government in the later Middle Ages. We see it on the municipal level, but even more on the territorial level, where the state—particularly in France and England—begins to take on a decidedly modern appearance.

This growth, like all change, brought with it conflict. France and England added intermittent combat to other forms of political antagonism during the

MAGIC AND FOLKLORE, WESTERN

Hundred Years War. Meanwhile the church, prey to schism and conciliar crisis, was in turmoil. To the stresses in the political and religious structures we must add the stress of the plague, which broke out repeatedly during this period and had negative effects in practically every sphere of life, from the demographic and economic to the spiritual.

All this conflict and uncertainty elicited some remarkable behavior from individuals, for which the embattled servants of church and state displayed little tolerance. Almost archetypal is the case of Joan of Arc, the Maid of Orléans, who hears voices, saves the French state, and is charged with sorcery and condemned (under political pressure) by the church—which later changes its mind and (in the twentieth century) canonizes her.

During this period the church's attitude toward superstition darkened substantially. Between the thirteenth and the fifteenth century the church's traditional analysis of sorcery was essentially repealed and replaced with a new theory that centered on devil worship. In other words, superstition was promoted to heresy.

The first stage in this evolution was marked by the publication of the pontifical constitution *Vox in Rama* of 1233. Already we have the basic charges that will be repeated again and again in the trials of magicians and sorcerers: homage to Satan in the form of the feudal *osculum* (but reversed since the devil's buttocks are kissed); meetings of a "sect" that indulges in debauchery (incest and sodomy); acts of infanticide and cannibalism.

The evolution of this new theory of sorcery hastened in the middle of the fourteenth century, favored very likely by the trauma of the Black Death. By the early fifteenth century, the witches' sabbath is well developed, although we do not get the name until around 1490, in the *Flagellum maleficarum* of the theologian Pierre Mamoris.

The old canon *Episcopi* proved a hindrance on the point of the witches' sabbath, since it held that such nocturnal excursions were only diabolical illusions designed to confuse simple souls. In the new analysis, however, the devil was no mere prankster; he was far too serious an adversary for that. The night riders would have to have corporeal reality.

A way around the venerable canon *Episcopi* was worked out by Jean Vineti, theologian and inquisitor, who suggested in his *Tractatus contra daemonum invocatores* that the devil worship at hand was a new phenomenon distinct from the old-time rustic sorcery, and much more dangerous. The canon *Episcopi* concerned traditional sorcery, but not this new form.

Finally, on 5 December 1484, Innocent VIII promulgated the bull *Summis desiderantes,* which accused sorcerers of abjuring their faith and fornicating with the devil. Shortly afterward, two inquisitors from the Rhineland, Henry Institoris and James Sprenger, published their *Malleus maleficarum.* This vast compendium of theology and inquisitorial practices took up the distinction between the old and the new sorcery, specifying that the change took place around the year 1400. With the *Malleus maleficarum* the foundations were fully in place for the witch hunts that covered almost all of Europe from the sixteenth to the eighteenth century.

As this new theory of sorcery evolved, it both influenced and was influenced by the study of natural science, which was benefiting from the importation of books by Arab authors who had preserved much of ancient Greek science. Scholars sought to distinguish carefully between "natural magic" and "black magic," whose effectiveness depended, it was believed, on an invocation of the devil. Thus Roger Bacon, in his *Epistola de secretis operibus artis et naturae et de nullitate magiae,* defended the natural magic that he was promoting at Oxford and opposed the false magic of those who invoked demons to satisfy their *curiositas* or even to achieve criminal ends.

The scholars had good reason to be nervous, because the church was moving to give jurisdiction over sorcery to the Inquisition. Indeed the rise of the polemics against sorcerers coincided with a lessening, even in certain regions a disappearance, of the danger of heresy. On the other hand, where churchmen still had heretics to fight, they were not overly scandalized by "superstitions," as Emmanuel Le Roy Ladurie has shown for the mountains of the Ariège, which were still infested with Catharism at the beginning of the fourteenth century.

Whatever the institutional imperatives, as soon as the church came to feel that sorcery could be a heresy, the Inquisition began to take charge. In 1258 and 1260, Alexander IV addressed two bulls to the Franciscan and Dominican inquisitors, authorizing them to recognize cases in which superstitious practices had "the odor of heresy." A few years later a *Summa de officio inquisitionis* that originated in the entourage of Bishop Benoît of Marseilles related in detail the *forma et modus interrogandi augures et ydolatras.* Bernard Gui, inquisitor at Toulouse from 1307 to 1323, likewise devoted a part of his inquisitorial manual *(Practica officii inquisitionis hereticae pravitatis)* to divination and spell-casting with "an odor of heresy." Finally, in 1326, John XXII took the definitive step in his constitution *Super illius specula*: from then on it was possible to apply the same repressive measures against sorcerers as against heretics, that is, transfer them to inquisitors, torture them, and eventually hand them over to the secular arm.

As the witch-hunts of later centuries show, there is no sharp break in folk culture between the Middle Ages and the modern period. The period from the revival of the eleventh century to the Industrial Revolution of the nineteenth century may be seen as a continuum. Of course, along this continuum there were periods of rapid change and periods of resistance to change. However, the endurance of the main elements of this culture is extraordinary. They give way only in the nineteenth century, when, along with its old adversary the church, folk culture loses many of its functions to the new, all-encompassing state and to the new media of mass communication.

BIBLIOGRAPHY

Peter Brown, *The Cult of the Saints: Its Rise and Function in Latin Christianity* (1981); Franco Cardini, *Magia, stregoneria, superstizioni nell'Occidente medievale* (1979); Claude Gaignebet, *Le carnaval* (1979); Carlo Ginzburg, *The Night Battles: Witchcraft and Agrarian Cults in the Sixteenth and Seventeenth Centuries,* John and Anne Tedeschi, trans. (1983); Jacques Le Goff and Jean-Claude Schmitt, eds., *Le charivari* (1981); Emmanuel Le Roy Ladurie, *Montaillou: The Promised Land of Error,* Barbara Bray, trans. (1978), *Carnival in Romans,* Mary Feeney, trans. (1979), and *La sorcière de Jasmin* (1983); Raoul Manselli, *La religion populaire au moyen âge* (1975), *Magia e stregoneria nel medio evo* (1976), and *Vita medioevale: La festa* (1978); Nicole Pellegrin, *Les bachelleries: Organisations et fêtes de la jeunesse dans le Centre-Ouest, XVe–XVIIIe siècles* (1982); Jean-Claude Schmitt, *The Holy Greyhound: Guinefort, Healer of Children Since the Thirteenth Century,* Martin Thom, trans. (1983); G. Storms, *Anglo-Saxon Magic* (1948); Keith Thomas, *Religion and the Decline of Magic: Studies in Popular Beliefs in Sixteenth- and Seventeenth-century England* (1971); Lynn Thorndike, *A History of Magic and Experimental Science,* 8 vols. (1923–1958); Richard C. Trexler, *Public Life in Renaissance Florence* (1980); Richard C. Trexler, ed., *Persons in Groups: Social Behavior as Identity Formation in Medieval and Renaissance Europe* (1985); Roger Vaultier, *Le folklore pendant la Guerre de Cent Ans* (1965).

JEAN-CLAUDE SCHMITT

[See also **Agriculture and Nutrition; Alchemy; Arthurian Literature; Astrology/Astronomy; Augustine of Hippo, Saint; Bacon, Roger; Beast Epic; Bestiary; Biology; Black Death; Botany; Burchard of Worms; Calendars and Reckoning of Time; Carnival; Cathars; Chrétien de Troyes; Class Structure, Western; Conciliar Theory; Confession; Dança General de la Muerte; Danse Macabre; Death and Burial; Family, Western European; Feasts and Festivals, European; Fortune; French Literature; Games and Pastimes; Geoffrey of Monmouth; Gerald of Wales; German Literature: Romance; Herbals, Western European; Heresies, Western European; Hrabanus Maurus; Hundred Years War; Iconoclasm; Inquisition; Isidore of Seville, St.; Italian Literature; Ivo of Chartres, St.; Joan of Arc, St.; John XXII; Lusignans; Mandeville's Travels; Medicine, History of; Penance and Penitentials; Regino of Prüm; Renard the Fox; Schism, Great; Science, Islamic; Unction of the Sick; Urbanism; Witchcraft, European; Ysengrimus.**]

MAGIC, BOOKISH (WESTERN EUROPEAN).

During the millennium that separated St. Augustine from Shakespeare, both learned and popular culture had a place for the practice of the magical arts. This essay treats the beliefs and practices of magic found in medieval books and briefly sketches their place in the wider intellectual life. This magic is called bookish to distinguish it from the popular practices and beliefs that were transmitted in oral form and were thus not dependent on literate communication—though, of course, some of the same ideas and actions appeared in both arenas.

A distinction is sometimes drawn between "high magic" and "low magic," but it is not useful here since those terms seem to imply a superiority of one type to the other, a derivation of one from the other, or a correspondence with social rank. In fact, even minimally literate people of lower social status had some access to bookish magic, and on the other hand, high-born folk, whether literate or illiterate, were not necessarily distant from popular magic. Jeffrey B. Russell uses the phrase "high magic" to denote as a group all the more technical, sophisticated, and literate occult arts and sciences, thereby subsuming in high magic both astrology and alchemy. Magic is taken here, however, in the strict sense, to separate it from astrology, alchemy, and divination.

In the common understanding from antiquity through the Renaissance, astrology interpreted the celestial causes of terrestrial events to give a limited and general knowledge of the future; divination tried to gain specific knowledge of the future by means of terrestrial signs, either naturally or with

MAGIC, BOOKISH

the assistance of demons; alchemy was practiced to transform base metals, such as lead, into the noble metals, gold and silver, sometimes combining this work with efforts to produce a spiritual ennoblement of the alchemist himself; and magic employed terrestrial processes, both human and physical, to effect favorable changes in things or to reveal hidden aspects of the past or future. A program for action, not deeper understanding, prompted resort to magic: even when knowledge was sought through magic, it was not the philosophical understanding of the natures of things, but the practical knowledge of, for example, a child's paternity, a woman's virginity, a lost object's location, an enterprise's success, or a disease's prognosis.

While the desired ends of popular magic were often the same as for bookish magic, there were important differences too. The magic recorded in books was transmitted by educated men, often clerics, who tended to derive their ideas from literate and remote sources, rather than oral and local ones. Whether they were authors or just compilers, their writings were rooted primarily in their privileged access to authorities. Their awareness of the wider world of nonmagical learning on occasion brought ideas from philosophy, science, and theology into their texts. Concepts from magic worked their way into philosophical discourse as well.

Before the seventeenth century Europeans saw no conflict between science (a study of nature's course) and magic (the practice of producing unusual and striking phenomena). These were different kinds of endeavor, not competing systems of thought. Magical writings worked within, and borrowed their conceptions directly from, the philosophical and theological analyses of man, nature, demons, angels, and God which dominated Western thought. They did not challenge the system nor create a rival system of their own.

The written record of medieval magic survives in many forms, which may be only outlined in this essay. Copies of ritual magic texts created for the private use of practitioners can still be read; they reveal both the aims and the processes of the magic art. In addition, there are numerous medieval collections of recipes, of which some are predominantly and others exclusively magical. These instructions for producing marvels and other magical effects often report only the ingredients without attention to spiritual preparation or to any ritual order. Scholars studying these fascinating manuscripts have not yet established much about the intentions of their compilers, the public to which they were addressed, or the audience who received, read, and perhaps attempted to follow the instructions. Scientific, philosophical, and theological writings have also preserved some information about medieval magic, both bookish and popular, and in many cases the reporting is sympathetic. Other accounts—some hostile, some sympathetic—appear in belles lettres, chronicles, legal proceedings, saints' lives, and in the images of the visual arts.

Underlying the many forms and characterizations of magic—white, black, natural, artificial, divine, demonic, real, illusory, and more—the central acknowledged attribute is that magic pursues and promises astounding feats. Whether or not success is gained, a magician's purpose is always some action or achievement. When the magician in Chaucer's Franklin's Tale makes the rocks on the seacoast vanish, medieval and modern people alike recognize this as a magician's work, whether they believe that an illusion was created or that the rocks "really" ceased to exist.

In the Middle Ages magical effects were taken by all to be every bit as real as the magicians' intentions and aspirations. The common modern usage by which we call something magical because it is impressive or purely imaginary and not physically real is only rarely in evidence before the sixteenth century.

The history of bookish magic—because of its dependence on literary transmission—closely follows the overall contours of the transmission of ideas and texts in general. In the early Middle Ages pagan magic texts as well as biblical, Greek, and Roman stories about magicians were inherited from antiquity. As in other areas of literate culture, some Germanic and pagan elements were absorbed, even while the Greek and Roman Christian cultures prevailed. After the twelfth-century Renaissance, the thirteenth century incorporated the novelties of the revived classical learning and also drew upon the newly accessible Arabic texts in ways that expanded the magic repertoire at the same time that it enriched the philosophical analyses of magic, giving it a more legitimate intellectual status. The fourteenth century consolidated and built on these gains. In the fifteenth century bookish magic shared in the general enrichment that resulted from humanism's revival of neglected aspects and texts of ancient philosophy, especially neo-Platonic and hermetic wisdom.

Before reviewing a few medieval accounts of magicians at work, we may briefly note the range of ac-

MAGIC, BOOKISH

tivities that in the Middle Ages were generally labeled magical when practiced to achieve purposeful effects: (1) rituals and incantations that were not part of divine worship; evocation of powerful names; words, sounds, gestures, characters, and symbols; (2) applications and mixing of natural substances where the ingredients, the recipes, or the effects were unusual or generally unknown; (3) mechanical contrivances whose workings were hidden or not generally understood; (4) sleight-of-hand and other illusionistic manipulations, including the use of mirrors and lenses; and (5) any other generally striking effect a person might create in which the causes were not recognized by others. Opinion varied from one authority to another and from one time to another as to which actions were superstitious, illicit, or dangerous to body or soul. Similarly, whether magical effects could be realized by purely human means or only through demonic aid was open to debate and received different answers over the centuries.

MAGICIANS AT WORK

While opinions about magic show great variation over the course of the Middle Ages, the range of magicians' actions—at least those known from textual sources—seems to change very little. While it would be wrong to imagine that practice survived unchanged for over a thousand years, the following examples selected from a large literature reveal various aspects of medieval magic that retained their currency from antiquity through early modern times.

Two episodes from biblical antiquity are illuminating because they were retold often in medieval literature and were illustrated as well in the visual arts of the day. In both cases the pagan magicians lose their contest to the devout, who are supported by God's miracles. Nonetheless, these stories illustrate the real power that magicians were thought to control. First, we read in the book of Exodus:

> So Moses and Aaron went to Pharaoh and did as the Lord commanded; Aaron cast down his rod before Pharaoh and his servants, and it became a serpent. Then Pharaoh summoned the wise men and the sorcerers; and they also, the magicians of Egypt, did the same by their secret arts. For every man cast down his rod, and they became serpents. But Aaron's rod swallowed up their rods. (Exod. 7:9–12)

Second, it was the performances of Simon Magus, more than the many other acts of magic in the early Christian era, that captured the medieval imagination. He is first mentioned briefly in Acts 8 as the Simon "who used sorcery and bewitched the people of Samaria," and who, when impressed by the apostles' powers to perform miracles, offered money to receive like power. Longer stories about Simon Magus appeared in the apocryphal *Acts of Peter* and the pseudo-Clementine writings, with further elaborations in the *Didascalia* and the *Apostolic Constitutions,* works that provided the basis for additional portrayals in patristic and scholastic literature and in medieval art. Although these accounts are antagonistic to magic, they nonetheless reveal much about the traditional appreciation of the scope of magicians' powers, many elements of which survive in countless other stories.

The difference between a marvelous feat that is a miracle and one that is a work of magic inheres in the morality of the actor and in the character of the agents; both actions are equally real, and no differentiation can be made by looking only at the act itself. This viewpoint, expressed by St. Augustine, would dominate medieval thinking about magic and miracles: "These miracles . . . were wrought by simple faith and godly confidence, not by the incantations and charms composed under the influence of a criminal tampering with the unseen world" (*City of God* 10:9). Augustine's dismissal of magic and his rebuke of its adherents do not, however, deny the reality of magical effects. For him, as for the Old Testament writer, the snakes produced by Pharaoh's magicians were no less real than Moses' snakes, only less powerful. Note, too, that while demons are not mentioned in Exodus, St. Augustine infers them:

> Since by means of [magic] arts wonders are done which quite surpass human power, what choice have we but to believe that these predictions and operations . . . are the pastimes of wicked spirits who thus seek to seduce and hinder the truly godly? (*City of God* 10:12)

In several accounts Simon Magus is shown specifically having the power to control demons who can carry him aloft. While not all magic was thought to require demons, precedents like these continually raised doubts that even those feats claimed to be due to natural magic were not really autonomous and orthodox, but were produced by demons, whether the magician admitted it or not.

Even though Augustine's denunciations provide us with little information on the magical practices he acknowledges as effective, he does picture magicians as performing "filthy cleansing by sacrilegious rites [to] see in their initiated state . . . certain wonderfully lovely appearances of angels or gods"

MAGIC, BOOKISH

(10:10). He reports, too, that "by the use of stones and herbs . . . they lay spells on people, and open [locked] doors, and do similar wonders," and that they "pester [the demons] only for the sake of finding a runaway slave, or acquiring property, or making a bargain of a marriage, or such things" (10:11). Fortunately, historians today need not rely only on Augustine's second-hand and hostile account, for among the many ancient magical papyri that survive, we find fourth-century instructions for just such a "filthy cleansing" as Augustine had in mind:

> Keep yourself pure for seven days, and then go on the third day of the moon to a place which the receding Nile has just laid bare. Make a fire on two upright bricks with olive-wood, that is to say thin wood, when the sun is half-risen, after having before sunrise circumambulated the altar. . . . Decapitate an immaculate, pure-white cock, holding it in the crook of your left elbow. . . . Hold the cock fast by your knees and decapitate it with no one else holding it. Throw the head into the river, catch the blood in your right hand and drink it up. Put the rest of the body on the burning altar and jump into the river. Dive under in the clothes you are wearing, then stepping backwards climb on to the bank. Put on new clothes and go away without turning round. After that take the gall of a raven and rub some of it with the wing of an ibis on your eyes and you will be consecrated. (Butler, *Ritual Magic,* p. 10)

With some variations, such procedures remained current in magical literature through the Renaissance, and beyond.

Another papyrus of the fourth or fifth century lists what a spirit can achieve. Notice the sometimes mundane aspirations of magical technique which Augustine mocked, for they characterize magical practices throughout the Middle Ages and well into the seventeenth century:

> This is the holy operation for winning a familiar spirit. . . . He will perform at once any commission you may give him. He will send dreams, he will bring you women and men without need for a material link; he will remove, he will subdue, he will hurl winds up from the bosom of the earth; he will bring gold, silver, bronze and give it to you, if you need it; he will also free from bonds the prisoner in chains, he opens doors, he renders you invisible, so that no human soul can see you; he will bring fire, carry water, bring wine, bread, and any other food you want: oil, vinegar, everything except fish, as many vegetables as you want; but as for pork, you must never command him to bring that. (Butler, *Ritual Magic,* pp. 16–17)

Magic rituals did not, however, always utilize demons in an explicit fashion. Great power was also attributed to specific materials, usually by virtue of an associative link between the agents and the intended outcome, that is, by the power of "sympathy." According to the doctrine of "signatures," a form of sympathetic magic, certain natural objects not only had special powers, but presented visible features that indicated their potential applications; for example, hepatica leaves bore the shape and color of the liver, thereby revealing their remedial value against liver ailments.

The following remedy "against a swelling" reveals a mingling of physical and symbolic elements that is typical of medieval magic; it comes from the large collection of magical recipes and charms surviving in Old English, where there is little recourse to spirits, even though Anglo-Saxon beliefs were highly animistic. "Take root of lily, sprouts of elder, and leaves of leek, and scrape them very small and pound them thoroughly, and put them [in] a thick cloth and bind [it] on [the swelling]" (Cockayne 3:9). Note that all three herbs have some swelling themselves which is destroyed by cutting and pounding.

In an Anglo-Saxon ritual to encourage a swarm of bees to relocate nearby and close to the ground (rather than in an inaccessible treetop), one was instructed to take earth, throw it up with the right hand, and then step on it where it falls with the right foot, saying:

> I catch it under my foot, I have found it. Lo, earth has power against all creatures, and against malice and against ungratefulness, and against the mighty tongue of man.

Then one is to throw a handful of loose sand over the swarming bees themselves and address them like this:

> Settle, victorious women, sink down to earth.
> You must never fly wild to the wood.
> Be as mindful of my welfare
> As every man is of food and home.
>
> (Storms, p. 133)

Whatever direct effect the tossed sand may have on the bees, the charm clearly gains its strength from the device of acting out a measure of control over the all-powerful earth, using the favored right hand and right foot. At the same time, the tossed earth imitates the moving swarm and also tries to enforce a limit on its height and distance. In the second action

MAGIC, BOOKISH

the sand encircles and encloses the swarm, symbolizing a restraint from wandering off.

The utilitarian ends of magic recipes encouraged the collecting and copying of large and diverse compilations. This was also promoted by the close connection between some charms and medical treatment, and was never inhibited by any large-scale hesitancy over magic's efficacy, but only over its morality in certain cases. In Latin as well as in the vernaculars, manuscript "books of secrets" abound from the later Middle Ages. The genre is hardly uniform, and it includes, sometimes indiscriminately, magical procedures, medical prescriptions, household formulas (whitening the teeth, removing stains, controlling vermin, preserving food), cookery, parlor tricks and practical jokes (itching powder, a clear water that turns the face black, invisible ink, creating the illusion that a bird is in the house), and theatrical effects (disappearing in a cloud of smoke, carrying fire without burning your hand).

The heterogeneous quality of such collections probably indicates that formulas of magic, like other recipes, were seen as potentially beneficial information and were thus copied along with other utilitarian procedures. Unfortunately for our understanding, scholars have been unable to ascertain much about the people who gathered these recipes into books, about their intentions, or about the people who recopied recipes, read them, or used them.

One Latin collection from the late thirteenth century circulated widely under an attribution to Albertus Magnus. Variously titled the *Secreta Alberti* or the *Liber aggregationis,* it was translated in the early modern period into English, French, German, Italian, and Spanish. It survives today in dozens of manuscripts and scores of early printed editions. Although it might best be termed a book of natural magic, for it makes little reference to spirits or demons, some of its procedures and ingredients must have circulated in black magic texts. The remarkable effects achieved would certainly have led many to suspect they were achieved only with demonic aid. The character of the recipes and the range of their intentions may be suggested by these few examples from among the roughly 200 formulas in the book:

> To know whether your wife is chaste. To be made invisible. To burn someone's hand without using fire. To make a perpetual, inextinguishable fire. To divine the future. To start a fire [using a lens]. To make an incombustible garment [using asbestos]. To make a sleeping man tell you what he has done. To make a rainbow appear [using a prism]. To generate love between two people. To make men seem headless. To make men seem to have dogs' faces. To make men seem to have three heads. To see what others cannot. To understand the speech of birds. To make a man impotent. To make a lamp that makes any man holding it fart until he sets it down.

From this and similar passages we can observe that unusual natural effects (lenses, prisms, asbestos wicks and cloths, sulfur dioxide bleaching, an accurate recipe for gunpowder for use in fireworks) are mixed with physiological and psychological effects (hallucinatory smokes, itching powders), with stage magic (coatings to protect the skin from flaming objects), and with fantasy and the power of suggestion (the language of the birds, induced farting, and the popular magic of love, potency, and impotence). In this text, instructions are largely limited to ingredients and manual operations, with no attention to ritual, except for brief instructions on astrological timing.

In addition to texts of magic, there circulated many stories about magicians beyond the accounts of Moses, Pharaoh's magicians, and Simon Magus mentioned above. Some of the most characteristic stories tell of the Roman poet Vergil, or more accurately, tell invented tales of "Vergil the Necromancer." Other legends about magical performances surrounded the historical figure Gerbert of Aurillac, who became Pope Sylvester II in 999 and died in 1003. Very well known to moderns is the Merlin figure of the Arthurian romances; but it should be noted that he is not typical of medieval magicians, for his powers derived not from any study or use of formal magical arts, but from his half-human status as the offspring of a woman and a devil.

Within the English tradition, a nameless cleric in Chaucer's *Canterbury Tales* illustrates the magician's powers, for he seems to make the rocky outcrops on the coast of Brittany disappear. Here in the Franklin's Tale, as elsewhere in medieval magic, the power of illusion and the power of effecting physical changes are not easily distinguished—either by historians or by medieval commentators themselves.

THE INTELLECTUAL SETTING FOR MEDIEVAL MAGIC

To appreciate the nature of magical powers, we need to consider the structure of the medieval Chris-

MAGIC, BOOKISH

tian cosmos and the natural philosophy that explained it; it may suffice to picture it as it was codified in the writings of the great scholastic scientists and theologians of the thirteenth and fourteenth centuries.

Clearly, at the top of the hierarchy stand the unlimited powers of God. This commonsense view of divine omnipotence, however, grew problematic with philosophical scrutiny, and the notion of God's infinite power came to be qualified by two important conditions. First, scholastics argued that even God could not perform a logical contradiction: even he could not create a square circle. Second, scholastics found it useful to distinguish between two aspects of his omnipotence, usually referred to as his "two powers." Late medieval theologians recognized that while he has the absolute potential to do, or to have done, anything at all (short of a contradiction), he did in fact choose to ordain or order this real world as a physical and historical creation in a certain way. This ordained power, though not limited by anything human or by the laws of physics (which were established by him), is limited by his having chosen to create the world as he did. The real world is thus based indirectly on an infinite and unfathomable power and directly on a limited, structured, and consistent ordaining of his power. In the ordained world, we can expect the sun to rise daily, we can expect people to be unable to fly, we can expect rabbits not to be born in magicians' hats, and we can expect a fatal illness to cause death—unless God chooses to act apart from the order of nature by causing a miracle.

Next in the hierarchy of powers are the angels, as well as the demons thought to play a role in magic. Demons had many powers not given to humans. They could fly, appear and disappear at will, speak diverse languages, and create many marvelous effects. Although some quite orthodox thinkers doubted the existence of demons from time to time, scholastic theology had by the late thirteenth century affirmed their reality and even made it a salient test of orthodoxy. In Thomas Aquinas' view, demons were capable of much, though they could not effect real transformations such as raising the dead, turning people into toads, or spinning straw into gold; they could, however, cause the appearance of such things by skillful use of their extensive scientific knowledge of the natural properties of things.

Following these supernatural powers come the heavenly bodies, whose powers are the highest of the natural causes, dominating all terrestrial things except the human intellect. (And even free human action is frequently dominated by celestial influence in virtue of the fact that most people follow the inclinations of their passions and these, as bodily functions, are subject to the stars and planets.) Because the positions of the heavenly bodies were thought to control not only the seasons, weather, and tides, but menstruation, the efficacy of medicines, and such processes as the growth of plants and animals, the smelting of ores, and the hardening of clay, astrology was naturalistic—an applied science rather than an occult art. Knowledge of it was useful in magic to help choose an astrologically appropriate time when natural processes would have their maximum effects.

The terrestrial world of nature operated by its own laws of physics; but unlike the modern conception in which nature's laws are inexorable and unbreakable, medieval thinkers regarded only common and spontaneous phenomena as natural. In their view, both mechanical devices and constraints upon natural tendencies (as, for example, the forced movement of a heavy body thrown upward) were regarded as preternatural, that is, beyond the laws of nature, but nonetheless possible and quite real.

People were physically, if not always morally, free to do many things to achieve their goals within God's ordained natural order. The laws of celestial influence and of terrestrial physics could be used in natural processes, or could be "broken" by unnatural processes. Magic operated, as did craft technology, within the realm of reactions, processes, and devices that were not routine or spontaneous—in short, in the realm of the "unnatural."

EVALUATION OF MAGIC BY MEDIEVAL THINKERS

Much of the intellectual discussion of magic in the Middle Ages attempted to refine, and in some cases redefine, the roles of the physical and the spiritual or demonic elements. St. Augustine, for example, made efforts to minimize the effectiveness of the natural, physical elements in magic and thereby to expand the role of demons (*City of God* 10:11). And Isidore of Seville in his great *Etymologiae* of the early seventh century provided a sinister portrait of magicians that was widely quoted and paraphrased well into the twelfth century: "*Magi* are those who are popularly called *malefici* or sorcerers on account of the magnitude of their crimes. They agitate the

MAGIC, BOOKISH

elements, disturb men's minds, and slay merely by force of incantation without any poisoned drink" (*Etymologiae* 8:9).

The longevity of this image is confirmed by the definition given in Robert Kilwardby's encyclopedia, *De ortu scientiarum,* dating from about 1250. It should also be noticed that magic differs here from philosophy, not because it is impotent fantasy, but because it is immoral and perilous to body and soul. The following is from chapter 67 of *De ortu scientiarum,* where Kilwardby is closely dependent upon chapter 15 of the seventh book of Hugh of St. Victor's *Didascalicon:*

> Magic is not accepted as part of philosophy since it teaches every iniquity and malice; lying about the truth and truly causing injury, it seduces men's minds from divine religion, it prompts them to the cult of demons, it fosters corruption of morals, and it impels the minds of its devotees to every wickedness.

In the thirteenth century, just at the time when Kilwardby was reconfirming the traditional view, some of his contemporaries in Western Europe were exploring a new philosophical vision of magic as applied knowledge, a view that emphasized the value of magic to humanity and de-emphasized its dependence on demons. This shift is evident in the writings of Roger Bacon and is especially strong in several passages in the writings of Albertus Magnus. As a comparable argument had appeared slightly earlier in the writings of William of Auvergne, bishop of Paris from 1228 to 1249, it is possible that Bacon, Albertus Magnus, and others were influenced by William; in any case, thirteenth-century scholars in general had better access to Arabic philosophy and to a more complete Aristotelian corpus than earlier Western scholars.

Where Albertus explained the Three Magi in his *Commentary on the Gospel of Matthew,* we read: "For magi are great men according to the etymology . . . . And the Magi are not sorcerers as some wrongly claim. For a magus is different from the astrologer, the enchanter, the sorcerer (or necromancer), and the other types of diviner, since properly a magus is only a great man who, having knowledge of all necessary things . . . sometimes produces marvels or gives advance notice of them." Albertus amplified his definitions of the several types of diviners and concluded that the magi did not practice those latter arts, but rather used the magical arts to produce or predict marvels, working solely by means of their knowledge of nature. He deemed this "praiseworthy."

The promotion of this new attitude in the thirteenth century apparently shows the particular influence of two works translated from the Arabic, both of which formulate magical operations as a necessary consequence of the structure of the cosmos: the *De radiis* (attributed to the ninth-century Islamic scientist al-Kindī) and the anonymous *Picatrix* (sometimes wrongly attributed to al-Majrīṭī). The former, one of the major naturalistic theories of magical effects, analyzes all forms of radiation that transmit "influence" through space, including astral influence and the effect of one mind on another. This *Book on Radiations or the Theory of Magic* argues that it is naturally flowing celestial influence, when properly tapped by magicians, that produces the unusual effects. Al-Kindī's naturalistic theory allowed no place for demons and for this reason evoked critical responses from certain quarters. But the Latin translation (made in the late twelfth or early thirteenth century) was widely dispersed in manuscripts, and al-Kindī's ideas influenced many later writers, including Roger Bacon in the thirteenth century, Nicole Oresme in the fourteenth, and John Dee in the sixteenth.

Picatrix was translated for Alfonso the Wise of Castile in 1256 from Arabic into Spanish and sometime thereafter into Latin. It is a comprehensive textbook of magic, presenting it as an applied science. After an opening chapter that establishes philosophy as the basis for magic, the second chapter offers this definition of magic:

> We call by the name necromancy all the things done by which the senses and spirits are brought to marvelous effects. . . . Necromancy is divided into two parts, theory and practice. Its theory is the knowledge of the positions of the fixed stars . . . , of the form of the heavens, and of the means by which they project their rays onto the self-moving planets. . . . And in this [theoretical part] is comprehended all of what the ancient sages related concerning the choosing of hours and seasons for the work of images [namely, talismans]. . . . And words, too, are a part of necromancy since speech has in itself the necromantic power. . . . Practice consists in the compounding of the three natures [animal, vegetable, and mineral] with the power of the influence of the fixed stars.

A third Arabic work that attracted widespread and enduring interest in the West, after being translated into Latin in the twelfth century (and again in

MAGIC, BOOKISH

the thirteenth), was the *Secretum secretorum,* purportedly a letter from Aristotle to Alexander on kingship and ethics. Originating probably in the tenth century, it grew by accretion, absorbing enough important scientific and occult material to achieve the status of an encyclopedia of learning and wise counsel. Its tenth discourse on the occult sciences includes recipes, material on talismans, herbs, and stones, as well as the theory of magic and the powers of the planets. Over 500 Latin manuscripts of this work are extant; its popularity is further attested by its medieval translations into Dutch, English, French, German, Hebrew, Italian, Spanish, and Welsh, and by an early modern rendering into Russian. Roger Bacon produced a well-known glossed version of this book.

As natural philosophy flourished and expanded in Europe in the thirteenth and fourteenth centuries, it came to include more and more magical effects among the phenomena it explained. Even critics of magic drew upon the naturalistic conception of magic found in texts like *Picatrix* and the *De radiis.* Nicole Oresme, for example, made a great effort to naturalize all magical phenomena. For most scientists of the late Middle Ages, however, credibility both of magical effects and of demons, which were assumed by the faithful to cause some of them, was accepted. Acknowledging the reality of God's miracles and of demonic actions did not, however, inhibit scholastics from elaborating novel scientific explanations for the magician's wonders: Albert thought that Pharaoh's rods-turned-into-snakes were simply a rapid instance of the process by which worms grow in rotting wood; Roger Bacon's explanation of the action of the evil eye *(fascinatio)* employed concepts from the newly recovered Aristotelian texts and the newly available philosophy of al-Kindī and Avicenna (Ibn Sīnā); and Oresme elaborated his theory of the configuration of qualities in order to explain a wide range of magical processes, including sympathetic action, attraction and repulsion at a distance, the power of enchanters' words and songs, and *fascinatio.*

When Albertus Magnus and Thomas Aquinas included magic in their understandings of the natural world, Albert tended to expand the role of celestial influence while reducing that of demons, while Thomas did the opposite. Siger of Brabant, a contemporary of Albert and Thomas, took the extreme position that from the point of view of reason, magical effects derive entirely from the powers of the heavenly bodies, that is, they take place because of the magician's scientific knowledge without any aid from demons—a position he developed with great philosophical skill and at great length. But Siger then proceeded to argue that reason has its limits and some of its conclusions must be denied by faith. In this way he espoused a role for demons and separated spiritual substances in magic. Siger's view resurfaced nearly three centuries later in the writings of Pietro Pomponazzi, especially in his book *On the Natural Causes of Effects; or, On Enchantments.*

A rather less sophisticated attempt to make sense of the processes of magical recipes in terms of the scientific principles available in the thirteenth century is seen in *A Book of the Marvels of the World,* often circulating as part of the above-mentioned pseudo-Albertus *Book of Secrets,* and likewise attributed to Albertus Magnus. This effort represents the usual approach taken by scientific writers of the Middle Ages toward magic: accept the phenomena as reported and then construct explanations of them. Rarely did the scientific writers challenge the credibility of the phenomena themselves, although they did argue at length about how great a role, if any, demons played in magic, and whether celestial or terrestrial forces were paramount in the process by which sympathy operated to accomplish remarkable effects.

In the second half of the fourteenth century, Nicole Oresme, the famous French mathematician and bishop, devoted several long works to challenging the credibility of some aspects of astrology and magic by naturalizing magic and marvels. To some phenomena he denied physical reality by asserting they were only illusions or deceptions of the observer's mind; for the others he accepted the phenomena as reported and proceeded to re-explain them only by natural causes without citing demons, God, or even—in most cases—celestial influence. He also argued that God's miracles were far less common in postbiblical times than they had been earlier and that it was therefore wrong for his contemporaries to attribute odd events to the direct hand of God. Yet Oresme, like all the medieval critics of magic, could at best reduce the scope of magic and could not—given the successful merger of Aristotelian natural philosophy and Christian theology—deny magic outright.

NEW TRENDS

Among late medieval thinkers, Oresme stands out for the vigor and sophistication with which he argued for the illusory character of magicians' achievements, but it seems possible that he was part of a

MAGIC, BOOKISH

more general development of his era, which challenged the easy identification of what seems to be with what really is.

This new attention to the relation between mental processes (especially illusions) and the operations of magic yielded two contrary tendencies which together would dominate the discussion of magic through the Renaissance and into the seventeenth century. One view emphasized artifice, that is, the illusions of hidden mechanisms and the wonders of mechanical devices, a theme that had long been part of European magic but without being taken as its central characteristic. Mechanical marvels are part of a long tradition evident in the ancient Greek works of Heron and the elaborate illustrated Islamic treatises on ingenious machines. The magic of mechanical devices played a prominent role both in stories, such as Chaucer's Squire's Tale and those about Vergil the Necromancer, and in late medieval and Renaissance pageants, morality plays, and stage dramas.

When sleight-of-hand and mechanical contrivances (which were acknowledged by many to have real human causes even though the means of working them were hidden from most people and were thus magical) were moved to center stage, the way was opened—and then widened by the general increase in use of mechanical technologies, including the new domestic clocks, in many areas of practical life—for seeing all magic simply as insufficiently explained natural phenomena rather than as productions of peculiar powers. This trend flourished during the Renaissance and blossomed fully in the seventeenth century with the mechanical philosophies of Galileo, Descartes, Boyle, and Newton.

Quite a different direction was taken in fifteenth-century Italy, where the powers of the mind, especially the imagination, were granted a new importance in magic. Rather than seeing magical effects as largely effects upon the mind, the assimilation of magic and imagination led to a new emphasis on the power of mind over external things. In this way Ficino and others constructed a new Renaissance magic of a predominantly intellectual and spiritual sort. They derived this largely from the newly available Platonic and hermetic texts translated by Ficino, but also from the theories of *Picatrix,* al-Kindī's *De radiis,* and those hermetic texts that had circulated in the Middle Ages. In particular, they took from the bookish magic of the Middle Ages the notions of man as a microcosm (in sympathetic relation with all other elements in nature), of celestial influences propagated by radiation and underlying all terrestrial phenomena, and of the powers of herbs, stones, fumigations, characters, numbers, symbols, and rituals.

BIBLIOGRAPHY

General studies. The best access to the materials on medieval magic is still Lynn Thorndike, *A History of Magic and Experimental Science,* 8 vols. (1923–1958). Also: Jurgis Baltrušaitis, *Le moyen âge fantastique: Antiquités et exotismes dans l'art gothique* (1955); Eliza M. Butler, *The Myth of the Magus* (1948) and *Ritual Magic* (1949); Edward Peters, *The Magician, the Witch, and the Law* (1978); G. Storms, *Anglo-Saxon Magic* (1948).

Ancient background. Marie-Thérèse d'Alverny, "Survivance de la magie antique," in Paul Wilpert, ed., *Antike und Orient im Mittelalter* (1962), 154–178; Geoffrey E. R. Lloyd, *Magic, Reason, and Experience* (1979); Karl Preisendanz, ed., *Papyri graecae magicae: Die griechischen Zauberpapyri,* 2 vols. (2nd ed. 1928–1931).

Magical texts. There are few reliable modern editions of medieval magic books. A handy edition of a sixteenth-century English translation of a popular medieval work attributed to Albertus Magnus is Michael R. Best and Frank H. Brightman, eds., *The Book of Secrets of Albertus Magnus of the Virtues of Herbs, Stones, and Certain Beasts; also, A Book of the Marvels of the World* (1973). Texts of Anglo-Saxon magic are found in Storms (cited above) and in Thomas Oswald Cockayne, ed., *Leechdoms, Wortcunning, and Starcraft of Early England,* 3 vols. (1864–1866). See also Nigel Barley, "Anglo-Saxon Magico-Medicine," in *Journal of the Anthropological Society of Oxford,* 3 (1972). The Latin translation of al-Kindī's *De radiis* has been edited by Marie-Thérèse d'Alverny and Françoise Hudry in *Archives d'histoire doctrinal et littéraire du moyen âge,* **41** (1974). An incomplete French version is found in Sylvain Matton, ed., *La magie arabe traditionelle* (1977). The medieval Latin version of *Picatrix* has been edited and analyzed by Vittoria Perrone Compagni, "*Picatrix* latinus: Concezioni filosofico-religiose e prassi magica," in *Medioevo,* **1** (1975). Also useful is *"Picatrix": Das Ziel des Weisen von Pseudo-Mağrīṭī,* trans. from Arabic into German by Hellmut Ritter and Martin Plessner (1962), which includes an English summary. Selections from an incomplete French version are in Matton's *La magie arabe,* which also includes texts by Ibn Khaldūn and Ibn Wahshīya. A number of versions and translation of the *Secretum secretorum* are available in Mahmoud A. Manzalaoui, ed., *Secretum secretorum: Nine English Versions* (1977); and in Roger Bacon, *Secretum secretorum cum glossis et notulis,* Robert Steele, ed., *Opera hactenus inedita,* fasc. 5 (1920). Seven valuable papers with references to the extensive literature on this work are collected in W. F. Ryan and Charles B. Schmitt, eds., *Pseudo-Aristotle, The Secret of Secrets: Sources and Influences* (1982).

Theatrical illusions and magical devices. William

Eamon, "Technology as Magic in the Late Middle Ages and the Renaissance," in *Janus,* **70** (1983); Laura Hibbard Loomis, "Secular Dramatics in the Royal Palace, Paris, 1378 and 1389, and Chaucer's 'Tregetoures,'" in *Speculum,* **33** (1958); Bruno Roy, "The Household Encyclopedia as Magic Kit: Medieval Popular Interest in Pranks and Illusions," in *Journal of Popular Culture,* **14** (1980); Wayne Shumaker, "Accounts of Marvelous Machines in the Renaissance," in *Thought,* **51** (1976).

Relations with natural science. Richard C. Dales, *The Scientific Achievement of the Middle Ages* (1973); Bert Hansen, "Science and Magic," in David C. Lindberg, ed., *Science in the Middle Ages* (1978), 483–506; Keith Hutchinson, "What Happened to Occult Qualities in the Scientific Revolution?" in *Isis,* **73** (1982); C. S. Lewis, *The Discarded Image* (1964).

Particular individuals. St. Augustine, *The City of God,* Marcus Dods, trans. (1948); Roger Bacon, "Epistola de secretis operibus artis et naturae et de nullitate magiae," in *Opera quaedam hactenus inedita,* J. S. Brewer, ed. (1859), 523–551, and *Opus maius,* John H. Bridges, ed., 3 vols. (1897–1900), trans. by Robert Belle Burke, 2 vols. (1928); Bert Hansen, *Nicole Oresme and the Marvels of Nature* (1985); Charles Edward Hopkin, *The Share of Thomas Aquinas in the Growth of the Witchcraft Delusion* (1940); Claude Jenkins, "Saint Augustine and Magic," in Edgar Ashworth Underwood, ed., *Science, Medicine, and History,* II (1953), 131–140; M. Manzalaoui, "Chaucer and Science," in Derek S. Brewer, ed., *Geoffrey Chaucer* (1974); Armand Maurer, "Between Reason and Faith: Siger of Brabant and Pomponazzi on the Magic Arts," in *Mediaeval Studies,* **18** (1956); Joseph Bernard McAllister, *The Letter of Saint Thomas Aquinas "De occultis operibus naturae ad quemdam militem ultramontanum"* (1939); A. G. Molland, "Roger Bacon as Magician," in *Traditio,* **30** (1974); Pietro Pomponazzi, *De naturalium effectuum causis; sive, De incantationibus* (1567), trans. by Henri Busson as *Les causes des merveilles de la nature; ou, Les enchantements* (1930); Lynn Thorndike, *Michael Scot* (1965).

From the Middle Ages to the early modern era. Jean Céard, *La nature et les prodiges: L'insolite au XVIe siècle, en France* (1977); Brian Easlea, *Witch Hunting, Magic, and the New Philosophy: An Introduction to Debates of the Scientific Revolution, 1450–1750* (1980); E. William Monter, *Ritual, Myth, and Magic in Early Modern Europe* (1983); Charles G. Nauert, Jr., *Agrippa and the Crisis of Renaissance Thought* (1965); Paolo Rossi, *Francis Bacon from Magic to Science,* Sacha Rabinovitch, trans., (1968); Keith V. Thomas, *Religion and the Decline of Magic* (1971); Daniel P. Walker, *Spiritual and Demonic Magic from Ficino to Campanella* (1958); Charles Webster, *From Paracelsus to Newton: Magic and the Making of Modern Science* (1982); Paola Zambelli, "Le problème de la magie naturelle à la Renaissance," in *Magia, astrologia, e religione nel rinascimento* (1974).

BERT HANSEN

[See also **Albertus Magnus; Alchemy; Aquinas, Saint Thomas; Astrology/Astronomy; Augustine of Hippo, Saint; Bacon, Roger; Kindi, al-; Magic and Folklore; Oresme, Nicole; Scientific Instruments; Siger of Brabant; Technology, Treatises on; Vergil in the Middle Ages; Witchcraft.**]

MAGISTER MILITUM (master of the soldiers), the supreme military commander of the Roman Empire from the time of Constantine. At first there were two *magistri,* one for the cavalry and one for the infantry. This was increased to five in the early Byzantine period, with each directly responsible to the emperor. A *magister equitum et peditum praesentalis* (chief of cavalry and infantry) resided at each of the two capitals and commanded the palace guards. In addition, there were three *magistri militum* in the eastern part of the empire: one for the Orient, one for Thrace, and a third for Illyricum. These had command over the *comitatenses* stationed in their areas as well as over the duces who led the *limitanei* (frontier troops). The title *magister militum* was sometimes given to barbarian challengers of the empire: Alaric was made *magister militum per Illyricum,* and Gainas, a Goth, became *magister militum praesentalis.*

BIBLIOGRAPHY

George Ostrogorsky, *History of the Byzantine State,* Joan Hussey, trans. (1957, rev. 1969).

LINDA C. ROSE

[See also **Alaric; Cavalry, Byzantine; Cavalry, European; Limitanei; Warfare, Byzantine.**]

MAGISTER OFFICIORUM (master of the offices), one of the most important Byzantine officials, having authority over a vast number of civil servants, especially the secretarial departments of the palace. As such he was an ex officio member of the imperial council or *consistorium.* He was responsible for the person of the emperor and commanded the imperial bodyguard even though he was a civilian. He was also the chief master of ceremonies of the imperial court; it was he who received foreign ambassadors and dignitaries and negotiated with them. And from the end of the fourth century he was also in charge of the postal service. He had, in effect, full control over the whole administrative structure of the empire. His own *agentes in rebus* were official couriers and provided information on all aspects of life: by the mid fifth century there were more than 1,200 of them in the eastern part of the empire alone. This office, which originated in the early fourth century, began to diminish in importance as its functions were gradually divided up among other officials, probably beginning in the seventh century.

BIBLIOGRAPHY

A. H. M. Jones, *The Later Roman Empire, 284–602,* 2 vols. (1964).

LINDA C. ROSE

[See also **Byzantine Empire: Bureaucracy.**]

MAGISTROS, a high official and later a dignitary of the Byzantine court. When the *magister officiorum* of the later Roman Empire was deprived of most of his administrative duties in the seventh century, the sources begin mentioning two "effective" *magistroi* who existed simultaneously and who acted as councilors of the emperor until the tenth century. The honorary title of *magistros,* bestowed for life, may have already existed in the eighth century and could be held by several persons simultaneously (in the tenth century Liutprand speaks of twenty-four *magistroi*). It disappears at the beginning of the twelfth century. The insignia of the *magistros* included a gilded chiton, a gold-plated tablion (shoulder strap), and a red belt decorated with gems.

BIBLIOGRAPHY

Arthur E. R. Boak and James E. Dunlap, *Two Studies in Later Roman and Byzantine Administration* (1924), 1–160; Nicolas Oikonomides, *Les listes de préséance byzantines des IXe et Xe siècles* (1972), 294.

NICOLAS OIKONOMIDES

[See also **Magister Officiorum.**]

MAGIUS. See **Maius.**

MAGNA CARTA (the great charter), sealed by King John at Runnymede in mid June 1215, has long been seen as a cornerstone of the British constitution, a source of the English people's liberties. In granting it, the king acknowledged that he was under the law and answerable to the community of the realm for his violations of the law. The charter is in the form of a free grant of concessions by King John, reissued in slightly revised form in the name of the young King Henry III in 1216 and 1217, then in its definitive version in 1225, and confirmed on many occasions down to 1416. In fact, King John did not grant the charter freely, but was coerced by the rebellion of a number of barons. They had broadened their base of support by adopting a reform program that appealed to the church and to lesser-ranking freemen as well as to the baronage. Although Magna Carta represented a peace treaty between king and baronage, it did not bring peace. Renewal of the rebellion followed (1215–1217) because of bad faith on the part of both king and baronage over the charter's implementation.

The 1215 version of the Great Charter consists of sixty-three articles, covering a wide range of topics. They can be grouped into five main areas. The first article, protecting the rights and liberties of the English church, stands apart from the others. A number of articles deal with financial concerns of King John's barons, such as their desire for limitations on his increasing demands for payments of reliefs and scutages on their fiefs and remedying abuses of the royal rights of wardship over and marriages of heirs to feudal holdings. A third group of articles deals with the royal courts and the Exchequer; for example, regulating how frequently the itinerant justices should visit the counties and defining methods for collection of crown debts. A fourth group, the last three articles, sought to guarantee that the king carried out his promises by providing for a committee of twenty-five barons to share power with him. Cooperation between the monarch and the twenty-five barons proved impossible, and civil war resulted. These articles were dropped from subsequent issues of the charter.

A final group of articles laid down general principles with lasting significance. These provisions at first applied mainly to the feudal landholding classes, but interpretations extended their protections to cover all the king's subjects by the mid fourteenth century. Most important is article 39 (29 of the 1225 Charter): "No free man shall be taken or imprisoned or disseised or outlawed or exiled or in any way ruined, nor will we go or send against him, except by the lawful judgment of his peers or by the law of the land." Other articles (12 and 14) set forth the principle that the king must obtain "the common counsel of the realm" before demanding scutages or feudal aids. It is not completely clear what that phrase meant in 1215, and the two clauses were omitted in 1225. It is often argued, however, that out of these articles grew the concept that the monarch must seek consent to any new taxation, an idea that was expressed more clearly in Edward I's 1297 Confirmation of the Charters.

Under the Yorkists and Tudors, Magna Carta receded into the background, but it came forward again under the early Stuart kings. Sir Edward Coke and other seventeenth-century common lawyers revived it as a weapon in their struggle against absolutism. They interpreted the document anachronistically, finding in it guarantees of the right to trial by jury, the right of habeas corpus, and Parliament's monopoly over the imposition of new taxes. Political thinkers in eighteenth-century Britain, because of doctrines of natural law, had less interest in Magna Carta as a historical or legal precedent for citizens' rights.

By the beginning of the twentieth century, the impact of nationalism and science brought another change in historians' emphasis. Interest in the growth of the civil service and central government caused scholars to reject the traditional view and to see Magna Carta as a feudal, reactionary document. They saw the feudal barons as standing for "feudal anarchy" and archaic localism, retarding the growth of strong national government. Scholars nevertheless recognize that although the charter was chiefly concerned with the baronial and knightly classes, in key clauses it went beyond a narrow class outlook. Furthermore, its protection was widened in the two centuries following 1215, as judicial rulings and parliamentary statutes extended it to all Englishmen. Magna Carta was a feudal document in that it applied the feudal notion that the lord had certain obligations to his vassals, and that they had the right to force him to fulfill those obligations. It moved beyond the feudal stage in applying this contract principle not only to the lord-vassal relationship but to the larger ruler-subject relationship. This principle found concrete expression in article 39 of the 1215 charter, which prohibited the king from arbitrary acts against his subjects, requiring him to follow "due process." The action of the barons in 1215 in taking up arms to force their ruler to act in accordance with the law was a precedent for later medieval rebellions, for the seventeenth-century struggles against the Stuarts, and for the American Declaration of Independence in the eighteenth century. Magna Carta's protection against arbitrary conduct by the king and his agents crossed the Atlantic with the Bill of Rights, incorporated in the first amendments to the United States Constitution.

BIBLIOGRAPHY

Herbert Butterfield, *Magna Carta in the Historiography of the Sixteenth and Seventeenth Centuries* (1969); James C. Holt, *Magna Carta* (1965) (appendixes give the 1215 Charter in Latin and English and the Latin version of the 1225 Charter, plus other related documents); J. A. P. Jones, *King John and Magna Carta* (1971); William S. McKechnie, *Magna Carta*, 2nd rev. ed. (1914); Harry Rothwell, ed., *English Historical Documents, III, 1189–1327* (1975), 310–349 (English translations of the Charters of 1215, 1216, 1217, 1225, with related documents); Faith Thompson, *The First Century of Magna Carta* (1925), and *Magna Carta* (1948).

RALPH V. TURNER

[See also **England: Norman-Angevin; Feudalism; John, King of England; Jury; Law, English Common; Parliament.**]

MAGNUS LIBER ORGANI (The great book of organum), the name generally given to the repertory of polyphonic liturgical music composed in Paris during the second half of the twelfth century and the first decades of the thirteenth. The name itself appears only once in medieval documents, in an account of the music of Paris written *ca.* 1275 by the English music theorist known today as Anonymous IV:

> Magister Leoninus was reportedly the best composer of organum, who made the great book of organum for the gradual and antiphonal, in order to enhance the divine service. This was in use until the time of the great Perotinus, who abbreviated it and made many better clausulae and puncta, for he was the best composer of discantus, and better [at discantus] than Leoninus. . . . The book or books of Magister Perotinus were in use until the time of Magister Robertus de Sabilone, and in the choir of the Paris cathedral of Notre Dame, and from his time up to the present day.

The writer describes the contents of Perotinus' libri in some detail, allowing us to identify several of his works in musical sources of the thirteenth century even though Perotinus' books themselves have not survived. Beyond this, circumstantial evidence suggests that Perotinus was active during the final years of the twelfth century and for perhaps ten or twenty years into the thirteenth century. Other remarks by Anonymous IV imply that Robertus de Sabilone was a teacher rather than a composer. About the music of the crucial figure of Leoninus, recently identified by Craig Wright as a canon of Notre Dame at the close of the twelfth century, nothing further is known with any degree of certainty; no specific compositions can be attributed to him with assurance, and no extant manuscript can be said to preserve the contents of his collection in anything like its original state.

Several manuscripts contain collections of music that correspond to Anonymous IV's liber in various stages of its history, most importantly and extensively: Florence, Biblioteca Medicea-Laurenziana, MS plut. 29.1 (copied in Paris, *ca.* 1250); Wolfenbüttel, Herzog August-Bibliothek, MS 628 Helmst. (copied at or for St. Andrews in Scotland in the late thirteenth or early fourteenth century, and often incorrectly thought to contain the work of Leoninus in its original form); and Wolfenbüttel, MS 1099 Helmst. (of unknown origin, copied *ca.* 1260–1280). Anonymous IV states that the liber was a collection of organa, but this is a term referring to polyphonic music in general and the Paris organa in fact include two genres. The first is a specific genre called organum—settings in two to four polyphonic lines of the responsorial chants of the Mass and Office (that is, the gradual and Alleluia of Mass and the great responsories of matins and vespers), pieces intended to follow Scripture readings in the service and to provide opportunities for reflection and meditation on them. The organa use the Gregorian plainchant melodies ordinarily sung at these points in the liturgy as cantus firmi over which elaborate, virtuoso lines were fashioned. Leoninus, Perotinus, and their contemporaries in Paris created a large cycle of such organa to embellish the principal feasts of the entire liturgical year, an extraordinarily ambitious achievement not to be matched until the work of Heinrich Isaac and William Byrd in the sixteenth century and J. S. Bach in the eighteenth. As Anonymous IV intimates they might, most of the Gregorian melodies set in polyphony adhere closely to the usage at the cathedral of Notre Dame de Paris.

The second main genre represented in the *Magnus liber* is the conductus—settings of newly written sacred poetry in from one to four voices, used in the service to accompany the reader to and from the lectern, at the end of the service as a replacement for or addition to the Benedicamus Domino, and at other points of action in the liturgical ceremony. Conducti are newly composed in all voices, not being based on already existing plainchant, and, unlike the organa, therefore, the individual lines tend to be similar in style and equal in importance. Both genres were intended exclusively for solo singers and are conceived on a scale unprecedented in European music history, their sheer size and brilliance "enhancing" in no small measure the splendor of the ceremonial at the newly built cathedral of Paris.

The repertory of the *Magnus liber* marks a crucially important turning point in the history of Western music. This is the earliest body of polyphonic music to have been conceived and circulated exclusively in writing, rather than being created extempore in improvization. Whereas earlier polyphony had been regarded primarily as extensions or embellishments of the plainchant on which it was based, the organa of Paris mark the beginning of composition in the modern sense; the newly created lines have a status of their own, and the cantus firmus, rather than shaping the composition, is in many respects shaped by the polyphonic treatment. It is significant, therefore, that this is the first repertory of polyphony for which the names of the composers are known. It is the earliest repertory to include music in more than two parts. It acted as the matrix in which a consistent system of consonance, dissonance, and counterpoint was developed, and in which the first coherent system of rhythm appeared in European music, along with a means for communicating it in notation. These developments helped establish the style of European art music for the next several centuries; the music of Paris circulated throughout Europe as the first body of "classical" music to appear since the Gregorian repertory four centuries earlier and laid the foundation for the emergence of local styles from England to Italy.

Leoninus' work, above all the organum, was subjected to recasting at the hands of Perotinus and others. Different manuscripts preserve the compositions in strikingly different versions, varying from totally different settings of the chant melody, to others in which some individual sections have been rewritten, to still others in which only rhythmic or melodic details have been changed. But it is not clear which represent the work of Leoninus and which that of Perotinus or of still other composers. All of the surviving manuscripts are late and none can be associated with any one composer. It is not certain what Anonymous IV meant when he referred to Pero-

MAGNUS LIBER ORGANI

tinus' work of "abbreviation"—whether he shortened the collection itself, which seems unlikely, or reduced the scale of individual works, which also seems improbable in view of the vast scale on which his known works are composed, or simply made a redaction (that is, an "edition") of Leoninus' liber, modernizing the notation in the light of changing rhythmic conceptions and recomposing sections that he found archaic. His "many better clausulae and puncta"—these terms refer to sections or phrases within a larger composition—appear to be incorporated to at least some extent into all surviving copies of the organa.

As Anonymous IV implies, most of these recomposed clausulae are in discantus style, in which the cantus firmus and newly composed voice move at more or less the same pace; other clausulae, in which the new voice sings in long melismatic flourishes over single, long-held notes of the chant, may have sustained rather less revision. The manuscripts Wolfenbüttel 628 and Florence 29.1 contain in addition separate collections of discantus clausulae; according to Ludwig's count 462 survive in the originally much larger Florence collection; these were presumably intended for substitution or interpolation into organa copied elsewhere in the same manuscript. Many are works of great technical skill and melodic or rhythmic sophistication; others, however, are simple and straightforward and may represent the work of local, less ambitious composers or the work of earlier generations. Revision and recomposition seem to have accompanied the organum repertory throughout the nearly 150 years that it was in use.

In one form or another the *Magnus liber* circulated throughout Europe. In the British Isles there were copies in the royal chapels of Edward I and Edward II; the Benedictine house of Bury St. Edmunds; St. Paul's Cathedral, London; and the Augustinian priory of St. Andrews. It was owned by the chapel of Pope Boniface VIII. It appeared in Spain in the mid thirteenth century, and the religious orders took it to Germany, Italy, and eastern Europe. A few smaller collections were created locally to supplement it. One such is the group of forty-seven organa in the last fascicle of Wolfenbüttel 628, modest works drawn from diverse sources, including Parisian ones, and intended for use at Marian Masses at St. Andrews. Another is the repertory of organa, conducti, and clausulae in the manuscript Paris, Bibliothèque Nationale, Latin 15139, a repertory seemingly associated in some way with the French royal family in the thirteenth century. The music in both collections is on a small scale in comparison with that of Leoninus and Perotinus. The notion of a cycle of polyphony for the church year was not new to Paris—the *Winchester Troper* of the early eleventh century is one earlier example, and Chartres Cathedral may have developed a cycle of responsorial chant settings in the late eleventh and twelfth centuries—but these were local creations, without the impact or the historical significance of the Parisian *liber organi.*

BIBLIOGRAPHY

Rebecca A. Baltzer, "Thirteenth-century Illuminated Manuscripts and the Date of the Florence Manuscript," in *Journal of the American Musicological Society,* **25** (1972); James H. Baxter, ed., *An Old St. Andrews Music Book (Cod. Helmst. 628)* (1931); Geoffrey Chew, "A *Magnus liber organi* Fragment at Aberdeen," in *Journal of the American Musicological Society,* **31** (1978); Luther A. Dittmer, ed., *Firenze, Biblioteca Mediceo-Laurenziana, pluteo 29.1,* 2 vols. (*Publications of Mediaeval Musical Manuscripts,* **10, 11** [n.d.]), and *Facsimile Reproduction of the Manuscript Wolfenbüttel 1099 (1206) (Publications of Mediaeval Musical Manuscripts,* **2,** [1960]); Rudolf Flotzinger, *Der Discantussatz im Magnus liber und seiner Nachfolge* (1969); Heinrich Husmann, ed., *Die drei- und vierstimmigen Notre Dame-Organa* (1940), "The Origin and Destination of the *Magnus liber organi,*" in *Musical Quarterly,* **49** (1963), and "The Enlargement of the *Magnus liber organi* and the Paris Churches St. Germain l'Auxerrois and Ste. Geneviève-du-Mont," in *Journal of the American Musicological Society,* **16** (1963); Peter Jeffery, "Notre Dame Polyphony in the Library of Pope Boniface VIII," *ibid.,* **32** (1979); Kenneth Levy, "A Dominican Organum Duplum," *ibid.,* **27** (1974); Friedrich Ludwig, *Repertorium organorum recentioris et motetorum vetustissimi stili,* 2nd ed., 2 vols., Luther A. Dittmer, ed. (1964–1978); Fritz Reckow, *Der Musiktraktat des Anonymus 4,* 2 vols. (1967), and "Das Organum," in *Gattungen der Musik in Einzeldarstellungen: Gedenkschrift Leo Schrade,* I, Wulf Arlt, ed. (1973); Edward H. Roesner, "The Origins of W_1," in *Journal of the American Musicological Society,* **29** (1976), and "The Problem of Chronology in the Transmission of Organum Duplum," in *Music in Medieval and Early Modern Europe,* Iain Fenlon, ed. (1981); Norman E. Smith, "Interrelationships Among the Alleluias of the *Magnus liber organi,*" in *Journal of the American Musicological Society,* **25** (1972), "Interrationships Among the Graduals of the *Magnus liber organi,*" in *Acta musicologica,* **45** (1973), and "Tenor Repetition in the Notre Dame Organa," in *Journal of the American Musicological Society,* **19** (1966); Jürg Stenzl, *Die vierzig Clausulae der Handscrift Paris, Bibliothèque Nationale Latin 15139 (Saint Victor-Clausulae)* (1970); William G. Waite, "The Abbreviation of the *Magnus liber,*" in *Journal of the*

American Musicological Society, **14** (1961), and *The Rhythm of Twelfth-century Polyphony* (1954).

EDWARD H. ROESNER

[See also **Anonymous IV; Clausula; Conductus; Leoninus; Music in Medieval Society; Music, Western European; Notre Dame School; Organum; Perotinus; Plainsong, Sources of.**]

MÁGUS SAGA JARLS. The tale of Earl Mágus, also known as *Bragða-Mágus saga* (Tale of the conjurer Mágus), is an anonymous *riddarasaga* (tale of chivalry) that derives from *Renaud de Montauban (Les quatre fils d'Aimon),* a chanson de geste belonging to the Carolingian cycle. The epic poem deals with a feud between Charlemagne and the four sons of Aimon. Although *Mágus saga jarls* corresponds in important details to *Renaud de Montauban,* it is not a direct translation of the epic poem, but either is based on an oral account of the tale or constitutes an Icelandic re-creation of the French version.

Two redactions of *Mágus saga jarls* are extant: the older was composed around 1300; a longer version dates from some fifty years later. The heart of both versions is the account that derives from *Renaud de Montauban:* Earl Ámundi (Aimon) has four sons—Vígvarðr, Rögnvalldr, Markvarðr, Aðalvarðr—and a daughter. Challenged to a chess game, Rögnvalldr defeats Emperor Játmundr of Saxland, named Hlöðvir (Charlemagne) in the later redaction, and thereby incurs his anger. When the emperor strikes Rögnvalldr, the latter's brother Vígvarðr avenges the insult by killing the emperor. The basic plot of the saga revolves around the ensuing clash between the emperor's son Karl and the four brothers. The latter are abetted during the feud by their brother-in-law, the conjurer Mágus, who is capable of assuming various disguises. The brothers are rescued time and again through his intervention, and in the end Mágus effects a reconciliation between the feuding parties.

In both redactions of the saga the main narrative is prefaced by a short tale of vengeance. Emperor Játmundr (Hlöðvir) imposes three seemingly impossible tasks on his wife as revenge for an apparent insult. By means of trickery she succeeds in regaining his affection. This segment of *Mágus saga* may once have existed as an independent tale. The younger redaction is supplemented by several *þættir,* short and relatively independent accounts that are frequently intercalated in a longer saga or appended as a continuation. The *þættir* are devoted to the deeds of Hrólfr Skuggafífl, Vilhjálmr Laisson, and Geirarðr Vilhjálmsson and function here as a continuation. The short narratives have only a tenuous connection to the saga about Mágus and the sons of Ámundi and presumably were not part of the original.

The younger redaction diverges from the older version of *Mágus saga jarls* not only by virtue of the appended *þættir* but also by reason of style. In the older redaction the classical, somewhat laconic style of the Icelandic sagas predominates, but the latter saga approximates stylistically the translated *riddarasögur.* Synonymous collocations, not infrequently alliterating, and the present participle are in evidence, and the author lingers over descriptions. He is a conscious manipulator of style, as is attested by an epilogue in which he explains the existence of variant versions by asserting that those who are skilled with words tend to augment stories that seem to them too briefly told. His redaction manifests a wide acquaintance with Icelandic literature in general, for example, in the account of Mágus, who, in his efforts to assist the sons of Ámundi, assumes three different guises—Skeljakarl, Viðförull, Hálfliti maðr—at the court of the emperor and fascinates his audience not only with various tricks and illusions, but also with his accounts of the heroes of old whom he has known. The author drew this material from such works as *Karlamagnús saga, Þiðreks saga,* and the *Saga af Hálfu ok Hálfsrekkum.*

That *Mágus saga jarls* has enjoyed considerable popularity in Iceland is evidenced by the fact that more than sixty manuscripts of the saga or parts thereof are extant, and of these manuscripts six date back to the fifteenth century and earlier. Most of these manuscripts are in the Arnamagnaean Institute and in the Kongelige Bibliotek (Royal Library) in Copenhagen, in the Kungliga Biblioteket (Royal Library) in Stockholm, and in the Landsbókasafn (National Library) in Reykjavík.

BIBLIOGRAPHY

Editions. Gustaf Cederschiöld, ed., "Mágus saga jarls," in *Fornsögur Suðrlanda* (1884), 1–42; Páll Eggert Ólason, ed., *Mágus saga jarls ásamt þáttum af Hrólfi skuggafífli, Vilhjálmi Laissyni og Geirharði Vilhjálmssyni* (1916); Gunnlaugur Þórðarson, ed., *Bragða-Mágus saga með tilheyrandi þáttum* (1858); Bjarni Vilhjálmsson, ed., "Mágus saga jarls (hin meiri)," in *Riddarasögur,* II (1949).

Studies. Eyvind Fjeld Halvorsen, "Mágus saga jarls," in *Kulturhistorisk leksikon for nordisk middelalder,* XI

(1966); Andrew Hamer, "Mágus saga: Riddarasaga or Fornaldarsaga," in *Fourth International Saga Conference, München, July 30th–Aug. 4th, 1979* (1979); Reinhold Köhler, "Zur Mágus-Saga," in *Germania: Vierteljahrsschrift für deutsche Alterthumskunde,* **21** (1876); Eugen Kölbing, "Zur älteren romantischen Litteratur im Norden, II," *ibid.;* Eugen Mogk, Review of Cederschiöld's *Fornsögur Suðrlanda,* in *Zeitschrift für deutsche Philologie,* **17** (1885); Hermann Suchier, "Die Quellen der Mágussaga," in *Germania: Vierteljahrsschrift für deutsche Alterthumskunde,* **20** (1875); Fredrik Wulff, *Recherches sur les Sagas de Mágus et de Geirard et leurs rapports aux épopées françaises* (1873–1874), 44.

MARIANNE E. KALINKE

[See also **Karlamagnús Saga; Riddarasögur; Þættir; Þiðreks Saga.**]

MAGYARS, name of the Hungarians and their language, derived from the name of a phratry in archaic Finno-Ugric times. Their Western name, *Hungari,* originated from the Magyars' having been part of the Onogur-Turkic empire in the eighth–ninth centuries (hence also their Byzantine name, *Tourkoi*). Linguistic and archaeological evidence suggests that the most ancient substratum of the Magyars left their original dwellings near the Oka River around 3000 B.C. and wandered south. From the fifth century on, they lived in the south Russian grassland steppe (though some remained in or returned to the north, where they were still encountered by Dominican travelers to Magna Hungaria in the early thirteenth century). The Magyars were part of various nomad empires, the last being that of the Khazars. Apparently in response to the Magyars' fighting in alliance with the Byzantines against them, the Pechenegs attacked the Magyars around 895 and forced them to move into the sparsely populated Carpathian basin. This resettlement may have involved some 400,000 seminomadic families, including members of non-Magyar tribes. The Slavs and the possible remnants of earlier settlers (perhaps Avars) were assimilated relatively soon, as were many of the Western knights and peasant-urban *hospites,* so that during the Middle Ages the Magyars were the ethnic majority in the kingdom of Hungary.

The Magyar language, essentially Finno-Ugric in structure but extensively enriched by loanwords from their neighbors and from Latin, appears up to the thirteenth century only in fragments. A written vernacular (lay spiritual) literature began to develop then, but as Latin remained the official language of Hungary until 1823, no major medieval historical source was written in the vernacular.

BIBLIOGRAPHY

Lóránd Benkő and Samu Imre, eds., *The Hungarian Language* (1972), esp. 15–36 and 327–347; Tamas Bogyay, "Research into the Origin and Ancient History of the Hungarian Nation After the Second World War," in *The Hungarian Quarterly,* **3** (1962); Pál Lipták, "An Anthropological Survey of Magyar Prehistory," in *Acta linguistica Academiae scientiarum Hungariae,* **4** (1954); Denis Sinor, "The Outline of Hungarian Prehistory," in *Cahiers d'histoire mondial,* **4** (1958)—see also the exchange of comments between Erik Molnár and Sinor, *ibid.,* **5** (1959). On Magna Hungaria, see Hansgerd Göckenjan, "Das Bild der Völker Osteuropas in den Reiseberichten ungarischer Dominikaner des 13. Jahrhunderts," in *Östliches Europa: Spiegel der Geschichte. Festschrift für Manfred Hellmann* (1977).

JÁNOS M. BAK

[See also **Hungary; Russian Nomads, Invasions of.**]

MAHDĪ, AL- (Abū ᶜAbd Allāh Muḥammad ibn ᶜAbd Allāh al-Mahdī; *d.* 785, after a reign of ten years), third caliph of the Abbasid dynasty. The eldest son of al-Manṣūr, Muḥammad, who was called al-Mahdī (the rightly guided), was sent as a boy to serve as governor of Khorāsān. The purpose of this appointment was to allow the young Abbasid to cut his political teeth in an important provincial setting. Given Muḥammad's tender age, it is clear that day-to-day affairs in Khorāsān were largely the responsibility of the young prince's political tutors and military advisers. In effect, the future caliph was given a base of power from which to support his claim to rule.

At first, al-Mahdī was the second heir apparent, after a much older cousin, ᶜĪsā ibn Mūsā, who had been a hero of the Abbasid revolution. ᶜĪsā had been a strong supporter of al-Manṣūr from his sinecure as governor of Al-Kufa. But al-Manṣūr, suspicious that ᶜĪsā, once caliph, would remove al-Mahdī in favor of his own progeny, set into motion a plan for son and nephew to exchange places in the line of succession. After considerable resistance, ᶜĪsā reluctantly agreed. Al-Mahdī returned from Khorāsān in 768 at the head of a triumphal procession. Everywhere he stopped, he distributed gifts to local functionaries—gifts that were matched by the caliph himself. They were meant to buy him support. Upon arriving at the capital, a public ceremony was held to reaffirm the caliph's decision and to allow the notables of the ruling house to pledge allegiance to al-Mahdī and then to ᶜĪsā ibn Mūsā. Not content with this arrangement, al-Mahdī later removed his cousin from the line of succession, thus guaranteeing that the dynasty would be maintained by his progeny alone.

Concurrent with the change in the line of succession, al-Manṣūr began construction of a major administrative center on unoccupied lands on the east side of the Tigris, across the river from Baghdad. The palace complex, which rivaled his own Round City, was designated the future residence of his son and served to give visual expression to al-Mahdī's newly established credentials. Following his father's death, al-Mahdī moved with a large retinue to the east side. The new administrative center, which was called al-Ruṣāfah, soon gave rise to extensive urban development in the adjacent areas of the east side.

Al-Mahdī's rule was marked by sound fiscal policies. Taking the advice of Abū ᶜUbayd Allāh Muᶜāwiya ibn ᶜUbayd Allāh, his vizier and an expert on taxation, the caliph changed the method of assessing agricultural lands. Previously, the assessment had been based entirely on the extent of land under production. Henceforth, taxes were levied (in kind) in proportion to agricultural output. The rationale for the new system was to protect farmers in times of bad harvest, when a tax geared to land would have been punitive. It also enabled the authorities to profit from a series of good harvests. Similarly, the caliph imposed a new system of taxation on the extensive markets of Baghdad. Merchants and artisans previously taxed according to the size of their establishments were now assessed relative to the wealth of the craft. In principle, the new system of taxation, also proposed by Abū ᶜUbayd Allāh Muᶜāwiya, guaranteed that those most able to sustain the tax burden did so. When he died, al-Mahdī reportedly left the imperial coffers full.

Al-Mahdī was not particularly innovative. For the most part, he continued the general policies of his father. The noble Abbasids from other branches of the family were returned to positions of prominence within the administration; but even then they did not exercise the dominant authority they had known in the past. On the contrary, al-Mahdī expanded the policy of utilizing clients and other confidants in positions of trust. The Barmakid family in particular extended its influence both in the capital and in the provinces.

One area in which the new caliph departed from his father's policies was in actively pursuing armed conflict with the Byzantines. Whereas al-Manṣūr had contented himself with border raids, al-Mahdī sought to acquire territory at the expense of the Christians, and huge expeditions were organized to that end. The expeditions led by his son Hārūn al-Rashīd in 780 and 782 were the largest and best equipped since the time of the Umayyads. The eastern frontier was also active during al-Mahdī's reign. Muslim armies pressed into Farghāna (in Transoxiana), forcing formerly independent rulers to acknowledge Muslim authority. Within the "abode of Islam," al-Mahdī was particularly severe with heretics. These included a charismatic leader from Khorāsān called "the Veiled One" (al-Muqannaᶜ), who successfully resisted the imperial armies for four years before being crushed. Abandoned by most of his followers, he died by his own hand.

Al-Mahdī had planned to leave the caliphate to his son Mūsā al-Hādī, but after some consideration he leaned to his son Hārūn. Before any change could be formally initiated, the caliph died, aged forty-three, allegedly the victim of poisoned fruit.

BIBLIOGRAPHY

Nabia Abbott, *Two Queens of Baghdad* (1946); Hugh Kennedy, *The Early Abbasid Caliphate* (1981); Jacob Lassner, *The Topography of Baghdad in the Early Middle Ages: Texts and Studies* (1970), and *The Shaping of ᶜAbbāsid Rule* (1980); Guy Le Strange, *Baghdad During the Abbasid Caliphate* (1900).

JACOB LASSNER

[See also **Abbasids; Baghdad; Barmakids; Hārūn al-Rashid; Manṣūr, al-, Abū Jaᶜfar.**]

MAHDI, THE. See **Millennialism, Islamic.**

MAI UND BEAFLOR is a rhymed legend of some 9,600 lines written in Middle High German, possibly during the second half of the thirteenth century. The unknown author of the poem asserts in the introduction to his work that he received his material orally from a "worthy knight," who had found it in a chronicle. The characterization of the Greek realm of Count Mai in the work appears to have as its point of reference a Greek dominion founded by the house of Villehardouin during the Fourth Crusade. The anonymous source, then, may well have been French. The tale is in any case an adaptation of a highly popular narrative motif, the slandering of an innocent queen, a motif perhaps best known in the Crescentia-Genoveva legend but treated in a variety of forms throughout the European Middle Ages.

Beaflor, daughter of the widower emperor of Rome, flees the incestuous advances of her father. With the help of a pair of faithful servants, she obtains a ship. She ultimately lands in the duchy of Count Mai, who marries the princess, a foreigner, despite the opposition of his mother. While Mai is absent on a crusade, the mother-in-law falsely accuses Beaflor of having given birth to an illegitimate son. Mai, informed of the accusation, sends orders that his wife be executed. The princess once again escapes by sea with the help of loyal vassals. Count Mai returns home and, enraged by his discovery of the truth of the matter, kills his mother. Beaflor in the meantime has safely reached Rome and is taken in by the servants who had aided her in her original flight. After eight years of penance for his misdeeds, Mai makes a pilgrimage to the Eternal City, seeking absolution. There he is forgiven, reunited with his wife and child, and crowned emperor of Rome.

The poem is essentially didactic, an exemplum of the rewards of patient suffering and Christian humility. Divine power vindicates the innocent heroine, who puts her trust in her Maker and abandons herself to his will despite a series of injustices and nearly unendurable trials. Her fortitude and faith bring grace, not only to herself but also to her erring husband and even to her sinful father, who is given absolution by the pope at the end of the tale. The poet's style is modeled on that of Hartmann von Aue and Gottfried von Strassburg, masters of the *ornatus facilis* (light style). The work, though at heart a Christian legend (the action being dominated by miracle rather than adventure), nevertheless successfully integrates the matter of romance into its structure. *Minne* psychology and courtly etiquette lend the religious poem a touch of secular elegance.

BIBLIOGRAPHY

Mai und Beaflor, Alois Joseph Vollmer, ed. (1848). Also: Fritz Peter Knapp, "Das Bild Griechenlands in der Verserzählung 'Mai und Beaflor,'" in *Beiträge zur Geschichte der deutschen Sprache und Literatur* (Tübingen), **98** (1976); Albert Leitzmann, "Zu Mai und Beaflor," in *Zeitschrift für deutsches Altertum,* **67** (1930); Ferdinand Schultz, *Die Überlieferung der mittelhochdeutschen Dichtung "Mai und Beaflor"* (1890); R. Sprenger and Ferdinand Schultz, "Zu Mai und Bêaflôr," in *Zeitschrift für deutsche Philologie,* **28** (1896); Otto Wächter, *Untersuchung über das Gedicht "Mai und Beaflor"* (1889).

JAMES F. POAG

[See also **Middle High German Literature.**]

MAIMONIDEAN CONTROVERSY is often used imprecisely in modern historiography in referring to several distinct episodes of Kulturkampf generated by the impact of the work of Moses Maimonides (*d.* 1204) and other philosophical writers upon traditional Jewish society in Christian Europe.

Conflict began during Maimonides' lifetime over the implications of theological statements in his codification of Jewish law, the *Mishneh Torah.* The assertion that the soul experienced a purely spiritual reward in the "world to come" immediately after death left critics in doubt about Maimonides' acceptance of the traditional doctrine of physical resurrection. Maimonides responded in an "Epistle on Resurrection" *(Ma*ᵓ*amar Teḥiyyat ha-Metim),* affirming his adherence to this belief.

The more encompassing conflict that erupted in the early 1230's involved some of the leading Jewish intellectuals of France and Spain. Rabbis from northern France were said to have placed a ban upon the first book of the *Mishneh Torah* and the *Moreh Nevukhim (Guide of the Perplexed).* Supporters and opponents of such a ban argued vigorously and acrimoniously over the legitimacy of Greek philosophy, the propriety of nonliteral interpretation of biblical verses and statements of rabbinic lore, the rational explanation of the commandments, and various aspects of eschatological doctrine. Apparently, opponents of Maimonides denounced his works before the newly established papal Inquisition, which is reported to have ordered copies of the books to be publicly burned in 1232.

The conflict that inflamed the Jewish communities of southern France from 1302 to 1305 was quite different. Maimonides was no longer at issue; both sides professed deep respect for his work, recognized the legitimacy of philosophy within certain bounds, and criticized the excesses of extreme rationalism. This conflict centered on an effort to prohibit Jews under age twenty-five from studying Greek and Arabic philosophical works, now accessible in Hebrew translations. The ban declared by the rabbinical court of Solomon ben Adret in Barcelona did not succeed in limiting the study of philosophy in southern France.

BIBLIOGRAPHY
Abraham S. Halkin, "Yedaiah Bedershi's Apology," in Alexander Altmann, ed., *Jewish Medieval and Renaissance Studies* (1967); Raphael Jospe, "Faith and Reason: The Controversy over Philosophy," in *idem* and S. Wagner, eds., *Great Schisms in Jewish History* (1980); Joseph Sarachek, *Faith and Reason: The Conflict over the Rationalism of Maimonides* (1935); Bernard Septimus, *Hispano-Jewish Culture in Transition* (1982); Daniel J. Silver, *Maimonidean Criticism and the Maimonidean Controversy, 1180–1240* (1965); Charles Touati, "La controverse de 1303–1306 autour des études philosophiques et scientifiques," in *Revue des études juives,* **127** (1968).

MARC SAPERSTEIN

[See also **Jews in Europe: After 900; Judeo-Arabic Literature; Maimonides, Moses; Philosophy and Theology, Jewish; Polemics, Christian-Jewish.**]

MAIMONIDES, ABRAHAM BEN MOSES (1186–1237). The leader (nagid) of the Egyptian Jewish community from 1205 to his death, Abraham Maimonides was an active scholar and judge of Jewish law, a defender of his celebrated father's rationalistic halakhic writings, a biblical and talmudic commentator, a court physician, and a would-be reformer, under Sufi influence, of Jewish ritual. He was also the author of an encyclopedic work, *Kifayāt al-ᶜabidīn* (Compendium [Guide] for the pious), extant in part, which advocates a Sufi-style pietism for Judaism.

BIBLIOGRAPHY
The High Ways to Perfection of Abraham Maimonides, Samuel Rosenblatt, trans., 2 vols. (1927–1938). Also: Gerson D. Cohen, "The Soteriology of R. Abraham Maimuni," in *American Academy for Jewish Research: Proceedings,* **35** (1967) and **36** (1968); S. D. Goitein, "Abraham Maimonides and His Pietist Circle," in Alexander Altmann, ed., *Jewish Medieval and Renaissance Studies* (1967).

ALFRED L. IVRY

[See also **Jews in Egypt; Maimonides, Moses.**]

MAIMONIDES, MOSES (also known as Rambam, the acronym of **R**abbi **M**oses **b**en **M**aimon) (1135 or 1138–1204), was one of the outstanding figures of Jewish history and had a profound and pervasive impact on Jewish life and thought. His epoch-making works in the central areas of halakhah and religious philosophy were extensively studied, meticulously annotated, frequently translated, and intensively interpreted. Their massive erudition and remarkable originality were unmistakable, and the extraordinary conjunction of halakhic authority and philosophic prestige was noted. Consequently, their influence, direct as well as indirect and reflected in the works of many authors who wrote in various genres, was global and unique.

The Maimonides family fled Córdoba in 1148 after the invasion of the fanatical Almohads, wandered through southern Spain and North Africa (1148–1158), and settled in Fēs for several years. In 1165 Maimonides resumed his wanderings, going from Morocco to the land of Israel, which was then the scene of the crusades—turbulent and inhospitable. After making his way southward from Acre through Jerusalem to Hebron, he eventually settled in Cairo. He began to practice medicine and became the house physician of Saladin's vizier. Simultaneously, he emerged as the untitled leader of the Jewish community but refused to accept any aid or remuneration, choosing instead to remain economically self-sufficient—a practice that reflected his religious-philosophical principles. His only son, Abraham, who was to become the official head (nagid) of the Jewish community and author of important exegetical and philosophical works, was born in 1186; by the time of Maimonides' death in 1204, Abraham had already managed to absorb an impressive amount of his father's teaching.

Maimonides was a prolific, versatile author, profound and original and, hence, authoritative. His youthful works, composed for the most part during his wanderings, include *Millot Higgayon* (a treatise on logic) and *Maᵓamar ha-Ibbur* (a treatise on astronomy and the Jewish calendar). His pioneering, comprehensive *Commentary on the Mishnah* (composed in Arabic), which was to engage his attention for about ten years (1158–1168), was intended both as an introduction to the Talmud and as a review of the Talmud. It is distinguished not only by close textual annotation and conceptual analysis but by many philosophical, scientific, and theological comments; it contains the equivalent of three important monographs, dealing with the doctrinal foundations of the oral law, the principles of Jewish belief, and the components of ethical theory, especially a definitive formulation of virtue as the golden mean. During the same period he completed two significant works that remained marginal in the later history of Talmudic literature: a brief commentary on three orders of the Babylonian Talmud and a compendium of laws found in the Palestinian Talmud. The most notable of his early letters and occasional pieces are the *Iggeret ha-Shemad* (Epistle on conversion) and the *Iggeret Teiman* (Epistle to Yemen)—both concerned with the vexing problems of persecution, conversion, catastrophe, false messianism, general demoralization, and the meaning of history.

His two most famous and enduring works are the *Mishneh Torah* (completed *ca.* 1178) and the *Moreh Nevukhim (Guide of the Perplexed),* completed between 1185 and 1190 and translated from the original Judeo-Arabic to Hebrew in 1204. The first, a work without precedent or sequel, is a fourteen-volume presentation of Jewish law distinguished by five major characteristics: (1) its codificatory form, which eliminated indeterminate debate and conflicting interpretation and generally formulated unilateral, undocumented decisions; (2) comprehensive scope, which obliterated accidental distinctions between the practical and the theoretical and insisted that the law in its totality be studied; (3) classification of the law in accord with a new topical-conceptual arrangement that departed from the sequence of the Mishnah and Talmud; (4) style and language, utilizing the Hebrew of the Mishnah rather than the Hebrew of the Bible or the Aramaic of the Talmud and developing a rich, flexible style characterized by precision, brevity, and elegance; and (5) fusion of halakhah and philosophy, that is, the unification of the practical, theoretical, and theological components of the law by summarizing the metaphysical and ethical postulates of Judaism.

In preparation for the *Mishneh Torah,* Maimonides wrote *Sefer ha-Mitzvot* (Book of commandments), which provided an exact, exhaustive list of the 613 commandments, thereby guarding against forgetfulness and omissions in the code; it also contains fourteen guiding principles *(shorashim)* that determine which laws should be included.

The *Moreh Nevukhim,* enigmatic in character, remains provocative and influential, though it is from one point of view hermeneutical, methodological, and interpretive; its raw material consists of difficult, often disconcerting passages from biblical and rabbinic literature interpreted in accordance with philosophic-scientific concepts. In essence, it covers a wide spectrum of philosophic problems: the claims of reason versus revelation; the existence, unity, and incorporeality of God; creation versus eternity of the world; problems of physics; miracles and natural law; prophecy; evil; providence; the reasons for the commandments. Maimonides was aware of the dangers of philosophy but also commited to its indispensability for religious perfection. As a result of his rigor and candor, his oeuvre marked the peak of medieval Jewish rationalism.

BIBLIOGRAPHY

Isidore Epstein, ed., *Moses Maimonides 1135–1204* (1935); Julius Guttmann, *Philosophies of Judaism* (1969); Abraham J. Heschel, *Maimonides,* Joachim Neugroschel, trans. (1982); Maimonides, *Crisis and Leadership: Epistles,* Abraham Halkin and David Hartman, trans. and eds. (1985); Shlomo Pines, "The Philosophic Sources of the Guide," in *Guide to the Perplexed,* S. Pines, trans. (1963); Isadore Twersky, *Introduction to the Code of Maimonides (Mishneh Torah)* (1980); Harry A. Wolfson, *Studies in the History of Philosophy and Religion,* 2 vols., Isadore Twersky and George H. Williams, eds. (1973–1977).

ISADORE TWERSKY

[See also **Aristotle in the Middle Ages; Cookery, European; Eckhart, Meister; Egypt, Islamic; Exegesis, Jewish; Historiography, Jewish; Judeo-Arabic Literature; Law, Jewish; Maimonidean Controversy; Philosophy and Theology, Jewish; Talmud, Exegesis and Study of.**]

MAINMORT was the custom whereby postmortem conveyance of chattels and real property to heirs of the body was denied or circumscribed. A person's liability to mainmort was in most areas of Europe, from the twelfth century on, a sign that he was a serf. Indeed, in many areas it was the condition that made him, juridically speaking, a serf.

When the word "mainmort," which means "dead hand" or, less literally, "dead power," is applied to chattels or movable goods, it describes a system in which a person's movables reverted on his death to his lord. The person to whom the goods reverted may be said, in some cases, to have proved personal lordship over the deceased by the latter's subjection to the system. The goods themselves were not necessarily physically removed to the lord's power. On the contrary, the "heir" would likely receive the goods under the same conditions as his predecessor in possession (formal reversion at death to the lord or his heir). How such a dependent relationship may have come into being depends on circumstances. A peasant, for example, might desire tools and animals to clear and work land, and he might secure those tools and animals from a person of wealth and influence on the condition that dominium over these goods remain to the grantor and his heirs. Once enough examples of this sort of dependency came into being, it became routine in some parts of Europe to impose mainmort on any laboring person who commended himself to a lord. Comparison with certain aspects of early medieval slavery suggests that another source for the custom of mainmort was the desire among lords to keep control over freed slaves by retaining power over their ability to transmit goods at death.

Even so, the regime of mainmort was not universal in Europe. Areas might be found where it was a minor aspect of the relationship of lords and their dependents. Moreover, traditions of inheritance among rustics and in towns mitigated the rigorous meaning attached to mainmort. Often the "best beast" was offered to the lord for permission to inherit. This mitigation served the needs of the lords: It gave them profit and emphasized their lordship without reducing laborers to poverty or inducing them to flee. Another form of mitigation was the privilege bestowed formally or informally on serfs to alienate a portion of their chattels by will to the church. In towns the restriction might be lifted entirely in order to stimulate commerce or in-migration, or to preserve order, for there is no doubt that the custom was considered debasing. Usually it was only when a serf had no heirs of the body and when collateral relations wished to succeed to their deceased relative's goods that there was a hardening of the practice of mainmort; stiff payments might be required for the privilege of succession.

When the word "mainmort" is applied to real property, it describes a system whereby land occupied by a person is returned to the possession of the lord on that person's death. The term might apply either to the land itself or to the occupant. In other words, it was possible for a free person to occupy and exploit land held under the liability of mainmort (in the same way that it was possible for a person liable to mainmort for his movable goods to possess some land freely and without restrictions). It was the late-twelfth- and thirteenth-century legists who frowned upon this situation. Their works contain evidence of the growing perception that residence on and exploitation of a mainmortable (servile) tenement for one year and one day by a free person would result in the degradation of the possessor to the status of a serf.

Mainmortability persisted in some places of rural Europe until the nineteenth century.

BIBLIOGRAPHY

Marc Bloch, "Liberté et servitude personnelles au moyen âge, particulièrement en France," in *Anuario de historia del derecho español* (1933), repr. in his *Mélanges historiques,* I (1963), and *Feudal Society,* L. A. Manyon, trans., I (1964), 206, 250–251, 263; *Histoire de la France rurale,* I, *La formation des campagnes françaises dès origines au XIVe siècle* (1975), 478–482, 493; Paul R. Hyams, *King, Lords, and Peasants in Medieval England: The Common Law of Villeinage in the Twelfth and Thirteenth Centuries* (1980), 69–70, 176–177.

William Chester Jordan

[See also **Class Structure, Western; Feudalism; Inheritance, Western European; Serf, Serfdom: Western European.**]

MAISTRE PIERRE PATHELIN is the best-known, the most complex, and one of the longest (1,599 lines) of the comic plays called farces that flourished in France from about 1450 to 1560. Written sometime between 1456 and 1469, its author is unknown, though some scholars have conjectured that it was Guillaume Alecis and others that it was one of the law clerks of the Basoche, a Parisian legal society that performed plays. The characters include Pierre Pathelin, a crafty, would-be lawyer; his wife and accomplice, Guillemette; Guillaume Joceaulme, a wealthy draper; Thibault Aignelet, a shepherd; and a judge. The main theme, common in farce, is that of the duper or trickster (Pathelin) who is outwitted by someone who appears to be less clever than himself (Thibault). In the play, which can be divided into eleven scenes, all the characters except the judge attempt to trick one another through guile, deceit, and a variety of ruses including feigned illness and stupidity, confusing use of dialects and language in general (for instance, double meanings), disguises, and outright lies. The humor hinges on puns, popular proverbs turned inside out, and visual tricks. First the draper, who wants to overcharge Pathelin for some cloth, and then Pathelin, who gets it on credit, are outwitted. Pathelin's undoing comes in the final scene when Thibault, who stands accused of having killed and eaten a number of the draper's sheep, is acquitted, largely on the grounds of incompetence, a defense contrived by Pathelin. Thibault then turns the tables on Pathelin by pretending to say only "bee" (sounding like a sheep) and refusing to pay him his fee.

Maistre Pierre Pathelin is a masterpiece rivaling Molière's early plays. Several expressions from the play continue to enrich the French language (for instance, *patelin/pateline, patelinage, pateliner,* and *revenons à [nos] moutons*).

BIBLIOGRAPHY

Sources. Editions include *Maistre Pierre Pathelin, farce du XVe siècle,* Richard T. Holbrook, ed. (1924, 2nd ed., rev., 1970); *Maistre Pierre Pathelin, reproduction en facsimilé de l'édition imprimée en 1489 par Pierre Levet,* Richard T. Holbrook, ed. (1953); *Four Farces,* Barbara Bowen, ed. (1967); *La farce de Maistre Pathelin et ses continuations Le nouveau Pathelin et Le testament de Pathelin* (1979).

Studies. E. Cazalas, "Où et quand se passe l'action de *Maistre Pierre Pathelin?*" in *Romania,* **57** (1931); L.-Émile Chevaldin, *Les jargons de la farce de Pathelin* (1903); Louis Cons, *L'auteur de la farce de Pathelin* (1926); Howard G. Harvey, *The Theatre of the Basoche: The Contribution of the Law Societies to French Mediaeval Comedy* (1941, repr. 1969); Richard T. Holbrook, *Étude sur Pathelin* (1917, repr. 1965), and "Pour le commentaire de *Maistre Pierre Pathelin,*" in *Romania,* **54** (1928); Rita Lejeune, "Pour quel public la *Farce de Maistre Pierre Pathelin* a-t-elle été rédigée?" in *Romania,* **82** (1961), and "Le vocabulaire juridique de *Pathelin* et la personnalité de l'auteur," in *Fin du moyen âge et Renaissance—Mélanges offerts à Robert Guiette* (1961); P. Lemercier, "Les éléments juridiques de *Pathelin* et la localisation de l'oeuvre," in *Romania,* **73** (1952); H. Lewicka, "Pour la localisation de la farce de *Me Pathelin,*" in *Bibliothèque d'humanisme et Renaissance,* **24** (1962); Emmanuel Philipot, "Remarques et conjectures sur le texte de *Maistre Pierre Pathelin,*" in *Romania,* **56** (1930); Bruno Roy, "La farce de *Maître Pathelin,* et autres oeuvres du fou Triboulet," in *Fifteenth-century Studies,* **3** (1980).

CHRISTOPHER PINET

[See also **Drama, French; Fabliau and Comic Tale; Farces.**]

MAITANI, AMBROGIO (*fl.* first half of fourteenth century), a Sienese architect and the brother of Lorenzo Maitani. Between 1298 and 1326 he was the

Church of S. Ercolano, Perugia. Ambrogio Maitani *et al.,* early 14th century. FROM R. A. GALLENGA-STUART, PERUGIA (1905)

Hell. Relief by Lorenzo Maitani from facade of Orvieto Cathedral, *ca.* 1310–1330. PHOTO: WIM SWAAN

city architect for Perugia, working on S. Ercolano and designing the facade and stairs for the Palazzo Pubblico. In 1337, along with his nephews Vitale and Antonio, he received payment from Orvieto for fortifications.

BIBLIOGRAPHY
Ulrich Thieme and Felix Becker, eds., *Allgemeines Lexikon der bildenden Künstler,* XXIII (1929), 582; John White, *Art and Architecture in Italy: 1250–1400* (1966).

ADELHEID M. GEALT

[See also **Gothic Architecture; Maitani, Lorenzo.**]

MAITANI, LORENZO (*d.* 1330), *capomaestro* of the Cathedral of Orvieto from 1310 until his death. His chief accomplishment was the design and supervision of construction of the lower part of the facade. How much earlier work he had to incorporate into his design is uncertain, but the existence of two divergent plans and of differing styles in the sculpture of the piers suggests a preceding campaign. Although not mentioned as a sculptor, Maitani probably was one; the lower reliefs of the Genesis and Last Judgment piers reflect his Sienese origins by their similarities to contemporary painting there.

BIBLIOGRAPHY
Enzo Carli, *Il duomo di Orvieto* (1965); Geza de' Francovich, "Lorenzo Maitani scultore e i bassorilievi della facciata del duomo di Orvieto," in *Bollettino d'arte,* 7 (1927–1928); Luigi Fumi, *Il duomo di Orvieto e i suoi restauri* (1891); Harald Keller, "Die Risse der Orvietaner Domopera und die Anfänge der Bildhauerzeichnung," in *Festschrift Wilhelm Pinder* (1938); John Pope-Hennessy, *An Introduction to Italian Sculpture,* I, *Italian Gothic Sculpture,* 2nd ed. (1972), 19–21, 188–189, pls. 40–45; John White, "The Reliefs on the Façade of the Duomo at Orvieto," in *Journal of the Warburg and Courtauld Institutes,* 22 (1959).

MICHAEL D. TAYLOR

[See also **Gothic Architecture; Gothic Art: Sculpture.**]

Genesis. Relief by Lorenzo Maitani from facade of Orvieto Cathedral, *ca.* 1310–1330. PHOTO: ALINARI

MAIUS (tenth century), the Spanish illuminator who signed (*ca.* 950, probably at S. Miguel de Escalada [León]) one of the earliest and most richly illustrated copies of Beatus' *Commentary on the Apocalypse* (New York, Pierpont Morgan Library, MS 644). He is usually identified with the Magius whose name appears in the Beatus *Commentary* of Tábara of 970 (Madrid, Archivo Histórico Nacional, codex 1097B).

BIBLIOGRAPHY

Wilhelm Neuss, *Die Apokalypse des hl. Johannes,* I (1931), 9–16; John Williams, *Early Spanish Manuscript Illumination* (1977).

J. WILLIAMS

[See also **Beatus Manuscripts; Manuscript Illumination.**]

MAJESTAS DOMINI (majesty of the Lord), Latin term for Christ seen as the ruler of the world, the

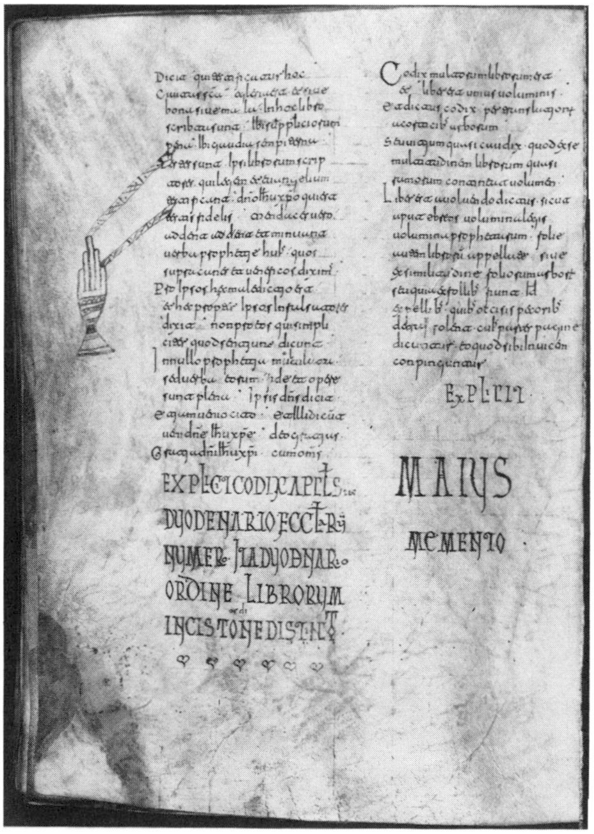

Signature of Maius from Beatus' *Commentary on the Apocalypse, ca.* 950. NEW YORK, PIERPONT MORGAN LIBRARY, MS 644, f. 233v

cosmocrator. A convention in Christian iconography, Jesus Christ is depicted as sitting on a throne, the world, or a rainbow. Typically, Christ is surrounded by a nimbus or mandorla and accompanied by cherubim, church fathers, and the evangelists or their symbols or the alpha and omega. In the Christian East, Christ is not normally shown enthroned, but seated on a rainbow. Hence confusion is avoided between Christ and the state sovereign, who rules the terrestrial kingdom in the name of the Lord.

BIBLIOGRAPHY

Ormonde M. Dalton, *Byzantine Art and Archaeology* (1911); André Grabar, *The Art of the Byzantine Empire: Byzantine Art of the Middle Ages,* Betty Foster, trans. (1966), and *Christian Iconography* (1968).

JENNIFER E. JONES

[See also **Byzantine Art; Lombard Art** (with illustration).]

MAJOLICA, a type of faience especially associated in the Middle Ages with Spain and Italy. Its manufacture begins with firing a piece of earthenware, then coating it with tin enamel, which forms a white, opaque, porous surface. A design is then painted on the white surface, a transparent glaze ap-

Majolica plate of reddish clay covered with white enamel and decorated in green and purplish black. Paterna, 13th–14th century. MUSEO NACIONAL DE CERÁMICA "GONZALEZ MARTÍ," VALENCIA

plied, and the piece is fired again. Beginning in the early fourteenth century, Spanish centers such as Manises and Paterna led production in the Mediterranean area for 150 years. The most common type of fourteenth-century Spanish majolica, which was exported all over the Mediterranean and influenced production in Italy, was decorated with either green or blue, and black or deep purple, on a white background. By the mid fourteenth century much majolica was painted with a metallic, reflective solution.

MARY GRIZZARD

[See also **Ceramics, European; Lusterware.**]

MALACHY, ST. (Mael Máedóc Ua Morgair, 1094/1095–1148). Malachy was the foremost figure in the twelfth-century ecclesiastical reform movement in Ireland. He was consecrated bishop of the two dioceses of Down and Connor in 1124. A strong advocate of Roman practices and customs, he was prevented for several years by anti-Roman supporters of hereditary primatial succession from taking up his appointment as archbishop of Armagh. He finally entered Armagh as archbishop in 1134. He resigned in 1137, satisfied that the hereditary line of succession had been broken, and returned to the see of Down. On his way to Rome in 1140, Malachy visited Clairvaux and struck up a close personal friendship with St. Bernard. Four of his companions, whom he left at Clairvaux to be trained, subsequently introduced the Cistercian order into Ireland. Malachy again set out for Rome in 1148, bearing the Irish church's formal request for the pallia for the metropolitan sees of Armagh and Cashel, but died at Clairvaux on 2 November. Malachy's feast day is 3 November.

BIBLIOGRAPHY

Bernard of Clairvaux, *The Life and Death of Saint Malachy the Irishman,* Robert T. Meyer, trans. (1978); Aubrey Gwynn, "St. Malachy of Armagh," in *Irish Ecclesiastical Record,* 5th ser., **70** (1948) and **71** (1949), and *The Twelfth-century Reform* (1968), 39–53; Tomás Ó Fiaich, "The Church of Armagh Under Lay Control," in *Seanchas Ard Mhacha* (Journal of the Armagh Diocesan Historical Society), 5 (1969); A. Brian Scott, *Malachy* (1976); John Watt, *The Church in Medieval Ireland* (1972), 15–26.

BERNARD CULLEN

[See also **Bernard of Clairvaux, St.; Celtic Church; Cistercian Order; Ireland: Early History.**]

MALALAS, JOHN (ca. 491–578), author of a Byzantine world chronicle in eighteen books ending at A.D. 565, was apparently an Antiochene and possibly the patriarch of Constantinople, John III Scholasticos (565–577). The work is important for the first half of the sixth century. The earlier parts are drawn from a variety of sources, often with naïve errors, and with a generally anecdotal and apologetic approach. The latter part has an Antiochene bias and, being favorable to the regime of Justinian, is a valuable supplement to Procopius. The whole work shows a taste for wonders and curiosities perhaps indicative of "popular" literature and is written in a lowbrow and colloquial Greek. It became the basis and model for later chronicles, especially that of Theophanes. The Greek text survives in one abbreviated Bodleian manuscript, and a fuller version exists in Church Slavonic.

BIBLIOGRAPHY

Edition is *Ioannis Malalae Chronographia,* Ludwig Dindorf, ed. (1831, repr. 1926). An English translation of the Church Slavonic version is *Chronicle of John Malalas, Books VIII–XVIII,* Matthew Spinka and Glanville Downey, trans. (1940).

R. Scott, "Malalas and Justinian's Codification," in E. M. Jeffreys and Ann Moffatt, eds., *Byzantine Papers* (1981); Z. V. Udalcova, "La chronique de Jean Malalas dans la Russie de Kiev," E. Voordeckers, trans., in *Byzantion,* 35 (1965), and "Mirovozrenie vizantiiskogo chronista Ioanna Malaly," in *Vizantysky vremenik,* 32 (1971); Kristen Weierholt, *Studien im Sprachgebrauch des Malalas* (1963).

AVERIL CAMERON

[See also **Byzantine Literature; Historiography, Byzantine.**]

MALATYA. See **Melitene.**

MALAZGIRT. See **Manazkert.**

MALCOLM I OF ALBA (*r.* 943–954) peaceably succeeded Constantine II of the alternate line as the king of Scots. King Edmund of Wessex attacked Cumbria-Strathclyde in 945 and commended it to Malcolm, who was to be his "helper by sea and land," though it is unclear against whom, since the Danelaw was now subject to Edmund. Perhaps Lothian was now effectively Scottish, for about 950 Malcolm made a cattle raid to the Tees. He also attacked Moray, perhaps rebellious, and was killed by the men of Mearns at Fetteresso in 954.

BIBLIOGRAPHY

A. A. M. Duncan, *Scotland: The Making of the Kingdom* (1975); A. P. Smyth, *Warlords and Holy Men: Scotland A.D. 80–1000* (1984).

A. A. M. DUNCAN

[See also **Danelaw; Scotland: History; Strathclyde, Kingdom of.**]

MALCOLM II OF SCOTLAND (*r.* 1005–1034), succeeded by killing the king of the alternate line. In 1006 the Scots were defeated in battle by the English, an event usually identified with a defeat of Malcolm at Durham (which may be a mistaken echo of a siege there in 1039); a Scottish account gives Malcolm victory over Earl Uhtred at "Burgum" in Cumbria, perhaps Burgh by Sands. In 1018 Malcolm again invaded Northumberland and defeated Uhtred at Carham; Uhtred was murdered on the orders of King Cnut, and his successor ceded Lothian to Scotland, generally taken as the final cession of a territory that the Scots had dominated since about 900. It is not certain, however, that Cnut was party to this cession. Certainly he invaded Scotland in 1031 and may have penetrated to Lindores, Fife, since a hoard of coins was buried there about 1030; Malcolm II submitted, probably doing homage.

Malcolm was accompanied at Carham by King Owen the Bald of Strathclyde, whose death (mistakenly placed by annals in 1015) must have followed soon after. Malcolm then had his grandson Duncan installed as king of Strathclyde, so that effectively the kingdom of Scotland took shape in Malcolm's reign.

Several rebellions and disturbances are mentioned in the laconic annals for the period, foreshadowing the later rule of the claimant from Moray, Macbeth. Malcolm effectively eliminated other possible claimants to his throne among his relatives in order to assure the succession of Duncan, his daughter Bethoc's son, the first succession in the direct line since the mid ninth century. This remarkable change in succession customs, which had hitherto favored a battle-tried male of an alternate line, gave Malcolm the unjustified reputation of introducing heritable succession by primogeniture.

BIBLIOGRAPHY

A. A. M. Duncan, *Scotland: The Making of the Kingdom* (1975), and "The Battle of Carham, 1018," in *Scottish Historical Review,* 55 (1976); William E. Kapelle, *The Norman Conquest of the North* (1979/1980); Bernard Meehan, "The Siege of Durham, the Battle of Carham, and the Cession of Lothian," in *Scottish Historical Review,* 55 (1976).

A. A. M. DUNCAN

[See also **Cnut the Great; Macbeth; Scotland: History; Strathclyde, Kingdom of.**]

MALCOLM III OF SCOTLAND (*r.* 1057–1093) probably gained Scotland by stages, defeating Macbeth in 1054, killing him in 1057, and slaying his stepson Lulach in 1058. About 1070 Edgar Atheling and his sister Margaret fled from William I the Conqueror to Scotland, and Malcolm married Margaret by 1071. Turgot's hagiographic life of Margaret shows her improving the cultural level of the court and influencing Malcolm to undertake ecclesiastical reform. Bishoprics remained vacant and Culdee minsters laicized, however. Their most notable achievement was the foundation of a Benedictine priory at Dunfermline with monks from Canterbury, while Margaret is said to have rebuilt and endowed the monastery of Iona.

Malcolm invaded England five times, once before 1066, which suggests that the other four were not pro-Anglo-Saxon incursions. William I in return invaded Scotland, and in 1072 at Abernethy Malcolm became his vassal. He broke his oath, however, and hence had to renew his homage to William I and William II Rufus. In 1091, after his fourth devastating attack on Northumbria, he reached agreement with William II, who promised him "in land and in everything all that he had had before under" William I. Rufus broke his agreement either by withholding English estates or by occupying Carlisle, and insulted Malcolm at Gloucester by refusing to speak to him (1093): hence Malcolm's final invasion of England, in which Malcolm and Edward, his oldest son by Margaret, were slain by the Northumbrians at Alnwick. He had a son, Duncan (II), by his first wife, and six sons and two daughters by Margaret. Three of these latter sons became kings of Scots: Edgar, Alexander I, and David I.

BIBLIOGRAPHY

G. W. S. Barrow, *The Kingdom of the Scots* (1973); A. A. M. Duncan, *Scotland: The Making of the Kingdom* (1975); William E. Kapelle, *The Norman Conquest of the North* (1979).

A. A. M. DUNCAN

[See also **David I of Scotland; England: Norman-Angevin; Macbeth; Scotland: History; William I of England.**]

MALCOLM IV OF SCOTLAND (*ca.* 1141–1165). Grandson and successor of David I, Malcolm IV was king of Scotland from 1153 to 1165. He continued the policy of encouraging settlement by Anglo-Norman and Flemish barons and knights in Scotland, and extended the new administrative structure with sheriffs and justices. Malcolm had to face rebellions by Somerled of Argyll and the MacHeth family; both were reconciled, the latter firmly, but the former rebelled again and was killed in 1164.

In 1157 Malcolm was compelled by Henry II of England to deprive his brother William of the earldom of Northumberland, though in compensation Malcolm received the earldom of Huntingdon. He served King Henry in the Toulouse campaign and was knighted but on his return faced a serious rebellion by native magnates who besieged him in Perth. Nonetheless he defeated them and one, Fergus, gave up his lordship of Galloway. In 1163 he visited Henry II again; falling gravely ill, he was put under pressure to concede castles in Lothian; Malcolm resisted but gave hostages as surety for peace. During his reign further unsuccessful attempts were made to obtain from the pope metropolitan status for St. Andrews, and he founded a Cistercian abbey at Coupar Angus. He died aged about 25 with a reputation as a virgin, hence his later nickname "the Maiden," taken to imply effeminacy. But Malcolm was an active knight strongly imbued with the chivalric virtues of his time.

BIBLIOGRAPHY

The Acts of Malcolm IV, Geoffrey W. S. Barrow, ed. (1960) (vol. I of *Regesta regum Scottorum*); Archibald A. M. Duncan, *Scotland: The Making of the Kingdom* (1975).

A. A. M. DUNCAN

[See also **David I of Scotland; Scotland: History.**]

MALI, a powerful black Islamic empire in sub-Saharan western Africa. Its heartland was along the Sankarani tributary of the upper Niger River, located in modern southwest Mali, near the border with Guinea. At its height in the fourteenth century it controlled the southern fringes of the Sahara from the Atlantic to well east of Timbuktu, and from there south to the Gambia and the sources of the Niger River.

Mali's kings adopted Islam in the eleventh century and some may have performed the pilgrimage to Mecca in the twelfth, but Mali achieved prominence only in the 1230's under Mārī Jāṭa, who is identified with King Sunjata or Suniata of oral tradition. Mārī Jāṭa/Sunjata conquered lands northward and westward from the Sankarani, established control over the southern termini of the western trans-Saharan trade routes, and is considered by most authorities to have established the permanent capital at Niani on the Sankarani. Niani remained the capital of Mali until the seventeenth century.

Mārī Jāṭa was succeeded by his son Mansā ('King') Ulī, who made the pilgrimage sometime during the reign of the Egyptian sultan Baybars (1260–1277). Mali declined under Ulī's successors, his two brothers and a nephew. The last was deposed by a freed slave, Sākūra, who expanded the empire and improved its commercial position, bringing many traders from Morocco and Ifrīqiya (Tunisia) to Mali. Sākūra was murdered on his return from a pilgrimage to Mecca, sometime around 1298.

Mali's greatest king was Mansā Mūsā (*r.* 1312–1337), grandson of a brother of Mārī Jāṭa. He made the pilgrimage in 1324, stopping in Cairo, where his munificent purchases and generosity caused the devaluation of gold. Under Mūsā and his brother Mansā Sulaymān (*r.* 1341–1360), Mali carried on active diplomatic relations with Morocco, and its kings were known in Europe (probably because of the gold trade). Caravan traffic was at its height, with active trans-Saharan routes to Morocco, Ifrīqiya, and Egypt.

Mali's decline may be dated from Sulaymān's death. Ibn Khaldūn reports that Mārī Jāṭa II (*r.* 1360–1374/1375) was oppressive and corrupt, depleted the treasury, and nearly destroyed the machinery of government. Later kings were mostly ineffectual. The royal family retained the throne, although power was often exercised by ministers.

By the 1440's Mali had lost control of most of its holdings in the commercial centers of the trans-Saharan trade. Yet in the fifteenth and sixteenth centuries it was still a considerable power in its southern regions, controlling gold-producing areas, the upper Niger, and the rivers emptying into the Atlantic. The king of Mali at the end of the sixteenth century was Mansā Maḥmūd (Niani Mansā Mamudu). He failed in his attempt to recapture Djenné, an important trading center between the Bani and the Niger, and lost the Bamako gold mines. Although these losses spelled the end of Mali's empire, Maḥmūd/Mamudu is remembered for his valor; all modern Mali chieftains trace their ancestry through him.

The chief sources of Mali's power and wealth were its control of the trans-Saharan trade and of gold mines close to the center of its empire. Commerce was left in private hands, with imposts on many types of commodities upon entering and leaving Mali's dominions. The kings found the gold mines more productive when left in the hands of non-Muslims and received all nuggets larger than about an ounce. The importance of this trade is not to be underestimated: at the height of Mali's power, two-thirds of the world's gold supply is said to have come from sub-Saharan Africa. Gold was exchanged for commodities such as salt, slaves, horses, copper, sugar, raisins, and dried dates and figs. Although a textile industry arose in Timbuktu and Djenné, clothing was also imported to Mali. Only a small portion of the populace was involved in commerce, however; the chief occupations were agriculture, fishing, and cattle breeding.

BIBLIOGRAPHY

Sources. Nehemiah Levtzion and J. F. P. Hopkins, eds., *Corpus of Early Arabic Sources for West African History,* Hopkins, trans. (1981); Salāḥ al-Dīn al-Munajjid, ed., *The Kingdom of Mali According to Muslim Geographers* (1963), in Arabic.

Studies. Nehemiah Levtzion, *Ancient Ghana and Mali,* 2nd ed. (1980), with updated bibliography, and "Mali," in *Encyclopaedia of Islam,* new ed. (forthcoming); Djibril T. Niane, *Sundiata: An Epic of Old Mali,* G. D. Pickett, trans. (1965), has traditional materials on the founding of the empire; G. T. Stride and Caroline Ifeka, *Peoples and Empires of West Africa* (1971).

SETH WARD

[See also **Baṭṭūṭa, Ibn; Blacks; Khaldūn, Ibn; Maghrib, Al-; Mining; Slavery; Trade, Islamic; Zanj.**]

MĀLIK IBN ANAS (708/715–795), renowned lawyer and traditionist, after whom the Maliki school, or rite, of Sunni Islam is named, was born and died in Medina, where he spent most of his life. Mālik studied with a number of Medina's well-known scholars and in time became a teacher in his own right whose fame attracted pupils from many parts of the Islamic world to his lecture sessions.

In 762, Mālik publicly supported a revolt led by an Alid claimant against the Abbasid caliph al-Manṣūr. Mālik himself took no active part in the revolt, but his reputation was such that many who might not otherwise have participated did so on the basis of his support. Although the revolt failed and the governor of Medina had Mālik flogged, this episode in no way diminished his standing as a scholar. In fact, he was apparently restored to royal favor; the next three caliphs, al-Mahdī, al-Hādī, and Harūn al-Rashīd, took a personal interest in his work, and in the last year of Mālik's life Harūn, while on a pilgrimage, even attended one of his lectures.

Mālik's contribution to the development of Islamic law is embodied in his only extant work, the *Muwaṭṭaʾ* (The leveled path), which is also the earliest surviving work of Sunni Muslim law. Its importance lies in the fact that in it Mālik integrated two areas of scholarly endeavor, Islamic law *(fiqh)* and the traditions of Islam *(ḥadīth).*

After the death of the prophet Muḥammad, the explicit legislation he had provided for the early Islamic community proved insufficiently complete for the needs of the expanding empire. Thus rulers who wished to ensure the Islamic character of their administrations, and individual Muslims who wished to lead more pious lives, turned for guidance to self-appointed religious specialists, whose knowledge of Islam and concern for its proper implementation made them also its first lawyers. They surveyed the existing legal institutions and practices with a view toward introducing religious and moral ideas into all aspects of public and private life. Scholars of Mālik's stature were frequently consulted about the legality or suitability of a particular act or point of view; in their consultative capacity they were called muftis, and their considered opinions were called *fatwā*s. Thus, in the case of the above-mentioned revolt against the caliph, Mālik gave a *fatwā* stating that allegiance to Manṣūr was not binding, since it had been obtained under compulsion.

In addition to these lawyers, another group of early specialists, known as traditionists, studied and collected traditions—biographical reports and anecdotes about the prophet Muḥammad, his family, and his contemporaries. Each tradition consisted of a text *(matn)* preceded by a chain of transmitters *(isnād),* that is, a list of people who had known Muḥammad or had themselves acquired reputations as religious authorities. Traditions were transmitted orally and in writing and were considered a major source of information on Muslim behavior, either as practiced or recommended by the Prophet. By Mālik's time, thousands of traditions were in circulation, some of them fabricated in support of various partisan causes. A major activity of traditionists was differentiating between genuine and false traditions, usually by considering the reliability of the transmitters in the *isnād.*

Before Mālik, two types of legal literature had evolved—compendia of decisions by lawyers on both theoretical and practical issues (none of these compendia survive, but they are often referred to and quoted in later sources), and compendia of traditions that provided authoritative guidelines for behavior. Mālik was both a lawyer and a traditionist. His achievement in the *Muwaṭṭaʾ* was to combine both branches of his scholarly activity by making use of traditions to provide a context for presenting legal doctrine.

The *Muwaṭṭaʾ* is arranged by subject matter in chapters that deal with the ritual, legal, and dogmatic concerns of the Muslim community. It includes, for example, chapters on prayer, the pilgrimage, fasting, marriage, inheritance, commercial contracts, free will, and predestination. In each area Mālik sets out the accepted doctrine of Medina as he and his scholarly contemporaries taught it and cites traditions to support Medinese practices and beliefs. However, despite the use Mālik makes of traditions, his method is not consistent. For one thing, he does not scrutinize *isnād*s carefully, and many traditions he relates have incomplete or faulty *isnād*s. For another, despite the weight he gives traditions, he does not hesitate to ignore them in favor of the overriding authority of the generally agreed-upon practice of Medina as it had evolved in the century and a half since the Prophet's death.

Mālik taught the *Muwaṭṭaʾ* for a number of years, by reading it aloud or reciting it. He did not always offer exactly the same text, and he often gave his pupils permission to teach it themselves without checking their versions carefully. Thus there existed at one time up to fifteen recensions of the *Muwaṭṭaʾ*. Only two survive in their entirety; fragments of others are available in a variety of sources. The prestige and enduring influence of the *Muwaṭṭaʾ* are due in part to the middle-of-the-road quality of Medinese doctrine and in part to the industry and geographical spread of successive generations of Mālik's pupils. These last gradually came to think of themselves as a group characterized by adherence to a distinctive Maliki doctrine and formed themselves into the Maliki school of Islamic law. The Maliki school predominates in upper Egypt, in North Africa, and in the other parts of Africa where Islam has prevailed.

Although Mālik's methods were not consistent, his constant reference to traditions in the *Muwaṭṭaʾ* was a major step in the development of Islamic legal theory. After Mālik, the incorporation of traditions into legal reasoning became a hallmark of this theory and persisted as one of its enduring features.

BIBLIOGRAPHY

The *Muwaṭṭaʾ* has been translated by Muḥammad Rahimuddin (1980). Also see Nabia Abbott, *Studies in Arabic Literary Papyri,* II (1967); Ignaz Goldziher, *Muslim Studies,* Samuel M. Stern, ed., *idem* and C. R. Barber, trans., II (1971); Joseph Schacht, *An Introduction to Islamic Law* (1964), and *The Origins of Muhammadan Jurisprudence* (1950); Fuat Sezgin, *Geschichte des arabischen Schrifttums,* I (1967).

SUSAN SPECTORSKY

[See also **Egypt, Islamic; Fatwā; Ḥadith; Law, Islamic; Medina; Sunna.**]

MALIKSHĀH (*r.* 1072–1092), the son of Alp Arslan and supreme ruler *(Sulṭan-i Aʿẓam)* of the Seljuk Empire. His reign marked the apogee of Seljuk power. It witnessed the extension of the empire's borders from eastern Turkistan to the Aegean, from Transcaucasia to Yemen. He was aided by the brilliant vizier Niẓām al-Mulk, to whom much of the greatness of his reign may be attributed. Niẓām al-Mulk furthered the transformation of the sultanate into a benevolent despotate along Irano-Muslim lines. This state, however, contained two contradictory elements that were never brought into harmony: an elaborate Irano-Islamic bureaucracy largely staffed by Iranians and backed by a multinational standing army of *ghulāms* (military slaves) and mercenaries; and the Turkoman tribes, the frequently slighted mainstay of the state and the most active force in the western parts of the realm. Persistent tension existed between the two.

Malikshāh periodically faced threats to his rule

MALORY, SIR THOMAS

from within his own family. Moreover, the Anatolian Seljukids never fully recognized his authority and, together with certain Turkoman begs, began to create their own political entities. Malikshāh had little direct control over events in Anatolia except to the extent that he encouraged Turkoman elements to move westward. He did, however, campaign extensively in Azerbaijan to further secure this area as a manpower reservoir for the Turkomans. He also fought the Georgians, promoting the wide-scale movement of Turkomans into that land (the *didi* $t^{c}urk^{c}oba$ or "great Turkish troubles" of the Georgian sources). In 1084 Malikshāh crushed the Kurdish Marwanids, gained control of Diyarbakir, and asserted his authority over various minor dynasties. His brother Tutush extended his Syrian holdings to Palestine in moves directed against their arch foes, the Fatimids. Seljukid military power also reached through Arabia to Yemen and Aden. At the time of his death, Malikshāh was considering the expulsion of the caliph from Baghdad and the proclamation of his own grandson (whose father was the reigning caliph) to that office.

BIBLIOGRAPHY

C. E. Bosworth, "The Political and Dynastic History of the Iranian World (A.D. 1000–1217)," in J. A. Boyle, ed., *Cambridge History of Iran,* V (1968); Claude Cahen, *Pre-Ottoman Turkey: A General Survey of the Material and Spiritual Culture and History, 1071–1330,* J. Jones Williams, trans. (1968); İbrahim Kafesoğlu, *Sultan Melikşah devrinde büyük Selçuklu İmparatorluğu* (1953), esp. xi–xxvi for a discussion of primary sources; Nodar Shengelia, *Selch*^{c}*ukebi da Sak*^{c}*art*^{c}*velo XI saukuneshi* (1968), with Russian summary. See also the historiographical survey in R. A. Guseinov, "Istoriografia istorii Zakavkaz'ia, XI–XII vv.," in *Tiurkologicheskii sbornik 1976* (1978).

PETER B. GOLDEN

[See also **Alp Arslan; Georgia: Political History; Iran, History: After 650; Niẓām al-Mulk; Seljuks; Turkomans.**]

MALORY, SIR THOMAS

THE AUTHOR

Sir Thomas Malory's authorship of *Le Morte Darthur* is attested in the two somewhat differing fifteenth-century forms in which that work is preserved: William Caxton's print of 1485 and the Winchester manuscript, prepared by two scribes, discovered by W. F. Oakeshott in 1934, and edited by Eugène Vinaver in 1947. Caxton names Malory as the author in his preface and again in his colophon; moreover, above the colophon is the author's own afterword, giving his name as "Syr Thomas Maleore, knyght," praying for his "good delyveraunce," and stating that the work was finished in 1469–1470 (9 Edward IV). In the Winchester manuscript at the end of several sections there are explicits embodying prayers for the writer's "delyveraunce," in one of which he speaks of himself as "a knyght presoner, sir Thomas Maleorré."

The urge to establish the historical identity of the author of so great a literary monument was, and remains, irresistible. The earliest efforts are those of John Leland and Bishop John Bale. Leland lists a Thomas Meilorius among Arthurian writers in his *Assertio inclitissimi Arturii* (1544), and much the same information appears in Bale's *Index Britanniae scriptorum* (1547 and 1548). Meilorius is there associated with the Welsh border country yet is not called a Welshman, although Sir John Rhys, in his 1893 edition of *Le Morte,* seeks to make him so. In 1897 a will signed by Thomas Malory of Papworth St. Agnes, Cambridgeshire, and dated 1469 came to light. The discoverer, A. T. Martin, believed this Malory to be the long-sought author, and he also accepted Rhys's argument as to his Welsh origins. But earlier in the same decade, H. Oskar Sommer and George L. Kittredge independently espoused another candidate, Sir Thomas Malory of Newbold Revell, Warwickshire, the candidate most widely favored until recently.

The Warwickshire Malory was a soldier in the forces of the Earl of Warwick; he once served in Parliament; and he was undoubtedly a knight, as proved by the inscription on his tomb in the chapel of St. Francis at the Grey Friars near Newgate in the suburbs of London. Possibly Malory found his Arthurian source-books in the library of the Grey Friars monastery across the road from Newgate. For many the clinching evidence of his authorship has been his prison record; he was for years a "knyght presoner." From 1443 to at least 1460, this Malory was charged with a variety of crimes, including cattle raids, robbery, extortion, rape, and attempted murder, and despite pleas of innocence he was several times committed to prison to await trial. No documents pertaining to actual trials or convictions have been found, yet the inquests and imprisonment indicate serious involvement. It has been suggested that, like others of his standing, Malory could have been caught up in the struggles between Yorkists and

MALORY, SIR THOMAS

Lancastrians and, as a partisan of the former, could have been arraigned on trumped-up charges. On the other hand, only one of the accusations, that of conspiring to murder the Duke of Buckingham, seems to relate directly to the political situation. Otherwise, he was charged with common felonies.

A number of scholars have long sensed a "moral paradox" in ascribing *Le Morte Darthur*, the classic English expression of late medieval chivalric idealism, to an unprincipled adventurer. To this consideration William Matthews adds his belief that the Warwickshire knight would in the 1460's have been much too elderly to undertake so extensive a literary labor. On the basis of a manuscript discovery that leads him to place Malory's military service at Calais in 1414 rather than 1436, he argues that Malory must have been born at least as early as 1393 or 1394. Also, Matthews maintains that physical conditions in Newgate were not conducive to literary composition. Beyond this, he rejects the earlier view that *Le Morte* is written in the dialect of Warwickshire. Rather, he finds throughout a substantial northern coloration in spellings and grammatical forms, and thus favors as author a younger man hailing from a northern county. Acknowledging that unassailable proof is not at hand, he finds these requirements met by Thomas Malory of Hutton and Studley, Yorkshire. The reference in *Le Morte* to imprisonment might reflect, Matthews suggested, incarceration in the honorable condition of prisoner of war in France, perhaps in a castle containing an Arthurian library.

Matthews' dismissal of Sir Thomas of Newbold Revell has seemed well founded to many, but the case for the Yorkshire Thomas has been less favorably received. The linguistic argument was not accepted by reviewers, and P. J. C. Field, after a study of the documentary evidence, concluded that Thomas Malory of Hutton is unlikely on several grounds, including the fact that he was not a knight. Field also rejects the Malory of Papworth on somewhat similar grounds, and in the end casts his vote for the knight of Newbold Revell.

More recently, however, a new champion of Thomas Malory of Papworth has come forward. Drawing on his careful genealogical and geographical investigations, Richard R. Griffith argues that this Thomas' residence in Cambridgeshire and his family connections account for a surprising number of place-names and other details appearing in *Le Morte* but not in its sources. Similar considerations help explain the northern speech forms and even the fact that Malory would have had access to a nearby Arthurian library, that of Richard Wydville, Earl Rivers. Richard was executed in 1469 and was succeeded by his son Anthony, Lord Scales, with whom this Malory almost certainly was associated. In fact, some scholars suggest that Anthony was the "one in specyal" mentioned in Caxton's preface as providing him with the text of *Le Morte.* Believing that the "knight prisoner" references may have been inserted after the completion of *Le Morte,* Griffith conjectures that Malory was kept under house arrest during the short period of the Earl of Warwick's ascendancy late in 1469, and that Anthony, Earl Rivers, by way of expressing gratitude for services rendered, conferred knighthood upon him at about that time. One cannot say that Griffith has as yet found full proof that the Malory of Papworth St. Agnes is the author of *Le Morte;* but as the search now stands, this Thomas Malory does seem the most likely candidate.

That a completely unchallengeable matching of the author to any Malory of record is yet to emerge is not of first importance to our appreciation of the work itself. Of greater relevance is a clear notion of the text as originally written. We do not have a text in Malory's handwriting, nor do we have the exemplar that Caxton used for his printing of the book. Caxton states that he divided the work into twenty-one "bookes"; and he further divided these "bookes" into chapters, doubtless to make for easier reading. Further, the Winchester manuscript includes a number of explicits which Caxton either deleted from or did not find present in his exemplar. Of greatest importance, however, in trying to determine just what Malory originally wrote is the fact that the account of Arthur's war against the Roman emperor Lucius is much longer in the Winchester manuscript than in Caxton's edition.

Eugène Vinaver, who in 1947 first edited the Winchester manuscript, maintained that it was Caxton who shortened this section, presumably as a part of his editorial effort to make the work seem more tightly unified. But James W. Spisak, citing unpublished papers by Matthews and Moorman, has advanced the much likelier explanation that the shorter version printed by Caxton resulted from Malory's own revision, which was present in Caxton's exemplar. The longer version in the Winchester manuscript is much closer in alliterative style to Malory's chief source, the Middle English alliterative poem *Morte Arthure,* than is the printed version. We know from prefaces in numerous other

MALORY, SIR THOMAS

works printed by Caxton that it was not his practice to make such major alterations in length and style without informing the reader of his changes. Further, some details taken from the sources are present in the shorter but not in the longer version. It seems unlikely that Caxton would have had these sources at hand; in fact, in his colophon Caxton says that *Le Morte* was "reduced into Englysshe" by Malory, which suggests that Caxton was not aware that Malory, in addition to his French sources, used sources already in English. Also, if Caxton as reviser for the shorter version was aiming at heightening the unity of the whole book, it seems strange to find omitted in the shorter version the opening sentence of the account of the Roman War in the longer version—"Hyt befelle whan Kyng Arthur had wedded Quene Gwenyvere and fulfylled the Rounde Table, and so aftir his mervelous knyghtis and he had venquyshed the moste part of his enemyes"—with its clear connection to the preceding section of the book. If, on the other hand, Malory had composed the longer version of the Roman War as his first effort toward writing an Arthuriad, as some scholars believe, it seems quite possible that he would later revise that section by removing much of the alliteration and the digressive material to make the account of the Roman War fit better in style and content with other parts of his book.

The conventional title of Malory's work—*Le Morte Darthur*—has also raised important issues. Whether the Winchester manuscript was left untitled is not known because the opening leaves are lost. Also, no formal title page is preserved in the two extant copies of Caxton's edition or in the known copies of Wynkyn de Worde's reprints of 1498 and 1529. But that Caxton had a title in mind is demonstrated by a passage in his colophon reading "Thus endeth thys noble and joyous book entytled le Morte Darthur." He then makes clear that he here refers to the whole of Malory's book rather than to the concluding account of Arthur's death by adding: "Notwythstondyng it treateth of the byrth, lyf, and actes of the sayd Kyng Arthur, [and] of his noble knyghtes of the Rounde Table."

Vinaver has argued that Caxton, by giving Malory's work the title *Le Morte Darthur*, by supposedly revising the account of the Roman War, by dividing the whole work into twenty-one "bookes," and by allegedly suppressing several incipits presumably in his exemplar, must accept responsibility for a long-lived misapprehension of Malory's real intention for his work. Caxton's title, *Le Morte Darthur*, did not come into use until Joseph Haslewood's reprint in 1816 of Stansby's edition of 1634. For the several editions of earlier date, lengthy titles suggested by Caxton's preface were used. But Vinaver's study of the explicits in the Winchester manuscript and of Malory's use of sources led him to the view that Malory intended and wrote a series of eight more or less separate Arthurian romances, which Vinaver denominated "tales," rather than a single unified Arthuriad. Thus Vinaver entitled his several editions of the Winchester manuscript *The Works of Sir Thomas Malory* rather than *Le Morte Darthur*. Lumiansky, Moorman, Brewer, Benson, and others have shown that Vinaver's argument is not convincing and that his use of *The Works* as a title for Malory's book is misleading. Thus, one must conclude that, despite the tremendous industry and learning which Vinaver exhibited in editing the Winchester manuscript and in studying the relation of Malory's work to its sources, Caxton's edition provides better representation of Malory's intended text than do Vinaver's editions of the Winchester manuscript.

THE *MORTE*

In considering Malory's text, however, we should recognize that dividing it into the eight consecutive parts, which are apparent from its relation to various chief sources and to the progress of its narrative, more clearly presents Malory's intention than does Caxton's division into twenty-one "bookes" or Vinaver's division into eight more or less separate tales. With that structure in mind, we turn now to an overview of Malory's book part by part, using titles not present in Caxton's edition or in the Winchester manuscript.

Part one, "The Coming of Arthur and the Round Table," comprises one-fifth of *Le Morte* and is drawn from various parts of the Old French *Suite du Merlin*. It narrates the familiar story of Merlin's magical arrangement whereby Uther spends the night with Ygerne, Arthur's birth and early years in Ector's household, his drawing the sword from the stone and his coronation, his adulterous begetting of Mordred, his marriage to Guenevere and the establishing of the idealistic society called the Round Table, the unfortunate Balin's slaying of his brother Balan, Merlin's fatal imprisonment, and Morgan le Fay's unsuccessful efforts to kill her brother Arthur. By the end of part one Arthur and his knights of the Round Table have brought stability to a formerly chaotic Britain, but that the seeds of coming diffi-

MALORY, SIR THOMAS

culties are present is made clear through Merlin's prophecies concerning Mordred's birth and the future liaison between Guenevere and Launcelot.

As was mentioned earlier, part two, "Arthur's War Against the Roman Emperor Lucius," is based upon the Middle English alliterative *Morte Arthure.* Both the longer version in the Winchester manuscript and the shorter version in Caxton's edition omit the final third of the Middle English poem. In place of presenting the Roman campaign as the last great achievement of British arms, which is immediately succeeded by Mordred's treachery, the final battle, and the death of Arthur, Malory follows another tradition by postponing the catastrophic conclusion and recounting Arthur's victory over the Romans and his crowning in Rome as emperor. This alteration of his main source seems to indicate clearly Malory's full knowledge of the whole Arthurian legend and his early formulation of his plan for a unified Arthurian epic. A second major alteration of his source here is Malory's considerable enhancement of the role of Launcelot. Thus part two presents Arthur's success in stabilizing Europe and introduces Launcelot in preparation for his role as central hero for Malory's book.

Part three, "Launcelot du Lake," the shortest of the major divisions in *Le Morte,* is drawn primarily from widely separated episodes in the Old French Vulgate Cycle of Arthurian romances. It firmly establishes Launcelot's place as Malory's central figure, and in it he performs impressive feats of knight-errantry by rescuing hostage knights and captive maidens. Mention is made of his love for Guenevere and of her high regard for him, but no evidence is presented at this stage in the book of an adulterous relationship.

"Sir Gareth of Orkney," part four, has no known source as a whole, although scholars have pointed to probable sources for some aspects of the narrative. Also, quite a number of analogous stories are to be found in medieval accounts of "fair unknowns," young men apparently of no standing or ability who come to court and are ridiculed, but who later perform outstanding deeds and whose noble birth is finally revealed. So it is with Gareth. He comes to court as an unknown young man whom Sir Kay scoffingly names "Beaumains," and he serves for a year as kitchen-boy. But then he is knighted by Launcelot, gains a series of victories against more experienced knights, and finally rescues the lady Lyones. After further knightly accomplishments his true identity becomes known to all, and he and Lyones are married. It would seem that Malory created the "Gareth" to show the Round Table in its full flowering and to present an example of "vertuous love" that will stand in sharp contrast to the imminent adultery of Launcelot and Guenevere. Also, in introducing Gareth here as Launcelot's protégé, Malory sets the stage for Launcelot's later inadvertent but catastrophic killing of Gareth.

Part five, "Sir Tristram of Lyoness," comprising about one-third of the entire book, is a highly original treatment of material mostly taken from the Old French prose *Tristan.* Malory recounts the hero's birth and *enfances* (childhood), his duel with Marhaus, his stay in Ireland with La Belle Isoud, his madness and exile from Mark's court, his outstanding feats in tournaments and jousts which make him second only to Launcelot in knightly prowess, his marriage in Brittany to Isoud la Blaunche Maines, and his becoming a knight of the Round Table. A constant theme here is the antagonistic relationship between Tristram and the pagan knight Palomides, which happily culminates in the former's assistance in the latter's baptism. Malory does not present the well-known tragic ending for this story; only later in his book does he refer briefly to Mark's treacherous murder of Tristram and to La Belle Isoud's death from grief. But Malory does include considerable material concerning other knights of the Round Table that connects his Tristram story much more closely with the Arthurian world than is the case in the earlier accounts. Most importantly, it is now made clear that Launcelot and Guenevere are involved in adultery; and toward the end of part five Malory includes the story of Launcelot and Elaine, whose son, Galahad, will become the chief Grail-knight in part six.

Some earlier critics saw the "Tristram" as formless, meandering, and of inordinate length, and felt that Malory would have done well to omit it. But more recent commentators have stressed the importance for both comparison and contrast of the Mark-Isoud-Tristram circumstance to that of Arthur-Guenevere-Launcelot.

Part six, "The Quest of the Grail," is a close rendering of *La Queste del saint Graal* in the Old French Vulgate Cycle. It begins with Galahad's introduction to the Round Table, his assumption of the Siege Perilous, the apparition of the covered Grail, and the vows of the 150 knights of the Round Table to seek the Grail in order to see it more openly. There follow the often mysterious and symbolic adventures of some of these knights, chiefly

MALORY, SIR THOMAS

Galahad, Launcelot, Percival, and Bors; others are killed or give up the quest in despair. At last an elect group penetrates Castle Corbenic, and there they are privileged to witness the celebration of Mass by Joseph of Arimathea, with the Grail as his chalice. At the consecration of the Mass wafer, Christ appears to the beholders as a child; thereafter he, bearing the wounds, emerges from the Grail to administer the Eucharist to the awestricken communicants. Following Galahad's healing of Pelles, the Maimed King, an act which restores the Waste Land surrounding the castle, the chosen knights—Galahad, Percival, and Bors—carry the holy vessel off to Sarras. Soon after, Galahad's soul is borne to heaven along with the Grail and the spear of Longinus; Percival enters the religious life, and when he dies his soul enters heaven; only Bors is left to return to Camelot.

Less concerned than the author of his source with expounding eucharistic doctrine, Malory nevertheless conveys the message of the Grail as a test of Arthurian chivalry. Most notably, Malory, concerned as always with his central hero, stresses that Launcelot's sincere effort to succeed in the quest, for which he is granted a sight of the Grail before he returns to Camelot, leads to his determination to end his liaison with Guenevere. And Galahad sends a message to his father by Bors that Launcelot should remember the vow he made during the quest to try to live more purely.

For part seven, "Launcelot and Guenevere," Malory used two sources: the *Mort Artu* from the Old French Vulgate Cycle and the Middle English stanzaic *Le Morte Arthur.* He placed his borrowing from these sources in direct continuity with the preceding Grail quest. Launcelot, remembering his vow during the quest, tries to refrain from a revival of the adultery but cannot. He demonstrates his preeminent knightly prowess in two legal duels to save Guenevere and in numerous tournaments. Despite Guenevere's rage over his hapless involvement with the Fair Maid of Astolat, he remains faithful to the queen, and in the healing of Sir Urry he exhibits a Grail-like power that points forward to his holy life near the end of the book. But Aggravain and Mordred, Arthur's nephews, are determined that Launcelot and Guenevere should be punished for their adultery.

Part eight, "The Death of Arthur," is based upon the same two sources that Malory used for part seven. It opens with an apostrophe to Spring, but almost at once catastrophe for the Arthurian society begins to unfold. Launcelot and Guenevere are ambushed in a damaging situation by a band of Round Table brethren led by Aggravain and Mordred. When Launcelot rescues the queen from being burned at the stake, his inadvertent slaying of his protégé Gareth, Gawain's brother, leads directly to the denouement. Incited by Gawain, Arthur feels obliged to wage war against Launcelot, persisting even after Launcelot's surrender of the queen. In the midst of his siege of Launcelot's castle on the Continent, Arthur is summoned home by word of Mordred's usurpation. In the first engagement with the traitor's forces, Gawain is mortally wounded, and his abject confession of his role in the nearly completed destruction of Arthurian society is touchingly related. The "wicked day of destiny" that follows depicts the death of Mordred and Arthur in the battle on Salisbury Plain and the end of the Round Table fellowship. Arthur is taken away to the Isle of Avalon to be healed, or perhaps he is buried at Glastonbury. Launcelot, summoned too late from France by Gawain's deathbed letter, mourns at Gawain's tomb. He then visits the repentant Guenevere at Almesbury, where she has become a nun. After a moving scene of renunciation, he departs to become a hermit and later a priest, eventually dying in the odor of sanctity.

Such is a glimpse of Malory's presentation of the rise and fall of Arthurian society. As earlier mentioned, Caxton's edition most probably reflects Malory's own revision of part two, and the exemplar from which Caxton printed may well have also presented the author's revision of many of the small variations to be found between the Winchester manuscript and Caxton's edition, including deletion of the several incipits. But it must be granted that there remain in Caxton's edition, as well as in the Winchester manuscript, numerous inconsistencies that further revision might have removed. Yet, significant though it is to an understanding of a great and often enigmatic work, conjecture about the unity or discontinuity of the narrative probably goes less directly to the heart of Malory's achievement and his timeless appeal than does an appreciation of his style, the "instinctive rhetoric" by which he evokes the spirit of a distant age. Few books in the English-speaking world have been so influential upon later novelists, poets, and playwrights. And year after year new adaptations of Malory's work appear.

Critics from the time of George Saintsbury (1845–1933) to the present day have paid tribute to Malory's prose. All marvel that he achieves his end with plain declarative sentences uncluttered by adjectives and subordinate constructions, and by a largely native English vocabulary. As noted by Field, Lambert, and others, direct narration comes most naturally to him, with few pauses for lengthy description or comment about a character's motives or state of mind. Yet he was capable of making his characters speak, injecting pathos or joy into his tale without the sacrifice of simplicity or dignity. Perhaps his most often quoted passage is Ector's eulogy of Launcelot near the very end of *Le Morte Darthur:*

> "A, Launcelot!" he sayd, "thou were hede of al Crysten knyghtes! And now I dare say," sayd Syr Ector, "thou Sir Launcelot, there thou lyest, that thou were never matched of erthely knyghtes hande. And thou were the curtest knyght that ever bare shelde! And thou were the truest frende to thy lovar that ever bestrade hors, and thou were the trewest lover, of a synful man, that ever loved woman, and thou were the kyndest man that ever strake wyth swerde. And thou were the godelyest persone that ever cam emonge prees of knyghtes, and thou was the mekest man and the jentyllest that ever ete in halle emonge ladyes, and thou were the sternest knyght to thy mortal foo that ever put spere in the reeste."

BIBLIOGRAPHY

Editions. Facsimile editions are *Le Morte Darthur,* printed by William Caxton (1485), and, with an introduction, by Paul Needham (1976), and *The Winchester Malory,* with an introduction by N. R. Ker (1976). See also R. M. Lumiansky, ed., *Le Morte Darthur* (1982, repr. 1986); Heinrich Oskar Sommer, ed., *Le Morte Darthur by Syr Thomas Malory,* 3 vols. (1889–1891); James W. Spisak, ed., *Caxton's Malory,* 2 vols. (1983); Eugène Vinaver, ed., *The Works of Sir Thomas Malory,* 3 vols. (1947, 2nd ed. 1973).

Studies. J. A. W. Bennet, ed., *Essays on Malory* (1963); Larry D. Benson, "Le Morte Darthur," in R. M. Lumiansky and Herschel Baker, eds., *Critical Approaches to Six Major English Works: Beowulf Through Paradise Lost* (1968), and *Malory's Morte Darthur* (1976); D. S. Brewer, "Form in the *Morte Darthur,*" in *Medium aevum,* **21** (1952); P. J. C. Field, *Romance and Chronicle: A Study of Malory's Prose Style* (1971), and "Thomas Malory: The Hutton Documents," in *Medium aevum,* **48** (1979); Richard R. Griffith, "The Authorship of *Le Morte Darthur* Reconsidered: A Case for Thomas Malory of Papworth St. Agnes, Cambridgeshire," in Toshiyuki Takamiya and D. S. Brewer, eds., *Aspects of Malory* (1981); Mark Lambert, *Malory: Style and Vision in Le Morte Darthur* (1975); R. M. Lumiansky, ed., *Malory's Originality* (1964); William Matthews, *The Ill-framed Knight* (1966); Charles Moorman, *The Book of King Arthur: The Unity of Malory's Morte Darthur* (1965); George D. Painter, *William Caxton* (1976); Elizabeth T. Pochoda, *Arthurian Propaganda: Le Morte Darthur as an Historical Ideal of Life* (1971); James W. Spisak, ed., *Studies in Malory* (1985); Edmund Reiss, *Sir Thomas Malory* (1966).

ROBERT W. ACKERMAN
R. M. LUMIANSKY

[See also **Arthurian Literature; Caxton, William; Excalibur; Grail, Legend of; Knights and Knight Service; Middle English Literature; Tristan, Legend of.**]

MALOUEL, JEAN (Jan Maelwael) (*fl.* late fourteenth–early fifteenth centuries, *d.* 1415), a painter from Nijmegen in Guelders who was court painter in Paris for Queen Isabeau of Bavaria (1396), and in Burgundy for Philip the Bold (1397–1404) and for John the Fearless (1404–1415). As court painter of the dukes of Burgundy he polychromed the *Well of Moses* of Claus Sluter (1401–1403) and painted panels for the Chartreuse de Champmol at Dijon. He was the uncle of the Limbourg brothers.

BIBLIOGRAPHY

Millard Meiss, *French Painting in the Time of Jean de Berry: The Limbourgs and Their Contemporaries* (1974); Erwin Panofsky, *Early Netherlandish Painting,* I (1953), 83–86; Margaret Rickert, review of Friedrich Gorissen, "Jan Malwael und die Brüder Limbourg" (in *Gelre,* **54** [1954]), in *Art Bulletin,* **39** (1957); Georg Troescher, *Burgundischer Malerei* (1966), 67–90.

ROBERT G. CALKINS

[See also **Dijon, Chartreuse de Champmol; Gothic Art: Painting; Limbourg Brothers; Sluter, Claus.**]

MÁLSHÁTTAKVÆÐI, an early-thirteenth-century poem by an unknown Norse skald, is often attributed to Bishop Bjarni Kolbeinsson of the Orkneys. It is preserved on the final folio of the Codex Regius of *Snorra Edda,* immediately following Bjarni's *Jómsvíkingadrápa.* The text is in part illegible. Its present title was given in the nineteenth century; other titles used include *Mansǫngskvæði, Fornyrðadrápa, Griplur,* and *Amatorium carmen.*

The poem is a *drápa* in twenty-nine stanzas and a concluding (defective) couplet. The meter is *runhent* with lines of seven syllables, ending on either one long or two short syllables. There are four stresses per line, and each line makes a complete sentence *(áttmælt).* The *drápa* falls into three sections of ten stanzas each. The central section contains four

Last communion and martyrdom of St. Denis. Panel painting at the Chartreuse de Champmol, Dijon, attributed to Jean Malouel, *ca.* 1414–1415. PARIS, LOUVRE. GIRAUDON/ART RESOURCE

refrain stanzas inserted at three-stanza intervals (stanzas 11, 14, 17, 20). The four-line refrain is: "Formerly that was no contagious disease; still, the Finnish girl drove Haraldr mad; to him she seemed as bright as the sun; now many a one experiences the same." The lamenting poet of this refrain recalls the lovelorn narrator of *Jómsvíkingadrápa;* with the exception of these two *drápur,* romantic refrains are not found in skaldic poetry.

The poem is a versified collection of one-line proverbs. The opening stanzas reveal that a woman has treated the poet badly, and that his unrequited love will reveal itself in his verse, which gathers together *forn orð* (old expressions). Some of the proverbs represent general wisdom: "All know what three persons know," "A hound has to bark," "A living man ever rejoices in a cow," "To love another's child is to love a wolf," "Dragons often rise on their tails," "Spears give a man his strength," "Outskerries are washed by waves," "Snakes creep out of their skin in spring," "Men say that the oars of a ship are short," "The mind of men seems wolfish." Other statements are based on legendary or mythological knowledge: "Bjarki had a brave heart," "Starkaðr felled many a host," "Hromundr seemed spirited and wily." There are only three real kennings in the poem, but the raw material of skaldic periphrasis is present in statements like "Mardǫll's crying was golden" and "Þjatsi spoke gold." The story of Baldr's death is represented by the names of Baldr, Hermóðr, Frigg, and Éljúðnir. Three of the heroes mentioned in *Málsháttakvæði*—Niðjungr, Sǫrli, and Brandingi—have not been identified, and may have had only a local reputation.

The anonymous author is ironic about his composition. He calls it "black-flecked" (stanza 22), motley—like a white sheep with black spots on it. He announces the imminence of the first refrain stanza

MALTA

by saying "Somewhat short in coherence is my verse" (stanza 11), and concludes the poem thus: "I have thrown it together without a rudder." Yet his intention was surely to create an illusion of incoherence, of a mind—unstrung by love-sorrow—still hanging on to the few certainties available to it: a variation on the poetic "discords" of the troubadours. *Málsháttakvæði,* although filled with proverbial wisdom, is not pedagogical in the way that *Hávamál* and *Hugsvinnsmál* are; if anything, its skald seems to mock the efficacy of the platitudes he so skillfully weaves together.

BIBLIOGRAPHY

Lee M. Hollander, *A Bibliography of Skaldic Studies* (1958); Finnur Jónsson, *Den norsk-islandske skjaldedigtning* (1912–1915), IIA, 130–136, and IIB, 138–145; Ernst A. Kock, *Den norsk-isländska skaldediktningen* (1946–1949), II, 73–78; Hermann Pálsson, "A Florilegium in Norse from Medieval Orkney," in *The Northern and Western Isles in the Viking World: Survival, Continuity, and Change,* A. Fenton and H. Pálsson, eds. (1984), 258–264; Jan de Vries, *Altnordische Literaturgeschichte,* 2nd rev. ed. (1964–1967), II, 68–71.

ROBERTA FRANK

[See also **Baldr; Bjarni Kolbeinsson; Jómsvíkinga Saga; Skaldic Poetry; Snorra Edda.**]

MALTA is the largest island in a central Mediterranean archipelago located 90 kilometers (about 58 miles) south of Sicily, 340 kilometers (about 220 miles) northeast of Tripoli, Libya, and 290 kilometers (about 180 miles) east of modern Tunisia; it includes Gozo, Comino, Cominotto, Filfla, and minor islets. The Romans took Malta from Carthage in 218 B.C. and held it until the Muslim conquest of 869/870. St. Paul converted the Maltese to Christianity in 58–60, and some of the population may have remained Christian through the Muslim period.

Malta's position made it important as a way station on the trade routes between the eastern and western Mediterranean and between Europe and Africa. Its proximity to Sicily and to the coasts of Ifrīqiya and Tripolitania gave it significance as a forward staging area and jumping-off place for naval and military attacks against any of those areas; since it is closest to Sicily, the history of medieval Malta is most closely tied to that island. Muslims, probably Aghlabids, conquered the archipelago in 869/870 as part of an expansion into the central Mediterranean. They controlled the archipelago until the Norman count of Sicily, Roger I, seized it in 1090, completing his conquest of Sicily. The Normans apparently lost control of Malta in the minority of Roger's son, Roger II, since the latter had to reconquer it in 1127.

Malta remained under titular Sicilian control until 1530, with sovereignty passing from the Normans to their Hohenstaufen successors under the Holy Roman emperor Henry VI in 1194. During the lengthy minority of his son and successor, Frederick II (1197–1220), Malta was ruled by a series of separatist counts, most of them Genoese, who served Genoese strategic interests and their own, rather than Frederick's. Seizing control over Italy in 1220, Frederick put an end to Maltese separatism and to the counts' use of the islands as a pirate base.

Frederick II died in 1250; his successors, Manfred and Conradin, were replaced in 1266 and 1268 in Sicily, and thus in Malta, by Charles of Anjou, brother of Louis IX of France. Angevin rule proved so onerous in Malta, as well as in Sicily, that the Sicilian Vespers (1282), which overthrew Charles and led the Aragonese king, Pedro (Pere) III, to conquer Sicily, seems to have been greeted with enthusiasm in Malta. Angevin forces held out in the Maltese citadel until at least February 1284 despite the Aragonese rout of an Angevin relief fleet in July 1283. The establishment of a separate Aragonese monarchy in Sicily (1296) under Frederick III, brother of the Aragonese king, led to the separation of Sicilian and Maltese fortunes from those of the Crown of Aragon for most of the fourteenth century (until 1380, when Pedro [Pere] IV reasserted Aragonese control). This period of separation saw Malta passed from hand to hand as a fief among the great barons of Sicily, who used it as a base from which to resist the power of the Sicilian and, later, the Aragonese monarchs.

The islands were reincorporated into the royal domain in 1397 on petition of the islanders. Although it remained a part of the domain of the Crown of Aragon throughout the fifteenth century, Malta suffered for that attachment through royal misgovernment and exploitation, Ifrīqiyan Hafsid reprisals for Aragonese raids on their territories, and a series of Genoese raids.

The archipelago became a strategic objective for the expanding Ottomans as early as 1488; thus Emperor Charles V's grant of Malta to the Knights Hospitalers in 1530 solved his defensive problem at the same time that it provided a refuge for the exiles from Rhodes.

BIBLIOGRAPHY
The best assessment of both European and Eastern sources remains Michele Amari, *Storia dei Musulmani di Sicilia,* 3 vols., 2nd rev. and enl. ed., Carlo A. Nallino, ed. (1933–1939). The best summary and discussion of modern scholarship is Anthony T. Luttrel, "Approaches to Medieval Malta," in Anthony T. Luttrel, ed., *Medieval Malta: Studies on Malta Before the Knights* (1975).

JAMES L. YARRISON

[See also **Aragon, Crown of; Frederick II of the Holy Roman Empire, King of Sicily; Islam, Conquests of; Roger I of Sicily; Roger II of Sicily; Sicilian Vespers; Sicily, Islamic; Sicily, Kindgom of.**]

MALTOLTE (maltôte) in medieval French originally meant an evil exaction and usually referred to indirect taxation. The best-known application of the term was to describe highly unpopular indirect taxes levied by Philip IV in the 1290's. The invidious connotation is less apparent by the mid fourteenth century, when the term was widely used in northern France to describe local or regional sales taxes. The term finally gave way to the word *aide* after royal indirect taxes by this name became common.

BIBLIOGRAPHY
John Bell Henneman, *Royal Taxation in Fourteenth Century France* (1971); Joseph R. Strayer and Charles H. Taylor, *Studies in Early French Taxation* (1939, repr. 1972).

JOHN BELL HENNEMAN

[See also **France; Taxation, French.**]

MALWIYA (Manāret al-Malwīya) denotes a type of helicoidal or spiral minaret which was briefly popular in ninth-century Islamic architecture produced in the orbit of Samarra, the Abbasid capital. It probably derived from the spiral ziggurats of ancient Mesopotamia and apparently carried royal associations for Muslims. The major surviving examples, all with external ramps, are those of the mosques of Samarra itself, Abū Dulaf nearby, and Ibn Ṭūlūn in Cairo.

BIBLIOGRAPHY
K. A. C. Creswell, *Early Muslim Architecture,* 2nd ed., I (1969); Ernst Herzfeld, "Mitteilung über die Arbeiten der Zweiten Kampagne von Samarra," in *Der Islam,* 5 (1914), 196–204; John W. Hoag, *Islamic Architecture* (1977).

ROBERT HILLENBRAND

[See also **Abbasid Art and Architecture; Islamic Art and Architecture; Samarra.**]

MAMIKONEAN. See page 78.

MAMLŪK (pl., *mamālīk*), an Arabic word meaning "one who is owned," hence a slave, is hardly ever used in its general sense, for which the usual word is ᶜ*abd.* Rather, it functions as a technical term, referring to a soldier who had been enslaved as a youth, trained to the profession of arms (and converted to Islam) under the supervision of his master (who was either the ruler or a senior military officer), and registered as a member of the standing professional forces of the realm. The obvious translation would thus be "slave-soldier," but this could be misleading, for in some Muslim states slave-recruits were manumitted on completion of their military training, while in others they remained in a state of formal servitude throughout their careers, however lofty the rank or office they might attain. Two matters of usage should be noted: (1) even a manumitted slave-recruit continued to be called a *mamlūk* and was hardly free to leave the service of his master of his own volition; (2) a free-born Muslim might often call himself *mamlūk* as a sign of deference to his prince.

In Islamic law a free man could be enslaved only if he were a non-Muslim residing outside the limits of Islamic territorial jurisdiction. Military slaves were imported from every region bordering the Islamic world: from sub-Saharan Africa (these were called ᶜ*abd* [pl., ᶜ*abīd*] instead of *mamlūk*); from Eastern Europe (the *ṣaqāliba*); from Anatolia and the Caucasus (Greeks, Armenians, Circassians); from India; and especially from the vast Turkic lands beyond the Oxus River. This great frontier zone was for many centuries (beginning *ca.* 850) the major reservoir of military manpower for Muslim rulers in the region between the Nile and the Oxus. The Turks were esteemed as military slaves for many reasons—their toughness, their racial pride and sense of solidarity, and their uncanny skill in the art of mounted archery.

The Ottoman sultans, like their predecessors, took military slaves from the non-Muslim lands around them (especially southern Russia and the Caucasus); however, in a striking departure from established Islamic tradition, they instituted a regular levy among the children of their Christian subjects in the Balkans and Anatolia. This child levy (the *devshirme*) lasted roughly from 1400 to 1700, but was very uncommon by the seventeenth century.

The *mamlūk* institution enjoyed an extraordinary importance in Islamic history from its first appearance in the mid ninth century; between the eleventh and eighteenth centuries there were very few Islamic polities in which a *mamlūk* corps did not play a major role. In a few states, military slavery was so central an element in the political system that the highest executive and military positions were normally open only to men who had begun their careers as *mamālīk*. Yet even in states like these it is a mistake to suppose that the entire army was composed of *mamālīk;* in one form or another, free-born Muslims were always a significant part of the armed forces of any Islamic state.

The origins of the *mamlūk* institution are still disputed. While early Islamic concepts of slavery, manumission, and clientage clearly provided the framework of law and custom within which military slavery could be instituted, they do not explain its appearance. Certainly the first clear case occurred under the Abbasid caliph al-Muᶜtaṣim (833–842). Seeking to undermine the existing military establishment, he aimed to create a new elite corps that would have no social or political links to anyone but himself. Even as heir apparent he had the governor of Transoxiana send him large numbers of Turkish youths who had been captured or purchased as a result of the incessant frontier wars of that region. Once brought to Iraq, these youths were housed in special barracks built in immediate proximity to the royal palace in Samarra. They were segregated from all regular contact with other elements of the army and the general populace and were even required to marry Turkish slave girls selected for them by the caliph. In these barracks they were taught the rudiments of Islam and given rigorous military training. At first the new *mamlūk* corps was simply the caliph's personal guard, but soon many of its members were promoted to high command. Down to the end of Abbasid independence, these Turkish *mamlūk* generals were among the most visible and powerful figures at the caliphal court. Al-Muᶜtaṣim's *mamlūk* regiment provided a powerful model for contemporary and later Muslim rulers, and the main features of his system endured throughout the subsequent history of the institution.

BIBLIOGRAPHY

Sources. C. T. Harley Walker, "Jahiz of Basra to al-Fath ibn Khaqan on the 'Exploits of the Turks and the Army of the Khalifate in General,'" in *Journal of the Royal Asiatic Society* (1915); Niẓām al-Mulk, *The Book of Government or Rules for Kings,* Hubert Darke, trans., 2nd rev. ed. (1978); al-Ṭabarī, *The Reign of al-Muᶜtaṣim,* Elma Marin, trans. (1951); al-Yaᶜqūbī, *Les pays,* Gaston Wiet, trans. (1937), 44–63.

Studies. There is still no full-length general study on the *mamlūk* institution; see, however, "Devshirme" and "Ghulam," in *Encyclopaedia of Islam,* new ed., II (1965). On the general institution of slavery in Islam, see "ᶜAbd," *ibid.,* I, 24–40. On the origins of the institution, there are two controversial studies: Patricia Crone, *Slaves on Horses* (1980); Daniel Pipes, *Slave Soldiers and Islam* (1981). See also David Ayalon, "Preliminary Remarks on the *Mamlūk* Military Institution in Islam," in Vernon J. Parry and M. E. Yapp, eds., *War, Technology, and Society in the Middle East* (1975). On the institution in its developed form, see David Ayalon, *L'esclavage du mamlouk* (1951), "Aspects of the Mamlūk Phenomenon," in *Der Islam,* 53 (1976), and *Studies on the Mamlūks of Egypt* (1250–1517) (1977). See also Clifford E. Bosworth, *The Ghaznavids* (1963).

R. STEPHEN HUMPHREYS

[See also **Abbasids; Circassians; Janissary; Muᶜtaṣim, al-; Slavery, Islamic World.**]

MAMLUK ART. The Mamluks, who ruled Egypt and Syria between 1250 and 1517, were formidable warriors renowned for their patronage of the arts. Lucrative trade routes between three continents passed through their lands and brought in vast revenues that the Mamluks used, in part, to finance an unprecedented flourish of artistic production. The products of this Mamluk renaissance continued to influence Islamic art up to the twentieth century.

Hundreds of religious and secular edifices were erected in Cairo, the capital, as well as in the provinces. Employing traditional plans, such as hypostyle mosques, four-*īwān* madrasas, and square mausoleums, the buildings were lavishly decorated with carved stone, stucco, and marble mosaics and panels. They were supplied with metal and wood furnishings, inlaid with precious materials. The most out-

Mirror decorated with signs of the zodiac. Mamluk metalwork, *ca.* 1340. İSTANBUL, TOPKAPI PALACE MUSEUM, 2/1786

standing features of Mamluk architecture are soaring tiered minarets, massive carved domes and entrance portals, and marble mihrabs. The elaborate floral and geometric patterns of the carved stonework give these structures their distinctly Mamluk character.

Patrons donated magnificent Korans to their religious establishments. These Korans, with exquisite calligraphy and dazzling illuminations, could be single volumes, two-volume sets, or thirty-volume sets. They were bound in leather and had stamped, tooled, and filigreed decorations. Illustrations in literary and scientific manuscripts were based on earlier traditions, whereas those in manuals on horsemanship, which were unique to the Mamluks, had original, though simple, compositions. The illustrations in late-fifteenth-century epic histories show the influence of artists who appear to have migrated to Mamluk territory from Baghdad and Shīrāz.

Brass bowls, basins, ewers, trays, and pen boxes inlaid with silver, gold, and copper are among the most celebrated works of Mamluk art. The decoration of earlier pieces relied on Ayyubid themes and employed figural compositions. Classical Mamluk style, which evolved around the 1330's, shows a predominence of inscriptions and heraldic blazons.

Enameled and gilded glass used the same decorative repertoire as metalwork. Artists created remarkable mosque lamps, bottles, bowls, and goblets. In ceramics, the figural compositions found on early Mamluk underglaze-painted wares soon gave way to concentric and radial designs. Lusterware ceased to be produced after 1400. Blue-and-white ware became popular. A ceramic type unique to the Mamluks was incised, slip-painted, and adorned with blazons and inscriptions.

Mamluk textiles and rugs were in great demand in the West. Striped and ogival silks woven with metallic threads were sewn into ecclesiastical vestments. Wool carpets with geometric designs, which appeared at the end of the fifteenth century, are among the oldest extant rugs.

Although Mamluk art was not radically innovative, the artists, stimulated by competitive patronage, produced some of the most spectacular examples of Islamic art and architecture.

BIBLIOGRAPHY

Esin Atıl, *Renaissance of Islam: Art of the Mamluks* (1981); K. A. C. Creswell, *The Muslim Architecture of Egypt,* II (1959); Hayat Salam-Liebich, *The Architecture of the Mamluk City of Tripoli* (1983).

ESIN ATIL

[See also **Ceramics, Islamic; Glass, Islamic; Islamic Art and Architecture; Lusterware; Manuscript Illumination, Byzantine and Islamic; Textiles, Islamic.**]

MAMLUK DYNASTY, the usual name for the line of rulers who governed Egypt and Syria (together with other adjoining regions from time to time) in the period 1250–1517. The regime is also sometimes referred to as the Mamluk empire and Mamluk sultanate. The term "dynasty" is actually a misnomer, for few of the major sultans in this long sequence were blood relatives. On the contrary, succession to the throne was normally determined by armed struggle among the regime's senior military officers, or emirs. The leading emirs, from among whom the sultans were typically chosen, were almost always

MAMLUK DYNASTY

men who in their youth had been military slaves (*mamlūks*—hence the name of the dynasty). Having been manumitted by some previous sultan on the completion of their training, they were then promoted by him to high military and executive office. In a real sense, therefore, the army was the state; soldiers determined policy and directed administration, while the senior officials of the realm retained not only military rank but also active field command. In the Mamluk state, civilian officials were mere functionaries, working under close military supervision and control.

Medieval Muslim authors never used the term "Mamluk" for this state. Normally they called it "the Turkish regime" *(dawlat al-atrāk),* because up until 1382 the sultanate was always held by a man of Kipchak Turkish origin, and Kipchak Turkish remained the principal language of the court and the military elite down to the very end, in 1517. After 1382, however, when the state was dominated by Circassian *mamlūks* recruited in the Caucasus, chroniclers sometimes used the term "the Circassian regime" *(dawlat al-jarākisa).* In official chancery usage, neither ethnic not territorial appelations were used: the government, personified by its head, was "The Noble Sultanate" *(al-salṭana al-sharīfa).*

The Mamluks legitimized their rule by a simple but compelling ideology that was not original to them. It had emerged with the rise of the Seljuks in the mid eleventh century, but through such media as official correspondence, epigraphy, architecture, and ceremony the Mamluks made it peculiarly their own. In the Mamluk view, the sultan is designated by the caliph, the head of the worldwide Muslim community, to be his executive agent in all matters pertaining to the well-being of Muslims in this life and the next. The sultan's authority has no territorial limits; it extends to whatever lands he can acquire and protect with his sword. The sultan is first of all a warrior in the path of God. As such, he defends Islam against the foreign infidel and strives to extend its sway; he also tramples down heresy and rebellion within his domains. To ensure that his subjects know and obey the divine commandments, the sultan must uphold sound religious scholarship and orthodox doctrine, which he accomplishes through close supervision and lavish patronage. It is the sultan's duty, finally, to bring justice to all who live in his dominions by the energetic enforcement of the *sharīᶜa* (sacred law), by whose provisions all receive their due and the weak are protected from oppression. The Mamluk sultan claims to be the preeminent king of his age, superior to all others in status and power; therefore he must show himself to be the very model of Islamic kingship.

This lofty ideology may appear to fit badly with the Mamluk dynasty's notorious political violence. But in most periods this violence was largely an intra-elite affair, and the major sultans usually tried to pay more than lip service to their professed ideals. Because the Mamluk state remained a formidable military power throughout its 267 years, the sultans were normally able to protect their central possessions of Egypt and Syria from foreign invasion. The sultans and their emirs were generous patrons of the institutional infrastructure of religion—mosques, madrasas, and Sufi convents—though few of them had any real understanding of Islamic doctrine and scholarship. Religious zealots were undoubtedly pleased by the state's ruthless pursuit of heresy and its humbling of the recognized Christian and Jewish minorities. Justice was a sometime thing, to be sure, but the Mamluks took the important symbolic step of creating a judicial system that gave official recognition to all four "orthodox" schools of jurisprudence (sing.: *madhhab*).

The claim of the Mamluk sultans to preeminence among Muslim monarchs is perhaps debatable, but the state that they headed was not only militarily powerful but also remarkably durable and well integrated. On a territorial level, traditionally fractious Syria was effectively subordinated to Cairo through a stable and tightly knit administrative hierarchy; the governors of Damascus or Aleppo may have tried to seize the sultanate in Cairo, but they never attempted to secede and create independent states. The concept of a centralized, unitary state comprising both Egypt and Syria was never challenged. Moreover, in spite of the almost constant violence among the political elite, the administrative machinery continued to function without a break. The Mamluk regime, in short, was a genuine state, not an ephemeral dynasty of the kind so common in medieval Islamic history.

On the debit side of the ledger, the Mamluk period saw a progressive economic and demographic decline, at least after the mid fourteenth century. To some degree this must be attributed to factors beyond the control of the Mamluk government, such as plague and the naval power of Venice and Genoa. Nevertheless, Mamluk policy clearly aggravated the situation; the fifteenth century especially was marked by rapacious and irregular taxation, attempts to monopolize the trade in various commod-

MAMLUK DYNASTY

ities, sporadic confiscation, and looting by uncontrolled bands of *mamlūks*. The regime's intolerance toward its Christian and Jewish subjects may have had some impact on the overall economy, although this is hard to assess; in any case, these groups had been vital and productive in Fatimid and Ayyubid times, but under the Mamluks they were driven into impoverishment and social marginality.

Formally the Mamluk state was an autocracy. All powers of administration, military command, and justice were conferred on the sultan by the caliph. (A shadow caliphate, with purely symbolic and ceremonial functions, had been established in Cairo in 1261 when the sultan al-Ẓāhir Baybars recognized an Abbasid refugee from Mongol-occupied Baghdad as the legitimate heir to this office.) The sultan in turn named such subordinate officials as he needed; these officials were his personal agents, answerable directly to him. He was expected to consult periodically with the great men of the realm in a council called the *mashwara,* but he was free to act without their consent.

In reality, however, the Mamluk state was a military oligarchy. The sultan was not a man apart from his senior emirs. On the contrary, he typically had been one of them and ruled by assembling a coalition of emirs who would support his regime against possible rivals. Such coalitions, based on personal ambition, gratitude for past benefits, and momentarily parallel interests, were difficult to assemble and inherently unstable; only very skilled politicians succeeded. During the crucial first years of his reign, the sultan had to move from the coalition that had put him in office to one that had a vested interest in keeping him there.

This situation helps to explain why the sons of sultans seldom established enduring regimes; since they did not belong to any of the military factions, they had no chance to create an effective coalition of their own or to control preexisting ones. Usually, they were only interim compromise candidates or the protégés of a particular faction—not necessarily the strongest one.

These factions were not mere congeries of ambitious individuals; rather, they were firmly rooted in the complex structure of the Mamluk army. Although troops recruited and stationed in Syria made up a substantial proportion (perhaps as much as one-half) of the empire's total forces, and although they did a great deal of the fighting, they were politically marginal. It was the forces permanently stationed in Cairo that were crucial to the struggle for power.

The regular Mamluk army in Cairo was made up of three elements: the sultan's *mamlūks*; the emirs' *mamlūks*; and a body of freeborn soldiers called the *ḥalqa.* (All these were calvary forces. Infantry was recruited on an ad hoc basis.) The sultan's *mamlūks* were the elite troops of the system, usually the largest single group in the army. In the famous reorganization of 1315, five-twelfths of Egypt's military revenues were set aside for their support. Because they were purchased and trained under the sultan's close supervision and housed in barracks within the citadel, they were much better placed than any other group for promotion to the emirate. Indeed, the great majority of the army's senior emirs had begun their careers as the sultan's *mamlūks*.

The sultan's *mamlūks* were by no means internally united and wholly reliable, however, for this group was divided within itself. Each sultan assembled a new *mamlūk* regiment of his own, which would typically be called by his throne name. (Thus the *mamlūks* of al-Ẓāhir Baybars were known as the Ẓāhirīya.) Such regiments did not break up on the death of their founder; on the contrary, a new sultan inherited more or less intact the several regiments established by his predecessors. However, the primary loyalty of an old *mamlūk* was to his own regiment. These old *mamlūks* had no reason to feel loyal to the new sultan and in fact were likely to be envious and fearful of the new *mamlūk* regiment that the new sultan would begin to form. Thus the inherited regiments were a constant source of tension and sedition, and an emir trying to overthrow the sultan could easily call upon the aid of his old regimental comrades. In short, the rival regiments among the sultan's *mamlūks* were the basis for political factions, though there was not any simple one-to-one correspondence between factions and regiments.

Although the emirs' *mamlūks*, in turn, were quite numerous, they were a subsidiary element in the political system for several reasons. They were much less well paid and trained than the sultan's men; their regiments were relatively small and isolated from one another; and, finally, when an emir died or fell from power, his regiment was broken up and its members distributed among the sultan and other emirs.

An emir supported his regiment from the revenues of lands assigned to him by the central administration, which, in turn, always maintained a careful supervision over them. These revenue assignments

MAMLUK DYNASTY

(iqṭāᶜ) were carefully ranked according to a three-tier hierarchy: emir of 100, emir of 40, and emir of 10. In this system, an emir of 100 was an officer who had been assigned an *iqṭāᶜ* capable of supporting 100 *mamlūks*, fully trained and armed, at a fixed rate of pay and allowances. The number of *mamlūks* named in the rank was the *minimum* number required from a holder of that rank; any emir who could garner extra revenues and thereby support more troopers would do so, since this would give him additional resources for the political melee.

In addition to the *mamlūk* units, the army had a very substantial number of freeborn soldiers, organized into a separate body called the *ḥalqa.* Many of the *ḥalqa* troopers were the sons of *mamlūks*, the so-called *awlād al-nās*—a group that retained its military status but was generally excluded from the higher ranks and offices. The origins of this body are still very obscure. In the thirteenth century, however, it was the largest group in the army, and its high-caliber soldiers were recruited from such sources as the remnants of the Ayyubid armies and Turko-Mongol refugees from Ilkhanid Iran. Even at its peak, however, it was never the equal in pay, training, or prestige of the sultan's *mamlūks*. From the opening years of the fourteenth century the *ḥalqa* declined rapidly; freeborn troops of high quality were now a rarity, and the fiscal reorganizations of sultans Ḥusām al-Dīn Lachin (1298) and al-Nāṣir Muḥammad (1315) squeezed the *ḥalqa* and the emirs' troops in favor of the sultan's *mamlūks*. The *ḥalqa* soon degenerated into an ill-paid militia of little military value. Ultimately it was penetrated by the sons of artisans and retailers, who valued the pay and privileges that even low military status conferred in Mamluk society.

The kernel of the Mamluk regime was the famous Baḥrīya regiment established by the Ayyubid sultan al-Ṣāliḥ Ayyūb (1240–1249). Composed of Kipchak Turkish *mamlūks*, the Baḥrīya corps was not large—some 1,000 men—but its rigorous training, loyalty to al-Ṣāliḥ, and segregation even from other segments of the army made it an extremely cohesive force. Both contemptuous and fearful of al-Ṣāliḥ's son Tūrān-Shāh, whom in fact they hardly knew, the Baḥrīya brutally murdered him within three months of his accession (1250). Al-Ṣaliḥ's widow, Shajar al-Durr, was named to succeed him—the only time in Islamic history that a woman ruled in her own name. But the new commander-in-chief of the army, ᶜIzz al-Dīn Aybak, became the sultan when he married Shajar al-Durr some three months later.

The new sultan, ᶜIzz al-Dīn Aybak, struggled bitterly to retain power during a turbulent seven-year reign, confronting a still considerable Ayyubid kingdom in Syria as well as countless internal factions. He was soon alienated even from his own Baḥrīya comrades and drove them into exile in Syria, where ironically they took service under the Ayyubid sultan al-Nāṣir Yūsuf II. In the end Aybak could not face down all the opposition; in 1257 he was murdered at the instigation of his wife, Shajar al-Durr. Again it fell to the senior emirs to determine the succession; as an interim measure they named the slain man's son ᶜAlī as sultan and a *mamlūk* of Aybak's, Sayf al-Dīn Quṭuz, as his regent and commander in chief. In light of ᶜAlī's youth, the looming Mongol danger, and continued factionalism in Egypt, it is hardly surprising that, in 1259, Quṭuz seized the sultanate in his own name.

Both the political violence of this decade and the ad hoc solutions to its crises may seem banal and degrading. However, these events provided the model for political action throughout the entire Mamluk period. Certainly the "electoral" role of the senior emirs, the nontransferability of loyalties from father to son, and the significance of the *mamlūk* regiment as the fundamental unit of politics are all clearly visible.

The usurper Quṭuz soon obtained a title of legitimacy far beyond that enjoyed by either of his predecessors. His army defeated the Mongols at the famous battle of ᶜAyn Jālūt in 1260 and drove them out of Syria. He used this splendid victory to establish his governors throughout Syria, thereby defining the territorial core of the Mamluk state for the rest of its history. After Quṭuz, the men of the new regime were no longer mere bloody regicides, but rather triumphant defenders of the lands of Islam against the infidel.

For his services Quṭuz received poor thanks. A month after ᶜAyn Jālūt he was murdered by the commandant of the still-lively Baḥrīya, one Baybars al-Bunduqdārī, who then induced or intimidated the other emirs into recognizing him as sultan. Baybars was a surprise: heretofore an unprincipled freebooter, he now became a brilliant ruler, in many ways the true architect of the Mamluk state.

The eighty-year span from 1260 to 1340 is defined by three long reigns—those of al-Malik al-Ẓāhir (Triumphant King) Baybars (1260–1277), his Baḥrīya comrade al-Manṣūr Qalaᵓūn (1279–1290), and the latter's son al-Nāṣir Muḥammad (1293–1294, 1299–1309, 1310–1341). Although it thus appears to have

MAMLUK DYNASTY

been an era of relative political stability, it was in fact filled with bitter infighting, and its long reigns simply attest to the skill with which these rulers manipulated the complex equations of power.

In spite of the events of the first Mamluk decade, the dynastic principle of succession still retained some plausibility. Baybars did everything he could (though in the end it was not enough) to assure the succession of his son, and Qalāʾūn did in fact found a dynasty that would rule until 1382. However, the Qalaunid succession was largely a fiction: his oldest son, al-Ashraf Khalīl, was murdered by the emirs in December 1293, and al-Nāṣir Muḥammad had to struggle for fifteen years to assure his grip on the sultanate. As to the latter's eight sons, two grandsons, and two great-grandsons, none was ever sultan in more than name.

Such political tensions should not obscure the great achievements of this period, however. The crusader states in Syria were eliminated in 1291, and the even more dangerous Ilkhanid Mongols of Iran were definitively checked by the first decade of the fourteenth century. The economic structures of Egypt and Syria must have been strained by the persistent warfare of the late thirteenth century: most of Syria's seaports were ruined by the Mamluks themselves, Mediterranean commerce was often disrupted by papal interdicts on trade with the infidel, and northern Syria was repeatedly ravaged by Mongol incursions. But the damage was not fatal, and after 1300 a brilliant efflorescence occurred: drainage and irrigation projects were undertaken in Syria, and extensive construction of all kinds took place in all the cities of the empire.

Indeed, it was under al-Nāṣir Muḥammad that medieval Cairo reached its apogee of population and wealth. On another level, the empire's military and administrative institutions took on their "classic" form in these decades, and al-Nāṣir Muḥammad's third reign came to be regarded by later generations as a golden age. Nevertheless, perhaps the glory of al-Nāṣir's reign was fool's gold; it has recently been argued that his grandiose projects hopelessly overextended the empire's resources and prepared the way for the dismal collapse that followed—a point still open to debate.

During the period from 1340 to 1382, the Mamluks remained the paramount Muslim power: the Ilkhanid regime in Iran was crumbling, and none of the petty principalities of Anatolia had as yet become a real force. The Armenian kingdom of Cilicia was finally absorbed in 1375, but Mamluk arms were by no means uniformly successful. The crusader Kingdom of Cyprus ruthlessly sacked Alexandria in 1365, and Cypriot fleets launched numerous destructive raids against the Syrian coast in the years following. Although humiliating, these assaults led to no losses of territory, and the Mamluk army remained fully intact.

Internally, these were decades of extraordinary stress on every level. The sultan ceased to be the effective master of the state; only three of the twelve monarchs reigned for as long as five years, and all were mere playthings in the hands of powerful but unstable military factions. The weakness of these sultans is not surprising; most of them were children when they mounted the throne. More striking is that none of the senior emirs was able to seize the throne for himself. The inability of the system to produce a strong ruler, unparalleled in previous Mamluk experience, remains a mystery, for the political history of these years is still little studied. Perhaps the long reign of al-Nāṣir Muḥammad prevented any emir from assembling a sufficiently powerful coalition to overawe his colleagues. Or possibly the terrible toll of the Black Death (1347–1349) made effective *mamlūk* coalitions hard to create and sustain.

The main social and economic fact of this period is certainly the Black Death itself, though its exact consequences are still—and probably will always be—a matter of speculation. The initial mortality in Egypt and Syria is likely to have been much the same as in Europe, perhaps one-third or more of the population. Nor was this only a momentary crisis, for severe outbreaks of plague recurred in Egypt and Syria for the rest of the Mamluk period. Though no class of the population was immune, three groups seem to have been especially hard hit: young women, children, and recently purchased *mamlūk*s. If this apparent incidence of mortality is valid, it means that the plague struck hardest at the future—high mortality among young *mamlūk*s would mean that the elite would have trouble replacing itself, and high mortality among children and women of childbearing age would depress the growth potential of the overall population.

During the thirty years from 1382 to 1412, the tensions of earlier periods exploded and nearly wrecked the Mamluk state. The period opens with the seizure of power by the Circassian *mamlūk* Al-Ẓāhir Barqūq. Even though he was an able and ruthless man, Barqūq had to struggle for a decade before he could secure his grip on the sultanate. He was succeeded by his son al-Nāṣir Faraj (1399–1405,

MAMLUK DYNASTY

1405–1412), who ascended the throne as a boy of ten. Faraj held on for a long time but never prevailed over the violent rivalries among the emirs. These struggles had an ethnic dimension: Barqūq had brought in large numbers of Circassian *mamlūks*, who were now contesting (victoriously, in the end) the traditional political supremacy of the Turks. Ultimately the young sultan was deposed and murdered, and after a brief interregnum one of the conspirators, the brutal al-Muʾayyad Shaykh, seized the throne. He proved strong enough to restore a modicum of order and predictability to political life during his reign (1412–1421).

Barqūq had faced no immediate foreign threats, but in his last years, as he became aware of the tremendous dynamism of the Turko-Mongol conqueror Timur (known in the West as Tamerlane), he undertook the restoration of Syria's fortifications. It was on the unfortunate Faraj that the storm burst. In 1400, Aleppo was overwhelmed, pillaged, and put to the torch. Faraj tried, ineffectually, to defend Damascus but was compelled to abandon the city to Timur's mercies. Damascus surrendered on terms, but even so was thoroughly pillaged; worst of all, many thousands of its people were deported to central Asia. At this juncture, Timur decided not to try to occupy Egypt; he turned north to Anatolia, and died in 1405 in central Asia without again attacking Mamluk territories. Far less important but still humiliating were the destructive naval raids of Marshal Jean Boucicaut on the port cities of Syria in the summer of 1403.

Faraj was not only an unlucky soldier but an inept and shortsighted administrator. An extremely low Nile in 1403 set off a monetary and economic collapse that was not righted for at least a decade and, in some respects, was never overcome. The initial disaster can hardly be charged to Faraj, for he had inherited a seriously weakened economy. But he proved utterly unable to restore a sound coinage, while his fiscal policies further disrupted the structure of trade and manufacturing. On every level, then, Faraj's successors were faced with urgent and very difficult challenges; it is remarkable that they resolved them even as well as they did.

The long period from 1412 to 1496 is in some ways comparable to the eighty years between 1260 and 1340. Mamluk arms recovered from the humiliation of Timur's invasions, as evidenced in al-Ashraf Barsbay's occupation of Cyprus in 1426 (the only successful naval expedition in Mamluk history) and the successful if hardly brilliant prosecution of a war against the Ottomans for paramountcy in central Anatolia in 1481–1491. The Mamluk cavalry, restored to a semblance of order by al-Muʾayyad Shaykh, was neither as numerous nor as highly trained as it had been in the early fourteenth century, but it was still the best force of its kind in the Middle East. Altogether, the mamluks were probably the leading Muslim power during these decades, though their position was momentarily challenged by the meteoric career of the Aq Qoyunlu sultan Uzun Ḥasan (1457–1478), and not only challenged but gravely endangered by the rise of the Ottomans after 1453.

In the economic sphere, Egypt and Syria never recovered the solid prosperity of the early fourteenth century, but a degree of order was restored. An acceptable silver currency was introduced by al-Muʾayyad Shaykh, and al-Ashraf Barsbāy minted a gold coin able to stay in circulation alongside the Venetian ducat. The benefits of relative monetary stability were largely negated, however, by an acute and unremitting fiscal crisis. The state's tax receipts were eroded by rural depopulation (presumably caused by the plague) and a radical decline in agricultural production. At the same time, the costs of maintaining an adequate army rose as a result of foreign wars, internal strife, and the decimation of younger *mamlūks* by plague. Moreover, the Mamluk elite was determined to retain its traditionally luxurious style of life whatever the cost.

Such circumstances warranted drastic action. Sultan Barsbāy began the process by making the spice trade with India a royal monopoly; thenceforth massive government manipulation of commerce and industry became a regular feature of economic life. These policies were frankly exploitative, adopted not to secure equitable prices and distribution but to maximize the current revenues of an administration that could not make ends meet any other way. That they were exceedingly destructive was fully recognized even by contemporary observers.

Political and military collapse might have come sooner than it did had it not been for the efforts of al-Ashraf Qāʾitbāy (1468–1496). Faced with a perpetually empty treasury, rampant *mamlūk* factionalism, and foreign crises, he nevertheless kept a modicum of public order, restored his empire's fortifications, and successfully confronted the external threats of his age. He was the first Mamluk sultan to establish a corps of harquebusiers, though this important military reform was quickly ended by the opposition of the *mamlūk* cavalry. He

MAMLUK DYNASTY

also tried with at least partial success to restore commerce and encourage international trade; his reign represents the last period of Egyptian domination of the India trade.

The final period of Mamluk rule, from 1496 to 1517, was one of constant crisis, coupled with a radically decreased capacity to cope with it. This was due to no failure of leadership; Qānṣūh al Ghawrī (1501–1516), the last major sultan, was an old man when he came to power, but he was energetic, courageous, and farsighted. His efforts to preserve the Mamluk state were crippled both by a lack of material resources and by the failure of those around him to grasp the true nature of the dangers they faced. The crises of this period were occasioned by two events: the Portuguese penetration of the Indian Ocean and the bitter struggle between the Ottomans and the new Iranian Safavid kingdom for control of central and eastern Anatolia.

The Portuguese navy attempted to choke off the Red Sea and Persian Gulf routes to India and to dominate the Indian ports themselves. In doing this the Portuguese ruined the Mamluk treasury, which was heavily dependent on the customs revenues yielded by the spice trade. The sultan's response was vigorous but ultimately ineffective. He refortified the Red Sea ports, equipping them with modern artillery, and outfitted a number of naval expeditionary forces. However, his fortifications were never really tested, and Mamluk ships were no match for the Portuguese.

The rise of the Safawids presented a more traditional kind of problem, but one which the weakened Mamluks were in no better position to face. The charisma of Shah Ismā^{c}īl I (1501–1524) among the Turkoman peoples of Anatolia, his astonishing conquests in Iran, and his radical Shiite ideology left the Mamluks fearful and indecisive but made the Ottoman sultan Yavuz Selim ever more determined to crush this menace once and for all. Selim's brilliant campaign of 1514, though it did no permanent damage to the Safawid state, neutralized it as a force in Anatolian politics for years to come.

Having secured his eastern frontiers, Selim then decided to move against the Mamluk empire as well, possibly fearing a Mamluk-Safawid alliance that would threaten his newly won position in Anatolia. He may also have calculated that the Ottoman Empire's long-term strategic interests could only be secured if it controlled the trade routes and grain production of the now moribund Mamluk state. Finally, he may have been impelled in part by ideology—a feeling that the lands of Islam must be as fully unified as possible in this time of worldwide struggle against Safawid heresy and the European infidel, and that only his state had the power to achieve such a goal.

Qānṣūh al Ghawrī was not unprepared for Selim's offensive. From the beginning of his reign he had striven to revitalize the *mamlūk* cavalry, and the army he led out of Cairo in the summer of 1516 was undoubtedly the best trained and equipped force the Mamluks had fielded for a century. On the other hand, its tactics and weapons were entirely traditional, whereas the Ottomans relied heavily on firearms, including field artillery. Qānṣūh al Ghawrī was aware of the value of firearms and had devoted vast sums to the casting of cannon, but these were naval and fortress guns, not mobile field pieces. Likewise, he had made a serious effort to reestablish a corps of harquebusiers. Some early efforts to equip black slaves with harquebuses had to be abandoned owing to *mamlūk* opposition, but in 1511 he founded a new regiment of free recruits, the so-called Fifth Corps. This unit was also bitterly resented by the *mamlūk* cavalry, however, and it was used exclusively in naval expeditions against the Portuguese.

Under the circumstances, the outcome of the struggle could not be in doubt. At Marj Dābiq, north of Aleppo, the Mamluk army was cut to pieces by Ottoman firepower in August 1516. Qānṣūh al Ghawrī died in the course of the fighting. A new sultan, Tūmān Bāy, showed vast energy in assembling a new army, outfitted this time with ample firearms. But it was too late, and the demoralized Mamluks were crushed again outside Cairo in January 1517. With this event the Mamluk dynasty came to an end. For the next four centuries Syria and Egypt would be Ottoman provinces.

BIBLIOGRAPHY

Bibliographies. Ira M. Lapidus, *Muslim Cities in the Later Middle Ages* (1967), 217–242; Hassanein Rabie, *The Financial System of Egypt, A. H. 564–741/A.D. 1169–1341* (1972), 198–227; Jean Sauvaget, *Introduction to the History of the Muslim East,* Claude Cahen, rev. and ed. (1965), 176–183.

Documents and archives. Muḥammad M. Amin, *Catalogue des documents d'archives du Caire de 239/853 à 922–1516* (in Arabic) (1981); Paul Balog, *The Coinage of the Mamluk Sultans of Egypt and Syria* (1964); Max van Berchem *et al., Matériaux pour un corpus inscriptionum arabicarum,* in *Mémoires de la mission archéologique française au Caire,* **19** (1894–1903), and in *Mémoires de l'institut français d'archéologie orientale au Caire,* **25,**

43–44, 52, 76–77 (1909, 1922, 1925–1927, 1930, 1955, 1956); Amnon Cohen and Bernard Lewis, *Population and Revenue in the Towns of Palestine in the Sixteenth Century* (1978); Étienne Combe *et al.*, eds., *Répertoire chronologique d'épigraphie arabe,* 17 vols. (1931–); Aḥmad Darrāj, *L'acte de waqf de Barsbay* (1963); Hans Ernst, *Die mamlukischen Sultansurkunden des Sinai-Klosters* (1960); Heinz Gaube, *Arabische Inschriften aus Syrien* (1978); Lapidus, *op. cit.,* 229–230; Jon E. Mandaville, "The Muslim Judiciary of Damascus in the Late Mamluk Period" (diss., Princeton, 1969); Robert Mantran and Jean Sauvaget, *Règlements fiscaux ottomans: Les provinces syriennes* (1951); Norman D. Nicol, Rafaat al-Nabarawy, and Jere L. Bacharach, *Catalog of the Islamic Coins, Glass Weights, Dies, and Medals in the Egyptian National Library* (1982); Rabie, *op. cit.,* 3–6, 8–10; André Raymond, *Artisans et commerçants du Caire au 18e siècle* (1973), xxii–xxiv; Jean Sauvaget, "Dècrets mamelouks de Syrie," in *Bulletin d'ètudes orientales,* **2, 3, 12** (1932, 1934, 1947–1948); S. M. Stern, "Petitions from the Mamlūk Period," in *Bulletin of the School of Oriental and African Studies,* **29** (1966).

Historiographical literature. Eliyahu Ashtor, "Some Unpublished Sources for the Baḥrī Period," in *Scripta Hierosolymitana,* **9** (1961); Jere L. Bacharach, "Circassian Mamluk Historians and Their Quantitative Economic Data," in *Journal of the American Research Center in Egypt,* **12** (1975); Ulrich Haarmann, *Quellenstudien zur frühen Mamlukenzeit* (1970); Donald P. Little, *An Introduction to Mamluk Historiography* (1970); Barbara Schäfer, *Beiträge zur mamlukischen Historiographie nach dem Tode al-Malik an-Nāsirs* (1971); Muḥammad M. Ziyādah, *al-Muʾarrikhūn fī Miṣr fī'l-Qarn al-Khāmis ʿAshar al-Mīlādī* (1949).

Texts and chronicles. Ibn ʿAbd al-Ẓāhir, "A Critical Edition of an Unkown Source for the Life of al-Malik al-Zahir Baybars," Ahmad A. al-Khowaitir, ed. and trans. (diss., London, 1960); Syedah F. Sadeque, *Baybars I of Egypt* (1956); Ibn Faḍlallāh al-ʿUmarī, *Masālik al-Abṣār fī Mamālik al-Amṣār,* Maurice Gaudefroy-Demombynes, trans. and ed. (1927); Richard Hartmann, "Politische Geographie des Mamlūkenreichs," in *Zeitschrift der Deutschen Morgenländischen Gesellschaft,* **70** (1916); and Klaus Lech, *Das Mongolische Weltreich* (1968); Ibn Iyās, *Histoire des Mamlouks Circassiens,* Gaston Wiet, trans., II (1945), and *Journal d'un bourgeois du Caire,* 2 vols. (1955–1960); Ibn Ṣaṣrā, *A Chronicle of Damascus, 1389–1397,* William M. Brinner, ed. and trans., 2 vols. (1963); Ibn al-Shiḥna, *Les perles choisies d'Ibn ach-Chihna,* Jean Sauvaget, trans. (1933) (this text should be studied together with Sibṭ ibn al-ʿAjamī, *Les trésors d'or,* Jean Sauvaget, trans. [1950]); Ibn al-Ṣuqāʿī, *Tālī Kitāb Wafayāt al-Aʿyān,* Jacqueline Sublet, trans. (1974); Ibn Taghrībirdī, *History of Egypt, 1382–1469 A.D.,* William Popper, trans., 8 vols. (1954–1963), and *Les biographies du Manhal Safi,* Gaston Wiet, ed. and trans. (1932); Khalīl al-Ẓāhirī, *Zubdat Kashf al-Mamālik,* Venture de Paradis, trans. (1950); Taqī al-Dīn al-Maqrīzī, *Histoire des sultans mamlouks de l'Égypte,* Étienne M. Quatremère, trans., 2 vols. (1837–1845), *Description topographique et historique de l'Égypte,* Urbain Bouriant, trans. (1900), continued by Paul Casanova (1906), and *Les marchés du Caire: Traduction annotée du texte de Maqrizi,* André Raymond and Gaston Wiet, trans. (1979); Mufaḍḍal ibn Abī Faḍāʾil in Edgar Blochet, ed. and trans., "Histoire des sultans mamlouks," in *Patrologia orientalis,* **12, 14, 20** (1919, 1920, 1929) (to be used with caution); Samira Kortantamer, *Ägypten und Syrien zwischen 1317 und 1341 in der Chronik des Mufaḍḍal ibn Abi al-Faḍāʾil* (1973); ʿAbd al-Qādir al-Nuʿaymī in H. Sauvaire, trans., "Description de Damas," in *Journal asiatique,* 9th ser., **3–7** (1894–1896); al-Qalqashandī, work analyzed by Walther Björkman, *Beiträge zur Geschichte der Staatskanzlei im Islamischen Ägypten* (1928), and Maurice Gaudefroy-Demombynes, ed. and trans., *La Syrie à l'époque des Mamelouks* (1923).

The Mamluk state. Aḥmad ʿAbd ar-Rāziq, "Le vizirat et les vizirs d'Egypte au temps des Mamluks," in *Annales islamologiques,* **16** (1980); David Ayalon, *L'esclavage du mamelouk* (1951), "Studies on the Structure of the Mamluk Army," in *Bulletin of the School of Oriental and African Studies,* **15, 16** (1953, 1954), *Gunpowder and Firearms in the Mamluk Kingdom* (1956), and "The Great Yāsa of Chingiz Khān: A Re-examination," in *Studia islamica,* **33, 34, 36, 38** (1971, 1972, 1973); Richard S. Cooper, "The Assessment and Collection of *Kharāj* Tax in Medieval Egypt," in *Journal of the American Oriental Society,* **96** (1976); R. Stephen Humphreys, "The Emergence of the Mamluk Army," in *Studia islamica,* **45, 46** (1977); Robert Irwin, *The Middle East in the Middle Ages: The Early Mamluk Sultanate, 1250–1382* (1986); Carl F. Petry, *The Civilian Elite of Cairo in the Later Middle Ages* (1981); William Popper, *Egypt and Syria Under the Circassian Sultans, 1382–1468 A.D.,* 2 vols. (1955–1960); Hassanein Rabie, *op. cit.;* Jean Sauvaget, *La poste aux chevaux dans l'empire des Mamelouks* (1941).

Particular reigns. Saʿīd A. ʿĀshūr, *ʿAṣr al-Mamālīk fī Miṣr waʾl-Shām* (1965); Aḥmad Darrāj, *L'Égypte sous le règne de Barsbay* (1961); R. Stephen Humphreys, *From Saladin to the Mongols* (1977); ʿAbd al-ʿAziz Khowaitir, *Baibars the First* (1978); Götz Schregle, *Die Sultanin von Ägypten* (1961); Gaston Wiet, *L'Égypte arabe* (1937).

Mamluk society. Eliyahu Ashtor-Strauss (see also Ashtor), "L'urbanisme syrien à la basse-époque," in *Rivista degli studi orientali,* **33** (1958); Eliyahu Ashtor, *Toledot ha-Yehudim be-Mizrayim ve-Suria tahat shilton ha-Mamlukim,* 3 vols. (1944–1970), and *Histoire des prix et des salaires dans l'Orient médiévale* (1969); Saʿīd A. ʿĀshūr, *al-Mujtamaʿ al-Miṣrīfī ʿAṣr Salāṭīn al-Mamālīk* (1962); Michael W. Dols, *The Black Death in the Middle East* (1977); Jean-Claude Garcin, *Un centre musulman de la Haute-Égypte médiévale: Qūṣ* (1976); Ira M. Lapidus, *op. cit.;* Nicola A. Ziadeh, *Urban Life in Syria Under the Early Mamluks* (1953).

Religion and culture. János Eckman, "The Mamluk-Kipchak Literature," in *Central Asiatic Journal,* **8** (1963);

R. Stephen Humphreys, "The Expressive Intent of the Mamluk Architecture of Cairo," in *Studia islamica,* **35** (1972); Henri Laoust, "Le hanbalisme sous les Mamlouks Bahrides (658–784/1260–1382)," in *Revue des études islamiques,* **28** (1960); Moshe Perlmann, "Asnawi's Tract Against Christian Officials," in Samuel Löwinger, Joseph Somogyi, and Alexander Scheiber, eds., *Ignace Goldziher Memorial Volume,* II (1958), 172–208; Maḥmud R. Salīm, *ᶜAṣr Salāṭīn al-Mamālīk wa-Nitājuhu al-ᶜIlmī waᵓl-Adabī,* 8 vols. (1947–1966); E. M. Sartain, *Jalāl al-Dīn al-Suyūṭī,* I (1975); Eliyahu Strauss (see also Ashtor), "L'inquisition dans l'état mamlouk," in *Rivista degli studi orientali,* **25** (1950).

Archaeology, art, and architecture. Esin Atil, *Renaissance of Islam: Art of the Mamluks* (1981); Keppel A. C. Creswell, *The Muslim Architecture of Egypt,* II (1959); Richard Ettinghausen, *Arab Painting* (1962), 143–160; Jean-Claude Garcin *et al., Palais et maisons du Caire,* I (1982); Duncane Haldane, *Mamluk Painting* (1978); Jean Sauvaget, "Inventaire des monuments musulmans de la ville d'Alep," in *Revue des études islamiques,* **5** (1931), and *Les monuments historiques de Damas* (1932); Karl Wulzinger and Carl Watzinger, *Damaskus: Die islamische Stadt* (1924).

Commerce and foreign relations. Eliyahu Ashtor, *Les métaux précieux et la balance des payements du Proche-Orient à la basse époque* (1971); Jere L. Bacharach, "Circassian Monetary Policy: Silver," in *Numismatic Chronicle,* 7th ser., **11** (1971), "The Dinar Versus the Ducat," in *International Journal of Middle East Studies,* **4** (1973), and "Circassian Monetary Policy: Copper," in *Journal of the Economic and Social History of the Orient,* **19** (1976); M. Canard, "Un traité entre Byzance et l'Égypte au XIIIᵉ siècle et les relations diplomatiques de Michel VIII Paléologue avec les sultans mamluks Baibars et Qalaᵓun," in *Mélanges Gaudefroy-Demombynes* (1935–1945), 197–224; Aḥmad Darrāj, *al-Mamālīk waᵓl-Firanj fīᵓl-Qarn al-Tāsiᶜ al-Hijrī, al-Khāmis ᶜAshar al-Mīlādī* (1961); Walter J. Fischel, "The Spice Trade in Mamluk Egypt: A Contribution to the Economic History of Medieval Islam," in *Journal of the Economic and Social History of the Orient,* **1** (1958); Subhi Y. Labib, *Handelsgeschichte Ägyptens im Spätmittelalter (1171–1517)* (1965); Robert Lopez, H. Miskimin, Abraham L. Udovitch, "England to Egypt, 1350–1500: Long-term Trends and Long-distance Trade," in Michael A. Cook, ed., *Studies in the Economic History of the Middle East* (1970); Kenneth M. Setton, *The Papacy and the Levant,* 4 vols. (1976–1984); Gaston Wiet, "Les marchands d'épices sous les sultans mamlouks," in *Cahiers de l'histoire d'Égypte,* 7 (1955).

R. STEPHEN HUMPHREYS

[See also **Abode of Islam—Abode of War; Aleppo; Aq Qoyunlu; Ayyubids; Barqūq; Baybars al-Bunduqdāri; Black Death; Cairo; Caliphate; Cavalry, Islamic; Cilician Kingdom; Circassians; Crusades and Crusader States; Cyprus, Kingdom of; Damascus; Diplomacy, Islamic; Egypt, Islamic; Emir; Genoa; Ilkhanids; Islamic Administration; Jean Boucicaut; Jihad; Mints and Money, Islamic; Ottomans; Portugal; Qāᵓitbay, al-Ashraf; Qalāᵓūn, al-Manṣūr; Qānṣūh al Ghawrī; Seljuks; Slavery, Slave Trade; Sultan; Tamerlane (Timur Leng); Taxation, Islamic; Venice; Warfare, Islamic.**]

MAMIKONEAN, the most distinguished family in early medieval Armenia after the royal Arsacid house. The lord *(tanutēr)* of the Mamikonean held the hereditary office of grand marshal *(sparapet),* commanding the entire Armenian army, and a number of members of the house also served as tutor *(dayeak)* to the king. The achievements of the family are set out by the Mamikonean historians Łazar Pᶜarpercᶜi and especially in the *Epic Histories* attributed to Pᶜawstos Buzand, whereas they are denigrated by the Bagratid historian Movses Xorenacᶜi. The persistent tradition that traced the Mamikonean lineage to China has no historical basis, and the family, which first appears in historical sources in 69 B.C., seems to have been of Armeno-Iberian origin, with its territorial base in the province of Taykᶜ. By the fourth century A.D., the Mamikonean had also acquired part of Tarōn in southwestern Armenia. In 437/439, Hamazasp Mamikonean received the western patriarchal domains as a result of his marriage to the Gregorid heiress Sahakanuyš. The Mamikonean were consequently the greatest territorial princes in Arsacid and Marzpan Armenia and they were able to raise a contingent of some 3,000 knights from their own lands. On numerous occasions, therefore, they exploited their power and their authority as *sparapets* to play the roles of royal advisers, regents, or even kingmakers. The almost supernatural prestige of the house, extolled in the *Epic Histories,* was further enhanced in the fifth century by the martyr's death of its *tanutēr,* the *sparapet* Vardan Mamikonean, at the battle of Avarayr while resisting the Sasanian attempt to impose Zoroastrianism on Armenia.

The general policy of the Mamikonean tended to be pro-Byzantine and anti-Persian, and they usually collaborated with the Gregorid patriarchs in the fourth century. After the establishment of the Marzpanate, Vahan and Vard Mamikonean made their peace with the Sasanians and served as *marzpans* (485–505), although the rebellion of 571 was once more spearheaded by Vardan II Mamikonean, who sought refuge in Byzantium after its failure. The prestige of the Mamikonean even survived the Arab conquest for a time, and a number of them held the title of "prince of Armenia" and curopalate.

The decline of the Mamikonean began with the unsuccessful attempt of Grigor Mamikonean to exploit the downfall of the Umayyad caliphate in the mid eighth century. It became increasingly visible in the eighth century as a result of the pro-Byzantine policy and the rise of the rival Bagratid house, especially after the death of Mušeł and Samuel Mamikonean, the instigators of the unsuccessful rebellion of 771/772 against the Abbasids. The hereditary Mamikonean title of *sparapet* had already increasingly been usurped by other houses. During the eighth and ninth centuries most of their domains were likewise lost, with most of Taykᶜ, Tarōn, and Bagrewand being seized by the Bagratids. One of Mušeł Mamikonean's daughters even sought safety in marriage with an Arab soldier of fortune who ruled her patrimony. Other territories passed to the Qaysite emirs. A number of Mamikonean descendants distinguished themselves in the service of Byzantium, and minor branches of the family survived in the border region of Sasun until the late twelfth century and even later elsewhere, but the Bagratids had replaced them as the dominant family in medieval Armenia by the end of the eighth century.

BIBLIOGRAPHY

Nicholas Adontz, *Armenia in the Period of Justinian,* Nina G. Garsoïan, ed. and trans. (1970); K. Mlaker, "Die Herkunft der Mamikonier und der Titel *Čenbakur,*" in *Wiener Zeitschrift für die Kunde des Morgenlandes,* **39** (1932); J. Muyldermans, "Le dernier prince Mamikonien de Bagrévand," in *Hantes amsoriya,* **40** (1926); Aram Ter Ghewondyan, *The Arab Emirates in Bagratid Armenia,* Nina G. Garsoïan, trans. (1976); Cyril Toumanoff, *Manuel de généalogie et de chronologie pour l'histoire de la Caucasie chrétienne* (1976), and *Studies in Christian Caucasian History* (1963).

NINA G. GARSOÏAN

[See also **Abbasids; Armenia, Geography; Armenia, History of; Arsacids; Bagratids, Armenian; Byzantine Empire: History; Gregorids; Sasanians; Umayyads.**]

MAMMEN STYLE. The Mammen style of Viking art is named for the silver inlaid ornament on an axe found at Mammen, Denmark. It developed from the Jellinge style during the mid tenth century and flour-

Mammen axe with silver inlaid ornament. PHOTO: DAVID WILSON. NATIONALMUSEET, COPENHAGEN

ished to around 1010. In the Mammen style the animal motif becomes more substantial, and plant tendrils are introduced from Western European art.

BIBLIOGRAPHY

Signe H. Fuglesang, *The Ringerike Style* (1980); David M. Wilson and Ole Klindt-Jensen, *Viking Art* (1980).

JAMES A. GRAHAM-CAMPBELL

[See also **Jellinge Style; Ringerike Style; Viking Art.**]

MAᵓMŪN, AL- (Abu'l-ᶜAbbās ᶜAbd Allāh ibn Hārūn) (*d.* 833, after a reign of twenty years), seventh Abbasid caliph. Al-Maᵓmūn (his royal name) was the son of Hārūn al-Rashīd and a Persian slave. In an effort to stave off a struggle for succession, Hārūn conceived of an elaborate plan in which three of his sons were named heirs. The eldest, the future caliph Muḥammad al-Amīn, was named heir apparent and given control of Baghdad, Iraq, and the western provinces. ᶜAbd Allāh al-Maᵓmūn, second in line, was named governor of Khorāsān and provinces to the east. A third son, al-Qāsim, was entrusted with northern Syria and the Byzantine frontier. As they were all lads at the time, the actual control of the provincial administration was in the hands of al-Rashīd's political and military officials who tutored the young princes. It would appear that the aim of this tripartite division of the empire was to decentralize lines of rule that had become unmanageable. At the same time it was thought that, by having at his disposal the enormous power of the army in the east, al-Maᵓmūn would be able to thwart any effort on the part of al-Amīn to dislodge him, hence assuring an orderly succession.

 MA⊃MŪN, AL-

After taking power, al-Amīn, influenced by his mentors in Baghdad, attempted what Hārūn al-Rashīd feared. He brought increasing pressure on al-Ma⊃mūn to leave his provincial capital at Merv in Khorāsān (now Mary, in the USSR) and to return to Baghdad. Aware of what this meant, al-Ma⊃mūn's advisers convinced the young governor to resist his brother's urgings. Civil war broke out, and after three years al-Ma⊃mūn's armies, having besieged Baghdad, forced al-Amīn to flee. He was apprehended and murdered in 813, thus ending the civil strife.

The conflict left badly ruffled feelings. The notables in Baghdad and the popular factions they influenced were not in a conciliatory mood. The issues that continued to separate them from the new caliph and his followers were not ideological, but were rooted in self-interest. It was feared that the Khorasanis would be given their prominent posts and that the eastern armies would receive the lion's share of military disbursements. In particular, the remnants of the military forces in Baghdad resisted a change in status; they proved a volatile element among the city's populace for many years thereafter.

Al-Ma⊃mūn thus decided to remain in Merv, ruling the occasionally turbulent capital and adjacent areas through viceroys. It was only six years later that he felt secure enough to return to Baghdad. He decided not to build a magnificent new palace complex, as his predecessors al-Manṣūr and al-Mahdī had done; nor did he take up residence, as did his father, al-Rashīd, in one of the existing great palaces. Instead, he built two new smaller palaces that became his domicile in the city. Al-Ma⊃mūn appears never to have felt comfortable in Baghdad.

The unstable conditions brought about by the war between the brothers gave rise to insurrections throughout the realm. The Alids profited from the political confusion and established themselves in Al-Kufa in 815; their rebellion proved short-lived when their leader Muḥammad ibn Ibrāhīm al-Ṭabāṭabā died the following year. A former supporter of the caliph, Abu'l-Sarāyā, who supported the Alid cause, took control of al-Basra, but he was freed to withdraw under pressure from government forces and was killed as the Alid revolt collapsed. In Baghdad, the caliph's viceroy, al-Ḥasan ibn Sahl, was driven from the city as the populace rioted. The city fell prey to roving bands of brigands before the people of Baghdad organized in defense of public order. Weary of the turbulent situation, they accepted the return of the caliph's viceroy.

Shortly thereafter, the caliph carried out an astounding change of policy. For reasons never explained, in 817 he declared ᶜAlī al-Riḍā, the sixth-generation descendant of ᶜAlī ibn Abī Ṭālib, the Prophet's son-in-law, to be his heir apparent and ordered that Alid "green" should replace Abbasid "black" as the color of the dynasty. In response, the Baghdadis, who had never favored the Alid cause, rose in rebellion and chose Ibrāhīm, the son of al-Mahdī, the third Abbasid ruler, to be caliph. Al-Ḥasan ibn Sahl was again forced to flee the city. Al-Ma⊃mūn's vizier, al-Faḍl ibn Sahl, the architect of the Alid policy, was mysteriously murdered and the caliph returned to Baghdad to take personal control of the situation. Soon afterward ᶜAlī al-Riḍā died, allegedly the victim of poisoned grapes. The two mysterious deaths allowed the caliph to put his marriage with the Alids behind him and to exert strong military and political pressure on the unruly Baghdadis.

To secure his hold on the troubled Abbasid domains, al-Ma⊃mūn relied heavily on the family of his able general, Ṭāhir ibn al-Ḥusayn, who, after serving as governor of Baghdad, took command of the eastern provinces. Although the caliph was leery of Ṭāhir, he invested him with great power. Ṭāhir soon took advantage of his position and laid the groundwork for the semiautonomous rule of his offspring in that region. The Tahirids proved capable and their independent ways were, no doubt, seen as a fair exchange for keeping Khorāsān free of more serious rebellions.

Toward the end of his reign, the caliph personally campaigned against the Byzantines and in Egypt, where his forces succeeded in quelling a number of local revolts. He was also responsible for recruiting the first group of Turkish slave soldiers. They would later become military commanders of the Turkish regiments formed by his successor, al-Muᶜtasim.

Al-Ma⊃mūn, unlike his predecessors, was a man of great learning and eclectic intellectual interests. He was a patron of scholars and encouraged broad-ranging scholarship. He was, in addition, a great proponent of the Muᶜtazilites and rigorously enforced their doctrine.

BIBLIOGRAPHY

Nabia Abbott, *Two Queens of Baghdad* (1946); Mohsen Azizi, *La domination arabe et l'épanouissement du sentiment national en Iran* (1938); Anwar G. Chejne, *Succession to the Rule in Islam* (1960), and "Al-Fadl b. al-Rabi: A Politician of the Early Abbasid Period," in *Islamic Culture,* **36**

(1962); Elton L. Daniel, *The Political and Social History of Khurasan Under Abbasid Rule* (1979); Francesco Gabrieli, "La successione di Hārūn al-Rašīd e la guerra fra al-Amīn e al-Maʾmūn," in *Revista degli studii orientali,* **11** (1926–1928), and *Al-Ma'mun e gli Alidi* (1929); Hugh Kennedy, *The Early Abbasid Caliphate* (1981); Jacob Lassner, *The Shaping of ʿAbbāsid Rule* (1980); Guy Le Strange, *Baghdad During the Abbasid Caliphate* (1900).

JACOB LASSNER

[See also **Abbasids; Alids; Hārūn al-Rashid; Muʿtazila, al-.**]

MAN OF SORROWS. See **Imago Pietatis.**

MANARAH. See **Minaret.**

MANAZKERT (Greek: Mantzikert; Turkish: Malazgirt). City twenty-five miles (forty kilometers) north of Lake Van (39°09′ N. × 42°31′ E.) on the border of the medieval Armenian provinces of Apahunikʿ and Harkʿ. It was probably founded in Parthian times but flourished particularly from the ninth century, when it was probably the site of a mint. Under the Qaysite Arab emirs in the ninth and tenth centuries, Manazkert was one of the main cities on the southern trade route crossing Armenia. Thereafter the fate of the city became more precarious, and it may have passed for a time into the hands of the Hamdanids of Mosul. Taken and razed by the Byzantines in 968/969, it was granted by them to the curopalate David of Taykʿ (or Tao), who captured it around 992–994 from the Marwanids, who had retaken it in the previous decade. Having returned to the Byzantine Empire as part of David's inheritance, Manazkert was the site of the momentous defeat of the emperor Romanos IV Diogenes by the Seljuk sultan Alp Arslan in 1071.

BIBLIOGRAPHY

Nicholas Adontz, *Armenia in the Period of Justinian,* Nina G. Garsoïan, ed. and trans. (1970); René Grousset, *Histoire de l'Arménie des origins à 1071* (1947); Heinrich Hübschmann, *Die altarmenischen Ortsnamen* (1904); Aram Ter Ghewondyan, *The Arab Emirates in Bagratid Armenia,* Nina G. Garsoïan, trans. (1976).

NINA G. GARSOÏAN

[See also **Alp Arslan; Armenia, Geography; Armenia, History of; David of Tao; Seljuks.**]

MANAZKERT, COUNCIL OF. This joint council of the Armenian and Syriac churches was held in 726 at Manazkert in Armenia. The purpose of the meeting was to resolve the Julian and Severian controversy concerning the corruptibility or incorruptibility of the body of Christ. At the council each side presented a profession of faith, and both sides agreed upon the formulation of the ten anathemas pronounced against the Aphthartodocetics and the Theopaschites. Both sides professed the incorruptibility of Christ's body, since the divine nature, united into one with the human, made him free of sin. However, Christ, as a perfect human being, suffered all of the human passions willingly (and not out of necessity). The doctrinal stand of the council differed from that of Julian of Halicarnassus in its emphasis on the union of the divine and human natures in Christ.

BIBLIOGRAPHY

Erwand Ter-Minassiantz, *Die armenische Kirche in ihren Beziehungen zu den Syrischen-Kirchen* (1904).

KRIKOR H. MAKSOUDIAN

[See also **Armenian Church, Doctrines and Councils; Monophysitism; Syrian Christianity.**]

MANDEVILLE'S TRAVELS. This most popular of late medieval books was composed in French around the middle of the fourteenth century. Its unknown author represents himself to the reader as a widely traveled English knight, Sir John Mandeville of St. Albans, who has returned home and set down his adventures, completing his book thirty-four years after he first set out on his travels. His account, soon translated into nearly every other European language, survives in more than 250 manuscripts. The immediate and continuing appeal of the *Travels*—indeed, its originality—lies in Mandeville's merging of two previously separate kinds of travel: religious pilgrimage and worldly exploration.

During most of the Middle Ages, pilgrimage was the most commonly approved form of journeying for Christians. Sanctioned places of worship like Jerusalem, Rome, Santiago de Compostela, and Canterbury were permissible worldly destinations because they had a significance that was not worldly. By Mandeville's time, however, the spiritual worth of pilgrimage had declined, and more frankly secular motives were inspiring medieval Europeans to travel abroad.

Mandeville's book neatly reflects these older and newer urges to travel. Roughly the first half of the work is a guide book for the Holy Land pilgrimage, full of information and practical advice for the pious wayfarer. Beyond Jerusalem, however, and in the remainder of the *Travels,* Mandeville turns a curious, worldly eye to the newly discovered non-Christian mysteries of Asia. Here we find not relics and miracles but worldly marvels: one-eyed peoples, the extravagant Great Khan of Cathay, the legendary Prester John, the Garden of Eden. This is the Asia that Marco Polo and intrepid missionaries like Odoric of Pordenone, John of Plano Carpini, and William of Rubruck had lately revealed to Western Europe; but Mandeville's alternately skeptical and amazed report of the region had a wider and more lasting effect on readers and on travel literature.

No travel book before Mandeville's had so subordinated the aims of pilgrimage to those of exploration, and none had suggested with such finality that a belief in the existence of God might well be implanted in all men by the light of natural reason. As Mandeville concludes, "No man scholde haue in despite non erthely man for here dyuerse lawes, for wee knowe not whom God loueth ne whom God hateth." This tolerant belief is related to Mandeville's firm opinion that the earth is not only round but inhabitable "vnder as above" and that, indeed, it is inhabited everywhere. His scientific proofs for this notion and his own plan to undertake a circumnavigation ("yif I hadde had companye and schippyng for to go more beyonde") were astounding for the time, and they explain why explorers and geographers of the next centuries—Columbus, Sir Walter Raleigh, and Martin Frobisher among them—were deeply influenced by Mandeville's *Travels* on their own voyages.

We know from modern scholarship that "John Mandeville" was in fact more of a reader of other travel books than a traveler, that his work was a fiction, not a reliable guide for travelers. It survived and was read because it altered the shape of earlier medieval travel writing and presaged the new world that succeeding thinkers and voyagers would encounter.

BIBLIOGRAPHY

Josephine W. Bennett, *The Rediscovery of Sir John Mandeville* (1954); Donald R. Howard, "The World of Mandeville's Travels," in *Yearbook of English Studies,* **1** (1971); Malcolm Letts, *Sir John Mandeville: The Man and His Book* (1949); C. W. R. D. Moseley, "The Metamorphoses of Sir John Mandeville," in *Yearbook of English Studies,* **4** (1974); Maurice C. Seymour, ed., *Mandeville's Travels* (1967); George F. Warner, ed., *The Buke of John Maundeuill* (1889); Christian K. Zacher, *Curiosity and Pilgrimage: The Literature of Discovery in Fourteenth-century England* (1976).

CHRISTIAN K. ZACHER

[See also **Crusades of the Later Middle Ages; Exploration; Jerusalem; John of Plano Carpini; Missions and Missionaries; Pilgrimage, Western European; Polo, Marco; Prester John.**]

MANDORLA, or almond-shaped aureole, is the enclosure of light around full-length figures of God or Christ that symbolizes the cosmos illuminated by divine nature, heavenly power, and majesty. Probably derived from the high god Ahura Mazda in Persia, it initially represented divine protection, but throughout the Middle Ages appeared most commonly in theophanies of Christ such as the Transfiguration, Descent into Hell, Ascension, and Last Judgment. Most frequently depicted as almond shaped, the mandorla also assumed round, oval, figure-eight, and polygonal forms in medieval art. The mandorla was extended ultimately to include the Virgin, the Evangelists, David, and other holy figures.

BIBLIOGRAPHY

W. S. Cook, "The Earliest Painted Panels of Catalonia, II," in *Art Bulletin,* **6** (1923–1924); André Grabar, *Christian Iconography: A Study of Its Origins* (1968), 116–119; Wilhelm Messerer, "Mandorla," in *Lexikon der christlichen Ikonographie,* III (1971).

MICHAEL T. DAVIS

[See also **Early Christian Art; Nimbus.**]

MANDYLION (literally, "facecloth"), the Holy Image of Edessa, according to legend a mantle sent by Christ to King Abgarus, of that city, to heal the king's malady. On the veil was impressed an image of Christ's face "not made by human hands" *(acheiropoietos).* It was presented to the public as an icon in 544 and sent to Constantinople in 944, when the Byzantine emperor Romanos I captured Edessa from the Muslims. It was taken by the crusaders in

1207. It is one of the many examples of a *volto santo,* as are the Veil of Veronica and the Shroud of Turin.

BIBLIOGRAPHY

Carlo Bertelli, "Storia e vicende dell'Immagine Eddessena," in *Paragone,* **217** (1968); Ernst von Dobschutz, *Christusbilder: Untersuchungen zur christlichen Legend* (1899); Kurt Weitzmann, "The Mandylion and Constantine Porphyrogennetos," in *Cahiers archéologiques,* **11** (1960).

BARBARA OEHLSCHLAEGER-GARVEY

[See also **Edessa; Relics; Vernicle; Volto Santo.**]

MANEGOLD OF LAUTENBACH (1030–1103), an antidialectician traditionally grouped with Peter Damian and Otloh of St. Emmeram, among others. Renowned throughout Europe for his scholarship and extensive knowledge of the liberal arts, he renounced dialectic (philosophy) and entered the monastery of Lautenbach shortly before 1084. He later entered the monastery of Marbach, where he became dean in 1094. According to Manegold, faith and dialectic are not compatible. Faith overwhelms mere human rationality, and whatever is true in dialectic originates in theology, that is, in biblical faith. He develops these ideas in his *Letter Against Wolfhelm.*

As human reason is subordinate to the Bible, so the emperor is subservient to the pope. Manegold expresses this political position in his *Letter to Gebhardt,* written during the controversy between Pope Gregory VII and Emperor Henry IV. More important than his idea of the overlordship of the pope, however, is his aside that a king and the people he rules are governed by the (natural) terms of a mutual pact or covenant. He thus anticipates Marsilius of Padua and other later theorists of populism.

BIBLIOGRAPHY

Joseph A. Endres, *Forschungen zur Geschichte der frühmittelalterlichen Philosophie* (1915); Ivo of Chartres, *Correspondance,* Jean Leclercq, ed. and trans., I (1949); Georg Koch, *Manegold von Lautenbach und die Lehre von der Volkssouveränität unter Heinrich IV* (1902, repr. 1965); H. Liebeschütz, "The Debate on Philosophical Learning During the Transition Period (900–1080)," in Arthur H. Armstrong, ed., *Cambridge History of Later Greek and Early Medieval Philosophy* (1967; 1970, repr. w. corrections); Manegold of Lautenbach, *Liber ad Gebhardum,* K. Francke, ed., in *Monumenta Germaniae historica: Libelli de lite,* I (1891), 308–430, and *Liber contra Wolfelmum,* Wilfried Hartmann, ed. (1972).

ARJO VANDERJAGT

[See also **Dialectic; Gregory VII, Pope; Henry IV of Germany; Investiture and Investiture Conflict; Otloh of St. Emmeram; Peter Damian, St.**]

MANFRED OF MAGDEBURG (*fl. ca.* 1010), teacher at Magdeburg in the reign of Henry II. He was associated with Arnold of St. Emmeram in Regensburg, at whose request he wrote the life of St. Emmeram *(De vita et virtutibus beati Emmerammi).* He is also probably the Manfred who wrote *Manfredi carmina,* a long calendar poem (941 hexameters) based on Bede's works.

BIBLIOGRAPHY

Patrologia latina, XCIV (1850), 641–655, and CXLI (1853), 970–986. See also Max Manitius, *Geschichte der lateinischen Literatur des Mittelalters,* II (1923), 574–576.

EDWARD FRUEH

[See also **Arnold of St. Emmeram; Bede; Latin Literature.**]

MANICHAEANS, adherents of a radically dualistic Gnostic religion. Its founder, Mani (Greek: Manes; Latin: Manichaeus), was born in northern Babylonia in 216. His father, Patēg, had emigrated from Hamadān in Media to Mesopotamia, and both his parents were reputed to be of noble Parthian stock. After settling in Babylonia, Patēg joined a Judeo-Christian baptizing sect, the Mughtasilas, who were followers of Elkesai. Mani was reared in this sect. In 228, when he was twelve years old, he received his first revelation from a spirit whom he called his Twin. From this time until his twenty-fourth year, Mani continued to receive enlightenment and guidance from his Twin. As the enlightenment progressed, so did his growing disagreement with his fellow baptists, from whom he began to distance himself and some of whom, including his father, he converted.

In 240, the Twin instructed Mani to take the now completed revelation to the world as the one, true, universal religion of redemption. He severed all ties with the baptists and traveled to northwestern India, where he preached and converted, among others, an Iranian vassal king. He returned to Babylonia, then continued through Parthia and Media. Mani converted two brothers of Šābuhr (Shāpūr) I, thereby gaining access to the Sasanian court and the approval of the king. He is also said to have accompanied Šābuhr on a campaign to the West, in either 242–244 or 256–260. For the next thirty years, Mani was able to proselytize inside the Persian Empire and send missionaries into Roman territory. At the accession of Bahrām I, his fortunes changed. Accused of heresy by priests of the still dominant Zoroastrian state religion, Mani found his activities sharply curtailed by Bahrām. In 277 he was summoned by the king and imprisoned at Gundēshāpūr, where he died.

Mani intended that his revelations be spread universally and unambiguously. Unlike the founders of earlier religions, who left no written works, he composed a canon of seven books written in Aramaic that set forth in exhaustive detail the myth and practice of Manichaeism. He also produced a picture book to illustrate his teachings. Only one work, the *Šābūhrāgān (Shapuragan),* addressed to Šābuhr I, was composed in Persian. Fragments of the canon have survived, none in the original Aramaic. From the first generation after Mani come the semicanonical Coptic books and the recently discovered Greek biography, all translated from Aramaic and containing quotations from Mani and his disciples, the *Tradition.* Fragments of Mani's own work, the *Tradition,* and later works survive in several Middle Iranian languages. There are similar texts in Chinese and Uighur.

Preeminent among the non-Manichaean sources are the anti-Manichaean polemics of Augustine of Hippo, who was a Manichaean for nine years. Also of great value are the *Acta Archelai,* a fictitious account of a disputation between Mani and a Christian bishop, and the polemical works of Ephraim the Syrian (fourth century) and Theodore bar Khonai (eight century), who attack Mani's teaching in Syriac, which is closely akin to Mani's Aramaic. Among the Muslims, Ibn al-Nadīm (tenth century) in his *Fihrist* gives a concise account of Manichaeism. A comparison of all these sources shows a remarkable consistency in the presentation of Manichaean doctrine and religious practices.

Mani divided the world into three ages: the beginning, the middle, and the end. In the first age, there are two coeternal uncreated principles, the Light and the Darkness, which coexist oblivious of each other. The Paradise of Light, ruled by the Father of Greatness, is composed of five Light Elements: Fire, Water, Air, Ether, and Light. It is orderly, intelligent, and spiritual. The Realm of Darkness, ruled by the Devil, consists of five Dark Elements, opposites of the Light Elements, each having male and female members engaged in continual lust and warfare. It is chaotic, ignorant, and material.

When, by chance, the Devil perceives the Paradise of Light, he lusts after it and tries to invade it. To protect the Light, the Father calls forth the First Evocation, the Mother of the Living, who in turn calls forth Primal Man. Primal Man is sent forth, armed with the five Light Elements, to drive back and subdue the Darkness. Instead, he is stunned and left senseless while demons swallow his Light.

Thus begins the middle age, the age of mixture, when the Father effects the rescue of Primal Man and the liberation of the trapped Light. To this end, the Mother of the Living beseeches the Father to save Primal Man, which he does through the Second Evocation: the Friend of Lights, the Great Builder, and the Living Spirit. The Friend of Lights unbinds Primal Man and the Living Spirit calls out to Primal Man, who answers. Call and Answer then come into being. Primal Man is lifted up and restored to the Paradise of Light.

It remains for the Light still trapped in Matter to be redeemed. To receive the liberated Light temporarily, the Great Builder prepares a New Paradise. The Living Spirit and his five sons then attack the Demons of Darkness, defeat them, and fashion ten heavens from their skin and eight earths from their flesh and excrement. From uncontaminated Light they make the sun and moon and three great wheels that will convey redeemed Light to them.

The stage is now set for the process of redemption that begins with the Third Evocation: the Third Messenger, the Maiden of Light, Jesus the Splendor, the Great Mind, and the Column of Glory. The Third Messenger starts up the wheels that convey the Light to the moon as it waxes to the full. As it wanes, the Light passes to the sun. From the sun it moves up the Column of Glory (visible as the Milky Way) to the New Paradise. The demons Greed and Lust struggle to sabotage the process. Through an involved series of sexual acts and cannibalism, they attempt to collect Light but are forced to abort and ejaculate, resulting in the formation of plants and animals. Two demons who devour the latter copulate, and bring forth Adam and Eve in the images of the Third Messenger and the Maiden of Light. Material creation, including the human body, is thus the result of sordid acts of the demons. Adam and Eve are oblivious of the Light within them, but Adam is awakened by Jesus the Splendor. Eve, after copulating with demons and bearing Cain and Abel, bears Seth to Adam because of their mutual lust.

Thus begins the series of procreations that the propagation of Mani's revelation will bring to a halt. In spite of man's mixed state, he will be the conscious vehicle for the redemption of Light. Before Mani, Prophets of Light have appeared: Zoroaster, the Buddha, and finally the docetic Jesus of history, who promises to send his Paraclete, Mani, the final prophet.

To accomplish his mission, Mani consciously organized his own church, leaving nothing to chance. Under a hierarchy composed of Mani and his successors assisted by 12 teachers, 72 bishops, and 360 elders, were two groups: the Elect and the Hearers. The Elect served as the collectors of the Light. They were an elite who lived austere lives, eating only fruits and vegetables, praying and fasting, and abstaining from sexual activity. At death their souls, which were pure Light, went directly to the New Paradise. The Hearers, who lived ordinary lives, devoted themselves to caring for the Elect, who were allowed no physical work. Hearers' souls were not liberated at death, but if they were faithful, they would return as Elect. If not, they returned as non-Manichaeans or animals. Those outside the sect who rejected the revelation were condemned to hell.

As the religion gains more adherents, and more and more Light is liberated, the amount of trapped Light will diminish and the physical universe will become more evil. In the final phase of the struggle, Jesus the Splendor will return and prepare for the final separation of the remaining Light. The five Sons of the Living Spirit, who maintain the firmament, will allow it to collapse, and a conflagration will refine out the last particles of Light. The New Paradise will rejoin the Paradise of Light. The Powers of Darkness will be imprisoned and sealed in forever by a great stone.

Manichaeism spread rapidly eastward throughout Iranian territory. It also spread westward into the Roman Empire through Syria and Palestine. By the end of the third century, it reached Upper Egypt from northern Arabia, where it was attacked by the Neoplatonist Alexander of Lycopolis, and in a Christian epistle. Through the fourth century it spread along the coast of North Africa. There is evidence of Manichaeism in Armenia, Asia Minor, Dalmatia, and Rome. It no doubt existed in other locales not clearly attested. Even under the pagan emperor Diocletian, Manichaeans were proscribed by an edict in 297. With the triumph of Christianity, their lot worsened, and they were subjected to punitive decrees under Constantine (326), Valentinian I (372), Theodosius I (381), and Justinian I (529). The tone of anti-Manichaean polemics had been set by the former Manichaean Augustine. By the first half of the sixth century, Manichaeism had disappeared in the West. Whether it simply ceased to exist or went underground in some places to reemerge in the so-called Neomanichaean sects of the later Middle Ages is undocumented. Just how numerous the Manichaeans were is difficult to assess. The evidence points to a wide dispersion, but a small number of adherents in any one place.

While Manichaeism was dying out in the West, it began to flourish in the East. Its situation in Sasanian Persia was similar to that of the Nestorian Christians: periods of peace interspersed with persecution and harassment instigated by the Zoroastrian clergy. Like the Nestorians, the Manichaeans took advantage of the overland trade routes and pushed their missionary enterprises across the Oxus into Turkistan, and thence to China when the silk routes were reopened in the late seventh century. From 762 to 840, the Turkish Uighur kingdom west of China took Manichaeism for its state religion. When the Uighurs were pushed into western China by the Kirgiz, they took their religion to the Turfan region in Sinkiang. It was this area that yielded a great cache of Manichaean writings together with some of their paintings. The tolerance shown to foreign religions under the T'ang dynasty gave way to proscription in 843, but pockets of Manichaeans survived along the borders of northern and western China until the thirteenth century, and in southeastern China until the fourteenth century.

In Mesopotamia, the center of Manichaeism, the advent of Islam brought a measure of tolerance to the communities who qualified as "people of a book." Since the end of the sixth century the Babylonian church had been cut off from the central Asiatic church by a schism that was not healed until the early eighth century. Mesopotamian Manichaeans, despite a savage persecution under the Abbasids, survived in Baghdad until the tenth century, when the leadership moved to Samarkand. After this, Mesopotamian Manichaeism disappeared from history.

BIBLIOGRAPHY

Sources. For selections of texts from Manichaean sources, see Jes Peter Asmussen, *Manichaean Literature: Representative Texts Chiefly from Middle Persian and Parthian Writings* (1975). Abraham V. Williams Jackson, *Researches in Manichaeism With Special Reference to the Turfan Fragments* (1932, repr. 1965), includes the text of Theodore bar Khonai. The recently discovered Greek biography, up to p. 92, is in *The Cologne Mani Codes (P. Colon. inv. nr. 4780 "Concerning the Origins of His Body")* (1979), which contains the Greek text edited by A. Heinrichs and I. Koenen, and translation by Ron Cameron and Arthur J. Dewey with a bibliography of articles about the codex. For St. Augustine's writings, see *The Anti-Manichaean Writings,* Philip Schaff, ed. (1956), 5–365. The Arabic text of Ibn al-Nadīm's *Fihrist,* with a German translation and extensive commentary, is in Gustav Flügel, *Mani, seine Lehre und seine Schriften* (1862, repr. 1969); for an English translation of the section on Manichaeism, see *The Fihrist of al-Nadīm,* Bayard Dodge, trans., II (1970), 773–825.

Studies. The best general surveys of Manichaeism are Francis C. Burkitt, *The Religion of the Manichees* (1925); Henri-Charles Puech, *Le manichéisme: Son fondateur—sa doctrine* (1949); Hans Jacob Polotsky, "Abriss des manichäischen Systems," in Pauly-Wissowa, *Real-encyclopädie der classischen Altertumswissenschaft,* supp. VI (1935), 240–271, also in Polotsky, *Collected Papers* (1971), 699–714. François Decret, *Mani et la tradition manichéenne* (1974), is a popular treatment with illustrations.

For extensive bibliographies, see Jes Peter Asmussen, *X^uāstvānīft: Studies in Manichinaeism* (1965); L. J. R. Ort, *Mani: A Religio-Historical Description of His Personality* (1967).

D. W. Johnson

[See also **Augustine of Hippo, Saint; Docetism; Dualism; Heresy.**]

MANIERA GRECA (the Greek manner) refers to the Byzantine stylistic contribution to Italian Dugento (thirteenth-century) painting. Coined by Vasari, the Renaissance art historian, it meant "monotonous rows of saints . . . drawn not painted." Vasari contrasts *maniera greca* to the variety of forms and modeling in gradations of color employed by Giotto and other early Italian painters. Only recently has the term lost its derisory connotation and Byzantine art been assigned a more positive influence on the proto-Renaissance.

BIBLIOGRAPHY

Ernst Kitzinger, "The Byzantine Contribution to Western Art of the Twelfth and Thirteenth Centuries," in *Dumbarton Oaks Papers,* **20** (1966); Giorgio Vasari, *Lives of the Artists,* George Bull, trans. (1966, repr. 1977), 46, 58.

Barbara Oehlschlaeger-Garvey

[See also **Byzantine Art; Giotto di Bondone; Italian Renaissance, Byzantine Influence on.**]

MANIÈRE DE LANGAGE, the name generally given to sets of model dialogues used in England in the late fourteenth and early fifteenth centuries for the teaching of French and applied in particular to a text written in Bury St. Edmunds about 1396. This *Manière de langage* recounts imaginary conversations of travelers journeying to Orléans and their subsequent dealings with merchants, innkeepers, and servants. The text provides vocabulary and expressions useful for travelers and merchants.

BIBLIOGRAPHY

Jean Gessler, ed., *La manière de langage* (1934); Kathleen Lambley, *The Teaching and Cultivation of the French Language in England During Tudor and Stuart Times* (1920); William Rothwell, "The Teaching of French in Medieval England," in *Modern Language Review,* **63** (1968).

Brian Merrilees

[See also **Anglo-Norman Literature; French Language.**]

MANNERED SCHOOL. See **Ars Subtilior.**

MANNYNG, ROBERT, of Brunne (Bourne) (*b. ca.* 1283), a canon of the Gilbertine order at Sempringham priory in Lincolnshire, is known for two lengthy works in Middle English verse: *Handlyng Synne* (1303) and *The Story of England* (1338). Both are fairly close translations from Anglo-Norman sources, with omissions and additions by Mannyng himself.

Handlyng Synne is based upon *Le Manuel des péchés,* a guide to confession by an Englishman writing in French (*ca.* 1260). William of Waddington, once thought to be the author, was probably a scribe and is otherwise unknown. *Handlyng Synne,* like its source, was intended to help penitents prepare for confession by teaching them to recognize and deal with the pervasiveness of sins in daily life. It is directed primarily to the laity, although there are frequent references to clergy, both sinful and virtuous. The Fourth Lateran Council (1215) and the episcopal decrees arising from it, all of which stressed the importance of confession, stimulated the writing of various works of instruction in the meaning and techniques of confession, including manuals that were practical rather than theoretical.

In his prologue, Mannyng sets forth his purpose and the organization of his treatise. The title, he explains, means that we "handle" sin in daily actions without realizing it and therefore must learn to "handle" our sins by careful examination in thought and then to cleanse ourselves by "handling" them in oral confession. He begins with the ten commandments, continues with the seven deadly sins and the sin of sacrilege, and the seven sacraments, the twelve points of shrift (confession), the twelve graces given by them, and concludes with counsel against despair, for God is merciful to those who confess completely.

The emphasis is upon sins rather than the imposition of penances. Sinners are advised to seek the appropriate penance from their priests after confession. Mannyng intended his work to be read aloud to laymen. To lead them away from the profane tales that they enjoyed at social gatherings, he illustrates his discourse on the sins with numerous tales (exempla), adding many of his own to those in the *Manuel,* some from written sources, others from local traditions, legends, and folklore. Although his purpose remains firmly didactic, the tales are notable for their lively narrative style and the variety of social types among the sinners.

Mannyng's *Story of England* is similarly addressed to a lay audience to instruct them in the history of their land and its rulers. His major source is the Anglo-Norman chronicle of Peter of Langtoft, a canon of Bridlington, but for the first part Mannyng chose to translate Wace's French version of Geoffrey of Monmouth because it is fuller and more detailed. He also uses Bede and other Latin historians. For the second part, which brings English history through the reign of Edward I (1282–1397), he translates Langtoft. The last section in both Mannyng and Langtoft on the Scottish wars of Edward I includes scraps of political verse expressing strongly partisan English feelings. In Langtoft these verses are written in both French and English, but Mannyng's verses are all in English and probably represent his own variants of popular songs.

BIBLIOGRAPHY

Sources. Thomas Hearne, ed., *Peter Langtoft's Chronical, as Illustrated and Improv'd by Robert of Brunne* (1725, repr. 1810); Robert Mannyng of Brunne, *The Story of England,* Frederick J. Furnivall, ed., 2 vols. (1887); *Robert of Brunne's "Handlyng Synne,"* Frederick J. Furnivall, ed. (1901–1903). See also John E. Wells, *A Manual of the Writings in Middle English, 1050–1400,* and later supplements (1919–1951); Rossell Hope Robbins, "Poems Dealing with Contemporary Conditions," in Albert E. Hartung, ed., *A Manual of the Writings in Middle English,* V (1975), 1400–1403.

Studies. Émile J. F. Arnould, *Le Manuel des péchés: Étude de littérature religieuse anglo-normande (XIIIme siècle)* (1940); Ruth Crosby, "Robert Mannyng of Brunne: A New Biography," in *PMLA,* 57 (1942); Mary Dominica Legge, *Anglo-Norman Literature and Its Background* (1963); William A. Pantin, *The English Church in the Fourteenth Century* (1955); D. W. Robertson, Jr., "The Cultural Tradition of *Handlyng Synne,*" in *Speculum,* 22 (1947).

HELAINE NEWSTEAD

[See also **Anglo-Norman Literature; Bede; Confession; Councils, Western (1215–1274); Edward I of England; Geoffrey of Monmouth; Historiography, Western European; Middle English Literature; Penance and Penitentials; Seven Deadly Sins.**]

MANRIQUE, JORGE (*ca.* 1440–1479), the last major Spanish poet of the Middle Ages, belonged to an aristocratic Castilian family and died in battle fighting for Queen Isabella; his uncle Gómez Manrique was also a significant poet.

Much of Jorge Manrique's poetry represents the best of the courtly love tradition as it developed its ingenious wordplay in fifteenth-century Castile: figuratively, woman is raised to a divine status; the lover is enslaved and takes joy in his suffering and lingering death. The god of love is a judge who rejects all appeal, love service is a religious order, and the lady is a fortress under siege of the lover. Short lyrical *canciones* alternate with longer narrative *decires.* There is also burlesque poetry: a rather indecent invitation to the poet's stepmother, for example.

In addition, Jorge Manrique is the author of one great poem, upon which his fame depends: his elegiac *Coplas por la muerte de su padre* (Stanzas on the death of his father). His father, Don Rodrigo Manrique, grand master of a military order, died in 1476; the poem was probably written two years later. It consists of forty twelve-line octosyllabic stanzas in which every third line is one-half of an octosyllable, known as "coplas de pie quebrado"; the rhyme scheme is *A B c A B c D E f D E f*.

The poem as a whole is organized with classical clarity of form. The first part (stanzas 1–24) consists of generalizations on life and death. Within this section, a brief prologue evokes the existential flow of time; an invocation, rejecting pagan gods, emphasizes the Christian orientation of the poem. The following stanzas (7–24) are based on *contemptus mundi* themes. First, there is a meditation on the vanity of perishable things in general: physical beauty, nobility, and wealth are contrasted with the permanence of the soul. Then, in a series of rhetorical questions (the ubi sunt motif), the poet evokes the common fate of the rich and the poor, of ancients and moderns, and in particular of the great figures of recent Spanish courts: the dances and love affairs, the music and poetry, the ornate clothing and jewelry have all disappeared.

The second part of the poem (stanzas 25–40) is devoted to the individual case of the death of Don Rodrigo. There is a eulogy of his character and of his great deeds as a warrior:

> ¡Qué amigo de sus amigos!
> ¡qué señor para criados
>   y parientes!
> ¡Qué enemigo de enemigos!
> ¡Qué maestro de esforzados
>   y valientes!

Then, in the final eight stanzas, his death is presented in a narrative with dialogue; Death comes and calls him to the fame and the immortality which he has won on earth and in heaven. Don Rodrigo responds in two stanzas, the first addressed to Death:

> "Y consiento en mi morir
> con voluntad placentera,
>   clara y pura,
> que querer hombre vivir
> cuando Dios quiere que muera
>   es locura."

His second stanza is a prayer of contrition to Christ. And in the final stanza of the poem the poet speaks calmly on behalf of the surviving family.

This poem is unique in medieval Spanish literature for achieving a classical tone of simple spoken language: there is no ingenious wordplay, no learned pedantry. And the flow and ebb of the long and short lines anticipate the complex rhythms of the Italian canzone. This poem was glossed as a religious text throughout the sixteenth century; it is still read and recited by speakers of Spanish today. Longfellow's translation (1833) gives English speakers some idea of its power.

BIBLIOGRAPHY

Jorge Manrique, *Poesía*, J. M. Alda-Tesán, ed. (1965). See also Anna Krause, *Jorge Manrique and the Cult of Death in the Cuatrocientos* (1937); Pedro Salinas, *Jorge Manrique; o, Tradición y originalidad* (1947, 2nd ed. 1952).

ELIAS L. RIVERS

[See also **Spanish Literature.**]

MANṢŪR, ABŪ JAᶜFAR ᶜABD ALLĀH IBN MUḤAMMAD Al- (*d.* 775, after a reign of twenty-one years), second Abbasid caliph. The son of the Abbasid patriarch, Muḥammad ibn ᶜAlī, and a Berber slave, he was chosen at the last moment to succeed his brother, the first dynast of the line, Abu 'l-ᶜAbbās al-Saffāḥ. In choosing al-Manṣūr, Abu 'l-ᶜAbbās passed over many traditionally better qualified candidates, including six uncles and a nephew, ᶜĪsā ibn Mūsā, all heroes of the revolution that brought the house of ᶜAbbās to power.

Al-Manṣūr's claim to the caliphate was soon contested by his uncle ᶜAbd Allāh ibn ᶜAlī, the conqueror of Syria and "extirpator" of the Umayyad line. To counter this threat, al-Manṣūr enlisted the aid of Abū Muslim, the creator of the dynastic army, and his nephew ᶜĪsā, who stood second in line of succession. ᶜAbd Allāh's Syrian-based forces were broken in battle and the caliphate was thus assured for al-Manṣūr. Moving swiftly to consolidate his rule, the new caliph now turned against Abū Muslim, whose independence as governor of Khorāsān was seen as a threat. Abū Muslim was lured to the caliph's quarters, believing that the two were about to settle their differences, and murdered. The governor's army retinue was then bought off. Several revolts were later invoked in Abū Muslim's name, but none of the incidents, about which we know very little, seems to have been of much consequence.

Once in power, al-Manṣūr sought to keep the rule

by future generations of the dynasty within his own house. To that end, he pressured his nephew ᶜĪsā to give way to his son al-Mahdī, and subsequent Abbasid caliphs were descended from his own blood. The Alids, whose resistance to the Umayyads had come to nought, were generally compliant. The exception was a serious revolt in 762–763, coordinated by Muḥammad and Ibrāhīm, sons of the militant ᶜAbd Allāh ibn al-Ḥasan. Despite some harrowing moments, the revolt was crushed and the Alids never again offered serious challenge to al-Manṣūr's rule, although the stigma of belonging to a family of rulers that lacked proper religious credentials in the eyes of the Muslim faithful continued to weigh heavily on al-Manṣūr.

To shore up his and his family's image, the caliph encouraged a revisionist historiography or, more correctly, a political hagiography, closely linked to official patronage. The particulars of his early life and career were rewritten to enhance his prestige. His alleged accomplishments mirrored those of more distinguished dramatis personae, such as his uncle and rival ᶜAbd Allāh ibn ᶜAlī and his nephew ᶜĪsā ibn Mūsā. The caliph also dramatized his claims to rule by encasing himself in monumental architecture and forming a highly stratified political and administrative bureaucracy.

To provide proper physical surroundings for his highly centralized rule, al-Manṣūr built Madīnat al-Salām, a magnificent round administrative center at the confluence of the Tigris River and the Ṣarāt Canal. The size of this center alone was greater than any Islamic city in Iraq. In time, an enormous urban area radiated from the Round City and came to be known as Baghdad (after an ancient Persian hamlet that had graced the site). As the center of a highly centralized authority, Baghdad dominated the surrounding landscape and served as the quintessential symbol of the caliph's rule.

In many respects, al-Manṣūr might be regarded as the real founder of Abbasid rule. It was he who established the incipient pattern of Abbasid government. He seriously curtailed the power of his paternal uncles by systematically removing them from positions of prominence. Through these measures, he made Islamic government less of a family concern. Relatives were often replaced with clients *(mawālī)*, tied exclusively to the caliph and his immediate family. As a result he managed to circumvent persons with direct ties to powerful interest groups. The pool of talent available to the caliph was considerable and included many veterans whose service dated to the days of clandestine activities against the Umayyads. Clients and other confidants were entrusted with the most sensitive posts. Certain positions were even passed along as family sinecures, thereby extending and strengthening the already existing ties between patron and client.

The army was remodeled to fit the caliph's concerns. The old Arab tribal forces, always riven with dissent and tribal animosities, were replaced by a professional standing army organized along regional lines and cultivated in a traditional fashion, by dispensing patronage in a manner beneficial to both subject and sovereign. The major regiments were subsequently settled in permanent cantonments of the capital city at some distance from the general populace. There they formed a standing reserve that could be sent to augment the provincial armies as the occasion demanded. Transplanted from Khorāsān to Baghdad, the new army established an esprit de corps by stressing the geographical affiliations of the past. The troops remained intensely loyal throughout al-Manṣūr's reign. Although he enjoyed a reputation for parsimony and austere behavior, it would appear that al-Manṣūr invested heavily in urban development. Toward the end of his life he gave orders to expand substantially the market areas of the capital, offering financial incentives to merchants and artisans. It is quite probable that al-Manṣūr meant to apply this commercial policy to other major settlements in the realm.

Upon his death, he bequeathed a viable state that appeared to rest on firm political foundations and the sound fiscal policy he had designed. The highly personalized way of exercising power nevertheless omitted the extent to which many innovations could be sustained after him.

BIBLIOGRAPHY

Hugh Kennedy, *The Early Abbasid Caliphate* (1981); Jacob Lassner, *The Topography of Baghdad in the Early Middle Ages: Texts and Studies* (1970), and *The Shaping of ᶜAbbāsid Rule* (1980); Farouk Omar, *The ᶜAbbāsid Caliphate, 132/750–170/786* (1969); M. A. Shaban, *The ᶜAbbāsid Revolution* (1970); Moshe Sharon, *Black Banners from the East* (1983).

JACOB LASSNER

[See also **Abbasids; Alids; Baghdad; Barmakids; Caliphate; Mahdi, al-; Saffāḥ, Abu'l-ᶜAbbās al-.**]

MANṢŪR, IBN ABĪ ᶜĀMIR AL- (938–1002), virtual ruler of Andalusia, who took his honorific title of al-Manṣūr bi-Allāh (conqueror with the aid of God) at the age of forty-three, was named at his birth Muḥammad ibn Abī ᶜĀmir. Christian Europe knew him as Almanzor.

Trained in the law, he rose by means of his native talents and the support of Princess Ṣubḥ, the wife of the caliph al-Ḥakam II and probably his mistress. Qadi (magistrate) of Seville when al-Ḥakam died in 976, Ibn Abī ᶜĀmir became the vizier (councillor) to Jaᶜfar ibn ᶜUthmān al-Muṣḥafī, the *ḥājib* or highest political officer in Córdoba, the capital of the Spanish Umayyad caliphate. The two defeated an attempt by the palace guard, made up of Slav mercenaries, to prevent the accession of Caliph Hishām II.

In 977 Ibn Abī ᶜĀmir led a military expedition through Christian Galicia and took the stronghold of Los Banõs. With the general Ibn ᶜAbd al-Raḥmān Ghālib, whose daughter Asmāᵓ he married, Ibn Abī ᶜĀmir overthrew al-Muṣḥafī, whom he then had thrown in jail and murdered. He assumed the office of *ḥājib.*

Ibn Abī ᶜĀmir's rumored liaison with the caliph's mother caused criticism in Córdoba, but he conciliated his critics by proving his devotion to the religious authorities and ostentatiously burning books considered unorthodox in the collection in the great Córdoban library of the Umayyad caliphs.

To reduce the caliph to a figurehead, Ibn Abī ᶜĀmir built a new government headquarters outside Córdoba in 978, al-Madīnat al-Zāhira. He then moved the leading officials of the administration there, where they were under his control. Hishām II became a powerless recluse in Córdoba.

For security reasons, Ibn Abī ᶜĀmir hired men from Christian Spain and from among the Berbers of North Africa, soldiers who became his personal army. They were a decisive factor when Ghālib, offended by the degradation of the old officer class, led a revolt against his son-in-law. Ghālib was defeated and killed in battle in 981.

That same year, Ibn Abī ᶜĀmir attacked the Christian kingdom of León. He defeated Ramiro III, who was deposed by his subjects. Bermudo II, who followed, took an oath of fealty to the conqueror. Ibn Abī ᶜĀmir then assumed the title al-Manṣūr bi-Allāh. Avoiding territorial adventures, he abandoned most of the caliphate's claims in North Africa, maintaining only Ceuta on the Strait of Gibraltar.

Al-Manṣūr's wars with the Christian states continued because they were on his northern border. In 985 he invaded Catalonia and sacked Barcelona. In 987 Coimbra in Portugal and Zamora in León suffered the same fate. In 997 he stormed Santiago de Compostela, the site of the great shrine of St. James, razed the cathedral, sparing only the tomb itself, and carried its bells back to Córdoba.

Meanwhile, he gave the office of *ḥājib* to his son ᶜAbd al-Malik in 991, only to take the title *al-malik al-karīm* (noble king) in 996. Still, he never attempted to replace the caliph. Perhaps fearing the reaction among the people of the caliphate, he was content to be the power behind the throne. He died at the age of 64, in the fullness of his power, while on yet another campaign in Castile.

BIBLIOGRAPHY

Titus Burckhardt, *Moorish Culture in Spain,* Alisa Jaffa, trans. (1972); Évariste Lévi-Provençal, *Histoire de l'Espagne musulmane,* II, *Le califat umaiyade de Cordoue (912–1031)* (1950); Jan Read, *The Moors in Spain and Portugal* (1974); Enrique Sordo, *Moorish Spain,* Ian Mitchell, trans. (1963); W. Montgomery Watt, *A History of Islamic Spain* (1965, repr. 1967).

VINCENT BURANELLI

[See also **Andalusia; Asturias-León; Caliphate; Catalonia; Córdoba; Santiago de Compostela; Spain, Christian-Muslim Relations; Spain, Muslim Kingdoms of.**]

MANUALS, ARTISTIC. Two types of handbooks served medieval artists. The craftsman's book contained descriptions of techniques and recipes for various processes; the iconographic manual provided descriptions of compositions to aid in the replication of images.

The four main craftsman's handbooks are the *Mappae clavicula,* Eraclius' *De coloribus et artibus Romanorum,* Theophilus' *De diversis artibus,* and Cennino Cennini's *Il libro dell'arte.* These derive ultimately from the antique tradition of technical books (Pliny, Vitruvius, and Theophrastus) but are more practical and comprehensive than their sources.

The collection of recipes known as the *Mappae clavicula* appears in an inventory of 821 (Reichenau); the versified treatise assigned to Eraclius seems to date from the late eleventh or early twelfth century. From the first half of the twelfth century is the important treatise *De diversis artibus* by Theophilus, sometimes attributed to Roger of Helmarshausen. It is especially valuable for painting, glass, and metal techniques. Cennini's *Libro,* in contrast, is richer in materials bearing on painting. Written in fifteenth-

MANUEL I KOMNENOS

century Florence, it betrays a Renaissance propensity to identify art with the liberal arts rather than the mechanical arts.

Iconographic manuals derive from a long tradition of descriptions of art works used to disseminate compositions or full programs. In 403, for instance, Paulinus of Nola sent to Sulpicius Severus detailed descriptions of the mosaics in the churches at Nola and Fundi "in case you should make a choice from the two for a painting in your newest church too." And from the early fifth century until the end of the Middle Ages *tituli* (descriptive captions) circulated as guides. It is only from the postmedieval period, however, that a comprehensive painter's manual survives, the well-known *Hermeneia* of Dionysios of Fourna, written between 1730 and 1734 on Mt. Athos. The *Hermeneia* incorporates earlier material but seems to be a phenomenon of the Turkish conquest, when Christian artists needed to preserve their artistic heritage.

BIBLIOGRAPHY

Cennino Cennini, *The Craftsman's Handbook,* Daniel V. Thompson, Jr., trans. (1933, repr. 1954); Dionysios of Fourna, The *"Painter's Manual,"* Paul Hetherington, trans. (1974); Heinz Roosen-Runge, *Farbengebung und Technik frühmittelalterlicher Buchmalerei* (1967); Theophilus, *On Divers Arts,* John G. Hawthorne and Cyril S. Smith, trans. (1979).

HERBERT L. KESSLER

[See also **Byzantine Art; Cennini, Cennino; Dionysios of Fourna; Early Christian Art; Iconography; Paulinus of Nola; Roger of Helmarshausen; Theophilus.**]

MANUEL I KOMNENOS (*ca.* 1123–24 September 1180) ruled the Byzantine Empire from 1143 until his death. He was the youngest son of John II, but when John was mortally wounded in Cilicia in April 1143, he allegedly designated Manuel emperor. Manuel was a clever but rash commander. Well educated, he enjoyed intellectual conversation; he liked Western Europeans ("Latins") who frequented Constantinople. But his court was licentious—Manuel had an illegitimate son by a niece.

Many of Manuel's conflicts were with Western Europeans. In 1147/1148, the Second Crusade, after experiencing difficulties with Byzantine guard forces, blamed their disasters at Turkish hands on Manuel's treachery. The Norman king, Roger II, took advantage of the crusade to seize Kerkyra (Corfu) and raid Corinth, Thebes, and other cities. Only in 1149 did Manuel expel the Normans. After Roger's death in 1154, Manuel sent several Byzantine armies to southern Italy (1155–1157). When they were defeated, he turned toward a policy of using the Normans and the papacy against the Germans.

Until the death of Conrad III in 1152, Manuel had maintained good relations with the Holy Roman Empire, but Frederick I Barbarossa was hostile to the Byzantines. During Frederick's struggles for Italy, Manuel supported the pope and the Lombard towns. He even hoped the pope would recognize him as the sole Roman Emperor of East and West.

The crusader states were one of the Komnenoi's lasting preoccupations. Cilician Armenia was closely tied to Latin Antioch. In 1158/1159, Manuel marched in force to this region and obtained the temporary submission of both states. In their need for assistance, kings Baldwin III (*d.* 1162) and Amalric I (*d.* 1174) of Jerusalem sought Byzantium's alliance; in 1169, Manuel sent a fleet to assist the crusaders in Egypt.

Serbia, under partial Byzantine control, was restive; it looked to Hungary for assistance. Manuel crushed the Serbs and Hungarians at the Tara River in 1150, but further campaigns were needed to impose Manuel's candidate, Béla III, on Hungary in 1172.

The Turks proved Manuel's severest problem. In 1146, he advanced on Ikonion, their capital, but was unable to take it; on his retreat his men suffered cruelly. In 1161 a peace treaty ended years of fighting. In 1174, however, alarmed by Turkish successes in eastern Asia Minor, Manuel renewed the conflict; during an advance on Ikonion, his army was almost annihilated near Myriokephalon (17 September 1176). Thus, Manuel's reign concluded in disaster.

Manuel I sought to impose theological uniformity on the church by suppressing dissident intellectuals. Members of the great families, linked to the Komnenoi by descent and marriage, predominated in the government. Despite Manuel's partiality for Latins, the Venetian merchants fell into disfavor; they were arrested and imprisoned on 12 March 1171.

Manuel I's heir, Alexios II, aged eleven, succeeded him on the throne of an exhausted realm. Neither he nor the empire would long survive.

BIBLIOGRAPHY

The essential bibliography is Joan M. Hussey, "The Later Macedonians, the Comneni and the Angeli, 1025–

1204," *Cambridge Medieval History,* IV, pt. 1, 2nd ed. (1966), 858–867, and, for Manuel's last years, Charles M. Brand, *Byzantium Confronts the West, 1180–1204* (1968), 14–30.

A new edition of a major source is Niketas Choniates, *Nicetae Choniatae historia,* J. A. van Dieten, ed., 2 vols. (1975), now available in translation as *O City of Byzantium: Annals of Niketas Choniatēs,* Harry J. Magoulias, trans. (1984). Another translated source is Ioannes (John) Kinnamos, *Deeds of John and Manuel Comnenus,* Charles M. Brand, trans. (1976).

On Manuel and the crusaders, see Odo of Deuil, *De profectione Ludovici VII in orientem: The Journey of Louis VII to the East,* Virginia G. Berry, ed. and trans., (1948), and William of Tyre, *A History of Deeds Done Beyond the Sea,* Emily A. Babcock and A. C. Krey, trans., 2 vols. (1943).

CHARLES M. BRAND

[See also **Byzantine Empire; Constantinople; Crusades and Crusader States: To 1192; Frederick I Barbarossa; Ikonion; John II Komnenos; Komnenoi; Myriokephalon; Roger II of Sicily.**]

MANUEL II PALAIOLOGOS (1350–1425), Byzantine emperor, the second son of John V Palaiologos and Helena Kantakouzene, was crowned co-emperor in 1373 and reigned as sole emperor from 1391 to 1425. He become involved in dynastic quarrels, siding with his father against his brother Andronikos IV and his nephew John VII (1373–1379). In 1382 he left for Thessaloniki, where he ruled as a virtually independent sovereign. Contrary to the official conciliatory policy, he adopted an aggressive attitude toward the Turks. Manuel took Serres after 1371 and in 1382–1383 established full control over the city and over some of the Macedonian countryside. In 1387 he fled Thessaloniki, which fell to the Turks after a long siege, then served as vassal in the Ottoman army, joining it on campaigns in Asia Minor.

In 1394 Constantinople was besieged by Bāyazīd I Yildirim, and Manuel tried to get help from Europe. He traveled to Italy, France, and England (1399–1403); but, although he impressed the Europeans, neither Charles VI of France nor Henry IV of England could give him aid.

After the Battle of Ankara (1402), there followed almost twenty years of relative peace (1403–1421) during the Turkish civil wars and the reign of Mehmed I. The Byzantine territories were extended to include part of Macedonia and Thrace, and Manuel took measures to augment public revenues and, thus, the army. He rebuilt the Hexamilion—fortifications at the Isthmus of Corinth (1415)—and tried to subdue the rambunctious nobles of the Morea. At the same time he pursued fruitless negotiations with the West for aid. The peace with the Ottomans was shattered in 1422, and with the treaty of 1424 Byzantium lost some of the possessions it had acquired in 1403, becoming once again vassal to the Turks.

Manuel II died under the monastic name Matthaios on 21 July 1425. A highly educated man, and a disciple of the scholar statesman Demetrios Kydones, Manuel left letters, a funeral oration for his brother Theodore, and several treatises. His trip to France is probably commemorated in miniatures of the *Très riches heures* of Jean, duc de Berry, and the *Grandes chroniques de France.*

BIBLIOGRAPHY

John W. Barker, *Manuel II Palaeologus (1391–1425)* (1969); George T. Dennis, S. J., *The Reign of Manuel II Palaeologus in Thessalonica, 1382–1387* (1960); Gustave Schlumberger, *Un empereur de Byzance à Paris et à Londres* (1916); Paul Wittek, "De la défaite d'Ankara à la prise de Constantinople," in *Revue des études islamiques,* **12** (1938).

ANGELIKI LAIOU

[See also **Ankara; Bāyazīd I Yildirim; Byzantine Empire; Demetrios Kydones; John V Palaiologos; Mehmed I; Thessaloniki.**]

MANUEL CHRYSOLORAS (*ca.* 1355–1415), a learned Byzantine noble and diplomat, in 1396 was appointed to the studium of Florence to teach Greek; his pupils included some of the leading early Italian humanists (Leonardo Bruni, Guarino da Verona, and Pier Paolo Vergerio). His was the first systematic teaching of Greek in the West ("since 700 years," according to Bruni), and in effect it began the intense and more methodical interest in Greek language and literature that flowered during the Renaissance. He also wrote the first Greek grammar for Western students, the *Erotemata.* Later Manuel taught at Pavia and Milan. Accepting the pope as head of the entire Christian church, he was appointed to attend the Council of Constance (1414), where his name was proposed for the papal office.

BIBLIOGRAPHY

Giuseppe Cammelli, *Manuele Crisolora,* in *I dotti bizantini e le origini dell'umanesimo,* I (1941); Deno J. Geanakoplos, *Greek Scholars in Venice* (1962), repr. as *Byzantium and the Renaissance: Greek Scholars in Venice* (1973).

DENO J. GEANAKOPLOS

[See also **Classical Literary Studies; Italian Renaissance, Byzantine Influence on; Translation and Translators, Byzantine.**]

MANUEL EUGENIKOS, a Constantinopolitan mural painter of the late fourteenth century. He signed himself Kyr Manuel Eugenikos and is known from paintings and an inscription in the Georgian church of Calendžiha, dated to the reign of Prince Dadiani Vameq I (1384–1396). Eugenikos' style is characterized by cool, clear colors; elongated, immaterial figures; and parallel gold hatching used for modeling. His work has been related to late-fourteenth-century icon painting from Constantinople.

BIBLIOGRAPHY

Hans Belting, "Le peintre Manuel Eugenikos de Constantinople en Géorgie," in *Cahiers archéologiques,* 28 (1979); Inga Lordkipanidze, *La peinture murale de Tsalendjikha: Peinture Kyr Manuel Eugenikos* (1977), 16.

BARBARA OEHLSCHLAEGER-GARVEY

[See also **Byzantine Art.**]

Holy women at the Tomb of Christ. From mural by Manuel Eugenikos for church of Calendžiha, *ca.* 1384–1396. © ÉDITIONS A. & J. PICARD, PARIS

MANUEL PANSELINOS (*fl.* late thirteenth–early fourteenth centuries) executed wall paintings in the Church of the Protaton on Mt. Athos in the early fourteenth century. His works are in the Palaiologan style and are considered the earliest and finest Byzantine wall paintings. He painted succeeding scenes in continuous units rather than using the strict framing devices of his contemporaries. Manuel enlivened the

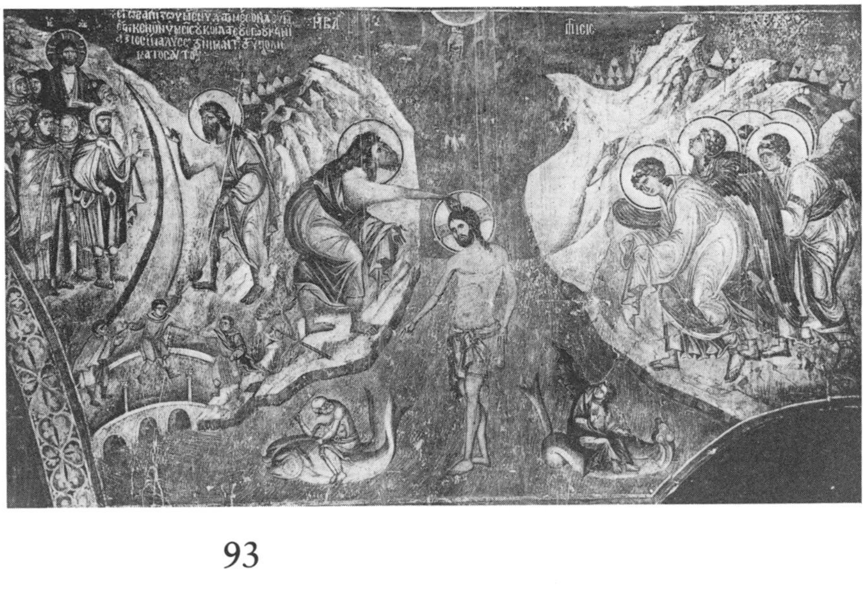

Preaching of John the Baptist and Baptism of Christ. Fresco by Manuel Panselinos from Church of the Protaton, Mt. Athos, early 14th century. PHOTO: G. MILLET

normally rigid feast scenes by giving saints individualized facial features and by introducing incidental genre motifs. He has been assigned to a Macedonian school, but his originality bespeaks connections with Constantinople.

BIBLIOGRAPHY

A. Embiricos, "Manuel Pansélinos," in *Le millénaire du mont Athos,* II (1964); Paul A. Underwood, "Manuel Panselinos," in *Archaeology,* **10** (1957); Andreas Xyngopoulos, *Manuel Panselinos* (1956).

BARBARA OEHLSCHLAEGER-GARVEY

[See also **Andronikos II Palaiologos; Athos, Mount; Byzantine Art; Fresco Painting; Thessaloniki.**]

MANUEL DES PÉCHÉS, an anonymous didactic work written in Anglo-Norman French around 1260 and translated three times into Middle English, most notably by Robert Mannyng. Its original parts formed a confessional manual for laymen, identifying various sins, describing how to make a good confession, and frequently employing exempla and references to everyday life. Added later were devotional prayers and discourses on such matters as the love of God and the power of prayer. William of Wadington may be author of part of the added material, a reviser, or a scribe.

BIBLIOGRAPHY

Editions. Roberd of Brunne's Handlyng Synne with the French Treatise on Which It Is Founded, le Manuel des Pechiez by William of Wadington, Frederick J. Furnivall, ed. (1862). A partial text is in *Robert of Brunne's "Handlyng Synne," A.D. 1303, with Those Parts of the Anglo-French Treatise on Which It Is Founded, William of Wadington's "Manuel des Pechiez,"* Frederick J. Furnivall, ed., 2 vols. (1901–1903).

Studies. Émile J. F. Arnould, *Le Manuel des Péchés* (1940); Charlton Laird, "Character and Growth of the *Manuel des Pechiez,*" in *Traditio,* **4** (1946).

ELLEN T. WEHNER

[See also **Anglo-Norman Literature; Mannyng, Robert.**]

MANUEL, DON JUAN (5 May 1282—13 June 1348), Spanish magnate, soldier, and writer; his father, Prince Manuel, was son of King Ferdinand III of Castile and León (S. Fernando, canonized in 1671), and brother of Alfonso X the Learned (Alfonso el Sabio). Before Don Juan Manuel was two years old, his father died; his mother, Beatriz of Savoy, died when he was eight. At the age of twelve he sent his army into battle against a Moorish force that attacked Murcia, where he was hereditary governor *(adelantado mayor).* A few months later, in September 1294, Don Juan Manuel met with his dying cousin, Sancho IV the Fierce, in Valladolid, and in early 1295, in Madrid, heard him unburden his conscience.

Sancho IV had battled against rival claimants to the throne during the reign of his father. The civil tumult broke out again during two minorities: Sancho's son, Ferdinand IV, was aged nine on his accession in 1295, and his son, Alfonso XI, was only one year old when Ferdinand died in 1312. Brothers, cousins, and other powerful royal relatives of Sancho either claimed the throne for themselves or sought profitable alliances. Don Juan Manuel was drawn into alliance with Prince Juan, one of the surviving sons of Alfonso X, and later with his son, also named Juan.

During the minority of Fernando, under the regency of the forceful queen mother María de Molina, Juan Manuel enlarged his territorial possessions in the region of Murcia and made political alliances with the pretender Alfonso de la Cerda, but avoided direct conflict with the crown. However, the preliminary contract (1303) for his second marriage (the first, in 1299, to Isabel of Mallorca, ended with her death in 1301) contained the provision that in the event of war between Aragon and Castile, Don Juan Manuel would remain neutral. Fernando IV, taking this as an affront, is said to have ordered Don Juan Manuel's assasination. In 1309 Castilians and Aragonese, remembering their common Moorish enemy, jointly besieged Algeciras, but Don Juan Manuel and Prince Juan withdrew their armies, and the campaign collapsed.

After the death of Ferdinand IV (1312), the aged María de Molina shared the regency with the princes Pedro and Juan, uncle and granduncle of the infant king Alfonso XI; but on the deaths of these regents in battle in 1319, Castile was plunged into anarchy. The regency was disputed by three princes—Felipe, Juan the Twisted, and Don Juan Manuel—who wrought devastation in the attempt to compel support from towns and lesser magnates.

The marriage of Don Juan Manuel and Constanza of Aragon was finally celebrated in 1312, when the princess attained the age of twelve. This alliance with Aragon was calculated to gain support should

MANUEL, DON JUAN

Juan Manuel wish either to oppose or to control the infant king of Castile. It was obvious to all that Don Juan saw himself called, by virtue of lineage and intellect, to be maker and molder of kings. In 1325 Alfonso XI's favorites exploited Don Juan Manuel's desires by arranging a marriage between his daughter Constanza and the young king, in order to prevent her marriage to Don Juan Manuel's ally and kinsman, Don Juan the Twisted.

As son-in-law of the king of Aragon, father-in-law of the king of Castile, and friend and brother-in-law of Prince Juan of Aragon, who was primate of Spain, archbishop of Toledo, and chancellor of Castile, Juan Manuel seemed to have all Spain within his grasp. Yet, within the same year (October 1325), he had an angry scene with the archbishop in the presence of King Alfonso, who had secretly negotiated marriages for himself with Maria of Portugal, repudiating Constanza, and for his sister Leanor with Alfonso IV, the heir to the Aragonese throne (a maneuver that Juan Manuel discovered only in April 1327). Juan the Twisted, summoned to an interview with the king, was slain in October 1326; Juan Manuel's wife and his father-in-law James II (Jaume in Catalan) both died in 1327. His political isolation appeared to be complete. When Alfonso had Juan Manuel's daughter Constanza imprisoned in October 1327, Don Juan withdrew his fealty and turned to his ally of last resort, the Moorish king of Granada. In the ensuing war Alfonso's advisers were killed. The general desire to prosecute the Reconquest led to peace in October 1329 and restitution of Don Juan Manuel's offices and titles in January 1330.

Relations remained difficult. As King Alfonso strengthened his hold on Castile, Juan Manuel continued to form alliances. In 1329 he married Blanca Núñez, the sister of Don Juan Núñez de Lara, his former enemy and one of the king's most reckless opponents, and five years later Don Juan had his daughter Constanza affianced to Pedro, the heir to the Portuguese throne. He then declared himself a subject of Aragon and the same year (1334) received the title prince of Villena. In 1336 Juan Manuel again renounced his fealty to Alfonso when the latter refused his daughter safe conduct to Portugal. But his Aragonese alliance no longer availed him. He faced a royal power that was overwhelming and had to flee to Valencia. Restored to his lands by the king, though at the cost of razing five castles, he was present at the Battle of Río Salado (1340), which repulsed the last of the incursions from Morocco, that of the Merinids, and at the siege of Algeciras (1344). His last years were spent mostly studying and writing in his castle at Peñafiel, where he established a Dominican monastery.

In spite of the personal care that Juan Manuel took to prepare a fair copy of all his works and deposit it in his Dominican foundation at Peñafiel, no authentic manuscript exists and only eight of the fourteen works survive: *Crónica abreviada* (*ca.* 1321), a digest of Alfonso X's *Crónica general; Libro del cavallero et del escudero* (1326–1327); *Libro de los estados* (1330); *Conde Lucanor* or *Libro de patronio* (1331–*ca.* 1335); *Libro infinido* (1336–1337), a manual of conduct for his son; *Libro de las armas* (after 1337), on the family's coat of arms; *Libro de la caza* (*ca.* 1325); *Tractado de la Asunción de Nuestra Señora* (probably after 1342).

Alfonso X and his teams of scholars made Castilian prose into a vehicle for serious intellectual matters, which previously had been expressible only in Latin or Arabic, thus forging new concepts and developing levels of discourse appropriate to law, philosophy of history, and natural science. His nephew, Don Juan Manuel, was the first prose writer in Castilian to develop a personal style within the somewhat severe syntactic structures available to him. If he pales before such other fourteenth-century masters of their own vernacular languages as Chaucer, Dante, or Boccaccio, it should be noted that conditions in Castile were not yet right for the development of those subtleties and ironies of detachment that an urban culture and its varied social currents made possible.

Don Juan Manuel was a powerful magnate, convinced of his right, with force at his command, in a world of limited motives. Although he could read Latin, there is no evidence that he could wield it and so impose its supple rhetoric upon the vernacular, as his great contemporaries did. He wrote, rather, like other soldiers, as Julius Caesar might have written had he lived into retirement, or like Kipling in his world of soldierly virtues. He carried over into the task of writing his knowledge that none was his equal in rank (except, of course, the king), and says as much in the *Libro infinido.* As in his political life, he felt free to make whatever pacts with literary forms and conventions he saw fit, and to put them aside without explanation.

Juan Manuel's writings are all more or less didactic, but they go beyond the terms of their didacticism. His best-known work is the collection of stories gathered under the title *El Conde Lucanor.* These fifty-one stories are of many different kinds:

folk tales, animal fables, anecdotes, events from the lives of historical characters—some elaborate, others very brief. Each story is told by the experienced counselor Patronio to his young master, Count Lucanor, in response to the latter's request for advice in a difficult situation. These situations, briefly explained, are the characteristic ones of a nobleman of that period: how to know if a former rival is sincere when he offers an alliance; how to know if a powerful neighbor is hostile; what to do about an ally who always has an excuse for not helping when he is needed—in short, the endless dilemmas of honor and loyalty and property, of religious obligations and the need to defend oneself sometimes with violence, sometimes with deceit.

These stories are told with vigor and seize the attention with their forceful economy. Their art is dynamic and internal, an art of motifs, of shifting balances and weight, rather than of stylistic elaboration or delicacy. The prologue states that the author wishes to help his readers to earn salvation for their souls and to protect their honor, their property, and their rank. The last stories stress the spiritual and moral obligations, but readers have not agreed on finding a controlling pattern of progression in the collection. What is clear is that these are not moralizing exempla in a conventional sense, because they are applied to situations of diplomacy, treachery, or survival in the society encountered by the author. Don Juan Manuel even intervenes as a character in the otherwise rather dull frame story.

Libro de los estados is perhaps the most complete medieval European treatise on the theory of the estates. It contains a reworking of the story of Barlaam and Josaphat; but what is memorable is the author's projection of himself into the narrative, on more than one level, and the way the discussions are made vivid with his own recollections and judgments of people and events.

Libro de las armas contains Juan Manuel's account of his visit, at age twelve, to the deathbed of his cousin Sancho IV the Fearless as the dying monarch, in between spasms, spoke of his violent life and finally regretted that he could not bless young Juan Manuel because Ferdinand III had not blessed his son Alfonso X, and thus there was no benediction to pass on. However, the Manuel line, as is stated in the same book, was blessed by a prophetic dream that came to Juan Manuel's mother.

Libro de la caza is no mere treatise on falconry; it is full of the author's pride in his prowess and that of his prize birds, and conveys his exhilaration in the chase and in the mountains and woodland around his castles.

Don Juan Manuel's public acts often appear to express little more than a petulant concern for having his own way and for getting back at his opponents. He argues in *Libro de los estados* for a strong central authority as the best assurance of order and tranquillity, but in his life he opposed the authority embodied in María de Molina and Alfonso XI. As a writer he expresses concern that vassals and servants should be sheltered and protected by lords, and no fault is so castigated as arrogance, yet the records show him carrying out arbitrary sentence and tell of delegations of vassals appearing before sessions of the cortes to complain of his harsh exactions and lawless treatment of them and their property. Such paradoxes can be largely resolved by considering the crises (of monarchy, of feudal authority, of agricultural production, of depopulation) through which he lived, and his strong belief in a Providence that would vindicate his line and his works.

BIBLIOGRAPHY

There is no modern edition of the complete works. Juan Manuel's *Obras,* in *Biblioteca de autores españoles,* LI (1860, repr. 1928), is incomplete and unreliable. See *El libro infinido,* José Manuel Blecua, ed. (1952); *Libro de las armas,* in José María Castro and Martín de Riquer, eds., *Obras de Don Juan Manuel,* I (1955); *El libro de los estados,* R. B. Tate and Ian R. Macpherson eds. (1974); *Libro del Conde Lucanor,* Reinaldo Ayerbe-Chaux, ed. (1983).

Studies include Daniel Devoto, *Introducción al estudio de Don Juan Manuel y en particular de "El Conde Lucanor": Una bibliografía* (1972); Andrés Giménez Soler, *Don Juan Manuel* (1932), with many letters and documents; Ian Macpherson, ed., *Juan Manuel Studies* (1977); H. Tracy Sturcken, *Don Juan Manuel* (1974).

PETER N. DUNN

[See also **Alfonso X of Castile, King; Aragon, Crown of; Castile; Spanish Literature: Instructional.**]

MANUSCRIPT BOOKS, BINDING OF: EUROPEAN. The invention and spread of the modern form of book, the codex, in the first centuries of the Christian era mandated a new method for binding and protecting the text. Technically speaking, any binding must overcome two problems: it must fasten together the various quires of which the pages are composed, and it must attach these quires to the

MS BOOKBINDING, EUROPEAN

book's cover. Both operations must be performed in such a way that the book opens easily and yet remains strong enough to resist breaking under the stress of repeated opening and closing. Modern sewn bindings effectively resolve this twin difficulty thanks to a long process of development that goes back to the days of the Roman Empire.

Extant manuscript books in codex form reveal two main approaches to these problems. The older approach, certainly developed in antiquity, seems to have been widely applied in the West as late as the seventh century, and remained typical of medieval bookbinding in the Byzantine sphere of influence. This technique consists of two distinct stages. First the quires are sewn to one another with one or two threads and stitches that vary according to the time and place of production. Because grooves were sawed across the spine of the quires at the point of stitching, the stitchwork lies flush with the spine of the book, whence the smooth spine characteristic of Byzantine bindings. The resulting sturdy but flexible group of pages is fastened to the book covers in a second operation, in which cords are passed through the stitchwork and then fastened to the book boards in various manners. The top and bottom of the book's spine are reinforced by elaborate headbands that project beyond the edge of the covers and lend the Byzantine binding its second obvious physical characteristic: the spine of the book is longer than the opposite edge.

The Western technique, on the other hand, addresses both technical problems of binding in one operation. Here the quires are sewn not to each other, but to several strips or bands of cord or leather; the bands are then fastened to the book boards or covers in various characteristic manners. Since, in the Western technique, no grooves are sawed out for the bands and stitchwork, the bands and stitching protrude from the spine of the book, producing the "ribbed" appearance characteristic of the spine of the Western medieval book. This technique seems to have emerged around the eighth century, and apparently presupposes the sewing frame, a device for holding the quires and bands tautly in place during the sewing.

Medieval book covers can be either soft (made of leather or parchment with soft backing) or hard (consisting of sturdy wood boards coverd with some other material, such as cloth, leather, or precious metals). Although soft-backed covers may well have been more common on some medieval library shelves, hard covers have resisted time better and are better known today. Such hard covers often comprise a number of functional metallic ornaments. For instance, one or both sides may be fitted with metal studs or bosses. This is because in a medieval library, books were not stacked on their edges, as they are today. Rather, they were laid on their sides and rested on the studs, which thus protected the cover from scraping or snagging on the shelf. The shape, number, and placement of the studs vary according to the workshop and era of production On the edges of the covers are clasps, intended to keep the books firmly shut when not in use. In Byzantium such clasps are generally of leather or cloth, while in the West they are frequently of metal. In the later Middle Ages it became customary to fasten strips of parchment with the book's title on the cover. There also were rings or other fasteners for chained books.

The prominent role of sacred books in the rituals of the Christian churches encouraged the development of spendid decorations for book covers, which were often the only part of the books that onlookers could see. These decorations seem to have encompassed the full range of late antique and medieval technical possibilities. Thus, the late antique Freer Gospels' wooden covers are decorated with encaustic portraits of the four evangelists. Brocades and silk were favorite materials for book covers, and richly decorated plates of silver or gold often sheathed the wooden boards of liturgical books. Many leather covers have survived from both East and West. Their stamped decorations were determined by the tools at the binder's disposal; their patterns and variety often reflect particular usages, and can facilitate localization and dating of the binding.

BIBLIOGRAPHY

Élisabeth Baras, Jean Irigoin, and Jean Vezin, *La reliure médiévale* (1978), is a good general introduction to modern, medieval, and Byzantine binding techniques, with a select, annotated bibliography and a useful multilingual glossary. The studies of Berthe van Regemorter are fundamental, particularly "La reliure des manuscrits grecs," in *Scriptorium,* **8** (1954), "Le codex relié depuis son origine jusqu'au haut moyen âge," in *Le moyen âge,* **61** (1955), and "La reliure byzantine," in *Revue belge d'archéologie et d'histoire de l'art,* **36** (1967). A useful classification of types and chronology is G. Pollard, "Describing Medieval Bookbindings," in *Medieval Learning and Literature: Essays Presented to Richard William Hunt* (1976). Léon Gilissen, *La reliure occidentale antérieure à 1400* (1983), marks a decisive advance. For illustrations and bibliography of decorated book covers to 1957, see Dorothy Miner, *The History of Bookbinding, 525–1950 A.D.: An Exhibition Held*

MS BOOKBINDING, ISLAMIC

at the Baltimore Museum of Art (1957), published by the Walters Art Gallery. See also F. A. Schmidt-Künsemüller, *Die abendländischen romanischen Blindstempeleinbände* (1985), with bibliography. For ongoing bibliography of medieval binding studies, see "Bulletin codicologique," published at the end of each issue of *Scriptorium,* and the annual index to that journal, under the entry *reliure.*

MICHAEL MCCORMICK

[See also **Chained Books; Codex; Codicology; Libraries; Quire.**]

MANUSCRIPT BOOKS, BINDING OF: ISLAMIC. In all of Islamic art there is perhaps no clearer case of the dependence of Islamic craftsmen on Western (or pre-Islamic) methods than is afforded by bookbinding. By the time the earliest Islamic manuscripts were being written, the format of the roll *(rotulus, volumen)* had long been superseded in the West by the codex, the ancestor of the modern book. It was this Western invention, itself derived successively from Roman tablets and diptychs, that was taken over by the Muslims, possibly via Ethiopian codices. This is not to say, however, that the *rotulus* was totally unknown to them. In the Christian and Muslim worlds alike, the roll form was employed spasmodically until the tenth century; but it is principally in the Islamic Near East that its influence on the codex form can be detected.

The preferred format employed for early Koran manuscripts is an extended oblong, stressing the horizontal rather than the vertical. The connection with the *rotulus* form is self-evident. Nevertheless, such manuscripts are in fact codices since they are bound within covers. Despite the prestige conferred on this format by its use for copies of the sacred book, its popularity was comparatively short-lived. Korans using the vertically conceived codex format were produced simultaneously with those in which the horizontal emphasis was dominant, and by the eleventh century the latter had died out. In the three centuries of its floruit this distinctively Islamic transitional form—part *rotulus,* part codex—generated what appear to be correspondingly original developments in binding technique and decoration. No description of these, however, can hope to be definitive in view of the almost total disappearance of so many kinds of early Islamic (and, for that matter, early Christian, Byzantine, and Coptic) manuscripts and bindings. The surviving samples derive principally from only two areas, Egypt and Tunisia, themselves very closely linked by style and technique as well as location, and thus cannot sustain any claim to be representative. It follows that features which seem to be original, or exclusively Islamic, may be nothing of the kind.

EGYPTIAN AND TUNISIAN BINDINGS

Before these early bindings of oblong format are examined with this caveat in mind, certain general remarks may be in order. All of these bindings appear to be Egyptian or Tunisian, and the vast majority of surviving pre-Islamic codex bindings are from Egypt too. Indeed, the history of the Islamic codex binding until the early thirteenth century must, insofar as it depends on surviving examples, perforce be based almost exclusively on Egyptian or Egyptian-influenced material. Ample literary evidence attests that bookbinding was widely practiced elsewhere in the Islamic world in this early period, notably in Spain and in Syria, Iraq, and Iran. While the names of these bookbinders and the places where they worked have been preserved, however, the records give no clue as to regional variations in bookbinding methods and ornament. Even in the period after 1200 it is hazardous to identify certain types of binding (those from Syria and Iraq, for example) on the basis of style alone. For many centuries it has been common practice to repair, renew, or even entirely to replace bindings, and it is therefore rash to assume that the binding of a dated manuscript will be contemporary with the text. Comparatively few Islamic bindings have been subjected to the detailed scrutiny, and occasionally even laboratory analysis, which should ideally underpin a dating attribution. Against a background of such lacunae, which are at once numerous and varied, generalizations are obviously risky.

The directly or indirectly Egyptian origin of so many early Islamic bindings means that the immediately pre-Islamic bindings of Coptic Egypt are the obvious starting point for a general survey of them. A great many of these Coptic bindings have survived, and they testify to the high technical quality that was reached and long maintained in monastery workshops. (A collection from the monastery of St. Michael's of the Desert can be found in New York, Pierpont Morgan Library.) The deliberate isolation of many of these monasteries fostered a notably conservative approach to this as to other crafts. Thus the ingrained expertise of Coptic bookbinders could be passed on virtually intact to their Muslim colleagues.

MS BOOKBINDING, ISLAMIC

It is not surprising, therefore, that many standard features of later Islamic bindings find their prototypes in this Coptic material, whose suggested dates range from the fourth to the ninth centuries. These features include: the preference for large geometrical designs filling most of the principal field; the contrasting plainness of the spine; the use of multiple borders, also of geometrical type; and the extension of the back cover to form a flap (though in Coptic bindings all four sides were so extended, whereas in Islamic bindings it is the right-hand side of the back cover which is so treated). The use of different designs for the front and the back of the binding, with the back cover being the simpler one, and of a blue linen backing pasted on the cover below the leather, are also features based on Coptic practice. Standard Coptic techniques are used to sew the leaves together—chainstitching is used, for example, to join the quires.

Coptic bindings also exhibit a wide range of technical devices that were borrowed and developed by Islamic craftsmen: the use of wooden boards covered in leather; sewn leather appliqué; painted, repoussé, stamped, incised, blind tooled, punched, and even inlaid fret and filigree work; stencil patterns; and painted vellum endpapers.

The only other substantial body of early Islamic bookbindings are those found by chance in a storage room of the Qayrawān Jāmi^{c} (Great Mosque). They totaled 179, of which fifty-eight were attributed to the ninth century, nineteen to the tenth, seventy-one to the eleventh, and thirty-one to the twelfth and thirteenth centuries. Their close relationship to Egyptian and ultimately Coptic bookbinding is patent. If these bindings are indeed local, Tunisian bookbinding was clearly an offshoot of that of Egypt. Wooden covers with fastening clasps are common. The leaves are fastened to the boards in Coptic fashion by threads passed through eyelets or by glued strips of cloth, the latter a technique not often found in Coptic bindings. In general, however, the technique of these Qayrawān bindings, and often enough their decorations, too, are closely dependent on Coptic work of the eighth and ninth centuries.

IRANIAN BINDINGS

Manichaean bindings from Turfan in central Asia, generally dated to the eighth and ninth centuries, can be recognized as very advanced for their time when compared to contemporary Egyptian work, for they employ such techniques as stamping, polychrome, and filigree work. It is highly likely that knowledge of these techniques percolated to Iran. With such correspondences in mind it is not surprising that the earliest Iranian bindings to survive do not seem to express a distinctively local style. A Koran cover in the Chester Beatty library dated 905 has a central knotted rosette easily paralleled in Tunisian or Egyptian bindings. Another in the same collection, dated 972, is unusual in that it has no flaps, but its lozenge grid with a circle at each vertical junction of the lozenges is in line with contemporary Tunisian work. Unfortunately, the dearth of eleventh- and twelfth-century Iranian bindings makes it impossible to be sure whether the close connection with Egyptian work continued, but the notable consonance between Egyptian and Iranian bindings throughout much of the fourteenth century, when both schools shared a preference for geometric designs, does suggest that the links were never broken. It is only in the later fourteenth century that Iranian bindings shed the taste for angular geometric patterns and begin to develop along lines alien to the Egyptian tradition. In the later medieval period the disparate traditions that had crystallized in Iran and Egypt remained the two dominant forces in Islamic bookbinding, and it was only in the bindings of Ottoman Turkey that a rapprochement between them was eventually achieved.

It is generally accepted that the high-water mark of Islamic bookbinding was reached in fifteenth-century Iran under Timurid patronage. The range of technique and ornament expanded dramatically in this period.

The "house style" favored bindings of dark brown kid; their cynosure was typically a central mandorla whose interior designs were repeated in miniature in the corner quadrants. Large expanses of smooth plain leather were set off by multiple borders packed with interlace, inscriptions, floral patterns, or combinations of these elements. Thus, the predominantly geometric quality of earlier book covers gave way increasingly to floral designs and arabesques, a process most clearly traceable in Shīrāz bindings of about 1400–1450.

Much of the ornament was executed in gold tooling (a process involving the impressing of designs on leather by applying heated tools to gold leaf—the earliest surviving examples of which are found on bindings coming from the Maghrib region of North Africa, as on the binding of a Koran copied in Marrakech about 1256 for an Almohad ruler).

Although Timurid bindings from Yazd, Shīrāz. Abarquh, and Isfahan have survived, it was Herāt that became the major center for bookbinding in the eastern Islamic world. Indeed, by the time that the Herāt scriptorium was reconstituted at Tabrīz by Shah Isma^cil in the early sixteenth century, the bookbinders were sufficiently important and independent to be organized in a guild, as their counterparts in Cairo had been for centuries.

Without doubt, the sharpest break with previous conventions afforded by Timurid bindings was the introduction of animals disporting themselves within a landscape, even if the latter was at times only suggested by profuse foliage. The choice of animals—for example, fabulous creatures like the dragon—betrays close dependence on Chinese designs, which presumably reached Iran through the media of textiles or paper. Humans and such animals as bears, deer, hares, foxes, and monkeys are frequently found in hunting and wrestling scenes. These echo contemporary miniatures and indeed bring the iconography of book painting (especially marginal decoration) onto the cover itself and often announce the content of the volume. This integration of text and cover is altogether novel and further indicates the great importance of Timurid bookbinding.

The introduction of figural motifs into Timurid bindings had a profound effect upon technique as well. The new motifs generated a new and laborsaving use of the metal block, which could be as large as the cover itself. One early result of the metal-block technique was a new emphasis on the third dimension, so that the design acquired the quality of an embossed relief, with the raised portions often picked out in gold. Further contrast was afforded by painting on leather and by filigree work with colored silk as a backing. Some of the later Timurid bindings in fact exhibit a polychrome splendor that surviving earlier Islamic bindings cannot match.

BIBLIOGRAPHY

For a bibliography to 1956 see Emil Gratzl, K. A. C. Creswell, and Richard Ettinghausen, "Bibliographie der islämischen Einbandkunst, 1871 bis 1956," in *Ars orientalis,* 2 (1957).

Other studies include Richard Ettinghausen, "Near Eastern Book Covers and Their Influence on European Bindings: A Report on the Exhibition 'History of Bookbinding at the Baltimore Museum of Art, 1957–1958,' " in *Ars orientalis,* 3 (1959); Basil Gray, ed., *The Arts of the Book in Central Asia* (1979), and *The Arts of India* (1981); *Islamic Masterpieces of the Chester Beatty Library,* David James, ed. (1981); *Islamische Buchkunst aus 1000 Jahren: Austellung der Staatsbibliothek Preussischen Kulturbesitz* (1980), an exhibition catalog; Martin Levey, Miroslav Krek, and Husni Haddad, "Some Notes on Chemical Technology in an Eleventh Century Work on Bookbinding," in *Isis,* **47** (1956); Martin Lings and Yasin Hamid Safadi, *The Qur'an* (1976), an exhibition catalog; Serrano Lopéz, *La encuadernación española* (1972); Jeremiah P. Losty, *The Art of the Book in India* (1982), an exhibition catalog; Theodore C. Peterson, "Early Islamic Bookbindings and Their Coptic Relations," in *Ars orientalis,* **1** (1954); Basil W. Robinson, ed., *Islamic Painting and the Arts of the Book* (1976).

ROBERT HILLENBRAND

[See also **Coptic Art; Islamic Art; Manuscript Illumination, Islamic; Timurids.**]

MANUSCRIPT BOOKS, PRODUCTION OF. For present purposes, "manuscript" means the handwritten codex on parchment or paper of the Latin West. It came into existence in the patristic world of late antiquity, replacing the papyrus roll (the characteristic medium of Greek and Roman pagan literature); and it continued as the dominant support for the written word until it was joined (*ca.* 1450) and gradually replaced (*ca.* 1550) by the product of the printing press.

Each individual manuscript was produced by the combination of two factors, physical and social: (1) the relatively fixed material framework—that is, the fact that all manuscripts are made up of sheets of parchment or paper formed into quires, on which people laid out texts and pictures, which were subsequently written and painted; and (2) the variety of environments in which manuscripts were produced—monastery, university, city, court. The procedures of production and the appearance of the product are, each of them, reflections of the time, the place, and the situation in which the manuscript was produced.

Broadly speaking, one may classify manuscripts into two groups according to their producers: individual or personal, that is, owner- or user-produced books, that were planned, laid out, and written (they were seldom decorated) by the person who was going to use them; and institutional or impersonal, that is, scriptorium- or atelier-produced books, books produced in monastic scriptoria, or from a stationer's exemplar, or by a secular workshop. Owner-produced books do not fit neatly into the patterns nor follow the rules applied to the formal, group-produced manuscripts, in the discussion

MS BOOKS, PRODUCTION OF

below. But whether one is considering a personal or a "professional" product, and whether a book of the ninth or of the fifteenth century, certain basic procedures in the making of a manuscript remain fixed.

The making of any manuscript involved a number of discrete steps or stages. First, the material base, parchment or paper, had to be prepared: If parchment, it had to be cut to size, be finished by sewing up holes and scraping with pumice to remove grease and ensure a smooth surface, and be folded into bifolia; if paper (increasingly the case, as the fourteenth century progressed), the size had to be selected and, again, the sheets folded to form bifolia. The amount of parchment or paper—that is, the number of quires required—will have been roughly calculated in advance, on the basis of the length of the text to be copied. The layout of the text on the bifolia also required prior planning: prose or verse, long lines or two columns, with or without gloss, with or without illustration; and the individual bifolia had to be ruled accordingly, with hard point (stylus), lead point, ink, or moldboard. The bifolia were then (or before, since these two stages did not have a fixed sequence) arranged loosely in quires—most commonly consisting of four, six, eight, ten, or twelve folios, but there was no real standard. In parchment manuscripts, the arrangement ensured, for aesthetic purposes, that the same side of the skin, flesh or hair, formed the surface for the two pages that faced one another, on each double-page opening.

The bifolia were then ready to be written on. The writer mixed a batch of ink from powder, cut a goose quill to a sharp edge, and transcribed the text. For the first half of the quire, he copied only the first folio recto/verso of each bifolium, carefully numbering the bifolium to preserve its place within the quire (*i*, *ii*, *iii*, and so on, or *a*, *b*, *c*, or the like) and then setting it aside, or hanging it up, to dry. When the first folio of the innermost bifolium was dry, the writer began the second half of the quire by completing the second folio of that bifolium, recto/verso, and then the second folio of the next bifolium, and the next, until he had written his way back "out" by completing the folio that was conjoint with the first folio of the quire—always setting aside or hanging up each completed bifolium to dry as he finished it. Having recorded the catchword at the bottom of the last verso, the scribe could then take up the second quire, and so on until he had copied the whole text. As he was writing through, the writer omitted those portions of the text that were to be written in a different color of ink, such as major initials, chapter titles, and running headings; he left blank what he judged to be an adequate space for this material, making a minute note in the margin as memorandum of the letter or words to be inserted. Once the scribe had finished the writing of the text, these unfinished portions could be completed, usually in red (whence the term "rubric"). This was normally done by the writer of the text himself, but it was not rare for the job to be given to another. Finally, in some situations—very commonly at the universities, for example—the finished and rubricated bifolia might have been proofread by a corrector, who often left his mark at the end of each gathering.

The art work represents another series of steps. In the case of a text manuscript, art work often involved very minor decoration—adding the initials, flourished or unflourished, in alternating red and blue, as well as the hundreds or even thousands of red and blue paragraph marks, and washing majuscule initials with yellow. Literacy was not required for this task. An illustrated romance or an illuminated book of hours was quite another matter, the work of specialists. After a base coat was applied to the surface, the design of the illustration, illuminated border, or historiated initial (containing a painted scene) would be sketched; gold was applied, in leaf form or in solution; colors were added, layer by layer, and each allowed to dry; and lastly the stipple or white penwork highlighting was applied.

Finally, the finished bifolia, perhaps loosely stitched together, were assembled into their quires, and the quires, assembled in sequence, were sewn onto bands that were attached to a cover—a limp vellum chemise or a formal hard cover of wooden boards covered with hide or leather.

These numerous stages could, in the case of a simple owner-produced book, be carried out successively by one person in his study; or, in the case of the product of a monastic scriptorium or commercial atelier, it could instead involve an elaborate distribution of labor organized by the head of the scriptorium or the contractor. In all times and places, the owner-produced book was the more individualistic or idiosyncratic, governed largely by the interests of the writer, and the less attractive, since the writer was generally not a professional. Books produced by an institution or a group, in contrast, were more orderly in their preparation (the layout of the whole, and the quality of the materials used) and in their execution (script, rubrication, decoration, and illus-

MS BOOKS, PRODUCTION OF

tration). While there were owner-produced books in every period, their proportion increased rapidly with the growth of the schools, the appearance of professional classes (parish priests, civil servants), and increase of literacy among the merchant classes in the fourteenth and fifteenth centuries. Although the owner-produced books are often the most interesting, the remainder of this article concentrates on the orderly world of institutionally produced manuscripts.

Manuscript books in the Middle Ages were produced in a variety of different settings. At times the results have been dichotomized as, on the one hand, books made within the monastic community for internal consumption and, on the other, books made in a commercial setting for external consumption—for sale. Such a division is misleading, because religious houses as well as secular shops produced manuscripts for commercial sale. It might be more meaningful, rather, to distinguish production within an ecclesiastical structure from production within a secular structure. Ecclesiastical production was the earlier of the two, and it enjoyed a revival at the end of the Middle Ages.

European book production was largely monastic in nature, from the late seventh century—when new books issued for the first time from northern monasteries such as Luxeuil in Burgundy and Wearmouth/Jarrow in Northumbria—until roughly the middle of the thirteenth century—when the monastic scriptoria of Europe gave way to the book production of the urban schools of Bologna, Paris, and Oxford. Books were produced as part of the internal work of the abbey, or for commission from the outside. Those of the monks or nuns who were able, either scribes or painters, spent a portion of each day, varying with the available daylight through the year, in copying texts. A certain minimum library was indispensable for any monastery or nunnery: the various volumes of Scripture (Pentateuch, prophets, psalter, gospels, epistles, and others), liturgical books, and the works of the church fathers and other authorities, for worship and instruction. The enormous revitalization and expansion of monastic houses that occurred in the late eighth and the ninth century as part of the Carolingian renaissance; and again in the tenth and eleventh centuries, associated with the Cluniac reform; and yet again in the twelfth and early thirteenth centuries, with the foundation and growth of the Cistercian order, meant that there was a recurring need for new books to supply the choirs and libraries of newly revitalized and newly established houses.

Lending order to the chaos left by the crumbling of ancient Roman civic education and book production, the Benedictine abbeys of the ninth century were essentially responsible for the transformation of the literature of Latin antiquity to the physical form in which it survives today, the parchment codex written in Carolingian minuscule. A total of only 1,800 manuscripts, many of them mere scraps of papyrus or parchment, survive from all the centuries prior to A.D. 800—while at least 6,700 survive from the ninth century alone. Of all the texts of all the ancient Latin authors, only Vergil rests essentially on surviving late antique manuscripts; all the rest are based on manuscripts of the ninth century or later. The Benedictine abbey of St. Martin of Tours on the Loire was a major early center of book production; its abbot Alcuin wrote of papyrus rolls in its library, and its scriptorium seems to have produced Bibles to supply other houses, copying over and over from an exemplar. In the twelfth century the Cistercians of Clairvaux produced libraries for each of their daughter houses; copies of the Clairvaux edition of the works of the Fathers made for this purpose can be seen today in a ten-volume set in the municipal library of Troyes. The voluminous writings of St. Bernard also had to be reproduced and circulated through the houses of the Cistercian order.

The great abbeys, however, also could produce superb monuments of illumination on commission for outsiders. Equipped with skilled writers and artists and with necessary material, abbeys such as Corbie, Tours, Reichenau, Echternach, Winchester, and St. Denis produced gospelbooks, psalters, or pontificals for kings, emperors, and bishops. Since they were able to supply steady employment and the materials of book production, such abbeys attracted artists and scribes renowned for their abilities; in early days, such artisans may have been accorded the status of lay brothers of the house, while later they simply worked on commission for the abbey.

The emergence and expansion of the schools in the eleventh and twelfth centuries was responsible for the growth of book production in urban abbeys associated with teaching—St. Pierre of Chartres; St. Aignan of Laon; Ste. Geneviève, St. Germain, and St. Victor of Paris; St. Frideswide and Osney in Oxford. The formalization of curricula by the middle of the twelfth century brought about the development of a new layout of the page—the great glossed page that, with the necessary variations, served in manuscripts of the *Glossa ordinaria* to the Scriptures, of Peter Lombard's *Sentences,* of Gratian's *Decretum,* and of Roman law. Wherever these large glossed books may have been produced—whether in the abbeys that sent monks to the schools or (more likely) in the abbeys at which the teaching was done—there appears to have been little difficulty in meeting the demand for these set texts.

The evolving of the many schools into the few universities, and the growth of the university-centered mendicant orders of Franciscans and Dominicans, spelled the end of the monastic era in book production. In the thirteenth century, abbeys sent their young men to houses of study at the universities; by the 1240's, even Clairvaux had succumbed and opened a house of studies at Paris. The great authors of the thirteenth century—Alexander of Hales, Bonaventure, Aquinas, Albertus Magnus—were not monks but mendicant friars; and the shelves of abbey libraries across Europe began to fill with manuscripts of their works (and a good many lesser items) produced in the uniform styles of Bologna, Paris, and Oxford. The local styles, which distinguished the great monastic scriptoria of the twelfth century and before, gave way to the nondescript red-and-blue flourished letters of the school books, written in the compressed letter forms of the university. No significant Benedictine or Cistercian houses were founded after about 1200–1250, and no great writers emerged from the ranks of black or white monks until the end of the Middle Ages; in a sense, monastic scriptoria simply ran out of things to do, while book production at the schools, on the contrary, was going full tilt.

The archetypal new books of the thirteenth-century university at Paris, concerned with pastoral care and the training of clergy, include the small one-volume "pocket" Bible, the portable handbooks of pastoral care such as Raymond of Peñafort's penitential *Summa,* collections of model sermons for the liturgical year, the verbal concordance to the Scriptures, and alphabetized collections of biblical distinctions—and, in the realm of theology, the commentary on the *Sentences,* the two *Summas,* and the lesser works of Thomas Aquinas. It is these last, in particular, that appear to have been responsible for fostering the one major change in the procedures of book production before print—namely, the appearance of the sworn university stationer who rented out books one *pecia* (that is, quire) at a time to students or masters who wished to make a copy. The procedure of making a single manuscript quickly, by distributing the quires among many scribes for copying, was a venerable one; the change represented by the *pecia* process was the fact that one could produce numerous copies simultaneously, with each scribe following along one after the other. The earliest university stationers of whom one has record—William of Sens (*fl.* 1270), Andrew of Sens (*fl.* 1296–1304), and Thomas of Sens (*fl.* 1313–1342)—were members of a single family, whose shop was adjacent to the Dominican house of St. Jacques in Paris and whose specialty was the works of St. Thomas, suggesting that the original impulse may in fact have come from the Dominicans, for their own convenience. The universities as they grew in strength, however, were increasingly able to regulate those trades that were essential to the universities' welfare, and at both Bologna and Paris this included the stationers, before the end of the thirteenth century. The publication of texts via dissemination in *pecia* enabled a given work to be reproduced in large numbers in a relatively short period of time, which greatly increased the initial impact that a new work might have. Created, it seems, to meet the demand for copies of the works of St. Thomas, the *pecia* system served the universities of Bologna and Paris well—but briefly. This interesting innovation seems to have been discarded by the middle of the fourteenth century, with the shrinkage of the market caused by the Hundred Years War and the Black Death.

The secular and commercial production of manuscripts emerged only in the later Middle Ages, since it depended upon the growth of a literate audience whose demand for books was larger than could be filled by the traditional book-producing capacity of the great abbeys. In contrast with the earlier audience of prelates, kings, and emperors—and the specialized audience of schoolmen—this new literate audience consisted of landed nobility, urban merchants, and civil servants, and of women as well as men. The books they commissioned were written not in Latin but in the vernacular, and written for the most part in the work-a-day running business scripts—*littera mercantesca, bastarda,* or *hybrida*—that their readers used in the exercise of their professions. While, particularly in the north, it might serve the nobility of the countryside, the commercial book trade was definitely centered in the cit-

MS BOOKS, PRODUCTION OF

ies: Milan, Florence, Rome, Naples, Paris, Rouen, Ghent, Bruges, London, and others. By the fourteenth century, this secular trade had largely replaced the great abbeys as the source for high-quality illuminated books. The courts of Europe, both secular and ecclesiastic, were by this date addressing themselves to the great commercial painters—and by the fifteenth century, they would be retaining scribes and illuminators of their own. The new secular and commercial book producers distinguished themselves from their ecclesiastical predecessors by leaving their names on the books they produced, wrote, and painted. The earliest secular book producers whom we know by name are people like William de Brailles on Cat Street in Oxford in the mid thirteenth century, or Herneis *le romanceeur,* who had a shop in the parvis in front of Notre Dame of Paris in the third quarter of the century, or Master Honoré and his son-in-law Richard de Verdun, who illuminated books on the rue Erembourc de Brie in Paris at the end of the century. This marks a vivid change from works known simply as "school of Tours" or the like.

This departure, from production within an ecclesiastical structure to urban lay production, was a major shift; and we have less precise knowledge about the process of this change than we might wish. Nevertheless, the shift was not as abrupt nor distinct as some scholars have thought. There is no need to postulate a new body of book producers emerging *ex nihilo.* The skilled craftsmen already existed, as laymen in the employ of the abbeys; and they simply adapted, gradually, to new demands and new opportunities. For a secular artist or scribe, there was little difference between working largely in the employ of St. Victor and working largely on his or her own. During the many decades of transition, artists and scribes must have sought work wherever they could get it, and fit with equal ease into both ecclesiastical and lay structures of book production.

The favorite books of the lay ateliers included the *Moralized Bible* of Guiart des Moulins, the *Great Chronicles of France,* the Arthurian and Alexander romances, and Froissart; but, increasingly, the leading stock-in-trade was the book of hours, the book of private devotions to the Blessed Virgin Mary. Replacing the psalter as the main book of private worship in the late thirteenth or early fourteenth century, the book of hours was an essential item in the households of fifteenth- and early-sixteenth-century landed nobility and, as a frequent betrothal gift, was a book often associated specifically with women.

The secular book trade of the later Middle Ages was a highly organized and specialized structure. Writers in London located around St. Paul's and the Inns of Court belonged to the Scriveners' Guild or Stationers' Company. Illuminators in Paris belonged to the Hôpital St.-Jacques-aux-Pélerins, and illuminators in Bruges belonged to the painters' and saddlemakers' Guild of St. Luke. Manuscripts, whether of romances, Chaucer, or books of hours, were made on commission for a buyer. The contractor might be the artist, or a seller of used books. Manuscript production, like cloth production, was a putting-out industry, in which the contractor tried to provide a steady flow of employment to those who subcontracted with him to work off various stages of production, probably working at their own homes. Rather than one scribe and one painter producing one manuscript, a given scribe or painter might be working on the text or the illuminations for several different manuscripts from different contractors or booksellers at a given time. The scribes in London who lived near the Inns of Court around 1400, for example, made their bread-and-butter income from legal work, writing contracts and wills; but they supplemented this meager amount by producing Middle English literary manuscripts—Gower, Hoccleve, Chaucer—for their wealthy clients at court. At Florence, in the second half of the fifteenth century, Vespasiano da Bisticci could lay on numerous scribes and illuminators to produce entire libraries, on demand. In Ghent and Bruges, what one might term "standardized" books of hours were produced for sale in London, their calendars and litanies completed with the universally celebrated saints, but with room having been left for specific local ones or patron saints to be filled in by the eventual purchasers.

The production of books was of course forever altered in the second half of the fifteenth century by the appearance of the printing press. While the press was, in itself, a singular agent for change and a unique invention, to fifteenth-century scholars it was simply a more efficient means of disseminating the written word. The press was invented—and, more important, printing survived—because the manuscript procedures were, at last, unable to satisfy the demand for new books. The printing press is the outgrowth of one last change in medieval manuscript book production, namely, the revival of the monastic scriptoria that is associated with the renewal movements fostered by the councils of Constance (1414–1418) and Basel (1431–1449) and the similar movements of Benedictine reform centered at Bursfeld and Melk. Nourished by the Carthusians, the Windesheim Congregation, and the Brethren of the Common Life, the so-called Modern Devotion, with roots that lay in the writings of Geert Groote, was a renewal that rested squarely on the written word, and the ability to read and interpret it. As a result, scriptoria that had lain dormant since the middle of the thirteenth century came back to life. The second half of the fifteenth century became, with the twelfth, the age of library construction. Books, printed and manuscript, came rolling in, quite literally, by the barrel load. It was largely the book buying of the reformed religious houses that kept the printing press alive in the fifteenth century and insured its survival.

Since the early printing press could not produce fine colored pictures, however, the hand-produced illuminated book of hours long survived the invention of printing. The manuscript book continued to be the vehicle for fine painting until the 1530's, when it finally succumbed, not to the press but to the Reformation.

BIBLIOGRAPHY

Bernhard Bischoff, *Paläographie des romischen Altertums und des abendländischen Mittelalters* (1979), especially part C, "Die Handschrift in der Kulturgeschichte," trans. into French by Hartmut Atzma and Jean Vezin as *Paléographie de l'antiquité romaine et du moyen âge occidental* (1985); Carla Bozzolo and Ezio Ornato, *Pour une histoire du livre manuscrit au moyen âge* (1980); Jean Destrez, *La pecia dans les manuscrits universitaires du XIIIe et du XIVe siècle* (1935); A. I. Doyle and Malcolm B. Parkes, "The Production of Copies of the *Canterbury Tales* and the *Confessio Amantis* in the Early Fifteenth Century," in Malcolm B. Parkes and Andrew G. Watson, eds., *Medieval Scribes, Manuscripts and Libraries: Essays Presented to N. R. Ker* (1978); James D. Farquhar, "Identity in an Anonymous Age: Bruges Manuscript Illuminators and Their Signs," in *Viator,* **11** (1980); Léon Gilissen, *Prolégomènes à la codicologie* (1977); Sandra Hindman and James D. Farquhar, *Pen to Press* (1977); G. S. Ivy, "The Bibliography of the Manuscript Book," in Francis Wormald and Cyril E. Wright, eds., *The English Library Before 1700* (1958); C. H. Talbot, "The Universities and the Medieval Library," *ibid.;* Wilhelm Wattenbach, *Das Schriftwesen im Mittelalter,* 3rd ed. (1896); Francis Wormald, "The Monastic Library," *The English Library Before 1700* (1958).

RICHARD H. ROUSE

[See also **Codex; Codicology, Western European; Ink; Libraries; Manuscript Illumination; Paleography; Paper, Introduction of; Parchment; Pecia; Scriptorium; Writing Materials.**]

MANUSCRIPT ILLUMINATION, EUROPEAN. The art of illustrating texts with images goes as far back as Egyptian times and the *Book of the Dead.* Later, Greeks and Romans illustrated mathematical, medical, and other scientific as well as literary texts. But the great tradition of medieval manuscript illumination is overwhelmingly religious and moralizing, using the codex (rather than *rotulus*) format of parchment pages. The relatively simple tempera painting methods, sometimes inks and dyes, and gold leaf or ground gold paint were used with breathtaking skill by the best artists of the Middle Ages to create small paintings unsurpassed in quality before or since.

The earliest extant biblical scenes are in a fragment of the Book of Kings, the *Quedlingburg Itala* (Berlin, Deutsche Staatsbibliothek, cod. theol. lat. fol. 485) made in Rome in the fourth/fifth century. An ansate cross filled with interlace ornament, combined with bird and plant forms, appears in a Coptic Acts of the Apostles (New York, Pierpont Morgan Library, Glazier Collection, MS 1) dated from the same early period. The existence of an early Jewish tradition of manuscript illumination—one perhaps even earlier than the Christian—has been postulated, but the earliest extant illuminated Hebrew manuscript is the Moshe Ben-Asher Codex of the Prophets (Cairo, Karaite Synagogue) executed in Palestine in 896. Stylistically, medieval Jewish illuminations generally follow the Christian or Muslim traditions of the place where they were made. The earliest extant Greek illuminated manuscripts are fragments of a gospelbook, *Codex Sinopensis* (Paris, Bibliothèque Nationale, suppl. gr. 1286), and a Genesis (London, British Library, Cotton Otho B. VI)—both dated fifth/sixth century but clearly based on earlier models. Thus, as fragmentary as are extant remains, it is clear that a vital tradition of Judeo-Christian manuscript illumination existed by about 500. The sixth- and seventh-century Mediterranean Christian tradition was, stylistically as well as iconographically (in terms of its dependence on existing pagan narratives and other forms of imagery), an extension of the forms of late antiquity (for example, the Vienna Genesis, Vienna, Nationalbibliothek, cod. theol. grec. 31).

Early medieval manuscript illumination was primarily a monastic art, although various court scriptoria also produced major monuments and styles. Interesting decorated letters and pages were produced in seventh- and eighth-century Frankish scriptoria, but it is in the British Isles, particularly in the Hi-

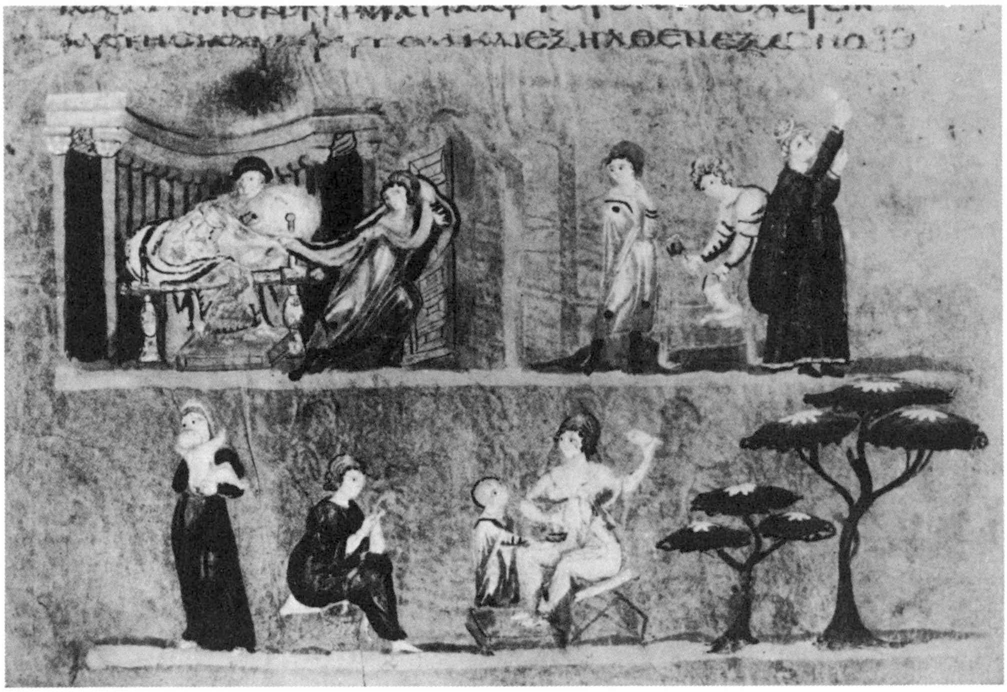

Joseph and Potiphar's wife. From Vienna Genesis, Syrian, 6th century. VIENNA, NATIONALBIBLIOTHEK, COD. THEOL. GREC. 31, fol. 16r

berno-Saxon areas as well as in continental Irish monastic foundations, that there developed during the seventh through ninth centuries one of the great art styles of all times. Using a vocabulary of interlace, stylized animals, scrolls and spirals, key patterns, and dot contours of antique, Byzantine, Coptic, Germanic, and Celtic origins, Hiberno-Saxon artists transformed canon tables, frames, Evangelist figures, cross pages, and decorated letters into marvelously intricate abstractions—as may be seen in the Book of Kells (Dublin, Trinity College). Southern English manuscripts of the same period are related in style to the Hiberno-Saxon, but are decidedly more "Mediterranean" in character.

The Carolingian tradition retained much of the Insular stock of ornament and design, and its manuscript illumination remained largely a monastic art. However, the key influences were generated by the taste of the royal or imperial scriptoria and their emphasis on the revival of the classical tradition and the imperial ideal in the Latin West. The first series of truly Carolingian illuminations begins with the rather abstract and two-dimensional Godescalc Gospels of 781–783, made in the court scriptorium of Charlemagne (Paris, Bibliothèque Nationale, nouv. acq. lat. 1203). This series soon reaches monumental grandeur in a number of sumptuous creations with more plastic and realistic—antique and Byzantine-like—forms. A second series, still associated with the court school of Charlemagne but characterized by a far more painterly style, is grouped around the Coronation Gospels (Vienna, Weltliche Schatzkammer).

A splendid example of the last phase of the Carolingian court styles is the sumptuously complex *Codex Aureus* of St. Emmeram (Munich, Bayerische Staatsbibliothek, Clm. 14,000), made for Charles the Bald in 870. Major monastic scriptoria also produced a distinguished array of illuminated manuscripts during this period, notably in Rheims, Tours, Metz, and St. Gall. The impressive Carolingian biblical image cycles were clearly developed from early Christian models and retain a distinctly late antique character. Another important contribution of Carolingian scribes and artists are a group of illuminated pagan literary and mythological/astronomical texts (moralizing texts combining elements from ancient science and pseudoscience, as well as from Christianity).

One of the last major Carolingian styles—the so-called Franco-Saxon or Franco-Insular—whose center is now generally placed in St. Amand, generally

MS ILLUMINATION, EUROPEAN

St. Matthew. From *Codex Aureus* of St. Emmeram, Court School of Charles the Bald, 870. MUNICH, BAYERISCHE STAATSBIBLIOTHEK, CLM 14,000, fol. 16r

eschews the dominant "neoclassical" trend in favor of ornaments and designs in the Insular mode. Nevertheless, in the monumental logic of its forms, largely frames and giant initials, even this style demonstrates at its best a firm hold on the principles of "classicism."

Following the disintegration of the Carolingian empire, the imperial spirit passed on to Ottonian Germany. There, under the influence of monastic reforms initiated at Cluny in early-tenth-century France, illuminated Gospels and liturgical books were produced in such major centers as Fulda, Trier, and Reichenau. Carolingian art provided an important, but not the sole, foundation for the Ottonian development. Thus, an important work of around 985, the *Codex Egberti* (Trier, Stadtbibliothek, codex 24), contains paintings by several hands, including an impressive series of scenes from the life of Christ that appears to be based directly on late antique–early Christian models rather than on Carolingian ones and also reflects some Byzantine influence. One of the classicizing illuminators of this book—the so-called Master of the *Registrum Gregorii*—was evidently also the creator of one of the most impressive of early medieval imperial portraits, that of Otto II or Otto III (single folio, Chantilly, Musée Condé).

But the late antique foundation, although an important factor, did not remain the key element for long. By around 1000, Ottonian illuminators had developed a unique, spiritually charged, expressionistic style, as in the superb Reichenau Gospels of Otto III (Munich, Bayerische Staatsbibliothek, Clm. 4453). The southern Germanic style of Reichenau was marked by a tight, flat linearism that immobilizes figures and objects into timeless abstractions on golden background; in northern Germany, notably Cologne, an equally expressionistic yet more painterly and fluid style became dominant. However, one cannot generalize too much about Ottonian illumination; not simply a blend of antique, Carolingian, and Byzantine elements, it was a varied and original art practiced in many centers besides Reichenau and Cologne—centers such as Regensburg, Mainz, Pommersfelden, Salzburg, and Echternach. Ottonian manuscript illumination is of critical importance in the study of the mainstream development of medieval art, for it forms an important link between the Carolingian and Romanesque traditions, and is indeed a key element in the foundation of Romanesque painting.

During the period corresponding to the flowering of Ottonian art, major traditions also developed in northern Spain and England. In the regions of León, Castile, and Navarre, a style often confusingly referred to as "Mozarabic" produced a distinguished series of works whose stylistic mix includes a base of Visigothic and North African elements overlaid with Carolingian and Islamic influences. In the best examples of the style, strikingly colored two-dimensional and curiously "modern" figures inhabit an exotically surrealistic mystical world. The dominant group of illustrated manuscripts is the distinguished series of Beatus of Liébana's *Commentary on the Apocalypse.*

In England, under the impetus of the cultural reforms of Alfred the Great and his successors, there developed a new tradition of manuscript illumination—notably at Winchester—that essentially rejected the earlier Hiberno-Saxon taste for convoluted abstractions. In such works as the *Benedictional* of St. Ethelwold (London, British Library, Add. MS 49,598), scenes with antique overtones, probably transmitted through Carolingian models,

MS ILLUMINATION, EUROPEAN

are set in elaborate frames with powerful decorative accents at the corners and mid sections. In Canterbury, a nervous linear style of multicolored ink drawing rather than painting was developed. All these elements were eventually fused and took hold in other important centers, such as Bury St. Edmunds.

Despite the dominance of architecture, sculpture, mural painting, and stained glass during the Romanesque and Gothic periods, manuscript illumination continued to develop as an important art form. The Romanesque, the first truly pan-European style, is so multifaceted as to defy simple definition. It is characterized by an enormous vigor and breadth of artistic activity and an awakening of regions that had long been artistically dormant. From Italy to Scandinavia and from England to Bohemia, monastic centers produced an impressive array of illuminated books, often very large and sometimes gigantic in size. Some illustrated liturgical works took on the guise of public art—notably the Italian exultet rolls, which were unfurled over the top of the altar during the Easter Mass to display their images to the congregation. A large range of types of legal documents and books were illuminated, but especially impressive are the Bibles, of which a number must be ranked among the art masterpieces of all time—for example, the English mid-twelfth-century Lambeth Bible (London, Lambeth Palace Library).

A strong taste for moralizing and encyclopedic writing is frequently reflected in illumination. For example, in bestiaries, animals are depicted as embodiments of theological concepts and are assigned vices or virtues. Even plants may become the objects of Christian moralizing lessons.

The sources of the Romanesque style are Byzantine, Carolingian, Ottonian, and Anglo-Saxon art. In the early stages, Romanesque illuminations strongly resemble one or the other of those earlier styles; and Byzantine inspiration continues to be an important factor thoughout the development of the style. Characteristic of the transformation to true Romanesque is the structuring of forms as additive, compartmentalized entities, as well as the building up of lines and color areas as strong, substantial elements—the colors themselves being dense and often bright. Compositions are structured according to highly ordered formulas. Movement is caught in curvilinear cell-like arabesques. Even when they retain a basically two-dimensional and abstract character, Romanesque miniatures decoratively project startling spiritual as well as material strength—as in the portrait of John the Evangelist in the Gospelbook of Abbot Wedricus, made at Liessies in northeastern France under English influence (Avesnes, Société Archéologique).

In its last phase, primarily influenced by the artistic tradition of the Meuse Valley (the Mosan school), the Romanesque style of manuscript illumination retains its additive, compartmentalized character, fluidity of line, and density of color, but rejects planar abstraction in favor of a three-dimensional sculptural solidity and realism. This quality is forcefully expressed in such works as the early-thirteenth-century Berthold Missal, made in the south German monastery of Weingarten (New York, Pierpont Morgan Library, MS 710).

Like the Romanesque, the Gothic period produced a multitude of regional stylistic variants throughout Europe, and only the main trends can be outlined here. From the late twelfth century on, the

Heraklios decapitating Chosroes. From the Berthold Missal, monastery of Weingarten, early 13th century. NEW YORK, PIERPONT MORGAN LIBRARY, MS 710, f. 114r

 MS ILLUMINATION, EUROPEAN

production of manuscripts shifted progressively but surely from monastic scriptoria to secular workshops, with Paris becoming a major center. The Ingeborg Psalter, made in the early thirteenth century, probably in Paris (Chantilly, Musée Condé, MS 1695), clearly exemplifies the "Style 1200" in miniatures, a style in which remarkably classical, fluidly chiseled forms act out on shallow stages the stories of Christ's entombment and the three Marys at the tomb. Although illuminated manuscripts continued to be overwhelmingly religious, some of the most important patronage emanated from the royal court and other aristocratic milieus. The "Style 1200" was short-lived and by about 1230 had already been replaced in Paris by a decorative, two-dimensional, sophisticated and abstract style reminiscent in some ways of the early Romanesque.

A major development in thirteenth-century manuscript illumination was the creation of the imagery of the moralized Bible, the *Bible moralisée,* a massive manuscript. Nevertheless, just as characteristically Gothic were the tiny books for private use, for example, the Psalter of Saint Louis of about 1256 (Paris, Bibliothèque Nationale, lat. 10,525), in which delicate abstract two-dimensional forms inhabit a fantasy world influenced by the decorative marvels of contemporaneous architecture and stained glass.

Although sources can be traced back as far as the seventh and eighth centuries, it is the Gothic period that produced the art of the *drolerie,* in which the marginal areas of serious religious imagery become populated by a fantastic array of insects, birds, apes, and decidedly satirical scenes. This fashion appears to have originated in England, but quickly spread to the Continent.

By the end of the thirteenth century, illuminators in the major centers had reintroduced figural modeling and combined it creatively with the decorative lyricism of the mid-century period—as can be seen in some fine works sometimes attributed to Master Honoré.

The critical factor in the evolution of manuscript illumination in the latter Middle Ages was the influence of the new spatial and figural realism developed by Italian painters in Florence and Siena. In the work of the early-fourteenth-century Parisian illuminator Jean Pucelle, especially, the new realism is combined with the earlier decorative mode to create pages on which fine script, three-dimensional scenes, friezelike *bas-de-page* illustrations and a medley of marginal *droleries* are combined into marvelous designs—as in the Belleville Breviary (Paris, Bibliothèque Nationale, lat. 10,483–10,484) completed before 1343.

Banquet scene from the January Calendar of the *Très riches heures.* Limbourg Brothers, 1416. CHANTILLY, MUSÉE CONDÉ, MS 1,284. GIRAUDON/ART RESOURCE

Late-fourteenth-century illumination is dominated by Flemish artists working in the courts of the king of France or the duke of Burgundy, notably Jean Bondol, André Beauneveu and Jacquemart d'Hesdin. However, the masterpiece of this Franco-Flemish tradition is the *Très riches heures* of the duke of Berry, on which Pol de Limbourg and his brothers Jehannequin and Hermann were still working when the duke died in 1416 (Chantilly, Musée Condé, MS 1284). Manuscript illumination continued well into the sixteenth century, but none surpassed the Limbourg brothers' masterpiece, in which the enchantingly detailed scenes of aristocratic and peasant life, illustrating the months of the year, her-

MS ILLUMINATION, HEBREW

ald the magic realism that became the hallmark of Early Netherlandish panel painting.

BIBLIOGRAPHY

François Avril, *Manuscript Painting at the Court of France: The Fourteenth Century* (1978); Walter Cahn, *Romanesque Bible Illumination* (1982); Robert G. Calkins, *Illuminated Books of the Middle Ages* (1983); David Diringer, *The Illuminated Book* (1967); Jacques Dupont and Cesare Gnudi, *Gothic Painting* (1954); André Grabar, *Byzantine Painting* (1953); André Grabar and Carl Nordenfalk, *Early Medieval Painting from the Fourth to the Eleventh Century* (1957), and *Romanesque Painting from the Eleventh to the Thirteenth Century* (1958); Joseph Gutmann, *Hebrew Manuscript Painting* (1978); Konrad Hoffmann *et al., The Year 1200: A Background Survey* (1970); Richard Marks and Nigel Morgan, *The Golden Age of English Manuscript Painting, 1200–1500* (1981); Florentine Mütherich and Joachim E. Gaehde, *Carolingian Painting* (1976); Bezalel Narkiss, *Hebrew Illuminated Manuscripts* (1969); Carl A. Nordenfalk, *Celtic Painting and Anglo-Saxon Painting: Book Illumination in the British Isles 600–800* (1977); Jean Porcher, *Medieval French Miniatures* (1959); David M. Robb, *The Art of the Illuminated Manuscript* (1973); Daniel V. Thompson, *The Materials and Techniques of Medieval Painting* (1956); Kurt Weitzmann, *Ancient Book Illumination* (1959), and, ed., *Age of Spirituality: Late Antique and Early Christian Art* (1979).

JACQUES GUILMAIN

[See also **Anglo-Saxon Art; Beatus Manuscripts; Beauneveu, André; Bestiary; Bible Moralisée; Bondol, Jean; Book of Hours; Breviary; Celtic Art; Codex Aureus; Drollery; Durrow, Book of; Early Christian Art; Exultet Roll; Gospelbook; Gothic Art: Painting; Honoré, Master; Initials, Decorated and Historiated; Jacquemart d'Hesdin; Kells, Book of; Limbourg Brothers; Lindisfarne Gospels (with frontispiece); Migration and Hiberno-Saxon Art; Mosan Art; Panel Painting; Paris Psalter (with frontispiece); Pre-Romanesque Art; Psalter; Pucelle, Jean; Romanesque Art; Très Riches Heures.**]

MANUSCRIPT ILLUMINATION: HEBREW. Extant Hebrew illuminated manuscripts of the Middle Ages date from the ninth through the fifteenth centuries; and other such manuscripts may already have existed in late antiquity. The existing manuscripts can be divided into four main schools: Eastern, Sephardi, Ashkenazi, and Italian. In none of them is there any evidence of a specific Jewish style, but they all show special Jewish characteristics in script, program of decoration, iconography, and special motifs.

Characteristics. The Hebrew script (like Arabic) has no capital letters, which would lend themselves to decoration. Hence, there developed instead the practice of decorating initial words within panels (although some artists in European schools, influenced by Latin illumination, did decorate initial letters). Another special feature of Hebrew illumination was the use of minute script (micrography) as outline for decoration and illustration. This was developed in the ninth century in eastern Islamic countries and was used, as well, by the European schools of Hebrew illumination.

Bible decoration was also developed in the East at that time. Like the Koran, a Bible is bound between decorative carpet pages, each book having a decorative opening or ending panel. Some carpet pages, related mainly to the Pentateuch, depict an array of Tabernacle and Temple implements. Pericope indicators, which were merely decorative in the East, came to be fully illustrated in Europe.

The program of decoration of daily and festival

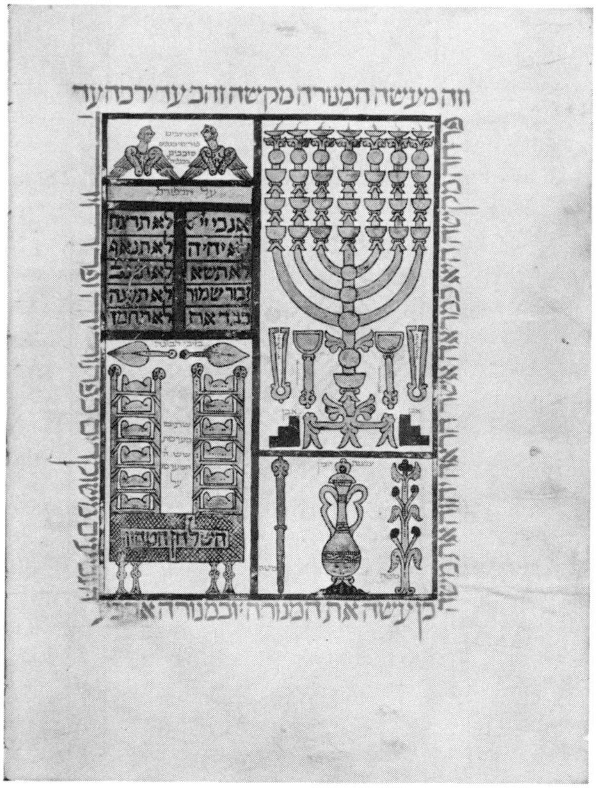

Carpet page from Sephardi Bible, decorated with sanctuary vessels from the Solomonic Temple. Perpignan, Aragon, 1299. PARIS, BIBLIOTHÈQUE NATIONALE, MS HÉBR. 7, fol. 12v

MS ILLUMINATION, HEBREW

prayer books adheres to the main divisions of daily and festival prayers, headed by panels embellishing initial words. In European manuscripts, text illustrations were added in the margins of prayer books, mainly in the Ashkenazi schools. In the fourteenth century the Haggadah, a ritual book for Passover eve, developed a very extensive scheme of decoration, including biblical, midrashic, ritual, and custom illustration. Sumptuous Spanish Haggadot contain a section of full-page biblical cycles similar to those in the Latin Psalters of the thirteenth and fourteenth centuries.

The most obvious special Jewish iconography, which is seen in all of the schools, is the use of midrashic interpretation added to biblical scenes. These midrashic themes, found in numerous examples of Jewish as well as general illumination throughout the Middle Ages, are similar to the iconography of Jewish art in the Hellenistic and Byzantine periods, as known from Jewish objects, the wall paintings of Dura Europos, and floor mosaics from other synagogues. Although there are no extant examples, some scholars suggest that Jewish manuscript illumination, as well, may have been in use in the earlier periods and that, in fact, it may have influenced medieval Christian, as well as Jewish, examples.

Schools of illumination. The Eastern school is the earliest and is the source of ninth- through thir-

The righteous celebrating in paradise. Note the leviathan, the wild ox, and the mythical bird Ziz (the food of the righteous). From the *Ambrosian Bible* of Ulm, 1236–1238. MILAN, BIBLIOTECA AMBROSIANA, MS B. 32, fol. 136r

teenth-century illuminated manuscripts from Iran, Mesopotamia, Palestine, and Egypt. From the fourteenth to the seventeenth centuries, schools were located in Yemen, Iran, Morocco, and Tunisia. Typical of their decoration is the use of contemporary Islamic motifs and style. As in Muslim illumination, it was forbidden to represent human figures and other living creatures in the sacred books. Being the earliest known, Eastern schools are the link that connects late antique and Byzantine synagogue decoration and lost Hebrew manuscripts with the later European schools.

The Sephardi school flourished in the Iberian Peninsula and southern France from the period of the Christian Reconquest in the thirteenth century to the expulsion of the Jews from Spain in 1492 and from Portugal in 1496/1497. No Hebrew illuminations survive from Muslim Spain. However, the program of decoration and iconography of Sephardi manuscripts may perpetuate an earlier Hebrew-Muslim tradition. The Sephardi illumination depends on French and Spanish Gothic styles and shows fourteenth-century Italian elements as well. The late-fifteenth-century Portuguese school is also related to Netherlandish illumination. Sephardi illumination is as eclectic as the Spanish Latin illuminated manuscripts, which were influenced by Muslim, French, Italian, and Flemish schools of illumination.

The Ashkenazi schools of illumination from the thirteenth through fifteenth centuries are located in England and Western European countries, mainly France, Germany, and northern Italy. The style conforms to the different local schools, but their iconography and manner of expression are varied and highly developed. In southern Germany during the thirteenth and fourteenth centuries, there developed a special stylistic motif in Hebrew illumination that used animal and bird heads on human figures.

The Italian Hebrew illumination follows the local style, with the typical Jewish decoration program in Bible and prayer books based on the Oriental, Spanish, and Ashkenazi decoration. The Italian Hebrew illuminations are the most aesthetic and sumptuous of all schools. Most of them were made for wealthy patrons who were, perhaps, anxious to keep up with their non-Jewish colleagues or with the rulers they served.

BIBLIOGRAPHY

Malachi Beit-Arié, *The Worms Maḥzor* (1986); Joseph Gutmann, *Hebrew Manuscript Painting* (1978); Elias Katz, ed., *Machzor Lipsiae* (1964); Bezalel Narkiss, *Hebrew Illuminated Manuscripts* (1969), and *The Golden Haggadah* (1970); Bezalel Narkiss, Aliza Cohen-Mushlin, and Anat Tcherikover, *Catalogue of the Hebrew Illuminated Manuscripts in the British Isles,* I (1982); Bezalel Narkiss and Aliza Cohen-Mushlin, *The Kennicott Bible* (1985); Gabrielle Sed-Rajna, *Le Maḥzor enluminé* (1983); Moshe Spitzer, ed., *The Birds Head Haggada* (1967).

BEZALEL NARKISS

[See also **Carpet Page; Dura Europos; Jewish Art.**]

MANUSCRIPT ILLUMINATION, ISLAMIC. The development of the Islamic tradition of book production, including manuscript illumination, relates directly to the history of the Koran, the divine revelations preached by the prophet Muḥammad during the first decades of the seventh century, and collected and codified in a volume of 114 suras, or chapters, during the reign of the third caliph, ᶜUthmān (644–656). Because of the Koran's sacred character as the word of God, its transcription was considered an act of piety. The high value placed on producing copies of this holy book and the consistent demand for other religious and secular works generated by a society very rapidly becoming literate soon elevated the copying and embellishing of texts of all types into a major art form.

The history of Islamic manuscript illumination has yet to be thoroughly traced; however, it is certain that the principal features of this art were formulated quite early in the Muslim era. The oldest surviving Korans, of the eighth–tenth centuries, contain virtually all of the characteristic forms of medieval Islamic illumination, incorporating a wide repertoire of geometric, floral, and vegetal patterns, and serving a variety of practical and aesthetic functions.

Small roundels dividing the text constitute the most common kind of illumination in early Koran manuscripts. These verse stops take diverse forms from a simple circle or a pyramidal arrangement of small circles to lobed rosettes and endless knots. Other devices in similar, as well as more complicated, shapes such as palmettes, diamonds, triangles, and teardrop medallions, are placed in the margins to indicate the fifth *(khāmisa)* and tenth *(ᶜāshira)* verses of a chapter and the divisions of the Koran into seven, thirty, and sixty parts *(ajzāᵓ)*. These ornaments also mark the passages after which ritual prostrations *(sajdāt)* should be performed. Long bands of braided, geometrical, and sometimes trellis or arcade design usually separate one sura from an-

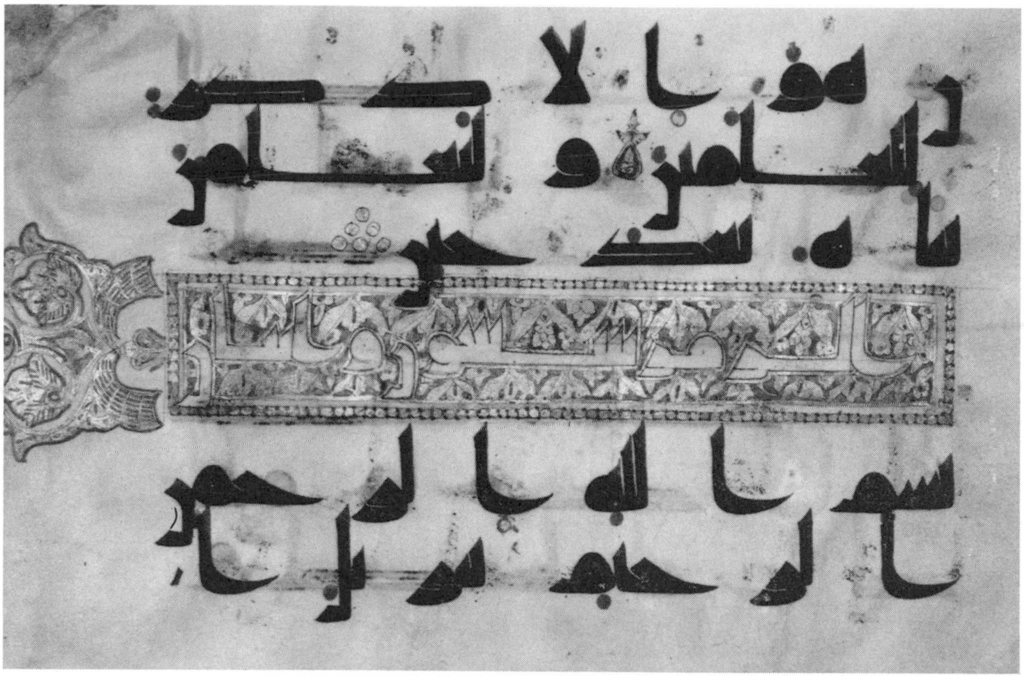

Folio from a Koran, suras 38–39. Eighth–ninth century. COURTESY OF THE FREER GALLERY OF ART, SMITHSONIAN INSTITUTION, WASHINGTON, D.C., 30.60.r

other. All such devices are invariably rendered in gold, with occasional touches of blue and sepia—the primary color scheme of early Islamic illumination.

The main function of these basic types of illumination is to signify the beginning and end of various parts of the text, and thereby to direct or assist the reader. Except for those marginal ornaments with notations for the number of Koranic verse or section, they contain no text. A second, and often more elaborate, form of illumination emphasizes or highlights specific lines of text, particularly the titles of the suras. In early Korans the chapter heading (*ᶜunwān*) is often written in gold or reserved in white against a background of gold blossoms, leaves, or arabesques, and framed in a beaded or braided gold border. Frequently a large palmette composed of fanciful floral and leaf motifs is attached to the end of an illuminated heading and projects into the margin. In a sense this is a superfluous element, since the sura title is already highlighted by the horizontal frame and gold pigment. However, it does draw further attention to the heading—almost like an exclamation mark—and suggests that an appreciation of the purely formal and aesthetic properties of ornament had developed in the formative phase of Islamic illumination.

This tendency is revealed even more fully in a third type of illumination found in early Korans. Many ninth- and tenth-century volumes open with full-folio frontispieces without any text. These compositions, often designed as double-page spreads, also appear at the beginning of the thirty main sections of the text or at the end of the volume as finispieces. Their function is to introduce, announce, or close the text, and their form is essentially an expanded version of the sura illuminations with a framed rectangle and a projecting marginal ornament. The decoration of the central field in these illuminations is always symmetrical, and may vary from simple floral scrolls to a complex series of intersecting and interlocking geometric units.

The most elaborate compositions contain interlaced circular, square, or oblong compartments of different, but proportionate, sizes surrounded by one or more braided bands. Often the center is punctuated by a large rosette. The marginal ornament is generally rendered as a large, encircled rosette. Like so many components in the visual vocabulary of early Muslim culture, certain elements in illuminated manuscripts were borrowed from the late antique world and adapted to specifically Islamic purposes. For example, the format used for both sura

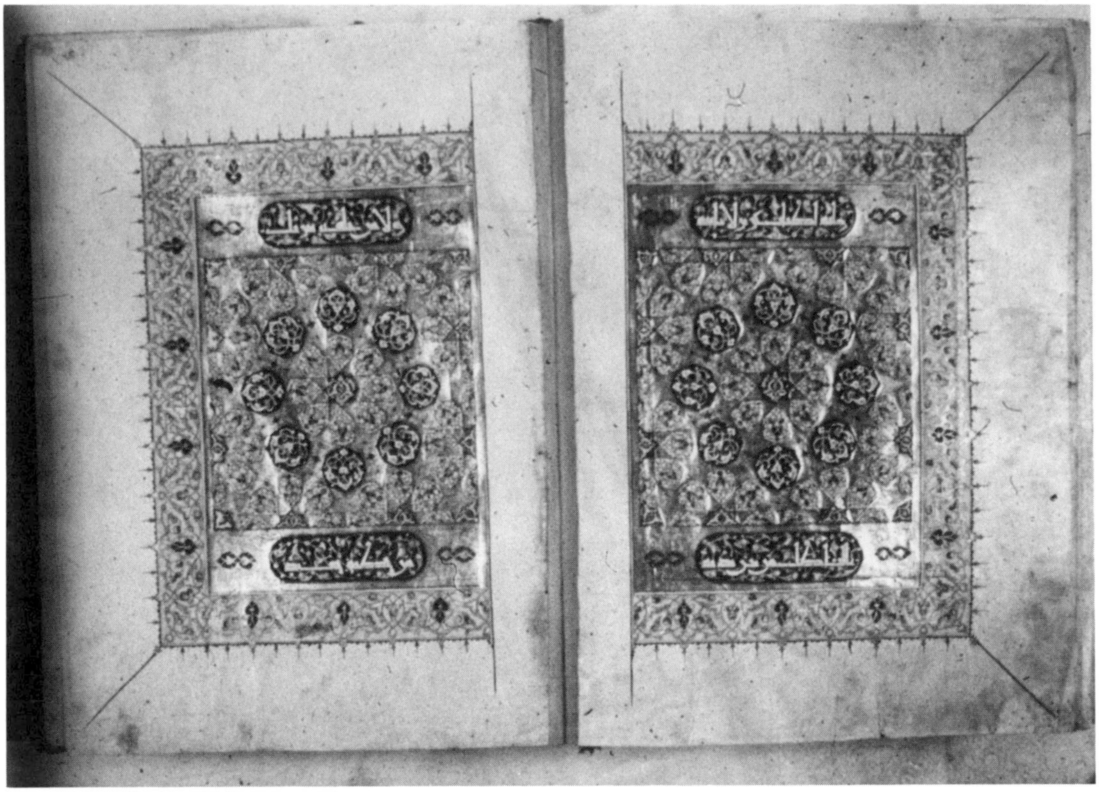

Double finispiece of Koran. Copied by Aḥmad al-Anṣārī al-Matatabbib, 1334. CAIRO, NATIONAL LIBRARY, 81, fols. 377b–378a

headings and full-page illuminations is thought to derive from the shape of a Roman inscription panel or writing tablet, and the style of the palmette from Sasanian or possibly Coptic art.

Illumination continued to develop new decorative themes for religious and secular manuscripts after the eleventh century while maintaining the basic forms and functions of earlier periods. In general the palette became more colorful, the units of composition more diversified, and the patterns more intricate. ᶜ*Unwan*s, for instance, typically consist of a central compartment inscribed with a title and flanked by two smaller units filled with arabesques, with a beaded or interlaced border to unify the separate elements. Often another, usually somewhat smaller, band of continuous geometric or floral designs is superimposed on the epigraphic section. Lines of text, especially those at the beginning of a manuscript, are frequently surrounded by cloud-shaped contour panels, and the interlinear spaces enhanced with scrolls and hatching.

The demarcation between written surface and margins is indicated by rulings that range from thin gold and colored lines to several wide bands of polychrome arabesque, often scalloped at the outermost edge. Marginal ornaments, headings, and borders are frequently outlined in spiky blue finials resembling a fleur-de-lis, further to enrich and unify the illuminated surface. The opening folio of a manuscript may be adorned with a large medallion containing the title of the text and the name of its author or the dedication to a patron. These motifs generally resemble a large spotlight or radiant sunburst (hence their name, *shamsa,* from the Arabic word for "sun"), although the actual shape may vary from a circular rosette to a twelve-pointed star. Other parts of a book, such as subheadings, colophons, and margins, are often enhanced with various types of decoration.

Illuminated manuscripts of considerable beauty were produced in many areas of the Islamic world from Spain to India, but the art as a whole may be said to have attained its technical and artistic apogee in Egypt and Syria during the Mamluk period (1250–1517). Perhaps the most spectacular sections of Mamluk manuscripts, and particularly of Korans

MS ILLUMINATION, ISLAMIC

and other works illuminated under court patronage, are the double-page frontispieces and finispieces that flash with gold, bright blue, and shades of other primary colors. The layout of these folios customarily consists of a vertical field divided into a large central unit and two narrower upper and lower panels, and surrounded by a continuous arabesque border and a blue finial outline. The pattern of the large central composition is invariably geometrical and may have a core, such as an eight-pointed star, from which radiate a series of polygons forming concentric rings, or may be based on the repetition of identical scalloped units to produce an infinitely expanding plane.

The overall effect of these works is undeniably striking, yet it is achieved less by the individual motifs than by the abstraction, symmetry, and harmony of the entire ensemble—design principles that persist throughout the centuries of Islamic manuscript illumination and give this art form its importance as a kind of "mother art" from which evolved the decorative programs of works in many other media.

Prior to the eleventh century, literary and material evidence for the decoration of secular texts with pictorial imagery is scant. (Muslim theological constraints would preclude the Koran and other religious books from being embellished with pictures.) That the history of representational illustration probably began in approximately the same period as that of abstract illumination is signified by the survival of a fragmentary folio from a love story, with a drawing of two tombs separated by a brightly colored fruit tree, datable on paleographic grounds to the late ninth or early tenth century. This work suggests that early Islamic illustrations were placed between lines of writing without any special background or frame, and that the images had a direct and close relationship to the surrounding text.

Such a straightforward and literal approach to pictorial representation also prevails in the earliest extant illustrated codex, a copy of al-Ṣūfī's *Kitāb ṣuwar al-kawākib al-thābita* (Treatise on the constellations of the fixed stars), dated 1009–1010. This work contains pictures of the constellations first represented in Ptolemy's *Almagest* (al-Ṣūfī's textual model), but with significant changes in nomenclature, iconography, and form. Instead of nearly nude mythological characters rendered in a three-dimensional, illusionistic manner, the stars are personified as fully clad figures with flat, linear contours. Their features are more oriental than classical, and their attributes include such Near Eastern devices as the scimitar and the turban. Several of the animal constellations have been similarly modified: Canis, for instance, looks like a Saluki hunting dog. Although the 1009–1010 al-Ṣūfī volume is an isolated example of early manuscript illustration, it typifies the common Islamic practice of recasting older themes and forms—particularly those derived from late antique painting traditions—into new artistic modes through the integration of Near Eastern subjects and motifs.

The process of artistic transfer and transformation remained in effect during the late twelfth and early thirteenth centuries, when the lands of the Fertile Crescent experienced an unprecedented burgeoning of representational imagery. This explosion seems to have been produced by the confluence of many cultural forces, among them the urbanization of medieval Muslim society, the growth of a prosperous middle class, and the increasingly active involvement in the arts of the urban educated, professional, and merchant classes. Copies of many different Arab literary and scientific works, ranging from animal fables to pharmaceutical manuals, began to boast extensive series of illustrations, including full-page frontispieces, that both explained and enlivened the text.

The basic sources for the themes and styles of Arab painting in this period can be traced directly to the Mediterranean Christian world, especially Byzantium, and secondarily to Sasanian Iran. However, the context of these inherited elements was radically altered as Arab artists responded to a new and distinctly original desire for representations of the settings, personages, and activities of the contemporary Islamic world. This predilection affected even the illustrations of scientific texts such as the *Kitāb al-ḥashāʾish fī hayūlāʾ al-ṭibb*, the Arabic version of Dioscorides' *De materia medica*, for which pictorial cycles had been well established in late antique art.

The expansion of compositions well beyond the dictates of the text through the injection of realistic and genre details occurs most notably in several volumes of the *Maqāmāt* (Assemblies) of al-Ḥarīrī, illustrated in Baghdad in the third and fourth decades of the thirteenth century. The ostensible subject of this renowned book is the peripatetic life of an old rogue named Abū Zayd; its actual purpose is to display the hero's (and thus the author's) virtuoso command of the Arabic language through a steady stream of rhetorical artifices and verbal conceits. Such a work, consisting as it does almost entirely of speeches with relatively little action, does not really require pictures or even lend itself very readily to

MS ILLUMINATION, ISLAMIC

Al-Ḥaris discoursing in a library. Miniature by al-Wāsiṭī from the *Maqāmāt* of al-Ḥarīrī, 1237. PARIS, BIBLIOTHÈQUE NATIONALE, MS ARABE 5,847, fol. 56

them. It is almost despite the *Maqāmāt*'s content that its illustrations portray the physical and human environment in which Abū Zayd's monologues were delivered and appreciated: the urban milieu of palaces, mosques, schools, houses, markets, taverns, and cemeteries populated by princes, governors, merchants, slaves, laborers, qadis, women, and children, all engaged in the complete spectrum of human activities from birth to death.

The illustrations in certain *Maqāmāt* volumes, most notably one by the scribe and artist Yahyā ibn Mahmūd al-Wāsitī, are often large and complex, sometimes even spreading across two facing pages to form double compositions, with several actions taking place simultaneously on multiple groundlines. The occupants of these dynamic pictures are invariably lively, occasionally even caricatured, figures who gesture broadly and display a wide range of emotions. The illustrated *Maqāmāt*s would seem to result from the prevalent taste for images of all sorts, manifest in various artistic media during the medieval Islamic period, that may be characterized as a kind of "art for art's sake" attitude. Be that as it may, these manuscripts may be credited with setting a standard for the illustration of Arabic literature of all types and for the representation of convincing three-dimensional, anecdotal scenes on the two-dimensional surface of a manuscript page.

This phase of Islamic manuscript illustration did not last long, however, as patronage of Arab art and literature soon shifted from the urban educated, professional, and merchant classes of Mesopotamia to the Mamluk courts of Egypt and Syria. The Mamluks apparently did not share the notion of book painting as a mirror of the visible world, preferring more static illustrations with minimal settings and immobile personages. These features, plus the abundance of strong primary colors and bright gold, and the repetition of stylized drapery patterns and overall geometric designs, suggest an interest in decorative and monumental effects, already observed in Mamluk illumination, rather than in lifelike vignettes.

Although one Persian poem with a unique series of illustrations, the *Varga va Gulshāh* of ᶜAyyūqi, has survived to give witness to the existence of book painting in the eastern realms of the Islamic world during the early thirteenth century, the actual development of this tradition can be documented only from the end of that century. Its uncertain origins notwithstanding, the art of the illustrated manuscript in Muslim Asia had an extraordinary history of innovation and experimentation occurring over a period of several hundred years and in numerous centers of production and patronage. A common thread uniting the many different, often coexisting, styles of book painting that emerged in Iran and neighboring territories was the preference for narrative literature, particularly poems and histories, as primary vehicles for illustration, and the formulation of rich pictorial cycles to convey the narrative events and to express the underlying literary themes.

Initial impetus for this important development in Islamic manuscript illustration came from the Mongol dynasty of the Ilkhanids (1256–1353). Most of the painted codices of this period are volumes of historical and epic texts written expressly for or revived by the Mongols. Among these the majority are copies of the great national epic, the *Shāhnāma* (Book of kings), which was to become the most popular text for illustration in the history of Iranian book painting. A celebrated example of the early epic genre, the so-called Demotte *Shāhnāma,* attributable to the Ilkhanid capital of Tabriz around 1330–1340, contains images that could be more accurately described as independent paintings rather than as text illustrations because of their varied formats (always framed between lines of text but often staggered at

MS ILLUMINATION, ISLAMIC

Prince Humay at the gates of Humayun's castle. Miniature by Junayd from the *Dīwān* of Khwāju Kirmāni, 1396. THE BRITISH LIBRARY, LONDON, MS ADD. 18,113, fol. 18b

the top or side), dramatic compositions, diverse physical and psychological treatment of human figures, and sensitive interpretation of the *Shāhnāma* themes.

Toward the end of the fourteenth century, Persian book painting began to undergo a shift in aesthetic sensibilities toward the idyllic style that would thereafter characterize its formal history and constitute its classical mode. This change coincided with the increased popularity of lyrical poems such as the *Khamsa* (Quintet) of Nizāmī and the *Dīwān* (collection of poems) of Khwājū Kirmānī, which inspired serene and romantic images quite different from the monumental and vigorous scenes appropriate to the *Shāhnāma.*

New features introduced into the painting repertoire at this time include high-horizoned landscapes filled with a profusion of flora and fauna, elaborate architectural structures covered with intricate tilework, and idealized personages dressed in princely attire—all rendered in bright colors, subtle brushwork, and delicate line. The overall proportions of the pictures also changed, often filling the entire folio and spilling out into the margins with lines of calligraphy incorporated into the painted surface, a significant revision of previous formulas of Islamic manuscript design and page layout. Such illustrations were not intended to represent the real world; they functioned instead as symbolic ensembles with landscapes, buildings, and figures conceived and arranged to create compositional harmony and to evoke paradisiacal illusions.

The artistic innovations initiated in the post-Mongol era were variously modified and refined by generations of Iranian artists working for numerous dynastic groups, such as the Jalāyirids (1336–1432), Tīmūrids (1370–1506), the Qara Qoyunlu (1380–1468) and Aq Qoyunlu (1378–1508), Shaybānids (1500–1598), and Safawids (1501–1732). Related traditions of book painting were fostered in Ottoman Turkey during the fifteenth through seventeenth centuries, and in Mughal (Mogul) India from the early sixteenth to the mid nineteenth century, each having a penchant for classical Persian literature and Iranian artistic conventions. Indeed, several painters from Safawid Iran helped establish and direct the first royal Mughal (Mogul) atelier, and a large group of their contemporaries are known to have worked at the imperial Ottoman painting studio *(nakkaşhane)* in İstanbul.

Yet each region soon developed its own distinctive style and pictorial themes. The Ottomans favored illustrated histories of all types, including genealogies of the ruling house, general chronicles of the empire, biographies of individual sultans, descriptions of specific military campaigns, and accounts of special festivals. This documentary genre is exemplified by a copy of the *Süleymanname* (Book of Süleyman), illustrated in 1558 with extremely accurate and detailed representations of all the notable ceremonies, battles, officials, and cities during the reign of Süleyman I.

A similar interest in realistic documentation prevailed in Mughal India and generated numerous illustrated copies of historical texts. In addition, Mughal patrons had a passion for nature studies, especially the many species of plants and animals in the subcontinent, and for individual and group portraits, some of which are masterpieces of natural observation and character portrayal. A fascinating variation on the portrait genre is a series of allegorical compositions based on the dreams of Jahangir and depicting the emperor in semidivine guise.

The Islamic traditions of manuscript illumination and illustration continued to flourish well past what is usually considered the medieval era in Western art. Over the centuries these twin arts inevitably lost a certain measure of creativity and quality. Yet they never ceased to be emulated, and even today are regarded as vital manifestations of Muslim visual culture.

BIBLIOGRAPHY

Illumination. Oleg F. Akimushkin and Anatol A. Ivanov, "The Art of Illumination," in Basil Gray, ed., *The Arts of the Book in Central Asia* (1979); Richard Ettinghausen, "Manuscript Illumination," in Arthur U. Pope, ed., *A Survey of Persian Art,* III (1939, 3rd ed. 1977); Martin Lings, *The Quranic Art of Calligraphy and Illumination* (1976), and, with Yasin Hamid Safadi, *The Qur'an* (1976), an exhibition catalog; David S. Rice, *The Unique Ibn al-Bawwāb Manuscript* (1955), 13–18, 29–36.

Illustration. Thomas W. Arnold, *Painting in Islam: A Study of the Place of Pictorial Art in Muslim Culture* (1928, 1965); Esin Atıl, ed., *Turkish Art* (1980), 137–238; K. A. C. Creswell, *A Bibliography of Painting in Islam* (1953); Richard Ettinghausen, *Arab Painting* (1962); Basil Gray, *Persian Painting* (1961, repr. 1977); Ernst Grube, ed., *Muslim Miniature Paintings from the XIII to XIX Century* (1962), an exhibition catalog; Jeremiah P. Losty, *The Art of the Book in India* (1982), an exhibition catalog; V. Minorsky and T. Minorsky, trans., *Calligraphers and Painters: A Treatise by Qādī Aḥmad,* Richard Ettinghausen, ed. (1959); Basil W. Robinson, ed., *Islamic Painting and the Arts of the Book* (1976); Marianna S. Simpson, *Arab and Persian Painting in the Fogg Art Museum* (1980).

MARIANNA S. SIMPSON

[See also **Bawwâb, Ibn al-; Iranian Literature; Islamic Art; Koran; Sasanian Art and Architecture.**]

MANUSCRIPTS, CELTIC LITURGICAL. The gradual suppression of Celtic liturgical practices from the seventh century on probably accounts for the scarcity of surviving Celtic liturgical books and certainly explains their fragmentary condition. All of them come from Irish monastic centers, either insular or continental.

The principal representative types of surviving books are missals (notably the Stowe and Bobbio missals) and sacramentaries (fragments only); antiphonaries (notably the Antiphonary of Bangor); psalters and gospels containing liturgical matter; and quasi-liturgical hymnals and devotional books. These books provide some of the earliest remains of Western liturgy—for the Roman rite in the missals and sacramentaries, and for the Gallican rite in the antiphonaries.

BIBLIOGRAPHY

Klaus Gamber, *Codices liturgici latini antiquiores,* 2nd ed. (1968), I, 130–152.

PATRICK P. O'NEILL

[See also **Celtic Church.**]

MANUSCRIPTS, HEBREW. Jewish books, written in Hebrew characters, were produced during the Middle Ages in many lands, owing to the wide geographical distribution of the Jews. Hebrew handwritten books were copied in Christian Europe, in Muslim Spain, North Africa, the Near and Middle East, and Byzantine Asia Minor and Greece. Although their script differs from those of Latin, Greek, Syrian, Arabic, or Persian manuscripts, their techniques may have been similar. Medieval Hebrew handwritten books reflect both Oriental and Occidental, Christian and Islamic civilizations. In Hebrew manuscripts, Latin, Greek, and Arabic paleography and *Handschriftenkunde* might find a tool for comparative intercultural study.

Our knowledge of Jewish bookmaking is inevitably restricted to late medieval texts because of the scarcity of dated manuscripts from the early Middle Ages. In fact, there is an almost total gap of about eight centuries between the time of the most ancient handwritten Hebrew books discovered—the Dead Sea Scrolls—and the earliest Hebrew codex, written in 894 or 895. Only a few small leather or papyrus fragments written during this period have been discovered.

The conditions under which Hebrew manuscripts were produced during the Middle Ages differ greatly from those for Latin or Greek manuscripts. There were no Hebrew scriptoria of the sort that facilitate research and typology in Latin and Greek paleography. The usual handwritten book was a product of either a private professional scribe or a learned man who copied the book for himself. Most Jews knew how to write, thanks to the communal educational system, and many people copied books for their per-

MSS, HEBREW

sonal use. Although a good many manuscripts were copied by more than one scribe, we have no information about any kind of institutional copying and production of books.

Nevertheless, archaeological study of Hebrew manuscripts reveals a certain striking local conformity as far as technical features are concerned, and a large variety of techniques, each of them employed in specific areas and, sometimes, periods. Codicological elements such as writing materials; composition of quires; means of preserving the order of quires, sheets, and leaves; ruling techniques; devices employed in producing even left margins; and other scribal practices, once classified, prove to be common in the same cultural area. Sometimes it is possible even to trace their emergence and shifts, and to date changes of technique.

Archaeological approach and codicological typology are vital to Hebrew paleography because of the exceptional historical conditions of the Jewish people. The wanderings of individuals and communities impeded the formation of distinct styles of local handwriting, and the frequent migrations of entire populations obscured the identifiable marks of different types of handwriting. At the same time and place we may find several types of script, since immigrant scribes continued to retain their native hand. In Italy, for instance, contemporaneous Hebrew manuscripts are found in Italian, German, and Spanish scripts. Under such conditions the role of script typology is weakened. Every element of the handwritten book becomes significant, for immigrant scribes, while retaining their native script, are found to change their technical practices and to adopt, at once or gradually, some or all of the local techniques.

The vast areas where Hebrew manuscripts were produced have been grouped into several distinct codicological entities. This grouping does not necessarily coincide with the late medieval political divisions, but mainly correlates with Jewish (and sometimes non-Jewish) cultural entities, some of which are rooted in older political structures. The codicological grouping is in full correlation with the grouping of the medieval Hebrew book scripts, thus forming a united paleographical typology. Like Hebrew scripts, Hebrew book techniques, once crystallized, were not transformed by non-Jewish political and cultural shifts.

The Islamic territories, sharing basically the same archetypes of Hebrew scripts, ductus, and writing instruments (made of reed), strongly influenced by the Arabic script and calligraphy, are explicitly divided into two codicological entities, an eastern and a western, employing completely different techniques.

The eastern entity is well known through the survival of manuscripts dated as early as the end of the ninth century and fragments found in the Cairo genizah (archive). All Hebrew manuscripts written throughout the Middle East (Yemen, Egypt, Palestine, Syria, Iraq, eastern Turkey, and Persia and its environs), an area unified under the Abbasid caliphate at the time of the earliest manuscripts, share the same scribal practices until the end of the Middle Ages.

Within this group two subentities are differentiated by some codicological elements (as well as by local scripts): Yemen and Persia and its neighborhood.

The western Hebrew codicological entity within the Islamic civilization, known to us only from later manuscripts, includes not only the Maghrib and Muslim Spain but the whole of Iberia, including regions beyond the Pyrenees. All late medieval Hebrew manuscripts written in the Iberian Peninsula, Provence, and Bas-Langedoc, and in North Africa, share the same technical, scribal, and graphic features, which were retained despite political and cultural transformations.

The Western European Christian territories, where the writing instrument was the quill and the influence of the Latin script was strong, are also divided into two codiocological entities. All manuscripts written in medieval central and northern France and medieval Germany share the same technical and graphic characteristics, and they form a united entity that should have included England. No Hebrew manuscript with an indication of an English place of writing has been traced, but since English Hebrew documents share the same cursive script with Franco-German cursive manuscripts, it is likely that some of the many unlocalized manuscripts of this entity were indeed copied in England. The small number of localized manuscripts within this entity makes it difficult to differentiate between France and Germany, though at this stage of our research it is already clear that in one technique, that of parchment manufacture, they differ, just as they differ slightly in their scripts.

The other Western codicological entity is Italy, where independent scribal practices (as well as scripts) have characterized Hebrew manuscripts from the earliest times. However, some correlation can be noticed between early Franco-German and Italian techniques (as well as scripts), which can easily be explained by the historical affinities between Franco-German and Italian Jewries. Chronologically, this affinity should have been channeled from Italy to Germany, but lack of early dated manuscripts, particularly from Germany and France, prevents this process from being followed exactly. Nevertheless, the techniques of preparing parchment, and of pricking and ruling, are common to early Italian and Franco-German manuscripts up to the middle of the thirteenth century, when Franco-German scribes started to employ very different techniques. On the other hand, the composition of quires differs from the first, though a few Italian manuscripts dating from the end of the thirteenth century share the Franco-German method.

Another independent late medieval group consists of manuscripts written in western Asia Minor, the Greek islands, the Balkans, Crete, and Rhodes, an area that constituted the late Byzantine Empire before its decline. Although dated manuscripts from these areas are rather late, and most of them were copied only during the Ottoman period, their common independent techniques, as well as scripts, show that they are rooted in Byzantine political and cultural structures and they were perhaps influenced by the Greek script and Byzantine book techniques.

BIBLIOGRAPHY

Malachi Beit-Arié, *Hebrew Codicology* (1977, rev. ed. 1981). Colette Sirat and Malachi Beit-Arié, *Manuscrits médiévaux en caractères hébraïques,* I (1972–).

MALACHI BEIT-ARIÉ

[See also **Codex; Codicology; Jews; Paleography; Quire.**]

MANZIKERT. See **Manazkert.**

MAP, WALTER, also known as Mapes (*ca.* 1140–*ca.* 1208), possibly a native of Herefordshire, studied in Paris (*ca.* 1155–1161) before returning to England, where he found favor with Henry II, for whom he worked as clerk and itinerant justice. Among other church offices, he held those of canon and precenter (after 1186, chancellor) of Lincoln, and—in 1197—archdeacon of Oxford.

Map was a well-traveled scholar and court satirist. Though the body of literature attributed to him has shrunk considerably, he is known to have written *De nugis curialium* (Courtiers' trifles) probably between 1180 and 1193, and a few scattered verses, some antifraternal. Evidence of his wit can be found in the works of his friend Gerald of Wales. Among the questionable attributions are Arthurian material, including the prose *Lancelot,* and a body of goliardic verse.

BIBLIOGRAPHY

Walter Map, *De nugis curialium,* Montague R. James, ed. (1914), and Montague R. James, trans. (1923), and *The Latin Poems Commonly Attributed to Walter Mapes,* Thomas Wright, ed. (1841, repr. 1968); Leopold Peeters, "Walter Map's 'De Gradone Milite Strenuissimo,'" in *Amsterdamer Beiträge zur älteren Germanistik,* 1 (1972); Lewis Thorpe, "Walter Map and Gerald of Wales," in *Medium aevum,* 47 (1978).

MARY-JO ARN

[See also **Gerald of Wales.**]

MAPHORION, a long, hooded cloak or tunic without sleeves. It may be related to a Hebrew garment, the *maforet,* which covered the hair and forehead. In Byzantine art it usually refers to that blue or purple garment worn by the Virgin Mary over her long-sleeved dress (chiton). The relic of what was believed to have been the Virgin's *maphorion* was transported to Constantinople during the reign of Emperor Leo I (457–474). He and Empress Verina built a church to house the relic near the Blachernes convent. Subsequently, the church became a pilgrimage site.

BARBARA OEHLSCHLAEGER-GARVEY

[See also **Costume, Byzantine.**]

MAPPA MUNDI, the main type of circular world map in medieval Western Europe. The medieval mappa mundi traces its origins back to Roman world maps, such as the first-century B.C. *orbis terrarum* of M. Vipsanius Agrippa, which were modified to conform with the Christian theology enunciated by Isidore of Seville, Kosmas Indikopleustes,

MAPPA MUNDI

CIRCA 1300

Mappa mundi from Hereford Cathedral, *ca.* 1300. Black ink, gold leaf, red and blue pigments on vellum; 52″ diameter. PHOTO: P. DEAN

and others. Thus, in the popular O-T schema, Jerusalem is placed at the center of a world subdivided into Africa, Asia, and Europe; and East, the direction of the earthly paradise, is installed in the place of honor at the top of the map. A vertical line divides Europe and Africa, intersecting with the horizontal line representing the diameter of the orb and thus forming a ⊥, as represented in the symbol on the spine of this volume.

The mappa mundi, of which over 1,100 examples are recorded prior to the sixteenth century, often includes religious or moralizing vignettes, illustrations of geographical myths and marvels culled from Pliny and bestiaries, as well as representations of contemporary sites. In such later maps as the Catalan map of 1375, a new spirit of critical realism entered medieval cartography, as portolanos (navigational charts) and travelers' accounts of journeys to Asia were employed to achieve greater accuracy.

BIBLIOGRAPHY

Gerald R. Crone, *The World Map by Richard of Haldingham in Hereford Cathedral, Circa A. D. 1285* (1954), "New Light on the Hereford Map," in *The Geographical Journal,* **131** (1965), and *Maps and Their Makers,* 5th ed. (1978); Marcel Destombes, ed., *Monumenta cartographica* *vetustioris aevi,* 1 (1964), 3–23; Georges Grosjean, *Mappamundi: Der katalanische Weltatlas vom Jahre 1375* (1977); Konrad Miller, *Mappaemundi: Die ältesten Weltkarten,* 6 vols. (1895–1898).

MICHAEL T. DAVIS

[See also **Geography and Cartography, Western European; Isidore of Seville, St.; Navigation.**]

MAQĀM, an Arabic musical term for "mode." Its origins and early meanings are obscure. Within the broad concept of mode, it is similar to the terms *jam*ᶜ, *jamā*ᶜ*a, shadd, dawr, āwāzāt, naghma,* and *laḥn.*

The first extant account of melodic modes that describes the periods of the orthodox caliphs (632–661) and the Umayyads (661–750) is Ibn al-Munajjim's (*d.* 912) *Risāla fī al-mūsīqī* (Treatise on music). Eight diatonic modes are discussed using a Pythagorean lute fretting of tones (204 cents), limmas (90 cents), and apotomes (114 cents). The modes are named after the *iṣba*ᶜ (finger that gives the tonic) and the *majrā* (course of notes, which determines the use of either a middle finger [minor] fret of 294 cents or ring finger [major] fret of 408 cents). In theory the major and minor frets were mutually exclusive. Transposing the modes to the key of C one gets seven species of octaves: cc′, dd′, ee′, ff′, gg′, aa′, bb′. The eighth mode is conjectural.

The tone system was greatly enlarged in the Abbasid era (750–1258). The lute of al-Fārābī (*d.* 950) extends to two octaves and adds three new frets between the middle finger and ring finger frets: a Persian middle finger fret of 302 cents, a middle finger fret of 354 cents introduced by the lutanist Zalzal (*d.* 791), and a variant of the Zalzal fret of 318 cents. (The approximate three-quarter tone that characterizes Arabic music was introduced about this time.) Furthermore al-Fārābī describes five frets anterior to the index finger frets with the values of 90, 98, 114, 145, and 168 cents, but adds that they are used not in the theoretical structure of a mode, but as ornamental notes in a performance or composition. Modes are given no names, and they use, in theory, either a ring finger fret or one of the four middle finger frets. There are seven octave species associated with each of the above-mentioned five frets. Finally, a mode may have a range of as little as a tetrachord plus a whole tone or as large as a double octave. In the latter case the two octaves may have identical notes or different notes.

Only minor changes to the tone system and modes occurred after al-Fārābī until Ṣafiyy al-Dīn al-Urmawī (*d.* 1294) revolutionized the whole theory. Taking as point of departure the fretting of al-Fārābī's *al-ṭunbūr al-khurasānī* (a long-necked lute)—limma (90 cents), limma, comma (24 cents)—Ṣafiyy al-Dīn integrated the Zalzal fret (318 and 354 cents) into the Pythagorean system and set it at 384 cents. He divided the whole tone into limma, limma, comma; the tetrachord into a combination of two whole tones and a limma; the octave scale into two tetrachords plus a whole tone. His modal system consisted of twelve primary modes *(shudūd),* six secondary modes *(āwāzāt),* and compound modes *(murakkabāt).* A mode had the concept of intervalic structure, melodic patterns associated with specific modes, and the concept of the importance of initial and final notes. Later medieval theorists followed Ṣafiyy al-Dīn's system with minor modifications.

BIBLIOGRAPHY

For the various and debatable meanings and origins of the term *maqām,* see Lois Ibsen al Faruqi, *An Annotated Glossary of Arabic Musical Terms* (1981), 169–170. For the tone system of Ibn al-Munajjim and the problematic transcription of modes, see Owen Wright, "Ibn al-Munajjim and the Early Arabian Modes," in *Galpin Society Journal,* 19 (1966); George Dimitri Sawa, "Music Performance Practice in the Early ᶜAbbasid Era" (diss., Toronto, 1983), 84–89. For an analysis of al-Fārābī's empirical tone system see Sawa, *op. cit.,* 90–106. A detailed analysis of Ṣafiyy al-Dīn's system is in Owen Wright, *The Modal System of Arab and Persian Music: A.D. 1250–1300* (1978). For an overview of the tone system and modal theory in medieval Arabic writings see Liberty Manik, *Das arabische Tonsystem im Mittelalter* (1969); and Amnon Shiloah, "The Arabic Concept of Mode," in *Journal of the American Musicological Society,* 34 (1981).

GEORGE DIMITRI SAWA

[See also **Fārābi, al-; Music, Islamic; Music, Middle Eastern; Musical Instruments, Middle Eastern.**]

MAQDISĪ, AL-. See **Muqaddasī, Muḥammad al-.**

MARBOD OF RENNES (Marbodus Redonensis, Marbodus Andecavensis) (*ca.,* 1035–1123), French writer, teacher, and churchman. Born of a good family in Angers, he attended the local school, after

MARBOD OF RENNES

which he became *cancellarius* (chancellor) of the city in 1069 and the successor to his own teacher Rainald as director of the cathedral school. He devoted himself to teaching and had several famous pupils, among them Geoffrey of Vendôme (*ca.* 1070–1132) and Rainald de Martigné. He also corresponded with several leading literary figures of his day, of whom the most interesting was the poet Baudri de Bourgueil (1046–1130). Marbod became successively archdeacon of Angers and bishop of Rennes, against his will, according to Bishop Ulgerius (1125–1148), who wrote his epitaph. He had several quarrels over doctrine, particularly with Robert d'Arbrissel and Rainald de Martigné. He was eighty-eight when he died, perhaps in the Benedictine convent at Angers.

Marbod was a prolific writer, but little of his prose survives—six official letters and some saints' lives. The latter are all lives of local figures: Licinius, bishop of Angers; Abbot Walter; Robert de la Chaise-Dieu; and Magnobod, bishop of Angers. His verse is much more extensive and varied in subject. The more commonplace of his works are those that offer no more than a versified form of Bible stories: Ruth in 220 lines and Jonah in 154 lines, for example. Not very different are the poems describing the sufferings of saints: *Passio sancti Laurentii* (235 rhymed hexameters); *Passio sancti Victoris Andegavensis* (482 rhyming hexameters); *Passio sanctae Thaisidis* (159 rhyming hexameters), the story of a famous prostitute, Thaïs, converted by the hermit Paphnutius, who, abjuring her life of luxury, obtains absolution through bitter penance (a story dramatized by Hrotswitha von Gandersheim, *d. ca.* 1001–1003); and *Passio sanctorum martyrum Felicis et Adaucti* (136 rhyming pairs), the story of Felix' proof of his power over pagan gods and of Adauctus' voluntary association with him in martyrdom. The *Vita beati Maurilii episcopi* is merely a versification of the deeds of a local bishop. The most powerful of these poems is the *Passio sancti Mauritii et sociorum eius* (219 rhyming hexameters), which tells the famous story of the Theban legion, martyred under Maximian, of Mauritius, who led and encouraged them, and of Victor, who voluntarily died with them.

Most of Marbod's poetry is in one way or another didactic, and enjoyed a great reputation. This is particularly true of the *Liber lapidum,* probably written about 1090. This work is preceded by a preface of 23 lines in which the author tells how he had used extracts from a book by a king of the Arabs, Evax, on the medical qualities of precious stones, knowledge that he believes should be confined to a few. The poem is in 734 hexameters and tells of sixty kinds of stones. The information is derived mainly from Isidore and Solinus, but the magical properties of the stones are ascribed to Evrax—even though the true source is apparently the same as that of Damigeron, *De lapidibus,* a work of late classical antiquity so popular that there are more than 160 manuscripts of the work and several translations into vernaculars. The *De ornamentis verborum* is a similar work. In 127 hexameters it takes verbal figures from popular rhetorical treatises, mainly the *Ad Herennium,* and illustrates each in three- to five-line pieces. The work was designed for Marbod's students, to one of whom it is dedicated. (Useful though the work was, they may have derived more pleasure from his fable of the wolf as monk.) Marbod's hymns, many written in rhyming stressed verse, show complete mastery of the imagery of the Christian hymn and of the antithesis and *annominatio* that are among its principal characteristics.

Marbod's greatest serious work, written at the age of sixty-seven, is the *Liber decem capitulorum.* The first of the ten chapters *(De apto genere dicendi)* deals with the proper way to approach writing (it must not be frivolous). The second *(De tempore et aevo)* is on the passage of human life and contrasts its sorrows and ephemeral nature with the joys of eternity. Two chapters on women follow. *De meretrice* (On the prostitute) is a long compendium of standard medieval antifeminine complaint, with the usual examples of evil women both real and imaginary (Chimaera, Charybdis), while *De matrona* cites such examples of feminine virtue as Lucretia and Alcestis from classical antiquity and figures from the Bible, urging that their virtues be valued as highly as those of men. These works are really compilations of *loci communes* on the topic. The fifth chapter, *De senectute* (On old age), puts forward the standard classical treatment of the topic as illustrated by Cicero's dialogue of the same name: old age has at least as many advantages as it has miseries. The sixth chapter, *De fato et genesi,* is really about astrology and superstition while the seventh, *De voluptate,* is an attack on Epicureanism as Marbod (wrongly) understood it. He sees only ill as the result of pleasure and praises moderation (as Epicurus did). In the eighth chapter, *De vera amicitia,* Marbod again turns to Cicero both for his subject and, to a large degree, for his treatment of friendship. He stresses the careful choice of friends more than does Cicero and places less stress on the mutual recognition of virtue as the true source of friendship. The ninth chapter, *De bono mortis,* emphasizes the inevitability of death and the folly of fearing it, thus leading naturally to the tenth, *De resurrectione corporum.* In it Marbod points out the great advantage Christians have over the pagans, whose works he has largely used up to now, since Christ has told Christians that they will rise again. Marbod describes the final resurrection vividly and animatedly.

These works show great technical skill, but we have left until last those that probably became most significant for later generations. Marbod wrote verse epistles to several noble ladies of his day, to Ermengarde, wife of Alanus Fergent, duke of Britanny, and to Matilde, queen of England. Here he employs all the resources of conventional panegyric to praise their qualities and particularly their beauty, but he indicates how ephemeral that beauty is. There can be little doubt that these poems deeply influenced the style in which later "praise of ladies" poems were written, both in Latin and in the vernaculars. Although its attribution to Marbod is disputed, the other work that had a significant influence on the future is *Historia Theophili* in 559 rhyming hexameters. This story of Theophilus, a disappointed cleric who sells his soul to the devil to take over a bishopric and then prays successfully to the Virgin to rescue him, became the subject of many medieval dramas in French and German and anticipates the Faust story.

Marbod, like Hildebert of Lavardin (*d.* 1133) and Baudri de Bourgueil, represents the peak achievement of medieval Latin poetry dependent on classical models and points the way to the great twelfth-century writers of rhythmic verse.

BIBLIOGRAPHY

Sources. The texts are in *Patrologia latina,* CLXXI (1854), 1457–1782. Selected hymns are in Guido Maria Dreves, ed., *Analecta hymnica medii aevi,* L (1907, repr. 1961), 388–403.

Studies. The best account of Marbod's life and work is in Max Manitius, *Geschichte der lateinischen Literatur des Mittelalters,* III (1931), 719–730. See also Frederic J. E. Raby, *A History of Christian Latin Poetry,* 2nd ed. (1953, repr. 1966), 273–277, and *A History of Secular Latin Poetry in the Middle Ages,* 2nd ed. (1957), 329–337; Léopold C. A. Pannier, *Les lapidaires français du moyen âge* (1882).

W. T. H. JACKSON

[See also **Baudri of Bourgueil; Hildebert of Lavardin; Hrotswitha von Gandersheim; Hymns, Latin; Latin Literature; Robert d'Arbrissel.**]

MARC, a unit of weight in France consisting of 8 onces or 64 gros or 160 estelins or 192 deniers or 320 mailles or 640 félins or 4,608 grains (244.753 grams) and equal to one-half livre poids de marc. This marc was used principally at Paris, whereas at Tours, Montpellier, Limoges, and Troyes it was 237.87 grams, 239.12 grams, 240.93 grams, and 260.05 grams, respectively. For gold transactions a marc was 24 carats of 32 grains each or 768 grains in all; for silver it was 12 deniers of 24 grains each or 288 grains in all. Etymologically it derived from Frankish *marka,* from Middle High German *mark, marke,* designating a half-pound of gold and silver.

RONALD EDWARD ZUPKO

[See also **Mints and Money, Western European; Weights and Measures, Western European.**]

MARCABRU (*fl.* 1128–1150), troubadour, poet, and composer. He was born in Gascony around 1100, and his known works were written between about 1128 and 1150. According to his *vidas,* which are of doubtful accuracy, he was also known as Marcabrun or Panperdut and as a child was a foundling in the care of the nobleman Aldric de Vilar. In his poem *Dirai vos senes doptansa* he calls himself the son of a lady named Bruna. In any case, the legend of low birth has adhered to his biography, and he represents, along with his contemporary Cercamon, an early phase of troubadour activity in which the poet was often a professional entertainer in the employ of a court establishment.

Some details about the life of Marcabru can be extracted from the texts of his own songs. He seems to have been resident at the court of William X of Aquitaine from 1128 until his patron's death on pilgrimage in 1137, an event mentioned in the well-known crusading song *Pax in nomine Domini.* The same song describes Marcabru as the author of both text and music: "Fetz Marcabrus los motz e.l son." He apparently sought employment in Portugal and Spain, finding a post in 1138 with Alfonso VII of Castile, self-proclaimed emperor of Spain, for whom he wrote the crusading song *Emperaire, per mi mezeis,* as well as the complaint *Emperaire, per vostre pretz,* in which he draws attention to Alfonso's lack of generosity. Marcabru returned to France in 1144 and around 1147 wrote *Cortezamen voill comensar* for the troubadour Jaufré Rudel.

Of the forty-three songs attributed to Marcabru, only four have extant music. His texts include the forms of pastourelle, sirventes, and canso; his subject matter is diverse. Marcabru was a master of *trobar clus,* the art of writing poetry whose meaning is reserved for those who comprehend the complexity of the poet's language; rare and obscure words are chosen, and certain key images may appear in several songs.

BIBLIOGRAPHY

Prosper M. Boissonade, "Les personnages et les évenements de l'histoire d'Allemagne, de France et d'Espagne dans l'oeuvre de Marcabru," in *Romania,* **48** (1922), 207–242; Marcabru, *Poésies complètes du troubadour Marcabru,* Jean-Marie Dejeanne, ed. and trans. (1909); Hans Spanke, *Untersuchungen über die Ursprünge des romanischen minnesange,* pt. 2 (1940).

MARCIA J. EPSTEIN

[See also **Cercamon; Courtly Love; Crusade Propaganda; Jaufré Rudel; Pastourelle; Sirventes; Troubadour, Trouvère, Trovador.**]

MARCADÉ, EUSTACHE. See **Mercadé, Eustache.**

MARCH, AUSIÀS (1397–1459), Valencian poet who wrote entirely in Catalan. A member of the minor nobility, he served under Alfonso V of Aragon and participated in a number of his military campaigns. One hundred twenty-eight of his poems survive, about 10,000 verses, on the themes of love and morality. Unlike most other poets of his time, he wrote about love in terms of its dual psychophysical nature—sensualility versus idealism—caused by his own conflicting spiritual pains. His work often has an abstract and analytic character, but at other times it takes on a licentious tone and expresses existential anguish with dark images and bold metaphors. His most important work is *Cant espiritual* (Spiritual song), a powerful confession of the religious problems that tormented him. Ausiàs March is the first poet who wrote poetry in Catalan without mixing in Provençal.

BIBLIOGRAPHY

Editions and translations include Ausiàs March, *Les obres d'Auzias March,* Amédée Pagès, ed., 2 vols. (1912–1914), *Poesies,* Pere Bohigas, ed., 5 vols. (1952–1959), *Selected Poems,* Arthur Terry, ed. and trans. (1976), *Obra poética: Selección y traducción,* Pere Gimferrer, ed. and trans. (1978), *Les poesies d'Ausiàs March,* Joan Ferraté, ed. (1979). See also Kathleen McNerney, *The Influence of Ausiàs March on Early Gold Age Castilian Poetry* (1982); Joan Fuster Ortells, *Ausiàs March* (1982).

PERE BOHIGAS

[See also **Aragon, Crown of; Catalan Literature.**]

MARCHETTUS OF PADUA (*fl.* 1305–1326), music theorist and composer. His reputation as the foremost Italian theorist of the fourteenth century is attested to by the mention of his name in the texts of several contemporary musical works of Italian and French origin, as well as by citations in treatises of his own and successive generations.

Information regarding Marchettus' life is minimal. He was most likely a native of Padua. The year 1274 has been suggested as a possible birthdate. Documentary evidence suggests that Marchettus was employed as *maestro di canto* at the Cathedral of Padua from 1305 through 1307. He apparently left Padua in 1308. The information that Marchettus was a practicing composer is revealed by an acrostic, reading "Marcum paduanum," contained in a motet text preserved in an early-fourteenth-century Paduan musical manuscript. A second acrostic contained in another voice part of the same work indicates that Marchettus may have composed the motet for the Feast of the Annunciation in 1305. Other biographical data are provided in the dedicatory proemia of Marchettus' theoretical works. His treatise on plainchant, entitled *Lucidarium,* was commissioned by Raynerius de Zaccaria de Urbeveteri, described as representative in Romagna for King Robert of Naples, who, as vicar of the pope, exercised power through his brother Giovanni, count of Gravina. The *Lucidarium* was completed within the years of Raynerius' tenure in Romagna, 1317–1318. A companion treatise on mensural music, the *Pomerium,* was composed in the household of Raynaldus de Cintiis, lord of Cesena from 1321 to 1326. No chronological information is provided in Marchettus' third treatise, the *Brevis compilacio.*

Marchettus is remembered primarily for his systematic presentation of the rules of *musica plana* and *musica mensurabilis* set forth in the *Lucidarium* and *Pomerium.* Although intended as practical, didactic works, the two treatises received a veneer of learned philosophy through the collaborative effort of a Brother Syphans, a Dominican friar of Ferrara. The *Lucidarium* is characterized by a traditional approach to the teaching of the system of the eight church modes. Marchettus' discussion of musical intervals is more innovative. The central feature of his theory was the division of the whole tone into five equal parts, or *dieses* (sing.: *diesis*). The rationale for the system was to enable the "fine-tuning" of vertical consonances in two-voice contrapuntal progressions. Two *dieses* (two-fifths of a tone) produced an enharmonic semitone, three *dieses* produced the diatonic semitone, and four *dieses* constituted the chromatic semitone. Marchettus' theory departed from the traditional Pythagorean division of the tone into two unequal parts (a major and minor semitone). He complemented his description of tonal division with a set of notational symbols that distinguished the various semitone types in written music. Examples of Marchettus' semitone notation survive in a few early-fourteenth-century Paduan musical sources. The notoriety of the *Lucidarium* extended well into the fifteenth century. The *Tractatus musice speculative,* composed by Prosdocimus de Beldemandis in 1425, contains an argument against Marchettus' theory of the five *dieses.*

The *Pomerium,* dedicated to King Robert of Sicily, is the most complete extant source of early-fourteenth-century Italian notational theory. Marchettus describes the hierarchical divisions of perfect and imperfect musical time, basing his concept of *tempus* on Franco of Cologne's definition of the term as "a minimum in fullness of voice." The perfect *tempus,* represented by the notational symbol of the breve, could be subdivided at the first, second, or third levels of division, which yielded three major semibreves, six or nine minor semibreves, or twelve minimal semibreves (minims), respectively. The divisions of the imperfect breve yielded two, four, six, or eight semibreves. Of particular interest to fourteenth-century musical theorists was the relationship between contemporary French and Italian systems of notation. Marchettus and his followers pointed to the divisions of the perfect breve into nine parts and the imperfect breve into six parts as primarily "French" in conception. In those cases, the Italian *divisiones novenaria* and *senaria* corresponded to the French ars nova mensurations of perfect and imperfect *tempus* and major prolation. According to Marchettus, music utilizing the French manner of division should be identified as such by placing the letter *g (gallica)* above the staff, while the Italian manner of division was to be indicated by the letter *y (ytalica).* Examples of these symbols are found in several compositions included in the northern Italian manuscript Rome, Vatican Library, Rossi 215. The extent to which Marchettus may have drawn upon the theoretical formulations of French ars nova notation made by Philippe de Vitry and Jehan des Murs in the early 1320's remains a matter for speculation. One manuscript source of the *Pomerium* refers to the French practice of red notation, an innovation generally ascribed to Vitry. However, elements of Marchettus' system that are without analogies in French notation (specifically, the divisions of the tempus into twelve or eight [minimal] semibreves) suggest an independent line of development.

Marchettus' last known treatise, the *Brevis compilacio,* is little more than a summary of the substance of the *Pomerium,* omitting the philosophical rationalizations that characterized the original work. The *Brevis compilacio* was, according to Marchettus, intended for beginners interested in absorbing the rudiments of the notational system. A fourth treatise, the *Rubrice breves,* is incorrectly ascribed to Marchettus in its manuscript source. Its contents reflect a considerably later stage in the development of Italian mensural notation than that described by Marchettus.

BIBLIOGRAPHY

F. Alberto Gallo, "Marchetus in Padua und die 'franco-venetische' Musik des frühen Trecento," in *Archiv für Musikwissenschaft,* **31** (1974); Marchettus of Padua, *Pomerium,* in Giuseppe Vecchi, ed., *Corpus scriptorum de musica,* VI (1961), and an imperfect edition of *Lucidarium,* in Martin Gerbert, *Scriptores ecclesiastici de musica sacra potissimum,* 3 vols. (1784); Nino Pirrotta, "Marchettus de Padua and the Italian Ars Nova," in *Musica disciplina,* **9** (1955).

MICHAEL P. LONG

[See also **Ars Nova; Franco of Cologne; Jehan des Murs; Musical Notation; Musical Treatises; Philippe de Vitry.**]

MARCO POLO. See **Polo, Marco.**

MÄREN

GENRE AND CANON

The German noun *das Märe* (pl., *die Mären*) is the generally accepted term for short, poetic narratives on fictional subjects written in German between roughly 1200 and 1500. The subjects are secular rather than religious, and the form is rhymed, octosyllabic couplets. The tales vary in length from about 150 to 2,000 lines; they are transmitted independently rather than forming part of a narrative cycle or collection; the personnel of the tales is entirely or predominantly human; and the action takes place within the real world. These formal and thematic criteria distinguish the *Märe* from drama, epic and romance, legend and miracle, historical poetry, strophic ballad, anecdote, monologue and dialogue, the tale forming part of a collection, the fable, and the supernatural story. Depending on one's judgment of marginal cases, some 200 to 250 *Mären* have survived to the present.

This definition of *Märe* is based on the seminal work of Hanns Fischer in the 1960's. Before that, several terms had been used to designate the short narrative of medieval Germany *(Novelle, Versnovelle, Erzählung, Schwank, Märe)*, but the body of literature in question was not defined with any precision. The editors of major collections, von der Hagen and Niewöhner, proceeded without systematic discussion of their principles of inclusion. Von der Hagen included legends and miracles as well as secular stories, while Niewöhner ruled out poetic exempla and *Mären* that, he believed, had their proper place in collective editions of their authors. Fischer's encyclopedia article, his edition of fifteenth-century *Mären* (a corpus virtually ignored by earlier editors), and his monograph provide a firm scholarly foundation for study of the *Märe.* The influence of his work on the introductory volume by Köpf is one measure of its importance.

Fischer's definition of the *Märe* and his canon have been questioned on several points. As Fischer expected, certain texts excluded by him have been championed by others, such as Schirmer and Schröder, and the independent character of differing versions of a story has been discussed. The most serious challenge to Fischer comes from Heinzle, who rejects his definition of the *Märe* because it purports to define a literary genre that was not understood to be such in the Middle Ages. The criteria established by Fischer are judged by Heinzle as too general and abstract to define a genre; Fischer's reliance on a principle of quantity to exclude very short tales is criticized as arbitrary; and Heinzle rejects Fischer's distinction between the exemplum *(bîspel)* and the *Märe,* on the grounds that all medieval comic literature was, in theory, didactic. Of these objections the most important is that of quantity, for Fischer is uncharacteristically subjective in deciding that stories of less than ninety to one hundred lines are "narratively too 'thin' to be *Mären.*" Scholars have reached no agreement on a typology of the *bîspel* or on the didactic force of comic literature in the Middle Ages. While Heinzle finds many questions for discussion in Fischer's concept of genre, it is unlikely that this concept will soon be replaced by one more consistent with medieval understanding and more helpful for modern study.

In this article the titles of *Mären* are those given by Fischer. Readers should consult his bibliography for editions of individual works and his useful plot summaries for a sense of the genre's content.

TYPES OF THE *MÄRE*

Fischer's criteria for the *Märe* admit both serious and amusing tales. Two main groups of the former are evident: those treating chivalric love and adventure and those explicitly propagating a moral lesson. Comic stories may be classified by the kind of events producing humor—including marital deceit, erotic naïveté, trickery, verbal wit, confusions, and misunderstandings. About four-fifths of the texts are comic, with chivalric stories far more numerous than didactic ones in the remainder. Although among the *Mären* pure examples of each type may be found, there are hybrids of many varieties, which show that medieval authors followed no strict norms in devising their stories: chivalric settings are combined with crudely sexual motifs (*Die halbe Birne, Die Nachtigall, Der Gürtel*), serious moral lessons are claimed for broad tales (*Der Wirt, Die Wolfsgrube*).

The comic stories have sometimes been called "realistic," and it is true that they are set in the world of familiar experience. Particularly by comparison with medieval romance, where the settings are often fanciful and the events fantastic, the *Mären* depict concrete events in daily contexts. The characters fight, lie, work, and copulate; they eat, drink, and eliminate. They wear trousers, ride donkeys, and use bathtubs, blankets, distaffs, money, and barrels. One gains a first impression of the enormous wealth and diversity of life, yet upon reflection one realizes that the plots and characters of *Mären* are strongly typified and that typification is a form of abstraction leading away from the particularity of things designated by the term "realism." Vulgar settings and events are no more "real" than lofty ones; that the comic *Märe* favors the former may be explained simply by the suitability of such settings for broad comedy. One sometimes finds realistically descriptive de-

MÄREN

tails, but they are of no consequence to the story line; aside from such passages it is doubtful that *Mären* should be termed "realistic."

In the comic stories, cleverness is the most admired attribute and obtuseness the most ridiculed failing. Though sexual adventures are described in about half the *Mären,* these stories too are focused on quickness of wit and sound understanding. No *Märe* appeals to prurience, though several deal bluntly with the genitals, and it is likely that the numerous adulteries, seductions, and tests of marital authority are basically stories in praise of practical intelligence, the settings and plots having been devised for the sake of suspense, tension, and ludicrousness.

To make these observations more immediate, synopses of five representative *Mären* follow.

Frauentreue. (Preserved in its entirety in four manuscripts and partially in two others, this *Märe* of some 420 lines has been convincingly analyzed by Ruh as a study in the conventions of courtly love.) A knight famed for his chivalry enters a city and asks a burgher who its most beautiful woman may be. The latter advises him to decide for himself at church the next day. He does so, falls in love with the burgher's wife, and lodges near their house. Noting his passion, the woman guards herself closely. The knight undertakes to joust with all comers, clad only in a silk robe; he is wounded, and the tip of the lance remains lodged in his body. Since he refuses to have the point withdrawn by any hand but the woman's, her husband obliges her to perform this service. The convalescing knight enters her bedroom one night and embraces her, against her wishes, so passionately that his wound opens and he bleeds to death. She secretly conveys the knight's body to his lodging, then attends the funeral mass. In the church she removes her outer clothing and places this on the casket as an offering; then, clad only in a robe like that in which he had jousted, she dies at the casket. The two are buried together.

Der Sohn des Bürgers (preserved in a single manuscript, 174 lines long). The spoiled son of a rich man lives a prodigal life. Hoping to improve him, his father gives him a share of his own wealth and arranges a marriage, but the son soon dissipates his property in the company of friends of high station and returns destitute to his father. The latter advises him to turn to his boon companions. He does so, but is rejected. The father then sends him to his own friends, where indeed he is liberally assisted. The father points out the lesson to be learned in the making of friendships, and the author concludes that prodigal persons are fools.

Der Ritter mit den Nüssen (preserved in its entirety in six manuscripts and partially in two others, about 200 lines). Because of a rainstorm a knight returns home earlier than expected, which upsets the rendezvous arranged by his wife with her paramour. She hides him behind the canopy of the bed and, before her husband's eyes, tosses nuts to him and vigorously claims to have secreted a lover. The husband doesn't want to seem gullible and refuses to look behind the canopy. She says she was only joking, but could in fact arrange for a lover to leave the house unnoticed even with her husband present. He asks how she would do this, and she playfully pulls his head under her clothing—whereupon the lover departs.

Der Reiher. (Preserved in two manuscripts, this tale of about 460 lines has been shown by Schirmer to contain elements of sophisticated parody.) A man has trained a tame rooster in the art of falconry and succeeds in hunting a crane in this manner. Delighted with his catch, he has it delicately prepared and goes to invite his lord to share the meal. In his absence, his wife and her friend consume the entire bird, and when he returns she denies all knowledge of it. The lord invites his would-be host to dine with him instead. The wife persuades her friend to take her place in the marital bed that night, with the result that this friend is badly beaten and has her braids cut off by the furious husband. The next morning, when his wife presents herself to him whole and unmarked, he is convinced he has gone crazy and begs her to cure him.

Der Preller. (Preserved in one manuscript and only eighty-eight lines long, it represents the shortest of the *Mären.*) To be sure that prospective husbands for their daughter are physically unblemished, a girl's parents arrange for each to bathe with her. Though many have failed this test, a wealthy and well-born youth passes it but for the girl's dismay at his erect *preller,* which seems disproportionately large. Her mother comforts her with the gift of a small scissors, suggesting she cut the *preller* to proper size. On her wedding night the girl wonders whether to use the scissors at night or in the morning and decides to wait so that she may have better light for her task. Events of the wedding night convince her, however, that the *preller* is well proportioned and that the scissors are not needed.

CHARACTERS AND ROLES

All strata of medieval society are reflected in the *Märe,* and a typification of roles occurs for several social groups. The highest feudal levels are present in such tales as *Konni, Der Striegel,* and *Die halbe Birne.* All are set in royal courts, simply, one feels, for the sake of anomaly. These settings contrast most strongly with the boorish and lewd motifs on which the plots depend. *Heinrich von Kempten* by Konrad von Würzburg purports to be historical truth, yet the value of the tale as entertainment lies partially in the surprisingly crude behavior of the hero when measured against the sophisticated norms of the emperor's court. In *Bürgermeister und Königssohn* by Heinrich Kaufringer the royal identity of the student is functionally unnecessary but serves to throw the prudence and generosity of the bourgeois mayor into sharp relief. By their very nature the *Mären* telling of chivalric love and adventure feature representatives of the high feudal classes (*Sociabilis, Wilhalm und Amalia, Der Bussard*), but with the exception of this group these classes appear only when they enhance the humorous or didactic conception of the author.

Persons high in the ecclesiastical hierarchy occur rarely in *Mären.* Two stories present romantic adventures of the provost of the cathedral in Würzburg (*Frau Metze* by Der arme Konrad, and *Der Bildschnitzer von Würzburg,* perhaps by Hans Rosenplüt), and a bishop plays a minor role in Heinrich Kaufringer's *Der verklagte Bauer.* Far more common in the *Märe* is the figure of the ritter, the knight.

Because *Mären* were composed throughout three centuries, in the course of which basic changes took place in the social and economic conditions of feudalism, the ritter of these stories do not constitute a homogeneous group. It is important to recall that in German lands from the twelfth century onward, the term was used for men who possessed horse, armor, and fighting skills but little more, as well as for wealthy and distinguished noblemen. As the example of *Frauentreue* has shown, the knight errant appears in the *Märe* as he does in chivalric romance, and in external respects the chivalric passerby who seduces the cloistered lass in *Der Sperber* is fully comparable. Knights owning substantial property are protagonists in both versions of *Die Nachtigall, Peter von Staufenberg, Der Nussberg* by Heinrich Rafold, and *Die Meierin mit der Geiss.* Other *Mären* identify as ritter persons without notable wealth, prowess, or dignity; these include *Der Liebhaber im Bade, Der Ritter unter dem Zuber* by Jacob Appet, and *Der Ritter mit den Nüssen.* Other tales tell of ritter in humble or unfortunate circumstances: a traveling knight, wet and chilled, asks for lodging and is involuntarily humiliated by his host (Stricker's *Der nackte Ritter*); a knight and the village priest are tricked by the knight's wife (*Der Hasenbraten* by Der Vriolsheimer); an old knight living in rustic circumstances is fooled by his wife and her lover (*Der betrogene Gatte* by Herrand von Wildonie); a knight is forced by poverty to marry his daughter to a blind man *(Der betrogene Blinde).* The latitude of reference of the term ritter in the *Mären* corresponds to the wide range of socioeconomic circumstances surrounding persons capable of functioning as cavalry in the conflicts of medieval Germany. It would be mistaken to suppose that a parodistic or socially critical intent must underlie texts in which the ritter play roles far removed from their traditional ones in the literature of chivalry. In the *Märe,* knights may be rich or poor, wise or foolish, respected or ridiculed, successful or failures, lovers or cuckolds.

Similar distinctions should be made when considering the bourgeois characters in *Mären,* who span a wide range of wealth and social dignity. Residents of towns and cities (the *burgaere*) play all possible roles, positive and negative, triumphant and futile. In the tales of Hans Folz, the most notable urban poet of the *Märe,* one finds a scale of bourgeois types and destinies that epitomizes that of the genre as a whole. *Der ausgesperrte Ehemann* draws all its characters from the town so that the dupers and duped have common origins; a merchant of Basel is cuckolded and fooled *(Die Hose des Buhlers);* there is stark social contrast in *Der arme Bäcker,* with a baker first humiliated by, then humiliating, a noblewoman; in *Der Köhler als gedungener Liebhaber,* a goldsmith entrusted with official business by the city of Cologne—and therefore one of the city's elite—must tolerate the witless and sensual behavior of his wife toward a charcoal burner—the dregs of society; the landlady of an inn in Bonn is fooled by three students *(Die drei Studenten).* For Folz, the bourgeoisie furnished instances of vice and virtue, cleverness and stupidity that expressed in microcosm the variety of human life.

Although many *Mären* cannot be dated with any precision, the growing importance of urban life during the later Middle Ages left its mark on the *Märe,* for the fifteenth century produced many tales of bourgeois adventure set more graphically in specific communities than those composed some two centuries earlier. Hans Schneider (*d.* 1513 or later) tells of a thief and the hangman in Bruges *(Dieb und Henker);* the same city is famed for its master thief *(Der Dieb von Brügge);* Heinrich Kaufringer (*d. ca.* 1400) sets his *Mären* in Erfurt and Strasbourg and twice in Augsburg; we hear of erotic adventures at a specific locale in Constance *(Liebesabenteuer in Konstanz);* Peter Schmieher (who probably lived in Augsburg around 1430) narrates the conflict between a student and a burgher of Prague regarding the latter's wife *(Der Student von Prag);* though not localized, *Der Bürger im Harnisch* places its readers in the church and adjoining streets of a German town.

The peasantry plays an important role in the *Märe* because the ignorance and simplicity attributed to it by higher medieval classes destined it to supply the fools in many tales. The drunken farmer who mistakes a thief for St. Martin and the stingy farmer who mistakes a thief for the devil (Stricker's *Die Martinsnacht,* Hans Folz's *Der Schinkendieb als Teufel*) exemplify a medieval bias against the illiterate and uncouth rural population. Peasants are often cuckolded or bewildered, or both, by their more clever wives and adversaries (priests, knights, students). Thus, the short comic tale *Des Weingärtners Frau und Der Pfaffe* depicts the vinedresser hard at work on the hillside while his wife entertains the village priest, and *Der Pfaffe im Käskorb* (by the Swiss Anonymous) tells of the same adultery committed while the peasant is away at the mill. Rural occupations are thus contrasted with erotic amusement. Within the peasantry, however, there are shrewd and wise individuals, such as the hired hand who exposes the misbehavior of the farmer's wife (Stricker's *Der kluge Knecht*), the maid who turns the tables on her mistress *(Das schlaue Gretlein),* and the peasant who outwits the village priest and magistrate (Heinrich Kaufringer's *Der verklagte Bauer*). In such cases, rural characters succeed through native wit and pragmatism; their social circumstances are less important than their inherent common sense. Fischer discerns an increasing sympathy for the peasant in the later *Mären,* which now and then present "peasant shrewdness" as a positive value.

Village priests are noted for their appetites, both of the palate and the genitals. The two lusts were connected in medieval understanding, which perceived sexual drive as resulting from rich and plentiful diet and the priesthood as faring far better nutritionally than the common lay classes. As the preceding comments on the peasantry reveal, priests are conspicuous as seducers of peasant women and frequently escape unscathed, a pattern that suggests that gullible and stupid men have no rights to the poetic justice of adultery punished. On the other hand, priests sometimes fall victim to drastic revenge on the part of men whose women they pursue. The pastor in *Der Hasenbraten* fears that he may suffer the typical punishment of lecherous priests, castration, and so flees the scene. Indeed, Heinrich Kaufringer tells of a priest castrated by the cuckold *(Die Rache des Ehemannes),* and Hans Rosenplüt contrives a plot in which the adulterous priest causes the mutilation of his genitals by an Egyptian vulture. Roles played by priests are highly conventional. *Der Hasenbraten,* in which the innocent priest fears castration and is unjustly convicted of gluttony in the mind of his host, is an exception that proves the rule.

Monks and nuns play main roles in about a dozen *Mären.* Their credulity in love is a favorite motif, whether they facilitate illicit love affairs (*Der Mönch als Liebesbote,* three versions) or prove personally naïve *(Das Gänslein, Des Mönches Not).* They may also behave with the darkest depravity: the head of a cloister seduces a widow's daughter by abusing his religious authority *(Der Guardian);* and three monks of different orders use the confessional in an effort to corrupt a pious young wife *(Die drei Mönche zu Kolmar).* Women in orders appear infrequently but are typically sensual and unprincipled (*Das Nonnenturnier, Die Nonne im Bade* by Peter Schmieher).

In contrast to the predominantly negative portraiture of religious persons, the *Märe* presents a very favorable picture of young men studying at university, or on their way to do so *(studenten, schuolaere),* and of those who have finished their studies and taken employment as clerks, secretaries, or scribes *(schrîbaere).* Schirmer has called them the one medieval social group in the *Mären* that can only succeed. They appear as lovers in seventeen tales, are never involved with peasants but always with women from the bourgeoisie or the nobility, and are generally characterized as well-bred, intelligent, and eloquent. Although France was the center of higher education for German speakers until the fifteenth century, and German society thus lacked firsthand experience with the crowds of students who filled Paris and Orléans and the routes of access, the positive stylization of the *student* and *schrîbaere* in the *Märe* cannot be explained as the result of ignorance of social realities—Germans as well as

MÄREN

French knew that students were a heterogeneous, irreverent, and frequently riotous population. Favorable stylizations in literature usually result from the efforts of authors to flatter the prejudices of their audiences or to shape these prejudices along the model of their own, hence we assume that students and clerks influenced the authorship and reception of *Mären.* But little direct evidence of this has been found.

THE LITERARY HISTORY OF THE *MÄRE*

The origins of the *Märe* are obscure. Fischer includes in his canon the curious romance *Moriz von Craûn,* which may have been written before 1200, but not all scholars agree with this inclusion; and *Moriz von Craûn* is far from a typical *Märe* in any case (it is nearly 1,800 lines long, with a 400-line prologue). The independent, short narrative emerges in Germany with the work of Der Stricker, a professional poet who flourished about 1220–1250.

Der Stricker—the meaning of this pen name may be "weaver [of words]"—tried his hand at many literary forms, including romance, fable, exemplum, pious tale, and monologue. The evidence suggests that his two romances, a revision of the German *Song of Roland* and an original Arthurian story, come from the earlier part of his career, while the large number of didactic and religious poems attributed to him cannot be dated with any certainty. It is plausible that he concentrated increasingly on short, didactic literature as his aptitude for such forms became clear. The sixteen texts of his that Fischer accepts as *Mären* may thus be dated between about 1230 and 1250.

With respect to form, Der Stricker wrote his *Mären* in octosyllabic couplets with pure rhyme and regularly alternating stressed and unstressed syllables; this form of German verse had emerged in the later twelfth century as the vehicle for chivalric romance and had been brought to technical sophistication by Heinrich von Veldeke and Hartmann von Aue. The *Märe* thus represents a branching but not an interruption of the formal tradition of courtly narrative. The contents of Der Stricker's tales are vignettes exemplifying strengths or weaknesses of moral behavior. Only occasionally does he narrate a comic predicament in which the texture of moral ideas is thin (for example, *Der nackte Ritter*). Since his large number of didactic and religious poems suggests a serious nature, Der Stricker may have "invented" the *Märe* as a means of treating earnest problems in an entertaining and thus broadly popular way, all in the poetic form of chivalric romance (which he himself had practiced). Even if one assumes that others had composed *Mären* before Der Stricker, these tales have not been preserved, and Der Stricker, for the purposes of literary history, may be considered the originator of the genre in Germany.

In other scholarship it is frequently asserted that the *Märe* derives from the French fabliau in a manner like the derivation of German Arthurian romance from French sources (notably the works of Chrétien de Troyes). Certain facts speak for this theory: fabliaux were common in France several decades before *Mären* were common in Germany; many cases exist in which a very similar story is told in a fabliau and a *Märe,* suggesting direct dependence; and in their medieval literary relations, France and Germany were generally connected as "lender" and "borrower" respectively. But for all the instances of narrative similarities, no direct dependence of *Mären* on fabliaux has been shown, and the theory of an inspirational role played by the latter in the development of the former remains, according to Fischer, "an axiom awaiting proof." Their plots and motifs connect the comic *Mären* to literature of amusement written in European and non-European languages before and after them, but these affinities shed no light on the emergence of the *Märe* as distinct genre in Middle High German.

Nearly 150 years elapse after Der Stricker's death before we can identify another poet who occupied himself to a comparable extent with *Mären.* Toward the end of the fourteenth century, Heinrich Kaufringer, probably a bourgeois from Landsberg, wrote thirteen *Mären* and fourteen other known poems, while Hans Rosenplüt (Nuremberg, *ca.* 1400–1460) and Hans Folz (Nuremberg, *ca.* 1435/1440–1513) wrote ten and twenty *Mären* respectively among a large number of other literary works. These four men are untypical of the authors of *Mären,* for of the thirty-six other Germans whose names appear in this list, only two are thought to have written more than two tales (Konrad von Würzburg wrote three and the Swiss Anonymous five). As a rule, the *Märe* was an occasional undertaking by men who specialized in other things, literary or nonliterary. Heinrich der Teichner (*d. ca.* 1377) wrote over 700 poems but just one *Märe;* Herrand von Wildonie (*ca.* 1230–1280) dabbled in poetry during an active political career and left two *Mären.* About half the *Mären* are anonymous; many of the others are attributed to persons of whom we known nothing, among whom there were no doubt many complete amateurs.

MÄREN

Yet, at least in the first half of its existence the *Märe* can lay claim to literary sophistication. Schirmer's analyses of stylistic and compositional features in *Mären* from this period have shown high levels of accomplishment in certain texts, suggesting familiarity on the part of their authors with principles of rhetoric and with the poetic masterworks of medieval Germany. Fischer has gathered the allusions in *Mären* to other works of literature, which tend to confirm that these short poems moved in the same social circles as chivalric romance and heroic epic. As he notes, however, explicit literary allusions are restricted to a scant 10 percent of the surviving texts, and stories from the fifteenth century are not to be found in this small number. It thus appears that the *Märe* was highly stratified between 1230 and 1400. Certain texts emanated from cultured authors and were initially intended for an audience of similar breeding; Konrad von Würzburg (*d.* 1287), after Gottfried von Strassburg the most elegant stylist of medieval German literature, left three such *Mären.* Others circulated anonymously and were revised and adapted at will. In the fifteenth century the literary niveau of the *Märe* was generally lower—the verse was written less carefully, complexity of structure and rhetorical sophistication were lacking, and there was little apparent moral or psychological content. Though the *Märe* was still a matter of interest in polite circles (one rather long story was written by Johannes Werner von Zimmern [1454–1495], the highly educated scion of a Swabian baronial family) its patronage was increasingly within less cultured classes where literary expectations were modest.

As a medieval genre, the *Märe* is said to end with the work of Hans Folz and the few other texts from around 1500 (for example, *Beringer,* preserved only in an incunabulum from 1495; *Dieb und Henker* by Hans Schneider). It is nonetheless true that the definitive criteria of the *Märe* fit a large number of compositions by Hans Sachs, shoemaker and poet of Nuremberg in the sixteenth century (1494–1576), as well as certain narratives by his contemporaries and successors. The question of continuity between the *Märe,* especially as practiced in the fifteenth century, and the comic tales of Hans Sachs has not yet been explored.

BIBLIOGRAPHY

The comprehensive bibliography in Fischer (1983), 280–437, is an invaluable guide for study of the *Märe.* In part *A,* it lists editions and scholarship on the *Märe* as a genre, as well as important works on relevant aspects of French literature, Latin literature, and folklore. In part *B,* it gives complete information on the manuscript transmission, printed editions, and scholarly studies for each tale in his canon, as well as for eight fragments. This bibliography is complete through 1981 and should be the starting point for all scholarly investigation. Only the most basic titles listed in it are repeated below.

Sources. Hanns Fischer, *Die deutsche Märendichtung des 15. Jahrhunderts,* 2nd ed. rev. by Johannes Janota (1983); Hans Folz, *Die Reimpaarsprüche,* Hanns Fischer, ed. (1961); Friedrich Heinrich von der Hagen, *Gesammtabenteuer,* 3 vols. (1850, repr. 1961); Heinrich Kaufringer, *Werke,* Paul Sappler, ed., 2 vols. (1972–1974); Heinrich Niewöhner, *Neues Gesamtabenteuer,* Werner Simon, Max Boeters, and Kurt Schacks, eds. (2nd rev. ed. 1967); Der Stricker, *Verserzählungen,* Hanns Fischer, ed. (1967), vol. I revised by Johannes Janota (3rd ed. 1973) and vol. II revised by Johannes Janota (3rd ed. 1984).

Translations into English and New High German. Hanns Fischer, trans., *Schwankerzählungen des deutschen Mittelalters* (1967), title varies in later editions; Ulrich Pretzel, trans., *Deutsche Erzählungen des Mittelalters* (1971); *Der Schwanritter: Deutsche Verserzählungen des 13. Jahrhunderts,* Hans J. Gernentz, trans. (1972); Herrand von Wildonie, *The Tales and Songs of Herrand von Wildonie,* John W. Thomas, trans. (1972).

Studies. Theodore M. Andersson, "Rüdiger von Munre's 'Irregang und Girregar': A Courtly Parody?" in *Beiträge zur Geschichte der deutschen Sprache und Literatur,* **93** (1971); David Blamires, "Recent Work on Medieval German 'Märendichtung'," in *Modern Language Review,* **65** (1970); Hanns Fischer, "Novellistik, mittelhochdeutsche," in Werner Kohlschmidt and Wolfgang Mohr, eds., *Reallexikon der deutschen Literaturgeschichte,* II (1965), and *Studien zur deutschen Märendichtung,* 2nd ed. (1983); Frauke Frosch-Freiburg, *Schwankmären und Fabliaux: Ein Stoff- und Motivvergleich* (1971); Joachim Heinzle, "Märenbegriff und Novellentheorie: Überlegungen zur Gattungsbestimmung der mittelhochdeutschen Kleinepik," in *Zeitschrift für deutsches Altertum und deutsche Literatur,* **107** (1978); Gerhard Köpf, *Märendichtung* (1978); Arend Mihm, *Überlieferung und Verbreitung der Märendichtung im Spätmittelalter* (1967); Heinz Mundschau, *Sprecher als Träger der "tradition vivante" in der Gattung "Märe"* (1972); Kurt Ruh, "Zur Motivik und Interpretation der 'Frauentreue,'" in Dietrich Schmidtke and Helga Schüppert, eds., *Festschrift für Ingeborg Schröbler zum 65. Geburtstag* (1973); Heinz Rupp, "Schwank und Schwankdichtung in der deutschen Literatur des Mittelalters," in *Der Deutschunterricht,* **14** (1962); Karl-Heinz Schirmer, *Stil- und Motivuntersuchungen zur mittelhochdeutschen Versnovelle* (1969); Werner Schröder, "Niewöhners Text des *bîhtmaere* und seine überlieferten Fassungen," in *Beiträge zur Geschichte der deutschen Sprache und Literatur,* **91** and **92** (1969 and 1970), *"Vom dem Rosen Dorn ein gut red,"* in Ursula Hennig and Herbert Kolb, eds., *Mediaevalia litteraria: Festschrift für Helmut de Boor zum 80. Geburtstag* (1971), "Das maere von dem toren," in Peter F. Ganz and Werner Schroder, eds., *Probleme mittelhochdeutscher Erzählformen* (1972), and "Additives Erzählen in der Mären-Überlieferung," in Karl-Heinz Schirmer and Bernhard Sowinski, eds., *Zeiten und Formen in Sprache und Dichtung: Festschrift für Fritz Tschirch zum 70. Geburtstag* (1972); Stephen L. Wailes, "Konrad von Würzburg and Pseudo-Konrad: Varieties of Humour in the 'Märe,'" in *The Modern Language Review,* **69** (1974), "Social Humor in Middle High German Mären," in *Amsterdamer Beiträge zur älteren Germanistik,* **10** (1976), and "Students as Lovers in the German Fabliau," in *Medium aevum,* **46** (1977).

STEPHEN L. WAILES

[See also **Bauernhochzeit, Die; Bussard, Der; Folz, Hans; Frauenlist; Herrand von Wildonie; Irregang und Girregar; Konrad von Würzburg; Middle High German Literature; Moritz von Craun; Rosenplüt, Hans; Sperber, Der; Stricker, Der; Wirt, Der.**]

MARGRAVE, MARQUIS (or **marquess**), a title of nobility throughout Western Europe. Both margrave (medieval Latin: *marcgravius*) and marquis (medieval Latin: *marchensis [comes]; marchio*) originally meant "count of a march or border area." As political and military units the marches and their counts came into prominence in the Carolingian period. Since the late Middle Ages, the title has described a nobleman ranking above an earl and below a duke.

The word "march" was used for a border area between Christian principalities or (more commonly) for a region of Christian settlement abutting unconverted territory. Both types of march were of strategic importance, and both suffered from high levels of violence. Partly the violence was organized, in the sense that it was an instrument of policy for the competing principalities (whether Christian or non-Christian). Partly, however, it reflected a level of criminality and brigandage incident to the instability of government in the war-torn and often rugged borderlands. Insofar as the men who were lords of marches were the first line of defense for the polities to which they owed their allegiance, they achieved a high dignity. (Hence, the honor accorded to the titles margrave and marquis.) Insofar as they were constantly combatting violence with violence (or manipulating violence for their own ends), they gained a reputation for being petty tyrants.

The lords of marches were frequently given special (regalian) privileges in order to carry out their defensive responsibilities, and sometimes in recognition of their success in doing so. Frequently they extorted further privileges as a condition of their military support. A consequence of these developments was the virtual immunity of some marches from royal or imperial authority, and the emergence of certain marches as powerful autonomous principalities. The Bavarian Ostmark (eastern march) of the ninth century, for example, ultimately became the duchy of Austria.

Among the most famous of the marches were those along the boundary of Scotland and England (the English marches) and Wales and England (the Welsh marches). Their history should be compared with that of the Angevin (we can no longer say Anglo-Norman) palatinates in England. The unruly lords of the march between Poitou and Aquitaine, appropriately known as the counts of La Marche, have been of considerable importance in French history. The marches along the changing line of German-Christian settlement in Slavic Eastern Europe continued their prominence beyond the Carolingian period as a result of the eastward expansion *(Drang nach Osten).* The most important of the Italian marches was that of Ancona, bordering the papal states. But perhaps the most famous march of all was the so-called Spanish March, which served as the buffer zone between Muslims and Christians in the Carolingian period and became the county of Barcelona.

BIBLIOGRAPHY

See Jan Frederik Niermeyer, ed., *Mediae latinitatis lexicon minus* (1976), *s.v.v.* "Marca," "Marcgravius," "Marchensis." Joseph Calmette treats the Spanish march in his rather idiosyncratic *La question des Pyrenées et la Marche d'Espagne au moyen-âge* (1947). Various aspects of the march of Ancona are examined in the reports of a scholarly conference on this territory, *Convengo di studi storici Federico Barbarossa, Ancona e le Marche* (1972). Geoffrey Barraclough, *The Origins of Modern Germany* (1957), places the history of the imperial marches in the general context of German political development. The English palatinates (marches of a special sort) are considered critically in James W. Alexander, "The Alleged Palatinates of Norman England," *Speculum,* **56** (1981).

WILLIAM CHESTER JORDAN

MARIA LEKAPENA (*d. ca.* 965) was a granddaughter of Emperor Romanos I and the wife of Czar Peter of Bulgaria, making her one of the first imperial princesses to be given in marriage to a barbarian ruler. The Bulgars had been formidable enemies of Byzantium under Czar Symeon, but following his death in 927, his son Peter made peace. As part of the treaty signed in that year, Maria became his wife, opening the way for enormous Byzantine influence in Bulgaria.

BIBLIOGRAPHY

George Ostrogorsky, *History of the Byzantine State,* Joan M. Hussey, trans. (3rd rev. ed. 1969).

LINDA C. ROSE

[See also **Bulgaria; Peter of Bulgaria.**]

MARIAN FEASTS. Feasts of the Virgin Mary during the Middle Ages in the West fall into two rough groups: those which were imported to Rome by a series of popes from the Christian East *ca.* 700, and those which evolved more or less haphazardly in the succeeding eight centuries. (Devotional expressions of Marian piety such as the Angelus and the Rosary are not considered here.)

With the possible exception of an obscure Gallican-Spanish observance in January, no Marian feasts seem to have been celebrated widely in the West before the late seventh century. Around that time certain commemorations seem to have become accepted at Rome: Mary's Purification (2 February), which was—and is—also celebrated as the Presentation of Christ in the Temple (cf. Luke 3); the Annunciation (25 March), celebrating the tidings of Christ's birth by the angel Gabriel (Luke 1); the Assumption (15 August), without definition as to its precise mode; and the Nativity of Mary (18 September). From Rome these observances spread, through the so-called Gelasian and Gregorian liturgical traditions, to Frankish and English areas of influence, and ultimately throughout the West. In each case the observance seems to have been Eastern in origin, and the early Latin collects for the feasts tend to be as much christological as mariological in approach, especially for the Purification and Annunciation.

The marked increase in Marian piety noticeable in the High Middle Ages and the sentimentalizing tone that develops subsequently are both reflected in further liturgical feasts. Of these the (Immaculate) Conception of 8 December is the most important, though it was always touched by the controversy surrounding the opinion (finally declared a doctrine in 1854) that Mary was conceived without the stain of original sin. The feast's origins seem to go back to eleventh-century England (perhaps ultimately from an Irish source), but its uniform observance by the late fifteenth century owed much to persistent Franciscan pressure. The second most widespread of these later feasts is the Visitation (of Mary to Elizabeth; cf. Luke 1), most often on 2 July with its primary impetus coming from efforts to heal the Great Schism. Feasts commemorating the Presentation of the Virgin (in the Temple at age three, according to apocryphal tradition), on 21 November, and her Compassion, sometimes on a Friday in Lent, came to have some currency during the fifteenth century as well. A few other small observances, such as ramifications of the Compassion into various feasts of the Sorrows of our Lady also originate in the late Middle Ages, but the great proliferation of Marian feasts is a phenomenon of the Counter-Reformation and its aftermath.

BIBLIOGRAPHY

Stephen Beissel, *Geschichte der Verehrung Marias in Deutschland während des Mittelalters* (1909, repr. 1972); Edmund Bishop, "On the Origins of the Feast of the Conception of the Blessed Virgin Mary," in his *Liturgica historica* (1918); B. Capelle, "La Fête de l'Assumption dans l'histoire liturgique," in *Ephemerides theologicae Lovanienses,* 3 (1926), and "La liturgie mariale en occident," in *Maria: Études sur la Sainte Vierge,* Hubert du Manoir, ed., I (1949); I. Deug-Su, "La festa della purificazione in Occidente (secoli iv–viii)," in *Studi medievali,* 3rd ser., **15** (1974); G. Frénaud, "La culte de Notre-Dame dans l'ancienne liturgie latine," in *Maria: Études sur la Sainte Vierge,* Hubert du Manoir, ed., VI (1961); Frederick G. Holweck, *Calendarium liturgicum festorum Dei et Dei Matris Mariae* (1925); M. Jugie, "La première fête mariale en Orient et en Occident: L'avent primitif," in *Echos d'Orient,* **22** (1923); Richard W. Pfaff, *New Liturgical Feasts in Later Medieval England* (1970); S. J. P. van Dijk, "The Origin of the Latin Feast of the Conception of the Blessed Virgin Mary," in *Dublin Review,* **118** (1954).

RICHARD W. PFAFF

[See also **Annunciation; Assumption of the Virgin; Byzantine Church; Christology; Church, Latin; Franciscans.**]

MARIANUS SCOTUS (1028–1082/1083), an Irish monk and chronicler known for his universal history. At the age of twenty-four, he entered the monastery of Mag Bile, where he was educated by the abbot Tigernach. Expelled for a minor fault in 1056, he entered the Irish monastery of St. Martin in Cologne, then traveled to Fulda, where he had himself walled in as a recluse. He was moved to Mainz in 1069, where he remained at the monastery of St. Martin, again walled in, until his death on 22 December 1082 or 1083.

Marianus' universal chronicle, covering the period from the Creation until 1082, provides important information on Irish monasteries in Germany during the tenth and eleventh centuries. It also had a significant impact on later historical writing. Sigebert of Gembloux used it extensively, and Robert of Losinga, bishop of Hereford (1079–1095), brought it to England, where he abridged and extended it. Perhaps through his influence, the Worcester chronicler used it to supplement the Anglo-Saxon Chronicle on continental affairs.

BIBLIOGRAPHY

Sources are Marianus Scotus, *Chronicon,* Georg Waitz, ed., in *Monumenta Germaniae historica: Scriptores,* V (1849), 481–568, also in *Patrologia latina,* CXLVII (1853), 623–802. See also Anna-Dorothee von den Brincken, "Marianus Scottus: Unter besonderer Berücksichtigung der nicht veröffentlichen Teile seiner Chronik," in *Deutsches Archiv für Erforschung des Mittelalters,* **17** (1961), including an edition of the preface and book I of the chronicle.

MARY LYNN RAMPOLLA

[See also **Anglo-Saxon Literature; Sigebert of Gembloux.**]

MARICA RIVER (also known as the Maritsa), in the southeastern Balkans, originates west of the ancient city of Philippopolis (modern Plovdiv) and, after flowing about 300 miles, empties into the Aegean Sea. On its banks at Klokotnica, John Asen II of Bulgaria defeated and captured Theodore of Epiros in 1230, thus establishing Bulgarian supremacy in this area. On 26 September 1371 the Serbian army, led by King Vukašin Mrnjavčević and his brother, Despot Uglješa, was defeated near Černomen by the Ottomans. Both leaders were killed, and many local princes became Ottoman vassals. The event is generally considered the most important battle of the early period of the Ottoman conquest of the Balkans.

BIBLIOGRAPHY

Rade Mihaljčić, *Kraj srpskog carstva* (1975); Georgije Ostrogorski, *Serska oblast posle Dušanove smrti* (1965), 137–146; also in his *Sabrana dela,* IV, *Vizantija i Sloveni* (1970), 603–614; George C. Soulis, *The Serbs and Byzantium During the Reign of Tsar Stephen Dušan (1331–1355) and His Successors* (1984).

BARIŠA KREKIĆ

[See also **Bulgaria; John Asen II; Philippopolis; Serbia.**]

MARIE DE CHAMPAGNE (1145–1198), first child of Louis VII of France and Eleanor of Aquitaine, believed to have been the patroness of several works about courtly love. She was betrothed in 1153 to Henry I the Liberal of Champagne, married to him in 1164, widowed in 1181, and was regent of Champagne on behalf of her son Henry from 1181 to 1187 and from 1190 to 1197. Living at a time of great prosperity for Champagne, derived principally from its fairs, and when the counts of Champagne were among the king's most powerful vassals, Marie seems to have made the court of Troyes a cultural center. In his *Chevalier de la charrette,* Chrétien de Troyes claims he obtained the subject matter of his story from her and attributes to her at least some of its thematic and structural orientation ("Matiere et san li done et livre," l. 27). Gautier d'Arras composed his romance *Eracle* for her, and several lyric poems are associated with her. In his *De amore,* Andreas Capellanus, chaplain at Marie's court, mentions her several times as an authority on matters of love casuistry.

BIBLIOGRAPHY

John F. Benton, "The Court of Champagne as a Literary Center," in *Speculum,* **36** (1961); Reto R. Bezzola, *Les origines et la formation de la littérature courtoise en occident (500–1200),* III (1967); June H. M. McCash, "Marie de Champagne and Eleanor of Aquitaine: A Relationship Reexamined," in *Speculum,* **54** (1979).

GLYN S. BURGESS

[See also **Champagne, County; Chrétien de Troyes; Courtly Love; French Literature; Gautier d'Arras.**]

MARIE DE FRANCE (*fl.* late twelfth century), the first poetess writing in French whose name has come down to us, is one of the most remarkable writers of her time. Whereas at that time most poetic activity was still anonymous, she signed her name: "Me numerai pur remembrance/Marie ai num, si sui de France" (I shall name myself in order to be remembered:/My name is Marie and I am from France; *Fables,* epilogue, ll. 3–4). She also named herself, simply as Marie, in two other works that consequently are

MARIE DE FRANCE

ascribed to her: at the outset of the *Lais* (*Guigemar,* l. 3) and at the close of *Espurgatoire saint Patrice* (l. 2,297).

Virtually nothing is known of Marie's person and her life. Many unverifiable hypotheses have been advanced. She has been identified with the illegitimate daughter of Geoffrey IV of Anjou (father of Henry II of England), abbess of Shaftesbury (1181–1216); with the abbess of Reading; with a daughter of Waleran de Beaumont; and with a daughter of King Stephen of England. She dedicated her *Lais* to a "noble King," and her *Fables* to a "Count William." Scholars have identified the *nobles rei* as either Henry II (1133–1189), or, less plausibly, as his son, the young king (crowned in 1170, *d.* 1226).

Several counts named William have been advanced, the most probable being either William of Mandeville, earl of Essex (*d.* 1189), or Guillaume Longespée (*d.* 1226), illegitimate son of Henry II. All that can be said with reasonable certainty is that Marie was a native of France (that is, either of the French kingdom or, more probably, of the Île-de-France; that she resided outside "France," probably in England; that she knew Latin and English; and that she was familiar with contemporary vernacular literature and the Ovidian tradition. Her *Lais* apparently enjoyed a considerable success. Denis Piramus, in his *Vie de seint Edmund le rei* (written before 1185), bitterly criticized the popularity of the "mendacious" *lais* composed by a *dame Marie.*

Marie's literary activity can be dated only approximately. Basing themselves chiefly on the considerations of literary influences—an apparent lack of direct borrowing from Chrétien de Troyes—scholars usually date the composition of the *Lais* as early as the 1160's. If they were dedicated to Henry II, they must have been composed before 1189. The *Lais* were followed by the *Fables* and the *Espurgatoire.* Dating this last work depends on the date of its Latin source, *Tractatus de purgatorio sancti Patricii,* in H. of Saltrey's version. This version has been dated as no earlier than 1208. Assuming the "Marie" of the three texts ascribed to her to be one and the same person, it is possible to conclude only that she wrote sometime during the last two decades of the twelfth and the first decade of the thirteenth century.

Marie's chief claim to fame rests on twelve short stories, written (like her other two works) in octosyllabic rhyming couplets and called lais. She states several times that she received the materials she utilized in her stories from Armorican minstrels: "Une aventure vus dirai/Dunt li Bretun firent un lai" (I shall tell you an adventure/Of which the Bretons made a lai; *Laüstic,* vv. 1–2) is typical of such claims. Together with many Celtic and English place-names and personal names, these references constitute not only indications of Marie's possible sources but also the conventional affirmations of the "authenticity" of her stories: "Issi avint cum dit vus ai;/Li Bretun en firent un lai" (It happened just as I have told you;/ The Bretons made a lai about it; *Deus amanz* [*Deux amants*], ll. 253–254, and *Équitan,* ll. 311–312).

Whether Marie introduced the lai to Old French literature, or whether she continued an existing genre, is still much debated. What is not debatable is that her lais constitute the finest achievement of the genre. Following are the lais commonly attributed to her: *Guigemar* (886 verses; the title, as in many lais, is the name of the protagonist), *Équitan* (314 verses), *Le fresne* (The ash tree, 518 verses), *Bisclavret* (The werewolf, 318 verses), *Lanval* (646 verses), *Deus amanz* (The two lovers, 254 verses), *Yonec* (558 verses), *Laüstic* (The nightingale, 160 verses), *Milun* (534 verses), *Chaitivel* (The unfortunate one, 240 verses), *Chievrefeuil* (The honeysuckle, 118 verses), and *Éliduc* (1,184 verses).

Adventure and love, in aristocratic settings, constitute the unifying themes of these various stories. Unlike the heroes of contemporary romances, the protagonists of the *Lais* do not really seek adventure; adventure seems to befall them. Love, sometimes happy *(Lanval),* often not *(Deus amanz, Laüstic, Yonec),* sometimes wise *(Le fresne),* sometimes foolish *(Chaitivel),* or even criminal *(Équitan),* is presented by Marie not as a coherent courtly doctrine but as a powerful, complex, and variegated motivating force in the lives of men and women.

Some lais *(Guigemar, Yonec, Lanval)* are impregnated with faerie supernatural or folkloric elements; some *(Équitan, Le fresne, Laüstic, Chaitivel)* are free of such elements. Marie moves from realistic details to a supernatural ambiance with ease and grace. *Bisclavret* (the only *lai* not having a love motif) has a realistic background, but its subject is a werewolf, sympathetically portrayed. *Chievrefeuil* narrates an incident in the *Tristan* legend. Delicate shades of emotion, expressed with restraint and brevity, permeate the art of Marie's *Lais.*

The Marie of the *Fables* claims this work is a translation of an English collection of mostly Aesopic stories translated from Latin by King Alfred. They are indeed a translation from an unidentified English version of the Latin *Romulus* and *Phaedrus*—which, ultimately, derive from Aesop's fables.

Marie's work is the first known example of the Old French *Isopets*. Her collection contains, in addition to a prologue and an epilogue, 102 fables. Each of these short (from 8 to 120 verses), simple stories leads to a terse moral. Occasionally they can be slightly ironic. Judging from the twenty-three extant manuscripts, they enjoyed great popularity.

The *Espurgatoire* (2,302 verses) is, as was noted, a translation from a Latin legend concerning its protagonist's descent to purgatory. In order to strengthen his people's faith in the afterlife, St. Patrick made it possible to visit purgatory, where the faithful could see the torments of the damned and the joys of the saved. An Irish knight named Owein makes this most perilous journey. He struggles against diabolic temptation by evoking the name of Jesus. He returns, purified, to tell his story. The *Espurgatoire,* a blend of romanesque, homiletic, and hagiographic literature, is one of the oldest vernacular examples of the immensely popular medieval tradition of works that present the visions of the afterlife, a tradition culminating in Dante's *Divine Comedy.*

BIBLIOGRAPHY

Sources. Die Fabeln der Marie de France, Karl Warnke, ed. (1898, repr. 1974); *The Espurgatoire Saint Patriz of Marie de France, with a Text of the Latin Original,* Thomas Atkinson Jenkins, ed. (1903, repr. 1974); *Das Buch vom Espurgatoire s. Patrice der Marie de France und seine Quelle,* Karl Warnke, ed. (1938); *Marie de France Fables,* Alfred Ewert and R. C. Johnston, eds. (1942), a selection of forty-six fables with excellent notes and commentary; *Les lais de Marie de France,* Jean Rychner, ed. (1966, repr. 1973), the best modern critical edition; *Marie de France: Äsop,* Hans Ulrich Gumbrecht, ed. (1973), Warnke's text with interesting commentaries and a facing German prose translation; *The Lais of Marie de France,* Robert Hanning and Joan Ferrante, eds. (1978), the most readable and scholarly translation, with commentary.

Studies. Glyn S. Burgess, *Marie de France: An Analytic Bibliography* (1977), lists 76 editions of Marie's works and 453 works on Marie published before the end of 1975; F. W. Locke, "A New Date for the Composition of the *Tractatus de purgatorio sancti Patricii,*" in *Speculum,* **40** (1965); Philippe Ménard, *Les lais de Marie de France: Contes d'amour et d'aventure du moyen âge* (1979), an excellent introduction to the *Lais* and to scholarship on Marie; Emanuel J. Mickel, Jr., *Marie de France* (1974), the best overall English introduction to all of Marie's works.

PETER F. DEMBOWSKI

[See also **Anglo-Norman Literature; Arthurian Literature; Breton Literature; Chastelaine de la Vergi, La; Espurgatoire St. Patrice; Fables, French; French Literature: To 1200; Jean de Liège (with illustration); Lai, Lay.**]

MARIGNY, ENGUERRAN DE (*ca.* 1275–1315), came from a respectable noble family of Normandy that was neither rich nor powerful. His father held a minor royal office in the province and had a small estate at Ecouis. Fortunately for Enguerran, one of his neighbors, Guillaume de Flavacourt, archbishop of Rouen and later a cardinal, was a remote cousin. It was probably the archbishop who presented Enguerran to Queen Jeanne, wife of Philip IV the Fair. The queen took a liking to the young man, married him to one of her goddaughters, and gave him a position in her household. Marigny served her well (she left him the large sum of 500 pounds in her will), and she and the archbishop probably secured his appointment as one of the king's chamberlains in 1304. As a chamberlain he was responsible for the finances of the royal household (including such great expenses as the building of the new royal palace of the Louvre), and he was a counselor and intimate of the king. He was certainly an influential member of the government but not yet a major maker of policy.

Marigny's rise to power was a result of his skill as a negotiator. Two problems were worrying the king in the latter part of his reign: the suppression of the Templars and the unwillingness of the count of Flanders, Guy of Dampierre, to observe the terms of a peace treaty made after the defeat of the Flemings in 1304. The guilt of the Templars, accused of heresy, idolatry, and homosexuality, was by no means certain, and the question of what to do with their property if they were condemned was still unresolved. Marigny certainly played a role in persuading the pope to abolish the order and transfer its holdings to other military orders. As for Flanders, the financial terms of the treaty were impossible to fulfill. Marigny made a good bargain; Lille and Douai were given to the king instead (1312).

These successes made Marigny the principal counselor of the king. A reform ordinance of January 1314 confirmed his complete control of royal finances. The death of Guillaume de Nogaret in 1313 removed the only other minister who had the king's ear. All accounts of the last two years of Philip IV agree that Marigny was, in effect, a prime minister and that he, and his aides, ran the government.

Such power naturally annoyed men who thought that they deserved to have some influence on the king. The person most offended was the king's brother, Charles of Valois. Marigny could be attacked on several grounds. He had built up a great estate in Normandy; therefore he had been robbing the king. The Flemings had not entirely fulfilled their agreements; the army had been called out twice to make them yield, and each time Marigny had made a truce; therefore Marigny was a traitor. While Philip the Fair lived, Marigny was in no danger, but his death in 1314 gave Charles of Valois a chance to turn his nephew, the young king Louis X, against Marigny. Marigny was arrested and charged with many offenses, including sorcery. No proof was offered and he was not allowed to defend himself. He was simply condemned by the king and his court, and was hanged on 30 April 1315.

BIBLIOGRAPHY

Jean Favier, *Un conseiller de Philippe le Bel: Enguerran de Marigny* (1963), is the only full-scale study. Joseph Petit, *Charles de Valois* (1900), has some useful material on the relationship between Charles and Marigny. There are some references to Marigny's diplomatic and financial activities in Joseph R. Strayer, *The Reign of Philip the Fair* (1980).

JOSEPH R. STRAYER

[See also **Chivalry, Orders of; France; Philip IV the Fair.**]

MARINIDS. The Marinids were a dynasty of Zanāta Berber tribal origin that succeeded the Almohads in Morocco. They emerged in the second half of the twelfth century as nomads of the Tafilelt in southeastern Morocco, migrating northward over the mountains into the Moulouya Valley for summer pasture. Their early history is obscured by flattering legend, but they appear to have been one of the peoples placed by the Almohads under the surveillance of more privileged tribal groups. Thus, when the agents of the Almohads, the ᶜAbd al-Wādids or Ziyanids, made themselves independent at Tlemcen in the 1230's, the Marinids allied with the tribes of northern Morocco in rebellion against them, as well as against the Almohad caliphs at Marrakech. In 1248 the Marinid chieftain Abū Yaḥyā Abū Bakr attacked and scattered the army of the caliph al-Saᶜīd as it returned, following the caliph's death, from an expedition against Tlemcen. Fortified with recruits from the defeated army, Abū Yaḥyā occupied Fēs, and by the time of his death in 1258 ruled over northern and eastern Morocco, including the Tafilelt.

Abū Yaḥyā was succeeded by his brother Abū Yūsuf Yaᶜqūb; their Almohad names are evidence of a deliberate attempt to supplant the dynasty of ᶜAbd al-Mu'min in Morocco. At Marrakech the caliph al-Murtaḍā was overthrown in 1266 by a rival, Abū Dabbūs, with Abū Yūsuf's aid. As the caliph al-Wāthiq, Abū Dabbūs was himself overthrown by Abū Yūsuf in 1269. The Marinid sultan occupied Marrakech, and received the submission of the peoples of southern Morocco. By 1274 he had crossed the High Atlas to defeat the Arab Maᶜqil tribes in the Draa Valley, and recover Sijilmāsa in the Tafilelt from his principal enemy, the Ziyanid emir Yaghmurāsin at Tlemcen. Yaghmurāsin himself was defeated, and Tlemcen besieged. Secure in Morocco, Abū Yūsuf turned to Spain. In 1275 he obtained the submission of Ceuta, and crossed the Straits to win a great victory over Castile in conclusion to a long raid up and down the Guadalquivir. He returned to Morocco as the new champion of Islam in the West.

After the capture of Marrakech, Abū Yūsuf had taken the title of *amīr al-Muslimīn* or Commander of the Muslims, which had belonged to the Almoravids. It distinguished his dynasty from that of the Almohad caliphs, while keeping the connection with Islamic empire and the defense of the faith. The Marinids further followed the Almoravids in claiming an Arab ancestry. A more concrete symbol of their power and authority was the city of Fās al-Jadīd (New Fēs), built on the high ground above the old town. Begun in 1276 with the labor of Christian captives from the Spanish campaign, it celebrated the victory of the previous year, and provided the dynasty with a grandiose new capital.

New Fēs comprised within its massive walls a palace and a great mosque, a quarter for the royal guard of Christian mercenaries, and a town with markets and bathhouses where ministers were required to build their residences. The palace was ruled by eunuchs and chamberlains. Ministers, with the title *wazīr* (vizier), were drawn from families of warrior nobles, whose ancestors had been the chief men of the founder of the dynasty, and whose offspring were trained in the palace with the royal children. Below them in the administration were the secretaries, with the title *kātib,* men of letters drawn from the learned class of religious scholars. The provinces were governed in the same way, by members of the royal or ministerial families. The Khalṭ or Khlot, military Arab tribes of various origins introduced under the Almohads, had their territories on the At-

MARINIDS

lantic plains; beyond the High Atlas, from the Tafilelt to the Sous, the Arab Maʿqil tribes dominated the valleys and oases, only intermittently interrupted by the expeditions of the sultans. The mountain Berbers were ruled or led by their own chiefs.

The Sous, Sijilmāsa in the Tafilelt, and especially the old capital Marrakech, remained potentially independent. The sultan ruled through a combination of authority and patronage; those whom he favored owed loyalty and military service in return for the right to tax. They retained much, if not most, of what they collected. Taxes and dues were calculated and recorded in detail at the source, but where they came to the sultan, they came as tribute. Regular troops were reviewed and paid every three months, but specific expenses of the palace, the army, and the fleet were normally met by specific persons from specific revenues. Thus the royal guard of Christian mercenaries was paid out of the tax upon the gardens of Fēs, while construction of the great mosque of New Fēs was assigned to the governor of Meknes, who used the income from the oil press of Meknes for the purpose. The chandelier of the mosque was paid for out of the poll tax on the Jews. In ways like this, the Jews of Fēs became increasingly associated with the finances of the regime. Such devolution of responsibility kept the need for a central bureaucracy to a minimum, and the bureaucracy itself small and subordinate.

The supreme test and final proof of the sultan's prestige and power was his ability to muster and lead an army to victory. Down to the early fourteenth century, government centered on almost annual campaigns. For the remainder of the reign of Abū Yūsuf Yaʿqūb, these campaigns were chiefly in Spain. The passage of the army was assured by a fine fleet based at Ceuta, Tangier, and Algeciras. There was no reconquest of the lost land of Al-Andalus, but the Marinid sultan won glory, booty, and influence over the politics of both Granada and Castile. Peace with Castile in 1285, however, was followed in 1286 by the death of Abū Yūsuf, and by dynastic revolts against his son Abū Yaʿqūb Yūsuf. An expedition to Spain in 1291 failed to prevent the fall of Tarifa to Castile in 1292. Abū Yaʿqūb turned instead to the Maghrib. He invaded Ziyanid territory in 1295, and in 1299 he laid siege to Tlemcen. The siege lasted for eight years, during which time the sultan's camp turned into a capital city, al-Manṣūra (the Victorious), from which Abū Yaʿqūb ruled the central Maghrib. When the sultan was murdered in 1307, however, the Marinids withdrew, the Ziyanids recovered their territories, and the formative period of Marinid history came to an end.

While the Ziyanids entered upon a period of prosperity and success, the Marinids, under Abū Yaʿqūb's brother Abū Saʿīd ʿUthmān II (1310–1331), were preoccupied at home. Castile captured Gibraltar in 1309 from the Muslims of Granada, and Ceuta, which had become the greatest port of Morocco, regained its independence in 1316. In 1315 the sultan was briefly deposed by his son Abū ʿAlī, who retained control of Sijilmāsa and the Tafilelt. Abū Saʿīd was saved largely by the ability of his elder son, Abū'l-Ḥasan. His reign, despite its problems, was one of culture; the dynasty finally lost its rude Berber character and surrounded itself with men of letters. The three madrasas that the Marinids founded in 1320–1323 in Fēs promoted this culture through the education of students from all over Morocco. They were, nevertheless, directed against the schools of the Al-Qayrawān and Andalusian mosques, and helped to perpetuate the uneasy relationship between New Fēs and the old city.

The Marinids needed Fēs as much as Fēs needed the Marinids to promote the commercial interests of the city: the wars with Tlemcen had a strongly economic character. But mutual distrust dated from the brutality of the original Marinid occupation (1248–1254), finding expression in the building of New Fēs and the rise of the *shurafāʾ*. The *shurafāʾ* (sing.: sharif, noble) claimed descent from the Prophet through Idrīs, the founder of Fēs, so that they represented a different and more venerable title to prestige, and possibly power, than those advanced by the Marinids. Their rise to become the aristocracy of Fēs was a long-term political defeat for the Marinids.

Abū'l-Ḥasan, who succeeded his father in 1331, the year of his marriage to a Hafsid princess, resumed the expansionism of the dynasty. After retaking Gibraltar in 1333, he besieged Tlemcen, taking it in 1337. In 1339 he prepared to reconquer Tarifa, and in 1340 he won a great naval victory over Castile. In the latter year, however, his lightly armed archers and cavalry were overwhelmingly defeated on the Río Salado by a Christian coalition that went on to besiege and finally capture Algeciras in 1344. Ousted from Spain, Abū'l-Ḥasan turned to Ifrīqiya, which he invaded in 1347, following the death of his father-in-law, the Hafsid caliph Abū Bakr, to claim the throne for himself. He occupied Tunis in the same year. In 1348 he was defeated by the Arab tribes of Ifrīqiya, whose privileges he had withdrawn, and he retired to Tunis. The defeat led to revolts by the Hafsids in Ifrīqiya and the Ziyanids at Tlemcen, but above all by his son Abū ᶜInān, who made himself sultan at Fēs. Abū'l-Ḥasan returned to Morocco in 1350 but failed to dislodge the usurper. He died in the High Atlas in 1351.

Despite the collapse of his father's empire, Abū ᶜInān found the authority and the strength for a second attempt. Taking for the first time the supreme title of the caliphs, *amīr al-muᵓminīn* (commander of the faithful), he reconquered Tlemcen and Bejaia (Bougie) in 1352–1353, suppressed the revolt of his brother Abū'l-Faḍl in southern Morocco during 1354–1355, and prepared to capture Tunis. The expedition of 1357, however, encountered the same opposition from the Arab tribes, and the Marinid army withdrew rather than continue the campaign. Further attempts were precluded by the death of Abū ᶜInān in 1358.

The period down to the death of Abū'l-ᶜAbbās, who ruled from 1374 to 1384 and from 1387 to 1393, was one of instability, in which rival viziers from the great ministerial families struggled to place their candidates on the throne with the help of Muḥammad V of Granada, whose influence became decisive. The Ziyanids were intermittently subjected, and Tlemcen was reconquered, but beyond the Atlas the Maᶜqil Arabs were effectively independent, while Marrakech was dominated by the Hintāta Berbers of the mountains. The Marinid right to the throne was not challenged; during the long reign of Abū Saᶜīd ᶜUthmān III (1399–1420), however, the princes of the dynasty divided Morocco among themselves, leaving the sultan as little more than the ruler of Fēs. In 1399 the Castilians sacked Tétouan, and in 1415 the Portuguese captured Ceuta.

In 1420 Abū Saᶜīd and his sons were murdered in the palace. The sole survivor, the infant ᶜAbd al-Ḥaqq, came into the hands of Abū Zakariyāᵓ Yaḥyā, governor of Salé and head of the Banū Waṭṭās, a family that had entered Morocco with the Marinids, and based itself in the Rif. As the effective ruler of northern Morocco, Abū Zakariyāᵓ installed his protégé at Fēs in order to make himself regent. His power was confirmed in 1437 by his victory over the Portuguese at Tangier; since the Portuguese would not surrender Ceuta, the hostage Prince Don Fernando was imprisoned at Fēs until he died in 1443. The victory was accompanied by the fortunate discovery at Fēs of the body of Idrīs II, the second founder of the city, and the ancestor of the principal *shurafāᵓ*. The discovery sealed the alliance between Abū Zakariyāᵓ and the leading group in the city, which lasted beyond his death in 1448, until that of his cousin and successor ᶜAlī ibn Yūsuf, in 1458. They were killed fighting against Arab tribes in eastern Morocco and on the Atlantic plains, respectively. The southern part of the Marinid dominions was now independent, ruled by the chiefs of the Hintāta, one of the old Almohad tribes of the High Atlas.

In 1458 the Portuguese captured El-Ksar es-Seghir, near Ceuta; the sultan ᶜAbd al-Ḥaqq murdered Yaḥyā, son of Abū Zakariyāᵓ and the third Wattasid regent, and took power. To contend with the surviving Wattasid, Muḥammad al-Shaykh, at Arzila, and to defeat the Portuguese attack on Tangier in 1464, ᶜAbd al-Ḥaqq increased his demands on Fēs, using Jewish officials from the Jewish community now established in the ghetto *(mallāḥ)* of New Fēs. In 1465 the populace revolted, ᶜAbd al-Ḥaqq was executed, and for several years the city was ruled by the leader of the *shurafāᵓ*. In 1472 Muḥammad al-Shaykh became sultan as the first of the Wattasid dynasty.

BIBLIOGRAPHY

Jamil Abun-Nasr, *A History of the Maghrib,* 2nd ed. (1975); Auguste Cour, *La dynastie marocaine des Beni Waṭṭas (1420–1554)* (1920); M. García-Arenal, "The Revolution of Fās in 869–1465 and the Death of Sultan ᶜAbd al-Ḥagg al-Marīnī," in *Bulletin of the School of Oriental Studies,* **41** (1978); Charles A. Julien, *History of North Africa,* rev. ed. by Roger Le Tourneau, John Petrie, trans., C. C. Stewart, ed. (1970); Georges Marçais, *Les Arabes en Berbérie du XIᵉ au XIVᵉ siècle* (1913); J. A. Robson, "The Catalan Fleet and Moorish Sea-power (1337–1344)," in *English Historical Review,* **74** (1959); Maya Shatzmiller, *L'historiographie mérinide* (1982); Henri Terrasse, *Histoire du Maroc dès origines à l'établissement du protectorat français,* II (1950).

MICHAEL BRETT

[See also **Fēs; Hafsids; Idrisids; Maghrib, Al-; Marrakech; Meknes.**]

MARIOTTO DI NARDO (*fl.* 1394–1431), Florentine painter, influenced by Jacopo di Cione, Niccolò di Pietro Gerini, Agnolo Gaddi, and Lorenzo Monaco. Mariotto was the prolific author of numerous altarpieces, many of which still survive. Important extant works include a *Madonna and Child with Saints* (Florence, S. Donnino di Villamagna), a *Co-*

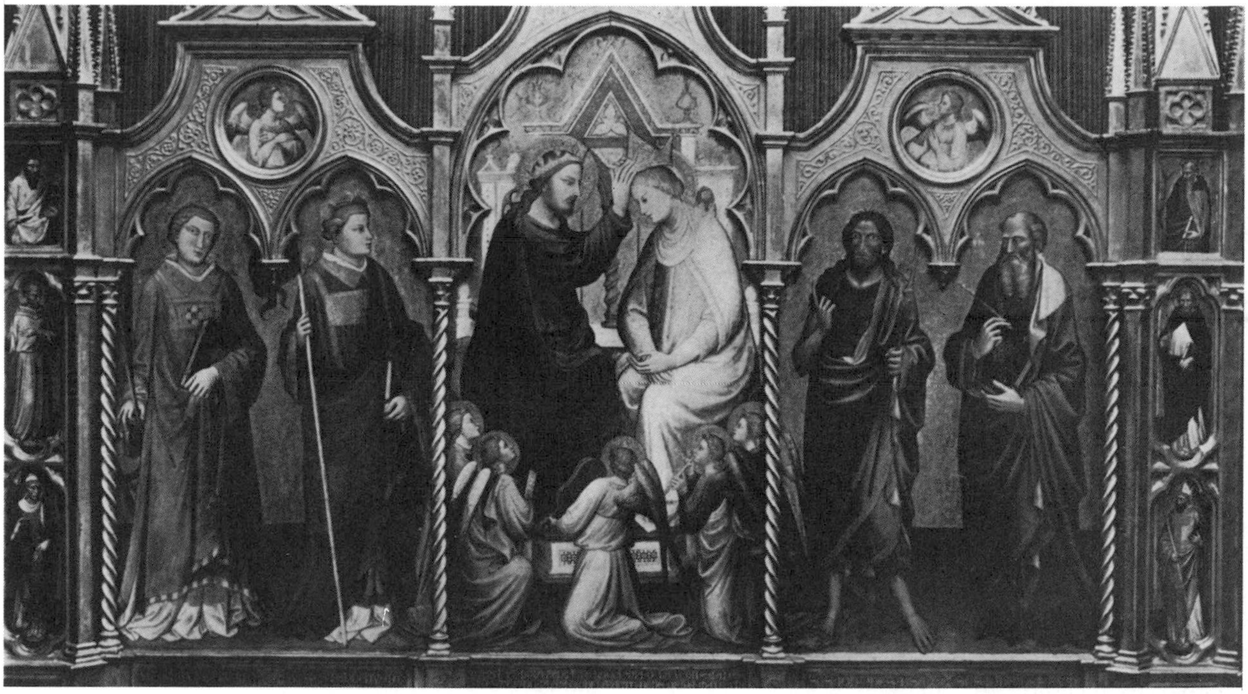

Coronation of the Virgin with Angels and Sts. Lawrence, Stephen, John the Baptist, and John the Evangelist. Altarpiece by Mariotto di Nardo, 1408. MINNEAPOLIS INSTITUTE OF ARTS, 65.37 (center panel), J. PAUL GETTY MUSEUM, MALIBU (wings)

ronation of the Virgin (Minneapolis Institute of Arts), an *Annunciation* (Pistoia, Museo Civico), and a fresco cycle depicting episodes from the life of Christ (Florence, Farmacia, S. Maria Novella). An eclectic figure, Mariotto echoes some of the stylistic impulses which took Florentine painting out of the hieratic traditions of the late trecento to the growing concern with volume and naturalism at the dawn of the Renaissance.

BIBLIOGRAPHY

M. Eisenberg, "*The Coronation of the Virgin* by Mariotto di Nardo" in *Minneapolis Institute of Arts Bulletin,* 55 (1966); Richard Fremantle, *Florentine Gothic Painters* (1975).

ADELHEID M. GEALT

[See also **Florence; Fresco Painting; Gaddi, Agnolo; Jacopo di Cione; Lorenzo Monaco; Niccolò di Pietro Gerini.**]

MARISCO, ADAM DE. See **Marsh, Adam.**

MARIUS VICTORINUS. See **Victorinus.**

MARJ DĀBIQ, a great plain near Dābiq (the Dabekon of Theophanes) on the Nahr al-Quwayq in northern Syria, about thirty-eight kilometers (twenty-four miles) north of Aleppo. There were numerous such meadows along the fringes of the arid Syrian steppe lands, and several of them were important meeting grounds for the Syrian tribes or the scenes of battles for control of the area. Marj Dābiq served as such a meeting ground in Umayyad times, and its location gave it additional importance as a headquarters for organizing expeditions against the Byzantines to the north. The caliph Sulaymān ibn ᶜAbd al-Malik used it as a staging area for his raid into Asia Minor in 717, and he died there the following winter. Some sources mention that Umayyad chieftains and others took refuge there when Syrian cities were stricken by the plague.

Marj Dābiq figured in a number of later events. The Abbasid caliph Hārūn al-Rashīd made his headquarters there for a time in 807. In 1064–1065 the Mirdāsid emir Rashīd al-Dawla Maḥmūd ibn Naṣr defeated his uncle ᶜAṭīya in a battle at Marj Dābiq, then went on to occupy Aleppo. During the crusades the plain was often a staging area for operations against the Franks; it also continued to serve, on occasion, as an encampment and battleground.

The plain is best remembered as the site of a great battle on 24 August 1516 between the forces of the Ottoman sultan Selim I and the Mamluk sultan Qānṣūh al-Ghawrī. The tripartite rivalry of the Ottomans, Mamluks, and the Safawid Shah Ismāᶜīl of Iran had by 1514 reached critical proportions. The Ottomans, fresh from a decisive victory over the Safawids at the Battle of Čāldirān (23 August 1514), resolved to punish ᶜAlāᵓ al-Dawla of Dhu'l-Qadr for refusing to assist them in this campaign. This move directly threatened the Mamluk position in northern Syria, and when the Ottomans defeated and killed ᶜAlāᵓ al-Dawla in the following year and annexed his domains, pressure from the Mamluk military establishment in Cairo and Aleppo obliged Qānṣūh al-Ghawrī to reinforce the area. Despite the critical economic situation of his empire, not to mention the flagrant challenge such a move would pose to the Ottomans, the Mamluk sultan set out for Syria with a large army in the spring of 1516.

Both the Ottomans and the Mamluks made peace proposals as tensions rose; but Selim I, with plans for renewed attacks on the Safawids in the near future, decided that he must first eliminate the potential Mamluk danger on his southern flank. The two armies finally clashed on the plain of Marj Dābiq, and the result was a near massacre of the Mamluk army. The Ottomans had introduced firearms into their army on a large scale, and the Turkish artillerymen and harquebusiers mowed down their opponents before they could use their lances, bows, and swords. Qānṣūh al-Ghawrī fell in the fighting. The carnage was of such magnitude that the battle gave the Ottomans immediate control of Syria, and facilitated their occupation, five months later, of Egypt as well. With this, the Mamluk sultanate came to an end. Even more important, this battle (as well as that of Čāldirān two years earlier) vividly demonstrated the vast superiority that firearms gave the Ottoman army over its more traditional rivals.

BIBLIOGRAPHY

David Ayalon, *Gunpowder and Firearms in the Mamluk Kingdom,* 2nd ed. (1978); René Dussaud, *Topographie historique de la Syrie antique et médiévale* (1927), 474; Guy Le Strange, *Palestine Under the Moslems* (1890), 426, 503; Stanford J. Shaw, *History of the Ottoman Empire and Modern Turkey,* I (1976), 79–85; Julius Wellhausen, *The Arab Kingdom and Its Fall,* Margaret Graham Weir, trans. (1927, repr. 1963), 263–266.

LAWRENCE I. CONRAD

[See also **Mamluk Dynasty; Ottomans; Qānṣūh al-Ghawrī; Selim I; Warfare, Islamic.**]

MARJ RĀHIṬ, a vast plain, slightly to the northeast of Damascus, on which was fought the decisive battle in one of the most important and far-reaching military campaigns of early Islamic history.

From the moment of his succession to the Umayyad caliphate in the summer of 684, as the Second Civil War was gaining momentum, Marwān I ibn al-Ḥakam found his authority challenged not only by the partisans of ᶜAbd Allāh ibn al-Zubayr, who retained the allegiance of Egypt, Iraq, and Arabia, but also, in Syria, by the Qays and other Syrian tribal groupings opposed to the Quḍāᶜa, the confederacy of Arab tribes (including the Kalb), on which the earlier Umayyads had relied for support. By aligning themselves with ᶜAbd Allāh upon Marwān's accession, the Qays and their allies posed an immediate and critical threat to Umayyad power at a moment of already grave difficulty. In the events that culminated in the battle of Marj Rāhiṭ, there hung in the balance not only the fate of Marwān's caliphate but also that of the Umayyad dynasty as a whole.

From al-Jābiya, the great tribal meeting ground (43 mi/70 km southwest of Damascus) where Marwān had been elected caliph, the Umayyad forces marched north against the Qays led by Ḍaḥḥāk ibn Qays. Marwān's army was heavily outnumbered, but several factors worked in the caliph's favor. The allies of the Qays in numerous instances had no interest in the establishment of a regime in Syria favorable to ᶜAbd Allāh, while the partisans of the Umayyads were firmly committed and had much at stake. At the same time, developments in Damascus were working against the Qays. As the city had been depleted of troops by the developing conflict over the succession, Ḍaḥḥāk's skeleton garrison was driven out with little difficulty by Ghassanid elements (from another great Arab tribe settled in Syria), who were friendly to Marwān. This had the immediate result of placing the treasury and considerable military stores at the caliph's disposal, and also made it impossible for the Qays to confront the Umayyads advancing from the south without exposing themselves to attack from Damascus, to the north. In order to avoid being caught between two hostile forces, the Qays awaited battle on the plain of Marj Rāhiṭ, where Ḍaḥḥāk seems to have had considerable landholdings. The final clash, which took place after some weeks of skirmishing and about three weeks after Marwān's accession, was a complete victory for the Umayyads. The Qays were utterly routed with great slaughter; almost all of their most important chieftains, including Ḍaḥḥāk, were killed.

The effects of the campaign were felt immediately. The rebellious districts of Syria quickly came over to Marwān; and through the remainder of the Second Civil War the Umayyads were never again so gravely threatened.

Marj Rāhiṭ had long-term consequences. To the tribes, it was not merely a clash between contenders for imperial power, but rather an intertribal battle that escalated the long-standing rivalry between the confederacies of Qays and Quḍāᶜa (Kalb) into a tribal feud. Kalb poets ranked Marj Rāhiṭ among the greatest of their tribe's "Battle Days" *(ayyām),* while the decimated Qays sought vengeance for the day that had seen the "extermination of the tribes." Instances of revenge and retaliation occurred with increasing frequency through the remainder of the Umayyad caliphate, and given the complex structure of alliances within Arab tribal society, it eventually became almost impossible for the tribes of Syria to avoid being drawn into the conflict.

But Marj Rāhiṭ was not the sole cause of this conflict. Pestilence, famine, Byzantine incursions from the north, and other similar factors served to hem in the Qays and to compel them to encroach on lands claimed by the older tribes of Syria (such as the Kalb). Such a situation was bound sooner or later to result in serious conflict. It was, however, Marj Rāhiṭ that drove the first and most irretractable wedge between the Umayyads and the Syrian tribes. The losses and bitter memories of the battle were thus instrumental in destroying the tribal accord and cooperation on which the stability of the Umayyad regime was dependent.

BIBLIOGRAPHY

For details on the various accounts of Marj Rāhiṭ in the sources, see Julius Wellhausen, *Das arabische Reich und sein Sturz* (1902), trans. by Margaret Graham Weir as *The Arab Kingdom and Its Fall* (1927). See also Frants Buhl, "Die Krisis der Umajjadenherrschaft im Jahre 684," in *Zeitschrift für Assyrologie und verwandte Gebiete,* **27** (1912); Henri Lammens, "L'avènement des Marwānides et le califat de Marwān Ier," in *Mélanges de l'Université Saint-Joseph,* **12** (1927), which is, however, highly romantic and speculative. These are all now superseded by the account in Gernot Rotter, *Die Umayyaden und der zweite Bürgerkrieg (680–692)* (1982), 133–152.

LAWRENCE I. CONRAD

[See also ᶜ**Abd Allāh ibn al-Zubayr; Marwān ibn al-Ḥakam; Syria; Umayyads.**]

MARK EUGENIKOS (*ca.* 1392–23 June 1444/1445), Byzantine theologian. After studying rhetoric and philosophy, he entered the monastic life in 1418. Involved in the emperor's efforts to assemble an ecumenical council of reunion, he was made metropolitan of Ephesus in 1437, and the following year joined the Greek delegation to the Council of Ferrara-Florence (1438–1439). There Mark discovered that theological differences with the Latins were deeper and less easily resolved than he had supposed. He refused to sign the council's final decree, and on his return to Constantinople became the center of opposition to the union. He died shortly after enduring a two-year imprisonment; he has since been honored as a confessor by the Orthodox church.

BIBLIOGRAPHY

Hans-Georg Beck, *Kirche und theologische Literatur im byzantinischen Reich* (1959), 755–758; Joseph Gill, *Personalities of the Council of Florence* (1964), 55–64, 222–232.

JOHN H. ERICKSON

[See also **Councils, Western (1311–1449).**]

MARKETS, EUROPEAN. In the Middle Ages, *mercatus* meant "marketplace" or "market right," but never referred to abstract commerce as it does today. A market was an institution that could be owned like a piece of land or a building. But market owners, such as bishops, nobles, monasteries, or towns, all had to obtain permission to run the market from the king or a high feudal lord. This permission was often purchased since markets produced profits in the form of rents, tolls, and fines.

Medieval markets served the needs of a local area. They met about once a week in rural settlements or more frequently (three to six times a week) in towns and cities. The basis of most markets was foodstuffs—grains, dairy products, fish, poultry, meat, and vegetables—brought into the market by peasant producers and sold either to local inhabitants or to traders for resale later. Some manufactures, such as iron implements, leather goods and pottery, and luxury commodities such as spices and fine cloth, were also exchanged in medieval markets, as were raw materials like wool and hides. These types of products were more often traded in town markets than rural markets.

With the decline of the Roman Empire in the fourth and fifth centuries and the intensification of

MARKETS, EUROPEAN

Cloth and dishware being sold in a covered market. Miniature from a 15th-century MS of the *Ethics* of Aristotle. Bibliothèque de la Ville de Rouen, MS I, 2 (927), fol. 145. GIRAUDON/ART RESOURCE

the Germanic invasions, European town life and trade contracted greatly. Market activity decreased as individuals and estates became more self-sufficient. But neither towns nor markets completely disappeared in the post-Roman era. Indeed, in some instances, new markets sprang up around monasteries and fortified castles to serve the needs of their inhabitants. Local market activity—the exchange of foodstuffs, raw materials, and occasionally simple manufactures—never entirely ceased, although long-distance and luxury trade dwindled considerably.

Markets became more numerous in the ninth century as commerce revived under the stable political regime of Charlemagne. Both Charlemagne and his grandson Charles II the Bald promulgated much market legislation and granted a great number of market charters. Originally the power to found a new market was a regalian right, but the privilege was increasingly usurped by the higher feudal lords who ruled over areas where royal influence was weak. Churches in particular received numerous royal concessions to establish markets within their domains. Several monasteries and bishops in tenth- and eleventh-century Germany, for example, obtained authority to raise markets on their estates and in their dioceses (sometimes as compensation for the royal appropriation of lands).

Feudal lords all over medieval Europe eagerly sought charters for new markets on their lands because of the potential profits to be had. The owners of markets could tax merchants who attended their markets and collect tolls from both buyers and sellers, as well as fines arising from the jurisdiction of market courts. In exchange for the right to hold a market, the lord was obliged to protect traders, guarantee proper weights and measures, maintain fair prices and quality control, and limit the exploitation of consumers and outsiders.

From the ninth to eleventh centuries many new markets grew up around places of settlement: by churches, abbeys, castles, suburbs, city gates, and by important crossroads. The churchyard frequently became the marketplace and Sunday was often the day of the market. (Sunday was actively discouraged as a market day by the church only from the thirteenth century on.) Markets usually took place weekly, fortnightly, or monthly; some were annual events. These markets, which commonly met on the occasion of a saint's festival or other religious holidays, often developed into the annual fairs of later centuries.

The generally infrequent meetings of markets in this period were a result of the low commercial demand of a still sparsely settled Europe. Agricultural produce remained the main object of rural markets from the ninth to eleventh centuries, although, with the expansion of settlement and the growth of towns in eleventh-century Italy and twelfth-century England, France, and Germany, town markets diversified and the products of craftsmanship and luxury items were increasingly traded.

In fact, the population expansion in medieval Europe, which began about the year 1000 and continued well into the thirteenth century, accounted for an increasingly complex and flexible system of trade. More land came under cultivation, new lands were settled (especially in Eastern Europe), and the resulting agricultural expansion produced greater agricultural surpluses for the market. Market exchange also provided the cash needed by the peasants for rents and taxes in an economy that was becoming more and more money oriented. The population growth and higher agricultural output also meant that the economy could support a greater number of nonagricultural workers (who were usually paid in cash). All these factors worked to augment greatly the number of markets in twelfth- and thirteenth-century Europe. In the prosperous thirteenth century alone, well over 3,000 market charters were granted in England by the king to various lay and ecclesiastical lords. Similar developments occurred on the Continent.

By the twelfth and thirteenth centuries, market charters were usually granted only after some kind

MARKETS, EUROPEAN

of investigation by royal agents into local conditions. In England the sheriff was responsible for discovering whether a new market would interfere with existing markets because of proximity in time or space. The thirteenth-century English lawyer Henry Bracton warned that neighboring markets held on the same or following day were harmful to each other. He also cautioned against markets that were spaced too closely together. In his opinion, markets less than six and two-thirds miles apart risked interfering with each other. (This figure was based on a day's journey, reckoned at twenty miles, which, when divided by three to account for the time it took to travel to the market, the time spent in the market, and the time returning, amounted to six and two-thirds miles.) Bracton's view was ignored by contemporaries and historians today no longer consider it valid. Nevertheless, medieval market holders, especially those who owned town markets, did voice objections to new markets established too close to their own. English towns such as London, Norwich, and Northampton obtained charters forbidding markets from being set up within a seven- to fifteen-mile range, and the royal inquisitions *ad quod damnum* regularly investigated the potential harm of newly established markets to older, neighboring markets. Similar practices occurred in continental Europe. In Saxony, for example, local codes forbade markets from being set up within a mile of one another.

The location of a new market depended on several factors. While some new market locations were chosen merely on the whim of owners, population density and the existing road networks were important factors. Population growth and settlement patterns directly affected the intensity of local market demand, which, in turn, accounted for the proliferation and distribution of medieval markets. Road networks and transportation problems greatly influenced not only the multiplication of markets but also their survival. Most of the markets that have survived to modern times lay on main roads while those that have decayed or disappeared were often located near small rural crossroads. In an age when inland transportation and travel frequently proved difficult and laborious, market towns and villages serviced by good road or river systems possessed a great advantage.

Many of the new markets were associated with the growth of towns. On occasion, markets even provided the nucleus for towns by attracting merchants and artisans to centers of exchange. The rise in specialized urban handicrafts and the development of industry and guild organizations also stimulated the expansion of market activity. Town markets quickly evolved to meet the more complex needs of thirteenth- and fourteenth-century trade. Market days increased in number from one to three and even six days a week depending on the size of the town. Special days or areas in the marketplace were set aside for certain merchandise such as cloth, wool, or cattle. Market halls were erected to protect goods from bad weather, such as Leadenhall in London. The construction of shops, stalls, and warehouses allowed for greater flexibility because of the advantageous retail and storage facilities they offered. Finally, market regulations were enacted and market officials were appointed or elected to ensure protection for consumers and traders alike in the form of price and quality control.

Protection and security in the marketplace were ensured first of all by the regulation of the time and place of commercial transactions. Generally, no buying or selling could occur before the first ringing of the market bell at "prime" (around dawn) or after the last ringing of the bell around late afternoon or nightfall. These rules ensured that all transactions took place openly, in broad daylight, thereby avoiding secret transactions that escaped market taxes and the supervision of market wardens.

Market authorities in both town and country also restricted the timing of commercial activities by fining those who engaged in such monopolistic practices as "forestalling" and "regrating." Forestallers intercepted goods coming to the market, generally before prime, and then sold the goods in the marketplace at a higher price. Regraters bought up goods early in the day and did not resell them until later, when shortages drove the price up. Both practices led to a restriction of competition, higher prices, and a loss of toll for the market.

Market owners, especially of town markets, also made efforts to stipulate the places where marketing could occur. Quality and price control, as well as the collection of market customs, were more easily guaranteed when transactions took place in the open marketplace in full view of all market-goers and the market officials. Town retailers, fishermen, and peasant producers were continually fined for setting up stalls or selling in illegal places—usually just outside the town gates or on the main approach to the marketplace. In this way they obtained first crack at those coming to market and also avoided market tolls. Town residents could also be fined for selling goods in their own houses (because they wanted to escape tolls and avoid quality and price regulations).

The majority of local and national marketing regulations focused on holding down prices, guaranteeing value, and securing adequate food supplies. For the most part these aims were realized through the evolution of such institutions as the assizes of bread, ale, and wine (for the enforcement of quality and maximum prices), the election or appointment of quality-control officers in the various trades represented at the market, and the punishment of market offenses in the town and village courts. Closely related to the concern for quality and price control was the enforcement of proper weights and measures. All towns and even some villages possessed official weights and measures in the marketplace. Privately owned measures had to be stamped or sealed by town or market officials; municipal authorities held regular assays of measures to ensure proper standards. The use of false measures, however, was apparently widespread amongst retailers of ale, wine, oats, flour, and salt.

Local market jurisdiction was aimed in particular at controlling the quality, supply, and price of foodstuffs. The lack of proper storage and refrigeration facilities made the consumption of spoiled victuals a constant hazard. The caprices of climate and the uncertainties of medieval agriculture contributed to an unreliable source of grains and other perishable produce. At the same time that supply was unpredictable, demand for food fluctuated erratically in response to such factors as rural immigration, disease, urban mortality, and the rise and fall of town or village fortunes. The highly urbanized regions of Flanders and Italy experienced special problems with food supply. Many of the large cities in these areas tried to maintain strict control over the supply, price, and organization of trade in such foodstuffs as wheat and other grains in order to avoid unfair prices and dearth in the marketing of victuals. On the other hand, the very frequency of complaints related to the sale of foodstuffs, as well as the regular occurrence of privately initiated suits in the courts concerning food-related market fraud, indicates that many of the urban markets did not adequately guarantee quality, price, and supply in the victual markets.

Market regulations were usually enforced in the courts of the town or village where the market was located. Some towns had special market courts that presented and fined those who committed market offenses. The courts judged commercial actions according to national statutes (for example, assizes of bread and ale or legislation on weights and measures), local codes, and "law merchant," which was a European-wide, generally uncodified system of legal usages and doctrines governing all mercantile dealings. This body of customary law evolved from the varying commercial practices of different regions and remained distinct from common law. Law merchant dictated the procedure for such commercial matters as the types of proof necessary in debt disputes and the method of dealing a bargain.

Fines that arose out of the jurisdiction of market courts belonged to the owner of the market, whether it be a town, ecclesiastical lord, or lay lord. Other profits accrued to market owners from a wide variety of tolls, customs, and other market exactions. Terrage (a tax for displaying goods on the ground), stallage (for using a market stall), peisage (for using the official weights and measures), through toll (for carrying marketable goods through the town or market), and pickage (for making holes in the ground to set up a stall) were only some of the tolls that a market owner was entitled to collect. Perhaps most profitable were the customs due on the sale or purchase of certain goods. In general, only foodstuffs purchased by consumers for immediate consumption were customs-free. Most goods bought for resale, export, industry, and nonfood use were taxable. Thus customs were due on cattle or pigs bought by a peasant as livestock, or on wood sold as fuel or for construction purposes. These customs and tolls were often collected at a tollbooth set up in the marketplace. Moreover, the right to collect certain customs and market tolls was frequently farmed out to individual merchants or traders.

Not all medieval people paid market exactions at the same rate. A person's personal or residential status often dictated whether or not custom was paid and in what amount. The aristocracy, local gentry, and privileged burgesses were exempt from many market customs. Individual towns also sought charters that excused their citizens from paying customs and other commercial exactions in the markets of other towns, regions, and even countries. In addition, individual merchants could also purchase special licences that released them from the payment of specific tolls and customs. Therefore, market charges fell most heavily upon the unenfranchised retail trader.

The wealthier people of medieval Europe probably visited the marketplace only rarely. Instead, they sent their servants to make their purchases or kept their own shops if they were well-off merchants. The marketplace itself, a bustling scene of activity, was usually located in a large open space (although some consisted of only a widening in the street). Temporary wooden stalls and display tables were erected in the larger markets and many towns had their own market halls. Peasants and poorer traders simply spread their wares on the ground or sold produce directly from their carts. Shops and stalls often lined the edge of the market and the streets leading to it. Specific areas were reserved for certain merchandise; thus livestock was sold in one part of the marketplace, foodstuffs in another, cloth and wool in still another. As the main meeting place in most towns and villages, marketplaces served social, as well as commercial functions. Guilds and other organizations performed plays in the marketplace, proclamations were first read aloud there, and the town or village stocks and gallows were often located there.

The marketplace therefore acted as the economic, commercial, and social center of most medieval communities. Furthermore, as the chief facility for the local exchange of goods, the market served as the basis for regional and long-distance trade in medieval Europe. Although in the fourteenth century the number of new markets declined drastically and many old markets disappeared because of the population decline caused by the famines and plagues, local markets not only remained the most important element of medieval commercial life, but also continued to grow in size and significance as the economy became increasingly money-oriented.

BIBLIOGRAPHY

R. H. Britnell, "The Proliferation of Markets in England, 1200–1349," in *Economic History Review,* 2nd ser., **34** (1981); R. J. Bromley, *Periodic Markets, Daily Markets, and Fairs: A Bibliography* (1974); James Lea Cate, "The Church and Market Reform in England During the Reign of Henry III," in *idem* and Eugene N. Anderson, eds., *Medieval and Historiographical Essays in Honor of James Westfall Thompson* (1938); Great Britain, Royal Commission on Market Rights and Tolls, *First Report of the Commission, and Report,* by C. I. Elton and B. F. C. Costelloe (1888); Paul Huvelin, *Essai historique sur le droit des marchés et des foires* (1897); Richard Koebner, "Dans les terres de colonisation: Marchés slaves et villes allemandes," in *Annales d'histoire économique et sociale,* **9** (1937), trans. without full bibliography as "German Towns and Slav Markets" in Sylvia Thrupp, ed., *Change in Medieval Society* (1964); Charles M. de La Roncière, *Florence: Centre économique regional au XIVe siècle,* 5 vols. (1976); Robert Latouche, *The Birth of the Western Economy,* E. M. Wilkinson, trans., 2nd ed. (1967); David Nicholas, "Structures du peuplement, fonctions urbaines et formation du capital dans la Flandre médiévale," in *Annales: Économies, sociétés, civilsations,* **33** (1978); Louis Salzman, "The Legal Status of Markets," in *Cambridge Historical Journal,* **2** (1928), and *English Trade in the Middle Ages* (1931), 121–141; T. Unwin, "Rural Marketing in Medieval Nottingham," in *Journal of Historical Geography,* 7 (1981); Charles Verlinden, "Markets and Fairs," in *Cambridge Economic History of Europe,* III (1963, repr. 1971).

MARYANNE KOWALESKI

[See also **Banking; Commune; Fairs; Food Trades; Guilds and Métiers; Mints and Money; Roads and Bridges; Trade; Trade, Regulation of; Travel and Transport; Urbanism; Weights and Measures.**]

MARKO (*d.* 1395), the greatest hero of Serbian epic, in which he is praised for nonhistorical exploits against the Turks, was in fact a Turkish vassal. He was the son of King Vukašin, the de facto ruler of most of Serbia from the early 1360's until his death fighting the Turks at Marica in 1371. Marko, designated as his father's successor, was crowned "Young King" during Vukašin's lifetime. He succeeded to the king's title immediately after his father was killed. Thus it is more accurate to call him King Marko than Marko the king's son *(Kraljević).* However, the Turkish victory over the Serbs at Marica forced Marko to become a Turkish vassal. At the same time other Serbian nobles immediately turned against him and seized the major portion of his family's lands, leaving him only part of western Macedonia, centered at Prilep. He was killed fighting for the Turks against the Wallachians at the Battle of Rovinj in 1395. After his death the Turks annexed his lands.

BIBLIOGRAPHY

John Fine, Jr., *The Late Medieval Balkans* (1987).

JOHN V. A. FINE, JR.

[See also **Serbia.**]

MARMION, SIMON (*fl.* 1449–1489), panel painter and illuminator, was a native of Amiens who lived in Valenciennes from 1458 to 1489. He worked for the Banquet of the Pheasant in 1454; painted a panel with the figures of Charles of Charolais (later Charles the Bold) and Isabelle of Bourbon before 1465; and painted altarpieces for several churches in

Valenciennes and Cambrai, as well as much heraldic decoration. He illuminated a sumptuous breviary for Charles the Bold between 1467 and 1470. Marmion was much admired, but no documented work survives; the nineteenth-century attribution of the St. Bertin Altar wings, and related paintings and manuscripts, is now recognized as being without documentary foundation.

BIBLIOGRAPHY

Chrétien Dehaisnes, *Recherches sur le retable de Saint-Bertin et sur Simon Marmion* (1892); Maurice Hénault, "Les Marmion (Jehan, Simon, Mille et Collinet), peintres amiénois du XVe siècle," in *Revue archéologique,* 4th ser., 9 (1907); Sandra Hindman, "The Case of Simon Marmion: Attributions and Documents," in *Zeitschrift für Kunstgeschichte,* **40** (1977); Edith Warren Hoffman, "Simon Marmion or 'The Master of the Altarpiece of Saint Bertin': A Problem in Attribution," in *Scriptorium,* **27** (1973).

ANNE HAGOPIAN VAN BUREN

MARMOUSETS (little boys), a term used in late medieval politics to belittle opponents as low-born upstarts. The word refers particularly to a political group at the French royal court in the late fourteenth century. The Marmouset party consisted of military and financial officers associated with the government of Charles V (1364–1380) and with his brother, Louis, duke of Anjou. In the 1380's the Marmousets opposed Philip the Bold, duke of Burgundy, in a struggle to lead the government of Charles VI.

Of the more than forty people who have been identified with the party, six were especially prominent: Olivier de Clisson, constable of France; Nicholas du Bosc, bishop of Bayeux; Bureau, lord of La Rivière; Jean le Mercier; Jean, lord of Montaigu; and Pierre de Villaines, count of Ribadeo. While three of these six came from nonnoble backgrounds, many of the less visible Marmousets were from distinguished noble families. They were long-time royal officers whose political base was the military aristocracy of northwestern France. In 1388 they seized power and drove the dukes of Burgundy and Berry from court, thereby inaugurating Charles VI's personal rule. Reviving the governmental traditions of Charles V, they promoted more frugal government and various ordinances of reform, and concluded a truce with England. In 1392, however, following an attempt on Clisson's life, the king became insane during a military expedition to Brittany. His uncle, Philip of Burgundy, quickly reassumed control, disgracing several leading Marmousets. The group lost its political cohesion and did not regain power.

BIBLIOGRAPHY

John Bell Henneman, Jr., "Who Were the Marmousets?" in *Medieval Prosopography,* 5 (1984); Ludovic Lalanne, *Dictionnaire historique de la France,* 2nd ed. (1877), 1233.

JOHN BELL HENNEMAN

[See also **Charles V of France; France.**]

MARNER, DER (*fl.* 1231–1276). Although the poet-musician known as Der Marner (the seaman) is mentioned in no historical document, certain biographical information can be obtained from his works. These show that he was well educated, earned a scanty living from his compositions, and probably had no permanent abode. Two songs that can be dated indicate that his career spanned, at the very least, the period from 1231 to 1267. References to him in the verse of his contemporaries reveal that he was widely known, was a Swabian, and was murdered—a blind, old man—sometime before 1287. In all likelihood, he was from a middle-class family.

Der Marner was one of the more prolific lyric poets of the thirteenth century, and his works appear in numerous manuscripts. He composed both minnesongs and didactic lyrics or *Sprüche,* in Latin as well as in German. The minnesongs include two dawn songs, two dance songs, four songs of courtly love (some of which may have been composed for dancing), but no songs of village maidens. These are all highly polished German works with sprightly rhythms and traditional language and contents. Their most distinctive characteristics are moderation of feeling—love evokes neither great joy nor deep sorrow—and a pronounced tendency to discuss ladies in general or love itself rather than tell of the passion for a particular lady. In spite of the detached air of the narrator, however, there is none of the parody and irony that many of Der Marner's contemporaries exploited in their amatory verse.

The poet's fifty-two German *Sprüche* are, on the whole, more original and subjective than his minnesongs. They comprise religious and political songs, songs of social criticism, lampoons of fellow composers, eulogies, short fables, proverbs, riddles, and one liar's song. The most numerous are the religious songs, which are of three kinds: those devoted to the praise of God or (more often) Mary,

MARONITE CHURCH

those concerned with man's sin and redemption, and those in which the poet uses the wondrous and commonplace phenomena of nature to show that each object and action plays a significant role in a divine cosmology, and is also a symbol of a spiritual truth. Except for frequent anaphora and alliteration, the expression is simple and unassuming. Permeating these works are the twin motifs of memento mori and *vanitas mundi.* The five Latin songs that are generally attributed to Der Marner include two eulogies, a discourse on the separate branches of knowledge, an attack on certain monastic orders, and a celebration of spring.

Like many German lyric poets of the mid thirteenth century, Der Marner uses complex strophic patterns. Particularly characteristic of his stanzas are rhyme responsion between *Aufgesang* (composed of two stollen) and *Abgesang,* interior rhyme, long stollen (even in the minnesongs), and long strophes. It was doubtless his virtuosity of form as much as the content of his verse that endeared him to the later meistersingers, who named him among the twelve old masters, often used his *Töne* (formal metrical and musical stanzaic structures), and honored one of them as the third of their four "crowned" *Töne.*

BIBLIOGRAPHY

The texts of Der Marner's songs, a catalogue of the manuscript sources, and a list of the significant secondary literature are in Philipp Strauch, ed., *Der Marner* (1965).

Studies include Christoph Gerhardt, "Perseus kristalliner schilt," in *Germanisch-romanische Monatsschrift,* 57 (1976); Gisela Kornrumph, "Eine Melodie zu Marners Ton XIV in Clm 5539," in *Zeitschrift für deutsches Altertum und deutsche Literatur,* **107** (1978); Ulrich Müller, *Untersuchungen zur politischen Lyrik des deutschen Mittelalters* (1974), 116–119, 522–524; Burghart Wachinger, "Der Marner," in Kurt Ruh *et al.,* eds., *Die deutsche Literatur des Mittelalters: Verfasserlexikon,* VI (1985).

J. Wesley Thomas

[See also **German Literature: Lyric.**]

MARONITE CHURCH. The Maronite church takes its name from St. Maron, a priest who led a solitary life near Apamea-on-the-Orontes (western Syria) in the late fourth and early fifth centuries. He had a great reputation for holiness and wisdom, and a considerable number of disciples gathered around him. When he died around 410, this group founded a monastery dedicated to his memory. Its members were active missionaries in their area and as they gained converts they established new monasteries, whose heads often acted as bishops for the region.

The early Maronites had a Syriac, not a Greek, liturgy, but were on good terms with the Greek Orthodox church. They opposed the Monophysite heresy, and, according to a letter sent to Pope Hormisdas in 517, hundreds of them were massacred by the heretics. There has been some doubt as to whether they were equally opposed to the Monothelites, and it does seem that they were a little less firm on this issue. The early Christians had debated whether Christ—fully human and fully divine—had both a human and a divine will. The Monothelites argued that there could be only a divine will. The Maronites said that there were two wills, but since they could not be in opposition, the result was the same as if there had been only one will. This subtle argument did not reach some Western writers at the time of the crusades. Relying on inaccurate sources, they considered the Maronites to be Monothelites. Rome, however, did not question their orthodoxy.

The Muslim expansion into Syria in the seventh century created new problems for the Maronites. The last Greek patriarch of Antioch was killed in 609; by 700 the leader of the Maronites was called patriarch of Antioch and the East. The monastery of St. Maron remained the center of the church until early in the tenth century, when it was destroyed by Muslims. Many Maronites had already taken refuge in the mountains of Lebanon; almost all of them were there by 939, which is the date given for the transfer of the patriarchate.

In Lebanon the Maronites were reasonably safe, and since the tenth century they have remained a large and influential group in the region. The patriarch was both the civil and religious head of the community; local landlords controlled the scattered villages. There was, for a while, little contact with the outside world, but the crusades reopened relations with the West. In spite of the doubts expressed by some chroniclers, the Maronites were accepted as fellow Christians by most of the crusaders. Relations between Maronites and Catholics grew closer throughout the twelfth century. They recognized Alexander III as rightful pope. The Maronite patriarch attended the Lateran Council of 1215 and after his return to Lebanon (1216) received the pallium from the pope. Maronites moved freely through the Christian principalities of the East; many emigrated to Cyprus. There was, of course, some friction—there was a Latin patriarch of Antioch as well as the Maronite patriarch, and it was awkward to have both a Catholic and a Maronite bishop in the same area. There were differences in liturgy, and in church law—the canon law of the West was completely foreign to the Maronites. Nevertheless, there was no break between the two churches, and the Maronites accepted the headship of the pope.

The destruction of the crusading states by the Mamluks in the late thirteenth century weakened the ties between Rome and the Maronites. The latinization of the Maronite church slowed and for some time there were few contacts between the pope and the Maronite patriarch. Relations became closer in the fourteenth and fifteenth centuries, thanks largely to the work of the Franciscan friars who were sent to encourage the remaining Christian communities in the former crusading states and to bring them into touch with Rome. The Maronites caused few problems, perhaps because they were such a small group. Differences in liturgy and canon law persisted, but of all the Eastern churches that were affiliated with Rome the Maronites were the only one that did not split into pro-Roman and anti-Roman sects.

BIBLIOGRAPHY

Pierre Dib, *Histoire de l'église maronite,* I: *L'église maronite jusqu'à la fin du moyen âge* (1930); Matti Moosa, *The Maronites in History* (1986).

JOSEPH R. STRAYER

[See also **Antiochene Rite; Lebanon; Monophysitism; Monothelitism; Schism, Eastern-Western Church; Syrian Christianity.**]

MARQUESS. See **Margrave, Marquis.**

MARQUETRY. In cabinetmaking, the gluing of a decorative pattern of wood or other material. Unlike inlaying, which sinks the secondary material into a prepared area, both field material and decorative patterning are applied as veneer of equal thickness. Wood of contrasting colors is most often used as decorative material, although ivory, bone, tortoiseshell, or metal is also employed.

BIBLIOGRAPHY

W. A. Lincoln, *The Art & Practice of Marquetry* (1971).

MARY GRIZZARD

MARRAKECH, properly Marrākush, appeared in European maps and literature as late as the nineteenth century as Marocco, thus giving its name to the country of Morocco. The city was founded about 1070 (not 1062, as in the traditional account) by the Almoravids as the headquarters of their army north of the High Atlas and close to Āghmāṭ, the existing center for trade across the mountains to the south. According to legend, the queen of Āghmāṭ, Zaynab, married first the Almoravid amir Abū Bakr, then his cousin Yūsuf ibn Tāshfīn, who made Marrakech the base for his conquest of Morocco and Muslim Spain. With the death of Abū Bakr in 1087, Yūsuf's city became the capital of the empire in the Sahara as well as the Maghrib. It was strategically placed on the plain of the Tensift River, just within the arc of the Atlas at the convergence of two major routes across the mountains, the one coming through the Tizi n'Test mountain pass from the Sous plain and following the Wad N'fis toward Marrakech, the other coming from the valley of the Wad Dra via Telouet through the Tizi n'Tichka pass. Rudimentary in the days of Yūsuf, the Almoravid city was largely the work of his son ᶜAli (ruled 1106–1143), who provided it with a wall and added a second palace to the Dār al-Umma or "House of the Community" built by his father. Both residences opened on to a large open space in the center of the city, of which the present Jāmaᶜ al-Fanā (Djemaa el-Fnā) is a vestige. In the northern quarter of the city, beyond the present Qayṣarīya or covered market, was the Great Mosque, the largest of all those built by the Almoravids (the nineteenth-century building on the site, the Ibn Yūsuf or Ben Youssef Mosque, is named after the creator of the original mosque, ᶜAlī ibn Yūsuf ibn Tāshfīn). The orientation was east-south-east; along the south wall was a fountain, and opposite the fountain a pool beneath a dome in the style of the Great Mosque of Córdoba, evidence of a strong Andalusian influence upon the Almoravid city.

Of this city, only the dome over the pool has survived. In 1147 Marrakech fell to the Almohads of the High Atlas, who made it the capital of their own still larger empire in North Africa and Spain. Even when the monarchs resided in Seville, the city was the center of the Almohad community with its shaykhs and regiments of troops called up for tours of duty from the mountains. The existing bridge was built across the Tensift to the north, putting an end, perhaps, to the prosperity of Āghmāṭ, still the chief commercial center under the Almoravids. The present circuit of walls and square towers in red pisé (mud concrete) was constructed. The great Almoravid mosque was abandoned, and a new mosque built by the Almohad conqueror ᶜAbd al-Muᵓmin, oriented south-south-east. To correct this orientation, a second mosque was promptly built against its south wall, oriented still further to the south. This second edifice alone survives as the Kutubīya Mosque. Built to the Almoravid plan of the Qarawīyīn Mosque of Fēs, it stands on the site of ᶜAlī ibn Yūsuf's palace; its minaret, completed about 1196, is the great landmark of Marrakech. The minaret is the earliest of three such tall Almohad mosque towers, the others being that of the Giralda in Seville and that of the unfinished Mosque of Ḥassān in Rabat.

The principal Almohad builder was Abū Yūsuf Yaᶜqūb al-Manṣūr (1184–1199), who came back to Marrakech after his father's years in Seville. He was largely responsible for the construction of the Casbah or royal precinct in the southern quarter of the city, with its great Bāb al-Kuḥl (now Bāb Agnāū or Gate of the Blacks or "Guineans") and its Mosque of the Casbah. The tiled decoration on the minaret of this mosque developed into the style of the later thirteenth and fourteenth centuries. The Almohad palaces, however, have disappeared. Meanwhile the walled Agdāl gardens, stretching for two miles south of the Casbah, began to be laid out. Water was brought to the city, for drinking and irrigation, by mainly subterranean canals from the mountains twenty miles to the south.

In 1220 the city witnessed the execution of five Franciscan missionaries. The Casbah, however, came to house a Christian militia, briefly provided with a church. In 1230 Marrakech was captured and the Almohad shaykhs massacred by the new caliph al-Maᵓmūn at the climax of a long quarrel between the shaykhs and the monarchy. The coup precipitated the disintegration of the empire, so that by 1250 the power of the dynasty was confined to the region of the city. Marrakech eventually fell to the Marinids of Fēs in 1269. For fifty years it was neglected by the new rulers as the home of a late Almohad culture associated with the caliph ᶜUmar al-Murtaḍā (1248–1266), which remained hostile to their pretentions; the school included the early fourteenth-century Ibn ᶜIdhārī al-Marrākushī, author of the major historical work, *Kitāb al-bayañ al-mughrib fī akhbār al-Andalus wa'l-Maghrib.* About 1320, however, Abū Ṣaᶜīd ᶜUthmān II, the great Marinid patron of Fēs, provided Marrakech with the Ibn Ṣālaḥ Mosque to the west of the Qayṣarīya, while about 1345–1349 a *madrasa* or college was built in the Casbah by the sultan Abū'l-Ḥasan.

As Marinid power declined after 1359, however, Marrakech fell gradually under the control of the amirs of the Hintāta Berbers of the High Atlas, who by the middle of the fifteenth century were effectively independent. Though Sufism was spreading, the tombs of holy men such as Abū 'l-ᶜAbbās al-Sabtī (Sidi Bel Abbès), who died in 1205 and is today the patron saint of the city, as yet received no especial veneration. The Jewish community, which despite Almohad intolerance survived until joined by refugees from Spain in 1492, remained inconspicuous. When Leo Africanus visited Marrakech about 1515, he found it ruinous. The Casbah was abandoned to squatters, the row of booksellers which had given its name to the Kutubīya Mosque had vanished, and one incompetent teacher alone remained in the *madrasa.* Only a third of the city was inhabited, while the rest of the area within the walls was cultivated in safety from the tribal bands who roamed to the gates, making agriculture in the Ḥawz or surrounding area largely impossible. Only after the nascent Saᶜdian dynasty captured the city in the course of its long campaign to reunite Morocco (1524/1525), did Marrakech become once again the capital, and enter a new period of greatness.

BIBLIOGRAPHY

Leo Africanus, *Description de l'Afrique*, A. Epaulard, trans., 2 vols. (1956); in English as *History and Description of Africa*, Robert Brown, ed., 3 vols. (1896); G. Deverdun, *Marrakech dès origines à 1912*, 2 vols. (1959); Derek Hill and Lucien Golvin, *Islamic Architecture in North Africa: A Photographic Survey* (1976); E. Lévi-Provençal, "La fondation de Marrakech (462–1070)," in G. Marçais, *Mélanges d'histoire et d'archéologie de l'Occident musulman*, II (1957), 117–120; G. Marçais, *Manuel d'art musulman: L'architecture. Tunisie, Algérie, Maroc, Espagne, Sicile*, 2 vols. (1926–1927); L. Massignon, *Le Maroc dans les premières années du XVIe siècle: Tableau géographique d'après Léon l'Africain* (1906); H. Terrasse, *Histoire du Maroc dès origines à l'établissement du protectorat français*, 2 vols. (1949), trans. into English by Hilary Tees as *History of Morocco* (1952).

MICHAEL BRETT

[See also **Almohads; Almoravids; Berbers; Fēs; Islamic Art and Architecture; Maghrib, Al-; Marinids; Mosque; Rauḍa.**]

MARRANOS. See **New Christians.**

MARRIAGE. See **Family.**

MARSEILLES, founded by the Greeks around 600 B.C. and a free city under the Romans, became in the Middle Ages the greatest Mediterranean seaport between Genoa and Barcelona. It was also a center of learning and piety in southern Gaul.

About 415 John Cassian founded in Marseilles the monasteries of Sts. Peter and Victor for men, and St. Savior for women; the former became a power in European monasticism. Marseilles flourished under the Visigoths after the fall of the Roman Empire, but declined under the more barbarous Burgundians, Ostrogoths, and Franks. Charles Martel stormed Marseilles (736 and 739) while extending (nominal) Merovingian authority over Provence.

The city revived mainly because of its seaborne trade, which, however, lapsed in the ninth century, when Islam dominated the Mediterranean. Muslim forces from Spain sacked Marseilles in 838. In 975, after William, count of Provence, captured the Muslim hilltop fortress at Fraxinet near Marseilles, one of his lieutenants became a viscount and the first of a long line to rule in Marseilles. The viscounts held the lower city, sharing power with the bishops in the upper city. A third urban area developed around the port where the commercial business of Marseilles was conducted.

The crusades led to a resurgence of Marseilles in Mediterranean trade. Its ships reached Tyre in 1187 and Acre in 1190, and a market was established in Jerusalem. It became a rival of Genoa and Venice.

In 1194 Marseilles had government by consuls. The city bought the viscount's seigneurial rights, and experimented with a rectorial system (1218) and an Italian-style podesta rule (1221). Caught in the duel between Raymond VII, count of Toulouse, and Raymond Berengar V, count of Provence, Marseilles accepted the overlordship of Raymond VII in 1230. It signed a treaty with Raymond Berengar V in 1243.

By 1249 both counts were dead and Charles of Anjou ruled in Provence. The Marseillais acceded to his authority in 1252. Charles needed them to support his adventures in Italy and Sicily. He therefore promoted stability in their city by letting an urban council function under his *viguier* (vice-regent).

After the massacre of the French in Palermo (the Sicilian Vespers, 1282), heralding the revolt against Charles, the decline of Angevin rule allowed Marseilles to gain some measure of freedom. Still, its trade diminished as the fall of Acre in 1291 left the Levant under Muslim control. An oligarchy arose that in 1348, despite the ravages of the Black Death, gained from Joan I, queen of Naples, the right to unify the three areas of the city.

In 1362 the abbot of St. Victor was elected Pope Urban V, and he became a patron of the city as it rebuilt its churches and widened the port. In 1385 Marseilles introduced government by syndics representing the oligarchy. Pro-Angevin Marseilles was sacked by the rival Aragonese in 1423. René I, abandoning Naples for Provence, restored prosperity in the 1440's, aided by the Lyons fair, the products of which passed through Marseilles. The galleys of Jacques Coeur, the wealthiest merchant in France, carried these products across the Mediterranean to markets in the Levant.

In 1475 the consulate was restored, three consuls being chosen from the council every three months. Six years later Charles III died, leaving Provence as a bequest to King Louis XI of France. A royal governor named in Paris governed Provence, and therefore Marseilles, after that.

BIBLIOGRAPHY

Edouard Baratier, ed., *Histoire de Marseille* (1973); Owen Chadwick, *John Cassian,* 2nd ed. (1968); Georges Lesage, *Marseille angevine: Recherches sur son evolution administrative, économique, et urbaine de la victoire de Charles d'Anjou à l'arrivée de Jeanne 1e (1264–1348)* (1950); Henri Pirenne, *Medieval Cities: Their Origins and the Revival of Trade,* Frank D. Halsey, trans. (1925, 1939, 1948).

VINCENT BURANELLI

[See also **Angevins: France, England, Sicily; Cassian, John; Trade, European; Trade, Islamic.**]

MARSH, ADAM (Adam de Marisco, *d.* 1259), first Franciscan regent master of theology at Oxford, exercised a significant role in the affairs of university, realm, and church during the reign of Henry III. Born near Bath, he took his arts degree at Oxford under Robert Grosseteste, whose friendship with the young scholar would eventually benefit the entire family. Attracted by the poverty of the Franciscans (Friars Minor) and prompted by the example of his aide and retainer, Adam Rufus of Oxford (or Exeter), Marsh joined the order at Worcester about 1233. He studied theology at Oxford under Grosseteste until the latter became bishop of Lincoln in 1235. Soon a leading English Franciscan, Marsh was a member of a commission that in 1241 urged the minister general not to mitigate the Rule of St. Francis. Grosseteste took Marsh as an adviser to the First Council of Lyons in 1245. Incepting in theology in 1245, or at least qualified to do so, Marsh succeeded Thomas le Waleys as lector to the Oxford Franciscans from about 1247 to 1250. Although reappointed by the Franciscans in 1252, it is doubtful he actually resumed teaching. In testimony of his friendship with Marsh, Grosseteste bequeathed his library to the Oxford Franciscans in 1253.

Marsh was assigned important commissions by Henry III; by the archbishop of Canterbury, Boniface of Savoy; and by Pope Alexander IV. It was probably in 1255 that, according to the *Lanercost Chronicle,* he prevailed upon the king to spare the lives of the Jews when they had been judged worthy of death. When the see of Ely became vacant the following year, king and archbishop unsuccessfully sought his appointment. In 1257 the king sent him abroad to test the climate for a peace settlement with France.

The 247 edited letters, dating mostly from 1250 to 1255, reveal Marsh's connection with the great of his day, among them Queen Eleanor, Simon and Eleanor de Montfort, St. Richard of Chichester, and St. Bonaventure. His correspondence marks him as an ecclesiastical reformer who saw in the shortcomings of the clergy and even of his own order a cause of spiritual decline, even as he argued upon them the work of preaching and evangelization of the Mongols, whose coming upon the European scene was a challenge to the Christian world view. Many letters contain pastoral counsel on the practice of virtue; others show concern for the poor and oppressed.

Recent studies have ascertained Marsh's collaboration with Grosseteste on the latter's *Concordance of Sacred Scripture and the Fathers,* which they furnished with an ingenious key of 400 symbols enabling the reader to locate the passages cited, and on his *Commentary on the Hexaemeron.* Marsh is now regarded as the probable author of a treatise on tides, *Quaestio de fluxu et refluxu maris,* formerly attributed to Grosseteste. Contemporary Franciscans mentioned his knowledge of natural science and of languages (Roger Bacon), and a commentary on Genesis (Salimbene). Marsh died 18 November 1259 and was buried at Lincoln Cathedral next to Grosseteste, who had called him "a wise and prudent man, fervent in zeal for the salvation of souls." Subsequent generations called him *Doctor illustris.*

BIBLIOGRAPHY

Marsh's letters have been published as "Adae de Marisco epistolae," in *Monumenta franciscana,* J. S. Brewer, ed., I (1858), lxvi–lxx, lxxvi–ci, 75–489; Davide Bigalli, *I tartari e l'apocalisse: Ricerche sull' escatologia in Adamo Marsh e Ruggero Bacone* (1971); Mary Anthony Brown, "Adam Marsh: The First Franciscan 'Magister regens' at Oxford," in *The Cord,* **14** (1964); Gustavus Cantini, "Adam de Marisco O.F.M.: Auctor spiritualis," in *Antonianum,* **23** (1948); Richard C. Dales, "Adam Marsh, Robert Grosseteste, and the Treatise on the Tides," in *Speculum,* **52** (1977); Decima L. Douie, "Adam 'de Marisco,'" in *Durham University Journal,* **32** (1940); A. B. Emden, "Marsh, Adam," in *A Biographical Register of the University of Oxford to A.D. 1500,* II (1958); Father Cuthbert [Hess], "Adam Marsh: An English Franciscan of the Thirteenth Century," in his *The Romanticism of St. Francis and Other Studies in the Genius of the Franciscans* (1924); R. W. Hunt, "Manuscripts Containing the Indexing Symbols of Robert Grosseteste," in *Bodleian Library Record,* **4** (1952–1953); Andrew G. Little, *The Grey Friars in Oxford* (1892), 134–139, and "The Franciscan School at Oxford in the Thirteenth Century," in *Archivum Franciscanum historicum,* **19** (1926); S. Harrison Thomson, "Grosseteste's Concordantial Signs," in *Medievalia et humanistica,* **9** (1955).

CONRAD HARKINS, O.F.M.

[See also **England: 1216–1485; Franciscans; Grosseteste, Robert; Henry III of England; Oxford University.**]

MARSHAL, an official in a baronial or princely household. In its earliest usages the word *mariscalcus* refers to a groom and reflects accurately the etymology "servant for the horses." The appropriate comparison is "constable" (count of the stable). In this sense and in the transferred senses that follow, the office of marshal is found throughout medieval Europe—in the Byzantine Empire, in some of the great fiefs of France, in German principalities like Saxony, and in royal France and England.

In later records (attested from 1047), the word sometimes refers to the official in charge of provisioning the army. The duties associated with this task necessitated that the marshal wield considerable power. In France and in England the marshal emerged as a military commander under the constable; but in England especially, the office of the marshal had a wider competence. The marshal assisted (later presided) at the court of chivalry wherein cases related to military precedence were adjudicated, and in the late Middle Ages the marshal's court exercised jurisdiction over war-related crime by right of martial law. The justice administered there has been described as "both savage and summary." The marshal, like other great officers of state in England, performed rather more personal services for the monarch, particularly keeping order in and regulating admission to the king's household (he was assisted by subordinate marshals). Out of this milieu emerged the Marshalsea Court or Court of the Verge, the court that adjudicated disputes among members of the royal household and among people in the vicinity (ultimately set at twelve miles) of the king's person, particularly with regard to relatively minor matters like debt. The procedures of this court were simple and swift; and, when possible, ordinary lay people not normally under its jurisdiction sought to have their claims adjudicated in this court.

Marshals were also used in various specialized capacities—and like all such officials, an array of adjectives and prepositional phrases describe the various offices. These were not always very high in status, and they are properly associated with the subordinate marshals rather than the great officer of state (hereditary in medieval England in the house of Pembroke). For example, in 1248 the "king's marshal came to the vill of Wantage and had the measures of the vill emended there, and by those measures he had the measures of Lambourn emended." Marshals also oversaw prisoners, especially debtors, in the late Middle Ages. It is from functions such as these that the modern signification of marshal as a police officer has emerged, while the meaning of marshal as commander of an army (French: *maréchal;* German: *Feldmarschall*) harks back to the idea of the marshal as the constable's right hand.

BIBLIOGRAPHY

Ferdinand Lot and Robert Fawtier, *Histoire des institutions françaises au moyen âge,* II, *Institutions royales* (1958), 53–54; Achille Luchaire, *Manuel des institutions françaises* (1892, repr. 1964), 527–528; Bryce D. Lyon, *A Constitutional and Legal History of Medieval England,* 2nd ed. (1980), 53, 155, 453; Marjorie McIntosh, "Immediate Royal Justice: The Marshalsea Court in Havering, 1358," in *Speculum,* 54 (1979); John Horace Round, *The King's Serjeants and Officers of State* (1911, repr. 1970). The quotation on the king's marshal at Wantage is taken from Michael T. Clanchy, ed., *The Roll and Writ File of the Berkshire Eyre of 1248* (1973).

WILLIAM CHESTER JORDAN

[See also **Constable of the Realm.**]

MARSHAL, WILLIAM. See **William Marshal.**

MARSILIUS OF PADUA (1275/1280–1342), Italian political theorist, was born Marsiglio dei Mainardini. After studying medicine at the University of Padua, he went to Paris, where he was rector of the university in 1313 and developed close associations with such leading Averroists as John of Jandun. He completed his monumental antipapalist treatise *Defensor pacis* (The defender of peace) in 1324. When, in 1326, his authorship of this work became known, he fled to Nuremberg, to the court of Louis of Bavaria, recently excommunicated by the Avignon pope John XXII. The following year the pope condemned the *Defensor* and its author as heretical. From 1327 to 1329, Marsilius accompanied Louis on his mission to be crowned emperor in Rome and was appointed his spiritual vicar. After Louis and his entourage were rejected by the people and forced to leave Rome, Marsilius spent the remainder of his life as physician to the court of Louis, together with William of Ockham. In 1342 he composed the *Defensor minor,* a pro-imperial summary of his major work.

The *Defensor pacis* was written to refute the partisans of papal "plenitude of power," such as Egidius of Colonna (Giles of Rome), who had claimed that the authority of the papacy was supreme in all matters: according to the papalists, secular rulers were completely subject to the pope and could be deposed by him at any time. Marsilius, by contrast, argued that the papacy and the ecclesiastical hierarchy must be wholly subordinate to the secular government, which derives its authority from the people.

The treatise is divided into three "discourses" *(dictiones),* the third of which is a brief summary of conclusions. The other discourses are concerned with the causes of civil peace and strife, since the civil authority cannot enable its citizens to attain "the sufficient life" without concord and peace. The first discourse, which leans heavily on the *Politics* of Aristotle, discusses the principles and institutions of good government. According to Marsilius' radically republican theory of government, the people make the laws and elect the ruler, who must govern in accordance with the laws and can be deposed and punished by the people for his failure to do so. The first discourse also considers the "general" causes of strife enumerated by Aristotle, while the second discourse is devoted to a "singular" cause of discord: the papal claim to plenitude of power. Marsilius' arguments against "this pernicious pestilence" invoke mainly Scripture and the history of the early church.

MARTIANUS CAPELLA

Marsilius concludes that the jurisdiction of the pope and the priests (who may own no property) is to be limited to the administration of the sacraments and the teaching of the divine law; even these rights are bestowed by the secular power, which may withdraw them at any time. Furthermore, the principal authority in all ecclesiastical matters, including the correct interpretation of Scripture, is the general council, a democratic assembly of priests and laymen. The general council retains the powers of excommunication, bestowal, and revocation of benefices, and appointment to ecclesiastical offices, including the election of the pope. This democratic theory of ecclesiastical government was widely influential at the time of the Reformation.

BIBLIOGRAPHY

Sources. The *Defensor pacis,* C. W. Previté-Orton, ed. (1928), is translated by Alan Gewirth as vol. II of *Marsilius of Padua, the Defender of Peace* (1956, repr. 1979). The *Defensor minor,* C. Kenneth Brampton, ed. (1922), is translated into French, together with the *De translatione imperii,* in *Marsile de Padoue: Oeuvres mineures,* Colette Jeudy and Jeannine Quillet, eds. and trans. (1979).

Studies. For the life of Marsilius, see C. K. Brampton, "Marsiglio of Padua: Life," in *English Historical Review,* 37 (1922). The fullest study in English of Marsilius' doctrines is Alan Gewirth, *Marsilius of Padua, the Defender of Peace,* I, *Marsilius of Padua and Medieval Political Philosophy* (1951, repr. 1979); this work contains a comprehensive bibliography. See also *idem,* "John of Jandun and the *Defensor Pacis,*" in *Speculum,* **23** (1948), which establishes the sole authorship of Marsilius; Ewart Lewis, "The 'Positivism' of Marsiglio of Padua," in *Speculum,* **38** (1963); Nicolai Rubinstein, "Marsilius of Padua and Italian Political Thought of His Time," in John R. Hale *et al.,* eds., *Europe in the Late Middle Ages* (1965); Michael Wilks, "Corporation and Representation in the *Defensor pacis,*" in *Studia Gratiana,* **15** (1972).

BERNARD CULLEN

[See also **Defensor Pacis; Egidius Colonna; Papacy, Origins and Development of; Plenitudo Potestatis; Political Theory, Western European: 1100–1485.**]

MARTIANUS CAPELLA (Martianus Minneus Felix Capella, *fl.* after 410), author of *De nuptiis Philologiae et Mercurii libri novem* (The marriage of Philology and Mercury), a North African, probably an advocate, possibly a proconsul of Africa, wrote after the Visigothic sack of Rome in 410 and possibly as late as the 470's. Nothing more is known of his life. His work is divided into nine sections, or books. Books 1–2 deal directly with the betrothal and marriage of the two allegorized figures. Books 3–9 present the seven liberal arts: Grammar, Dialectic, Rhetoric, Geometry, Arithmetic, Astronomy, and Music. Each has a prose-meter introduction and a summary of the respective discipline by a serving maid of the bride, Philology. Each maid has an appearance suggestive of the art she represents.

Martianus' limitation of the arts to seven, although he mentions Architecture and Medicine without allowing them to speak, was among the more important precedents, along with Boethius and Cassiodorus, for the canonization of seven as the number of liberal arts. The restriction to seven along with the internal order of contents of *De nuptiis* show conscious structuring rather than accidental results. The arrangement of the text reflects the order of the cosmos: a macrocosm-microcosm parallel appears in the work; the seven arts chosen represent the three Latin arts plus the four Greek arts; and the conclusion of the work with Music (book 9) is appropriate to a text within which harmony on many levels is a leitmotiv.

In books 1–2 Mercury decides to marry and looks for a suitable wife. Various deities are considered but are unavailable, and a mortal, Philology, suggested by Apollo, is chosen and carried to the heavens for the wedding. She is purged and given immortality. A trip through the heavenly spheres, paralleling that of human souls, leads to the company of the gods and the completion of the nuptials. Mercury presents to Philology the seven liberal arts as a gift. According to Remigius of Auxerre in the ninth century, Philology responds with a gift of the seven mechanical arts to Mercury. Each personified liberal art, subsequently describing her subject matter, offers no more than a preliminary handbook, following a long tradition of late antiquity. Among these seven, the presentations by Astronomy and Music are the most competent.

Representing values of *ca.* 400, *De nuptiis* offers a perspective on pagan classical learning which Christians could easily adopt. While the seven liberal arts appear primarily as accumulations of erudition and as a defense of the classical tradition, they take their larger value from their place in the allegory, whose focus is Philology's ascent and apotheosis. Martianus derives this account from the ritual practices of contemporary mystery cults with various Orphic, Neopythagorean, and Chaldean elements. He writes as a priest with secret knowledge.

MARTIANUS CAPELLA

The allegory considers classical learning in successive guises. The deity Mercury, a Latin Hermes, carries his traditional learning lightly so that it does not obtrude. Philology, in whom learning is at first essential and weighty, must eject her classical—even her Egyptian—learning before becoming immortal. The seven liberal arts, a sum of classical learning, then return to her as handmaidens given by Mercury at the close of the nuptial allegory. Classical culture is thus circumscribed and made strictly subordinate to the higher, spiritual ends of the soul.

During the Middle Ages the figures of Mercury and Philology were consistently identified with eloquence and disciplined reason, respectively. This medieval identification saw the marriage as a clothing of truth *(sapientia, studium rationis, philosophia)* by attractive words *(eloquentia)* and was traced back to Cicero and Quintilian. The apex of this medieval view is found in the twelfth-century commentaries.

The use of *De nuptiis* appears minor until the ninth century. In 534 a Roman rhetor, Securus Felix, emended *De nuptiis* (but perhaps only books 1–2, or even book 1 alone) from exemplars he labeled "extremely corrupt." Cassiodorus could not locate a copy of *De nuptiis* when writing his *Institutiones.* Gregory of Tours referred to Martianus as one who set standards for eloquence. Isidore of Seville made very slight use of *De nuptiis.* From Isidore into the ninth century (for example, Hrabanus Maurus), Cassiodorus, and Isidore were the standard authors on the liberal arts. The revival and spread of *De nuptiis* was a Carolingian phenomenon, especially under the influence of Irish masters in France, from the 840's onwards, when the work became a basic manual for Carolingian culture.

From Fleury, Soissons, and Laon east to St. Gallen, Freising, and Corvey, the manuscripts of the ninth and tenth centuries show a rapid spread with many apparent connections. More than half of all extant manuscripts of the complete text of *De nuptiis* are from the ninth and tenth centuries. Interest in the complete text declines from the eleventh to the fifteenth century, when there is some revival of interest with the Italian humanists. Books 1–2 appear separately with great frequency from the twelfth century on. Book 8 (astronomy) is the single book most often appearing alone in surviving manuscripts, with by far the greatest number in the twelfth century. Book 8 retains something of a reputation as an adequate introduction to astronomy, even after the twelfth century, at lesser schools like the Dominican convent of Auxerre.

For commentaries on *De nuptiis* the ninth century is again the greatest century, with commentaries by Remigius of Auxerre, Johannes Scottus Eriugena, and either Heiric of Auxerre or Martin of Laon. Remigius' commentary remained the standard commentary and was actively copied through the twelfth century. Of the presently identified medieval commentaries, only one after the ninth century covers all nine books. Two on book 8 alone have been discovered. By far the most popular section for commentary was the allegory of books 1–2, with nine distinct commentaries identified. Prior to 1600, *De nuptiis* was printed in eight editions, the first in 1499, which may be compared with thirty-four editions of Macrobius' *Commentary on the Dream of Scipio* during the same period.

The text of *De nuptiis* has often been considered to have provided the program for medieval pictorial representations of the seven liberal arts. However, before the twelfth century there is no consistent set of images for the liberal arts. With the twelfth century there emerges a tradition unconnected to the earlier images, a new invention on other bases. In the fifteenth century, illustrations of the liberal arts in manuscripts of *De nuptiis* are designed with closer similarity to the literary descriptions in the work.

BIBLIOGRAPHY

Sources. Martianus Capella, James Willis, ed. (1983), the latest edition; critically reviewed with authoritative commentary in *Classical Philology,* **81** (1986), by Danuta Shanzer. William H. Stahl and Richard Johnson, eds. (with E. L. Burge), *Martianus Capella and the Seven Liberal Arts,* 2 vols. (1971–1977), provide detailed summary and commentary (vol. I) and a complete translation (vol. II); an essential review with many corrections appears (in English) in *Beiträge zur Geschichte der deutschen Sprache und Literatur,* **104** (1982). Cora E. Lutz, "Martianus Capella," in *Catalogus translationum et commentariorum,* **2** (1971), gives a very useful list of commentaries through the sixteenth century, including all known manuscripts and printed editions.

Studies. Pierre Courcelle, *Late Latin Writers and their Greek Sources,* Harry E. Wedeck, trans. (1969), 211–219; Bruce Eastwood, "The Chaster Path of Venus *(orbis Veneris castior)* in the Astronomy of Martianus Capella," in *Archives internationales d'histoire des sciences,* **32** (1982); Michael W. Evans, "The Personifications of the *Artes* from Martianus Capella up to the End of the Fourteenth Century" (diss., Univ. of London, 1971); Cora E. Lutz and

John J. Contreni, "Martianus Capella: Addenda et corrigenda," in *Catalogus translationum et commentariorum,* 3 (1976); William H. Stahl, "To a Better Understanding of Martianus Capella," in *Speculum,* **40** (1965), and "The *Quadrivium* of Martianus Capella: Its Place in the Intellectual History of Western Europe," in *Arts libéraux et philosophie au moyen âge* (1969), 959–967.

BRUCE STANSFIELD EASTWOOD

[See also **Arts, Seven Liberal; Boethius; Cassiodorus; Gregory of Tours; Hrabanus Maurus; Isidore of Seville; John Scottus Eriugena; Macrobius; Remigius of Auxerre.**]

MARTIN OF BRAGA, ST. (Martinus Bracarensis, *ca.* 515–579), bishop and writer. Born in Pannonia (part of modern Hungary) and educated in Greek as a monk, Martinus reached Galicia by ship from the Holy Land about 550. He founded a monastery at Dumium and in 556 was ordained first bishop of Dumium. He consecrated the new Basilica of St. Martin of Tours there in 558. Martinus represented Dumium at the First Council of Braga (561) and, in his capacity as metropolitan bishop, presided over the Second Council of Braga (572). About 100 pages of his writings are extant.

BIBLIOGRAPHY

Claude W. Barlow, ed., *Martini Episcopi Bracarensis: Opera omnia* (1950), and trans., *Iberian Fathers,* I (1969) (vol. LXII of *The Fathers of the Church*).

JAMES T. MCDONOUGH, JR.

[See also **Monasticism.**]

MARTÍNEZ DE TOLEDO, ALFONSO, Spanish prose writer (1398–1468). He was probably born in Toledo, and likely took his bachelor of canon law degree at Salamanca. His best-known work is the *Arcipreste de Talavera* (popularly called *El Corbacho,* or Whip), a tract that condemns the sin of lust and that is titled after Martínez' principal ecclesiastical benefice. Martínez was also the author of the *Atalaya de las corónicas* (Watchtower of the Chronicles, composed between 1443 and 1453), a digest of Iberian peninsular history culled from early Castilian chronicles and covering the period from the Visigoth king Walia to the reign of John II. Two hagiographies have also been attributed to him: the *Vida de San Isidoro* and the *Vida de San Ildefonso* (both completed in 1444). The latter contains a notable Castilian translation of Ildefonso's *De virginitate Sanctae Mariae contra tres infideles.* Several works thought to be his (the *Invencionario de todas las cosas* and the *Vencimiento del mundo*) have since been proven spurious.

Aside from being the archpriest of Talavera de la Reina, an important medieval agricultural and commercial center near Toledo, Martínez held numerous important benefices in the cathedral of Toledo. In his youth he traveled extensively through the Iberian Peninsula, but especially through Aragon. He spent two years in Italy (1431–1433) under the aegis of Juan de Casanova, Cardinal San Sixto. The latter half of his life was devoted to Castilian church affairs and his literary interests. After 1436 he appears in documents as chaplain to John II; later he also became chaplain to Henry (Enrique) IV. Although little is known of his family background, his successful accumulation of lucrative ecclesiastical benefices and his favor at the Castilian court and among the Aragonese church hierarchy seem to point to influential origins, perhaps, as his coat of arms suggests, even a connection with a distant branch of the Álvarez de Toledo family (the family of the dukes of Alba).

His *Arcipreste de Talavera* (1438) is considered an important forerunner of Spanish Golden Age imaginative prose. The vividly realistic vernacular language and direct speech of the characters in the exempla, as well as the expository rhetoric of the doctrinal parts of the work, have their foundations in the learned and popular sermon tradition. The theme of the work centers on human accountability for sin and the moral and physiological consequences of concupiscence. A satirico-didactic tract divided into four parts, it examines and reproves amatory beliefs and conventions associated with courtly love in fifteenth-century Spain. Part II is the best-known section of the work. It contains raucous, often bawdy exempla depicting feminine foibles. Adopting an unmistakably mysogynistic tone, notwithstanding his stated desire to praise virtuous women, the author intimates that the female sex is the deciding factor in man's perdition.

The principal sources of *Arcipreste de Talavera* are Andreas Capellanus' "De reprobatio amoris" (book III of his *De amore*), Boccacio's *De casibus virorum illustrium,* the pseudo-Aristotelian *Secreta secretorum,* and various ecclesiastical and patristic writings (particularly the Old Testament, the *Clementine Constitutions, Gratian's Decree,* the *Extra Decrees* of Gregory IX, and St. Augustine's *De doctrina christiana* and *De libero arbitrio*).

BIBLIOGRAPHY

Editions. El Corbacho: Arcipreste de Talavera; o,Corbacho, Michael Gerli, ed. (1979). *Atalaya: Atalaya de las corónicas,* James B. Larkin, ed. (1983); Inocencio Bombín, "La 'Atalaya de las corónicas' del Arcipreste de Talavera (diss., Toronto, 1976); Raúl A. del Piero, *Dos escritores de la baja Edad Media castellana (Pedro de Veragüe y el Arcipreste de Talavera, cronista real)* (1970), containing a small section of Atalaya, with an introductory study; *San Ildefonso: San Ildefonso de Toledo a través de la pluma del Arcipreste de Talavera,* José Madoz y Moleres, ed. (1943).

Studies and bibliography. E. Michael Gerli, *Alfonso Martínez de Toledo* (1976), and "The Burial Place and Probable Date of Death of Alfonso Martínez de Toledo," in *Journal of Hispanic Philology,* **1** (1976–1977); Erich von Richthofen, "Alfonso Martínez de Toledo und sein *Arcipreste de Talauera,*" in *Zeitschrift für romanische Philologie,* **61** (1941); David J. Viera, "An Annotated Bibliography on Alfonso Martínez de Toledo: Arcipreste de Talavera," in *Kentucky Romance Quarterly,* **24** (1977).

E. MICHAEL GERLI

[See also **Ildefonsus, St., Spanish Literature; Toledo.**]

MARTINI, SIMONE. See **Simone Martini.**

MARTINUS GOSIA (*ca.* 1100–1160), one of the "four doctors," disciples of Irnerius, who continued his teaching in Bologna and made theirs the leading school of law in Europe. He is remembered especially as the forerunner of a current of juridical interpretation whose antithesis was that of Bulgarus and his followers. This divergence, which had its antecedents in Roman legal history and whose analogue exists in all legal systems, not only lasted throughout the lives of the two doctors but was destined to divide the school until its end.

The contrast crystallized around the question of the role of equity, with Martinus advocating a predominant role for it while Bulgarus asserted the desirability of a more literal interpretation of the law. While both doctors sought a renewed understanding of the Roman legal system in its entirety, Martinus pursued this goal not only through a search for the connection existing among the different norms but also by the isolation of general ideas that revealed the organic nature of the *Corpus iuris civilis.* These ideas could also serve as the means of resolution of the antinomies that could arise among the different specific legal norms.

The dissension between these two doctors gave rise to the literary genre known as *dissensiones.* Martinus was also the author of glosses, *quaestiones disputatae,* an exordium, and an apparatus to the *Institutes* (part of the *Corpus iuris civilis*). Some of his glosses are in the form of distinctions; this also was to become a separate literary genre. He also wrote a treatise *de jure dotium* and, in the form of a long gloss, a *computatio graduum.* In this latter work, Martinus referred to norms of both civil and canon law. This novel approach again brought to the fore the question of the reconciliation of antinomies; the solution adopted was to choose in each case the more reasonable norm from either of the two systems. This may mark the beginning of the jus commune.

BIBLIOGRAPHY

Hermann Kantorowicz with William W. Buckland, *Studies in the Glossators of the Roman Law* (1938, repr. 1969); Bruno Paradisi, *Storia del diritto italiano: Le fonti del diritto nell'epoca bolognese,* I, *I civilisti fino a Rogerio* (1962).

GIULIO SILANO

[See also **Bologna, University of; Bulgarus; Corpus Iuris Civilis; Glossators; Irnerius; Law, Schools of.**]

MARTORELL, BERNARDO (*fl. ca.* 1429–1452). A leading figure in Catalan painting of the International Gothic Style during the second quarter of the fifteenth century, he was known for many years as the Master of St. George after his large altarpiece of St. George, *ca.* 1434–1438 (Art Institute of Chicago; Louvre). Several of his later paintings depart from International Style formulae and show his interest in space, texture, and light—characteristics of the Hispano-Flemish period.

BIBLIOGRAPHY

Mary Grizzard, *Bernardo Martorell: 15th-century Catalan Artist* (1985).

MARY GRIZZARD

[See also **Gothic, International Style.**]

MARTYRDOM, CHRISTIAN

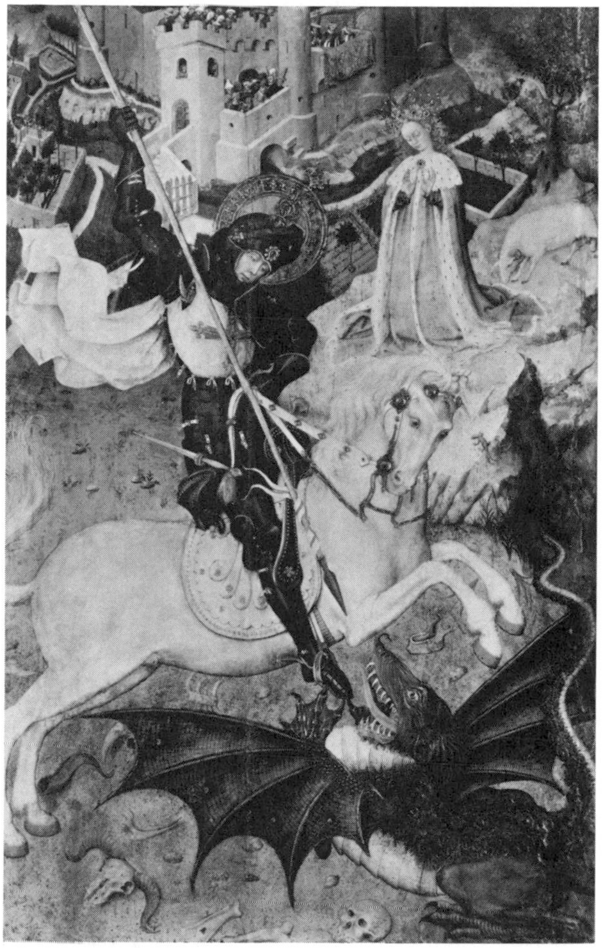

St. George and the Dragon. Central panel of retable by Bernardo Martorell, *ca.* 1434–1438. ART INSTITUTE OF CHICAGO, 33.786

MARTYRDOM, CHRISTIAN. Martyrdom is suffering death for one's religious beliefs. Its great prestige during the Middle Ages was an inheritance from the early church, which regarded martyrdom as the perfect completion of a Christian life. The cult of the martyrs was linked to their remains, and the practice of translating relics assured the continuation and development of the cult as Christianity moved north from Rome and Constantinople. The annual celebration of the martyrs' feasts and pilgrimages to their shrines helped keep alive a respect, and even a desire, for martyrdom.

Although the number of martyrs in the Middle Ages was relatively small, the rapid spread of their cults shows that martyrdom had remained a Christian ideal. When the missionary Boniface was murdered by the pagan Frisians in 754 his fame soon extended through northern Europe from Fulda, where his relics were enshrined. The concept of martyrdom was applied quite elastically. In England a popular local cult to William of Perth, a pilgrim murdered by robbers in 1201, developed at Rochester. Conflicts between church and state also produced martyrs. The most popular in the Western church was Thomas Becket, who was murdered at Canterbury in 1170 as a result of his opposition to the ecclesiastical policies of Henry II. The political aspects of Thomas' death made him even more popular. He was canonized in 1173, and his magnificent shrine became one of the most celebrated goals of medieval pilgrims. Although his claim to be considered a martyr can be questioned, Thomas' death had earlier parallels, such as those of Stanislaus (*d.* 1079) at Cracow, and, much earlier, Pope Martin I (*d.* 655), and the philosopher Boethius (*d.* 524). Another popular saint, Peter Martyr, was a victim of heretics. He was canonized in 1253, only one year after his death at the hands of the Cathari. Martyr's honors were also readily given to Christian rulers who died fighting the heathen or for the church, such as Hermenigild (*d.* 585), Oswald of Northumbria (*d.* 642), Edmund of East Anglia (*d.* 870), and Olaf II of Norway (*d.* 1030).

Martyrdom was discussed by Thomas Aquinas (*d.* 1274) under the general heading of fortitude. According to him, a martyr is rightly regarded as a perfect Christian, not primarily because his courage is great, but because his motive is a total love for God, whom he prefers even to life itself. The intensity of the martyr's love removes sin and all its consequences so that, even if he be a great sinner or unbaptized, he will enter heaven directly after his death. While Aquinas recognized that martyrs could be put to death for many reasons, he saw them all rooted in faith, viewed as the source of every virtuous act. Thus, John the Baptist, one of the most popular saints of the medieval church, is rightly honored as a martyr although he was executed not directly for his faith but because he condemned the sin of adultery.

The strong identity of church and state that characterized Eastern Christianity produced a feeling of religious veneration for the ruler. In the Balkans and Russia this resulted in an application of the title "martyr" to victims of political assassinations. The most popular of these martyrs in the medieval Russian church were the brother princes Boris and Gleb (*d.* 1015), sons of St. Vladimir, the first Christian duke of Kiev. Accounts of their death emphasize their meekness and their conscious imitation of Christ in voluntarily sacrificing their lives. Their cult was encouraged in the eleventh and twelfth centuries by the rulers, partly at least, to foster their people's loyalty.

Crusaders who died in battle were not martyrs, but they were popularly regarded as such because they had died for the Christian faith. Furthermore, the indulgence they were eligible for, if its conditions were properly fulfilled, assured them of an immediate entry into heaven. But the failure of the Second Crusade and the subsequent difficulties of the Latin kingdoms in the Holy Land redirected the desire for martyrdom to an older substitute, the ascetical life.

After the age of the early persecutions, ascetics had viewed themselves as a new sort of martyr because, by their austerities, they gave up their lives for Christ, not by a single act, but nonetheless completely. Bernard of Clairvaux (*d.* 1153) described three types of martyrdom: in will and act, such as the protomartyr, St. Stephen; in act alone, such as the Holy Innocents; and in will alone, such as St. John the Evangelist. The last type was the model for monks. A long tradition, going back to the earliest ascetics in the desert of Egypt and beyond, called a life of asceticism a "white martyrdom." Among the Irish monks the term "white martyrdom" was applied to those who had given up what was most precious to them for the love of God; "green martyrdom" was used of those who suppressed their passions by severe and continual penance. In the Middle Ages these ideas had become structured into a way of life formed particularly by the three vows of religion: poverty, chastity, and obedience.

A striking example of this ascetical "martyrdom" is Francis of Assisi (*d.* 1226), who had invited actual martyrdom by a journey to Muslim countries as a missionary and peacemaker. In his desire to conform as closely as possible to the crucified Christ he embraced a life of extreme asceticism, which culminated in his receiving the stigmata in 1224. His life was described by his follower Bonaventure (*d.* 1274) as an expression of a desire for martyrdom, which produced in Francis an identification with Jesus Christ. Like a martyr, the true ascetic is called upon to renounce the world and ascend, though more slowly, to Christian perfection. From his mystical experiences, Francis became convinced that the suffering of an ascetic, or martyr, like Christ's own, would be salvific for others. This intensely personal piety appears in the Devotio Moderna school of spirituality of the late fourteenth century. Its typical expression is found in the spiritual classic of Thomas à Kempis, *The Imitation of Christ,* which describes the entire life of Christ as a martyrdom.

BIBLIOGRAPHY

For a general treatment of the subject see R. Hedde, "Martyre," in *Dictionnaire de théologie catholique,* A. Vacant, E. Mangenot, and E. Amann, eds., 15 vols. (1903–1950), and James E. Sherman, *The Nature of Martyrdom* (1942). See also E. Randolph Daniel, "The Desire for Martyrdom: A *Leitmotiv* of St. Bonaventure," in *Franciscan Studies,* **32** (1972), and David Knowles, *Thomas Becket* (1971). For an important discussion of martyrdom by Thomas Aquinas in the original Latin with a good English translation and copious notes see his *Summa theologiae,* Anthony Ross and P. G. Walsh, eds. and trans., XLII (1964–1966), esp. 40–59.

DANIEL CALLAM

[See also **Aquinas, St. Thomas; Becket, Thomas, St.; Bernard of Clairvaux, St.; Bonaventure, St.; Boniface, St.; Byzantine Church; Canonization; Church, Early; Church, Latin; Crusades; Francis of Assisi, St.; Indulgences; Russian Orthodox Church; Thomas à Kempis.**]

MARTYRDOM, JEWISH. The commandment of martyrdom *(kiddush ha-shem)* is incumbent upon a Jew under any one of three circumstances, which are sometimes termed "persecution," "public action," and "the three inviolables." For the sake of clarity they will be discussed in reverse order.

First, should a Jew be told under the threat of death to worship idols, commit murder, or engage in incestuous or adulterous intercourse, he must choose death. Whether the crime demanded is to be committed publicly or privately is irrelevant. The inherent severity of these transgressions precludes their commission at all times, in all places, and at all costs. Second, should it be demanded of him that he violate publicly (that is, in the presence of at least ten other Jews) any other religious restriction (such as eating nonkosher food) he must again choose death. Were this demand to be made "privately" (in the presence of fewer than ten of his coreligionists), he would be permitted to yield to his coercer. Third, should it be demanded of him during a period of religious persecution to commit the most minute religious infraction, he is enjoined to suffer martyrdom. In many opinions, in times of religious persecution, even a demand for change in something only symbolically associated with Judaism (distinctive national garb, for example) must be resisted, even if the demand is, technically speaking, religiously insignificant.

Voluntary martyrdom is problematic. In the Maimonidean view choosing martyrdom in instances where it is not required is tantamount to suicide. Northern European communities throughout the Middle Ages frequently chose such martyrdom, and in the course of centuries a strong case was made for its permissibility, possibly even its commendability. It is this view that generally prevailed.

Committing suicide so as to avoid being tortured into changing one's religious allegiance would appear to be forbidden. But again northern European Jewry did so frequently, and post-facto justifications were found.

Christianity, with its doctrine of the Trinity, was viewed as a form of polytheism and fell within the definition of "idolatry." Islam was viewed as being strictly monotheistic, but since the Koran abrogated the authority of Jewish law, acceptance of Islam constituted heresy and fell within the prescription of martyrdom.

Jewish communities of Islamic countries submitted more frequently to forced conversions. This different pattern of conduct may in part be attributable to the fact that while heresy was legally equivalent to idolatry it had none of the latter's repugnant force, and in part perhaps to the more lenient concept of martyrdom in the surrounding Islamic culture, as expressed in the principle of the *takiya.*

BIBLIOGRAPHY

S. Eidelberg, ed. and trans., *The Jews and the Crusaders: The Hebrew Chronicle of the First and Second Crusade* (1977); J. Katz, *Exclusiveness and Tolerance* (1961), chap. 7; B. Lewis, *Jews in Islam* (1985); Moses Maimonides, *Mishneh Torah, Book of Knowledge,* M. Hyamson, ed. and trans. (1965), chap. 5, Laws Concerning the Foundation of Torah; H. Soloveitchik, "Halakah and Rhetoric: Maimonides' Iggeret Ha-shemad," in L. Landman, ed., *Rabbi Joseph H. Lookstein Memorial Volume* (1980).

HAYM SOLOVEITCHIK

[See also **Jews** (various articles).]

MARTYRIUM (from the Greek *marturion* for [place of] witness), a structure erected to commemorate a martyr's grave or relics, or the site of an event in Christ's life. Rooted in the *heroa* (semitemple, semimausoleum) of antiquity, the earliest preserved martyrium lies under St. Peter's in Rome and is a sec-

Martyrium over the tomb of St. Agnes, originally erected as a mausoleum for Constantine's daughter. Rome, Sta. Costanza, *ca.* 350. PHOTO: GERMAN ARCHAEOLOGICAL INSTITUTE, ROME

ond-century shrine above the presumed tomb of St. Peter. Pre-Constantinian martyria were varied in form; but from the fourth century, a centralized plan, apparently adapted from Roman mausoleums, was favored.

BIBLIOGRAPHY

André Grabar, *Martyrium: Recherches sur le culte des reliques et l'art chrétien antique,* 2 vols. (1943–1946); Richard Krautheimer, *Early Christian and Byzantine Architecture,* 3rd ed. (1979), 11–14, 29–30, 36–41.

LESLIE BRUBAKER

MARTYROLOGY, a list of the feasts of saints and other fixed celebrations organized in calendrical order. Martyrologies differ from liturgical calendars in that the occurrence of a name in a martyrology does not necessarily imply a liturgical commemoration of the saint, and most martyrologies contain an entry on every day of the year, often with several notices for individual saints or groups on a single date. Furthermore, martyrologies have a historical aspect lacking in calendars, for even in their simplest form they usually refer to a place associated with the feast mentioned, normally the location of the saint's death or burial.

The most famous and influential martyrology of the Middle Ages was the *Martyrologium Hieronymianum (MH).* Compiled from local calendars or martyrologies originating in Rome, Africa, and the Christian East, *MH* was the first general or "universal" martyrology. Falsely attributed to St. Jerome, this ultimate source of all later Western martyrologies acquired its final form in Gaul about the end of the sixth century. The historical element in *MH* goes beyond simple topographical references, for this text contains brief narratives about some of the saints commemorated, but these are overshadowed by the vast majority of notices that include nothing beyond the names of persons and places.

The first "historical" martyrology properly so called is that of Bede, which contains 114 historical notices and formed the basis for all later historical martyrologies. (As applied to martyrologies, the term "historical" refers to their narrative rather than to their factual character, for much of the information in these texts is legendary.) The flowering of historical martyrologies occurred in the Carolingian age. Prompted by monastic reform that specified the daily reading of the martyrology at chapter and by a hagiocentric piety that emphasized large numbers of saints, numerous new compilations appeared. In this development a direct line of descent leads from Bede through an anonymous text from Lyons and the martyrologies of Florus of Lyons and Ado of Vienne to Usuard, whose work formed the basis of the modern Roman martyrology compiled by Caesar Baronius in the sixteenth century.

The major martyrologies of the East Frankish region also date from the Carolingian period. These include the work of Hrabanus Maurus and the poetic martyrology by Wandalbert of Prüm. Some texts from Germanic Europe, such as that by Notker Balbulus, combined several branches of the martyrological tradition by drawing materials from both Ado and Hrabanus, but none of the German compilations equaled the popularity of Ado's or of Usuard's. Insular martyrologies drew upon the continental tradition, but with the exception of Bede's work, they contributed little to it. Nevertheless, these texts include the earliest examples of vernacular martyrologies, in both Irish and English. Post-Carolingian martyrologies on the Continent consist for the most part of abbreviations or minor expansions of the Carolingian texts. Usuard's work proved the most adaptable, and in the High Middle Ages, various religious orders developed standardized martyrologies based on his composition.

BIBLIOGRAPHY

René Aigrain, *L'hagiographie: Ses sources, ses methodes, son histoire* (1953); Baudouin de Gaiffier, "De l'usage et de la lecture du martyrologe: Témoignages antérieurs au XIe siècle," in *Analecta Bollandiana,* 79 (1961); Hippolyte Delehaye, *Cinq leçons sur la méthode hagiographique* (1934), 42–74; Jacques Dubois, *Les martyrologes du moyen âge latin* (1978), with supplemental 'Mise à jour' (1985); Regina Hausmann, *Das Martyrologium von Marcigny-sur-Loire: Edition einer Quelle zur cluniacensischen Heiligenverehrung am Ende des elften Jahrhunderts* (1984); H. Leclercq, "Martyrologe," in *Dictionnaire d'archéologie chrétienne et de liturgie,* X, 2 (1932), 2532–2619; Henri Quentin, *Les martyrologes historiques du moyen âge* (1908); R. Stieger, "Martyrologien," in *Lexikon für Theologie und Kirche,* 2nd ed., 7 (1962).

JOHN M. MCCULLOH

[See also **Bede; Feasts; Florus of Lyons; Hrabanus Maurus; Notker Balbulus; Usuard.**]

MARTYROLOGY, IRISH. Martyrologies grew out of the early church calendars annotated with brief entries to commemorate the early martyrs. To these were gradually added commemorations of other men and women revered by the church. Since the formal process of canonization had not yet been established, early medieval martyrologies varied considerably in their rosters of saints.

The tradition of early Irish martyrology is preserved in four works, in manuscripts dating from the twelfth to the seventeenth century. Three of these, the martyrologies of Tallaght, Óengus, and Gorman, are medieval compositions, while the fourth, the martyrology of Donegal, is a later product compiled from medieval sources.

The martyrologies of Tallaght and Óengus are closely connected in time and place, but quite different in execution. The monastery of Tallaght (near Dublin) was founded by Máel Rúain (*d.* 792), a promient figure among the ascetic monastics known as the Céli Dé. The martyrology of Tallaght survives in the twelfth-century manuscript known as the Book of Leinster and in an abstract in a seventeenth century manuscript. The entries for continental saints' days suggest a Hieronymian model. The martyrology of Tallaght begins on 25 December and uses the Roman dating system of Kalends, Nones, and Ides. There is a prose Latin list of continental saints, mostly Roman, and festivals for each day, with a separate list in mixed Irish and Latin prose of Irish saints following it. The redactor of the martyrology of Tallaght could not have been familiar with the continental material in his exemplar. There are frequent duplications and errors in the dates assigned to the saints, and continental place and road names are sometimes mistaken for personal names.

The martyrology composed by Óengus, a monk at Tallaght and a student of Máel Rúain's, sometime between 797 and 808 clearly drew upon the martyrology of Tallaght since it repeats many of the errors. However, it abandons the prose list format in favor of the native Irish verse form called "rinnard," a six-syllable-line quatrain. There is a 226-stanza prologue to the martyrology on the victorious rise of Christianity in history, and a text of 365 stanzas, one for each day of the year beginning with 1 January. To the Roman dating used in the martyrology of Tallaght, Óengus adds the dominical letters and notes on the names of the months, the latter probably borrowed from Bede. Óengus consistently sacrifices content to form, mentioning only as many saints and feasts as a quatrain will accommodate. The complicated schemes of alliteration, assonance, and rhyme in the martyrology of Óengus make it a very valuable text for linguistic studies. The poetic text is accompanied by copious notes in Irish and Latin which supply many insights into contemporary church practices, features of daily life, and legends and folklore about the saints. This work is preserved in several manuscripts; the earliest is the fourteenth-century Leabhar Breac.

The third medieval text was composed by Máel-Muire hua Gormáin (Marianus Gorman[us]), abbot of Cnoc-na-nApstol (Knock, Co. Louth), who probably began working on it about 1167 and prior to 1174. His martyrology survives only in a seventeenth-century copy now in the Bibliothèque Royale in Brussels. His text is also composed in verse, but utilizes the more flexible "rinnard mor," which allows a variation in the length of the stanza (4, 6, 8, 10, 12, 14 lines). In his prologue Gorman takes Óengus to task for omitting too many saints, Irish and foreign, from his martyrology and for the numerous errors in dates, though he concedes that the blame rests on his model, the martyrology of Tallaght. Gorman adds about one hundred Irish and foreign saints to the Tallaght roster in his composition. He also begins with 1 January and uses Arabic numbered days as well as the Roman dates and dominical letters. The original entries in Gorman's martyrology have been heavily glossed with material similar to the notes added to the martyrology of Óengus.

The last of the Irish martyrologies is not itself a medieval composition. It was compiled in 1630 by the noted scholar Michael O'Clery for the monastic community of Donegal. His work is very useful, for it utilized a number of medieval sources which have not survived, notably the Calendar of Cashel. Thus, his martyrology became a summation of medieval lore, legend, and historical tradition concerning the Irish saints. The martyrology of Donegal is in Irish prose and deals exclusively with Irish saints. Many citations from various hymns and poems, as well as genealogical information, have been included in the individual entries.

The various martyrologies have entries that record as little information as a date and name for some saints, and paragraphs for others. Since the martyrologies thoroughly meld fact and folklore they are difficult to use as primary historical sources. However, they do provide a valuable insight into popular hagiographic tradition and the medieval cults of saints in Ireland.

BIBLIOGRAPHY

Richard I. Best and Hugh J. Lawlor, eds., *The Martyrology of Tallaght* (1931); Paul Grosjean, "Le Martyrologe de Tallaght," in *Analecta Bollandiana,* **51** (1933); J. Hennig, "Studies in the Latin Texts of the *Martyrology of Tallaght,* of *Félire Oengusso,* and of *Félire Húi Gormáin,*" in *Proceedings of the Royal Irish Academy,* **69** (1970); James F. Kenney, *The Sources for the Early History of Ireland,* I (1929, repr. 1968); Whitley Stokes, ed., *The Martyrology of Gorman* (1895), *The Martyrology of Oengus* (1905); James H. Todd and William Reeves, eds., *The Martyrology of Donegal* (1864).

DOROTHY AFRICA

[See also **Hagiography, Western European.**]

MARWĀN I IBN AL-ḤAKAM (*ca.* 622–685), the fourth Umayyad caliph and progenitor of the dynasty's Marwanid line. Though he reigned less than a year, Marwān played a decisive role in the restoration of Umayyad power in the Second Civil War.

The future ruler was born at about the time of Muḥammad's hegira to Medina (A.D. 622). With the accession of ^{c}Uthmān ibn ^{c}Affān to the caliphate in 644, Marwān, who was ^{c}Uthmān's cousin, became his secretary, and in this capacity he seems to have been a powerful adviser. He was severely wounded during the attack in which ^{c}Uthmān was assassinated in Medina in 656, and was wounded again at the Battle of the Camel later that year. By the time the First Civil War had been won by his kinsman Mu^{c}āwiya I ibn Abī Sufyān, he was clearly one of the most influential members of the Umayyad family, serving several times as governor of Medina and the Hejaz, and acting as a highly regarded political adviser.

By the time of Mu^{c}āwiya's death in 680, Marwān's standing had risen so high that he was regarded as the logical successor. Indeed, Mu^{c}āwiya is said to have feared his ambitions in the later years of his own caliphate. But Marwān still lacked the support of the Syrian tribes on which Umayyad power rested, and thus was passed over in favor of Mu^{c}āwiya's son and designated successor, Yazīd I. Marwān cooperated with the new caliph, and again served in various advisory capacities.

In 683, Yazīd I suddenly died as his armies were about to crush the rebellion of ^{c}Abd Allāh ibn al-Zubayr in the Hejaz. The Umayyad forces then returned to Syria. Yazīd's sickly son and successor, Mu^{c}āwiya II, also died within several months, and Egypt, Arabia, and Iraq acknowledged Ibn al-Zubayr as caliph. In Syria, dissension over the succession fragmented the ranks of the Syrian tribes, with the Quḍā^{c}a confederacy championing the Umayyad line against its tribal opponents, led by the Qays. At this moment, in the summer of 684, at the great tribal meeting ground of al-Jābiya, the Umayyad chieftains and their allies elected Marwān as caliph.

Marwān's forces marched north from al-Jābiya and inflicted a crushing defeat on the Qays and other Syrian rivals at the battle of Marj Rāhiṭ, near Damascus. Umayyad control of Syria was thus restored, and the caliph was shortly thereafter able to check a threat by Ibn al-Zubayr against Palestine, and to turn his attention elsewhere. Egypt was reoccupied with little difficulty, and with this development Ibn al-Zubayr, whose forces were centered in the Holy Cities, was cut off from an important source of grain supplies. Marwān also sent military forces south toward Medina and east into Mesopotamia. The first effort was premature and ended in defeat, and before the second could produce any results, the aged caliph died.

Despite the brevity of his reign and the attempts by medieval historians to blacken his reputation, Marwān appears to have exhibited great political acumen in dealing with the restive tribes that buttressed the Umayyad polity. Equally impressive were his skill and quickness in dealing with the sensitive matter of the succession. At al-Jābiya he had been obliged to accept as his successor Yazīd's young son Khālid, who enjoyed little support among the tribal allies of the Umayyads. After Marj Rāhiṭ, he moved swiftly to nullify the agreement (which had been rather informal) and established his own son ^{c}Abd al-Malik as heir to the throne. The wisdom of this choice was proved by ^{c}Abd al-Malik's success in finishing the difficult task his father had begun.

BIBLIOGRAPHY

Julius Wellhausen's *Das arabische Reich und sein Sturz* (1902), trans. by Margaret Graham Weir as *The Arab Kingdom and Its Fall* (1927), is still of great value; see also Henri Lammens, "L'avènement des Marwānides et le califat de Marwān Ier," in *Mélanges de l'Université Saint-Joseph,* **12** (1927), very detailed, but extravagant and often mistaken; Patricia Crone, *Slaves on Horses: The Evolution of the Islamic Polity* (1980), 34–36. The era of Marwān has now been thoroughly studied by Gernot Rotter, *Die Umayyaden und der zweite Bürgerkrieg* (1982), especially pp. 119–26.

LAWRENCE I. CONRAD

[See also **^{c}Abd Allāh ibn al-Zubayr; Caliphate; Marj Rāhiṭ; Marwān, ^{c}Abd al-Malik ibn; Mu^{c}āwiya; Syria; Umayyads; Yazīd I ibn Mu^{c}āwiya.**]

MARWĀN II IBN MUḤAMMAD (*d.* 750), the last of the Umayyad caliphs, was about sixty when he came to power in 744. His grandfather was Marwān ibn al-Ḥakam; his father, Muḥammad, was governor of Armenia and northern Mesopotamia and a prominent general in the frontier wars with the Byzantine Empire. Marwān soon gained renown as a soldier. In 732, the caliph Hishām appointed him governor of al-Jazira (in upper Mesopotamia), Armenia, and Azerbaijan, primarily to deal with the threats posed there by incursions of Turkish Khazars.

Within five years Marwān had driven back the Khazars and restored order to his provinces. These and other campaigns made him an experienced leader with a seasoned army, which he completely reorganized. Dispensing with tribal contingents, he levied troops as regular paid soldiers under professional officers. He also abandoned rigid battle lines, and divided his troops into compact units, which gave him a fast-moving and maneuverable army.

Marwān was in a very powerful position when Hishām died in 743. Hishām's successor, al-Walīd II ibn Yazīd, was a partisan of the Qays tribal confederacy, and proved to be a poor ruler with little political sense. Within a year the Qays's great adversary, the Kalb, revolted in Syria, killed al-Walīd, and proclaimed Yazīd III ibn al-Walīd I caliph. Yazīd died shortly thereafter and was succeeded by his brother Ibrāhīm. In this period of rapid successions, Marwān at first maintained his distance, but after the accession of Ibrāhīm he threw his support behind the claims of the sons of the slain al-Walīd II. Upon entering Syria, ostensibly on their behalf, his army was joined by Qays tribesmen. He easily defeated a Kalb army at ᶜAyn al-Jarr, and soon occupied Damascus. Al-Walīd II's sons were murdered before Marwān reached the capital, Damascus, and in December 744 he proclaimed himself caliph.

In consideration of his Qays power base, Marwān moved the capital to Ḥarrān in northwestern Syria; only months later this move, coupled with other unpopular moves, provoked a Kalb revolt, which Marwān's veterans quickly crushed. The caliph then marched to bring Iraq under his control, but had to return to deal with an uprising by Syrian levies within the army itself. After much bloodshed, this rebellion was also crushed. Although by the summer of 746 Syria was at peace, in almost every other respect it lay in ruins. The accord of its tribal groupings had collapsed and the region had proved to be so unreliable that Marwān leveled the walls of most of its major cities. Also, plague frequently raged between 744 and 749, bringing with it severe famine.

Meanwhile, rebellions in other parts of the empire broke out. The Shaybānī Kharijites asserted their authority over Iraq and Mesopotamia, seizing Al-Kufa and most of al-Jazira in 745 and capturing Mosul the next year. Marwān's army proved more than a match for them. Their leader al-Ḍaḥḥāk ibn Qays al-Shaybānī was killed in battle as they lost al-Jazira in 746, and in 747 Umayyad forces crushed Kharijite power in Iraq as well.

In 744 the Shīᶜa of Al-Kufa, led by ᶜAbd Allāh ibn Muᶜāwiya, rebelled. Forced out by other anti-Umayyad elements, Ibn Muᶜāwiya withdrew to southwestern Iran and for a time ruled over a large domain—but only until Marwān's military power could be brought to bear. The uprising was crushed in 748 and Ibn Muᶜāwiya fled eastward, where Abū Muslim ᶜAbd al-Raḥmān ibn Muslim, leader of the expanding Abbasid rebellion, had him killed.

While these conflicts wracked the east, Egypt was afflicted by army mutinies and peasant revolts, which Marwān's forces could not keep subdued. In southwestern Arabia, the Ibadite sect (an offspring of the Kharijites) acclaimed its leader Ṭālib al-Ḥaqq as caliph in 746. The rebellion engulfed the entire area and in the following year the Ibadites captured Mecca and Medina. Marwān's Qays force crushed the revolt in 747, amid great slaughter.

These clashes distracted Marwān from repeated pleas for help from eastern Khorāsān, where his governor, Naṣr ibn Sayyār, was finding it increasingly difficult to contain Abbasid agitation and propaganda. In 747 the long-feared revolt was finally declared, and within months the Umayyads had lost control of the region. In 748 the rebel Abbasid army began to move westward. This force the embattled Marwān proved unable to stop. In 749 the rebels captured the leading city of Iraq, Al-Kufa, where the Abbasid Abu'l-ᶜAbbās ibn ᶜAbd Allāh al-Saffāh, the great-great-grandson of al-ᶜAbbās, the uncle of the Prophet, was proclaimed caliph. In January 750 Marwān suffered a devastating defeat on the upper Zāb River near Mosul, and the remnants of his once-great army scattered. He fled through Syria to Egypt, and several months later was surprised and killed in the Nile delta village of Būṣīr (Busiris).

BIBLIOGRAPHY

E. Amélineau, "Les derniers jours et la mort du khalife Merouân II d'après l'histoire des patriarches d'Alexandrie," in *Journal asiatique,* 11th ser., **4** (1914); Margaret B. Bíró, "Marwān ibn Muḥammad's Georgian Campaign," in *Acta orientalia (ASH),* **29** (1975); Daniel C. Dennett, Jr., "Marwān ibn Muḥammad: The Passing of the Umayyad Caliphate" (diss., Harvard, 1939); Marshall G. S. Hodgson, *The Venture of Islam* (1974), I, 272–279; Hugh Kennedy, *The Early Abbasid Caliphate* (1981), 46–48; M. A. Shaban, *Islamic History, A.D. 600–750 (A.H. 132),* (1971), 153–189; Julius Wellhausen, *Die religiös-politischen Oppositionsparteien im alten Islam* (1901), ed. and trans. by Robin C. Ostle and S. M. Walzer as *The Religio-Political Factions in Early Islam* (1975), 79–91, 161–167, and *Das arabische Reich und sein Sturz* (1902), trans. by Margaret Graham Weir as *The Arab Kingdom and Its Fall* (1927), ch. 7.

LAWRENCE I. CONRAD

[See also **Abbasids; Caliphate; Hishām ibn ᶜAbd al-Malik; Kufa, Al-; Syria; Umayyads.**]

MARWĀN, ᶜABD AL-MALIK IBN

MARWĀN, ᶜABD AL-MALIK IBN (646/647–705), the fifth caliph of the Umayyad dynasty (*r.* 685–705) and one of its greatest rulers. Born in Medina in 646/647, ᶜAbd al-Malik was from the days of his youth caught up in the political and social turmoil that characterized most of his own caliphate. As a boy he witnessed the onset of the First Civil War, when the caliph ᶜUthmān was killed in Medina (656), and when only sixteen he was appointed by the caliph Muᶜāwiya to a high military position in the city.

ᶜAbd al-Malik came to power in a moment of grave crisis. His father, Marwān ibn al-Ḥakam, had succeeded in a reign of less than a year in reestablishing Umayyad control in Syria and Egypt. Outside this core area, ᶜAbd al-Malik enjoyed the support of few of the many factions contending for power in the chaotic conditions prevailing at the time. A Kharijite rebellion by the Najdīya in Arabia had spread through most of central Arabia, while another more extreme Kharijite sect, the Azraqites, had seized control of the territories of al-Ahwāz in southwestern Iran. The Byzantines were becoming increasingly troublesome on the northern Syrian frontier. ᶜAbd Allāh ibn al-Zubayr had been proclaimed caliph in Mecca, and had won at least nominal recognition from most of the provinces. But even his authority was extremely precarious, as the revolt of al-Mukhtār, who in 685 rose against the Zubayrids and seized control of Al-Kufa and most of northern Iraq and northwestern Iran, very quickly demonstrated. Elsewhere, pro-Zubayrid, Alid, and Umayyad factions and clans were locked in combat in a number of regional conflicts. Plague in Iraq and Syria further compounded the general disorder.

After concluding a truce with the Byzantines in 689, ᶜAbd al-Malik set out to recover the rebellious provinces. An abortive revolt in Damascus forestalled operations for a time, but by late 691 ᶜAbd al-Malik's forces had crushed resistance in northern Mesopotamia and were poised to enter Iraq proper, which had already been exhausted by the strife between the partisans of Ibn al-Zubayr, al-Mukhtār (defeated and killed by the Zubayrids in 687), and the Kharijites. The province fell quickly, and ᶜAbd al-Malik lost no time in sending one of his ablest commanders, al-Ḥajjāj ibn Yūsuf, to Arabia to deal with Ibn al-Zubayr himself. Mecca was besieged for six months, and in late 692 Ibn al-Zubayr was killed in battle and his rebellion (frequently referred to as the "anti-caliphate") crushed.

This victory brought the Second Civil War to a close, but Umayyad authority remained tenuous. The revolt of the Najdīya in Arabia was suppressed in 692, but the Azraqites in Iran represented a grave danger until ᶜAbd al-Malik transferred al-Ḥajjāj to the governorship of Al-Kufa in the following year. Eradication of this tenacious and fanatical Kharijite sect required three years of hard fighting and the introduction of reinforcements from Syria. Even then, Kharijite sentiment remained a latent threat to the Umayyad order in Iraq and other eastern provinces. And the menace of the Azraqites had no sooner been contained than internal dissension again threatened the empire. Turmoil in Khorāsān in northeastern Iran in 697 prompted ᶜAbd al-Malik to add this vast region to the already substantial governorship of al-Ḥajjāj, and in 700 the revolt of Ibn al-Ashᶜath once again fomented rebellion in the east against Umayyad rule. This rising was crushed by al-Ḥajjāj in 701 with the aid of Syrian troops, and in ᶜAbd al-Malik's last years the empire was finally restored to peace and order.

The conflicts in ᶜAbd al-Malik's caliphate indicated the rising disaffection with the emerging political and social order that the Umayyads represented. The regime was thoroughly Arab in orientation, and it had neither the flexibility nor the inclination to assimilate or accommodate the vast non-Arab populations over which it ruled. But even more serious at this early date was the fact that it was by no means agreed within Arab ranks that the Umayyads had a more legitimate claim to the caliphate than representatives of other Arab factions or families. The Umayyads remained, however, the most powerful cohesive force in the empire, and ᶜAbd al-Malik was able to destroy his enemies one after the other while they quarreled and fought among themselves. The empire was thus unified by force rather than through resolution of the fundamental issues under dispute.

ᶜAbd al-Malik was clearly under no illusions concerning this point. He was a shrewd politician and autocrat who viewed centralization as the only counter to the destructive factional tendencies of Arab tribalism. Ready to use whatever means necessary to maintain the Arab empire and the position of the Umayyads, he condoned the heavy-handed manner in which some of his governors, most notably al-Ḥajjāj, ruled their provinces. He became increasingly reliant on Syrian troops to maintain order in the eastern provinces; the southern Iraqi city of Wāsiṭ, founded by al-Ḥajjāj in 702 after the defeat of Ibn al-Ashᶜath, was in fact a Syrian garrison camp from which Iraq was ruled more as an enemy territory than as an integral part of the empire. Henceforth, the eastern provinces tended to equate Umayyad rule with Syrian occupation. Not surprisingly, later writers were to describe ᶜAbd al-Malik as the "progenitor of tyrants" and a primary culprit in reducing the caliphate to mere kingship.

In fact, ᶜAbd al-Malik's rule was no less Islamic than it was Arab, and his actions and policies can only be understood in light of his conception of Islam as a religious system that had inseparable bonds to Arabism. It is worth noting that ᶜAbd al-Malik was one of the first caliphs to have been raised from birth in the Islamic faith, and that he was, and remained, a Medinan closely associated with its circles of religious piety and learning. He was very fond of and well versed in pre-Islamic poetry, but was also keenly interested in the life of the prophet Muḥammad and the early history of the Islamic community. Some of the earliest extant fragments of Arab historical writing are narratives by a Medinan scholar replying to queries addressed to him by ᶜAbd al-Malik. The caliph adopted Arabic as the language of administration, replacing the languages in use in pre-Islamic times (Greek in Syria, Pahlavi in Iran, and Coptic and Greek in Egypt). This measure was surely intended to centralize the machinery of government along Arab lines, but was no less seen as an islamizing reform as well, since it henceforth became easier for Muslims to gain posts in the government bureaucracy. Similarly, ᶜAbd al-Malik's new gold coinage replaced Byzantine motifs with Arabic inscriptions, which also had important religious ramifications, since these inscriptions were Koranic phrases stressing the main tenets of the faith. Of even more pointedly spiritual orientation were such projects, undertaken under ᶜAbd al-Malik's supervision, as the reedition of the Koran to produce an unambiguous voweled text, and the erection of the magnificent Dome of the Rock in Jerusalem.

After a reign of twenty years, ᶜAbd al-Malik died, leaving the empire perilously close to the brink of yet another civil war. Wishing the caliphate to pass to his own sons, he tried to exclude from succession his brother ᶜAbd al-ᶜAziz, who had been named by their father to succeed him. Disaster was avoided when ᶜAbd al-ᶜAziz died only months before ᶜAbd al-Malik himself, allowing the latter's son, al-Walīd I, to assume power without incident.

BIBLIOGRAPHY

The fundamental assessment of ᶜAbd al-Malik's caliphate remains Julius Wellhausen, *Das arabische Reich und sein Sturz* (1902), trans. by Margaret Graham Weir as *The Arab Kingdom and Its Fall* (1927), chaps. 2 and 3. A recent more revisionist view is in M. A. Shaban, *Islamic History, A.D. 600–750 (A.H. 132)* (1971). The detailed study by ᶜAbd al-Ameer ᶜAbd Dixon, *The Umayyad Caliphate: 65–86/684–705* (1971), is a useful history of ᶜAbd al-Malik's caliphate. Marshall G. S. Hodgson, *The Venture of Islam* (1974), I, 217–267, assesses the background to ᶜAbd al-Malik's rule. All these works are superseded by Gernot Rotter, *Die Umayyaden und der zweite Bürgerkrieg (680–692)* (1982).

LAWRENCE I. CONRAD

[See also **Abbasids; ᶜAbd Allāh ibn al-Zubayr; Caliphate; Dome of the Rock; Ḥajjāj ibn Yūsuf, al-; Koran; Medina; Mints and Money, Islamic; Syria; Umayyads.**]

MARY OF BURGUNDY, MASTER OF (*fl. ca.* 1470–*ca.* 1480), Flemish illuminator. His painterly style gives a narrative expression to the style of Hugo van der Goes; his pictorial borders present new spatial relationships between illuminations and the text area; and his innovative compositions were imitated by Ghent followers in the 1480's and the later Ghent-Bruges school. The chronology of the works now recognized as his (*Breviary of Margaret of York,* St. John's College, Cambridge; *Hours of Mary of Burgundy,* Nationalbibliothek, Vienna; *Hours of Engelbert of Nassau,* Bodleian Library, Oxford; and *Horae* in the Biblioteca Nacional, Madrid) argues against the older identification with Alexander Bening, but his identification with Claeys Spierinc remains a possibility.

BIBLIOGRAPHY

Antoine De Schryver, *Gebetbuch Karls des Kühnen, vel potius Stundenbuch der Maria von Burgund* (1969); Gerard I. Lieftinck, *Boekverluchters uit de Omgeving van Maria van Bourgondië, c. 1457–c. 1485* (1969); Otto Pächt, *The Master of Mary of Burgundy* (1948); Anne H. Van Buren, "The Master of Mary of Burgundy and His Colleagues: The State of Research and Questions of Method," in *Zeitschrift für Kunstgeschichte,* 38 (1975); Friedrich Winkler, *Die flämische Buchmalerei* (1925).

ANNE HAGOPIAN VAN BUREN

[See also **Flemish Painting; Gothic Art: Painting (with illustration); Spierinc, Claeys.**]

St. George Altarpiece by Andrés, Marzal de Sax, *ca.* 1400. VICTORIA AND ALBERT MUSEUM, LONDON

MARZAL DE SAX, ANDRÉS, painter active in Valencia *ca.* 1394–1410. He is attributed one of the most important works in Valencian painting, the large, International Style St. George Altarpiece (*ca.* 1400) in the Victoria and Albert Museum, London. Crossbows on the frame suggest the patron was the Centenar de la Pluma, a Valencian militia. Sax may refer to Saxony as a place of origin, while the artist's gaunt figures, with exaggerated postures and expressions, are similar to those of German painting.

MARY GRIZZARD

MARZPANATE. The name given to the period of Armenian history between the end of the Arsacid dynasty in eastern Armenia or Persarmenia (428) and the Arab conquest of the mid seventh century. It is derived from *marzpan* (Pahlavi: *marz[o]bān),* that is, "warden of the marches," the title of the Sasanian governor or viceroy of the region. The *marzpan*s governed the major part of Greater Armenia, leaving only Armenia Minor and about a quarter of the territories east of the Euphrates to Byzantine overlordship during most of this period, although the area under their jurisdiction was sharply reduced for a time by the eastward shift of the Byzantine-Iranian frontier in 591. The seat of the *marzpan* was at the former royal capital of Dwin.

Although the Armenian *naχarar*s rebelled against the *marzpan*s on a number of occasions, most notably against the attempt to reimpose Zoroastrianism on Armenia in 450 and again under Vardan II Mamikonean in 571, and the Sasanian rulers occasionally interfered in the affairs of the Armenian church, Persian rule does not seem to have been insufferably hard. A number of the *marzpan*s were chosen from among local Armenian princes, and the *naχarar* social structure of Armenia remained unimpaired. The Armenian cavalry served regularly in the Persian army, the Armenian nobles loyally sided with the legitimate Sasanian heir Xusrō II against the rebellion of Vahrām Čobēn in 591, and some Armenian sources even praise the later Sasanian rulers, whom they inaccurately portray as crypto-Christians. The growing authority of the autonomous Armenian church, replacing the crown as a focus for native loyalties, the preservation of traditional institutions, and the development of a vigorous literature in the native language made of the marzpanate a period of crucial cultural evolution and increasing self-awareness despite the restlessness resulting from the absence of political independence.

BIBLIOGRAPHY

Nicholas Adontz, *Armenia in the Period of Justinian,* Nina G. Garsoïan, ed. and trans. (1970); Paul Goubert, *Byzance avant l'Islam,* I (1951), 164; René Grousset, *Histoire de l'Arménie des origines à 1071* (1947).

NINA G. GARSOÏAN

[See also **Armenia: History of; Armenia, Social Structure; Armenian Church, Doctrines and Councils; Armenian Church, Structure; Arsacids/Aršakuni, Armenian; Dwin; Naχarar; Sasanians; Xusrō II Abarwēz.**]

MASACCIO, TOMMASO CASSAI (1401–1428), Tuscan painter, was born in Castel San Giovanni (modern San Giovanni Valdarno). He matriculated in the Arte dei Medici e Speziali in 1422 and joined the Compagnia di San Luca two years later. He died in Rome.

A figure who stands apart from and beyond his own time, Masaccio created a monumental and spatial idiom that profoundly influenced painters of the late fifteenth and early sixteenth century. His oeuvre is small. The earliest surviving work generally attributed to him is the San Giovenale triptych, the *Madonna and Child with Saints* (1422), now in the Uffizi, Florence. Sometime after 1422, Masaccio must have executed his Sant' Ambrogio altarpiece, the *Madonna and Child with St. Anne,* perhaps with Masolino, also in the Uffizi. Masaccio's Pisa altar, documented 1426, is now dispersed among the National Gallery, London; the Museo di Capodimonte, Naples; the Berlin Staatliche Museen; the Museo Nazionale, Pisa; and the J. Paul Getty Museum, Malibu.

Masaccio's major fresco cycle, painted *ca.* 1427 for the Brancacci Chapel of S. Maria del Carmine (Florence), depicts the life of St. Peter. Masaccio's contribution includes the *Expulsion of Adam and Eve, St. Peter Healing with His Shadow, The Distribution of Communal Goods and the Death of Ananias, The Tribute Money,* and parts of the *Resurrection of the Son and Theophilus and St. Peter Enthroned.* Additional scenes were painted by Masolino and the cycle was finally completed by Filippino Lippi later in the century. The exact sequence of the division of labor between Masaccio and Masolino remains unknown. Masaccio's other major fresco is his *Trinity and Donors with Skeleton,* painted *ca.* 1427 for S. Maria Novella (Florence).

The Tribute Money. Fresco from the Brancacci chapel cycle by Masaccio, *ca.* 1427. ALINARI/ART RESOURCE

All of Masaccio's works are revolutionary. His San Giovenale triptych shows his understanding of the dynamic use of space. The dramatically foreshortened angels, seen from behind, and the tipped-up throne create an aggressive space that is also more cohesive than space had been in Tuscan painting for nearly a century.

Masaccio's *Madonna and Child with St. Anne* explores these tendencies further, while his Pisa altarpiece is a dramatic departure in its figural conception and in its use of architectural and spatial perspective. Earlier and contemporary painters drew their figures using the picture plane as a guide for scale and as a surface to which the figures could align themselves, thereby reinforcing the viewer's perception of the picture plane. Masaccio drew figures that obeyed the laws of dimension only. He drew figures that were independent of the picture plane and used lines that did not adhere to the picture surface but gave the remarkable illusion of volume and depth. With this departure, Masaccio created a new language of form, which did not rely on older formulas, but introduced a new realism based on natural observation. Much of that observation was focused on the effects of light and shadow on forms and may have been the result of Masaccio's intense study of Donatello's sculpture and perhaps Brunelleschi's architecture.

The Madonna in Masaccio's Pisa altar has no clear ancestor in earlier painting, nor would she be fully appreciated until much later in the century. A solid and convincingly dimensional form, she is the monumental ancestor for the epic Madonnas by Luca Signorelli, Fra Bartolommeo, and Michelangelo. A grave and sober personality, Masaccio's Madonna exhibits none of the grace and elegance that characterize Tuscan Madonnas of the late fourteenth and early fifteenth century.

Masaccio's frescoes were similarly conceived. The drama is solemn and dignified, the figures are massive and bold. The settings are sparing, yet convincingly real. Masaccio employed light, air, and architecture to achieve an illusion of depth and spatial consistency. His grandiose vision stands apart from the ephemeral decorative norm of contemporary Tuscan painting. Masaccio's style shaped the future more than his present. Without his genius, the powerful styles of later Renaissance painters would have been impossible.

BIBLIOGRAPHY

Bruce Cole, *Masaccio and the Art of Early Renaissance Florence* (1980).

ADELHEID M. GEALT

[See also **Brunelleschi; Donatello; Florence; Masolino.**]

MASEGNE. See **Dalle Masegne, Pierpaolo and Jacobello.**

MASHHAD (the place of martyrdom), an Iranian city in the province of Khorāsān located on the frontiers of Turkish- and Persian-speaking peoples in northeast Iran at the confluence of the Soviet Union and Afghanistan. By the sixteenth century it had gradually replaced the city of Ṭūs (razed by the Mongols) as the administrative and cultural center of the region. But its rise to prominence began as early as the "martyrdom" of Imam Rezā (more fully ᶜAlī al-Riḍā), the eighth of the twelve Shiite imams. Mashhad is the holiest city in Iran itself and draws pilgrims from throughout the Twelver Shiite world.

Mashhad has its roots in infamous events of Shiite-Sunni contentions during the Abbasid caliphate. According to Twelver Shiite tradition, the celebrated caliph Hārūn al-Rashīd was responsible for the murder of Imam Rezā's father. Some years later Hārūn al-Rashīd died on campaign and was buried in a garden of Sanābād near Ṭūs. Ironically ten years later, in 818, Imam Rezā was murdered by the succeeding Abbasid caliph and came to be buried at the same spot, which, in his honor, was thereafter referred to as Mashhad, the site of his "martyrdom."

By the tenth century the adjacent tombs were surrounded by a fortified wall. A mosque, houses, and a market were built nearby. The area was inevitably subjected to the political upheavals of succeeding centuries, and the shrine buildings underwent various periods of destruction and restoration.

In 1389 Timur (Tamerlane) destroyed what was left of Ṭūs, and the survivors fled to nearby Mashhad, where his successors focused their attention and patronage. Most notable is the monumental mosque, which was commissioned by Queen Gauhar-shād in 418 and is still the ornament of the shrine complex.

With the coming of the Safavids (1501–1722) Twelver Shiisim became the state religion. The prestige of Mashhad grew accordingly and the shrine became a pilgrimage site to rival those of the Shiite shrines controlled by the Ottomans. In this new era of patronage, the wealth of the shrine and its endowed properties grew to support its philanthropy and influential seminaries. In the process Mashhad became a major center of international trade.

BIBLIOGRAPHY

Dwight M. Donaldson, *The Shiᶜite Religion* (1933), 152–187; Guy Le Strange, *The Lands of the Eastern Caliphate* (1930), 388–391.

CAROLINE J. BEESON

[See also **Imam; Islam, Religion; Pilgrimage, Islamic.**]

MASHRABĪYA, a projecting latticed window characteristic of traditional Egyptian domestic architecture. The lattice, usually made of unpainted turned wood, shuts out or modulates the glare of the sun yet freely admits air to the interior. It also provides privacy, enabling one to see out without being seen from the street.

JONATHAN M. BLOOM

[See also **Islamic Art and Architecture.**]

MASO DI BANCO (*fl. ca.* 1325–1350), Florentine painter and perhaps the most gifted pupil of Giotto di Bondone. Maso is an important transitional figure whose monumental, sparing style strongly influenced Nardo di Cione and Orcagna. His principal works include the polyptych with half-length *Madonna and Child with Saints* (Florence, S. Spirito), the half-length *Madonna and Child with Saints* (Berlin, Staatliche Museen), a fragmented fresco depicting a *Coronation of the Virgin* (Florence, S. Croce Museum), and the partially restored fresco cycle depicting episodes from the legend of St. Sylvester in the Bardi di Vernio chapel of S. Croce, dated roughly 1336.

BIBLIOGRAPHY

Bernard Berenson, *Italian Pictures of the Renaissance: Florentine School,* 2 vols. (1963); John White, *Art and Architecture in Italy, 1250–1400* (1965); David Wilkins, "Maso di Banco and Cenni di Francesco: A Case of Late Trecento Revival," in *Burlington Magazine,* **111** (1969).

ADELHEID M. GEALT

[See also **Florence; Fresco Painting; Giotto di Bondone; Nardo di Cione; Orcagna;** and illustration overleaf.]

MASOLINO, Tommaso di Cristoforo Fini or Tommaso da Panicale (1383?–1440/1447). A Florentine painter, Masolino enrolled in the guild in 1423, which is also the year of his only dated panel: *Madonna of Humility,* in the Bremen Kunsthalle. His career was far-flung. In 1424, Masolino was paid for a now destroyed *True Cross* fresco cycle for the church of S. Stefano at Empoli, and the following year probably executed the *Man of Sorrows* in the town's Collegiata. After 1425 he may have been in Hungary, while in 1428 he was back in Florence. His chief Florentine work is part of the undated fresco cycle illustrating the life of St. Peter, Brancacci

St. Sylvester subduing the dragon and resuscitating two magicians. Fresco by Maso di Banco from the Bardi de Vernio chapel of S. Croce, Florence, *ca.* 1336. UFFIZI, FLORENCE, SGF 25,573

Chapel, S. Maria del Carmine (in connection with Masaccio). Sometime after 1428 he probably executed his fresco cycles for Castiglion Olona in Lombardy and the church of S. Clemente in Rome. Masolino's style, based on the reserve and elegance of Lorenzo Monaco, may also owe a debt to Gentile da Fabriano or, like Fabriano, trace back to Altichiero.

BIBLIOGRAPHY

Emma Micheletti, *Masolino da Panicale* (1959); Maria Bianchini, *Masolino da Panicale* (1965).

ADELHEID M. GEALT

[See also **Altichiero; Florence; Fresco Painting; Gentile da Fabriano; Masaccio, Tommaso Cassai; Rome.**]

MASONS AND BUILDERS. The construction of cathedrals and castles in medieval Europe raises many questions, not all of which are easy to answer. Financial records for the construction of many churches and castles have survived, particularly in England, but these usually do not contain satisfactory information on building techniques, and they provide only scanty information regarding the professional and personal lives of the builders—masons, carpenters, glaziers, and other craftsmen. Surprisingly, medieval scholastics who wrote voluminously on scientific and technical as well as theological topics did not pay much attention to architecture. There are no scholastic treatises on medieval building which compare with Vitruvius' *De architectura* from Roman antiquity, or Leon Battista Alberti's *Ten Books on Architecture* from Renaissance Italy. Medieval chroniclers and biographers sometimes did notice prominent building construction, but their accounts devoted far more attention to the role of the patrons than to the craftsmen. Nor did the craftsmen themselves provide written or graphic evidence about their work before the thirteenth century, and most of the documents from their own hands come from the fifteenth century. One is grateful for these late Gothic documents, but we would like to know more about builders and techniques during the twelfth and thirteenth centuries, which saw the culmination of Romanesque building and the origin and flowering of Gothic construction. Furthermore, medieval documentary

MASONS AND BUILDERS

St. Peter raising Tabitha. Detail from fresco by Masolino for Brancacci chapel, *ca.* 1428. GIRAUDON/ART RESOURCE

sources are more copious regarding building craftsmen of England and Germany than for other parts of Europe. For this reason, the following account will be geographically weighted toward these countries; there will be no attempt here to deal with Byzantine or Moslem builders.

SOCIAL-ECONOMIC STATUS OF MASONS AND BUILDERS

Scholastics considered building construction to be one of the mechanical arts, and thereby lower on their scale of values than the liberal arts and theology. Likewise, builders belonged to the artisan class, which was considerably down the social scale from the feudal and ecclesiastical nobility. In the towns, masons and carpenters ranked lower than the greater, or even lesser, merchants. Building craftsmen did not develop strong guilds to compete with merchant guilds or other craft guilds, and this effectively left them out of the mix of politics, economics, and social status which characterized guild life in medieval towns.

The masons' craft was necessarily itinerant, for masons had to seek work where there was stone construction currently underway. This could be an abbey, castle, or manor house in the countryside; in an urban setting it might be a cathedral, city or parish church, town house, or the surrounding walls of the town. Economic, political, and social status were most often derived from the holding of property in the form of feudal or ecclesiastical benefices, or houses, shops, and lots within a town. The itinerant nature of the masons' craft worked against the accumulation of properties, which would have given masons the physical and capital basis for social status.

Not every mason had to be itinerant. A few could earn their living on successive building projects in a particular town. Or a mason might become the master mason of a very large project such as a cathedral. He could then buy a house and settle down for the rest of his life in that cathedral town. But it is interesting that these men who ranked high in their craft seldom assumed important roles in the political life of the town. Without the support of fellow craftsmen through the institutional life of the guilds, these masons lacked a power base for moving up the political and social ladder of town life.

When masons did hold office or perform official duties in urban political life, it generally was associated in some way with their technical competency in building construction. Thus they might serve on commissions to survey town defenses, bridges, or drainage systems. One of the major civic responsibilities in London was the maintenance of London Bridge, and several master masons performed official duties relating to the bridge. Henry Yevele, one of the most famous of all English master masons, was bridge warden for many years in the latter part of the fourteenth century. This was a fairly important post and earned him a fee of £10 per year. As the king's master mason, Yevele was constantly involved in royal projects, for which he served as designer or consulting architect. He was also an active building contractor, a merchant of building materials, and something of an entrepreneur in various other enterprises. He held several properties in London, and certainly was a well-known figure there. Yet he never became an alderman or served in other major civic offices. Political power simply was not a likely culmination of a career as a master builder, even for one so prominent as Yevele.

But if masons could not expect to achieve high political and social status, the greatest masters of the

MASONS AND BUILDERS

craft could acquire personal prestige. Again, Yevele nicely illustrates this point. He was the personal guest of the bishop of Winchester several times when the bishop was contemplating new construction at Winchester Cathedral. On another occasion he dined at high table in New College, Oxford, with two other prominent master craftsmen, presumably for consultation with the fellows about construction at the college. On one occasion the king sent Yevele a special selection of wine, and in 1369 he was issued black cloth for the funeral of the queen because he was considered to be an esquire of minor degree.

Medieval cathedrals and castles were built by craftsmen who worked long hours at low pay compared to their twentieth-century counterparts. This difference is reflected in the difficulties which modern European societies encounter in finding and paying for the skilled labor needed to maintain medieval monuments. Building in stone was expensive then, as now, but a much greater share of that expense was borne by the craftsmen, who worked for very low wages relative to the personal income of the royal officials, feudal lords, bishops, abbots, and merchants who commissioned those buildings. If one wonders how medieval society could afford to build so many beautiful churches, abbeys, and castles, the answer lies in part in the distribution of wealth, which made available a low-paid work force of skilled craftsmen and unskilled laborers to carry out the building ambitions of royal, feudal, ecclesiastical, and merchant patrons.

The values of that society are further reflected in the higher economic standing, relative to building craftsmen, of the stewards, clerks, lawyers, and bureaucrats, who served at the pleasure of the wealthier classes. The situation of Henry Yevele can again illustrate this point. When he became the king's master mason in 1360 he received a fee of 1*s.* per day and an annual robe. The king's master carpenter, chief smith, sergeant plumber, and sergeant glazier received the same fee. But the king's clerk of the works, responsible for administrative and financial aspects of royal building, obtained a fee of 2*s.* per day. Furthermore, a clerk of the works who performed his duties well could expect royal advancement to an important ecclesiastical benefice or to a higher-paid office in the royal service. The king's master craftsmen, on the other hand, were at the top of their trades and careers.

There was no set scale of wages for journeymen masons, carpenters, and other builders in England, although occasionally royal and London officials tried unsuccessfully to fix rates of pay. In the fourteenth century, masons' daily wages varied from 2*d.* to 5*d.*, and these rose in the fifteenth century to a more uniform 6*d.* per day. Master masons' pay also varied widely. It seems to have been set as a function of journeymen rates, and could range from 2*d.* to 8*d.* more per day than the going rate for journeymen. But often the master mason enjoyed the advantage of a weekly salary rather than daily wages, so that he was paid the same regardless of weather or holidays. The derivation of the master mason's salary from the masons' wages constrained the income of the masters and reflected the societal view that even those master masons who were widely known for their design and supervising abilities were, after all, artisans and building craftsmen. To be sure, the great masters of the craft like Yevele could develop much larger incomes than lesser masters by accepting multiple commissions and appointments, by serving as paid consultants, and by engaging in contract work for both materials and construction. But very few of these men climbed out of the artisan class to found mercantile families in the towns, let alone gentried families in the countryside.

In social and economic terms, then, masons and other builders of whatever rank or personal prestige continued to be identified as members of their particular craft. The range of income and professional status between, for example, a rough layer and the king's master mason could be quite broad, but it was on the same scale. That the greatest architects of the period did not strive to escape from their crafts into higher professional and social classes had important consequences for Gothic design and construction, as we shall see.

EDUCATION OF MASONS AND BUILDERS

The social status of the building craftsmen, as well as the technical requirements of their crafts, had an important bearing on the education and training which they received for their occupation. Clearly in the later Middle Ages some master craftsmen were literate in their vernacular language and a few in Latin as well. While literacy among the laity was certainly increasing during this period, scattered evidence suggests that less than a majority of English master masons were literate. Presumably even fewer journeymen masons would have known how to read and write one or more of the three languages (Latin, French, and English) used in fourteenth-century England.

Some boys who were preparing for the masons'

MASONS AND BUILDERS

craft would have acquired literacy in the vernacular language in petty schools, and a few would have attended grammar schools, where the language of learning was Latin. But it is highly unlikely that a future master mason would have attended a university, for the curriculum there offered little of interest or use to the building trades. For example, Vitruvius' *De architectura* held no place in the curriculum, and even Euclid's *Elements* assumed only a minor slot, and that late in the baccalaureate program. Besides, a young man attending the university would have been seeking a clerical or ecclesiastical career, higher in social status than that of a master craftsman. He might have expected to become clerk of the works, but not master of the masons.

In fact, literacy was not an essential element in the education of a mason, even of one wanting to become a master mason. Rather, it was oral transmission of the traditions of the craft which constituted the primary mode of education. During the fourteenth and fifteenth centuries this was formalized in the institution of apprenticeship, but the educational process had been in use for centuries, as fathers and uncles taught the next generation of masons the necessary knowledge and skills of the craft. In this process the young man or boy often began in the quarry and then worked his way through all the stages of building in stone. He would serve a period of time as a rough layer, then as a setter of finely carved stones. He could then be placed at a banker or bench in the masons' lodge, where he learned to carve stones to the shapes of templates designed by the master mason. A promising young apprentice, or the more advantaged son of a master mason, would be apprenticed to a master, from whom he would learn the design techniques necessary to become a master of the craft.

The result of this educational process was that building designers, the master craftsmen, acquired a vast knowledge of every aspect of building in stone, wood, iron, lead, and glass. Theirs was not a bookish or academic knowledge, for there were no books which contained their learning nor academies which taught it. Rather it was the practical and technical knowledge of materials and the skills needed to work those materials into a completed building that was the object of their education. This knowledge came from several sources. One was the craft traditions which had accumulated through the experiences of generations of building craftsmen, and which were passed by word of mouth and sleight of hand from one generation to the next. A second source was the actual monuments built by previous generations, and from which the astute master could learn much about what to do and not do in his own designs. The third source was his own personal experience as a working mason, carpenter, or glazier. Having spent years in mastering the physical techniques of shaping and placing stones or timber or leaded glass, designers knew from their own experiences what could be wrought and how best to go about it. Finally, the role of the patron in the education of master masons and other building masters should not be overlooked.

It is doubtful that more than a handful of master craftsmen were sufficiently skilled in Latin to have read classical or scholastic treatises written in that language. Yet the design programs of church sculpture and windows were demonstrably influenced by literary traditions. Access to these traditions was most likely through ecclesiastical patrons who knew that literature and could transmit its substance to the master builders, who in turn transformed literary themes and allusions into monumental forms. Again it was oral transmission which played a key role in this part of the education of master builders.

MASONS' ORGANIZATIONS

Masons were slower than other craftsmen to develop formal organizations, largely because of the itinerant nature of their work. Town merchants were the first to organize into guilds, and these provided the pattern for the development of craft guilds. Merchant and craft guilds were aimed at the monopolistic control of commerce and industry within a particular town. Since masons moved from one town to another to work on different projects—or were employed in the countryside in building abbeys, castles, or manor houses—the localized, monopolistic mode of merchant and craft guilds did not readily lend itself to the masons' craft. Eventually masons who resided more or less continuously in the largest cities did form guilds, such as the London Masons' Company, but even in London this did not occur until the late fifteenth century.

Masons found that their more natural organizational unit was the building lodge attached to a major building project, usually a cathedral or large city church. Ordinances of the masons' lodge at York Minster have survived from 1370, and references in the late-fourteenth-century English document known as the "Articles and Points of Masonry" suggest that the institutional organization of masons at the local project was not uncommon. The

MASONS AND BUILDERS

lodge itself was the shed or house in which masons worked at their benches in cutting stones for the building. But it served as the organizational center for both setting and cutting masons, since all the masons ate meals, rested, and took naps in the lodge. Both the York Minster regulations and the "Articles and Points of Masonry" contained detailed regulations about the behavior of the masons in the lodge and on the building project. These "customs" governed the relationships of the masons to each other, to the master mason, to the apprentices, and to the patron or patrons of the project. While some customs were local, most were common with the "ancient customs of the craft" to which these documents frequently refer.

Enforcing these customs was a problem for the masons. Their craft lacked the tight monopolistic control of the urban guilds, and the coming and going of masons in the local building lodges did not provide the craft with an effective means of disciplining masons who broke or defied the general customs of the craft. The "Articles and Points of Masonry" refer to regional assemblies or congregations of masons who were to meet with governmental officials of the region—lords and sheriffs—as well as the mayor and aldermen of the town in which the assembly was held. The purpose of the assembly was to regulate the craft in that region. However, the document is vague about the authority of the assembly, and there is very little evidence that such assemblies were ever held in England.

German masons were somewhat more succcessful in establishing regional authority over their craft. The pattern of craft organizations was similar to that in England. There were a few urban guilds, for example at Trier and Erfurt, but German masons found this form of craft organization to be no more suitable than did their English fellow masons. The local building lodge *(Bauhütte)* was the better focus of organization for them as well. In particular the *Bauhütten* of several German cathedrals became famous in the fifteenth century for the importance of their projects. These lodges developed their own rules and customs, though of course there were many similarities in practice. During the 1450's masons of southern Germany began discussing ways to coordinate and codify these common elements. Meetings were held in Speyer and Strasbourg, and in 1459 a large session was held in Regensburg, where the masons drew up an ordinance *(Ordnung)*, the particulars of which were called points and articles *(Punkte und Artikel)*. The major *Bauhütten* received a copy of the book *(das Buch)* containing the ordinance, and the master mason of each lodge assumed the responsibility for keeping the book from unauthorized copying or persons. He was also charged to see that the book was read aloud to the lodge masons at least once a year.

While each *Bauhütten* was responsible for maintaining the ordinance in its own locale, special eminence of certain lodges was recognized, and these were granted somewhat vague jurisdictional authority and privileges over the other *Bauhütten* within their region. But the Regensburg ordinance did not establish a firm organizational structure to regulate the masons of these various *Bauhütten*. Instead, it produced a rather loose-knit and voluntary association of building lodges which individuals joined by an oath of obedience to the brotherhood *(Bruderschaft)* of masons. Since there was minimal centralized authority for enforcing either this oath or the ordinance, it remained for the local *Bauhütten* to regulate the professional lives of the masons within the points and articles of the ordinance.

In spite of the efforts of the German masons to establish a broader organizational pattern, the local building lodge remained the key element in shaping and maintaining the character of the masons' craft. At least two important features of medieval building and architecture can be attributed to the functioning of the building lodge. On large projects like cathedrals the traditions of the lodge maintained continuity even through changes in design and construction as the decades and centuries rolled past. This can be visually perceived today in the large and beautiful architectural drawings which were carefully preserved in the *Bauhütten* at Strasbourg, Regensburg, and Vienna, and which are still extant. These drawings preserved the design concepts of the master who drew them, and the church could be built to those designs long after the originating master had departed. But successive generations of builders were not rigorously bound to execute those designs in every detail. Over the decades changes could be made, but these generally developed as variations on the received tradition. The work of predecessors was respected, even while different forms or up-to-date stylistic devices and building techniques were introduced. This flexibility within continuity was an essential element of Gothic design.

The dynamics of the masons' lodges produced another important characteristic of Gothic architecture, and that was the transference of design concepts and building practices whenever the master

MASONS AND BUILDERS

mason or a crew of masons migrated from one lodge to another. This ability of design concepts to leapfrog, sometimes at a considerable distance, makes the study of medieval architecture endlessly fascinating, as historians try to reconnect the links between building lodges which produced stylistically related buildings.

ROLES OF THE MASTER MASONS

The central figure in the connections between building lodges and in the transfer of design concepts and building practices was the master mason, who carried responsibilities that are now assumed by several different persons in modern building practice. He was the architect and supervisor of construction, and on some projects he might function as a building contractor, a design or building consultant, or an inspector of the work of other masters. He was also the vital link between the patrons, who maintained the cultural traditions of the ruling classes of society, and the craftsmen, who carried on the technical traditions of building construction. The strength of the master mason's position lay precisely in the fact of his being a craftsman himself. The greatest masters knew virtually everything there was to know about design and construction within their particular building traditions. They held the respect of their fellow craftsmen on the one hand, while on the other they were absolutely essential to the patrons, who might know what they wanted in their buildings but who did not have the technical ability to get or to produce it themselves.

As the architect, the master mason was responsible for the overall design as well as minute details of the building. By the beginning of the fourteenth century it was common for master masons to draw building plans and elevations in order to show their overall design to both patrons and the building craftsmen. But these were not blueprints in the modern sense, for they did not contain a scale or specific dimensions to guide the masons in their work. Another crucial element was required, which was also the master mason's responsibility to provide. This was the design of the masons' molds or templates. Normally these were cut from boards by a carpenter, although there are references to the use of canvas and parchment for templates. Larger templates might require boards to be nailed or glued together. The function of the templates was to provide specific, full-scale directions to the stone carvers, who could easily translate the straight lines, curves, and points on the two-dimensional plane of the template into the three-dimensional forms of the stones which they were carving.

On larger projects the master mason would set out his designs for the templates in his "tracing house," where a plastered floor or walls provided space for full-scale rendering of larger components, such as doors or windows. From this large "tracing" the master mason then derived the several templates needed for individual stones in the component. The master mason thus had three basic devices for developing his design concepts: overall plans and elevations, full-scale setting out of particular elements, and templates for individual stones. A major difference between medieval and modern design practices is that the modern architect is expected to work out all the design concepts and details in advance of actual construction, and to express these in blueprints and building specifications. These documents are so detailed that in principle the building can be constructed without the architect's presence. But on medieval projects the master mason was needed on site for completing the design process as it advanced from one stage to the next, for it would have been unfeasible to design all the templates in the beginning.

It was not just details that could wait, for within this design process significant decisions could be delayed until construction reached a point where they had to be made. One of the fascinating aspects of the constructional history of medieval buildings where written records are available is to perceive the uncertainties, conflicts of opinion, and techniques of resolving design problems by the parties involved. The best-known of these situations unfolded in the late fourteenth century at Milan Cathedral, where Italian, French, and German master masons, as well as cathedral and city officials, argued bitterly with each other for several years over the design and building of the huge new cathedral, even after it had reached an advanced stage of construction.

The Milan story illustrates another characteristic of medieval building, the use of consultants to settle disputed design questions. The master mason was highly regarded within his craft, but he was not so authoritative that patrons hesitated to call in other masters for consultation if a serious design problem could not be solved by the project's own master builder. From contemporary reports on these consultations we get rare glimpses into the jargon and concepts which builders applied to their technical problems of design and construction.

In addition to designing the building, the master

MASONS AND BUILDERS

mason was also responsible for the technical supervision of its construction. The clerk of the works kept the account books, disbursed funds, and played a large role in the administrative tasks necessary on a large project. But the master mason directed the actual building procedures. On very large projects, such as the royal castle-building of Edward I in Wales, this involved hundreds of men, both skilled craftsmen and unskilled laborers. Three major centers of activity required the masters' attention: the quarry, the building lodge, and the building fabric itself. The work of craftsmen and laborers in all three of these centers had to be carefully coordinated by the master mason, so that the rough-hewn stones moved steadily from the quarry past the masons' benches in the lodge to the singular spot in the monument where the multiple faces of each stone had to fit perfectly against the faces of the surrounding stones.

The logistical problems of directing and coordinating all of these tasks would certainly have overtaxed even the best master masons had they not been able to rely upon the craftsmen to use their own deep knowledge and skills with a minimum of individual supervision. This was another advantage of the architect and construction boss also being a master of the masons' craft, for it meant that the designer and executors, the supervisor and workers, could all speak the same technical language, think the same thoughts, imagine the same forms, and otherwise get on together in the complex business of designing and building in stone. Even then the master mason could not do all the necessary supervising on large projects, in which case he was assisted by one or more undermasters, who were skilled craftsmen on their way to becoming master masons themselves.

Masons building a crenellated tower. From a 13th-century window donated by the masons' guild for Bourges Cathedral. PHOTO: WIM SWAAN

Another role for master masons emerged in the later Middle Ages as some of these men developed into building contractors. In earlier centuries building was accomplished by a direct labor system: the patron hired masons, carpenters, ironworkers, glaziers, and masters of these various crafts, and paid each of them directly for their daily work. In England during the thirteenth century employers sometimes paid for the task accomplished, and out of this taskwork there emerged the building contractor, who was paid for the tasks accomplished by other craftsmen working directly for him. Several masons with their own crews might contract part of the structure under the supervision of a master mason in charge of the entire project. Eventually some contractors established enough capital so that they could contract with the patron to produce the entire building for a previously agreed-upon price. The separate roles of the master mason as architect and as contractor were not sorted out during the Middle Ages. It remained for modern building practices to establish the distinctive responsibilities of the professional architect and the building contractor.

THE ART OF GEOMETRY AND THE SECRET OF THE MASONS

The English "Articles and Points of Masonry" claimed "that among all the crafts of the world of man's craft, masonry has the most notability and most part of this science of geometry." This was probably correct, if one understands the special character of that geometry. It was not Euclidean geometry; there were no axioms or proofs, and almost no mathematical formulas or calculations were involved in the work of the masons. It can more properly be called "constructive geometry," for it consisted almost entirely of the construction and manipulation of geometrical figures. Constructive geometry was essentially arbitrary, for it moved step by step through lengthy procedures which could only be memorized in order to be repeated. One could not rationally or mathematically reconstruct the steps of the procedures.

MASS, LITURGY OF THE

practice of the church was that Jews, heretics, and those under instruction were blessed, then left the church, after the Old and New Testament lessons.

The Nicene-Constantinopolitan Creed, commonly used at Mass, is a statement of belief of the faithful, and hence perhaps belongs within the Mass of the faithful, the second major part of the Mass. But before it was used as a Mass creed, it was a baptismal creed used in the East and placed in the Mass after the prayer of the faithful by Timothy I, patriarch of Constantinople (511–517). From the East the creed as part of the Mass seems to have gone to Spain, where in 589 the Third Council of Toledo ordered that, to counter Arianism, it be said in masses directly before the paternoster—that is, later in the Mass of the faithful. The use of the creed in the Mass spread very slowly, first in the Frankish and Beneventan rite territories, and it was not until 1014, when Emperor Henry II ordered Pope Benedict VIII to use it, that it was said in Rome—and then only on Sundays and feasts mentioning parts of the creed.

Originally the creed was a people's song, and hence very simple chants were used with it. But eventually even this became too burdensome, and the clergy and choir assumed its singing by the tenth century. At this time the creed seems to have taken the place of the sermon in some areas.

During the creed there was a genuflection at the words *et incarnatus est,* an old practice that Peter the Venerable (*d.* 1156) says was observed almost everywhere. Also, at the name of Jesus heads were bowed, a practice legislated by the Second Council of Lyons (1274).

Until the fifth century in the Roman rite there were, at this point, the prayers of the people, spoken of by Prosper of Aquitaine (*d. ca.* 463) as celebrated in the whole world. Similar formulas existed in Gaul and Spain, and the Gallican *Expositio brevis* says that after the homily there are *preces pro populo,* a *collectio post precem,* and the dismissal of the catechumens. A remnant of these old prayers perhaps remained in the Roman rite, where before the offertory the celebrant said *Dominus vobiscum,* with people responding, and then *Oremus,* which would have preceded a now lost or transferred prayer. Perhaps a type of this prayer continued to exist in the Milanese rite as the *Ovatio super sindonem.*

When the Roman rite spread north of the Alps, there was introduced a general prayer of the church. By the late ninth and early tenth centuries the canonist Regino of Prüm noted that after the sermon on Sundays and feast days the celebrant was to recommend to the people a general prayer for various needs. This tradition survived in pre-Conquest England in "bidding prayers"; in France in the *prières du prône* with a little office of prayers, psalms, paternoster, Ave Maria, and the like; and in Norman England and Germany in a similar little office.

STRUCTURE AND DEVELOPMENT: MASS OF THE FAITHFUL

Offertory. The offertory rites in the Mass, sometimes called the "little canon" because several of its texts are similar to the canon proper, derived from the ceremonies of the people's—more particularly the faithful's—presentation of their gifts for blessing and consecration by the celebrant.

The items offered by the people varied according to the century and the location of the church. It is often said that in the ancient church not only bread and wine were brought for the offertory, but also oil, cheese, and olives. From the early Middle Ages on, however, occasional regulations stated that they were to be presented at other times than the offertory. Throughout the later Middle Ages, at certain special masses, traditional offerings in kind could be made—for instance, pigeons, doves, and other birds at canonization ceremonies. Despite all of these types of offerings, the two major substances offered were those used at the Last Supper, bread and wine. From the eleventh century on, when the bread and wine were offered principally by clerics and monks, the laity was reduced to substituting money for their traditional offerings in kind. This process was accelerated by the use of Mass stipends.

From early frescoes and painted representations, it appears that in the ancient church round leavened loaves with a cross notched in them were used. Eventually these loaves were stamped with decorative designs.

By the ninth century in the West it appears that both leavened and unleavened bread were being used. By the mid eleventh century, however, the Western church used unleavened bread (azymes) exclusively. This had come about for two reasons. First, the size of the hosts decreased dramatically because of the decline in the number of communicants. Thus, for communicants the celebrant needed only smaller hosts or particles, which could be made before the Mass. Second, the discussion with the Eastern church leading to the schism of 1054 forced the Western church to argue for the use of azymes against the Easterners, who continued to use leavened bread. Among the arguments the Westerners used to support their practice were that just as Christ's body was free from corruption, so the bread should be free of the corruption of leaven; that Christ warned of the "leaven of the Pharisees"; and that at the Last Supper, Christ used unleavened bread. To this the Easterners countered: "The kingdom of God is like leaven"; to use bread without leaven is like saying Christ had no soul, an Apollinarian heresy; unleavened bread is lifeless, and so to share Christ's body without life is a useless practice; and salvation and the Eucharist are types of deification, so how can one be deified without partaking of a life-filled (leavened) host? As a result of the schism, the West continued to insist on the use of azymes.

The making of the bread or hosts had its own liturgical forms, especially in the monasteries. There was a kernel-by-kernel selection of the grain; certain rules had to be followed regarding cleanliness; at least three of the monks were to be in the diaconate or higher orders; and psalms were to be sung while working. And, like the Eastern bakers, Western makers of bread and hosts came to use decorative stamps with letters, crosses, and images of Christ.

Aside from a regulation at the Synod of Winchester (1076) forbidding the use of water alone or beer, there was little regulation in the Middle Ages regarding the type or color of wine to be used. Red was probably preferred because white might be confused with water; it was only in the sixteenth century, when the use of purificators became widespread, that white was preferred because it left less obvious stains on the linen.

The practice of adding water to the wine went back to the ante-Nicene church. Cyprian, Ambrose, and others, who were often quoted in the Middle Ages on the point, argued that the mingling of water and wine signified either Christ and his people or the blood and water that issued from Christ's side.

As was the case with the substances offered, the manner of presentation of offerings varied according to century and location. Nonetheless, the presentation was generally within the context of a procession and chant, and, after the procession died out, the context of a chant alone.

In Gallican-rite territories the offering by the people was made before the Mass, according to Gregory of Tours, the gifts being placed in the sacristy. To carry the offerings to the altar there was at the beginning of the Mass of the faithful a procession during which the *sonum* was sung. In other rites the people presented their offerings together with those of the clerics.

In the ancient and early medieval church, when offerings in kind were presented, not all were used for consecration; what was not used went to the poor. In the eighth and ninth centuries, when unleavened hosts began to take the place of bread, the loaves and excess wine were placed behind the altar. At the end of the Mass they were blessed for distribution to the poor.

As the presentation of offerings took place, a choir chanted the *offertorium* or *offerenda.* The earliest accounts of this chant come from North Africa, and perhaps it was used by the early fifth century in Rome, where a signal was given to conclude the chant when all the gifts had been presented. In Rome the *schola* seems originally to have performed the chant in antiphonal style.

Until about 1000 the congregation took part in the offertory. The psalm verses numbered from one to four, and were interspersed with refrains and other embellishments sufficient to fill the time needed for the offertory. In the eleventh century, with the decline of the offertory procession, the offertory verses began to disappear from the manuscripts.

Originally it seems that the celebrant placed the oblations on the altar, then said a silent prayer followed by the *oratio super oblata* (the secret, in Gallican Mass books). This simple procedure was extended by a complicated rite of preparing the altar, placing the oblations on it, silent prayers, washing of the hands, and incensing before the secret was said.

By the late ninth and tenth centuries a series of private prayers was added as the oblations were placed on the altar and were offered to God. By the early eleventh century the deacon handed the paten with host to the celebrant, who then said the prayer *Suscipe sancte Pater.* In *Ordo Romanus I* the deacon also handed the celebrant the chalice, into which he had poured wine while tracing the shape of a cross. According to Bonizo of Sutri (*d. ca.* 1095), the celebrant himself should add the water. The celebrant then prayed an ancient Christmas prayer, *Deus qui humanae substantiae,* and offered to God the chalice on his own behalf, and that of the deacon who had given it to him, with the prayer *Offerimus tibi, Domine, calicem* (which in the tenth century had come at the beginning of the offertory). After bowing, the celebrant said the prayer *In spiritu humilitatis,*

MASS, LITURGY OF THE

which had in the tenth century been part of the *Hanc oblationem.* He called down blessings on the oblations with the prayer *Veni Sanctificator.*

Amalarius of Metz, the first to mention censing at the conclusion of the offertory, says it was unknown at Rome. By the early eleventh century one or more prayers were said as the incense was put into the thurible, including *Incensum istud* and *Per intercessionem beati Gabrielis.* According to Remigius of Auxerre, during the censing the celebrant repeated Psalm 140 (said in the tenth century at the offering of incense). The censing of the altar was left to the deacon. As the ministers were censed, the text *Accendat in nobis* was said.

Originally the lavabo, the washing of hands, may have preceded the oblation (after the *Oremus*) as well as followed the reception of the gifts. Eventually the first lavabo was omitted and only the second, immediately after the censing, remained.

At this point in the non-Roman Western rites there was a reading of the names *(nomina)* of the living and dead inscribed on local lists. In Rome, Pope Innocent I objected to this practice, saying that these lists should come within the canon. The custom of reading the diptychs remained, however, in Spain and Milan. Charlemagne attempted to suppress it in his realm in 789.

The diptychs, referring to the offerers both present and dead, were related to the intentions of the Mass. Hence, it was very difficult to suppress them, and there quickly came into use the prayer *Suscipe sancta Trinitas*, with its lists of saints and intentions, as a substitute. Other prayers for various persons—the king, the dead, all saints, the church—could be added to the *Suscipe.*

By the end of the ninth century, in Frankish territories it was thought fitting that the secret not be said without a preface, so the *Orate fratres* (in some manuscripts *et sorores*) was added. It was said in a slightly louder voice after the altar had been kissed and the celebrant had turned to face the people. There was a response by the clerics or people, which might be the *Suscipiat Dominus* (or another form), after which came the secret, the most important of the offertory prayers. So important was it in some places, according to Guillaume Durand, that a *Dominus vobiscum* and an *Oremus* was placed before it; and in a St. Gall codex of *Ordo Romanus VII* there is the suggestion that the canon starts with the secret.

In Rome the secret was called the *oratio super oblata* and was said audibly. It is first called secret in Gallican-rite territories (Bobbio Missal), where it was perhaps said silently.

Canon. During the Middle Ages the canon, which went under a variety of names, was recognized as the core of the Mass. The concentration on the oblations the people had just offered was shifted to the action in which the offerings became the body and blood of Christ.

Over the course of the Middle Ages the canon was of varying lengths. In the Gelasian Sacramentary and in the *Missale Francorum* the title *Incipit canon actionis* was placed before the introductory dialogue beginning with *Sursum corda.* By the time of *Ordo Romanus I,* however, the term "canon" was reserved for the *Te igitur* and beyond. The end of the canon was thought by some writers to be at the Amen before the paternoster; by others, at the paternoster itself; and by others at the Agnus Dei.

Much has been made of the way the canon was recited. Originally it was probably sung or spoken; but by the late eighth century the celebrant was directed to change his voice so that only those around the altar could hear, and by the ninth century it was said silently *(tacito).*

The emphasis given to the canon by the change in voice or silence was heightened in the Middle Ages by the use of swinging censers, Sanctus candles, and a variety of gestures. For example, the subdeacon held the paten aloft; the celebrant held his arms in an orant position for all of the canon except the *Supplices;* he bowed during the Sanctus and from the *Supra quae* and *Supplices* to the end of the petition, according to Amalarius; and there was a flurry of crosses noted in manuscripts as early as the eighth century.

The great prayer of the church, the canon, was introduced with much more solemnity than the others. Hence, there was not simply the salutation *Dominus vobiscum* but also *Sursum corda* and a response by the people. To early medieval commentators it was very clear that something important was about to happen when the words *Dominus vobiscum* were uttered; several of the most popular of their *expositiones* were entitled *Dominus vobiscum.*

The preface is the great prayer beginning with the words *Vere dignum,* attested to in the *Apostolic Tradition* and Cyprian. Ornately illuminated in manuscripts—the letters *V* and *D* include the *Maiestas Domini*—this prayer went under several names:

MASS, LITURGY OF THE

contestatio, immolatio, or *illatio* in the Gallican rite; *illatio* in the Mozarabic rite; and *prefatio* in the Roman rite.

In the West the preface originally varied throughout the year, and in the Roman and other rites there were great numbers of them. In the *Sacramentarium Veronense,* for example, there are 267. But by the *Sacramentarium Hadrianum* they had been reduced in the Roman books to fourteen. Shortly thereafter, in the supplemented *Hadrianum,* however, additional prefaces were restored, only to be reduced by the time of Burchard of Worms (*d.* 1025) to nine for the various liturgical seasons.

The Sanctus (*Tersanctus,* from Isa. 6:3) was perhaps in use by the first century in Rome, and by the fourth century it was being overlaid with Trinitarian significance, an interpretation lasting into the Middle Ages. It was originally a song for the people, so the accompanying chants were uncomplicated. Eventually the singing of the Sanctus was assumed by the choir and embellished with tropes. Nonetheless, the tradition that the Sanctus was a people's chant lasted well into the twelfth century.

By the time of Caesarius of Arles (*ca.* 470–542), the Benedictus had been added to the Sanctus. In the eleventh century, according to Bernard of Cluny, the sign of the cross was made here because, as John Beleth later pointed out, the Benedictus came from the Gospels.

The first intercession of the canon, beginning with the words *Te igitur* and existing probably since the fourth century, mentioned the gifts and oblations, which were signed with crosses. Then there was a series of intercessions, not unlike the old *orationes sollemnes.* Among those persons in the church first mentioned was the pope *(papa),* although this was subject to various interpretations because *papa* could be any bishop; in fact, some non-Italian manuscripts specified other bishops until it came to be accepted that only the pope's name was to be used. Then came the orthodox bishops, emperors, and kings, although the names of some of these latter, inserted in the manuscripts from 800 to 1100, were erased after the investiture controversy.

The "memento of the living" was an intercession very much like the diptychs. It was early read by the deacon. Although the practice was soon dropped, when the Roman rite reached Frankish territories in Carolingian times, the names were read out.

The *communicantes,* grammatically an incomplete prayer, followed the memento of the living and reinforced it. A long list of heroes of the faith is named; and on Christmas, Epiphany, Maundy Thursday, Easter, Ascension, and Pentecost the prayer might be proper to the day. The names in the *communicantes* could vary according to rite and location in the West, but usually they were Mary, the twelve apostles, and twelve martyrs (including six bishops, of whom five were popes, and two pairs of clerics and two of laymen). In Milan and Frankish territories local heroes of the faith could be mentioned.

The final part of the first intercession, *Hanc igitur,* emphasizes those for whom the offering is made. From early times there was great flexibility in the number of individuals named. In the Gelasian Sacramentary, for example, there are forty-one. Those prayed for could be candidates for baptism, virgins to be consecrated, and the like. Pope Gregory I apparently decided to do away with all the intentions, and introduced a general commendation. But for such important days as Easter, Maundy Thursday, and Pentecost, and for the consecration of bishops, special formulas were kept.

In the West the epiclesis—a call for the power to make the bread and wine the body and blood of Christ—was said at this point. Called the *Quam oblationem,* it is mentioned in Ambrose's work and in its developed form is in the Gregorian Sacramentary. During the *Quam oblationem* five signs of the cross were made over the bread and wine, in remembrance of the five wounds of Christ.

The text beginning *Qui pridie,* the central part of the canon, is an account of Christ's institution of the Eucharist at the Last Supper. At base the text consists of the biblical narrative, but there are distinct changes. For example, there is a Roman insistence on balance: the words *in sanctas ac venerabiles manus suas* are used for both the bread and the wine. Also, some of the biblical text, such as *quod pro vobis datur,* is missing. Further, there are "theological" additions, such as the words *mysterium fidei* (perhaps an early acclamation by the deacon over the chalice).

In this central part of the Mass there was a clear tendency for the celebrant to imitate Christ's actions: a ceremonial taking of the bread and wine, lifting his eyes to pray, bowing at the words *gratias agens,* and crossing himself as a sign of blessing at the word *benedixit.* Added to these dominical gestures of the celebrant were actions bespeaking the heightened reverence for the sacrament in the eleventh century and later. These gestures included, by at least the late twelfth century, the elevation of the

MASS, LITURGY OF THE

host and the chalice; the kissing of the host and the kneeling of everyone at the consecration (by at least 1201 at Cologne); the bowing of the celebrant; genuflection by the deacon and subdeacon (by 1201 in Cologne); and the striking of the breast and the making of the sign of the cross. Also, at the consecration the host was censed, and bells were rung (at Cologne by 1201). Special prayers and formulas, such as *Adoro te devote* or *Ave verum corpus,* could be said.

Immediately following the consecration came a return to the general prayer, in which there is a memorial *Unde et memores* of the salvific works of Christ: his passion, resurrection, and ascension. The oblation was then signified by *hostiam puram, hostiam sanctam,* and *hostiam immaculatum,* with a series of five crosses over the host and chalice.

Next there were two prayers, the *Supra quae* and the *Supplices,* that lingered on the external performance of the sacrifice and asked for acceptance (even though the gifts had already been consecrated). In the latter part of the *Supplices* there was a Communion epiclesis asking that the reception be for the good of the communicants, so that they might be filled with every heavenly benediction and grace. From as early as the ninth century, during this prayer the host and chalice were crossed, and from the twelfth century a sign of the cross was made at the word *benedictione.*

The "memento of the dead" *(memento mortuorum)* does not seem to have been a permanent part of the Roman canon, and is missing in many early medieval manuscripts. The reason for this is that it was not used in solemn episcopal masses on Sundays and feasts, when the names of the dead were not to be read, but only in daily and private masses. When the Roman canon was copied in northern manuscripts, however, the names of the dead were to be read from the diptychs by a deacon, just as they would have been recited in the Gallican *nomina* earlier in the Mass. In fact, in some manuscripts the title *Super diptycia* is written above the *memento etiam.* Nonetheless, the Carolingians insisted that the *nomina* not be said on Sundays and feasts; hence their absence from some manuscripts. To symbolize the bowing of Christ's head at his death, the celebrant bowed his head.

The *Nobis quoque* was a natural continuation of the *memento mortuorum.* It contains a long list of saints resembling closely those of the *communicantes.* The list undoubtedly developed slowly, with saints being added and dropped; but by the time of Pope Gregory I they were stabilized: John the Baptist (often confused with John the Evangelist in the Middle Ages); seven men hierarchically arranged—the apostolic figures Stephen, Matthias, and Barnabas, the martyr bishop Ignatius, the shadowy figure Alexander, the presbyter Marcellinus, and the exorcist Peter; and seven women—the Roman Felicity, the North African Perpetua, the Sicilians Agatha and Lucy, the Romans Agnes and Cecilia, and the Oriental Anastasia.

With the *per quem haec omnia* the canon was interrupted to bless some of the produce of the earth: wine, cheese, oil, and the like. Grapes were blessed on 6 August, new beans on the Ascension, and water, milk, and honey for neophytes following baptism. For these special blessings the ancient sacramentaries provided a plethora of benedictions.

With the praise of God in the Trinity *(per ipsum et cum ipso et in ipso),* there was a flurry of crosses and the minor elevation. The number of crosses grew from two to five, and they were assigned a variety of meanings. The minor elevation was not to show the people the holy gifts but to raise them to God in oblation. By the twelfth century this elevation was advanced to the *omnis honor et gloria,* thus making it seem that the final *Per omnia saecula saeculorum, Amen* was a preface to the paternoster.

Communion. The history of the parts of the Communion is especially complicated because their position and interpretation changed drastically from the fourth to the ninth century. Originally the preparation for Communion seems to have been the fraction or confraction, and in the Gallican and Mozarabic rites the creed seems to have been used as a type of chant during the fraction. In Rome, until the sixth century, the fraction probably took place at this point, but Gregory I insisted that the paternoster be said before the fraction. He argued that since the canon, a prayer composed by men, was said over the oblation, it was not proper that the paternoster, a prayer of Christ, should be said after the fraction or during the time when the celebrant had left the altar to preside over this action.

But despite Gregory's view, the paternoster had very early been connected with the Communion by virtue of several of its petitions. The *panem nostrum* was understood, at least from the time of Ambrose, as referring to the sacramental bread; and the *dimitte nobis debita nostra* was interpreted as signifying reconciliation of brethren before Communion or the fulfillment of Christ's command to reconcile oneself to one's brothers. Moreover, it was the first prayer neophytes learned, and hence it was appropriate to say it before Communion.

In Gallican-rite territories the paternoster was sung by the people, whereas in Rome, Milan, and Spain it was said by the celebrant with either the people's response Amen after the entire prayer or, in the Mozarabic rite, a variable response after each petition. During the paternoster, even as early as the ninth century, the people were expected to prostrate themselves, except on festal days; and the celebrant elevated the chalice and host at the words *Pater noster.*

The final petition of the paternoster, *Libera nos a malo,* was in the West developed into an interpolated prayer, called an embolism, asking for deliverance from evil.

After the paternoster in the non-Roman rites there was a blessing over the people. It seems to have been a dismissal of the faithful who did not intend to remain for Communion. In *Ordo Romanus I* the noncommunicants seem to have left after the commingling and before the Communion when the archdeacon announced the next station; in Gaul there was a solemn episcopal benediction. The deacon first said *Humiliate vos,* to which the people responded *Deo gratias,* after which the bishop gave a solemn blessing. This blessing was popular in Gallican territories, and there were special benedictional manuscripts containing them. In the mid eighth century Pope Zachary spoke out against these Gallican blessings as not being of apostolic tradition. He could not suppress them, however, and they were added to manuscripts of the Gelasian Sacramentary of the eighth century and to the supplemented *Sacramentarium Hadrianum.* In Italy (but not in Rome) they were used into the eleventh century. In Spain the tradition also lasted, although there the benediction was given after the *commixtio.*

In the early Roman rite there were two comminglings of the bread and wine. The first of these, the *commixtio,* came after the *Pax Domini* and consisted of placing some of the *sancta* or *fermentum* (bread consecrated at an earlier Mass) into the chalice. In the early Roman church the pope, as bishop, sent to priests in the titular churches pieces of bread in sign of the unity of the church. These they put into their chalices. Some of the *fermentum* was placed in the chalice during the papal Mass, presumably to signify the unity of the Mass in time. The second commixture, called the *inmixtio,* came after the fraction of the bread when the pope, having communicated the bread, put into the chalice held by the archdeacon a particle he had bitten off.

Outside Rome the custom of the *fermentum* was hardly known or at least was not practiced, and hence the first commixture was confused with the second. To the second, then, was attached the *Pax Domini,* which placed the commixture after the fraction.

The words *Pax Domini,* said before the first commixture, was the signal for the faithful to exchange the kiss of peace *(pax).* Moreover, it was an acting out of the clause in the paternoster *sicut et nos dimittimus.* In several non-Roman rites the *pax* occurred before the consecration of the elements, as a sign of peace among the faithful, but in Rome, according to Pope Innocent I, it signified acquiescence of the people to all that had been done in the mysteries.

In the early church the kiss was exchanged, men with men and women with women, a rule that held into the late Middle Ages. The kiss was a stylized action of bowing, touching of fingers, or light embrace. Also a pax-brede was used in some places at least from the thirteenth century. Although in some instances the *pax* was used by the laity throughout the Middle Ages, it came to be generally reserved to the celebrants. Eventually, though, the celebrant substituted for the *pax* between ministers a kiss of the altar or items on it. It was, however, delayed until after the fraction and commixture, and was accompanied by acclamations of peace among the participants.

At the time of *Ordo Romanus I* the fraction was extremely important, and there are detailed instructions as to how it should be carried out. Acolytes carried the bread in linen bags to the bishops and presbyters to break, and the deacons began the fraction over the pope's paten, held by subdeacons.

Eventually the fraction dwindled in significance, becoming little more than a symbol, and was slipped into the conclusion of the embolism and the *Pax Domini* because, as Amalarius argued, Christ, whose risen body is seen in the commingling, rose before he brought peace to heaven and earth. The celebrant broke only the host destined for his own Communion, the other little hosts or particles having been broken beforehand for consecration and Communion by the people.

To accompany the original long and meaningful fraction of the bread, the Agnus Dei was sung, its *dona nobis pacem* complementing the earlier *Pax*

Domini. Originally the chant at the fraction was variable in Rome, as it was at Milan, but by the time of Pope Sergius I (687–701) the Agnus had become the fixed form in Rome.

The Agnus, originally a popular chant, had simple melodies, but the tendency from the ninth century on was for the *schola* to sing it, sometimes with tropes. It could be sung as many times as necessary to cover the long fraction, but as the long fraction declined, it was limited to three times.

The original response to the Agnus Dei was *Miserere nobis,* but by at least the eleventh century *dona nobis pacem* was inserted to complement the *Pax Domini* and the kiss of peace. By the eleventh century this had been altered for requiems to *dona eis requiem.*

The second commingling in the Roman church, the *inmixtio,* became the more important because outside Rome the first commixture with the *fermentum* was not used. The action of commingling, accompanied by a prayer, was interpreted in two ways: both species together represent one sacrament and one Christ, or the commingling represents Christ's body after the resurrection.

Originally it was expected that anyone who had stayed to this point would communicate, and Communion was even taken to some who were absent. But eventually it came to be primarily the celebrants who communicated. This was because the Communion was progressively perceived as consisting of two parts, the Communion of the celebrants and the Communion of the people, after which a few prayers and liturgical actions followed.

In *Ordo Romanus I* there are elaborate instructions for the Communion of the clergy. Basically it was done by rank. The pope bit off a piece of bread and commingled a particle with the wine, after which he was "confirmed" or given the wine, which he presumably drank through a liturgical straw. Thereafter the bishops communicated from the pope, and so on down the line.

Originally there do not seem to have been prayers for the celebrant at Communion, but in Frankish and Gallican territories they were added both before and during his Communion. Also added were sumption formulas. For one of those formulas, *Domine non sum dignus,* the breast was to be struck three times in humility when it was repeated.

Until the fourth century it was commonly the rule that the people should communicate at every Mass. But after the fourth century, if one may judge by canonical strictures, there was a decline in lay Communion. In Carolingian times there was an attempt to reintroduce Communion for the people each Sunday (although everyone was urged to communicate daily if possible), but the improvement was only temporary. Only in monasteries did Sunday Communion remain the rule, and then among monks, not lay brothers. By the Fourth Lateran Council (1215), matters had declined to such a state that Communion came to be obligatory for everyone only on Easter.

Scholars have suggested a number of reasons for the continuous decline, all of them bearing some truth but none is sufficient in itself. It is sometimes said, for example, that the decline came in those countries, such as Spain and southern Gaul, where the struggles with Arianism had led to an emphasis on Christ's divinity. As a result, the humanity of Christ receded into the background, saints took Christ's place, and the Mass became the *mysterium tremendum.* Others argue that penitential discipline requiring confession before Communion and an insufficient corps of confessors led to the decline. Still others say that sexual purification regulations and fasting practices were the cause. During the twelfth century, with the rise of new eucharistic piety, gazing on the host replaced consuming it; the notion that the celebrant represented the entire people in his Communion had the same result. Finally, during the later Middle Ages other devotions, such as the Little Hours, tended to replace the Mass and Communion.

Originally the Communion of the faithful followed directly on that of the clergy. Again, especially in Gallican and Frankish-rite territories, a series of preparatory prayers was said.

In the Roman rite the clergy brought Communion to the laity, first to the men's side and then to the women's. In the Gallican rite the people went up to the altar, and in Carolingian times the gates were opened and the people went as far as the altar.

Throughout the Middle Ages the position assumed by the laity in receiving Communion varied widely. In the ancient and early medieval churches, the rails around the altar seem to have been so high that people outside them would have had to stand for Communion. From the eleventh century on, the practice of spreading a cloth on which the communicant kneeled was common, although because of the danger of spillage, one stood to receive the chalice.

Before entering the church the communicant washed his or her hands. On approaching Communion he or she lowered the eyes and perhaps covered the hands with a cloth. The priest's hand or foot might be kissed, or there might be a threefold bow. The communicant also genuflected.

From at least the fourth century, the right hand was held atop the left as a "throne" to take the host. But perhaps by the fifth century, and certainly by the ninth, it became the practice to place the host directly into the communicant's mouth, perhaps to prevent its being taken home as a talisman. Undoubtedly the use of azymes, from the ninth century on, encouraged the practice.

The laity regularly received the chalice at least until the twelfth century, and beyond that on certain special occasions, such as coronations. Lay Communion with the chalice began to disappear as sacramental theologians began to stress that the entire body of Christ was in both species.

In the early Middle Ages and until the twelfth century, a small amount of the consecrated wine was poured into larger chalices, serving to consecrate the wine there. The people drank from the chalice either with a liturgical straw or directly. Outside Rome intinction was used but, after its similarity to Judas' sop was pointed out in the eleventh century, it fell out of favor.

The chalice was administered by the deacon according to the most ancient tradition. Occasionally subdeacons were permitted to do this, and there are reports of women's doing it, although, except in emergencies, this was treated as an abuse.

Since the time of Ambrose, writers stressed the importance of the communicant's response, Amen, on receiving the sacrament. In Frankish territories a blessing was given as Communion was administered.

To cover the long period of silence when Communion was being made, a chant was introduced. In many of the Western rites Psalm 33 *(Gustate et videte)* was the earliest of these chants. Bt the ninth century time the Agnus Dei was being extended into the Communion and became the Communion chant, thereby making the *communio* a form of post-Communion.

After Communion a great variety of prayers for the celebrants and the faithful was introduced. These prayers can be found in such early sacramentaries as the *Sacramentarium Veronense* and *Missale Gothicum.* While they were being said, the vessels were cleansed and arranged.

After Communion had been completed, there was usually some of the consecrated species left. Over the centuries this excess was handled in a variety of ways. Up to the thirteenth century it was at times burned. The Council of Mâcon (585) directed that it be given to innocent children. But most often it was consumed by clerics. In the ancient and early medieval church it might also be given to the faithful, to be consumed at home or reserved there. On the other hand, the *sancta* might be preserved in the church itself, in a *conditorium.*

The *capsa* or *pixa* with its reserved host might be kept in the sacristy, the altar, a suspended tabernacle, a wall tabernacle, or, from the twelfth century, a eucharistic house, such as are seen in German churches.

After the remnants of the elements had been reserved or disposed of, there were two ablutions accompanied by prayers. The first was that of the mouth, a practice dating back to the fourth century. A bit of water or bread was taken so that none of the sacrament would be ejected from the mouth with spittle. This practice lasted into the High and later Middle Ages; but wine rather than water or bread was used. Moreover, as early as the ninth century not only the celebrant but also the laity could take a drink of water or wine as an *ablutio oris* immediately after Communion, a custom that was widely practiced. The second ablution, that of the hands or fingers, dates back at least to the eighth century and varied considerably in practice. Usually the celebrant cleansed his fingers over the chalice with wine and water, after which he drank the contents of the chalice. Occasionally prayers were said during both ablutions, and the eyes were touched with the fingers after the second ablution, in imitation of Christ's healing the blind. Because the drinking of the ablution wine and water could serve the same function as the *ablutio oris,* it tended to supplant it in the later Middle Ages.

Thanksgiving and post-Mass ritual and prayers. The earliest descriptions of the Mass admonish the faithful to give thanks after Communion. Hence there developed the post-Communion collect. Like all important prayers in the Mass, this was preceded by *Dominus vobiscum* and *Oremus.* The prayers, which are called *ad complenda* or *ad completa* in the Gregorian sacramentaries and post-Communion in the Gelasian, varied from feast to feast. Basically they began with a thanksgiving for the sacrament received, followed by a petition for some need or bodily welfare, and finally a petition for the aid of the saints.

There was a doublet to the post-communion but said only on limited days. Called *Orationes super*

MASS, LITURGY OF THE

populum these prayers were probably originally the bishop's blessing over public penitents enrolled during Lent who had remained in the church but had not had Communion. Hence the prayers were a type of substitute Communion.

The formal close of the Mass came with the dismissal, which in the various Western rites went under a variety of names and forms, such as *consummatio* in the Gallican, *Missa acta est* in the Mozarabic and Celtic rites, and *Procedamus cum pace* in the Milanese rite. In the Roman rite the dismissal was introduced by *Dominus vobiscum* with the response *Et cum spiritu tuo.* The deacon or celebrant then said *Ite missa est,* probably meaning "the Mass is over" or " the dismissal is here," and the people responded with *Deo gratias.* In the Gallican liturgy the words *Benedicamus Domino* were used, a formula that was introduced into the Roman rite and repeated on days when the Gloria was not said. At funeral masses from at least the twelfth century, the words *Requiescant in pace* replaced the festive *Ite missa est.*

While the *Ite missa est* or *Benedicamus Domino* may have been the formal close of the Mass, a plethora of additional ceremonies and prayers followed it in the Middle Ages. The altar might be kissed once more. From the eleventh century on, two additional prayers were said at this point, one of them being the tenth-century *Placeat.*

As early as the seventh century, it was thought that an abrupt departure of the clergy at this point was not fitting; hence a final blessing should be given to all who had stayed. The giving of this blessing was originally restricted to bishops, but gradually priests were allowed to give it as well. Nonetheless, there was maintained a distinction that bishops blessed with their hands, whereas priests used objects such as crucifixes, patens, or corporals.

By the twelfth century the prologue to John's Gospel had become so important a text that it was used as a blessing over animals, the sick, and newly baptized children, and for the weather. Hence it came to be a final blessing in the Mass. In the Dominican *Ordinarium* of 1256 there is mention of its being said in the sacristy, but gradually it was said at the altar, sometimes rounded off with an oration. Although it was technically a reading, it was recited by rote, and hence was not really a Gospel. By the early sixteenth century there was a genuflection at the words *Et verbo caro,* perhaps paralleling the genuflection at the *Et incarnatus est* in the creed.

After the last Gospel there was a recession in which the vessels were carried out with great pomp. So as not to leave this act without words, the *Benedicite* and Psalm 150 were said, not unlike the *Judica* at the beginning of the Mass. Other material might be added, such as the paternoster, kyrie, and various short prayers.

BIBLIOGRAPHY

Arnold Angenendt, "Missa specialis. Zugleich ein Beitrag zur Entstehung der Privatmessen," in *Frühmittelalterliche Studien,* **17** (1983); Paul De Clerck, *La "prière universelle" dans les liturgies latines anciennes: Témoignages patristiques et textes liturgiques* (1977); George Every, *The Mass: A History of Liturgical Evolution* (1978); Andrew Hughes, *Medieval Manuscripts for Mass and Office* (1982); Josef A. Jungmann, *Missarum sollemnia* (1948, 5th ed. 1968), translated by Francis A. Brenner as *The Mass of the Roman Rite,* 2 vols. (1951–1955); Aimé-Georges Martimort, *L'eglise en prière: Introduction à la liturgie,* 3rd ed. (1965), section on Mass translated and edited by Austin Flannery and Vincent Ryan as *The Church at Prayer,* 2 vols. (1973), and *The Church's Prayer* (1985); Nathan Mitchell, *Cult and Controversy: The Worship of the Eucharist Outside Mass* (1982); Jaroslav Pelikan, *The Growth of Medieval Theology: 600–1300* (1978); Richard W. Pfaff, *Medieval Latin Liturgy: A Select Bibliography* (1982); Niels Krogh Rasmussen, "An Early 'Ordo Missae' with a 'Litania Abecedaria' Addressed to Christ (Rome, Bibl. Vallicelliana, Cod. B. 141, XI. Cent.)," in *Ephemerides liturgicae,* **98** (1984); Roger E. Reynolds, "Image and Text: A Carolingian Illustration of Modifications in the Early Roman Eucharistic Ordines," in *Viator,* **14** (1983).

ROGER E. REYNOLDS

[See also **Agnus Chant; Agnus Dei; Altar; Amalarius of Metz; Antiphon; Antiphonal; Apostolic Constitutions; Architecture, Liturgical Aspects; Azymes; Bangor, Rite of; Bells; Benedicamus Domino; Benedictional; Benedictions; Beneventan Rite; Berengar of Tours; Cantatorium; Celtic Church; Chalice; Cistercian Rite; Cluniac Rite; Collectarium; Colors, Liturgical; Communion Chant; Communion Under Both Kinds; Corpus Christi, Feast of; Creeds, Liturgical Use of; Dalmatic; Easter; Furniture, Liturgical; Gallican Rite; Gloria; Gospelbook; Gradual; Holy Week; Hymns, Latin; Incense; Introit; Ite Chant; Jubilus; Kyriale; Kyrie; Laudes; Lectionary; Lincoln, Rite of; Liturgy, Celtic Church; Liturgy, Stational; Liturgy, Treatises on; Lyonese Rite; Manuscripts and Books, Celtic Liturgical; Mass Cycles; Masses, Votive; Milanese Rite; Missal; Mozarabic Rite; Narbonne Rite; Offertory; Ordinale; Ordines Romani; Pontificals; Premonstratensian Rite; Processions; Psalter; Ratramnus of Corbie; Reservation of the Sacrament; Responsory; Rouen, Rite of; Sacramentary; St. Peter Liturgy of; Sanctus; Sarum Rite; Troyes, Rite of; Vestments; York Rite**]

 MASS CYCLES, EARLY POLYPHONIC

MASS CYCLES, EARLY POLYPHONIC. It was in the fourteenth century that the term "Mass," as referred to in a musical context, received the specialized meaning it has today: a composition consisting of the five sections of the Ordinary (Kyrie, Gloria, Credo, Sanctus, and Agnus Dei). It was also in the fourteenth century that polyphonic Mass cycles first appear. These polyphonic Masses were clearly a significant innovation, leading to the musically unified Mass cycles of the Renaissance, the most important large-scale compositions of that period.

Polyphony was not new to sacred music in the fourteenth century. During the previous centuries it was common practice to provide polyphonic elaboration for the responsorial chants for the Proper of the Mass. The Ordinary sections, though, were sung in monophonic plainsong.

The shift to polyphonic elaboration of the Ordinary resulted from the increasing precision and specificity of musical notation with regard to rhythm. Polyphonic responsorial chant in earlier times involved solo voices primarily. The Ordinary portions of the Mass, originally intended as the response of all the worshipers, came to be sung only by the clergy and the choir, which was able to benefit from the more precise rhythmic notation to read and coordinate the multiple vocal lines of polyphony.

The only complete cycle of the Ordinary written by one composer that survives from the fourteenth century is the *Messe de Nostre Dame* by Guillaume de Machaut (*d.* 1377). Machaut obviously considered this work to be very important. In the manuscripts of his poetry and music that were prepared under his supervision at the end of his life, the Mass was copied several times.

The *Messe de Nostre Dame* was composed in four parts at a time when most polyphonic composition was for two or three parts. The cycle includes the five sections of the Ordinary plus a motet-style setting of the Ite missa est. Machaut set the long texts of the Gloria and Credo in conductus style—that is, the text syllables are sounded simultaneously in all four voices and the music is in chordal or note-against-note style. A feeling of stylistic unity was achieved, however, by composing the closing amens of the Gloria and Credo in the same motet style of the Kyrie, Sanctus, Agnus Dei, and Ite missa est.

Although there are no fourteenth-century cycles other than the Machaut Mass which were indisputably composed as a musical entity by one composer, there are five fourteenth-century manuscripts which contain a compilation of Mass movements suggesting that the pieces, which are often unrelated stylistically, were intended to be performed as a liturgical and musical entity. The collectors of repertoires and copyists of these manuscripts were apparently responding to the growing practice in the fourteenth century of having the entire Ordinary performed as a musical unit during the celebration of the Mass. Four of these so-called Mass cycles are apparently of French origin; the fifth is of Italian origin.

The Sorbonne Mass. A collection of Mass movements called the Sorbonne Mass (the manuscript is presently at the Institut de Musicologie de l'Université in Paris) lays some claim to being a cycle composed or compiled by one composer. The name Johannes Lambuleti appears in the middle of the Kyrie, and therefore this Mass has been attributed to him. It would not, however, be appropriate to refer to Lambuleti as the composer in the same sense in which this can be said of Machaut, because all of the movements, which unfortunately are only fragmentary, are arrangements of other known Mass movements.

Borrowing musical material from existing compositions was common in the fourteenth century. This practice became a special feature called "parody" in the fifteenth and sixteenth centuries, when composers based Mass movements on secular chansons and madrigals. However, the technique in the Sorbonne Mass does not achieve the same degree of purpose. Although the Sorbonne Mass demonstrates serious concern for musical unity, it still remains essentially a collection of arrangements of earlier music rather than a new composition.

The Mass of Barcelona. The Barcelona Mass (the manuscript is in Barcelona's Biblioteca Central, shelf number M. 946) is the most unusual and the most interesting of the early examples of Mass cycles with which no composer's name is associated. In musical style this cycle seems to have been put together as a compendium of existing musical practices, encompassing the simultaneous style of the conductus, the popular secular song style, motet style, and the new mixed style that is a precursor of the fifteenth-century Mass.

The Mass of Tournai. This Mass is found in the manuscript Tournai, Bibliothèque de la Cathedrale, Voisin IV. Though this cycle of movements of the Ordinary, including the final Ite missa est, was clearly chosen by the manuscript compiler for performance as a liturgical unit, the style of the musical movements indicates that a time span of perhaps fifty years separated the composition of the various movements.

The Kyrie, Sanctus, and Agnus Dei are in note-against-note style employing the notational practice of modal rhythms from the late thirteenth century. The other three movements employ the rhythmic and notational innovations of Philippe de Vitry (*d.* 1361) found in his treatise *Ars nova.* The Gloria is undoubtedly the most advanced in musical style, displaying cadential features that are not commonly found until the latter part of the fourteenth century.

The Mass of Toulouse. The large manuscript in which this Mass cycle is preserved (Toulouse, Bibliothèque municipale, MS 94) was compiled in the first half of the fourteenth century and is devoted mainly to plainchants and texts of the Mass. Many years later, perhaps at the very beginning of the fifteenth century, some copyist filled in blank spaces in the manuscript with polyphonic movements that are now identified as the Mass of Toulouse. It is clear that these polyphonic movements of the Ordinary were intended to be performed as a liturgical unit because the compiler indicates at the end of the Agnus Dei where the Ite missa est can be found. This cycle lacks a Gloria and therefore may have been designed for performance during Lent, when the Gloria is replaced by a solemn Tract. The Credo is incomplete, showing only the tenor part from the Crucifixus onward. This Credo, however, was well known; it appears in a number of other manuscripts.

The Italian cycle. The five Mass movements (Gloria, Credo, Sanctus, Agnus Dei, and Benedicamus) in the Italian manuscript Paris, Bibliothèque National, fonds italien 568 are the only sacred pieces in that manuscript. They were copied on the last folios and were obviously intended to be performed as a liturgical unit. The Kyrie is missing from the cycle because it was not common to give the Kyrie a polyphonic setting in Italy at the time. The compiler of the manuscript seems clearly to have chosen a collection of Mass movements by Italian composers closely associated with the Capponi family of Florence. Four composers are identified: Gherardello for the Gloria and Agnus Dei, Bartholus for the Credo, Lorenzo for the Sanctus, and Paolo for the Benedicamus.

The five movements are written in the Italian fourteenth-century style and display particularly the mid-century secular practice found in the madrigals. The first four movements have two parts only; Paolo's Benedicamus is the only three-voice piece in the cycle, and it is based on a plainchant melody.

BIBLIOGRAPHY

Sources. Leo Schrade, ed., *Polyphonic Music of the Fourteenth Century,* I (1956), contains the music for the masses of Tournai, Toulouse, and Barcelona; the music of the *Messe de Nostre Dame* may be found in volume III of the same work.

Studies. Kurt von Fischer, "The Mass Cycle of the Trecento Manuscript F-Pn568(Pit)," in Jerald C. Graue, ed., *Essays on Music for Charles Warren Fox* (1979); Richard H. Hoppin, *Medieval Music* (1978); Billy Jim Layton, "Italian Music for the Ordinary of the Mass, 1350–1450," (diss., Harvard, 1960); Hanna Stäblein-Harder, *Fourteenth-century Mass Music in France* (1962).

GORDON K. GREENE

[See also **Agnus Dei; Ars nova; Creeds; Gloria; Kyrie; Machaut, Guillaume de; Mass, Liturgy of the; Melisma; Music, Western European; Musical Notation, Western; Musical Treatises; Notre Dame School; Philippe de Vitry; Sanctus.**]

MASS CYCLES, PLAINSONG. The idea of compiling cycles of chants for the so-called Ordinary of the Mass (Kyrie, Gloria, Credo, Sanctus-Benedictus, Agnus Dei, and sometimes Ite missa est or Benedicamus Domino) is a development of the later Middle Ages. The texts themselves were added to the Roman liturgy at widely separated dates (from no later than the seventh century for the Kyrie to the eleventh for the Credo) and a variety of melodies were composed for them throughout this period and beyond. At first, the melodies were simple, mainly syllabic, settings, suitable for congregational singing, but as these chants gradually became the prerogative of clergy and choir, more elaborate versions appeared, for the Kyrie beginning in the tenth and eleventh centuries, and for the Sanctus-Benedictus and Agnus Dei in the eleventh and twelfth centuries. (The Gloria and Credo retained their syllabic character.)

During the period of their adoption, it is clear that the chants of the Ordinary were not considered together as a group, and the choice of melodies at any given Mass was entirely at the discretion of the precentor. Until recently, in fact, scholars regarded the plainsong Ordinary cycles of late manuscripts and modern editions as applications to plainsong of a conception of unity first developed in the polyphonic Ordinary settings of the fifteenth century. Although there is as yet no evidence that musically united plainsong cycles of the Ordinary occur before the early fifteenth century, set groupings of the chants, whether implied or specified, are found as early as the eleventh century.

The first groupings were accomplished by means of tropes added to the texts of Ordinary chants to make them proper to a given feast. In the manuscripts, the chants might appear interspersed among the Propers in the Temporale or Sanctorale, or in a separate section or book among troped Propers arranged in liturgical order. These troped Ordinary chants would not be musically related, but their specific assignment to individual feasts implies a fixed grouping. Later, in the twelfth century, elaborate new Sanctus and Agnus Dei melodies were composed; these were sometimes paired and assigned to feasts of a designated liturgical rank, as were Kyrie and Gloria chants.

The inspiration to group all four chants into a cycle seems to have come in the thirteenth century from the new religious orders, the Dominicans and Franciscans. For example, in the Franciscan Gradual, dated by Van Dijk and Walker to 1251, the section containing the Ordinary chants (the Kyriale) is arranged in ten complete Masses of Kyrie (sometimes Gloria), Sanctus, Agnus Dei, and Ite missa est or Benedicamus Domino. (The Credo is not included, since it was usually sung to a single plainsong melody in the Middle Ages.) Each complete cycle is assigned to a specific rank of feast. Once again, the chants of the cycles are not musically related, except for the Ite missa est, which is often a variation of the Kyrie melody. The same musical disunity is evident in the fourteenth-century polyphonic cycles. The idea of composing a true musical cycle of the Ordinary seems to have been a product of the early fifteenth century, applied, at about the same time, to both plainsong and polyphony.

BIBLIOGRAPHY

Bruno Stäblein, "Messe, A," in *Die Musik in Geschichte und Gegenwart* (1961), includes most of the early studies in his bibliography.

For more recent work, see Willi Apel, *Gregorian Chant* (1958); Dominique Catta, "Aux origines du *Kyriale,*" in *Revue grégorienne* 34 (1955); Kurt von Fischer, "Neue Quellen zum einstimmigen Ordinariumszyklus des 14. und 15. Jahrhunderts aus Italien," in *Liber amicorum Charles van den Borren* (1964); S. J. P. Van Dijk and J. Hazelden Walker, *The Origins of the Modern Roman Liturgy* (1960).

Richard H. Hoppin, *Cypriot Plainchant of the Manuscript Torino, Biblioteca Nazionale J.II.9* (1968), 81–99, is an especially useful and balanced discussion.

DIANE L. DROSTE

[See also **Agnus Dei; Ambrosian Chant; Antiphonal; Gloria; Gradual; Gregorian Chant; Kyriale; Kyrie; Monophony; Music in Medieval Society; Musical Performance; Plainsong, Sources of; Sanctus; Tropes to the Ordinary of the Mass.**]

MASSES, VOTIVE. The formularies of masses kept in the missals of the Catholic church are made up, as a whole, of four definite groups. First, the temporale—that is, the formularies used on Sundays of the liturgical year, to which Lent time should be added. Second, the sanctorale—that is, the special formularies intended for use in a number of feasts of saints. Third, the common of saints, which concerns those saints who do not appear in special formularies. And, finally, the votive masses, which are the subject of the present article.

The idea at the origin of these special, "votive" formularies can already be found in the way the formularies of the sanctorale appeared. In the early church, the Eucharist was essentially and only a Sunday paschal celebration, commemorating on the Day of Our Lord (Sunday) the resurrection of Christ, with the feasts of the Jewish Passover as a background. This became the temporale. But, as far back as the fourth century, formularies of masses appeared "in honor" of the saints, the martyrs first of all, considered as intercessors by virtue of the communion of saints. This led to the sanctorale, quickly followed by the common. Some time later, in the sixth century, the idea germinated of celebrating mass either "in favor" of various persons, alive or dead, or, on the occasion of difficulties or calamities, to ask the Lord to put an end to them. This body of formularies came to be called "votive" masses, which simply means that they expressed a wish *(votum)* to see a particular prayer answered.

Such masses seem to have been very popular from the early Middle Ages onward. One of the oldest Roman sacramentaries known today, the "old Gelasian," which dates from the late seventh century and was intended for the *tituli* (the parish churches in Rome), contains as many as fifty-nine votive formularies, fifteen of which are for the dead. In Gaul, one century later, the sacramentaries compiled on the occasion of the liturgical reform supported by

Pepin III and his son Charlemagne—called the "eighth-century Gelasians"—offer no fewer than ninety-six votive texts, including nineteen for the dead. Finally, in the ninth century, at the peak of the Carolingian reform, new votive formularies multiplied in such a way that, around the year 900, a hardly believable number of 278 votive masses, including fifty-six formularies for the dead, could be found in the various sacramentaries of that time which have come down to us. Such a number shows the popularity of this kind of devotion in the Christian world at that time.

Jean Deshusses, the learned editor of these masses, divides the formularies into the following seven groups:

1. *Masses in honor (forty-one formularies).* These are very particular masses, to call attention to and focus prayer on one of God's attributes, or a special aspect of redemption, or the intercession of saints. So, among them, we find formularies referring to the Holy Trinity, God's wisdom, the Holy Spirit, the cross, the Virgin Mary, the angels, and the saints in general or some particular saint, such as St. John the Baptist, St. Peter, St. Stephen, or St. Martin.

2. *Masses in favor of certain persons (sixty-two formularies).* Among them we find masses for the pope, bishops and their flocks, kings, priests, monks, and nuns.

3. *Masses that request particular favors (thirty-five formularies).* This heterogeneous group includes masses to ask for charity, peace in the community, the grace of the Holy Spirit, patience and humility; and masses with prayers for intimate friends, benefactors, and also physically or mentally suffering persons.

4. *Masses for certain public needs (forty-four formularies)*—particularly in cases of war, persecution, or epidemics affecting people or animals. Other mass intentions deal with such topics as the gathering of crops and the need for rain or fair weather.

5. *Masses for certain private circumstances (twenty-nine formularies)*—for example, the forgiveness of sins, penitents, travelers, sailors, childless women, and the sick.

6. *Masses for the dead (fifty-six formularies)*—bishops, abbots, priests, monks, and lay persons, anniversary masses, masses in cemeteries, and masses for the dead in general.

7. *"General" masses (eleven formularies),* which include, as the word suggests, prayers for all the living and the dead.

It is during the Carolingian era that votive masses seem to have multiplied most, and it is clear that in the second half of the Middle Ages (the tenth to the fifteenth centuries), the church used this body of votive masses without adding to it significantly. In fact, there was a marked tendency to reduce the number of votive masses contained in a missal. For example, the famous missal of St. Pius V (in fact that of Innocent III with slight changes), which was published in 1570, contains only seventy-five such formularies, with only six for the dead.

BIBLIOGRAPHY

Antoine Chavasse, *Le sacramentaire gélasien* (1958); Jean Deshusses, *Le sacramentaire grégorien, ses principales formes d'après les plus anciens manuscrits,* II, *Textes complémentaires pour la messe* (1979).

ROBERT AMIET

[See also **Alcuin of York; Benedict of Aniane; Carolingians and the Carolingian Empire; Church, Latin: To 1054; Gelasius I, Pope; Gregory I the Great, Pope; Innocent III, Pope; Magic and Folklore, Western European; Mass, Liturgy of the; Missal; Pepin.**]

MASSINGHAM, JOHN (*fl.* 1409–1450), a sculptor, he probably came from an established London family of carvers and carpenters, and he certainly left a son, also named John, in the trade. Between 1429 and 1438 he is mentioned in Canterbury in minor contexts, and he may have carved the four outer kings on the screen in Canterbury Cathedral. Between 1438 and 1442 he worked with his son and another assistant at All Souls, Oxford. At All Souls his chief glory was the chapel reredos, of which no sculpture survives. In the later 1440's he was probably based in London. In 1448–1449 he made an expensive image of the Virgin for the old church at Eton College. He could have been involved with Henry V's chantry at Westminster Abbey. He certainly worked on Richard Beauchamp's monument at St. Mary's, Warwick, about 1450, and he may have designed the effigy.

BIBLIOGRAPHY

John Harvey, *English Mediaeval Architects: A Biographical Dictionary Down to 1550* (1954); Lawrence Stone, *Sculpture in Britain: The Middle Ages,* 2nd ed. (1972), 206–209.

BARRIE SINGLETON

[See also **Canterbury Cathedral; Westminster Abbey.**]

MASTARA. The seventh-century Armenian church of St. Yovhannēs at Mastara near Erevan (Ałc) is dated through its architectural details and a reference to the contemporary Bishop Theodore of the Gnuni family in one of several inscriptions in Armenian. Another is in Greek.

Mastara is a large, cruciform, central-plan church with four projecting semicircular apses. The central square bay is surmounted by a polygonal drum which supports a spacious dome through the use of squinches in an unusual manner. A variant of free-standing seventh-century cruciform churches in Armenia (Lmbat, Karmrawor at Ashtarak), Mastara served as a model for other contemporary ones (Oskepar, Art'ik) and a tenth-century example (Kars).

BIBLIOGRAPHY

Architettura medievale armena (1968); Sirarpie Der Nersessian, *The Armenians* (1969), and *Armenian Art* (1977, 1978), 42; Tommaso Fratadocchi, "La cattedrale di S. Giovanni a Mastara," in *XX Corsi di cultura sull'arte ravennate e bizantina* (1973); Varaztad Harouthiounian and Morous Hasrathian, *Monuments of Armenia* (1975); Josef Strzygowski, *Die Baukunst der Armenier und Europa,* I (1918); N. Tokarskii, *Arkhitektura armenii IV–XIV vv.* (1961); Tʿoros Tʿoramanian, *Nyutʿer haykakan čartarapetutʿyan patmutʿyan,* 2 vols. (1942–1948).

LUCY DER MANUELIAN

[See also **Armenian Art.**]

MASTER ECKHART. See **Eckhart, Meister.**

MASTER OF. See next element of name.

MAŠTOCʿ, ST. (360/370–439/440), an Armenian monk who invented the Armenian alphabet at the end of the fourth or the beginning of the fifth century. The Armenian historians of the postclassical period also refer to him as Mesrob, a name that is unattested in his biography, which was written by his pupil and associate Koriwn. The latter states that Maštocʿ was from the village of Hacʿekacʿ in Tarōn (the plain of Mush). The date of his death is usually placed on 17 February 439 or 440, depending on calendrical calculations. He is buried in the village of Ošakan (in present-day Soviet Armenia), where his grave is still a major pilgrimage site.

Maštocʿ was the son of a certain Vardan who is said to have been a *karčazat,* a word that indicates a humble social status, perhaps that of a peasant tied to the soil. Despite such a lowly origin, Maštocʿ must have acquired enough education to be able to join the divan of the royal army and attain a minor military rank. His inclination toward spirituality led him to leave the army and join a monastic order or a skete. At an unspecified date, probably as head of a killion, he led his pupils to Gołtʿn in southeastern Armenia (in the present-day Nakhichevan Autonomous SSR) for missionary work. There he conceived the idea of inventing an alphabet for Armenian in order to translate the Bible and the liturgical books of the church into Armenian. His major collaborators were Bishop Sahak, the head of the Armenian church, and King Vṙamšapuh. After the failure of their initial efforts to adapt an already existing script, Maštocʿ went to Edessa to find a solution. He succeeded in his mission. Modern scholars are of the opinion that the Armenian alphabet was invented in the town of Samosata sometime between 393 and 412, the commonly accepted date being 406.

During his stay in northern Syria, Maštocʿ began to translate the Bible, presumably from a Syriac original. After his return to Armenia, he was engaged in founding schools and in missionary work that took him to Gołtʿn and Siwnikʿ in southeastern Armenia, and to Georgia, where he invented an alphabet for Georgian. In order to get permission to establish schools in Byzantine Armenia, he went to Constantinople, where he met Emperor Theodosius and Patriarch Atticus. After returning from Byzantium he went to Caucasian Albania, where he invented a script for Albanian. After the fall of the Arsacid dynasty of Armenia in 428 and the dethronement of Bishop Sahak, Maštocʿ was probably forced to restrict his missionary activities. He devoted his remaining years to the supervision of the translation of the works of the Greek and Syriac church fathers. After Sahak's death in 438 or 439, Maštocʿ succeeded him as the overseer of spiritual matters, a position that was not officially recognized by the Sasanian government.

Modern scholars attribute to Maštocʿ the *Yačaxapatum caṙkʿ,* a collection of twenty homilies; the "Teaching of St. Gregory," which is the second part of Agatʿangełos' *History of the Armenians;* and several hymns on penance. Nikolai Adontz has tried to identify him with the *chorepiskopos* Mastoubios, a friend of Theodore of Mopsuestia, who is mentioned in the *Bibliotheka* of Photios.

Maštocʿ was greatly honored as a saint. Three years after his death, his pupil Prince Vahan Amatuni raised a martyrium over his grave, and soon after that Koriwn wrote his biography, which is the first hagiographical work in Armenian.

BIBLIOGRAPHY

Source. Koriwn, *Vark^c Maštoc^c i* (Life of Maštoc^c) (1985), photoreproduction of the 1941 Erevan ed. with a modern translation and concordance, and a new introduction by Krikor H. Maksoudian.

Studies. H. Ačaṙyan, *Hayoc^c grerě* (1984); Nikolai Adontz, *Maštoc^c ew nra ašakertnerě ěst ōtar ałbiwrneri* (Maštoc^c and his pupils according to non-Armenian sources) (1925); Nerses Akinian, *Der hl. Mashtotz Wardapet, sein Leben und sein Wirken. Nebst einer Biographie des hl. Sahak. Mit einer deutschen Zusammenfassung* (1949); P. Ananean, "Vark^c S. Mesrop Maštoc^c i" (Life of St. Mesrop Maštoc^c), in *Bazmavep,* **120** (1962) and **122–127** (1964–1969); Josef Markwart, *Über den Ursprung des armenischen Alphabets in Verbindung mit der Biographie des hl. Maštoc^c* (1917).

KRIKOR H. MAKSOUDIAN

[See also **Agat^c angełos; Alphabets; Armenian Church, Doctrines; Armenian Literature; Armenian Saints; Sahak, St.**]

MAS^c ŪDĪ, AL- (Abū'l-Ḥasan ^c Alī al-Mas^c ūdi), (*ca.* 896–956), Islamic historian. He was the son of al-Ḥusayn, son of ^c Alī, son of ^c Abdallah. Born in Baghdad, of a Kufan family, he traced his descent to ^c Abdallah ibn Mas^c ūd, a companion of the prophet Muḥammad. Al-Mas^c ūdī studied under and had scholarly contact with some of the most prominent savants of his age.

Generally known as a humanist, but famed as an outstanding historian and geographer, al-Mas^c ūdī journeyed extensively throughout the ancient world as a scholar and a researcher. Such places as Persia, Armenia, India, Ceylon, the China Sea, Zanzibar, and Oman came under his scrutiny. Spurred again by yearning for knowledge and pleasant adventure, al-Mas^c ūdī traversed the southern shore of the Caspian Sea and back to the Syrian frontier towns and Palestine, until he finally settled in Egypt, where he died.

In the judgment of the philosopher Ibn Khaldūn (*d.*1406), numerous historical writings in which al-Mas^c ūdī depicted the "state . . . genius and usages of the nations" established him as "the prototype [imam] of all historians to whom they refer, and the authority on which they rely in the critical estimate of many facts." Al-Mas^c ūdī's receptive and perceptive mind, his penchant for accuracy and integrity of procedure, his comprehensive and engaging erudition, and his warm rendition of impressions and opinions that embrace the past and reflect on the present merited him the appellation "Herodotus of the Arabs." Like the Greek historian, he combined ethnography and geography with history. And as Nicholson observed:

> His work, although it lacks the artistic unity which distinguishes that of the Greek historian, shows the same eager spirit of enquiry, the same openmindedness and disposition to record without prejudice all the marvelous things that he had heard or seen, the same ripe experience and large outlook on the present as on the past.

A reconstruction of a list of al-Mas^c ūdī's historical and other works with a description of their contents, gleaned mostly from scattered references to them by the author himself, places the number at thirty-six, with five additional doubtful titles. Seven of these works comprise a historical series presumed to be the earliest and the largest of his writings. Of the few extant works of al-Mas^c ūdī, the following two are the most illustrious and enduring: *Kitāb murūj al-dhahab wa-ma^c ādin al-jawhar* (The book of the meadows of gold and mines of gems) and *Kitāb al-tanbīh wa 'l-ishrāf* (The book of admonition and recension). The authenticity of one published volume (1938) of *Kitāb akhbār al-zamān* (The history of the ages), believed to be his largest work, is questioned by many scholars. The *Murūj al-dhahab* and *al-tanbīh wa 'l-ishrāf* are generally assumed to be abridgements of larger and now lost works.

Stylistically and thematically, the *Murūj* figures as the epitome of al-Mas^c ūdī's genius and erudition. The author completed the writing of this work in 943 and then finished revising it in 947. It is fundamentally a universal history that begins with the Creation and ends with the year of its completion. However, its 132 chapters, which treat everything "terrestrial and celestial," are also replete with observations that include accounts of the peoples, empires, and lands on the periphery of Islam; Arab astronomy, augury, divination, and physiognomy; Muslim and non-Muslim sects and beliefs; and demons, sea serpents, and rhinoceroses.

Kitāb al-tanbīh wa 'l-ishrāf is a comprehensive survey of history that supplements previous compilations. Characteristically, the author digresses into such diverse topics as the principles of astronomy or a description of the physical qualities of each caliph and the inscription on his seal.

As a versatile humanist whose knowledge of science, philosophy, theology, ethics, politics, history, geography, and ethnography enlivened and embellished medieval Arab scholarship, al-Masᶜūdī is considered an ingenious offspring of that tenth-century intellectual efflorescence appropriately referred to as the renaissance of Islam.

BIBLIOGRAPHY

Sources. Kitāb murūj al-dhahab wa-maᶜādin al-jawhar, trans. by Charles Barbier de Meynard and Abel Pavet de Courteille as *Les prairies d'or,* 9 vols. (1861–1877), and revised and corrected by Charles Pellat, 5 vols. (1962–1971), and *Kitāb al-tanbīh wa 'l ishrāf,* trans. by Bernard Carra de Vaux as *Le livre de l'avertissement et de la revision* (1896). The first seventeen chapters of the *Murūj* were translated by Aloys Sprenger as *El-Masᶜūdī's Historical Encyclopedia* (1841).

Studies. Celebrations commemorating the millennium of al-Masᶜūdī's death were held at Aligarh Muslim University, India, in January 1958. International scholars presented numerous articles later published in *Al-Masᶜūdī Millenary Commemoration Volume,* S. Maqbul Ahmad and A. Rahman, eds. (1960). See also S. Maqbul Ahmed, "Travels of Abu'l Hasan ᶜAli b. al-Husayn al-Masᶜūdī," in *Islamic Culture,* 28 (1954); Tarif Khalidi, *Islamic Historiography: The Histories of Masᶜūdī* (1975); Reynold A. Nicholson, *A Literary History of the Arabs,* 2nd ed. (1930, repr. 1962); Ahmad M. H. Shboul, *Al-Masᶜūdī and His World* (1979).

MANSOUR J. AJAMI

[See also **Antiquarianism and Archaeology; Arabic Literature, Prose; Historiography, Islamic; Travel and Transport, Islamic.**]

MĀTAKDĀN Ī HAZĀR DĀTASTĀN *(The Book of One Thousand Judgments),* also called, for convenience, the Sasanian Law-Book. It was probably compiled in the city of Gōr by Farraxvmart, son of Vahrām, around 620, during the reign of Xusrō II Parwēz (Abarwēz) rather than in the ninth century, as was formerly believed. The last document included is dated in the twenty-sixth year of Xusrō II (or 615), and the work contains no evidence direct or indirect pointing to a period later than the Sasanian era. The work has survived in only one fragmentary and badly damaged manuscript copied in Iran before 1637. This manuscript was subsequently divided into two parts, of which T. D. Anklesaria brought twenty folios to Bombay in 1872, while fifty-five more folios were identified in the library of M. L. Hataria and likewise brought to Bombay. The surviving folios, which comprise about 40 percent of the original work, are now in the possession of the K. R. Cama Oriental Institute in Bombay. Facsimile editions of the two surviving sections were published in 1901 and 1912.

The *Book of One Thousand Judgments* is neither a law code nor a legal treatise. It is the only surviving example in Pahlavi of a collection of *responsa,* or legal decisions, and was presumably intended as a manual of judicial procedure. The material is set out in "articles" containing legal cases and the decisions regarding them. These articles are grouped in chapters bearing titles usually reflecting the main subject treated in them. The authorities cited are first the legal *nasks,* or divisions, of the Zoroastrian sacred scripture, called the Avesta; the Pahlavi commentaries on these *nasks,* called *čāštak;* the *Dātastān-nāmak* (Book of judgments) compiled under Xusrō I Anōšarwān; the *Aβyātkār* (Memorial) of the high priest Veh Šāhpuhr; the opinions of other heads of the clergy, usually cited by name; and chancellery regulations.

The surviving portion of the *Book of One Thousand Judgments* deals mainly with private law, with only sporadic references to public administrative law. The book contains a wealth of material on property, contractual relations, social forms and institutions, criminal law, and legal procedure, as well as instructions on the formal drawing up of official documents. The elaborate system of succession, real rights, and judicial procedure in the Law-Book sheds considerable light on other late Pahlavi texts such as the religious text called the *Dēnkard* and the *Dātastān-ī dēnik.* Reaching beyond the Zoroastrian community, this work is also of great importance for the study of the Christian Sasanian *Law-Book of Išōᶜ bōxt,* the *Babylonian Talmud,* and subsequent Islamic legislation.

BIBLIOGRAPHY

Sources. The first attempt at a transcription is A. G. Perikhanian, *Sasanidskiy sudebnik* (1973). This also contains a Russian translation and commentaries. A revised edition, with an English translation, has been prepared by A. G. Perikhanian and N. G. Garsoïan and awaits publication. A German translation is also in process.

Studies. See the relevant articles of Christian Bartholomae in the *Sitzungsberichte der Heidelberger Akademie der Wissenschaften* (Philosophisch-historische Klasse): 1910, Abhandlung 11; 1917, 11; 1918, 5 and 14; 1920, 18;

1922, 5; 1923, 9. Other works of interest by Bartholomae are "Beiträge zur Kenntnis des sasanidischen Rechts," in *Wiener Zeitschrift für die Kunde des Morgenlandes,* **27** (1913), and *Die Frau im sasanidischen Recht* (1924).

See also Antonino Pagliaro, "L'anticresi nel diritto sāsānidico," in *Rivista degli studi orientali,* **15** (1935), and "Aspetti del diritto sāsānidico," in *Rivista degli studi orientali,* **24** (1949); A. G. Perikhanian, "Agnaticheskie gruppy v drevnem Irane (Agnatic groups in ancient Iran)," in *Vestnik drevnei istorii (Journal of Ancient History),* **105** (1968), with English summary, "On Some Pahlavi Legal Terms," in *W. B. Henning Memorial Volume* (1970), "Chastnye tselevye fondy v drevnem Irane i problema proiskhozhdeniya *vakfa* (Private endowment funds in ancient Iran and origin of the *Waqf*)," in *Vestnik drevney istorii (Journal of Ancient History),* **123** (1973), with English summary, "Le contumace dans la procédure iranienne et les termes pehlevis *hačašmānd* et *sraδ*," in *Mémorial Jean de Menasce* (1974), and "Iranian Society and Law," in *Cambridge History of Iran,* III.2 (1983).

NINA G. GARSOÏAN

[See also **Avesta; Dēnkard; Pahlavi Literature; Sasanians; Xusrō I Anōšarwan; Xusrō II Abarwēz; Zoroastrianism.**]

MATHEMATICS. From the primitive technique of reckoning with the fingers to the sophisticated theory of an arithmetic of ratios, mathematics in the Middle Ages consisted of a broad and varied array of practices and learned traditions that stemmed from different times and were carried on in different settings. At first, the Germanic peoples that took over Europe from the Romans in the fifth century were innumerate as well as illiterate. Like most primitive cultures, they did not deal with the world in precise quantitative terms, and hence possessed neither elaborate systems of numbers, weights, and measures, nor sophisticated techniques for calculating with these quantities and recording the results. Still less did they have any notion of mathematics as an abstract system of logical relations underlying techniques of measurement and calculation. They had to learn these things from the people who had cultivated them.

Circumstances made learning a long and arduous process. The Romans, from whom the Europeans took their common language, literature, and liturgy, had pursued mathematics only at the most basic, practical level of commercial transactions, architectural measurements, and civil and military surveying. Practitioners learned their craft from masters rather than textbooks, and very few thought to set down what they knew in writing. Romans whose taste ran to the philosophical studied theoretical mathematics in its original language, Greek. The absence of any reported translations of Greek mathematical texts into Latin before the sixth century testifies to how select that philosophical audience was, even at the height of the empire. By the time Boethius tried to save Greek learning for Latin posterity, the audience had disappeared. From the mathematics of the Romans, the Europeans could learn only rudimentary techniques and a smattering of unconnected theory.

Hence, when introduced in the twelfth century, the elementary and advanced geometry of Euclid, Archimedes, and Ptolemy, together with the written arithmetic and the algebraic problem-solving techniques of the Arabic writers, caught European culture by suprise. Even without such complications as variant translations and corrupt texts, Latin scholars would have had difficulty assimilating the unfamiliar ways of thinking set forth in the new books that lay before them. With few exceptions, none of the texts had been composed for self-study; rather, all assumed an initiated reader or a teacher at hand. Lacking the requisite initiation, medieval mathematicians spent most of their effort on studying and commenting on what had already been done, rather than on adding new results to it. Moreover, they tailored their study to their own intellectual setting: mathematics became a subject of the arts curriculum of the medieval university and a tool for the scholastic explication of philosophical and theological authorities.

These circumstances define the standards for originality and achievement in medieval mathematics. Restoring a garbled passage or supplying a missing proposition certified hard-won command of the subject of a text. So too did wide-ranging commentary on difficult points or skillful unmasking of the mathematical flaws in an opponent's argument. Innovation meant devising a mathematical model to illustrate a philosophical point. Mathematics was seldom pursued for its own sake in the Middle Ages; rather, it was put to use in other realms of thought. On occasion, the combination of incomplete understanding of the text and of concern for application to essentially unrelated problems led to creative new insights, such as the doctrine of "ratios of ratios" in the fourteenth century. But on the whole, European mathematicians did not pick up where the Greeks had left off until Renaissance humanist translations made emulation of ancient thought both possible and desirable. Even then, the most fruitful developments of the early modern period would spring from the wedding of the two different traditions of Greek and medieval mathematics.

THE ROMAN HERITAGE:
ABACUS AND AGRIMENSOR

Until the end of the twelfth century, Europeans entered the realm of numbers along two main routes. The *De institutione arithmetica* of Boethius (*d.* 524/525) or chapter 7 of the *De nuptiis philologiae et Mercurii* of Martianus Capella (*d.* 440) offered the rudiments of Pythagorean number theory as set forth by Nicomachus of Gerasa (*fl. ca.* 100): even and odd numbers; prime and composite numbers; perfect, abundant, and deficient numbers; figurate numbers; names and classes of numerical ratios; arithmetical, geometric, and harmonic means. But the treatment scarcely went beyond definition of terms and enunciation of elementary theorems; neither of the works, nor any others based on them, taught readers how to add, subtract, multiply, and divide the relatively large numbers—not to mention the many fractional parts of Roman weights and measures—encountered in commerce or administration. In the ancient world, computation was a matter of technique, not of learning, and hence had no literature.

Two systems were commonly used in the Middle Ages, even after the introduction of written arithmetic: finger reckoning and the abacus. Tradition credits the Venerable Bede (*d.* 735) with the introduction of finger reckoning into Europe, but he composed his *De computo vel loquela digitorum* probably to teach monastic audiences in writing what more worldly circles of the ancient Mediterranean had long learned by oral tradition. The technique had the capacity in any of its several variants to express and to calculate with numbers from 1 to 9,999, although its actual use seldom involved values of more than two digits, as in computing the movable date of Easter *(computus).* Combining larger numbers required a level of mental computation that defeated the purpose of the technique. For big tasks, Europeans turned to the abacus, using their fingers to carry out intermediate calculations on the device.

The abacus is the answer to the canard that multiplication and division were all but impossible in the Roman number system. The board, whether slotted for sliding counters or simply lined in colums for the *calculi* that gave operations with numbers their generic title, translated the sequence of denominations I, X, C, M, . . . into a decimal place-value array, often dividing the columns horizontally and using the upper portion to record the groups of five expressed in the number system by V, L, D. . . . Thus, for example, the written number MCMLXXXIV, or MDCCCCLXXXIIII (1984), became the array shown in Figure 1. Clearly, addition and subtraction on the abacus required no more than setting down the addends and regrouping the resulting columns that exceeded nine, or picking up the subtrahend from the minuend, borrowing and regrouping when columns lacked enough counters. Multiplication was reduced to repeated addition by the following procedure: having laid down the factors at the top and bottom of the board, the abacist began with the highest (usually leftmost) digit of the multiplicand and multiplied it by each digit of the multiplier in descending order. Each multiplication consisted of two steps: determining the absolute value of the product (using repeated addition on the abacus itself, a 9 × 9 multiplication table, or finger reckoning) and determining the column into which it should be placed (for instance, tens column × hundreds column = thousands column). The lowest digit of the full subproduct replaced the now multiplied digit of the multiplicand, and the operation was repeated on its next lower digit, the subproduct being added to that of the previous step in the appropriate columns. So, for example, DCLXXII times XXXVIII (672 × 38) took the sequential form, as shown in Figure 2.

Division was slightly more complicated than multiplication and followed either of two patterns: "golden" division worked directly with the divisor, while "iron" division supplemented the divisor to the next power of ten and then added the product of the supplement times the subquotient to the remainder before dividing the next column. Since in practice fractions arose from the division of measured quantities, the abacist usually referred to the elaborate duodecimal system of Roman weights and measures to convert fractions into units of common de-

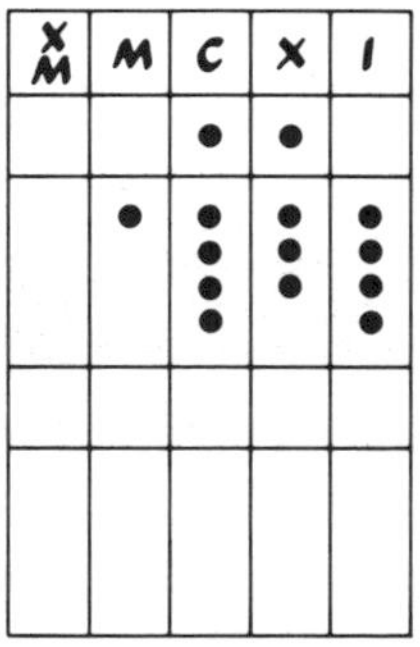

Fig. 1

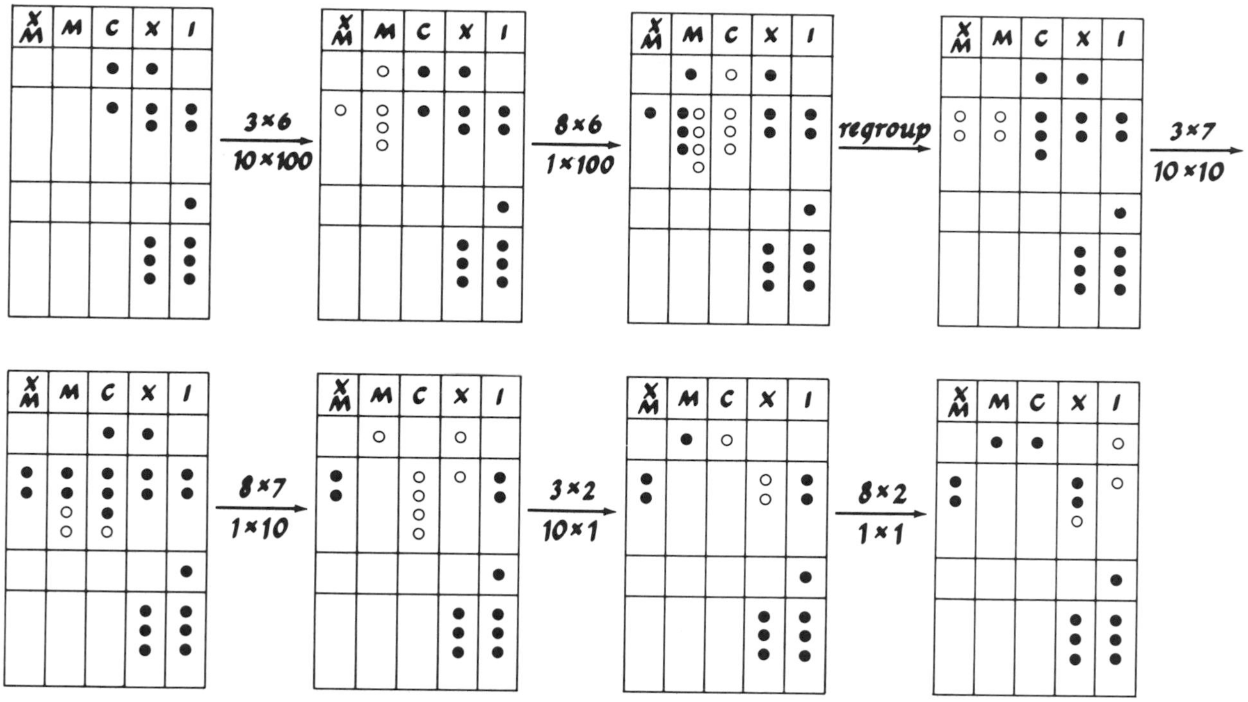

Fig. 2

nomination, which were then treated as ordinary integers on the board. Depending on the elaborateness of the abacus being used, regrouping occurred at various levels and determining the products of columns became quite complicated.

The first medieval texts on the abacus date from the late tenth century, and through their common form and shared emphases reveal both their origin in oral modes of instruction and the points at which the guidance of a master was most needed. Saying little about addition or subtraction, or even 9 × 9 multiplication, the various tracts concentrate on decimal carrying and on the products of columns (that is, decimal place-value multiplication); for the latter they often include elaborate tables. These features of the abacus derived from the decimal structure of Roman numeration, a structure that the notation obscured and for which existing mathematics lacked an adequate theoretical language. Still more did it lack the foundations for explaining carrying and multiplication of columns for nondecimal counting systems, such as those encountered when calculating with Roman fractions. The treatises took no steps toward establishing those foundations; they aimed at teaching a practical technique and used whatever examples and metaphors they could devise to that end.

Among the earliest treatises is the *Regulae de numerorum abaci rationibus* of Gerbert of Aurillac, composed about 980. In it the future Pope Sylvester II introduced, possibly from Spanish Muslim sources, a variation on the Roman abacus, replacing the identical counters by *apices* bearing a numeral (in the West Arabic form) from 1 to 9. Thus, 1984 was expressed by *apices* with the numerals 1, 9, 8, and 4 placed in the thousands, hundreds, tens, and units columns, respectively. Whatever the economy of counters thereby achieved, the new form required the abacist to carry out all single-digit calculations, even addition and subtraction, in his head, and made the abacus an instrument more for keeping track of computations than for computation itself. Although Gerbert's abacus pointed toward the written arithmetic soon to be introduced from Arabic sources, it did not make the Roman device more efficient, and hence did not replace it in common use.

In the directly Roman tradition, geometry consisted of the body of mensurational techniques known as the *ars gromatica* (from *groma,* surveyor's pole) and practiced by the *agrimensores* (field measurers). Roman practitioners had learned their art, as Roman abacists had learned theirs, by oral tradition, supplemented in the late empire by occasional handbooks and compilations. Largely by way of the latter, in particular a work by two otherwise unknown writers, Epaphroditus and Vitruvius Rufus, medieval Europeans inherited rudimentary procedures for determining the areas of regular and irregular plane figures and the volumes of several common solids. Not all of the recipes were precisely correct, and none rested on any theoretical derivation or justification. To find the area of a regular hexagon of side 10, for example, an author related: "I multiply this one side by itself; it makes 100. This I multiply by 4; it makes 400. From this I subtract twice the side; it makes 380, of which the half taken is 190. So many feet is the area of this hexagon" (Tannery, *Mémoires scientifiques,* V, 65).

Some theoretical geometry did exist in Latin. Cassiodorus attests to Boethius' having translated Euclid's *Elements* in full; and detached portions of that work, culled from various Greek sources, lay scattered in the writings of the encyclopedists. Lotharingian scholars of the early eleventh century knew that this material somehow belonged with the practical tradition. Two compilations that circulated under the title *Geometria Boethii* stem from their school. Both join to the gromatic precepts the definitions, postulates, axioms, and propositions (but generally not the proofs) of the first four books of the *Elements,* evidently as translated by Boethius. One version, which dates back to the eighth century, also contains geometrical excerpts from the writings of Cassiodorus (*d. ca.* 575) and Isidore of Seville (*d.* 636), along with sections of Boethius' *Arithmetica;* the other supplements Euclid and the *agrimensores* with a version of Gerbert's abacus and a discussion of Roman fractions.

Yet the juxtaposition of arithmetic and geometry suggests that the compilators did not discern the relation of Greek theory to Roman practice, and the writings of other eleventh-century scholars confirm that impression. Even with Euclid's theorems at hand, they viewed geometry as a matter of direct measurement and calculation, not as a theory of measure based on the concept of congruence and transformation of areas. Thus Gerbert had to explain to his student Adelbold, later bishop of Utrecht, why an equilateral right triangle of side 30 does not have as its area the triangular number of the same side. So too Ragimbold of Cologne and Radulf of Laon puzzled each other with such questions as what could be meant by the "exterior angle" of a triangle, whether 7:5 or 17:12 is the correct ratio of the diagonal of a square to its side, and what the metrologers could have had in mind by "linear feet," "square feet," and "solid feet." So too Franco of Liège began his *De quadratura circuli* (*ca.* 1050) by explaining wherein the problem of finding a square equal to a circle lies. Confessing his uncertainty about how anyone could have first determined that a circle of 14 feet in diameter has an area of 154 square feet, he nonetheless accepted that measure as accurate and puzzled, rather, over the difficulties of constructing a square of the same area, that is, of transforming a 14×11 rectangle into a square. His discussion rests on the notion of direct measurement, that is, of computing $\sqrt{154}$ as the side of the square, and hence the treatise ends with a section on Roman fractions. Although Franco apparently knew of the "Boethian" compilation, he did not see that theorems in it supplied the transformation he was seeking.

With the introduction of Greek and Arabic learning into twelfth-century Europe, scholars soon grasped geometry in the Euclidean mode as they learned to do arithmetic on paper. But the culture as a whole did not abandon practical geometry, any more than it gave up the abacus. Roman notions of the nature and purposes of mathematics persisted throughout the Middle Ages, conditioning the assimilation of the Greek model and defining lines of development peculiar to the Europeans.

THE NEW LEARNING: ALGORISM, GEOMETRY, AND ALGEBRA

Translations from Arabic texts opened three new areas of mathematics to Europeans in the twelfth century: Hindu-Arabic arithmetic, Euclidean geometry, and algebra. The subjects belonged to different traditions stemming from diverse origins. Hence, they posed different problems of initial comprehension and of eventual accommodation with the Roman heritage.

Around 825 the Muslim mathematician and astronomer Muḥammad ibn Mūsā al-Khwārizmī set forth in his *Treatise on Calculation with Hindu Numerals* a way of writing numbers that captured in symbols the decimal structure of Arabic counting. It used distinct symbols for the numbers 1–9 and expressed powers of ten by serial order from a first position on the right; a tenth symbol denoted an empty rank in that order. Translated into Latin sometime before 1143, the *De numero indorum* became the prototype for a series of texts expounding decimal place-value numeration and computation, which for several centuries bore the designation *algorismus* (whence the modern "algorithm") after al-Khwārizmī.

As noted above, the new system did not arrive totally unannounced in Europe. Gerbert's abacus embodied its basic principle, and many of the early techniques of written computation had their origin in the procedures of the abacist. For example, multiplication began with the highest digits and worked down, altering previous results when required to carry over to the left. Doubling was treated as a separate operation; it began with the lowest digit and added 5 to the right when an odd digit was encountered (an especially simple operation when using an abacus that groups at 5). Most revealingly, the earliest algorists erased or wrote over intermediate steps and, in generating a product or quotient, progressively eliminated the multiplicand or the dividend, as if the calculator were picking up and laying down counters. For example, computation of 672 × 38 took place in the following sequence (italic numerals represent the developing product):

672	→	*18672*	→	*22872*	→
38	3 × 6 = 18	38	8 × 6 = 48	38	shift
22872	→	*24972*	→	*25462*	→
38	3 × 7 = 21	38	8 × 7 = 56	38	shift
25462	→	*25522*	→	*25536*	
38	3 × 2 = 6	38	8 × 2 = 16	38	

Variant twelfth-century translations of al-Khwārizmī's text gave way in the early thirteenth to two Latin recensions that became the standard algorisms for the next three centuries. Alexander de Villa Dei cast the new system into verse for pupils in monastic and cathedral schools; his *Carmen de algorismo* (*ca.* 1225) joined his *Doctrinale puerorum* and *Massa compoti (computus)* as staples of the early arts curriculum. John of Holywood (Sacrobosco) wrote his *Algorismus vulgaris* (*ca.* 1240) for the secular audience of the new universities, describing the operations in added detail, increasing the number of illustrative examples, and even including some number theory from Boethius' *Arithmetica.* Enhanced in 1291 by Peter Philomena of Dacia's extensive commentary, Sacrobosco's text was the source of most educated people's knowledge of arithmetic until the mid sixteenth century.

During the thirteenth century scholars learned that in dealing with fractions, written arithmetic bypassed the difficulties inherent in the abacus. The growth of commerce and administration was making it hard to avoid calculation with common fractions, and algorism lent itself to methods of combining them directly, without reduction to a conventional system such as Roman measures, or the use of special apparatus. Jordanus de Nemore (*fl. ca.* 1220) began the development of new techniques in his *Tractatus minutiarum* and *Demonstratio de minutiis;* but the standard notation (numerator over denominator, separated by a bar or *virgula*) and terminology stem from Gernardus' *Algorismus de minutiis* by way of the later and more widely read text of the same title by John of Lignères (*ca.* 1340). Written as part of an introduction to the use of astronomical tables, John's work included the sexagesimal arithmetic of the "physical" or "philosophical" fractions (degree, minutes, seconds) used by astronomers.

Although a translation directly from the Greek of Euclid's *Elements* existed in the Middle Ages, the versions that scholars used to learn theoretical geometry came to them by way of Arabic—indeed, by way of two Arabic traditions. The first of these stemmed from the two translations, one complete and the other an abridgment, done by al-Ḥajjāj under the caliphs Hārūn al-Rashīd and al-Maʾmūn in the early ninth century. The second tradition originated toward the end of that century with the complete and close rendering of Euclid into Arabic by Isḥāq ibn Ḥunayn and its revision by Thābit ibn Qurra. Although the eminent Gerard of Cremona (*ca.* 1114–1187) made an accurate translation of the Isḥāq–Thābit text, few people appear to have used it. Instead, medieval scholars read the *Elements* in one of several Latin versions of al-Ḥajjāj's abridged edition, translated first by Adelard of Bath (*fl.* 1116–1142) and later by Hermann of Carinthia (*fl. ca.* 1150). Adelard's translation circulated in three different recensions, of which the best-known retained Euclid's enunciation of the theorems but replaced his proofs with sketches and commentaries on how proofs might be constructed, should the reader wish to do so. This truncated version, together with one that gave the full proofs as well as commentaries on them, formed the basis of the thirteenth-century recension by Campanus of Novara (*d.* 1296), which quickly became the standard edition and remained so until the Renaissance.

Despite the hazards of passing successively through two languages at the hands of translators to whom the subject was initially unfamiliar, Euclid's text remained remarkably intact. Only a few propositions were lost along the way, and in most cases their absence was soon noted and remedied. Changes in the order of propositions occurred, but on the whole for consciously pedagogical reasons; elegance suffered, but not coherence. With the notable exception of the theory of ratios, to be discussed below, medieval scholars seldom misunderstood the intent of Euclid's theorems, and the few lapses were inconsequential.

Yet, the spirit of the *Elements* proved more elusive than its letter. With no tradition to guide them, Europeans read the work in the context of Aristotle's *Organon,* the "new logic" introduced at about the same time through translations from the Greek and the Arabic. Aristotle frequently used geometrical examples to illustrate points of logic, and the *Elements* in turn conforms closely to the canons of demonstrative science as set forth in the *Posterior Analytics.* Hence, teachers and commentators tended to view Euclidean geometry as an extended exercise in logical reasoning rather than as a body of mathematical techniques or as a general theory of measure. Commentaries on propositions focused more on their logical structure than on the range of their applicability, additions to the text aimed more at filling in axioms than in branching out into corollaries, independent inquiry explored more the metaphysics or metalogic of basic concepts than the mathematics that followed from them.

The medieval *Elements* echoes the language of the classroom, where students prepared less for problem solving than for disputation. Addressing the reader in the second person, the text carefully instructs him in drawing a diagram, outlines the structure of the proof to follow, relates the proposition and its mode of proof to other theorems and constructions, explains unusual aspects of the demonstration, and anticipates objections that the student might encounter in debate: "Perhaps an adversary will say . . . " or "An adversary will be led in the same way to a contradiction if. . . ." In general, the form of argumentation was of greater concern than the content of the mathematics, which interested scholars largely through the assistance it rendered in understanding ancient authorities and in explicating philosophical questions. Taught in this fashion, many medieval writers took their mathematical problems from Aristotle and expounded them in the dialectical style of the *questio;* the range and cleverness of the arguments adduced pro and con counted for more than did the solution, which more often than not was well known.

The didactic tone and philosophical purpose conditioned the reception of what little was known of other Greek mathematical writers, in particular Archimedes. His works arrived piecemeal, beginning in the twelfth century. From the fragmentary Arabic tradition came his *Measurement of the Circle* and some theorems of his *On Spirals,* the latter by way of a mensurational treatise known as the *Verba filiorum,* after its authors, the Banū Mūsā. Perhaps from Byzantium came a paraphrase of book I of the *Sphere and Cylinder,* latinized as the *Liber de curvis superficiebus Archimenidis,* of Johannes de Tinemue. These selections remained the most common source of Archimedean learning even after William of Moerbeke translated almost all of the extant corpus from the Greek in 1269; only a few Parisian mathematicians of the fourteenth century and several writers in the fifteenth used this full collection.

Yet, whether borrowing one proposition for a *quadratura circuli* (an effort most commonly stimulated by Aristotle's works) or paraphrasing an entire treatise, medieval writers treated Archimedes' mathematics as a school-room exercise. His style as a working mathematician gave them ample room for filling in the details of his arguments, not only pointing to lemmas and propositions found elsewhere in his writings but also supplying the propositions he assumed his readers would know from the *Elements.* Thus, for example, the author (perhaps Jehan des Murs) of a *Circuli quadratura* written in 1340 showed his sophistication by recognizing that the first eighteen propositions of *On Spirals* could be used to supply the straight line equal to the circumference of a circle that was called for by proposition 1 of *Measurement of the Circle.* But even those who knew Archimedes' works well enough to make such connections between them still achieved no creative advance beyond them.

The works of Euclid and Archimedes did not supplant the earlier surveying tradition, but, rather, gave substance to the distinction between theoretical and practical knowledge that was common among inherited classifications of learning. Besides constituting the theoretical science of geometry, the Greek texts enabled medieval scholars to work out a theoretical structure for the practices of the *agrimensor,* to fill in its foundations, and to improve the practices. Not all writers followed precisely the same lines of development, but gradually three main themes emerged: new instruments; Euclidean foundations; more precise measures, taken largely from Archimedes.

Hugh of St. Victor (*d.* 1141) first extended the

MATHEMATICS

general distinction between theory and practice to the specific case of geometry. In his *Didascalicon* (before 1125) he divided the science into a theoretical, speculative part that proceeds "by rational consideration alone" *(sola rationis speculatione),* and a practical, active part that "uses some instruments and measures by deriving some things from others via proportions." His *Practica geometrie* gave name and form to the resulting genre: It set forth the measurement of lengths *(altimetria),* areas *(planimetria),* and spherical volumes (*cosmimetria;* generalized by later writers to *stereometria* and applied to a wide range of solids). The instruments—Hugh cited the astrolabe, right triangle, various staffs, mirror, and gnomon—pertained to altimetry. When a length or height could not be measured directly (for instance, by stepping it off or by laying down a cord), the instruments provided a proportional model (usually through similar triangles) by which to measure it indirectly. Altimetry consisted of the construction and use of such tools. Planimetry and stereometry, by contrast, involved no instruments but, rather, comprised the computational recipes by which various linear elements of plane and solid figures were combined to yield their areas and volumes.

Although Hugh apparently first added the astrolabe to the art's tools, he could add no theoretical depth to the old surveying precepts. Neither, it seems, could Johannes Anglicus of Montpellier a century later, when he introduced another instrument of Arabic origin, the quadrant. For example, his procedure for describing the curved lines that mark the twelve "artificial" hours of the day between sunrise and sunset required the construction of an isosceles triangle, given the base, one (indefinitely extended) side, and the angle between them. Yet, far from citing the propositions of books I and III of the *Elements* that yield that construction, Johannes referred only to manipulating the compasses and spoke in a way suggesting that he himself had proceeded by trial and error. Similarly, he instructed his reader to divide the circular rim of the quadrant first into halves, then each half into thirds, then each third into thirds, and finally each of the last parts into fifths. However, he did not say how all this should be carried out, nor did he show any awareness that the bisection of an angle and its division into five parts pose challenges of quite different sorts.

Although an anonymous practical geometry of 1193 (incipit: "Artis cuiuslibet consummatio ... ") made an effort to justify theoretically a few of the mensurational precepts it set forth, not until the first half of the fourteenth century did Euclid's *Elements* and Archimedes' works have substantial influence on the style and content of the surveying art. Dominicus de Clavasio's *Practica geometrie* (1346) reveals a novel emphasis on the theoretical foundations of its techniques. Since, for example, use of the instruments rests ultimately on similar triangles and on calculating proportions, Dominicus opened with four *suppositiones* about proportions and about solving for unknown terms in them. These suppositions, together with theorems cited by number from the *Elements,* underpinned the "proof of this practice" that he supplied for each application of the various devices.

While Dominicus concentrated his attention on altimetry, he sought also to link the recipes of planimetry and stereometry to their theoretical roots. The effort was far from thorough and did not always hit the mark. In construction 15 of book II, for example, he confused the determination of the area of a regular polygon, given one of its sides, with the construction of a similar polygon by means of *Elements* VI.18. Yet, he apparently appreciated why Euclid had used a special form of demonstration for *Elements* XII.2, proving that the areas of circles are as the squares on their diameters: Circles cannot be measured directly: "The ratio of the circumference of any circle to its diameter is a triple sesquiseptimate [ratio], or thereabouts ... because there is no definite demonstrated ratio of the circumference to the diameter. Therefore, when I speak of measuring a circle with a square, I do not mean to speak demonstratively but only to teach how to find the area such that no sensible error remains" (II. def. 5).

Such methods of approximation had been Archimedes' forte, and, working both from his treatises themselves and from traces of them contained in translated Arabic surveying texts, thirteenth-century scholars had already begun to improve the recipes for curvilinear areas, surfaces, and solids. But Jehan des Murs's *De arte mensurandi* (*ca.* 1344) first gave the techniques, new and old, a fully Archimedean treatment with proofs, cross-references, and exact determination of the limits of precision.

Dominicus' and Jehan's works are the culmination of the tradition of practical geometry initiated by Hugh of St. Victor and rooted in the Roman *ars gromatica.* New techniques being introduced in the fourteenth century required calculation of relations more complex than the direct proportionality of similar figures. Dominicus reserved for a "special treatise, viz. on shadows and radii" the measurement of lengths by means of angles, which demanded the determination of the chord subtending a given angle in a circle of given radius. The tables of values and the techniques for computing them belonged to the astronomers, who learned them from Ptolemy's *Almagest* or from compilers of astronomical tables; not until the fifteenth century did the methods take shape as the branch of mathematics called trigonometry.

A third new form of mathematics introduced into Europe in the twelfth century was algebra. As in the case of Hindu-Arabic arithmetic, al-Khwārizmī composed the text that served as prototype for Arabic and Latin treatments of the subject and that incidentally provided its European name. The Arabic *Kitāb al-mukhtaṣar fī-ḥisāb al-jabr wa'l-muqābala* (Compendious book on calculation by completion and balancing) became in Latin simply *Liber algebre.* As the title was broken up, so too was the treatise itself; only two of its three parts were transmitted to Europe, and they arrived separately. Latin scholars took time to reestablish the connection between them.

At first the term "algebra" applied only to the first part, translated by Robert of Chester in 1145 and by Gerard of Cremona several decades later. It set forth solution paradigms for six types of problems expressed in modern symbolism by the equations (1) $ax^2 = bx$, (2) $ax^2 = b$, (3) $ax = b$, (4) $ax^2 + bx = c$, (5) $ax^2 + c = bx$, and (6) $bx + c = ax^2$, where a, b, and c are all positive rational numbers. Al-Khwārizmī employed no symbolic notation; indeed, he even wrote out the numbers in words. Instead, he used a special technical vocabulary in formulaic style to state his procedures in general before illustrating them with specific examples: *shay*ᵓ (thing) and *jidhr* (root) denoted the unknown quantity; *māl* (wealth), its share; and *dirham* (a common coin), the constant.

The paradigms had an ancestry reaching back to Babylonian times, and the word problems used as examples each had its own long, cross-cultural history. To justify and explain the paradigms for forms (4) through (6), al-Khwārizmī added geometrical demonstrations stemming ultimately from book II of the *Elements.* He also devoted considerable attention to the multiplication of binominals, both for numbers written explicitly as the sums of tens and units (whether to reinforce the concept of decimal arithmetic or to show that algebra is a form of arithmetic, is not clear) and for sums and differences of numbers and "things." The first part concluded with the "rule of three" for solving problems by finding the fourth proportional to three given values ("if five cost three, how much do seven cost?").

The second part of al-Khwārizmī's treatise was not transmitted directly but through an expanded version of it by Abraham bar Ḥiyya (Savasorda in Latin), translated by Plato of Tivoli in 1145 as the *Liber embadorum* (Book of areas). Belonging to the Arabic tradition of ᶜ*ilm al-misāḥa* (science of measurement), it resembled in many aspects a practical geometry of the Latin tradition. But it included a more sophisticated mathematics, especially by adding algebra to the techniques of the *mensurator* and by using it to solve problems of dividing areas and volumes into parts having a given relation, and of determining lengths from various combinations of dimensions. An otherwise obscure Abū Bakr made even more extensive use of algebra in a similar text translated by Gerard of Cremona as the *Liber in quo terrarum et corporum continentur mensurationes* (Book in which are contained the measurements of lands and bodies, soon shortened to *Liber mensurationum*). The third part of al-Khwārizmī's algebra treated the division of inheritances. Although portions of it may have found their way into the writings of Leonardo Fibonacci, the section as a whole remained untranslated.

Despite algebra's association both with the author of the new algorism and with the popular subject of practical geometry, the new art evoked little response from European scholars of the thirteenth and fourteenth centuries. Few manuscripts of the works just cited exist, and, more tellingly, few mathematicians before the fifteenth century show any familiarity with them. The knowledge of al-Khwārizmī and Fibonacci that Jehan des Murs displayed in part 3 of his *Quadripartitum numerorum,* or of Abū Bakr, as shown in chapter 5 of *De arte mensurandi,* is as exceptional among his contemporaries as is his familiarity with Archimedes. It is certainly uncharacteristic of the mathematical texts being produced by masters of the arts curriculum in the universities. Algebra did not appear in the curriculum until it was taught at Leipzig in the late fifteenth century, a time when new texts on the subject began to spring up. Before then, if knowledge of algebra spread at all, it did so by oral tradition among merchants and surveyors, to whom it offered practical utility and intellectual recreation. Although practical geometry did have a literary form aimed at giving it a theoretical structure, mensurational techniques evidently continued to circulate by oral tradition. Near the end of the fourteenth century a *Geometria culmensis* made Dominicus de Clavasio's treatise available to a German-speaking audience of practitioners.

EUROPEAN ACHIEVEMENTS

When set against the efforts of someone like Franco of Liège, the works of Leonardo Fibonacci and Jordanus de Nemore (or Nemorarius), composed in the early thirteenth century, show how much mathematics became available to interested Europeans during the intervening 150 years and how adeptly they could learn to handle it. Born about 1170, the son of a wealthy Pisan merchant, Leonardo followed his father's trade around the Mediterranean littoral, learning not only commerce but also practical and theoretical mathematics from Greek and Arabic sources. Around 1200 he settled at home in Pisa, where he composed his works and, apparently, taught mathematics and advised the city government. He died sometime after 1240.

Despite the title, Leonardo's *Liber abbaci* (1202, revised 1228) focused on Hindu-Arabic reckoning and was meant to introduce the system into Italy. In it, he illustrated the mechanics of decimal place-value computation by means of a rich collection of mercantile and recreational problems solved by various arithmetical techniques (such as rule of three, single and double false position, reverse calculation) and by elementary algebra. Using theorems from book II of the *Elements* as "keys," he turned to the arithmetic of binomial surds, both to justify his techniques for determining square and cube roots, and to lay the foundations for al-Khwārizmī's six basic forms and their solution paradigms; again, specific examples from many sources backed up the general precepts.

The same varied mix of practice and theory characterizes Leonardo's *Practica geometriae* (1220/1221). There theorems from Euclid and Archimedes ground the procedures of the *ars gromatica* and the *ᶜilm al-misāḥa,* pointing as well to more esoteric exercises, such as the duplication of the cube by Archytas, Plato (as reported by Eutocius via the *Verba filiorum*), and Philo of Byzantium, or the division of figures (from Euclid's work of that name by way of the *Liber embadorum*). Similarly, algebra and Arabic adumbrations of trigonometry widen the scope of the mensurator's instruments while stimulating such subtleties *(subtilitates)* as finding the sides of a pentagon or decagon from the diameters of inscribed and circumscribed circles.

Leonardo's originality as a mathematician shows most clearly from two small algebraic treatises written around 1225. His *Flos* treats the equation (here transcribed in modern notation) $x^3 + 2x^2 + 10x = 20$, which appears in the *Algebra* of ᶜUmar Khayyam. After demonstrating that the solution is not an integer or (as he skillfully argued from *Elements* X) a quadratic irrational, Leonardo presented without derivation or demonstration the sexagesimal solution $x = 1;22,7,42,33,4,40$, which is too great by 1.5 parts in 60. Leonardo's *Liber quadratorum* briefly revived the number-theoretical algebra of Diophantus of Alexandria in determining the general solution in rationals of the system $x^2 + 5 = y^2$, $x^2 - 5 = z^2$, or $y^2 - x^2 = x^2 - z^2 = 5$. In replacing the particular value 5 by a parameter on which he set conditions of solvability, Leonardo showed a facility in number theory unmatched until the seventeenth century.

Identified only by the informed and expert treatises that bear the name Jordanus, the thirteenth century's second most accomplished mathematician is shrouded in obscurity. The shadows hide more than the lines of life and career that tie Jordanus to the sources on which he evidently drew but that did not circulate widely. Also lost from sight are the stimuli that gave rise to his original treatments of those sources. For example, his largest work, *De numeris datis* (On given numbers), sets out the linear and quadratic techniques of the Arabic algebraists and of Leonardo in a form reminiscent of Euclid's *Data.* Moreover, to the traditional modes of algebraic exposition—rhetorical precept and numerical example—Jordanus added a partial system of alphabetic notation. Though neither technically nor conceptually as complete as the later system of François Viète's *In artem analyticem isagoge* (1591), Jordanus' literal symbolism nonetheless pointed in that direction. Proposition I.9 illustrates the new style and its limitations:

> [If a given number be divided into two parts] and a given number result[s] from [adding] the product of the whole times the difference [of the parts] to [that of] the greater [part] times itself, each [of the parts] will also be given.
>
> Let *ab* be divided into *a* and *b,* of which the difference is *c,* and let *d* be *ab* times *c,* and *e* be *a* (which is the greater [part]) times itself; and the whole *de* will be given. But also let *ab* times itself be *f,* whence the whole *def* will be given. But, because *abc* is twice *a, df* will be the product of *ab* times twice *a;* therefore, *df* will be the product of twice *ab* times *a.* And so, therefore, *def* will be the result of [adding] *a* times itself [to *a*] times

twice *ab*. And since *def* is given, as is 2*ab*, *a* will also be given, as will *b*.

For example, let *x* times the difference of the parts, plus the greater part times itself be *lvi;* to which let *c* be joined, and there will result *clvi,* of which the double is *cccxii,* which is doubled and will make *dcxxiiii,* to which is added the square of *xx,* which is twice *x,* and *mxxiiii* will result; the root of this is *xxxii,* from which is taken *xx* and there remains *xii,* of which the half is *vi.* This is the greater portion of *x,* and the other is *iiii.*

This proposition has two parts, of which only the first employs the new notation in showing that the given conditions reduce to a known form of quadratic problem. The second follows out the rhetorical solution paradigm of that form for a specific numerical example; paradigm and reduction are unrelated.

In contrast to later symbolic algebra, Jordanus' notation gives only a faint glimpse of the structure of the problem and of the transformations it undergoes in reduction to canonical form. For example, the statement that *abc* is twice *a* carries no self-evident justification but relies on some tacit theorem; the manner in which it entails that *df* is the product of *ab* and 2*a* is similarly unclear. Jordanus set out no rules for operations on the symbols, much less symbolic operations. The juxtaposition of *a* and *b* did not denote symbolic addition but simply the conjoint whole; no symbolic form reversed the conjunction, and hence no means existed for substituting into *abc* the value c = difference of *a* and *b,* as in the modern schema: $a + b + c = a + b + a - b = 2a$. Again, no operative symbolism readily factored a conjunction of two products into a product of two conjoint wholes, as in the modern sequence $(a+b)^2 + (a+b)c = (a+b)(a+b+c) = (a+b) \times 2a$. Manipulation remained tied to rules expressed rhetorically rather than symbolically. So, a fortiori, the second part of the proposition followed a pattern of solution unrelated to the symbolic equation $a^2 + 2a(a+b) =$ *const.*

Nonetheless, coming less than a century after Hugh of St. Victor showed himself unable to label a figure properly, Jordanus' abbreviatory symbolism displayed an informed originality. So too did his other works, which included a *Demonstratio de . . . algorismo* in the style of al-Khwārizmī's, an *Elementa super demonstrationem ponderum* (Elements for the demonstration of weights) setting forth statics on the Euclidean-Archimedean model but including concepts from the less common tradition of pseudo-Aristotelian *Mechanical Problems,* two treatises on fractions, and a geometry titled *De triangulis.* This last work, based on some of the same sources as Leonardo's *Practica geometriae,* focused more on theoretical topics, including (IV.20) the trisection of the angle (two solutions taken from the Banū Mūsā and one of his own based in part on a proposition from Ibn al-Haytham's *Optics*), Hero of Alexandria's theorem for the area of a triangle from its three sides, two solutions to the problem of determining two mean proportionals (IV.22), and a quadrature of the circle differing essentially from the Archimedean model. Finally, Jordanus' best-known work, his *Arithmetica,* opened the substance of Euclid's arithmetical books (*Elements* VII–IX) to readers theretofore dependent on Boethius' much less technical book.

Yet, Leonardo and Jordanus stand out among their contemporaries in part because they stand alone, as do their works over the next two centuries. Neither man attracted a following or established anything akin to a school or tradition. By as yet undetermined, possibly oral, filiations the algorismic sections of Leonardo's *Liber abbaci* did shape the teaching in Italian *scuole d'abbaco* in the fourteenth century; and excerpts from his works found their way into various problem texts compiled by anonymous practitioners. But his systematic exploration of algebraic techniques and his inventive efforts to widen their scope lay essentially untouched until taken up again by Italian algebraists of the fifteenth century. They grafted them onto the less sophisticated, practical tradition that had given itself the name *arte della cosa* and that was turning the abbreviations of such technical terms as *res, census,* and *cubus,* translated literally from the Arabic *shayʾ, māl,* and *kaʿb* into a form of symbolic notation.

Similarly, Jordanus' treatise on statics prompted several expanded recensions, and enough copies were made of his other works to ensure their survival. But real interest in Jordanus' original achievements first emerged during the Renaissance. Among his contemporaries and immediately succeeding generations, mathematics attracted attention along lines different from that of skilled emulation of Greek and Arabic authors. On one level, mathematics provided instruments of commerce and administration; on another, it served the needs of teaching and exegesis, the prime concerns of the medieval university and the context for autonomous mathematical development in the Middle Ages. The theory of ratio and proportion offers perhaps the best example, both of the special circumstances that provoked independent development and of the peculiar lines it followed.

Euclid took into his *Elements* two theories of ratio and proportion, a limited one for numbers in book VII and a broad one for continuous magnitudes in book V. The former stemmed from Pythagorean doctrine and was grounded in the definition of number (integer) as a collection of units. Common to all numbers, the unit served to determine the equality of two ratios, or proportion, by a finite counting procedure (*Elements* VII. def. 20): "Numbers are proportional when the first is the same multiple, or the same part, or the same parts, of the second that the third is of the fourth." That is, the ratio of A to B, or $(A,B) = (C,D)$ if and only if when (for some integers m and n) $mA = nB$, then $mC = nD$. Because A and B are numbers, there will always exist some pair m, n establishing the first equality, as Euclid showed in VII. def. 4.

The second theory arose in response to the existence of quantities having no common measure and hence standing in ratios not expressible in numbers, such as the diagonal and side of a square, or the diameter of a circle and the side of an inscribed decagon. Eudoxus of Cnidus varied the principle that underlay his famous "method of exhaustion" to make a useful definition out of the fact that the Pythagorean method for determining equality of ratios would lead to an endless search for a suitable pair m, n (*Elements* V. def. 5): "Magnitudes are said to be in the same ratio, the first to the second and the third to the fourth, when, if any equimultiples whatever be taken of the first and third, and any equimultiples whatever of the second and the fourth, the former equimultiples alike exceed, are alike equal to, or alike fall short of, the latter equimultiples respectively taken in corresponding order." That is, $(A,B) = (C,D)$ if and only if, for all m and n, $mA \gtreqless nB$ if [and only if] $mC \gtreqless nD$. This criterion and its inverse secured the central theorems of book V, hurdling at once the barriers of the infinite, the continuous, and the incommensurable by using a potentially infinite set of discontinuous elements to narrow in on a common measure. It was one of the most brilliant achievements of Greek mathematics.

For the most part, Arabic and European mathematicians could not fathom the theory's subtlety, nor, unaccustomed to reading the *Elements* as a historical document, could they understand the reason for the presence of two theories. Some Arabic writers assailed the difficulty of V. def. 5 and proposed other, seemingly simpler criteria. European mathematicians had less choice. The texts transmitted to them omitted the original definition in favor of one that was not equivalent and that directed attention elsewhere; in Campanus' version: "Quantities that are said to have continuous proportionality are those of which equimultiples are either equal or equally exceed or fall short of one another without interruption." In this one important instance, the pattern of logical analysis and commentary described above did not reveal the flaw and correct it. Attentive dissection of various theorems in book V should have produced an accurate version of the definition. For example, Campanus understood its inverse for unequal ratios; in the notation being used here, $(A,B) > (C,D)$ if and only if there exist integers m and n such that $mA > nB$ but $mC \leqq nD$.

Instead, commentators deepened the flaw by drawing on Boethius' *Arithmetica*, and thus on the Pythagorean theory of *Elements* VII, though in grosser form. "Those ratios are equal," they wrote, "of which the denominations are equal," According to Jordanus' brief tract *Liber de proportionibus*, "the denomination of the ratio of this to that is what results from dividing this by that." Campanus agreed verbatim in his *De proportione et proportionalitate*, although he did worry about this arithmetical notion in the geometrical domain of *Elements* V. As he commented there on definition 16, "[Euclid] could not define identity of ratio by identity of denomination, as the arithmetician does, since, as has been said, the denominations of many ratios are simply unknown." Yet, Thomas Bradwardine, who knew his *Elements*, wrote in his *Geometria speculativa* (*ca.* 1328): "Proportion, just as is said in arithmetic, is the similitude of ratios, whence it demands at least two ratios. Ratios, moreover, are said to be similar, of which the denominations are the same, as double, double; triple, triple; sesquialterate, sesquialterate; and so on for the class of rational ratios . . ." (Molland, ed.).

Denomination assigned names to ratios according to a system of classification, and thus fitted well the encyclopedic tradition from which medieval scholars drew their first acquaintance with mathematics. According as $A \gtreqless B$, the ratio (A,B) was called a "ratio of greater inequality," a "ratio of equality," or a "ratio of lesser inequality." Within the first category, if $A = mB$ for some integer m, (A,B) was, in general, a "multiple ratio" and, in particular, an "m-tuple ratio." If A contained B once with a remainder of 1, (A,B) formed a "superparticular ratio"; specifically, (3,2) was a "sesquialterate ratio," (4,3) a "sesquitertian," (5,4) a "sesquiquartan," and so forth. If *A* contained *B* once with a remainder greater than 1, (*A*,*B*) constituted a "superpartient ratio"; specifically, for example, (7,5) was a "superbipartient fifths," (10,7) a "supertripartient sevenths," and so on. When *A* contained *B* more than once with a remainder, their ratio fell into the general categories of "multiple superparticular" and "multiple superpartient," with specific names formed analogously to the preceding. Denomination was a commonplace of medieval mathematical literature, and the use of names rather than numbers to denote ratios continued through the seventeenth century.

In theory, assigning to ratios denominations based on an ordering different from that of numbers reflected the distinction between ratios and numbers, and, by extension, emphasized the peculiar nature of ratio as a relation *(habitudo)* between quantities rather than a quantity itself. In practice, denomination overrode the distinction, and gradually led medieval mathematicians to combine arithmetic and geometry in ways unthinkable to the Greeks. Thinking of ratios as relations of numbers that, when divided one by the other, yield the ratios' denominations ultimately made the denominations numbers too. For example, in *De numeris datis* II.2, Jordanus multiplied one term of a ratio by the ratio's denomination to find the other term, and in II.3 he divided 1 by the denomination of a ratio to determine the denomination of the inverse ratio. Through denomination, the transformation of ratios so carefully formalized by Euclid in *Elements* V was assimilated to the arithmetic of fractions. In the short run that arithmetization conduced to the neglect of the subtler aspects of the theory of ratio and proportion. In the long run it pointed toward the extension of the concept of number to include fractions as ratios to the unit and, ultimately, to include any quantity linked to a unit quantity by a ratio or relation definable in specified ways.

Working in the dominant genre of commentary and exegesis, medieval mathematicians could largely evade the conflicts inherent in combining denomination with the theory of *Elements* V. The profound incommensurability of, say, rectilinear and curved magnitudes as found in Archimedes' works lay on the fringes of scholastic interest, and hence did not force Euclid's techniques on the Schoolmen. The simpler examples they could not avoid, such as Aristotle's frequent allusion to the incommensurability of the diagonal of a square to its side, they couched as problems in denomination. Some maintained that ratios among such quantities had no denomination. Others followed Thomas Bradwardine in distinguishing between the mediate denomination of irrational ratios and the immediate denomination of rational ones; the ratio of the diagonal of a square to its side he called "half a double ratio," whence his definition of proportion cited above continued, "and as half a double, half a double for the class of irrational ratios." Yet, the nomenclature appears to have lacked evident operational meaning. Nicole Oresme followed Bradwardine in the matter, but identified contrary parts of the name as the mediate and immediate denominations. Naming things did not entail insight into their mathematical structure.

The theory that Nicole Oresme (*d.* 1382) took from Bradwardine and developed further also had its origins in the mixing of Euclid's *Elements* with extraneous sources. In this case, the combination of two minor definitions in book V, Boethian music theory, and a theorem of Menelaus' *Sphaerica* transmitted through Arabic sources produced the concept of "compound ratio" or "ratio of ratios." Oresme's exploration of the subject perhaps best illustrates the medieval penchant for sophisticated analysis directed toward essentially nonmathematical ends.

Euclid had mentioned the compounding of ratios only in passing: In a continued proportion (*A*,*B*) = (*B*,*C*) = (*C*,*D*), the ratio (*A*,*C*) is the duplicate of ratio (*A*,*B*), and (*A*,*D*) is its triplicate (V. defs. 9, 10); and "equiangular parallelograms have to one another the ratio compounded of the ratios of their sides" (VI.23). There he left the notion. Mathematical astronomers had used it more extensively in comparing elements of plane and spherical triangles; Ptolemy employed it in the *Almagest,* and his remarks stimulated comments from Greek and Arabic writers. But in Europe only Leonardo Fibonacci was familiar with the larger context of the idea. In culling it from Arabic sources, Jordanus and Campanus couched it in the language and style of the Euclidean-Boethian theory of ratios. "To produce or compound a ratio from ratios," wrote Jordanus, "is to produce the denomination of the ratio by multiplying the denominations of the ratios by one another." The conceptually unclear "compounding" of two relations to form a third thereby became the simple operation of multiplying two fractions. By means of denomination, compound ratio followed simple ratio out of the domain of geometry and into that of arithmetic, not to return until the emergence of trigonometry in the fifteenth century.

Medieval scholars liked to probe ideas to their

limits, and in the new setting compound ratios stimulated two wide-ranging explorations: Bradwardine's use of the new relations to explicate a troublesome point in Aristotle's *Physics* and Oresme's construction of a theory of commensurability parallel to Euclid's theory for simple ratios. The later of the two, Oresme's study survives in greater detail and aids in understanding Bradwardine's.

In the long treatise *De proportionibus proportionum,* Oresme assumed that his reader knew how to determine the equality of two ratios (A,B) and (C,D), and had learned from Euclid that two ratios (A,B) and (B,C) formed the compound ratio (A,C). Oresme even used the term "addition," and hence the modern expression $(A,B) + (B,C) = (A,C)$ translates his words without substantial anachronism. Since, for any value C between the terms of a ratio (A,B), $(A,B) = (A,C) + (C,B)$, compounding had an inverse operation $(A,C) - (B,C) = (A,B)$; Oresme even called it "subtraction." That some C exists between any unequal pair A and B, at least in the realm of magnitude, was the common, explicit assumption of all writers since Campanus. It follows immediately that any ratio may be increased by addition or decreased by subtraction: for instance, to increase any (A,B), take some $C > A$ or some $D < B$; then $(C,D) > (C,B) > (A,B)$. To compound, or "add," any two ratios (A,B) and (C,D), Oresme determined the quantity E such that $(C,D) = (B,E)$, or the quantity F such that $(A,B) = (F,C)$; again the existence of a fourth proportional was commonly assumed by medieval mathematicians. Then $(A,B) + (C,D) = (A,B) + (B,E) = (A,E) = (F,C) + (C,D) = (F,D)$. "Subtraction" followed the obvious inverse procedure.

Clearly, a ratio may be added to itself any number of times; hence one may define the "n-tuple" of (A,B)—that is, $n(A,B)$—as the sum $(A,B) + (A,B) + \ldots + (A,B)$ for n terms. Similarly, the determination of $m - 1$ means proportionals between the terms of any ratio (A,B) gives precise meaning to its "sub-m-tuple," $1/m$ of (A,B). Conjointly the procedures define the expression n/m of (A,B). But n and m themselves stand in a ratio (n,m). Therefore, if

$$(C,D) = \frac{n}{m}(A,B) = (n,m)(A,B),$$

then (n,m) constitutes the "ratio of the ratios" (C,D) and (A,B); that is, $(n,m) = [(C,D), (A,B)]$. According to Oresme's modern intepreter, Edward Grant, (C,D) is immediately denominated by (A,B) and mediately denominated by (n,m).

Throughout his discussion Oresme played on the comparison of quantities under addition and ratios under compounding. Because continuous quantity is infinitely divisible, so too is any ratio of continuous quantities; because numbers (integers) are only finitely divisible, so too are ratios of numbers. Ratios may be rational or irrational; the former if their terms are commensurable, the latter if they are not. So too ratios of ratios may be rational or irrational, according as the ratios constituting them are or are not commensurable. To establish criteria for this last condition, Oresme looked to books VII and X of the *Elements,* where Euclid set forth tests for the commensurability of discrete and of continuous quantities, respectively.

Fundamental to Euclid's criteria are the notions of "part" and of "unit." He called a quantity A a "part," or an "aliquot part," of quantity B if and only if for some integer n, $nA = B$. A is "parts" of B if and only if there exists some quantity C that is a part of A and a part of B; that is, C is a "unit" common to both A and B. Euclid called A and B commensurable if and only if one of them is part or parts of the other. Compound ratios as set forth by Oresme invited closely analogous definitions: (A,B) is part of (C,D) if and only if, for some n, $n(A,B) = (C,D)$, or if and only if the ratio of the ratios (C,D) and (A,B) is a multiple ratio. (A,B) is parts of (C,D) if and only if there exists a unit ratio common to them both—that is, if and only if there is some (E,F) such that $(A,B) = m(E,F)$ and $(C,D) = n(E,F)$; whence $(n,m)(A,B) = (C,D)$. Two ratios are commensurable if and only if one is part or parts of the other.

With these criteria established, Oresme went on to determine the ways in which rational and irrational ratios can be decomposed, and then the conditions under which rational ratios are commensurable with one another. He leaned heavily on Jordanus' *Arithmetica* and on *Elements* VII–IX for theorems concerning the existence and number of proportional means between integers. Although he might have continued the exercise for a similar set of criteria for irrational ratios, Oresme turned from mathematics to pursue two outside lines of argument.

The first stemmed from Bradwardine (as did the main elements of the mathematical theory). In his *Tractatus de proportionibus,* Bradwardine considered the apparent conflict between Aristotle's accounts of forced motion in book IV, chapter 8, and in book VII, chapter 5, of the *Physics.* In the former he seemed to suggest a direct proportionality between the speed of a body's motion and the force

MATHEMATICS

moving it, and an inverse proportionality between the speed and the resistance of the medium through which the body is moving. In the latter, however, he set boundaries on the proportionality: No motion will occur if the force applied is less than or equal to the resistance encountered. The relations immediately suggested by the first passage, $(v_1, v_2) = (F_1, F_2)$ and $(v_1, v_2) = (R_2, R_1)$, fail to satisfy the second since they leave open the possibility that $v > 0$ even if $F \leqq R$. Other, more complicated relations proposed by Greek and Arabic commentators also failed the joint test of the two passages. In their stead Bradwardine suggested that the ratio of the velocities follows that of the ratios of the forces and resistances; that is, in the symbolism being used here, $(v_1, v_2) = [(F_1, R_1), (F_2, R_2)]$.

Bradwardine placed special emphasis on the manner in which this compound relation set a lower limit on the amount by which a force producing motion in a given medium could be diminished before motion stopped altogether. For if a given force F_1 and a given resistance R stand in a ratio of greater inequality (that is, $F_1 > R$), then any force $F_2 > F_1$ must also stand to R in a ratio of greater inequality, else (v_1, v_2) will be undefined (that is, v_1 will stand to v_2 in no definable ratio). As Bradwardine demonstrated in his treatise, no value n suffices to multiply a ratio of equality into a ratio of greater inequality or, a fortiori, to raise a ratio of lesser inequality into one of greater inequality.

Bradwardine's interests here were more exegetical than mathematical or physical. He proposed the new relation as an interpretation of Aristotle's meaning, not as a correction or refutation of it. He had no empirical basis for asserting the relation to hold true in nature. Nor, apparently, did he have any interest in the mathematical theory beyond what he needed to carry out the interpretation. It was left to Oresme to fill in the details and to give Bradwardine's "law," to which Oresme devoted chapter 4 of his treatise, its full development.

But Oresme's interest also stemmed from purposes beyond mathematics. The condition he established for commensurability among rational ratios seemed so to limit the number of such ratios—for instance, (3,1) is incommensurable with (2,1), as are (5,1), (6,1), (7,1), and so on—that, as he wrote in Proposition III.10, "Given two unknown ratios, it is likely *(verisimile)* that they are incommensurable; because if many unknown [ratios] are proposed it is most likely *(verisimilimum)* that any [one] is incommensurable to any other." Hence, Oresme concluded, it seemed most unlikely that the as yet unknown ratios of planetary motions would turn out to be commensurable. But the cycles of conjunction and opposition that are the foundations of astrology rest on the commensurability of those ratios. Therefore, astrology is at best scientifically dubious.

For roughly a century after Oresme, mathematics continued in the patterns described above. In the marketplace and among the trades, people learned to compute and to measure by practical techniques taught orally and only occasionally committed to writing in a collection of problems. In the school and university, students read Sacrobosco, the *Algorismus de minutiis,* the commentaries on Euclid, and the many brief *questiones* that used mathematics to argue about philosophy. Astronomers fostered the special techniques needed for their discipline. Very few individuals proceeded beyond those confines, either to explore advanced topics such as those found in the works of Archimedes and the commentaries on them by people like Jehan des Murs, or to work out the further details of original medieval theories, such as that of ratios of ratios.

The patterns changed only toward the end of the fifteenth century, and the changes reflected the general transition from medieval to Renaissance culture. Mercantile arithmetic, algebraic problem solving, and mensurational techniques began to appear in treatises and textbooks, both Latin and vernacular, and to replace the university texts as authorities. The works of Archimedes circulated in new translations, first by Jacob of Cremona in manuscript and later by Federigo Commandino in print; soon added to the classical library of mathematics were printed Latin translations of the extant writings of Apollonius, Diophantus, and Pappus. Read and interpreted by people who valued the problem-solving efficacy of algebra, and who had been conditioned by elements of the medieval tradition to merge what the Greeks had carefully kept separated, that library soon gave rise to a new genre of theoretical algebra, renamed "analysis" at the end of the sixteenth century. Several of the algebraists, such as Johanes Regiomontanus in the fifteenth century and François Viète in the sixteenth, joined with astronomers in developing the mathematical techniques of Ptolemy and his commentators, combining them with other sources to lay the foundations of trigonometry.

In general, learned mathematics left the precincts of the university. Needs felt in various sectors of society for improved techniques of mathematical problem solving shifted the treatment of the subject from didacticism and philosophical application toward internal development along several lines. But that shift marked the end of the medieval history of mathematics.

BIBLIOGRAPHY

General histories of mathematics usually have a section about the Middle Ages. Still the most detailed (and, when used together with the emendations published in the third series of *Bibliotheca mathematica,* as yet unsuperseded) is Moritz Cantor, *Vorlesungen über Geschichte der Mathematik,* 3rd ed. (1907, repr. 1965), I and II. A. P. Yushkevich, *Istoriia matematiki v srednie veka* (1961), German trans. as *Geschichte der Mathematik im Mittelalter* (1964), places European mathematics against the backdrop of Chinese, Indian, and Islamic developments. *Dictionary of Scientific Biography,* 16 vols. (1970–1980), sets out the careers and works of individual authors and includes the current bibliography about them; a superb index links the authors with the subjects they treated and, hence, with one another. Johannes Tropfke's *Geschichte der Elementarmathematik,* 2nd ed., 7 vols. (1921–1924); 3rd ed., I–IV (1930–1940); 4th rev. ed., I (arithmetic and algebra), Karl Vogel *et al.,* eds. (1980), contains a wealth of detail organized by subject, but by its nature lacks any consideration of medieval mathematics in its cultural context. Alexander Murray, *Reason and Society in the Middle Ages* (1978), sets some of that context, as does John E. Murdoch, "From Social into Intellectual Factors: An Aspect of the Unitary Character of Late Medieval Learning," in John E. Murdoch and Edith D. Sylla, eds., *The Cultural Context of Medieval Learning* (1975). For an overview of Greek mathematics, see Thomas L. Heath, *History of Greek Mathematics,* 2 vols. (1921); and Barteel L. van der Waerden, *Science Awakening,* Arnold Dresden, trans., 2 vols. (1954).

On the Roman heritage, see Gottfried Friedlein's edition of Boethius' *Arithmetica, Anicii Manlii Torquati Severine Boetii De institutione arithmeticae* (1867); and the edition of Martianus' *De nuptiis* by Adolfus Dick (1925, repr. 1969) and its translation in William H. Stahl, *Martianus Capella and the Seven Liberal Arts,* I (1971). The classical source of these works is Nicomachus of Gerasa's *Introduction to Arithmetic,* Martin Luther d'Ooge, trans. (1926). Karl W. Menninger, *Zahlwort und Ziffer* (1958), translated by Paul Broneer as *Number Words and Number Symbols* (1969), II, 3–25, gives a full account of finger reckoning, including the many allusions to the technique in the writings of classical authors and of the church fathers. Elisabeth Alföldi-Rosenbaum, "The Finger Calculus in Antiquity and in the Middle Ages: Studies on Roman Game Counters I," in *Frühmittelalterliche Studien,* 5 (1971), offers interesting pictorial documentation of the system. Bernhard Bischoff, "Wendepunkte in der Geschichte der lateinischen Exegese im Frühmittelalter," in his *Mittelalterliche Studien,* I (1966), argues for Bede's having introduced finger reckoning into medieval Europe; Bede's treatise is printed in *Patrologia latina,* XC (1850), 295–298.

On the abacus, consult Menninger, II, 102–238. Tenth- and eleventh-century treatises by Gerbert, Abbo of Fleury, Walter of Speyer, Heriger of Lobbes, and an anonymous writer on fractions are included in Nicolaus Bubnov's *Gerberti . . . opera mathematica* (1899, repr. 1963), 1–22, 197ff. Editions of other treatises are scattered through the journal literature; for a partial list see Gillian R. Evans, "Duc oculum: Aids to Understanding in Some Mediaeval Treatises on the Abacus," in *Centaurus,* **19** (1975). Evans' article emphasized the pedagogical nature of the early texts and the difficulties of conveying in writing skills theretofore learned by personal instruction.

On early medieval geometry, Oswald A. W. Dilke, *The Roman Land Surveyors: An Introduction to the Agrimensores* (1971), complements Moritz Cantor's classic, but more narrowly focused, *Die römischen Agrimensoren und ihre Stellung in der Geschichte der Feldmesskunst* (1875, repr. 1968). The still standard edition by Friedrich Blume, Karl Lachmann, and Adolf Rudorff, *Die Schriften der römischen Feldmesser,* 2 vols. (1848–1852, repr. 1967), is supplemented by appendixes 4 and 7 of Bubnov's ed. of Gerbert and by Paul Tannery, "Un nouveau texte des traités d'arpentage et de géométrie d'Epaphroditus et de Vitruvius Rufus," in his *Mémoires scientifiques,* V (1922). Menso Folkerts, *"Boethius" Geometrie II: Ein mathematisches Lehrbuch des Mittelalters* (1970), considers the two compilations that circulated under Boethius' name and gives a critical edition of the second of them; concurring with Bubnov and with Tannery, Folkerts establishes that II is from the hand of some Lotharingian compiler of the early eleventh century, perhaps the one who linked Boethius to the *apices* introduced by Gerbert.

Gillian R. Evans, "The 'Sub-Euclidean' Geometry of the Earlier Middle Ages, up to the Mid-twelfth Century," in *Archive for History of Exact Sciences,* **16** (1976), examines the fragments of Euclid's *Elements* that survived in popular literary sources but were separated from their theoretical underpinnings by their use in illustrating essentially nonmathematical points. Tannery's studies remain the best source for the mathematical efforts of the Lotharingian schools; see, in vol. V of his *Mémoires scientifiques,* "La géométrie au XIe siècle," "Une correspondance d'écolâtres du XIe siécle," "Notes sur la Pseudo-Géométrie de Boèce." These articles discuss the examples cited in the present article, except for the Gerbert–Adelbold correspondence published by Bubnov (41–45). Franco of Liège's tract has been edited by Menso Folkerts and A. J. E. M. Smeur: "A Treatise on the Squaring of the Circle by Franco of Liège, of About 1050," in *Archives internationales d'histoire des sciences,* **26** (1976).

For the technical details of medieval arithmetic and algebra, along with a digest of the most common practical and recreational problems and a full bibliography, consult Tropfke's *Elementar-mathematik,* 4th rev. ed., Kurt Vogel *et al.*, eds., I; see also Louis C. Karpinski, *History of Arithmetic* (1925, repr. 1965). G. J. Toomer sets out what is known of al-Khwārizmī in *Dictionary of Scientific Biography*, VII; see also Julius Ruska, "Zur ältesten arabischen Algebra und Rechenkunst," in *Sitzungsberichte der Heidelberger Akademie der Wissenschaften*, Phil.-hist. Kl. (1917), sec. 2; A. P. Yushkevich, "Arifmeticheskii traktat Muchammeda ben Musa Al-Chorezmi,“ in *Trudy instituta istorii estestvoznaniia i techniki*, I (1954), and "Über ein Werk des Abu ᶜAbdallah Muhammad ibn Musa al-Huwarizmi al-Magusi zur Arithmetik der Inder," in *Schriftenreihe für Geschichte der Naturwissenschaften, Technik und Medizin*, Beiheft 1964 (1964).

The oldest translation of al-Khwārizmī's arithmetic seems to be the unique Cambridge MS text beginning "Dixit Algorizmi . . . ," a thirteenth-century copy of an original predating 1143; it has been twice edited: by Baldassare Boncompagni, *Trattati d'aritmetica*, I, *Algoritmi de numero indorum* (1857); by Kurt Vogel, *Mohammed ibn Musa Alchwarizmi's Algorismus* (1963). The second version, *Liber Ysagogarum Alchorizmi a Magistro A. compositus*, exists in five MSS and has been edited by Maximilian Curtze, "Über eine Algorismus-Schrift des XII. Jahrhunderts," in *Abhandlungen zur Geschichte der Mathematik*, 8 (1989); and by A. Nagl, "Über eine Algorismusschrift des XII. Jahrhunderts und über die Verbreitung der indisch-arabischen Rechenkunst und Zahlzeichen im christlichen Abendland," in *Zeitschrift für Mathematik und Physik*, hist.-lit. Abt., 34 (1889). The third version, *Liber algorismi de practica arismetrice*, generally ascribed to John of Seville, was edited by Baldassare Boncompagni (1857); at least seven MSS copies survive.

Gillian Evans discusses aspects of the new system's introduction in "From Abacus to Algorism: Theory and Practice in Medieval Arithmetic," in *British Journal for the History of Science*, **10** (1977). Alexander de Villa Dei's *Carmen de algorismo* was first published by James O. Halliwell in his *Rara mathematica* (1839, 2nd ed. 1841, repr. 1977), and later with an early English exegesis titled "The Crafte of Nombryng" by Robert Steele, in *Earliest Arithmetics in English* (1922). Steele's collection also includes "The Art of Nombryng," an English version of Sacrobosco's *Algorismus*, of which the Latin is available in the critical edition of Maximilian Curtze, *Petri Philomeni de Dacia in Algorismum vulgarem Johannis de Sacrobosco commentarius. Una cum algorismo ipso . . .* (1897). On the spread and influence of these works, see Guy Beaujouan, "L'enseignement de l'arithmétique élémentaire à l'Université de Paris aux XIIIᵉ et XIVᵉ siècles," in *Homenaje à Millás-Vallicrosa*, I (1954). H. L. L. Busard gives a brief survey of the texts and techniques of fractions, together with an edition of the *Algorismus de minutiis*, in "Het rekenen met breuken in de Middeleeuwen, in het bijzonder bij Johanes de Lineriis," in *Mededelingen van de koninklijke Vlaamse Academie voor Wetenschappen, Letteren en schone Kunsten van België, Klasse der Wetenschappen*, **30**, pt. 7 (1968).

John E. Murdoch sets out the complex textual history of the medieval *Elements* in "Euclid: Transmission of the Elements," in *Dictionary of Scientific Biography*, IV. For greater detail of the concomitant changes and differences in the content of the text, see Marshall Clagett, "The Medieval Translations from the Arabic of the *Elements* of Euclid, with Special Emphasis on the Versions of Adelard of Bath," in *Isis*, **44** (1953); John E. Murdoch, "The Medieval Euclid: Salient Aspects of the Translations of the *Elements* by Adelard of Bath and Campanus of Novara," in *Revue de synthèse*, **89** (1968). Campanus' recension served for the first printed edition of the *Elements* by Erhard Ratdolt (1482) and was reprinted several times over the next century. Of the other medieval Latin versions, only that of Hermann has been published in a modern edition: H. L. L. Busard, *The Translation of the Elements of Euclid from the Arabic into Latin by Hermann of Carinthia (?)*, 2 vols, (1968–1977). John E. Murdoch has published an early translation from the Greek: "*Euclides graeco-latinus:* A Hitherto Unknown Medieval Latin Translation of the *Elements* Made Directly from the Greek," in *Harvard Studies in Classical Philology*, **71** (1966).

On the nature of medieval interest in geometry, see, besides the already cited articles by Murdoch: Gillian R. Evans, "*More geometrico:* The Place of the Axiomatic Method in the Twelfth-century Commentaries on Boethius' *Opuscula sacra*," in *Archives internationales d'histoire des sciences*, **27** (1977); A. G. Molland, "The Geometrical Background to the 'Merton School': An Exploration into the Application of Mathematics to Natural Philosophy in the Fourteenth Century," in *British Journal for the History of Science*, **4** (1968), and "An Examination of Bradwardine's Geometry," in *Archive for History of Exact Sciences*, **19** (1978).

The first three volumes of Marshall Clagett's *Archimedes in the Middle Ages—I, The Arabo-Latin Tradition* (1964), II, *The Translations from the Greek by William of Moerbeke*, (1967), III, *The Fate of the Medieval Archimedes 1300–1565*, pt. 1, *The Moerbeke Translations of Archimedes at Paris in the Fourteenth Century*, pt. 2, *The Arabo-Latin and Handbook Traditions of Archimedes in the Fourteenth and Early Fifteenth Centuries*, pt. 3, *The Medieval Archimedes in the Renaissance 1450–1565* (1978)—contain editions of and commentaries on the texts, fragments, and traces that constituted the medieval corpus. Vol. IV, *A Supplement on the Medieval Latin Traditions of Conic Sections, 1150–1566* (1980), collates the remnants of Apollonius' *Conics* and of texts derived from it. Vol. V, *Quasi-Archimedean Geometry in the Thirteenth Century*, pts. 1 and 3 (1984), analyzes Gerard of Brussels' *De motu* and Jordanus' *De triangulis* for their use of Archimedean methods. See also Sabetai Unguru, "Pappus in the 13th Century in the Latin West," in *Archive for*

History of Exact Sciences, **13** (1974), and "A Very Early Acquaintance with Apollonius of Perga's Treatise on *Conic Sections* in the Latin West," in *Centaurus,* **20** (1976); Shuntaro Ito, "On the Medieval Latin Translation of the Data of Euclid," *Japanese Studies in the History of Science,* **5** (1966).

Clagett's *Archimedes,* III, pt. 2, contains a useful survey of practical geometry, especially as a repository of Archimedean mensurational paradigms; for greater detail, along with an edition of the anonymous tract of 1193, see Stephen K. Victor, ed. and trans., *Practical Geometry in the High Middle Ages: Artis cuiuslibet consummatio and the Pratike de geometrie* (1979). For other aspects and texts of the tradition, see Roger Baron, "Sur l'introduction en Occident des termes 'geometria theorica et practica,'" in *Revue d'histoire des sciences et de leurs applications,* **8** (1955), and "Hugonis de Sancto Victore Practica geometriae," in *Osiris,* **12** (1956), repr. in *Hugonis de Sancto Victore opera propaedeutica* (1966), 3–64; Paul Tannery, "Le traité du Quadrant de Maître Robert Anglès (Montpellier, XIIIe siècle): Texte latin et ancienne traduction grecque," in his *Mémoires scientifiques,* V; Frances Nan Long Britt, "A Critical Edition of Tractatus Quadrantis" (diss., Emory Univ., 1972)—Britt argues to Victor's satisfaction the identification of the author as Johannes and not Robertus; Hubert L. L. Busard, "The *Practica Geometriae* of Dominicus de Clavasio," in *Archive for History of Exact Sciences,* **2** (1962–1965), and "L'algèbre au moyen âge: Le 'Liber mensurationum' d'Abū Bekr," in *Journal des savants,* **153** (1968).

Besides linking practical geometry and algebra, Busard's last-cited article offers some idea of the sources and continuity of the algebraic tradition by means of concordances of problems found in the texts of the Babylonians, al-Khwārizmī, Abū Bakr, and Abraham bar Ḥiyya; see also Solomon Gandz, "The Sources of al-Khowārizmī's Algebra," in *Osiris,* **1** (1936). The Arabic text of al-Khwārizmī's treatise (pt. 1) was published with a direct translation by Frederic Rosen, *The Algebra of Mohammed ben Musa* (1831, repr. 1969); for the Latin version, see Louis C. Karpinski, *Robert of Chester's Latin Translation of the Algebra of al-Khowarizmi* (1915), repr. in Louis C. Karpinski and John G. Winter, *Contributions to the History of Science* (1930, repr. 1972).

As a measure of the learning of a well-informed fourteenth-century mathematician, Jehan des Murs's *Quadripartitum numerorum* and *De arte mensurandi* would reward full editing and commentary. Of the former, only extracts of book II—A. Nagl, "Das *Quadripartitum numerorum* des Johannes de Muris," in *Abhandlungen zur Geschichte der Mathematik,* **5** (1890)—and the verse preface and portions of book III—Louis C. Karpinski, "The *Quadripartitum numerorum* of John of Meurs," in *Bibliotheca mathematica,* 3rd ser., **13** (1912–1913)—have been published. Clagett, *Archimedes,* III, pt. 1, presents portions of the *De arte mensurandi* and gives the rather full literature containing other selections and discussing the text's multiple authorship.

Hans Mendthal edited the German translation of Dominicus' practical geometry: *Geometria culmensis. Ein agronomischer Tractat* (1886). For a study of the mathematics not set down in writing in the Middle Ages, see Lon R. Shelby, "The Geometrical Knowledge of Mediaeval Master Masons," in *Speculum,* **47** (1972).

Two major studies of Fibonacci are Baldassare Boncompagni, *Della vita e delle opere di Leonardo Pisano* (1852), Joseph Gies and Frances Gies, *Leonard of Pisa and the New Mathematics of the Middle Ages* (1969), though the latter is largely nontechnical. An admirable analytic précis of Fibonacci's works is Kurt Vogel's article in the *Dictionary of Scientific Biography,* IV. Baldassare Boncompagni edited the writings in two volumes, *Scritti de Leonardo Pisano* (1857–1862).

Barnabas B. Hughes, "The *De numeris datis* of Jordanus de Nemore: A Critical Edition, Analysis, Evaluation and Translation" (diss., Stanford Univ. 1970), contains an extensive introduction setting out what is known of Jordanus' life. Text and translation of the treatise on statics are in Ernest A. Moody and Marshall Clagett, eds., *The Medieval Science of Weights* (1952), For Jordanus' other work, see Edward Grant's article on him in the *Dictionary of Scientific Biography,* VII.

On the role of mathematics in medieval natural philosophy, see John E. Murdoch, "*Mathesis in philosophiam scholasticam introducta:* The Rise and Development of the Application of Mathematics in Fourteenth Century Philosophy and Theology," in *Arts libéraux et philosophie au moyen âge* (1969), along with the articles of Murdoch and Molland cited above. John E. Murdoch, "The Medieval Language of Proportions: Elements of the Interaction with Greek Foundations and the Development of New Mathematical Techniques," in Alastair C. Crombie, ed., *Scientific Change* (1953), is the basis for much of the discussion of the subject in the present article, which also draws from Molland's "Geometrical Background." Other pertinent sources are H. L. L. Busard, "Die Traktate *De proportionibus* von Jordanus Nemorarius und Campanus," in *Centaurus,* **15** (1970), and "Der *Tractatus proportionum* von Albert von Sachsen," in *Oesterreichische Akademie der Wissenschaften, Math.-Naturw. Kl., Denkschriften,* **116**, no. 2 (1971); Stillman Drake, "Bradwardine's Function, Mediate Denomination, and Multiple Continua," in *Physis,* **12** (1970), and "Medieval Ratio Theory vs. Compound Medicines in the Origins of Bradwardine's Rule," in *Isis,* **64** (1973); Nicole Oresme, *De proportionibus proportionum, and Ad pauca respicientes,* Edward Grant, ed. and trans. (1966).

Richard of Wallingford (*ca.* 1291–1336) is perhaps the major exception to the claim that trigonometry was largely a creation of Renaissance mathematics. His *Quadriparti-*

tum, "the first comprehensive medieval treatise on trigonometry to have been written in Europe," according to John D. North, is included in North's edition of the complete works, *Richard of Wallingford: An Edition of His Writings with Introductions, English Translation and Commentary,* 3 vols. (1976).

On some of the themes that mark the new mathematics of the later sixteenth century, consult Michael S. Mahoney, *the Mathematical Career of Pierre de Fermat* (1973), chaps. 1–2.

MICHAEL S. MAHONEY

[See also **Abraham bar Ḥiyya; Adelard of Bath; Arabic Numerals; Archimedes in the Middle Ages; Aristotle in the Middle Ages; Bede; Boethius; Bradwardine, Thomas; Calendars and Reckoning of Time; Computus; Exchequer; Franco of Liège; Gerard of Cremona; Hermann of Carinthia; Hugh of St. Victor; Isidore of Seville, St.; Jehan des Murs; Martianus Capella; Oresme, Nicole; Roman Numerals; Sylvester II, Pope; Translation and Translators; ᶜUmar Khayyām; William of Moerbeke.**]

MATHIEU D'ARRAS (*d.* 1352), French master mason trained at Narbonne and called from Avignon to Prague by Charles IV of Bohemia in 1344 to design a new cathedral (that of St. Vitus). Mathieu adopted a French ambulatory-and-radiating chapel plan based on Narbonne, but including more complex decorative elements. Mathieu died in 1352, when only the radiating chapels were completed, and was followed by Peter Parler, who modified his designs.

Bust of Mathieu d'Arras from choir of Prague Cathedral, mid 14th century. ART RESOURCE/FOTO MARBURG

BIBLIOGRAPHY

Paul Frankl, *Gothic Architecture* (1962), 161–163; Henri Stein, *Les architectes des cathédrales gothiques,* 2nd rev. ed. (1929), 107.

CARL F. BARNES, JR.

[See also **Gothic Architecture; Masons and Builders; Parler, Peter.**]

MATILDA OF TUSCANY (1046–24 July 1115), ruler of the marches of Tuscany and Lombardy-Emilia, was the primary Italian political and military supporter of the reforming popes during the investiture conflict. She inherited extensive allodial lands, imperial titles, and tithes from her father, Boniface of Canossa, and from her mother, Beatrice of Lorraine, a niece of Emperor Conrad II. The marriage of Matilda's parents represented the high point of a pro-imperial strategy of the house of Canossa by which Boniface gained the March of Tuscany in 1028.

After the death of Conrad II in 1039, the Canossans steadily moved to establish a political position independent of the later Salian emperors. On the death of Boniface, Beatrice married her cousin, Godfrey of Lorraine, another opponent of Emperor Henry III. Relations between Lorraine and the Canossans were further strengthened in 1069 when Matilda married her stepbrother, Godfrey the Hunchback. These marriages to relatives of the reforming popes Leo IX and Stephen IX put Beatrice and Matilda firmly in the reform party. After the deaths of Beatrice and Godfrey the Hunchback, both in 1076, Matilda's closest advisors were Pope Gregory VII and Bishop Anselm of Lucca. The famous meeting of Henry IV and Gregory VII in 1077 took place in the heart of Matilda's allodial lands at the castle of Canossa. Under Gregory's influence Matilda agreed (1078–1080; reconfirmed in 1102) that at her death her allodial lands should pass to the papacy. In 1089 she further alienated the emperor by marrying the young Welf of Bavaria. The marriage was short and unhappy; by 1097 the couple had separated and Welf made his peace with the emperor.

While always a devout reformer, Matilda's actions increasingly reflected a concern to maintain intact her Canossan dominions in northern and north-central Italy. For a time (1099–1108) she designated count Guido Guerra of Tuscany as her heir, although ultimately he inherited nothing. Yet by 1100 it was clear that the Canossan dominions would not survive as they had been. Even Mantua and Ferrara, the two towns most traditionally and completely controlled by the Canossans, were virtually independent. Probably in recognition of this, Matilda began to donate or return lands and tithes to a number of churches and monasteries throughout her domain; she freed her vassals to do the same. After the death of Emperor Henry IV, Matilda defended her own territories, but did not, as previously, aid the papal party in other parts of Italy.

In 1111, Matilda was reconciled with Henry V and her imperial titles, removed in 1081, were returned. It seems likely that at this time Matilda decided to give her allodial lands to the emperor instead of the pope. She died in 1115 and was buried in S. Benedetto Polirone, a monastery founded by her grandfather. Her body was later transferred to St. Peter's in Rome, where it lies in a tomb designed by Bernini. Matilda's allodial lands in Tuscany, Lombardy, and Emilia, which Emperor Henry V claimed shortly after her death, initially without any opposition, remained a bone of contention between the popes and emperors until the mid thirteenth century.

BIBLIOGRAPHY

A contemporary biography was written by Donizone di Canossa, *Vita Mathildis,* Luigi Simeoni, ed., new ed. (1940); an Italian translation is *Matilde e Canossa: Il poema di Donizone,* Ugo Bellocchi and Giovanni Marzi, eds. (1970). The best introduction to recent studies on Matilda and the fortunes of the house of Canossa is Convegno di studi matildici, 3rd, 1977, *Studi matildici* (1978), esp. 3–53. See also Nora Duff, *Matilda of Tuscany* (1909), badly dated; Niccolo Grimaldi, *La contessa Matilde e la sua stirpe feudale* (1928); Alfred Overmann, *Grafin Matilde von Tuscien* (1895, repr. 1965).

DUANE J. OSHEIM

[See also **Canossa; Donizo; Investiture and Investiture Conflict.**]

MATRIMONY. See **Family.**

MATTEO RAVERTI. See **Raverti, Matteo.**

MATTER OF BRITAIN, MATTER OF FRANCE, MATTER OF ROME. Since the end of the twelfth century, the principal subjects of medieval romance and legend have been conveniently classified as the matters of Britain, of France, and of Rome. The Matter of Britain is a vast body of legend, chronicle, and romance clustering around King Arthur. Charlemagne is the center of the Matter of France, composed of epic narratives known as chansons de geste. No single figure dominates the Matter of Rome, which includes the classical legends of Troy and Thebes, as well as the stories of Aeneas and Alexander the Great. These cycles developed in France during the twelfth century and spread over most of Europe through translations and adaptations into other vernaculars and even into Latin, and their influence lasted well beyond the Middle Ages. The appeal of this material owed much to its connection, real or fancied, with the historical past, an interest fostered by the medieval belief that Western Europe was a continuation of the Roman Empire and by the tradition of its Trojan origin. The narrative action is set in the past, although there is little genuine history, and the stories are presented in terms of medieval life and its social and religious conventions.

THE MATTER OF BRITAIN

The Matter of Britain includes not only the life of Arthur but also romances about the knights of the Round Table and the huge cycle of Grail legends. During the thirteenth century these heterogeneous stories were combined with pious legends about the supposed evangelization of Britain by Joseph of Arimathea to form a compilation blending the history of the Grail with the rise and fall of Arthur's kingdom.

The historic Arthur, not a king but a military leader, was probably a Romanized Celt who led the British forces about A.D. 500 to a decisive victory over the Saxon invaders. His memory was cherished in Wales, the territory of the Britons; and in early Welsh literature he became the hero of fabulous adventures in which he encounters not the Saxons but supernatural foes and friends, many derived from Celtic myth. He leads a daring raid upon the Celtic Otherworld to capture a magic cauldron and accomplishes similar feats with the aid of companions endowed with supernatural skills.

In the view of Roger Sherman Loomis and his followers, such stories reached the Continent, beginning about 1100, through the medium of bilingual Breton *conteurs,* professional storytellers fluent in

 MATTER OF BRITAIN, FRANCE, ROME

French as well as their native Breton, a tongue closely related to Welsh. Largely through their activities as entertainers in courts wherever French was understood, the legends of Arthur and his knights were disseminated in Western Europe, as French poets developed their romantic and fantastic possibilities.

Arthur's prestige was further enhanced by the *Historia regum Britanniae* (*ca.* 1136), composed in Latin prose by Geoffrey of Monmouth, a cleric associated with Oxford and London, who claimed to have translated it from an ancient book in the British language. Since no such document has ever been discovered, Geoffrey's book seems to be a composite of material drawn from well-known Latin sources, local legends, Celtic oral tradition, and his own imagination. It purports to relate the early history of Britain from its founding by Brutus, a descendant of the Trojan Aeneas, to Cadwallader, the last British king. The central narrative deals with the reign of Arthur, whose career is modeled upon Charlemagne's. After defeating the other kings of Britain, Arthur expands his empire to the Continent, but just as he is about to conquer Rome, he is summoned back to Britain because of Mordred's treachery. Arthur kills Mordred and, gravely wounded, is transported for healing to the isle of Avalon.

Geoffrey's largely fictitious history spread Arthur's fame in learned circles and became the authoritative source for the early history of Britain until its authenticity was challenged during the Renaissance. Arthur's military exploits, however, are not the subject of the French romances. His court becomes the center from which individual knights set forth to test their valor, chivalry, and fidelity in love. The earliest of these romances, by Chrétien de Troyes, written between 1170 and about 1185—*Érec et Énide, Cligès, Lancelot, Yvain,* and *Perceval*—draw upon quite different Celtic traditions circulated orally by the Bretons. Knights depart from Arthur's court on mysterious adventures, encounter marvels, engage in single combats with foes (some of them supernatural), rescue ladies, and return to Arthur's court in triumph. Chrétien's romances were widely imitated and translated; and his treatment of love themes, derived from Ovid and the Provençal lyric, set the fashion for later poets.

The interest in love probably drew into the Arthurian orbit the originally independent tragic romance of Tristram and Isolt, whose doomed love led to their destruction and death. The most important texts, by Béroul (*ca.* 1190) and Thomas of Britain (*ca.* 1160) in French, and by Gottfried von Strassburg (*ca.* 1210) in German, survive only in fragments, but translations and redactions into Norse and German enable scholars to reconstruct the whole story.

Chrétien's unfinished *Perceval (Le Conte du Graal),* the earliest Grail romance, relates how the youth Perceval reaches an understanding of suffering through the quest for the Grail. The work was continued by four other poets, but Wolfram von Eschenbach's *Parzival* (1200–1210) achieves the fullest realization of the Grail quest by extending the Arthurian world to the Orient and developing the significance of humility and compassion as chivalric values.

The mysterious forms of the Grail and its varied, miraculous powers inevitably suggested a Christian interpretation, which dominated the French cycle of five prose romances known as the Vulgate, composed by various authors at various times in the thirteenth century. In the earliest group, the prose *Lancelot,* the *Queste del Saint Graal,* and the *Mort Artu* (1215–1230), Lancelot, the paragon of Arthurian chivalry, is the father of the destined Grail hero, the sinless Galahad, and the Grail quest begins the dissolution of Arthur's kingdom, which ends with Arthur's death and the retirement of the survivors to a life of religious penitence. To complete the fusion of the Grail story with the Arthurian legend, two other romances were added: *Estoire del Saint Graal,* a prologue about the supposed role of the Grail in the evangelization of Britain, and the prose *Merlin,* which extends the chronology to the early years of Arthur and the Round Table. The Vulgate influenced the idealization of chivalry in later romances in France, Italy, the Netherlands, Spain, and England. It was the principal source of Sir Thomas Malory's *Le Morte Darthur* (1469–1470), the version most familiar to English readers through Caxton's printed edition (1485) and the modern adaptations of Tennyson, T. H. White, and others.

THE MATTER OF FRANCE

The central figure in the Matter of France is the mighty Charlemagne, king and emperor (742–814), whose historical achievements are abundantly documented, in contrast to the obscurity enshrouding the historic Arthur. In the legends that rapidly developed about Charlemagne, he appears chiefly as defender of Christendom against its enemies, a tradition that, with clerical encouragement, stimulated the circulation of such legends along the great pilgrimage routes of the Middle Ages. A lively vernac-

MATTER OF BRITAIN, FRANCE, ROME

ular tradition of oral songs and stories also contributed significantly to the later epics, the chansons de geste.

In the earliest and most famous of these, the *Chanson de Roland* (*ca.* 1100), Charlemagne is not only the defender of Christendom but also the king of France, who leads the people chosen by God to accomplish this mission. The spirit of the crusades is apparent in its insistence upon the necessity of war against the infidel and the glory of martyrdom for the faith. The historical nucleus of the poem is the only defeat recorded by Einhard in his life of Charlemagne (830/833). It was inflicted on 15 August 778, by Gascon mountaineers, who attacked the rear guard of Charlemagne's army in the Pyrenees and fled with plunder after killing all the men, including Roland, count of Brittany.

This event is transformed into the Battle of Roncevaux, the central episode of the poem. Charlemagne is a majestic, patriarchal figure, 200 years old, the awesome leader of the Christian world, and Roland is his nephew. Treacherous Saracens are the enemy; they first offer peace but soon conspire with Ganelon, Roland's stepfather, to ambush the rear guard at Roncevaux in order to destroy Roland, the object of Ganelon's hatred, and so to injure Charlemagne. Roland is the last to die after a heroic defense with his greatly outnumbered forces. Summoned by Roland's horn, Charlemagne returns to Spain, exacting a terrible vengeance upon the infidels and converting their queen to Christianity. Ganelon's fate is decided not by Charlemagne but by God in a judicial combat. After the victory of Roland's champion, Ganelon is ignominiously put to death. The poem ends without joy as Charlemagne learns from the Angel Gabriel that he must resume the struggle.

The conflict between Ganelon and Roland that is beyond Charlemagne's control represents a theme developed in later epics, such as *Doon de Mayence, The Four Sons of Aymon,* and *Ogier the Dane,* that deal with rebellious vassals and the feuds of powerful families. Another group of epics focuses upon the family of William of Orange, relating not only the exploits of the hero himself, but also those of his father, his nephew, and other relatives.

The Carolingian legends spread into Germany, the Netherlands, Scandinavia, England, Italy, and Spain through compilations and translations. In Italy the numerous feuds were reduced to a conflict between the two families of Clermont and Mayence, Charlemagne receded into the background, and the heroes of Clermont were Orlando (Roland) and Rinaldo (Renaud de Montauban). Ganelon, of course, was the head of the enemy family. This tradition, popularized by minstrels in Italian cities in the fourteenth and fifteenth centuries, was a major source for two masterpieces of the Renaissance, Matteo Boiardo's *Orlando innamorato* (1494) and Ludovico Ariosto's *Orlando furioso* (1532), both of which also drew upon the Arthurian romances.

THE MATTER OF ROME

The Matter of Rome is primarily of literary origin. The three long narrative poems dealing with classical antiquity—the *Roman de Thèbes,* the *Roman d'Enéas,* and the *Roman de Troie*—seem to have been composed in that order between 1150 and 1185. The *Roman de Thèbes,* based upon the Latin *Thebaid* of Statius, begins with the story of Oedipus and ends with the battle of the Seven against Thebes. The poet adapts the story to the tastes of his courtly audience, modeling scenes of battles and feasts upon the chansons de geste and giving some prominence to love affairs. The *Enéas* is a rather free adaptation of the *Aeneid* that minimizes the hero's political mission and contrasts the illicit love of Dido with the virtuous love of Lavinia for Aeneas. The poet also draws upon Ovid for the lengthy monologues analyzing various states of love that are a distincitive feature of his work. The *Roman de Troie,* by Benoît de Ste. Maure, is based not upon Homer, who was considered unreliable in the Middle Ages, but upon the medieval tradition established by two brief Latin chronicles supposedly written by eyewitnesses, Dares the Phrygian (sixth century) and Dictys of Crete (fourth century). Benoît used these, as well as other classical and medieval sources, to develop a long chivalric romance with vivid accounts of the entire war and four love stories elaborated from hints in the Latin chronicles. The most famous of these is the story of Troilus, the basis of Boccaccio's romance *Filostrato* (*ca.* 1335–1340), which Chaucer transformed into his masterpiece *Troilus and Criseyde* (*ca.* 1385). An abbreviated paraphrase of Benoît, the *Historia destructionis Troiae* (1287), by a Sicilian judge, Guido delle Colonne, became the authoritative historical version of the Trojan War in later times largely because it was written in Latin prose without acknowledgment of its origin in vernacular fiction.

The Matter of Rome also includes the vast legendary material about Alexander the Great (356–323 B.C.), his career of conquest from Greece to India,

 MATTER OF BRITAIN, FRANCE, ROME

and his untimely death. A biography known as the Pseudo-Callisthenes (earliest Latin version *ca.* A.D. 300) is the nucleus of the legendary developments in Latin and many other languages of Europe and Asia. The twelfth-century *Roman d'Alexandre,* written in twelve-syllable lines (hence alexandrines) by Lambert le Tort, Alexandre de Paris, and others, with interpolations of various independent texts, relates not only Alexander's military exploits and love affairs, but also such fabulous adventures as his descent to the bottom of the sea, his visits to the exotic East and its marvels, and his ascent into the sky in a conveyance powered by griffins. Alexander as a legendary figure became renowned for his liberality as well as for those qualities of valor and prowess that defined him as a conqueror.

The massive contribution of the three matters to medieval culture extended beyond literature to the other arts. The figures and scenes appear in sumptuously illuminated manuscripts, sculptures, tapestries, and paintings. Despite changing tastes, these stories continued to stimulate the imagination of poets, artists, and even composers of opera down to our own time.

BIBLIOGRAPHY

Sources. Benoît de Ste. Maure, *Le roman de Troie,* Léopold Constans, ed., 6 vols. (1904–1912, repr. 1968); Béroul, *The Romance of Tristram,* Alfred Ewert, ed., 2 vols. (1963–1970), full commentary in vol. II; Robert de Boron, *Merlin, roman du XIIIe siècle,* Alexandre Micha, ed. (1980); Chrétien de Troyes, *Cligès,* Alexandre Micha, ed. (1957, repr. 1968), *Le chevalier de la charrette,* Mario Roques, ed. (1965), *Érec et Énide,* Mario Roques, ed. (1969), *Le chevalier au lion,* Mario Roques, ed. (1968, 1972), *Le conte du Graal,* Félix Lecoy, ed., 2 vols. (1972–1975)—translations available in *Arthurian Romances,* W. Wistar Comfort, ed. and trans. (1914, repr. 1928); *The Continuations of the Old French Perceval of Chrétien de Troyes,* William J. Roach, ed., 5 vols in 6 (1949–1983); Eilhart von Oberg, *Tristrant,* Franz Lichtenstein, ed. (1877, repr. 1973), trans. into English by J. W. Thomas (1978); *Enéas: Roman du XIIe siècle,* J.-J. Salverda de Grave, ed., 2 vols (1925–1929, repr. 1977); Geoffrey of Monmouth, *The "Historia regum Britanniae"...,* Acton Griscom, ed. (1929), *Historia regum Britanniae: A Variant Version,* Jacob Hammer, ed. (1951), and *The History of the Kings of Britain,* Lewis Thorpe, trans. (1966, 3rd ed. 1973); Gottfried von Strassburg, *Tristan und Isolde,* Friedrich Ranke, ed. (1930, 1949, rev. by Eduard Studer 1958); Guido delle Colonne, *Historia destructionis Troiae,* Nathaniel E. Griffin, ed. (1936), also in English, Mary Elizabeth Meek, trans. (1974), with valuable introduction and notes.

Lancelot: Roman en prose du XIIIe siècle, Alexandre Micha, ed., 4 vols. (1978–1979); *The Works of Sir Thomas Malory,* Eugène Vinaver, ed., 3 vols. (1947); *The Medieval French Roman d'Alexandre,* Edward C. Armstrong *et al.,* eds., 6 vols. (1937–1976); *La mort le roi Artu,* Jean Frappier, ed., 3rd ed. (1964); *La queste del Saint Graal,* Albert Pauphilet, ed. (1923, repr. 1949), also in English as *The Quest of the Holy Grail,* Pauline M. Matarasso, trans. (1969, repr. 1971); *Le roman de Thèbes,* Guy Raynaud de Lage, ed., 2 vols. (1966–1968); *The Saga of Tristram and Ísönd,* Paul Schach, trans. (1973), translation of the Norse saga text; *The Song of Roland: An Analytical Edition,* Gerard J. Brault, ed., 2 vols. (1978), introd. and commentary in vol. I and Oxford text and English translation on facing pages in vol. II; Thomas of Britain, *Le roman de Tristan,* Joseph Bédier, ed., 2 vols (1902–1905, repr. 1968), full commentary in vol. II, and *Les fragments du roman de Tristan,* Bartina H. Wind, ed. (1960, 2nd ed. 1963); *The Vulgate Version of the Arthurian Romances,* H. Oskar Sommer, ed., 8 vols. (1909–1916, repr. 1969); Wolfram von Eschenbach, *Parzival,* K. Leachmann, ed., 7th ed. rev. by Eduard Hartl (1952), also translated by Helen M. Mustard and Charles E. Passage (1961).

Studies. Joseph Bédier, *Les legends épiques,* 3rd ed., 4 vols. (1926–1929); *Bulletin bibliographique de la Société internationale arthurienne,* annual (1949–); George Cary, *The Medieval Alexander,* D. J. A. Ross, ed. (1956, repr. 1967); Edmund K. Chambers, *Arthur of Britain* (1927, repr. 1964); John H. Fisher, ed., *The Medieval Literature of Western Europe* (1966), 131–148, 160–162; Jean Frappier, *Étude sur La mort le roi Artu* (1936, 2nd ed., rev. and enl., 1961), *Les chansons de geste du cycle de Guillaume d'Orange,* 3 vols. (1955–1983), *Chrétien de Troyes: L'homme et l'oeuvre* (1957, 3rd ed. 1968), translated by Raymond J. Cormier as *Chrétien de Troyes: The Man and His Work* (1982), and *Chrétien dé Troyes et le mythe du Graal* (1972); Rosemarie Jones, *The Theme of Love in the Romans d'antiquité* (1972); Roger S. Loomis, *Arthurian Tradition and Chrétien de Troyes* (1949), *The Development of Arthurian Romance* (1963), and *The Grail: From Celtic Myth to Christian Symbol* (1963); Roger Sherman Loomis, ed., *Arthurian Literature in the Middle Ages* (1959), the most comprehensive and authoritative work on Arthurian literature, with chapters written by specialists and bibliographical notes; Roger S. Loomis and Laura Hibbard Loomis, *Arthurian Legends in Medieval Art* (1938, repr. 1966); Paul Meyer, *Alexandre le Grand dans la littérature français du moyen âge,* 2 vols. (1886, repr. 1970); Alexandre Micha, *Étude sur le "Merlin" de Robert de Boron* (1980); Gaston Paris, *Histoire poétique de Charlemagne,* Paul Meyer, ed. (1865, 2nd ed. 1905, repr. 1974); Jean Rychner, *La chanson de geste: Essai sur l'art épique des jongleurs* (1955, repr. 1967); Gertrude Schoepperle, *Tristan and Isolt: A Study of the Sources of the Romance,* 2 vols. (1913, 2nd ed., enl., 1960); Jonathan Burke Severs, ed., *A Manual of the Writings in Middle English, 1050–1500,* fasc. 1 (1967), 224–256 (Arthurian legends), 256–266 (Charlemagne legends), 268–278 (Matter of Rome); John S.

P. Tatlock, *The Legendary History of Britain: Geoffrey of Monmouth's "Historia regum Britanniae" and Its Early Vernacular Versions* (1950).

HELAINE NEWSTEAD

[See also **Alexander Romances; Arthurian Literature; Benoît de Ste. Maure; Boccaccio, Giovanni; Chansons de Geste; Charlemagne; Chaucer, Geoffrey; Chrétien de Troyes; Enéas, Roman d'; French Literature; Geoffrey of Monmouth; Gottfried von Strassburg; Grail, Legend of; Malory, Sir Thomas; Roland, Song of; Tristan, Legend of; Tristan, Roman de; Troy Story; Wolfram von Eschenbach.**]

MATTHEW OF AQUASPARTA (*ca.* 1238–29 October 1302), Franciscan friar, theologian, and cardinal, was born in Aquasparta, a little village near Todi, in Umbria. He was a descendant of the noble Bentivenghi family and brother of Cardinal Bentivenga (*d.* 1289). He studied theology at the University of Paris, which in 1268 awarded him the degree of *baccalarius biblicus* (lecturer on the Bible). Between 1270 and 1273 he commented on the *Sentences* of Peter Lombard at Paris. After receiving the doctorate in theology in 1273, he lectured and engaged in disputation at Bologna, then at Paris, and finally at the Roman Curia. From 1277 to 1279 Matthew held the post of regent master at the Franciscan studium in Paris, and from 1279 to 1287 functioned as the official theologian of the pope and of the Roman Curia with the prestigious title of *Lector sacri palatii.*

At the chapter of Montpellier (1287), Matthew was elected minister general of the Franciscan order. In that capacity he acted as a prudent moderator and peacemaker between feuding factions within the order. He restored freedom to the persecuted Spirituals and appointed their leader, Peter John Olivi, to the chair of theology at the Franciscan studium of Sta. Croce in Florence.

In May 1288, Pope Nicholas IV (1288–1292) created Matthew cardinal priest, with the title of S. Lorenzo in Damaso, but he continued to moderate the Franciscan order until the next chapter, held at Rieti in 1289. In the same year he was appointed director of the Sacred Apostolic Penitentiary, and in 1291 was promoted to the bishopric of Porto and S. Rufina.

The rest of Matthew's life was spent in the service of the Holy See. On behalf of Pope Boniface VIII (1294–1303) he acted as papal legate to Lombardy, Romagna, and Tuscany. He attempted to reconcile the Guelphs and Ghibellines, and played a prominent part in the conflict between the pope and Philip IV the Fair, king of France (1285–1314). Matthew wholeheartedly supported the claim of Boniface VIII to supreme power *(plenitudo potestatis)* in matters both spiritual and temporal. It is very likely that he had a hand in the preparation and redaction of the controversial bull *Unam sanctam,* issued 18 November 1302, only twenty days after Matthew's death at Rome.

Matthew was a very prolific writer. If all his works were published, they would fill about 15,000 octavo pages. He wrote in an easy, fluent, and correct Latin that is far superior to the Latin of most contemporary scholastic authors. He treated every problem he proposed to solve fully and with admirable lucidity. Besides his voluminous commentary on the *Sentences* of Peter Lombard, Matthew wrote disputed and quodlibetic questions on a wide variety of philosophical and theological problems, exegeses of several books of the Bible, and more than 200 sermons.

Matthew was thoroughly familiar with all the writings of St. Augustine and made extensive use of them. He also had a fair knowledge of the principal works of Aristotle and his commentators. After St. Augustine, his most trusted guide was St. Bonaventure, but he also borrowed frequently from Thomas Aquinas.

In treating theological problems, Matthew's main concern was to uphold, clarify, and defend the authentic teaching of the Roman Catholic Church according to the directions of the magisterium. In philosophy he is best known for his epistemology, which is elaborated—as might be expected—in the Augustinian-Bonaventurian tradition. In the acquisition of knowledge of the material world, Matthew agreed with Aristotle that nothing enters the mind except through the senses. Objects and mind are partial causes of knowledge, but the mind is the principal cause. External objects are represented to the senses by sensible species and to the intellect by intelligible species. In reality only singular objects exist, but singulars of the same kind share a common nature that is the foundation of universal concepts. In order to arrive at perfect, evident, and necessarily true cognition, the mind needs a special divine assistance called "illumination," which originates from the divine ideas and is distinct from grace and revelation. The soul has a direct knowledge of itself. Ideas of purely immaterial entities, such as that of God, angels, the good, and first principles, are innate

 MATTHEW OF EDESSA

or impressed in the soul, and are not abstracted from the outside world.

God is the first being and the first principle. He exists necessarily, and created the universe out of nothing. God is eternal, but he created the world in a moment of time and rules it by his providence. Matthew rejects the idea of an eternal world.

BIBLIOGRAPHY

Sources. Victorin Doucet describes Matthew's works (and the MSS that contain them) in great detail in his critical introduction to Matthew's *Quaestiones disputatae de gratia* in Bibliotheca Franciscana Scholastica Medii Aevi, XI (1935), xi–clxiii. The same series contains Matthew's writings on disputed questions of faith and cognition in vol. I (also in 2nd ser., 1957); on the Incarnation and original sin (vol. II); on creation and divine providence (vol. XVII); and on the fate of the souls of the dead (vol. XVIII). His questions on the soul in this life have been published in A. J. Gondras, "Les Quaestiones de anima VI," in *Archives d'histoire doctrinale et littéraire du moyen âge,* **24** (1957). His sermons on the Blessed Virgin and on St. Francis have been published in the series Bibliotheca Franciscana Ascetica Medii Aevi, IX and X (1962).

Studies. Helen Marie Beha, "Matthew of Aquasparta's Theory of Cognition," in *Franciscan Studies,* 2nd ser., **20** (1960), and **21** (1961); Giulio Bonafede, *Matteo d'Acquasparta,* 2nd ed. (1968); John D. Dowd, "Matthew of Aquasparta's *De productione rerum* and Its Relation to St. Thomas Aquinas and St. Bonaventure," in *Franciscan Studies,* 2nd ser., **34** (1974); Zachary Hayes, *The General Doctrine of Creation in the Thirteenth Century, with Special Emphasis on Matthew of Aquasparta* (1964); S. P. Marrone, "Matthew of Aquasparta, Henry of Ghent and Augustinian Epistemology After Bonaventure," in *Franziskanische Studien,* **65** (1983); Pasquale Mazzarella, *La dottrina dell'anima e della conoscenza in Matteo d'Acquasparta* (1969); G. R. Payne, "Cognitive Intuition of Singulars Revisited (Matthew of Aquasparta Versus B. J. Lonergan)," in *Franciscan Studies,* 2nd ser., **41** (1981).

GEDEON GÁL, O.F.M.

[See also **Augustine of Hippo, St.; Bonaventure, St.; Boniface VIII, Pope; Franciscans; Philosophy and Theology, Western European; Plenitudo Potestatis.**]

MATTHEW OF EDESSA (Armenian: Matt^{c}ēos Uṙhayec^{c}i) (*ca.* 1070–*ca.* 1144) is the author of a chronicle, the last recorded events of which are from 1138. This fact has led scholars to assume that the author died soon thereafter. He may have perished during the sack of Edessa in 1144. There is no information about the life of Matthew, except for the fact that he was a monk. His superior knowledge and detailed descriptions of events that took place in and around Edessa indicate that he lived in or near that city.

Matthew's only known work is the *Chronicle,* a most valuable source on the events of the tenth, eleventh, and the first half of the twelfth centuries in Armenia and in the neighboring lands. The first book of the *Chronicle,* which covers the period from 952 to 1051, was compiled during the period 1113–1121. This section is basically about the Bagratids of Ani and their relations with Byzantium, the Muslim powers, and the other Caucasian principalities and kingdoms. The author has included a letter of the Byzantine emperor John Tzimiskes addressed to King Ašot III of Armenia. The authenticity of this document, in which Tzimiskes gives information about his conquests in Syria, Lebanon, and Palestine, has been questioned by some scholars, but some of the expressions in it presuppose a Greek original. Matthew's text may have derived from an original in the archives of the Bagratid kings of Ani.

The second book of Matthew's *Chronicle,* which was compiled during the period 1121–1128, covers the years from 1051 to 1101, and contains information about the disintegration of the Bagratid kingdom as well as the dispersion of the Armenian feudal families as a result of the Seljuk invasions. After a hiatus of ten years (1128–1138), Matthew compiled the third book of the *Chronicle,* which covers the events of the period from 1101 to 1138.

Matthew of Edessa was an eyewitness to many of the events narrated in the *Chronicle.* For the contemporary period he also consulted the oral testimony of other eyewitnesses. His lack of learning and indiscriminate use of sources, however, are often responsible for the inclusion of untrustworthy evidence in his work. It has been shown that some of his information on the tenth and the early eleventh centuries is more valuable than hitherto assumed by scholars, since he used as a source the lost *Chronicle* of Yakob, vardapet of Sanahin, a historian who had access to the patriarchal and royal archives at Argina and Ani. It has also been suggested that Matthew also made use of Fulcher of Chartres's *Gesta Francorum* in those sections of the *Chronicle* where he gives information on the crusades.

The *Chronicle* of Matthew was continued by Grigor the Priest (Grigor *erēc^{c}*), who was from K^{c}esun. Even less is known about him than about Matthew. Gregory's work, which is written in the same style as that of Matthew, covers the period from 1137 to 1162/1163. Both writers are extremely anti-Byzantine and usually well disposed toward the Franks. They both present the historical events from a local or provincial point of view.

BIBLIOGRAPHY

Sources. Patmutᶜiwn Mattᶜēosi Uṙhayecᶜwoy (History . . .) (1869); Mattᶜēos Uṙhayecᶜi, *Žamanakagrutᶜiwn* (Chronicle) (1898). Translations include *Chronique de Matthieu d'Edesse (962–1136) avec la continuation de Grégoire le Prêtre jusqu'en 1162* . . . , Édouard Dulaurier, trans. (1858). See also *Recueil des historiens des Croisades: Documents arméniens,* I (1869, repr. 1967).

Studies. Manuk Abełean, *Hayocᶜ hin grakanutᶜean patmutᶜiwn* (History of Armenian literature), II (1946); H. Ačaṙean, "Mattᶜēos Uṙhayecᶜi," in *Handes amsoriya,* **67** (1953); Nikolai Adontz, "La lettre de Tzimiscès au roi Ashot (Ašot)," in *Études arméno-byzantines* (1965); Joseph Laurent, "Dès Grecs aux Croisés: Étude sur l'histoire d'Edesse entre 1071–1098," in *Études d'histoire arménienne* (1971); Anneliese Lüders, *Die Kreuzzüge im Urteil syrischer und armenischer Quellen* (1964); L. Xačᶜikyan, "Hakob Sanahnecᶜi, žamanakagir 11-rd dari" (Hakob Sanahnecᶜi, a chronicler of the eleventh century), in *Banber Erevani hamalsarani* (1971), no. 1.

KRIKOR H. MAKSOUDIAN

[See also **Armenia: History of; Armenian Literature; Historiography, Armenian.**]

MATTHEW OF VENDÔME (*ca.* 1130–*ca.* 1200). Matthew is known today for his *Ars versificatoria,* a text for writing descriptive Latin poetry. The *Ars* has four sections, the first of which deals with the writing of descriptions, the second with elegant diction, the third with figures and tropes, and the fourth with the execution of material and the correction of students' work. Matthew treats the threefold elegance of verse: polished words, figurative expression, and inner sentiment. He sets forth a theory of descriptions based upon assigning attributes to a person or an action, and illustrates his principles with model descriptions.

The *Ars,* written about 1175 and the earliest of the twelfth- and thirteenth-century arts of poetry, differs considerably from the treatises of Geoffrey of Vinsauf, Everard the German, and John of Garland. It does not discuss difficult and facile ornamentation, nor does it treat amplification and abbreviation; it is also set apart by its tone, which is often personal, abusive, and obscene.

In his day Matthew was famous principally for *Tobias,* a verse paraphrase of the Book of Tobit. He also wrote *Milo,* an Oriental romance; *Pyramus and Thisbe;* and *Epistolarium,* a collection of model letters.

Much of what is known of Matthew's life and works comes from autobiographical details in his poems. Born in Vendôme, he moved to Tours and was raised by his uncle, the archbishop, after his father died. At Tours he studied under Bernard Silvester. From there he went to Orléans, where he taught grammar and wrote the *Ars versificatoria.* Matthew next moved to Paris, where he lived for ten years and studied logic. He died near the end of the century.

BIBLIOGRAPHY

The text of the *Ars versificatoria* is in Edmond Faral, *Les arts poétiques du XIIe et du XIIIe siècle* (1924, repr. 1962). It has been edited by Ernest Gallo, "Matthew of Vendôme: Introductory Treatise on the Art of Poetry," in *Proceedings of the American Philosophical Society,* **118** (1974), in which Gallo summarizes parts II and III, and by Aubrey E. Galyon, *Matthew of Vendôme: The Art of Versification* (1980). For Matthew's other works, see James J. Murphy, *Rhetoric in the Middle Ages* (1974). Matthew's works are being reedited by Franco Munari: *Mathei Vindocinensis opera* (1977–).

AUBREY E. GALYON

[See also **Ars Poetica; Dictamen; Latin Literature; Rhetoric.**]

MATTHEW PARIS (*ca.* 1200–1259), a prolific English chronicler, hagiographer, and artist who spent all his adult life as a monk at the Benedictine abbey of St. Albans in Hertfordshire. He was the author of five historical works in Latin: *Chronica majora, Historia Anglorum, Flores historiarum, Abbreviatio chronicorum,* and *Liber additamentorum.* The first, his major work, is a revision and continuation of the *Flores historiarum* of a St. Albans colleague, Roger Wendover; his contribution is a straightforward but lively account of events in Britain, continental Europe, and the East for the period 1236–1259. The next three works are essentially abridgments of the *Chronica majora,* while the *Liber additamentorum* provides a documentary supplement to the main work and includes two subsidiary texts of importance for the history of St. Albans, the *Gesta abbatum* and the *Vitae Offarum.*

Matthew also wrote in French and added four saints' lives to the stock of Anglo-Norman literature: *La vie de St. Auban, La estoire de St. Aedward le rei* (Edward the Confessor), *La vie de St. Edmond* (Edmund Rich of Abingdon), and *La vie de St. Thomas de Cantorbéry* (surviving in a fragment), all of them in verse. An accomplished artist, Matthew illustrated some of his texts with drawings and paintings, diagrams, maps, and itineraries.

BIBLIOGRAPHY

Sources. Historia Anglorum and *Abbreviatio chronicorum Angliae,* Sir Frederic Madden, ed., 3 vols. (1866–1869); *Chronica majora,* Henry R. Luard, ed., 7 vols. (1872–1884, repr. 1964); *Fragments d'une vie de Saint Thomas de Cantorbéry,* Paul Meyer, ed. (1885); *Flores historiarum,* Henry R. Luard, ed., II (1890); "La vie de Saint Edmond, archevêque de Cantorbéry," A. T. Baker, ed., in *Romania,* 55 (1929); *La vie de Seint Auban,* Arthur R. Harden, ed. (1968); *La estoire de Seint Aedward le rei,* Kathryn Y. Wallace, ed. (1983).

Studies. David Knowles, *The Religious Orders in England,* I (1948, repr. 1962), 292–298; Mary Dominica Legge, *Anglo-Norman Literature and Its Background* (1963); Richard Vaughan, *Matthew Paris* (1958).

BRIAN MERRILEES

[See also **Chronicles; Vie de St. Auban.**]

MAURICE, EMPEROR (*ca.* 539–602), Byzantine emperor from 582 to 602, whose reign—during which there were wars against the Persians, Avars, and Slavs, as well as important internal changes—represented the last real attempt to preserve the territorial gains made under Justinian I in the mid sixth century.

Maurice's wife was the daughter of Tiberius II (578–582); his own origins, by contrast, are obscure. Some sources say he was a Cappadocian; others claim that he was Greek or Armenian. Nevertheless, he was by all accounts an excellent ruler and a soldier who personally led an expedition against the Avars while he was emperor.

Maurice's greatest administrative reform was the creation of the exarchates of Ravenna and Carthage (or Africa) in an attempt to improve control over the empire's western possessions. The exarchs were essentially military rulers who also had authority over all civil functions with virtually unlimited power. Civilian officials continued to exist, but they were subordinate to the exarch.

Maurice came to the throne in the midst of a war with Persia, which in turn was in the throes of internal strife. In 589, Huns and Turkic tribes attacked the Persians and were defeated, but there ensued a rebellion against the Persian ruler Hormizd (Ohrmizd) IV in which he was killed. His heir, Xusrō II Abarwēz, fled and asked for help from Maurice, who received him as his adopted son. The Byzantine army moved east, joined with elements of the Persian army loyal to Xusrō, and helped restore him to his throne, thereby forging strong links between Byzantium and Persia. In 591 the two rulers signed a treaty that moved the imperial frontier eastward, giving Byzantium a large part of Persian Armenia, an important source of manpower for the Byzantine army, and canceling the Byzantine contribution for the joint defense of the Caucasian passes. The treaty greatly strengthened Byzantium's eastern frontier.

Once the war with Persia was over, Maurice was free to turn his attention to the Slavs and Avars who threatened the Danube frontier. At first the Byzantines were victorious, but as the war dragged on, dissatisfaction among the troops increased. When the army was ordered to take up winter quarters across the Danube, the troops rebelled and raised Phokas, one of the centurions, on a shield and marched on Constantinople. In the capital the demes rose, and the Blues handed the city over to the rebels. Maurice was overthrown and executed together with his sons. His death resulted in a disastrous war with Persia, since Xusrō used his claim to avenge Maurice to overrun the eastern provinces of the Byzantine Empire and take Jerusalem.

BIBLIOGRAPHY

Paul Goubert, *Byzance avant l'Islam,* 2 vols. (1951–1956); George Ostrogorsky, *History of the Byzantine State,* Joan Hussey, trans., 2nd ed. (1969).

LINDA C. ROSE

[See also **Armenia: History of; Armenian Church, Doctrines and Councils; Demes; Exarchate; Georgia: Political History; Phokas; Sasanians; Xusrō II Abarwēz.**]

MAXIMILIAN I, EMPEROR (1459–1519), German king from 1486, became Holy Roman Emperor-elect in 1493. He never actually received papal confirmation of the imperial title. The son of Emperor Frederick III, he married Mary of Burgundy (1457–1482) in 1477, thus laying the groundwork for Habsburg expansion in Western Europe. The consummation of this policy came in 1495, when Maximilian arranged a marriage for his only surviving legitimate son, Philip I the Handsome, to the Spanish infanta Juana. A series of deaths among the male members of her family made her and her Habsburg husband heirs to the crown of Castile.

Ambitious and imaginative to a fault, Maximilian labored to enhance both imperial and dynastic interests. His efforts to centralize the administration of the empire and to ensure regular funding for its armies met with mixed results or outright failure. The German princes, led by Berthold von Henneberg, archbishop of Mainz, were his chief opponents. However, Maximilian's creation of ten imperial circles to enforce public peace would endure, as would the imperial chamber court *(Reichskammergericht).*

Maximilian pursued the same goals of administrative efficiency and greater personal authority within his Austrian patrimony. This he ruled undivided after Archduke Sigismund of the Tyrol turned that territory over to his nephew in 1490, in return for 50,000 gulden and lifetime hunting and fishing rights. His territorial estates, however, liked his policies no more than did their imperial counterparts. Particularly resented were his attempts to staff the administrations of these lands with personnel drawn from throughout the Habsburg possessions rather than locally. At his death, the Habsburg holdings, especially Lower Austria, openly rebelled against these arrangements.

The German and Austrian estates were able to thwart their ruler in part because he depended heavily upon them for financial aid. Maximilian went to war many times. From 1495 until his death, he participated regularly in the Italian conflicts precipitated by Charles VIII of France's invasion of the peninsula in 1494. Maximilian was also locked in hostilities with the kings of France and the Flemish townsmen of Ghent and Bruges over his Burgundian claims. Finally, he was deeply involved in the defense of Eastern Europe against the Turks and a vain attempt to capture Hungary in 1490 on the grounds of a succession agreement concluded in 1463 between his father and the Magyar ruler Matthias Corvinus. A great step toward this last-named goal, however, was taken in 1515. The betrothal of one of Maximilian's grandsons—either Charles or Ferdinand—and their sister Mary to Anna and Louis, the offspring of King Ladislaus of Bohemia and Hungary, paved the way for the Habsburg acquisition of those kingdoms in 1526.

Cultivated in his taste for the arts and utterly undisciplined when indulging it, Maximilian ranked among the great Renaissance patrons of learning, painting, and music. Some of the finest contemporary composers—Heinrich Isaac, for example, and his student Ludwig Senfl—wrote for the imperial chapel in Vienna. Endowed with a flair for self-advertisement, Maximilian participated in the composition of two autobiographical epics, *Theuerdank,* an allegory of his courtship of Mary of Burgundy, and *Weisskunig,* a wide-ranging narrative of his life, especially his military exploits. His most monumental testament to himself was his outsize tomb in the Franciscan church in Innsbruck, completed long after his death. He is not buried there, however, but in the Chapel of St. George in Wiener Neustadt.

BIBLIOGRAPHY

Gerhard Benecke, *Maximilian I (1459–1519): An Analytical Biography* (1982); Louise Cuyler, *The Emperor Maximilian I and Music* (1973); Glenn E. Waas, *The Legendary Character of Kaiser Maximilian* (1941, repr 1966); Hermann Wiesflecker, *Kaiser Maximilian I,* 4 vols. (1971–1981).

PAULA SUTTER FICHTNER

[See also **Austria; Germany, 1254–1493; Germany: Idea of Empire; Habsburg Dynasty.**]

MAXIMS, LEGAL. Maxims, or rules of law *(regulae iuris),* were an important part of medieval jurisprudence. Jurists used them to establish general rules or principles covering many different areas of law. In the early twelfth century the glossators of Roman law learned what they knew about rules of law from Justinian's *Digest,* which formed part of the *Corpus iuris civilis.* Roman jurisconsults had created many "rules of law," and their learning was summarized by the compilers of Justinian's *Digest,* in Book 50, title 17, under the title *De diversis regulis iuris antiqui* (Concerning various rules of old law).

The compilers of the *Digest* included a wide variety of rules among the 211 fragments under this title. Some had a broad and general application, such as "He who can consent must be able to refuse" (50.17.3) or "In doubtful matters the more favorable interpretation ought to be adopted" (50.17.56). Others are narrow statements of law and are clearly applicable to only one field of law: "No one can die partly testate and partly intestate" (50.17.7).

Medieval lawyers were generally more attracted to the maxims that pronounced general principles than to those defining limited cases. Bulgarus (*d.* 1166) was the first to comment on the *regulae* in a treatise he wrote for Haimeric, chancellor of the papal curia from 1123 to 1141. He selected seven rules from the title in the *Digest* and explained each. Later he wrote a complete series of explanations for each fragment in the title. Placentinus (*d.* 1192), Johannes Bassianus, and others continued Bulgarus' tradition of treating the title separately from the main body of the *Digest.*

The canon lawyers also discussed the Roman rules of laws and were responsible for developing many of the most innovative uses of maxims. By the end of the twelfth century, Roman and newly formulated rules were incorporated into canonical collections. Bernard of Pavia (*d.* 1213) appended a small selection of maxims to his decretal collection of 1189–1192, later known as *Compilatio prima.* Raymond of Peñafort (*ca.* 1176–1275) included eleven rules in the decretals of Gregory IX (1234). Finally, in 1298 Pope Boniface VIII (1294–1303) presented eighty-eight rules of law in the last title of his *Liber sextus.* Dinus Mugellanus (1253–*ca.* 1300) wrote an extensive commentary on the title shortly afterward.

The first rule in the *Digest* was taken from the Roman jurisconsult Julius Paulus (*fl.* late second and early third centuries), and defined what a rule was: "Law is not derived from a rule, but a rule is formed from existing law." Medieval lawyers debated whether the ultimate source of any rule was the gathering together of several cases *(causae)* decided in the same way (Placentinus) or whether a rule emerged from underlying principles or reason that governed individual cases (Bassianus). The authoritative author of the *Glossa ordinaria* to the *Corpus iuris,* Accursius (*d. ca.* 1263), accepted Bassianus' contention that principles shaped rules and took it one step further. In cases that had not yet been decided, he wrote, but in which one finds the same principle *(equitas),* a rule makes law. Accursius only codified what had already become practice. The commentaries of the glossators, canonists, lawyers in various kingdoms like the Englishman known as Henry de Bracton (*d.* 1268), and papal decretals abound with maxims justifying legal decisions or doctrines. In the fourteenth century Baldus degli Ubaldi (1327–1400) could even write that a litigant who could cite a rule in his favor was in the right, unless the other party specifically demonstrates that the rule is not applicable.

Some of these maxims obtained a status in the intellectual life of the Middle Ages that transcended the discipline which spawned them. A rule that Boniface VIII included in the *Liber sextus* (VI 5.13.29), "Quod omnes tangit debet ab omnibus approbari," or *Q.o.t.* (What touches all ought to be approved by all), was found, in slightly different form, in Justinian's *Code* (5.59.5.2), where it governed the relationship of several tutors holding joint administration. The Roman jurists did not recognize this obscure passage as a rule of law, but the medieval canonists began to use it as a rule embodying a general principle. They defined the legal relationship of a bishop to his chapter of canons with it and argued, more broadly, that lesser members of the ecclesiastical hierarchy should have the right to participate in the governance of the church. It became a constitutional principle. By the early thirteenth century, canonists declared that even laymen should be summoned to church councils because what touches all should be approved by all. During the next two centuries kings all over Europe were summoning representative assemblies of their noblemen, clergy, and townsmen with the same words. *Q.o.t.* became an important part of the theory supporting parliamentary institutions. The maxim was well known beyond the fields of law and constitutional theory. The philosopher William of Ockham used it in his *Dialogus* to buttress an argument that women could participate in a general council (although he was probably indulging in irony), and Giovanni Boccaccio referred to *Q.o.t.* in a tale of his *Decameron.*

Maxims like *Q.o.t.* are examples of medieval man's search for general principles. During the fifteenth century the humanist lawyers began to doubt the universal validity of rules of law. They pointed out the shortcomings of Justinian's rules and criticized earlier lawyers' uncritical acceptance of them. They observed that these rules were drawn from a single legal system and could not, therefore, claim general applicability.

BIBLIOGRAPHY

The best general treatment of rules of law is Peter Stein, *Regulae iuris: From Juristic Rules to Legal Maxims* (1966). A detailed study of twelfth- and thirteenth-century developments is Severino Caprioli, "Tre capitoli intorno alla nozione di *regula iuris* nel pensiero dei glossatori," in *Annali di storia del diritto,* **5–6** (1961–1962), in which he has appended editions of many important texts. See also Yves M.-J. Congar, "Quod omnes tangit, ab omnibus tractari et approbari debet," in *Revue historique de droit français et étranger,* 4th ser., **35** (1958), and Kenneth Pennington, "A Note to *Decameron* 6.7: The Wit of Madonna Filippa," in *Speculum,* **52** (1977).

KENNETH PENNINGTON

[See also **Azo; Bologna, University of; Boniface VIII, Pope; Corpus Iuris Civilis; Decretals; Decretists; Gloss; Glossators; Gratian; Irnerius; Law, Canon; Law, Civil; Law**

Codes: 1000 to 1500; Law, Schools of; Martinus Gosia; Placentinus; Raymond of Peñafort.]

MAXIMUS THE CONFESSOR, ST. (*ca.* 580–662), theologian, ascetic, and mystic who is generally considered the most brilliant and creative thinker of the late patristic period.

Born into a family connected to the imperial court of Constantinople, Maximus received an excellent education and eventually became, at a relatively early age, a secretary to Emperor Heraklios (610–641). As early as 613/614, he abandoned his secular career and entered a monastery in Chrysopolis (modern Üsküdar), the Asiatic suburb of the capital. After 626, as Constantinople was besieged by Persians, Avars, and Slavs, he began a life of travel and of active involvement in theological debates. In 632 he was in Carthage, where he met another eminent monk, Sophronius, who shared his opposition to the heresy of Monoenergism promoted by the imperial government.

As conceived by Sergios, patriarch of Constantinople (610–638), and endorsed by Emperor Heraklios—and also by Pope Honorius—Monoenergism interpreted the Chalcedonian definition of the "two natures" of Christ as compatible with the idea that Christ possessed only one "energy," or existential manifestation. In the light of Monoenergism, Christ was not distinctively divine and human, but had a single "divine-human energy" (an expression found in the writings of Pseudo-Dionysius). The promotion of this view aimed at appeasing the Monophysites, who considered that any real distinction between the two natures of Christ implied a division of his unique person, or "nature." Forcefully opposed by Sophronius, who in 634 had become patriarch of Jerusalem, Sergios had Heraklios sign the *Ekthesis* (638), an imperial edict forbidding discussion of the "energies" and instead affirming Monothelitism: Christ had only one will. The change was suggested in letters of Pope Honorius to Sergius, but it was equally unacceptable to Sophronius.

Although the Muslim Arabs had conquered most of the Middle East, so that agreement with the Monophysites was, in any case, unattainable, Emperor Constans II (641–668) persisted in promoting Monothelitism by force, with Maximus now standing up as the main spokesman for orthodoxy. Before 645, in Carthage, he held a successful debate with Pyrrhus, a former Monothelite patriarch of Constantinople, and was instrumental in provoking the condemnation of the imperial policy by several African synods. In 646 Maximus was in Rome, enjoying the support of Pope Theodore I (642–649) and, particularly, Pope Martin I (649–655). Shortly after Emperor Constans published a new decree, the *Typos* (648), forbidding further discussion of the "will" or "wills" of Christ, the Roman Council of the Lateran (649), at which Maximus was the most prominent theologian, affirmed the doctrine of "two wills"—the divine and the human—in the one person of Christ.

In 653, on orders from the emperor, the Byzantine exarch of Ravenna had both Pope Martin and Maximus arrested and taken to Constantinople. The pope was tried and exiled to the Crimea, where he died in 655. Maximus, tried in May 655 on political charges (purported cooperation with Arab invaders of Sicily), was exiled to Bizya in Thrace. An unsuccessful attempt was made in 656 to induce him to accept communion with the Monothelite patriarchate of Constantinople. In 662 Maximus was again brought to the capital and a new attempt was made to break his resistance. Condemned by a council, together with his disciples, he was delivered to secular authorities for punishment: His tongue and right hand were amputated. Exiled to Lazica, on the eastern shore of the Black Sea, he died there on 13 August 662.

Maximus' confession and martyrdom were followed by posthumous victory. Not only was his doctrine of the two wills in Christ endorsed by the Sixth Ecumenical Council (Constantinople, 680), but his thought influenced the development of Byzantine theology. Furthermore, his example of uncompromising resistance to Constans II made it difficult for later generations to interpret Byzantine imperial power in caesaropapistic terms.

The thought of Maximus the Confessor is recognized today as a coherent system, built upon conscious argument with the Christian Neoplatonism of Origen and incorporating the major theological and christological achievements of the Greek fathers. The system, however, is proposed in a very unsystematic way. The writings of Maximus include the following: (1) essays explaining selected passages of Scripture, of Gregory of Nazianzus, or of Pseudo-Dionysius (*Questions to Thalassius,* and particularly the very important collections generally referred to as *Earlier Ambigua* and *Later Ambigua*); (2) spiritual and ascetic writings (a commentary on the Lord's Prayer, and collections of short sentences, known as *Centuries on Love* and *The Century on Theology and Economy*); (3) meditations on the eucharistic liturgy *(Mystagogy)*; (4) polemical treatises related to the christological controversy *(Opuscula theologica et polemica)*; (5) letters to individuals.

The position taken by Maximus on the question of Monothelitism was not a polemical ad hoc attitude; it was based not only on the Chalcedonian definition but also on philosophical convictions clearly expressed before the beginning of the controversy.

According to Maximus, created nature has a dynamic existence, which implies movement *(kinesis)* or action *(energeia)*; therefore, humanity "exists in acting," pursuing a purpose implied for it by the Creator. Consequently, without a distinctly human energy, or will the humanity of Jesus cannot be truly human. Maximus always interprets energy or will as a necessary attribute of nature *(thelema physikon)*. However, in fallen humanity this "natural" will is distorted by the misuse of personal freedom, or gnomic will *(thelema gnomikon)*, which acts not in accordance with the God-established dynamism of nature, but on the basis of self-love *(philautia)*, which breaks apart the harmony and unity of the world created by the divine Word, or Logos. The incarnation of the Logos-Christ restores this harmony, reintegrates human will into the natural order of things, and thus saves humanity and the entire creation from disintegration and death. Nature can truly be faithful to itself when its dynamism not only conforms externally to the will of the Creator but also is in true communion with Him, while remaining fully itself. Thus, according to Maximus, the doctrine of deification *(theosis)*, inherited from the Greek fathers, safeguards the identity and integrity of created nature distinct from God.

BIBLIOGRAPHY

Sources. Maximus' writings are in *Patrologia graeca*, XC (1860) and XCI (1860). See also *The Ascetic Life: The Four Centuries on Charity*, Polycarp Sherwood, ed. and trans. (1955).

Studies. Hans Urs von Barthasar, *Kosmische Liturgie: Das Weltbild Maximus des Bekenners*, 2nd ed. (1961); S. L. Epifanovich, *Prep. Maksim Ispovednik i vizantiiskoe bogoslovie* (1917); Juan M. Garrigues, *Maxime le Confesseur: La charité, avenir divin de l'homme* (1976); Alain Riou, *Le monde et l'église selon Maxime le Confesseur* (1973); Lars Thunberg, *Microcosm and Mediator: The Theological Anthropology of Maximus the Confessor* (1965); Walther Völker, *Maximus Confessor als Meister des geistlischen Lebens* (1965).

JOHN MEYENDORFF

[See also **Caesaropapism; Christology; Constans II, Emperor; Ekthesis; Heraklios; Monothelitism; Sergios I.**]

MAYOR (Latin: *major,* greater), the chief municipal administrative and judicial official, in England and France, from the twelfth century onward. The *major* appears often in French documents of the Merovingian period as any man or woman *(majorissa)* who supervised others in tasks within a lord's household or on his land. At this time the appellation *major* was used to describe many different offices. It was often followed by a specific term to define a mayor's particular duties, for example, *major domus, major equorum.* The most exalted position reached by an official bearing the title *major* was that of mayor of the palace.

Officials designated *major* continued to function at a more local level, in various capacities, as the agents of their lords. These mayors are frequently mentioned in northern French documents of the eleventh, twelfth, and thirteenth centuries concerning seigneurial administration. The *major* or *majorissa* appears most often as the steward of a particular villa. His or her office was known as a *majoria,* was often hereditary, could be partible, and could be held by a serf as well as by a free man.

The first French communal charters (late eleventh and early twelfth centuries) speak of the offices of mayor and *scabini* (*échevins* or aldermen) as political institutions already in place in northern towns at the time of the grant of communal status. Towns that did not receive privileged status (as did communes and *villes franches*) had their recognized mayors and aldermen as well. The charters, which often, though not always, accompanied early grants of privileged status to a town, are not precise in their description of either the mayor's duties or the method by which he was chosen. Both his duties and his selection varied: in Amiens in the twelfth century, for example, he was elected by his fellow burghers; in Rouen he was chosen by the duke from among three candidates presented to the duke by a hereditary group of patricians. In some towns the judicial powers of the mayor and the aldermen included "high justice," in others the judgment of violent crimes was reserved to the town's seigneur or, later, to the king. In addition to his judicial duties, the mayor's activities might include the summons of the aldermen to discuss town affairs, organization of the night watch, administration of the town's finances. Among other perquisites including often a small salary and a portion of fines and of taxes on weights and measures, the mayor's travel expenses were paid by the town and included in the town accounts. King Louis IX, upon review of the town accounts, found these expenses to be excessive and issued ordinances in 1262 to regulate the mayors' activities and expenditures. In France by the mid-thirteenth century, the mayor was drawn from an entrenched patriciate, and had often served more than once as an alderman or already as mayor.

In England, boroughs began to receive general municipal charters under Kings Richard I and John in the late twelfth century, a century later than in France (though the English towns had already been granted particular privileges by the king). The office of mayor emerged correspondingly late. An English town did not need a mayor in order to be incorporated as a borough. Many boroughs were administered by sheriffs and bailiffs. A dozen English towns borrowed the idea of a mayoral office from the Continent and began electing their own mayors in the first two decades of the thirteenth century. Evidence concerning the election of mayors in England, though limited, suggests that in the early years the mayor was elected by the whole community. The king merely reserved the right of veto. The king granted to very few boroughs the formal right to elect a mayor. London was the first to receive this privilege in 1215; no such grant was made again until 1284, when Nottingham obtained this privilege. As in France, the mayor's powers and perquisites varied: for instance, Salisbury's mayor did not receive a salary until 1420–1421.

By the fifteenth century in France the mayors' powers and those of the communes had declined, as a result of urban financial difficulties and of the increasing involvement of royal officials in urban affairs. In England, the mayor, though chosen by the townsmen or town council, was always closely allied with the royal administration, which had long had a strong presence in the towns. The mayor's power, perhaps more stable than in France from the start, increased in the later Middle Ages, especially in its ceremonial aspect. By the fifteenth century he was supported by a growing bureaucracy of clerks, bailiffs, coroners, and others; with them he supervised a municipal staff of sergeants, gate keepers, street cleaners, even minstrels. The mayor's position was established and secure.

BIBLIOGRAPHY

For the mayor in England, see Helen M. Jewell, *English Local Administration in the Middle Ages* (1972); Betty R. Masters, "The Mayor's Household Before 1600," in A. E. J. Hollaender and William Kellaway, eds., *Studies in London History* (1969), 95–114; Colin Platt, *The English Medieval Town* (1976); Sir Frederick Pollock and Frederic William Maitland, *The History of English Law* I, 2nd ed. (1895, repr. 1968), 656–662; Susan Reynolds, "The Rulers of London in the Twelfth Century," in *History,* 57 (1972); James Tait, *The Medieval English Borough* (1936).

For the mayor in France, see *Histoire de la France urbaine,* II, Jacques Le Goff, ed., *La ville médiévale* (1980), 274–280; William Chester Jordan, "Communal Administration in France, 1257–1270," in *Revue belge de philologie et d'histoire,* 59 (1981); Charles Petit-Dutaillis, *Les communes françaises* (1947), also in translation for the medieval period but without notes or bibliography as *The French Communes in the Middle Ages,* Joan Vickers, trans. (1978).

JANE CUYLER BORGERHOFF

[See also **Aldermen; Borough (England-Wales); Commune; Échevin; Podestà; Urbanism, Western European.**]

MAYOR OF THE PALACE. In the Roman and barbarian territories the *maior* was the highest ranking servant in a household. In the royal Merovingian household, the *maior* was the most important free member of the king's followers and by the sixth century was the leader of the king's personal followers *(antrustiones).* Gregory of Tours (*ca.* 538–*ca.* 594) is the first author to speak of a *domus regiae maior,* or mayor of the palace (*History of the Franks,* 6.9).

Like those of other Merovingian officers, the exact duties of the mayor of the palace are unclear. Apparently they included powers of control and justice over the persons—aristocrats, servants, and others—who surrounded the royal palace. In the absence of the king the mayor apparently presided over royal councils. He was in charge of royal finances and supervised the royal fisc. He also controlled the appointment of provincial officials.

Into the first half of the seventh century, mayors seem to have been selected from the aristocracy by the king. However, as royal power faded, the mayors themselves and the factions which they represented came increasingly to control their appointment. Moreover, rather than serving as the first administrators of the king, the mayors appropriated to themselves real control of the Merovingian kingdoms.

This process had begun already in 614 when Chothar II had to swear to the Burgundian *maior domus* Warnachar that he would never remove him from his office. Increasingly in the seventh century both the Austrasian mayoral office and that of Neustria-Burgundy tended to become a hereditary position within certain aristocratic families. This was particularly true of the allied Austrasian Arnulf and Pepin families who, with the battle of Tertry in 687, established themselves as the mayoral family not only in Austrasia but in Neustria. Although the authority of this family was jeopardized during the wars of succession which followed the death of Pepin II in 714, the *maior domus* Charles Martel ultimately emerged as the undisputed ruler of the heartlands of Francia.

Through the first half of the eighth century, the Arnulfingian mayors of the palace conducted themselves not as royal agents but as rulers. Charles Martel presided over his own court, disposed freely of fiscal land, and issued in his own name charters prepared in the form of royal diplomas. Following the death of the puppet Merovingian king Theuderich (Theodoric) IV in 737, he continued to rule without replacing him until his death in 741. Only when his sons Pepin III and Carloman were threatened by revolts in Aquitaine, Alamannia, and Bavaria, whose leaders used the interregnum as an excuse for their separatist activities, did they establish one last Merovingian as king, Childeric III (743–751). When finally the papal-Carolingian alliance made possible the elevation of Pepin III to the Frankish kingship in 751, the Carolingians abolished the position of mayor of the palace.

BIBLIOGRAPHY

Werner Bergmann, "Untersuchungen zu den Gerichtsurkunden der Merowingerzeit," in *Archiv für Diplomatik,* 22 (1976); Heinrich Brunner, *Deutsche Rechtsgeschichte,* II, rev. ed. (1928), 142–148; Paul J. Fouracre, "Observations on the Outgrowth of Pippinid Influence in the 'Regnum Francorum' After the Battle of Tertry (687–715), in *Medieval Prosopography,* 5 (1984); Archibald R. Lewis, "The Dukes in the *Regnum Francorum,* A.D. 550–751," in *Speculum,* 51 (1976); Heinz Löwe, *Deutschland im fränkischen Reich* (1973); Josef Semmler, "Zur pippinidisch-karolingischen Zukzessionskrise 714–723," in *Deutsches Archiv,* 33 (1977); Herwig Wolfram, *Intitulatio,* I, *Lateinische Königs- und Fürstentitel bis zum Ende des 8. Jahrhunderts* (1967).

PATRICK J. GEARY

[See also **Antrustiones; Carolingians; Charles Martel; Mayor; Merovingians.**]

MAZDAKITES. Mazdak was a Zoroastrian heresiarch who flourished in the reign of the Sasanian king Kawād (488–531) but was killed with his followers by Kawād's son, the crown prince Xusrō. According to the Byzantine historians Pseudo-Joshua the Stylite, Agathias, and Procopius, Kawād became a hostage of the Hephthalites following the defeat of his father, Pērōz, in 484. Under Pērōz's brother Balāš, who seems to have introduced into Iran foreign practices that the priests and nobles condemned, the empire was tributary to the Hephthalites, too poor to pay the army, and divided against itself. Soon after his accession to the throne in 488 Kawād was overthrown by a noble faction and imprisoned in the Fortress of Oblivion; he managed to flee to the Hephthalite court, where he married the king's daughter, and was soon returned to the Sasanian throne with the aid of his father-in-law's army. For most of his subsequent reign, Kawād favored the sect of Mazdak, which enabled him to suppress for a time his opponents in the nobility and to allow the impoverished and priest-ridden populace to express their grievances without immediate threat to the throne.

Mazdak was the son of a Persian, Bāmdād, from a town called Fasā or Nasā. According to several Islamic sources, Mazdak received the teachings he later preached to Kawād from an earlier sect of the Zoroastrian priesthood called Zarduštagān after its founder, the priest Zardušt ī Khwarragān. The origins of the sect may go back still further to a Persian, Bundos, called a Manichaean by Malalas of Antioch, who preached in the reign of Diocletian, in both Rome and Persia, a new teaching called "pure religion" (Middle Persian: **drist-dēn*); Kawād received the same epithet as a Mazdakite, suggesting that the sect may have been several centuries old when Kawād accorded it favor.

The theological teachings of Mazdak are described by the Islamic Persian writer Šahristānī (*d.* 1153). There were in the beginning the three elements of fire, water, and earth, which commingled to produce two cosmic Managers, of Good and Evil. The first was wise and endowed with sense, but the second was ignorant and blind. The Manager of Good ordered the world through four powers: Reason, Intelligence, Memory, and Joy—corresponding

MAZDAKITES

to the four chief officials of the king of kings, named as the High Priest *(Mōbadān Mōbadh),* Judge (here called *Hērbad*), Commander of the Army *(Spāhbad),* and Chief of Entertainments *(Rāmišgar).* These command seven viziers: the *Sālār* (Chief), *Pēškār* (President), *Bārwar* (Bearer?), *Parwān* (Commissioner), *Kārdān* (Expert), *Dastwar* (Counselor), and *Kūdag* (Servant). In turn, the viziers act in concert with the following spiritual forces: *Xwanandag* (Caller), *Dahandag* (Giver), *Sitānandag* (Taker), *Barandag* (Bearer), *Xwarandag* (Eater), *Dawandag* (Runner), *Xīzandag* (Ariser), *Kušandag* (Killer), *Zanandag* (Striker), *Kunandag* (Actor), *Āyandag* (Comer), *Šawandag* (Goer), and *Pāyandag* (Stayer). The world is now held to be in a mixed state because of the collision by chance or accident of the two primary Managers, and in consequence Fate and Fortune alone govern the course of events. Mazdak taught that men should not dominate each other, but should extend hospitality to all, enjoy the pleasures of life in moderation, abstain from bloodshed, and hold all property in common.

In the Sasanian empire, property was kept in the hands of powerful families through elaborate laws governing inheritance and through the Zoroastrian system of *χwēdōdād,* next-of-kin marriage; polygamous marriage served to affirm dynastic alliances and to concentrate power in the royal house. Mazdak therefore proposed that women should be held in common by the entire community, thereby leveling at one stroke the entire structure of property and power. This policy gained Mazdak the greatest notoriety among later writers as the epitome of his radical social philosophy, and because of it the Mazdakites were conveniently condemned as lascivious—but the latter charge was brought against many heresies of medieval faiths, and is not inherently justifiable in the case of Mazdakism.

Unlike the other great heresy based upon Zoroastrian dualism, that of Mani, Mazdakite doctrine does not negate the world; although several Zoroastrian sources accuse Mazdak of self-mortification, his ascetic practices (such as abstention from meat, mentioned by Ibn al-Athīr) seem to stem from nonviolence and the rejection of individual material gain, rather than from Manichaean denial of the material world as evil.

The doctrine of Mazdak is at variance with Zoroastrianism in that it attributes the origin of the present, mixed state of good and evil in the world to chance, rather than to a conscious strategy of the good God, Ohrmazd. The latter, orthodox scheme invests the present battle, despite its reversals and sufferings, with the powerful promise of the ultimate triumph of Good. But the suggestion that Good and Evil meet by accident, and have a neutral, common origin (the three elements of matter, in Mazdakism), removes the certainty of the sovereignty and ultimate triumph of the good and replaces it by fatalism. Although the Mazdakite cosmology seems outwardly to reproduce the hierarchical scheme of the Zoroastrian cosmos, and is even modeled on the Sasanian court, the various beings, with the exception of the two Managers, do not embody moral or spiritual qualities, like the *Aməša Spəntas* (Holy Immortals) of Zarathustra's revelation, but are merely physical forces. Mazdakite doctrine is therefore materialistic in essence, and in its cosmogonical scheme is virtually identical to Zurvanism. The latter sect believed both the good Ohrmazd and the wicked Ahriman to have originated from Zurvān or "Infinite Time" (in orthodox Zoroastrianism the two spirits are coeternal and irrevocably opposed to one another); Ahriman came into being because Zurvān doubted whether Ohrmazd would be born. Although the Mazdakites attributed to mischance the mixture of good and evil, rather than the origin of the latter, the operation of the world in both sects is a matter of fate rather than design. The Zurvanite heresy conformed to Zoroastrian orthopraxy and became the official ideology of the middle Sasanians, eventually to be expunged from the faith. But in the catastrophic conditions of the late fifth century, Mazdakism developed from a materialist philosophy into a powerful, communistic social movement.

It has been suggested that Bīrūnī, in claiming that the Manichaeans were called *zandīks*—heretical reinterpreters of the Avesta—meant only metaphorically to imply that the predecessors of Mazdak, such as Bundos and Zardušt, were the real *zandīks* whom the early Sasanians persecuted with zeal. But in the early Sasanian period the only heresy that assumed wide enough support and influence to alarm the Sasanians was Manichaeism. It seems, rather, that Mazdakism, so similar to Zurvanism in its theological tenets, came to be attacked as a pernicious heresy only when it emerged as a social program championed by Kawād, who, according to Agathias, violated the established customs and order of Iran. Zaehner considered as a survival of Zurvanism in early Islamic Iran the *Dahriyya,* fatalistic believers in the principle of morally neutral Time. In the same period the heterodox Islamic sect of the *Xurramdī-niyya* (those of joyous religion), who are called Mazdakites in various Islamic sources, believed in recurrent cycles of time, that is, in endless time, as opposed to the bounded, linear time of the Zoroastrian revelation. The very similarity of Mazdakism to the then-acceptable sect of Zurvanism might have led Zoroastrians to abjure Mazdak as the *ahlomō-ghān ahlomōgh* (heretic of heretics) (*Dēnkard* 7.7.21), while equating him for his pernicious disruption of social order with Aždahāg, the fabulous monster in Zoroastrian lore who comes to embody tyranny and chaos in the state.

The Mazdakite movement strengthened Kawād for a time against his enemies among the nobility, but its attacks on Iranian institutions grew to threaten first the Zoroastrian church and finally the king himself: according to al-Mutawakkilī (ninth century), Mazdak ordered all fire temples abolished except for the three principal shrines of Persia, Media, and Parthia. Although many poor Iranians must have welcomed the reform as relief from the oppressive burden of a bloated clergy, the *mōbadān* were also the local bureaucrats and judges of Iran, and the administrators of many pious foundations for the assistance of the poor. Mazdak's reform thus severed the hand of royal administration and cast the nation deeper into economic disorder.

Given the power of the Mazdakites and their presence at court, the element of surprise was used to disarm them: Xusrō, rather than his closely watched father, laid the plans for a banquet at which they were suddenly set upon and massacred (in 524). According to one account, the dead were then planted head downwards in the garden, and Mazdak, the last to appear for the dinner, was invited to behold the forest of his followers before he himself was slain. Surprise slaughters at formal dinners are a commonplace of historical epic fantasy, and the banquet, if it ever took place, has received gleeful and grisly embellishment at the hands of authors hostile to Mazdak. But Xusrō's persecution of the Mazdakites earned him the epithet of *Anōšarwān* (of immortal soul) from grateful Zoroastrians; and his career after Kawād's death demonstrates his superior skill in reckoning with the power of the Iranian nobility.

The third century of Islam, with its economic and social unrest, witnessed a recrudescence of Mazdakism among the followers of Abū Muslim and various other revolutionary Islamic sects in Khorāsān, although not in the Zoroastrian strongholds of western Iran, which tended to support the Umayyad caliphate. The neo-Mazdakites alloyed the social doctrines of the old teaching with various heterogeneous ideas, many apparently Buddhist, such as a belief in metempsychosis. In recent times, Mazdakism has received considerable attention among socialist scholars as an early form of communism, and its social theories have accordingly been stressed, perhaps at the expense of the study of the heresy as one of several related philosophical schools in Iran whose rejection of orthodox Zoroastrianism led them to materialist formulations. In these, absolute morality was compromised by chance, and the hierarchy of heaven and earth, described by physical processes rather than ruled by divine principles, was left to degenerate into a chaos called equality.

BIBLIOGRAPHY

Arthur E. Christensen, *Le règne du roi Kawādh I et le communisme mazdakite* (1925); Otakar Klima, *Beiträge zur Geschichte des Mazdakismus* (1977), and *Mazdak, Geschichte einer sozialen Bewegung im sassanidischen Persien* (1957, repr. 1979); J. R. Russell, "Aždahak," in *Encyclopaedia Iranica* I (1986); Gholam H. Sadighi, *Les mouvements religieux iraniens au IIe et au IIIe siècle de l'Hégire* (1938); Ehsan Yarshater, "Mazdakism," in *Cambridge History of Iran,* III.2 (1983); Robert C. Zaehner, *Zurvan: A Zoroastrian Dilemma* (1955, repr 1971).

JAMES. R. RUSSELL

[See also **Manichaeans; Mōbadān Mōbadh; Xusrō I Anōšarwān; Zoroastrianism; Zurvanism.**]

M^{c}BIN. See **Nisibis.**

MC^{c}XET^{c}A, now a small city twenty kilometers (about twelve miles) west of the Georgian capital Tbilisi. During Hellenistic and Roman times it was a significant political-cultural center and the capital of East Georgia (Greek/Latin: Iberia/Hiberia; Georgian: K^{c}art^{c}li). Excavation of the Armaztsikhe acropolis (Bagineti), palaces, and the necropolis on its outskirts has yielded an astonishing abundance of gold artifacts, numismatic materials, and epigraphic monuments.

In the fifth to seventh centuries the gradual transfer of the administration to Tbilisi and its final emergence as the capital of Georgia diminished the significance of Mc^{c}χet^{c}a, although it remained the seat of the *kat^{c}ołikos;* and even during the domination of the Arabs and the installation of the emir at Tbilisi, Mc^{c}χet^{c}a continued to play an important role. Numerous churches were built, including Gersemania, Antiochia, and the church of St. George in Kaloubani. The best-preserved are two churches in Djvari, a small one built by Erismtavar Guaram the Great and a larger one built by his son Stephanos I (586/587–604/605), and two colossal churches: the cathedral of Sveti Cχoveli (Life-spending pillar) and Samt^{c}avro. Sveti Cχoveli, the largest religious building preserved in Georgia, was commissioned by Kat^{c}ołikos Melḫisedek and built by the mason Arsukisdze (1010–1029). It is a cruciform domed building with an east-west elongation having galleries on three sides. The interior murals of the church, which were whitewashed in the nineteenth century, are now being cleaned. The architectural sculpture, concentrated on the exterior wall, consists of figural and intricate plant and geometric motifs within continuous blind arcades.

Located close to Sveti Cχoveli is the cathedral Samt^{c}avro, built in the first half of the eleventh century. Its plan is similar to that of Sveti Cχoveli, but it displays a certain innovation reflected in the renunciation of the galleries, shortening the east-west axis and moving the dome toward the eastern apse, thus creating a more compact interior space. The sculptural decorative effect is heightened by lavish plant and geometric motifs and sumptuous window frames. This church is very well preserved in its original form except the drum, the upper part of which was restored in the thirteenth to fourteenth century.

BIBLIOGRAPHY

R. Mepisashvili and V. Tsintsadze, *The Arts of Ancient Georgia* (1979), 116, 117, 162, 163; R. Schmerling, "Samtavro pamiatnik XI go veka," in *Ars georgica,* **1** (1942), 49–76, published by the Institute of Georgian Art in Tbilisi (Academy of Sciences of Georgian SSR); N. Severov and G. N. Tshubinashvili, *Mtskheta* (1946).

WACHTANG DJOBADZE

[See also **Djvari; Georgian Art and Architecture; Sveti Cχoveli.**]

MEAD is an alcoholic beverage of fermented honey and water. In medieval Europe, mead was usually flavored with herbs, spices, or fruits and varied in alcoholic content depending upon the proportion of honey used and the amount of time in fermentation. Mead was especially prevalent in areas of northern Europe where grapes for wine could not be grown.

MARYANNE KOWALESKI

[See also **Brewing; Honey.**]

MECCA (Arabic: Makka) has been the site of pilgrimage and a focal point of prayer for Muslims since the seventh century, prior to which it had been a pagan Arab shrine for several centuries. The Alexandrian geographer Claudius Ptolemaeus referred to it in the second century as Macoraba, and its existence as a major commercial crossroad linking Asia, Africa, Mesopotamia, and the Mediterranean may well be much older. It is situated in western central Arabia in a wadi between parallel ranges of steep hills. The surrounding terrain is desiccated, relieved only by the well known as Zamzam and harsh rains in the winter. The combination of burning heat in summer and violent rainstorms in winter made it a less than pleasant place to visit or inhabit until its development and urbanization in the eighth century. The fame of Mecca "the Honored" lay rather in ritual and symbolic associations which, by the Middle Ages, were drawing Muslims in great numbers annually from Spain, North Africa, and western, central, and southern Asia to fulfill the religious obligation—the hajj—established by Muḥammad.

Even in pre-Islamic times, when travel to and worship in Mecca was mostly confined to the Arabs living in or traveling to central Arabia, it was also the focus of thriving commerce and festive cultural activities. Indeed, the commercial, cultural, and religious aspects of Mecca were closely linked and interdependent, and thus found to be most conspicuous during the annual ingathering of pilgrims. The central object of attention was the Kaaba, a cube-shaped house *(bayt)* of idols representing the deities of clans in association with the tribal chieftains of Mecca. Counterclockwise circumambulation around the Kaaba appears to have been the most ancient form of homage.

During the first half of the seventh century, the Arab conquests of Syria, Mesopotamia, Iran, and Egypt led to the growing internationalization of Mecca. Although nearby Medina began to lose its significance as the capital of the nascent Islamic empire already by midcentury, Mecca remained important as the place of orientation of the daily canonical prayers, for the presumed alignment of mosques, and as the destination of pilgrims. Mecca and the hajj served as a powerful means of communication throughout the world of Islam after the decline of the Abbasid caliphate ended hope of political unity. Despite the hazardous journey, Indians, Turks, Iranians, Berbers, and Arabs experienced, in making the hajj, opportunities to exchange and foment political ideas, develop commerce, and study with noted Muslim savants at Mecca or at important cities and teaching mosques along the way.

The early caliphs of the Umayyad dynasty (661–750) were born in Mecca, and Mu^{c}āwiya, the founder, saw to the building and upkeep of the shrine and city. During the reigns of his successors, the effects of the harsh climate, erratic rain, and simplicity on pilgrims and other visitors were ameliorated by the regulation of water supplies, the development of agriculture, and the burgeoning of cultural life associated with local poetic traditions and the pilgrimage cult. The Kaaba itself was the subject of rebuilding and protection from the flash floods which came with the winter rains. Umayyad times also saw abortive attempts by ^{c}Abd Allāh ibn al-Zubayr to secure the political independence of Mecca (and the Hejaz) from the ruling Umayyads.

The Abbasid caliphs, who ruled (750–1285) from Iraq, continued the Umayyad prerogative of appointing a prince or governor over each of the Arabian *ḥaramayn* (the two sacred cities Mecca and Medina). By the tenth century, Abbasid control was slipping into the hands of Alid (Shiite) princes and other rulers, such as the Buyids of Iran and the Fatimids of North Africa and Egypt. Thereafter Mecca was governed by local Alid rulers known as sharifs. Even in the eighth and ninth centuries, Alid brigands were able to disrupt the annual pilgrimage caravans to the holy cities, so much so that various ploys, such as appointing Alid governors over the cities, were adopted, for example, by the caliph al-Ma$^{\supset}$mūn (*r.* 813–833). A century later, a relatively small band of Qarmatians—a radical Shiite sect from eastern Arabia—entered Mecca, killing thousands of its inhabitants and removing the sacred Black Stone to Bahrain. It was returned two decades later, in 950.

By the second half of the tenth century, Alid control of western Arabia was a virtual fact. By the mid tenth century, Mecca came under the control of Alids, whose dynastic periods of rule were known collectively as the sharifate. The Abbasid caliphs' waning influence, even in their own capital of Baghdad, deprived them of the means and perhaps the interest to reexert their control over the *ḥaramayn.* The Fatimid caliphs of Egypt (969–1117) were another matter. A Shiite dynasty, the Fatimids showed more interest than the Abbasids in subduing the pretensions of the Meccan sharifs, and did so from time to time when the pilgrimage routes were threatened. The Meccan economy was dependent upon imports from Egypt and hence the Fatimids were able to exert as much leverage through economic boycotts as through the sending of troops. At issue for Muslims generally was the right to visit the holy places in and around Mecca and Medina annually. What motivated the Fatimid caliphs in particular was the Islamic tradition of mentioning the name of the caliph by local rulers during the Friday prayer (longsince withheld from the Abbasid caliphs). In the eleventh century, the Meccan sharifs sought to sell the right to have the name of the caliph mentioned to rulers other than Egypt's, which occasioned a serious Fatimid boycott. During the eleventh and twelfth centuries, however, internal strife among the Alids of western Arabia chiefly occupied the sharifate. After the fall of the Fatimids in 1171 and of the Baghdad caliphate to the Mongols in 1258, the chief outside influence was the Mamluks of Egypt. They were replaced in 1517 by the Ottomans of Anatolia, who in their capacity as rulers of Egypt intruded into local Meccan affairs by preempting the prerogative of the grand sharif of Mecca to appoint the chief Muslim judge (qadi) of Mecca.

What effect did the often turbulent and unstable history of political control of Mecca by the sharifate have upon Mecca as an international city of religious pilgrimage? The noted twelfth-century Spanish traveler Ibn Jubayr visited Mecca in 1183–1184. Like most travelers, Ibn Jubayr wrote for the consumption of his own sovereign patrons—in this case the Muslim Almohads of North Africa and Spain—and thus did not disguise his contempt for the way "foreign" Muslims were treated by the Alid grand sharifs. His lengthy descriptions of Mecca and its holy sites as well as of pilgrims' experiences constitute a valuable resource on Mecca in the Middle Ages. In 1332, another well-known Muslim traveler, Ibn Baṭṭūṭa, visited Mecca, but his account is less interesting. Their travelogues make clear that pilgrims from virtually every land inhabited by Muslims trekked annually to Mecca, despite political intrigues by local sharifs and the occasional interventions by Egyptian rulers.

Mecca's major economic resource was the hajj itself. Throughout the centuries Meccans provided lodgings, tended the shrines and holy places, and led the observance of appropriate rites for thousands of visitors who were charged fees for their services. It was a mark of prestige, especially for Muslims from afar, to linger in Mecca after the pilgrimage ceremonies were completed in order to study the Islamic religious sciences with a noted scholar. Many academic pedigrees in Muslim religious circles began in Mecca. Together with its symbolic role as the navel of the Muslim universe and its profound associations with the prophet Muḥammad and the origins of Islam, Mecca exerted renown throughout the Middle Ages.

BIBLIOGRAPHY

The most valuable collection of historical materials is Heinrich F. Wüstenfeld, *Die Chroniken der Stadt Mekka,* 4 vols. (1857–1861). A useful summary of these and other primary source materials is found in the article on "Makka" in *The Encyclopaedia of Islam,* 1st ed. (1960). W. Montgomery Watt, *Muhammad at Mecca* (1953), provides a detailed account of Mecca in the seventh century. For the medieval period, Ibn Jubayr, *The Travels of Ibn Jubayr,* Ronald J. C. Broadhurst, trans. (1952), though based on a corrupt Arabic manuscript, contains many pages of descriptions of Mecca, its inhabitants, and its shrines.

RICHARD C. MARTIN

[See also ᶜ**Abd Allāh ibn al-Zubayr; Alids; Arabia, Pre-Islamic; Arabia, Islamic; Baṭṭūṭa, Ibn; Islam, Religion; Kaaba; Muḥammad; Pilgrimage, Islamic; Quraysh; Zaydis.**]

MECHTHILD VON MAGDEBURG (1212–1281/1301), greatest German woman mystic of the Middle Ages. Little is known about the external facts of her life. She was almost certainly of noble descent and lived the life of a beguine in Magdeburg before joining the Benedictine cloister of Helfta near Eisleben in southern Germany in 1268. She is last documented as being alive in 1281, and spoken of as being already dead in 1302.

Mechthild has the distinction of being the first German mystic on record to have composed her works in the vernacular, perhaps by default because she did not master Latin. Her visions and dialogues with God, collected and written down by her spiritual counselor, Heinrich von Halle, became famous throughout the Middle Ages under the title *Das fliessende Licht der Gottheit* ("The Flowing Light of the Godhead," composed before 1268). Unfortunately, there is no extant manuscript of the Low German original, only a translation into Middle High German by Heinrich von Nördlingen (*ca.* 1344) and a Latin translation with the title *Revelationes* (*ca.* 1300).

German literary historians and theologians consider Mechthild's work a milestone in the development of the vernacular literature and place Mechthild herself at the beginning of the intellectual/religious movement known as "die deutsche Mystik." *Das fliessende Licht der Gottheit* contains visionary revelations about deceased contemporaries, about hell, purgatory, and paradise. It also offers apocalyptic prophecies about judgment day as well as poignant, often stinging, comments about contemporary political personalities. But through it all runs a unifying strand: the *unio mystica,* that is, the attainability of the union with God while still being alive in this world. This theme is presented in a dithyrambic, highly metaphorical and allegorical, almost "expressionistic" language that has to be judged by the standards of courtly society to be fully appreciated. Mechthild's vocabulary and her style are intimately tied to the conventions of minnesong. Such knightly concepts as *mâze, êre, zuht* are superposed on her nuptial mysticism, which has its origin in St. Bernard's interpretation of the *Song of Songs,* according to which Sulamith no longer is identified with the personalized church but rather with the soul (the "bride") of the nun or beguine who passionately longs to be united with Christ (the "groom"). Mechthild's experience of this union is an emotional, sensual one: it takes place in the heart, not in the seat of the intellect. She is the *Gefühlsmystikerin* (mystic of sentiment) par excellence, but the descriptions of her personal *Brautminne* (bridal song) are never pathological reflections of sexual frustration; rather, they are the product of a finely tuned, healthy mind that is in touch with the aristocratic sensibilities of the time.

The guiding principle that permeates all her writing is *mâze* (Old French: *mésure*), which can be only inadequately circumscribed as "knowing and acting within the limits of the acceptable norms (of courtly society)." A reflection of the admiration which she evoked in the Middle Ages is the fact that Dante gave her immortality as Matelda in the *Purgatorio,* cantos 27–33.

BIBLIOGRAPHY

Sources. There are reliable editions of *Das fliessende Licht der Gottheit* by P. Gall Morel (1869); Sigmund Simon (1907); Wilhelm Oehl (1922); and Wilhelm Schleussner

(1929). In English: Lucy Menzies, *The Revelations of Mechthild of Magdeburg* (1953).

Studies. Jeanne Ancelet-Hustache, *Mechthild de Magdebourg* (1926); Grete Lüers, *Die Sprache de deutschen Mystik des Mittelalters im Werk der Mechthild von Magdeburg* (1926); Hermann Taigel, "'Minne' bei Mechthild von Magdeburg und bei Hadewijch" (diss., Tübingen, 1955); Heinz Tillman, *Studien zum Dialog bei Mechthild von Magdeburg* (1933); Friedrich-Wilhelm Wentzlaff-Eggebert, *Deutsche Mystik zwischen Mittelalter und Neuzeit* (1969), with an extensive bibliography.

ERNST H. SOUDEK

[See also **Beguines and Beghards; Middle High German Literature; Mysticism, Christian: Continental (Women).**]

MEDIATIO, or mediation, in psalmody, the musical inflection marking the caesura in the verse. The median cadence may be either cursive (set to the final few syllables of successive half-verses without change) or accentual (adjusted by means of one or two inserted notes to reinforce the last, or the last two stressed syllables).

TERENCE BAILEY

[See also **Modal Notation; Mode; Psalm Tones.**]

MEDICI. An illustrious family whose great wealth, political power, and artistic patronage indelibly influenced the history of Florence as well as of the Italian Renaissance. The branch of the Medici from which Cosimo (1389–1464) and Lorenzo the Magnificent (1449–1492) descended arrived in Florence from the nearby valley of the Mugello in the early thirteenth century. The Medici clan amassed wealth through trade and considerable social distinction through participation in civic life. Between 1282 and 1399, fifty-three members of the clan were selected for the Signoria, the city's highest magistracy. But the depiction of the Medicis' past by family panegyrists as an uninterrupted ascent toward greatness does not accord with historical fact. In the mid fourteenth century the Medici were wracked by internal dissension and experienced economic decline. Five Medici were convicted of murder in this period, while other members of the clan were condemned for assorted crimes of violence.

The foundations for Medici ascendancy in the fifteenth century were laid by Giovanni di Bicci de' Medici (1360–1429), a shrewd merchant and founder in 1397 of the Medici bank. An offshoot of the bank established by Vieri di Cambio de' Medici (1323–1395), Giovanni's distant cousin, the Medici bank combined money changing and local deposit banking with dealings in bills of exchange and international financial transactions. These financial activities were facilitated by branches in Rome, Venice, Milan, Pisa, Avignon, Geneva, Bruges, and London. The organizational structure of the Medici bank at this time resembled a modern holding company with a central partnership owning shares in subsidiaries or branches. Besides banking, the Medici invested in workshops manufacturing woolen and silk textiles and profited from dealings in spices, jewelry, silver plate, and other goods. The Medici's principal source of profits derived from their role as banker to the papacy. The profits for the years 1397 to 1420 totaled 151,820 florins, half of which was earned by the Rome branch. Giovanni's share of these profits amounted to 113,865 florins. At the time of his death, Giovanni had accumulated a vast fortune—his household ranked as Florence's third wealthiest in a tax survey of 1427—which he bequeathed to his sons, Cosimo and Lorenzo (1394–1440).

Like his father, Cosimo was a first-rate banker, but he was also a skillful actor on the treacherous stage of Florentine politics. Since the late fourteenth century, Florence had been dominated by contending coalitions of rich mercantile and aristocratic families and their allies. These coalitions sought to protect and advance their collective interests by granting political leadership to one family: the Albizzi. When the Albizzi leadership faltered after a costly and disastrous military campaign to conquer Lucca, they made a final bid to save power by engineering in 1433 the exile of their archrivals, the Medici-led coalition. One year later the Albizzi and their supporters fell victim to their own excesses. They suffered banishment and confiscation of property, while Cosimo de' Medici returned in 1434 in triumph, no longer just the chief of a family coalition, but the first citizen of the republic of Florence.

The ascendancy of Cosimo de' Medici has both fascinated and puzzled historians for many centuries. In his *History of Florence,* Machiavelli observed that the Florentines "needed money; and no one else was able to provide it." Patriotism was also profitable. Between 1430 and 1432 Cosimo and his allies advanced the staggering sum of 560,000 florins to the city, expecting to receive interest as high as 30 percent or more, as well as the return of the principal.

Acknowledging that the very solvency of Florence may have depended upon the Medici's financial resources, modern historians tend to give more credit to the effective performance of the "Medici party," which comprised kinsmen and especially a loyal band of allies and clients who provided the pro-Medici majorities in the city's councils. Once in power, Cosimo immediately acted to avoid the fate of his rivals. He shunned personal displays of his preeminence by comporting himself like other leading citizens and holding only those offices for which he was selected. Behind this facade he ultimately determined which citizens would be selected for office through manipulation of the electoral system. He kept his allies and clients happy by satisfying their incessant requests, ranging from pleas for small loans to intercession with the pope. And he pleased the majority of the citizenry by scoring diplomatic triumphs over Milan and Venice. His crowning diplomatic achievement was the Peace of Lodi in 1454, which formalized the partition of Italy among Milan, Venice, Florence, the Papal States, and Naples.

Cosimo is perhaps best remembered as the foremost patron of Renaissance culture. Tutored by Roberto de' Rossi, one of the first Florentines to learn Greek, Cosimo profoundly appreciated and actively supported the revolutionary accomplishments of the humanist Leonardo Bruni, the bibliophile Niccolò Niccoli, the Hellenist Marsilio Ficino, the architects Filippo Brunelleschi and Michelozzo Michelozzi, and the sculptor Donatello. He poured more money into building than did his contemporaries in other parts of Italy or in Florence. The Medici palace, the church of S. Lorenzo, the Dominican friary of S. Marco, and the Laurentian Library, which preserves hundreds of precious manuscripts that Cosimo personally collected, commemorate Florence's leading family.

Cosimo's consolidation of power and the assimilation of almost the entire ruling class into his ranks not only thwarted political opposition but also paved the way for the succession of unofficial rule from one Medici to another. Piero, Cosimo's invalid son (1418–1469), rebuffed threats to his short-lived regime (1464–1469), and Lorenzo, his more famous grandson, became unofficial ruler of Florence without friction at the remarkably young age of twenty. Lorenzo followed Cosimo's precedent of ruling through a network of allies and clients. However, Lorenzo barely escaped being deposed when Florence's second wealthiest family, the Pazzi, with the support of Pope Sixtus IV, wounded him and assassinated his brother Giuliano in front of the altar of the Cathedral of S. Maria del Fiore during the Mass on Sunday, 26 April 1478. The citizens of Florence rallied to the Medici, and within a few hours the bodies of the conspirators were hanging head down from the upper windows of the Palazzo Vecchio, Florence's town hall.

Like Cosimo, Lorenzo proved to be adept in foreign affairs. He prevented the conquest of the Florentine dominion by persuading the king of Naples to switch alliances. He enlarged his patronage network beyond the borders of Tuscany and took the unprecedented step, for a Medici, of marrying into the nobility by taking as his bride Clarice Orsini, daughter of one of Rome's most powerful baronial families. When Pope Innocent VIII elevated Lorenzo's thirteen-year-old son Giovanni (1475–1521) to the cardinalate (he later became Pope Leo X, 1513–1521) the Medici were on the way to becoming an Italian dynasty. Giuliano (1478–1534), Lorenzo's nephew, was Pope Clement VII (1523–1534).

Highly educated and intelligent, Lorenzo had no difficulty in participating in the colloquia of Greek and Latin scholars. His verses rank among the finest examples of Italian poetry. Although he was well acquainted with outstanding artists and men of letters, Lorenzo lacked the financial resources to match Cosimo's investment in culture as well as his personal commitment to profit. He invested instead in a lavish style of life, worthy of a scholar-prince, while leaving the affairs of the Medici bank in the hands of lackluster managers. It is not surprising that the bank went bankrupt in the troubled economic climate of the late fifteenth century.

When Piero di Lorenzo (1471–1503) succeeded his father in 1492, it seemed as if Medici rule would last forever. The invasion of Italy in 1494 by Charles VIII of France shattered that illusion, and eventually what remained of the Florentine republic. The forty-three years from Piero's exile in 1494 to the installation in 1537 of a new line of Medici as hereditary dukes represent one of the most turbulent periods in Florentine history.

BIBLIOGRAPHY

Source. Lorenzo de' Medici, *Lettere,* Nicolai Rubinstein, ed., 4 vols. (1977–).

Studies. John R. Hale, *Florence and the Medici* (1977); Dale Kent, *The Rise of the Medici Faction in Florence:*

1426–1434 (1978); Raymond de Roover, *The Rise and Fall of the Medici Bank: 1397–1494* (1963); Nicolai Rubinstein, *The Government of Florence Under the Medici: 1434–1494* (1966).

JULIUS KIRSHNER

[See also **Banking, European; Florence; Italy: Fourteenth and Fifteenth Centuries; Libraries.**]

MEDICINE, BYZANTINE. Byzantine medicine was an extension of Hellenic and Hellenistic medicine and was based on the works of the philosophers and physicians of those cultures. Plato's conception of anesthesia, which meant the absence of sensation; Aristotle's observations on anatomy (his comparative study of the uterus in various animals and his description of the stomach as well as of the embryonic development of the chick); Theophrastus' analysis of the therapeutic properties of herbs—all exerted an influence on Byzantine medicine.

It was, however, particularly the classical medical texts that inspired Byzantine medicine. Hippocrates' (*b. ca.* 460 B.C.) treatises on surgery were studied until modern times; his recognition that an individual's constitution determines the nature of certain diseases as well as his emphasis on the healing powers of nature made his work a source of reference for many centuries. Herophilos of Chalcedon (*b. ca.* 300 B.C.) was the first physician to dissect the human body and made many discoveries in anatomy. Erasistratos of Chios (*b. ca.* 290 B.C.) was the father of physiology and advanced beyond Herophilos' anatomical obervations. Herakleides of Tarentum (*b. ca.* 160 B.C.) was the leading empirical physician of the pre-Christian era. He contributed to several branches of medicine, including pharmacology, the identification of poisons, therapy, and dietetics. Galenos, or Galen, of Pergamum (*b. ca.* 130) excelled in diagnosis and prognosis, in physiology and anatomy, which he advanced through experimentation. His reverence for the human body, his ardent belief in God ("everything manifests God's glory"), and his religious attitude toward the ailing person all contributed to the development of Byzantine medicine.

It has been rightly observed that in no other scientific field is the Byzantine contribution greater than in medicine. The Byzantines preserved the high conception of the art of healing of both Hippocrates and Galen. Hippocrates wrote in the *Precepts:* "Where there is love of man there is also love of the medical art." The term *philanthropia,* in the sense of love for the human being, was used widely in Byzantine literature, including medical literature. Byzantine medicine was concerned with the health of the whole human being.

The Byzantines were never monolithic in their attitude toward disease and the art of healing. Some viewed illness as a punishment sent by the divinity; others saw it having natural causes—food, occupation, climate, and environmental factors. Some physicians followed medical practices of the past dogmatically, but a number of them were innovative and progressive. While some physicians and patients made a rational analysis of a disease and sought a logical and natural therapeutic approach, others confused the logical with superstition, the rational with the irrational. Diet, baths, exercises, and drugs were all prescribed along with religious faith, incubation of the patient in church, and other religious formulas. The physician was expected to be *aristos* (excellent) but also *philosophos* and *philanthropos.* Hospitals were built next to churches, and there were no hospitals without chapels. Religion and medicine were catalysts in Byzantine life and civilization.

The *Corpus Hippocraticum,* as well as the writings of Galen and of the other Greek physicians of antiquity, was commented upon extensively and preserved. Thus the following branches of medicine were studied and practiced: anatomy, surgery, dermatology, gynecology, hygiene, neurology, obstetrics, ophthalmology, otolaryngology, pathology, parasitology, pediatrics, pharmacology, physiology, physiotherapy, stomatology, toxicology, urology, as well as prognostic, prophylactic, diagnostic, and therapeutic medicine.

The history of Byzantine medicine can be divided into three periods. The first (330–650) relies heavily on antiquity; not much is known about the second (650–1050); the third (1050–1453) produced some innovative physicians who added to existing medical knowledge both theoretically and empirically.

The most important physicians of the first period are Oreibasios of Pergamum (*b. ca.* 325), Aetios of Amida (*b. ca.* 502), Alexander of Tralles (*b. ca.* 525), and Paul of Aegina (*b.* 625). Each remained influential in later centuries.

Oreibasios compiled an encyclopedia of medicine in which he preserved the works of many physicians of antiquity. His original work included seventy books but only twenty-seven of them have survived, including extracts from Antyllos, Dioscorides, Archigenes of Apamea, and Galen. His work *Euporista* (common, family medicines) and his treatises on dietetics, hygiene, and other medical themes were for the education of the public. He followed a rational approach on medical issues, excluding superstition and magic, and displayed a reverence and admiration for traditional Greek medicine, Galen's work in particular.

Aetios was the first Christian physician of importance. His writings reflect both rational Greek inquiry and Christian mysticism and faith. His *Sixteen Books on Medicine* is a compilation from Galen and other masters of antiquity, but it demonstrates the acute clinical observations of the author as well. He possessed the power to provide detailed and sound descriptions of epidemics, diphtheria, poisons, infections of the eyes, intestinal worms, and other maladies. He provides information and counsel on obstetrics, gynecology, and anatomy; his writings on surgery manifest some originality and an effort to depart from traditional medicine. He is considered the best ophthalmologist of antiquity.

Next to the influence of Hippocrates and Galen, that of Alexander of Tralles was the greatest in the Middle Ages in both the East and the West. His writings were translated into Syriac, Arabic, Hebrew, and Latin. His *Twelve Books on Medicine* has been described as a masterpiece and became a required textbook at the University of Paris in the High Middle Ages. He was more original than his predecessors and maintained an independent judgment based on great learning and personal observation. He advised that "choice of drugs should be guided by reason but even more by experiment."

Paul of Aegina was the last of the great physicians of the early Byzantine period. He is the author of a seven-book encyclopedia, which provides information on surgery, pediatrics, lung diseases, gout, sclerosis of the kidneys, encephalitis, and other illnesses. His book on surgery was a prescribed textbook at the University of Paris for many years. He wrote on catheterization, tracheotomy, excision of tonsils, nasal polyps, lithotomy, hemorrhoidectomy, and several other forms of surgery. He had extracted cataracts and had operated for trichiasis, cysts, and staphyloma, among other maladies. His work, too, was translated into Arabic and had a considerable influence on Arabic medicine, especially in the areas of gynecology and surgery.

As to the middle Byzantine period, it seems that between about 690 and 1050 there was little original work done in medicine and few influential physicians. But medicine was taught in Constantinople by physicians like Stephen of Athens, a certain Nicholaos, and a monk named Meletios of Phrygia. The most important philosopher-physician *(iatrosophistes)* of the ninth century was Leo, surnamed the Mathematician, who wrote an *Epitome of Medicine* and *On the Characteristics of Human Beings.* Photios, too, the ninth-century intellectual and patriarch, was well versed in medicine and devoted several chapters of his *Bibliotheca* to medical subjects. A certain physician of the tenth century named Niketas is a source of surgical practices. He collected several older surgical treatises and preserved thirty plates illustrating the Hippocratic therapy of bond dislocations and sixty-three smaller cuts illustrating Soranos' method of bandaging. Niketas' collection of surgical illustrations was used by Italian medical schools in Florence and Bologna. Under the patronage of Emperor Constantine VII Porphyrogenitos, Theophilos Protospatharios, a tenth-century physician, compiled a medical encyclopedia that depends greatly on the work of Oreibasios.

Medical education entered into a new phase in the second half of the eleventh century along with the revival of classical learning. Michael Psellos wrote a dictionary of diseases, a work on medicine, and another on baths and embellished his *Didaskalia pantothape* (Various teachings) with medical and physiological information. Symeon Seth's importance for Byzantine medicine lies in the description of many oriental drugs, translated into Greek for the first time, and the discussion of the healing powers of various foods that he provides in his *Lexicon on the Properties of Foods.*

Medical teaching in twelfth-century Byzantium is best understood in the light of a very important hospital built by John II Komnenos and his wife Irene in 1136. The hospital at the Pantokrator monastery, which has been studied by several scholars, served as a center for medical education. Michael Italikos and Kallikles are described as *didaskaloi iatron* (instructors of physicians). Nepotism prevailed in the medical profession; the children of the hospital's thirty-two physicians were trained in medicine. Women, too, were allowed to study and to practice medicine. A well-disciplined system prevailed among the physicians, who were well remunerated for their services.

Medical studies in the Palaiologan era, the third period, were pursued with far greater vigor and propensity for innovation than before. In addition to the ancient legacy of Hippocrates and Galen, the masters of the early and the middle Byzantine periods, such as Oreibasios, Aetios of Amida, Alexander of Tralles, Paul of Aegina, and John the Alexandrian, remained the authorities for the study of the healing arts. But the period also produced some distinguished physicians of its own, namely Nicholaos Myrepsos, Demetrios Pepagomenos, and John Aktuarios. Myrepsos compiled 2,656 pharmaceutical recipes for several illnesses. He emphasized the application of mercurial ointments for skin problems and the use of common salt. A Latin translation of his *Pharmacopoieia* remained the standard work on the subject in Western Europe, particulary Paris, until the seventeenth century.

For illnesses like gout, Demetrios Pepagomenos, the personal physician to Emperor Michael VIII Palaiologos (1259–1282), was more original. He wrote "a very sensible treatise on gout." The illness was diagnosed as "a diathesis caused by defective elimination of excreta." In the middle of the fourteenth century, John Aktuarios wrote "an excellent medical treatise" and "an unusually comprehensive treatise on urine." The second work was extensively used. It has been described as an important contribution to medieval uroscopy. Aktuarios is also credited with identifying a parasite of the human intestine called *trichocephalus dispar,* or whipworm. In addition to these contributions, Aktuarios, who served as court physician to Andronikos III Palaiologos (1328–1441), wrote a work dealing with psychopathology and pneumatism. He described the powers of the mind and their effects on the body and proposed rules for psychosomatic hygiene.

Joseph Bryennios (*fl.* 1387–1405) expressed his distress and puzzlement at the decline of medicine after Aktuarios. Byzantine medicine passed on to other hands. Nevertheless, the advice of Byzantine physicians was followed in the Greek as well as in the Latin world for several centuries. Demetrios Pepagomenos' recommendations for the prevention of gout were repeated by John Choumnos, who prescribed a strict diet, eliminating salted and smoked food, fried fish, eggs, milk and milk products, and spices. He also urged moderation in drinking and emphasized physical exercise such as walking, horseback riding, and swimming. If advised by a physician, the patient should not refuse to undergo surgery for the removal of a damaged part.

The medical profession in the Byzantine Empire was not limited to lay persons, and the contribution of churchmen to medicine cannot be overlooked. Throughout the Byzantine era many monks, priests, bishops, and even patriarchs received a medical education and practiced the profession. They should not be confused with popular healing saints such as Therapon, Panteleimon, Kosmas and Damianos, Kyros and Ioannes, Sampson and Diomedes, and other heroes of popular piety, whose names are cited even to the present day in services of the Orthodox church.

Church fathers such as Basil the Great, the founder of the first major hospital of the Middle Ages, Eusebios of Caesarea, Nemesios of Emesa, and John the Eleemon, patriarch of Alexandria, described epidemics such as smallpox and diphtheria and made important contributions to clinical medicine and physiology, including a description of the nervous system. Many churchmen used their medical knowledge in establishing hospitals, leprosariums, and other philanthropic instutitions.

Physicians ordained clergymen were highly respected. For example the physician Pausikakos of Apameia in Bithynia (Asia Minor) was ordained a priest by Patriarch Kyriakos of Constantinople (595–606) in order to practice the act of healing on "bodies and souls." Politianos, patriarch of Alexandria in the eighth century, continued to offer his medical expertise even as a patriarch. At the request of Hārūn al-Rashīd, the caliph of Baghdad, he traveled there in order to treat one of Rashīd's wives. In the twelfth century the famous hospital of Pantokrator included physican-priests among its medical staff.

BIBLIOGRAPHY

Demetrios J. Constantelos, "Physician-Priests in the Medieval Greek Church," in *Greek Orthodox Theological Review,* 12 (1966–1967), and *Poverty, Society, and Philanthropy in the Late Medieval Greek World,* pt. 4, chap. 9, "Hospitals and Health Services" (1986); A. Hohlweg, "Johannes Aktuarios Leben-Bildung und Ausbildung—De Methodo Medendi," in *Byzantinische Zeitschrift,* 76 (1983); Herbert Hunger, *Die hochsprachliche profane Literatur der Byzantiner,* I (1978), 285–320; Ralph H. Major, *A History of Medicine,* I (1954), 207–218; Timothy S. Miller, *The Birth of the Hospital in the Byzantine Empire* (1985); Georgios Pournaropoulos, *Sӱmvole eis ten historian tes Byzantines iatrikes* (1942); John Scarborough, ed., "Symposium on Byzantine Medicine," in *Dumbarton Oaks Papers,* 38 (1984); Owsei Temkin, "Byzantine Medicine: Tradition and Empiricism," in *Dumbarton Oaks Papers,* 16 (1962); K. Vogel, "Byzantine Science," in J. M. Hussey, D. M. Nicol, and G. Cowan, eds., *The Cambridge Medieval History,* IV, pt. 2 (1967), 288–294.

DEMETRIOS J. CONSTANTELOS

[See also **Herbals, Byzantine and Arabic; Hospitals and Poor Relief, Byzantine; Leo the Mathematician; Pharmacopiae; Photios; Psellos, Michael.**]

MEDICINE, HISTORY OF. The history of medicine in the Middle Ages is customarily and indeed not inconveniently divided into the stages by which Greek medicine was introduced to the West through Arabic intermediaries, first by Constantine the African in Italy in the late eleventh century and then by a variety of translators throughout Europe in the twelfth and thirteenth centuries. But this by no means implies the absence of Hellenistic medicine from Western Europe in the early Middle Ages. Cassiodorus' *Institutiones* (about 562) recommended to his monks at Vivarium the reading "of Hippocrates and Galen translated into Latin—that is, the *Therapeutics* of Galen addressed to the philosopher Glaucon—and an anonymous treatise assembled from various authors; then Caelius Aurelius' *De medicina,* and Hippocrates' *On Herbs and Cures,* and various other works on the art of healing which, with God's help, I have gathered together for you in my library." Translations of other Greek works—Oribasius' *Synopsis,* Hippocrates' *Aphorisms*—were also available in the sixth century, together with a number of late Roman therapeutic collections.

Eventually, in Carolingian times, something of a flexible medical collection seems to have come into use, embodying theoretical and practical sections. The most commonly used theoretical works typically included Galen's *Ad Glauconem* and *De sectis,* the *Aphorisms* with an anonymous commentary, and two treatises deriving from Caelius Aurelianus' translation of Soranus—one concerned primarily with acute diseases and ascribed to "Aurelius," the other dealing with chronic diseases and attributed to "Esculapius." The corresponding texts of a practical nature are less easy to assign to particular classical sources. They deal most often with dietetics, materia medica, phlebotomy, and bathing, and are often falsely assigned a Greek authorship: the *Sapientia artis medicine* and the Pseudo-Dioscoridean *Ex herbis femininis* may serve as examples.

We know of the existence and association of these texts from the remains of the great Carolingian monasteries: Corbie, Reichenau, St. Gall, and others. There was certainly some lay practice of medicine in Europe during the early Middle Ages—particularly in Italy, where the tradition seems to have remained strong—but after the seventh century the clerical element predominated. The early Christian church had originally tended to leave healing to God, but this soon changed, as the medical section of Isidore of Seville's *Etymologies* (seventh century) shows. Hrabanus Maurus, two centuries later, insisted that clerics must not be ignorant of how to use medicines to treat disease. Thus, monasteries not only housed medical texts, they also put them to use. Someone had to take charge of the sick brethren; at St. Gall, buildings were projected to house the ill and to provide for the bloodletting that was a regular feature of the monastic routine. A monastery's *medicus* would often treat the secular clergy and the laity as well as his fellows; among the patients treated by Notker of St. Gall (Teutonicus) in the tenth century were the bishop of Constance, the duke of Bavaria, and the emperors Otto I and II.

In the tenth and eleventh centuries, the secular clergy also began to play a considerable role in medicine. It was possible to pursue medical studies at the cathedral schools as an adjunct to the seven liberal arts: Richer of Rheims tells of traveling to Chartres about the year 990 to read the *Aphorisms* with the cleric Heribrand and of going on to study more specialized subjects there. Such studies kept alive a knowledge of classical texts of theory—at Rheims, Gerbert (later Pope Sylvester II) had even studied Celsus' *De medicina,* a text almost unread during the Middle Ages—but the actual medical practice of the secular clergy was still empirical rather than theory-dominated, concerned with sensible dietary regimen, phlebotomy, and reputable simple or compound purges and other drugs.

Toward the end of the eleventh century, Salerno and the nearby Benedictine abbey of Monte Cassino in southern Italy began to become the centers of a new and different medical tradition. Salerno had had a reputation as a center of skilled practitioners in Richer's day, though we have no evidence of formal instruction in medicine there and know the names of no members of the "school" at that time. In the course of the next hundred years, however, Salernitan physicians seem to have started to produce their own medical literature, perhaps implying the beginnings of more formal learning. Many of the texts that have been assigned to Salerno in this period are still controversial—the work of Trotula, for example—but it seems likely that the *Passionarius* of Gariopontus (or Guarimpotus) was indeed completed there by 1050; this compilation was wholly deriva-

MEDICINE, HISTORY OF

tive from the collections of Greco-Latin medical literature that had evolved by the ninth century—Aurelius, Esculapius, the *De sectis,* and so forth—but in its generally systematizing approach to a mixture of materials it suggests a new interest in medical theory at Salerno.

CONSTANTINE THE AFRICAN AT SALERNO

Perhaps as early as 1065, Constantine the African had come to Salerno from North Africa and, at the encouragement of Archbishop Alfanus, had begun to translate medical works into Latin from Arabic. Shortly thereafter he became a Christian and entered the monastery at Monte Cassino, where medical studies were already being carried on. During the next twenty years Constantine continued to translate from the Arabic while teaching medicine to a generation of disciples. Many of the texts that he translated were works of Greek physicians, which had been rendered into Arabic by Ḥunayn ibn Isḥāq (also known as Johannitius) and others in the ninth century. One story has it that his first translation was of the *Ars medica* or *Tegni* of Galen; others included Hippocrates' *Aphorisms* and *Prognostics* with Galen's commentaries, and a summary version of Galen's *Megategni.* Perhaps more important in the long run for European medicine were the translations Constantine made of Arabic authors—treatises on diet, fever, and urines by Isaac Israeli and the *Pantegni* of Haly Abbas (ᶜAli ibn al-ᶜAbbas). Constantine seems to have been convinced of the connection between medicine and philosophy: These latter works have a strongly theoretical and philosophical orientation, new in medieval Europe, which came eventually to mark Salernitan medicine.

The European physicians in Constantine's day may initially have been suspicious of Arabic influence; at any rate, the earliest writings of twelfth-century Salerno do not seem to show the influence of the new translations but continue the empirical orientation of earlier medieval medicine. But it was not too long before Constantine's work led to the formation of a new collection of medical translations that gave shape to Western medicine for a century and a half, the *Articella* or *Ars medicinae.* This set of texts apparently crystallized around the *Isagoge* of Johannitius, an Arabic introduction to medicine translated by Constantine (of which a manuscript still survives at Monte Cassino); as it had become established by 1150 or so, the corpus of writings included: (1) the *Isagoge;* (2) Hippocrates' *Aphorisms* and (3) *Prognostics;* (4) Theophilus, *De urinis;* and (5) Philaretus, *De pulsibus.* Subsequently Galen's *Ars medica* and (in the thirteenth century) Hippocrates' *De regimine acutorum* were added to the collection. To assume that the creation of the *Articella* was due purely to Constantine's efforts must be mistaken, for only the translation of the *Isagoge* can be assigned to him with real security, but his example was surely responsible for the production of the other texts.

It was not long before these translations became the basis for a new sort of medical education at Salerno that foreshadowed the scholastic forms of the later Middle Ages. Much of the surprisingly extensive literature of the twelfth-century school reveals a background in actual teaching, and particularly noteworthy are several early commentaries on a variety of locally authored texts: European medicine was beginning to pass definitively from a practical to a more theoretical orientation. Subsequently the works of the *Articella* became the authoritative heart of a curriculum, for we have sets of commentaries on this collection by two different Salernitan physicians of the second half of the century, Bartholomeus of Salerno and Maurus.

Paul Kristeller has called attention to the frequency with which the new term "physicus" was coming to replace "medicus" at this time and has suggested that the terminology reflects a rising conviction that the fully trained physician should be something of a natural philosopher as well. The label was applied after his death in 1214 to Maurus, a figure whose writings are among the earliest medieval treatises to reveal a knowledge of and interest in the *libri naturales* of Aristotle. It can be applied even more appropriately to Maurus' younger colleague, Urso of Calabria (*fl. ca.* 1200): Urso has left a number of works upon standard areas of medical practice, but he also composed several important works of a more theoretical nature that attempted to give Hellenistic medicine a solid grounding in Aristotelian natural philosophy by linking the four elemental qualities systematically to medicinal activity. Maurus was still attempting to subordinate Aristotle to traditional forms of medical education; Urso was willing to consider the two as equals.

Something of this same movement toward a more formal, more structured presentation of medical knowledge is apparent in the Salernitans' work in anatomy, a field which in effect they recreated. They had inherited virtually no anatomical literature from the classical past, a situation changed only by Constantine's translation of the *Pantegni* with its anatomical chapters. By this time a tradition of a public

MEDICINE, HISTORY OF

anatomization of a pig had already been initiated at Salerno, witnessed to by the late-eleventh-century *Anatomia porci* attributed to Copho, which provides a description of the contents of the neck, chest, and abdomen. Thereafter, however, the various anatomical texts proceeding from the school in the twelfth century (attributed by Morris Saffron to Bartholomeus, Maurus, and Urso) show the influence of the Arabic tradition in their language and fuller treatment, as well as an increasing tendency to organize anatomical information along scholastic lines. It should perhaps be emphasized that the Salernitan anatomies are all of the pig, not of man.

TWELFTH- AND THIRTEENTH-CENTURY TRANSLATIONS

The trends apparent in twelfth-century Salerno became characteristic of European medicine generally in the thirteenth century, under the influence of a second group of medical works translated into Latin. As is well known, Constantine the African's work stands at the beginning of a century of intense translating activity by Latin scholars in Sicily and Spain. In its first stages, however, the texts translated were almost entirely astronomical, mathematical, or philosophical. It was only after about 1150 that additional medical writings were rendered into Latin, from both Arabic and Greek. In Italy, Burgundio of Pisa (*fl.* 1136–1193) translated from Greek at least ten of Galen's works, including the *De regimine sanitatis, De sectis, De differentiis febrium,* and the *Compendium pulsuum.* But the accomplishment of Gerard of Cremona (*ca.* 1114–1187) at Toledo is even more remarkable. The list of translations from the Arabic attributed to him by his disciples includes no fewer than two dozen works on medicine. Nine of these were by Galen: most importantly, perhaps, the *De elementis, De complexionibus,* and *De simplici medicina* (books 1–5); the brief *De malicia complexionis diverse;* the *Methodus medendi* (part of which Burgundio had also translated); and the *Tegni* or *Ars medica,* with commentary by "Haly" (ᶜAlī ibn Riḍwān). Almost all the remainder were of works by the outstanding figures in Islamic medicine: seven works by Rhazes (Abū al-Rāzī), including both his great medical compilations, the *Liber almansoris* and the *Continens;* the *Canon* of Avicenna (Ibn Sīnā); the *Breviarium* of Serapion; and the *Chirurgia* of Albucasis (Abū al-Kāsim al-Zahrāwī).

The importance of these new materials for Western medicine is not easy to overestimate. The remarkable medical encyclopedias of the Arabs, in particular the *Canon,* confirmed Western physicians in their belief that medicine should be studied as a rational system with close ties to philosophy, grounded in logical order and susceptible of methodical investigation. The works of Galen offered them more detailed discussions of both clinical and preclinical material, cast again in a form easily accommodated to Aristotelian natural philosophy, and the more specialized Arabic texts introduced the West to fields in which Islamic physicians had advanced well beyond Galen—that is, surgery, materia medica, and theoretical pharmacy.

Surgery for removal of hemorrhoids, nasal polyps, and cataracts. Miniature from a surgical MS of the School of Salerno, late 12th century. BY PERMISSION OF THE BRITISH LIBRARY, LONDON, MS SLOANE 1975, fol. 93r

The establishment of medical faculties within the new universities of the thirteenth century ensured the importance of these Greco-Arabic texts, though they did not immediately supplant the Constantinian translations as the foundation for education. Medical faculties of some importance were established at Paris and Montpellier early in the thirteenth century, but they continued to base their curricula upon the older material. At Paris, for example, the statutes of the medical faculty drawn up in the 1270's still listed the *Articella* texts as necessary reading for their students. Montpellier, a community with a considerable Jewish population, which began after 1200 to replace Salerno as the center of medical studies, has always been supposed to have been particularly receptive to the new Arabic science, yet the commentaries that survive from the school make it clear that here too medical instruction continued throughout much of the century to be based upon the *Isagoge* and the rest of the *Articella,* not on Galen and Avicenna. Only in 1309 were the newer texts—*De complexionibus,* Galen's *De crisi,* the

Canon—established as the basis of the curriculum at Montpellier.

If we read through the heavily schematic *Isagoge,* it will serve us as an introduction to Galenic medical theory, as it did so many students in the Middle Ages. We learn first about the *res naturales,* whose normalcy constitutes health: the four elements; the four primary qualities; the four humors or bodily fluids; the body's internal powers, the faculties and their functions; and the spirits. These "things natural" provide the basis for understanding the physiological and psychological activity of the body, and thus health: Every body, indeed every member of the body, has its own normal balance or proper temperament of qualities and humors, and illness arises when imbalance is so great as to distort function. The six nonnaturals, of which we learn next, are the causes external to the body that we or the physician can manipulate to preserve or sometimes to restore health: air, food and drink, excretion, exercise, sleep, and the emotions. Finally we learn of pathology: of disease, its causes and consequences (etiology and semiotics)—the *res contra naturam.* Diseases are classified sometimes by the part of the body they affect, sometimes by the symptoms they manifest, and sometimes by their supposed cause.

Only a very small portion of the *Isagoge* summarizes medical practice for the beginning student: "The practice of medicine deals with the right ordering of the nonnaturals, with giving of drugs, and with surgery"—to be essayed in that order, no doubt, by the consulting physician; of these, the administration of drugs, mostly botanical, seems to have dominated medical practice. The herbal of classical antiquity—for example, Dioscorides'—had disappeared as a literary form; instead, medieval physicians systematized their knowledge of remedies in medico-botanical lexica like the *Circa instans* of (Johannes?) "Platearius," works that supplied the medicinal properties of the plants they named but did not attempt to describe them. These works could be supplemented in practice by the many collections of recipes and prescriptions, one of which, the *Antidotarium Nicolai,* had acquired a special authority by the end of the thirteenth century. Physicians could employ time-tested recipes or, if they chose, could compound their own medicines, ordinarily trying to act on the patient in one or two fundamental ways—by bringing a qualitative imbalance back to normalcy by administering a drug of the opposite quality, or by eliminating humoral excess with a purge (as scammony was used to purge red bile).

Some historians have viewed the medical literature produced by the thirteenth-century schools as disastrously sterile, a scholastic regression from the more practical tradition of previous centuries; and certainly there is no doubt that the tendencies already plain in Maurus and Urso are even stronger in slightly later writers such as Gilbertus Anglicus—the attempt to accommodate medical data to the categories of Aristotelian thought, for example, and the consistent interpretation of facts in the light of philosophical reasoning. Yet this critical appraisal is too severe. Even apart from the context of medieval academic life, the emphasis of medieval physicians was bound to have stressed systematization as a route to assimilation. Thirteenth-century medicine had suddenly to master a new literature and terminology, a new pathology, a new therapeutics, which as a whole held out the promise of making medicine the intelligible subject it once had been in classical times.

What positive results such efforts could yield is illustrated by the career of Peter of Spain (Petrus Hispanus, *ca.* 1205–1277). A student in arts and theology at Paris in the 1220's, he received medical training perhaps at Montpellier and went on to teach medicine (at Siena, 1246–1250) before being made cardinal-bishop of Frascati (Tusculum) and eventually Pope John XXI. Peter's works tie up the whole spectrum of learning: they include an enormously influential treatise on elementary logic (the *Summulae logicales*); commentaries on the new Aristotelian psychology as well as on the old *Articella;* and works of general therapeutic importance (the famous *Thesaurus pauperum*). Such all-encompassing concerns reveal the ambitions thirteenth- (and fourteenth-) century physicians had for a fully developed scientific medicine.

THIRTEENTH-CENTURY SURGERY

The branch of thirteenth-century medicine that has received most praise for its empirical and "progressive" quality is surgery, though even here the influence of the schools can certainly be seen. The first medieval compilation on the subject was the so-called *Bamberg Surgery* of the early twelfth century, brought together at Salerno from classical sources and the *Pantegni;* it was supplanted by the text of Roger Frugardi, fifty years later, which in Guido d'Arezzo's rearrangement of 1170 dealt with certain operations, the treatment of wounds, fractures, and dislocations in a systematic and widely useful fashion. The works of early-thirteenth-century surgeons—the "Four Masters" of Bologna, William de

MEDICINE, HISTORY OF

Congenis of Montpellier—prove how central Roger's text was to surgical instruction until the new Arabic translations of Gerard of Cremona began to infiltrate the West. We gradually see in the important line of north Italian surgeons—Bruno Longoburgo, Hugh of Lucca and his son Theodoric, and William of Saliceto, all of Bologna, and Lanfranc of Milan—the penetration of Arabic teachings, of Avicenna, and particularly of Albucasis.

This thirteenth-century surgical literature is plainly marked by the immediacy of direct experience, on the battlefield or in urban practice, which unquestionably led to some concrete advances. For example, against the traditional view that pus should be produced in all wounds, artificially if necessary, Hugh and Theodoric began to teach that wounds would heal best if left without interference or merely washed with wine. Henry of Mondeville, who practiced and taught surgery at Montpellier in the first decade of the fourteenth century, was one of the first to try to introduce into France this proven technique of wound treatment. His *Chirurgia,* begun in 1306, was illustrated with thirteen figures meant to depict anatomical structures as actually observed. Yet Henry's obvious debt to empiricism was coupled with a commitment to scholastic form and wide mastery of medico-philosophical learning that today tend to strike historians as inconsistent. We should probably acknowledge, however, that there was not always an unbridgeable gulf between surgery and the medicine of the medieval schools. The professional relation between surgery and medicine in the Middle Ages is still not entirely clear. Certainly no formal distinction between the two was in force at Salerno, but at the new universities there seems to have been a growing feeling that scientific medicine should rank higher than manual surgery. The Montpellier statutes of 1239 exclude surgeons from the university, and by the fourteenth century medical masters were being forbidden the study of surgery there: Henry's conscious scholasticism no doubt reflects a desire to associate his practical subject with the higher prestige enjoyed by academic medical writers. Within the Italian universities, however, surgery remained a part of the curriculum, integrated as a respected branch of medical education.

MEDICAL SCHOOLS IN THE FOURTEENTH CENTURY

It is in the Italian schools, especially Padua and Bologna, that the core of fourteenth-century medicine is to be found. The real origins of scholastic medical teaching in northern Italy are perhaps to be fixed at Bologna in the 1260's with Taddeo Alderotti (*d.* 1295), his students, and his younger associates. Some of this teaching is reflected in scholastic commentaries (by no means all important masters chose to publish commentaries; those of Taddeo, Gentile da Foligno [*d.* 1348], and especially Jacopo da Forli [*d.* 1413] were most widely read), which were now on the Gerardian translations of the *Canon* and *Liber almansoris* as well as on older *Articella* texts like the *Aphorismi.* The dozens of Galenic works translated directly into Latin from Greek by Nicholas of Reggio in the first half of the fourteenth century further enlarged the schools' opportunities for discussion and analysis of texts. Gradually, within the general trend in the medieval universities, particular *questiones* began to be isolated for study and debate. In the Italian *studia* medical education was integrated with arts teaching, and this practice made it natural that the physicians should have investigated issues closely related to natural philosophy; often they show an awareness of contemporary discussions by philosophers at Paris and Oxford. They seem to have wanted from the beginning to associate medicine with the other sciences (though preserving its autonomy) by stressing that it was demonstrable from first principles that were rooted in philosophy. The general science available in the arts faculty often had a real bearing upon medical matters: astrological theory, for example, was regularly invoked to help illuminate the cause of an illness, or to determine the critical days in the course of a disease. And of course the biological writings of Aristotle (readily available by the mid thirteenth century) had to be assimilated to medicine.

This last practice led to some problems when the curricular study of the Galenic works (and later of Avicenna and of Averroës' *Colliget*) made it clear that in at least two respects Aristotle and Galen were sharply divided, and forced physicians to try to reconcile the two authorities in some manner. Aristotle had believed that the heart was the principal and primary organ in the body, from which the sensation, the intellect, and indeed the nerves derived, while the brain's function was merely to cool or regulate the heat arising in the heart. Galen had argued that there were four principal organs—heart, brain, liver, testicles—each of which had its own particular function: specifically, the brain was the origin of the nerves and the source of the psychic faculty, while the heart's vital faculty nourishes and heats the body. The teaching of the Italian masters generally favored

Galen on this point but supported Aristotle on the other controversial issue, the nature of conception: Aristotle had concluded that conception can be likened to implantation, and that male sperm contributes the form to the passive matter provided by the female's retained menstrual blood, whereas Galen assigned an active role to both male and female sperm, each of which he understood to make both a material and a formal contribution to conception, now interpreted as a mixing or fusing.

What we might regard as the more practical aspects of the physician's task do not seem to have received quite the same attention at the Italian schools. Medical writers acknowledged repeatedly the importance of experience, but the information they could acquire from their regular practice was limited and had always to be brought back and united to a theoretical framework. The collections of late medieval *consilia* (which can be traced back at least to Taddeo) illustrate this fact very well. *Consilia* were judgments and advice offered in individual cases, and they seem sometimes to approach the case history. Yet the theoretical element in the *consilia* bulks very large, and they were widely used as teaching aids. They were often organized around the arbitrary framework of the Galenic nonnaturals, not by spontaneous and individual appraisal, and indeed were often drawn up at a distance, a famous consultant's response to a colleague about patients of the latter's who remained unseen. Similarly, Taddeo's student Mondino de' Liuzzi is often praised for his pioneering work on human anatomy, completed in 1316, which drew upon actual dissections of the human cadaver (which had been initiated at Bologna in the late thirteenth century); Mondino's teaching established direct human-anatomical demonstrations in the Bologna curriculum, and perhaps at Padua as well. Still, his *Anatomia* is solidly Galenic and often reflects the doctrines of the *De iuvamentis membrorum,* even where they are in error.

Much the same generalization can be offered for the other important medical school in fourteenth-century Europe, that of the University of Montpellier. Practical experience was without question an important part of the professional activity both of its teachers and of its students. From its earliest days, students were required to interrupt their classes for extramural practice, eventually totaling eight months; and, after 1340, a biennial academic dissection was required to be held there. The Montpellier masters of the time composed an impressive number of works aimed expressly at helping the novice physician begin his practice (like Gerard of Solo's *Introductorium iuvenum*) or at helping patients regulate their own health (like the numerous *regimina sanitatis*); but their practical advice was virtually always governed by the structure of medical theory learned in their books: the *regimina,* for example, almost always organize their advice to patients by the various *res non naturales.*

Such markedly rationalized organization is characteristic of more general works as well (such as Bernard of Gordon's *Lilium medicine* of 1303–1305) and, along with the development of the commentary and *questio*—of which Montpellier produced its share—indicates the sense in which late medieval medicine was becoming "scholastic." So too does Montpellier's interest (apparently originating with Arnald of Villanova in the 1290's) in pursuing the logical and scientific implications of the arts faculty's natural philosophy within its own work on both medical theory and practice—Gerard's *Introductorium,* for example, spends considerable time discussing the technical features of a mathematical model for pharmacy worked out by Arnald a generation before. Thus, though Montpellier and the Italian schools developed independently, they evolved a generally similar system of medicine.

MEDICAL PRACTICE

But what sort of medical practice did this system actually inform? The medieval physician could use superficial signs, quality of pulse, blood and urine, and symptoms to diagnose an illness in essentially Galenic terms. He could provide a prognosis; but he could do little more in treatment than Hippocrates could have. *Regimina* kept the patient healthy; but if they failed, the physician had to turn to bloodletting (as permitted by the current zodiacal sign) and to a wide range of compounded and uncompounded (simple) medicines: some whose effects followed rationally from Galenic theory, others whose occult virtues had to be learned empirically, on a case-by-case basis. The influx of Arabic writings had enlarged the number of drugs known by name to the medieval physician, including some mineral remedies, though he had still to trust to his apothecary for their availability; but it had not significantly enhanced the physician's chance of therapeutic success. The vade mecum of the ordinary university-trained practitioner published by Charles Talbot illustrates this routine and its limitations very well. But we

MEDICINE, HISTORY OF

should not forget that patients cared for by learned physicians were probably healthier than others, relatively speaking; their therapy was generally moderate and sensible and did not go to the heroic extremes of, say, the early nineteenth century, and, what is most important in any age, it afforded real psychological support and confidence.

There were still some clerics with an important medical practice at the beginning of the fourteenth century, but medicine was now a predominantly secular occupation. The emergence of medical schools had had something to do with this; so had the limitations placed on clerical activity by canon law. Of this latter confusing subject the most recent summary is Darrel Amundsen's, which concludes that after 1163 monks and canons regular were forbidden to leave their cloisters to study medicine, as a violation of their vow of stability, and that in 1219 this prohibition was extended to secular clergy in major orders (in order to encourage instead their study of theology). The practice of medicine, to be sure, was forbidden in neither case: the one restriction is canon 18 of the Fourth Lateran Council, which prohibits subdeacons, deacons, and priests from practicing "that part of surgery involving burning or cutting" but implicitly leaves them free to perform other surgical tasks such as setting fractures, applying medicines to external wounds, and so forth. But the net result must certainly have been to take the church out of the nascent profession.

Nevertheless, health care continued to be stamped by the Christian tradition. The church's continuing concern for medical practice is obvious in other canons of Lateran IV, which prohibited patients from "having recourse to sinful means for the recovery of bodily health" and required physicians to insist that their patients make confession before beginning to treat them. At a different level, secular society organized and administered medical aid as an act of Christian charity through the establishment of hospital care specifically for the sick poor *(pauperes infirmi).* At first such sufferers had been cared for by physicians contracted to a municipality (like the surgeon Hugh of Lucca in Bologna in 1214), but from the late thirteenth century on larger urban centers like Florence or Valencia developed and expanded a system of hospitals whose function was now one not of offering food and lodging to travelers and the destitute but of providing medical services to the needy. Florence's hospital of S. Maria Nuova, for example, was founded in the 1280's and by 1400 was the largest of four in the city dedicated to the sick poor, employing two or three physicians (and a large staff of attendants) to care for perhaps 250 patients.

Many of these features of medieval medicine can be observed in the physicians' response to the Black Death, or bubonic plague, which arrived in Italian ports in late 1347 and within three years had enveloped the entire continent, killing perhaps one European in three. The unpleasant, inexorable, and usually deadly character of the disease encouraged an unprecedented outpouring of medical writings devoted to this one topic, most of them spontaneous but one commissioned. Philip VI of France ordered the medical faculty at Paris to explain the plague and its treatment, and the document that emerged from their discussions in October 1348 gave an authoritative statement of its origin—the conjunction in Aquarius of Jupiter, Saturn, and Mars in March 1345 had generated evil, pestilential vapors, and this corrupted air was the immediate cause of the epidemic. Writers generally agreed that the best precaution was to flee from the disease if you could, and if you could not, to carry a pomander and take theriac as prophylactics against the poison, while maintaining a regimen of moderate food, drink, and activity. Prevention played a much greater role in these treatises than cure, but there was some consensus upon bleeding, purging, and digestive cordials as possibly useful treatments. The disease may have been unique, but the physicians' response seems to have been of a piece with their routine practice.

The writers in whose works we have traced the development of medicine in the Middle Ages were at the head of their profession in status: literate and university-trained men who could hope to serve as physicians to kings and popes, as well as to nobles, clerics, and townsmen. But throughout the Middle Ages they were a small minority of those individuals actually offering medical counsel or care, even though the learned medicine that they practiced was an ideal accepted by the majority. Among full-time *medici* (both physicians and surgeons), the academically trained were very few before the fourteenth century, and even then many successful practitioners continued to be trained by apprenticeship. Apothecaries and barbers, too, could be routinely involved in health care, but their participation in the learned tradition was necessarily derivative and limited, although they were forced to acknowledge their dependence upon it: in the kingdom of Aragon, for example, the right to practice medicine was by the

1330's made dependent—in theory—upon training in a medical faculty, and twenty years later both apothecaries and barbers had been made subject in their own practice to the new learned medical profession.

Practitioners of a still lower order also existed, working in the country and (in general) among the poor. In many cities the professional physicians attempted to eliminate these unqualified or borderline practitioners, with the support of both secular and ecclesiastical authority, while apothecaries (who were natural sources of medical advice of the public) were brought more closely under their supervision. Many of these were well known to have successfully treated patients for whom regular physicians could do nothing—Jacqueline Félicie de Almania, for example, was excommunicated and fined sixty Parisian pounds in 1322 for having provided (successful) medical treatment. But the frequent prohibitions of such unauthorized practice make it clear that it was very common, and that most unlicensed practitioners in the Middle Ages were—unlike the unfortunate Jacqueline—never brought to trial.

Given these various forms of medical practice, how widely available was health care of some sort by the fourteenth century? Sketchy data for urban centers like Paris, London, or Valencia suggest that, in the years just before the Black Death, one would have found three "professional" physicians and as many surgeons for every 10,000 of city population, and perhaps twice as many of both barbers and apothecaries: that is, eighteen full-time practitioners of all sorts per 10,000 population, with unlicensed or irregular practitioners increasing this figure to an indeterminable degree. Full-time practitioners tended (then as now) to concentrate in cities, and consequently the level of medical personnel was much lower for the population as a whole, but it may have been on the order of 4:10,000—always remembering that the unlicensed or casual part-time healers who have left few traces probably supplied the need for medical care in the medieval countryside.

BIBLIOGRAPHY

Darrel W. Amundsen, "Medieval Canon Law on Medical and Surgical Practice by the Clergy," in *Bulletin of the History of Medicine,* **52** (1978); Gerhard Baader, "Die Schule von Salerno," in *Medizinhistorisches Journal,* **13** (1978); Vern L. Bullough, *The Development of Medicine as a Profession* (1966); Anna M. Campbell, *The Black Death and Men of Learning* (1931); Luke E. Demaitre, *Doctor Bernard de Gordon* (1980); Dietlinde Goltz, "Mittelalterliche Pharmazie und Medizin," in International Society for the History of Pharmacy, *Veröffentlichungen,* n.s. **44** (1976); Danielle Jacquart, *Le milieu medical en France du XIIe au XVe siècle* (1981); Pearl Kibre, "The Faculty of Medicine at Paris, Charlatanism, and Unlicensed Medical Practices in the Later Middle Ages," in *Bulletin of the History of Medicine,* **27** (1953), repr. in *idem,* ed., *Studies in Medieval Science* (1984); Paul O. Kristeller, "The School of Salerno," in *Bulletin of the History of Medicine,* **17** (1945), repr. in his *Studies in Renaissance Thought and Letters* (1956); Brian Lawn, *The Salernitan Questions* (1963); Loren C. MacKinney, *Early Medieval Medicine* (1937); Per-Gunner Ottosson, *Scholastic Medicine and Philosophy* (1984); Katharine Park, *Doctors and Medicine in Early Renaissance Florence* (1985); "Salernitan Anatomists," in *Dictionary of Scientific Biography,* XII (1975); Heinrich Schipperges, *Die Assimilation der arabischen Medizin durch das lateinische Mittelalter* (1964); Nancy G. Siraisi, *Taddeo Alderotti and His Pupils* (1981); Charles H. Talbot, "A Mediaeval Physician's Vade Mecum," in *Journal of the History of Medicine,* **16** (1961), *Medicine in Medieval England* (1967), and "Medicine," in David C. Lindberg, ed., *Science in the Middle Ages* (1978); Owsei Temkin, *Galenism* (1973).

MICHAEL MCVAUGH

[See also **Arnald of Villanova; Barbers, Barber-Surgeons; Black Death; Constantine the African; Gerard of Cremona; Herbals; Hospitals and Poor Relief; Insanity, Treatment of; Leprosy; Notker Teutonicus; Pharmacopeia; Plagues; Râzi, al-; Sinâ, Ibn; Trota and Trotula.**]

MEDICINE, SCHOOLS OF. Three major aspects may be distinguished in a survey of medieval medical schooling. First, in the rather sparsely documented early centuries and along the broad spectrum of intellectual history, we discern various centers where medicine was taught either as part of a comprehensive program or as a subject in its own right. A second aspect, interwoven with the emergence of universities in the late twelfth century, illuminates the formation of medical faculties as corporations of scholars for the regulation of teaching and practice. Third, without clear chronological boundaries but with a narrower focus in the history of medicine, comes the recognition of "schools" as bearers of particular traditions or orientations in doctrine and didactic method. This third aspect can only be touched upon here; its elucidation awaits further systematic study of medical writings to expand the existing knowledge about both preceding aspects of the history of universities and early medieval learning.

Throughout the fifth and sixth centuries, in Rome

MEDICINE, SCHOOLS OF

as well as in Ostrogothic Italy, Visigothic Spain, and in cities such as Bordeaux, Arles, Lyons, and Marseilles, lay physicians continued to teach their art as a literate, theoretical subject, distinguished from the actual practice of their craft. Also, in keeping with various traditions of late antiquity, they occasionally addressed audiences beyond the narrow circle of their students in order to enrich popular knowledge and to supplement the shortage of fully trained practitioners. Some of this teaching may have taken place in municipal schools or even in public lectures on Hippocrates and Galen, as perhaps in Ravenna until the eighth century. However, most medical instruction was apparently individualized and carried out in conjunction with an apprenticeship or as continuation of more basic studies. During the same period, while general education became the domain of the clergy, medical lore was also included by several nonphysicians in the liberal arts program and fostered by others for the benefit of the monastic infirmary.

Although this picture does not allow us to identify definite schools of medicine as such, it suggests the survival of medical teaching in various school milieus, and it points at the channels through which at least a nucleus of the classical and especially the Hippocratic-Galenic tradition was transmitted. This nucleus comprised not only doctrines on the nature and treatment of disease but also principles of deontology. The continued place of medicine among the disciplines, underlined in the sixth and seventh centuries by such influential authors as Cassiodorus and Isidore, is further attested to by library lists and compilations in more than eighty extant eighth- and ninth-century manuscripts. Most of these codices come from the great abbeys, including Monte Cassino, St. Gall, and Reichenau, but some have their provenance in cathedral towns such as Troyes and Chartres.

Two of these centers, Chartres and Monte Cassino, played an important role in the development of medical schools until the twelfth century, when they were both overshadowed by nearby beneficiaries, Paris and Salerno respectively. By 1050 the school of Chartres was producing royal physicians, among whom John "the Deaf" administered to the Capetian Henry I, and Baldwin served both Edward the Confessor and William the Conqueror. As a center of medical teaching Chartres had itself been the beneficiary of the Rheims school of Gerbert of Aurillac during the last quarter of the tenth century. Three alumni of this school brought to Chartres their rudimentary background and active interest in medicine: Bishop Fulbert, the physician Heribrand, and the historian Richer of Rheims.

Richer, having come to Chartres for this avowed purpose, pursued his medical studies first by reading the Hippocratic *Aphorisms* and *Prognostics* and then by requesting from Heribrand "a lecture on that book which is inscribed *De concordia Ypocratis Galieni et Surani*" (Concerning the harmony of Hippocrates, Galen, and Soranus). This book was perhaps an alphabetical compendium similar to the thirteenth-century *Concordantiae,* as Loren MacKinney has suggested, or a handbook listing acute and chronic diseases in a head-to-toe order, as Paul Diepgen and Karl Sudhoff have assumed. However, it may have been a dialectical arrangement of authoritative texts and thus a link in the evolution of the scholastic method of medical instruction. If so, the medical collection on which Heribrand lectured would antedate the better-known compilations in law and in theology that were similarly indebted to masters of Chartres, most notably Ivo (1040–1117) and Bernard (*d. ca.* 1130). There is indeed other evidence of an early French interest in the essence of scholastic medicine, which, as in the original Alexandrian mold, revolved around authoritative canons and dialectical methods while stressing the relevance of all the liberal arts and natural philosophy. Such an interest is revealed, for example, in a poem by the humanist Baudri of Bourgueil for William the Conqueror's daughter Adèle.

The dynamism of northern schools in teaching the medical art is further indicated in anecdotes and allusions that compared their accomplishments favorably, albeit somewhat chauvinistically, with those of the most renowned southern health center, in Salerno. Thus, around the turn of the millennium, Richer told of a public debate between two "eminent experts in the art of medicine." In this tournament a French bishop proficient in "the literary arts" had bested a Salernitan physician who was long on practical experience and natural talent, but short on "knowledge of letters." A half century later Rodulfus Mala Corona, after completing his studies in Chartres, traveled to Salerno, where, allegedly, he could not find "his equal in medicine." The obvious provincialism in these anecdotes is less significant than its complement, the stimulating interaction between northern and southern centers of medical teaching before 1100. The exposition of authoritative writings with the aid of the liberal arts, which initially gave the French a tactical advantage, be-

MEDICINE, SCHOOLS OF

came a prominent feature of Salernitan education. On the other hand, the practical instruction of the healing art as an end in itself, on which Salerno concentrated, was to be an essential component in the transalpine genesis of medical faculties. Our awareness of this European interaction in the teaching of medicine should serve to counteract the often one-sided emphasis on sudden or external factors in the rise of Salerno and in the emergence of other centers.

The introduction of Arabic writings, especially in the translations and arrangements by Constantine the African during the last quarter of the eleventh century, tends to eclipse the importance of previous and concomitant developments in the area. It is worth noting that Constantine started his career as transmitter under the aegis of two outstanding humanists, namely Alphanus, the archbishop of Salerno who had translated at least one Greek work on natural philosophy, and Desiderius, the abbot of Monte Cassino (and later Pope Victor III) who was in close contact with the Norman network. Moreover, the Salernitan masters already had access to the substance of Galenic theory, for example through the *Quaestiones medicales* or *Isagoge* ascribed to Soranus; and their own scholarly activity is evident in the systematic compilation of textbooks both for therapeutics, such as the *Antidotarium Nicolai,* and also for pathology, most notably the *Passionarius* attributed to Gariopontus. Perhaps Salerno's most valuable contribution to medicine, the pursuit of anatomical studies, was epitomized under the name of Copho in treaties that were contemporary with the work of Constantine yet virtually unaffected by it.

Twelfth-century writings, including the popular *Trotula de passionibus mulierum* with a woman as legendary author, reflect a gradual assimilation of the Constantinian contributions. The exact value and influence of these contributions may have to be reassessed in the light of the publication of new critical editions. In any event, this was a golden age for the Salernitan physicians, who practiced under the official protection of the Norman kings from 1140 on, maintained the lay character of their schools, and developed both the content and the form of their teaching. Several among the masters emerge more clearly as individual authors. Their works evince an increasing cultivation of the trivium (especially grammar and logic) as well as of natural philosophy or *physica.* This philosophy was formulated in a Galenic and, benefiting from new translations after 1150, in a more explicitly Aristotelian vein; it culminated in the speculations of Urso of Calabria (*d.* 1225). Meanwhile, didactic techniques facilitated—and potentially also corrupted—the learning of theoretical and practical medicine. Among these techniques, which in themselves had a long history, Salerno applied, in particular, mnemonic versification, catechetic *quaestiones,* dialectic disputations, and exegetic commentaries. The subject matter of instruction coalesced around a body of texts, first under the name *ars medicinae* and, by the advent of printing, under the title *Articella,* which was to provide the core of medical curricula throughout Europe for over four centuries. Though eventually supplemented with Constantinian translations, the heart of this corpus was primarily the fruit of earlier interactions between northern, southern, and eastern Europe. The constituent works, most of which were translated directly from the Greek, were the Hippocratic *Aphorisms* and *Prognostics,* Galen's *Ars parva* or *Tegni (Technē iatrikē)* with an introductory outline or *Isagoge* by Johannitius, and two Byzantine treatises on diagnostics—one on urines by Theophilus, the other on pulses by Philaretus. This was the corpus on which Salerno's leading masters, especially Bartholomaeus and Maurus, wrote commentaries during the second half of the twelfth century.

In the same period stronger Salernitan influences spread beyond the Alps. They entered Montpellier shortly before 1150 and reached Chartres in the same decade. They were introduced in Paris about a generation later and had crossed into England by the end of the century. These influences turned the tables in the old rivalry and also figured in the broader changes in the development of medical education. They may have enhanced a trend toward secularization that (though not becoming universal until much later) was further boosted by ecclesiastical injunctions against the practice and teaching of medicine by monks or by the clergy for the sake of gain. Such prohibitions were issued, for example, at the Councils of Clermont (1130) and of Tours (1163). In any event, the accelerating pace of change is vividly illustrated in the critique and controversy that grew rather intense after midcentury. An earlier visitor to Montpellier, Archbishop Adalbert of Mainz, had observed in 1137 that medicine was studied there "not with the object of making money from these matters but only in order to learn to understand the deeply hidden meaning of things"; more jaundiced views were soon to be expressed about the aim and nature of medical studies. Thus, in 1159 John of Salisbury censured the students who, "discovering their failure in philosophy," sought refuge with the physicians in Salerno or in Montpellier only to return "stuffed with fallacious observations" to practice what they had learned, to "show off Hippocrates and Galen," and to spout aphorisms and "unheard-of words." In the last quarter of the century Gilles de Corbeil, ardent alumnus of Salerno, reviled Montpellier as quarrelsome and puffed up with error after he had felt forced to flee from there to Paris, where he found a more receptive audience. Gilles also warned against the medical novices who rushed into practice intoxicated by the ability to untie a few knots of *physica* and lured by the promise of wealth.

The charge of greed, leveled at physicians in general throughout the ages, was now aimed at those trained in the schools of Salerno or Montpellier. The poet Guiot de Provins (*ca.* 1200), for example, complained that they commanded the highest fees. "Mercenary healers" is what Alfred of Sareshel called these physicians in his work *De motu cordis* (*ca.* 1210), scoffing that they were mere practitioners *(medici)* rather than the scientists *(physici)* they claimed to be. He further singled out "those of Montpellier and Salerno" in his allegation that they neglected the natural philosophy of Aristotle and studied only Johannitius and the Hippocratic aphorisms. This critique is in marked contrast to the attitude of Alexander Neckham, to whom, ironically, Sareshel's work on the heart was dedicated. Neckham boasted of having attended lectures on Hippocrates and Galen in Paris; he further included the Constantinian version of the *ars medicinae* in his own syllabus proposal; and he cited Salerno and Montpellier as models of schools where healing skills were taught "in the service of the public welfare."

Several recurring themes in these references underline certain directions that were taking shape toward 1200. Increasingly visible as a group were the physicians who, schooled in the *ars medicinae,* faced the challenge of proving themselves adequate both in empirical training and in the knowledge of natural philosophy. Most of them, however, had learned the art of medicine less for the sake of intellectual speculation than for the purpose of practicing a career. This particular orientation was enhanced by the dual prospect of personal prosperity and public service. These directions, sharpening the need for group protection and self-regulation, signaled the emergence of medicine as a profession; and they reached their logical fulfillment in conjunction with the more general movement of teachers and students toward the organization of guilds or universities. The medical guilds were strengthened, and their concerns with

Medieval physician (Bernard de Gordon or Guy de Chauliac) lecturing at Montpellier, late 13th century; before him pass Hippocrates, Galen, and Avicenna. BIBLIOTHÈQUE NATIONALE, PARIS, MS LAT. 6,966, fol. 4r

protection and regulation were sanctioned by official privileges and charters. These charters were granted by both ecclesiastical and secular authorities, even though the latter had previously supervised practice while preferring an open market in teaching. Due, at least in part, to the impetus of this guild movement and official support, the magnetism of Salerno was gradually replaced by the drawing power of urban centers such as Montpellier, Paris, and Bologna. Within the nascent universities, however, the medical schools were generally slow to develop their own corporate identity and autonomy or to reach academic equality with other higher disciplines.

The curricular and organizational demarcations between the study of medicine proper and that of the liberal arts, a common prerequisite for the aspiring medical student, are particularly elusive. Even though physicians were mentioned as distinct groups in early-thirteenth-century university documents, in most places, from Padua to Oxford, they belonged to the faculty of arts or to a joint university of arts and medicine until much later. The first medical faculty to appear as a patently separate entity was in Montpellier, where "the universtiy of physicians, masters as well as students," received a teaching constitution from the papal legate in 1220. Nevertheless, even here the situation remained paradoxical and confusing. When this constitution, which later (in 1242) provided the model for the charter of the arts faculty, was confirmed and extended to the regulation of medical practice in 1239, it still classified medicine *among* the liberal arts. The need for clear-cut separation was still present a century later, when new statutes not only prohibited bachelors from accepting a master of arts degree after incepting in medicine but also enjoined medical faculty from teaching grammar, logic, or natural philosophy.

The new statutes of 1340 may reveal another encroachment upon the original preeminence of medicine at Montpellier. Since these statutes were drawn up by teachers of jurisprudence, they suggest that the medical faculty was succumbing to the hegemony of other faculties, a pattern that was characteristic from the beginning at most other universities as well. At Paris, for example, university protocol expressly ranked medicine after theology and law, and until 1452 the statutes required celibacy of one with the status of regent master in the medical faculty. At Bologna, the prestige and power of the law teachers long overshadowed the academic standing of the physicians. The aspiration to gain full academic respectability and to achieve equality with the inherently intellectual and politically influential professions intensified the university physicians' growing preoccupation with bookish learning or *doctrina.* They obviously also preferred the guild title of *magister* over the more common labels such as *medicus* or *physicus,* and they virtually monopolized the teaching title par excellence of doctor. Furthermore, the time required to earn the teaching license and the master's degree was increased more markedly in medicine than in the other faculties. Thus, between 1240 and 1350 at Montpellier and at Paris, the minimum period of study was extended from about five years (six for candidates without the master of arts degree) to more than eight years. This increase was both the cause and the effect of a parallel expansion in instructional matter that was fed by the influx of new translations from Spain and Italy and by the proliferation of the masters' own writings, although the *ars medicinae* remained the cornerstone of the official curriculum.

The years of medical education fell into two phases. During the first the student, who could claim the title of *scholaris* only upon being assigned to the governance of a regent master, worked toward the baccalaureate. In order to acquire this status, which was not really a degree until later in the fourteenth century, the student had to attend classes for a period that varied from twenty-four to forty-eight months, to pass one or more examinations, and finally to defend a thesis in a "determination."

During the second phase of study the new bachelor and prospective master faced a program that seems both more varied and more hectic, perhaps because it is better documented. He continued to attend classes until he had heard most of the *ars medicinae* expounded three times in all. On the basis of the morning and afternoon lectures conducted regularly *(ordinarie)* by regent masters from October to April, he himself had to teach during the "free" hours and days (*cursorie* or *inordinarie*). He was required to offer at least one course on a medical work from each of the following categories: classical sources, which consisted primarily of Hippocratic works and a steadily growing number of Galenic treatises; commentaries, which might include the most recent literature; and practical compendia or parts of summas, among which the *Canon* of Avicenna (Ibn Sīnā) and the *Liber Almansoris* of Rasis (al-Rāzī) gained prominence after 1300. Furthermore, the bachelor was expected to participate in disputations on course topics and on a variety of random questions *(de quolibet).* Such *quaestiones* on medical theory and practice occur separately and in collections throughout the manuscripts, so that their didactic and paradigmatic importance—misleadingly peripheral if one focuses on curricular treatises—apparently equaled their ritual role in the student's promotion. A veritable battery of questions, in public *responsiones* to each regent master, in a private examination, and in a solemn debate of the candidate's dual lecture on theoretical and practical medicine, preceded the granting of the license to teach and to practice *ubique terrarum*. Finally, an almost orchestrated question-and-answer test highlighted the "inception" ceremony in which the licensee received the master's degree after pledging his loyalty to the university and his commitment to lecture in the faculty for two more years.

The compulsory term, which detained the new master from a full-time career in practice, was crucial to the structure and stability of the medical faculty. Physicians were apparently less cohesive in their corporations than their colleagues in other disciplines, and their schools long lacked the permanence of a shelter in dramatic contrast with the medical centers that may tower over modern campuses. Public lectures and faculty assemblies were held in churches. Classes or *scholae* were conducted in houses owned or rented by individual teachers, a domestic setting that did not, however, entail familiarity between the students, who humbly sat on low benches if not on the floor, and the lecturer, who presided from the cathedra. Some professors might be upstaged by the book on which they lectured, but others immortalized their teaching in the pedagogic subtleties of their own treatises.

The acquisition of books was a growing expense to aspiring physicians, who at the time of promotion to master might be required to possess some ten major works. Although texts were copied laboriously not only by scribes but also by bachelors and even by masters, there was an ever-growing need for communally accessible volumes in excess of the number that remained chained in the classroom or circulated informally. This need was met in part by the libraries of monasteries, courts, or other faculties; it also stimulated the establishment of the first medical libraries in the "colleges of physicians." From their earliest foundations around 1370, these colleges housed not only classrooms and living quarters but also facilities for research, at least in the bookish sense. In addition, by providing occasional treatment in the in-house infirmary and by offering the large hall or aula as a most appropriate setting for anatomical demonstrations, the college boosted practical experience and scientific observation in the teaching of medicine.

Considering the magisterial character of the faculty, the emphasis of the statutes on bookish and dialectical prowess, and the speculative penchant of the writing masters—who represent, it should be noted, a minority among university-trained physicians—it is all the more significant that experience and observation were integral parts of medical education. Even the earliest constitutions stipulated that bachelors must interrupt their class sessions for a stint at clinical work. Paris students had the option of either two summers outside the city or two years in town under a master's supervision. Montpellier candidates were obliged to spend the term, which was extended from a half year (1240) to a minimum of two summers or eight months (1309), out of town and thus presumably without constant guidance. In Vienna, a latter provision (1389) prescribed a one-year term of service in the company of a master. The minimum requirements mentioned in the statutes can be supplemented with written and iconographic evidence scattered throughout diverse sources, which indicates that bachelors not only routinely assisted their masters as apprentices in patient care but also visited hospitals, even though these were not institutionally linked with universities until later.

Although clinical work must surely have enriched the student's knowledge of diagnostics and therapeutics, it may have lacked educational effectiveness insofar as it remained insufficiently correlated to classwork and examinations. However, within the classroom, the lecture format, including the study of pictures, slowly gave way to observation in the areas of anatomy and surgery. Early in the thirteenth century the Italian schools, expanding Salerno's legacy, moved from the Alexandrian schemata of systems (labeled *Fünfbilderseries* by Karl Sudhoff) to human topography in the so-called *anatomia vivorum* that was later attributed to Galen. Around 1300 this approach, boosted by a parallel interest in embalming procedures and judicial autopsies, led to the reintroduction of dissection for teaching purposes. Bologna and later Padua retained the leadership in anatomical studies from Mundinus to Vesalius, while classroom dissections entered transalpine schools at an uneven pace. In Montpellier, for example, they were sanctioned by the 1340 statutes, whereas in Paris they may not have occurred until the end of the century. The frequency of these demonstrations reflected the degree not only of observation in anatomy and pa-

MEDICINE, SCHOOLS OF

thology, but also of rapport between medicine and surgery.

The social distance between academic physicians and artisan surgeons widened as one moved northward, although it did not preclude scholarly interaction. Mutual requests and collaborations produced treatises and translations. Textbooks on surgery were regular features in medical libraries, and many teaching physicians displayed a more than bookish understanding of such operations as lithotomy or suturing, contrary to the notion that they universally disdained manual work. At the same time master surgeons, in emulation and at the urging of professional doctors, promoted the inclusion of medical literature in the training of their apprentices. Among a dozen thirteenth- and fourteenth-century authors of summae on surgery, many cannot be classified as nonphysicians, several had studied with university masters, and some presumably taught in affiliation with a faculty of medicine. These active but undefined exchanges between physicians and surgeons remind us that many aspects of teaching were not covered by the statutes.

The institutional framework of the university is transcended even more broadly by the world of traditions and trends or of "schools" in medicine, a complex world that awaits further exploration. Initial steps have been taken in essays on methodological trends, whether didactic as in the influence of the liberal arts and in the compilation of summae, or heuristic as in the quantification of qualities and in the classification of diseases; studies of doctrinal traditions have uncovered themes such as fevers and reproduction, as well as paradigms such as the radical moisture and the nonnaturals. Additional paths have been opened to orientations that were predominantly Hippocratic, Aristotelian, Galenic, or Avicennan, and to local or personal spheres. Local specialties are outlined in a particular academic or social context: thus, in Bologna clinical *concilia* echoed the lawyers' briefs, in Paris discussions of *physica* drew upon the theologians' debates, and in Montpellier dietary and pharmacological tracts were inspired by the spice trade. Personal followings have been identified around teachers such as William of Saliceto, Taddeo Alderotti, and Gentile da Foligno. Deeper in the sources loom circles whose teaching either favored one approach, for example prevention over therapeutics, cultivated a particular subject area, ranging from uroscopy to ethics, or relied on other disciplines, among which astrology became increasingly fashionable. Although most of these trends and traditions overlap, they can be broken down into many more areas. A better comprehension of their diversity, together with continued study of the famous and the more obscure universities, and with further reconstruction of the earlier centuries, is bound to underscore the vitality of the European schools of medicine during the Middle Ages.

BIBLIOGRAPHY

In addition to the titles listed below, pertinent materials may be found in works and current bibliographies on the history of universities, medicine, and science.

General works. Guy Beaujouan *et al.*, *Médecine humaine et vétérinaire à la fin du moyen âge* (1966); Loren C. MacKinney, "Medical Education in the Middle Ages," in *Cahiers d'histoire mondiale,* **2** (1955); Charles D. O'Malley, ed., *The History of Medical Education* (1970), 3–87; Charles H. Talbot and E. A. Hammond, *The Medical Practitioners in Medieval England: A Biographical Register* (1965); Charles H. Talbot, *Medicine in Medieval England* (1967); Ernest Wickersheimer, *Dictionnaire biographique des médecins en France au moyen âge* (1936), with *Supplément,* Danielle Jacquart, ed. (1979).

Early centuries. A. Z. Iskandar, "An Attempted Reconstruction of the Late Alexandrian Medical Curriculum," in *Medical History,* **20** (1976); Loren C. MacKinney, *Early Medieval Medicine, with Special Reference to France and Chartres* (1937); Henry E. Sigerist, "The Latin Medical Literature of the Early Middle Ages," in *Journal of the History of Medicine and Allied Sciences,* **13** (1958); L. G. Westerink, "Philosophy and Medicine in Late Antiquity," in *Janus,* **51** (1964); Ernest Wickersheimer, *Les manuscrits latins de médecine du haut moyen âge dans les bibliothèques de France* (1966).

Salerno. Walter Artlet, "Die Salernoforschung im 17., 18., und 19. Jahrhundert," in *Sudhoffs Archiv,* **40** (1956); Francesco Gabrieli, "The Arabian Medicine and the School of Salerno," in *Salerno,* **1** (1967); Eugene H. Guitard, "Les attaques de Guiot de Provins contre les praticiens instruits à Montpellier au XIIe siècle," in *XVIe Congrès international d'histoire de la médecine: Résumé des communications* (1958), 78; Paul O. Kristeller, "Bartholomeus Musandinus and Maurus of Salerno and Other Early Commentators of the 'Articella,' with a Tentative List of Texts and Manuscripts," in *Italia medioevale e humanistica,* **19** (1976), and "The School of Salerno: Its Development and Its Contribution to the History of Learning," in *Bulletin of the History of Medicine,* **17** (1945); Pascal Parente, ed. and trans., *The Regimen of Health of the Medical School of Salerno* (1967); A. Pazzini, "Sull' origine e sulla didattica della scuola medica di Salerno," in *Pagine di storia della medicina,* **2** (1958); Gernot Rath, "Gilles de Corbeil as Critic of His Age," in *Bulletin of the History of Medicine,* **38** (1964); Morris H. Saffron, trans., *Maurus of Salerno: Twelfth-century "Optimus Physicus,"* *with His Commentary on the Prognostics of Hippocrates* (1972); Heinrich Schipperges, "Die Schulen von Chartres unter dem Einfluss des Arabismus," in *Sudhoffs Archiv,* **40** (1956); Ernest Wickersheimer, "Autour du Régime de Salerne," in *Scalpel,* **50** (1952).

Universities. Vern L. Bullough, *The Development of Medicine as a Profession: The Contribution of the Medieval University to Modern Medicine* (1966), and "Achievement, Professionalization, and the University," in Jozef Ijsewijn and Jacques Paquet, eds., *The Universities in the Late Middle Ages* (1978); Luke Demaitre, *Doctor Bernard de Gordon: Professor and Practitioner* (1980); Louis Dulieu, *La médecine à Montpellier,* I (1975); Luis García Ballester, *Historia social de la medicina en la España de los siglos XIII al XVI* (1976); Edward F. Hartung, "Medical Regulations of Frederick the Second of Hohenstaufen," in *Medical Life,* **41** (1934); Pearl Kibre, "Cristoforo Barzizza: Professor of Medicine at Padua," in *Bulletin of the History of Medicine,* **11** (1942), "The Faculty of Medicine at Paris, Charlatanism, and Unlicensed Medical Practices in the Later Middle Ages," *ibid.,* **27** (1953), and "Dominicus de Ragusa, Bolognese Doctor of Arts and Medicine," *ibid.,* **45** (1971); Dean P. Lockwood, *Ugo Benzi: Medieval Philosopher and Physician (1376–1439)* (1951); Nancy G. Siraisi, *Arts and Sciences at Padua: The Studium of Padua Before 1350* (1973), and *Taddeo Alderotti and His Pupils* (1981); F. A. Sondervorst, "L'histoire de l'ancienne faculté de médecine de Louvain," in *Louvain médical,* **96** (1977); Ernest Wickersheimer, "Les médecins de la nation anglaise (ou allemande) de l'université de Paris aux XIVe et XVe siècles," in *Bulletin de la société française d'histoire de la médecine,* **12** (1913).

Curriculum and libraries. Luke Demaitre, "Scholasticism in Compendia of Practical Medicine, 1250–1450," in *Manuscripta,* **20** (1976); Stephen D'Irsay, "Teachers and Textbooks of Medicine in the Medieval University of Paris," in *Annals of Medical History,* **8** (1926); Richard J. Durling, "An Early Manual for the Medical Student and the Newly-fledged Practitioner: Martin Stainpeis' *Liber de modo studendi seu legendi in medicina* ([Vienna] 1520)," in *Clio medica,* **5** (1970); Pearl Kibre, "Hippocratic Writings in the Middle Ages," in *Bulletin of the History of Medicine,* **18** (1945), "Hippocrates Latinus: Repertorium of Hippocratic Writings in the Latin Middle Ages," in *Traditio,* **31–36** (1975–1980), and "Arts and Medicine in the Universities of the Later Middle Ages," in Jozef Ijsewijn and Jacques Paquet, eds., *The Universities in the Late Middle Ages* (1978); Brian Lawn, *The Salernitan Questions: An Introduction to the History of Medieval and Renaissance Problem Literature* (1963), and ed., *The Prose Salernitan Questions: An Anonymous Collection Dealing with Science and Medicine Written by an Englishman c. 1200, with an Appendix of Ten Related Collections* (1979); A. Louis, "Analyse des bibliothèques de deux médecins malinois du 15e siècle," in *Janus,* **53** (1966); Heinrich Schipperges, *Die Assimilation der arabischen Medizin durch das lateinische Mittelalter* (1964); James A. Weisheipl, "Classification of the Sciences in Medieval Thought," in *Mediaeval Studies,* **27** (1965).

Theory and practice—anatomy and surgery. Mary N. Alston, "The Attitude of the Church Towards Dissection Before 1500," in *Bulletin of the History of Medicine,* **16** (1944); Darrel W. Amundsen, "Medieval Canon Law on Medical and Surgical Practice by the Clergy," in *Bulletin of the History of Medicine,* **52** (1978); Walter Artelt, "Die ältesten Nachrichten über die Sektion menschlicher Leichen im mittelalterlichen Abendland," in *Abhandlungen zur Geschichte der Medizin,* **34** (1940); George W. Corner, *Anatomical Texts of the Earlier Middle Ages* (1927); Luke Demaitre, "Theory and Practice in Medical Education at the University of Montpellier in the Thirteenth and Fourteenth Centuries," in *Journal of the History of Medicine and Allied Sciences,* **30** (1975); Stephen D'Irsay, "The Black Death and the Medieval Universities," in *Annals of Medical History,* **7** (1925); Ynez V. O'Neill, "The Fünfbilderserie Reconsidered," in *Bulletin of the History of Medicine,* **43** (1969), "An Anatomical Mystery with Global Dimensions," in *Actes du XXVe congrès international d'histoire de la médecine* (1976), and "Innocent III and the Evolution of Anatomy," in *Medical History,* **20** (1976); Henry E. Sigerist, "A Salernitan Student's Surgical Notebook," in *Bulletin of the History of Medicine,* **14** (1943); Ernest Wickersheimer, "Les secrets et les conseils de maître Guillaume Boucher et de ses confrères: Contribution à l'histoire de la médecine à Paris vers 1400," in *Bulletin de la société française d'histoire de la médecine,* **8** (1909), "Les maladies épidémiques ou contagieuses et la faculté de médecine de Paris, de 1399 à 1511," *ibid.,* **13** (1914), and "Médecins et chirurgiens dans les hôpitaux du moyen âge," in *Janus,* **32** (1928).

Schools of thought. Thomas S. Hall, "Life, Death, and the Radical Moisture: A Study of Thematic Pattern in Medieval Medical Theory," in *Clio medica,* **6** (1971); Pearl Kibre, "Giovanni Garzoni of Bologna (1419–1505): Professor of Medicine and Defender of Astrology," in *Isis,* **58** (1967); Michael R. McVaugh, "Quantified Medical Theory and Practice at Fourteenth-century Montpellier," in *Bulletin of the History of Medicine,* **43** (1969), "Theriac at Montpellier, 1285–1325," in *Sudhoffs Archiv,* **56** (1972), and "The Humidum Radicale in Thirteenth-century Medicine," in *Traditio,* **30** (1974); John H. Randall, *The School of Padua and the Emergence of Modern Science* (1961); Lelland J. Rather, "The 'Six Things Non-natural': A Note on the Origins and Fate of a Doctrine and Phrase," in *Clio medica,* **3** (1968); Owsei Temkin, *Galenism: Rise and Decline of a Medical Philosophy* (1973).

LUKE DEMAITRE

[See also **Alphanus of Salerno; Barbers, Barber-Surgeons; Constantine the African; Fachschrifttum; Hospitals and Poor Relief; Ivo of Chartres, St.; Neckham, Alexander; Textbooks; Trivium; Universities.**]

MEDINA, from the Arabic *madinat al-nabi* (city of the Prophet), the name given to the old Arabian town of Yathrib sometime after Muḥammad and his followers from Mecca settled there in 622. For the next decade until the Prophet's death in 632, the emigrants *(muhājirūn)* from Mecca and the more hospitable "helpers" *(anṣār)* among the residents of Medina cooperated with him and his closest companions to establish the foundational community of believers of Islam, the *umma.* The Islamization of much of Arabia, accomplished in large part by 632, and the conquests of the Fertile Crescent and Persia, complete by midcentury, were directed first by Muḥammad from Medina and after him by four successor heads of the *umma,* known as Rightly Guided caliphs. After 661 the dynastic political centers of power shifted first to Syria under the Umayyads (661–750) and then to Iraq under the Abbasid caliphs (750–1258). Medina remained, however, a focal point of pilgrimage, second only to Mecca some 200 miles to the southwest, and a favorite place for teachers and the pious to gather for periods before or after the hajj to Mecca. The center of religious attention in Medina has been the shrine complex, the famous green-domed mosque that houses the remains of the prophet Muḥammad and purportedly was built on the site of his original home.

Muslim historians in the Middle Ages provided lists of the governors appointed to rule Medina by the Umayyad and Abbasid caliphs. In addition, travel literature (the *riḥla*) and geography texts provide some information about the social and cultural aspects of life in the city. By and large, however, Medina played less of a political role than did Mecca, except in the period from the Prophet's emigration to the rise of the Umayyads. Associated with Medina are a number of neighboring sites, such as Uḥud and Badr, where the Muslim *umma,* under Muḥammad's leadership, had fought with the Meccan forces. Along with Mecca and Jerusalem, Medina has been regarded as one of the three holy cities of Islam and today is still visited annually by pilgrims on the hajj to Mecca.

BIBLIOGRAPHY

Ibn Baṭṭūṭa, *The Travels of Ibn Batuta,* Samuel Lee, trans. (1829); Ibn Jubayr, *The Travels of Ibn Jubayr,* R. J. C. Broadhurst, trans. (1952); William Montgomery Watt, *Muhammad at Medina* (1956); Heinrich F. Wüstenfeldt, *Geschichte der Stadt Medina* (1860).

RICHARD C. MARTIN

[See also **Arabia; Islam, Conquests of; Islam, Religion; Muḥammad; Pilgrimage, Islamic.**]

MEDWALL, HENRY (1461–150?), author of *Fulgens and Lucres* and *Nature,* is the earliest vernacular English dramatist known by name. He is the first of the Tudor dramatists and author of the first vernacular play to issue from an English press.

Medwall was born on or about 8 September 1461. In 1475 he left his home in Southwark for Eton College, remaining until 1480, when he entered King's College, Cambridge. Here he witnessed, and perhaps participated in, "disguisings," or theatrical entertainments, produced by fellows of the college. He vacated his scholarship on 13 June 1483, the day his prospective patron, John Morton, bishop of Ely, was arrested by the future Richard III. Evidently Medwall was already Morton's protégé.

Following Henry VII's accession in 1485, Morton became archbishop of Canterbury (1486) and lord chancellor (1487); in 1493 he became cardinal. Medwall served as one of Morton's Lambeth Palace notaries from 1490 at the latest. By 1500, the year of Morton's death, Medwall had personal control over the archbishop's papers and documents. During his tenure as notary, Medwall received a degree in civil law from Cambridge, entered minor orders, and accepted the benefice of Balinghem, in the pale of Calais. Following his resignation from this benefice in 1501, his name disappears from the records.

Medwall most likely wrote his two plays in the early 1490's to entertain Morton's household and guests, probably during Christmas holidays. Both plays are divided into two parts, each part lasting about ninety minutes. Part one was presented during a midday dinner, part two during an evening supper the same day.

Fulgens and Lucres is the earliest English play on a purely secular theme and is based on Buonaccorso da Montemagno's *Controversia de vera nobilitate* (*ca.* 1428), which was translated into English by John Tiptoft, earl of Worcester, around 1460 and printed in 1481 by Caxton with Cicero's *Of Old Age.* The play concerns Lucres (Lucrece), daughter of the Roman senator Fulgens, who must choose her mate in marriage from between Publius Cornelius, a noble rake, and Gayus Flaminius, a virtuous commoner. With apologies to the nobles in her audience, Lucres chooses the commoner. This consideration of the true nature of nobility is varied by a secondary plot in which nameless servants (A and B) gain employment with the suitors and vie for the hand of Lucres' maid Jone (Joan). Their wooing involves jests (often scatological), a three-part song, and physical combat; the primary plot incorporates a *bassedanse* performed to minstrel music by a troupe of dancers.

Nature exemplifies the morality play as it flourished during the fifteenth and early sixteenth centuries. Nature, the medieval goddess, introduces Man to Mundus (World) and consequently to Worldly Affection and the Seven Deadly Sins. Sensuality encourages Man to sin, while Reason encourages Man to seek the protection of the seven remedial virtues. After a youthful fall Man briefly reforms, but then relapses until Age makes him impotent. At the end of his life Man is abandoned by vice to the protection of the Virtues and thus finds salvation. The play is characterized by lively descriptions of urban vice.

Fulgens and Lucres was printed between approximately 1512 and 1516 by John Rastell, and *Nature* around 1530 by William Rastell, his son.

BIBLIOGRAPHY

Alan H. Nelson, ed., *The Plays of Henry Medwall* (1980), brings together all relevant scholarship. *Fulgens and Lucres* has been edited by Frederick S. Boas and Arthur W. Reed (1926). See also Sheila Lindenbaum, "The Morality Plays," in Albert E. Hartung, ed., *A Manual of the Writings in Middle English, 1050–1500,* V (1975); and Arthur W. Reed, *Early Tudor Drama* (1926).

ALAN H. NELSON

[See also **Drama, Western European; Everyman; Middle English Literature; Morality Play.**]

MEGINHART OF FULDA (Menginhardus Fuldensis) (*fl. ca.* 850), a monk associated with Hrabanus Maurus, abbot of Fulda from 822 to 842 (*d.* 856). At the request of Gunther, bishop of Cologne, he wrote the life of Sedulius Scottus, a treatise on the symbolism of the apostles, and a defense against heretics. For Adager, abbot of Fulda, he wrote a panegyric on St. Ferrutius. He also completed the *Translatio S. Alexandri* begun by Rudolf of Fulda (*d.* 851).

BIBLIOGRAPHY

Monumenta Germaniae historica: Epistolae, VI (1925), 163; *Monumenta Germaniae historica: Scriptores,* XV (1963), 148; Max Manitius, *Geschichte der lateinischen Literatur des Mittelalters,* I (1911), 668–673.

NATHALIE HANLET

[See also **Fulda; Hrabanus Maurus; Rudolf of Fulda; Sedulius Scottus.**]

MEHMED (MUḤAMMAD) I (Chelebi ibn Bāyazīd), Ottoman sultan who ruled during 1413–1421. He ended the anarchy of the interregnum following the death of his father, Bāyazīd I, in 1403, and later, in 1413, reunited the fragmented state. In Anatolia, Tamerlane's victory had reduced the Ottoman borders to approximately those of 1389. Rival factions of Turkomans, *ghāzi*s, *kapıkulu*s (slaves of the Porte), and Christian vassals competed for power in the succession struggle. Fortunately for the Ottomans, the European powers were too divided to take advantage of this situation.

Mehmed Chelebi, with the support of the Turkomans and *ghāzī*s, elements opposed to the centralizing forces associated with the *kapıkulu*s, bested his brothers Süleymān (*d.* 1411) and Musa (*d.* 1413) to gain the throne. To a certain extent, Mehmed may have represented a backlash to Bāyazīd's policies. Nevertheless, he retained ties with Byzantium and recognized that the strength of his state lay in Europe with both the Turkoman *ghāzī*s and the *kapıkulu*s of the *devshirme* (child-levy). The hostility of the Anatolian beys to the Ottomans and the unease which the Turkoman *ghāzī*s felt in fighting fellow Turkish Muslims would ultimately incline the dynasty toward the *kapıkulu*s.

Limited in his actions by the Timurids, Mehmed nonetheless forced the Mentesch beylic in Anatolia to recognize his overlordship in 1415 and in the following years made encroachments on Karaman, Saruhan, and Aydin. In 1418, he defeated the Jandarids, taking part of their lands. In Europe he restored some measure of Ottoman authority to Albania and Wallachia and raided the Morea, Bosnia, and Hungary. Venice, however, defeated the fledgling Ottoman fleet in 1416. Far more serious was the domestic discord which marked his later years: the bid for power of the "Pretender Mustafa," who claimed to be a son of Bāyazīd. Defeated, Mustafa fled to Byzantium in 1416 (only to surface after Mehmed's death). Despite setbacks, Mehmed persevered during his rule and began the work of Ottoman restoration.

BIBLIOGRAPHY

John W. Barker, *Manuel II Palaeologus (1391–1425)* (1969); Dukas (Ducas, Doukas), *Historia Turco-byzantina,* V. Grecu, ed. (1958), translated into English as *Decline and*

MEHMED (MUḤAMMAD) II

Fall of Byzantium to the Ottoman Turks, Harry J. Magoulias, trans. (1975); İsmail Hakkı Uzunçarşılı, "Mehmed I," in *İslām Ansiklopedisi,* VII, 496–506, and *Osmanlı tarihi,* I (1972); Hans J. Kissling, "Das Menāqybnāme Scheich Bedr ed-Dīns, des Sohnes des Richters von Samāvna," in *Zeitschrift der deutschen morgenländischen Gesellschaft,* **100** (1950); Paul Wittek, "De la défaite d'Ankara à la prise de Constantinople," in *Revue des études islamiques,* **12** (1938), and *Das fürstentum Mentesche* (1934).

PETER B. GOLDEN

[See also **Anatolia; Bâyazid I, Yildirim; Ghâzī; Karamania; Ottomans; Tamerlane.**]

MEHMED (MUḤAMMAD) II (reigned 1444–1446, 1451–1481), Ottoman sultan, in Turkish *Fâtih Mehmed,* Mehmed the Conqueror, a distinction earned by his conquest of Constantinople. His father, Murād II (1421–1444, 1446–1451), brought him to the throne at the age of fifteen in the hope of averting the customary succession struggle. Internal discord and the Crusade of Varna (1444), however, obliged Murād to resume the sultanate.

Ascending the throne again in 1451, Mehmed immediately set about undermining the powerful grand vizier Halil Pashsa Çandarlı (Candarlı), who represented the old Turkish beys and who had gained some measure of control over the Janissaries. Given the increasing role of classical Islamic institutions in the Ottoman state, control of the Janissaries would be crucial.

Mehmed, wishing to establish his authority, undertook a feat that would make him undisputed master not only among Turks but also within the larger Muslim world: the conquest of Constantinople. Despite considerable opposition from Halil Pasha and the "peace" party, the Byzantine capital was taken on 29 May 1453, completing the transformation of the Ottoman state from a Turkish principality founded by religious warriors to a world empire. The conquest set in motion a series of ideological claims regarding the dynasty's place in the world. Mehmed encouraged a glorification of his family's Turkic heritage, which was aimed at Genghisid and Timurid elements as well as Turkoman chiefs and beys. Following old Turko-Mongolian traditions of the *Qaghan* as the fount of law, he began the codification of Ottoman "secular" law (as opposed to religious and family, which remained in the hands of the caliph). These ideological claims extended beyond the borders of the Turko-Muslim world. In effect, Mehmed had succeeded to the throne of the Greco-Roman emperors and was to be considered the ruler of a universal empire.

It was Mehmed's vision of his role as *khan* (emperor of the Turkic nomadic steppes), *ghāzī* (fighter for Islam), and *basileus* (Byzantine emperor) that made possible the millet system that protected the ethnoreligious minorities. This same vision also required the removal of all challenges to his authority. Domestically, this meant the accession of Zaganos Pasha (from the *devşirme:* tribute of children) to the vizierate, replacing Halil Pasha Çandarlı, and the closer binding of the Janissaries to the sultan. Abroad, it signaled a policy of converting onetime vassal territories into provinces of the empire. Mehmed campaigned incessantly in the Balkans, Danubian Europe, and Anatolia, and on the sea against Venice (with which he fought a sixteen-year war ending in 1479). At the end of his reign, most of Serbia, Albania, Herzegovina, and parts of Bosnia and mainland Greece (including Athens and the Peloponnese) had been taken. The Karaman beylik (in southeastern Anatolia) and Trebizond, all that remained of the Byzantine Empire on the Black Sea, had been extinguished, and Uzun Ḥasan of the Aq Qoyunlu (in eastern Anatolia) had been badly defeated. Venice recognized the Ottoman hold on the Balkans and paid tribute. The way was prepared for Turkish advances into Danubian Europe, and the vassal Crimean khanate would be used against Poland and Muscovy. At Mehmed's death, assaults against Italy and the island of Rhodes were under way.

The constant warfare constituted an enormous burden that nullified Mehmed's attempts to improve the economy. It led to the debasement of coinage, the farming out of state-created monopolies, and a sharpening of social problems.

BIBLIOGRAPHY

Sources. Ducas (Doukas), *Istoria turco-byzantina,* Vasile Grecu, ed. (1958), trans. by Harry J. Margolias as *Decline and Fall of Byzantium to the Ottoman Turks* (1975); Kritovoulos, *Fragmenta historicorum Graecorum,* C. Müller, ed., I (1883), 52–164, trans. by Charles T. Riggs as *The History of Mehmed the Conqueror by Kritovoulos* (1954).

Studies. For detailed bibliographies of Turkish sources, see the journal *Fātih ve İstanbul Dergisi.* See also Franz Babinger, *Mehmed the Conqueror and His Times,* Ralph Mannheim, trans., William C. Hickman, ed. (1978); Halil İnalcik, *Fātih Devri Üzerinde tetkikler ve vesikalar* (1954); Stephen Runciman, *The Fall of Constantinople* (1965); Salahaddin Tansel, *Osmanlı Kaynaklarına göre Fātih Sultan Mehmed'in Siyasī ve Askerī Faāliyeti* (1954).

PETER B. GOLDEN

[See also **Byzantine Empire, History; Constantinople; Janissary; Murād II; Ottomans; Seljuks.**]

MEILYR BRYDYDD (*fl. ca.* 1100–*ca.* 1137), chief court poet *(pencerdd)* to Gruffudd ap Cynan, ruler of Gwynedd (North Wales), at Aberffraw. He is traditionally regarded as the earliest of the *Gogynfeirdd,* the professional court poets who composed eulogies and elegies in honor of the Welsh princes of the twelfth and thirteenth centuries. Three poems ascribed to him survive: an elegy to his patron, Gruffudd (*d.* 1137); a deathbed song *(marwysgafn);* and an elegy to Trahaearn ap Caradog and Meilyr ap Rhiwallon (both slain in 1081). The authorship of the latter is doubted, as both its meter and its prophetic content belong to a lower grade of poet than *pencerdd.*

In his elegy to Gruffudd ap Cynan, Meilyr set the example that the poets of the other princes were to follow. Continuing the ancient tradition, Meilyr extols the same heroic ideal of kingship as the earliest Welsh poetry, upholding the dominant virtues of bravery and generosity and rejoicing in his close relationship with his patron. These themes, however, are presented in a far more detailed form than by earlier poets, and are embellished by complex metrical devices and expressed in a deliberately archaic diction. Thus Meilyr achieved a new degree of dignity in praise poetry that befitted the resurgent dynasty in Gwynedd. The *marwysgafn* gave Meilyr a vehicle for expressing his personal feelings and individuality. With refreshing sincerity he confesses his sins and begs God's mercy, recollecting the worldly rewards that mortal kings formerly gave him. The poem ends with a wish to be buried on Bardsey, described in lines of great beauty.

Meilyr's son, Gwalchmai, succeeded him as *pencerdd* at Aberffraw, and his grandsons also composed verse—one of the few examples in Wales of a family of poets. As part payment of their court duties, Meilyr and his son could expect to be given land, which may explain the Anglesey place-names Trefeilyr and Trewalchmai.

BIBLIOGRAPHY

Alexander French, "Meilyr's Elegy for Gruffudd ap Cynan," in *Études celtiques,* **16** (1979); A. O. H. Jarman and Gwilym Rees Hughes, eds., *A Guide to Welsh Literature,* I (1976), 157–188; David Myrddin Lloyd, *Rhai Agweddau ar Ddysg y Gogynfeirdd* (1976, 1977); John Ellis Caerwyn Williams, *Canu Crefyddol y Gogynfeirdd* (1977), and *The Poets of the Welsh Princes* (1978).

RHIAN M. ANDREWS

[See also **Gruffudd Ap Cynan; Welsh Literature.**]

MEINLOH VON SEVELINGEN (*fl. ca.* 1170–1180), an early minnesinger, seems to have been a member of a family from Söflingen near Ulm. The family is documented from 1220, and one Meinloh is attested in 1240. Meinloh's songs are preserved in two manuscripts, *B* (*ca.* 1300) and *C* (*ca.* 1325); the former contains eleven strophes and the latter fourteen. Numerous parallels in verse form (long-line couplets), rhyme technique (slant rhymes), language, and some of the themes and roles (especially in the three woman's songs) between Meinloh's songs and those attributed to Der von Kürenberg, the Burggraf von Regensburg, and (to an extent) Dietmar von Aist have led scholars to assume a Danubian school flourishing in the third quarter of the twelfth century. Since Meinloh was clearly acquainted with Provençal song and his technique of content, presentation, and development was more intellectual than that of Der von Kürenberg and less so than that of Reinmar von Hagenau, he has been considered a transitional figure and his songs have been dated from the decade 1170 to 1180. According to some scholars, several songs contain borrowings from Andreas Capellanus, which would date them toward the end of the century, if not later. However, the similarities between Meinloh and Andreas may stem from a common desire to explore a wide range of love situations. Several references to the suitor as a childish man and an outspoken desire for love as a horizontal pastime lend an individual accent to what is basically conventional love poetry.

The fourteen strophes in *C* have been interpreted by Schweikle as four triads (with formally heterogeneous strophes) plus a two-strophe song—other scholars have rearranged (and sometimes rewritten) the strophes to arrive at other cycles and/or at multiple-strophe songs. Schweikle's advocacy of *C,* which includes a hypothesis that the rhyme modernization often found in this manuscript reflects the singer's acceptance of prevailing fashion, discounts the sporadic disdain for meter exhibited by the *C*-scribe (who does not restrict his innovations to the rhymes). Nevertheless, *B* does tend to support the order in *C*, and Ittenbach's rejection of multiple-strophe songs or groups of strophes does not take into account that individual strophes, though they may be ideationally autonomous, are scarcely long enough to stand by themselves as courtly entertainments. The best critical approach may be to eschew editorial rearrangements and emendations, but to admit that alternative performance situations would have changed an audience's perceptions of the strophes' meaning.

BIBLIOGRAPHY

Max Ittenbach, *Der frühe deutsche Minnesang: Strophenfügung und Dichtersprache* (1939); Elisabeth Lea, "Die Sprache lyrischer Grundgefëge: MFr. 11, 1–15, 17," in *Beiträge zur Geschichte der deutschen Sprache und Literatur,* **90** (1968); Hugo Moser and Helmut Tervooren, *Des Minnesangs Frühling,* 2 vols. (1977); Karl-Heinz Schirmer, "Die höfische Minnetheorie und Meinloh von Sevelingen," in Karl-Heinz Schirmer and Bernhard Sowinski, eds., *Zeiten und Formen in Sprache und Dichtung: Festschrift für Fritz Tschirch zum 70. Geburtstag* (1972); Gunther Schweikle, *Die mittelhochdeutsche Minnelyrik* (1977); Franz Taiana, *Amor purus und die Minne* (1977); Helmut Tervooren, *Bibliographie zum Minnesang und zu Dichtern aus "Des Minnesangs Frühling"* (1969).

HUBERT HEINEN

[See also **Capellanus, Andreas; Der von Kürenberg; Dietmar von Aist; Minnesingers; Reinmar von Hagenau.**]

MEINZO OF CONSTANCE (*fl.* mid eleventh century) was a teacher of mathematics at Constance and a pupil of Hermann of Reichenau (1013–1054). He is known only as the author of a letter to Hermann (dated 1048) asking for a more detailed explanation of the relationship between the diameter and the circumference of a circle.

BIBLIOGRAPHY

Ernst Dümmler, "Ein Schreiben Meinzos von Constanz an Hermann den Lahmen," in *Neues Archiv der Gesellschaft für ältere deutsche Geschichtskunde,* 5 (1880), 202–206; Claudia Kren, "Herman the Lame," in *Dictionary of Scientific Biography,* VI (1972), 301; Max Manitius, *Geschichte der lateinischen Literatur des Mittelalters,* II (1923), 786–787.

W. T. H. JACKSON

[See also **Herman of Reichenau; Mathematics.**]

MEISTER BERTRAM. See **Bertram, Meister.**

MEISTER ECKHART. See **Eckhart, Meister.**

MEIT, CONRAD (*fl.* 1496–1550), German sculptor. A native of Worms, Meit was a refined carver of both stone and luxury materials. He was a favorite in the imperial courts of both Germany and the

Judith. Alabaster statuette (29.5 cm/11.6 in high) by Conrad Meit, *ca.* 1510–1515. BAYERISCHES NATIONALMUSEUM, MUNICH

Netherlands, especially in that of Margaret of Austria (1520–1530) at Malines (southern Netherlands). A signed alabaster *Judith* (*ca.* 1510–1515) is an early indication of the full-bodied, sensuous nudes that recall those of Albrecht Dürer—also active at the imperial courts—and are typical of Meit's Italianate forms. He also produced portrait busts; his magnum opus is a marble and alabaster tomb complex for Margaret at Brou (St. Nicolas de Tolentin, 1526–1532).

BIBLIOGRAPHY

Josef Duverger, *Conrat Meijt* (1934); Constance Lowenthal, "Conrad Meit's *Judith* and a Putto at Brou," in *Marsyas,* **16** (1972–1973), and "Conrad Meit" (diss., NYU, 1976); Jörg Rasmussen, "Eine Gruppe kleinplastischer Bildwerke aus dem Stilkreis des Conrat Meit," in *Städel-Jahrbuch,* **4** (1973); Georg Troescher, *Conrat Meit von Worms* (1927); Wilhelm Vöge, "Konrad Meit und die Grabdenkmäler in Brou," in *Jahrbuch der königlichen preuszischen Kunstsammlungen,* **29** (1908); Friedrich Winkler, "Konrad Meits Tätigkeit in Deutschland," in *Jahrbuch der preuszischen Kunstsammlungen,* **45** (1924).

LARRY SILVER

MEKNES (Arabic: Miknās/Miknāsa; French: Méquinez), a town of medieval origin located in north-central Morocco at the intersection of routes between Salé (and Rabat) and Fēs and between the Tafilalt oasis, beyond the Atlas mountains in the south, and the northern coastal cities on the Atlantic Ocean. The medieval city was situated on the side of a ridge commanding the eastern end of a plateau separating the last of the Middle Atlas range in the south from the Zarhūn mountains to the north. The river that supplies the town and waters the surrounding countryside is a tributary of the Sebou and is known now as the Wādī Bū Fikrān. The area around Meknes is among the most fertile and best watered in Morocco and long has been known for its olives, fruits, cereals, vegetables, and flax, although not all these crops are grown today.

Meknes lies nineteen miles (thirty kilometers) south of Volubilis, the important inland town of the Roman province of Mauretania Tingitana. The ancient Greeks had known of that area of Morocco for its exotic animals and plants, but the Romans developed it into a producer of cereals, olives, olive oil, and grapes; Flavius Josephus labeled Mauretania one of Rome's granaries. While no evidence exists for a settlement of Meknes during the Roman period, its proximity to Volubilis and its position commanding an avenue of approach to latifundia for raiders from the interior make it likely that at least an outpost existed then.

The Meknes area appears to have been inhabited continuously and to have remained under fairly regular agricultural exploitation into medieval times. The Muslim geographers Ibn Ḥawqal (late tenth century) and al-Bakrī (mid eleventh century) do not mention specific settlements in the Meknes area, but both mention the Miknāsa Berbers, from whom the town later took its name. The first mention is by al-Idrīsi, who in the mid twelfth century identifies a town called "Taqarart" between Fēs and Salé, which is inhabited by Miknāsa. "Taqarart" appears to have been one of several tribal settlements located close to one another in the area, which were united by the erection of a citadel late in the eleventh century, after the Almoravids had conquered the area and its people. Ibn Tūmart, the spiritual founder of the Almohads, passed through Miknāsa, by then a town, in 1120–1121 en route from Fēs to Marrakech and is said to have met with a poor reception there. His successor, ᶜAbd al-Muᵓmin, ordered the walled town to be besieged in the 1140's and after a siege lasting a reputed seven years, Meknes fell to the Almohads in 1150.

The Almohads sacked and leveled the town, and many of the remaining inhabitants were enslaved. In a departure from usual Muslim practice, many Jews, who had lived in the area since Roman times, were forced to convert to Islam. The Almohads rebuilt the city, but sovereignty over it was contested by the Marinids, who conquered the city in 1247–1248. The Marinids, too, appear to have persecuted the Jews with great severity.

The Marinid emir Abū Yūsuf Yaᶜqūb ibn ᶜAbd al-Ḥaqq (*r.* 1258–1286) around 1275 initiated the construction of a fortified, walled complex that included a citadel and a mosque. This and other construction programs throughout the Marinid period raised the city to the rank of first importance in Morocco (reaching a peak in the seventeenth century when the Sharifian ruler, Mawley Ismāᶜīl, made it his capital). But the importance of Meknes throughout the medieval period was due to the rich agriculture of the surrounding area. While its cereal crops and olive groves suffered frequently from the depredations of marauders and conquerors, the agricultural wealth of the city made it a favorite prize. In addition, the nearness of Meknes to Fēs and its geographical position astride the routes to the Atlantic ports made its control indispensable to the rulers of Fēs.

BIBLIOGRAPHY

Maurice Besnier, "La géographie économique du Maroc dans l'antiquité," in *Archives marocaines,* 7 (1906); Charles-André Julien, *History of North Africa: Tunisia, Algeria, Morocco,* R. Le Tourneau, ed. and rev., John Petrie, trans., C. C. Stewart, ed. (1970).

JAMES L. YARRISON

[See also **Almohads; Fēs; Maghrib, Al-; Marinids.**]

MELCHITES. A term used to designate those Christians from Syria, Palestine, and Egypt who adhered to the decrees of the Council of Chalcedon (451). In Greek, the designation for this group by their Monophysite opponents was *basilikos,* that is, imperialists, those who supported the religious settlement espoused and enforced by the imperial governments of the emperor Marcian and his orthodox successors. At some point, *basilikos* was translated into Syriac as *malkāyā,* from *malkā* (meaning "king" or "emperor"). The earliest recorded use of the word is by Dionysius bar Salibi about 1160. It was used in the thirteenth and fourteenth centuries by Syriac authors to embrace all members of the Greek and Latin churches. Around the twelfth century, the Syriac word was borrowed by Greek writers who transcribed the letter *kaf* with a *chi,* thus producing the Greek form, *Melchitai.*

After the Arab conquest of the Near East, the Melchite party, shorn of imperial support and opposed by the Monophysite majority, began to decline. Except for brief periods when the Byzantines regained lost territory, as at Antioch from 969–1078, the old patriarchates of Antioch, Jerusalem, and Alexandria lost their significance and became increasingly dependent on Constantinople. The patriarchs were often shadowy figures and many of them never resided in their sees. Following the Great Schism of 1054, the Melchites maintained communion with Constantinople and removed the pope's name from the diptychs. By the beginning of the thirteenth century, Antioch, Jerusalem, and Alexandria had replaced their local liturgies with that of Constantinople. The term Melchite is no longer used to designate Eastern Orthodox, but instead designates the Greek Catholics of Syria, Palestine, and Egypt.

BIBLIOGRAPHY

A. Fortescue, *The Uniate Eastern Churches* (1923).

D. W. JOHNSON

[See also **Byzantine Church; Councils (Ecumenical, 325–787); Monophysitism; Syrian Christianity.**]

MELFI, CONSTITUTIONS OF. The code of laws promulgated by the Hohenstaufen emperor Frederick II for the kingdom of Sicily in 1231 remained the fundamental law of the kingdom until the Napoleonic period. Compiled by Piero della Vigna, judge of the royal court, and other legal experts, this collection is divided into three books. Book one deals with the origins of royal authority and the functions of royal officials. Book two covers civil and criminal procedure, including penalties for their violation. Book three contains feudal law, regulations of professions and crafts, and the punishment of criminal acts. Based on Roman, Byzantine, Lombard, and Norman law, as well as on the canon law of the church, the Constitutions of Melfi were designed to support the strong monarchy envisioned for the kingdom of Sicily by Frederick II, who saw in it the linchpin of his imperial program in Italy. His laws are striking for their effort to systematize the structures of his government, particularly the royal courts. He attempted to break through the network of local authorities impeding effective royal administration and worked to preserve the integrity of the royal demesne and the rights of the crown. Of particular interest is his public health legislation, probably the first of its kind in Western Europe. This *Liber Augustalis,* as modern scholars have often termed it, stands as a major witness to the legal revival of the twelfth and thirteenth centuries.

BIBLIOGRAPHY

Hermann Conrad *et al., Die Konstituzionen Friedrichs II. von Hohenstaufen für sein Königreich Sizilien* (1973); Hermann Dilcher, *Die sizilische Gesetzgebung Kaiser Friedrichs II.: Quellen der Constitutionen von Melfi und ihrer Novellen* (1975); James M. Powell, trans. and ed., *The Liber Augustalis; or, Constitutions of Melfi* (1971).

JAMES M. POWELL

[See also **Frederick II of the Holy Roman Empire; Germany; Sicily, Kingdom of.**]

MELIOR ET YDOINE, an anonymous Anglo-Norman debate poem surviving in an early-fourteenth-century manuscript. The ladies Melior and Ydoine discuss whether it is better to love a knight or a clerk. Acting as their champions, two birds bring the debate before a turtle-dove acting as judge and fight a judiciary duel. The outcome favors the clerk, as in most of the medieval debate poems on the same topic.

BIBLIOGRAPHY

For the text, see Paul Meyer, *"Melior et Ydoine,"* in *Romania,* 37 (1908). See also Charles Oulmont, *Les débats du clerc et du chevalier dans la littérature poétique de moyen âge* (1911).

ELLEN T. WEHNER

[See also **Anglo-Norman Literature; Débat.**]

MELISMA, a Greek word meaning "song" applying strictly to vocal music. Medieval singing was, at one extreme, "syllabic," the inflected recitation of language, with one note per syllable, and at another, an extended flow of melody on a single phoneme. Any such span of melody sung on a single phoneme is called a melisma. In the case of syllabic singing (such as the tones for the singing of the psalms) melody was strictly in the service of the text. In melismatic singing (such as the long vocalise or jubilus of an alleluia) the expressive and, in appropriate situations, ritual purposes of the song were served directly by the melody itself. Thus St. Augustine wrote that singing without words expressed a joy too deep for words.

Among the identifying characteristics of the genres of liturgical chant in all medieval traditions are the degree to which the chants of the genre are melismatic or syllabic and the normal place of melismas within the chant. And given conventions about the positioning of melismas, the genres developed specific standard melismas. These could be transferred from one chant to another and, ironically, were sometimes separated from their chants and provided with a new text in a syllabic setting. Such fixed melismas were also used throughout the Middle Ages in the West as grounds, or tenors, for the construction of new polyphonic compositions. So what had started as a rather free and expressive melodic practice, ended as a building block in a formalistic compositional practice.

BIBLIOGRAPHY

Richard L. Crocker, "Melisma," in *New Grove Dictionary of Music and Musicians,* XII (1980), 105–106; Michel Huglo, *Les tonaires* (1971).

LEO TREITLER

[See also **Ars Antiqua; Clausula; Motet.**]

MELITENE (Turkish and Arabic: Malatya), a city in Asia Minor (38°22′ N. × 38°18′ E.). The ancient strategic and commercial importance of Melitene was increased in the first century, when it became the base of a Roman legion. In late antiquity, it was a capital of Armenia and the seat of orthodox and Jacobite (Monophysite) archbishops. Refortified by Anastasius and Justinian, it was burned by Xusrō I in 575 and first attacked by the Arabs in 635. Under Arab rule (656–934), Melitene was a major garrison town, the headquarters for raids against the Byzantines and thus an object of their retaliation. It was frequently damaged and restored before enjoying a long period of prosperous Byzantine rule (934–1074), when it was the seat of the commander of the southeastern frontier. After the city was captured and burned by Turks in 1058, the emperor Constantine X Doukas had its fortifications rebuilt, but to little avail, as the population failed to resist the invaders. During a chaotic period (1068–1102), Melitene was defended by Armenians against Greeks, Turks, and crusaders, until it fell to the Danishmendids, who maintained themselves through bitter struggles until finally yielding to the Seljuks in 1178. New elements appeared with the attacks of Turkoman tribes in 1185 and the Mongols in 1231. After 1243, the city was generally ruled by the Mongols through Seljuk princes until shortly before it was taken and devastated in 1315 by the Mamluks, who made it the headquarters of a frontier province. Although Bāyazīd I captured it in 1391 and Tamerlane in 1400, Melitene was mostly ruled by the Dulgadir Turks under Mamluk suzerainty until the final Ottoman conquest in 1516.

Melitene was a great center of Syriac culture, the home of the historians Michael the Syrian (1126–1199) and Bar Hebraeus (1226–1286). Numerous destructions have left little of the medieval city beside the Byzantine walls, which incorporate those of the Roman camp, and the Great Mosque of the thirteenth century.

BIBLIOGRAPHY

Claude Cahen, *Pre-Ottoman Turkey,* J. Jones-Williams, trans. (1968); Albert Gabriel, *Voyages archéologiques dans la Turquie orientale* (1940); Friedrich Hild and Marcell Restle, *Tabula imperii byzantini,* II, *Kappadokien* (1981).

CLIVE FOSS

[See also **Armenia, Geography; Bar Hebraeus; Danishmendids; Michael the Syrian; Monophysitism; Seljuks of Rum.**]

MELKITES. See **Melchites.**

MELODY. Most medieval music was monophonic, a single line of pure melody; accompaniment, if any, was extremely simple and probably extemporized, and thus can be ignored here. Any understanding of medieval music, then, must be based on an appreciation of melodic styles of the period. Since harmony, accompaniment, and (usually) rhythm are lacking, theorists have always found it extremely difficult to describe how melody works, especially when the customs of the time allow, perhaps entail, ornamentation and variation of a tune, often connected with an oral transmission in which there is no written form of the melodies from which to derive a rational analysis. Variation and rearrangement of formulas were common methods of adapting one tune to serve another purpose, and deciding when a tune changes into a different tune in this process is usually a matter of musical intuition. So too is any detailed attempt to separate ornament from structure, to distinguish stable pitches from those that need resolution in some sense, and to relate all these factors to some system of tonal organization. Notation, phrasing, method of performance, and the manner in which the text is set, no doubt have at least a psychological effect on the perception of melody, but not on its ultimate reduction to a series of pitches.

We can distinguish five melodic styles, roughly associated with (1) plainsong of the so-called standard repertory, (2) secular song, (3) the prosa or sequence, (4) the hymn, and (5) later plainsong. Plainsong is generally thought to meander, to use a pejorative modern term. It rarely moves in one direction for more than a note or two, and prefers movement by step and by third, with very few large leaps. This circling may originate in decoration of a monotone reciting pitch. A step and a third in the same direction outline a fourth and are part of the pentatonic scale, which seems to underlie much medieval melody. The range is small, fundamentally a seventh; the octave is not an important pitch. In general, melodies move in an archlike form with few noticeable points of musical articulation. Both exact and sequential repetition within a tune, even of small motives, are always avoided. The repertory consists essentially of melodies of fundamentally oriental quality transformed, through the Christian church, from an orally transmitted form to a Western, written form. To categorize these melodies, theorists evolved a system of modes, partly using Greek examples. Defining a reciting pitch, a final pitch, and a range with respect to them, these theoretical patterns match the actual repertory more or less well for most tunes. Some melodic motives are associated with specific modes, and some with more than one mode; thus each mode has an audible melodic character. The restraint and lack of articulation and direction contribute to a sense of ineffable worship.

Secular songs, of which few are known before the twelfth century, are not categorized by the modal system, even by medieval theorists. Some are like plainsongs; a few are known to have been adaptations of plainsong, and thus the same melodic styles occur in this repertory. But there are also other methods of organizing the pitches: successive thirds in the same direction, later called a triad, are noticeable, and cause the third and the fifth to be stressed somewhat more; the modern major scale, with its stress on the fifth and octave, is almost as common as the pentatonic scale; in addition, chains of thirds in the same direction (such as D-F-A-C) seem to form the skeletal structure of some melodies. Repetitive melodic motives and phrases occur, and open and closed phrases strengthen a feeling of directed movement, so that articulation by means of cadential patterns is sometimes clear. These and other qualities of secular tunes are thought by some scholars to be characteristics more of European folk music in contrast to the oriental qualities of plainsong. When these qualities are found in plainsong, we may have evidence for the separation of a later layer of plainsong.

Hymns are known to be compositions of Western origin; prosae melodies mostly date from between the ninth and thirteenth centuries. Their different melodic style, long recognized, has not been analyzed much. Although the two genres have some similarities in melodic style, some differences can be observed. Both have clearly articulated phrases, and thus clear cadences, which lend a strong sense of direction. The cadence form, especially in the prosa, consists of a step up to a repeated pitch, quite different from the descending cadence of plainsong. As with secular song, phrases and motives of these genres are often the same as those of plainsong. Some hymns can easily be assigned to one of the plainsong modes; many cannot, and seem to have characteristics of the secular style. In others, modal phrases seem to have been transposed to unusual pitches, sometimes phrase by phrase, so that each phrase is independently modal and the whole tune has conflicting modal effects. In the prosa fewer phrases have a true modal flavor, and some prosae cannot properly be assigned to a mode; this is perhaps because the genre is so predominantly syllabic in its text setting that the modal formula has become unrecognizable when changed from an ornamental group of notes, in which many are subordinate, to a series of individual pitches, each more or less equal in strength (Ex. 1). Each phrase has quite a small range, as in the hymn, but in contrast to the hymn, successive phrases are often in quite distinct ranges, so that the total range of the composition is larger.

In the later compositions of plainsong, from the twelfth century concentrated in proper offices, many of the characteristics of secular music, hymns, and prosae are incorporated into a melodic framework which is essentially that of modal plainsong, and clearly recognizable as such. All the plainsong modes occur, although often with greatly extended range, and the major scale is also frequent; the modal formulas are retained, although now used in a clearly articulated series of phrases. Larger leaps are more common, and some tunes are very extravagant; the range of individual phrases is often distinct, although the overall arch shape is usual. All of these characteristics create a genre recognizable as plainsong, but with a clarity of form, direction, and tonal assignation that makes it explicit, and thus quite different from the circuitous, circumlocutory, and symbolic style of the standard repertory. The character of the texts is one factor responsible for this change in style.

As the Middle Ages gradually moved into the Renaissance, polyphonic music occupied the attention of composers more and more, and composition of all kinds of monophony decreased. Since polyphonic forms are outgrowths of plainsong, their melodic style was originally dependent on plainsong. At first, composers were concerned with harmony and rhythm, essentials of polyphony, and accepted the current melodic styles where that was possible, or merely allowed the melody to be dictated by the needs of the harmony, so that it had little integrity of its own. Only when the other fundamentals of polyphony were mastered did composers begin to consider how their harmonic compositions might be made melodically attractive. A case can be made that melodic beauty, as we know it, appeared in part music only with Guillaume Dufay and John Dunstable in the early fifteenth century.

BIBLIOGRAPHY

Andrew Hughes, *Medieval Music: The Sixth Liberal Art,* in *Toronto Medieval Bibliographies,* IV (1974, rev. ed. 1980); Curt Sachs, "Primitive and Medieval Music: A Parallel," in *Journal of the American Musicological Society,* 13 (1960).

ANDREW HUGHES

[See also **Hymns; Mode; Monophony; Music, Popular; Plainsong, Sources of; Rhymed Offices; Sequence.**]

MEMLING, HANS (Memlinc) (*ca.* 1433–1494), Flemish painter, was considered "the most accomplished and excellent painter of the whole Christian world" by his contemporaries. He was born in Seligenstadt in the Rhineland and was influenced by Rogier van der Weyden, for whom he may have worked as an apprentice-assistant in Brussels sometime between 1460 and 1465. In that year he moved to Bruges, where he soon established himself as the leading painter. His early works (*Adoration of the Magi* triptych, Madrid, Prado) are dependent on compositions learned in van der Weyden's shop, but gradually he tempered Rogier's expressive monumentality with the richness and refinement of van Eyck's detailed realism. Memling repeated a number

Example 1

hypothetical
Ma-ri - a Vir-go
Vic- ti - me Pas-cha - li lau - des im - mo - lent Chris - ti - a - ni

Mystical Marriage of St. Catherine. Panel painting by Hans Memling for the Hospital of St. John, Bruges, 1479. ART RESOURCE

of his compositions with the Madonna and Child enthroned in an elaborate loggia with two angels, one usually playing a musical instrument, standing on either side (Berlin, Florence, London, Washington). His most famous works were painted for the Hospital of St. John in Bruges. A huge triptych dedicated to the two St. Johns with the *Mystical Marriage of St. Catherine of Alexandria* as a centerpiece is an elaboration of the enthroned Madonna and Child compositions. The Shrine of Saint Ursula (Bruges, St. John's Hospital) has six panels illustrating the legend of Ursula placed on the sides of a church-like reliquary. Memling was also renowned for his elegant portraits, which were sometimes paired with a representation of the Madonna and Child. By the time of his death, he was one of the wealthiest citizens of Bruges. He had many followers.

BIBLIOGRAPHY

Max J. Friedländer, *Early Netherlandish Painting,* Heinze Norden, trans., VI (1971); Kenneth B. McFarlane, *Hans Memling* (1971).

JAMES SNYDER

[See also **Flemish Painting; Weyden, Rogier van der.**]

MENA, JUAN DE (1411–1456), one of the two great Castilian poets of the first half of the fifteenth century—Iñigo López de Mendoza, marquess of Santillana, was the other—and among contemporaries the more admired of the two. A dedicated intellectual, Mena studied at Salamanca, and possibly at Rome, and became an accomplished Latinist with a first-hand knowledge of Vergil and Lucan, authors whose works influenced him. He joined the court as the king's secretary for Latin letters and was later appointed one of the chroniclers in charge of writing the history of the reign. This chronicle he never wrote; instead, in his *Laberinto de Fortuna* (1444), he wrote what he wished John II to accomplish during his reign: a government in keeping with the imperatives of the four cardinal virtues, the peaceful coexistence of the Christian princes within the peninsula, and the completion of the Reconquest.

From the point of view of its structure, the *Laberinto* probably surpasses in complexity anything written up to that time in the vernacular languages of Western Europe. The action progresses simultaneously on both a fictional and a historical level: the historical one is contemporary Castile, while the fictional one corresponds to the poet's imagined experience, which is in itself an interpretation of history—an exploration of past and present with the hope of influencing the future.

As history and fiction are synthesized in the *Laberinto,* light and darkness (easy and difficult poetry) appear combined in a poem titled precisely *Claroescuro,* and calamity and glory in another one written to honor Iñigo López de Mendoza, *La coronación del Marqués de Santillana.* The title of the latter is also known as *Calamicleos,* from the Greek *cleos* (glory) and the Latin *calamitas.* The frequent use of Latin syntactic constructions and Latin words in these poems confirms the author's concern with binary oppositions and with the possibility of reducing or even canceling them. The same concern is suggested by his use of two recognizable styles: the so-called second style would belong to the poems already mentioned, while the first and easier one would belong to his love songs and *cancionero* poems written in strict accordance with contemporary poetic convention.

This preoccupation of Mena's with synthesis and dualities may reflect the schizoid nature of his time, when a new poetic manner imported from Italy was beginning to conflict with the established one, and when aspirations of future glory made many feel that imperial Rome and its Latin had to be projected upon Castile and its language. A poem entitled *Coplas de los siete pecados mortales* (Verses concerning the Seven Deadly Sins), begun late in life, was left unfinished. The fact that it is almost free of latinisms suggests that he may have awakened from his Castilian dreams of glory before he died.

Mena is not an important prose writer. He did however, make a translation of the *Ilias latina* known as the *Homero romanceado,* and a commentary to his *Calamicleos.*

BIBLIOGRAPHY

Luis Beltrán, "The Poet, the King, and the Cardinal Virtues in Juan de Mena's *Laberinto,*" in *Speculum,* **46** (1971); María Rosa Lida de Malkiel, *Juan de Mena, poeta del prerrenacimiento español* (1950); Inez Macdonald, "The *Coronación* of Juan de Mena: Poem and Commentary," in *Hispanic Review,* 7 (1939); Florence Street, "La vida de Juan de Mena," in *Bulletin hispanique,* 55 (1953).

LUIS BELTRÁN

[See also **Castile; Santillana, Marqués de; Spanish Literature; Vergil in the Middle Ages.**]

MENANDER PROTECTOR (*fl.* second half of sixth century), early Byzantine historian whose *History* has been preserved only in fragments. In the preamble Menander described his life in detail and emphasized his change from laziness and dissolute behavior to scholarly activity, a change that he ascribed to the beneficial influence of the emperor Maurice (582–602) and his court. The title of *protiktor* implies that Menander received the position of palace guardsman. Encompassing the period 558–582, the *History* was designed as a continuation of the historical work of Agathius (*ca.* 531–*ca.* 580). The preserved fragments deal mostly with the relations between the empire and its neighbors (Persians, Huns, Avars, and others). Menander widely used official and semiofficial documents, such as the relation by Peter the Patrician (*d.* 565) of his diplomatic missions. Unlike Procopius, whom he admired, Menander was a loyal supporter of the imperial regime; he remained, however, lukewarm toward Christianity and tolerant of heterodox opinions.

BIBLIOGRAPHY

The History of Menander the Guardsman, R. C. Blockley, ed. (1985), English trans. with commentary. See also B. Baldwin, "Menander Protector," in *Dumbarton Oaks Papers,* **32** (1978).

ALEXANDER P. KAZHDAN

[See also **Agathius; Historiography, Byzantine; Procopius.**]

MENDICANT ORDERS. Those religious orders (Augustinians, Carmelites, Franciscans, and Dominicans) which, when founded in the early thirteenth century, were committed by vow to a life of absolute evangelical poverty in voluntary imitation of the poverty and humility of Christ and the Apostles. So called from *mendicare* (to beg), they had to work or beg for their food and clothing; and unlike monks, they were itinerant preachers, not bound to one convent by a vow of "stability." Their privilege of preaching and hearing confessions without having to seek episcopal consent aroused fierce hostility from the bishops and secular clergy, until its scope was limited by Boniface VIII in 1300.

BIBLIOGRAPHY

Bonaventure, *The Works of Bonaventure,* IV, *Defense of the Mendicants,* José de Vinck, trans. (1966); Rosalind Brooke, *The Coming of the Friars* (1975), which contains valuable bibliographical notes and documents in translation; Decima L. Douie, *The Conflict Between the Seculars and the Mendicants at the University of Paris in the Thirteenth Century* (1954); Lester K. Little, *Religious Poverty and the Profit Economy in Medieval Europe* (1978), 146–169.

BERNARD CULLEN

[See also **Augustinian Friars; Beguines and Beghards; Carmelites; Church, Latin; Dominicans; Franciscans.**]

MENOLOGION, a series of biographies of saints arranged in liturgical order, one for each day of the year, often accompanied by pictures. Most illustrated menologia appear after Metaphrastes' textual edition of the second half of the tenth century, though the pictures often seem to rely on earlier models provided by either individual vitae or synaxarion collections. In menologia, extensive pictorial cycles detailing a saint's life occasionally appear (as in Mount Athos, Esphigmenou codex 14), but because of the length of the text, illustrations were normally limited to one image at the beginning of the life and/or one at the end. Portraits and scenes of martyrdom are the standard illustrations, as in the Menologion of Basil II (Vaticanus graec. 1613).

BIBLIOGRAPHY

Sirarpie Der Nersessian, "The Illustrations of the Metaphrastian Menologium," in Kurt Weitzmann, ed., *Late Classical and Mediaeval Studies in Honor of Albert Mathias Friend, Jr.* (1955).

LESLIE BRUBAKER

[See also **Symeon Metaphrastes; Synaxarion.**]

Martyrdom of St. Eleutherius. Miniature from the Menologion of Basil II, *ca.* 986. ROME, BIBLIOTECA APOSTOLICA, VAT. COD. GR. 1613, p. 246

MENORAH, a seven-branched lampstand, which, according to Exodus 25:31–40 and 37:17–24, supposedly was in the Wilderness Tabernacle. This menorah, in fact, stood in the Second Jerusalem Temple, destroyed by the Romans in A.D. 70, and it was depicted on the triumphal arch of Titus in Rome. An important symbol of Judaism found in early synagogues and catacombs, it is now the official emblem of the State of Israel.

BIBLIOGRAPHY

Joseph Gutmann, ed., *No Graven Images: Studies in Art and the Hebrew Bible* (1971), 36–38, and *The Temple of Solomon: Archaeological Fact and Mediaeval Tradition in Christian, Islamic, and Jewish Art* (1976), 125–145.

JOSEPH GUTMANN

[See also **Jewish Art.**]

MERCADÉ, EUSTACHE (*d.* 1440). Prominent during his lifetime primarily as a rhetorician and theologian, Mercadé (or Marcadé), an official of the abbey of Corbie and dean of the faculty of ecclesiastical law in Paris, is today chiefly known for a mystery play attributed to him, the *Passion d'Arras.* Arras, Municipal Library MS 697, in which the *Passion* is followed by a play signed by Mercadé *(La vengeance de Jésus-Christ),* contains evidence that makes this attribution highly probable. The *Passion d'Arras* is the first surviving passion play by a single author. Its length (24,945 lines) appears to be a novelty, and it is the first passion to take four days for its performance: (1) Christ's Birth and Childhood, (2) Public Life, (3) Passion, and (4) Resurrection and Ascension. Mercadé's training is evident in the *Procès de paradis,* a debate framing the play, and in the incorporation of theological discourse throughout.

BIBLIOGRAPHY

Eustache Mercadé, *Le Mystère de la Passion,* Jules-Marie Richard, ed. (1893, repr. 1976). See also Maurice Accarie, *Le théâtre sacré de la fin du moyen âge: Étude sur le sens moral de la* Passion *de Jean Michel* (1979); Omer Jodogne, "La tonalité des mystères français," in *Studi in onore di Italo Siciliano* (1966); Émile Roy, *Le Mystère de la Passion en France du XIV*[e] *au XVI*[e] *siècle: Étude sur les sources et le classement des mystères de la Passion* (1903–1904, repr. 1974).

T. S. FAUNCE

[See also **Drama, French; Mystery Plays; Passion Plays, French.**]

MERCHANTS. See **Trade.**

MERIGARTO (Meregarto), the name given to parts of a late-eleventh-century cosmographical poem in German that survive on two parchment leaves now in Donaueschingen. The author, drawing upon school learning embellished with anecdote, describes the Red Sea, the "liver sea," and various springs, lakes, and rivers notable for miraculous properties. One passage, however, is based on a firsthand account of a visit to Iceland by one Reginpreht, who had sailed to that country, perhaps on a trading voyage. Reginpreht was known to the author as "an upright priest" he had met in Utrecht while exiled there in consequence of an episcopal feud. Neither the author nor Reginpreht has been identified. The title *Merigarto* was given to the text by H. Hoffmann in 1834.

BIBLIOGRAPHY

Sources. Wilhelm Braune, ed., *Althochdeutsches Lesebuch,* 16th ed., rev. by Ernst A. Ebbinghaus (1979), 140–142; Karl Müllendorf and W. Scherer, eds., *Denkmäler deutscher Poesie und Prosa aus dem VIII–XII Jahrhundert,* 4th ed. (1964), I, 93–100 (text), and II, 188–197 (commentary).

Studies. Ernst A. Ebbinghaus, "A Note on the Merigarto, " in *Journal of English and Germanic Philology,* **64** (1965); Gustav Ehrismann, *Geschichte der deutschen Literatur bis zum Ausgang des Mittelalters,* II, pt. 1 (1954), 231–234; Johannes A. Huisman, "Utrecht im Merigarto," in *Beiträge zur Geschicte der deutschen Sprache und Literatur,* **87** (1965), with facsimile.

D. R. MCLINTOCK

MERLIN. See **Arthurian Literature.**

MERLÎNÚSSPÁ is an Old Norse verse translation of Geoffrey of Monmouth's *Prophecies of Merlin (Propheciae Merlini),* a prose work that occurs as a two-chapter interpolation in Geoffrey's *Historia regum Britanniae* (VII, 3–4). *Merlínússpá* is preserved only in *Hauksbók,* a fourteenth-century manuscript, where it is inserted in the correct place in a text of *Breta sǫgur,* the Icelandic version of

Geoffrey's *Historia,* and is attributed to Gunnlaugr Leifsson, monk of Þingeyrar, who died around 1218. *Merlínússpá* is not found in AM 573 4°, the other redaction of *Breta sǫgur,* which mentions Gunnlaugr's poem at the appropriate place and explains its omission by the assertion "many know that poem by heart."

Although his Latin original was in prose, Gunnlaugr's translation is in a very regular form of the Eddic meter *fornyrðislag,* with some stanzas in *kviðuháttr* and some couplets in *runhent* or end-rhyme, used mainly to highlight the poet's battle descriptions. The length of Gunnlaugr's stanzas is variable; most have eight, but some have ten or even twelve lines. Gunnlaugr tends to follow his Latin text closely, but occasionally inserts stanzas and half-stanzas of his own devising. Two such passages (I, 33–36; II, 65–69) elaborate Geoffrey's battle scenes in traditional skaldic style.

Editions present *Merlínússpá* as two separate poems of 68 and 103 stanzas respectively, with each poem based on one of the two sections of the *Prophecies.* For reasons that are unclear, the order of the two sections is reversed. The beginning stanzas (1–4) of the first poem stress the wisdom of Merlin and the importance of old lore, insisting that the verse to follow will be clear and simple; the poem concludes (62–68) with a prayer to God for salvation. In between are found such prophecies as that a hedgehog will fortify the town of Winchester with five hundred towers (19); that stones will speak and the English Channel become so narrow that voices will be audible from land to land (23); that a death-dealing snake will be born whose tail will encircle all London (46); and that a great war will devastate the earth (51) until all is empty: "The sea rages and flings itself into the air: such is terrible for the sons of men; such is terrible to relate, the old earth will be devoid of men" (61).

The beginning stanzas of the second poem (1–20) relate the historical background of the *Prophecies* and the struggle between the Britons and the Anglo-Saxon invaders; this material, along with other details in the poem, suggests that Gunnlaugr knew Geoffrey's entire *Historia* and not just the two sections he versified. After giving the final prophecy—that monks in their cowls will be forced to marry and that their laments will be heard on the cold peaks of the Alps (92)—the second poem pauses to confirm the truth of what has been related, cites Daniel's dreams and David's prophecies, and ends with a stanza resembling the final lines of the Eddic *Hávamál:* "Hail to all men who have listened to this poem."

In his choice of both meter and of diction, Gunnlaugr shows the influence of Eddic poetry. There are numerous echoes of *Vǫluspá,* whose Sibyl performs a role similar to Merlin's, as well as verbal similarities with the Helgi poems, *Fáfnismál,* and especially with *Grípisspá.* Gunnlaugr employs more kennings than are usual in Eddic poetry, however, and shows himself to be conversant with skaldic conventions, even if we have no other poetry from his hand.

BIBLIOGRAPHY

J. S. Eysteinsson, "The Relationship of *Merlínússpá* and Geoffrey of Monmouth's *Historia,*" in *Saga-Book of the Viking Society for Northern Research,* **14** (1953–1957); Lee M. Hollander, *A Bibliography of Skaldic Studies* (1958); Finnur Jónsson, *Den norsk-islandske skjaldedigtning,* II: A, B (1915); Ernst A. Kock, *Den norsk-isländska skaldediktningen* II, (1949); E. O. G. Turville-Petre, *Origins of Icelandic Literature* (1953).

ROBERTA FRANK

[See also **Breta Sǫgur; Eddic Meters; Eddic Poetry; Geoffrey of Monmouth; Grípisspá; Helgi Poems.**]

MEROBAUDES (*d. ca.* 460). A member of the senatorial aristocracy of southern Spain and probably of Frankish descent, Flavius Merobaudes had a distinguished career both as a rhetorician and as a soldier. In 435, after moving to Italy and becoming a court poet and a count, he was granted a statue in Trajan's Forum in Rome. Shortly thereafter, perhaps in 437, he was made a patrician, and in 443 he was sent as master of soldiers to Spain to fight the Bacaudae, a group of ruined peasants. Despite marked success, he soon was recalled.

Aside from his poem on Christ *(De Christo),* his extant works exist only in fragments. These include parts of four descriptive poems or *ekphrases,* and two panegyrics. The first is in prose and of uncertain purpose; the other is in hexameter verse and was delivered on 1 January 446 in honor of the third consulate of Flavius Aëtius.

BIBLIOGRAPHY

Texts of the *Carmina, Panegyrici,* and *Carmen de Christo seu Laus Christi* appear in *Monumenta Germaniae historica: Auctorum antiquissimorum,* XIV, Friedrich Vollmer, ed. (1905). See also Frank M. Clover, "Flavius Merobaudes: A Translation and Historical Commentary," in *Transactions of the American Philosophical Society,* n.s. **61**.1 (1971).

RALPH W. MATHISEN

[See also **Latin Literature.**]

MEROVINGIAN ART. See **Migration and Hiberno-Saxon Art.**

MEROVINGIANS. The first Frankish royal family had its origins as chieftains of the Salians, one of the diverse groups of romanized Germanic peoples who inhabited the lower Rhine on the northern border of the Roman Empire and who collectively came to be called the Franks. The early Merovingians, particularly Merovich and Childeric I (*d.* 481), had served as faithful allies of the Romans against the Saxons and Visigoths and by the middle of the fifth century were established around Tournai and within the remnant of the empire in Gaul. Thus, when in 486 Childeric's son Clovis defeated Syagrius, the so-called "king of the Romans" at Soissons, the event was less the conquest of the Roman province by barbarians than a coup d'etat in an isolated and strongly barbarized Roman kingdom by the commander of its Frankish army.

While reserving for their Frankish followers the most important positions in the kingdom and significant allocations of land, Clovis and his successors essentially continued and incorporated much of the Roman tradition they inherited. Administratively, this included the imperial fiscal system and the provincial chancellery. Clovis cultivated the image of defender of Roman traditions and enhanced this image by his baptism into orthodox Christianity (the Franks had been pagans) probably in 496 or 498. This conversion was also in part responsible for the imperial recognition he received in 507, when an

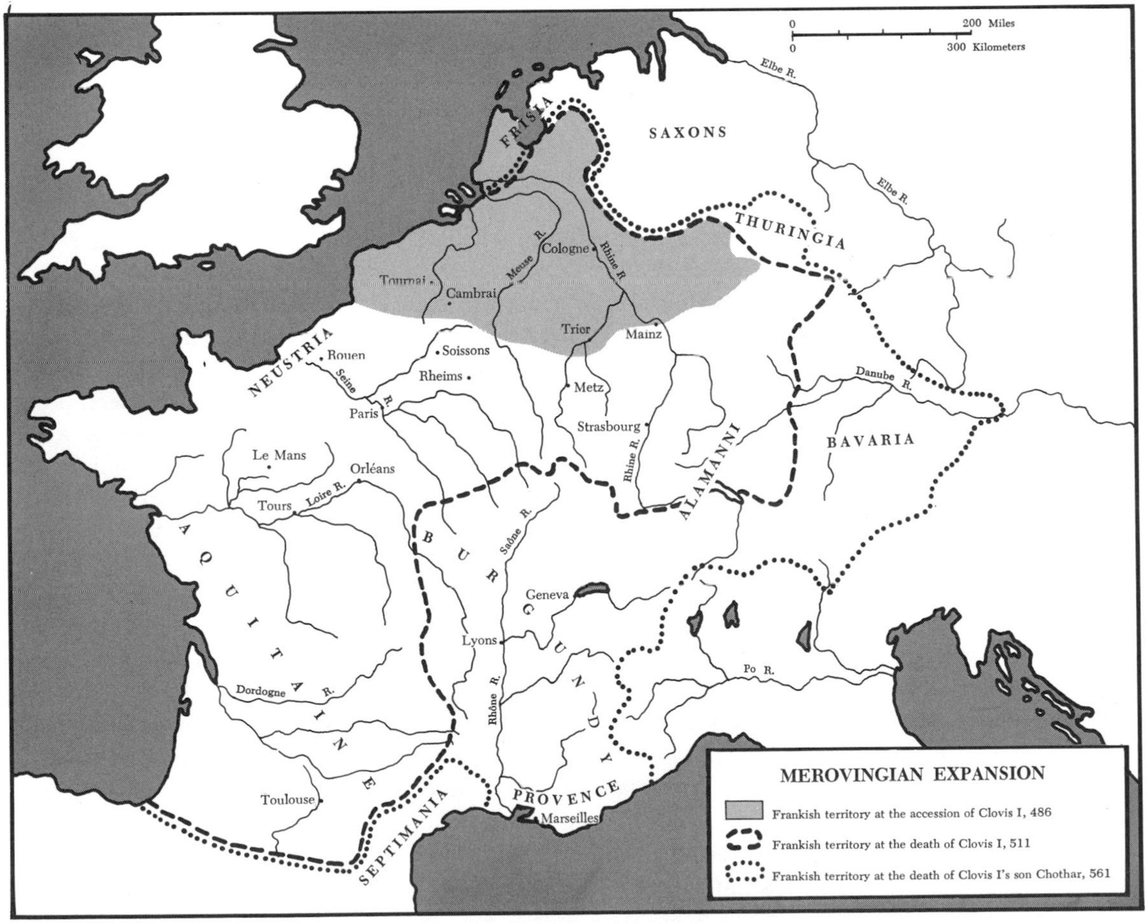

MEROVINGIANS

embassy from the emperor Anastasius apparently brought him the regalia of honorary consul. In return, Clovis assured the interests of the Roman church through the canons of the Council of Orleans held in 511. The *lex salica,* probably prepared by Roman jurists around the end of Clovis' reign, presents the image of a powerful king exercising his control both over his Frankish followers and over the Roman inhabitants of his kingdom. As a result of these policies toward the empire and Roman traditions, the Frankish and Gallo-Roman societies merged fairly early and fully in the old kingdom of Soissons and, as the kingdom expanded, this merger took place elsewhere as well.

Once established in Syagrius' kingdom, Clovis began to push southward against the Alamanni and then the Visigoths, whose kingdom of Toulouse he conquered. In the north, he eliminated the other kings of Frankish tribes around Cologne, Cambrai, and Le Mans. His sons continued this expansion (which was the fruition of older Roman ambitions in the west) with the absorption of Thuringia, Burgundy, Provence, and Bavaria.

Following Clovis' death in 511, his kingdom was divided among his four sons, each of whom received a portion centered on a Roman city within the old kingdom conquered from Syagrius. While this division was in accordance with Frankish inheritance customs, it introduced one of the major problems the Frankish kingdom would face into the tenth century—the division of the kingdom as personal inheritance among royal children. This practice led to continual civil war and fratricide in the Merovingian family since every male, regardless of his mother's status, was by birthright a king and would seek to secure his share at the expense of his kinsmen. These conflicts and divisions led ultimately to the establishment of three major divisions of Francia: northwestern Neustria, northeastern Austrasia, and southeastern Burgundy, each of which had its own king and court.

In the latter part of the sixth century the internal conflicts among members of the royal family were exacerbated by a growing conflict between the kings and their service nobility drawn from various elements of Frankish and Roman society on the one hand, and the old Frankish aristocracy that had risen with Clovis on the other. Particularly in Austrasia, where Brunhilde, a Visigothic princess and queen and later queen mother, attempted to reinstate the old Roman system of taxation and, in general, to reintroduce Roman fiscal and administrative machinery to the benefit of her sons and grandsons, these efforts met powerful and ultimately successful opposition. In 613 Brunhilde was defeated by the Burgundian and Austrasian aristocracies and was handed over to Chothar II of Neustria for execution.

With the help of this same aristocratic alliance, Chothar was able to unite the entire kingdom under his rule and to pass it intact to his son Dagobert I. In return for this assistance, Chothar assured local magnates that they would maintain control of their local counties. He also used the chief opponents of his late enemies, Warnachar of Burgundy and the Arnulfings of Austrasia (so named after Arnulf of Metz), as his closest advisers and administrators. In order to balance this aristocratic power, Chothar and later Dagobert increased their reliance on bishops and on abbots of major monasteries (especially that of St. Denis), whose appointments the king could control and thus exercise through them some local control throughout the kingdom. In addition, the kings encouraged noble families to send their youth to be educated at court in order to develop among the local aristocracies strong personal loyalties to the king. Finally, royal propaganda sought to emphasize the difference between the royal family and the aristocracy on which it was increasingly dependent by ascribing to the former a sacred, quasi-mystical image based on both mythic pagan traditions and Christian teaching.

Under Dagobert I, the Merovingian kingdom reached its apogee. Following his death in 638, a series of royal minorities destroyed the balance between king and aristocracy, and the Merovingians fell under the control of the nobility. Increasingly the struggle became one not between king and noble, but rather between rival factions within the nobility for control of the king as source of legitimacy, specifically between the Austrasian Arnulfings and the Neustrian aristocracy. However, contrary to the popular image largely created by Arnulfingian propagandists, the last Merovingians were not all do-nothing kings (*rois fainéants*). Several were capable and independent, if ultimately unsuccessful, sovereigns. In time, nevertheless, the Arnulfings defeated the Neustrians at Tetry in 687 and then, with brief interruptions, strengthened their control over the kingdom to the extent that in 751 Pepin III could, with papal support, send the last Merovingian, Childeric III (743–751), to a monastery and have himself made king.

BIBLIOGRAPHY

One contemporary source, a vivid account of the early Merovingian kingdom, is Gregory of Tours, *History of the Franks,* Ormonde M. Dalton, trans. (1927). Studies include Samuel Dill, *Roman Society in Gaul in the Merovingian Age* (1926); Patrick J. Geary, *Aristocracy in Provence: The Rhône Basin at the Dawn of the Carolingian Age* (1985); Peter Lasko, *The Kingdom of the Franks* (1971); John M. Wallace-Hadrill, *The Long-haired Kings and Other Studies in Frankish History* (1962), and *The Frankish Church* (1983); Patrick Wormald, *et al.,* eds., *Ideal and Reality in Frankish and Anglo-Saxon Society* (1983).

For an excellent guide to the enormous literature on the Merovingians see the bibliographies in Heinz Löwe, *Deutschland im fränkischen Reich* (1982).

PATRICK GEARY

[See also **Carolingians; Clovis; France.**]

MERSEBURGER ZAUBERSPRÜCHE. See **Charms, Old High German.**

MERURE DE SEINTE ÉGLISE (Mirror of Holy Church), religious treatise composed possibly before 1220 by St. Edmund of Abingdon, archbishop of Canterbury (1234–1240). It was once believed that the treatise was originally written in Anglo-Norman French and subsequently translated into Latin, but recently it has been demonstrated that the original most likely was written in Latin under the title *Speculum religiosorum* and then translated around the middle of the thirteenth century into Anglo-Norman French. This French version, usually known as the *Merure de Seinte Église,* was then retranslated three times into Latin, these retranslations being generally known as the *Speculum Ecclesie.* Both the French and the retranslated Latin versions were then translated several times into Middle English.

A popular work extant altogether in some eighty manuscripts, the treatise was revised in some versions for a lay audience but was originally intended for the religious as a guide to living a perfect life. Drawing heavily on Hugh of St. Victor, it discusses how God should be contemplated in his creatures, in the scriptures, and in himself.

BIBLIOGRAPHY

Edmund of Abingdon, *Speculum religiosorum and Speculum Ecclesie,* Helen P. Forshaw, ed. (1973); Alan D. Wilshere, ed., *Mirour de Seinte Eglyse (St. Edmund of Abingdon's 'Speculum Ecclesiae')* (1982).

ELLEN T. WEHNER

[See also **Anglo-Norman Literature.**]

MESEMBRIA (modern Nesebūr, Bulgaria) was an important Byzantine administrative and economic center situated on a peninsula on the southwest coast of the Black Sea. Built upon the site of an ancient Thracian city, it possessed strong fortifications and a major harbor. A constant bone of contention between the Byzantines and the Bulgars, it was taken by the Bulgar khan Krum in 812; in addition to gold and silver, Krum captured an important supply of Greek fire, an early incendiary weapon, along with the bronze tubes necessary to release the fire. Over the next several centuries Mesembria changed hands between Byzantium and the Bulgars many times.

BIBLIOGRAPHY

Cambridge Medieval History, IV, pt. 1 (1966), 97, 333, 490–491, 591–592.

LINDA C. ROSE

[See also **Bulgaria; Greek Fire; Krum.**]

MESROB, ST. See **Maštocᶜ, St.**

MESSIANISM, JEWISH. See **Apocalyptic Literature and Movement, Jewish.**

MESTA, or *honrado concejo de la mesta* (Honorable Council of the Mesta), was the guild or *hermandad* of the Spanish shepherds, cowboys, and owners of livestock engaged in transhumance (the seasonal migration of livestock between mountains and lowlands). The word *mestas* also describes the local gatherings of shepherds when they met to settle disputes over strays, grazing rights, and other matters related to the transhumance. In earlier usage, *mestas* were also the seasonal grazing lands used by the livestock. In addition the *mesta* is the general term given to the entire pattern of transhumance of livestock in the Iberian peninsula and southern Italy.

This annual movement of livestock had a long history in Spain because of the sharp climatic contrasts between north and south, mountain and plain. It predated Roman times and reached important dimensions under Visigothic rule. The range of the transhumance was limited in the early Middle Ages because of the Muslim threat, but it increased rapidly as new lands opened to Christian settlement. One cannot overemphasize the importance of ranching in a frontier society. Herds could be protected from Muslim raids by removing them far from the threatened area in a way in which agricultural goods and land itself could not. With the expansion of Castile into Estremadura (late twelfth and early thirteenth centuries) and Andalusia (first half of the thirteenth century), the transhumance now reached from the northern mountains of the Bay of Biscay, the Asturian region, and the Pyrenees into the temperate grazing lands of the south. The herds moved through the peninsula's cultivated and barren lands by preestablished routes, the *cañadas* in Castile, veritable highways or sheep walks for the migrating animals. In the mid thirteenth century, three such routes served the needs of the four great *mestas* of León, Segovia, Soria, and Cuenca. Beginning in each of these areas, the *cañadas* led to the newly conquered lands of Estremadura, Andalusia, and La Mancha.

In 1273 Alfonso X granted his protection to the different *mestas,* exempted them from most of the taxes levied on them by the municipalities and seignorial and ecclesiastical lords, and brought together the diverse guilds into one general council, a national *mesta.* Whatever Alfonso's aims were, either to foment a textile industry in Castile, as Sánchez-Albornoz maintains, or to seek new revenues, as argued by Vicens Vives, after the 1270's the *mesta* played an ever-increasing role in the financial life of Castile. Nevertheless, the economic and political troubles of the late thirteenth and early fourteenth centuries prevented the crown from fully exploiting the *mesta.* As the flocks passed through different areas, taxes were collected by the owners of the lands around the *cañadas.* During the reign of Alfonso XI (1311–1350), these taxes, *portazgo* (a toll tax) and *montazgo* (originally a payment for unauthorized use of grazing lands), became a generalized tax, *servicio y montazgo,* collected mainly by the crown. In fact, the taxes collected from the *mesta* became the crown's main source of income for the next three centuries.

The transhumance acquired greater importance in the early fourteenth century with the introduction of a new breed of sheep, the merino, which, as Robert S. Lopez has shown, had been brought from North Africa by Genoese merchants. Although the *mesta* had always included a variety of livestock (horses, cows, goats), the marked improvement in the quality of the wool from the merino had dramatic results. The sheep herds increased in number from around 1.5 million head in the early fourteenth century to over 3 million head in the late fifteenth. After 1350 wool became, and remained for the next three centuries, the basic staple for Castile and, later on, Spain. Moreover, its export to the textile centers in Flanders created important economic ties with that area long before the marriage of Joanna the Mad and Philip the Handsome. Around the same time (1347) Alfonso XI renewed the royal protection over the *mesta* by establishing the so-called *cabaña real,* which brought not only the royal herds but all the *mesta* livestock under the king's protection. The flocks were granted the right to graze freely along the *cañadas* as long as they did not damage the cultivated lands.

By the fourteenth century the *mesta* shepherds and owners had begun to meet twice a year in a great assembly, one in the south and the other in the north, to settle their internal problems and discuss matters related to the transhumance. Historians have written many pages since Julius Klein's *The Mesta* (1920) arguing for or against the democratic nature of these meetings, which brought many small owners together against a few powerful ecclesiastical and lay lords. It suffices to say that from the late thirteenth century on, the head of the *mesta* (the *alcalde entregador mayor*) was always a magnate, and after 1454, a member of the royal council.

In addition to these high officials, the *mesta* had a fairly complex judicial and financial organization. At the lowest level, each *cabaña* or herd had two *alcaldes de la mesta,* who judged the disputes occurring within their jurisdiction. Appeals from their decisions were heard by four *alcaldes de alzada* or *alcaldes de apelaciones. Procuradores del puerto,* also agents of the *mesta,* collected the tax on the transhumance at specific places (usually mountain passes) along the route. *Alcaldes entregadores,* representatives of the king, protected the rights of the *mesta* against the encroachment and attacks of the

MESTER DE CLERECÍA

towns and others. As one might expect, conflicts between towns, farmers, and the *mesta* were frequent and often violent as each tried to expand its jurisdiction at the expense of the other. Moreover, the claims of the *mesta* over strays, even of those herds that did not migrate (the *estantes*), were an added reason for conflict.

The debate on the impact of the *mesta* on Castilian agriculture and society is lively. Although the *mesta* has been indicted since the sixteenth century as responsible for most of the ills of Spain, and although Julius Klein's influence on the historiography of the *mesta* has not yet been successfully challenged in its entirety, the triumph of the transhumance did not ruin the rural economy of Castile and Spain. The *mesta* succeeded because the basic agricultural and economic structure of Castile was weak and underdeveloped before and after the expansion of the transhumance, and therefore it could not oppose what then seemed a profitable and rational alternative.

BIBLIOGRAPHY

Charles Bishko, "The Castilian as Plainsman: The Medieval Ranching Frontier in La Mancha and Extremadura," in *The New World Looks at Its History,* Archibald R. Lewis and Thomas F. McGann, eds. (1963); Miguel Caxa (Caja) de Leruela, *Restauración de la abundancia de España* (1975), see notes to Jean-Paul Le Flem's introduction; Julius Klein, *The Mesta: A Study in Spanish Economic History, 1273–1836* (1920, repr. 1964); Jean-Paul Le Flem, "Las cuentas de la Mesta (1510–1709)," in *Moneda y crédito,* **121** (1972), and "La ganadería en el Siglo de Oro XVI–XVII: Balance y problemática con especial atención a la Mesta," in Gonzalo Anes Álvarez, *et al., La economía agraria en la historia de España* (1978); Robert S. Lopez, "The Origin of the Merino Sheep," in *The Joshua Starr Memorial Volume* (1953); Claudio Sánchez-Albornoz, *España: Un enigma histórico,* 2 vols. (1956); Jaime Vicens Vives, *An Economic History of Spain,* Frances M. López-Morillas, trans. (1969).

TEOFILO F. RUIZ

[See also **Agriculture and Nutrition; Castile.**]

MESTER DE CLERECÍA is a term that serves to classify a literary craft widely cultivated in Spain in the thirteenth and fourteenth centuries by clergymen and other erudite poets. The dominant form used by these poets was the *cuaderna vía* (fourfold way), a quatrain of fourteen- (later sixteen-) syllable lines with each line divided by a caesura into two equal hemistichs, and with one consonantal rhyme throughout. The French alexandrine provided the model for the line, while medieval Latin verse likely inspired the stanza. The close association of the two terms *mester de clerecía* and *cuaderna vía* has caused their frequent—though mistaken—use as synonyms; the former refers to the style, content, and intended audience of a work, while the latter applies solely to the poetic form used.

This poetry displayed the erudition and elegance normally expected of clergymen and other learned authors yet had moral and didactic aims that led to its public recitation before wide audiences. Its typically universal themes came from religion, romance, history, and legend, both ancient and medieval. Despite its deliberately cultured nature, *clerecía* poetry coexisted harmoniously with the popular *mester de juglaría* (minstrels' craft). No real barriers existed between them and, in competing for audiences, there were many reciprocal borrowings and influences, both stylistic and thematic. *Clerecía* poets used a blend of popular and learned language and some called themselves minstrels. Even the progressive decay of the originally rigid *clerecía* verse form reveals that, by the fourteenth century or earlier, irregular *juglaría* verse had made *clerecía* poets relax their strict compliance with inflexible rules. Some recent scholarship advocates widening the limits of *clerecía* poetry to include debate poems, religious narratives, and certain other texts which, despite their *juglaría* forms, contain enough erudite elements to place them in the *clerecía* category.

Twenty-one *clerecía* poems in *cuaderna vía* survive and others probably existed. Ten extant works (four saints' lives, three doctrinal works, and three poems about the Virgin Mary) are by Gonzalo de Berceo (*ca.* 1196–*ca.* 1264). *Clerecía*'s supreme masterpiece is the *Libro de buen amor* (1330; expanded in 1343), a fascinating literary parody by Juan Ruiz (*ca.* 1283–1351), archpriest of Hita. The last major work of the group is the *Libro rimado del palacio* (1367–1403), a confession and social satire by Pero López de Ayala (1332–1407).

The nine remaining poems are anonymous and comprise two epics (*Libro de Alexandre, ca.* 1240, and *Poema de Fernán González, ca.* 1250); one romance (*Libro de Apolonio, ca.* 1260); three works of wisdom literature (*Castigos y ejemplos de Catón, ca.* 1265, and *Proverbios de Salamón* and *Libro de miseria de omne,* both *ca.* 1375); one saint's life (*Vida de San Ildefonso, ca.* 1333); and two scriptural accounts—biblical and koranic—of Joseph, which, though written in Spanish, are transliterated respectively into Hebrew (*Coplas de Yoçef, ca.* 1330–1350) and Arabic script (*Poema de Yûçuf, ca.* 1350–1400). The great success of the *mester de clerecía* is evident in that its characteristics transcended boundaries of ethnicity, genre, and theme, as revealed by this diversity of works.

BIBLIOGRAPHY

Pedro Luis Barcia, *El mester de clerecía* (1967); John D. Fitz-Gerald, *Versification of the Cuaderna Vía* (1905); Gerald B. Gybbon-Monypenny, "The Spanish *Mester de Clerecía* and Its Intended Public," in Frederick Whitehead *et al.,* eds., *Medieval Miscellany, Presented to Eugène Vinaver* (1965); Francisco López Estrada, "*Mester de clerecía:* Las palabras y el concepto," in *Journal of Hispanic Philology,* 2 (1977–1978), and *Introducción a la literatura medieval española,* 4th ed., rev. (1979), esp. 300–326, 367–379; Nicasio Salvador Miguel, "El mester de clerecía," in José María Díez Borque, ed., *Historia de la literatura española,* I (1974), and *El mester de clerecía: Teoría e historia de un género literario* (1986).

STEVEN D. KIRBY

[See also **Cuaderna Vía; Ruiz, Juan; Spanish Literature.**]

MESTER DE JUGLARÍA, the craft of minstrel poet, differentiated from that of *mester de clerecía,* the craft of clergymen, in that the latter has been thought of as more learned. In 1116 Queen Urraca of Castile identifies *juglares* as a profession of tainted social standing by including them in the group that had caused an urban revolt at Sahagún: "Let be gone now all these jongleurs and knaves, tanners and cobblers who usurped my rule and denied you proper respect."

From the beginning of the twelfth century onward the profession called *mester de juglaría* was widely exercised by members of the three major religious groups of Iberia—Jews, Moors, and Christians—as well as by other nationals resident in Spain, especially the French and Italians. According to Ramón Menéndez Pidal, important schools for *juglares* were formed in Arabic Spain, for example, in Úbeda and Játiva, as well as in Sahagún and other cities of the Christian north.

Because the profession was loosely defined and underwent constant change, it is difficult to determine what kind of training *juglares* received or what common elements defined their activity. Poetic differences between the *juglares* and the *mesters de clerecía* were that the *juglares* did not use the *cuaderna vía* and did not count their syllables. Rather, poetic assonance and metric irregularity are themselves poetic characteristics of compositions in the *mester de juglaría.* Scholars of medieval Spanish poetry have in fact traditionally divided the two *mesteres* along these broad lines, and although the two tendencies cannot be called poetic schools in the modern sense, they certainly marked two different trends in medieval Spanish poetics. This one area of distinction, however, should not be seen as having established a rigid line of separation between the two groups. Gonzalo de Berceo (1196?–1264?), a poet of *clerecía,* calls himself "joglar," as does Juan Ruiz (*ca.* 1283–1351), who spent a good part of his poetic life writing compositions for *juglares.* Likewise the proud author of the literary manifesto of the *mester de clerecía, Libro de Alexandre* (*ca.* 1240), probably Berceo himself, speaks of "*un yoglar de grant guisa,* sabía bien su mester, / ombre bien razonado que sabía bien leer" (a jongleur of great accomplishment, well he knew his craft, / a learned man who knew how to compose well). And yet, these authors who called themselves *juglares* are considered masters of the *mester de clerecía,* suggesting that we cannot draw positive conclusions about the nature of the two *mesteres* based exclusively on their poetic techniques.

Several poets of *juglaría* used a wide range of meters (regular and irregular) and a high degree of poetic sophistication and technical skill that seem to contradict the assignment of poetic informality as the primary identifying feature of the *mester de juglaría.* For this reason we might better see the *mester* as a poetic quality, a mood or a tone, that characterizes a poet or a composition, rather than as a poetic school, as that term is applied to the *mester de clerecía.* The attitude of the jongleur's work is manifested in, or characterized by, a certain poetic freedom and flexibility, exempt from many of the learned restrictions of technique, genre, theme, and style. The sardonic smile with which Juan Ruiz closes his masterpiece, the *Libro de buen amor,* points up his unpretentious approach to poetry: "*Señores,* hevos *servido* con poca sabidoría,/ por vos *dar solaz* a todos, *fablévos en juglaría*" (Good sirs, I have entertained you with little book learning. / So as to please you all, I have spoken in the manner of a jongleur).

Fablar en juglaría in this context would seem to indicate the poet's desire to accommodate his work to a wide popular audience gathered in the streets and squares of towns and villages, as opposed to the select audiences of the castles and royal courts. But it also means to speak in jest, as he does when he mixes the most unexpected themes: *serranillas,* prayers, praises of the Virgin Mary, tales, fables, *cantigas d'escarnho* (ditties of mockery), portraits of bourgeois life, parodies of traditional *gestas* and religious ceremonies, as well as the constant combination of comedy and tragedy, mimicry and gentleness. This disparity made up the body of the *mester de juglaría*'s repertoire. The relaxed style of the poetry helped them reach a wider audience, and reaching out was the basic tenet of the *juglares'* art.

BIBLIOGRAPHY

Alan D. Deyermond, "Mester es sen pecado," in *Romanische Forschungen,* 77 (1965); Ramón Menéndez Pidal, *Poesía juglaresca y orígenes de las literaturas románicas,* 6th ed. (1957).

H. SALVADOR MARTÍNEZ

[See also **Berceo, Gonzalo de; Joglar; Ruiz, Juan; Spanish Literature.**]

METALLURGY, the technique of extracting metals from their ores, along with refining and preparing these metals for use, may have had its earliest medieval demonstration at the battle of Adrianople, around 400. There, the heavy cavalry of the Goths, wielding their spathas, or double-edged broadswords, annihilated the Roman army. After Adrianople (now Edirne, Turkey), the Romans adopted the arms of the Goths, Alans, and other riders of the steppes due to their superiority. These pattern-welded spathas, which could cut armor, were probably made by Celtic smiths in the Goths' employ. Because Celtic metalworking had been brought to Denmark and Scandinavia by the Goths before their wandering to the Black Sea shores, the Alamans, the armies of Charlemagne, and the Vikings also used similar swords.

The Ripuarian Franks were the first to wear *brunia* (brunies, or coats of mail) made of strips cut from iron sheets. Then came tight-fitting sleeves of protochain mail material and greaves of overlapping metal plate. The quality of Frankish weaponry was so high that for security's sake Charlemagne forbade its exportation. When the Frankish host entered Pavia, Italy, in 773, the people cried in dismay, "Iron, iron everywhere," at the pageant of an armored corps.

The richest spathas and scramasaxes, short one-edged swords, were adorned with gold and garnets. The Franks used, for decorating iron, a damascening technique inherited from the *barbicarii* (foreigners) mentioned in documents of the fifth century. Their iron belt-buckles were encrusted with strips of brass or silver tapped down in incised patterns. In the "tarsia" (intarsia) method, a sheet of silver was hammered on a striated or spiky ground. Plating in silver, engraved with interlaces—occasionally nielloed—characterizes Viking swords of the ninth and tenth centuries.

BRONZE

Bronze casting, used in barbarian fibulae, was revived on a scale as great as in Roman times by the Carolingians. The "Frankish" and "antiquizing" grilles of the cathedral at Aachen and its double doors with their lion mask ring handles date to the last decade of the eighth century. The "throne of Dagobert," from Saint Denis, is a Merovingian or Carolingian copy of a consular folding stool.

Bronze doors are a main feature of Ottonian art. Those of Archbishop Willigis at Mayence and of the Augsburg cathedral were cast in one piece as were those at Aachen. The bronze doors of Saint Michael, in Hildesheim, Germany, were cast in an open mold (1015). After the beeswax models had been run off by heating, the core was discarded and the negative mantle of the coated mold was turned over in a container of clay. Metal was poured, forming the back of each wing when it attained its level. For the column at Hildesheim, the twenty-eight episodes of the life of Christ, a spiral about fifty feet (nearly sixteen meters) long, was cast in one piece with the shaft of Bernward's column at Hildesheim. The column was cast standing, the metal poured through a tube coated with a loam core—a method which kept the temperature relatively constant during the process. The craftsman-monk Roger of Helmarshausen ("Theophilus," if he is the author of the *De diversis artibus,* 1110–1140) was concerned with the making of small objects, their materials, and tools. His treatise is an invaluable source for the techniques of metalworking. The third book covers the activities of the goldsmith and of the metalworker. It describes the forge, the anvils, tongs and hammers, punches, tools for engraving and for making nails, stamps and dies for repeating designs on metal sheets, an iron implement for swaging filigree, and a machine for cutting the ground of iron spurs before their damascening. He acquaints us with the methods for punching, raising, and repoussé, and with recipes for preparing niello (a black alloy of silver, lead, and sulphur) and for blackening brass with an application of heated linseed oil. The casting of a bronze censer in the lost-wax technique is the first written description of the process. Four chapters are consecrated to the construction of a furnace for melting bell metal (smelted copper to which is added a fifth of tin), the casting of bells, and the scaling of small bells. Distinctions are established among coarse brass *(aes),* out of which are made cauldrons, kettles, and basins and which cannot be gilded, refined copper *(torridum),* which is purged of lead and is used for working—in repoussé—vessels and figures before their gilding, and a bronze with a low content of lead and addition of calamine, which can also be gilded. Calamine is a zinc carbonate abounding near Liège. The gilt doors of the abbey church of Saint Denis, melted in 1793, must have been made by Mosans with the same ingredients given by Theophilus. The ingredients correspond to those of the baptismal font made by Rainer of Huy for Notre Dame at Liège (1107–1118), where the proportion of zinc varies from 17 percent in the vat to a low of 7.2 percent in the teams of bronze oxen supporting it. (See "Mosan Art" for illustration.)

Bronze doors of Saint Michael, Hildesheim, 1015. PHOTOGRAPH BY HERMANN WEHMEYER, HILDESHEIM. FROM *PROPYLÄEN KUNSTGESCHICHTE,* BAND 5. © 1969 Propyläen Verlag, Berlin

Mosan craftsmen made the foot of the great cross at Saint Denis—a bronze base decorated with scrolls and dragons like those of a fragment in the Rheims Museum and of candelabra in the cathedrals of Braunschweig (Brunswick) and Milan. Following the destructions of the Reformation, only the altar candlestick (1104–1113) from Gloucester in the Victoria and Albert Museum remains to give an idea of English bronze candelabra mentioned in texts and today lost—like the one presented to Cluny by Queen Mathilda, and the one in Durham Cathedral, which was "as high as the vaults of the aisles."

Only the left wing of the Gniezno Cathedral doors (in central Poland) was cast in just one piece. For it, the melting was done on the spot, without calamine, by a Mosan workshop. However, the doors, commissioned about 1152 by Alexander of Plock for the cathedral (today at Hagia Sofia, Novgorod), were made in Magdeburg of panels separately cast. Three of the panels represent the casters and their tools. The doors at San Zeno, Verona, are a hodgepodge of forty-eight panels, in two styles, enframed within moldings of pierced work. Related to the first (older) San Zeno style is a rare statuette in bronze of a kneeling woman signed Lagerinus (Val Lagerina), formerly in the Von Hirsch collection, which was sold in 1978. The six doors signed by Bonannus of Pisa and Barisanus of Trani in the last decades of the twelfth century are all made of bronze panels separately cast, then enframed in a framework nailed on wooden boards. Barisanus used matrixes and sand casting to produce, in series, the elements of his frames.

In the second half of the eleventh century were imported into south Italy, at Amalfi, Monte San Angelo, Atrani, Salerno, and San Paolo fuori le Mura in

Gilt bronze candlestick from Gloucester Cathedral, 1110. VICTORIA AND ALBERT MUSEUM, LONDON. NR. 7649.1861

Rome, Constantinopolitan bronze doors inlaid in silver (for the flesh tones) and damascened in silver (for the draperies). Oderisius of Benevento executed in the same technique the doors of the main portal of Troia Cathedral, in Benevento.

IRON

The medieval methods for hardening, tempering, and annealing iron are mixed with folklore in *Von Stahel und Eisen,* published in 1539. The smith had to beat into rods and bars the rough blooms received from the furnace. Water-powered drop hammers appeared during the twelfth century and developed into hydraulic helve hammers, which in the fifteenth century led to the standardization of suits of white armor made of tightly adjusted plates. Steel, called *acer* since the mid twelfth century, was imported in osmunds from Sweden and Spain. It was valuable for welding edges on tools and weapons, knitting chain mail, and sharpening picks and wedges. Spurs and stirrups were formed in the separate trade of the spurrier. Blast furnaces—in which a draft of air was blown by water-powered bellows—born in the Liège region and Rhineland, are reported in Weardale in 1418. Cannon were sometimes cast in iron before they became mass produced in bronze. Cast iron was used for fireplace furnishings, with the finest German firebacks coming from the Eifel region of the "Stückofen" (shaft furnaces).

Wrought iron, used for hinges, roof finials, and weathercocks, as well as for tying together courses of ashlar and stone tracery, entered art history with the iron-work decorating wooden doors and coffers, and wrought iron screens and grilles. The basic motifs of hinge strapwork and scrollwork shown in tenth- and eleventh-century illuminations and existing in situ at the portals of Romanesque French and English churches—C-shaped bars, scrolls, and palmettes—were hammered out of red-hot bars bent by blows on a rounded anvil, the stake. Details of the strapwork on the doors of the western portals of Notre Dame de Paris, in the thirteenth century, the vine pattern of a chest at St. Jacques, Liège, the ironwork door stamped by the smith Gilebertus at St. George's Chapel, Windsor (*ca.* 1245), and the Eleanor hearse at Westminster Abbey (1294)—were all struck while the wrought iron was red-hot, in dies of steel or hardened iron.

Catalonia gave its name to a type of forge for smelting iron that remained in use in remote spots of Europe until modern times. In the Catalan furnace a blast pipe inclined downwards penetrates the brick

METALLURGY

wall of an open hearth and concentrates the draught on the base of a charge of sifted ore and fuel lying on burning charcoal. The malleable iron thus yielded allowed the production of fine grilles in Spain, the earliest being that separating the Santa Cruz chapel from the cloister in Pamplona Cathedral.

Comparable work exists at the pilgrims' gate in Winchester Cathedral and in the screens inserted by the Knights Templar between the columns of the Dome of the Rock in Jerusalem. In the greatest ensemble—the grilles before the twenty chapels in the cloister of Barcelona Cathedral—the scrolls were replaced by spaced vertical bars and the decoration was concentrated on the flowers blossoming on the crest. In England, a similar evolution toward a sense of structural verticalism was influenced by the perpendicular style in architecture, with its partitioning into panels. It led to the "joiner's style" of ironwork in the fifteenth century.

In the early stage of Italian grilles, the iron framework was grooved to receive sheet iron. Panels of openwork quatrefoils were constantly used in the fourteenth century. In the fifteenth century, these quatrefoils were built into iron framing, surmounted by a cut-out frieze and heraldic shields like those in the chapel of the town hall of Siena (1445).

The German bronze founders created such monumental masterpieces as the crowns of light, symbolic of the Heavenly Jerusalem, at Hildesheim and Aachen, the imperial throne at Goslar, and the four kneeling figures supporting the reliquary altar named Crodoaltar. A great number of church candelabra and bases for crosses were produced in the Meuse valley and in Saxony, at Fritzlar, and in Westphalia.

BRASS

Aquamanilia, when not shaped into human busts, followed a style inspired by Islamic bronze animals. Sepulchral brass sheets engraved with the image of the deceased made sporadic appearances in Germany between 1187 and 1231. After the second third of the thirteenth century, northern France was the center of diffusion of the brass tomb toward England, the Low Countries, and western Germany. Brass alloy is described by Albertus Magnus (*ca.* 1206–1280) in his *Book of Minerals.* Copper is permeated by zinc vapor emanating from a heated mixture of calamine ore, charcoal, and shavings of copper. The temperature is then raised, and some tin (to modify the color) and "oil of glass" (to impart brilliance) are added. Cologne exported undecorated brass sheets, usually cast in sand trays. Local artists engraved these sheets with chasing tracers and burins. The brass sheets then were set in a flat stone indented enough to receive the brass flush with the surface of its frame. Thousands survive in England as an alternative to more expensive sculptured effigies. In the duchy of Burgundy, the stone mourners of the tombs at Dijon were imitated in brass statuettes representing a procession of relatives, as in the tombs of Louis II de Male, Joan of Brabant, and Isabella of Bourbon. In the late fifteenth century, English engravers tried to imitate relief on their brass tombs by shading with crosshatching.

Dinanderie—a word derived from the ware produced at Dinant, in the Meuse valley—applies to brass dishes, jugs, cooking vessels, chandeliers, and candlesticks of the pricket and socket types. The sack of Dinant in 1466 forced many brass founders to emigrate to France and England. Monumental works in dinanderie produced in the last third of the fifteenth century are the baptismal font at 's Hertogenbosch in the Netherlands and the *tref*—a screen bearing candles—thirteen meters long at St. Victor in Xanten, Westphalia (both founded by Aerts of Maastricht), Renier van Thienen's paschal candelabrum, over six meters high at St. Leonard, Léau, and the Van Trichts' eagle lectern in the Metropolitan Museum, New York, in which the lost wax technique and the sand piece mold process seem to have been combined.

Lead was essential in architecture to cover roofs and spires and to channel water. In the fifteenth century, gargoyles were sometimes made in lead. Slabs were cast on inclined sand trays, a process resurrected by the French architect Deneux in the restoration of Rheims Cathedral after World War I. These slabs could not be too long or too wide because of the propensity of lead to expand or shrink according to temperature. In order to avoid the formation of white lead, they had to be laid on timber completely purged of sap. Lead, easy to cast because of its low melting point and its stability when cooling, was used to fashion a number of baptismal fonts in Romanesque France and England. Badges worn by pilgrims back from visiting shrines were made of lead or tin. More lead flagons are represented in fifteenth-century painting than there are surviving objects.

PEWTER AND TIN

Fine pewter does not contain lead. It is an alloy of 90 percent tin with red copper and antimony.

Common pewter contains from 10 percent to 20 percent of lead. Tin was mined in Cornwall since antiquity and also in Saxony and Bohemia from the fourteenth century on. The oldest medieval art objects in tin are tripod candlesticks ornamented with horsemen in chain mail (in the Bruges and The Hague museums).

BIBLIOGRAPHY

Albert Boeckler, *Die Bronzetür von Verona* (1931); Philippe Boucaud, *Les étains* (1978); Wolfgang Braunfels, "Karls des Grossen Bronzewerkstatt," in *Karl der Grosse: Lebenswerk und Nachleben,* III, *Karolingische Kunst* (1965); Arthur Byne and Mildred Stapley, *Spanish Ironwork* (1915); Suzanne Collon-Gevaert, *Histoire des arts du métal en Belgique* (1951); Jadwiga Irena Daniec, "The Bronze Door of the Gniezno Cathedral in Poland," in *The Polish Review,* **11** (1966); Giulio Ferrari, *Il Ferro nell'arte italiana* (1910); Albert France-Lanord, *La fabrication des épées damassées aux époques mérovingienne et carolingienne* (1949); John Starkie Gardner, *Ironwork,* I, *From the Earliest Times to the End of the Medieval Period,* rev. by William W. Watts (1927); Adolph Goldschmidt, *Die deutschen Bronzetüren des frühen Mittelalters* (1926), *Die Bronzetüren von Nowgorod und Griesen* (1932), and *Die Bronzetüren von Bonannus von Pisa und Barisanus von Trani* (1953); John H. Harvey, *Mediaeval Craftsmen* (1975); John G. Hawthorne and Cyril S. Smith, eds. and trans., *On Divers Arts: The Treatise of Theophilus* (1963, repr. 1979); Otto S. Homburger, *Der Trivulzio-Kandelaber* (1949); Anton Legner, "Die Rinderherde des Reiner von Huy," in *Rhein und Maas, Kunst und Kultur 800–1400,* II (1973); Mary P. Merrifield, ed., *Original Treatises,* I (1849); Édouard Salin, *La civilisation mérovingienne,* III, *Les techniques* (1957); Édouard Salin and Albert France-Lanord, *Rhin et Orient,* II, *Le fer à l'époque mérovingienne* (1943); Jacques Stiennon, "La Pologne et le pays mosan au moyen âge: À propos d'un ouvrage sur la porte de Gniezno," in M. Walicki, ed., *Drzwi Gnieznienskie,* 2 vols. (1956–1959), and *Cahiers de civilisation médiévale,* **4** (1961); Daniel V. Thompson, "Trial Index to Some Unpublished Sources for the History of Mediaeval Craftsmanship," *Speculum,* **10** (1935); Berthie Trenteseau, *La damasquinure mérovingienne en Belgique* (1966); Francis J. Tschan, *Saint Bernward of Hildesheim,* II, *His Works of Art* (1951); Philippe Verdier, "La grande croix de l'abbé Suger à Saint-Denis," *Cahiers de civilisation médiévale,* **13** (1970); Eugène E. Viollet-le-Duc, "Plomberie," in *Dictionnaire raisonné de l'architecture Française du XIe au XVIe siècle,* 7 (1864), and "Serrurerie," *ibid.,* 8 (1866); Otto von Falke and Erich Meyer, *Romanische Leuchter und Gefässe, Giessgefässe der Gotik* (1935); Hermann W. Williams, Jr., ed. and trans., "A Sixteenth-century German Treatise: *Von Stahel und Eysen,*" in *Technical Studies in the Field of the Fine Arts,* **4** (1935); George Zarnecki, *English Romanesque Lead Sculpture: Lead Fonts of the Twelfth Century* (1957).

PHILIPPE VERDIER

[See also **Arms and Armor; Bells; Bronze and Brass; Metalsmiths, Gold and Silver; Metalworkers; Mosan Art; Theophilus.**]

METALSMITHS, GOLD AND SILVER. Throughout the Middle Ages the artisans who worked with gold and silver were usually known as goldsmiths, a fact reflected in the name of the livery company in London that has controlled the craft of working in precious metals since its incorporation by royal charter in 1327—the Worshipful Company of Goldsmiths of London. Only in recent times does the title "silversmith" appear to have become common, and the *Oxford Dictionary of English Etymology* gives an Old English origin for "goldsmith," but fails even to mention "silversmith."

The goldsmiths of the early Middle Ages, in the towns of the Mediterranean area which survived the breakup of the Roman Empire, were no doubt subject to organized control. Craft guilds had existed in the Roman Empire and large numbers of surviving pieces of silver plate are stamped with control marks, which attest the weight and/or purity of the silver. This type of control—essentially an early form of hallmarking—continued in the workshops of the Byzantine Empire of the East, whose products were familiar to the barbarians in the West, even if they did not understand the significance of the control stamps. For example, at the Sutton Hoo burial site, there was found in the grave of the East Anglian king Raedwald (who died *ca.* 625) a large silver dish with a control stamp of the emperor Anastasius.

However, in early medieval northern Europe, no such organization or control is known to have existed. As a result, the goldsmith was dependent on the patronage of the nobility, and the only control exercised on the craft was the satisfaction given to very powerful customers. Among the barbarian tribes that established kingdoms which were the successors of the Roman Empire in Italy, France, Spain, and England, the tribal organization was such that society was bound together by the obligations of one class to the next. At the top of the pyramid was the king, who sustained his immediate following by the giving of gifts, normally of personal jewelry or richly ornamented weapons. The goldsmith played

METALSMITHS, GOLD AND SILVER

an essential role in this process by making the precious donatives for the ruling classes.

Virtually nothing is known of the status of the goldsmith in the very early Middle Ages, but two facts are clear. First, the most skilled smiths could rise to high positions in the social hierarchy and become very powerful men in their own right; and second, at this period the goldsmith was also an expert in the working of other nonferrous metals, such as lead, pewter, bronze, and brass, and possibly also in the working of iron. The evidence for the varied skills of the smith is to be found in the mythology of the period and in the assemblages of tools from a number of graves.

That goldsmiths could rise to positions of power is demonstrated by the career of Eligius, in France. He was apprenticed to a goldsmith and mintmaster by the name of Abbon in the early seventh century, and subsequently the excellence of his work brought him to the notice of the Frankish king Clotaire II (613–629), for whom he made two gold thrones. Eligius continued to be patronized by Dagobert I (629–639), who made him master of the mint, and a number of Merovingian coins survive with Eligius' name on them. In 641, Eligius was consecrated bishop of Noyon. He died in 660, having combined great offices of church and state in a way which was to become increasingly common in the Middle Ages. The names of many Merovingian moneyers or mintmasters are known from the gold coinage of the seventh century, but, with the exception of coinage, other works of art were not signed and their creators are thus known only from chance mentions in wills and other documents. Thus the will of Perpetuus, bishop of Tours, who died *ca.* 477, bequeathed to his church two gold chalices and a gold cross, which had been made by a certain Mabuinus.

With the rise of the church as an important feature of daily life, the goldsmith acquired a new patron, as not only did churches require gold and silver liturgical plate, but the dignitaries of the church required jewelry, in the form of rings and pectoral crosses, to mark their status.

It has often been suggested, especially for the early Middle Ages, that most artists were in fact monks, but this cannot be proved and is certainly not true from the twelfth century on. Nevertheless, it may be significant that Eligius founded the monastery of Solignac, near Limoges, in which he assembled monks who were skilled in all the arts and whose job was the production of objects for ecclesiastical use. In this way, monasteries, which were an organized and regulated group of craftsmen, were the forerunners of the fraternities and guilds which later on existed in the towns.

Although both church and state patronized the goldsmith in the early Middle Ages, surviving examples of gold and silver are heavily weighted to-

Angilbert presenting the golden altar to St. Ambrose, and Ambrose blessing Wolvinus. Roundels from the doors of Wolvinus' golden altar of S. Ambrogio, Milan, 9th century. ALINARI/ART RESOURCE

METALSMITHS, GOLD AND SILVER

ward those produced for the church. Secular works of art did not receive the same reverence as the ecclesiastical ones and were much more likely to be melted down by subsequent owners.

One of the earliest works of art to be signed by a goldsmith in the Middle Ages is the magnificent gold altar in the Church of St. Ambrose in Milan, which was executed in 835 by Wolvinus (or Vuolvinus) on the orders of Archbishop Angilbert II. Two embossed scenes on this altar show, respectively, St. Ambrose receiving the golden altar from the hands of Archbishop Angilbert and St. Ambrose blessing Wolvinus himself. The depiction of a donor on a work of art is quite common, but it is unusual at this time for a goldsmith to sign his work.

Fashion in metalwork was no less important than in architecture, and the result was that the best goldsmiths were sometimes imported from other countries to manufacture important pieces. Hence, Constantinople was a source of goldsmiths for Italian and German patrons in the tenth and eleventh centuries.

That the tradition of successful monastic goldsmiths rising to high office continued is demonstrated in the tenth century by Dunstan, who became archbishop of Canterbury, and in the eleventh by Bernward, who became bishop of Hildesheim. But, to the historian of technology, the most important ecclesiastical goldsmith lived in the late eleventh and early twelfth century and is known by the pseudonym of Theophilus. The real identity of this artisan is unknown, although he has been identified with the Benedictine monk and metalworker Roger of Helmarshausen, but his importance lies in the treatise on glassmaking and metalwork which he wrote, probably in the period 1110–1140.

Although Theophilus' book is, in part at least, a compilation from other sources, its importance is to demonstrate that the goldsmith also worked in other nonferrous metals, particularly copper, bronze, and brass. Chapters are included which tell the goldsmith how to make and maintain tools for himself. He is then instructed in refining his own silver before converting it into an object. The treatise also deals with the making of solder and soldering, and with techniques of decoration such as gilding, enameling, engraving, and inlaying niello.

The manufacture of chalices in both gold and silver is described, as is the lost wax casting of a brass censer. But besides these techniques for the manufacture of small objects, the treatise also deals with the manufacture of organs and the casting of bells, and this latter activity is attested for at least one goldsmith, Edward Fitz Odo of Westminster, who died in 1264/1265. With the growth of towns, the secular goldsmith became more common and the necessity of controlling the craft and its products became evident.

It is known that the goldsmiths themselves had formed a fraternity in London by the late twelfth century at the latest, because in 1179–1180 they were fined the large sum of forty-five marks for operating without a license from the king. This fine, equivalent to more than four years' wages for a master craftsman, must indicate that the goldsmiths were already a well organized and powerful, if illegal, organization.

The reason is not difficult to see, in that the precious metals, gold and silver, were the basis of economic exchange. Hence, the most successful of those who dealt in these materials were often able to amass fortunes. As a result, the craft of goldsmiths often ran in families, and the Edward Fitz Odo who cast bells at Westminster in the thirteenth century was a member of a family of prominent goldsmiths and mintmasters between 1100 and 1300 who probably traced their ancestry back to a certain Otto the Goldsmith mentioned in Domesday Book. These rich and powerful families provided mayors and sheriffs for the City of London and were well placed to petition the king for a royal charter, which was granted in 1327.

This date may seem far removed from 1180, but there are occasional hints at an organized guild in the intervening years, as in 1273 when Geoffrey de Ambresbure, goldsmith, founded a chantry and put it in the care of the wardens of the fraternity of St. Dunstan, the patron saint of English goldsmiths.

The crown's willingness to grant a charter was linked to the necessity of controlling the craft—in particular the quality of the wares produced by the artisans—and of maintaining a regular supply of coin of the realm. The king issued the coin via authorized mints and guaranteed the quality of the silver. But the refining of the silver, the cutting of dies, the assaying of the metal, and the overall overseeing of the operation were probably in the hands of goldsmiths.

The crown also depended on goldsmiths for another activity—the checking and exchanging of foreign coin when it was imported into the country. The expansion of trade in the thirteenth century brought into London all manner of continental coins of alloy inferior to that of the English silver

METALSMITHS, GOLD AND SILVER

pennies, and Edward I made several vigorous attempts to control the situation. The effect on the goldsmiths was felt in 1238 and 1241, when the king ordered that all wares of gold and silver should conform to standards of purity laid down by the crown, and then in 1300 Edward I stipulated that silver should not be less than 92.5 percent fine and that all articles should be assayed and hallmarked with a punch in the shape of a leopard's head before being sold. These rules applied to all goldsmiths, and those in provincial towns had to observe the same standards. Strangely, however, the standard laid down for gold wares remained 80 percent fine.

The assaying and hallmarking were put in the hands of the goldsmiths and the manufactured articles were brought to the wardens of the craft for testing. However, the wardens also visited goldsmiths' workshops and had the power to destroy substandard wares. Nevertheless, the reforms of Edward I were short-lived, and the goldsmiths themselves sought a royal charter in 1327 to confirm their powers with a view to putting their own house in order. In this year, six goldsmiths either were aldermen of the city of London or had just relinquished or were about to take up office. The regulations imposed by the charter were concerned not only with the quality of the metal, but expressly forbade the setting of imitation (glass) gemstones in precious metal or the gilding of brass. They limited the selling of plate either to the goldsmiths' area (now Cheapside) or to the Royal Exchange, and regulated the apprenticeships for the good of the craft.

The regulations of the Worshipful Company of Goldsmiths of London indicate that the craft was now becoming more specialized, although in the last decade of the thirteenth century the casting in bronze of the funeral effigies of Henry III and Eleanor of Castile had been put in the hands of William Torel, goldsmith of London. Clock making was another, and expanding, branch of metalworking which was sometimes carried on by goldsmiths, but by the fifteenth century, metalworking was, on the whole, very specialized. The wide range of these specialities is demonstrated by the illustrations of craftsmen at work in the list of "brothers" of an almshouse for elderly men in Nuremberg.

Besides the organization of a guild in London, similar associations evolved in other countries. In 1260, the provost of Paris issued a code of statutes for the goldsmiths there, and it was the French standard of 80 percent (19.2 carats) fine for gold alloys which was adopted in England, where it was known as the "touch of Paris." In 1355 the French king, John II, ordered that each goldsmith should have a distinctive punch to mark his wares, and the same practice was introduced in England in 1363 by Edward III. The date/letter hallmark was introduced in the fifteenth century as a means of identifying the wardens responsible for the assay in case a piece of plate was subsequently found to be substandard. In England, the date/letter was changed on St. Dunstan's Day, 19 May, when the new wardens were elected.

In 1477, Edward IV increased the responsibility of the wardens and made the Goldsmiths Company responsible for their actions, with the result that, in 1478, a full-time salaried assayer was first appointed. He had three methods of testing gold and silver available to him, although, in practice, only two of them seem to have been used. The oldest method was fire assay, in which a small sample of the gold or silver is removed from the article, weighed, and heated in a special crucible with some lead. The lead and any alloying elements are oxidized in the furnace and the oxides absorbed by the crucible, leaving behind the gold and/or silver, which is reweighed. When gold articles are assayed there is a second stage to the process, known as parting, in which the silver is dissolved away in nitric acid to leave behind pure gold. This process was probably in use as early as the second millennium B.C. in the eastern Mediterranean area.

The second method was the use of the touchstone, which was known to the Greeks in the sixth century B.C. This is a piece of smooth black stone on which gold can be rubbed to leave a yellow streak. The color of this streak is compared with marks made on the same stone by alloys of known composition until a match is found. By this technique, the medieval goldsmith could assay gold with an accuracy of about plus or minus 2 percent. The touchstone was also used for testing silver containing copper, although probably with somewhat reduced accuracy.

The third method was to measure the density of a gold object by Archimedes' method. However, although the principles of the method were understood by the beginning of the Middle Ages, there is very little evidence that it was actually in routine use for quantitative assaying.

Little or nothing can be written about the workshops of the goldsmiths in the early medieval period, and it is not even known with certainty whether they were sedentary, or whether they migrated from one patron to another. However, by the twelfth century a workshop had evolved which would be instantly recognizable to the craft goldsmith of today. At the actual bench, there were virtually no changes in the period from 1000–1500, and probably very few in the previous 500 years.

BIBLIOGRAPHY

Rupert L. S. Bruce-Mitford, *The Sutton Hoo Ship-Burial: A Handbook,* 2nd ed. (1972); Wilfred J. Cripps, *Old English Plate* (1881); Erica C. Dodd, *Byzantine Silver Stamps* (1961); John H. Harvey, *Mediaeval Craftsmen* (1975); Hugh Honour, *Goldsmiths and Silversmiths* (1971); M. Jules Labarte, *Handbook of the Arts of the Middle Ages and Renaissance* (1855); Jean Lafaurie, "Eligius Monetarius," in *Revue numismatique,* 6th ser., **19** (1977); Thomas F. Reddaway and Lorna E. M. Walker, *The Early History of the Goldsmiths' Company* (1975); David Sherlock, "Silversmiths and Silversmithing," in Donald Strong and David Brown, eds., *Roman Crafts* (1976); Theophilus, *On Divers Arts,* John G. Hawthorne and Cyril S. Smith, eds. and trans. (1963, repr. 1979), and *The Various Arts,* C. R. Dodwell, ed. and trans. (1961); Wilhelm Treue *et al., Das Hausbuch der Mendelschen Zwölfbrüderstiftung* (1965).

W. A. ODDY

[See also **Exchequer; Metallurgy; Metalworking; Mints and Money; Theophilus.**]

METALWORKERS. By the end of the medieval period in Europe, the majority of metalworkers, from goldsmiths to blacksmiths, were craftsmen whose activities were controlled by guilds; thus they were no different from the members of numerous other trades. However, this was not always the case. There is some evidence that 1,000 years earlier the metalworker was an exalted member of the community, the result of tradition handed down from the Bronze Age, when the smith was in the forefront of the advance of technology; there is also little doubt that the idea of a smith-god originated in the Bronze Age. By the Iron Age the Greek pantheon included a smith-god, Hephaistos, whose Hindu equivalent was Viśvakarma. The tradition passed into Roman mythology with Vulcan. Norse folklore has the god Thor, and it is with this god and the mythological smiths, Wayland and Regin, that we enter the medieval period proper.

In the early Middle Ages, the power of the smith was associated with that of kingship. The grave of the East Anglian king Raedwald, who died around 625, contained not only a symbolic axe-hammer with a wrought iron haft, but also a scepter in the form of a huge whetstone to symbolize the king's mastery over the weapons of his followers.

The importance of the smith lay above all in his ability to make weapons, especially swords, which were not just weapons but also symbols of authority. Some mythological swords, such as Excalibur in the stories of King Arthur and Charlemagne's Joyeuse, were even believed to possess magical powers. The sword was the emblem par excellence of the warrior. A number of magnificent specimens from the early-medieval period in Europe survive, attesting to the prowess of the blacksmith and the jeweler. Many of these craftsmen must have held the same sort of exalted positions in the numerous royal or chieftains' households at this period as the alchemists did at the close of the Middle Ages.

THE SOCIAL POSITION OF THE SMITH

Grave finds are the most important source of evidence for the social position of the smith and for the extent of his tool kit in the early Middle Ages. Forty-five known graves in Scandinavia from this period each contained at least one item of metallurgical equipment—the most usual being hammer, tongs, or a file. In twenty-six of the graves only one tool was present, usually accompanied by one or two farming implements and the weapons of the dead man. This suggests that many men were capable of carrying out basic smithing operations, such as repairs to household and agricultural equipment. Nevertheless, some graves contained more extensive assemblies of tools as well as weapons, probably indicating that their owners were full-time smiths who occupied key positions among a warrior class near the top of the social scale.

Occasionally the contents of a grave suggest a degree of specialization within the generalized craft of metalworking. At Schönebeck in Germany, Poysdorf in Austria, and Kunszentmárton in Hungary, there are graves that have been interpreted (by Schmidt and Werner) as those of goldsmiths. The graves in Austria and Hungary contained matrices for impressing designs on metal (gold?) foil, and hammers and tongs, which could be used for other metalworking operations; and the grave at Kunszentmárton contained a balance and weights. The graves also contained weapons, indicating warrior-smiths, as did a grave at Hérouvillette in Normandy (described by Decaens), which also contained a large number of tools. The presence of some mercury in the latter is almost certainly an indication that the

METALWORKERS

smith was a maker of jewelry and decorative metalwork, since mercury was used in the process of gilding silver and bronze.

The rich contents of royal or princely graves, such as that at Sutton Hoo in England, which dates from about 625, suggest that the most skilled smiths and jewelers worked under the patronage of the king. In the mythology of the period, Wayland the Smith served a royal master to the extent of having his Achilles tendons cut so that he could not run away. Wayland's fame as a smith encompassed the use of both iron and nonferrous metals. He is reputed to have revenged himself on the king by killing the ruler's two sons and making richly ornamented drinking cups out of their skulls. These must have resembled the well-known ornamented drinking horns of the period, which often had their rims decorated with gilt-silver mounts and the outside covered with embossed silver or gold foil.

While the mutilation of the mythological Wayland implies that he was not a freeman, the master smith Eligius at the seventh-century Merovingian court rose from humble origins to serve two royal patrons as goldsmith, as master of the mint, and as bishop of Noyon. The career of Eligius is perhaps the best indication of the social position of the smith in that period. At the lowest level, many of the freemen in the village community were probably able to carry out simple metalworking tasks, while the more difficult operations were taken to the local smith, whose craft, by analogy with modern ethnographic parallels, was probably often hereditary. The more skilled would earn a reputation that would take them into the ranks of the warrior class or, with the

Wayland the Smith. Detail from the whalebone box known as the Franks Casket, Northumbrian, late 7th century. BY COURTESY OF THE TRUSTEES OF THE BRITISH MUSEUM, LONDON

growth of a more settled society, into the households of the nobility, where they exercised their skills under princely patronage. We know from Italian documents, as cited by Bóna, that the "Lombard smiths . . . were distinguished men of great importance . . . [who] bought land to give additional emphasis to their noble status."

In the early Middle Ages there is little evidence for specialization among the numerous metalworking skills, and the first great division that manifests itself (and that may have been already in existence for some time) is between workers in iron and those who made things of the other metals of antiquity (gold, silver, copper, tin, lead, and alloys such as pewter, bronze, and brass). The division is brought about by the fact that, until the fifteenth century, iron was not normally obtained in the molten state during the extraction process, because of limitations to the temperature that could be reached in the contemporary furnaces. As a result, iron objects were not made by casting until the very end of the Middle Ages. Military necessity eventually provided the stimulus for technological advance: the development of the blast furnace owed much to the need for casting cannon solid, rather than making them out of strips of wrought iron hooped together like barrels. The other metals, however, known collectively as nonferrous metals, had been cast since the Bronze Age.

Although the basic difference between the blacksmiths and the nonferrous metalsmiths is one of technique, it resulted in the gradual development of a social scale in which the gold- and silversmiths considered themselves far superior to the workers in other metals, and the blacksmiths were regarded as the most inferior. These social differences have developed to such an extent in the Indian subcontinent that the various types of smiths belong to different castes and do not intermarry. While we have no evidence for such an extreme position in medieval Europe, there is no doubt that a social scale existed, fostered by the guilds into which the craftsmen formed themselves.

Craft specialization on a large scale is a product of a developed economy and, in particular, of the growth of towns. Thus the evidence for specialization between different metalworking techniques, which is available for the Roman period, is more or less lacking for the early Middle Ages, but reemerges with the rise of medieval towns. Wilhelm Treue discusses a fifteenth-century Nuremberg manuscript that illustrates artisans at work in many different trades, several of them being specialized metalworkers such as goldsmith, wire maker, nail maker, knife maker, armorer, armor polisher, and blacksmith. This type of specialization must have emerged gradually, being spurred on by the consumer demands of a rapidly increasing population and by military necessity. Thus the widespread use of mail for protection in battle on the one hand, and the need for carding brushes for an expanding wool industry on the other, are both said to have been important factors in the development of the manufacture of iron wire as a specialized craft, and in the harnessing of waterpower to do the actual drawing.

In the later medieval period, the metalworkers probably occupied certain areas of the towns, as did the other trades, but little is known about the craftsmen of earlier centuries. Smiths are often said to have been itinerant from the Bronze Age onward, and certainly there is an ancient tradition in Europe of wandering gypsies who made a living by tinning or retinning the inside of copper cooking vessels or by sharpening knives. Nevertheless, an early medieval site at Helgö in Sweden has revealed that jewelry-making operations there were carried out on a large scale over many years, and that the products of the smiths must have been disseminated by trade. On the other hand, the late Saxon levels at the deserted medieval village site of Netherton in Hampshire have produced evidence for bronze-casting and decorating techniques on a small scale, probably to satisfy purely local requirements. It is impossible to generalize about the organization of metalworking in the early Middle Ages beyond saying that every community would require the services of a blacksmith and a coppersmith, but whether the needs for items of decoration were filled by means of trade or by a wandering smith setting up his bellows under a convenient tree is impossible to say. Pending further research, we must be content with the few isolated representations, usually carvings, that have survived of smiths at work, such as the eighth-century representation of Wayland at his anvil on a small whalebone box in the British Museum.

THE WORKING OF IRON AND STEEL

Until almost the end of the medieval period iron was produced from its ore as a lump, known as a "bloom," which was very porous and was mixed with slag, charcoal, and unreduced ore. Blooms were relatively small in size, reaching a maximum of about fourteen kilograms (or thirty-one pounds) by the time that the introduction of the blast furnace enabled much larger "pigs" (or ingots) of cast iron to be produced.

The blooms as such were useless to the smith because of the high content of impurities mixed with the iron, so they had to be reheated and hammered on a smithing hearth to eliminate the slag and to turn them into a wrought-iron ingot. This was probably the form in which the iron was traded to the blacksmiths, who made it into weapons, tools, and all the other household paraphernalia. In Scandinavia and Eastern Europe, the form of the ingot seems to have been long and thin, resembling the so-called currency bars of the Iron Age.

Wrought iron is relatively soft and ductile, but it differs from steel only in the amount of carbon that is incorporated in the alloy. The blooms, in fact, usually had a highly variable carbon content, which could be increased or decreased during ingot production on the smithing hearth. The smiths exploited the differences between wrought iron and steel for both utilitarian and decorative purposes. A wrought-iron tool is too soft to use and will bend, but a steel one is too brittle and will break; therefore, smiths found that more serviceable tools could be made by hammer-welding a strip of steel onto the cutting edge of a wrought-iron implement. Hence, they could exploit the properties of both materials and, at the same time, conserve stocks of the more valuable steel. This process was taken to the extreme by swordsmiths and makers of other weapons. They hammer-welded together strips of steel and wrought iron to produce sword blades that would neither break nor bend in battle, and in the very best blades these strips were often twisted together and folded over during the manufacturing process so that the steel and iron were intimately mixed. If the surface of such a blade is carefully polished and then etched with a dilute acid, the structure of the metal shows up as a pattern, the complexity of which reflects the amount of twisting and folding of the original strips. This process is known as pattern welding. It is not, therefore, surprising that the best swords were believed to have magical properties and that the men who made them achieved well-deserved acclaim.

Pattern welding seems to have been on the decline by the end of the Viking period, and the later medieval sword seems to have had a more homogeneous carbon content, although it was often still made of strips of iron welded together. The cutting edges or outer surface were hardened either by the addition of strips of steel or by introducing more carbon in the fire, a process known as case hardening.

In this later period, when sword blades were not themselves decorative, wires of copper, silver, or brass were often inlaid into grooves cut into the iron, to form either decorative patterns or inscriptions and marks to indicate the place of origin of the blade. Inlaying of iron was not new—it is a process that had been known by the Romans—but in the early Middle Ages it was used on jewelry rather than on weapons. The Merovingians, particularly, made iron buckles that were inlaid with silver wires to form very complicated patterns. This was done by either cutting or hammering grooves into the surface of the iron and then hammering silver wires into the grooves. In this way whole areas of a surface could be covered with silver by cutting parallel grooves close together in the iron so that when the silver wire was hammered in, some of it would spread over the adjacent surface, giving the appearance of a continuous sheet. Unlike pattern welding, inlaying with silver also flourished under the Vikings; many superbly decorated Viking weapons have survived.

With the fourteenth-century development of plate armor—to supplement the coat of mail as a means of protection for the soldier—the smith acquired a new field for the exercise of decorative metalworking skills, many of which seem to have developed expressly for the purpose of providing the superb etched, gilded, and embossed parade armor of the Renaissance. However, the development of these decorative techniques was only just beginning to emerge by the end of the fifteenth century, with small areas of etched decoration and the extensive use of fluted decoration embossed into the iron. Like everything else, armor varied in quality: that which was mass produced for the common soldier was made of wrought iron and so was far inferior in the protection it would afford, while the armor produced on commission for the nobility was made to measure and was likely to have been carefully hardened on the surface.

Apart from weapons and armor, the blacksmith was principally engaged in the production from wrought iron of articles for domestic, agricultural, or architectural use, and in this the smith exercised skills that had first been developed in the later Iron Age. Decorative wrought iron has survived in sufficient quantity from the pre-Christian era to testify to the skill of the smiths, whose principal tools were the hammer, tongs, anvil, and hot chisel. From the early medieval period, a number of wrought-iron masterpieces have been preserved, one of the most famous being the seventh-century decorative chainwork from which a cauldron was suspended, found in the Anglo-Saxon royal burial site at Sutton Hoo. Since most of the surviving early medieval artifacts have been found in graves, there are virtually no remains of domestic ironwork, such as spits, firedogs, bucket handles, fittings for carts, and so forth. Architectural ironwork survives in an ever-increasing amount from the tenth century onward. Window grilles and decorative door hinges are our main evidence for the skill of the blacksmith in the period up to the fourteenth century, a period that has been called "the age of the blacksmith."

From the fourteenth century, however, a change takes place in the blacksmith's workshop. Instead of relying exclusively on the working of wrought iron when hot with only the help of a hammer (and chisel), the smith began also to shape the iron when cold. To do this, smiths introduced the file, saw, drill, and vise and began to shape iron components that were then riveted together, or tenoned and mortised, instead of hammer-welded. It is probably at this time that the skills of the blacksmith began to diversify and that smiths began to specialize in the production of one type of object, such as swords and knives, or iron locks and keys. Some idea of the degree of specialization can be obtained from the guild records (one of the most useful of these records is the above-mentioned Nuremberg manuscript, which illustrates the various artisans at work). Indeed, the diversification of skills and the growth in the demand for iron, especially for use in warfare, was so great that the fourteenth and fifteenth centuries have been called "the age of the locksmith and armorer."

THE WORKING OF NONFERROUS METALS

By comparison with the coppersmith and goldsmith (a title that included the working of silver), the blacksmith had a very limited repertoire of techniques and a relatively small range of tools—at least until near the close of the Middle Ages, when iron began to be decorated by engraving, embossing, and tinning, and, for armor especially, bluing and gilding. Nonferrous metals were different because they could be cast to shape as well as forged hot or cold, and because they were used much more for decorative purposes, either on their own or to adorn an object made of iron. Thus the best swords had bronze or brass (or even silver or gold) pommels, and iron spurs were often tinned by dipping in a bath of the molten metal.

Just as the techniques of the blacksmith continued from the earlier period, so there is no evidence for change in the technology for working nonferrous metals. Vessels were usually made by hammering (known technically as raising) from a suitably shaped cast ingot, and the surviving bronze, brass, silver, and, occasionally, gold vessels testify to the skill of the workers. Jewelry was usually made by casting, as were handles and other fittings for the hammered vessels. Two casting techniques were in use. One was to make a model in wax of the object to be cast and then to build up layers of clay around this to form the mold. An opening was left at a suitable point so that when the clay dried, the wax was melted and poured out, the clay was baked, and molten metal was poured in to take the place of the wax original. Using this technique, which is known as the lost-wax or cire perdue method, the mold can be used only once, as it must be broken to release the casting. However, it is possible to make a series of almost identical castings by using pattern molds to create the wax original. Using the cire perdue technique, castings of great complexity can be made, although considerable skill was necessary to ensure that the metal completely filled the mold before it solidified and to ensure that no air bubbles were trapped in the mold, thus preventing the access of molten metal to every part. Lost-wax casting has a history going back to the Bronze Age, and it is still used today, particularly in the jewelry industry.

The other method of casting is with a reusable mold. This was either a simple "open" mold usually cut in a suitable stone or made out of a block of clay, or a piece mold consisting of two (or more) pieces that fit together during casting, but that could be separated for the removal of the finished object and then used again. Surviving fragments of baked clay molds are not common and it is usually difficult to distinguish between a broken piece mold and a discarded cire perdue mold, unless a join is visible indicating the former. One site that has produced hundreds of early medieval mold fragments, which appear to be broken piece molds, is Helgö near Stockholm, where bronze jewelry was manufactured in the pre-Viking period.

The coppersmith or goldsmith, unlike the blacksmith, used solder as a method of joining composite parts of single objects and for attaching decoration in the form of filigree and granulation—techniques of jewelry decoration that did not survive into the later Middle Ages. They were replaced by enameling as a means par excellence for adorning the highest quality jewelry or plate. In fact, enameling developed during the medieval period from the simple filling of single cloisonné cells, built up on the surface of a piece of jewelry, to the covering of larger areas of a surface with translucent enamels melted together to make exquisite works of art.

Gilding was commonly applied to silver or base metal and the technique used was invariably that of fire gilding, in which the gold was dissolved in mercury to make a mixture that was soft (like butter) and that could be rubbed onto the surface of the object. This was then heated over a fire to evaporate the mercury and leave behind a firmly bonded layer of gold. In addition, the nonferrous smiths excelled at engraving, embossing, and inlaying with precious stones or with niello.

The only important metalworking technique that was invented in the millennium following the collapse of the Roman Empire in the West, apart from the casting of iron (which was the result of furnace development), was the invention of wiredrawing. The origins of this process are obscure. It has been claimed as a Roman, or even Iron Age, invention, but in Britain, for instance, gold wire was certainly not drawn before the end of the Roman period. The process was known by early Viking times, as attested by a number of wiredrawing dies that have survived in Scandinavia.

The nonferrous smiths made much use of punches and matrices for the application of repeated designs to their products and these techniques were readily adapted for the manufacture of dies for the production of coinage. The growth of towns and the development of trade demanded an abundant coinage, which was manufactured in special workshops, known as mints, that were usually under royal control. From the ninth century on, the designs on the dies were made with punches, and therefore the resulting portraits were stylized, bearing little or no relation to the actual ruler. It was not until the fifteenth century that dies were engraved in the antique manner, which resulted in real portraits on the coins. Each coin required the use of two dies, one for the obverse and the other for the reverse. The coins were struck from discs of silver, usually cut with a pair of shears, by placing them between the two dies and striking the upper one with a heavy hammer while the lower one was embedded in a large block of wood. In this way, the designs were impressed onto both faces of the coin at the same time. This process is the only example of real mass production before the Industrial Revolution.

METALWORKERS

METALWORKING TOOLS

For the study of medieval tools we have three sources of information: (1) the actual tools that have survived, especially in the graves of the pagan period, (2) illustrations in manuscripts or carvings on architectural reliefs or gravestones, and (3) descriptions in the literature of the period.

As a whole, these sources show that metalworking tools have remained unchanged for centuries and many modern hand tools can be paralleled throughout the Middle Ages. The Mästermyr chest, from the Viking period, contained a set of seven hammers of different sizes and types, together with tongs, files, shears, punches, an anvil, a saw, a wiredrawing die, and a nail-making iron. The number of hammers shows how this most basic of tools had developed specialized forms to suit particular jobs. It is noticeable that one of these seven hammers has the hole for the haft at one end of the head, rather than in the center. An identical hammer is shown in a fifteenth-century manuscript illustration of a goldsmith.

Another find, from Viborg in Jutland, has four different types of hammer and three different types of tongs, one of which is probably for gripping wire when pulling it through a drawplate, while a warrior grave from Vestly in Roganland includes a hand drill in the tool kit. Apart from these tools, a vast range of different types of punches are known or are attested from the impressions they have left on medieval metalwork. Similarly, although only a few matrices are known for embossing designs on thin foil, large numbers of pieces of embossed foil survive, usually as applied decoration on larger objects. Goldsmiths used delicate tweezers in addition to the more robust tongs, and were often buried with a balance and weights, and occasionally with a touchstone for assaying gold. This touchstone is a small piece of fine-grained black stone on which the gold is rubbed to make a yellow mark, the color of which is then compared with the marks made by a number of alloys of known composition. Besides the use of the touchstone for assaying gold, documentary sources such as the *Mappae clavicula* indicate that Archimedes' method was also used—a method that involves measuring the density of the alloy to be tested by weighing it in air and then reweighing it when immersed in water.

The one tool that does not survive in the archaeological record is the bellows, because they were made of wood and leather. They are, however, well illustrated on a number of early medieval carvings and in manuscripts for the later period, from which it can be seen that bellows were always used in pairs to give a continuous blast.

Most of the tools mentioned so far are for the hot working of iron or the cold (or hot) working of nonferrous metals, but the smith also needed a supply of crucibles, master molds, wax, and clay for his casting operations. Many crucibles have survived but, as yet, no significant petrological studies have been carried out on their composition, although Theophilus, writing in the twelfth century, tells us that they were made from finely ground white clay, which was tempered with crushed fragments from broken crucibles. The wax used for making the models was beeswax, but modern parallels suggest that it was probably blended with rosin (a natural resin from pine trees). Similarly, eventual examination of surviving fragments of molds will probably show that the clay was mixed with organic material, such as chaff, which burnt away when the mold was fired, thus rendering it sufficiently porous so that the air could escape during the casting operation.

The other source of inestimable value, both for tools and techniques, is the literature of the period. Surprisingly, four technological treatises have survived from the eighth to twelfth centuries, but the next important preserved treatise dates from as late as the end of the fifteenth century, when the first of a number of books on mining, assaying, and metal-

Fifteenth-century goldsmith, depicted in the *Hausbuch* of the Mendelsche Zwölfbrüder Stiftung, 1431. NÜRNBERG STADTBIBLIOTHEK, AMB. 317. 2°, fol. 51r

METALWORKERS

working was produced. Of the four books from the medieval period, three contain mainly recipes, giving details of alloys, solders, methods of refining precious metals, and ways of coloring metal surfaces. The fourth treatise is a handbook written by a practicing craftsman, a part of which deals with the working of nonferrous metals.

This book, *De diversis artibus,* which was written by a monk known as Theophilus, probably between 1110 and 1140, is the single most valuable source for the history of metal technology during the Middle Ages. It starts with a description of how to equip a workshop, which includes the building of the forge, construction of bellows from the skins of rams, and manufacture of anvils and tools. Numerous different hammers are listed, together with all the types of tools that are known from grave finds. In addition, Theophilus mentions a soldering iron, a burnisher, a scraper, a brass wire-brush, a pestle and mortar, a swage block for making beaded wire, awls, scribers, tracers, and engraving tools. The latter, together with the files, are hardened either by rapid quenching in water—which was sometimes preceded by heating while covered in a mixture containing burnt ox horn—or while wrapped in strips of old leather and clay.

Theophilus then describes the techniques of raising, lost-wax casting, soldering, gilding and inlaying with niello, enameling, embossing, and repoussé work, including in his narrative practical details about the tools and how they were used.

Another tool that has not survived is the lathe, but like the bellows it was made of perishable materials. Theophilus describes its use for turning a wax pattern for the lost-wax casting of a pewter vessel, rather than for actual work on metal, although the lathe was certainly used in the Middle Ages as a method of finishing symmetrical objects as it had been in the Roman period.

BIBLIOGRAPHY

Leslie Aitchison, *A History of Metals,* 2 vols. (1960); A. K. Anteins, "Structure and Manufacturing Techniques of Pattern-welded Objects Found in the Baltic States," in *Journal of the Iron and Steel Institute,* **206** (1968); Thomas W. Becker, *The Coin Makers* (1969); Mavis Bimson, "Coloured Glass and Millefiori in the Sutton Hoo Grave Deposit," in Rupert Bruce-Mitford, ed., *The Sutton Hoo Ship-Burial,* III, 2 (1983); István Bóna, *The Dawn of the Dark Ages,* László Boros, trans. (1976); Rupert Bruce-Mitford, ed., *The Sutton Hoo Ship-Burial,* II (1978) and III (1983); Karin Calissendorff, *et al., Iron and Man in Prehistoric Sweden,* Helen Clarke, ed. and trans. (1979); Hilda R. E. Davidson, *The Sword in Anglo-Saxon England* (1962); J. Decaens, *et al.,* "Un nouveau cimetière du haut moyen âge en Normandie, Hérouvillette (Calvados)," in *Archéologie médiévale,* **1** (1971); Charles R. Dodwell, ed. and trans., *Theophilus: The Various Arts* (1961); Franz Maria Feldhaus, *Die Technik der Antike und des Mittelalters* (*ca.* 1931, repr. 1971); Robert James Forbes, *Studies in Ancient Technology,* 2nd ed., VII (1963), VIII (1971), and IX (1972); John Starkie Gardner, *Ironwork from the Earliest Times to the End of the Mediaeval Period,* I (1893); John Harvey, *Mediaeval Craftsmen* (1975); John G. Hawthorne and Cyril S. Smith, eds. and trans., *On Divers Arts: The Treatise of Theophilus* (1963, repr. 1979); Wilhelm Holmqvist, *et al.,* eds., *Excavations at Helgö,* IV, *Workshop,* Part I, (1972); Otto Johannsen, *Geschichte des Eisens* (1935); K. Lamm, "Early Medieval Metalworking on Helgo in Central Sweden," in W. A. Oddy, ed., *Aspects of Early Metallurgy* (1980); K. Lamm and A. Lundström, eds., *Excavations at Helgö,* V, 1, *Workshop,* Part II (1978); *Made of Iron* (1966)—a catalog of an exhibition by the University of St. Thomas Art Department, Houston, Texas; Michael Müller-Wille, "Der frühmittelalterliche Schmied im Spiegel skandinavischer Grabfunde," in *Frühmittelalterliche Studien,* **11** (1977); W. A. Oddy, "The Production of Gold Wire in Antiquity," in *Gold Bulletin,* **10** (1977), and "Gilding and Tinning in Anglo-Saxon England," in Oddy, *op. cit.;* Andreas E. Oldeberg, *Metallteknik under Förhistorisk Tid,* 2 vols. (1942, 1943), and *Metallteknik under Vikingatid och Medeltid* (1966); Horst Ohlhaver, *Der germanische Schmied und sein Werkzeug* (1939); Jan G. T. Petersen, *Vikingetidens Redskaper* (1951); Radomír Pleiner, *Základy slovanského železářského hutnictví v českých zemích* (1958), and *Staré evropské kovářství* (1962); Frederick W. Robins, *The Smith* (1953); Marc Rosenberg, *Geschichte der Goldschmiedekunst auf technischer Grundlage* (1910, repr. 1972); Édouard Salin and Albert France-Lanord, *Le fer a l'époque mérovingienne* (1943); Berthold Schmidt, "Kunst und Metallwerkstätten bei den Thüringern der Völkerwanderungszeit," in *Early Medieval Studies,* **7** (1973); Charles Singer, *et al., A History of Technology,* II (1956), III (1957); Cyril S. Smith and John G. Hawthorne, "Mappae Clavicula: A Little Key to the World of Medieval Techniques," in *Transactions of the American Philosophical Society,* n.s. **64** (1974); Wilhelm Treue, *et al., Das Hausbuch der Mendelschen Zwölfbrüderstiftung zu Nürnberg* (1965); Ronald F. Tylecote, *Metallurgy in Archaeology* (1962), and *A History of Metallurgy* (1976); Leslie E. Webster and John Cherry, "Medieval Britain in 1978," in *Medieval Archaeology,* **23** (1979); Joachim Werner, 'Waage und Geld in der Merowingerzeit," in *Sitzungsberichte der Bayerischen Akademie der Wissenschaften* (1954), and "Zur Verbreitung frühgeschichtlicher Metallarbeiten," in *Early Medieval Studies,* **1** (1970).

W. A. ODDY

[See also **Arms and Armor; Cannon; Engraving; Gems and Jewelry; Sutton Hoo; Theophilus; Tools.**]

METAMORPHOSIS. See **Transfiguration.**

METAPHRASTES, SYMEON. See **Symeon Metaphrastes.**

METEḪI, a church on the ancient citadel in Tbilisi, Georgia, dedicated to the Mother of God. According to tradition, it was a court church erected by King Waχtang I in the fifth century. During the invasion of the Mongols in 1235, the church was burned down along with the adjacent palace. From 1278 to 1289 Waχtang's building was replaced by a new church, which is a centrally planned domed structure with projecting apse and pastophories. The main doorway, emphasized by a porch, is on the northern side. The exterior walls are embellished by decorative carvings, applied on the east facade and on the window frames. These carvings, although characterized by precision of execution, are lifeless and schematic, lacking the creativity of the previous centuries. Through these symptoms, the Meteḫi foreshadows the beginning of a new era in Georgian architectural sculpture and a new decorative system of church facades. The exterior walls of the church are essentially preserved in their original form; the interior, however, underwent considerable restoration from the sixteenth century on.

Church of Meteḫi, apse. Tbilisi, 1278–1289. © 1977 EDITION LEIPZIG. PHOTO: ROLF SCHRADE

The Meteḫi generally reflects the architectural tradition of medieval Georgia, yet it reveals significant departures from contemporary domed churches. For instance, the dome is supported by four free-standing pillars instead of the two customary after the eleventh century—for example, at Mcᶜχetᶜa. Other departures from tradition are the semicircular projections of the eastern apse and the pastophories, as well as the transfer of the main doorway to the north side. Vakhtang Béridzé believes that these departures could be explained by the masons' adherence to the plan of the original church when it was fundamentally rebuilt in the thirteenth century.

According to tradition, the diaconicon houses the remains of St. Šušanik, whose *bios* (life) contains valuable insights into the struggle of Christianity against the rise of Zoroastrianism in fifth-century Georgia.

BIBLIOGRAPHY

Vakhtang V. Béridzé, L. Rtsheulishvili, R. Schmerling, *Tbilisis meteḫis tadzari* (1969), in Georgian with summaries in Russian and French; R. Mepisashvili and V. Tsintsadze, *The Arts of Ancient Georgia* (1979), 178, 213, 215.

WACHTANG DJOBADZE

[See also **Georgian Art and Architecture.**]

METELLUS OF TEGERNSEE (*fl.* second half of the twelfth century), a Bavarian poet and imitator of Horace and Vergil who still remains unidentifiable. No contemporary or later documents mention him or record his death. The name Metellus (known from the Roman past) may have been a pen name for a man of letters, possibly a Benedictine monk of Tegernsee, proud of Bavarian traditions, and an admirer of St. Quirinus, patron of the monastery of Tegernsee. Attempts to identify him with Abbot Erbo of Prüfeningen, the canon Hugh Metellus of Toul, Wernher of Tegernsee, and others failed. On the basis of the manuscript tradition of his *Quirinalia* and of allusions to contemporary events in them, he can be assigned with certainty to the period around 1165.

His long poetic work, the *Quirinalia,* consists of two series of panegyrical-hagiographical poems dealing with the life, martyrdom, and miracles of the Roman St. Quirinus (*d.* 308 and not 370 as suggested by Metellus in his work). This work is unique in the history of medieval Latin poetry and appears in the manuscripts in two different versions, both of which are the work of Metellus. In the older version (between 1165 and 1175), twenty-two odes may have been the original nucleus of the *Quirinalia.* The second, expanded version is recorded partially in an autographic copy written by Metellus himself.

The contents of the *Quirinalia* are drawn from older hagiographical sources. (Local traditions perpetuated the belief that Tegernsee possessed authentic relics of St. Quirinus.) Their undiluted source could not have been the three-century-old "primitive" passion, but rather some secondary version, partially supplemented either through oral (local) traditions, or by considerations of Metellus due to political pressures exerted on Tegernsee by the powerful Bishop Otto von Freising, famous uncle of the Holy Roman emperor Frederick II Barbarossa. Even if the contents have interesting features, it is the form of the poems making up the *Quirinalia* that renders them unique. They consist of two main parts, followed by a poetic appendix (eleven narratives written in hexameters) dealing chiefly with the deeds or misdeeds of judges and advocates (lawyers). These narratives as well as the poems of the preceding parts are introduced by brief prose summaries.

In the first main part (consisting of four sections, corresponding to the books of Horace's odes) the Horatian meters dominate seventy odes on Quirinus. The first twenty-two odes imitate the verse form of the corresponding Horation odes in the order as found in Horace. Parts of the other odes borrow meters from Prudentius and Boethius, others are written in stanza forms probably created by Metellus himself. The contents of the other odes are typically "medieval," but the Horatian influence goes deeper than the use of Horatian meters alone. Konrad Bursian demonstrated that Metellus not only uses the language (and style) of Horace but also makes efforts to imitate other aspects of the Horatian odes in details. In other instances, the Horatian influence is minimalized.

The second, "Vergilian," part of the *Quirinalia* consists of imitations of Vergil's *Eclogues,* of a "prologue," and ten bucolic poems. The prologue deplores the decay of poetry and arts and contrasts the contemporary decadence with the golden age of poetry under Augustus. Metellus attributes this decline to the "mercantile" spirit of his age, dominated by "businessmen." The eclogues make use of Vergil's traditional eclogue figures (Meliboeus, Tityrus, Menaclas, and Dameta). In this part, too, Metellus attempts to add Vergilian flavors to his poems and uses Vergilian passages and phrases. The concluding part employs leonine hexameters *(retrogradi).* The use of Vergilian eclogue traditions is less striking than the imitation of Horace by Metellus in this not fully explored work.

The same Codex 267 of Admont from the twelfth century which contains the *Quirinalia* preserves the versified version of the history of the First Crusade (1096–1099) by Robert of St. Rémy. It consists of 4,845 hexameter lines. This poetic *Expeditio Ierosolimitana* was unedited and anonymous until recently. The editor, Peter Christian Jacobsen, ascribes this as well to Metellus and suggests that this was written soon after the composition of the *Quirinalia.*

BIBLIOGRAPHY

Wilhelm Fink, "Abt Erbo II. von Prufening, der Verfasser der sog. Quirinalien-Metellus," in *Studien und Mitteilungen,* 60 (1946); Peter Christian Jacobsen, *Die Quirinalien des Metellus von Tegernsee* (1965), "Die Admonter Versifikation der Kreuzzugsgeschichte Roberts von St.-Remi," in Alf Önnerfors, *et. al.,* eds., *Literatur und Sprache im europaischen Mittelalter: Festschrift für Karl Langosch* (1973), and, ed., *Expeditio Ierosolimitana* (1979); K. Langosch, "Metellus von Tegernsee," in *Verfasserlexikon,* III (1943) and V (1955); Karl Weyman, *Beiträge zur Geschichte der christlich-lateinischen Poesie* (1926).

JOSEPH SZÖVÉRFFY

[See also **Latin Literature.**]

METEORA, meaning "in the air," is the name given to a group of monasteries built on the summits or in caves of huge rocks that rise out of the plain of Thessaly east of Stagoi (modern Kalabáka). The earliest monks in the area lived in the caves and formed a skete in the style of desert fathers. The first cenobitic monastery, the Great Meteoron, perched atop the Broad Rock, was founded about 1350 by Athanasios, a hesychast monk from Mt. Athos. The Serbian rulers who conquered Thessaly in the fourteenth century encouraged further development; the monastery

The Great Meteoron seen from the Monastery of Barlaam. FROM A DRAWING BY VISCOUNT EASTNOR (PUBLISHED 1849)

of the Presentation (Hypapanti) is one of four built under their patronage. John Uroš (1372–*ca.* 1422), son of the Serbian emperor Symeon, abdicated his throne and became the monk Joasaph, Father of the Great Meteoron, whose church he rebuilt in 1388.

Thessaly was overrun by the Turks in 1393, and its rock monasteries, accessible only by ropes and ladders, became secure strongholds of the Christian faith. Those of St. Nicholas, Holy Trinity (Hagia Triada), and St. Stephen were built in the fifteenth century; those of Barlaam and Rousánou in the sixteenth. At one time there were at least twelve monasteries, as well as countless hermitages in the surrounding caves. They were endowed by the Orthodox rulers of Wallachia and Moldavia, and were granted valuable landed estates in those countries.

The meteora fell on hard times after the seventeenth century, and the six monasteries that are inhabited or accessible today are sparsely populated. Some of their former wealth can be seen in their treasures and libraries (still to be fully catalogued), and their churches are rich with frescoes in the Byzantine tradition.

BIBLIOGRAPHY

Donald M. Nicol, *Meteora: The Rock Monasteries of Thessaly* (1963, 2nd ed. 1975).

DONALD M. NICOL

[See also **Monasticism, Byzantine.**]

METGE, BERNAT (1340/1346—1413), Catalan prose writer, translator, and humanist; son of Guillem Metge, a Barcelona apothecary patronized by the royal family of Aragon. His stepfather, Ferrer Sayol, prothonotary to Queen Eleanor of Sicily and translator of Palladius' *De re rustica,* had a profound influence on Metge and was responsible for introducing him as a notary to the royal chancellery. Metge became a scribe to the future John I (*r.* 1387–1395), son of Peter IV the Ceremonious, in 1375; he was accused of corruption (1388) but retained royal favor and became secretary to John I and Queen Violant de Bar in 1390. His duties led him to travel throughout the kingdom, and he also acted as royal ambassador to the papal court at Avignon. After John I's death in 1395, he found himself again in trouble and was probably imprisoned, but he soon found favor with King Martín I. He married twice and left five legitimate children.

Metge is known primarily for his translations from the classics, although his allegorical work, *Llibre de Fortuna e Prudència* (1381), was medieval in orientation. It was written in verse, as were two minor works, a satirical sermon and a parody of prescriptions for love potions *(A tot mal),* possibly inspired by his knowledge of pharmaceutical remedies. He was responsible for the first translation in Spain of Petrarch's version of *Història de Valter e Griselda,* noteworthy for its elegant style.

His main contribution to Catalan letters, *Lo somni* (1399), uses the literary device of a dream framework in which King John appears to the author in prison. Books I and II show the king in purgatory, where he has been sent to repent of his excessive love of hunting, music, and magic, and for his part in the papal schism. Metge indulges in a philosophical dialogue with the king on such subjects as the immortality of the soul and the attitudes of Christians, Jews, and Moors, drawing heavily on Boccaccio, Cicero, Valerius Maximus, and the church fathers. Books III and IV allow the author to show the value of classical literature through the king's two companions, Orpheus and Tiresias, and include a diatribe against women, which Metge rebuts in the same exaggerated way by praising women, including Catalan queens. No doubt here he hoped to win the favor of Maria de Luna, the reigning monarch's wife, and to dissociate himself from Violant de Bar. The fact that he wrote *Lo somni* in Catalan can also probably be explained by his desire for self-justification before the king and other important readers.

Metge's work is important, as it is the first humanistic prose in the Iberian peninsula, and although his style in *Lo somni* owes much to classical rhetoric, the themes he deals with serve as a mirror of contemporary customs, many of which the author describes in a picturesque but ironic tone. There is no doubt that his prose is superior to that of his contemporary, Francesc Eiximenis, while his ability to question and make use of rational arguments to support his views clearly places him as a precursor of the Renaissance.

BIBLIOGRAPHY

Bernat Metge, *Obras,* Martín de Riquer, trans. (1959), *Obras completas,* Lola Badia and Xavier Lamuela, eds., 2nd ed. (1975), *Lo somni,* Marta Jordà, ed. (1980), and *Lo somni,* Josep Maria de Casacuberta, ed., 3rd ed. (1980). See also Manuel de Montoliu, *Les grans personalitats de la literatura catalana,* IV (1960).

J. R. WEBSTER

[See also **Aragon, Crown of (1137–1479); Catalan Language; Catalan Literature; Catalan Narrative in Verse; Eiximenis, Francesc.**]

METHODIOS. See **Cyril and Methodios, Sts.**

METROPOLITAN, a title designating the bishop of a provincial capital *(metropolis)* in the Christian Roman Empire. According to the canonical legislation of the fourth century, particularly the council of Nicaea in 325, the metropolitan is the president of the council of bishops convened biannually in each province (canons 4 and 5) for the election of bishops and the settling of disputes. The metropolitan carries the right of approving all decisions of the council. In the West, after the barbarian invasions and the disintegration of the Roman provincial system, the title was used more loosely to designate regional primates. In the East, the original meaning was preserved longer, but the title tended to become honorary in the late Byzantine period.

JOHN MEYENDORFF

[See also **Byzantine Church; Church, Latin: Organization; Nicaea, Councils of; Patriarch.**]

METZ, USE OF. For most of the Middle Ages the liturgical use or practice of the city of Metz (in present-day northeastern France), like the uses of most other churches in the West, was largely an adaptation of the Roman rite. Nonetheless, scholars often refer to the "use of Metz" because its liturgical practices, especially in the Carolingian period, were distinctive and widely admired. Before a trip to Rome by Bishop Chrodegang (712–766) in 753, it would seem that Metz had its own distinctive liturgical use and was renowned particularly for its *schola cantorum.* It is reasonable to think that this early Metzine rite had characteristics of the Gallican liturgy practiced widely north of the Alps. When Bishop Chrodegang returned after his visit to Rome and had enjoyed the companionship of Pope Stephen II (*r.* 752–757) on the latter's sojourn to Frankish territories from 753 to 754/755, the Roman rite and Roman chant were firmly implanted into the liturgical practice of Metz. For example, the Roman practice of stational liturgy became a fixture of Metz, and it is known that clerics from as far away as England came to Metz to learn Roman practices. Moreover, Metz provided liturgical practitioners for such cities as Lyons, which had distinguished liturgical traditions of their own. Nonetheless, we know that there continued to be local peculiarities in Metz because when the famous liturgical specialist and commentator Amalarius of Metz (*ca.* 775–*ca.* 850) formulated his version of the antiphonary, he noted specifically those practices that were used in Metz, those in Rome, and those of his own invention. Moreover, it is known from the *Ordines romani* used in Metz that what was basically a Roman order of services was modified to conform to the situation in Metz. This same phenomenon can be seen in the depiction of liturgical practices on the ivory cover of the Sacramentary of Drogo, the ninth-century bishop of Metz. Even after the Carolingian period, Metz, like other cities, continued to have its own local liturgical customs. This can be seen in calendars and liturgical books produced in or for the churches of Metz and in the ecclesiastical officers and hierarchy of the church at Metz.

BIBLIOGRAPHY

L. Cherpin, *Essai sur l'historie de l'Ordo missae dans les trois diocèses de Metz, de Toul, et de Verdun* (1900); H. Leclercq, "Metz," in *Dictionnaire d'archéologie chrétienne et de liturgie,* XI (1933); Jean Baptiste Pelt, *Études sur la cathédrale de Metz: La liturgie,* I (1937); Otto Gerhard Oexle, "Die Karolinger und die Stadt des heiligen Arnulf," in *Frühmittelalterliche Studien,* 1 (1967), 250–364; Roger E. Reynolds, "A Visual Epitome of the Eucharistic 'Ordo' from the Era of Charles the Bald: The Ivory Mass Cover of the *Drogo Sacramentary,*" in *Charles the Bald: Court and Kingdom. Papers Based on a Colloquium Held in London in April 1979,* Margaret Gibson and Janet Nelson, eds. (1981).

ROGER E. REYNOLDS

[See also **Amalarius of Metz; Carolingians; Divine Office; Gallican Rite; Lyonese Rite; Ordines Romani; Pepin; Stephen II, Pope.**]

MICHAEL III, EMPEROR (*r.* 842–867), was six when he came to the Byzantine imperial throne; he was to be the last emperor of the Amorian dynasty. The traditional view of him, derived from sources favorable to his successor Basil I, is of an ineffective ruler and a drunkard, but more recent works have emphasized his positive achievements. He wrested power from his mother, Theodora II, in 856 (*d.* 867) aided by his uncle, the caesar Bardas (*d.* 865). With Bardas and the future patriarch Photios, he established the university at the Magnaura Palace.

Michael III won an important victory over the Arabs in 863 as part of the renewed Byzantine offensive. He sponsored Boris, the Bulgarian tsar (*r.* 852–889), at his conversion to Christianity in 864, after which Boris took the name Michael. In 866 Michael III made his favorite, Basil the Macedonian, co-emperor; a year later he was dead at Basil's hand.

BIBLIOGRAPHY

H. Grégoire, "The Amorians and Macedonians, 842–1025," in *Cambridge Medieval History,* IV, pt. 1 (1966); George Ostrogorsky, *History of the Byzantine State,* Joan Hussey, trans. (1957, rev. ed. 1969), 222–232.

LINDA C. ROSE

[See also **Amorians; Bardas Caesar; Basil I the Macedonian, Emperor; Boris; Byzantine Empire: History; Theodora II, Empress.**]

MICHAEL VIII PALAIOLOGOS (1224/1225–1282), first Byzantine emperor (*r.* 1259–1282) of the Palaiologan dynasty, was a consummate diplomat and emperor who restored Constantinople to the Byzantines in 1261 after fifty-seven years of Latin occupation following the Fourth Crusade. As ruler of Byzantine Nicaea (in Asia Minor) Michael opened the way to the Greek reconquest of Constantinople by defeating, at the battle of Pelagonia in 1259, a coalition of powers—William of Achaia, Manfred of Sicily, and Michael II of Epiros. After recovering Constantinople and beginning the desolated city's restoration, Michael was faced by the newly crowned king of Sicily, the formidable Charles I of Anjou (*r.* 1266–1285), who nurtured the overriding ambition of seizing the city for himself. The diplomatic duel between the two rulers involved most of Europe, as Charles organized an enormous coalition of powers against Michael, including finally even the papacy and Venice.

Using diplomacy as his chief instrument, Michael VIII offered religious union of the Greek and Latin churches to the papacy if, as suzerain of Sicily, the pope would order Charles to desist from his planned conquest of Constantinople. Union between the two churches was signed at the Second Council of Lyons in 1274, but the Byzantine population overwhelmingly refused to accept it. Finally, after the collapse of the papacy's efforts to reunite the two churches, Charles persuaded Pope Martin IV (1281–1285) to excommunicate Michael (1281), and Charles then launched a land expedition across the Adriatic against the fortress of Berat (in present-day southern Albania). But Charles's troops were crushed, which forced him to turn instead to a naval campaign against Constantinople. Before the great expedition could be launched, however, the revolt of the Sicilian Vespers broke out in Palermo (30 March 1282), as a result of which Charles had to abandon his entire expedition. It was the greatest triumph of Michael's career, for he had probably played a major role in organizing the great conspiracy (with Charles's Hohenstaufen enemies in Sicily and with King Pedro III of Aragon) which helped lead to the success of the uprising.

BIBLIOGRAPHY

See especially Deno J. Geanakoplos, *Emperor Michael Palaeologus and the West, 1258–1282: A Study in Byzantine-Latin Relations* (1959, repr. 1973), with bibliography, and *Byzantium: Church, Society, and Civilization Seen Through Contemporary Eyes* (1984). For a succinct discussion of the Palaiologan renaissance in art, see John Beckwith, *Early Christian and Byzantine Art* (1970, 2nd ed. 1979), 301–302.

DENO J. GEANAKOPLOS

[See also **Aragon, Crown of (1137–1479); Byzantine Art; Byzantine Empire: History; Constantinople; Epiros, Des-**

potate of; Michael II of Epiros; Nicaea, Empire of; Pelagonia; Sicilian Vespers; Sicily, Kingdom of.]

MICHAEL I OF EPIROS (*r.* 1205–*ca.* 1215), founder of the independent Byzantine state in Epiros after the Fourth Crusade, was a cousin of the emperors Isaac II Angelos (*r.* 1185–1195, 1204) and Alexios III Angelos (*r.* 1195–1203). In 1205 he made himself master of the northern Greek territory between Dyrrachium and Naupactus (later Lepanto), with his capital at Arta. There is no evidence for the tradition that he held the imperial title of despot. By diplomacy and warfare he preserved the independence of Epiros from the Venetians—to whom it had been allotted after the conquest of Constantinople in 1204—and from the crusaders, who had occupied Thessaloniki.

BIBLIOGRAPHY

Donald M. Nicol, *The Despotate of Epiros* (1957); Lucien Stiernon, "Les origines du despotat d'Épire," in *Revue des études byzantines,* 17 (1959).

DONALD M. NICOL

[See also **Angelos; Byzantine Empire: History; Crusades and Crusader States: Fourth; Epiros, Despotate of; Isaac II Angelos.**]

MICHAEL II OF EPIROS (*r.* 1230–*ca.* 1267) was a bastard son of Michael I of Epiros. He held the imperial title of despot and ruled Epiros until his death. His ambition to emulate his uncle Theodore (*r.* 1224–1230), who had briefly reigned as emperor at Thessaloniki, was never fulfilled. But he became the major rival of the Byzantine emperor in exile at Nicaea, by whom he was finally defeated in battle at Pelagonia in 1259.

BIBLIOGRAPHY

Donald M. Nicol, *The Despotate of Epiros, 1267–1479* (1984).

DONALD M. NICOL

[See also **Byzantine Empire: History; Epiros, Despotate of; Michael VIII Palaiologos; Pelagonia; Thessaloniki.**]

MICHAEL ASTRAPAS (*fl.* 1295–1320). A Greek painter who, with Eutychios, first frescoed the Peribleptos church (St. Clement) at Ohrid in 1295 and the Bogorodica Ljeviška at Prizren (1307–1309) before becoming a court artist for King Milutin of Serbia, a position Michael held until at least 1320. His early work provides one of the best preserved examples of the "heavy" style characteristic of Con-

Meeting of Joachim and Anne and Birth of the Virgin. Fresco by Michael Astrapas from the Peribleptos church, Ohrid, 1295. PHOTO: JACQUELINE LAFONTAINE-DOSOGNE

stantinopolitan artists at the time, with massive, cubic forms painted in cold colors and dissected by hard, smooth lines; later products such as the frescoes at Staro Nagoričino (1316–1318) are increasingly mannered and provincial.

BIBLIOGRAPHY

Otto Demus, "The Style of the Kariye Djami and Its Place in the Development of Palaeologan Art," in Paul Underwood, ed., *The Kariye Djami,* IV (1975), 146–150; Richard Hamann-MacLean and Horst Hallensleben, *Die Monumentalmalerei in Serbien und Makedonian vom 11. bis zum frühen 14. Jahrhundert,* I (1963).

LESLIE BRUBAKER

[See also **Byzantine Art; Eutychios.**]

MICHAEL ATTALEIATES (before 1030–*ca.* 1080), Byzantine historian, jurist, and high governmental official. His *Historia* chronicles the troubled late Macedonian dynasty from 1034 to 1079, concluding with a panegyric for the emperor Nikephoros III Botaneiates (*d.* 1081). Attaleiates' brief law treatise, derived from the Basilics, contains an unusual statute concerning the monastery and poorhouse that he founded; it is also important for its listing of the monastery's art objects.

BIBLIOGRAPHY

Michael Attaleiates, *Historia,* Immanuel Bekker, ed., in B. G. Niebuhr, ed., *Corpus scriptorum historiae Byzantinae,* XXXIV (1853); Alexander Kazhdan, *Studies on Byzantine Literature of the Eleventh and Twelfth Centuries* (1984); Agostino Pertusi, "Per la critica del testo della 'storia' di Michele Attaliate," in *Jahrbuch der österreichischen byzantinischen Gesellschaft,* 7 (1958), with corrections of typographical errors in the Bekker work.

BARBARA OEHLSCHLAEGER-GARVEY

[See also **Basilics; Byzantine Empire: History (1025–1204); Byzantine Literature; Historiography, Byzantine.**]

MICHAEL KEROULARIOS (*ca.* 1000–1059), patriarch of Constantinople (1043–1058) involved in the conflict with the Roman legates in 1054. As were several other Byzantine patriarchs, Keroularios belonged to the ruling aristocratic class; before ascending the patriarchal throne, he was engaged in unsuccessful political opposition against Emperor Michael IV (1034–1041). Forced into exile, he accepted monastic tonsure, an action which normally signified the end of a political career. Under Constantine IX Monomachos (1042–1055), however, he again acquired great influence at the court and, on 25 March 1043, was elected patriarch. In this position he showed uncompromising authoritarianism but also authentic zeal for the good of his church.

No formal communion existed at that time between the sees of Rome and Constantinople. The name of the pope had been dropped early in the eleventh century, during one of the numerous political upheavals in Rome. At the time of Keroularios this general estrangement turned into open conflict, connected with competing Roman and Byzantine jurisdictions in southern Italy. Under Pope Leo IX (1049–1054), the growing influence of the Frankish clergy—inspired by the reform movement in the church—tended to associate Greek customs and church discipline with immorality (because the Greek clergy was married) and with simony. These attacks by the Franks on Greek churches in Italy provoked Michael's retaliation. Latin churches in Constantinople were closed. Through the initiative of Emperor Constantine IX, however, an effort at reconciliation was made. Papal legates, led by Humbert of Moyenmoutier, cardinal of Silva Candida, arrived in Constantinople in 1054. But mutual intolerance led to mutual anathemas (16 and 24 July 1054).

In the following years, Patriarch Michael continued to play an active role in the policies of the empire. He contributed to the overthrow of Emperor Michael VI Stratiotikos (1056–1057) and the enthronement of a military leader, Isaac I Komnenos (1057–1059). Invoking in his own favor as bishop of "New Rome" the text of the spurious *Donation of Constantine,* he obtained from the new emperor the exclusive administration of the "Great Church" (Hagia Sophia), and made him promise to guarantee the interests of the church. Eventually, however, Michael was forced to leave the patriarchate. Isaac I had him arrested in November 1058, and while journeying to his trial in Madytus, in Thrace, Michael died.

BIBLIOGRAPHY

Jules Gay, *L'Italie méridionale et l'empire byzantin . . . (867–1071)* (1904); Anton Michel, *Humbert und Kerullarios,* 2 vols. (1924–1930); Steven Runciman, *The Eastern Schism* (1955); Nicolai Suvorov, *Visantiiski papa* (1902).

JOHN MEYENDORFF

[See also **Byzantine Church; Byzantine Empire: History; Church, Latin: to 1054; Constantine IX Monomachos; Donation of Constantine; Humbert of Silva Candida; Leo IX, Pope; Schisms, Eastern-Western Church.**]

MICHAEL OF CANTERBURY (*fl.* 1275–1323), master mason and principal architect of Edward I, executed important royal commissions, especially the Cheapside Eleanor Cross (1291–1294, fragments in the Guildhall Museum, London) and the earlier parts of St. Stephen's Chapel, Westminster Palace (1292–1298 and 1319–1326, mostly destroyed by fire 1834). He is sometimes seen as the originator of the Perpendicular Style and also of the innovative London School of tomb sculpture.

BIBLIOGRAPHY

Paul Biver, "Tombs of the School of London at the Beginning of the Fourteenth Century," in *Archaeological Journal,* 67 (1910); Jean Bony, *The English Decorated Style: Gothic Architecture Transformed* (1979); John H. Harvey, "St. Stephen's Chapel and the Origin of the Perpendicular Style," in *Burlington Magazine,* **88** (1946); J. Maurice Hastings, *St. Stephen's Chapel and Its Place in the Development of Perpendicular Style in England* (1955).

STEPHEN GARDNER

[See also **Gothic Architecture; Masons and Builders.**]

MICHAEL SCOT (*b.* before 1200–*d. ca.* 1235), translator and writer on scientific subjects, and famous as a magician. He was even accorded a place in Dante's *Inferno* and an anecdote in Boccaccio's *Decameron.* Although he later resided in Sicily, he began his career as a translator in Spain, producing his first translation in Toledo about 1217. Among his translations are Latin versions of two of Ibn Rushd's (Averroës') commentaries on Aristotle: the *Great Commentary on the De caelo* and the *Great Commentary on the De anima.* During the last years of his life, Michael received the patronage of Emperor Frederick II, for whom he is said to have acted as court astrologer. It was to Frederick that he dedicated his tripartite work *Liber introductorius, Liber particularis,* and *De secretis naturae,* dealing with such subjects as astronomy, astrology, human reproduction, and physiognomy (interpretation of character by examining the shapes of various bodily parts).

Although Roger Bacon and Albertus Magnus were scathingly critical of Michael's translations and ideas, nearly 200 thirteenth- and fourteenth-century manuscripts of his works (mainly his translations) survive to testify to his great popularity.

BIBLIOGRAPHY

The indispensable account of Michael's *opera omnia* is Lorenzo Minio-Paluello, "Michael Scot," in *Dictionary of Scientific Biography,* IX (1974). Other studies include Charles H. Haskins, *Studies in the History of Mediaeval Science,* 2nd ed. (1927); Lynn Thorndike, *A History of Magic and Experimental Science,* II (1923), 307–337, and *Michael Scot* (1965). For a study of a specific work by Michael, see F. Albert Gallo, "Astronomy and Music in the Middle Ages: The *Liber introductorius* by Michael Scot," in *Musica disciplina,* **27** (1973). See also J. Ward Brown, *An Enquiry into the Life and Legend of Michael Scot* (1897).

ELAINE GOLDEN ROBISON

[See also **Astrology; Astronomy; Frederick II of the Holy Roman Empire; Magic, Bookish; Translation and Translators.**]

MICHAEL THE SYRIAN (1126–1199), the Jacobite patriarch of Antioch from 1166 to 1199, was a historian and a liturgist. He was born in Antioch, the son of a Syriac priest by the name of Elias. As a young man he entered the priesthood and became the prior of the monastery of Bar-ṣaumā near Melitene.

During his three decades on the patriarchal throne, Michael proved himself to be a prolific writer and an active churchman. Besides his literary pursuits, he organized the Jacobite church and strengthened its administrative setup by appointing priors for the monasteries and new bishops for the Jacobite communities in various cities. He himself traveled from place to place in order to attend to his flock. Like the Armenians, Michael was also approached by the Byzantine emperor Manuel I Komnenos in 1169 for a dialogue on church unity. He was invited by the Armenian *katᶜołikos* Nersēs Šnorhali (1166–1173) to participate in the theological discussions with the representative of the Byzantine emperor. Michael sent delegates but acted very cautiously toward the Byzantines.

Michael's patriarchate was marked by a schism. In 1180 his pupil Theodore bar Wahbōn was made an antipatriarch by some of the bishops who opposed Michael. Michael at first tried to depose Theodore, but the latter succeeded in escaping to Cilicia, where he was ultimately given official recognition by the Armenian prince Leo II (later King Leo I).

Despite the turbulent times and his close encounters with the Muslim potentates of the period, Michael distinguished himself as a great builder of monasteries and churches and as a great champion for the cause of Monophysitism. He wrote and edited several works, including liturgical texts, theological treatises, a poem, and hagiography. His best known work, however, is the renowned *Chronicle,* which begins with the creation of man and ends with the year 1195/1196. This work, which consists of twenty-one books, covers three different sets of events arranged in chronological order in three separate columns: the first one contains a record of secular events, the second of ecclesiastical events, and the third, miscellanea. The dating is arranged according to the Seleucid era. Michael followed the *Chronicon* of Eusebius of Caesarea and made ample use of earlier historians' works, which he frequently quoted verbatim. For the history of the twelfth century it is a most reliable source, and it is also a very important source for the history of Syria, the Byzantine Empire, Cilicia, Armenia, and Mesopotamia. Besides the Syriac original, there are two Armenian versions that have additional passages of historical interest, and also an Arabic version.

BIBLIOGRAPHY

The *Chronique de Michel le Syrien, Patriarche Jacobite d'Antioche,* was edited and translated by Jean B. Chabot, 3 vols. (1899–1910). The reprint of 1963 contains the Syriac text in a fourth volume. The Armenian versions were published in Jerusalem in 1870 and 1871.

See also Ignatius Ortiz de Urbina, *Patrologia syriaca* (1958); Judah B. Segal, "Syriac Chronicles as Source Material for the History of Islamic Peoples," in Bernard Lewis and P. M. Holt, eds., *Historians of the Middle East* (1962); William Wright, *A Short History of Syriac Literature* (1894, 2nd ed. 1966).

KRIKOR H. MAKSOUDIAN

[See also **Bar Hebraeus; Monophysitism; Syria; Syrian Christianity.**]

MICHEL BEHEIM (*ca.* 1420—1472/1479), German poet and composer. Son of a weaver, he was induced to become a poet/composer by Konrad von Weinsberg, archchamberlain of the Holy Roman Empire and his feudal lord. From Beheim's remarkable "career song" (no. 24 of the "Gedichte": "Von Michel Pehems gepurt und Seinem her chomen in dis lannd"), which is extant in several redactions, it is possible to determine that he served several high-ranking patrons, among them Emperor Frederick III (1415–1493). Municipal patronage is also attested. In stark contrast with the recognition Beheim received during his lifetime is the censorious or perfunctory evaluation of his achievements in literary histories. One consistent source of offense was his employment of the adage "Whose bread I eat, his song I sing" in the *Pfälzische Reimchronik* (*ca.* 1471). It gave rise to charges of rank opportunism, especially since the chronicle was composed for Frederick's rival, Count Palatine Frederick I the Victorious (1425–1476). Not until 1968–1972 did the critical edition of the poet's 452 "Gedichte" and the historical poem *Buch von der statt Triest* appear.

Until recently Beheim's poetry held interest for its extraliterary content, and the curious aspects of his work attracted the most attention. His verses on the historical Dracula, the Romanian Vlad the Impaler (Vlad Tepes, *fl.* 1456–1462), may serve as a case in point. With the accessibility of Beheim's song corpus and discoveries concerning his artful union of text and musical form has come a dramatic reversal in appreciation. He is now recognized as one of the major political poets and authors of the fable in the fifteenth century.

Determined to bring forth a musical and poetical summa, Michel Beheim tried his hand at religious songs, moral and ethical poetry, political and historical writings, autobiographical verse, love songs, and songs on the theory of art. His active involvement in manuscript recording of his own song poems is documented. An important literary theme in his work is the status of the inventive song composer. At the same time Beheim espoused reverence for the past, and was both intellectually and artistically conservative. His literary sources are wide-ranging and his method eclectic; not all model texts have been identified. Source texts from two spheres proved crucial: the Prague "Kulturkreis" (Johann von Neumark [*ca.* 1310–1380], Heinrich von Mügeln, and Heinrich Suso), and the theologians of the "Viennese School" (Henry of Langenstein, Thomas Peuntner [*d.* 1439], and Nikolaus von Dinkelsbühl). Beheim was also much indebted to Muskatblüt (*fl.* 1424–1434), his admired predecessor. Beheim versified and set to music Scripture, sermons, and prose tracts; even his historical poems and chronicles can be sung. His striving for homogeneity and a common artistic base also is reflected in the frequently dim boundaries between song types and literary genres.

Michel Beheim contributed to a patristic, specifically Augustinian, revival that he sought to promote as a means of educating the laity. Contrary to a still widespread belief, he was no Meistersinger but, rather, an aphorist *(Spruchdichter)* committed to biblical humanism.

BIBLIOGRAPHY

Annemarie Altpeter, *Die Stilisierung des autobiographischen bei Oswald von Wolkenstein und seinen Zeitgenossen Hugo von Montfort, Muskatblüt und Michel Beheim* (diss., Tübingen, 1950); Hans Gille, *Die historischen und politischen Gedichte Michel Beheims* (1910), and "Michel Beheims Gedicht 'Von der statt Triest': I. Teil," in *Zeitschrift für deutsche Philologie,* 77 (1958), 258–281; Dagmar Kratochwill, "Die Autographe des Michel Beheim," in *Litterae ignotae, Beiträge zur Textgeschichte des deutschen Mittelalters: Neufunde und Neuinterpretationen* (1977), 109–124; William C. McDonald, "Michel Beheim Reconsidered: On Imagery in His *Erzgräberbîspel,*" in *German Quarterly,* **48** (1975), and *"Whose Bread I Eat": The Song-Poetry of Michel Beheim* (1981); Ulrich Müller, *Untersuchungen zur politischen Lyrik des deutschen Mittelalters* (1974), and "Michel Beheim," in *Die deutsche Literatur des Mittelalters: Verfasserlexikon,* I, 2nd ed. (1978), 672–680; Christoph Petzsch, "Zur Notierungsweise im Beheimkodex cgm 291," in *Archiv für Musikwissenschaft,* **23** (1966), and "Michel Beheims 'Buch von den Weinern': Zum Gesangsvortrag eines spätmittelalterlichen chronikalischen Gedichts," in *Anzeiger der philosophisch-historische Klasse der Oesterreichischen Akademie der Wissenschaften,* **109** (1973), 266–315; Ingeborg Spriewald, "Grundzüge des Werkes von Michel Beheim. Ein Beitrag zur Problematik der Reimdichtung im 15. Jahrhundert," in *Wissenschaftliche Zeitschrift der Martin-Luther-Universität Halle-Wittenberg* (1961), 947–950.

WILLIAM C. McDONALD

[See also **German Literature: Lyric; Heinrich von Mügeln; Henry of Langenstein; Suso (Seuse), Heinrich; Middle High German Literature.**]

MICHEL COLOMBE. See **Colombe, Michel.**

MICHELOZZO DI BARTOLOMEO (*b.* 1396–*d.* 1472), Florentine architect and sculptor. He assisted

Palazzo Medici-Riccardi, Florence. Michelozzo di Bartolomeo, 1444–1459. ALINARI/ART RESOURCE

and collaborated with three major Florentine sculptors: Lorenzo Ghiberti, Donatello, and Lucca della Robbia. Between 1417 and 1424 he assisted Ghiberti on the first bronze doors of the Florence Baptistery and between 1419 and 1422 worked on the statue of St. Matthew for Or San Michele. Michelozzo shared a studio with Donatello from 1425 to 1433 and was his partner in three commissions: the Baldassare Coscia monument in the Florentine Baptistery; the Cardinal Brancacci monument (1428, Naples, S. Angelo a Nilo); and the Aragazzi monument in the Duomo of Montepulciano (1427–*ca.* 1437, fragments found in Montepulciano and London, Victoria and Albert Museum).

A brilliant architect, Michelozzo's patronage derived mainly from the Medici, for whom he designed the massive Palazzo Medici-Riccardi (1444–1459), his most famous and influential work. From 1446 to 1451 he was capomaestro of the duomo in Florence, succeeding Filippo Brunelleschi.

BIBLIOGRAPHY

Harriet M. Caplow, "Michelozzo at Ragusa: New Documents and Revaluations," in *Journal of the Society of Architectural Historians,* XXXI (1972); Ottavio Morisani, *Michelozzo, architetto* (1951); John Pope-Hennessy, *Italian Renaissance Sculpture* (1971), 268–269; Charles Seymour, Jr., *Sculpture in Italy: 1400 to 1500* (1966).

ADELHEID M. GEALT

[See also **Baptistery; Brunelleschi, Filippo; Donatello; Ghiberti, Lorenzo; Medici.**]

MICON OF ST. RIQUIER (*d.* 865), monk and teacher at the Benedictine abbey of St. Riquier, in northern France, and master of grammar and prosody. By the time of his death, he had achieved fame as a poet and anthologist. His works include original, short poems written between 825 and 853, among them "De natali Domini," "Musa de corpore Christi," "De Epiphania," and "De festa S. Martini." Micon compiled a *Florilegium (Flores poetarum),* with marginal notes, and the *Exempla diversorum auctorum,* and wrote *De primus syllabis,* an introduction to prosody.

BIBLIOGRAPHY

"Carmina centulensia," in *Monumenta Germaniae historica: Poetae latini aevi carolini,* III (1896), 265–368, 753–754, 780–789; Max Manitius, *Geschichte der lateinischen Literatur im Mittelalter,* I (1911), 469–476.

EDWARD FRUEH

[See also **Latin Literature.**]

MIDDLE AGES. The idea of the Middle Ages was first adumbrated by the humanists of the fourteenth century. Petrarch and his followers became conscious of the cultural and chronological gap that separated their own time from that of the Greeks and Romans they most admired. To describe it they added to the traditional schematic divisions of world history (the four ages ending with the Roman, or the six monarchies, both derived from Augustine's *De civitate Dei*) a new one both less clear and more suggestive. They argued that human culture had reached its zenith in the ancient world, had collapsed, like the Roman Empire, with the onset of Christianity and barbarism, and had only revived in their own time.

In the next century scholars like Lorenzo Valla (1406–1457) and artists like Lorenzo Ghiberti (1378–1455) made this scheme as all-inclusive as the older ones. They claimed that language, literature, philosophy, and art had all suffered a sea change at around the time of the fall of Rome, and that the culture that came between the fall of Rome and their own day was distinctively different from and worse than either the classical culture that preceded it or the classical revival of their own time. Their dates for the beginning and end of the Middle Ages were vague and shifting, but their estimate of the period was clear indeed. By the early sixteenth century classical scholars regularly referred to "experts in the middle period" and to poets and documents of "middle antiquity"; in normal usage such phrases implied a negative assessment of the period.

As early as the fifteenth century, however, a new notion came into being that enriched and revised the original one. Historians like Leonardo Bruni (1369–1444) and Flavio Biondo (1388–1463) saw the Middle Ages as a distinct interval between ancient and modern times; but unlike the purists they viewed the interval with approval. They praised the political achievements of the medieval communes and the spiritual ones of the medieval church, treating both as unclassical but nonetheless valuable. They thus suggested the notion that medieval civilization as a whole was only different from, not worse than, classical civilization.

Many scholars of the sixteenth and seventeenth centuries accepted and expanded upon this benign point of view. French, English, and German intellectuals belonged to nations that lacked classical pasts. All tended to magnify the achievements of their medieval ancestors, to appreciate Gothic architecture and vernacular poetry, as well as the institutions of the medieval state and church. Religious controversy intensified interest on all sides. Protestant divines looked energetically for earlier religious rebels; Catholic scholars looked equally energetically for documents supporting the sanctity of saints and the temporal powers of popes.

By the mid seventeenth century scholars not only admired the Middle Ages in general but understood an enormous amount about the history of Latin and the vernacular languages, and about the development of medieval society. The greatest reference book of the age, Charles du Fresne, sieur du Cange's *Lexicon,* aimed to trace the historical development of medieval Latin and to shed light on the general history of medieval society and culture. Meanwhile, the standard seventeenth-century textbooks by Christoph Cellarius (Kaller, author of *Historia medii aevi*) and Georg Horn (author of *Arca Noae*) treated the Middle Ages as a central and complete period in world history, one crucial to the development of Europe. Although *philosophes* of the Enlightenment used "feudal" and "medieval" as terms of abuse, even they added to the stock of knowledge about medieval literature and institutions. Since the beginning of the nineteenth century even adjectives like "medieval" have, for all educated people, lost their pejorative connotations. The Middle Ages are, for them, what they were for the best scholars of early modern times: a distinct period with a distinct and valuable Christian civilization.

BIBLIOGRAPHY

Frank L. Borchardt, *German Antiquity in Renaissance Myth* (1971); David C. Douglas, *English Scholars, 1660–1730* (1951); Nathan Edelman, "The Early Uses of Medium Aevum, Moyen Age, Middle Ages," in *Romanic Review,* 29 (1938); Wallace K. Ferguson, *The Renaissance in Historical Thought* (1948); George Gordon, *Medium Aevum and the Middle Age* (1925); Lionel Gossman, *Medievalism and the Ideologies of the Enlightenment* (1968); Denys Hay, "Flavio Biondo and the Middle Ages," in *Proceedings of the British Academy,* 45 (1959); Donald R. Kelley, *Foundations of Modern Historical Scholarship* (1970); May McKisack, *Medieval History in the Tudor Age* (1971).

ANTHONY GRAFTON

[See also **Historiography, Western.**]

MIDDLE ARMENIAN. See **Armenian Language.**

MIDDLE ENGLISH LANGUAGE. "Middle English" defines that period of the language between Old English, or Anglo-Saxon, and Modern English. The time boundaries at either end are necessarily arbitrary. The Norman Conquest of 1066 led to important changes in English, but not immediately. Chaucer's death in 1400 is rather more significant for literary than for linguistic history; the Great Vowel Shift of about 1450 affected only a part of a part of the language—the pronunciation of the long vowels; and Caxton's introduction of printing into England in 1476 was only the beginning of the influence of spelling on pronunciation. This article will deal with the English language between about 1100 and 1500, allowing for the great events of 1066 and 1476 to have had some effect.

After the Conquest the upper classes spoke French; the rest, English. More and more French words were borrowed into English, including some important grammatical ones such as "except." Even more people might have come to speak French but for the loss of Normandy in 1204; landowners had to choose between their English and their French possessions. Those who chose to stay in England necessarily had less contact with the Continent than before. English began to gain lost ground, replacing French in both the law courts and the schools during the fourteenth century.

The introduction of printing froze spelling. We spell essentially the way Caxton did and almost exactly like certain Elizabethan printers. Before printing, spelling followed a little behind phonological developments, trying to mirror them. Also, people speaking different dialects spelled accordingly. Since printing came to be common, the fact that words have continued to be spelled the same way has probably slowed changes in pronunciation—it certainly has led to the reintroduction of some old pronunci-

MIDDLE ENGLISH LANGUAGE

ations, such as sounding the "t" in "often." In addition, people everywhere soon learned to spell the same way, following the system they saw in print: that of London English.

Old English resembles present-day German and differs from present-day English in at least two obvious ways: discrete elements are commonly strung together to make words, and there are many inflections. Take the opening of *Beowulf:*

> Hwæt, we Gardena in geardagum
> þeodcyninga þrym gefrunon.

Literal: Lo, we Spear-Danes in yore-days people-kings' might heard of.

Free: Lo, we Spear-Danes heard of the might of the kings of the people in days of yore.

The Old English has three inflections for case (genitive plurals *Garden*a and *þeodcyning*a, and dative plural *geardag*um); the literal modern English equivalent, one (people-king*s'*); the free modern English equivalent, none. Aside from the special name for the Danes, the Old English has two compounds; the free modern English, none. The work done by compounding or inflecting in the Old English is now sometimes done by prepositions (for instance, "*of* the kings *of* the people" for *þeodcyninga*), sometimes allowed to lapse (the dativeness of the dative plural inflection *-um* of *geardagum* is not included in the simply plural inflection *-s* of "days").

But though Modern English does not have nearly as many inflections as Old English did, it may still be as capable of forming compounds as its ancestor, even if the capability is not exercised to the same degree; the literal translation above of the opening lines of *Beowulf* is at least possible, and understandable, albeit forced. Also, Modern English has many disguised compounds (for instance, "college student") written as two words. In Old English, any separable modifier preceding a noun would be inflected, and any uninflected modifier is printed by modern editors of Old English texts as the first element of a compound, either run in without division or hyphenated.

The *Beowulf* passage quoted above and the free Modern English equivalent also differ in the order of the fundamental sentence elements. *Beowulf* has SOV (subject-object-verb); the Modern English, SVO. But Old English also commonly used SVO, as well as VSO and other orders. Its greater number of inflections allowed Old English (like Latin) to be relatively free in word order. Modern English, with fewer inflections, depends more on the fixed position of a word to indicate meaning. (In the *Beowulf* passage, the direct object *þrym* is uninflected and is unaccompanied by any demonstrative pronouns or adjectives, which would have been inflected; but it is already clear that *we* must be the subject of the sentence.)

The first stages of Middle English can be seen in two types of text: late copies of Old English works and new compositions. Old English texts continued to be copied as late as the thirteenth century, often with great fidelity to the original, though in general with increasing change (often termed "corruption" or "deterioration").

An anonymous Old English homily on the phoenix survives in two copies: one from the second half of the eleventh century in Corpus Christi College, Cambridge MS 198, the other from the middle of the twelfth century in British Library, MS Cotton Vespasian D.xiv. Brief extracts follow for comparison:

> Þonne se monaþ in cymeð . . . þær is se
> fæȝere wuduholt þe is on bocum ȝehaten
> Radiansaltus. Þær is ælc treow swa riht
> swa bolt and swa heah . . . (MS 198)

> Þonne se monð . . . þær is se
> fægere wudeholt þe is ȝenemmed
> Radionsaltus. Þær is ælc treow swa riht
> swa bolt and swa heh . . . (Vespasian D.xiv)

> When the month comes in . . . there is the
> fair forest which is (in books) named
> Radiansaltus. There each tree is as straight
> as a bolt and so high . . .

The differences between the two texts are minimal but not without significance. In respect to orthography, Old English and Middle English scribes used both *þ* (called "thorn") and also *ð* ("edh" or "eth") for the "th" sound, voiced or unvoiced. (No writer ever used one for the voiced sound, as in "then," the other for the unvoiced, as in "thin," as is often stated.) The letter *ð* fell out of use in the fourteenth century, but *þ* continued into the sixteenth, and later, having merged in shape with *y* (and giving rise to such misconceptions as "ye olde tea shoppe"). On the other hand, Old English scribes used only one letter, *ȝ* (yogh), where Middle English scribes at first used two, *ȝ* and *g*, representing different guttural sounds, and later *y, gh, hg,* and other combinations. (The Old English *ȝ* is usually printed *g* by editors—as in the *Beowulf* passage above—since there is no contrast to be made between the two. Similarly, the *p*-

MIDDLE ENGLISH LANGUAGE

shaped letter "wynn" or "wen"—like *þ* a survival from the runic alphabet—is usually printed *w.*)

As for pronunciation—as indicated by spelling, at least—in the Vespasian manuscript unaccented vowels have merged in a single pronunciation rendered by *e,* and then some of them have been syncopated *(monaþ/monð, cymeð/cumð, wudu-/wude-);* and an accented diphthong has become one sound *(heah/heh).* There is evidence, however, that all three of these developments took place in at least some dialects of Old English before the Conquest. But Old English, too, developed a rigid spelling system used all over the country in the later tenth and eleventh centuries, called late West Saxon, which hid many phonological changes.

The only change in vocabulary in the Vespasian version of the homily, *genemmed* replacing *gehaten* (named), is in the direction of Modern English. Old English had both words, but nothing close to *hatan,* the past participle of which is *gehaten,* has survived. The verb "name" comes from the Old English noun *nama,* which is related to the verb *nemnan,* or *nemman,* the past participle of which is *genemmed.*

An early composition in Middle English is from the entries made in the Peterborough Chronicle between 1132 and 1155, showing more sweeping changes than Vespasian D.xiv:

> On þis gær [1154] wærd þe king Stephne ded
> and bebyried þer his wif and his sune wæron
> bebyried. . . . þa þe se king was ded, þa
> was þe eorl beionde sæ, and ne durste nan
> man don oþer bute god for þe micel eie of him.
>
> In this year became the king Stephen dead
> and buried where his wife and his son were
> buried. . . . When the king was dead, then
> was the earl beyond the sea, and no one dared
> do other than good for the great fear of him.

Here almost all Old English diphthongs have become monophthongized (**gear* > *gær, wearð* > *wærd, dead* > *ded*), but new diphthongs have arisen, with the *g* of the Old English **ege* becoming vocalized as *eie.*

More striking is the relative absence of inflection in the Peterborough Chronicle: only the nouns *sune* and *eie,* the verb *durste,* and the prepositions *beionde* and *bute* have inflections—all final *-e*—that subsequently were lost. Even Chaucer might have inflected the nouns and verb this way, though not the prepositions. The final *-e* was not lost everywhere in English until just after Chaucer's death, at the beginning of the fifteenth century, and there have not been any further losses of inflection from the language since.

In line with the great reduction of inflection is the merging of the many declined forms of the two Old English demonstrative pronouns into one invariable form for the singular and one for the plural. Whereas Old English declined the singular *se* (the, that) according to three genders (masculine, feminine, neuter) and as many as five cases (nominative, accusative, genitive, dative, instrumental), Middle English used only *the;* similarly, the Old English plural forms—nominative and accusative *þa,* genitive *þara,* and dative *þæm* or *þam*—all merged into *tha* (later *tho*). The same thing happened with the Old English demonstrative pronoun *þes* (this), the neuter nominative singular *þis* became extended to all singular functions, and the nominative and accusative plural *þas* superseded the genitive and dative forms *þissa* and *þissum.* The neuter nominative singular form of *se* was *þæt,* which developed into an emphatic pronoun, *that,* as *the* came to assume the functions of a definite article. By Chaucer's time, *tho* had become the plural only of *that,* and *the* was the invariable definite article, singular or plural. After Chaucer's time a final *-s* was added to *tho,* on the analogy of nouns, giving *thos* (modern English: "those"). Meanwhile, the older *thos,* from the Old English *þas,* had been superseded by the new formation *thise,* or *these,* as the plural of *this.*

The vocabulary of the Peterborough passage quoted is wholly native, or at least pre-Conquest. *Eorl* was introduced by the Vikings and took over some of the functions of the Anglo-Saxon word *ealdorman;* all the rest of the words in the passage go directly back to Germanic through the Anglo-Saxons. The absence of French words may, at least in part, reflect the subject matter—a simple narration of simple facts. After all, even today, all of the 100 commonest words in English go back to Old English.

Middle English is often thought of as the period par excellence for diversity of dialects. Chaucer's Parson in the *Canterbury Tales* says he "kan nat geeste 'rum, ram, ruf' by lettre," referring as much to the (to London ears) crudeness of the Northern and Western dialects as to the alliterative, versus rhymed, style. The first explicit statement about, or admission of the existence of, English dialects is from William of Malmesbury, who, writing in the earlier twelfth century, claimed he could not understand the language spoken north of the Humber,

MIDDLE ENGLISH LANGUAGE

particularly in York ("sane tota lingua Nordanimbrorum et maxime in Eboraco, ita inconditum stridet, ut nichil nos australes intelligere possimus").

No Anglo-Saxon writer, in Latin or English, refers to fellow countrymen speaking any differently from himself, but we know that they did. Certainly before the onset of late West Saxon, any Old English text of sufficient length can be assigned on the basis of its spelling to one of four major dialects: Northumbrian, Mercian, Kentish, or West Saxon. Within each of these areas it is also clear from the surviving evidence that there were subdialects, though the paucity of texts does not allow us to begin to say how many or to locate them very well.

There are hundreds of times as many texts in Middle English as in Old English; accordingly, some experts believe that they can locate a Middle English text to within an area having a radius of five miles or even less. Equally, linguists carefully mapping the country have discovered significant differences of pronunciation, as well as of vocabulary and even of syntax, from one English village to another; the same is true, though to a lesser degree, in the United States and Canada.

It is highly plausible that after the Angles, Saxons, and Jutes invaded England and were settled, the speech of each village became ever more particularized and the number of distinguishable dialects or subdialects increased. On the other hand, the different invading Germanic tribes may have spoken dialects whose differences, at least at first, broke down in England, yielding the national language, English, with characteristics as a whole that set it off from its continental sister languages and their dialects.

If English, throughout Anglo-Saxon and into Middle English times, increased in geographical dialectal diversity, when did the trend stop and begin to recede? In the twentieth century it has become clear that dialects are becoming less distinct and that English is becoming more homogeneous, both worldwide and within each country. The trend toward diversity may have stopped as early as the fourteenth century, when English once again became the language of government and the ruling class; or not until the introduction of printing; or perhaps not until the advent of radio and television.

Whenever London English made its way to other parts of the land, at first speakers must have learned it like any other foreign language and continued speaking their own dialect without modification. But sooner or later the London dialect would affect the local one, at first through the occasional visitor and book, finally through six hours or more a day of television.

In the fourteenth century there is explicit testimony that books had to be, in effect, translated from one dialect into another. A scribe of the *Cursor mundi* wrote of that work:

> In sotherin Englis was it draun,
> And turnd it have I till our aun
> Langage o northrin lede,
> That can nan other English rede.
>
> In southern English was it written,
> And I have turned it into our own
> Language of Northern people,
> Who cannot read any other English.

A modern reader can sympathize with this view after reading the openings of two of the greatest English literary works of the fourteenth century, the anonymous alliterative poem *Sir Gawain and the Green Knight,* thought to have been written in northwestern England, near Chester, and Chaucer's *Canterbury Tales,* written in London:

> Sithen the sege and the assaut watz sesed at Troye,
> The borg brittened and brent to brondes and askez,
> The tulk that the trammes of tresoun ther wroght
> Watz tried for his tricherie, the trewest on erthe . . . .
>
> Since the seige and the assault were ceased at Troy,
> The town broken up and burned to brands and ashes,
> The man who there wrought the tricks of treason
> Was tried for his treachery, the truest on earth . . . .
>
> Whan that Aprille with his shoures soote
> The droghte of March hath perced to the roote
> And bathed every veyne in swich licour
> Of which vertu engendred is the flour . . . .

Though both works date from the last quarter of the fourteenth century, Chaucer's is very much easier for any modern reader—in spelling, pronunciation, vocabulary, and syntax—because his or her dialect, descended from or through the centuries, has been greatly influenced by London English.

Traditionally, Middle English has been divided into three great dialects: Northern, Midland, and Southern, with dividing lines at the Humber and the Thames. Southern was further divided into Southwestern (Old English's West Saxon dialect) and Southeastern (Old English Kentish), and Midland into East Midland and West Midland. A more recent approach has been to draw as many isoglosses as possible, the number of dialects, and their characteristics and affinities, being indicated accordingly.

An isogloss marks the boundary between a linguistic feature, *a,* on one side of the line and not-*a* on the other side. For example, one of the most important isoglosses for Middle English, affecting many words, indicates the realization of the Old English *y* (pronounced *ü*) in stressed syllables. In the Southwest and West Midlands, words with the Old English *y,* such as *kyng* (earlier *cyning*), are often spelled with *u;* in the Southeast, with *e;* and elsewhere, including London, with *i*—hence the modern standard English "king."

Isoglosses can also be drawn for differences of inflection, vocabulary, and syntax, as well as for spelling and pronunciation. The third-person-singular verb inflection *-(e)s,* for instance, began in the North in Old English times and became established in London speech, ousting *-(e)th,* only after the Middle English period. Chaucer uses the *-s* inflection twice in rhyme, so it was recognizable, but must have been perceived as a dialectism. Middle English (and modern) dialects also differ widely in vocabulary, even with such common words as prepositions, for instance, the southern *to* versus the northern *til(l).* As for syntax, the northern dialect of Middle English preserved an older habit, never common in the South, of using both a demonstrative and a possessive pronoun with a noun.

Another well-known phonological isogloss of Middle English forms the outline of a thumb sticking up into England from the south, centered on the Isle of Wight (but not including that island) and extending almost as far as the Humber. Within the thumb the Old English *eag* became *iȝ.* London lies just outside the thumb, Chaucer usually writing *eigh* and *eye,* but occasionally *ye.* London English of the fourteenth century partook of features found all over the country, but had closest affinities with the dialects of the East Midlands, to the north and east and not cut off from the city by any important natural barriers such as the Chilterns or the Thames.

BIBLIOGRAPHY

J. A. W. Bennett and G. V. Smithers, eds., *Early Middle English Verse and Prose* (1966, 2nd ed. 1968); Karl Brunner, *An Outline of Middle English Grammar,* Grahame Johnson, trans. (1963; repr. 1970); R. W. Chambers and Marjorie Daunt, eds., *A Book of London English 1384–1425* (1931); Norman Davis, *et al.,* comps., *A Chaucer Glossary* (1979); Hans Kurath, Sherman M. Kuhn, Robert E. Lewis, John Reidy, *et al.,* eds., *Middle English Dictionary* (1952–); Tauno Mustanoja, *Middle English Syntax* (1960); Kenneth Sisam, ed., *Fourteenth Century Verse and Prose* (1921, repr. 1959).

DAVID YERKES

[See also **Anglo-Saxon Literature; Chaucer, Geoffrey; Dialect; Grammar; Old English Lanugage.**]

MIDDLE ENGLISH LITERATURE. The major genres of English literature between 1100 and 1500 are treated below in a general survey, **Middle English Literature,** and three specialized essays: **Alliterative Verse; Lyric; Prosody and Versification.** Related articles are cited in cross-references at the end of each section.

MIDDLE ENGLISH LITERATURE. The Middle English period of language and literature may be dated between the demise of the last version of the Anglo-Saxon Chronicle in 1154 and the establishment of Caxton's press in 1476. Such dates are, of course, merely bench markings in a continuous flow. Long before 1154 the last entries in the Peterborough Chronicle had begun to lose the grammatical features of Old English, and in the Signet letters of Henry V (*d.* 1422) features of regional dialect had already disappeared.

The principal characteristic of Middle English literature is that it was produced in an era in which the official and cultivated languages of England were Latin and French. Before the Norman Conquest, England had created the earliest vernacular literature in Europe, with a rich tradition of legal, learned, and literary documents. This movement was suspended in 1066 by the Norman Conquest. That political event produced a trilingual society that lasted for more than three centuries. French was the colloquial language of the Norman rulers and so became the language of government, law, and business. At the time of the Conquest, Latin was still regarded as the correct way to write French, and was the language of record. From 1066 until after 1350, all writing in England for men of power and men of learning was in French and Latin. The Anglo-Norman court, dividing its time between France and England, patronized some of the outstanding French poets—

MIDDLE ENGLISH LITERATURE

for example, Bernart de Ventadorn, Marie de France, Wace, Chrétien de Troyes—while English scholars writing both in England and on the Continent—for example, John of Salisbury, Walter Map, Geoffrey of Monmouth, Richard of St. Victor, Roger Bacon—testify to the vitality of the Latin tradition.

In contrast to the internationality and cultivation of the French and Latin traditions, writing in English between 1066 and 1350 was predominantly local and domestic. It was always the work of authors and scribes who had been educated in Latin and French. With no vernacular standard before them, and addressing unlettered local audiences, writers in English simply transliterated the sounds of their local speech, with the result that everything written in English is in regional dialect. Until the second half of the fourteenth century, writings in English fall into two broad categories: religious educational materials produced by Latin-trained clerics for the edification of an unlettered laity, and popular literature such as romances, chronicles, and songs intended to entertain the common people. Although the latter need not have been created by learned authors, a surprising proportion of what has survived has sources or analogues in French. Only with the advent of Chaucer, Gower, the *Pearl* poet, and others after 1350 do we begin to find sophisticated literature composed in English for cultivated audiences, although much of this writing still continues to be based upon originals in French and Latin.

The most comprehensive handbook for the study of Middle English literature is John Edwin Wells's *A Manual of Writings in Middle English, 1050–1400* (1916). The majority of the titles in the following discussion are given in the forms that appear in the *Manual.* Only one work of major importance has been added to the canon of Middle English literature since the publication of Wells's original volume, *The Book of Margery Kempe,* discovered in 1934. Wells, like other bibliographies and histories of Middle English literature, treats the writings by genre—for example, romances, chronicles, homilies, legends, and so forth. It has seemed preferable in this survey to treat them chronologically to observe the changes in ambiance that produced changes in style and subject matter over the course of three centuries.

FROM *ANCRENE RIWLE* TO JOHN WYCLIF

The outstanding example of literature in English produced during the earliest period is the *Ancrene Riwle* (*ca.* 1220). This is a devotional manual composed for the guidance of three noble women of English descent in the west of England, who had withdrawn from the world to live as recluses. It has eight parts: (1) Devotions, (2) Custody of the Senses, (3) Regulation of Inward Feelings, (4) Temptations, (5) Confession, (6) Penance, (7) Love, and (8) External Rules. The text reveals keen psychological insight and broad acquaintance with the writings of the great mystics and theologians. The advice is benign and the style witty and idiomatic. There is much specific information about the daily lives not only of cloistered nuns but of middle-class householders in general. The *Ancrene Riwle* exists in English, French, and Latin versions, the English and French so similar that there has been disagreement about the language in which it was originally composed. The existence of two different translations into French appears to support the view that the original was in English. However, there are also two early versions in English, the one called by modern editors *Ancrene Riwle,* intended for the three recluses, the other called by modern editors *Ancrene Wisse,* possibly by the same author, adapted for the spiritual guidance of a convent of nuns.

The *Ancrene Riwle* throws light on the audience for vernacular writing in the twelfth and thirteenth centuries. Its many redactions (the last printed by Wynkyn de Worde in 1493) perpetuate the Anglo-Saxon homiletic tradition. R. W. Chambers argued for the persistence of a cultivated vernacular prose tradition throughout the Middle English period in sermons and devotional treatises intended for members of an English-speaking gentry, many of them women. Discussions since 1960 have tended to minimize the influence of the *Riwle* and to present Modern English prose as a re-creation modeled on French and Latin. However one may feel about the argument about continuity, it is a fact that some of the most effective Middle English prose is devotional, in the tradition of the *Ancrene Riwle.* Even Chaucer's prose in the Parson's Tale is more lucid and idiomatic than his attempts at philosophical and scientific exposition. The lives of St. Katherine, St. Juliana, and St. Margaret, and the homilies *Hali Meidenhad* and *Sawles Warde,* all in the same dialect and style as the *Ancrene Riwle,* show that the *Riwle* was not an exception but the member of an identifiable tradition. Collections of prose homilies like those in the Bodley, Lambeth, and Vespasian manuscripts (all between 1100 and 1200), Bible renderings in both prose and verse, allegories like the prose *Debate Between the Vices and Virtues* (*ca.* 1200), and

MIDDLE ENGLISH LITERATURE

other devotional manuals continue the tradition. This corpus of vernacular writing is but the tip of the iceberg. Most of the legendaries, sermon collections, and confessional manuals are in Latin—sourcebooks from which the clergy were expected to adapt materials for ex tempore sermons and discourses. Only infrequently were these vernacular adaptations written down.

One such English adaptation is the *Ormulum* (*ca.* 1210), preserved in a unique holograph. Orm, evidently a canon in an Augustinian monastery in Carlisle or Lincoln, projected a collection of 242 homilies, one for each day of the liturgical year. The 20,512 septenary lines preserved represent only about one eighth of his plan. Neither Orm's matter nor his manner holds interest for the modern reader, but his systematic spelling is of some importance. Orm clearly envisaged his text's being read aloud, and he attempted to help the reader pronounce the words by doubling consonants after short vowels and marking the long vowels. Orm's is the earliest attempt at phonetic transcription in English—unless all writing of English dialect with Latin characters be considered phonetic. There are many other cycles of materials arranged for use on holy days throughout the church year. The *South English Legendary* is mostly in septenaries, the *Northern Homily Cycle* in couplets. Both of these exist in many manuscripts, altered and augmented from the thirteenth through the sixteenth centuries. John Mirk's *Festial* (*ca.* 1400) is in prose. Such collections are often enlivened by snatches of poetry, stories, fables, and other forms of illustration.

The poetic form and entertaining illustrations show the affinity between preaching and entertaining. Indeed, we may conclude that preaching was a form of entertainment in the Middle Ages. The lyrics from before 1350 that have come down to us are nearly all from collections of sermon material. Many of these seem to have been compiled by friars of the Franciscan order, which reached England in 1224. St. Francis was himself a jongleur to Our Lady, as he said. In Italy his followers early began to set religious words to popular tunes to enhance their evangelical ministry. They carried this practice with them to France and to England. The earliest Middle English Lyrics were gospel songs, some of them preserved with musical notation. They are learned productions, many from originals in Latin and French, composed by priests to wean the folk away from their secular frivolities. Beside more than 150 of these religious lyrics, there are no more than nineteen secular English lyrics from before 1400 (excluding Chaucer), and many of these are also learned productions. Seven of the nineteen are preserved in a famous early-fourteenth-century anthology of English, French, and Latin poetry, British Library MS Harley 2253. But genuinely popular songs and poems of the early Middle Ages are a genre entirely lost to us. Not until the fifteenth century do we find an efflorescence of secular poetry, and much of that is preserved in transcriptions made in the seventeenth and eighteenth centuries.

Earlier than the lyrics are the moralistic poems from the school tradition. The oldest, *Poema morale* (*ca.* 1150), in septenary couplets (from which developed the 4/3 ballad stanza), is *in fine* a religious begging poem, lamenting the vanity of human affairs and exhorting the rich man to give alms. It exists in seven versions containing 270 to 398 lines. The *Proverbs of Alfred* (*ca.* 1180) and the somewhat later *Proverbs of Hendyng* offer the same sort of versified moralization, deploring the uncertainty of life, the fleetingness of worldly possessions, and the fickleness of women and friends. The debate poems, like their prose counterparts, grow out of medieval pedagogical method. Disputation was the audio-lingual system by which spoken Latin was taught in the lower schools, and by which dialectic philosophy was taught in the universities. This pedagogical method grew into a literary genre. *The Owl and the Nightingale* (*ca.* 1200) is the most successful English example of the type. It is the first English poem written in French octosyllabic couplets, the form so favored by later English poets. The ironic voice and skillful rhetoric, also modeled on French and Latin debate poems, was later brought to perfection by Chaucer. The real question is, why was this poem composed in English at all? The anthropomorphic characterization of the birds and their habits is delightful, but the legal terminology and subtle argument would have been most appreciated by a learned audience who knew the French and Latin models. The poem appears to be occasional, but there is no indication as to the occasion. It ends by recommending for promotion one Master Nicholas of Guildford, possibly the author. The subject of the debate is as obscure as the occasion. Modern critics have interpreted it as an argument between secular and monastic life, art and philosophy, or erotic and religious poetry. In spite of the obscurity, the wit and specificity of the language make the piece a continuing delight.

The Thrush and the Nightingale (*ca.* 1275) is

MIDDLE ENGLISH LITERATURE

more obvious. The Nightingale argues that women are always gracious and true; the Thrush, citing authorities, that they are not to be trusted. The shape of the Latin school exercise can be discerned behind the argument, and troubadour prosody behind the complicated stanza form. *The Cuckoo and the Nightingale* by Chaucer's friend Sir Thomas Clanvowe is a love debate; the *Body and the Soul* and the *Good Man and the Devil* are moralistic; and there are other examples in both verse and prose listed in Wells.

Another monument of the early Middle English period is Layamon's *Brut* (after 1189), the first Middle English chronicle. Like the *Ancrene Riwle,* this sophisticated poem was written in the west of England, where the native tradition survived longest. Its subject matter implies a genteel audience not acquainted with French or Latin. Although the author claims to be translating Bede and Geoffrey of Monmouth, his only written source appears to be Wace's French version of Geoffrey. Layamon's continuity with the Anglo-Saxon tradition appears to be deliberate. Not only did he write his poem in alliterative long lines but he used the Anglo-Saxon poetic vocabulary, avoiding the French words in his source. The 16,095 lines begin with the founding of Britain by Brutus and end with Aethelstan driving the Britons into Wales (*ca.* 689). Lines 9,000–14,000 tell the story of Arthur. Layamon expanded his sources, introducing material from Celtic oral tradition, and changed Wace's chivalric French romance into a vigorous Germanic epic, full of violence and bloodshed. Although it was not influential in the subsequent development of the Arthurian legend, the *Brut* stands beside the *Ancrene Riwle* as one of the most significant productions in English before Chaucer.

The least didactic form of literature in English before 1350 was the romance, although many romances are in fact works of courtesy literature, designed to help inculcate the knightly virtues. Four from the early period deal with pre-Conquest subject matter: *King Horn* (*ca.* 1225), the *Lay of Havelok* (*ca.* 1280), *Guy of Warwick* (*ca.* 1300), and *Sir Beues of Hamtoun* (*ca.* 1300). Two others are Arthurian: *Arthour and Merlin* (*ca.* 1250) and *Sir Tristrem* (*ca.* 1280). Two are continental: *Floris and Blauncheflour* (*ca.* 1250), *Amis and Amiloun* (*ca.* 1290). Although they must have been intended for an English-speaking populace, these pieces show no connection with Anglo-Saxon. They are all in French metrical and stanzaic forms and even those dealing with Danes and Britons appear to be adaptations from Anglo-Norman originals. Other popular pieces are the *Land of Cockaygne* (*ca.* 1300), ninety-five couplets satirizing the luxury of monastic life, and *Dame Siriȝ* (*ca.* 1270) and *A Peniworþ of Witte* (*ca.* 1325), the only fabliaux in English before Chaucer's. *The Bestiary* (*ca.* 1250), a combination of alliterative verses and rhyme, straddles instruction and entertainment, as does the only Middle English beast fable outside of Chaucer, the *Fox and the Wolf* (*ca.* 1250).

The pieces dated between 1300 and 1350 differ little from what had gone before. The *Cursor mundi* (*ca.* 1300) is an encyclopedic retelling of Bible stories from the Creation to Doomsday in some 30,000 lines of varying meters. It begins by observing that people love to hear rhymes and read courtly romances, but the Virgin is the best lover and this poem is written to honor her. Although largely from the Vulgate, the poem includes material from Wace, Grosseteste, the *Legenda aurea,* and other French and Latin sources. The material is well organized and the voice is sprightly, but the narrative is all distant and exemplary, without immediacy that captures the interest of the audience. Robert Mannyng of Brunne's *Handlyng Synne* (*ca.* 1303) is much more effective in this respect. F. E. Furnivall remarked that it tells the best stories in English before Chaucer. Like the author of the *Cursor mundi,* Robert tells us that he is writing for the common people, who love to hear rhymes at feasts and in the alehouse, so he will translate the *Manuel des péchés* to rescue them from sin and folly. He handles his source very freely, omitting six stories, adding fourteen new ones, and adapting the doctrinal instruction to give it more life.

Handlyng Synne is the most interesting English example of the penitential manuals inspired by the requirement laid down by the Fourth Lateran Council (1215–1216) that every Catholic must confess and be absolved at least once a year, and that the clergy must instruct their congregations about the sacraments and the vices and virtues. This promulgation led to the creation of manuals in Latin for use by confessors and preachers, and eventually to vernacular treatises to enable devout laypeople to examine their own consciences. In England the decrees of the Lateran Council were reinforced by a series of synods and episcopal decrees. The most influential Latin treatises were St. Raymond of Peñafort's *Summa de casibus poenitentiae* (*ca.* 1235) and William Peraldus' *Summa de vitiis et virtutibus* (*ca.* 1260). The most important adaptation of the material in a ver-

MIDDLE ENGLISH LITERATURE

nacular treatise for personal use was Friar Lorens Gallus' *Le somme le roi* (*ca.* 1279), dedicated to King Philip of France. The Anglo-Norman *Manuel des péchés* (*ca.* 1260), sometimes attributed to William of Waddington, began the practice of introducing exempla to illustrate the sins. This literary innovation was developed further by Robert Mannyng. The other English treatises on the vices and virtues, most notably the *Pricke of Conscience* (*ca.* 1350), formerly attributed to Richard Rolle (extant in more than 100 manuscripts), and Dan Michael of Northgate's *Aȝenbite of Inwyt* (The backbiting of conscience) (1340), are fairly direct translations of the *Somme* without the enlivening exempla. Like the *Ormulum,* the *Aȝenbite* holograph is most important as a linguistic document—a dated and localized example of pure Kentish dialect. The most important literary influence of the penitential tradition was upon the writings of John Gower and Geoffrey Chaucer.

Thirty-five years after completing *Handlyng Synne,* Robert Mannyng of Brunne completed his *Rimed Story of England* (1338), a chronicle beginning with Noah and the Flood and ending with the death of Edward I (1307). The first 8,365 lines, to the death of Cadwallader, are based on Wace's *Brut;* the latter 9,000 lines are based on the Anglo-Norman chronicle of Peter Langtoft, with additions from other sources. The time had not yet come when historians thought of actually composing in English. However, some of them did begin to supplement the legendary history with first-hand information. For example, the *Chronicle* (*ca.* 1290–1310) that goes under the name of Robert of Gloucester supplements Geoffrey of Monmouth's account with genuine history gleaned from Henry of Huntingdon and other Latin historians and annalists, and with a firsthand account of a town-gown riot in Oxford (1263) and of the battle of Evesham (1265). Likewise, John de Trevisa's 1387 translation of Hygden's enormously popular Latin *Polychronicon* amplifies the contemporary material in the original. John Barbour's *Bruce* (1375) represents the earliest historical work composed in English as it recounts the wars between the English and the Scots in the time of Robert Bruce (1290–1332). Although scholars cavil at Barbour's factual errors, his poem is evidence of the growth of an influential audience ignorant of Latin and French. Of these chronicles only Trevisa's is in prose. If we can assume that verse exposition normally implied a listening audience and prose a reader, then Trevisa's translation marks a watershed, foreshadowing the prose chronicles of John Capgrave, the Monk of Malmsbury, and John Warkworth in the fifteenth century, and Edward Hall, Hollinshed, and others in the sixteenth.

The evolution of prose to be read—in contrast to verse to be recited—owes much to the fourteenth-century mystics. Up to the middle of the fourteenth century ecclesiastical writing in English had been largely conventional and derivative. This is true even of such masterpieces as the *Ancrene Riwle* and *Handlyng Synne.* But with Richard Rolle (*d.* 1349) we begin to see the emergence of original composition in English. Rolle was a learned man and most of his writings are in elaborately decorative Latin prose, but for the edification of his female disciples—the same sort of audience as that of the *Ancrene Riwle*—he wrote three English treatises on the mystical life, the *Form of Perfect Living* for a recluse named Margaret Kirkby, *Ego dormio et cor meum vigilat* for a nun at Yedingham, and *A Commandment of Love to God* for a nun at Hampole. These pieces are not translations but prose poems that express with clarity and feeling the *calor, canor, dulcor*—heat, melody, sweetness—of Rolle's spiritual ecstasy.

The rhythms of Rolle's prose show affinity with the unrhymed long lines of the alliterative poems coming into vogue at about the same time. The anonymous *Cloud of Unknowing* (*ca.* 1370) and other pieces by the same author lack the music of Rolle's prose, but they provide more analytical descriptions of the progressive stages of mystical experience, whose profundity has attracted the attention of modern psychologists. The author of the *Cloud* addressed his treatise to a male disciple, but Walter Hilton (*d.* 1395) again addressed his *Scale of Perfection* to a female recluse. The ideas in this guide to spiritual development come from Rolle and the *Cloud of Unknowing.* The tone is solicitous, but Hilton's works lack the human interest of the *Ancrene Riwle,* the poetry of Rolle, and the profundity of the *Cloud of Unknowing.*

Alongside the Middle English treatises written by men for the guidance of women, we have personal accounts of the spiritual experiences of two women. Some of the early lyrics purport to be by women, but the *Revelations of Divine Love* of Julian of Norwich (*d.* 1416/1423) and the *Book of Margery Kempe* (*d.* 1438) are the first pieces we can be sure were composed by women. In the *Revelations of Divine Love* Julian meditates on the significance of sixteen mys-

MIDDLE ENGLISH LITERATURE

tical visions of Christ's passion she experienced during a desperate illness in 1373. Her use of arithmetical sequence in ordering her statements and the analytical form of argument are hard to associate with an illiterate woman dictating to an amanuensis. In spite of the statement in the sixteenth-century Paris manuscript that "this revelation was made to a symple creature unlettyrde levyng in deadly flesh," one must suppose either that the complexity of the style was contributed by the scribe or that the demurral is conventional (like those by Chaucer and Caxton) and that the educated author held the pen in her own hand. If the latter is true, the *Revelations of Divine Love* would be the first piece in English actually written by a woman.

The *Book of Margery Kempe* has more human interest, if less spiritual profundity, than the *Revelations.* It is the spiritual autobiography of a middle-class housewife, mother of fourteen children, who after the birth of her first child began to suffer what modern medicine would call postpartum neuroses. This led her to spend the rest of her life in various forms of hysterical religious exhibitionism, pilgrimages, and contention with civic and religious authorities. The candor of the account is breathtaking; there is nothing else like it in English until Pepys' *Diary.* Its lack of inhibition is the more surprising when we read about Margery's problems with her scribes. But in spite of being read back and forth and several times revised, the style preserves spontaneity and the impress of a strong personality.

The development of English prose in the second half of the fourteenth century is further evidenced by the writings of John Wyclif and his followers. As with Rolle, the bulk of Wyclif's writings are in Latin. Indeed, there is a question whether any of the English works attributed to him were by his own hand. Most are abridgments of his Latin works. The sermons appear to be briefs intended for the poor priests who carried his doctrine to the people. The Wyclif Bible owes nothing to him but inspiration. It is the work of Nicholas Hereford, John Purvey, perhaps John Trevisa, and others. Wyclif's followers wrote Bibles, sermons, and tracts that disseminated his ideas throughout England. In the process they created the first Middle English written standard, which combined in the fifteenth century with the court standard developing in London to produce the Modern English written standard. Little is known about the activities of the poor priests, called Lollards, who disseminated Wyclif's doctrine of dominion throughout England in the 1370's. This doctrine asserted that temporal lordship was conditional upon righteousness, and that if that condition was violated, the unrighteous might be deprived of their property. Wyclif intended the doctrine to apply only to the clergy, but the Lollards applied it to the secular aristocracy and used it to justify the Peasants' Revolt of 1381.

ALLITERATIVE REVIVAL

The alliterative revival has likewise been associated with resistance to French-tinctured aristocratic rule. Many of the alliterative poems deplore contemporary conditions, but the genre also includes romances, chronicles, and moralistic poems. Several of these are translations from French, but there was little interrelation between the alliterative poems and the courtly poems being created by Chaucer and the metropolitan poets in London. Nor do we know the names of any of the alliterative poets. They inhabit the same sort of shadowy anonymous world as the Lollard priests. No poems in unrhymed alliterative long lines have survived from the period between Layamon's *Brut* (*ca.* 1190) and the grail romance *Joseph of Arimathie* (*ca.* 1350), although Gerald of Wales in his Latin *Descriptio Kambriae* (*ca.* 1200) reports that English and Welsh poets continued to prefer to write alliterative poetry, and gives examples of alliterative lines from poems that have not survived. If there was continuity of the alliterative tradition in the thirteenth century it was deeply submerged. The reason for its revival after 1350 is moot. If linguistic nationalism was not involved, it is hard to understand why after more than 150 years of nearly exclusive concentration on French forms, between 1350 and 1425 some thirty-five poems were written that eschew French prosody and vocabulary (even when translating the French) and return to the traditional English form—usually the unrhymed line with four stresses, two on each side of the caesura. Unstressed syllables are not counted, and ideally the stressed syllables are linked by alliteration. After about 1425 the movement died out in England, but it was continued by William Dunbar, Robert Henryson, and other Scottish poets to the end of the fifteenth century.

The most important poem of the alliterative revival is *Piers Plowman.* It exists in three versions: *A* (*ca.* 1370) in seventeen manuscripts, *B* (*ca.* 1377) in sixteen manuscripts, and *C* (before 1388) in nineteen manuscripts. The prosody of the poem is extremely loose. There is so much variation in the syllable count and the alliterative patterns that it reads more like rhythmic prose than like verse. This prosaic

MIDDLE ENGLISH LITERATURE

style is appropriate to the meditative, autobiographical tone of the work, which blends criticism of society with an individual quest for perfection. As with so many other poems of the period, the frame is a series of visions, here moving from moral and political allegory in the first seven passus (or steps) to spiritual and anagogical allegory in the eighth through the twelfth passus in the *A* version—the twentieth or twenty-third passus in *B* and *C*. The dreamer falls asleep in the Malvern Hills and finds himself looking down on a "field full of folk" representing society, lying between the Tower of Truth on the hill and the Valley of Death below. He observes the political fable of the belling of the cat and the moral allegory of the marriage of Lady Mede (money). In Passus V the personified Seven Deadly Sins make their confessions; in VI Piers Plowman (Piers = Peter, Pope, Church) appears and offers to guide the company to the shrine of St. Truth. The vision of the world then begins to shade into the vision of the search for Do-Well, which in the *B* and *C* versions is extended to the search for Do-Better and Do-Best. John Matthews Manly in 1906 suggested that the three versions were the work of different authors, but modern scholars have generally concluded that they represent the lifework of a single author, William Langland, whose views changed and matured, but whose text became disordered as he continued to revise it and as it was misunderstood and emended by the many copyists.

Piers Plowman draws upon medieval homiletic and devotional traditions, but it also shows connections with Latin satiric works such as Bernard of Cluny's *De contemptu mundi* (Rejection of the world) or Nigel of Longchamp's *Speculum stultorum* (Mirror of fools). This scholastic tradition is reflected even more clearly in other satiric poems of the alliterative revival. *Wynnere and Wastoure* (*ca.* 1350) is an allegory criticizing the handling of the war with France and social unrest in England. The *Parlement of the Thre Ages* (of about the same date and in much the same style) is a dispute between Youth, Middle Age, and Old Age in the tradition of the school disputations. Both are dream visions in style and language not unlike that of *Piers Plowman,* but more aristocratic in their subject matter. *Wynnere and Wastoure* begins with a vision of two armies drawn up for battle, and the *Parlement* includes an informed description of a deer hunt. *Pierce the Ploughman's Crede* (*ca.* 1394) is even more angry in its criticism of the mendicants than *Piers Plowman.* Both *Pierce the Ploughman's Crede* and *Wynnere and Wastoure* make use of the motif of making the rounds of the courts and religious orders in search of assistance only to be disappointed by their futility, like the ass Burnellus' search for a longer tail in the *Speculum stultorum. Richard the Redeless* is addressed to Richard after his fall in 1399, telling him what he did wrong. *Mum and the Sothsegger,* possibly by the same author, is an attack on the household of Henry IV written after 1402.

The unpretentious manuscripts in which the alliterative poems have come down to us tell us something about their ambience. The author of the romance *William of Palerne* (*ca.* 1350) says that he is translating the poem at the command of Humphrey de Bohun, earl of Essex; however it was not for the earl himself but "for hem that knowe no Frensche." The poem, composed in the dialect of Gloucestershire, was evidently intended for the edification of the Earl's Gloucestershire dependents. The Thornton manuscripts, which contain some of the best poems of the alliterative school, are commonplace books compiled over the years by a country gentleman in Yorkshire. MS Cotton Nero A.x., which preserves the unique texts of the *Pearl, Sir Gawain and the Green Knight, Patience,* and *Purity* (all *ca.* 1360–1395), well illustrates the nonprofessional character of the alliterative manuscripts. Its hand is clear and careful, but not that of a professional scribe, and the illuminations are amateurish. But there is nothing amateurish about the poems it contains. They are as polished and sophisticated as anything written in the century. One wonders under what circumstances such cultivated poems were composed in an outlandish dialect and preserved in a unique manuscript that evidently had no circulation. Manchester is not so far from Haworth, and there is much in the *Pearl* and *Gawain* collection that suggests the Brontë household five hundred years later.

Patience and *Purity* are verse homilies in unrhymed alliterative lines. *Patience* teaches the virtues of humility through the tale of Jonah, drawing on Latin poems by Tertullian and Bishop Marbod and a hymn by Prudentius. The dramatic expansion of Jonah's monologues and the descriptions of the storm and the belly of the whale reveal the poet's creative power. *Purity* teaches the virtue of obedience with illustrations from various Bible stories, in particular Belshazzar's Feast. The description of the Dead Sea is from Mandeville's *Travels,* and the author himself identifies an allusion to the *Roman de la Rose.*

Although they reveal the poet's wide reading,

MIDDLE ENGLISH LITERATURE

these two poems are pale beside the masterpieces. The *Pearl* and *Sir Gawain and the Green Knight* are the finest poems of the alliterative revival and rival Chaucer's as among the best in the fourteenth century. Form and content marvelously reinforce one another. Each poem comprises 101 stanzas and begins and ends with similar lines. The *Pearl* is in intricately interwoven twelve-line stanzas whose lyric expression complements the narrative argument: the complexity of the prosody reflects the complexity of thought and emotion. *Gawain* is in the same unrhymed long lines as *Purity* and *Patience* except that they are marked off into paragraphs of varying length by a rhyming five-line "bob and wheel" refrain. Alliteration deftly points up the rhythm and the rhetorical emphasis in all of the poems. Although they occur in the same manuscript, there is no objective evidence of common authorship, but the technique and the vocabulary indicate that if the poems are not by the same author they must be by an intimate circle. *St. Erkenwald* and the *Becket* prophecy in the Hatton MS have sometimes been attributed to the same circle.

Pearl begins as an elegy on the death of an infant daughter but soon, like Milton's *Lycidas* and Tennyson's *In Memoriam,* broadens from the expression of personal grief to consider some of the fundamental questions of contemporary theology. The poet-dreamer falls asleep on a grassy mound where his lovely Pearl has slipped away from him into the grass. He finds himself in a glistening land resembling Paradise. There he encounters a beautiful maiden, his Pearl grown older, with whom he discusses the efficacy of baptism, divine grace, and the equality of heavenly rewards. These were questions that had preoccupied theologians since St. Augustine, which John Wyclif and Thomas Bradwardine were writing about in the fourteenth century. There has been discussion by scholars of the orthodoxy of the Pearl's position, but there can be no doubt of the exquisite skill with which the poet blended personal sentiment with abstruse argument, spiritual epiphany with the abasement of the courtly lover to his lady.

The resemblance of Pearl as a spiritual instructress to Beatrice in the *Divine Comedy* has been noted, and of the situation in this elegy to Boccaccio's eclogue on the death of his daughter in the *Olympia.* But neither of these poems voices the rebellious personal anguish of the *Pearl,* although as analogues they again suggest the breadth of the poet's background. His transformation of chivalric "courtaysye" into Christian charity may be compared to Chaucer's transformation of the courtly convention of dying for love into elegy in the *Book of the Duchess.* Clearly, in the hands of English poets in the end of the fourteenth century, the themes and motifs of courtly love were undergoing the same sort of refinement as they had a century and a half earlier in the hands of the Italian poets of the *dolce stil nuovo.*

In *Gawain and the Green Knight* commonplace chivalric adventures are invested with mythic significance. Scholars are still debating whether the beheading and the temptation plots, which are found separately in various French and Irish romances, were first combined by the English author, but in none of these analogues does the plot line provide the sort of sensitive study of the chivalric ideal found in *Gawain.* The rich descriptions of action, architecture, furniture, clothing, the seasons, hunting, and the behavior and psychological reactions of Gawain and the other characters make this a cynosure among medieval romances.

The other romances of the alliterative revival are of some interest. The *Gest Historiale of the Destruction of Troy* (*ca.* 1350), the longest of the group, is a versification of Guido delle Colonne's *Historia destructionis Troiae.* The *Morte Arthure* (*ca.* 1360) may be a sort of allegorical commentary on Edward III's wars in France, and may have suggested to Malory the parallel between the fall of Arthur's empire and the demise of the chivalric ideal. There are three Alexander poems that exemplify the futility of temporal ambition. And *De tribus regibus mortuis, Summer Sunday,* and the *Awntyrs of Arthure* are three versions of a moralistic exemplum in which the hero comes face to face with putrefying apparitions that warn him of the horrors of death. In all of the romances of the alliterative revival, battle and conquest tend to be subordinated to moral and spiritual didacticism. In this respect they may be said to be morally superior to Malory.

The regional dialects and traditional prosody of the alliterative poems indicate their separation from the poetry being composed for the royal court and the Inns of Court during the second half of the fourteenth century. Whether this separation was merely geographical or whether it was also cultural and political remains moot. Nevertheless, the appearance of the alliterative revival in poetry and the Lollard movement in prose in conjunction with the political resistance exemplified by the Peasants' Revolt is hardly coincidental. They represent an attack on

MIDDLE ENGLISH LITERATURE

both the foreign aristocracy that had dominated England since 1066 and the growing centralization of power in London and Westminster. Outlandish clergy and poets had been the only ones writing in English before 1350, while the court and government wrote in Latin and French. It was the function of Chaucer and other courtiers and civil servants to revive the native tradition in the heart of government. Without exception the metropolitan authors were bi- or even trilingual, continuing to carry on their official business in French and Latin while writing for the entertainment of the court circle in English, which by 1350 must have become its vernacular.

CHAUCER, GOWER, MANDEVILLE

The key figure in this innovation was Geoffrey Chaucer. His career was modeled on that of the French civil-servant poets, Machaut and Deschamps. He began in the 1360's and 1370's to translate and emulate their themes and forms and gradually enriched his own poetry and the English tradition with material from the Latin classics, the Italian Renaissance, university treatises, satire on the estates, and contemporary manners. Whereas the writings of the alliterative revival, like those of Dante, epitomize the medieval tradition, Chaucer's works, like those of Boccaccio and Petrarch, introduce humanism. This view of Chaucer was set forth by scholars at the beginning of the twentieth century. Since the publication of C. S. Lewis' *Allegory of Love* (1936) critics have tended to stress Chaucer's continuity with the Middle Ages rather than his innovation. Chaucer was not an existentialist, a naturalist, an egalitarian, or a proto-protestant. He was a dualist who believed that the chief end in life was the search for salvation in a hierarchical society. But his concern for philosophical and psychological interpretations of behavior is in sharp contrast to the spiritual and theological interpretations of the *Pearl* and *Piers Plowman.*

Chaucer's *Book of the Duchess* (1369), *Parliament of Fowls* (*ca.* 1377), and *House of Fame* (*ca.* 1380) are dream visions in the manner of the *Roman de la Rose* and so many other French and Latin poems of the period. It has been suggested that the popularity of this convention in the later Middle Ages may be one aspect of the passage from literature to be recited, in which the delivery of the speaker can direct the response of the audience, to literature to be read, in which direction for audience response must be incorporated into the text. The reactions of the dreamer-persona in the dream vision became a technique for directing the audience how to respond. In his early poems we see Chaucer progressively enriching the courtly allegory of love with scientific and philosophical ideas, after the fashion of Jean de Meun's continuation of the *Roman de la Rose.* The *Book of the Duchess* and *House of Fame* are in French octosyllabic couplets of the sort that had been naturalized in English since the *Owl and the Nightingale.* In the *Parliament of Fowls* Chaucer introduced into English the pentameter line, which has also become so important in English poetry. Although the French poets used pentameter in some of their ballades, there seems little doubt that Chaucer's trip to Italy in 1373 and observation of the effective use of the hendecasyllabics by Dante and Petrarch is what convinced him of the value of this conversational meter for narrative. The *Parliament of Fowls* and *Troilus and Criseyde* are in seven-line stanzas, a typical form in the French ballades, but in the *Legend of Good Women* (*ca.* 1386), Chaucer moved to the pentameter couplet, which remained his favorite form throughout the rest of his career. (Some of the stanzaic pieces in the *Canterbury Tales* probably date from the period of the mid 1380's, when he was experimenting with the ballade stanza forms.)

Troilus and Criseyde is Chaucer's most finished poem, carefully planned and polished. Its principal characteristic is tension between the medieval and modern. The brilliant psychological characterization and dramatic interplay have led some critics to call it the first modern novel, but the motivation is quintessentially courtly—*la belle dame sans merci* and the passive lover right out of Chrétien's *Chevalier de la charrette.* This has led other critics to argue that what Chaucer really did was to move Boccaccio's naturalistic novella back in the direction of romance. In spite of Chaucer's attempts to reconcile these opposing principles through the imaginative application of Boethian philosophy, the poem remains ambiguous. Such conceptual ambiguity disappears from the *Canterbury Tales.* What ambiguity there is in them is purely structural. We may not know what order to read the tales in, or even whether all of the tales are assigned to their proper tellers, but the dramatic frame absolves the author of responsibility. We accept each tale as an extension of its teller and revel in the variety of Chaucer's human comedy.

The *Canterbury Tales* represent a crowning achievement of Middle English literature. The idiomatic ease of the General Prologue and the twenty-

MIDDLE ENGLISH LITERATURE

four links and tales has served as a model for all subsequent English poetry. Their psychological verisimilitude looks forward toward the shift in preoccupation away from the soul to the psyche. But it should be borne in mind that in spite of the modernity of treatment, the *Canterbury Tales* are rooted in the penitential tradition of *La somme le roi* and *Handlyng Synne.* In addition to encouraging penitential handbooks, the promulgations of the Fourth Lateran Council had led to an efflorescence of preaching. One category of sermons, designated *sermones ad status,* were those addressed specifically to the various classes, for example to the clergy, to knights, to merchants, to women. These sermons gave rise, in turn, to the literary tradition of "satire on the estates," that is, poems criticizing the behavior of the various classes in society. One of the most famous examples of this genre is Sebastian Brant's *Das Narrenschiff* (Ship of fools, 1494), and it is reflected in the "field full of folk" in Passus V of *Piers Plowman.* Chaucer's great poem is a brilliant adaptation of the medieval satire on the estates, anticipating Ben Jonson's comedy of humors and modern psychological conceptions of personality. The Parson's Tale is itself a penitential manual, summarizing and reflecting on the vices and virtues earlier presented in dramatic form. One especially interesting aspect of Chaucer's achievement is the immediacy of its depictions of character and behavior in the absence of any specific allusions to contemporary events or personalities. The verisimilitude for which the *Canterbury Tales* are so famous is totally a stylistic, linguisitic achievement.

John Gower, who wrote in three different languages, was much more a man of the Middle Ages than his friend Chaucer. Like the *Canterbury Tales,* his poems combine technique and materials from the penitential tradition. The French *Mirour de l'omme* (*ca.* 1378) begins with the fall of Lucifer, the conception and birth of Sin by Lucifer himself, his infatuation with his own daughter upon whom he begets Death and the Seven Deadly Sins, the marriage of the Seven Sins to the classes in society, and their manifestations in the behavior of the classes. The similarity to Milton's allegory of the begettal of Sin and Death in Book II of *Paradise Lost* is striking but has not been found to be directly related to the allegory in the *Mirour.* Gower's Latin poem *Vox Clamantis* (*ca.* 1385) begins with a vivid allegorical vision of the sack of London by the revolting peasants in June 1381, and then traces the manifestation of the Seven Deadly Sins in the various classes of society in much the same fashion as in the *Mirour.* Finally Gower's English poem *Confessio Amantis* (*ca.* 1390) adapts the penitential format to confession by the Lover of his guilt in the Seven Deadly Sins of love. Like the *Somme,* the *Mirour* and *Vox* present their criticism of society without illustrative exempla, whereas, like *Handlyng Synne,* the *Confessio* illustrates each sin with a series of stories.

The thematic connections between Gower's poems lead one to admire the comprehensiveness of his vision. His direct criticism of Richard II and other magnates of church and state lead one to admire his probity and independence. Individual tales in the *Confessio Amantis* are told with skill and grace. Gower's language and prosody are very nearly as facile as Chaucer's. Yet Gower's writing never achieves the immediacy of Chaucer's, or even of *Handlyng Synne.* In spite of the many references to contemporary characters and events—exactly the sort of references lacking in Chaucer—his poems lack human interest.

The *Travels of Sir John Mandeville* is evidence of the continuity of the French tradition in England. It and Gower's *Mirour de l'omme* are the last important works composed in Anglo-Norman, but unlike the *Mirour, Mandeville* was one of the most influential books of the Middle Ages and one most anticipatory of the Renaissance, when the idea of travel as pilgrimage gave way to the idea of travel as exploration. The Anglo-Norman version, evidently written about 1356, exists in twenty manuscripts, ten from the fourteenth century. Before 1371 it had been copied into Parisian French, and before the end of the century it had appeared in two, possibly three, independent English translations (not to mention Latin, Italian, Spanish, German, Dutch, Danish, and Czech). This popular account belongs to the literature of romance rather than the literature of travel. One cannot tell whether the author himself ever stirred from home because the details are derived wholly from the immensely popular pilgrimage/adventure literature dealing with the crusades and travels to the Holy Land and shrines throughout Europe. The marvels of the East in the Alexander legends and the few accounts of journeys into Central Asia and China bear witness to the spirit of adventure that underlay even the most pious accounts. To the extent that travel literature is one of the sources of the modern novel, the English translations of *Mandeville,* extant in thirty-six manuscripts and seventeen editions before 1700, are part of the history of the English novel.

MIDDLE ENGLISH LITERATURE

THE FIFTEENTH CENTURY

Chaucer, Gower, Langland, the *Pearl* poet, Wyclif, and their contemporaries made the second half of the fourteenth century the first golden age in English literature. It was followed by a century in which there is only one acknowledged masterpiece, Malory's *Le Morte Darthur.* Yet the fifteenth century is important for the spread of literacy and the development of popular literature. During this century business began to be carried on in English rather than in Latin and French. Writing spread from the ecclesiastical scriptoria and official chancelleries to the homes and offices of merchants and the gentry. Dialectal forms began to disappear from written documents and grammar and orthography to grow more standard. The first standardization is found in the Signet correspondence of Henry V (*r.* 1413–1422). Thence it spread to the other government offices and to the writing of scriveners and private individuals throughout England. The earliest notable collections of private papers are the Stonor Letters and Papers (1290–1483, the first English letter in 1420), the Paston Papers (1440–1486), the Cely Letters (1472–1488), the Plumpton Correspondence (1461–1551), and the Trevelyan Papers (1446–1643). By the end of the century the scope and quantity of this sort of administrative writing had so increased that since the sixteenth century these utilitarian genres have fallen out of the purview of what we call English "literature."

In the area that we today regard as "literature" much of the fifteenth century was spent trying to cope with the innovations introduced by Chaucer, which were not fully naturalized until the time of Thomas Wyatt and the Earl of Surrey. John Lydgate and Thomas Hoccleve, at the beginning of the century, tried mightily to emulate Chaucer's achievement. Lydgate (*d. ca.* 1449), even more a poet laureate than Chaucer, spent his life writing an enormous body of poetry on commission by Henry V and VI, by members of the court, and by wealthy bourgeoisie like Thomas Chaucer and the Pastons. In addition, he wrote and directed mummings for the court and municipalities, helped stage festivities to welcome Henry V to both London and Paris, served on the administrative staff of John, duke of Bedford, while he was regent of France (1426–1428), and otherwise busied himself with promoting the literary life both of the court and of the country. In nearly every poem, he pays homage to Chaucer as his role model. His earliest pieces are dream visions. His first major work was the *Troy Book* (1420), another rendering of Guido delle Colonne. Another important work is *The Fall of Princes* (1440), translated from a French rendering of Boccaccio's *De casibus virorum illustrium.* In addition, he made many other translations and wrote satires, saints' lives, religious and didactic verse, and occasional pieces for royal birthdays and weddings. His most personal expressions are his many digressions advocating peace and moderation. Although he is full of admiration for the achievements of Henry V and his brothers who ruled as regents during the infancy of Henry VI, it is clear that he did not view bloodshed and violence as chivalric virtues—as did Froissart and Malory. Lydgate recognized Chaucer's innovations in technique but lacked his master's genius for achieving idiomatic expression within the formulae. His vocabulary tends to be artificial and his syntax stiff. However, he was linked with Chaucer and Gower by commentators throughout the fifteenth and sixteenth centuries as one of the innovators of the new poetry.

Thomas Hoccleve (*d. ca.* 1437), a clerk in the Privy Seal office for some thirty-five years, is most interesting for the autobiographical references in his poems. Whether or not they are genuine, they create a persona rivaled only by Chaucer's. In this respect *La male regle* (The undisciplined rule, 1406), recounting his irregular life in Westminster and London, is the most revealing. In *De regimine principum* (1411–1412) he describes the difficulties of a scrivener's life. In his *Complaint* (1422) he describes his nervous breakdown. His poems were addressed to Henry V and others of the court circle, but on a much less intimate basis than those of Lydgate. While Lydgate's poems are mostly commissioned, Hoccleve's are mostly begging poems. *De regimine,* addressed to Henry while he was still Prince of Wales, was Hoccleve's most popular work. After an autobiographical introduction and complaint about the social ills of the time, the poem is a conventional collection of exhortations and examples directed to a ruler, taken from the *Secreta secretorum* and similar mirrors for princes. In these and many ballads and didactic poems, Hoccleve acknowledges the example of Chaucer, but like Lydgate he has problems with writing idiomatic lines in which the metrical stress reinforces the rhetorical. Of some historical interest is the formulary he compiled toward the end of his career in the Privy Seal (*ca.* 1425). Although this was just the period when the government offices were beginning to write in English, and Hoccleve himself was a poet in English, this collection of official documents for all occasions is all in Latin and

MIDDLE ENGLISH LITERATURE

French. Clearly Hoccleve did not foresee the emergence of English as an official language.

There is other English poetry in the fifteenth century, but none of it successful. The writing of poetry may have been discouraged partly by the rapid changes taking place in the language. The great vowel shift was making rhyming uncertain, and the loss of final *-e* and syncope of *-es* and *-ed* was making meter uncertain. The most interesting poet comes at the end of the century, John Skelton (*d.* 1529). He occupied in the court of Henry VII something of the place Lydgate had occupied in that of Henry V, and thought of himself as a translator and a poet in the aureate tradition, following in the footsteps of Chaucer and Lydgate. But his fame rests not on his serious poetry but on his humorous "Skeltonic" verse. This is a four-stress rhyming line with an indeterminate number of unstressed syllables harking back to the alliterative tradition. It has been preserved in the rhythm of nursery rhymes, and it has influenced the experiments of later poets such as Gerard Manley Hopkins and W. H. Auden. In this meter, toward the end of his life, Skelton produced a series of humorous satires against the corruptions in court, ribald drills like *The Tunnyng of Elynour Rummynge,* and tender conceits like *The Death of Philip Sparrow.*

More than any of the English poets, the Scottish poets of the fifteenth century managed to maintain a high standard of versification. It should be borne in mind that their language was not changing as rapidly as southern English, though the state of the language alone is no explanation for the lack of genius. The *Kingis Quair,* attributed to James I while he was a prisoner of England (1406–1423), is a dream vision in the manner of Chaucer's early poems detailing the narrator's capture and imprisonment and eventual union with his lady. Scholars no longer accept the attribution to James, but the poem, in rhyme royal, in northern dialect, is another example of the long shadow Chaucer cast over the poetic endeavors of the fifteenth century. Robert Henryson (*d.* 1508), a schoolmaster attached to Dunfermline Abbey, came closest to achieving a Chaucerian tone. His thirteen beast *Fables,* satirizing ecclesiastical and civic corruption, are, however, much more specific in their references than Chaucer's Nun's Priest's Tale. The *Testament of Cresseid* in seventy-nine rhyme royal stanzas is a male-chauvinist sequel to Chaucer's *Troilus and Criseyde* in which Cresseid is punished for her defection. She is afflicted with leprosy, and Troilus, returning victorious from battle, not recognizing her, tosses her a coin as she sits begging by the roadside. Henryson's verse is assured and effective, without the stiffness of Skelton's aureate poetry nor the ribald colloquialism of his humorous verse.

Although William Dunbar (*d.* after 1513) occupied a position in the household of James IV of Scotland similar to Chaucer's, Lydgate's, and Skelton's under their respective monarchs, he cannot be called a "Scottish Chaucerian." His is one of the most distinctive voices in medieval poetry. His *Lament for the Deth of the Makkaris* (after 1490), canonizing the great poets of the past, has a somber solemnity. His *Flyting of Dunbar and Kennedie* (*ca.* 1500) reminds one of *The Owl and the Nightingale,* as well as of the *tensos* and *sirventes* of the troubadours. *The Tretis of the Tua Mariit Wemen and the Wedo* (*ca.* 1490) in 530 unrhymed alliterative lines continues the tradition of the debate as well as of the alliterative revival. There are more than a hundred other poems attributed to him, many no longer than five or ten lines. They deal with all aspects of court, town, and religious life, with a characteristically satiric point of view and a vigorous obscenity of language.

Gavin Douglas (*d.* 1522), another Scottish court poet of the time of Jameses III and IV, is remembered chiefly for his translation of Vergil's *Aeneid* into heroic couplets. In the prologues to the books, Douglas discussed the theory of translation, Chaucer, Caxton, the evils of the day, and Christian interpretations of the poem. The *Palice of Honour* is an allegory on the various routes to honor, modeled on Chaucer's *House of Fame. King Hart* (heart), an allegory on the life of man, is no longer attributed to Douglas. There is no evidence as to the dates of composition of any of the poems; they exist only in manuscripts or editions after Douglas' death. Douglas' verse is less idiomatic than Henryson's and Dunbar's, but still more effective than that being written by his English contemporaries.

Although court poetry did not thrive in England in the fifteenth century, three popular genres emerged: the drama, the carol, and the ballad. Perhaps the most important development in Middle English studies since 1950 has been the new assessment of the importance of the mystery plays. Until the 1950's the literary and dramatic qualities of the plays were ignored or discounted and they were discussed as merely a stage in the evolution from ritual to drama. What was chiefly valued was their realistic and comic touches, which were viewed as foreshadowing the techniques of the Elizabethan drama.

MIDDLE ENGLISH LITERATURE

Since the 1950's a spate of studies and theatrical revivals have asserted the effectiveness of the mystery plays as drama in their own right, not as precursors to something better. The mystery plays, dramatizing episodes from the Bible from Creation to Doomsday, are largely found in four great cycles: Chester, York, Wakefield, and the *Ludus Conventriae* (performed not at Conventry, but at Lincoln or Durham or somewhere else). There are parts of cycles from Newcastle and Norwich and several unattached plays. These cycles were produced by the guilds and municipal corporations in connection with the celebration of the feast of Corpus Christi, some eight weeks after Easter. The miracle plays and saints' plays, dealing with stories extrinsic to the Bible, are thought of as subtypes under the mystery plays. The morality plays are dramatized allegories, like *Everyman, Wisdom,* and *Nature.* These are adaptations of the teachings in sermons and penitential manuals and the allegories on the life of man popular in the thirteenth and fourteenth centuries. Since they were independent of Biblical narrative and concerned with the psychological conflict inherent in the struggle between vice and virtue, this type developed into the Tudor interludes and eventually affected the structure and characterization of plays like Marlowe's *Dr. Faustus,* Shakespeare's *Macbeth,* and the Jonsonian humor plays.

Secular lyrics, carols, and ballads of the later Middle Ages were adjuncts to popular song and dance. Popular entertainment of this sort must always have existed, but since recording was in the hands of the clergy, who disapproved of it as frivolous if not actually sinful, only sentiments of disapprobation have come down to us, not the songs themselves. Much of what is now dated in the fifteenth century comes from seventeenth- and eighteenth-century manuscripts and transcriptions from oral tradition. Some 475 carols have been preserved, many of them gospel songs like the earlier lyrics. But there are some carols on marriage, amorous carols, and political and satiric carols. The characterisic form of the carol is a stanza to be sung by the leader and a refrain to be sung by the group. In contrast to the aureate poems of the period, the carols are notable for the ease and directness of their expression.

Only six ballads have been preserved in sources before 1500. The *Geste of Robyn Hood,* possibly from Caxton's press, was reprinted by both Wynkyn de Worde and Pynson before 1500. The fact that many of the ballads are in northern dialect and that they deal with Scottish subjects attests again to the vigor of the Scottish poetic tradition in the fifteenth century, when poetry in England was at a low ebb.

It is fitting that this survey of Middle English literature conclude with Malory and Caxton. Sir Thomas Malory of Newbold Revell in Warwickshire (*d.* 1471) has been traditionally identified as the author of the *Book of King Arthur and His Knights,* called by Victorian editors the *Morte Darthur.* However, the scandalous career of this knight so contrasts with the avowed idealism of the book that it has caused discomfort to the critics. Few have had occasion to remark that what Roger Ascham called the "open mans slaughter and bold bawdrye" of the book does indeed accord with the Warwickshire Malory's indictments. Other Malorys have been proposed whose careers are less at odds with the theme of the book. Authorship aside, the *Book of Arthur* provides a fitting conclusion to the chivalric literature of the Middle Ages. It blends the heroic tradition of the English alliterative and stanzaic romances with the chivalric tradition of the French prose romances to encompass the Whole Life of Arthur with digressions on the Tale of Lancelot, the Tale of Sir Gareth of Orkney, the Book of Sir Tristram, and the Tale of the Sankgreall.

The *Book of Arthur* is the last major work that takes the chivalric code seriously; thereafter the code is treated allegorically, satirically, or as an antiquarian ideal. Until the discovery in 1934 of the manuscript in Winchester College, the only text was Caxton's edition, which presents the account as a unified whole. The confusion in chronology, characterization, plot, and transition were attributed to Malory's naïveté as a writer. The Winchester manuscript, however, presents the text as six separate romances, each with its own explicit. The first explicit refers to the author as a knight prisoner; the last asks for his deliverance. These references to imprisonment have been taken to confirm the identification of the author as Malory of Newbold Revell, and the nature of the Winchester manuscript led Eugène Vinaver to edit the work as a cycle of romances. Much of the discussion since the 1950's has been devoted to the question of the structure and unity of the work. Somewhat less has been devoted to the intrinsically more important question of the way in which the fall of Arthur's kingdom symbolizes the end of the Middle Ages.

Just as the career of Thomas Malory and the fall of Camelot may be viewed as icons of the waning of the Middle Ages, so the achievement of William Caxton may be seen as ushering in the modern era.

We have remarked that one of the important cultural movements that marked the end of Middle English was the creation of a standard written language and the employment of this language for official and intellectual purposes. Caxton played a key role in these developments: he himself translated some twenty-four works from French and Latin into English. In so doing he gave wide dissemination to the developing forms of chancery usage upon which the modern standard is based. Caxton had a clear view of his middle-class audience. Unlike continental printers, the majority of whose books were in Latin and Greek, Caxton never printed a classic in the original. But his printing of Chaucer, Gower, Lydgate, Trevisa, Malory, saints' lives, and prose romances and his selection for translation of such classics as the *Troy Book*, the *Disticbes of Cato, Eneydos*, Ramon Lull's *The Order of Chivalry*, Christine de Pizan's *Fayttes of Armes*, and *Reynard the Fox* mark the journalistic bent that would extend literature beyond the purview of the church and the court to a much wider lay public. With Caxton, English literature moved into the domain of the middle class, where it developed until the advent of the mass media in the twentieth century.

BIBLIOGRAPHY

The most comprehensive handbook is John Edwin Wells, ed., *A Manual of the Writings in Middle English, 1050–1400* (1916), with nine supplements that bring the bibliography to 1951. The *Manual* is being revised in a series of separate volumes extending the coverage to 1500. By 1986, six volumes had been published in sixteen sections: vol. I, J. Burke Severs, ed., *I: Romances* (1967); vol. II, *idem*, ed., *II: The Pearl Poet, III: Wyclyf and His Followers, IV: Translations and Paraphrases of the Bible and Commentaries, V: Saints' Legends, VI: Instructions for Religious* (1970); vol. III, Albert E. Hartung, ed., *VII: Dialogues, Debates, and Catechisms, VIII: Thomas Hoccleve, IX: Malory and Caxton* (1972); vol. IV, *idem*, ed., *X: Middle Scots Writers, XI: The Chaucerian Apocrypha* (1973); vol. V, *idem*, ed., *XII: Dramatic Pieces, XIII: Poems Dealing with Contemporary Conditions* (1975); vol. VI, *idem*, ed., *XIV: Carols, XV: Ballads, XVI: John Lydgate* (1980).

General bibliographies. Robert W. Ackerman, "Middle English Literature to 1400," in John H. Fisher, ed., *The Medieval Literature of Western Europe: A Review of Research, Mainly 1930–1960* (1966); John H. Fisher, "English Literature," in Thomas D. Cooke, ed., *The Present State of Scholarship in Fourteenth-century Literature* (1982); Modern Humanities Research Association, *Annual Bibliography of English Language and Literature* (1920–); Modern Language Association of America, *MLA International Bibliography* (1921–, international in scope since 1957); William L. Renwick and Harold Orton, *The Beginnings of English Literature to Skelton*, 2nd ed. (1952); *The New Cambridge Bibliography of English Literature*, George Watson, ed., I (1974).

Special bibliographies. Carleton F. Brown and Rossell Hope Robbins, *The Index of Middle English Verse* (1943), with a *Supplement*, Rossell Hope Robbins and John L. Cutler, eds. (1965); A. J. Colaianne, *Piers Plowman: An Annotated Bibliography of Editions and Criticism, 1550–1977* (1978); Frieda Elaine Penninger, *English Drama to 1660 (Excluding Shakespeare): A Guide to Information Sources* (1976); Beryl Rowland, ed., *Companion to Chaucer Studies* (1968, rev. ed. 1979); Michael E. Sawyer, *A Bibliographical Index of Five English Mystics* (1978), which covers Richard Rolle, Julian of Norwich, the author of *The Cloud of Unknowing*, Walter Hilton, and Margery Kempe; Lena L. Tucker and Allen R. Benham, *A Bibliography of Fifteenth-century Literature* (1928); Robert F. Yeager, *John Gower Materials: A Bibliography Through 1979* (1981).

Studies. Albert C. Baugh, *et al., A Literary History of England*, 2nd ed. (1967); Thomas Cable and Albert C. Baugh, *A History of the English Language*, 3rd ed. (1978); Henry S. Bennett, *Chaucer and the Fifteenth Century* (1947, repr. 1958), useful on the book trade; Edmund K. Chambers, *English Literature at the Close of the Middle Ages* (1945, repr. 1964); Raymond W. Chambers, *On the Continuity of English Prose from Alfred to More and His School* (1932); Christopher R. Cheney, *English Synodalia of the Thirteenth Century* (1941), provides background for penitential and homiletic traditions; Eric J. Dobson, *The Origins of Ancrene Wisse* (1976); Mary Dominica Legge, *Anglo-Norman Literature and Its Background* (1963); Jill Mann, *Chaucer and Medieval Estates Satire* (1973); Thorlac Turville-Petre, *The Alliterative Revival* (1977).

JOHN H. FISHER

[See also **Anglo-Norman Literature; Arthurian Literature; Ballads; Carols; Drama, Western European; Preaching and Sermons; Seven Deadly Sins; Troy Story; Virtues and Vices; Visions;** and individual authors and works.]

MIDDLE ENGLISH LITERATURE: ALLITERATIVE VERSE. The alliterative poetry of the Middle English period cannot be discussed without reference to its antecedents, and the prehistory of English alliterative verse takes us back to the end of the first century. At that time, according to Tacitus' *Germania*, the Germanic tribes of which he knew used the alliterative line as a formal principle of literary composition. It seems certain that the poetry of the early Germanic tribes was universally cast in the form of alliterative verse. The earliest example to survive may be a runic inscription on a bronze ferrule found in a bog near the village of Süder-Brarup, northeast of Schleswig in modern Germany, in the home territory of the dominant tribe of the area, the Anglii—those Anglians who were later to colonize England and from whom the English took their name. The date of this inscription is said to be between A.D. 250 and 300.

OLD ENGLISH ALLITERATIVE VERSE

Almost 30,000 lines of alliterative verse in Old English survive—nearly three times as much as that preserved in various languages by all other Germanic tribes. The striking facts about it are its ubiquitousness and its persistence. Nowhere in the whole corpus of Old English literary verse—religious or secular, in heroic poems or in elegies, in biblical paraphrases or in gnomic verses—is there an example of an author writing or attempting to write in a verse form other than the traditional alliterative meter. The fundamental principle of that meter requires that either one or two stressed syllables of the first half-line must alliterate with the first stressed syllable of the second half-line. That principle is sustained on the larger, Germanic time scale over a period of 800 years (beginning with the alliterative long line engraved in runes on the Süder-Brarup ferrule), and in England for more than 300 years, from the earliest datable English poem, Cædmon's *Hymn,* which survives in a copy of about 740, to the poem on the death of King Edward entered in the Anglo-Saxon Chronicle under the annal 1065.

In the course of the 30,000 lines and 300 years the identifiable examples of poetic license are so few that they can be listed in a single paragraph. There is, most notably, the unique case of the *Riming Poem* in the Exeter Book, where a poem of eighty-seven lines has, in addition to alliteration, a complete scheme of rhyme (the first half-line rhyming with the second); such a scheme is also found at the beginning of the epilogue to Cynewulf's *Elene* (lines 1,236–1,250); rhyme is elsewhere found in addition to alliteration in *Beowulf* (line 1,014), *Vainglory* (line 33), *Andreas* (line 1,587), and *Battle of Maldon* (line 282). In *Maldon* (line 271) rhyme is used as a substitute for alliteration, as it is also used sporadically in the poems that appear in the Anglo-Saxon Chronicle under the annals for 959, 975, 1036, and 1086. The versified homily *Seasons of Fasting,* the short poem *Deor,* and the fragment *Wulf and Eadwacer,* while in other respects regular alliterative poems, display a stanzaic structure and the last two have refrains.

The Old English alliterative meter is, then, not merely a dominant meter (like the Roman hexameter or the pentameter in post-Renaissance England), it is the only meter and one sustained by more than 300 years of universal acceptance. In such a case alliteration must be seen not so much as a literary device as a cultural phenomenon; and it is generally held that it took a cultural revolution—the arrival of the Normans under Duke William in 1066—to displace it. However, that is too simple a view. There is evidence that the strictness of the metrical rules governing Old English verse was beginning to be relaxed before the end of the Anglo-Saxon period, evidence that appears in a number of poems found in the Anglo-Saxon Chronicle over the 150-year period between 937 and 1086.

Some of these poems—that which celebrates the victory of the West Saxons and the Mercians over the Vikings and the Scots at Brunanburh in 937; the poem on the freeing of the Five Boroughs (942); those on King Edgar's coronation (973) and his death (975); and that on the death of Edward the Confessor (1065)—follow the form of classical Old English verse. A larger group (occurring in the annals for 959, 975, 979, 1011, 1036, 1057, 1067, 1075, 1076, and 1086) are characterized by very wide divergences from the classical meter and in addition display variations among themselves. Thus, under the year 975 there are two short poems, one (nine lines) with alliteration, assonance, and a rhyming couplet, the other (ten lines) with only sparse alliteration and some assonance. Two longer poems under the years 1036 and 1086 display a mixture of irregular but alliterating long lines and unambiguous rhymed couplets. Those under 959 and 1057 are more like rhythmical prose than verse, with frequent but unsystematic alliteration and a scattering of rhymes and assonance.

Given the commonly held assumption that all Old English verse would be classical if it could, the usual view of the second group of poems is that they are the result of the technical incompetence of their authors or that they represent a debased popular taste. It is an argument not easy to sustain in the face of the certain attribution to Wulfstan (*d.* 1023) of the second short poem in the annal for 975 and that in the annal for 959; this archbishop of Worcester and York was a man skilled in rhetoric, an orator, and a self-conscious stylist in the writing of vernacular prose. In the license they display—unsystematic alliteration, rhyme, assonance—Wulfstan's poems are representative of the other so-called "popular" poems in the Anglo-Saxon Chronicle. But in view of his authorship they must surely be ascribed to bold experiment rather than to technical incompetence, an experiment analogous to Wulfstan's and Aelfric's experiments (if not to their achievements) in writing rhythmical alliterative prose. And the whole group of nonclassical poems may be seen as the attempt of imaginative men to break out of the straitjacket of an inherited poetic, to demonstrate that there are alternatives to the suffocating inevitability of the traditional form.

If the association of Wulfstan with nonclassical alliterative use suggests caution in condemning it, there remains the question why so few examples have survived, since it is not reasonable to assume that he alone explored new possibilities for the native meter. The explanation may lie in the conditions under which nonclassical Old English verse has survived. All the poems are on historical subjects and all are to be found in a single historical source, the Anglo-Saxon Chronicle. More precisely, they are found in only two of the five extant copies of the Anglo-Saxon Chronicle—the Worcester Chronicle, containing copies of ten of the eleven nonclassical poems, and the Peterborough Chronicle, with copies of seven. But the Worcester copy of the Chronicle was in fact kept up at York and did not leave there until the end of the eleventh century, and the Peterborough copy is also northern in its affiliations until it came to Peterborough via Canterbury in 1120. The three southern copies of the Anglo-Saxon Chronicle between them preserve copies of only two of the nonclassical pieces—a total of eight lines found in one of the two Abingdon versions.

Furthermore, there seems to have been a policy on the part of the compilers of the two northern chronicles, Worcester and Peterborough, to exclude poems in the classical meter: instead of inserting the poem on the battle of Brunanburh under the annal for 937 the Peterborough scribe dismisses it in a single sentence of prose; the poem on the crowning of Edgar (973) appears in Worcester and Peterborough only in a brief prose summary; for the long poem on the death of Edgar (975) they substitute a shorter nonclassical poem, and Worcester adds a second short poem in the same place. It is difficult not to conclude that such filtering and substitution is a conscious exercise of editorial taste.

By the same token it is arguable that the appearance of nonclassical poems in the two northern versions of the chronicle is attributable not to historical accident but to cultural preference—an established taste for nonclassical over classical Old English verse or even a dislike of classical verse. And the absence of nonclassical verse in the extant collections of Old English literary verse may be explained by the opposite cultural preference, since those collections survive in manuscripts of southern affiliations, though for this there may be a simpler explanation. The four great codices in which most Anglo-Saxon poetry survives were written about 1000; the Worcester copy of the Anglo-Saxon Chronicle was copied about 1050; and the Peterborough copy is not earlier than 1021. Only three of the nonclassical poems, those under the annals 959, 975, and 979, celebrate events earlier than 1011, and it is accepted that Wulfstan is the author of two of them; yet it is unlikely that he was in a position to introduce these two poems into a copy of the chronicle kept at York until he was appointed archbishop in 1002. At any rate, if the nonclassical verse represents a conscious attempt to break with the traditional forms of Anglo-Saxon verse, the impetus seems to have come from northern areas, and its experiments seem to have been found little sympathy in a West Saxon and culturally conservative south; and the experimental forms seem to have developed in the first half of the eleventh century, too late to find a place in the surviving collections of Old English verse.

The attraction of this hypothesis is that it allows for a new and more affirmative view of the development of alliterative verse in the late Anglo-Saxon period, one that better fits the evidence of the early Middle English period. Instead of the assumption that the arrival of the Normans in 1066 destroyed Anglo-Saxon culture as it destroyed the Anglo-Saxon political hegemony, and that the tradition of classical Old English verse was lost as a consequence, the alliterative meter surviving only in a debased popular form in culturally backward areas, it can be argued that in the last fifty years of the Anglo-Saxon period, certainly in the north and perhaps in other non–West Saxon areas of England, enterprising and imaginative minds were trying to emancipate themselves from the oppressive conservatism of traditional alliterative verse forms. What the Normans destroyed was not Anglo-Saxon culture but the West Saxon cultural hegemony and the concomitant authority of the old rules. The Conquest freed English poetry to seek new forms and new voices.

THE EARLY MIDDLE ENGLISH PERIOD

On this view what we should expect to find in English verse of the post-Conquest period is evidence of experiment, of poets struggling to find alternatives to the old ways against a cultural background that for 500 years had deemed alternatives scarcely thinkable. And that is the case. But it was a long and laborious process; as in all experiments, success was not guaranteed.

Success, indeed, proved singularly elusive for nearly 250 years. It should come as no surprise that experiment is more in evidence than accomplishment in the surviving works that employ the alliterative long line or some version of it. There are not many more than a dozen such works all told, only four of which (*The Departing Soul's Address to the Body, The Proverbs of Alfred, The Bestiary,* and Layamon's *Brut*) run to more than a handful of lines. Alliterative poetry after the Conquest became a dispersed tradition caught between a cultural past that (because of the political collapse of Wessex) had lost the power to support it, and the alien present of the usurping Normans that lacked either the interest or the means to nurture it. It was a tradition in which the individual poet's conception of verse form was bound to be an accidental product of his particular, local experience.

Such conditions do not lend themselves to neat evolutionary patterns of change. And considered in the light of the paucity of the remains, dates of composition spread over more than 200 years, the variety of kinds the works represent, and the different cultural backgrounds from which they emerge, it follows that the history of alliterative verse in the early Middle English period is muddled and inconsequential. Nonetheless, although there is not much evidence before about 1230, and not all of it is trustworthy, it is possible to chart some of the confused currents in the vernacular poetry of the period. One can validate the figure of the native poet as a man working in isolation from other poets. Maintaining a powerful sense of a tradition that was, however, increasingly difficult to accommodate to rapidly changing linguistic conditions, he was forced to seek individual and local solutions to common and often intractable technical problems.

Thus, within forty years of the Conquest we find a poet writing in or near Durham in the far north of England, composing between 1104 and 1109 a short poem about the city *(The Site of Durham)* in Anglo-Saxon verse of the classical type that adheres rigorously to traditional metrical principles and practices systematic alliteration, while avoiding end rhyme, run-on lines, and any excess of unstressed syllables. Also around 1100, 200 miles away in Worcester in the West Midlands, is composed a vivid little poem of twenty-three lines that laments the replacing of native English teachers—Bede, Aelfric, bishops (he names thirteen)—by Normans. It is in a very variable alliterative meter, four lines in the middle are in prose, three lines in a regular syllabic meter without alliteration, and there are a number of run-on lines. But from Worcester seventy or eighty years later, around 1170, comes a macabre piece *(The Grave)* which plays imaginatively with the idea of the grave as a house. It is alliterative verse of a wholly traditional (that is, Anglo-Saxon) type—metrically regular, with systematic alliteration, no end rhyme (though there is one example of assonance), no run-on lines, and no excess of unstressed syllables. In Durham about the same time three short verses associated with Godric, hermit of Finchale (*d.* 1170), are in a strict syllabic meter (no doubt on the model of Latin hymns) with rhyming couplets, and some merely decorative alliteration. Thus, around 1100 we have a poet following the traditional model of classical Anglo-Saxon poetry in Durham and another in Worcester exploring the old forms for new possibilities. Seventy years later the case is reversed: Worcester produces the traditional styles and manner, Durham the experiment.

How widespread the appetite for experiment was at the end of the twelfth century can be seen from two other examples. Contemporary with the second pair of poems just mentioned (*ca.* 1180) is the so-called *Death Fragment*—twenty-four half-lines in free (and probably corrupt) alliterative verse, seven of them without alliteration, the rest alliterative but following no regular system, with rhymes (sometimes medial) and assonance, written in the northwest Midlands; and far to the south in Sussex a collection of moralizing proverbs *(The Proverbs of Alfred),* a mixture of alliterative long lines without rhyme, alliterative long lines with rhyme and assonance, couplets with alliteration and couplets without alliteration, relatively few run-on lines but a higher incidence of lines with extra unstressed syllables and consequently a longer line than usual in traditional practice.

In the first half of the thirteenth century metrical experiment continued unabated and on an immeasurably larger scale. An eleventh-century metrical version of the Bestiary in Latin was translated probably between 1200 and 1250 in the northeast Midlands, perhaps Norfolk, and the energetic translator produced a version that follows the Latin in its use of a variety of meters often in the same passage. His very free mixture includes regular alliterative long lines, alliterative lines with internal rhyme, alliterative lines as couplets, lines without alliteration or rhyme, octosyllabic couplets, and quantities of lines in common meter and in the Latin septenary measure. Early in the century, on the other side of the country, Layamon, parish priest of Areley Kings on the Severn near Stourport, Worcester, wrote an immense poem of more than 16,000 lines tracing the early history of Britain (hence the title *The Brut*). It is also in a free alliterative meter (although nearly a third of the lines do not alliterate) with much rhyme and assonance—seldom allied with alliteration—linking the two half-lines, and frequent extensions of the length of line by the addition of extra unstressed syllables, but seldom run on.

There is evidence from about the year 1200 that the vigorous interest in the possibilities of metrical form was not restricted to the alliterative poets. In the first decade of the century Orm, a monk of Elsham Priory in north Lincolnshire, adjacent to the area to which the Bestiary is assigned, was composing a vast collection of metrical English sermons extending in its unfinished state to 20,000 lines; he uses neither alliteration nor rhyme but the most rigid syllabic regularity in a line based on the Latin septenarius and having invariably fifteen syllables, no more or less. Almost contemporaneous with Orm, in Surrey south of the Thames, Nicholas of Guildford was at some time between 1189 and 1216 writing his delightful *Owl and the Nightingale,* nearly 2,000 lines in a free octosyllabic verse with rhyming couplets, displaying only incidental use of alliteration and only for decorative purposes.

The ferment extends beyond English and beyond verse. About 1180, at Credenhill near Hereford (not very far from Layamon in Areley Kings), a lighthearted, witty, and independent Anglo-Norman writer, Hue de Rotelande, an especially skillful and stylish versifier in octosyllabic couplets, was at work on his romances *Ipomedon* and *Protheselaus.* And also near Hereford, no more than a generation later (*ca.* 1220), a group of imaginative clerics—almost certainly contemporaries of Orm, Layamon, and Hue de Rotelande—were busy composing English works of piety and edification. They wrote works about saints' lives, homiletic treatises, meditations, and rules for living. Among the latter the most considerable is the rule for anchoresses known as *Ancrene Riwle,* which exists in English, Latin, and French versions—cast in a serviceable and self-confident rhythmical prose in which alliteration is systematically and ubiquitously employed.

MIDDLE ENGLISH VERSE: 1230–1340

It is unnecessary to plot in any detail the story of alliterative verse between about 1230 and 1340. It continued to be written and showed a comfortable and marked propensity to come to terms with syllabic verse and the rhyme, which for the century and a half before 1230 it had found such difficulty in assimilating. The traditional accentual and unrhymed alliterative long line ceased to be cultivated. Having found a workable mode, poets seemed content to stay within it and produced a smoother, technically more accomplished verse that lacks the disturbing energies and the disconcerting variety of some of the earlier Middle English poetry.

Why does it survive at all? There is no simple answer. The early post-Conquest history of alliterative verse does not encourage any appeal to "tradition," for if tradition survived the coming of the Normans it very rapidly fossilized into an antiquarian nostalgia, elements of which are to be seen in Layamon's *Brut,* accounting perhaps for the curiously archaic flavor that seems to characterize his verse. The case made by R. W. Chambers in 1932 (and still fashionable, though in a much qualified form) that explains the continuity of Middle English alliterative verse in terms of its oral transmission, and the argument for a submerged popular tradition, remain unconvincing.

The explanation may be that alliteration exists in Middle English not as a traditional and self-consciously literary phenomenon but as an autochthonous cultural habit, an ever-present fact of verbal consciousness accessible to the poet and attractive to him because of its universally recognized association with the idea of what poetry should be. As we have seen, the Roman Tacitus at the end of the first century remarks on the use by Germanic tribes, precursors of the English, of alliteration as a formal principle of composition; more than a thousand years later, about the year 1200, Giraldus Cambrensis (Gerald of Wales) remarks on the Englishman's love of alliteration. The examples Giraldus quotes by way of illustration are all proverbial sayings, and proverbs, as the expression of the racial wisdom, lie close to the very foundations of human consciousness. The use in English of alliteration as a device to encapsulate that wisdom establishes it as part of the aboriginal fabric of the English imagination and guarantees it a sort of immanent presence in the minds of poets (and of preachers, liturgists, lawyers, and others, the evidence makes clear). Alliteration represents for them an instinctive, instantly accessible resource that exists at a level too deep to be more than superficially controlled by considerations of literary tradition or stylistic decorum.

Such a view may help to explain a great deal that is puzzling about the history of alliterative verse in the Middle English period. It enables us to approach much nearer to an understanding of its persistence and waywardness, its recalcitrance and its adaptability. It explains the impossibility of fitting the existing remains into a satisfactory chronology and accounts for the arbitrariness of their geographical distribution. It explains the existence of alliterative prose alongside the poetry. It illuminates such stylistic eccentricities as Richard Rolle's "Liquidum licebit non labar in lutum, lachrimis iam lotus libenter laboro in laude letari ac liquescere in lumen letificans levatos" (from his *Melos Amoris,* and not unrepresentative); such anomalies as Chaucer's lapse on two, but only two, occasions (Knight's Tale, 2,602ff; *Legend of Good Women,* F. 637ff) into alliterative verse; and the bursting into vigorous and extravagant flower in *Song Against the Blacksmiths* (*ca.* 1325) of the unrhymed alliterative long line after it had lain dormant for nearly a hundred years. Last of all and most importantly, it helps account for that otherwise baffling phenomenon, the so-called "Alliterative Revival," by removing the need to establish continuity between the unrhymed alliterative verse of the second half of the fourteenth century and the poetry of the Anglo-Saxon period, and excusing us from the requirement of finding an explanation for the meter of *Piers Plowman* and *Sir Gawain and the Green Knight* in terms of conventional categories—tradition, sources, influence—which in most respects they so resolutely refuse to be explained by.

MIDDLE ENGLISH VERSE: AFTER 1340

Sometime around 1340, probably in the neighborhood of Hereford, was compiled a very miscellaneous anthology of religious and literary pieces including religious works in Latin prose and verse, saints' lives, fabliaux and poems in Anglo-Norman, and in English the romance of *King Horn, The Proverbs of Hendyng,* some of the earliest political poems in the language, and a group of short lyrics. The anthologist was clearly a man of catholic interests and cultivated taste. To the extent that his taste is reflected in the collection of English lyrics (more than thirty in number), the so-called Harley Lyrics, to which the volume owes its chief fame, his choice is interesting for the historian of alliterative verse in the Middle Ages. The generous and eclectic interests represented in the composition of the volume and evident also in the selection of lyrics (which include both secular and religious poems, courtly, pious, and comic subjects, and a variety of forms—carol, pastourelle, and reverdie, for example) are apparent in his evenhanded choice of metrical forms.

The collection illustrates the consolidation of syllabic meters and stanzaic forms that had developed since about 1230. Yet alliteration is very freely employed throughout and in poems of all kinds; three poems are cast in a version of the native alliterative line and two show alliteration in every line. The interest of this collection is twofold—first, that a settled, mature, and sophisticated taste of about 1340 should show such a confident appetite for alliteration. Second, given the wide variety of alliterative forms displayed in the poems, there is little to prepare us for the coming tidal wave of alliterative poetry cast in a singular and brilliant mutation of the native line. It was about to break at almost exactly the moment the anthologist was working, and nowhere more powerfully than in areas in and adjacent to that in which the collection was being assembled.

The mutation is in essence very simple. It lies in restoring the use of alliteration (long reduced to the function of decoration) as a structural principle by firmly relating it to the pattern of stressed syllables (usually no more than four) within a line, two on either side of a medial pause. The alliteration normally falls on both stressed syllables before the medial pause and on the first of the two stressed syllables after it. The full line may be of variable length, shorter or longer, depending on the number of syllables without stress or with diminished stress found in it; and stressed and unstressed syllables are disposed without reference to any pattern of regular alternation characteristic of syllabic meters. Such a line can, if necessary, accommodate both rhyme and a regular pattern of stanzaic forms without any serious weakening because the avoidance of any regular pattern of syllabic alternation ensures that rhyme and stanza, if employed, are subordinate to the principles of its own internal alliterative economy.

The benefit to the poet of such a system is that it gives him authority over the syntax and movement of his verse, authority that in strict syllabic and rhyming verse is to a large extent sacrificed to an arbitrary and often mechanical metrical pattern. It allows him to mold a line to a precise verbal configuration, to respond to local and very particular imaginative needs, and in practice makes it possible for him to achieve an immense range of subtle, sophisticated, and often surprising effects. Such verse is a pipe on which many tunes can be played, and if the best of them are played by the *Gawain* poet and Langland—the Mozart and Beethoven of alliterative poetry—that is not to diminish the more modest claims of much other alliterative poetry of the late fourteenth and the fifteenth centuries, claims which, since few of the poems have attracted serious critical attention, for the most part remain to be pressed.

Readily apparent is the great variety of subjects of the alliterative poets of the fourteenth and fifteenth centuries, subjects for which alliterative verse served as a more or less satisfactory vehicle—historical chronicles in the epic manner on native subjects *(Morte Arthure)* and classical subjects *(Alisaunder of Macedoine, Alexander and Dindimus, The Wars of Alexander, The Destruction of Troy)*; romances—sentimental *(William of Palerne)*, moralizing *(Cheuelere Assigne, The Awntyrs of Arthure)*, and chivalric *(Sir Gawain and the Green Knight, Golagros and Gawane, Rauf Coilȝear)*; semi-religious and pseudo-historical *(Joseph of Arimathie, The Siege of Jerusalem)*; religious and political satire *(Pierce the Ploughman's Crede, Richard the Redeless, Mum and the Sothsegger)*; religious polemic (the texts associated with the antimendicant *Jack Upland, Friar Daw's Reply* and *Upland's Rejoinder*); social and religious allegory *(Piers Plowman, Death and Life, Wynnere and Wastoure, The Parlement of the Thre Ages)*; a group of poems on a variety of religious and generally edifying themes *(Pearl, Patience, Purity, St. Erkenwald, The Pistill of Susan, The Quatrefoil of Love)*; and a group of Scottish works (*The Buke of the Howlat, Scottish Field,* two *Scottish Prophecies*) and pieces by Douglas, Dunbar, Henryson, Lyndsay, Montgomerie, one of which, Dunbar's *Tretis of the Tua Mariit Wemen and the Wedo,* is the most elaborate of alliterative jokes. As this list suggests, these fourteenth- and fifteenth-century works are too heterogeneous in mode and subject matter and too various in style to be accounted a "school" except in the loosest sense, but apart from their use of a basic alliterative line a number of other features commonly appear.

Most striking are the distinctive poetic diction and formulaic phraseology found particularly in poems such as *Sir Gawain and the Green Knight* associated with the northwest Midlands, the area between Shropshire and Lancashire. Nearly 200 years earlier, a vocabulary peculiar to his poetry and not found in the written prose of the period had characterized Layamon's style in *The Brut;* in that case it was modeled on the diction of Old English poetry and was in part derived from it—as in the numerous synonyms for "man"—and it may have been a conscious effort to give an antique flavor to the work.

No such motive seems to underlie the special vocabulary of the fourteenth-century poems and it is, indeed, easier to describe it than to account for it. It is used especially in technical descriptions of one sort or another, such as the arming of a knight, the protocol of a banquet, in describing the architecture of a castle or the physical features of a landscape or the weather. The style is particularized and the diction concrete and material. Words of Scandinavian origin are especially prominent and are usually, in the narrowest sense, dialectal. They are seldom found outside of fourteenth-century alliterative poetry and are characteristically found in alliterating positions; it is likely that it was because of their usefulness in such positions that they became part of the literary vocabulary in the first place.

A distinctively alliterative diction is much less widespread in some works, such as *Joseph of Arimathie* and *Cheualere Assigne,* and its absence is particularly noticeable in works from the area of the southwest Midlands. *Piers Plowman* and the texts associated with that poem are strikingly free from it; and whatever the reason for that, it resulted in a much wider audience for *Piers Plowman* than for any other alliterative poem. More than fifty complete or almost complete manuscripts of the poem survive, and they were copied in places as widely distributed as Sussex, Durham, Shropshire, Norfolk, London, and Ireland.

Many of the fourteenth- and fifteenth-century alliterative poems express a rather solemn conviction of their own importance and are on a scale commensurate with it: ten of the unrhymed alliterative poems are between 1,000 and 7,000 lines long; one, *The Destruction of Troy,* is 14,000. Stanzaic and rhyming works are on the whole shorter, though many run to several hundred lines.

It is generally held that the so-called "Alliterative Revival" began around 1350 and had petered out by about 1450. Yet most of the Scottish alliterative works are demonstrably late—the prologue to book

VIII of Douglas' *Aeneid* was finished in 1513, and the poem entitled *The Scottish Field* celebrates the battle of Flodden, of the same year. *The Wars of Alexander* survives in two manuscripts, both dated between 1450 and 1500; the unique manuscript of *The Destruction of Troy,* the longest of all the alliterative poems of the period, was copied around 1550, that of *Death and Life,* around 1650. The orthodox view that they are late and corrupt rests on two comfortable assumptions: that while copies of works preserved in fourteenth-century manuscripts derive from originals composed not long before the date of the manuscripts in which they appear, copies of works found in late-fifteenth- or sixteenth-century manuscripts derive from originals composed very much earlier than the date of the manuscripts in which they appear. It is far from certain that this must necessarily be the case. More compelling arguments than have yet been advanced seem desirable before these assumptions, and with them the chronology they imply, can be allowed the canonical authority often claimed for them.

BIBLIOGRAPHY

Sources. J. A. W. Bennett and G. V. Smithers, eds., *Early Middle English Verse and Prose* (1966); George L. Brook, ed., *The Harley Lyrics* (1948, rev. 1956); Bruce Dickins and R. M. Wilson, eds., *Early Middle English Texts* (1951); Elliott V. K. Dobbie, ed., *The Anglo-Saxon Minor Poems* (1942), 16–26; Joseph Hall, ed., *Selections from Early Middle English, 1130–1250* (1920); Layamon, *Brut*, printed by George L. Brook and R. F. Leslie (1963 and 1978), and *Selections from Laȝamon's Brut,* George L. Brook. ed. (1963)

Studies. James P. Oakden, *Alliterative Poetry in Middle English* (1930–1935, repr. 1968), though less rigorous in its selection and method than is now thought desirable, remains indispensable because it is the only comprehensive treatment of the subject. The questions of the survival of alliterative verse after 1066 and its revival after 1350 were much influenced by Raymond W. Chambers, *On the Continuity of English Prose from Alfred to More and His School* (1932, repr. 1966). Representative of the older views are Dorothy Everett, "Laȝamon and the Earliest Middle English Alliterative Verse," in her *Essays on Middle English Literature,* Patricia Kean, ed. (1955); Charles Moorman, "The Origins of the Alliterative Revival," in *Southern Quarterly,* 7 (1969). Representative of newer views are N. F. Blake, "Rhythmical Alliteration," in *Modern Philology,* 67 (1969–1970); Angus MacIntosh, "Early Middle English Alliterative Verse," a lecture delivered in the Faculty of English, Cambridge University (1974); Derek A. Pearsall, *Old English and Middle English Poetry* (1977), 57–84; Elizabeth Salter, "The Alliterative Revival," pts. 1 and 2, in *Modern Philology,* **64** (1966 and 1967).

Studies that discuss other issues include Marie Borroff, *Sir Gawain and the Green Knight: A Stylistic and Metrical Study* (1962); Seymour Chatman, *A Theory of Meter* (1965); George Kane, "Music, 'Neither Unpleasant nor Monotonous,'" in P. L. Heyworth, ed., *Medieval Studies for J. A. W. Bennett* (1981); Robert W. Sapora, *A Theory of Middle English Alliterative Meter* (1977); Thorlac Turville-Petre, *The Alliterative Revival* (1977); Ronald A. Waldron, "Oral-Formulaic Technique and Middle English Alliterative Poetry," in *Speculum,* **32** (1957).

P. L. HEYWORTH

[See also **Ancrene Riwle; Anglo-Norman Literature; Anglo-Saxon Literature; Brut, The; Cædmon; Chaucer, Geoffrey; Douglas, Gavin; Dunbar, William; Gawain and the Green Knight, Sir; Hue de Rotelande; Langland, William; Middle English Literature; Old English Language; Owl and the Nightingale, The; Pearl; Scottish Literature, Gaelic.**]

MIDDLE ENGLISH LITERATURE: LYRIC.

"But saye me, felowe, what is your use,
To do in contr' aftyr the none.
And what is the custome of your hous,
Tille men to souper shalle gone?"

"Sir, somme men jouste with sper and shelde,
And somme men carol and singe gode songes,
Some shote with dartis in the feelde,
And somme play at Chesse amonge."

(Hausknecht, ed., *The Romaunce of the Sowdone of Babylone, ca. 1390)*

BACKGROUND

In a curious sense, Middle English "lyric" did not come into existence until the early twentieth century. During the Middle Ages there were instead songs, carols, treatises, prayers, charms, and other kinds of short poems, from all of which modern editors and scholars created the inclusive category of Middle English lyric. As late as 1890, Henry Morley, author of the nineteenth century's most ambitious history of English literature, identified medieval "songs" of several kinds—profane, popular, devotional, and the like—and discussed them in various parts of his voluminous work; but he acknowledged no single lyric genre. By 1916, however, when John Edwin Wells issued his *Manual of the Writings in*

Middle English, 1050–1400, he devoted a chapter to "Pieces Lyrical in Impulse or in Form," both "secular" and "religious"; and the same presumption of genre is, expectably, evident in the revision of Wells currently being published under the editorship of Albert E. Hartung. Like "courtly love," which was actually conceived by Gaston Paris about 1883 to account for certain medieval literary phenomena, Middle English lyric is also a modern concept, not a medieval one. Although it is useful as a catchall for certain diverse kinds of poems, the reader must not approach most of these poems with the expectations that the word "lyric" often arouses.

Indeed, the meaning of lyric in our literature as a whole is notoriously imprecise. The word entered English from French and the classical languages only in the 1580's. Its earliest general use in antiquity, at Alexandria, referred to poems composed to be sung; in consequence it has usually retained a vaguely musical connotation—at least in theory—in its English incarnation. However, other, quite different criteria are as often invoked as well. A popular notion is that "personal emotion of the poet" is the most characteristic feature of the lyric. But this is exceptionally difficult to demonstrate, and, on the contrary, it is now widely accepted that most lyric poetry embodies literary conventions quite like those of other genres—that the lyric personae of, say, Shakespeare's sonnets are as much an artifice as the dramatic personae of his plays. Lyric verse is not so much "personal emotion" as the imitation or illusion of personal emotion. Failure to understand this distinction—a Romantic heresy—has impeded both the appreciation of older verse and the composition of new. C. Hugh Holman adds the Romantic categories of imagination and unity, defining lyric as "a brief subjective poem strongly marked by imagination, melody, and emotion, and creating for the reader a single, unified impression." J. W. Johnson's long article on lyric in the *Princeton Encyclopedia of Poetry and Poetics* surveys much modern thinking on the subject. Johnson acknowledges the many types of poetry that are likely to be called lyric but considers their musical element the "irreducible denominator." In contemporary usage, he believes, "a lyric is a type of poetry which is mechanically representational of a musical architecture and which is thematically representational of the poet's sensibility as evidenced in a fusion of conception and image."

Such modern definitions reveal by their abstractness and artificiality how distant actual poetical practice can be from accepted critical theory. In fact, current functional (as distinct from theoretical) usage, with its indifference to traditional genres, regards any short poem as a lyric, thus precluding a search for arbitrary, elusive, or ambiguous qualities such as "music," "imagination," "subjectivity," and "unity." This realistic approach serves eminently well for the Middle English lyric specifically, as in the work of the anthologist R. T. Davies: "By a 'lyric' is meant simply a shorter poem, and the word is used only because it is shorthand which is understood by most people in this general sense."

Indeed, insofar as the supposed characteristics of lyric can be identified in actual poems, they are, in some sense, correlatives of the poems' brevity, which naturally invites a relatively "unified impression," some illusion at least of "subjectivity," certain conspicuous repetitions of sound and stress that seem to be what literary critics mean by "music," and so forth. It remains an open question whether the "lyrical impulse" induces a poet to write a relatively short poem, or whether his wish to compose such a poem awakens his lyrical impulse. It is enough to assert that—for whatever reasons—many or most short poems seem to aspire toward those features regarded as lyric; that such features generally appear more distinctly in short than in long poems; and that, finally, to define lyric as "a shorter poem," unsatisfying as such a definition is conceptually, makes sense on formal as well as inductive grounds. If one uses these common-sense, inclusive criteria, the familiar question, whether Old English verse produced lyrics, is readily answered: yes, of course, though only a few survive. Accordingly, such poems as *Seafarer, Wife's Lament,* and *Deor* are manifestly lyric and it is only our difficulty in relating ourselves to their personae which sometimes leaves us in doubt.

POETRY AND CULTURE

At the heart of all poetry is style. Part of style—the more arresting part, no doubt—is the deposit of individual genius or talent, which is not subject to historical classification, as distinct from critical analysis. But style includes as well the imprint of the particular culture that has nourished the poet; that element accounts for the prevailing differences between religious lyrics of the thirteenth or fourteenth century and those of George Herbert or Gerard Manley Hopkins, or between certain of the Harley lyrics and the love poems of Shelley or Yeats. It is culture, too, that accounts for the fact that most of Middle English lyrics of all kinds, including most of the best ones, are by poets now nameless. We are unlikely, for example, ever to know the autnor ot the following memorable poem, which has come down to us, with music, on a flyleaf bound into an early-thirteenth-century manuscript in the Bodleian Library. (All quotations of Middle English lyrics are from the edition by Luria and Hoffman.)

Mirie it is while sumer ilast
With fugheles song—
Oc nu necheth windes blast
And weder strong.
Ey! ey! what this nicht is long,
And ich wid wel michel wrong
Soregh and murne and fast.

Merry it is while spring lasts
With birds' song—
But now draws nigh wind's blast
And weather strong.
Ey! ey! how long this night is,
And I with very much wrong
Sorrow and mourn and fast.

This poem is compact with intense, "personal" emotion; yet, like many comparable pieces, it comes to us anonymously. This is not merely an accident of transmission; nor is it because artistic ego was not very assertive in early-thirteenth-century England. Rather, the sentiment of the poem was felt to be not so much personal as typical or representative. Not the unique sentiment, uniquely expressed, of a unique sensibility that a modern reader might expect, it was the common property of many sensibilities and therefore had the authority or truth—we should, alas, probably be tempted to say "relevance"—of the common, instead of the novelty of the particular. Medieval culture differs radically from modern culture precisely with respect to this matter. Moderns seek poetic truth and beauty in the individual and eccentric, in the "original," whereas medievals distrusted whatever lacked the sanction of commonly held tradition and authority. (A parallel cultural bias explains why the most distinguished of our identifiable authors of medieval lyric—Chaucer, of course—wrote his lyric verse almost exclusively in the French genres of ballade, envoi, and *complainte,* lavishing his superb art on the elegant and refined expression, in traditional forms, of traditional ideas and feelings.)

The energies of medieval culture, especially in the northern countries, tended to discourage the identification of particular lyric voices with particular poets, as later ages would associate certain kinds of expression with Donne or with Wordsworth. And the authority of received ideas and familiar feelings—and, especially in courtly circles, of received continental genres—was more powerful than the attraction of the novel. So too the pervasively Christian orientation of cultural life at all levels of society rendered the distinction between "religious" and "secular" poetry less absolute than it would be in later periods. This is obviously true of the great chefs d'oeuvre, where the categories are, indeed, scarcely meaningful. Is *Beowulf* a religious poem? Is the *Canterbury Tales* or *Troilus and Criseyde* a secular one? To be sure, there is much manifestly religious poetry among the surviving Middle English lyrics; it constitutes, in fact, the larger part of our lyric literature. By the same token, there are drinking songs and bawdy rhymes with no religious content or implications. But there is a considerable body of work, including some of the finest poems, in which this distinction is more elusive, as with the verses quoted above. In their expression of unease at the approach of winter, they contain no explicitly religious sentiment; but the poem is found in a manuscript of devotional writings. There can be no doubt that the sorrow it adumbrates has reference to Christian apprehensions of sin and damnation and that the poem, with its traditional metaphors of winter and night and its skillful choice of diction and rhythm, expresses a condition of spiritual anxiety. Nevertheless, it is also meaningful on its literal level, as a statement of foreboding at the approach of winter, a familiar theme in medieval poetry. Are these verses "religious" or "secular"? The answer must be "both" or "neither," for they come from a culture in which material phenomena were often regarded as emblems of spiritual realities. To the allegorically oriented mind of the Middle Ages, winter of the body readily suggested winter of the soul, that is, sin in this world, damnation beyond it. No special effort of imagination was needed to see the life of the spirit shadowed by the life of the flesh.

Let us, then, summarize what chiefly distinguishes Middle English lyrics from later lyric verse. Even as we cannot generally relate specific medieval poems to specific authors, so the "subjective" or "emotional" component of medieval work, in contrast with modern practice, is likely to express a conventional rather than a novel perspective, accessible to all readers or listeners and coming from accepted literary, religious, or other cultural sources. Moreover, certain distinctions of content, such as religious and secular, which have great relevance for later periods, and which many critics have imposed on the medieval poems as well, must be used cautiously, owing to the ascendance of religion and the allegorical mode in medieval culture.

CLASSIFICATIONS

In seeking to classify Middle English lyrics one can make an essential distinction between those that are imitations of continental (especially French) genres—that tend to be self-consciously literary in diction and aspire to elevation of tone, and whose authors are sometimes known to us—and those simpler, more direct poems that have come to us anonymously through popular oral channels and social matrices. Ignorant of French forms, these latter often display remnants of native allegorical meter. The distinction is not, of course, categorical, but with the noteworthy exceptions of the short poems of Chaucer and some few others, it is among these native or popular poems (if we may so distinguish them from more self-consciously literary ones) that we find the finest, the most arresting Middle English lyrics. Related to them are two cognate genres. The ballad is a traditional narrative song with elaborate stanzaic patterns and verbal repetitions. And the carol is a type of lyric originally designed for social singing; it corresponds to the French *chanson à carole* but is wholly English in content and distinguished structurally by its burden or chorus appearing at the beginning of the poem as well as after each uniform stanza.

Although this varied and copious body of verse, dating from the thirteenth to the sixteenth centuries, constitutes one of the great lyric literatures of the world, it is certain that much of what once existed has been lost, and it is possible in fact that a native lyric literature flourished in England in the twelfth century, and perhaps even earlier. One of the oldest surviving Middle English lyrics, and today the best known of all, serves as a reminder that though the large bulk of our thirteenth-century lyrics is in the devotional or meditative mode, there were also poems of simple rejoicing.

Sumer is icumen in,
Lhude sing, cuccu!
Groweth sed and bloweth med
And springth the wude nu.
Sing, cuccu!
Awe bleteth after lomb,
Lhouth after calve cu,
Bulluc sterteth, bucke ferteth.
Murie sing, cuccu!
Cuccu, cuccu,
Wel singes thu, cuccu.
Ne swik thu naver nu!
Sing cuccu nu, sing cuccu!
Sing cuccu, sing cuccu nu!

Spring has come in,
Loudly sing, cuckoo!
Seed grows and meadow blooms
And now the forest springs.
Sing, cuckoo!
Ewe bleats after lamb,
Cow lows after calf,
Bullock leaps, buck farts.
Sing merrily, cuckoo!
Cuckoo, cuckoo,
Sing well, cuckoo.
May you never stop!
Sing cuckoo now, sing cuckoo!
Sing cuckoo, sing cuckoo now!

This charming little celebration of the return of spring—it suggests the French genre of reverdie—is the only English song, among others in French and Latin, found, with music, in a monks' commonplace book compiled at Reading Abbey and now in London, British Library, MS Harley 978. Nothing else in medieval poetry and little since possesses its unreflective, exuberant celebration of nature's vitality, seemingly so indifferent to cultural distinctions. Apart, indeed, from language, it is not even especially medieval, but rather speaks of universal human experience.

Other short poems of comparable subject and merit have come down from this early period. However, they inevitably juxtapose their images of natural animation with a Christian perception of sin and imperfection, obliging the reader to reflect on the ironic coexistence of beauty and life with corruption and death in a world at once divine and fallen. "Mirie it is while sumer ilast," discussed above, is such a poem. Here is another:

Foweles in the frith,
The fisses in the flod,
And I mon waxe wod.
Mulch sorw I walke with
For beste of bon and blod.

Birds in the wood,
The fishes in the river,
And I must become mad.
Much sorrow I walk with
On account of best (beast?)
of bone and blood.

This subtly modulated poem about man's alienation from the rest of nature embraces its complex subject in a few compressed, fruitfully ambiguous words and images. Man, it may be saying, is (and knows that he is) a "beast" of bone and blood. Moreover, to be human is to sorrow, and if a Christian, to sorrow for the "best" of bone and blood—for Christ and the metaphysical tragedy of the crucifixion. As Edmund Reiss has put it, the narrator "carries on his shoulders the weight of human sin and its resultant sorrow." The ambiguity and ominous mystery (with ballad echoes) of the last three verses express at once the largeness of the theme and the oppressive disharmony of the narrator's inner life.

NONDEVOTIONAL THEMES

Several other Middle English lyrics also join images from nature with melancholy emotions, but directly and without irony—and with decidedly less affecting intensity and hard lapidary objectivity.

Winter wakeneth all my care;
Now this [these] *leves waxeth bare;*
Ofte I sike [sigh] *and mourne sare* [sorely]
When it cometh in my thoght
Of this worldes joye how it geth all to noght.

The poem, of which this is the first of three stanzas, appears in the most important manuscript collection of Middle English lyrics, London, British Library, MS Harley 2253. The collection includes most of the early nondevotional lyrics, including nearly all the best. The origin of this varied anthology of materials in Middle English, French, and Latin (partly written in the late thirteenth century, partly in the early fourteenth) has not been determined. It has been surmised that the manuscript was assembled for the library of a fourteenth-century dignitary, possibly Thomas de Charlton, bishop of Hereford from 1327 to 1344 and chancellor of Ireland from 1337 to 1340. The best recent scholarship, that of Isabel Aspin, dates it about 1338.

The forty-eight English poems in the Harley Manuscript include a dozen that treat sexual love and related emotions with a sympathy, earnestness, formality, and sophistication that indicate the influence of the continental romance lyric and its courtly conventions. These are virtually the only love poems we have before the latter part of the fourteenth century that are entirely without Christian reservations or Marian typologies, and they are perhaps the most celebrated of the Harley lyrics. Loaded with verbal and rhetorical encrustation, leisurely and formal, they reveal many evidences of French influence. They are, however, remarkably varied in their perspectives and styles. In "Lenten is come with love to toune," the description of spring's return (reverdie) is followed by a concluding rueful reflection on the contrasting phenomenon of female reluctance:

Wormes woweth under cloude,
Wimmen waxeth wounder proude,
So well it wol hem seme.
If me shall wonte wille of on,
This wunne weole I wole forgon
And wight in wode be fleme.

Worms make love under ground,
Women grow exceedingly proud,
So well it will suit them.
If I shall lack the pleasure of one,
This wealth of joys I will forego
And quickly be a fugitive in the woods.

"Ichot a burde in a bour ase beryl so bright" (I know a maiden, in a bower, as bright as beryl, sometimes called "Annot and John") is a series of intense similes glorifying the lady, extravagantly artificial and mannered, more rhetorical than emotional. The same theme appears in several other Harley lyrics with greater restraint, most notably in "A wayle whit as whalles bon" and "Most I riden by Ribbesdale" ("The Fairy of Ribbesdale"). The most conspicuous motif in these lyrics is the sorrow of the disdained lover. One such poem begins:

With longing I am lad—
On molde I waxe mad—
A maide marreth me.

With longing I am afflicted—
On earth I become mad—
A maid injures me.

Another starts by evoking the *locus amoenus* or emblematic garden of love, an image related to the reverdie and familiar to all readers of medieval verse:

When the nightegale singes,
The wodes waxen grene:
Lef and grass and blosme springes
In Averil, I wene [reckon];
And love is to min herte gon
With one spere so kene:
Night and day my blod it drinkes;
Min herte deth me tene [grieves].

The motif of love's sorrow appears in the Harley lyrics in various shapes: a charming carol ("Blow, northerne wind, / Send thou me my sweting!"); a dialogue of almost Mozartian delicacy between a clerk and his reluctant inamorata, whose reluctance is not, however, impermeable ("My deth I love, my lif ich hate," known as "De Clerico et Puella"); a poem in which a knight encounters a shepherdess—like the preceding, a variation of the French pastourelle but less colloquial and more deliberate ("In a frith as I con fare fremede"; In a wood as I did walk, unfamiliar). Probably the finest of these poems of lovesickness is "Bitwene Mersh and Averil" ("Alysoun"), a lyric of tenderness and refinement:

Nightes when I wende and wake—
Forthy min wonges waxeth won—
Levedy, all for thine sake
Longinge is ilent me on.

Nights when I turn and wake—
Therefore my cheeks become pale—
Lady, all for thy sake
Has longing come upon me.

The same motif occurs in a few early-fourteenth-century poems outside the Harley group, notably the lovely carol "Als I me rode this endre day," and a superbly simple, moving piece—one of the best of the lyrics—for which there is haunting music:

Brid one brere, brid, brid one brere!
Kind is come of love, love to crave.
Blithful birid, on me thu rewe,
Or greith, lef, greith thu me my grave.

Bird on briar, bird, bird on briar!
Nature has come because of love,
to beg love.
Blithesome bird, pity me,
Or make ready, dear one,
make ready for me my grave.

It continued to be exploited through the fourteenth and fifteenth centuries, though with diminishing freshness and emotional authenticity and increasing literary self-consciousness. (This later work may be represented at its best by Chaucer's admirable "Compleynt unto Pite.") And yet no Middle English lyric of love, however ambitious or accomplished, surpasses an enigmatic quatrain in which the art is virtually invisible but the music quite unforgettable:

All night by the rose, rose,
All night by the rose I lay;
Darf ich nought the rose stele,
[I dared not steal the rose,]
And yet ich bar [bore] *the flour away.*

As early at least as the thirteenth century, however, there were English poems that satirized sexual love and the adoration of women. One of the oldest of these is "Somer is comen with love to toune" ("The Thrush and the Nightingale"), a flyting, or poem of abusive debate, in which the thrush provides, in effect, a catalog of clerical complaints about women. Antifeminism was, indeed, a significant factor in later medieval thought and literature, deriving (at least ostensibly) from belief in the primal sin of Eve, and serving as a medium for the assertion of fundamental Christian values with regard to marriage and sexuality, while often expressing (at times, no doubt, playfully) certain biases of the celibate masculine ecclesiastical establishment. Its literary locus classicus was the enormously influential thirteenth-century allegorical satire, *The Romance of the Rose.* We have a number of poems in English, especially from the fourteenth and fifteenth centuries, in which complaint about woman's unapproachability has turned into abuse of her character or condemnation of her very nature, and warning young men against marriage. These pieces are certainly not elegant or refined. They are direct and hearty, jocular and playful and represent, obviously, a drastically different perspective on sexual love from the poems discussed above.

Whan netilles in winter bere roses rede,
And thornes bere figges naturally,
And bromes [shrubs] *bere appilles in every mede,*
And lorelles bere cheris in the croppes [tree-tops] *so hie,*
And okes bere dates so plentuosly,
And lekes geve hony in their superfluens—
Than put in a woman your trust and confidence.

Sexuality itself is the subject of a small group of humorous lyrics, mostly carols, which treat it in the earthy, sometimes cynical spirit of fabliau. There is no sentiment or tender emotion in these unpretentious verses, redolent of coarse male conviviality and reeking of the ale house; there is, rather, rollicking and unqualified sensuality, as in "I have a newe gardin":

The fairest maide of this town
Preyed me
For to griffen her a grif
Of min pery tree.

When I hadde hem griffed
Alle at her wille,
The win and the ale
She dede in fille.

And I griffed her
Right up in her home;
And be that day twenty wowkes,
It was quik in her womb.

The fairest maid of this town
Begged me
To graft on her a shoot
From my pear tree.

When I had grafted it
[literally, "them"]
All at her will,
[With] wine and ale
She filled me up.

And I grafted her
Right up in her membrane;
And by twenty weeks from that day,
It was alive in her womb.

Issuing, we may suppose, from essentially the same broad folk sensibility and speaking to the common person's experience are a substantial number of mnemonic rhymes, charms, recipes, and the like, at least one of which—"Thirty dayes hath November"—has remained, with only minor changes, part of the stock of verse known to nearly everyone who speaks English. Others provide cures for sore eyes or nightmare, deafness or menstrual flow; warnings against prodigality and poverty; and much other useful information. We have, too, imaginative descriptions of noisy blacksmiths and of the man in the moon, and a haunting, balladlike rhyme whose music is as memorable as its meaning is elusive:

Maiden in the mor lay,
In the mor lay,
Sevenight fulle, sevenight fulle.
Maiden in the mor lay,
In the mor lay,
Sevenightes fulle and a day.

One other group of popular (as distinct from literary or courtly) Middle English lyrics must be noted: the genial drinking songs, of which there are many fine specimens. Although generally carols, often occasioned by the conviviality of Christmas, they are otherwise untouched by religious sentiments. (Indeed, the "holly and ivy" motif in some of them is believed to hark back to pre-Christian folk traditions in symbolizing the principle of male-female strife.) We know from such romances as *Sir Gawain and the Green Knight* how elaborately the great feasts of the Christian calendar, especially Christmas, were celebrated in noble houses. These mirthful songs of good cheer show us holiday festivity in less exalted environments.

Now is Yole comen with gentil chere,
Of merthe and gomen [amusement] *he has no pere;*
In every londe where he comes nere
Is merthe and gomen, I dar wele say.

Mende the fire, and make gud chere!
Fill the cuppe, Ser Botelere [Sir Butler]*!*
Let every mon drinke to his fere [companion]*!*
Thys endes my carol, with care awaye.

RELIGIOUS THEMES

In turning, finally, to that most numerous body of Middle English lyrics that treats explicitly religious themes, we find as wide a variety of styles as we find among the lyrics of worldly love and life. Here, too, the finest pieces are likely to be relatively brief, relatively simple, and anonymous, perhaps the happy distillation, in the mind of a talented poet, of some oral folk tradition. Among the many poems treating the paradox of the Incarnation or the melancholy of the Crucifixion, no other is more memorable than the mysterious and unforgettable "Corpus Christi carol" of the late fifteenth or early sixteenth century:

Lully, lulley; lully, lulley;
The faucon hath born my mak [mate] *away.*
He bare him up, he bare him down;
He bare him into an orchard brown.
In that orchard ther was an hall,
That was hanged with purpil and pall.
And in that hall ther was a bede;
It was hanged with gold so rede.
And in that bed ther lithe a knight,
His woundes bleding day and night.
By that bedes side ther kneleth a may,
And she wepeth both night and day.
And by that beddes side ther stondeth a ston,
Corpus Christi *wreten theron.*

This magnificent poem, stately in its grave simplicity, well represents the genius of the folk tradition. It has been found by collectors of folksongs in several versions (this, the standard one, is from a sixteenth-century commonplace book), and inevitably makes one think of a ballad, with its deliberate, incremental development. There is no scholarly consensus as to its meaning. R. L. Greene thinks it contains Tudor allegory; others find in it Arthurian Grail symbolism. It is certainly enigmatic, and was perhaps intended to be. The diction is simple, the rhythms straightforward, but the poem has undeniable poignance.

In conceiving Jesus metaphorically as a knight, the "Corpus Christi carol" exemplifies one of the most arresting features of a number of lyrics about Christ, as well as of certain of the many lovely poems in which the profound devotion accorded the Virgin in the later Middle Ages found expression. It should be noted, by way of explanation, that ecclesiastical authorities were always eager to turn the widespread taste for song and poetry to Christian use. (Even the manuscript of "Sumer is icumen in" was at some time furnished with alternative devotional verses in Latin.) From the thirteenth century, the Franciscan order of friars was especially active in this endeavor, and recent scholarship suggests that Franciscan influence was in fact a major factor in the development of the Middle English lyric, including the carol. Thus, it is not surprising to find the language and imagery of love lyric and romance used to express religious themes—again demonstrating how inadequate is the unqualified division of Middle English lyrics into religious and secular. One of the thirteenth-century Harley poems about Jesus begins with a stanza that in each of its details, even its diction, is pure love lyric:

When I see blosmes springe
And here foules song,
A swete love-longinge
Min herte thourghout stong,
All for a love newe,
That is so swete and trewe,
That gladieth all my song;
Ich wot all mid iwisse
[I know quite certainly]
My joye and eke [also] *my blisse*
On him is all ilong.
[Are wholly caused by him.]

Although most of the lyrics that express devotion to Maid and Mother, Queen and Virgin, do so in relatively traditional (though often intense and hyperbolic) ways, there are, as we have noted, startling exceptions, in which the Virgin is perceived as though the object of sexual love. For example, one of the Harley lyrics begins thus:

As I me rod this ender day
By grene wode to seche play,
Mid herte I thoghte all on a may,
Swetest of alle thinge.
Lithe, and ich you telle may
All of that swete thinge.

As I rode out a day or two ago
By green woods to seek pleasure,
With my heart I thought all on a
maiden,
Sweetest of all persons.
Listen, and I may tell you
All about that sweet person.

One of the most moving of our Marian lyrics, and a felicitous use of the conventions of love lyric to express a religious theme, is the celebrated "In a tabernacle of a toure," better known by its Latin refrain, "Quia amore langueo" (Because I languish for love), taken from the Song of Songs 2:5, the biblical book which is itself an enigmatic, allegorical love poem. This poignant lyric embodies elements of the love complaint (familiar to readers of Middle English from Chaucer's skillful specimens of the genre) and also of the *chanson d'aventure,* a type of French love narrative. Both the erotic tone and the elevated diction of late medieval love lyric are to be found here:

I bid, I bide in grete longing,
I love, I loke when man woll crave;
I pleyne for pite of peyning;
Wolde he aske mercy, he shuld it have.

I pray, I wait with great longing,
I love, I look for the time when man will beg;
I lament with pity on account of suffering;
If he would ask mercy, he should have it.

And the poem's ending forms an apt climax to its metaphorical merger of loves: "Take me for thy wife and lerne to singe, / *Quia amore langueo.*"

Equally remarkable is the early-fifteenth-century "I sing of a maiden," a poem of exquisite delicacy in which the conception of Christ is imaged as Mary's receiving a secret visit from a young man in her chamber:

He cam also stille
To his moderes [mother's] *bowr*
As dew in Aprille
That falleth on the flour.

Like the "Corpus Christi carol," this poem combines mystery and directness, repetition and increment, so as to suggest the folk ballad. One notices, again, that the most luminous achievements of Middle English lyric are very likely to be poems of apparent simplicity emerging from native forms. As a final example, we may cite a much-commented quatrain of the early thirteenth century, about Mary's sorrow, in which we find at once brevity and homeliness, complexity of tone and ambiguity:

Now goth sonne under wod:
Me reweth, Marye, thy faire rode.
Now goth sonne under tree:
Me reweth, Marye, thy sone and thee.

Now goes sun under wood:
I feel pity, Mary, for thy fair face.

Now goes sun under tree:
I feel pity, Mary, for thy son and thee.

MORTALITY

The subject most often encountered in Middle English lyrics, however, is not love at all, either worldly or spiritual, but rather mortality: sin and death, the fear of damnation, contempt for the pleasures of the passing world, reflection upon the transiency of human life itself. *"Ubi sunt?"* these poems often ask: "Where are they now?" Thus, one well-known thirteenth-century poem begins: "Where beth they biforen us weren? / Houndes ladden and hawkes beren" (Where are they who came before us? / They led hounds and carried hawks). And another: "Fare well, this world! I take my leve for evere." If these poems about man's ultimate fate (which are often prayers imploring Christ's intercession) hardly ever reach the level of art attained by some of the work already surveyed, they can yet be pithy and colloquial and fresh, memorable for all their grimness:

When the turuf is thy tour,
And thy put is thy bour,
Thy wel and thy white throte
Shulen wormes to note.
What helpet thee thenne
All the worilde wenne?

When the turf is thy tower,
And thy pit is thy bower,
Thy skin and thy white throat
Shall worms have for their use.
What will help thee then
All the world's bliss?

Another poem of sin and death contains this indelible image:

Welawey! nis king ne quene
That ne shel drinke of dethes drench.
Man, er thu falle off thy bench,
Thu sinne aquench!

Alas! There is not king nor queen
Who shall not drink of death's draught.
Man, before you fall off your bench,
Quench your sin!

Though medieval men were often frightened of death, they were not reluctant to talk about it. These poems of mortality, along with those others of love and devotion, conviviality and melancholy, celebration of the sacred and rejoicing in the created, give a more lively sense of what went on in men's minds during the medieval centuries than can be derived from any other branch of medieval literature. If (as is true of all other human artifacts) only a handful of the Middle English lyrics have formidable merit as poetry, a great many of them are filled with a great deal of life. It is for this reason, above all, that they continue to command our interest.

BIBLIOGRAPHY

Manuscripts. For information about manuscripts in which specific Middle English lyrics appear, two works are most useful: Carleton Brown and Rossell Hope Robbins, *The Index of Middle English Verse* (1943); Rossell Hope Robbins and John L. Cutler, *Supplement to the Index of Middle English Verse* (1965). See also Edmund K. Chambers, *English Literature at the Close of the Middle Ages* (1945, repr. 1957), 218–221; Albert E. Hartung, ed., *A Manual of the Writings in Middle English, 1050–1500,* IV–VI (1973–1980); Neil R. Ker, ed., *Facsimile of British Museum MS. Harley 2253* (1965); Rossell Hope Robbins, "Middle English Lyrics: Handlist of New Texts," in *Anglia,* 83 (1965); John E. Wells, *A Manual of the Writings in Middle English, 1050–1400* (1916), chap. 13, and *ibid.,* (1919–1951), supplements 1–9; Richard M. Wilson, *The Lost Literature of Medieval England,* 2nd ed. (1970), 159–186.

Editions. The standard editions are listed; beginning students should turn first to an anthology, such as Davies or Luria and Hoffman. George L. Brook, ed., *The Harley Lyrics* (1948, 4th ed. 1968); Carleton Brown, ed., *English Lyrics of the Thirteenth Century* (1932), and *Religious Lyrics of the Fifteenth Century* (1939); Carleton Brown and G. V. Smithers, eds., *Religious Lyrics of the Fourteenth Century* (1924, 2nd ed. 1957); Edmund K. Chambers and F. Sidgwick, eds., *Early English Lyrics: Amorous, Divine, Moral, and Trivial* (1907, repr. 1926); Reginald T. Davies, ed., *Medieval English Lyrics* (1963); Douglas Gray, ed., *A Selection of Religious Lyrics* (1975); Richard L. Greene, ed., *The Early English Carols* (1935, rev. 1977), and *A Selection of English Carols* (1962); Neil R. Ker, *op. cit.;* Maxwell Luria and Richard L. Hoffman, eds., *Middle English Lyrics* (1974); Henry Person, ed., *Cambridge Middle English Lyrics* (1953); Rossell Hope Robbins, ed., *Secular Lyrics of the Fourteenth and Fifteenth Centuries,* 2nd ed. (1955), *Historical Poems of the Fourteenth and Fifteenth Centuries* (1959), and *Early English Christmas Carols* (1961); Siegfried Wenzel, ed., *Verses in Sermons: Fasciculus Morum and Its Middle English Poems* (1978); Thomas Wright and James O. Halliwell, eds., *Reliquiae antiquae,* 2 vols. (1841–1843).

Music. The essential collections of musical settings are J. F. R. Stainer and Cecie Stainer, *Early Bodleian Music,* 2 vols. (1901); John E. Stevens, ed., *Mediaeval Carols,* 2nd ed. (1958). For discussion of musical backgrounds, see Frank L. Harrison, *Music in Medieval Britain* (1958), 135, 141–144, 153, 273, 283–284, 290, 416–424.

Studies. Albert C. Baugh, ed., *A Literary History of England,* 2nd ed. (1967), 208–224; Cecil M. Bowra, *Mediaeval Love-song* (1961); Sabino Casieri, *Canti e liriche medioevali inglesi* (1962); Edmund K. Chambers, "Some Aspects of Medieval Lyric," in Chambers and F. Sidgwick, eds., *op. cit.,* 259–296, and *English Literature at the Close of the Middle Ages* (1945, repr. 1957), 66–121; Henry J. Chaytor, *The Troubadours and England* (1923), ch. 1–3; Peter Dronke, *Medieval Latin and the Rise of European Love-Lyric,* 2 vols. (1965–1966), and *The Medieval Lyric* (1969); Douglas Gray, *Themes and Images in the Medieval English Religious Lyric* (1972); David L. Jeffrey, *The Early English Lyric and Franciscan Spirituality* (1975); Stephen Manning, *Wisdom and Number: Toward a Critical Appraisal of the Middle English Religious Lyric* (1962); Arthur K. Moore, *The Secular Lyric in Middle English* (1951); Raymond Oliver, *Poems Without Names: The English Lyric, 1200–1500* (1970); Edmund Reiss, "A Critical Approach to the Middle English Lyric," in *College English,* **27** (1965–1966), and *The Art of the Middle English Lyric* (1972); Rossell Hope Robbins, "The Authors of the Middle English Religious Lyrics," in *Journal of English and Germanic Philology,* **39** (1940), and "Middle English Carols as Processional Hymns," in *Studies in Philology,* **56** (1959); Leo Spitzer, "*Explication de Texte* Applied to Three Great Middle English Poems," in *Archivum linguisticum,* **3** (1951, repr. in Anna Hatcher, ed., *Essays on English and American Literature by Leo Spitzer* [1962]); Robert D. Stevick, "The Criticism of Middle English Lyrics," in *Modern Philology,* **64** (1966); Richard M. Wilson, *The Lost Literature of Medieval England* (1952, 2nd ed. 1970), 135–208; Rosemary Woolf, *The English Religious Lyric in the Middle Ages* (1968).

MAXWELL LURIA

[See also **Anthologies; Antifeminism; Ballade; Ballads, Middle English; Carols, Middle English; Chaucer, Geoffrey; Commonplace Books; Complainte; Envoi; Fabliau and Comic Tale; Music, Popular; Pastourelle; Reverdie; Sumer Is Icumen In.**]

MIDDLE ENGLISH LITERATURE: PROSODY AND VERSIFICATION. Between the time of the Norman Conquest of 1066 and the introduction of printing by Caxton into England in 1476, Middle English poets developed two differing prosodic systems and a wide range of versificatory patterns. Most early Middle English poets, influenced by their native Old English heritage, resorted to the alliterative tradition—a tradition destined to reach a new artistic zenith in the fourteenth century and thereafter to suffer eclipse in Britain. The majority of poets, however, many of whom were multilingual, imitated the alien features of rhyme and stanzaic patterning familiar to them in medieval Latin, French, Anglo-Norman, and Italian poetry; and in the process they established the accepted conventions of versification that have come to dominate English poetry down to the present day.

NATIVE ALLITERATIVE VERSE

Old English poetry was based on a system of lines subdivided by a caesura into nonrhyming half-lines, each (with some exceptions) containing two stressed syllables. Each line was bound together by the initial alliteration (of identical consonants, or any one of *sc/st/sp* with its identical cluster, or of any vowel with itself or any other vowel) between at least one syllable in the first half-line and at least one syllable in the second half-line, as in *Beowulf* (lines 2,602–2,603, here marked with A for alliteration and X for nonalliteration):

A X	A X
Wígláf was haten,	Wéoxtánes sunu,
A A	A X
léoflíc lindwiga,	léod Scylfinga.

Wígláf was his name, the son of Wéohstán, a cherished shield-warrior, a tribesman of the Swedes.

In Old English poetry the predominant pattern of alliteration was AA/AX. In Middle English poetry, however, new freedoms appeared, so that any one of the nine possible combinations between either *AA* or AX or XA in the first half-line is linked with either AA or AX or XA in the second half-line. Furthermore, there are sometimes two new combinations that would have been unacceptable in Old English: AA/BB, where each half-line alliterates only with itself, and XX/XX, where only the beats and the caesura are maintained and the requirement of alliteration is completely ignored.

Even without these new liberties, the taut, formal Old English line of *Beowulf* was doomed to disappear because of dramatic changes in the patterns of the English language. Thus, to cite a typical example, a phrase such as *Wéoxtánes sunu* (quoted above) became in Middle English the equivalent of the Modern English "the son of Wéohstán." The resultant shift in the movement of Middle English alliterative verse away from a dominantly iambic beat (stress, unstress) toward a line in which unstressed prepositions, definite articles, and indefinite articles almost submerge the main beats can best be exemplified by a quotation from Layamon's *Brut* (*ca.* 1200, Southwestern dialect, ll. 28,589–28,591):

X A A X
Arthur was for-wunded wunder anė swithė.
A A X A
Ther to him com a cnavė the wes of his künnė.
A X X A
He wes Cadores sunė, the eorles of Cornwailė.

Arthur was mortally wounded, grievously and severely. To him there came a youth who was of his kin. He was the son of Cador, the earl of Cornwall.

In the hands of poets somewhat more talented than Layamon, alliterative verse gained a new kind of flexibility, and it also acquired a new kind of melody, especially since the Middle English vocabulary gradually adopted many words of French origin; in these the stress did not necessarily, as is so often the case in Old English, fall on the initial syllable. Thus the new movement in William Langland's *Piers Plowman* (*B*, Southwestern dialect, *ca.* 1377–1379, passus XVIII, ll. 424–425):

A A A A
Tyl the dayė dawed, this damaiselės dauncėd,
A A
That men rongen to the Resu-rexioun;
A X
and right with that I waked.

These damsels danced till the day [Easter] on which men rang in the Resurrection dawned; and therewith I awoke.

The anonymous author of *Sir Gawain and the Green Knight* (West Midland dialect, *ca.* 1390, lines 1–2) uses a somewhat more conservative line than Langland's, but it also displays a similar flexibility:

A A A A
Sithen the sege and the a-ssaut was sesėd at Troyė,
A A
The burgh brittenėd and brent |
A A
to brondės and askės . . .

After the siege and the assault had ceased at Troy, the town destroyed and burnt to brands and ashes . . .

NATIVE ALLITERATIVE VERSE COMBINED WITH OPTIONAL RHYME

Even in the Old English period poets had begun to add continental end rhymes to their alliterative lines (as in *The Riming Poem* in the Exeter Book, *ca.* 975). Understandably, therefore, when Layamon translated the rhyming octosyllabic couplets of Wace's Anglo-Norman *Roman de Brut* (1155) into Middle English alliterative verse, he himself felt drawn toward the addition of rhyme as an optional decoration. Hence, for instance, in the passage quoted (Arthur's address to Constantin), Anglo-Norman rhymes (italicized) transcend English alliteration:

X X
And witė minė Brütt*es* | *a*
X X
a to thines lif*es,* *a*
X X
And haldė heom allė tha l*aghen* | *b*
X X
tha habbeoth i-stonden a minė d*aghen* *b*
A X
And allė tha laghen g*odė* | *c*
A X
tha bi Utheres daghen st*odė.* *c*

And guard my Britons ever in your lifetime, and on their behalf keep all the laws that existed in my days and all the good laws that in Uther's days existed.

The pervasive and irresistible influence on Layamon of Wace's octosyllabic rhyme is clear, as can be illustrated from a corresponding passage in the *Roman de Brut* (ll. 13,691–13,692):

X X X X
Al fil Cador de Costent*in* *a*
X X X X
De Cournuaill(e), un sien cos*in,* *a*
X X X X
Livra son rainė, si li d*ist* . . . *b*

To Cador the son of Constantine of Cornwall, a cousin of his, he yielded his realm and told him . . .

Other, more profound influences of the rhyming tradition later became more pronounced, most notably in the work of the "Gawain poet." Thus, in *Sir Gawain,* already cited as exemplifying the traditional alliterative line, the poet did not, as did Langland or the composer of *Beowulf,* deploy his lines in an unbroken sequence of symmetrical, alliterative, stichic (recurrent) one-line units; instead, uniquely, he divided his lines into groups consisting of 101 stanzaic units (varying in length from 12 to 38 alliterative lines), which are sectioned off by the use of a rhyming "bob and wheel" consisting of 5 lines rhyming *a b a b a.* The one-line "bob" contains one stress; each of the four lines of the "wheel" contains generally two or three stresses and at least two alliterations. Thus, the last alliterative line and the concluding "bob and wheel" of the second stanza of *Sir*

Gawain scan as follows (with correct alliteration of the cluster *st* in the Old English manner):

A A A X
I schal telle hit as-tit, | as I in toun herde,

With t*onge;* *a*
A A
As hit is stad and st*oken* *b*
A A A
In story stif and str*onge,* *a*
A A A
With lel lettres l*oken,* *b*
A A
In londe so has ben l*onge.* *a*

I shall tell it now in my own tongue just as I heard it in town, in the same way that it is set down and written out in a bold and stark story, linked together in faithful alliteration, as in the land it has been for long.

RHYMING VERSE WITH OPTIONAL ALLITERATION

Some Middle English poetry may be described as employing obligatory rhyme as its informing system and alliteration as its decoration. In particular, *The Pearl* (attributed to the "Gawain poet," West Midland dialect, *ca.* 1380) displays a prosodic complexity unmatched in its particular kind of virtuosity before or since. The poem consists of 101 stanzas, each containing 12 octosyllabic lines, rhyming *ababababbcbc,* and totaling 1,212 lines (in keeping with the numerological symbolism of the poem); more than two-thirds of the 1,212 lines are decorated with alliteration.

A typical stanza of *The Pearl* (XVIII) begins as follows:

X X X X
As John hym wrytes yet more I s*yghė:* *a*
A A X X
Üch pane of that place had thre y*ates;* *b*
X A X A
So twelve in poursent I con assp*yé* . . . *a*

As John himself writes, still more did I see: each side of that city had three gates; thus twelve in the encompassing wall I descried . . .

In this unique poem, moreover, each group of five stanzas (or six stanzas in XV) repeats the *c*-rhyme in every one of the stanzas in the tenth and twelfth lines; each group's *c*-rhyme is also echoed internally in the first line of the first stanza of the next group; and the very last line of the poem echoes the first line, so that *The Pearl* is actually concatenated like an endless string of pearls.

Technically speaking, no other English poet has ever achieved the artistry reached by the "Gawain poet" within the self-imposed limits of his highly original patterns. Outside of the West Midland area, where alliterative poetry throve, however, the majority of poets in the Middle English period moved more and more toward the perfection of fixed-stress lines united by rhyme, whether distributed in couplets or in stanzas. These Middle English poets for the most part borrowed their new patterns from French and Italian models.

RHYMING COUPLETS

In the early Middle English period poets experimented with foreign metrical models, often without lasting success. So, for instance, the English redactor of *King Horn* at times resorted, in his highly irregular verse, to couplets that might be classified as a^3a^3.

Layamon, on the other hand, in the twelfth century had Wace's octosyllabic couplet as a model even though he imitated only its rhyme and not its strict pattern; Wace's particular couplet a^4a^4 with optional use of masculine or feminine endings (which had been used in France as early as the tenth century) remained popular in nonalliterative English poetry for many purposes, whether popular or sophisticated, far beyond the bounds of the Middle English period. A distinguished early example is provided by *The Owl and the Nightingale* (Southwestern dialect, *ca.* 1198–1216); later examples are provided by Chaucer, who used the octosyllabic couplet with extraordinary fluency and variety during the earliest stages of his career (first in *The Romaunt of the Rose*—if his—and in *The Book of the Duchess, ca.* 1369–1370).

Chaucer had imitated the five-beat line (first in his stanzaic ABC, *ca.* 1369) familiar to him through French and Italian models; his predilection for this line led him to become the first master of the iambic pentameter couplet, a^5b^5, which Dryden later (1693) called the "heroic couplet." The famous prologue to the *Canterbury Tales* (1387) exemplifies Chaucer's brilliant instinct in selecting the five-beat couplet form as one especially suited to the patterns of the English language, for his newly adopted measure avoids not only the monotonous jog trot peculiar to the octosyllabic couplet but also the loose canter peculiar to the popular ballad meter:

X X X X X
Bifel that in that sesoun on a d*ay* *a*
X X X X X
In Southwerk at the Tabard, as I l*ay* *a*
X X X X X
Redy to wenden on my pilgrym*agė* *b*
X X X X X
To Caunterb(u)ry with ful devout cor*agė* . . . *b*

It happened that in that season one day as I lay in Southwark at the Tabard ready to travel on my pilgrimage to Canterbury with a fully devout heart . . .

The ballad meter, in contrast, was never adopted by the discriminating Chaucer. It consists of a seven-beat couplet a^7a^7, variously known as the "septenary," "heptameter," "fourteener," or—especially when it is printed in four lines instead of two ($x^4a^3x^4a^3$)—as "ballad meter" or "common [hymn] meter."

The Latin *septenarius,* which is fundamentally trochaic, should not be confused with the ballad meter, which is fundamentally iambic, but both share the same 4/3 pattern and end rhyme, displayed typically in goliardic verse:

x x x x x x x
Omnibus in Gallia | Anglus Goli*ardus* *a*

x x x x x x x
obediens et humilis frater non bast*ardus* . . . *a*

To all in France, an English goliard, an obedient and humble brother, and no bastard . . .

In its most peculiar Middle English form, the ballad meter was used uniquely by Orm in his *Ormulum* (East Midland dialect, *ca.* 1200); each of the more than 20,000 lines of his pious work contains an eight-syllable, four-beat half-line followed by a hiatus and then by a seven-syllable, three-beat half-line with a feminine ending. This unstressed ending always contains the vowel *e*, but, since the *e* is usually followed by a final consonant or consonants, it does not provide normal rhyming couplets:

x x x x
Icc hafė sett her o thiss boc |
x x x
amang goddspelless wordess,
x x x x
All thurrh me sellfenn, manigh word |
x x x
the rimė swa to fillenn.

I have placed here in this book among the words of Gospel, entirely on my own, many a word so as to fill out the meter.

The same meter, when provided with end rhyme carried by stressed syllables, appears, for instance, in the *Poema morale* (Southwestern–West Midland dialect, *ca.* 1175, ll. 14–15):

x x x x
Ich em nu alder then(e) Ich wes |
x x x
a Wintrė and a l*arė.* a^7
x x x x
Ich weldė marė then(e) Ich dedė; |
x x x x
Miwit ahtė bön m*arė.* a^7

I am now older than I was in winters and in experience; I control more than I did; my intelligence should be greater.

This potentially lighthearted meter, so readily adapted to music, became the favorite not only for traditional English ballads but also for vernacular carols and hymns, and it became as popular in its way as a^4a^4 and a^5a^5.

RHYMING STANZAIC VERSE

The couplet is a stanza that is limited to two lines. The numerous stanzaic forms extending beyond two lines that are used in Middle English may comprise any number of lines from three to twelve or even more, and may interweave two or three different rhymes; and stanzas may be linked to one another by rhyme that carries from one to the next.

The three-line stanza $a^5b^5a^5$ $b^5c^5b^5$ (and so on) is the famous terza rima, a sequence introduced by Dante in his *Divine Comedy.* Chaucer early in his career (*ca.* 1370) experimented with it only once (in lines 14ff. of "Complaint to His Lady"); other Middle English poets avoided it, presumably because they found it alien to the patterns of the English language.

The much more workable four-line stanza, such as $a^4b^4a^4b^4$, occurs particularly in popular works such as *Thomas of Erceldoune* (Northern dialect, *ca.* 1388–1401), where the lines run on consecutively *abab cdcd* (and so on):

x x x x
Of the Baylliols(e) blod so sall it f*all(e):* *a*
x x x x
It sall be lyk(e) a rotyn(e) tree. *b*
x x x x
The Comyns and the Barlays *all(e)* . . . *a*

Of the Baliols' blood, likewise it shall befall; it shall be like a rotten tree. The Cumyns and the Barclays all . . . (II, ll. 21–23)

Sometimes English poets varied the length of individual lines within the stanza by the introduction of a recurrent rhyming short line, generally called a tail rhyme, as in the six-line tail-rhyme stanza $a^4a^4b^3c^4c^4b^3$, notably avoided by Chaucer except in his Tale of Sir Thopas, which parodies the style of the popular romances:

x x x x
He priketh thurgh a fair for*est* *a*
x x x x
Therinne is many a wildė b*est*— *a*
x x x
Ye, bothė bukk(e) and h*arė*! . . . *b*

He spurs through a fair forest wherein is many a wild beast—yes, both buck and hare! . . . (ll. 43–45)

At the conclusion of the Clerk's Tale (*ca.* 1393–1400), Chaucer introduced a much more distinguished five-beat, six-line stanza, modeled on the French envoi, in which all six of the stanzas carry the same set of rhymes (here, for that reason, marked with capitals) $A^5B^5A^5B^5C^5B^5$ throughout, so that the identical A-rhyme, for instance, occurs a total of twelve times within thirty-six lines.

Chaucer and his contemporaries, however, seldom attempted such difficult displays of virtuosity, for, as he remarked in his later years (in *The Complaint of Venus*), "rhyme in English hath such scarcity" that he found difficulty in recapturing the "*curiosité*"—that is, the intricacy—of his French models. So he excusably avoided the challenge set, for instance, by Eustache Deschamps—a poet much admired by Chaucer—in his ballade "En dimanche, le tiers jour de decembre" (*ca.* 1365). It consists of three nine-line stanzas rhyming $A^5B^5A^5B^5C^5C^5D^5C^5D^5$ and a six-line envoi rhyming $C^5C^5D^5C^5C^5D^5$, so that the *C*-rhyme occurs a total of thirteen times within thirty-three lines.

Chaucer did, however, adopt from the French a seven-line, five-beat stanza, $a^5b^5a^5b^5b^5c^5c^5$, which in his hands proved to be admirably suited to the genius of the English language, whether for short lyrics such as "The Complaint to Pity" (*ca.* 1369–1372) or for his magisterial romance *Troilus and Criseyde* (1385–1386), which extends to more than 8,000 lines. This stanzaic form, later known as the "rhyme royal" because of its use in *The Kingis Quair* (*ca.* 1423, ascribed, probably wrongly, to James I of Scotland), was later used in works such as Thomas Hoccleve's *Regement of Princes* (*ca.* 1412) and Robert Henryson's *Testament of Cresseid* (*ca.* 1470). Its popularity continued into the Renaissance.

Other long stanzas appear sporadically in Middle English, two of them worthy of some note. One is the eight-line, five-beat stanza rhyming $a^5b^5a^5b^5b^5c^5b^5c^5$, which Chaucer introduced in his "ABC" and in his Monk's Tale, and which William Dunbar later used in his "Resurrection of Christ" (Northern dialect, *ca.* 1500–1512).

The other long stanza deserving mention, though rather as a tour de force than as a common measure, is displayed in Chaucer's "Compleynt of Anelida" (contained within his unfinished *Anelida and Arcite, ca.* 1372–1380). Inspired, like his other early experiments, by the French ballade form, it contains a one-stanza, nine-line proem $a^5a^5b^5a^5a^5b^5b^5a^5b^5$; then a strophe containing four similar nine-line stanzas, a sixteen-line stanza $a^4a^4a^4b^5$, $a^4a^4a^4b^5$, $b^4b^4b^4a^5$, $b^4b^4b^4a^5$, and a concluding nine-line stanza; then a matching antistrophe of four nine-line stanzas, a sixteen-line stanza, and a concluding nine-line stanza; then a nine-line conclusion, the last line and *a*-rhyme of which echo the first line and *a*-rhyme of the proem.

Technical virtuosity can never, of course, of itself produce great poetry; but clearly, during the formative period examined here in the two different modes of poetry—the native and the foreign—the "Gawain poet" and Chaucer stand preeminent not only as versifiers but also as poets.

BIBLIOGRAPHY

Albert C. Baugh, "Improvisation in the Middle English Romance," in *American Philosophical Society: Proceedings,* **103** (1959); Larry D. Benson, *Art and Tradition in Sir Gawain and the Green Knight* (1965); Charles W. Dunn and Edward T. Byrnes, eds., *Middle English Literature* (1973); Tauno F. Mustanoja, "Chaucer's Prosody," in Beryl Rowland, ed., *Companion to Chaucer Studies* (1968, rev. ed. 1979); Rae Ann Naeger, "English: Bibliographical," in William K. Wimsatt, ed., *Versification: Major Language Types* (1972); James P. Oakden, *Alliterative Poetry in Middle English,* 2 vols. (1930–1935); George E. B. Saintsbury, *A History of English Prosody,* I (1906, 2nd ed. 1961), and *Historical Manual of English Prosody* (1910, repr. 1930); J. Burke Severs and Albert E. Hartung, eds., *Manual of the Writings in Middle English, 1050–1500* (1967–), a revision of Wells; John E. Wells, ed., *Manual of the Writings in Middle English, 1050–1400* (1916), and *Supplements* I–IX (1923–1952).

CHARLES W. DUNN

[See also **Anglo-Norman Literature; Anglo-Saxon Literature; Ballads, Middle English; Beowulf; Brut, The; Chaucer, Geoffrey; Gawain and the Green Knight, Sir; Henry-**

son, Robert; Hoccleve, Thomas; Kingis Quair; Langland, William; Ormulum; Owl and the Nightingale, The; Pearl, The; Wace.]

MIDDLE FRENCH. See **French Language.**

MIDDLE HIGH GERMAN LITERATURE

THE TIME FRAME

The "national" literatures of the European Middle Ages evolved in a process of gradual emancipation from Latin as the language of the written word. German was the second vernacular, after Anglo-Saxon, to begin this process, and around 1050 it entered the second major stage—Early Middle High German. After the death of Notker III of St. Gall (also known as Notker Labeo and Notker the German) in 1022, the newly literate vernacular remained curiously silent for more than a generation. Suddenly there was vigorous movement again, in several different places at once, in different intellectual contexts, and in notably greater variety of form and purpose. At the same time, the graphemics of this written language began to reflect changes that set it apart from Notker's advanced Old High German.

Where Middle High German literature ends is far less clear. For one thing, there is much less agreement between literary and linguistic evidence. Phonetic criteria and the presence of supraregional dialects in adminstration and commerce put the beginning of New High German in the decades after 1350, but many of the established "medieval" literary genres and practices continued into the sixteenth century. To complicate matters further, the impact of the Italian Renaissance on German literature (as distinct from literature in Germany) was much lighter than might be expected. The usual cutoff date of 1500 is an awkward compromise illustrated felicitously by the Janus-headed figure of the emperor. Maximilian I (1459–1519) founded the Academy in Vienna and secured for it the services of the "arch-humanist" and *poeta laureatus* Conrad Celtis, who was born in the same year as Maximilian, but Maximilian himself wrote nostalgic allegorical romances in German and commissioned the peerless retrospective collection of poetic texts known as the *Ambraser Heldenbuch* (1516).

All discussion of the internal chronology of Middle High German literature builds on the assumption of a "classical" (courtly) period centered around 1200. One of its chief characteristics,is a group-specific, supraregional poetic language usually referred to as Classical Middle High German. The line between this courtly state and Early Middle High German is usually drawn around 1170, although such a line tends to disguise a good deal of overlap caused by diverse regional developments.

The period that has attracted by far the most scholarly attention and talent (and about which most has been learned) since about 1960 is Late Middle High German. Exactly where it begins and what additional dates might be helpful in charting the course of literary activity during this large span of roughly 250 years have been the subject of much debate. By adopting 1220/1230–1300, 1300–1430, and 1430–1500 as the most relevant dividing lines the present article follows recent thinking, which has given preference to internal criteria such as the rise and fall of literary genres and forms rather than external, political, or sociological ones.

EARLY MIDDLE HIGH GERMAN: 1050–1170

During the Early Middle High German era, production and dissemination of literature remained where they had been throughout the Old High German period: in the hands of the church. The contexts and aims of this activity changed, however. The majority of the 100 or so texts in question, most of them written in verse, probably originated in monastic communities, and some were obviously intended for the sole use of the religious. Many, however, were composed by the secular (or cathedral) clergy and addressed more or less directly to the laity, which in this time was the male nobility, frequently addressed as *herren.* The cathedral schools—in conjunction with other religious institutions clustered in the cities—must have had something to do with this shift of audience. In the first generation Bamberg, an episcopal see established in 1007, provides an excellent example of concentrated yet varied preoccupation with German. Williram von Ebersberg, who later wrote a paraphrase of the Song of Songs, headed the cathedral school in the 1040's; Ezzo, who composed the first (and one of the most durable) of the great religious poems of the age, was one of his successors. Gunther, bishop since 1057, probably commissioned Ezzo's *Cantilena* (the *Ezzolied*), but he was also well known as a connoisseur of the native heroic tradition, encouraging recitals at his court. Wille, composer of the melody for Ezzo's poem and later abbot

MIDDLE HIGH GERMAN LITERATURE

of Michelsberg, may have been a student in Bamberg at that time. And it is quite likely that two of the most ambitious pieces of early catechetical prose, *Bamberger Glaube und Beichte* and *Himmel und Hölle,* originated there as well, in the 1070's or 1080's.

In the wake of religious reform movements emanating from Cluny, notions of ascetic *contemptus mundi* (disdain for the things of this world) are common in this literature, but almost as strong seems to be the desire to confront social, even political, issues of the day. Typically in Early Middle High German, sermonlike, rhymed exhortations *(Reimpredigten)* unfold a range of themes from basic social justice (in the early Alemannic *Memento mori*) to the proper organization of society so that peaceful coexistence between the various estates and professions might be achieved (*Vom Recht,* perhaps *ca.* 1140) and to the social conventions of the secular ruling class (Heinrich von Melk's *Memento mori, ca.* 1180).

Histories appeared—Christian histories connecting the present with the past in order to define the individual's place in God's larger plan for the salvation of mankind. They paved the way for progressively more mundane accounts of historic adventure in faraway lands, featuring not only the Greek Alexander (after a French source) but also Duke Ernest and King Rother, heroes of native legend cast in the role of crusaders.

Thus the 1150's and 1160's saw a decisive shift away from Latin as the immediate source or inspiration of all vernacular writing. On the other hand, that relationship had never been one of lavish dependence of the latter on the former. Of course the Vulgate, learned exegesis, and the school authors stand behind most of what was written before 1150, be it straight biblical narrative, primarily from the Old Testament; the more independent accounts of the lives of Christ and of Mary, the former by Frau Ava (*ca.* 1120), the first identifiable woman writing in German; or the theological tracts and allegories, such as *Die Hochzeit* of about 1160, that seek to elucidate essential truths and dogmas of the Christian faith. However, the poetics of this religious poetry (as distinct from its content) owe surprisingly little to Latin prototypes. As they opened up totally new dimensions of religious, historical, and aesthetic experience to the laity and those in religious orders who were not learned, its (typically anonymous) authors created their own forms and forged German as a literary language—a language capable of literate interpretation of the world and, to some extent, of the self. In that sense their work constitutes one of the truly original contributions made by the German-speaking regions to medieval European literature.

Unlike their ninth-century forebears they had no official use for the old Germanic verse pattern, a long line composed of two half-lines with two strong lifts in each, held together and (rhythmized) by alliteration. The twelfth-century poets' versification works with end rhyme or (originally) assonance and (fairly irregular) short lines with three to five lifts, which makes them much more compact metrically than the Germanic half-lines. While narrative-historical genres employ these short lines in rhymed couplets, direct forerunners of the more regular courtly couplet, others string them out in long lines divided by a caesura which rhymes with the end of the line. Grouping lines of either type in loose, strophic arrangements is quite common practice in all genres. Chant may be one reason for this, particularly in the shorter poems written in long-line stanzas. After all, Ezzo's *Cantilena* was chanted. But memories of indigenous verse forms probably lingered on as well. Very definitely that appears to be the case with the evocative and relatively unmannered indigenous love lyric that flourished, mostly in the southeast, around 1150 and for a short while afterward. It is written in (end-rhymed) long-line stanzas that are highly reminiscent of, and in one case (Kürenberg) identical with, the stanza form employed by the poet of the *Nibelungenlied.*

The explanation for all of this must lie in the lively undercurrent of oral poetry in the traditional manner. The clergy was duty-bound to denounce as irrelevant what was obviously a prime subject of such poetry: the heroic Germanic past. This genre did not surface in writing until secularization had advanced further, but its long existence left clear traces in the language, style, and metrics of the poetry that was designed, at least in part, to replace it. The most striking example of this is a balladesque strophic composition from the early twelfth century known as the older *Judith.* It depicts Judith's victory over Holofernes very much in the manner of the heroic lay.

Not much Early Middle High German prose has survived, and most of it is utilitarian: ministration of the faith (prayer, catechization, homily) and health care (charms and recipes). But two paraphrases, with commentary, of the Song of Songs are among the landmarks in the history of German prose style: Wil-

MIDDLE HIGH GERMAN LITERATURE

liram's at the beginning of the period and that of an anonymous monk, perhaps of Admont in Styria, at the end.

The author of the latter, the mystical *St. Trudperter Hohelied,* knew and used Williram's work. The Vorau version of Ezzo's *Cantilena* begins with a "history" of the poem. Around 1126 a copy of the Rhenish *Annolied* (1077–1081) was taken to Ratisbon, where it was later used in the composition of the *Kaiserchronik.* Sometime around the middle of the twelfth century, a group of Rhenish poems seems to have migrated to the southeast, to be reworked in Bavarian and eventually to be incorporated into the great Vorau collection. All this shows that in spite of the relative barrenness of the landscape, a network of diachronic and synchronic relationships developed, and even something like a historical perspective—essential elements of a history independent of Latin.

The Vorau codex, put together around 1180 as a summa of religious and historical verse in German, probably with an eye to the landed gentry in Styria, preserves much of what was still current while the west and north had already succumbed to the new vogue of French romances and novels of antiquity, and noble amateurs in the Hohenstaufen retinue were learning new tunes and sentiments from the troubadours of Provence.

CLASSICAL MIDDLE HIGH GERMAN: 1170–1220/1230

Against the background of the preceding centuries, the outstanding characteristics of the so-called classical period appear to be secularity and the movement toward secular courts as centers of literary activity. Although the way had been paved, the swiftness with which this transition occurred is amazing. German poets and their patrons wanted to catch up with what was already a major European movement. Deliberate efforts were made to redefine ideals of conduct and achievement in the terms of a small secular ruling class, and to this end patrons and poets turned to the Romance literatures for ready-made examples and models, at least for the lyric and the courtly novel, the major modes of courtliness. Thus, German literature in the following two generations was to a very large extent a literature of creative adaptation.

Unlike Anglo-Norman England and (later) France, Germany did not have a central court to nourish and focus such ambitions and activities. That is not only because the royal/imperial household traveled from palace to palace in pursuit of its business and spent a good deal of its time in Italy as well, but also because the Hohenstaufen, who with short interruptions ruled from 1138 to 1250, were inclined to favor homage in Latin, certainly until the 1230's. In this (rather important) sense the often-used handbook designation of the period as *Staufische Klassik* is misleading. Patronage of the vernacular was left to territorial interests (often at odds with those of the Hohenstaufen)—regional overlords having permanent residences: the landgraves of Thuringia in Eisenach and the dukes of Austria in Klosterneuburg/Vienna, to name the most visible ones. No doubt some have disappeared entirely from our ken. Some were not secular in the technical sense at all: Wolfger von Erla, bishop of Passau at the time, patronized Walther von der Vogelweide and in all probability the *Nibelungenlied* poet as well. The most powerful adversaries of the Hohenstaufen were the Welfs, but their literary influence tended toward the noncourtly. It was important chiefly for the period between 1140 and 1170, and the only later work that can be tied directly to Henry the Lion's main residence, Brunswick, is the (pathbreaking) prose translation of the *Elucidarium* of Honorius Augustodunensis. Entitled *Lucidarius,* it was completed in 1190–1195.

The royal/imperial court under Frederick I and his son, Henry VI, was nevertheless responsible for some of the conditions that made this general reorientation possible. For one thing, their administration of *ministeriales* (powerful but technically unfree noblemen), their social activity (most widely acclaimed was the Mainz festival of 1184), and their regular sojourns in Italy spawned the kind of amateur poet who dominated the first generation of minnesingers in the Romance vein.

Love, adventure, and manners were the topics, but it does not follow that concerns with the hereafter disappeared. Only the perspective changed. How can man live a full life on earth without forfeiting the eternal life of his soul? That is the kind of question with which much of courtly literature approached its self-imposed task of redefining the human condition.

In actual literary practice that redefinition assumed many different guises, depending, not least, on genre. New narrative (romance) patterns recall and actualize exemplary social behavior and norms of personal virtue from a distant, ideal past enshrined in a body of texts that deal mostly with the *matière de Bretagne.* The lyric, on the other hand,

MIDDLE HIGH GERMAN LITERATURE

idealizes with an eye to the here-and-now, drawing on a rich fund of ritual poses and gestures with which to articulate and dignify the relationship between the sexes. Refinement of sentiment, dress, and speech are some of the lower common denominators, and the highest is the fulfillment of self in ultimate (shared) joy and bliss, clearly the secular analogue to eternal salvation. A few key terms such as *mâze* (moderation) and *triuwe* (loyalty and faith) are grouped loosely around the idea of *ritterschaft* (chivalry), a direct translation of the Old French *chevalerie.* There never was such a thing as a "system" of courtly values independent of the text, but the nobility saw itself mirrored in such texts—in the (prescriptive) medieval sense that the mirror suggests an ideal form. Part of this sublimation of human existence was art itself; public, communal consumption of literature became an essential part of life at court, and along with the literary sublimation and formalization of manners went systematic formalization and refinement of expression in rhyme, meter, style, and structure. What it all amounted to is the discovery of poetic reality.

These are themes and ethical and aesthetic tenets that nobody who wanted to be part of the literary scene could ignore. They provide the context for Gottfried von Strassburg's ethical and aesthetic skepticism as well as for Heinrich der Glîchzaere's (*fl. ca.* 1180) biting satire of feudal institutions, and they guide the *Nibelungenlied* poet, whose generic predisposition is almost diametrically opposed. The smooth, four-stress rhymed couplets and the new poetic language—sleek as well as expressive, and capable of modes ranging from highly stylized to colloquial—proved seductive in the treatment of religious subjects as well. Some of the most courtly lyrics are devoted to the Virgin Mary. Religious narrative still thrived in the same circles that turned to romance for entertainment and emotional nourishment. Priester Wernher's precocious *Maria* (1172) was adorned with an equally precocious cycle of colored pen drawings in a manuscript of the early thirteenth century, and Konrad von Fussesbrunnen, author of the *Kindheit Jesu* (*ca.* 1200), was one of the better poets in this time of abundant talent. Hagiography, a relative newcomer, experienced its first flowering in German in the style and spirit of courtly narrative, with verse legends by Heinrich von Veldeke, Ebernand von Erfurt (*Heinrich und Kunigunde, ca.* 1220), and Reinbot von Durne (*Georg,* after 1231), and hybrids such as Hartmann's legends and Meister Otte's *Eraclius* (*ca.* 1205).

The first German poet who, as far as is known, tried his hand (and succeeded) at several different genres, including minnesong, was Heinrich von Veldeke, and he was a professional at least to the extent that his writing did not go unremunerated. Hartmann von Aue and Wolfram von Eschenbach probably led similar, semiprofessional lives. Like Heinrich they were men of noble birth who depended on more fortunate members of their class for part of their livelihood, perhaps not much more than room and board. While noble amateurs continued to practice the art of the performed lyric to the very end of the Middle Ages, some minnesingers in the second generation of court poets seem to have had relatively stable employment as entertainers. Walther von der Vogelweide was different. He and many after him clearly lived the lives of itinerant minstrels, depending on their wits and exposed to the winds of political and aesthetic change.

Many, even most, of these professionals may have had some sort of education, but since the culture of the lay nobility to which they catered was still largely oral, that is by no means an automatic assumption in every case. Hartmann and Wolfram were highly conscious of their role in the propagation of a new lay literature and played down their own learning in order to identify themselves more closely with the class for which they wrote. Clerics with or without office continued to function as authors—of religious texts, but probably also of romances (Ulrich von Zazikhoven and possibly Gottfried) and even heroic poetry (*Nibelungenlied*). To replace the old-fashioned rhyme sermon they also created a type of didactic verse tract of which there are early (Wernher von Elmendorf, 1170–1180) as well as late examples (Thomasin von Zerclaere, 1215–1216).

A typical audience must have included clerics. The primary target group was, however, the lay aristocracy. Conventional wisdom has it that the men in this group were largely illiterate while more and more women were able to read, at least in the vernacular. Such increase in female literacy was probably one of the major causes of the rapid growth of this lay literature, since so many texts seem to be addressed specifically to female audiences. The growth of female literacy does not mean, however, that private reading became a major factor. In principle, vernacular literature remained performance literature. *Lied, Spruch,* and *Leich* were sung poetic forms; narrative and the longer didactic poems (*Reden*) were recited before relatively small groups gathered for

MIDDLE HIGH GERMAN LITERATURE

the occasion. Dance, playacting, and other social activities, including the viewing of pictures in illuminated copies of the text, which became increasingly common in the course of the thirteenth century, contributed to this process of public communal consumption. Unfortunately, unlike their French-speaking counterparts, the German poets on the whole say little about these matters—the circumstances of their own lives, their patrons, the performance and transmission of their work. Only one aspect of professional life provoked more than occasional auctorial comment: artistic rivalry.

Behind this tradition of self-serving comments and critical attacks that culminated in the famous feuds between Walther and Reinmar der Alte, Walther and Neidhart von Reuental, Wolfram and Gottfried, and Wolfram and Hartmann may lie concrete struggles for a place in the sun of princely favor; but in effect these assertions of aesthetic values, ethical norms, and proper content have to do as much with poetics and the poet's role in society as they do with earning a living. Kürenberg stakes out artistic turf when the lady in one of his stanzas proclaims that she has fallen in love with a knight who sang a song in "Kürenberg's tune." And so does Gottfried when, without mentioning names, he lets his audience know in no uncertain terms that his *Tristan* is told in more advanced technique than Eilhart von Oberg's. Lyricists can put down a rival as much through musical and metrical parody as through verbal response, and Walther and Reinmar were particularly good at such parody. Narrative poets tend to be less subtle. Wolfram on one occasion refers directly to Hartmann as the master of Arthurian romance, only to threaten him with reprisals if he should interfere with Parzival's progress, and in another context he sets up his own character, Sigune, as an example of everything Hartmann's character Lunete (in *Îwein*) is not. But there are also some telling and touching tributes, as when Walther pays Hartmann the supreme compliment of borrowing images and phrases from *Îwein* in his elegiac swan song known as the *Elegie.* Walther also wrote a conciliatory epitaph for Reinmar, which may have initiated the practice among thirteenth-century lyricists of celebrating their predecessors in song.

The correlative of such intense rivalry is intense intertextuality. The most remarkable achievement of these two generations of court poets is that they created a textually coherent body of literature in a largely illiterate environment. In doing so, they created, for the first time in the history of the vernaculars, something like a literary public that, in spite of the geographic fragmentation of this artistic activity, would understand and appreciate these allusions and references.

None of that could have happened without at least a temporary lowering of dialect barriers. Most participants in this chorus of poetic voices retained some of the flavor of their native dialect, but at the same time they collectively developed a literary koine that enabled authors and texts to travel and to appeal to audiences everywhere in the German-speaking regions. This is classical Middle High German—not nearly so consistent and pure in its phonetics and graphemics as the standard editions of the major authors would lead a reader to believe, but effective nevertheless as the vehicle of this revolutionary and short-lived movement toward a national literature.

In this revolution all kinds of earlier native impulses were cut short or suppressed because they were unable to cross the new taste barrier. In some cases superficial remakes in the courtly vein assured survival; in others it was the still lively undercurrent of oral tradition and popular convention that kept topics and materials afloat until their time came. For some it had already come. Walther almost singlehandedly raised the *Sangspruch* to the level of high art and made it a force in the affairs of men by marrying this ancient type of didactic verse to the strophic forms of minnesong. The story of the Niflungs crossed the divide between oral and written, and so did one or two others. Orally transmitted heroic legend must have been very much in vogue among the same people who listened to the court poets, or Walther could not have referred, tongue in cheek, to his ladylove as Hildgund, a character associated with the legend of Walther—of Aquitaine. Wolfram, in *Willehalm,* advertises his own realism by pointing to battle descriptions in stories about Dietrich von Bern that obviously were notorious for their hyperbole.

Scholars have often warned against treating this period as too much of a monolith of artistic values, ideology, and social dogma. There is good reason for such a view, but it must also be said that no other moment in the history of German literature saw such a degree of tacit consensus among patrons, authors, and audiences as to what literature should be about, and a literary public of such social and ideological homogeneity. The lofty construct of an ideal life on earth for a small, privileged social elite, a construct at which the Germans seem to have worked

MIDDLE HIGH GERMAN LITERATURE

with somewhat greater earnestness than the French, was finally brought down as much by criticism from within (such as the late work of Walther and Wolfram) as by the centrifugal forces of change in society at large.

LATE MIDDLE HIGH GERMAN I: 1220/1230–1300

The rest of the thirteenth century was essentially a time of experimentation against this background. To understand this properly, a very clear distinction must be made between two aspects of the situation. First, ideals of courtliness, the main themes of courtly literature, and the language of courtly ideality remained highly influential to the end of the Middle Ages. This was a heritage to be passed along and enjoyed. Fundamentally more important is that lay literature, a literature by the laity for the laity, had arrived. This was a heritage to be divided and reinvested.

Naturally, lyric and romance were the primary conduits of courtliness. Even when the production (if not the transmission) of Arthurian novels was suspended temporarily in the last quarter of the thirteenth century, a type of romance appeared in their place that grafted the characteristic themes and sentiments onto Greek, Hellenistic, or otherwise exotic subjects. The satirical frolickings of Neidhart and Tannhäuser at the Babenberg court in the 1230's and 1240's, Neidhart's role playing with his own persona and peasant voices, even Ulrich von Lichtenstein's reenactment of his career as courtly lover and poet, all reflect on the past in innovative, forward-looking ways.

The unifying tendencies of classical Middle High German can still be recognized in the avoidance of gross deviations from what had become the norm of literary expression, but on the whole the decades after 1230 show more regional variety again. At the same time, the institutions of patronage and social interaction began to change character and to fall into new patterns. The extended but sparse network, with a few centers in the southeast, the southwest, the central region, and the northwest, was expanded, particularly toward the east and north, and became much more dense. In addition, several much more broadly based regional concentrations can be traced. The well-documented southwest must suffice as an example.

The "Swabian School," a group of noble minnesingers, conservative politically as well as aesthetically, was clustered around the *ministerialis* Ulrich von Winterstetten and displayed considerable diversity of social rank. Swabia was also the homeland of the Hohenstaufen family, and the two young sons of Frederick II, Henry and Conrad, maintained close ties not only with this group but also with some of the novelists of this first postclassical and last Hohenstaufen generation, notably Rudolf von Ems (*d.* around 1250), another Swabian nobleman. While Rudolf's substantial oeuvre harked back increasingly to the precourtly genre of *historia,* the Swabian minnesingers experimented freely with courtly forms and themes, and in this they provided a bridge, no doubt, to patrician interests in the cities of Zurich and Constance, which led to the codification of all available minnesong and *Sangspruch* around 1300. The city changed the literary climate somewhat. An array of sponsors—city aristocracy, landed gentry in town houses, high clergy, and others—offered the writer more choice and thereby promoted diversity in content and form. Konrad von Würzburg, a "Gottfriedean" who died at Basel in 1287 and was the most prolific and, next to the Stricker, most versatile author of the century, worked in the city and for the patrician ruling class for most of his professional life. Conservatism in taste and life-style and new configurations in institutional and personal patronage represent a combination for which there is no good name; "bourgeois" is definitely inappropriate.

Intensified active participation of the laity in lettered discourse began to fill the void that had existed for so long between the Latin, written culture of the clerk and the oral culture of the people. New subject areas opened up and new literary forms appeared, sometimes seemingly out of nowhere. Along with the further development of lyric and romance, they set the stage for the next two centuries, while what was left of the precourtly tradition seems to have petered out in the early fourteenth century. The following paragraphs will outline the more consequential among these initiatives.

Minnesong attracted amateurs, but those who took their cue from Walther's political and didactic poetry became (migrant) professionals—Reinmar von Zweter, Der Marner, and many others. To them lay literacy meant that the lay poet acquired, through his learning, a mandate to educate that was analogous to that of the clerk. They pursued this goal with almost missionary zeal and intensity, and with self-consciously erudite, increasingly formalistic artistry. Their medium was the *Sangspruch,* an open-ended strophic composition with melody that can accommodate any number of strophes on any

MIDDLE HIGH GERMAN LITERATURE

number of subjects; it is symptomatic of their art that the *Sangspruch* repertoire of the thirteenth and fourteenth centuries includes so many strophes that expound the poet's calling and the principles of his craft, and show him in competition with others. The *Sangspruch* poets are the most clearly delineated group of literary entertainers in the thirteenth century.

The man who called himself *Stricker* (knitter) flourished between 1220 and 1250, apparently in Austria, and was without a doubt the most innovative and versatile German author of the thirteenth century. He was also a professional, but he worked in a different medium. He stands in the middle of what amounts to an eruption of ideas concerning the use of the regular rhymed couplet as the courtly period had established it. The *Märe* is one of his forms, a short novelistic verse narrative of secular content, obviously a new alternative to the novel. The *Märe* (from MHG *maere;* compare Old French *conte*) does not stand alone, however. It is a member of a larger family of short narrative forms that also includes the *bîspel,* an exemplary tale, originally always a fable, followed by a short moral; the fable, which had made only sporadic and marginal appearances, and now occurs in the *bîspel* in early Stricker manuscripts; and various kinds of religious and moral tales, cousins of the Latin exemplum and of the legend.

Many times these forms cannot be distinguished too clearly from one another, but as a group they stand together against another type of short or medium-length poetry in rhymed couplets, the *Rede* (from MHG *rede;* compare Old French *dit*). Very short *Reden* are often referred to as *Spruch,* particularly in the fifteenth century, and modern scholarship uses the pleonastic term *Sprechspruch* to indicate that, unlike the *Sangspruch,* it is nonstrophic and not sung. The *Rede* is also nonnarrative, concentrating on argument, expostulation, and explanation rather than on action in the flow of time. Most prominent are religious, moral, or political tracts and the *Minnereden* (discourses on love), which, especially when they include allegory, have some narrative content as well.

Not all of these options were new in the thirteenth century, and some are more typical of the fourteenth or fifteenth, but overall the thirteenth century can be called the cradle of this kind of literature. It fills volume after volume in fourteenth- and fifteenth-century collections and must have constituted one of the more readily available (and certainly one of the cheapest) forms of literary entertainment. Usually the intent is didactic—to teach religious subjects and attitudes, moral behavior, a particular doctrine of thought or decorum, and, later, all kinds of practical skills as well. At the same time, some forms, particularly the *Märe* and certain kinds of parodistic or obscene *Reden,* became vehicles of comedy. With the exception of Wolfram's *Parzival,* sustained comedy had been notably absent from German literature. Here, too, Stricker broke new ground. Within a few decades the *Märe* and the *Rede* were to prove that they could even manage vigorous and artistically sophisticated political and social protest: in Wernher's *Märe vom Helmbrecht* and in the cluster of *Reden* that goes by the name of Seifrid Helbling.

After the early success of the *Nibelungenlied* just after 1200, the undercurrent of oral-traditional narrative poetry concerned with the Germanic past finally surfaced in written texts in the first half of the century. That also happened in the southeast, but among a clientele whose taste might be called rustic-conservative and somewhat escapist by comparison. The "heroic epic" that emerged and was to remain popular for centuries to come looked to the past, but unlike the Old French chansons de geste it did not envision a national past. Nor could it be called heroic in any strict sense. Most of the time essential generic conventions such as anonymity of the author, the use of traditional long-line stanza forms, and, it can be supposed, the use of recitative chant in performance (a few melodies have survived, albeit in different, later contexts) were adhered to. But the legends themselves had undergone numerous transformations, involving countless anecdotal accretions, and their new guardians added rich doses of thirteenth-century sentiment and sentimentality as well as themes and motifs from courtly romance. Even the courtly meter, four-stress couplets, was used occasionally. The central character of much of this literature is Dietrich von Bern (Verona), that is, Theodoric the Great, and much of the action takes place in northern Italy. Serialization of this material went on for more than 200 years, and a small selection of texts was eventually printed as the *Heldenbuch,* with reprints to the end of the seventeenth century.

Meanwhile the landed gentry along the middle and lower Rhine, where, as was often said in the south, chivalry was practiced with superior skill and refinement, seems to have adopted a game that implies a new understanding of the courtly which was

 MIDDLE HIGH GERMAN LITERATURE

to become more widespread as time passed. The small corpus of occasional *Reden* lumped together under the designation "Pseudo-Zilies von Sayn" casts contemporaries, members of the audience, as protagonists in historical and histrionic happenings.

Nothing, however, surpassed the rise of prose in implications for the future. In contrast with what happened in France, it was still fairly rare for prose to replace verse in traditionally poetic genres—the Rhenish *Prosa-Lanzelot* of about 1250 appears to have been the only courtly novel in prose before the fifteenth century, and even chroniclers mostly stuck to verse. Rather, the growth of prose was the result of an extension of vernacular writing into the preserves of oral tradition and Latin. Two areas in particular contributed to this: law and administration, and theology and religious devotion.

The early masterworks of expository and descriptive prose are all from the northern sector of central Germany. The precocious *Lucidarius* has already been mentioned; the others are Eike von Repgow's (illustrated) codification of Saxon law, the *Sachsenspiegel* (*ca.* 1225), the anonymous *Sächsische Weltchronik,* sometimes also attributed to Eike, and Mechthild of Magdeburg's revelations, *Das fliessende Licht der Gottheit* (1250–1265).

This last work, among the most splendid flowers of German mysticism, followed a general reorientation of religious life that took place in the early decades of the century. Mechthild's struggle to communicate personal experience in vernacular writing is symptomatic of the yearning for a new spirituality in the laity, especially among women, the best-educated segment of the nobility. This yearning inspired not only new forms of devotion and new religious organizations, such as the Beguine communes in which Mechthild lived most of her adult life, but also the demand for a language to serve the spiritual needs of this semiliterate laity. During the same time the newly founded Franciscan and Dominican orders made preaching a primary concern. The ensuing interplay brought forth an ever-widening stream of homiletic, devotional, theological, and revelational literature. This is the second most important move, after the secularization of writing in the two preceding generations, toward ultimate emancipation of the vernacular.

It has been estimated that, in sheer bulk, religious prose alone accounted for 70 percent to 80 percent of the total literary production (and reproduction) in late medieval Germany. Naturally it is impossible even to adumbrate this subject adequately in the present article; it will continue to focus on mysticism, since German is native, as it were, to this movement, whereas elsewhere in religious prose it is often defined by its ancillary function to Latin.

The first substantial sermon collection of the thirteenth century, the *St. Georgener Prediger* (perhaps *ca.* 1235), still bears the imprint of Cistercian monasticism, and Lamprecht von Regensburg's adaptation of Thomas of Celano's *Life of St. Francis* (around 1238) was still in verse. But the collaboration between the preacher Berthold von Regensburg and his companion, David von Augsburg (both *d.* 1272), changed that situation for good. Compilations such as the *Baumgarten geistlicher Herzen,* which was distributed through an early Franciscan clearinghouse in Augsburg, provided the first systematic impetus toward a new form and language of religious didactics and devotion. The second, Dominican mysticism, was not far off.

Taken as a whole, the thirteenth century fashioned the repertoire of Middle High German literary forms that can, at this point, briefly and roughly be described as follows:

First, prose—traditionally homiletic and catechetical, now also encyclopedic and legal/administrative, and in the process of acquiring many more functions in the sphere of religious thought and practice.

Second, verse in strophic composition serving two main modes, both associated with music. The first is the lyric in three basic types, *Lied, Sangspruch,* and *Leich.* The first two are largely based on the (imported) canzone form, and the kinds of melodies used are therefore similar in some essential respects. The main difference between *Lied* and *Sangspruch* lies in content. The *Leich* is a much more complicated textual and musical construct, a virtuoso piece reserved for very special occasions and subjects (often the Virgin Mary). The second mode is narrative in the form of the traditional (heroic) epic. The stanzas are native and completely different from the canzone, but also associated with music (chant). On the basis of this musical link, presumably, occasional borrowing from the *Lied* occurred, for example, in the *Eckenlied.* On one occasion Wolfram modified the heroic stanza type to treat a courtly subject *(Titurel).* It was an isolated incident with resounding repercussions, for the resulting *Titurelstrophe* remained a popular medium of courtly narrative and allegory to the end of the era.

Third, verse in rhymed couplets (in principle octosyllabic with four lifts). Refined and promoted by

MIDDLE HIGH GERMAN LITERATURE

courtly romance, it governs major religious narrative (hagiography, biblical poetry), the various types of short narrative (religious and secular) that sprang up around the Stricker, and moral and religious didactics in tracts of sometimes considerable length, such as Hugo von Trimberg's *Renner* (1300; 24,500 lines). The latter are a form of *Rede,* which subsequently appeared in a variety of shorter forms as well and picked up new topics.

LATE MIDDLE HIGH GERMAN II: 1300–1430

The fourteenth century is still the least understood of the late medieval centuries and in some respects the least attractive. There are very few outstanding personalities and texts, a general drift toward the pragmatic and didactic, and a loss of generic identity among the established forms. Since sociological or stylistic labels like "bourgeois" and "realism" do not fit nearly as well as was once thought, it would appear that organic cohesion is not the outstanding characteristic of the 130 or so years after 1300. Diversity is a feature of this era. There were new beginnings (such as "organized" mysticism) and there were comings and goings (such as the literature of the Teutonic Knights). Possibilities indicated in the preceding decades were played out during this period. The circle of players widened dramatically and literary coverage extended into more and more areas of life. The city asserted itself as the environment in which all these changes could take place most naturally. Prose expanded its domain and matured as a vehicle of scholarly, religious, and artistic expression.

Franciscan preaching was directed toward the general public; David von Augsburg was the only mystic among the early Franciscans. But in 1264 the monastic communities became the special wards of the Dominicans, and by 1300 an entirely different constellation was in place. More than eighty religious communities of women, in which the level of intellectual receptivity and education was considerably higher than in the general public, had been incorporated, and mysticism—ranging in actual expression from philosophical speculation to extreme ascetic practice—became the common bond between preacher and congregation. Their interaction is best observed in the Alamannic region, including Swabia and Alsace, and along the Rhine (the *studium generale* of the Dominicans was in Cologne).

Homily and sermon are heart and soul of this new partnership, and all the other prose forms to which it gave rise—instructional or devotional tract, the *Sendbrief* (epistle), spiritual (auto)biography—are deeply indebted to them. They serve as rhetorical and structural models; they translate dogma and abstract truth into images and metaphors; and under the mantle of suasion they unite philosophical speculation with the language of the people. This is not to say, however, that the surviving examples should be taken as direct records of the spoken word. In all but a few cases some sort of redaction has taken place, and collections were often intended more for readers than for listeners. Sermonizing was very much part of the growing literary enterprise.

It was a quite traditional awakening. Underneath the obvious differences in content, tone, and style between Meister Eckhart's speculative and Heinrich Suso's sentimental mysticism or Johannes Tauler's pragmatic ethical preaching lie similarities that mark the whole movement as essentially courtly and elitist, both in the sociological and in the systematic-systemic sense. The great majority of teachers, preachers, and conventuals were of noble birth. In their striving for a state of higher bliss on earth, to be achieved through contemplation and catharsis, they exhibit the same desire for analogous salvation as their forebears, who had sought fulfillment in more worldly constructs. Similar things could be said of their language. While each of the major mystics created his or her own language, the notion that systems of interdependent key concepts and terms—*kere, warheit, wesen, vernunft, grund der sele, einvalteceit*—will identify and bring within reach one central goal, the birth of God, the Logos, in the depths of the individual soul, is reminiscent of courtly idealism.

There is a fundamental difference as well. It is not just that the vernacular had gained perceptibly both in power to abstract and conceptualize and in sensitivity to explore the inner recesses of the self, but that it was now anchored in experience rather than in poetic reality. Suso put it well when he explained why he had recorded his visions in German: that was the language in which God had granted them to him.

Visionary experience, the counseling of the mendicants, and perhaps the work of Mechthild, which was passed around in these circles, freed creative energies that generated—still in the first half of the century—what might be called a first body of women's literature in German. Some of these women, for example, Elisabeth von Kirchberg, described the ascetic lives of older or deceased sisters. Some formed lasting spiritual unions with their mentors, and among the fruits of such friendship are the earliest major works of spiritual autobiography in German: Suso's *Vita* in Elsbeth Stagel's redaction, Heinrich von Nördlingen's letters to Margareta Ebner and her namesake Christine Ebner, and Margareta's *Revelations,* addressed to Heinrich.

The eventual trivialization of this movement, Tauler's teaching in particular, by the gifted and unscrupulous Rulman Merswin (*d.* 1382) of Strassburg transferred it into the intellectual milieu of the town and put it before a wider public. It also demonstrated that the basis for the reading of German religious prose had broadened a good deal and that—at least among the mystics and their followers—it had become quite divorced from its Latin background and conscious of its own history. In a different context the same consciousness is apparent in a new collection of saints' lives known as *Der heiligen Leben.* Composed in Nuremberg around 1400, this largest of several medieval German legendaries in verse and prose, even more influential than the German versions of the *Golden Legend,* relies not only on the standard Latin sources but on a good many German ones as well, reaching back as far as the hagiographic poetry of Hartmann and Ebernand.

The bulk of scholastic prose—moral-theological, encyclopedic, catechetical—the true dimensions of which are only beginning to be appreciated, is of course not "popular." The social contexts were the monastery, the major courts, the academy, and combinations of them in the larger cities, and often these translations and adaptations were intended merely as crutches for the handicapped professional. In some cases, however, this academic bilingualism appears in more complex configurations with more creative effects on the vernacular. A few examples from a large number of individual bilingual oeuvres may illustrate this.

Eckhart the academic teacher wrote Latin, while Eckhart the mystic spoke and wrote German. In the case of the pivotal Heinrich von Mügeln (*fl.* 1346–1372), whose German oeuvre is probably the largest and certainly the most diversified in the fourteenth century (history and theological commentary in prose, allegorical *Reden,* a very large number of didactic and religious *Sangsprüche*), Latin learning linked up with the trend toward "masterly" poetry in strophic form through which at least one sector of the laity—those who "know"—claimed a voice in the propagation of religious truth and learning. Johann von Neumarkt (*d.* 1380), chancellor to Emperor Charles IV, translated the pseudo-Augustinian *Soliloquia animae ad deum* in a deliberate attempt to fashion a new, highly rhetorical, artistic prose style. It is this particular combination of Latin-German bilingualism, the academic atmosphere of court and university at Prague, and the cultivation of artistry in prose that underlies what is arguably the pinnacle of German prose writing in the late Middle Ages, the *Ackermann aus Böhmen* (*ca.* 1400) by the trilingual Bohemian Johannes von Tepl.

Konrad von Megenberg (*d.* 1374), one of the more versatile scholars of the time, was headmaster of the School of St. Stephen in Vienna for a while, a post that prompted his most notable excursion into the vernacular, the *Buch von den natürlichen dingen* (1348/1350), adapted from Thomas de Cantimpré. It was the most comprehensive encyclopedic treatment of the natural world available in German, and hence one of the cornerstones of the semiacademic and nonacademic literature usually referred to as *Fachprosa* or *Fachschrifttum*—manuals and short instructional texts providing access to the liberal, mechanical, and magical arts. There was less need, initially, for translations in the first category, since a student of the liberal arts had to know Latin anyway, but in the fourteenth century there was extensive writing on subjects in the "lesser" arts: surgery and medical science in general (the major work in this very old and broad tradition is Ortolf's *Arzneibuch,* before 1348); veterinary medicine, horticulture, and oenology; alchemy, hunting, and cooking; dyeing of cloth, astrology, and travel. The first translation of John Mandeville's *Travels* dates from 1388–1393; that of Ordorico of Pordenone's account of his travels in the East appeared in 1359; and several original German travelogues were published before 1430.

There are no written instructions in the art of poetry and versification—not even in the fifteenth century. The only theoretical discussion of verse making occurs as an aside in Heinrich von Hesler's *Apocalypse* (*ca.* 1300). The early *Fachschrifttum* does, however, include the odd manual in verse—on health care, dreams, or fencing with swords. One of the truly original poets of the fourteenth century, who used the curious pseudonym "König vom Odenwald," descends frequently into the sphere of this literature as he makes points about the practice of bathing, untidy households, or the virtues of various household animals.

Secular narrative in prose was still not very frequent and remained confined to subjects of epic length. A good example is the story of Alexander; another, that of Troy: apart from eight different

MIDDLE HIGH GERMAN LITERATURE

translations of Guido delle Colonne's *Historia,* there are two independent redactions that combine several sources, including the late-thirteenth-century verse poem by Konrad von Würzburg. Several of these can be dated around 1400. For the most part, however, readers of romance simply continued to use what had been available since the late twelfth and thirteenth centuries.

The verse epic enjoyed continued (and anachronistic) popularity and continued to be produced in the order of the Teutonic Knights during the first half of the fourteenth century. Systematic organization of this production from composition (by members for members) through standardized scribal convention to methods of book manufacture resulted in enormous quantities of mostly biblical and hagiographic verse, rarely inspired but almost always of solid quality. Most influential inside as well as outside the order and most clearly indebted to courtly and postcourtly romance was the anonymous author of two legendaries, *Väterbuch* and *Passional* (before and around 1300, respectively), which replaced these worldly diversions with edifying table reading for the knights. A member of the Templars who represents the ideals of the order very clearly, although he never lived in Prussia, was Hugo von Langenstein, author of *Martina,* the longest Middle High German verse legend (1293; 32,588 lines). As the order finally turned to prose after 1350, Klaus Kranc translated the Prophets from the Vulgate. It is the most distinguished Bible translation before Luther.

In some sense the growth of prose in every area except secular narrative undoubtedly reflects the conviction expressed first in the *Lucidarius* prologue and later in many others that verse indicates fiction, while prose has an automatic claim to accuracy and factual truth. On the other hand, familiar clichés of intellectual and literary polemics are recognized in such statements. Of the two nondramatic genres in which the old rhymed couplet continued in sole use and that grew during the fourteenth century and beyond, only one has to do with fiction: the secular *Märe,* represented chiefly by comic tales, many of them occasional pieces. The other, broadly defined as *Rede,* is nonfictional in most of its subcategories, and its basic stance of authoritative prescription and description assures the continuity of spoken verse as the proper medium even for the most serious message. In this category are, for instance, the voluminous satires that divide and discuss mankind in accordance with the doctrine of the three estates and their subdivisions in all walks of life. They extend from Konrad von Ammenhausen's *Schachzabelbuch* (1337), one of several adaptations of Jacobus de Cessolis' famous allegorical chess book, to the very original, anonymous *Teufelsnetz* (*ca.* 1420). Apart from that, messages conveyed in *Reden* might also be nonreligious—almost anything from personal hygiene to the praise of princes.

Increased concentration on these shorter forms of nonlyrical poetry is evidence of a marked change in literary taste that may also explain the increasingly frequent mention of a special kind of performer, the *Sprecher,* a traveling professional who recited such poetry in public. A *Sprecher* might also write part or all of his repertoire. A case in point is Heinrich der Teichner (*d.* 1377), whose vast oeuvre of mostly very short *Reden* on every conceivable subject of moral didactics is also an oeuvre of freely interchangeable parts to be regrouped and recombined to meet the demands of individual occasions. In the production and dissemination of this poetry an oral element again plays an important, albeit not easily definable, role. This is true especially of the encomiastic lament, a subgenre of the secular *Rede* brought to perfection by the *Sprecher*-poet Peter Suchenwirt (*d.* after 1395), who composed, among many other works, *Ehrenreden* (panegyrics) for at least eighteen deceased members of the high nobility, mostly Austro-Bavarian. Also courtly in orientation is the *Minnerede,* which includes some of the finer examples of sustained allegory in Middle High German and in a sense replaced minnesong as the purveyor of doctrine and decorum in matters of love.

Minnesong in the classical manner (and canzone form) seems to have lain dormant while other, mostly simpler forms of the secular lyric, among them the popular ballad, were gaining ground. The early religious *Lied* appears to be connected with quite specific situations and groups of users, and form and content vary accordingly, from the mystic sequence *Granum sinapis* (The mustard seed), boldly speculative and hauntingly beautiful, to quasi-liturgical, congregational hymns and the paraliturgical processional chants of the flagellants. After 1350 spiritual and secular song came together in the rich (and often polyphonic) oeuvre of the so-called Mönch von Salzburg, and before long, aristocratic amateurs began to take up the craft once again: Hugo von Montfort (1357–1423), who also mixed secular with spiritual lyrics, many of them highly personalized, and Oswald von Wolkenstein (*d.* 1445), at once the last of the chivalric *Lied* singers and a

MIDDLE HIGH GERMAN LITERATURE

personality shaped by the historical forces around 1400. Both Hugo and Oswald left "collected works," a new idea in German letters. These collections are hardly comparable with earlier systematic collections of their own work by French professionals like Machaut, but along with moves in the same direction by German professionals such as Heinrich der Teichner and Peter Suchenwirt, they reflect a new overall consciousness of the poet's individuality and artistic persona.

It is difficult to tell whether this self-consciousness may have anything to do with the rise of the so-called masters (*Meister,* not to be confused with his fifteenth-century cousin, the *Meistersinger*). The idea of the master, the magisterial singer-poet, is actually a thirteenth-century one. Although "masterly" views are manifested in other genres, *Sangspruch* poets are usually spoken of in this connection. Their poetry is often esoteric and dull to the modern reader, but the contribution of these masters to musical and literary life and to the general intellectual climate was no doubt great. It is one of the chief topics of current research in Late Middle High German.

The Colmar *Liederhandschrift* of about 1460, the most voluminous of the manuscripts that gather the masters' production together, preserves 4,380 strophes in 108 different tunes. Most renowned among later generations were Regenbogen and Frauenlob (Heinrich von Meissen), both active around 1300; at the end of the line stands Muskatblüt (*d.* after 1438), who, like Frauenlob, was, for a time, in the employ of the archbishop of Mainz. Heinrich von Mügeln is the central figure in the middle, with almost 400 *Sangsprüche* on cosmology, the arts, the Virgin Mary, astronomy, the Old Testament, and other subjects.

A special and especially potent poetic tradition that energized other genres originated in the lyrical poetry of Neidhart von Reuental. He had cast himself in the role of aristocratic adversary of the peasants, and later generations built upon this fictional relationship a whole corpus of antirustic comic tales in song, drama, and epic narrative. One of the two secular plays that survive in fourteenth-century manuscripts is a Neidhart play, and the most colorful flower of this "village poetry" *(dörperliche Dichtung)* is one of the few timeless gifts of the comic muse to medieval Germany, Heinrich Wittenwiler's mock-heroic epic, *Der Ring* (*ca.* 1400).

Under Charles IV (1347–1378) the imperial court took a certain interest in German letters, especially after contacts with the fledgling Italian humanism and its chief exponent, Petrarch (Francesco Petrarca), had been established. Certainly the preeminence of Prague as a literary center in the second half of the fourteenth century reflects in part the presence of the imperial court and its chancery. However, a comprehensive survey of the situation in Prague, Vienna, Würzburg, Erfurt, and many other cities of the realm would reveal that momentum had begun to shift toward the cities. Patronage remained in the hands of the traditional powers—the lay nobility, the cathedral clergy, and the monasteries, to name only the most obvious—but these institutions now tended to appear increasingly in new configurations involving an urban environment. Often these sources of inspiration and material support had existed in relative physical (and intellectual) isolation; now the growing cities brought more and more of them together, adding new ones at the same time: monasteries, cathedrals and their chapters, episcopal administrations, secular courts, the landed gentry with residences in town, the upper middle class of the bourgeoisie, and the universities and schools. None of this means that aesthetic or ethical norms changed dramatically in favor of bourgeois ideals or that, with the possible exception of drama, specifically urban patterns of literary engagement developed; but there was change in another, less tangible but no less consequential, way. The institutions may not have changed, but they now operated in a common environment, and their originally different clienteles could not fail to mingle to some degree. Once again, something like a literary public was created. It was much broader, socially as well as intellectually, than what existed, briefly, around 1200—and it lasted.

Not coincidentally, more or less official city chronicles began to appear, from Magdeburg to Limburg and Strassburg to Cologne. One of the first of the chroniclers to incorporate the ancient concept of the "common good" *(gemein nutz)* into vernacular civic didactics was the lawyer and theologian Johannes Rothe (*ca.* 1360–1434), town clerk of Eisenach, canon, and school principal. He wrote local (Thuringian) as well as world history, hagiographic verse, and several didactic *Reden* identifying rights and responsibilities of the bourgeoisie and certain sectors of the aristocracy.

LATE MIDDLE HIGH GERMAN III: 1430–1500

As the fifteenth century progressed, forms of literary activity appeared that belong to the city in the much more narrow sense that they are structured

MIDDLE HIGH GERMAN LITERATURE

around social or administrative organizations specific to urban life. The imperial city of Nuremberg became an unrivaled literary center. Meanwhile, some courts entered a stage of nostalgic revival of chivalric ideals that did not, however, preclude the promotion of the modest German humanism that now began to appear. Herein lies one of the chief causes of the eventual prosification of secular narrative.

Seasonal public theater was easily the most accessible and popular entertainment from about 1450 well into the sixteenth century. Such theater includes the drama of the church, with heavy concentration in the Easter season and plays of the Passion and Resurrection that might require a hundred or more actors and last several days, as well as secular drama, mostly short farces *(Fastnachtsspiele)* performed during Shrovetide, with suspension of practically all sexual and hygienic taboos. Records of performances go back as far as the twelfth century, yet only about a dozen complete texts survive from before 1400. This scarcity must be attributed in part to the open, improvisational form of the drama—often there was no written text at all or only a set of guidelines to be filled out in performance. But another reason is probably that drama did not in fact reach maturity until the mid fifteenth century, when more urban communities—from Sterzing in the south to Lübeck in the north—were large and secure enough, and had the administrative and financial capability, to stage and supervise major spectacles, and when the lower middle class had become sufficiently confident and sophisticated to assume, mostly through the guilds, the stewardship of carnival comedy.

Like the sermon, religious drama became a mass medium when and where it had divorced itself from Latin and moved outside the church and into the market square. Although it could never shed its liturgical ties, it incorporated more and more extraneous (mostly comic) material to facilitate the process of identification and empathy that it was designed to promote. Shrovetide plays were performed indoors—in private homes, inns, and town halls—and some Neidhart plays and others seem to have required an open-air setting outside the town walls. Despite its coarse humor and slapstick burlesque, the comedy is often highly verbal, requiring considerable mental agility on the part of the audience. The medium for all drama is the rhymed couplet (except for hymns and songs in the plays of the church). It is illusionary, non-Aristotelian epic theater in close touch with its audience. Characters in the play address the spectators; spectators and actors may pray and sing together before the play of the Passion begins; a comedy in the local pub may conclude with a dance to be joined by all.

As institution and content, Late Middle High German drama inspired a strong sense of bourgeois identity. The same can be said of *Meistergesang.* The Meistersinger look back to the masters, but they are not their direct descendants. Institutionalized singing and poetic competition of the kind associated with Meistersinger practice is not nearly as old, at least in Germany, as the Meistersinger themselves believed; the earliest unequivocal reference to the founding of a "singing school" dates from 1450 in Augsburg. Basically it was a fifteenth/sixteenth-century phenomenon. These schools were guilds of practitioners of the old *Sangspruch* technique, taught by local masters or traveling professionals such as the incredibly prolific Michel Beheim (1416–1474/1478). They borrowed their ideology of "learned" and "measured" poetry from literary models. The Nuremberg school appears to have been the liveliest in the early years, especially after the barber-surgeon and printer Hans Folz of Worms (*d.* 1513) acquired citizenship there in 1459. With his successful defense of the liberal Nuremberg practice of allowing aspiring masters to compose their own tunes rather than rely on the twelve canonical old masters, he saved subsequent *Meistergesang* from total sterility.

Hans Rosenplüt (*d.* 1470), another Nuremberg craftsman and poet, and Folz contributed a large share of the some 100 extant Nuremberg Shrovetide plays; both wrote *Mären*, and both composed *Reden* about, among many other bourgeois topics, the city and its institutions, as did Rosenplüt's pupil, the clothier Kunz Has (*d.* before 1527).

The works of Hugo von Montfort and Oswald von Wolkenstein, among others, show that privatization (as opposed to representation) was no prerogative of the bourgeoisie. Privatization does, however, characterize rather well the way in which the secular *Lied*, sung to the accompaniment of instruments, existed in fifteenth-century cities and towns and survived in collections made for private use in individual households. Owners of such collections ranged from prosperous professionals such as Hartmann Schedel, town physician of Nuremberg, to municipal officials such as Jacob Kebicz in the little Swabian town of Wemding. Most of these *Liederbücher* are part of larger codices that contain other types of short poetry as well as household and family notes

 MIDDLE HIGH GERMAN LITERATURE

(as in that of Klara Hätzlerin), and most lack the melodies (the most conspicuous exception being the famous *Lochamer Liederbuch* of about 1460, also from Nuremberg), which were probably well known anyway in many cases. In a mixture that varies greatly from case to case, these collections preserve a wide spectrum of what was current and, in the main, considered popular at the time: love poetry of all sorts (imitation minnesong, the much-loved *Tagelied* [aubade], personalized greetings and letters), ballads, historical songs, some *Sangsprüche,* and other forms.

No place in Germany or, for that matter, in Europe conveys a better impression than the imperial city of Nuremberg of what literary life could be like in a fifteenth-century city, and how rich it could be. Even outsiders like Albrecht von Eyb (1420–1475), canon of Bamberg and Eichstät, were eager to pay homage. Albrecht, one of the first Germans with close ties to fifteenth-century Italian humanism, dedicated his first major work in German, the *Ehebüchlein* (printed at Nuremberg, 1472), to the city fathers and the community at large, "to support their government and civic institutions." In its actual manifestations this literary life may be more characteristic of Nuremberg than of other cities, but it exemplifies very well that (and how) the bourgeois milieu modernized medieval literature without taking away its essential character. Obviously verse, be it through drama, *Märe, Meistergesang,* or *Rede,* maintained a key position.

Church drama apart, the emphasis was on short forms. Something like a popular culture evolved, in which the old and the new, tradition and individual creation, were often indistinguishable—merging, as it were, in repeated acts of creative reproduction. A similar (and often noted) phenomenon is that one and the same subject—above all the subject of human folly, perhaps the most pervasive theme of the age—could now be treated in almost any one of those forms and that, conversely, demarcations between the various verse genres became severely blurred. Another example of this mixture of genres is the anonymous compilation of a large corpus of songs about Neidhart and the peasants and a few other lyrics to form a continuous verse narrative of *Neidhart Fuchs* (in print since 1491), one of a series of cyclical, comic chapbooks, still mostly in verse and based largely on older material, that satirize and ridicule the human condition through the machinations of a central hero who cleverly and often unscrupulously manipulates society around him. Similar examples are Philipp Frankfurter's *Pfarrer vom Kahlenberg,* in print since 1473; or, in Low German, Hermann Bote's *Ulenspiegel,* in print since 1510 or 1511, and the anonymous German version of Renart, *Reinke de Vos* (1498). The city acted as a melting pot, not only in social terms.

The courts in both the north and the south, on the other hand, leaned more toward the preservation of clearly delineated traditions, at least in some conspicuous instances. Only a short while after the most ambitious *Heldenbuch* of the fifteenth century was put together for Duke Balthasar of Mecklenburg around 1472, Ulrich Fuetrer (*d.* 1496) wrote his *Buch der Abenteuer* (1473–*ca.* 1480) for Duke Albrecht IV, of the Munich branch of the Wittelsbachs, recasting many of the old verse romances in one comprehensive narrative. The recasting was not, however, in prose, as Malory and his French predecessors had done, but in Wolfram's *Titurelstrophe!*

At the same time the courts became eager promoters of narrative prose. Isolated earlier examples notwithstanding, secular narrative prose is a phenomenon of the fifteenth century after about 1430. The rapidity with which it spread and found readers in all strata of society can be linked to several interrelated causes: the increased desire of a better-educated public to read (and to be read to), the invention of the printing press, and (not least) the fact that, not for the first time in German literary history, most publications drew on preexisting texts. In the first generation, from the 1430's to the 1460's, the sources were primarily French romances and chansons de geste, both in prose and in verse, and major authors were members of high society (Elisabeth von Nassau-Saarbrücken [*d.* 1456] and Eleonore von Oberösterreich [*d.* 1480]) or close to it (Thüring von Ringoltingen [*d.* 1483; *Melusine,* 1456]).

The Latin-Italian novella was the next major reservoir to be tapped, mainly in the 1460's and 1470's, often seen as the time of early German humanism. In this context German prose took on an unmistakably academic hue and involved a new type of author. The men who reaped the benefits of (still mostly aristocratic) patronage were bourgeois professionals who also wrote: doctors, lawyers, theologians, city clerks. They all had some contact with Italian humanism, and they saw a sociocultural mission for themselves.

Johannes Hartlieb (*d.* 1468) of Munich, physician to Albrecht III, is an early example, although he remained tied to the more traditional prose of the arts. Albrecht von Eyb, lawyer and theologian, has al-

 MIDDLE HIGH GERMAN LITERATURE

ready been mentioned. His *Guiscard und Sigismunda* (after Boccaccio, via the Latin of Leonardo Bruni) and *Marina* (after an anonymous Latin author), and his translations of Plautus, are masterpieces of early literary German prose. The Ulm physician Heinrich Steinhöwel (1412–1477/1478), who also was personal physician to Count Albrecht of Württemberg, was one of at least five Germans who adapted Boccaccio's story of Griselda from the *Decameron* (via Petrarch's Latin version, in 1461/1462), and his rendering became one of the most popular works of the time. Niclas von Wyle (*ca.* 1410–1478), town clerk of the imperial city of Esslingen and later chancellor of the counts of Württemberg, wielded his pen as an educational tool by insisting on more or less literal translation and deliberate imitation of Latin grammar and style. He was nevertheless enormously successful, especially with *Euryalus und Lucretia,* the first of his eighteen *Translatzen,* a series begun in 1461 and printed together for the first time in 1478. The Latin *Euryalus* of 1444, by Enea Silvio de Piccolomini (later Pope Pius II), the chief propagator of Italian humanism in the north, was already the classic love story of the Renaissance, and this was its first vernacular version.

The social and artistic milieu in which this new prose grew was distinctly different from that described in conjunction with Nuremberg. It involves the city, too, but more the type of city with a princely residence. Through family relationships among the sponsors and personal contacts among the authors, as well as through their common bond in education, a supraregional network of literary communication and shared, forward-looking interests came into being that reached from Vienna and Innsbruck through Munich to Swabia and Württemberg, where the widowed Countess Mechthild, femme fatale of her generation, held court at Rottenburg. These interests were still medieval enough to encourage someone to pen an original large-scale narrative in traditional mold and poetic form (which might eventually even be printed), but only, it can be suspected, if this was done in high good humor, tongue in cheek, and with the elegance of a Hermann von Sachsenheim (1366/1369–1458). His parodistic *Minnerede, Die Mörin* (1453; first printing 1512) is a dazzling revue of time-honored conventions with a great deal of name-dropping that attests not only to Hermann's wide reading and wit but also to the ability of his audience to look at medieval literature with new eyes, the eyes of collectors and connoisseurs—Renaissance eyes.

The general public and the printers who cared for verse had less patience with long narratives. In the final three decades of the century, when publishers reached, almost as a last resort, into the rich grab bag of indigenous poetic texts that were still being copied in scribal workshops in order to satisfy the public's hunger for reading material, these texts were shortened and rendered in prose (sometimes via an intermediate Latin prose version). Almost invariably these chapbook versions were the only form in which a long medieval secular verse tale managed to leap the hurdle of print and survive into subsequent centuries. Eilhart von Oberg's *Tristan,* including its established cycle of illustrations, did so (1484); Gottfried von Strassburg's did not.

There is one outstanding original prose narrative of the late fifteenth century, the chapbook *Fortunatus,* written at Augsburg and first printed there in 1509 (with woodcuts by the older Jörg Breu). Drawing on fairy tale and recent travel literature, it is in the main a tale of fantastic adventure involving two generations of Cypriot merchants, but it concludes with a moral that projects the self-consciousness of the class of international traders who dominated cities such as Augsburg: the tragedy that ultimately befalls the family could have been avoided had the patriarch chosen wisdom over riches.

The invention of printing with movable letters had met, rather than created, a demand. By speeding up the publication boom that had been under way since inexpensive paper had begun to replace parchment, it helped bring about, among other things, the phenomenon of the instant best seller. Sebastian Brant's *Narrenschiff* (1494), the last of the great satirical *Reden,* is the first of these, and it was unsurpassed for centuries. Only four years later the foremost preacher of the age, Johannes Geiler (1445–1510), of Kaysersberg near Strassburg, began a series of sermons on the *Narrenschiff,* a profane text in the vernacular. In a sense, then, the vernacular had arrived. It must also be said, though, that the international success of the *Narrenschiff* and its fame among humanists rested on Jakob Locher's translation into Latin (1497).

BIBLIOGRAPHY

Useful for preliminary bibliographical orientation are three volumes in the series Handbuch der deutschen Literaturgeschichte, Abt. II, Bibliographien: II, Michael Batts, *Hohes Mittelalter* (1969); III, George F. Jones, *Spätes Mittelalter (1300–1450)* (1971); and IV, James E. Engel, *Renaissance, Humanismus, Reformation* (1969). The best and most up-to-date general reference work is Kurt Ruh *et al.*, eds., *Die deutsche Literatur des Mittelalters: Verfasserlexikon,* 2nd ed. (1978–).

For questions of periodization see especially Joachim Heinzle, "Wann beginnt das Spätmittelalter?" in *Zeitschrift für deutsches Altertum und deutsche Literatur,* **112** (1983); Johannes Janota, "Das vierzehnte Jahrhundert—ein eigener literaturhistorischer Zeitabschnitt?" in Walter Haug *et al.*, eds., *Zur deutschen Literatur und Sprache des 14. Jahrhunderts* (1983); Hugo Kuhn, *Entwürfe zu einer Literatursystematik des Spätmittelalters* (1980); Dieter Wuttke, *Deutsche Germanistik und Renaissance-Forschung: Ein Vortrag zur Forschungslage* (1968).

There are only two brief treatments of Middle High German literature in English, both of them quite out of date for the time after 1250: Paul Salmon, *Literature in Medieval Germany* (1967); Maurice O'C. Walshe, *Medieval German Literature: A Survey* (1962). An excellent comprehensive account in German with good introductory bibliographies is Max Wehrli, *Geschichte der deutschen Literatur vom frühen Mittelalter bis zum Ende des 16. Jahrhunderts* (1980). The standard history is Helmut de Boor and Richard Newald, eds., *Geschichte der deutschen Literatur,* I; Helmut de Boor, *Die deutsche Literatur von Karl dem Grossen bis zum Beginn der höfischen Dichtung, 770–1170,* 9th ed. (1979); II: *Die höfische Literatur: Vorbereitung, Blüte, Ausklang, 1170–1250,* 10th ed. (1979); III: *Die deutsche Literatur im späten Mittelalter,* pt. 1, *Zerfall und Neubeginn, 1250–1350,* 4th ed. (1973); IV: Hans Rupprich, *Die deutsche Literatur vom späten Mittelalter bis zum Barock,* pt. 1, *Das ausgehende Mittelalter, Humanismus und Renaissance: 1370–1520* (1970). See also Ingeborg Glier, ed., *Die deutsche Literatur im späten Mittelalter,* II (1987).

Aimed primarily at students is the new history compiled under the general editorship of Joachim Heinzle, *Geschichte der deutschen Literatur von den Anfängen bis zum Beginn der Neuzeit* (1984–).

MICHAEL CURSCHMANN

[See also **Alexander Romances; Beast Epic; Biblical Poetry, German; Drama, German; Fachschrifttum; German Language; German Literature: Allegory, Lyric, Romance; Mären; Minnereden; Minnesingers; Mysticism, European: Germany; Nuremberg;** and individual authors and works.]

MIDGARD SERPENT. In Scandinavian mythology, the midgard serpent (Old Norse *miðgarðsormr*) is the great enemy of the god Thor. *Snorra edda (Gylfaginning,* chaps. 19–20) states that the serpent is the son of Loki and the giantess Angrboða; his brother is the Fenris wolf and his sister the death figure Hel. Odin cast the serpent into the sea, where it surrounds the earth *(miðgarðr),* and from this it has its name. Another name is *Jǫrmungandr* ("powerful magic being"), but in most cases it is referred to simply as the serpent.

Thor fights the serpent three times in the mythology. The best-known occasion is when he hooks it on a fishing line and pulls it up to the boat's gunwale. According to some sources he then kills it (Úlfr Uggason, *Húsdrápa;* probably also *Hymiskviða*); in other sources the giant accompanying Thor cuts the line, and the serpent escapes (Bragi Boddason, *Ragnarsdrápa; Snorra edda, Gylfaginning,* chap. 32). The heart of the story seems to be not the outcome but the moment when Thor and the hooked serpent glare at one another; scholars have identified this scene on the Altuna stone (Sweden) and Gosforth cross (Cumberland, England).

In Thor's journey to Útgarða-Loki, told only in *Snorra edda (Gylfaginning,* chaps. 26–31), Thor attempted to lift the serpent, believing it to be a cat. He nearly succeeded.

Vǫluspá 50 and, following it, *Snorra edda (Gylfaginning,* chaps. 38–39) describe Thor's third encounter with the serpent, at Ragnarǫk. They kill one another, but Thor staggers back nine paces before dying, perhaps indicating a small victory over his foe.

The serpent girdling the earth is known to many cultures. According to Erich Neumann, it represents a psychological archetype of the *uroboros,* "devouring its tail." When the hero slays it, he frees his ego from the influence of parental figures. Within Indo-European tradition, the closest analogue to the serpent is the dragon Vritra, in Indic tradition killed by Indra, said to be a cognate figure to Thor. Influence from Leviathan and similar figures is also possible.

BIBLIOGRAPHY

Aage Kabell, "Der Fischfang Þórs," in *Arkiv för nordisk filologi,* **91** (1976); Erich Neumann, *The Origins and History of Consciousness* (1954); Jan de Vries, *Altgermanische Religionsgeschichte,* Grundriss der germanischen Philologie, **12** (1956).

JOHN LINDOW

[See also **Bragi Boddason the Old; Eddic Poetry; Fenris Wolf; Gylfaginning; Hel; Loki; Odin; Scandinavian Mythology; Snorra Edda; Thor; Úlfr Uggason; Vǫluspá.**]

MIDRASH. See **Exegesis, Jewish.**

MIÉLOT, JEAN. See **Jean Miélot.**

MIGRATION, INTERNAL. See **Reclamation.**

MIGRATION AND HIBERNO-SAXON ART

MIGRATION ART

The period of the great migrations of Germanic peoples was one of uncertainty and disorder. By the third century the Roman Empire was in full decay. Its army, composed mainly of Germanic and Oriental elements, was disintegrating. Through the desperate years of the fourth century it managed to shield the frontier against Persians and barbarians until the Huns, an especially fierce enemy from the east, drove before them displaced Germanic tribes as they advanced deep into the western provinces. The peoples of the Germanic territories, stretching from the Black Sea northward into Scandinavia, experienced a continuous and protracted pressure—a movement toward lebensraum in western and southern Europe. Thus, the Visigoths of the Black Sea region, yielding to Hunnic force, settled first in Italy and then in Spain. They were followed into Italy by the Ostrogoths, who in turn were replaced by another Germanic people, the Lombards.

In the north, a confederation of tribes living on the west bank of the Rhine, the Franks, traveled southward into western Germany and Gaul. The Frankish kingdom that they established eventually brought about that synthesis of Germanic and Latin culture which was to give shape and life to an emergent Christian medieval civilization. Scandinavia, though on the periphery of this continental turbulence, played an important role in the movement of peoples, for it was from Jutland as well as Germany that the Angles, Saxons, and Jutes invaded Britain in the fifth century. However confused the details of the restless movements of groups or of whole peoples, the outcome is known: by the close of the sixth century, unstable, often ephemeral barbarian kingdoms had replaced the central authority of the Roman imperium in western Europe.

Never a homogeneous nation, being composed of many national groups with diverse customs and traditions, the Germanic peoples yet shared certain fundamental characteristics. Long nomadic, they gradually took to farming, though always preferring, it seems, maritime commerce and fishing. Archaeological evidence reveals a prevailing aversion to the monumental arts. Stone architecture produced by subject populations remained alien to the tribal groups until they had long settled an area. Except for the Scandinavian picture stones, the same holds true for sculpture in stone. By contrast, the tombs of the barbarians were filled with weapons, tools, and jewelry, often magnificently decorated. Indeed, the art of the Germanic peoples is almost exclusively one of personal adornment, a portable art that followed men and women into their graves. From first to last, it was intended to ensure survival in the next world and to protect the living from evil forces emanating from the dead.

Aristocratic burials could be remarkably sumptuous. The tomb of a sixth-century Frankish queen, discovered beneath the crypt of the abbey church of St. Denis, permits a rare glimpse of the rich variety of articles interred with the deceased. The body of the queen rests on a red woolen blanket within the stone coffin, dressed in a linen shift beneath a violet silk tunic held in place by an elegant leather girdle. A dark red silk gown ornamented with gold thread at the cuffs covers the tunic and is fastened at the neck and waist by two splendid gold brooches set with garnets. An equally beautiful long gold pin passes through the upper left side of the gown, and a silken veil is held in place by two gold pins. The queen also wears earrings, silver belt ends, and buckles. Stockings, leather garters, and leather slippers complete the royal attire. A large belt buckle decorated with garnets, undoubtedly a burial gift, was also found in the coffin.

Two styles dominate the history of barbarian art: the polychrome style, whose origins are to be found among the Goths of the Black Sea, and the animal style, which reaches its zenith in Scandinavia, north Germany, and Anglo-Saxon England. More restricted geographically, and of shorter duration than the polychrome style, the animal style is perhaps of greater importance, for it is characteristically and quintessentially Germanic, an exquisitely sensitive barometer of the vitality and originality of barbarian art.

The polychrome style. During the second century a taste for richly chromatic effects—a love of gold inscribed and inlaid with precious stones—found expression in the goldsmith's art practiced by the Goths and other Germanic peoples of south Russia. Without doubt, these barbarians borrowed techniques and motifs from Roman provincial sources,

MIGRATION PERIOD ART

yet the origin of the polychrome technique is not Roman but seems to depend on inspiration from inner Asia and the Near East. For centuries gold polychrome objects had been made by the Scythians of the Black Sea; the Sarmatians perpetuated this tradition well into the second century. Undoubtedly, by carrying polychrome objects out of the Asian heartland, the Huns increased the popularity of the technique.

The Gothic polychrome style appears in mature form in the famous fourth-century treasure of Petrossa in Romania. Two variants, sometimes used to adorn the same object, are employed. In the first, rounded stones—garnets or almandines—are raised above the surface. Spaces are left between settings in order to allow the gleam of polished gold to set off the richly colored jewels. The second style at Petrossa introduces flat, highly polished stones into closely fitted cells of wire or metal strips. This cloisonné technique is applied to broad areas of surface. Both styles figure in the decoration of the great gold eagle fibula from Petrossa (*Fig.* 1). Along the edge and center, heart-shaped cloisonné cells enclose flat garnets, but round, raised stones are also set into the piece, so that it takes on a heavy, ponderous look. Such lavish excess, to the point of obscuring the glittering gold background, distinguishes much of the Petrossa material from later, more restrained Germanic jewelry.

The Goths of south Russia combined Eastern polychrome techniques with traditional Greco-Roman metalwork craftsmanship. Adding filigree and granulation ornamentation, they carried an enriched polychrome style to Italy, the south of France, and Spain. Among the Ostrogoths and Visigoths the fashion for polychrome jewelry centered on cloisonné; they applied the technique to a variety of weapons and objects of personal adornment. A superlative example is the Ostrogothic eagle fibula from Cesena, Italy, now in Nuremberg (Germanisches Nationalmuseum). Of rare quality itself, it underlines the ubiquity of fibulae, the dress-fasteners, clasps, and brooches of the migration period. It seems probable that such work had liturgical significance. Totemic symbols are prominently featured on Alamannic examples, and the horse forms of certain Merovingian fibulae have been interpreted as bearers of the soul after death. The eagle runs like a leitmotiv through early migration art and was perhaps understood as a solar symbol. Whatever his symbolic intent, the goldsmith who fashioned the Cesena gold eagle imbued it with magisterial dig-

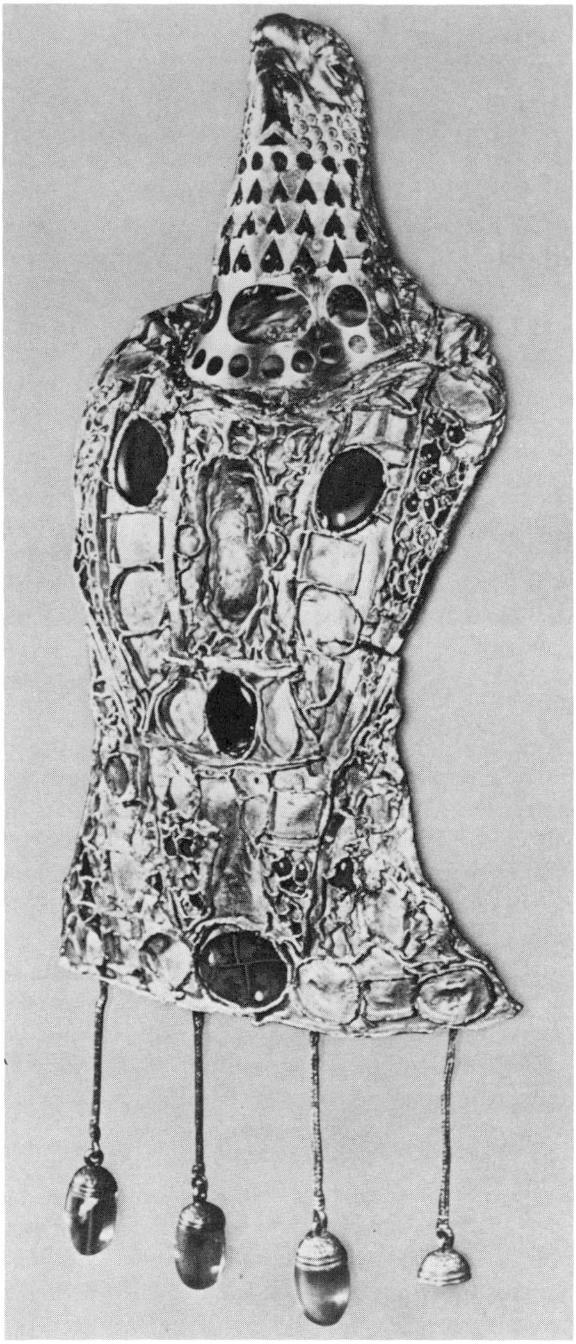

Fig. 1. Fibula from Petrossa, late 4th century. NATIONAL MUSEUM, BUCHAREST

nity. Flattening the shape of the creature but preserving its essential outlines, he set his brooch with exquisitely cut, closely spaced almandines of alternately round and rectangular contour.

During the fifth century the cloisonné style became increasingly fashionable in central and south-

MIGRATION PERIOD ART

ern Europe. Though possibly the work of a Gothic craftsman, the cloisonné jewels found in the tomb of the Frankish king Childeric I testify to the spread of this style beyond the Alps. The beautiful sword from the tomb (now in Paris, Bibliothèque Nationale) is decorated in a manner characteristic of the evolving polychrome style of the late fifth century. Flat garnets are confined in rows enclosing strips framing an elaborate central design—this in place of wide zones of cloisonné ornament.

The animal style. Until the sixth century the polychrome style was largely confined to the barbarians settling Italy, Spain, and Gaul. It was, in effect, a southern style with limited appeal for the Scandinavians and northern Germans engaged in the creation of the extraordinary animal ornamentation we think of as giving Germanic art its definitive character. Bernhard Salin, who pioneered the study of zoomorphic decoration in the early twentieth century, divided animal art of the period from 400 to 900 into three successive phases—Scandinavian styles I, II, and III. This chronology, modified by reassessments and later discoveries, remains essentially valid. For the migration period, Salin's first two categories are of particular interest.

Style I first appears in fifth-century northwest Europe. Contemporary scholarship tends to view its origin as partially in the art of the nomadic peoples of the Asiatic steppes and Near East—and certainly individual motifs such as birds' heads and griffins display strong affinities with Scythian, Sarmatian, and Parthian examples—but mainly in the simple, rigid animal figures of late Roman provincial art. Vital to its inception was the introduction of chip carving, a technique of light-catching wedge-shaped incisions most likely developed from the cire perdue method of casting. Applied to bronze and, with finer result, to silver, this distinctive treatment accompanied the earliest evidence of animal ornament in northern Germany, Denmark, and Scandinavia. Chip-carved forms (scrolls, spirals, rosettes, animal heads, human facial masks, and animal friezes made up of relatively naturalistic but stiff figures) at first almost indistinguishable from late Roman types, increasingly depart from these sources. Whereas in the provincial works marginal animals, heads, masks, and foliate details preserved a semblance of reality and plasticity, in barbarian metalwork such elements are subjected to a process of stylization and abstraction of breathtaking novelty. Animals once complete are twisted, distorted, and segmented. Component parts are reassembled as bizarre patterns of fluid outline inserted into every available area of surface or border. Once begun, this system of dismemberment and reformation inspired greater and greater feats of contortion, exaggeration, and surreal invention until, finally, animal forms became nearly unrecognizable linear configurations. At its best this northern style was capable of intense surface energy, startling abstract cadences, and compositions of dazzling fecundity.

Style I is most clearly observed in the large Scandinavian silver gilt fibulae. These magnificent objects employ chip carving, but also inlaid black niello, to set off the zoomorphic patterns. Perhaps most impressive of the group of finest fibulae is the example from Fonnås, Norway (*Fig.* 2). Almost seven inches (17 cm) long, it features three red stones in its rec-

Fig. 2. Fibula from Fonnås, 6th century. UNIVERSITETETS OLDSAKSAMLING, OSLO, C nr. 8154

MIGRATION PERIOD ART

tangular head plate. Animal ornamentation spread everywhere over the surface is most powerfully realized along the borders. Typical of Style I and giving it much of its expressiveness are the contour lines that sharply define and emphasize the limbs, thighs, paws, and jaws of the partially or fully disjointed creatures.

In Scandinavia, Style I is associated with a filigree technique which, employed in a group of gold collars variously dated from the first half of the fifth to the second half of the sixth century, achieves an unmatched level of delicacy and richness. A collar from Ålleberg, Sweden, is representative (now in Stockholm, Historiska Museet). Small molded rings adorned with filigree encircle ribbed tubes. Masks, human and animal figures similar to those on the fibulae, have been cut from heavy gold plate and inserted between the tubes. These figural elements are themselves embellished with gold grains and filigree wire. Buried in a time of danger, these large, heavy Swedish collars speak of an age of great wealth. Their beauty and skillful execution exemplify the exalted level of Scandinavian craftsmanship during the first centuries of the migration period.

From about 600, Style I was everywhere in retreat before the advance of a new animal style, Salin's Style II. Although not untouched by Mediterranean influence and distributed over the greater part of the Germanic territories—in southern as well as northern Europe—Style II achieves its greatest artistic triumphs in Scandinavia and Anglo-Saxon England. Displacing the fragmented beasts of Style I, elongated, interlaced animals cover surfaces and create flowing, often symmetrical patterns. The effect is altogether calmer, more stable, and more coherent than that of the earlier animal style.

Fine examples of Style II patterns enrich the horse mounts of grave twelve at Vendel, Sweden (now in Stockholm, Historiska Museet). Diagonally symmetrical ribbons with added tails, limbs, and heads, in tendril-like fashion, move slowly across surfaces. Chip carving continues to impart a dramatic and luminous quality. A variant of the style displayed at Vendel, in which the ribbons are thinner and more nervously articulated and which employs considerable knotwork, appears toward the middle of the seventh century. It characterizes the animal decoration of the Germanic jewelry found in the boat burial at Sutton Hoo, East Anglia, including the remarkable Anglo-Saxon solid-gold belt buckle from

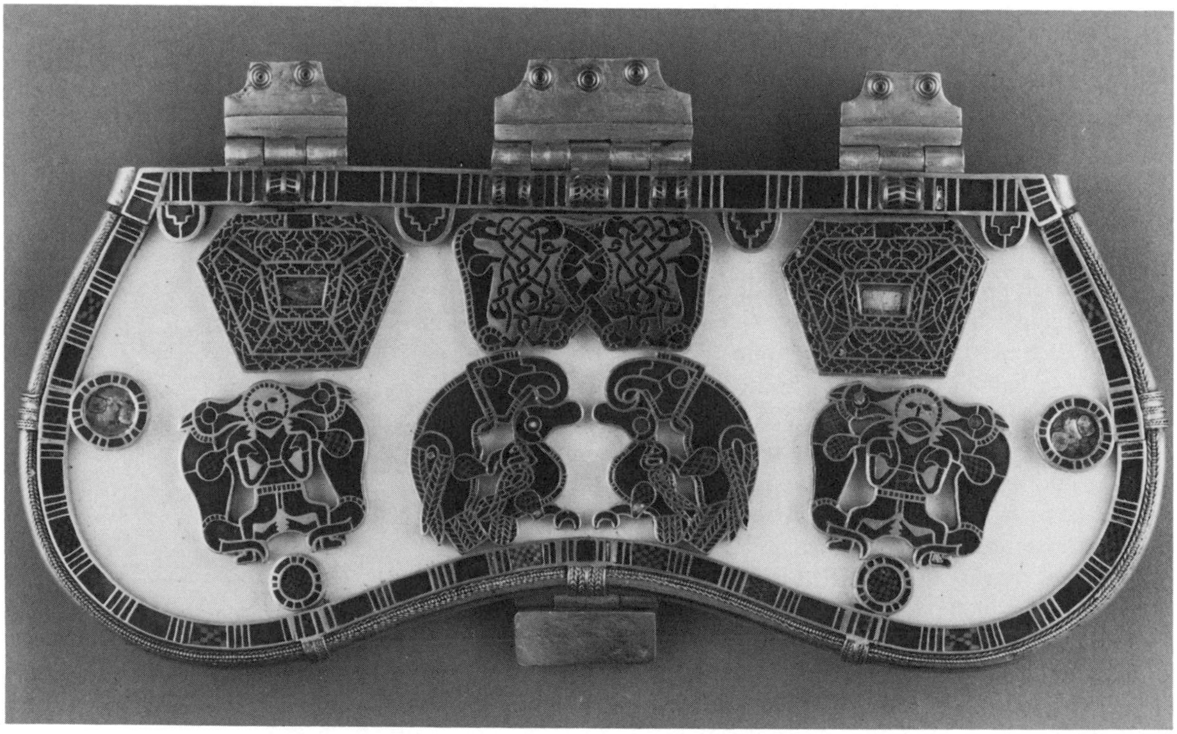

Fig. 3. Gold purse lid (restored) from Sutton Hoo, before 625. BY COURTESY OF THE TRUSTEES OF THE BRITISH MUSEUM, LONDON, 1939.10-10.2

MIGRATION PERIOD ART

about 625 (now in London, British Museum). Tiny circles and lines and dots of inlaid niello outline the ornament. Besides profile birds' heads, biting animal heads, and a tiny, complete animal framing the buckle, flat, interlaced, snakelike creatures swarm over its surface. These snakelike beasts and similar dragonlike animals are thought to be symbols of the dead. Appearing and disappearing in a seemingly endless ballet of movement, they are born and die and are resurrected—intermediaries between the world of the living and the nether regions.

At Sutton Hoo, Style II animal ornament is combined with cloisonné in such variety and with such vitality as to constitute a native Anglo-Saxon contribution to both the polychrome and the animal style. Nowhere is this more apparent than in the decoration of the great purse lid (*Fig.* 3). The white background is new; the border of twisted wire filigree, the seven decorated plaques inlaid with garnets and colored glass, and the four circular studs originally would have been attached to leather or ivory. In the central plaque of the upper row, complex interlacings of Style II animals are achieved by curving and enlarging garnets. This unusual technique of enlargement is found nowhere else in barbarian Europe.

On the outer pair of lower plaques of the Sutton Hoo purse is a representation of a man spreadeagled between rampant beasts. This "man between monsters" theme, a favorite of Scandinavian artists, introduces a not-inconsequential aspect of Germanic art, its interest in figural scenes and human representations. In the sixth century, mainly because of the impact of late antique and early Christian models, barbarian artists began to execute figural arrangements of outstanding value. Inspiration for the lancer on the famous Frankish gold-disk brooch of about 700 from Pliezhausen probably came from Mediterranean images of mounted saints, but the most striking effect achieved is that of extreme abstraction and stylization (*Fig.* 4). A fallen adversary who plunges his sword into the warrior's horse appears at the left. A war demon is seen at the right. Costume is Germanic; the curiously squat proportions of the figures, the emphasis on patternization, segmentation, and linear assonance recall the treatment of animal forms in Style II ornament.

A group of large carved stones from Gotland, Sweden, provides us with interesting examples of migration-era figure work. These picture stones display a wealth of episodic images difficult to decipher but undoubtedly based on the Nordic sagas. Lively

Fig. 4. Gold-disk brooch form Pliezhausen, *ca.* 700. WÜRTTEMBERGISCHES LANDESMUSEUM, STUTTGART

silhouettes, the figures stand in profile; they lack mass and are presented with no attempt at spatial recession. Scenes appear as horizontal bands read downward from the top. In a stone from Lärbro, dating from about 700, the iconography centers on the death of the hero and his funeral. At the top, the hero falls beneath his horse, a scene followed by the funeral procession, the hero now prone atop his horse. In the third zone the hero enters the harbor of the next world and finally, below, a great square-rigged ship sails toward Valhalla.

Christian art. Represented on the Gotland picture stones are ancient Nordic subjects, but elsewhere in the Germanic territories Christian iconography had become paramount. Through the early centuries of the migration period, one institution, the Christian church, emerged to fill the void left by the withered power and authority of the Roman state. Its order and cohesion, its supranational character, and above all its spiritual attraction made it the most influential medium for the preservation of what little remained of classical culture and the creation of a new medieval civilization. As conversion of the Germanic tribes of western Europe and Britain neared completion toward the end of the seventh century, the church became an increasingly important sponsor of works of art—of richly embellished liturgical objects and illuminated manuscripts produced in monastic workshops. Increasingly sensitive to direct Mediterranean influence, the visual arts record a slow but relentless disintegration of Germanic forms and motifs.

As might be expected, the barbarians of the south—the Lombards in Italy and Visigoths in Spain—responded most energetically to Christian styles, especially to the art of the dominant Byzantine culture, while more remote northern peoples reacted more slowly and with greater reluctance. Curious conjunctions of pagan Germanic and Christian Mediterranean forms appear. An example is the decoration on a Merovingian round gold fibula from Linon (Auvergne) of about 650 (now in Paris, Bibliothèque Nationale). Small garnets and Style II animals ornament the rays and aureole surrounding the central head of Christ framed by Alpha and Omega.

In Merovingian monastic scriptoria, illustrated books, icons, textiles, ivories, and metalwork imported from the older cultural centers—from Rome, Constantinople, Antioch, Alexandria, and the monasteries of Coptic Egypt—began to enlarge and enrich the vocabulary of Frankish artists. Thus in the Gelasian Sacramentary, a codex of about 750 from a scriptorium near Paris, the painter, though not eschewing Germanic figurative and decorative elements, displays neither the metallic precision nor the schematized animal ornament of Style II (*Fig. 5*). Rather we are presented with a style delighting in light, bright colors—red, green, and yellow—and rapid, sprightly, if somewhat coarse, drawing. Human figures appear occasionally in Merovingian books, but quadrupeds, birds, and especially fish based on Eastern Mediterranean examples are preferred as ornament—lively creatures used to construct large letters at the beginning of chapters.

Monastic workshops produced splendid liturgical objects—jeweled book covers, altar frontals, vessels, and reliquaries—more directly reflective of the tradition of pagan Germanic metalwork than manuscript illumination.

We may assume that by the late seventh century Germanic craftsmen trained in alien techniques of stonemasonry were participating in the erection of monumental buildings in the conquered territories. Except for those in Visigothic Spain, these structures, though often impressive, seem somewhat deficient in independent character. In Visigothic architecture we are made aware of a vision beginning to free itself from slavish imitation of Mediterranean models. Visigothic churches are relatively small but are characterized by a high level of craftsmanship,

Fig. 5. Cross, initial, and decorated letters from Gelasian Sacramentary, *ca.* 750. BIBLIOTECA APOSTOLICA, VAT. REG. LAT. 316, fol. 132

spatial complexity, and an abundance of sculptural decoration. Intricate, rectangular ground plans avoiding curves even for apses are the rule. For example, the church of S. Pedro de la Nave in Zamora has a plan of interlocking squares and rectangles. As interesting is its use of large, beautifully dressed ashlars, barrel vaulting, and relief sculpture. Carvings cover capitals, column bases, and friezes. The crossing of nave and transept is marked by four columns with heavy capitals carved with figural scenes, including two from the Old Testament—Daniel in the lion's den and the sacrifice of Abraham. These reliefs are quite shallow and lack true modeling; but traces of color suggest an original richness now lost. Capitals with figural subjects—historiated capitals—are usually considered the invention of the proto-Romanesque sculptors of the tenth and eleventh centuries. Their employment at S. Pedro de la Nave

MIGRATION PERIOD ART

underlines the originality of the Visigothic contribution to early medieval art and architecture.

HIBERNO-SAXON ART

In the British Isles, Germanic traditions fused with those of the Celts to engender the style known as Hiberno-Saxon. It was a style whose unique system of abstract ornamentation characterized the art of England up to the time of the Viking invasions and persisted in Ireland well into the Romanesque age.

The Celtic peoples of Britain had already been converted to Christianity when, in the fifth century, heathen Angles, Saxons, Jutes, and Frisians arrived and drove them into mountainous retreats in Wales and Cornwall. The Celts of Ireland, never conquered by the Romans, were not greatly troubled by the Germanic invaders settling in east and southeast England. Left alone, they created a Christian culture in advance of any in northwest Europe before the Carolingian period. With its dioceses, bishops, and priests, traditional Christianity proved antithetical to the simple tribal society of these Celtic-speaking people and was supplanted by monasticism. Born in Egypt in the third century, the fervently ascetic monastic movement took firm root in Ireland, so that by the sixth century Celtic monasteries were in a position to sponsor an extraordinary restoration of Latin learning and scholarship, and an art of extreme virtuosity, freedom, and verve.

Evangelization was the propelling force of Celtic Christianity; St. Columba was at the center of this impassioned missionary activity. Around 563 he brought Irish monasticism to Iona, a tiny island off the west coast of Scotland, the first of a congress of foundations from which Christianity was carried to the heathen Picts of Scotland. Columban monks came to Northumbria in 635 to found a monastery on the island of Lindisfarne. From there they converted the north of England. Rome had already begun the conversion of the Anglo-Saxons in the south with a mission to Kent in 577. Differing on important ecclesiastical and liturgical issues, the Irish and Roman churches clashed over the date of the celebration of Easter at the Synod of Whitby in 664. The Irish were defeated and withdrew from Lindisfarne to Iona. Anglo-Saxon England, brought under the firm control of the Roman church, was beguiled by the richness and authority of the Mediterranean culture introduced in its wake. Irish tastes and traditions, though sometimes slighted, were never ignored for long, however, and continued to have a profound effect on English culture well into the ninth century.

The Celts who brought Ireland to its preeminent intellectual and artistic position remain elusive. Their ancestors had learned ironworking by the eighth century B.C.—a technological advance that explains their dominance over a large part of central Europe. Ancient historians record their movements in Spain and Asia Minor, their sack of Rome in 390 B.C., and their attack on Delphi a century later. And we have an imperfect picture of their gradual retreat to the more remote corners of Europe, including Britain and Ireland, as the empire of Rome grew in power and size.

Archaeology has revealed La Tène in Switzerland as an important center of Celtic Iron Age culture. There, Celtic craftsmen subjected the classical motifs on luxury goods imported from distant Mediterranean lands to intense stylization and subordination to an art of swelling, serpentine curves. In Britain by the third century B.C. and in Ireland shortly afterward, this La Tène style of *S*-shaped and scroll forms, spirals, and pelta and triskele shapes found expression in ornamental metalwork of great beauty. These objects very often were enriched by glass decoration—glass pressed in a semiliquid state into shallow recessions to form champlevé enamel; and millefiori, sectioned rods of colored glass. Diluted by a flaccid Roman provincial art, the La Tène style in Britain began to weaken and disintegrate after 200; even in Ireland, for reasons difficult to fathom, the style fell into long decline but did not entirely disappear. When, in the sixth and seventh centuries, the church began to manifest an interest in elaborately ornamented altar vessels, reliquaries, and jewelry, the La Tène style was brilliantly revived.

The artistic heritage of La Tène metalworking dominated the arts in early Christian Ireland, and, indeed, even as other traditions were introduced, metalworking long remained the medium in which the most advanced and sophisticated ideas were formulated. Among the most important objects of Christian Celtic workmanship are the so-called hanging bowls, vessels based on a type used by the Romans and in the sixth century given a liturgical function by the church. Three Celtic hanging bowls were found in the ship burial at Sutton Hoo. Each employs rings for suspension, and each has several bronze plaques covered in champlevé and decorated with variants of traditional La Tène motifs. Tiny

MIGRATION PERIOD ART

stylized animal heads form nuclei from which swelling curves—spirals, pelta and trumpet shapes—emerge and are linked. Millefiori designs also appear on the plaques. With the champlevé, they effect a graceful, fluid conjunction of multicolored glass and miniature metalworking.

In order to spread the word of God, the Irish missionaries needed books—bibles, gospels, psalters. The introduction of these books from foreign centers and their transcription proved to be most decisive to the creation of the Hiberno-Saxon style. Almost from the first, even as they developed a script known as Celtic half-uncial, Irish artists began to embellish their texts. Though still tentative and rather crude, this system of calligraphic decoration can be seen in the late-sixth- to early-seventh-century Cathach, a psalter which traditionally is connected with St. Columba himself (now in Dublin, Royal Irish Academy). Initials do not stand apart from the body of the text as in classical books. Instead they are joined to the text by clusters of letters which follow and gradually diminish in size. This is accompanied by a concomitant simplification of the ornament introduced into and around the initials. The Cathach initials are still relatively severe. Hollow and elastic, they end in small spirals or sometimes in animal heads and are set off by red dots. The Cathach scribe has borrowed his spirals and scrolls from Celtic enamels and preserved something of the excitation, the sense of endless movement, of the metalworkers' La Tène motifs. But it is his revolutionary approach to book decoration—his use of progressively diminishing decorated initials—that will have the most lasting impact on the evolution of early medieval manuscript illumination. (See "Celtic Art" for illustration.)

Following the creation of the Cathach of St. Columba, book decoration became progressively more varied and complex. Carpet pages—folios completely given over to ornament—were inserted. The repertoire of ornamental motifs expanded to include not only the curvilinear designs directly appropriated from Celtic metalwork, but also interlace, geometric patterns, and elaborate zoomorphic compositions. Inspiration for the carpet pages, the interlace patterns, and various of the geometric motifs came from the eastern Mediterranean, probably from Coptic Egypt. Animal ornament, a minor aspect of Celtic metalwork, suddenly appeared in new and elaborate form, undoubtedly an Anglo-Saxon contribution to the nascent Hiberno-Saxon style.

The first definitive statement of this new style is made by the scribe-artist of the oldest of the complete Gospelbooks from the British Isles, the Book of Durrow. Written at a Columban monastery affiliated with Iona (or perhaps written at Iona itself) during the second half of the seventh century, the manuscript is a large, luxury codex undoubtedly intended for altar or lectern. Each gospel opens with a symbol of its Evangelist framed at the center of the page. Two pages follow, a carpet page at the left facing an ornamented text page with one or two large and ornate capitals accompanied by smaller, still elaborate letter groups, themselves followed by one or more lines of embellished script, and finally the undecorated text—an amplification of the system of decorative embellishment seen in the Cathach of St. Columba.

Folio 3v at the opening of the book is one of the most impressive of the carpet pages. (See "Durrow, Book of" for illustration.) Within a heavy interlace border is a La Tène pattern of two large and four smaller spiral-filled medallions linked by trumpet forms. The page has the hard, sharply outlined, and brightly colored aspect of enamel work; metalwork inspiration is equally apparent in the ornamentation of folio 192v, the carpet page introducing St. John's Gospel (*Fig.* 6). Here, surrounding a medallion of pure knotwork, are six rectangular compartments filled with interlaced animals given extended biting jaws—variants of Salin's Style II beasts, and similar to those in the frame of an Anglo-Saxon gold-enameled clasp from Sutton Hoo and those on the Sutton Hoo purse lid. Found only on folio 192v, the biting beast chains suggest recent admission. Indeed, the Celtic, Germanic, and Mediterranean ornamental elements employed in the Durrow codex, which combine to shape the character of the Hiberno-Saxon style, are still relatively isolated from one another. Broadly drawn, often confined to separate pages, the various Durrow ornamental patterns stand at the beginning of the mature phase of Hiberno-Saxon illumination. They are quickly superseded by the composite, microscopic, incredibly dynamic designs we have come to think of as most perfectly embodying the spirit of Hiberno-Saxon art.

Unlike the Book of Durrow, the Lindisfarne Gospels has a certain provenance and date. Its colophon informs us that it was written by Eadfrid when bishop of Lindisfarne, that is, between 698 and 721. Judiciously building upon the Durrow ornamental system, Eadfrid introduced new motifs (the bird and dog replace the Style II creatures of the earlier codex), richer and far more subtle pigments includ-

MIGRATION PERIOD ART

Fig. 6. Carpet page from the Book of Durrow, *ca.* 675. COURTESY OF THE BOARD OF TRINITY COLLEGE, DUBLIN, MS A.4.5 (57), fol. 192v

ing blue and purple, and a minuteness of touch and perfection of detail unknown before. The carpet page beginning the Gospel of Matthew is an excellent example of this new virtuosity (*Fig.* 7). A cross composed of central circle and five campanular protrusions dominates the composition. Circular millefiori studs reproduced at the center of the cross units exemplify the continuing and fundamental debt owed to metalwork techniques and motifs. Interlacings of birds and quadrupeds create suave symmetrical patterns within and surrounding the cross. With its rigid and powerful vertical and horizontal accents and emphatic compartmentalization, the structure of the cross carpet page establishes a sense of balance and order contrasting with and thereby intensifying the savage energy of the strange creatures swarming within.

For all their fantastic vivacity, the patterns formed by the animals of the Lindisfarne Gospels cross carpet page seem to depend on the example of late antique foliate scrolls. Such influence is emblematic of the involvement of the Roman church in Northumbria following its victory at the Synod of Whitby. The reorganization of the church in England after 669 by such men as the Greek Theodore of Tarsus (St. Theodore of Canterbury) and the North African Hadrian of Niridanum had profound consequences, not the least of which was the encouragement of the Anglo-Saxon nobleman Benedict Biscop to found the monasteries of Wearmouth (674) and Jarrow (682). Benedict made a number of trips to Rome to secure books and works of art.

The language of the late Roman pictorial world, suddenly made available to Hiberno-Saxon artists in Northumbria and obliquely registered in the ornamental patterns of the Lindisfarne Gospels, is directly recorded in that manuscript's Evangelist portraits, for the latter are closely based on sixth-century Italo-Greek prototypes. Without vitiating the humanistic essence of the original, Eadfrid sympathetically translated its classical, seminaturalistic forms into his own flatter, more linear and metallic style. This we know from a comparison between the Lindisfarne Matthew portrait (see "Lindisfarne Gospels") and the portrait of Ezra in the Codex Amiatinus, a Bible written at Jarrow in the late seventh or early eighth century (before 716) and dependent on the same imported model. Though a native Anglo-Saxon, the Amiatinus painter was far less submissive to the Hiberno-Saxon koine than Eadfrid. He reproduced his Italian picture page with considerable fidelity, respecting its use of antique modeling, subtle colors, and gold ground, and even duplicating the cast shadow of the ink bottle in the original.

Mediterranean influence is as strongly marked in a group of stone crosses of Northumbrian workmanship and late-seventh- and eighth-century date. The most classical of these monuments is the cross now standing in the church of Ruthwell in Dumfriesshire, Scotland. More than seventeen feet (five meters) high and lacking any trace of Hiberno-Saxon decoration, it features a complex program of Christian subjects and decorative vine scrolls inhabited by birds and beasts, all within panels and carved in high relief.

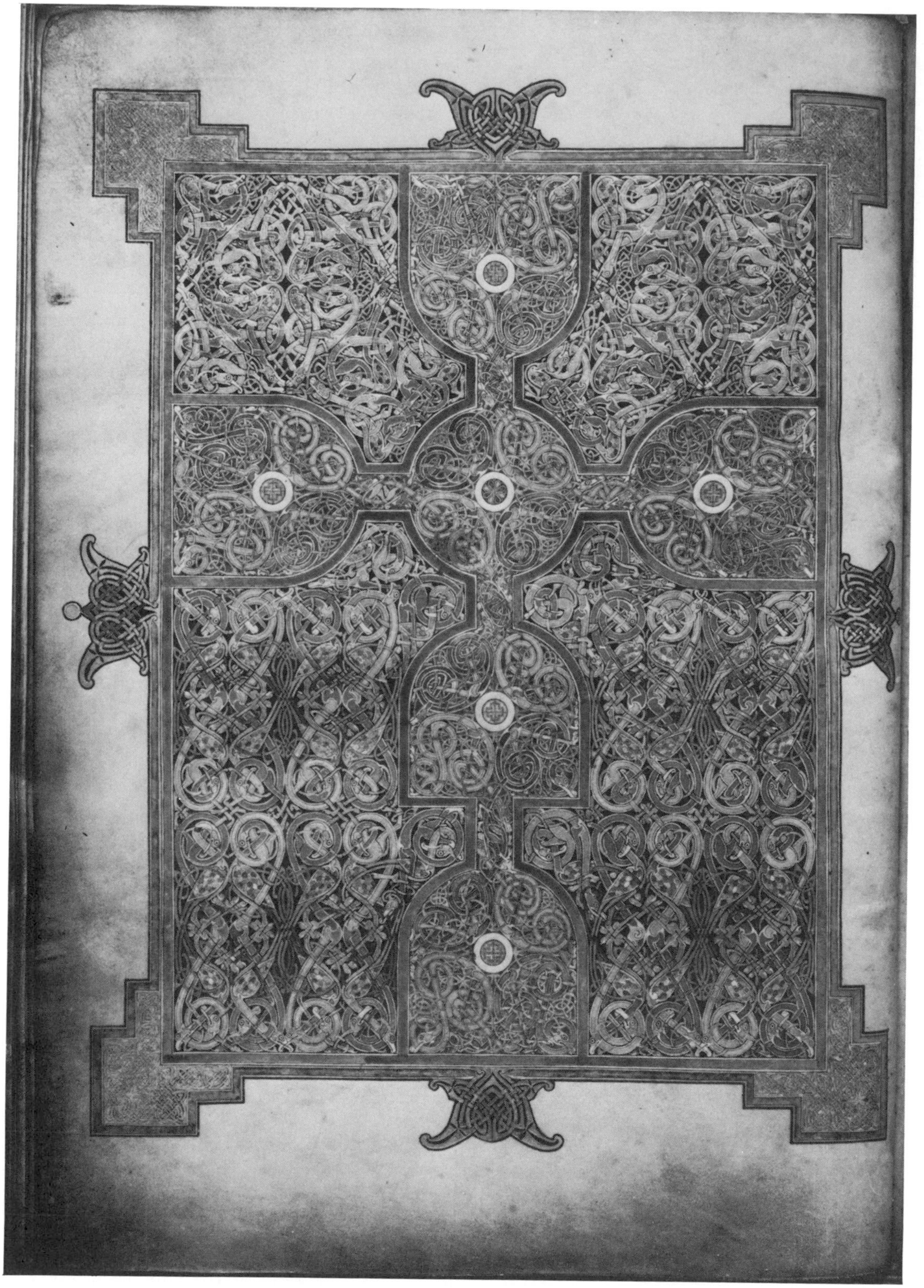

Fig. 7. Cross carpet page from the Lindisfarne Gospels, early 8th century. BY COURTESY OF THE TRUSTEES OF THE BRITISH MUSEUM, LONDON, COTTON MS NERO D. IV, fol. 26v

The Northumbrian assimilation of classical modes made a lasting impression on the treatment of the human figure by Hiberno-Saxon artists but did not inhibit their genius for decorative inventiveness. If anything, there was an eighth-century resurgence of interest in virtuoso feats of microscopic perfection and delicacy. Ancient Celtic metalworking techniques achieved unmatched levels of miniaturization and variety; and new techniques were introduced, including gold filigree, to impart a scintillation and sparkle to surfaces already incredibly elaborate. Among the most beautiful examples of Hiberno-Saxon metalwork are a series of large and profusely ornamented ring (penannular) brooches, none more magnificent than the Tara Brooch (now in Dublin, National Museum), a work in gilded bronze with added details in amber, gold, silver, and copper (see "Celtic Art"). Its richly varied ornamentation includes studs of blue and red, cast reptile and birds' heads, gold filigree animals, interlace and key patterns, confronted human masks of dark glass with enigmatic Celtic faces, bands of inset amber, and heavy panels of chip-carved trumpet spirals in niello. The baroque exuberance of all this decoration, the crowding of detail and movement into the tiniest areas, the application of a variety of goldwork techniques, all testify to the religious intensity Hiberno-Saxon artists were able to bring to the creation of pure ornament.

In quality, the Tara Brooch is rivaled, perhaps surpassed, only by the Ardagh Chalice (see "Celtic Art"). Probably a Holy Communion vessel (the names of the apostles are engraved on the bowl), it draws together almost all the skills available to the eighth-century metalworker. Ornament sumptuously applied in a wide range of materials and techniques, including chip carving, filigree, cloisonné, and rock crystal, is restricted to certain areas—the handles, a band below the rim of the cup, the stem, a band around the base, and a section of the underside of the base. Filled with scrolls, spirals, pure interlace, frets, and animal interlace, these panels and bands are sensitively contrasted with the simple, unbroken outlines of the chalice and its broad areas of beaten silver. The effect of this juxtaposition, although considerably more austere than that made by the Tara Brooch, is no less compelling and intense.

This wonderfully skillful metalwork style is reflected in the development of eighth-century stone sculpture. For many centuries the Irish had set up wooden crosses in their monastic enclosures. These were now translated into stone and covered with the intricate patterns of the goldsmith. One such cross, at Ahenny, County Tipperary, Ireland, stands on a pyramidal base covered with figural relief and has an oblong shaft and arms and a large open ring at the crossing. It exhibits the fret patterns, trumpet spirals, and closely woven interlace of contemporary jewelry. Even rivet-head bosses and the wire twists marking metalwork junctions are faithfully replicated.

With the ninth century, the great, creative age of Hiberno-Saxon art approaches its end. The disruptions of the Viking raids, followed by a growing reliance on continental styles, contributed to the weakening of the rather fragile fabric of conventions necessary to sustain the uncompromisingly nonrepresentational art of Ireland and north England. The Vikings first sacked Lindisfarne, then turned their attention to the Hebrides. Iona was assaulted. The subsequent flight of its abbot and large party of monks in 807 may directly bear on the history of the most richly decorated of Hiberno-Saxon manuscripts, the Book of Kells. There is much to recommend the thesis that the codex, perhaps begun during the late eighth century on Iona, was thence carried to Kells in Ireland by the departing Iona clergy, there to receive further decoration, but never to be completed. Whatever may be the truth of its origin, this large and sumptuous Gospelbook presents an endless and fantastic display of the techniques and motifs evolved and elaborated during the eighth century. Several painters were employed to execute the incredible number of animal, foliate, and geometric designs interspersed in the text, large and small initials freely and ingeniously detailed, portraits of the Evangelists, and full-page figural subjects. Everywhere detail is piled upon detail with a joyousness and charm especially poignant in a work which stands at the end of a glorious artistic tradition.

Writing was regarded with mystical reverence by the Irish church. This attitude, expressed in the increasing enlargement and embellishment of the initials opening important texts, is visually presented most dramatically in a page bearing Xρ (the Greek initials for Christ) introducing the genealogy of Matthew in the Book of Kells (*Fig.* 8). Indeed, Hiberno-Saxon precedent hardly prepares the reader for its splendor, its mazelike intricacy and chimerical inventiveness. At first glance, the page seems a wild conglomeration of varieties of ornament, but closer inspection reveals its careful balance: the

Fig. 8. Chi-rho page from the Book of Kells, *ca.* 900. COURTESY OF THE BOARD OF TRINITY COLLEGE, DUBLIN, MS A.I.6 (58), fol. 34

Fig. 9. Virgin and Child. Miniature from the Book of Kells. COURTESY OF THE BOARD OF TRINITY COLLEGE, DUBLIN, MS A.I.6 (58), fol. 7v

shape of the great swinging *X* at the top together with the inverted *L*-shape below creates a certain sense of order, and even greater unity is achieved by the regular distribution of endless patterns over the surface. Fantastic animals, interlaced ribbons, spirals and other geometric designs, and foliate forms—many smaller than the eye can see without the aid of magnification—compel a nervous shifting of glance from place to place. Here and there human figures and animals are depicted with humor and fidelity to nature, yet nothing is allowed to interrupt the ceaseless movement, the electric ebb and flow capable of charging the smallest area, the tiniest detail, with vibrant energy.

The picture of the Virgin and Child is the first of the full-page illustrations in the Book of Kells (*Fig.* 9). Based on an early Christian model in which the Greco-Roman tradition, though diluted, retains some force, it is anything but classical in appearance. The intense training of the painter in the abstract, linear style of the Hiberno-Saxon scriptoria, with its disregard for natural appearance, enabled him to convert the enthroned Virgin and Child and the angels of his prototype into bizarre yet sophisticated patterns. Faces, draperies, and throne are turned into ornamental shapes without a trace of highlighting or shadowing. Everything seems to be made of some flat metallic substance—a substance embracing even the birds in the heavy frame and the interlaced men in the half circles intruded into the central field. The effect is similar to that of openwork ornament in bronze or iron seen against a neutral ground. Successive early medieval styles would be marked by the tension between the two traditions here conjoined, that of the northern barbarians with their passionate love of complicated and rhythmic abstract patterns, and that of the Christian Mediterranean world with its legacy of antique materialism.

On the edge of reality, or perhaps parallel to it, the art of the Hiberno-Saxon golden age conjured up

MIGRATION PERIOD ART

a world of marvelous and incredible creatures, of strange plants and exquisite geometric designs, a world animated by its own magical sense of genesis and maturation. It is a place where things are rarely what they seem, where all is extension, accretion, metamorphosis. Paradoxically, the church employed this obsessive and savage art to express the holiness of the Christian message. Intuitively, perhaps, it responded to the spell of magical incantation and otherworldly association clinging to ornamental patterns that many centuries earlier, and even into Christian times, possessed symbolic and ritualistic meaning. In any event, there can be no doubt that Hiberno-Saxon art achieved its greatest triumph and made its most lasting contributions when, brought into the monastic scriptorium, it shaped itself to the form and substance of the Christian Gospelbook, the bearer of the word of God. Words and letters became supports for mysterious, exquisitely beautiful veils of ornament. This idea of text embellishment must have represented to the Hiberno-Saxon artist everything grand, splendid, and sacred. Its evocative power was not lost on the manuscript illuminators of the Middle Ages.

BIBLIOGRAPHY

General. Nils Åberg, *The Occident and the Orient in the Art of the Seventh Century,* 3 vols. in 1 (1943–1947); Philip Dixon, *Barbarian Europe* (1976); André Grabar and Carl Nordenfalk, *Early Medieval Painting from the Fourth to the Eleventh Century* (1957); Jean Hubert *et al., Europe of the Invasions,* Stuart Gilbert and James Emmons, trans. (1969); Elias A. Lowe, *Codices latini antiquiores,* 11 vols. and supplement (1934–1971); David Talbot Rice, ed.,*The Dawn of European Civilization* (1965); Helmut Roth, *Kunst der Völkerwanderungszeit* (1979); David M. Wilson, ed., *The Northern World* (1980); E. H. Zimmermann, *Vorkarolingische Miniaturen,* 5 vols. (1916–1918).

Migration art. Peter Anker, *The Art of Scandinavia,* I (1970); Julius Baum, *La sculpture figurale en Europe à l'époque mérovingienne* (1937); Friedrich Behn, *Römertum und Völkerwanderung* (1963); Hans-Joachim Diesner, *Die Völkerwanderung* (1976); Günther Haseloff, "Die germanische Tierstil," in *Atti del convegno internazionale sul tema: La civiltà dei Langobardi in Europa* (1974), and *Die germanische Tierornamentik der Völkerwanderungszeit,* 3 vols. (1981); Wilhelm Holmqvist, *Germanic Art During the First Millennium A.D.* (1955); Gyula László, *The Art of the Migration Period* (1974); Geneviève Aliette Maillé, *Les cryptes de Jouarre* (1971), and *Les manuscrits à peintures en France du VIIe au XIIe siècle,* 2nd rev. ed. (1954); Lawrence Nees, *From Justinian to Charlemagne, European Art, 565–787: An Annotated Bibliography* (1985); Eric Graf Oxenstierna, *The World of the Norsemen* (1967); Pedro de Palol Salellas, *Early Medieval Art in Spain* (1966); Marvin C. Ross, *Arts of the Migration Period in the Walters Art Gallery* (1961); Bernhard Salin, *Die altgermanische Thierornamentik,* 2nd ed. (1935); Édouard Salin, *La civilization mérovingienne d'après les sépultures, les textes, et le laboratoire,* 4 vols. (1949–1959).

Hiberno-Saxon art. Jonathan J. G. Alexander, *Insular Manuscripts: Sixth to the Ninth Century* (1978); Christopher F. Battiscombe, ed., *The Relics of Saint Cuthbert* (1956); Rupert L. S. Bruce-Mitford, "Anglo-Saxon and Irish Art," in *Encyclopedia of World Art,* I (1959); Rosemary J. Cramp, *Early Northumbrian Sculpture* (1965); Liam De Paor and Máire De Paor, *Early Christian Ireland* (1958); *Evangeliorum quattuor Codex cenannensis* (Book of Kells), I and II: facsimile, III: text by Ernest H. Alton *et al.* (1950–1951); *Evangeliorum quattuor Codex durmachensis* (Book of Durrow), I: facsimile, II: text by A. A. Luce *et al.* (1960); *Evangeliorum quattuor Codex lindisfarnensis* (Lindisfarne Gospels), I: facsimile, II: text by T. D. Kendrick *et al.* (1956–1960); A. M. Friend, Jr., "The Canon Tables of the Book of Kells," in *Medieval Studies in Memory of A. Kingsley Porter,* Wilhelm R. W. Koehler, ed., 2 vols. (1939); Françoise Henry, "Les débuts de la miniature irlandaise," in *Gazette des beaux arts,* **37** (1950), *Irish High Crosses* (1964), and *Irish Art,* 3 vols. (1965–1970); Walter Horn, "On the Origins of the Medieval Cloister," in *Gesta,* **12** (1973); *Kolloquium über frühmittelalterliche Skulptur,* 2 vols. (1969–1970); Lloyd Laing, *The Archaeology of Late Celtic Britain and Ireland* (1975); Harold G. Leask, *Irish Churches and Monastic Buildings,* I (1955); Carl Nordenfalk, "Before the Book of Durrow," in *Acta archaeologica,* **18** (1947), "An Illustrated Diatessaron," in *Art Bulletin,* **50** (1968), "The Diatessaron Miniatures Once More," in *Art Bulletin,* **55** (1973), and *Celtic Painting and Anglo-Saxon Painting* (1977); Meyer Schapiro, "The Religious Meaning of the Ruthwell Cross," in *Art Bulletin,* **26** (1944), and with his seminar, "The Miniatures of the Florence Diatessaron," in *Art Bulletin,* **55** (1973); George Speake, *Anglo-Saxon Animal Art and Its Germanic Background* (1980); Harold M. Taylor and J. Taylor, *Anglo-Saxon Architecture,* 2 vols. (1965); Charles Thomas, *The Early Christian Archaeology of North Britain* (1971); *Treasures of Early Irish Art: 1500 B.C. to 1500 A.D.* (Exhibition catalogue, Metropolitan Museum of Art, 1977); Otto K. Werckmeister, *Irisch-northumbrische Buchmalerei des 8. Jahrhunderts und monastische Spiritualität* (1967); Martin Werner, "The *Madonna and Child* Miniature in the Book of Kells," in *Art Bulletin,* **54** (1972), and *Insular Art: An Annotated Bibliography* (1984); David M. Wilson, ed., *Archaeology of Anglo-Saxon England* (1976); David H. Wright, *The Vespasian Psalter* (1967).

MARTIN WERNER

[See also **Anglo-Saxon Art; Animal Style; Barbarians, Invasions of; Bede; Benedict Biscop, St.; Bible; Carpet Page;**

Celtic Art; Chip Carving; Columba, St.; Durrow, Book of; Evangeliary; Fibula; Gospelbook; Hanging Bowl; Initials, Decorated and Historiated; Kells, Book of; Lindisfarne Gospels (with frontispiece); Manuscript Illumination; Manuscripts, Celtic Liturgical; Metalworkers; Monasticism; Parthians; Pre-Romanesque Art; Psalter; Romanesque Art; Sarmatians; Sutton Hoo; Theodore of Canterbury, St.; Viking Art; Vikings; Whitby, Synod of.]

MIGRATION PERIOD. See **Barbarians, Invasions of.**

MIḤRĀB. In conventional Islamic usage the word *miḥrāb* signifies a prayer niche that indicates the direction of prayer. The exact meaning of the word is not quite clear. It admits of several parallel meanings not all of which are relevant to the context of the mosque. A clue to the original significance of the *miḥrāb* as a feature of mosques is supplied by its location when first introduced into the Mosque of Medina in 709–710. There the *miḥrāb* was placed asymmetrically in the south (qibla) wall, on an axis with the place where the Prophet used to stand while leading the prayer. It may be suggested then that its purpose was to symbolize the place of the Prophet as the first imam (leader of prayer). Textual evidence supports such an explanation. Al-Nawāwī and al-Zarkhashī, for instance, explain the *miḥrāb* of the Prophet as the station where he used to stand while leading the prayer.

BIBLIOGRAPHY

Maḥmūd ᶜAli Ghūl, "Was the Ancient South Arabian *MDQNT the Islamic Miḥrāb?*" in *Bulletin of the School of Oriental and African Studies,* **25** (1962); Oleg Grabar, *The Formation of Islamic Art* (1973), 120–121; J. Horovitz, "Bemerkungen zur Geschichte und Terminologie des Islamischen Kultus," in *Der Islam,* **16** (1927); George C. Miles, "Miḥrāb and ᶜAnazah: A Study in Early Islamic Iconography," in *Archaeologia orientalia in Memoriam Ernest Herzfeld* (1952), 156–171.

GHAZI I. BISHEH

[See also **Abbasid Art and Architecture (with illustration); Islamic Art and Architecture (with illustration); Medina; Mosque; Qibla.**]

MIHRANIDS. See **Chosroids.**

MILAN. The medieval history of Milan begins with the barbarian invasions. In the summer of 452 the Huns sacked and plundered the city. The rebuilt cathedral was reconsecrated by Bishop Eusebius in October 453.

OSTROGOTHS AND LOMBARDS (489–774)

The Po Valley was invaded by the Ostrogoths in the summer of 489. Their king, Theodoric, secured ten years of peace under a stable government that aimed to reconcile Goths and Romans. This wise policy won the support of Cassiodorus and Boethius as well as the bishops Eustorgius II and Laurentius. At the beginning of the sixth century Milan was again a center of intellectual life. Its most notable figure was Ennodius.

A new period ensued with the Gothic War (535–553), which began when Justinian I, the Byzantine emperor, attempted to reconquer Italy. No sooner had Milan been occupied by the Byzantines in the summer of 538 than it fell to the Goths and Burgundians in March 539. Uraias ordered the massacre of all Milanese citizens; the women were given over to the Burgundians as spoils of war.

The victories of the Byzantine generals Belisarius and Narses ended Gothic domination of Italy. Byzantine rule (553–569) was marked by oppressive taxation. The region also suffered from the poverty and devastation caused by the war, incursions by the Franks and Alamanni, disease, and famine.

The Lombards entered the scene in the spring of 569, when, guided by King Alboin (*ca.* 565–572), they crossed the Julian Alps. In a few months they took over the principal cities of the Po Valley. Only Pavia (Ticinum) resisted, sustaining three years of siege before surrendering in 572. In Milan there was a massive exodus; the city notables took refuge in Genoa—which was still Byzantine—as did the majority of the clergy.

The Italy that had been unified in language, law, and government by the Romans was broken by the Lombard invasion, which came to a halt to the north of Lazio. The division, ethnic and linguistic, is still apparent today. Instead of Milan, the capital of the Roman era, the Lombards preferred to establish Pavia as the seat of their king, the royal court, and the military command.

The Lombard duchy experienced civil war; Alboin and Cleph (572–574) successively fell victim to conspiracy. After the death of Cleph the dukes did not elect a successor; each duke was king in his city. The next ten years (574–584) were ones of violence and disorder. Exploiting this situation, Byzantium, offering payment in gold, persuaded the Franks to cross the Alps and attack the Lombards. To confront the threat, the Lombard dukes elected as their king Authari (584–590), the son of Cleph, and to him they ceded half of their lands for the maintenance of the court. To administer these estates Authari appointed royal officers (gastaldi) who could also check the power of the dukes. The royal seat at Pavia became the center of the administrative organization of the Lombard kingdom.

At this time the Lombards were mostly pagan, and those who had been baptized were Arians. In order to gain an alliance with the Bavarians, however, Authari took for his wife a Catholic, Theodolinda, the daughter of Garibald, duke of Bavaria. Pope Gregory I the Great wrote to his "daughter" Theodolinda, and through her sought to render the Lombard government less ferocious. When King Rothari (636–652) conquered Genoa and the rest of Liguria, the bishop of the Milanese, Giovanni Bono, restored his seat to Milan.

The first written law of the Lombards, the *Edictum Rotharis regis* (643), published in 388 chapters, was a sign of gradual civilization. King Aripert I (653–661), a Catholic of Bavarian origin, favored the conversion of the Lombards to Catholicism and abolished Arianism as the official sect. During the seventh century the Catholics maintained one bishop and the Arians another in the Lombard cities. King Cunicpert (688–700) called a synod to Pavia in 698 that put an end to a schism and established the unity of the Catholic faith in Lombardy.

During the reign of King Liutprand (712–744), Milan was restored to new life; after centuries of silence, a written record of the life of the city returned in the form of the seventy-two lines of the *Versum de Mediolano ciuitate,* written between 738 and 744 and including an account of a Lombard expedition to Provence (739) to help Charles Martel in his war against the Saracens. King Aistulf (749–756) took Ravenna in 751, overthrowing the Byzantine exarchate there.

When Aistulf sought to follow up this conquest by annexing the duchy of Rome and seizing the domains of the Roman church, Pope Stephen II made an alliance with the Carolingians. To defend Rome against the invasions of King Desiderius (757–774), Pope Adrian I asked Charlemagne for aid. Charlemagne and his army besieged Pavia for ten months, finally entering the city on 7 June 774. The Franks thus ended the reign of the Lombards in Italy, but the Lombards remained even though Franks entered into the nobility of the region. Pavia remained the administrative capital, but Milan regained the political preeminence it had held in the sixth century over the other northern cities. One sign of this preeminence is the conservation of the rite of St. Ambrose in Milan, while in all the other churches in his domains Charlemagne abolished the other rites and introduced the liturgical books of Rome. In 784 Archbishop Peter founded in Milan the Benedictine abbey of St. Ambrose next to the basilica of the same name, which he commenced to reconstruct. The Carolingian renaissance was political, economic, cultural, and religious. One of its foremost artistic monuments is the golden altar by Wolvinius (840–850) for the tomb of Ambrose.

EMPERORS AND ARCHBISHOPS (774–1277)

For the archbishops of Milan, the dissidence among Charlemagne's successors enabled them to assume a political function. For having assumed authority during the reign of King Bernard, Archbishop Anselm was exiled in 818, but Angilbert II (824–859) made peace between the emperor Louis I the Pious and his son Lothair (later Emperor Lothair I). Anspert (868–881) was named *missus,* that is, imperial representative for judicial questions. On the death of the emperor Charles the Bald (877), in a situation of political confusion, Anspert led the Italian nobles in resisting Pope John VIII, who wanted to make a Carolingian from France king of Italy. Not even papal excommunication could move the bishop to relent. In order to affirm the priority of Milan over Pavia, Anspert wrote a new biography of St. Ambrose; to this period also belong ambrosian miniature psalters. Anspert also provided for the restoration of the city's walls.

During the anarchy that followed the deposition of the emperor Charles the Fat (887), Milan was contested by Berengar of Friuli, Arnulf of Carinthia, and Guy and Lambert of Spoleto. Meanwhile the Hungarians made continual incursions into Lombardy. Castles of refuge were constructed in many places. Archbishop Manasse was given the authority to mint money in 949 by King Lothair. In 960 Archbishop Walpert went to Germany to seek the aid of Otto of Saxony, who journeyed to Italy in 961 and was crowned emperor at Rome in 962 as Otto I.

A major increase in population and economic activity in Milan characterized the Ottonian era. There was much new construction, both in the city and its surroundings, and ancient buildings were restored.

New donations of land were made by Otto to the archbishop. A pro-imperial party was able to secure the election of its candidates for the office of archbishop. In 979 an uprising drove Archbishop Landulf II from Milan; in return for support he distributed church lands as fiefs to his supporters, who became powerful feudatories known as the *capitanei.*

Emperor Henry II came to Italy in 1004, and the archbishop of Milan, Arnulf II, crowned him king of Italy at Pavia on 14 May. Following a revolt of the Pavians against the emperor and his soldiers, Henry moved to Milan. The tenure of the archbishop Aribert of Intimiano (1018–1045) saw the height of the political power of the archbishops. When the succession to Henry appeared uncertain and divisive, Aribert went to Germany and in the name of the nobles of Italy promised fealty to the German king Conrad II. Conrad arrived in Italy in 1026 and was crowned king of Italy by Aribert—not at Pavia but at Milan. During these years Pavia, Lodi, and Cremona had to recognize their dependence on Milan.

Complying with an invitation from Conrad, Aribert went to France in 1034 with an army to reconquer Burgundy for the emperor. In 1035 minor vassals (vavasors) revolted against him and the *capitanei,* asking for help from the emperor and describing the archbishop as responsible for anti-German violence. Aribert was able to avoid their attempts to arrest and return him to Milan. After besieging Milan, Conrad conceded to the vavasors the rights enjoyed by the nobility in the *constitutio de feudis* issued in 1037. Aribert raised a coalition of Milanese around the carroccio—the insignia of Lombardy—against the imperial decree. But when Conrad was succeeded by his son Henry III, Aribert went to Germany at Easter in 1040 to conclude a compromise peace.

The next act in Milan saw artisans and merchants, led by Lanzone de Corte, rebel against the nobility. In 1042 they forced Aribert and his noblemen friends to leave the city. The threat of imperial intervention persuaded the different classes to come to an agreement in 1044; and this was the prelude to the formation of the Milanese commune. During the tenure of the archbishop Guido of Velate (1045–1071) a furious civil war arose. Preachers of reform contemptuously called *patarini* ("ragpickers") by the nobles and high clergy denounced simony and demanded the restoration of the obligation of celibacy for bishops and priests. In December 1057 two Roman legates, Anselm of Baggio (later Pope Alexander II) and the monk Hildebrand (the future Pope Gregory VII), came to Milan and concluded a truce and condemnation of Guido's simony. The truce was broken in June 1066 when the deacon Ariald, head of the Patarines, was killed. Guido was forced to resign in 1067 and sold his office to Goffredo da Castiglione, who was confirmed by Emperor Henry IV. The Milanese, in protest against Goffredo, elected Attone as archbishop in 1072; his election was confirmed by the pope.

This episode marked the beginning of the investiture controversy between pope and emperor. Clashes and uproar continued in Milan; in June 1075 the murder of Erlembaldo, head of the Patarines, seemed to indicate the failure of their revolution. Henry appointed Tedaldo archbishop of Milan, replacing the discredited Goffredo, and in January 1076 declared Gregory deposed. Gregory responded by excommunicating Henry, who in January 1077 was forced to go to Canossa and ask absolution from Gregory. The Gregorian reform slowly prevailed in Milan. At the end of the eleventh century the polemics gave rise to various writings—the oldest books of Milanese history. While Arnulf of Milan contributed well-informed history for the period from 925 to 1077, Landulf Senior's abstruse books (covering 375–1085) pile up slander and fables.

A sign of the stability now reestablished was in 1100 the taking up of the cross by many thousands of Lombards, led by Archbishop Anselm of Bovisio (1097–1101), for the Holy Land. The challenge of the Patarines had put an end to the excessive power of the Milanese archbishops. Around 1097 the three classes of citizens—*capitane, vavasors,* and *borghesi* (the bourgeoisie)—joined together to form the *commune civitatis,* a group composed of their representatives which in turn elected consuls—that is, city administrators. Peace resulted in great economic growth, making necessary free passage along roads leading south and across the Alps. This led to war against Lodi (destroyed in 1111), Cremona, and Pavia. At the end of a long war, in 1127, Como also submitted to Milan.

Emperor Frederick I Barbarossa responded to the protests and laments of Lodi, Como, Pavia, and Cremona by intervening against Milan. The first siege invested Milan in August 1158; the city spent 50,000 silver marks to reinforce the walls but surrendered in a month and paid a large indemnity. The second siege ended in March 1162 with the surrender and destruction of the city.

The opposition of Pope Alexander III to Barbarossa favored the revival of Milan. In April 1167 the communes of Bergamo, Brescia, Cremona, and Mantua formed the Lombard League, and Milan quickly joined. The victory of the league at Legnano at the end of May 1176 overturned the imperial policy and affirmed the liberty of the communes, which was recognized in the Peace of Constance (1183). Milan set on a course of great enterprises, such as the Grand Canal (1179), which provided the countryside with irrigation from the waters of the Ticino River.

The Milanese factions were reborn at the end of the twelfth century; the minor nobility and wealthy merchants belonged to the *Motta,* while the lesser merchants and artisans composed the Credenza of St. Ambrose (1198). In order to bridge the conflict, the government was entrusted to an outsider, the podesta, in 1213, and customary law was codified. A second Lombard League was formed in 1226 over the protest of Emperor Frederick II. After being defeated at Cortenuova (1237), the Milanese entrusted their defense to Pagano della Torre, captain of the Credenza of St. Ambrose, in 1240.

The early thirteenth century was also characterized in Milan by the rise of the Cathars, who, like the Albigenses in France, became a subversive element. The podesta Oldrado da Trezzeno had several Cathars or heretics burned at the stake about 1233. The Dominican inquisitor Peter of Verona (St. Peter Martyr) was killed at Seveso, near Milan, on 6 April 1252. The struggle between the nobles and the people became more bitter, and the Peace of St. Ambrose concluded in 1258 soon collapsed. The archbishops Leon of Perego (1241–1257) and Ottone Visconti (1262–1295) supported the Ghibelline party, composed of nobles and conservatives, while the Della Torre family (Martino, Filippo, Napoleone) championed the Guelphs, made up of artisans and the bourgeoisie. For years the Della Torre kept Ottone Visconti from entering the city, until the Battle of Desio (20 January 1277).

THE VISCONTI AND SFORZA (1277–1535)

The outcome at Desio ushered in the rule of the Visconti (1277–1447) as *signori* (lords or despots). Ottone Visconti's good administration won the support of all classes and fostered industry and commerce. In 1287 Ottone's grandnephew Matteo I was made captain of the people and podesta (1287–1322). The rule of the Visconti was extended over Mortara, Novara, Vercelli, and Vigevano as well as Milan. In 1302 a revolt organized by the Della Torre forced Matteo into exile. In 1310 he returned in the entourage of Emperor Henry VII and was nominated imperial vicar. Matteo extended Milan's sway over Pavia, Piacenza, Tortona, Bergamo, Como, and Alessandria, while successfully defying excommunication by Pope John XXII. The Florentine Giovanni Villani described Matteo Visconti as "like a great king in Lombardy."

Matteo's son Galeazzo (1322–1328) succeeded him as imperial vicar by appointment of the emperor Louis IV of Bavaria. With Bavarian aid, Galeazzo defeated the papal offensive led by Cardinal Bertrand of Poggetto and supported by Philip of Valois (late King Philip VI of France). Azzo (1328–1339), Galeazzo's son, bought for 25,000 florins the title of imperial vicar and defeated an uprising by his cousin Lodrisio in the Battle of Parabiago (1339), famous because in that encounter the Visconti chroniclers saw an apparition of St. Ambrose on horseback. Among the many buildings constructed during Azzo's reign, the most notable was the bell tower of S. Gottard. During these years also the prosperous silk industry was established.

Azzo's successors were Luchino (1339–1349) and his brother, the archbishop Giovanni (1349–1354), who extended the rule of the Visconti over Bologna (1350) and Genoa (1353). He bought papal recognition from the Avignon pope Clement VI. He founded the Carthusian monastery of Garegnano and invited Petrarch to Milan; the poet made his residence there from 1353 to 1361.

The successors to Giovanni were his nephews. Galeazzo II (*d.* 1378) settled in Pavia, while Bernabò (1319–1385) resided in Milan. The son of Galeazzo II, Gian Galeazzo (1351–1402), in 1385 imprisoned Bernabò in the castle of Trezzo' Adda and became sole ruler of the Visconti domain, which was extended over Verona, Padua, Pisa, and Siena. Gian Galeazzo began the construction of the Milan Cathedral and the Carthusian monastery of Pavia, where he built a bridge over the Ticino and expanded the university. An able diplomat, he opposed outside interference in his realm. In 1389 he married his daughter Valentina to Louis, duke of Orléans. Valentina's son, Charles of Orléans, was to become father of King Louis XII of France, destined to claim rights over Milan. In payment to Emperor Wenceslas of 100,000 florins, Gian Galeazzo was given the title "duke" in 1395.

Civil war and anarchy were brought about by the division of the duchy among the three sons of Gian Galeazzo. Filippo Maria (1412–1447) succeeded in reconstructing the duchy in great part. Politically

MILAN

broadminded, Filippo Maria married in 1412 Beatrice, widow of condottiere Facino Cano, bringing him not only Cano's private army but also 400,000 gold ducats and about one-tenth of the city. In 1418 he had her executed on the pretext of adultery and in 1428 married Maria of Savoy. In 1427 the Visconti army was defeated at Maclodio by Venetian and Florentine troops. This last reckless enterprise forced Filippo Maria first to deal with and then to hire the condottiere Francesco Sforza, giving to him in marriage his natural daughter Bianca Maria.

When Filippo Maria died without heir in 1447, the Ambrosian Republic was proclaimed, but it lasted only three years. Bad administration and war with the Venetians obliged the Milanese to seek the aid of Sforza, who became the new ruler of Milan (1450–1466). The able Sforza made agreements with Venice, Florence, Rome, and Naples. A federation of Italian states, the Italian League, was proclaimed in March 1455; it secured forty years of peace.

Agriculture and the wool and iron industry, ruined in Filippo Maria's war, revived, as did commerce. Sforza used his means to build on a grand scale; among the works to benefit in this period were the Castello Sforzesco, the cathedral, the Maggiore hospital, and the Carthusian monastery of Pavia. Architects, painters, musicians, and poets flocked to his court. Sforza also summoned to Milan expert Florentine bankers like the Medici and Spini; they helped him extend Milanese commerce over the Alps with Germany and with Mediterranean lands by way of Genoa. The silk and arms industries brought considerable wealth to the city, and the brilliant court became one of the leading centers of Renaissance culture.

At the height of his fortune, Francesco Sforza died on 8 March 1466. His widow, Bianca Maria, succeeded in securing the succession for her young son Galeazzo Maria (1466–1476). Cicco Simonetta, the duchy's secretary-chancellor, continued in office. Although dissolute and despotic, Galeazzo Maria fostered agriculture by constructing canals and introducing the cultivation of rice. He was assassinated in December 1476 and succeeded by his young son Gian Galeazzo II Maria under the regency of his mother, Bona of Savoy, with the assistance of the faithful Cicco Simonetta.

In 1478 Genoa rebeled against Milan while the Swiss occupied the Ticino River valley. Ludovico il Moro, younger brother of Galeazzo Maria, asked Bona for permission to reenter Milan and free her from the influence of Simonetta. When Bona refused, Ludovico prepared to assault the city. In September 1479 Bona surrendered the regency in favor of her brother-in-law. On reaching power, Ludovico had Simonetta beheaded on the charge of treason, while Bona was relegated to the castle of Abbiategrasso.

The ambiguous policies pursued by Ludovico ended in being fatal to him and to Milan. In 1491 sumptuous ceremonies celebrated the marriage of the nearly forty-year-old Ludovico to the fifteen-year-old Beatrice d'Este. In 1494 he succeeded in obtaining a promise of recognition from Emperor Maximilian I as duke of Milan, a title that properly belonged to his nephew Gian Galeazzo II Maria, exiled in Pavia. Gian Galeazzo died in 1494, enabling Ludovico to assume the title. Ludovico, in order to forestall a claim to the duchy by the king of Naples, the father of Gian Galeazzo's widow, allied himself with King Charles VIII of France, who claimed the right to rule Naples. Charles entered Naples in February 1495, but the emperor, the pope, the king of Spain, and the Venetian league all joined against him. Ludovico first sided with the Venetians but then made peace with Charles.

On Charles's death in 1498, he was succeeded by Louis XII, grandson of Valentina Visconti. Louis proclaimed himself the legitimate duke of Milan and invaded Italy in the summer of 1499. Ludovico fled over the Alps. Louis sent to France many of Milan's art works and the entire Visconti-Sforza library of Pavia. Ludovico reoccupied Milan for two months in 1500, but he was defeated once and for all at Novara in April; imprisoned in France, he died in 1508. The twenty years of rule under Ludovico were splendid for building and reconstruction. He summoned to Milan Donato Bramante and Leonardo da Vinci. Industry was greatly developed. At his court lived about 100 artists, scientists, painters, historians, musicians, poets, and printers. Milan was then one of the richest cities of Italy. It exported tapestries, velvet, cotton and linen cloth, silk, wrought iron, gold and jewelry, and arms.

The first period of French domination (1500–1512) was followed by a brief return of the Sforza under Massimiliano, Ludovico's older son. Then in October 1515, by virtue of the victory of Francis I at Melegnano, Milan returned to the French. The interminable war between Francis and Emperor Charles V was fought especially in Lombardy; it ended with the Battle of Pavia in February 1525. The younger son of Ludovico, Francesco II Sforza, was restored as duke of Milan from 1529 to 1535, when

Charles V took possession of the dukedom. Milan remained Spanish for almost the next 200 years.

BIBLIOGRAPHY

The fullest account of the medieval history of Milan is the first eight volumes of the *Storia di Milano* by the Fondazione Treccani degli Alfieri per la storia de Milano, 17 vols. (1953–1966). Still useful is Giorgio Giulini, *Memorie spettanti alla storia, al governo ed alla descrizione della città e campagna di Milano, ne' secoli bassi,* 2nd ed., 7 vols. (1854–1857). A bibliography can be found in Alfredo Bosisio, *Storia di Milano* (1958).

Although there is no English-language scholarly history of Milan, the following works are useful for aspects of Milanese history in the medieval period: Jan T. Hallenbeck, *Pavia and Rome: The Lombard Monarchy and the Papacy in the Eighth Century* (1982); Gino Luzzatto, *An Economic History of Italy from the Fall of the Roman Empire to the Sixteenth Century,* Philip Jones, trans. (1961); Lauro Martines, *Power and Imagination: City-States in Renaissance Italy* (1979); Lucien Musset, *The Germanic Invasions,* Edward and Columba James, trans. (1975).

ANGELO PAREDI

[See also **Alexander II, Pope; Alexander V; Ambrose, St.; Ambrosian Chant; Angilbert of Milan; Arianism; Arms and Armor; Arnulf of Milan; Barbarians, Invasion of; Carroccio; Cathars; Commune; Condottieri; Constitutio de Feudis; Frederick I Barbarossa; Gothic, International Style; Gregory VII, Pope; Guelphs and Ghibellines; Heresies, Western European; Inquisition; Investiture and Investiture Controversy; Irrigation; Italy, Fourteenth and Fifteenth Centuries; Italy, Rise of Towns in; Lombard League; Lombardy, Kingdom of; Ostrogoths; Peter Damian, St.; Petrarch; Podestà; Roman Empire, Late; Sforza; Theodoric the Ostrogoth; Visconti; Wolvinus of Milan.**]

MILAN CATHEDRAL was founded in 1386 to replace the double cathedral of Sta. Tecla (fourth century) and Sta. Maria Maggiore (ninth century). Nave, aisles, choir, and crossing dome were erected by about 1500; but ornamentation and facade were not completed until the nineteenth century. Milan Cathedral is the best-known Lombard Gothic building, most famous for the well-recorded confrontations between local architects and French and German consultants over its design.

BIBLIOGRAPHY

James S. Ackerman, "'Ars sine scientia nihil est': Gothic Theory of Architecture at the Cathedral of Milan," in *The Art Bulletin,* 31 (1949); Giacomo C. Bascapè and Paolo Mezzanotte, *Il Duomo di Milano* (1965); Maria Luisa Gatti Perer, ed., *Congresso internazionale, Milano: Il Duomo di Milano,* 2 vols. (1969); Angiola Maria Romanini, *L'architettura gotica in Lombardia* (1964).

DALE KINNEY

[See also **Gothic Architecture** and illustration overleaf.]

MILANESE CHANT. See **Ambrosian Chant.**

MILANESE RITE, often called the Ambrosian rite from the legend of its foundation by St. Ambrose of Milan (bishop 374–397), is a distinct liturgical practice of the archdiocese of Milan with its own calendar and repertory of prayers, lections, and chant for both Mass and Office. The liturgy of Milan, originally a regional rite closely related to other early Italian liturgies and also sharing traits with the Gallican, Old Spanish, and even Greek liturgies of the early Middle Ages, has been able to preserve many of its distinctive features and avoid the eclipse that other regional rites suffered, its conservatism and the authority of its supposed origin effectively counterbalancing the cultic influence of the Romano-Frankish liturgy. Major periods in the development of the liturgy include its adoption of hymns and antiphons under Ambrose, the attempted curtailment of its geographic range by the Carolingians, and the sixteenth-century reform of the liturgy by St. Charles Borromeo with the first official publication of its books and its acknowledgment as an exception to post-Tridentine uniformity.

The earliest sources for the study of the Milanese liturgy, dating from late antiquity, include the *De sacramentis* and *De mysteriis* of Ambrose, liturgical references in the *Liber notitiae sanctorum Mediolani,* and the antiphons and hymns introduced by Ambrose. The earliest complete liturgical books are the Sacramentary of Bergamo (Bergamo, Biblioteca di S. Alessandro in Colonna) and the Sacramentary of Biasca (Milan, Biblioteca Ambrosiana, A 24 bis inf.) from the late ninth or early tenth century. Early Milanese sacramentaries often contain the Epistle and Gospel lections of the Mass, though the preceding Old Testament reading continued to be found in a separate book. The earliest books of the Office, called the *manuale,* are preserved in two Milanese manuscripts of the tenth and eleventh centuries (Bib-

Milan Cathedral, apse, with "populated" pinnacles, before 1500. PHOTO: WIM SWAAN

lioteca Ambrosiana, T 103 sup.; Biblioteca del Capitolo Metropolitano, 2,102), the latter edited by Marco Magistretti. The tenth-century pontifical of the Milanese church (Biblioteca del Capitolo Metropolitano, DI, 12) and the noteworthy book of Ordines compiled by the twelfth-century Milanese liturgist Beroldus have also been edited by Magistretti. The chant for both Mass and Office was contained in a single book: the first noted antiphonals of this type are two twelfth-century manuscripts, one for the winter season (London, British Library, MS Add. 34,209; reproduced in facsimile in *Paléographie musicale,* V–VI) and the other for the summer season (Bedero di Val Travaglia, Church of S. Vittore).

The Milanese liturgical year is structured, as is the Roman, around the central events of Christ's life: Christmas, with a period of preparation; Epiphany; Easter, preceded by a penitential period and followed by a time of celebration; Pentecost; and a series of Sundays between Pentecost and the start of the next cycle. In the medieval Milanese church, the arrangement of the year had several differences in detail that were based principally on the physical requirements of the semiannual alternation between the "winter" church, the cathedral itself, and the "summer" church, the nearby Church of St. Thecla: The manuscript sources of the rite are divided into a *pars hiemalis* and a *pars aestiva* to correspond. Several major feasts were provided with Masses for both churches; the transition from one church to the other at Easter and the dedication of the "winter" church on the third Sunday of October were marked by processions.

The first part of the liturgical year varies from the Roman in having six Sundays, instead of four, in Advent; the week before Christmas was dedicated to Mary; and St. James was included among the saints of Christmas week. Lent began on the Monday after Ash Wednesday, which was not observed in Milan. The Sundays of Lent before Palm Sunday were named for the Samaritan woman, Abraham the man born blind, and Lazarus, after the distinctive, non-Roman, Gospel readings from John on each Sunday. Scrutinies, or stages in the instruction of the catechumens, were conducted during Lent, leading to the teaching of the creed on the Saturday before Palm Sunday and baptism on Holy Saturday. In the seasons following Easter, special features included three Rogation Days before Pentecost and the naming of the Sundays following Pentecost: "I–XV after Pentecost," "I–V after the Beheading of John the Baptist," "I–II of October," "III of October" for the dedication of the major church (the day of changeover from the "summer" to the "winter" church), and "I–III after the dedication."

The structure of the Milanese Mass corresponds for the most part to that of the Roman Mass: A preliminary Mass of the catechumens with a series of instructive biblical readings is followed by the principal Mass with its offering of the gifts, their consecration, the Communion, and a closing. The Mass of the catechumens begins with an entrance antiphon *(ingressa),* the Gloria in Excelsis, the kyrie, the canticle *Benedictus,* and a proper collect. In the readings that follow, the Milanese liturgy retains the first lection from the Old Testament that was dropped in late antiquity for most feasts of the Roman church. The prophetic reading is followed by the *psalmellus;* an alleluia comes after the Epistle; and a homily, the *tractatus,* follows the Gospel. After a triple kyrie and an antiphon *post evangelium,* the Mass of the faithful began. In the modern rite the offertory begins with a procession bearing the gifts, during which the antiphon *post evangelium* is sung. A deacon says the invitation for a kiss of peace, now simply the phrase *Pacem habete,* but probably following the offertory, and the reading of the diptychs, or memorials, in the early Milanese church. After the gifts are brought to the altar, they are set down and covered by a cloth (the sindon) as the priest says the prayer over the sindon *(oratio super sindonem).* Then the choir sings the *offerenda* as two old men and two old women from the distinguished order of the *vecchioni* (twenty old men and women) bring forward the gifts of the congregation in a second procession. The offertory closes with the prayer over the gifts. The great variety of prefaces to the consecration, suppressed in the Tridentine Mass, have been preserved in the Milanese liturgy. During the consecration the medieval Milanese canon included a section beginning *Mandans quoque* after the Roman *Qui pridie.* For the Communion, the breaking of the bread and the mixing of the wine and water take place before the paternoster; the Communion itself is accompanied by the singing of the *transitorium.* Following the prayer after Communion, the Mass closes with a triple kyrie, a blessing, and the dismissal.

The distribution of psalms for matins differs from the Roman: In Milan, two weeks are required for the recitation of Psalms 1–108 instead of one. On Saturdays and Sundays, the canticles of Isaiah, Anna, and Jonah are sung in place of the psalms. Lauds consists of canticles, Psalms 148–150, and the Gloria in Excelsis. Vespers, in which the remaining psalms (109–147) are repeated in a weekly cycle, is distinguished especially by its opening chant, the *Lucernarium,* also found in the Gallican and Old Spanish liturgies.

BIBLIOGRAPHY

Sources. Beroldus, sive Ecclesiae Ambrosianae mediolanensis kalendarium et ordines, Marco Magistretti, ed. (1894, repr. 1968); Klaus Gamber, *Codices liturgici latini antiquiores* (1963, 2nd rev. ed., 1968), nos. 050–067, 501–595; Cyrille Vogel, *Introduction aux sources de l'histoire du culte chrétien au moyen âge,* 2nd ed. (1975), 230–231.

Studies. Robert Amiet, "La tradition manuscrite du missel ambrosien," in *Scriptorium,* **14** (1960); Edmund Bishop, *The Mozarabic and Ambrosian Rites* (1924); Pietro Borella, *Il rito ambrosiano* (1964); Archdale A. King, *Liturgies of the Past* (1959).

RICHARD GYUG

[See also **Ambrose, St.; Ambrosian Chant; Gallican Rite; Lectionary; Mass, Liturgy of the; Mozarabic Rite; Offertory; Sacramentary.**]

MILE, a measure of length in the British Isles. It had the following variations during the Middle Ages: 5,000 feet (about 1.52 km) or 1,000 paces of 5 feet each; 5,000 feet or 8 furlongs of 125 paces each, the pace containing 5 feet; 6,600 feet (about 2.01 km) or 10 furlongs of 220 feet each; and the Old English mile of 1,500 paces, the pace varying in size from one region to another. During the Tudor period it was standardized under Elizabeth I at 5,280 feet (1.609 km) or 1,760 yards, equal to 8 furlongs of 40 perches each, the perch containing 16.5 feet. Etymologically it was derived ultimately from Latin *milia* (miles), from *milia passuum* (thousands of paces), plural of *mille* (mile), from *mille passūs* (thousand paces), from *mille* (thousand).

RONALD EDWARD ZUPKO

[See also **Weights and Measures.**]

MILLEFIORI. See **Enamel.**

MILLEFLEURS. See **Tapestry, Millefleurs.**

MILLENNIALISM, CHRISTIAN. "Millennialism" can be used with either a limited or a more general meaning. In the limited sense millennialism is the belief originating in the Book of Revelation (Apocalypse), chapter 20, that Christ would come again to reign with the saints on earth for 1,000 years before the Last Judgment and the end of the world. This belief had currency among early Christians, but it was condemned by the Fathers of the fourth and fifth centuries and thereafter was never publicly espoused in all its details throughout the Middle Ages. But millennialism can also mean the more general belief in the imminent coming of sweeping change for the better brought about by supernatural forces. In this more general sense, millennialism was rarely expressed in Western Europe in the early Middle Ages. It emerged, however, as an important aspect of Western European thought in the twelfth century, and thereafter became a main theme of medieval European thought about the future. It is often believed that millennialism was a subversive doctrine, but in the High and later Middle Ages it served conservative more often than revolutionary purposes. The term "chiliasm" should be considered as an exact synonym for millennialism because it has the same etymology: millennialism comes from the Latin for one thousand years (*millenarium*) and chiliasm from the Greek for the same number of years (*chiliad*).

The entire New Testament is permeated with an eschatological message, but only Revelation (probably written about A.D. 90) foretells the coming of a future glorious kingdom *on earth.* Most of Revelation describes a series of woes, but ultimately Christ appears in chapter 19 to lead a heavenly host in victory against the army of the "beast." This victory accomplished, an angel descends in chapter 20 to bind Satan for a thousand years, during which time the souls of the elect are to reign with Christ on earth. The text of Revelation explicitly states that those who were martyred for Christ during the prior persecutions would reign with Him as kings, judges, and priests; it also seems to imply that those who had lived through the previous trials without having wavered in their faith would receive the same reward. The earthly millennium is then followed by a final struggle between the forces of Christ and of evil (Gog and Magog), a Last Judgment, and the descent of the heavenly Jerusalem.

Revelation's vision of an earthly millennium had its detractors and its supporters among Christians of the following few centuries. Some Christian fathers,

MILLENNIALISM, CHRISTIAN

most notably Origen in the third century, found the idea of an earthly millennium too materialistic to be acceptable, especially because Christ had said, "My Kingdom is not of this world" and "The Kingdom of God is within you." Others, such as Irenaeus (second century) and Lactantius (fourth century), accepted the idea and elaborated on it. According to Lactantius, during the time of the millennial kingdom children would play with serpents, rocky mountains would drip with honey, and streams and rivers would flow with wine and milk.

After the conversion of Constantine, millennialism increasingly fell into disrepute among Christian theologians. Not only had the antimaterialist strain of Christianity gained ground, but apparently the triumph of Christianity in the Roman Empire altered the views of Christian spokesmen about the advisability of promising a better earthly future. As long as Christianity was a proscribed minority faith, the promise of an earthly millennium might have inspired steadfastness in the face of persecution, but once Christianity prevailed and became inseparable from Rome there could be no reason for ecclesiastical authorities to say that a better earthly condition loomed in the near future.

Accordingly, after the time of Constantine a growing number of attempts were made to discredit a literal reading of chapter 20 of Revelation. One approach was to deny the canonicity of Revelation altogether, but this failed because the assumption that Revelation's author was John the Evangelist had become too deeply entrenched to be uprooted. Another approach, that of Constantine's panegyrist, Eusebius, was to refer Revelation's millennium to the present instead of to the future, and make Constantine stand for the reigning Christ. But this extreme of emperor worship was not widely accepted.

Ultimately the solution that triumphed in the medieval West was that put forth by St. Augustine (*d.* 430) in the *City of God* (XX, 7–9). Augustine sharply rejected the view that there would be a coming earthly kingdom of "material feasts." Instead he presented a figurative interpretation that referred the millennial kingdom to the present. Unlike Eusebius, however, Augustine did not make this a political kingdom. Rather, he said that the events of Revelation 20 referred to the "resurrection" of souls that had been taking place since Christ's resurrection by means of faith and baptism. Thus, those who were saved by faith and baptism were already reigning with Christ on earth in the Church, or as Augustine summed up: "Therefore the Church at this moment is the Kingdom of Christ and the Kingdom of Heaven." Furthermore, not only would there not be an earthly millennial future, but there would be no significant earthly progress before the Last Judgment of any sort.

Since Augustine was joined in his rejection of literal millennialism by other influential Latin fathers, the combined result was a cessation of fully literal readings of Revelation 20 throughout the Middle Ages. Moreover, Augustine's position that the last really significant events in world history before the Last Judgment (that is, the Incarnation and Resurrection) had already transpired became so dominant in Western Europe in the early Middle Ages that there were hardly any recorded expressions of hope for any better earthly future at all. Nonetheless, two traditions did emerge from the early Middle Ages to provide the bases for the developed millennialism of the twelfth century. These may be labeled "political" and "theological" millennialism, or the hope for a future "conquering hero" and the hope for a future "refreshment of the saints."

The political or conquering hero theme grew out of late Roman and Byzantine messianic imperialism. In the *Tiburtine Sibyl* and the *Revelations* of Pseudo-Methodius, originally written in the fourth and seventh centuries respectively (in both cases, without any knowledge of St. Augustine's strictures about the future), a last great Roman emperor would rally Christianity and inaugurate a wondrous time of happiness and plenty before the reign of Antichrist and the end of the world. Both of these texts were certainly millennarian in the general sense, but they were delayed in becoming known to the Latin-speaking West. The *Tiburtine Sibyl* was not known in the West until the middle of the eleventh century, and although the *Revelations* of Pseudo-Methodius was translated into Latin in eighth-century Gaul, the Latin text did not circulate very widely until the twelfth century. The tenth-century West Frankish monk Adso of Montier-en-Der was the only early medieval Westerner known to have expressed "conquering hero" millennialism. (It is uncertain whether he learned of this from Pseudo-Methodius or via some other Eastern route.) Adso's millennial statement, however, is very brief: all it says is that in the last days a Frankish king will unite the Roman Empire, become the greatest of all rulers, and reign happily before laying down his scepter in expectation of Antichrist.

In contrast to the silence of the early Middle Ages on the subject, political millennialism became extremely popular in the West after about 1100 and remained so until 1500 and beyond. Explanations for the change are related to the emergence of the crusading movement and the rise of dynastic publicism. The idea of a coming conquering hero, who would unite the world for Christianity and become the greatest ruler of all time, accorded well with crusading expectations and was extremely suitable for the purposes of dynastic propaganda. Accordingly, not only did the *Tiburtine Sibyl* and Pseudo-Methodius begin to circulate in hundreds of copies, but new prophecies imitative of them were written in the West to fit specific propagandistic aims more precisely. For example, around the time of the Second Crusade a French prophet altered the *Tiburtine Sibyl* to predict that the reigning Louis VII of France would conquer the entire East after the manner of Cyrus; similarly, in 1281 a prophetic text circulated to support the imperialistic ambitions of Charles of Anjou.

A particularly large number of political millennial prophecies were applied to real or expected German rulers named Frederick and French rulers named Charles. These often included the predictions that the conquering hero would not only unite the world and inaugurate a reign of marvelous peace, but also that he would reform the clergy. When these prophecies failed in their application to one ruler, they were usually reapplied, with or without alterations, to another. Thus, a French "Charles" prophecy, originally written in 1380 to apply to Charles VI, was reapplied to Charles VII and Charles VIII of France, the Emperor Charles V, and later to Charles II of England.

The expectation of a conquering hero had one major limitation from the point of view of an optimistic interpretation of future history: namely the qualification that the reign of the glorious conqueror would come before the triumph of Antichrist, when all good Christians would be frightfully persecuted. This limitation was not present in the "theological" millennialism of the "refreshment of the saints" variety, a strain of millennialism that had its origins in the biblical exegesis of St. Jerome. Even though Jerome was a strong opponent of millennialism, his exegesis of the Book of Daniel forced him to conclude that there would be a surplus period of forty-five days between the death of Antichrist and the end of the world. Jerome's view was reaffirmed by the subsequent early medieval exegetes, Bede (*d.* 735) and Haimo of Auxerre (mid ninth century), who added the interpretation that the forty-five days were to be understood as an approximate rather than as an exact number, although they believed the period would still be a very brief one. All three commentators conceived of a very limited purpose for the extra time. Either it was meant for the further testing of the elect after the testings under Antichrist (Jerome), or it was a very brief foreshadowing of otherworldly rest (Bede), or it was granted for the penance of the elect who had wavered in their faith during Antichrist's persecutions (Haimo).

Since the biblical commentaries of Jerome, Bede, and Haimo were all accepted as standard, the prediction of a brief final time on earth after the death of Antichrist was transmitted to the high Middle Ages as an exegetical commonplace. But it was left for twelfth-century writers to transform the idea into a more truly millennarian expectation. Most likely this transpired in the twelfth century because only then did real historical change and progress seem obvious; people therefore must have found it easier to believe or hope that more progress was still to come. Whatever the explanation, different twelfth-century theorists, such as Otto of Freising, Hildegard of Bingen, and Gerhoch of Reichersberg, extended the limited conception of a brief period for testing, rest, or penance into an expectation of a time meant for "the refreshment of the saints," the conversion of the heathen and the Jews, and the reformation and purification of the church.

The culmination of these twelfth-century developments came in the work of the Calabrian abbot and seer Joachim of Fiore (*ca.* 1135–1202). Joachim transformed the early medieval exegetical commonplace about a brief time on earth after the death of Antichrist into a new theory of steady historical progress typified by the progressive unfolding of the Trinity. According to Joachim, the time after Antichrist would be a fully developed future historical "status," guided by the Holy Spirit, just as there had once been a first "status" of the Father (the time of the Old Testament) and as there was presently a second "status" of the Son. Joachim was also bold enough to say that the time after Antichrist, or third status of the Holy Spirit, was the same as the thousand-year kingdom of Revelation. In making this equation Joachim implicitly rejected Augustine's view that Revelation 20 referred to the present, not the future. (But Joachim was still by no means a literal millennarian because he did not take the figure of one thousand years literally, and because he did not expect Christ himself to reign during that first period.) Joachim expected the final age to be partic-

MILLENNIALISM, CHRISTIAN

ularly wondrous, not only because it would be characterized by peace, the conversion of unbelievers, and the final evolution of ecclesiastical forms, but also because men would then be granted the highest possible earthly state of spiritual insight.

Joachim was probably the most original and imaginative millennial theorist of the entire medieval period, and his work definitely had great subsequent influence, but there is no doubt that even without Joachim's accomplishment millennialism would have been widespread and deeply rooted in the West after 1200. This may be said with assurance because while many later prophecies were written with knowledge of some of Joachim's contributions, many others were not. Some of the prophecies written between 1200 and 1500 continued to elaborate on the "refreshment of the saints" theme in different ways, providing greater lengths for the final period (Joachim still believed it would be short), and adding different details about how it would bring humanity to the heights of earthly perfection. Others united the "conquering hero" to the "refreshment of the saints" theme, either by having a great conqueror help bring in the final wondrous period after Antichrist, or else by having two wondrous periods: one dominated by the hero before the reign of Antichrist and the other coming afterward. Still another new variant, which first appeared in the late thirteenth century, was the prediction of a future "angelic pope," who would act either alone or together with a "conquering hero" to inaugurate a wondrous final dispensation on earth.

Among the most elaborate late medieval millennial predictions were those of the mid-fourteenth-century French Franciscan prophet John of Rupescissa (French: *Roquetaillade*). Rupescissa foretold that after terrible imminent woes a conquering French hero, together with an angelic pope, would ultimately triumph over Antichrist. The two then would inaugurate a wondrous reign of peace that would last literally for a thousand years. This was the closest any medieval writer came to returning to literal millennialism, but even Rupescissa fell short of reviving all the details of Revelation 20 insofar as he did not state that the millennium would see the earthly return of Christ.

Depending on what one means by "revolutionary," it is possible to find some revolutionary millennialism in the period between 1200 and 1500. Many prophecies predicted violent chastisement for the clergy. These were conservative rather than revolutionary insofar as they conceived of a purification of existing institutions rather than the introduction of substantially new ones, but they may be considered revolutionary insofar as they approved of violent punishment of reigning authorities in the near future. A few prophecies went further in including details about altered economic and social relationships. For example, around 1248 a Dominican, Brother Arnold, predicted that the emperor Frederick II would inaugurate a time of peace and justice when the poor would receive back all the goods that had been taken away from them by the rapacious clergy, and the prelates who had robbed them would be forced to stand trial. Also outstanding in its concern for the poor was a prophecy that circulated in Germany around 1348 that Frederick II would miraculously return to inaugurate a new age of equality in which poor girls and women would be married to rich men, and rich women would be married to poor men. Such prophecies, however, did not call upon the poor to rise up to create their own new order; rather they assured them that their wrongs would be righted by supernatural powers.

Most likely the closest approach to a truly revolutionary ideology in the medieval period was made during the period of the Hussite Revolution in Bohemia. Faced with possible defeat and demoralization in the winter of 1419–1420, the most militant Hussites helped bolster their spirits with millennial prophecies that came closest to being truly revolutionary for two reasons. First, the Hussites went the farthest in conceiving of imminent material as well as spiritual betterment; not only would there soon be "no sin, no scandal, and no abomination," but there also would be no hunger or thirst, no taxes or tithes, and not even any pain for women in childbirth. The Hussites were unique in believing that they could not wait for the new age to occur by purely supernatural means: Christ would come to triumph, but they themselves would first have to help destroy Christ's enemies by fire and sword.

Despite these examples, most high- and late-medieval millennial prophecies served conservative rather than revolutionary purposes. Above all, millennial prophecies appear to have served the function of instilling hope and fortitude during times of disaster. Millennial prophecies were customarily inspired by meteorological portents or by calamities such as the onslaught of the Mongols, the fall of the Holy Land, the spread of the Black Death, or the outbreak of the Great Schism. Prophetic texts that circulated on such occasions stated in one way or another that God was angry and that present chastise-ments would get worse, but that ultimately the woes would have an end and would be followed by wondrous times of "peace and tranquillity." Thus millennial prophecies gave comfort by offering certainties in the face of uncertainty and helped frightened people get about their work by assuring them that there would be a better future.

BIBLIOGRAPHY

Sources. Two excellent collections of translated sources that contain basic millennialistic texts are Bernard McGinn, *Apocalyptic Spirituality: Treatises and Letters of Lactantius, Adso of Montier-en-Der, Joachim of Fiore, the Franciscan Spirituals, Savonarola* (1979), and *Visions of the End: Apocalyptic Traditions in the Middle Ages* (1979).

Studies. Paul J. Alexander, *The Byzantine Apocalyptic Tradition* (1985); Howard Kaminsky, "Chiliasm and the Hussite Revolution," in *Church History,* **26** (1957); Robert E. Lerner, "Refreshment of the Saints: The Time After Antichrist as a Station for Progress in Medieval Thought," in *Traditio,* **32** (1976), "The Black Death and Western European Eschatological Mentalities," in *American Historical Review,* **86** (1981), and *The Powers of Prophecy* (1983); Bernard McGinn, "Apocalypticism in the Middle Ages: An Historiographical Sketch," in *Mediaeval Studies,* **37** (1975), "Angel Pope and Papal Antichrist," in *Church History,* **47** (1978), "Awaiting an End: Research in Medieval Apocalypticism, 1974–1981," in *Medievalia et humanistica,* n.s., **11** (1982), and *The Calabrian Abbot: Joachim of Fiore in the History of Western Thought* (1985); Marjorie Reeves, *The Influence of Prophecy in the Later Middle Ages* (1969), and "The Originality and Influence of Joachim of Fiore," in *Traditio,* **36** (1980).

ROBERT E. LERNER

[See also **Antichrist; Joachim of Fiore.**]

MILLENNIALISM, ISLAMIC, found expression chiefly in the expectation of the coming of the Mahdi, a messianic Restorer who would "fill the earth with justice as it has been filled with oppression." The specific idea of a reign of justice and peace lasting a thousand years was unkown in Islam. The belief in the Mahdi (the divinely guided one) has no foundation in the Koran. It arose first during the Second Civil War (681–692), reflecting the hopes of the Shīʿa for a Deliverer from the House of the Prophet and of conservative Sunnites for a restoration of the early Caliphate of Medina. Shiites in Kufa proclaimed Muḥammad ibn al-Ḥanafiyya, a son of Muḥammad's cousin ʿAlī, the Mahdi, in 686. After the failure of the restoration movement of ʿAbd Allāh ibn al-Zubayr, which extended from 681 to 692 (the year of his death), conservative Sunnites considered the pious Umayyad caliph ʿUmar II (717–720) as the Mahdi. Under Shiite influence, however, later Sunnism adopted the doctrine that the Mahdi must be a member of the House of the Prophet.

Prophecies ascribed to Muḥammad about the Mahdi were received in the Sunnite canonical collections of *ḥadīth* and thus provided a firm basis for the popular belief in his coming, which, though not considered essential to the Sunnite creed, was only exceptionally rejected. According to these prophecies and uncanonical elaborations, the Mahdi's name was to be identical with that of the Prophet, and he would come from Medina to Mecca, where his followers would pledge allegiance to him. He would defeat his Umayyad opponent, the Sufyānī, conquer Constantinople and Rome, and reign over the whole world. He would apply strictly the law of Islam. According to some traditions, he would discover copies of the original version of the Torah and the Gospel in Antioch and would rule Jews and Christians in accordance with them. His age would be a time of unprecendented prosperity, and he would pour out money in heaps for his followers.

While most traditions do not relate the coming of the Mahdi to eschatology, and some envisage his being succeeded by a line of caliphs descended from him, others connect him with the descent of Jesus from heaven and his killing of the Dajjāl (deceiver), a kind of antichrist, just before the end of the world. Belief in the descent of Jesus and the Dajjāl was older than the idea of the Mahdi, though also un-Koranic, and thus was integrated into it. Although offered leadership in the prayer of the Muslim community by the Mahdi, Jesus would at first pray behind him and thus acknowledge the abrogation of Christianity by the law of Islam. The Mahdi would then aid him in the killing of the Dajjāl. This eschatological role of the Mahdi was sometimes attributed to a second Mahdi expected to come long after the first.

A later development in the beliefs about the Mahdi originated in Andalusian Sufi circles in the twelfth century. They spread traditions predicting the appearance of the Mahdi from the mountain Māssa in southwestern Morocco. He would lead an army of Berber tribes to Andalusia and conquer seventy Christian towns. These traditions are subsequent to the activity of the Almohad Mahdi, Muḥammad ibn Tūmārt (*d.* 1130), which they reflect.

Among many of the Shīʿa, messianic hopes were intense and belief in the Mahdi a vital aspect of faith.

The Deliverer was often called the *qāʾim* (the riser) of the House of the Prophet, who was usually identified with the Mahdi. The meaning of the name was commonly connected with the promise that he would rise with the sword against the illegitimate rulers of the world or, more rarely, that he would rise from the dead. The Ismailis distinguished between the *qāʾim* and the Mahdi and viewed the former as the Lord of the *qiyāma,* the Resurrection, thus turning him into an eschatological figure. Widespread among the Shīʿa was also the belief in a period of absence or occultation (*ghaiba*) of the Mahdi before his second appearance in glory to rule the world. This belief had arisen around Muḥammad ibn al-Ḥanafiyya, who, after his death, was held to be alive, hiding in a mountain near Medina. It attached itself during the following centuries to many descendants of Muḥammad among small Shiite groups, which recognized one or the other as the Mahdi. The Twelver Shīʿa considered their "twelfth imam" as living in occultation after his disappearance as an infant and awaited his return as the Mahdi. Shiite expectations about the role of the Mahdi were generally similar to those of the Sunnites. The Mahdi would, however, enforce the Shiite form of Islamic law also against Sunnite Muslims. Those Muslims unwilling to accept the Shiite faith would be subjected to payment of the *jizya* tax like Jews and Christians. Some radical, especially Ismaili, Shiites held that the Mahdi would abrogate the law of Islam and replace it with a new, final law or a state of pure spirituality in which no law was needed.

Millenarian hopes have at times played a major part in the political history of Islam. The Abbasid revolutionary movement was supported with predictions attributed to Muḥammad that an army with black banners coming from Khorāsān would be the vanguard of the Mahdi. The first Abbasid caliph, Abū 'l-ʿAbbās, was given the messianic name al-Saffāḥ, the generous (*r.* 749–754). The second Caliph, Abū Jaʿfar, adopted another messianic name, al-Manṣūr (*r.* 754–775), and gave his son, whose name was identical with that of the Prophet, the regnal name al-Mahdī (*r.* 775–785), presenting him as the promised Restorer. This was in reaction to the abortive rising of a descendant of Muḥammad through his daughter Fāṭima and grandson Ḥasan who also bore the name Muḥammad ibn ʿAbd Allāh and, in accordance with the prophecies, had appeared in Medina claiming to be the Mahdi. The Fatimid caliphate in North Africa represented the millenarian aspirations of the Ismaili movement. The first caliph, ʿUbayd Allāh, bore the regnal name al-Mahdī (*r.* 909–934), the second, al-Qāʾim (*r.* 934–946). Ismaili religious propaganda taught that the predictions about the Mahdi would be gradually fulfilled by the Fatimid caliphs. A strictly Sunnite millenarian movement was that of the Almohads originating in southwestern Morocco. Its founder, Muḥammad ibn Tūmart (*d.* 1130), claimed to be a descendant of Muḥammad and the Mahdi. As such he stressed his infallibility in his teaching aimed at a purification of Islam.

BIBLIOGRAPHY

D. S. Attema, *De Mohammedaansche opvattingen omtrent het tijdstip van den jongsten dag en zijn Voorteekenen* (1942); Ignacz Goldziher, *Vorlesungen über den Islam* (1910), 230–233; Ibn Khaldūn, *The Muqaddimah,* Franz Rosenthal, trans., II (1958); David S. Margoliouth, *On Mahdis and Mahdiism* (1916).

W. MADELUNG

[See also **Abbasids; Abu Jaʿfar; Almohads; Caliphate; Fatimids; Ḥadīth; Ismāʿiliya; Mahdi, al-; Qāʾim, al-; Sects, Islamic; Shiʿa; Sunna; Sunnites.**]

MILLET. See **Grain Crops.**

MILLS. Industrial mechanization is one of the most characteristic and significant achievements of the West. An essential discovery upon which it is based is that forces existing in nature can be tapped and transformed into mechanical power. The water mill and the windmill were the first practical engines to utilize natural power. Their exact points of origin remain obscure, but it was in medieval Europe that each received its basic mechanical designs and was first applied to a variety of manufacturing and other work processes.

THE WATER MILL

The first known attempt in the West to harness the energy of running water for practical industrial purposes was the water-powered grain mill, which appeared in the late first century B.C. There was a contemporary development of water-powered machinery in East Asia, but no proven connection between the two, either in the general concept or in any critical mechanical detail. The West can be shown, in fact, to have already possessed by the late first century B.C. some of the requisite conceptual and technical elements employed in the hydraulic milling devices that emerged there at that time. With respect to the manufacture of flour, the rotary grindstone was by then effectively used in Roman hand-powered and animal-powered mills. As for the utilization of water power, the noria, a vertical irrigation wheel fitted with paddles and buckets, lifted water from the current that turned it. Likewise, Greco-Roman engineering had conceived various hydraulic automata in which running water turned wheels, the object being, as temple tricks, the turning itself or the noise produced. These precedents are significant, but they do not obviate the inventive inspiration by which the energy of the stream was transmitted from the wheel and utilized by a grinder. The earliest certain Western evidence of this comes from the writings of Antipater of Thessaloniki, Strabo, and Vitruvius, as well as from some carefully studied archaeological remains.

No clear description of the machinery involved is provided by either Antipater or Strabo. Archaeology and Vitruvius, however, provide clear evidence, respectively, of the horizontal and the vertical water mill, the two basic forms to which all subsequent developments are related.

Horizontal water mill. Excavations at Bolle, Jutland, reveal traces of two dam sites dating from the beginning of the Christian era that include clear evidence of the dams, reservoirs, and races. Analysis of silt deposits indicates the presence of mills of the horizontal type—that is, there was no gearing; the power was transmitted directly along a vertical axle from the horizontal waterwheel to the grinder.

In a typical medieval form, the horizontal mill was contained in a small covered structure, built from local materials and composed of an upper and a lower room. The vertical axle extended through the floor that separated the basement, through which the current passed, from the upper room containing the grinding stones surmounted by the hopper mechanism. The lower part of the axle, resting directly in the bed of the stream or on a bearing, had several paddles mortised into it, thus forming a rimless horizontal wheel against which the current, often narrowed by a slanting trough, struck. The upper end of the vertical axle passed through the lower, solidly emplaced bed stone and was attached by a rynd in the central eye of the upper runner stone; one revolution of the waterwheel and axle thus produced one revolution of the runner stone, the diameter of which did not normally exceed two to three feet. Provisions for adjustment are not clear from the medieval evidence; the most that might be suspected, based upon some later survivals, is a sluice gate to control the current, and the resting of the axle's bearing on a movable beam that could be lifted or lowered to change the space between the stones, and thus to determine the grade of the flour produced.

The simplicity of the horizontal mill encourages the assumption that it was the earliest, and remained the most common, type. However, firm descriptive evidence of it during the late classical and medieval periods is exceptionally rare. The earliest example, that revealed by the Jutland excavation, does not appear to antedate the late-first-century-B.C. vertical mill of Vitruvius. The next firm testimony is from early-tenth-century Ireland, and the next from thirteenth-century Tuscany. The records remain silent then until the fifteenth century, when the horizontal waterwheel is illustrated not only as activating wood-pipe borers (1437, *ca.* 1472–*ca.* 1485) but also as being studied by Leonardo da Vinci in regard to its turbine principles. The paucity of evidence for the horizontal mill during the early centuries of its Western existence is particularly striking when compared with the wide distribution of the device from early modern times to the present: Ireland, the British Isles, Scandinavia, Germany, France, Italy, Spain, eastern Europe, Greece, and the Holy Land. The truth is probably that the horizontal mill, less efficient than the vertical mill but relatively simple and cheap to build, diffused widely and unheralded through less affluent, more primitive medieval societies in isolated areas, particularly rugged regions where small, fast streams facilitated its use.

Vertical water mill. In essence, the vertical mill consisted of a vertical waterwheel with a horizontal axle geared to a vertical axle that communicated the drive to the runner stone; such a wheel could receive the water as it flowed below (undershot) or as it was fed from above (overshot). The gears made it possible to adjust the rotation of the stone to a speed not limited absolutely by the revolution of the waterwheel (a limitation of the horizontal mill). The weight of the water gave the overshot mill greater power, but the need for a launder, along which the water was led to the necessary elevation, must inevitably have involved more effort and expense; the choice, once the alternatives were known, was doubtless made according to the nature of the current, the condition of the river bank, and the available resources.

Vitruvius, a Roman engineer writing no later

than 14 B.C., carefully describes a vertical undershot mill, including the essential gearing; gearing had been known in the Hellenistic world since the third century B.C., but Vitruvius' mill represents its first industrial use and marks a decisive step in the development of power mechanisms. The vertical overshot mill was used by the fourth century at Barbegal near Arles, in southern Gaul, producing flour for the imperial legions there, and by the fifth century in the eastern Mediterranean, where the Athenian agora provided a lucrative locus for such an installation. From this time on, through the Romano-Byzantine period and into the Middle Ages in Europe, the vertical grain mill spread with the main concentrations of Christian culture.

Virtually no cartulary fails to document this spread; and no single source testifies to it more spectacularly than the Domesday Book, which lists 5,624 mills just in those counties surveyed and reported in 1086. Typical of these was a vertical grain mill of the undershot or overshot type, located along the banks of a stream, and housed, along with the miller and his family, in a structure made of local materials. The mill parts were fashioned largely from wood and joined by dowels or treenails. The few contemporary illustrations normally depict the medieval mill with its waterwheel exterior to the building, its horizontal axle passing through the wall and

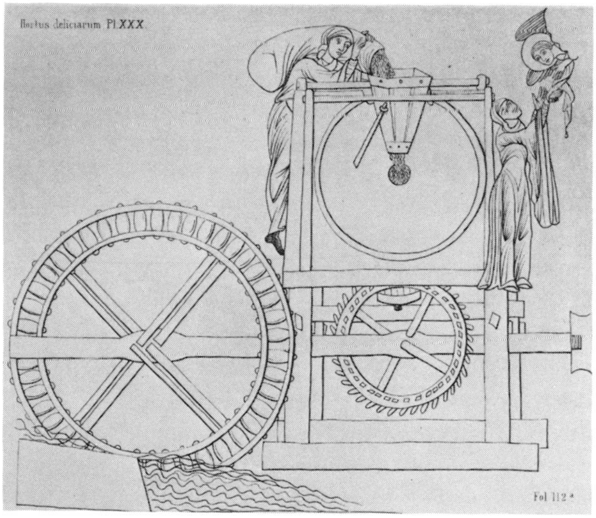

Internal mechanism of a corn mill. From a sketch in the *Hortus deliciarum* by Herrad von Landsberg, abbess of Hohenburg (*d.* 1195), for the instruction of her nuns. THE NEW YORK PUBLIC LIBRARY, GENERAL RESEARCH DIVISION ANNEX, ASTOR, LENOX, AND TILDEN FOUNDATIONS

equipped with a cogged pit wheel that engaged the lantern gear of the vertical axle, which terminated in the rynd attaching it to the runner stone. The stones, made variously of hard sandstone, granite, or quartz, and dressed with radial furrows and lands, sheared the grain as the rotation forced it outward from the eye of the runner stone, where it had been discharged from the hopper mechanism.

Adjustments included tentering of the stones by raising or lowering a beam (the sole tree) upon which the vertical axle rotated; quickening the discharge of grain by lowering a slanting shoe through which the grain passed from the hopper to the eye of the stone; causing a vibration of the hopper by a clapper stone, or by a flexible stick attached to the hopper and rubbing on the surface of the runner stone; and controlling the current where a sluice or launder was involved. The scale in medieval illustrations is unreliable, but waterwheels appear to be 8 to 10 feet in diameter; as for the stones, considerable efficiency may be gotten from stones 4 feet in diameter rotating at 125 to 130 rpm. The 16 overshot mills of the fourth-century milling complex at Barbegal are estimated to have produced 28 tons of flour in a 10-hour day, somewhat more than 1.5 tons per mill. There is no reason to expect any lesser or greater efficiency from a similarly constructed medieval mill.

Boat mill and bridge mill. To avail themselves better of the stream, millers had learned by the early sixth century to put their mills afloat, and by no later than the eleventh century they were constructing them in association with bridges. The boat mill (ship mill or floating mill) took one of two forms: a single hull supporting one or more vertical waterwheels and the grinding mechanism(s), or a vertical waterwheel suspended between two hulls and supplying power to the grinding mechanism(s) located in one or both hulls. Notwithstanding problems relating to access, to river obstruction, and to damage caused by mills that lost their moorings, the boat mill appeared with growing frequency from its first mention in Rome shortly after the Goths' siege of the city in 537.

A bridge mill was not a boat mill incidentally moored to a bridge but, rather, a stationary vertical mill utilizing the architecture and/or currents of passenger bridges. Less common, as the obvious danger and extant laws against it attest, was the mill attached substantially to the piers of the bridge itself. More common was the mill built on pilings in an arch, normally not directly under the roadway, or built on pilings slightly upstream or downstream, thus utilizing the current accelerated by the arch and cutwaters. Access to such mills could be by boat, the roadway of the bridge, or, most frequently, roadways built over the pilings. Problems and litigation occurred as a result of damage to the bridge and obstruction of the river, especially when a mill included the addition of a millrace and a sluice gate, formed from pilings, and a dam built obliquely across the river to direct the current toward the arch containing the mill. Mill bridges—bridges built specifically to support mills and provide access to them—had similar attractions; by the later twelfth century such installations began to appear, adding to the industrial utilization of rivers.

Tide mill. There is evidence from the Middle Ages that where streams were not available or suitable in coastal areas, tidal action was sometimes harnessed. Tide mills were first discussed and illustrated by Mariano di Jacopo Taccola in his *De ingeneis* (1433) and Faustus Verantius in his *Novae machinae* (1615). In both cases the current is formed by tidal water returning down a sluice from a pool, natural or man-made, in which it was trapped at high tide; Taccola prescribes a vertical wheel and Verantius a horizontal one. Medieval references to tide mills are far less explicit in their mechanical detail and leave open the possibility that the pond and sluice were less critical to the definition of a tidal mill than the fact that tidal action was the essential fact of its operation. Hence, the earliest European evidence of tidal mills may well be the floating mills, cited in 1044 and in 1078, in the salt marsh around Venice, changing their location with the flood and ebb of the tidal current. Another possible variation is the mill, built probably between 1067 and 1082, that Domesday Book establishes at the harbor entrance to Dover and that, "by the great turbulence of the sea," endangered ships and men; a major tidal milling operation located on the end of a breakwater or pier could wreak such havoc and excite such notice.

Technical ambiguities persisted from the eleventh-century examples until Taccola's treatise of the early fifteenth century, but the existence of tidal mills in Western Europe during the period cannot be doubted. The evidence accumulates from the early decades of the twelfth century, especially in Britain and France, and ongoing research points to a viable tradition thenceforth of tidal water mills along the Atlantic coast at least from Portugal to the Low Countries and in Britain.

INDUSTRIAL ADAPTATIONS OF THE WATER MILL

The preparation of flour by grinding remained a central function of the water mill throughout the Middle Ages. It is a mark of the medieval European technological genius that a vastly broader application of waterpower to practical purposes than Greco-Roman technology ever achieved occurred during the period. Among the activities and industries affected were those relating to food other than flour—beer, oil, and sugar—textiles, paper, metallurgy, woodworking and building construction, and irrigation and drainage. In many of these, the critical function remained the transmission of the rotary motion of the waterwheel to that of some working part. Crucial to the revolutionary versatility of medieval waterpower, however, and long before the fifteenth-century appearance of the compound crank with connecting rod, was the employment of cams on the horizontal axle of the vertical mill in order to translate the rotary motion of the waterwheel into the reciprocating motion required in some industrial processes. This marriage of the cam and waterwheel cannot seriously be doubted in the hammers *(pilae)* of the beer mills depicted in the architectural plan of St. Gall (*ca.* 820) or disputed as indispensable to the water-powered mills for fulling cloth, first mentioned as *batatoria* in the Dauphiné about 990, and associated with the Bavarian town of Schmidmühlen (smithy or forge mill) by about 1028.

These examples and all subsequent evidence, which includes more precise terms, such as *molendinum brasium* (beer mill), *molendinum fullonarium* (fulling mill), and *molendinum ubi fabricatur ferrum* (iron mill), suggest that the European water-powered hammer was first established in the Alpine regions and, along with related reciprocating devices, such as the water-powered bellows that appears in the Tridentine Alps in the early thirteenth century, diffused in all directions. It is yet to be proved that the medieval pounder was most typically a recumbent trip-hammer or vertical-beam stamp. Both types are included in the notebook of the anonymous "Hussite Engineer" (*ca.* 1472–*ca.* 1485), which contains the earliest illustrations of each. Clearly, in any case, the medieval water mill came to have the capacity both to transmit rotary power from the turning waterwheel and to translate the wheel's rotary motion into reciprocating action, two functions that can be shown to have appeared in various industries during the Middle Ages.

Food. Although hand-powered and animal-powered mills continued in use for the preparation of flour, the water-powered grain mill achieved nearly universal dominance in medieval Europe; recognized for its efficiency, the mill's operation also constituted a lucrative monopoly, in which the tolls and banalities associated with the lord's soke rights encouraged legal enforcement of its use by all people under the lord's jurisdiction. Waterpower was employed in the manufacture of beer mash from the early ninth century on, with the pounder proving more effective than grindstones in the production of the malt. The use of the animal-powered edge roller, common since Greco-Roman antiquity in the preparation of oils, continued through the Middle Ages; nor is there evidence of water-driven edge-rollers until the seventeenth century. From the early twelfth century on, however, there were in the western part of Europe water mills, doubtless employing pounders and/or grinders, producing oils made not only from olives but also from mustard, poppy seed, hemp seed, and nuts. The sugar industry was introduced into Sicily and the Iberian peninsula by the Arabs, but there is no indication that they initiated the use of waterpower in the manufacturing process. All the evidence, however, points to the fact that the Christians did. Whether employing pounders or flat-rotating grindstones, a sugar mill existed in Norman Sicily in 1176; crusaders had water-powered sugar mills at work in the Middle East by the mid thirteenth century, and the Portuguese and Spaniards are known to have carried the technique to the Madeiras, Canaries, and West Indies.

Textiles. The most significant utilization of waterpower in the medieval textile industry was to activate the hammers of fulling mills and hemp mills, both of which were in operation in the Dauphiné and northern Italy by the beginning of the eleventh century. Extensive mechanization, especially of the fulling industry, followed in many parts of Europe; within a few decades of its appearance in England in 1185, for instance, a major industrial and demographic migration occurred as wool production moved from the old urban communities of the eastern lowlands to the rural regions of the northern and western uplands, with their more suitable watercourses. Related activities involve the use of grindstones and hammers in the reduction of tanning agents, first reported from northern France in 1138, and, by the mid fourteenth century, for the preparation of dyestuffs used in the textile industry.

Paper. Europeans learned how to make paper from the Arabs, who acquired the knowledge from the Chinese in the mid eighth century. There is no proof that waterpower was used in the process until the second half of the thirteenth century, when Christian papermakers in Spain and Italy, already familiar with the hydraulic hammer from other industries, adopted the device to prepare pulp. From its origins in Italy and Spain, the paper mill spread throughout Europe during the next three centuries, and although pride continued to be taken in especially fine handmade papers, major Western papermaking installations employed waterpower.

Metallurgy. The earliest use of waterpower in metallurgy was almost certainly to drive forge hammers, a technique that was known in Bavaria by about 1028, diffused slowly though widely through the eleventh and twelfth centuries, and had penetrated all the major mining regions of Europe by the thirteenth century. During that century this mechanization came to include not only hammers but also bellows. Mechanized bellows made possible the enlargement of smelting furnaces and the generation of more intense heat. When these improvements were combined with the proper mixture of ores and fuel, cast iron could be produced in quantity; this was achieved in Liège by 1384, thus marking the first firm evidence of the blast furnace. The metallurgical industry also employed waterpower for sharpening and polishing metal (from the early thirteenth century), stamping ores (from the early fourteenth century), and drawing wire (by no later than the fifteenth century).

Woodworking and building construction. Medieval woodworkers and construction engineers made varied use of waterpower, not counting the indirect benefits they received from hydraulic technology, such as more and better tools and rope. Hydraulic wood saws appeared by 1204, in Normandy, and diffused widely thereafter. The water-powered lathe is another medieval invention; present evidence reveals turning mills in the Dauphiné from the mid fourteenth century on. Ingenious Bavarian and Styrian builders were using waterpower to prepare mortar and gravel in the fourteenth century and, by the mid fifteenth century, to bore wooden pipe.

Irrigation and drainage. The history of hydraulic water-raising devices during the Middle Ages shows that the noria, if not common throughout most of Europe, was utilized extensively in Spain by both Muslims and Christians. Elsewhere in Europe, interest in water-raising machinery centered primarily on the drainage of mines; this became a particularly pressing matter in the later medieval period, when shafts became sufficiently deep to require major draining operations. Although the more efficient suction pump was not put into practical use until the sixteenth century, water-driven chain devices were, beginning in the early fourteenth century, employed in the mines of Eastern Europe.

THE WINDMILL

The history of the windmill in the Middle Ages is far less extensive and complex—in chronology, mechanical development, and industrial applications—than that of the water mill. The notable sophistication and variety both of design and of utilization that the windmill eventually achieved trace most dramatically in Europe from the sixteenth century on. Yet the medieval period marks the crucial beginnings of the windmill, just as the device testifies further to the remarkable ingenuity of medieval technology.

Windmills first appeared in Europe in the late twelfth century. The mill *(molendinum ad ventum)* at Wigeton Parva, Leicestershire, in 1137 is the earliest for which the date is certain. Rapid proliferation in England, for instance at Weedly, Yorkshire, in 1185, at Oseney Abbey by 1189, and at Bury St. Edmonds in 1191/1192, is particularly evidenced by the imposition there of tithes on the device, pronounced in a papal decretal of Celestine III datable between 1191 and 1197. By the 1190's, German crusaders were building windmills in Syria, and by the late thirteenth and early fourteenth centuries they were known to most Europeans. What inspired their development is not certain. Vertical-axle windmills with vanes on the horizontal plane existed in Persia in the tenth century and in China by the thirteenth century. As surviving illustrations show, however, the Western medieval windmill employed vanes on a vertical plane turning on a horizontal axle. Mariano Taccola's sketch, in his *De ingeneis* (1433), of the Eastern vertical-axle type is the first known reference to one of its kind in Europe. The distinctive Western model appears to have been an independent invention, possibly suggested by the mechanical principles and efficient production associated with the familiar water mill in which the vertical wheel turned the horizontal drive shaft.

Post mill. The earliest and dominant medieval windmill design was that of the post mill. In it the small, wooden-framed building (the buck), with roof of thatch or tile, and vertical or horizontal sideboards forming its walls, was wholly supported by and pivoted upon a large, upright beam. The central transverse timber (the crown tree) of the buck's floor received a bearing (the pintle) from the vertical beam, which was held up by quarter bars resting on crosstrees. Pivoting on the bearing, the buck could be turned, bringing the vanes into the wind, by walking the end of a long tail pole, which attached at its top to the buck, in a circle. The buck was entered by a ladder.

The light vanes, formed into frames by longitudinal spars and transverse sail bars, had as wind surfaces strips of canvas woven in and out through the sail bars. The spars of the vanes were mortised to the horizontal axle (the wind shaft), which held a cogged wheel that meshed with the lantern gear, which in turn transmitted the power down the vertical axle to the runner stone. The cogged wheel on the windshaft eventually became the great brake wheel, but there is no evidence that the medieval windmill had any braking mechanism. The internal machinery and the wooden construction techniques were essentially the same as those of contemporary water mills, except that the vertical axle usually led down to the grinder from the horizontal drive shaft rather than upward to the stones, as in most water mills.

Tower mill. Appearing by the end of the fourteenth century, the tower mill consisted of a rigid tower, built of brick or masonry (or of wood, as distinguished the nearly contemporary smock mill), surmounted on its flat top (the curb) by a rotating cap that carried the vanes and could be moved around the curb, thus bringing the vanes into the wind. Distinct advantage was gained from the larger working area afforded by the permanent tower and from the lighter mobile unit, so much easier to turn.

The employment of the windmill. There is no available evidence that the windmill was used industrially during the Middle Ages except for grinding grain. This is not surprising, since the characteristic medieval device—the small, fully contained, rotating post mill—could hardly be used for such heavy industrial activities as fulling or smelting and forging metal. The first new practical employment of the windmill of which there is evidence is its use to power water-drainage scoop wheels, beginning in the early fifteenth century and thereafter becoming crucial especially in the Low Countries. It was principally in this region, in fact, that major efforts to use wind power in other industries were ultimately made—for example, the sawmills and oil mills appearing there in the later sixteenth century. None of this detracts from the importance that the windmill achieved in its actual grain-grinding function from the late twelfth century on. Nor does it deny the extent to which the then familiar windmill had stimulated technical imagination by the end of the Middle Ages. A manuscript of 1327, attributable to Walter de Milemete, includes a proposal for using a windmill to throw beehives over the wall of a besieged town. In an unpublished manuscript of 1335 (Paris, Bibliothèque Nationale, N.S. lat. 11015, fol. 14 v.), Guido da Vigevano describes a wheeled fighting vehicle propelled by wind vanes. And an early-fifteenth-century sketch in Konrad Kyeser's *Bellifortis* presented a plan for a wind-powered elevator.

BIBLIOGRAPHY

A.-M. Bautier, "Les plus anciennes mentions de moulins hydrauliques industriels et de moulins à vent," in *Bulletin philologique et historique,* **2** (1960); Richard Bennett and John Elton, *History of Corn Milling,* 4 vols. (1898–1904, repr. 1966); Bradford B. Blaine, "The Enigmatic Water-Mill," in Bert S. Hall and Delno C. West, eds., *On Pre-modern Technology and Science* (1976); Marc Bloch, "Avènement et conquêtes due moulin à eau," in *Annales d'histoire économique et sociale,* **7** (1935); Marjorie N. Boyer, *Medieval French Bridges* (1976), chap. 9; R. J. Forbes, "Power," in Charles J. Singer *et al.*, eds., *A History of Technology,* II (1956); Bertrand Gille, "Le moulin à eau: Une révolution technique médiévale," in *Techniques et civilisations,* **3** (1954), and "Machines," in Singer, *op. cit.;* Walter Horn, "Water Power and the Plan of St. Gall," in *Journal of Medieval History,* **1** (1975); Edward J. Kealey, *Harvesting the Air: Windmill Pioneers in Twelfth-century England* (1986); Walter Kuhn, "Das Spätmittelalter als technisches Zeitalter," in *Ostdeutsche Wissenschaft,* **1** (1954); W. E. Minchinton, "Early Tide Mills: Some Problems," in *Technology and Culture,* **20** (1979); John Muendel, "The Horizontal Mills of Medieval Pistoia," *ibid.,* **15** (1974); Joseph Needham, *Science and Civilisation in China,* IV, pt. 2 (1965); Frank D. Prager and Giustina Scaglia, *Mariano Taccola and His Book "De ingeneis"* (1972), 15, 86–87, for illus. and trans. of text; John Reynolds, *Windmills and Watermills* (1970); Terry S. Reynolds, *Stronger Than a Hundred Men: A History of the Vertical Water Wheel* (1983); Rex Wailes, " A Note on Windmills," in Singer, *op. cit.;* Lynn White, Jr., *Medieval Technology and Social Change* (1962), chap. 3, and "Medieval Uses of Air," in *Scientific American,* **223** (August 1970).

BRADFORD B. BLAINE

[See also **Agriculture and Nutrition; Bread; Brewing; Grain Crops; Irrigation; Metallurgy; Mining; Paper, Introduction of; Technology, Western; Textile Technology.**]

MILO OF ST. AMAND (*ca.* 810–872), monk, poet, and teacher. Born in Picardy, he was closely tied to the court of Charles the Bald (823–877) as tutor to the king's two sons: Pepin and Drogon. In 855 Milo wrote both a metrical and a prose life of St. Amand (Amandus, *d.* 679), the founder of his monastery, St. Amand-les-Eaux, in Elnone near Lille. Milo also dedicated a poem on sobriety to Charles the Bald: *De sobrietate,* which incorporates all the virtues found in Prudentius' *Psychomachia.*

There are a number of sermons attributed to Milo, as well as the epitaphs for Drogon and Pepin, both of whom died before their father. Milo died in Flanders.

BIBLIOGRAPHY

Monumenta Germaniae historica: Poetae latini aevi carolini, III (1896), 557–684; *Patrologia latina,* CXXI (1852), 927. Ernst R. Curtius, *European Literature and the Latin Middle Ages,* Willard R. Trask, trans. (1963); Max Manitius *Geschichte der lateinischen Literatur des Mittelalters,* I (1911), 577.

NATHALIE HANLET

[See also **Carolingian Latin Poetry; Carolingians and the Carolingian Empire; Prudentius.**]

MÍMIR (Mímr, Mími) in Scandinavian mythology is an unclear being or several beings of uncertain meaning and relationship. According to Snorri Sturluson, when the Æsir and Vanir made peace after the first war in the world, they exchanged hostages. Hœnir and Mímir went to the Vanir; Njǫrðr, Freyr, and Kvasir, to the Æsir. When Hœnir was unable to make a decision without Mímir's counsel, the Vanir slew Mímir and sent his head to Odin, who preserved it and said spells over it so that it would give him wisdom. A strophe of *Vǫluspá* (46) tells that Odin consults the head; *Sigrdrífumál* (strophe 14), that it talks.

According to *Vǫluspá* 28, the famous well of Mímir hides Odin's eye; strophe 27 implies that the well conceals Heimdalr's hearing or ear and is located under Yggdrasill, the world tree. Mímir drinks each day "from the pledge of Odin." Snorri cites strophe 28, noting that Mímir is full of wisdom, because he drinks from the well with Gjallarhorn (Heimdallr's horn). Odin pledges his eye for a drink from the well (*Snorra edda, Gylfaginning* chap. 8).

Fjǫlsvinnsmál 19 and 22 seem to equate *Míma-*

meiðr (the tree of Mími) with Yggdrasill. This may have to do with the location of Mímir's well under the tree, but the form Mími is attested nowhere else.

Mím(i)r may be a giant. His well is situated near the root of Yggdrasill that runs among the frost giants, and at Ragnarǫk his sons play (do battle) (*Vǫluspá* 46).

A single conception cannot easily unify these disparate elements. Common to them, however, are the notion of wisdom and an association with Odin. The exchange of Kvasir for Mímir in *Ynglinga saga,* Odin's pledge for a wisdom-giving drink from Mímir's well, and the possibility that Mímir is a giant suggest an association with the mead of poetry, which was also possessed by giants and obtained by Odin.

BIBLIOGRAPHY

E. F. Halvorsen, "Mímir," in *Kulturhistorisk XI* (1966), 629–630; Jacqueline Simpson, "Mímir: Two Myths or One?" in *Saga-Book of the Viking Society* (1962); Jan de Vries, *Altgermanische Religionsgeschichte,* I (1970), 245–248.

JOHN LINDOW

[See also **Æsir; Freyr; Hœnir; Njǫrðr; Snorra Edda; Vanir; Vǫluspá.**]

MINAI WARE, a Persian ceramic ware whose polychrome effects closely imitate miniature painting, was produced at Kashan in the late twelfth century. Blue, purple, and green pigments were laid onto a hardened glaze and refired. White, red, and brown color agents were then applied, and the object was fired again at lower temperatures. Sometimes a final firing followed for gold leaf.

BIBLIOGRAPHY

Arthur Lane, *Later Islamic Pottery: Mesopotamia, Egypt, and Persia* (1971); Oliver Watson, "Persian Lustre-painted Pottery: The Rayy and Kashan Styles," in *Transactions of the Oriental Ceramic Society,* **40** (1973–1975).

MARINA D. WHITMAN

[See also **Ceramics, Islamic;** and frontispiece to volume VI.]

MINARET. The conventional meaning of the term "minaret" is a high tower attached to a mosque and used for the call to prayer. The Arabic words for minaret, with their very different etymologies, inspire the various theories proposed as to the origins of the form. *Manār(a)* ("place of light" or "place of fire") suggests a derivation from lighthouses, and indeed many minarets in coastal or desert regions performed this function. *Miʾdhana* ("place of the call to prayer") is surprisingly rare for a term so naturally appropriate to the main function of the building. *Ṣawmaʿa* ("monk's cell"), a term used principally in the al-Maghrib, points to the formal ancestry of the minaret in the lofty square church towers of pre-Islamic Syria. The very early Islamic practice of making the call to prayer from the roof of the mosque never totally died out and was even revived in certain areas in later medieval times, when minarets became increasingly rare. Thus, minarets are not obligatory, and many smaller mosques lack them. Diminutive "sentry-box" minarets, the staircase minarets of Saharan and western Africa and the Persian Gulf, and the open-plan aedicules *(guldastas)* perched on the roofs of post-Seljuk mosques in Iran, all owe something to the pristine simplicity of early Islamic ritual.

No monumental minarets survive from pre-Abbasid times, and the evolution of the genre may well have begun no earlier than the later eighth century. Probably the earliest surviving major minaret is that of the Qayrawān Mosque in Tunisia (836), in form three superposed cubes of diminishing size. Another ninth-century type popular in the orbit of Samarra, the Abbasid capital, was apparently inspired by Babylonian helicoidal ziggurats. Pronounced regional variations quickly developed. North African minarets perpetuated the model of Christian campaniles. Very tall cylindrical minarets—so high that the muezzin's call to prayer proclaimed from their summits would have been inaudible—characterized eastern Islamic architecture from the eleventh century onward. The tallest, those of Jam (213 ft.) and Delhi (238 ft.), were raised in the twelfth and thirteenth centuries in newly islamized territory, presumably as victory monuments and symbols of the faith. Egypt experimented with multistory minarets with stages successively square, octagonal, and finally cylindrical, the entire shaft articulated by balconies and windows. In Ottoman Turkey, cylindrical minarets girdled with tiers of balconies and with a pencil-shaped crown were the norm.

The earliest monumental minarets suggest in their location—at the far end of the courtyard opposite the sanctuary, or even outside the mosque proper, and on the axis of the *mihrab*—a processional emphasis and thus a desire to invest the form with associations of political power. Later they were sited laterally in a corner of the courtyard, or non-axially outside the mosque. In later medieval architecture, especially in Anatolia and the eastern Islamic world, multiple minarets—flanking entrances or demarcating perimeter walls—became popular as a decorative, and no longer liturgical, feature. They were added in a similar spirit to mausolea and madrasas.

Most varieties of minaret display elaborately decorated surfaces—brick ornament in high relief, thickly encrusted stone carving or intarsia work, glazed tilework—and virtually all have interior ramps or staircases, usually of the spiral type.

BIBLIOGRAPHY

K. A. C. Creswell, "The Evolution of the Minaret, with Special Reference to Egypt," in *Burlington Magazine,* **48** (1926), and *Early Muslim Architecture,* I: *The Umayyads* (1932); Robert Hillenbrand, "Manāra," in *Encyclopaedia of Islam,* new ed. (1986); A. Husain, *The Manara in Indo-Muslim Architecture* (1970); André Maricq and Gaston Wiet, *Le minaret de Djam: La découverte de la capitale des sultans ghorides (XIIe–XIIIe siècles)* (1959); Ghazi R. Muhammad, "The Minaret of Ibn Tulun," in *Sumer,* **23** (1967); Myron B. Smith, "The Manars of Isfahan," in *Athār-e Irān,* **1** (1936); Herman Thiersch, *Pharos, antike, Islam, und Occident* (1909); David Whitehouse, "Staircase Minarets on the Persian Gulf," in *Iran,* **10** (1972).

ROBERT HILLENBRAND

[See also **Islamic Art and Architecture; Mosque.**]

MINBAR (mimbar), a high, stepped pulpit used in mosques. The word, which is probably borrowed from the Ethiopic, comes from the root *NBR,* which means a high or an elevated thing.

The minbar was introduced into the mosque during the lifetime of the Prophet. Originally, it consisted of two steps and a seat, and was made of tamarisk wood. Textual evidence indicates that during the first two centuries of Islam, the minbars continued to be small and portable. This original form of minbars may have been copied from the so-called "judges' seats" from Aksum, Ethiopia, rather than from Christian pulpits. Such raised seats were in general use among the pre-Islamic Arabs, and both minbar and staff were symbols of judicial powers. In early Islam the minbar became a symbol of sovereignty and political authority.

Minbar from the Mosque of the Andalusians. Fēs, Morocco, 980. INSTITUT DES HAUTES-ÉTUDES MAROCAINES, RABAT

BIBLIOGRAPHY

Keppel A. C. Creswell, *Early Muslim Architecture,* I (1932, 2nd ed. 1969); Joseph Schacht, "An Unknown Type of Minbar and Its Historical Significance," in *Ars orientalis,* **2** (1957).

GHAZI I. BISHEH

[See also **Aghlabid Art; Islamic Art and Architecture; Miḥrāb; Mosque; Qayrawān, Al-.**]

MINING. The extraction of metalliferous ores from the crust of the earth began at the end of the Neolithic Age. The first metal to be worked was almost certainly copper, followed by tin and iron. Next to be mined were two other base metals, lead and zinc. At an early stage, however, the precious metals gold and silver were discovered and played an important role in the development of mining. Some base metals were by-products of silver mining, and in all probability would not have been worked on their own account. With the exception of gold, these metals occurred in chemical combination with other elements. They were not easily recognized, and smelting was necessary in order to obtain the pure metal. This was, however, impossible in the case of zinc. Although used in the later Middle Ages to produce the alloy brass, zinc was not actually produced industrially until the beginning of the nineteenth century. The problem was that the temperature at which it separates out is above its boiling point; it thus separates out as a vapor. The practice developed of adding the ore calamine (zinc carbonate) to molten copper. The metal was absorbed, leaving the waste as a scum. This was the method used in the fifteenth century at Dinant (on the Meuse River, Namur Province) and elsewhere.

Other metallic ores were obtained during the Middle Ages, including cinnabar, the source of mercury; stibnite, the source of antimony; and mispickel (arsenopyrite), the source of arsenic. These ores were mostly the by-products of the mining of other and more important minerals, and they were chiefly used in alchemy and as pigments in paints and glassmaking.

DISTRIBUTION OF ORES IN MEDIEVAL EUROPE

The ores of the common metals were, with the exception of those of iron, highly localized. They had been intruded into the earth's crust in zones of weakness, so that one of them was usually accompanied by several others. Silver, for example, was almost always found in association with lead and often with zinc. There were thus a number of mineralized zones within which most of the nonferrous mining took place during the Middle Ages. Nine such regions can be distinguished, though there were many metalliferous deposits, some of them of great economic importance, outside these areas.

The hills of western Britain formed one of the richest and best-documented medieval mining areas. They included the tin deposits of Cornwall and Devon, together with related copper and other nonferrous metals. Throughout the Middle Ages, Cornwall and Devon held a near monopoly of European tin production. Farther north were important lead deposits in the Mendip Hills of Somerset and in the Pennine Chain and Lake District hills.

The Spanish Meseta was an even larger and more richly endowed mining region. Its wealth had attracted miners early in the Bronze Age, and the Romans, according to the elder Pliny (*Natural History,* III), made great use of it. Prominent among the minerals worked were the copper ores of Tharsis in the southwest, the silver-lead of the southern parts of the plateau, and mercury from Almadén. Mining was interrupted during the Germanic invasions but was revived by the Arabs, who discovered a means of extracting copper from waters that had become impregnated with copper salts by using a simple chemical reaction with iron. To the extent that this procedure was used, underground mining became temporarily less important. Spain also produced tin in the mountains of the northwest, although on a much smaller scale than Devon and Cornwall.

France was notably lacking in deposits of nonferrous metals, though it had abundant ores of iron. There were, however, important deposits of lead-zinc in the Ardennes. These gave rise to the metal industry of Dinant, whose *dinanderie* was made from local zinc alloyed with copper imported from the Harz region.

The Harz Mountains formed a small but richly mineralized region. About 960, argentiferous lead ores were discovered in the Rammelsberg, the mountain that rises above Goslar. The Saxon emperors, who controlled the area, made great profit from the silver that was mined on their behalf. Mining spread into the interior of the Harz, and in the early thirteenth century revealed large deposits of copper, second only to those of Tharsis, near Mansfeld in the eastern (Lower) Harz.

In the later Middle Ages, Saxony became the preeminent mining region of Europe, and the name "Saxon" became almost synonymous with "miner." Not only were the Erzgebirge of Saxony a very important source of metalliferous ores; they were also a training ground for miners who carried their craft to Poland, Bohemia, the Carpathian Mountains, and southeastern Europe, as well as to Scandinavia. Silver-lead ores are said to have been found near Freiberg before 1200 after a flood had scoured the soil from a steep hillside. Other discoveries quickly followed on both the Saxon and the Bohemian sides of the mountains, at Annaberg, Schneeberg, and, above all, at Jáchymov (German: Joachimsthal), where the *Thäler* (thaler, taler) began to be minted from locally produced silver about 1517.

Bohemian ore deposits were geologically related to those of Saxony, and their exploitation followed naturally from that of the Erzgebirge. Again the minerals exploited were in the main the ores of silver and lead, with copper of lesser importance. Two areas proved to be outstanding. The first, Příbram, lay to the southwest of Prague; the other, Kutná

Hora (German: Kuttenberg), lay to the east and became noteworthy for the city, with its richly decorated churches, that grew up there.

The even richer deposits of Slovakia were opened up in the thirteenth and fourteenth centuries, and their exploitation continued beyond the sixteenth century. The most important were at Kremnica (German: Kremnitz), Stiavnica (German: Schemnitz), and Baňská Bystrica (German: Neusohl); lesser deposits were scattered through the mountains of Upper Hungary and Transylvania. These mines were greatly expanded in the sixteenth century by the Fuggers, the Welsers, and other German entrepreneurs.

The eastern Alps and the Balkans held considerable mineral wealth, which included, in addition to silver-lead and mercury (especially in Idrija), some reserves of gold, which was always in great demand but rare in Europe. Although these resources had been exploited by the Romans, they were of little importance during the Middle Ages. At about the time the Saxons might have been expected to begin to work them, the region was overrun by the Turks, and development was postponed until modern times.

Scandinavia was the last significant mining region to be opened up. Its resources were great in both volume and variety, but the physical obstacles to their exploitation were formidable. Most lay in the far north, beyond the range of mining until the nineteenth century. Apart from iron, the only ores to be worked during the Middle Ages were of copper and silver. These were discovered about 1280 in the Stora Kopparberg area of central Sweden. Mining became increasingly important during the later Middle Ages, and the sale of copper became a major source of revenue to the Swedish crown.

Although most medieval European mining activity took place in these nine regions, mines were found beyond their limits—in central Italy, the Massif Central of France, Brittany, and the Vosges—but in most of these mining was short-lived and of no great importance.

Iron mining differed from that of the nonferrous metals because the ore occurred in many chemical forms and under a wide range of geological conditions, from intrusive veins in the older rocks to nodules secreted in the swamps of northern Europe. All were used, however uneconomic their processing might have been. No part of Europe was without iron ore of some kind, and few were the areas where it was not extracted and smelted. Certain areas acquired a more than local importance, chiefly because the ore obtained there lent itself to easy smelting or produced a metal of superior quality. Among these were the hills that bordered the lower Rhineland, especially the Eifel and the area around Siegen. Other such areas were Burgundy and Champagne, where a good-quality ore was found close to the surface; the eastern Alps, where massive ore bodies could be quarried rather than mined; the Pyrenees; and Tuscany.

CONDITIONS OF MINING

Most nonferrous and some ferrous ores occurred in lodes or veins, which rose like the trunk and branches of a tree through the crust from the deep magma chamber where they originated. Lodes varied in thickness from a fraction of an inch to several feet. Sometimes they split into threads that enclosed masses of the country rock; at other times they expanded to fill vast cavities in the crustal rock. The lode was commonly made up of a number of minerals among which those of economic importance formed only a small part. The lode material thus had to be crushed and by some means—usually an application of the gravity principle—the metalliferous material had to be separated from the rest. The grade of an ore, or percentage of metal it contained, was important. Low-grade ores were more expensive, in terms of labor, to mine and process. They also required far more fuel for smelting, and thus tended to be avoided.

Most ores are unstable when separated from the lodes in which they occur, and are quickly dispersed in solution. Insofar as medieval mining is concerned, there were two important exceptions: gold and tin. Gold occurs in lodes in its pure or "native" state, usually in small particles. These are dispersed as the lode erodes, and much of the gold finds its way into valley sands and gravels. (Although little gold was found in Europe during the medieval period, all the gold that was found was obtained by panning the river valley deposits of ore-bearing regions.) Cassiterite, the only important ore of tin, is also a stable mineral. Worn from the ore-bearing lodes, it is carried into the valleys, where its great weight tends to hold it in the river deposits. Part, possibly a large part, of the Cornish tin production came from such alluvial workings.

Difficulties of transportation made it desirable to smelt the ore as close as possible to the mines from which it was extracted. It was, however, not unusual for the amount of fuel used to be ten times that of the ore. The supply of charcoal—coal was not used for primary smelting—was thus of crucial importance. As most of the ore-producing regions were hilly and forested, the supply of fuel did not become a serious problem. But in some regions, such as parts of Spain and Italy, the lack of forests greatly hindered mining and smelting activities.

Some of the mineral-bearing lodes rose to the surface, where they were likely to be discovered. The sixteenth-century Cornish writer Richard Carew (*d.* 1620) describes how the tin miners traced the lumps of lode material in the soil back to the parent lode. Once discovered, the lode was followed along its tortuous path into the crust. The tools and methods used at the end of the Middle Ages differed little from those employed by the Romans. Explosives were not used in mining before the seventeenth century, but fire setting came into use late in the Middle Ages. A fire of brushwood was kindled against the rock, and the heat of the fire, with or without the addition of water, cracked the rock so that the metal could be removed by hand. Most of the tunneling through the rock was accomplished by means of pick, hammer, and chisel, as it had been since classical times.

In contrast with smelting and metalworking, mining was rarely illustrated in medieval manuscripts and bas reliefs. An exception is the Kutná Hora Gradual of the late fifteenth century, now in the Österreichische Nationalbibliothek, Vienna, in which there is a panoramic painting of both surface and underground operations in a silver-mining community at Kutná Hora. The lower part of the picture, a section through the workings, shows a large number of miners, clad in white, burrowing through narrow cavities in the rock, their way lighted by small oil-burning lamps. The rock is being broken with picks, then loaded into baskets or small, low carts that are pulled through the tunnels before being winched to the surface. The miners use ladders to descend and ascend. At the surface the winch is operated by a horse. Nearby, the lode material is being broken up with hammers and washed to separate the ore from the lighter waste. The Kutná Hora Gradual, supplemented by other Bohemian book illustrations and, as at Rožňava, wall paintings, gives an intimate picture of life in one of the most important mining districts in the later Middle Ages.

One important feature of medieval mining is absent from the Kutná Hora painting: no pumps to remove water from the mine are shown. Water constituted one of the major problems in medieval mining. It was sometimes possible in mountainous

Silver mining at Kutná Hora, Bohemia. Watercolor miniature by Matthias Illuminator, 1490. VIENNA, ÖSTERREICHISCHE NATIONALBIBLIOTHEK, COD. 15501. PHOTO: LICHTBILDWERKSTÄTTE ALPENLAND

areas like the Harz and the Erzgebirge to drive an adit into the hillside to intersect the workings and thus to draw off the water. This, however, called for surveying techniques that were beyond the scope of most medieval miners. The alternative was to use a variety of primitive mechanical devices, the best of which could lift only small quantities of water a very short vertical distance. Most used of these devices was an endless chain, turned by a wheel, which dipped into the workings. It might be fitted with a series of buckets or, alternatively, it might be made to rise through a leather pipe into the bottom of which the water was made to pass. Balls of rags, fastened at intervals to the chain, lifted the water within the pipe. This rag-and-chain pump, illustrated by Agricola in his *De re metallica* of 1556, became one of the most important devices for keeping the mines dry. Such machines, however, were very inefficient, and the presence of water set a limit on the depth of mining until the steam engine began to be used in the eighteenth century.

HISTORY OF MINING IN THE MIDDLE AGES

It is probable that mining was brought to an end in most parts of the Roman Empire by the Germanic and barbarian invasions. There is an allusion in a seventh-century life of St. John the Almsgiver to a merchant who sailed from Egypt to Cornwall and returned with a cargo of tin, but there is no other evidence for the continuance of mining in this area. Except for iron, most metals in use could be recovered and reused. There must have been a large store of the precious metals in the form of currency and artwork, and there is evidence that it continued to be recoined and reworked until the increase in population and the revival of trade required it to be supplemented with fresh metal. The same was true of lead, although there is little evidence for any continuing demand for it during the early Middle Ages. Iron, however, corrodes, and the store of it had always to be supplemented with freshly smelted metal. There is good evidence for iron mining and smelting in Merovingian France, and ironworking certainly continued in Italy, Spain, and Central Europe.

It is evident that all branches of mining revived and expanded in the eleventh and twelfth centuries, but just when is far from clear. The famous Rammelsberg mine was opened about 960 for the extraction of silver ore. At about the same time iron mining, which had probably never ceased entirely, began to expand in the Alps, especially in Savoy and Styria. Peter the Venerable, for example, showed a not inconsiderable knowledge of the iron mining carried on in his day in the neighborhood of Allevard, near Grenoble. Silver mining spread eastward through the Harz Mountains, and in the second half of the twelfth century (*ca.* 1170) silver ores were discovered near Freiberg in Saxony.

It is uncertain when the Cornish tin-mining industry revived, but from about 1160 it is well documented because the ores were held to belong to the king, who derived an income from the metal smelted.

It is unlikely that mining would have spread as far and as fast in central Europe if silver had not been an important component of the ores. It was silver and the occasional trace of gold that attracted the prospector and miner, not the base metals that accompanied them. The precious metals were in increasing demand, as trade expanded, for the minting of coins, and it was chiefly in this form that they moved about Europe. The discovery of gold was the ultimate objective of the prospector, as it was of the alchemist. Since Europe held few reserves of this metal, much of the new stock of gold that entered into circulation came from West Africa, in particular the medieval state of Ghana.

The base metals—tin, lead, copper, and zinc—were used, some in alloys, for the manufacture of goods in everyday use. Tin and lead were used to make pewter, which came into widespread use in the later Middle Ages. Copper and tin yielded bronze, and the addition of the zinc ore calamine to copper produced brass. The chief European source of copper was at first the Harz Mountains. From here it was transported to supply the metalworkers of the south German cities and of the lower Rhineland and central Belgium. The Venetians were able to obtain some copper from the mines in the Balkan peninsula. Lead had an important use in its unalloyed state. Beaten into thin sheets, it was used for roofing large buildings, especially churches and castles. Building accounts from the thirteenth century on contain much evidence of the purchase of loads, or fothers, of lead for this purpose.

Although the statistical evidence is lacking, mining activity increased from the tenth to the thirteenth century. It suffered, however, from the recession that began during the middle years of the latter century. The Black Death and subsequent plagues decimated the population of many mining centers. In southwestern England tin production fell by a half as a result of the plague. Output then remained low in most of the mining areas of Central Europe at least until the mid fifteenth century, while in Bohemia silver mining at Kutná Hora suffered severely during the Hussite wars.

During the second half of the fifteenth century, conditions for mining began to improve. Demand for silver rose, and new mines were opened in Saxony and Bohemia. The most rapid expansion appears to have been in the mountains of northern Hungary. The immigrant Germans not only opened mines of the silver-lead ores, but also founded such small mining towns as Kremnica and Banská Bystrica. Early in the sixteenth century the mining and smelting of silver passed under the control of financiers from south Germany, as already discussed. Silver production continued to mount until the 1540's, but soon afterward the import of bullion from the New World brought about a sharp decline in European production.

A new mining frontier developed in the later Middle Ages in Scandinavia. Its mineral wealth was, nevertheless, abundant. Bog-iron ore had been dredged from the floors of Swedish lakes since prehistoric times, and sometime during the twelfth century ore began to be mined from rock. This activity increased in volume and relative importance, so that by the end of the Middle Ages, Sweden was an important source of bar iron, called osmund *(osemund),* for Western Europe. Exports from Stockholm to Lübeck came to exceed 1,000 tons a year.

Silver and copper were also produced in Sweden during the later Middle Ages. The silver from Silvberg was of no great importance, but the copper from Stora Kopparberg, mining of which was under way in the thirteenth century, grew to be one of Sweden's most important mineral products.

Iron-ore mining and ironworking probably declined less in the fourteenth century and recovered more quickly than that of other minerals. Demand for the metal increased during the later Middle Ages as more uses came to be found for it.

MEDIEVAL MINING LAW

The question of ownership of the mineral wealth beneath the soil arose at an early date, and a system of mining law, varying from mineral to mineral and from place to place, gradually took shape. Ownership of minerals and the right to mine them were first defined by the Romans. They were held to belong to the imperial authority, and the right to extract them had to be conceded and, in some way, paid for. The Roman system of controlling mining broke down in most of Europe during the fifth century. For several centuries there was no recognizable mining law, and local communities exploited whatever mineral resources they possessed in whatever way they chose. Echoes of this primitive system survived into modern times in some remote areas, such as Vicdessos in the eastern Pyrenees, where the indigenous population alone had the right to prospect for minerals and to organize their extraction and processing.

As the feudal principle—that there was no land without its lord and that ultimate authority over it rested in the prince or king—began to prevail, however, rights over minerals within the land were gradually clarified. In this process, the influence of Roman law was felt, though it seems likely that royal claims to all minerals derived from the assertion of the prince's authority over the waste and unsettled areas where most of them were found.

This claim to ownership of economic minerals and to control over their exploitation was restricted at first to gold and silver. In 1158 Emperor Frederick I Barbarossa claimed such a regalian right for the German emperors. Mining of precious metals could be carried on within the empire only with permission and on payment of a royalty to the emperor. In theory, intermediate territorial lords had no right to interfere with activities that were so beneficial to the emperor. In reality, however, the fragmentation of political power in the thirteenth century made such imperial pretensions unrealistic. The regalian right devolved upon the territorial princes, both lay and ecclesiastical, and even on the imperial cities. The regalian law assumed various forms. In some territories attempts were made to extend its scope to base metals. This was not difficult in the case of lead, since it usually occurred in close association with silver. One metal that never came within the scope of the regalian law was zinc, since its metallic nature was not recognized during the Middle Ages and it was classed as an "earth."

A unique extension of regalian rights was the control that the English kings exercised over tin mining in Cornwall and Devon. The legal system that evolved permitted any prospector to "bound" or stake out a claim on anyone's land, whether cultivated or waste. He had, however, to work the claim within a year, paying compensation for any damage caused, a small toll (tin) to the local landowner, and a much larger royalty, called coinage—so named from the practice of striking off the corner of a tin ingot for assay purposes. It was in the king's interest that the tin be mined, even if local interests suffered in the process. Indeed, the courts heard numerous cases relating to the damage caused by miners. The most common source of complaint was not the sinking of the mines, but the construction and operation of the primitive hydraulic works associated with them. The practice in the silver-mining regions of Central Europe was broadly similar to that in the tin-producing areas of southwestern England.

Whereas in the empire the regalian right came to be fragmented among the territorial princes, in France such rights were first claimed and exercised by the princes, notably the dukes of Burgundy. In the course of the fifteenth century, the French kings began to assert a regalian right and succeeded gradually in claiming control over mining and the profits that flowed from it. As a general rule, however, the regalian principle was successfully applied only to the precious metals, and the complete control exercised in England over tin mining must be regarded as the exception rather than the rule.

Mining tended to be carried on in remote and sparsely populated areas by communities that engaged in few other economic activities. Mining, furthermore, was an activity in which disputes were frequent but cooperation essential. It is not surprising, therefore, that such communities developed their own codes of practice for both working the mines and settling disputes. The earliest such code known is that embodied in the Aljustrel tables, prepared for the Vispasca mines in Portugal during the second century. Such codes were sometimes developed by the miners, sometimes imposed upon them by their territorial lords. Late in 1185 the bishop of Trent formulated a code for the miners within his diocese. In the middle of the next century (*ca.* 1249) a code was imposed by the king of Bohemia on the miners of Jihlava (German: Iglau) in the south of the country. The "laws" of Jihlava were adopted and adapted in other mining areas of Central Europe.

Such codes were written. Where, however, the miners themselves gradually created a code of practice, it was more likely to remain an unwritten body of customary practice. Such was the case in Cornwall, where the elaborate practices that had evolved during the Middle Ages were not codified until the seventeenth century. This was, of course, in keeping with the contemporary development of the common law. Written or customary, the codes required courts for their interpretation and enforcement. These were, as a general rule, the courts normally held by the territorial lords. In England the royal courts settled many of the disputes that arose in the course of mining. But there were other courts that existed to hear only cases between miners, cases that by their technical nature were ill-suited to the ordinary courts. Best-documented and best-known of such courts was the stannary court of the tin miners of southwest England. In 1201 these miners were granted a charter by King John, later revised and extended, that not only confirmed their traditional practices but also removed them from the jurisdiction of the local courts and placed them under that of their own warden and his stannary courts.

THE SOCIAL HISTORY OF THE MEDIEVAL MINER

In classical antiquity mine workers were usually slaves or condemned criminals. During the Middle Ages they were, almost without exception, free men. There are frequently references to "free miners," and the status of miner was generally held to confer personal freedom. Nevertheless, miners formed a far from egalitarian society. The illustration in the Kutná Hora Gradual shows the scantily clad miners and the more lavishly dressed supervisors who checked the ore as it was brought to the surface. With the increasing scale of mining in the later Middle Ages, social cleavages became more strongly marked. By the end of the Middle Ages, most miners were wage earners in a capitalistically organized industry, and there are instances from the early sixteenth century of miners revolting against the harsh conditions in which they worked.

The scale of mining operations grew steadily during the later Middle Ages. The increasing depth of mines made more complex pumping and winding devices necessary. Water-powered machines were introduced for crushing the ore. All this necessitated an ever increasing capital investment in mining. Small, weakly capitalized mines, worked by a handful of men, were still the rule in iron mining and occasionally in other types of mining. But by the end of the fifteenth century, mining companies were taking shape, their share capital commonly divided into 128 or more parts *(kuxen)*. Expansion was paid for by making calls on each shareholder, much as in the "cost-book" partnerships that became common in the Cornish tin-mining industry. It was by participating in such companies that the Fuggers, Welsers, and others established their dominance in the Central European silver-mining industry during the sixteenth century.

It is difficult to form an estimate of the numbers employed in the mining industry. John Nef, citing the estimate of Emperor Charles V (1525), thought that there could not have been less than 100,000 at the beginning of the sixteenth century. In Cornwall there may have been 2,000 or 3,000 miners at this time. Many, however, worked only part-time. Much of the nonferrous mining was carried on in mountainous or hilly areas, where there was only a scanty indigenous population. The work force was, therefore, largely recruited by immigration. Germans, for example, developed the mines in Bohemia, Silesia, and Hungary, and were even brought to England in the late sixteenth century to develop the mining of copper. Most miners lived in communities in which agriculture, restricted in many instances by the physical conditions of the land, was limited to the production of the barest necessities. Many such settlements disappeared with the exhaustion of the deposits on which they were based. In a few instances, notably in Saxony, Bohemia, and the mountains of northern Hungary, small mining towns arose. In them were established the administration of the mines and commercial activities associated with the smelting of the ore and sale of the metal, as well as with the provisioning of the miners. Many of these towns have survived the decline of mining and are lasting evidence of the wealth the early miners extracted from the earth.

BIBLIOGRAPHY

Agricola, *De re metallica* (1556), Herbert C. Hoover and Lou H. Hoover, trans. (1912, new ed. 1950); C. N. Bromehead, "Mining and Quarrying to the Seventeenth Century," in Charles Singer *et al.*, eds., *A History of Technology,* II (1956); Oliver Davies, *Roman Mines in Europe* (1935); R. Dietrich, "Untersuchungen zum Frühkapitalismus in mitteldeutschen Erzbergbau und Metallhandel," in *Jahrbuch für die Geschichte Mittel- und Ostdeutschlands,* **7–9** (1958–1960); Richard Ehrenberg, *Capital and Finance in the Age of the Renaissance,* H. M. Lucas, trans. (1928); R. J. Forbes, "Metallurgy," in Charles Singer *et al.*, eds., *A History of Technology,* II (1956); John W. Gough, *The Mines of Mendip* (1930, rev. ed. 1957); John W. Gough, ed., *Mendip Mining Laws and Forest Bounds* (1931); J. Janáček, "L'argent tchèque et la Méditerranée," *in Mélanges Fernand Braudel,* I (1973); P. Jeannin, "Le cuivre, les Fugger, et la Hanse," in *Annales de l'École S-C,* **10** (1955); Jan Kořan and Vaclav Vaňeček, "Czech Mining and Mining Laws," in *Cahiers d'histoire mondiale,* **7** (1962); *Le fer à travers les âges, Annales de l'Est* (1956); George R. Lewis, *The Stannaries* (1924); John U. Nef, "Silver Production in Central Europe, 1450–1618," in *Journal of Political Economy,* **49** (1941), and "Mining and Metallurgy in Medieval Civilisation," in *Cambridge Economic History of Europe,* II (1952).

NORMAN J. G. POUNDS

[See also **Bronze and Brass; Dinanderie; Metallurgy; Mints and Money; Technology, Western.**]

MINISTERIALS (*ministeriales* in Latin, *Dienstmänner* in German), were members of an estate (ministerialage) whose common characteristic was, as their name suggests, their obligation to serve their lord. The ministerialage was an institution unique to the kingdom of Germany. Largely of servile origin, the ministerials were employed in a number of capacities, including bailiffs, knights, court and household officials, territorial administrators, and castellans. They attained their greatest political importance in the twelfth century, when they became the chief instruments in the Hohenstaufen's efforts to rebuild the power of the German monarchy after the investiture conflict and in the princes' similar attempt to create their own states. There was considerable variation in the status of the ministerials, since their rights and social position were determined by the power and prestige of their lord. After 1200 they coalesced with the surviving minor noble families to form the knighthood of the later Middle Ages.

Roman aristocrats and Celtic and Germanic chieftains had surrounded themselves in antiquity and in the early Middle Ages with bodyguards of lowly origin who posed less of a threat to their masters than wellborn individuals. A vassal had originally been such a servile retainer, but the vassals had risen in status through service to the Merovingians. When the Carolingians demanded homage from members of the nobility in the eighth century in order to bind them more closely to the crown, vassalage was transformed into an honorable relationship, and the vassals became part of the Frankish aristocracy. While the ranks of the nobility were constantly being replenished throughout Europe from below, the unusual aspect of Germany's social development in the post-Carolingian era was the magnates' turning to the servile population on a far greater scale than elsewhere in Europe to create a new estate of servile warriors and officials, who remained distinct from the nobility for centuries.

The church in Germany took the lead in promoting this development. At the beginning of the tenth century, Germany was exposed to raids by the Northmen and Magyars. As the danger from these invasions subsided in the course of the century, the Saxon kings imposed an increasingly heavy military burden on the church. The bishops and abbots had originally attempted to fulfill these obligations and to administer their extensive properties and households by using their kinsmen, but the gradual disintegration of the large noble clans centered around a magnate reduced the size of the prelates' noble entourage. At the same time vassal ties were never as important in Germany as in France, since the nobles possessed numerous allods and generally regarded any form of subordination as demeaning. The prelates were thus forced to turn to their serfs, whose personal servitude made them more reliable than the nobles. There has been considerable controversy about the precise stratum of the servile population from which the prelates recruited their warriors and household and manorial officials, but the best answer probably is that the prelates chose whoever was willing and able to serve them.

The bishops and abbots provided their servile retainers with both allods and fiefs, increasingly held by hereditary tenure, so that they could perform their responsibilities. These *servi, servientes, servitores, famuli, clientes, homines de familia, familiares, ministri,* and *ministeriales,* as they were variously identified in documents of the tenth and eleventh centuries, formed a quasi-hereditary estate by the middle of the eleventh century. This fact is evidenced by the ministerial code *(Dienstrecht)* of the ministerials of the bishops of Bamberg written about 1060. The Bamberg ministerials were permitted to have their own courts, to be judged by their peers, to clear themselves by compurgation, to inherit fiefs from collateral relatives, and to be free from their obligations to serve if the bishop failed to supply them with a fief.

Conrad II (*r.* 1024–1039), the first of the Salian monarchs, followed the example of the prelates as part of his program to develop a counterweight to the power of the nobility. He and his successors tried to create a strong royal domain in Saxony and Thuringia, garrisoned and administered by servile warriors. These measures were a major factor in precipitating the Saxon revolt of 1073–1075 during the reign of Henry IV (1056–1106), and in turning the Saxon nobility into the most embittered opponents of the Salians during the investiture conflict (1075–1122). The ministerials became instead the staunchest supporters of Henry IV and Henry V (*r.* 1106–1125).

The investiture conflict provided a major impetus for the ministerials' further upward social mobility. Their military might proved to be of decisive importance during the fifty years of civil war. It was during this period that the lay princes as well as many comital and noncomital noble families acquired their own ministerials. The ministerials' growing importance is revealed in two ways. First, they began to adopt surnames around 1100, and, like the nobles themselves, often took the name of a castle. The adoption of a name was both a symptom and a cause of the ministerials' growing family consciousness and contributed to the formation of distinct lineages among them. Second, *ministerialis* became the standard designation for a member of the estate. The word had been used in the Carolingian period for the holder of an office *(ministerium),* regardless of his personal legal status. While the word continued to be employed in this fashion in France, the German magnates' reliance on a hereditary group of servile officials helps to explain why the word acquired a more precise meaning in Germany. The new term had the added advantage, as far as the ministerials were concerned, of placing less emphasis upon their servile ancestry than words like *servus* (serf).

The imperial ministerials, who were first called *ministeriales regni* in 1128, reached the peak of their power and prestige during the reigns of Frederick I Barbarossa (*r.* 1152–1190) and Henry VI (*r.* 1190–1197). They served as the kings' most trusted advisers, supplied the manpower for the Hohenstaufen's Italian campaigns and their forces in the Third Crusade, and garrisoned and administered the imperial domains in Germany and Italy. In exchange for such services, the Hohenstaufen amply rewarded their retainers. On his deathbed in 1197, Henry appointed, for example, the most famous imperial ministerial, Markward of Anweiler (*d.* 1202), who had been the king's own tutor and whom he had formally manumitted and created duke of Ravenna and the Romagna and margrave of Ancona, regent of the kingdom of Sicily. They played a decisive role in the subsequent struggle for the German throne, but their influence declined during the absentee rule of Frederick II (*r.* as emperor 1220–1250). After the collapse of the Hohenstaufen empire, the imperial ministerials formed the unruly estate of the imperial knights *(Reichsritterschaft).*

The princely ministerials played a similar role in the formation of the individual German territories in the High Middle Ages. Powerful princes, like the archbishops of Salzburg or the Babenberg dukes of Austria and Styria, sought their ministerials' advice; employed them as castellans, soldiers, judges, and officials; and settled them on uncleared land, where the ministerials were able to procure sizable holdings and develop their own lordships. These princes benefited from the fortuitous extinction of most of their noble rivals in the twelfth and thirteenth centuries and often forced the few surviving lesser noble families to enter the princely ministerialage. But the princes' dependence on their ministerials also posed a threat to the ruler's authority. Collectively, the ministerials were more powerful than the prince, especially in a period of crisis. For instance, after the death of the last Babenberg duke, Frederick II, in

MINISTERIALS

1246, the Styrian ministerials claimed the right to select his successor. It was not until 1292 that the first Habsburg duke, Albrecht I (duke of Austria, 1282–1298; king of Germany, 1298–1308), managed to reassert his authority. The Hohenstaufen effort to rebuild the power of the monarchy with the aid of the ministerials must thus be judged a failure, and the princes' similar efforts only a partial success.

The basic problem was that the ministerials were in fact becoming the new German nobility and behaving accordingly. The imperial ministerial Werner II of Bolanden (*fl. ca.* 1160–1194/1198), who served Frederick I Barbarossa, was, for example, himself the vassal of forty-five different lords, the possessor of seventeen castles, and the lord of 1,100 knights. The telltale marks of the ministerials' servile origins persisted, however, until at least the thirteenth century. It remained customary until then to distinguish between nobles and ministerials in the witness lists of documents, to restrict the ministerials' right to alienate their allods, except to ministerials of their own lord or to his proprietary churches, and to divide the children of ministerials of different lordships who had intermarried. The tension between the ministerials' actual position in society and their legal status was reflected in German courtly literature, often written by poets of ministerial ancestry, which stressed that nobility was a matter of conduct rather than birth, a concept which accompanied the Arthurian legends from France to Germany. The chivalric culture of the Hohenstaufen period helped in part to bridge the gap between the ministerials and the nobles. The word "knight" (*miles, Ritter*) replaced *ministerialis* in many areas as the standard designation for a ministerial, for example, after 1230 in the ecclesiastical principality of Cologne.

How rapidly the ministerials were finally accepted, if at all, as the equals of the old nobility depended on the individual principality and family. A few of the most powerful imperial and princely ministerials, like the Bolanden or the Styrian Liechtensteins, entered the ranks of the high nobility, the estate of lords (*Herrenstand*). These families were distinguished by their wealth and political power, exercised various seigneurial rights, and had often married women of noble ancestry. The remaining ministerial families slowly combined with the minor noble families to form the estate of knights (*Ritterschaft*). The handful of surviving Austrian and Styrian noble families had coalesced, for example, by 1300 with the ducal ministerials to form the *Herrenstand* of the two duchies; the other ducal ministerials, the ministerials of other nobles, and the ministerials' own knights made up the knighthood. The nobility remained separate from the ministerialage in Westphalia, on the other hand, until the end of the Middle Ages. The absence of strong princely authority in Westphalia helps to explain this; as a result the Westphalian ministerials lacked the prestige of their Austrian counterparts. There were limits, however, to the ministerials' rise. A few of the most exalted noble families, like the Habsburgs, always carefully avoided sullying their bloodlines by marrying ministerials; and the most exclusive religious foundations, such as the cathedral chapter of Cologne, remained closed to persons of ministerial origin until after 1400.

Not all of the ministerial families, or even a majority of them, made the transition into the ranks of the nobility. Many of them, especially those who had only been manorial officials, remained at best wealthy peasants. More important, many ministerials settled in the towns as castellans, judges, toll collectors, market overseers, supervisors of the lord's mint, and members of the town councils. Others sold the surplus agricultural commodities from their estates and became merchants. These urbanized ministerial families composed a sizable segment of the patriciate in such cities as Frankfurt, Nuremberg, Trier, and Worms. In many cases they retained their rural property and knightly life-style. Finally, many ministerial families died out at an early date. One hundred and sixty-seven ministerial families have been identified in the area around Bamberg in the High Middle Ages; only seventy-eight were still in existence by 1300. This rapid decline in the number of ministerial families can be explained by their violent life style, excessive interbreeding within a limited group of families, deliberate measures to limit the number of possible heirs, and the placement of cadets in religious foundations.

The proliferation of monasteries in Germany in the twelfth and thirteenth centuries can be directly linked to the rise of the ministerials. The Cistercians, Premonstratensians, Austin Canons, Teutonic Knights, and to a lesser extent the Dominicans and Franciscans, recruited their members from this stratum of German society. Indeed, it was not uncommon by 1300 for ministerials to become bishops. The emergence of this new class of nobles from the ranks of the dependent population was a major factor in the transformation of German society between the tenth and thirteenth centuries.

BIBLIOGRAPHY
Benjamin Arnold, *German Knighthood 1050–1300* (1985); Karl Bosl, *Die Reichsministerialität der Salier und Staufer,* in *Monumenta Germaniae historica, Schriften,* X (1950–1951), *Frühformen der Gesellschaft im mittelalterlichen Europa: Ausgewählte Beiträge zu einer Strukturanalyse der mittelalterlichen Welt* (1964), and "'Noble Unfreedom": The Rise of the *Ministeriales* in Germany," in Timothy Reuter, ed. and trans., *The Medieval Nobility: Studies on the Ruling Classes of France and Germany from the Sixth to the Twelfth Century* (Europe in the Middle Ages: Selected Studies, XIV [1979]), 291–311; Joachim Bumke, *The Concept of Knighthood in the Middle Ages,* W. T. H. Jackson and Erika Jackson, trans. (1982); John B. Freed, "The Origins of the European Nobility: The Problem of the Ministerials," in *Viator,* 7 (1976), and "The Formation of the Salzburg Ministerialage in the Tenth and Eleventh Centuries: An Example of Upward Social Mobility in the Early Middle Ages," in *Viator,* 9 (1978).

JOHN B. FREED

[See also **Allod; Antrustiones; Class Structure, Western; Crusades, Political; Feudalism; Germany: 843–1137; Hohenstaufen Dynasty; Investiture and Investiture Conflict; Nobility and Nobles; Swabia; Tenure of Land, Western European.**]

MINNEALLEGORIE. See **Middle High German Allegory.**

MINNEBURG. The Middle High German *Minneburg* is an anonymous allegory of love that probably dates from the second quarter of the fourteenth century (*ca.* 1340). Dialect peculiarities (especially in certain rhymes) have prompted suspicions that the poet's home may have been in the diocese of Würzburg. *Die Minneburg* survives in three forms: (1) a long version in rhymed couplets, preceded by a stanzaic prologue (three twenty-line strophes); (2) a shorter verse recension that agrees with the long text for lines 80–3,118 but has a completely independent beginning and end; and (3) a prose redaction of the short form, in which the account has been supplemented with materials drawn from a manuscript of the longer text. Linguistic evidence leaves no doubt as to the priority of the long version, but the two later recensions bespeak the work's continuing popularity during the fourteenth and fifteenth centuries. Unfortunately, the most complete manuscript of the oldest version (Heidelberg, Universitäts Bibliothek, Codex Palatinus Germanicus 455) becomes illegible following line 5,488 and breaks off entirely twenty-four lines later. Because the other two texts replace the concluding love-trial sequence with a totally different final section, they are of no help in reconstructing the outlines of the lost portion.

In terms both of size and structural complexity, *Die Minneburg* is the most imposing of the Middle High German allegories. The narrative centers on the familiar siege of love's castle, but the poet does not appear to have modeled his depiction after any known source. Indeed, the arrangement of materials is highly unusual for a work of this kind.

The poet divides his account into five chapters, marking these junctures with brief summaries (both retrospective and anticipatory). Each transition explicitly delimits the numbered sections—for example: "Ir habt gehort daz erste capitel,/Wie ich daz fur geleget han./Nu hebt sich hie daz ander an" (vv. 352–354; see also vv. 664–666, 2,285–2,286, 3,178–3,179). The textual divisions correspond to subject changes in the account, each chapter being devoted to a major topic.

This system of division offers an important point of reference for estimating how much of *Die Minneburg* has been lost. On two different occasions the poet states that chapter 5 is "daz letzte capitel" (ll. 3,188 and 3,597). The long version ends with a trial presided over by *fraw Mynne.* The poet himself appears before the bar in the guise of a certain *edelkneht,* whom *fraw Truwe* represents as legal counsel. When the text breaks off, his appeal for recompense from a harshly cool lady seems to lack little more than the final summation and a favorable judgment by the court. Even allowing for the poet's increasing verbosity, the account probably did not continue very far beyond the present ending.

The style of *Die Minneburg* is extremely excursive. In addition to the chapter divisions, the poet distinguishes between the *materge,* the main allegorical narrative, and the *underbint,* lengthy autobiographical inserts that disrupt the flow of the account. Although the poet frequently pauses to reflect upon his own unrequited love, only three such outpourings of personal sentiment are deemed long enough to warrant separation as *underbint.* Even stylistically these sections stand out by virtue of a much heavier use of complex rhetorical figures. It was the *underbint* that later provided obvious points for abbreviating the text. The shorter verse redaction eliminates only the third *underbint,* but the prose redaction omits all three.

BIBLIOGRAPHY

Source. Die Minneburg, Hans Pyritz, ed. (1950). Pyritz's introduction has provided the point of departure for all subsequent discussions of the text.

Studies. Walter Blank, *Die deutsche Minneallegorie* (1970), 216–223; Tilo Brandis, *Mittelhochdeutsche, mittelniederdeutsche und mittelniederländische Minnereden: Verzeichnis der Handschriften und Drucke* (1968), 191–192; Ingeborg Glier, *Artes amandi: Untersuchung zu Geschichte, Überlieferung und Typologie der deutschen Minnereden* (1971), 127–156, the best introduction to *Die Minneburg,* both comprehensive and totally reliable.

R. WILLIAM LECKIE, JR.

[See also **German Literature: Allegory; Minnereden.**]

MINNEREDEN. As a literary genre *Minnereden,* or discourses on love, figure prominently in late medieval German literature. Similar traditions developed in France and the Netherlands, but were mostly absent in other European countries.

In Germany discourses on love are part of a huge complex of short poems in rhymed couplets *(kleine Reimpaargedichte)* that includes discourses and narratives on a wide variety of topics. Among narratives there are saints' lives, tales of miracles, novellas *(Mären),* fables, and exempla. The scope of discourses is even wider: by the end of the fourteenth century almost any topic, ranging from the obscene to the spiritual and from the pragmatic to the sublime, could be treated in a discourse.

Two main reasons support considering the *kleine Reimpaargedichte* as a literary complex with some unity, albeit with a wide variety of genres. First, poets felt free to use certain literary conventions across genre divisions and also created many texts that blend the features of individual genres. Second, medieval text collectors and scribes conceived of these genres as related and combined them freely in groups that ranged from small clusters to large collections.

Although the *kleine Reimpaargedichte* have attracted considerable scholarly interest over the past several decades, much basic research has still to be done in many areas before we can fully determine their importance in literary and cultural history.

Thus far *Minnereden* have been more comprehensively researched than other kinds of discourses. We know more than 500 texts that still exist. Hence *Minnereden* outnumber by far any other genre of discourse, except perhaps religious ones (which, however, have not been cataloged). The great majority of *Minnereden* were written in rhymed couplets. However, an interesting small group was composed in an elaborate form, the *Titurelstrophe,* that derives from the stanza Wolfram von Eschenbach created for his *Titurel.*

Thematically, discourses on love have much in common with minnesong, or love songs. In both the dejected lament over unrequited love and the exuberant praise of the beloved lady or woman are repeated in many variations over and over again. *Minnereden* and minnesong also share values, among which *triuwe* (loyalty or reliability) ranks uppermost. Honor, perseverance, generosity, restraint, decency, kindness, and humility likewise play dominant roles, often appearing as full-fledged personifications. But even though the demise of minnesong proper around 1300 coincides with the rise and flourishing of *Minnereden,* the later genre did not historically "substitute" for the earlier one. One can maintain, however, that in the fourteenth century all serious and sophisticated discussion of matters of love was carried on in discourses and not, as previously, in songs and romances. The popularity of *Minnereden* continued to the beginning of the sixteenth century. *Minnereden* then died out, as did most genres of short poems in rhymed couplets. The reasons for this shift remain a subject for further research.

PRECURSORS

Reflections and debates on love were a staple of the courtly romance, beginning with Eilhart von Oberg's *Tristrant* and Heinrich von Veldeke's *Eneide.* In addition, small books or tracts on love, called *Büchlein,* appeared sporadically before 1260. These *Büchlein* could be either independent texts or parts of larger works, and they may be considered forerunners of *Minnereden.*

The first extant independent *Büchlein* is an anonymous poem called *Der heimliche Bote* (The secret messenger; *ca.* 1170–1180?) after its first-person speaker, who instructs women on how to choose a lover prudently and insists above all on secrecy in love. The second part of the poem advises on chivalrous and courtly behavior in general. The author must have had some knowledge of Latin literary traditions; he even refers the reader to *Facetus moribus et vita,* a Latin poem on morals and manners, for further information. But the poem remains isolated in its time.

The same holds true for Hartmann von Aue's *Büchlein* or *Klage* (Lament; *ca.* 1180?), which shows quite different patterns. Here a first-person speaker (who calls himself Hartmann) complains about unrequited love. Yet instead of using a monologue, Hartmann creates an elaborate debate between Body and Heart. Mindful of its own comfort, the Body argues for abandoning the struggle and service for the beloved lady. Yet the Heart finally prevails, and Heart and Body are reunited in unswerving devotion, regardless of how the beloved, who is addressed directly in the last part of the poem, will respond. No source or model for this *Büchlein* has been discovered so far. Hartmann might well have combined elements from Latin (debate), Romance *(salut d'amour)*, and German (minnesong) literary traditions.

Büchlein seem to have enjoyed a moderate popularity until approximately 1260. The so-called *Zweite Ambraser Büchlein* (1220–1250?) is couched as a message to the beloved lady throughout. It discusses love in adversity and the separation of the lovers, which only *triuwe* (loyalty) can overcome. Despite occasional passionate outbursts of the first-person voice, the reasoning follows recurring logical patterns which suggest that the anonymous author must have had some training in formal debates. Ulrich von Liechtenstein included three shorter *Büchlein* in his *Frauendienst* (Service of ladies; *ca.* 1255). In this pseudo-autobiographical narrative, *Büchlein*—like love songs and objects—serve as presents to the lady. Like Hartmann, Ulrich uses dialogues to discuss matters of love. He demonstrates even more clearly than Hartmann that *Büchlein* were hybrid forms which could tend more toward either treatise on love or love letter. In his second work, *Frauenbuch* (Book of ladies; *ca.* 1257), Ulrich stresses repeatedly that he has composed the whole poem as a service for his beloved lady. The body of the work consists of a dialogue in which a knight and a lady debate whether men or women are responsible for the loss of joy in courtly society. Each accuses the other sex and describes decadent court life at times in vivid detail. Finally the first-person narrator joins them and decides that women are not to blame and ought always to be praised.

Der Stricker, an older contemporary of Ulrich and a great innovator of genres, discusses similar themes in his *Frauenehre* (Honor of ladies; first half of thirteenth century). Yet he chooses a different form, a first-person monologue that freely touches on a variety of topics, occasionally using allegory. Der Stricker extols women who maintain the honor and joy of courtly society; he encourages those men who serve women and condemns those who abuse them. Above all Der Stricker was thoroughly aware of creating a new form to discuss women and love. His claim that this form would remain "new" for a very long time proved indeed to be prophetic.

Der Stricker's *Frauenehre* and Ulrich's *Frauenbuch* anticipate basic patterns of later *Minnereden,* although no direct influence can be demonstrated. One of these basic patterns is the first-person monologue, in which the speaker—almost always a man—laments his suffering from love, and/or praises the beloved, and/or reflects and advises on matters of love. This comes closest to the love song, but is often carried on over hundreds, even thousands, of lines. In another basic pattern the first-person narrator becomes an involved witness. He usually describes a walk into the woods or a wilderness *(Spaziergangseinleitung)*—the scenery can vary greatly—where he overhears or meets characters or personifications lamenting, debating, even engaging in love tribunals *(Minnegericht).* He can be called upon to decide the outcome of a debate or to carry back a present to his beloved, more often a message to people in general. This pattern in particular allows for many variations and was widely popular. It also demonstrates that discourse and narrative elements were blended in many different ways, ranging from thin didactic tale to sophisticated allegory.

EARLY *MINNEREDEN*

There seems to be a historical gap between the earlier *Büchlein* and the later *Minnereden.* Thus far hardly any discourses on love can be dated with certainty to the second half of the thirteenth century. But some that are transmitted in early-fourteenth-century manuscripts may stem from that period. The majority of all *Minnereden* have come down to us anonymously, which makes dating in many cases a guessing game at best.

Between approximately 1300 and 1340 a number of rather unusual discourses on love originated along the Rhine. They are unusual in that most of their characters are historically documented aristocrats. The poet known to us as Pseudo-Zilies von Sayn (*ca.* 1300), who presumably served the counts of Katzenelnbogen, may have been the author of the two oldest of these discourses, *Minnehof* (Court of love) and *Ritterfahrt* (Chivalrous expedition). He also wrote historical poems on two major battles of the time and eulogies on groups of aristocrats residing in the area. The two discourses on love employ popular narrative (or allegorical) patterns, namely love tribunals and the siege of a castle. Two later anonymous discourses, *Minne und Gesellschaft* (Love and friendship; *ca.* 1325) and *Die Schule der Ehre* (The school of honor; 1331–1340), use debate and dialogue to assess whether love or friendship is superior, or to praise former students in a school of honor and replace them with new ones. In each case the authors are discussing aspects of love as well as paying tribute to aristocrats who might have been their patrons or members of their audience. Since such direct personal references are more common in French discourses of the time than in German ones, they were perhaps inspired by French models, a rare instance for such an influence on *Minnereden.*

Guillaume de Lorris and Jean de Meun's *Roman de la Rose,* which had a great impact on French and Dutch discourses on love, left hardly any traces in *Minnereden.* The authors of *Minnereden* rely more on native traditions with a few borrowings from Latin literature here and there. Johann von Konstanz's *Minnelehre* (The art of love; *ca.* 1300) is a case in point. Instead of giving abstract rules and advice, Johann presents this first comprehensive German art of love as an exemplary tale. The first-person narrator recounts how he fell in love with, courted, and won a charming young woman. Roughly a third of the poem is dedicated to the narration of a dream in which the narrator meets first Cupid and then Lady Venus/Minne. Cupid is naked, blind, and winged; wears a crown; carries a torch and a lance; and stands on a richly decorated golden pillar above the burning shores of a lake filled with blood. As he explains to the narrator, all of this indicates allegorically the qualities, effects, and dangers of love. The sumptuous appearance of Venus is also related in detail, but not allegorically explained. When she shoots an arrow into the narrator's heart, this only reinforces allegorically his having fallen in love. At the end of the dream she leaves him with two succinct precepts, namely to write letters to the beloved and to persevere. Thus the dream represents an initiation into the nature and effects of love. Only then does the narrator begin to court the woman, first by writing letters, then by meeting with and talking to her until she finally agrees to making love. Then both promise to remain loyal to one another and keep their happiness a secret. Johann had a talent for creating genre scenes. He was also well versed in the German courtly literature of the preceding century. He differs from most other authors of *Minnereden,* however, in freely using the Latin tradition (mythographs, handbooks for letter writing, Ovidian material), which also colors his conception of love.

THREE ARTS OF LOVE

Three comprehensive German arts of love stem from the second quarter of the fourteenth century. They are all allegories, but even though they were written very close together in time, they employ allegory in very different ways. All three poems share basic themes: they explore the nature of love, and they instruct—as does Johann von Konstanz's *Minnelehre*—on how a man should or might win a woman's love and retain it.

The anonymous author of the *Minneburg* (The castle of love) gives the most scholarly definition of love in all of the *Minnereden:* love is *ein vernunfticlich /Wirklich wirkunge dez willen* (a rational, active working of the will; 1. 630f). He tells an elaborate allegorical narrative culminating in the birth of a child, the *Minnekind,* love personified. This *Minnekind* shares features, such as beauty, strength, and increasing blindness, with the traditional figure of Cupid, yet it is also the most original and flexible personification of love in all of the *Minnereden.* What the *Minnekind* stands for changes as the allegorical narrative progresses: it represents first the beginning of love, then a love that becomes aware of itself in a long dialogue with a sage. Leading an army of personifications to storm a castle, the *Minnekind* personifies the courtship of a young man. When the *Minnekind* is settled with his beloved in the castle, yet has to defend both of them against outside intruders, he stands for a happy and mutual, if somewhat incautious, love. Transformed into Lady Love, the *Minnekind* finally presides over a tribunal of love.

For courtship to succeed, so the author of the *Minneburg* claims on the one hand, a young man has to possess a formidable array of good manners and virtues. But when he employs them rightly, he will win the woman he loves. This demanding, yet basically optimistic, conception of love is counterbalanced in the poem by a darker view: throughout, the first-person narrator laments his own suffering from unrequited love in ingenious monologues which he calls *underbint* (interpolated discourses) as opposed to the *materge,* the allegorical narrative. Unfortunately we do not know whether the author succeeded in resolving this tension, because the end of the poem is missing.

Hadamar von Laber took a different allegorical approach in his poem *Die Jagd* (The hunt). He also

MINNEREDEN

developed a conception of love that differs markedly from that of the *Minneburg,* since he was less of a scholar and more of a poet. Furthermore he apparently introduced a new metrical form, the *Titurel* stanza, to the *Minnereden.* This stanza is a sophisticated form and encouraged an elegiac and hermetic style of writing. Hadamar rises to its challenge, but some of his followers in the fifteenth century drift into obscurantism.

The ethical standards the *Jagd* sets for lovers are just as high as those of the *Minneburg.* But Hadamar does not envision a happy end for courtship. Several forces are working against it. One is the malicious interference of society. Another is the "paradoxical" urge of the lover/hunter to extend indefinitely the moment just before the surrender of the beloved/game. A third seems to be that the lady finally becomes indifferent or even fickle. Yet despite these negative forces that cause suffering, the lover remains nobly committed to love, an endurance that is even projected beyond the end of his life and the end of the poem. Not surprisingly, Hadamar insists several times on the analogy of human and divine love, a view that is strongly shared by the author of the *Minneburg,* but usually as strongly rejected by contemporary authors of religious allegories.

The author of *Das Kloster der Minne* (The cloister of love) projects a similar analogy, but handles it in a more playful way. To conceive of lovers as belonging to a quasi-religious order is not unique to this poem. It is a recurring theme in *Minnereden* and serves as a framework for two other discourses: *Die Sekte der Minner* (The sect of lovers; early fourteenth century?) and *Das weltliche Klösterlein* (The little worldly cloister; 1472), which exploit the parodistic, even blasphemous potential of the theme more than does *Kloster der Minne.* This cloister is an allegorical haven for lovers, male and female, whose lives conform to the demanding old codes of chivalry and courtliness. Only gossip, bragging, and disloyalty are severely punished. Shunning those, however, members of the community share a life of rigorous chivalric exercise and spirited feasting in an earthly paradise. The darker aspects of suffering, on which Hadamar increasingly concentrated, are entirely absent.

Hence the anonymous author of the *Minneburg* is more inclusive in his approach than either Hadamar von Laber or the author of *Kloster der Minne,* since his art of love covers the whole gamut from suffering to happiness as well as from scholarly analysis to feasts of rhetoric.

OTHER WORKS

Hadamar and the author of *Minneburg* must have known quite a few shorter *Minnereden,* because they incorporated many of their features and patterns into their more comprehensive works. The author of *Minneburg* even quotes on several occasions with admiration one Egen von Bamberg, who is presumably identical with the author of two shorter discourses on love, *Die Klage der Minne* and *Das Herz* (The complaint of love, The heart; *ca.* 1320–1340). Their themes are conventional—lament of unrequited love, praise of the beloved lady—but Egen apparently introduced a highly ornate style, called *geblümter Stil,* into *Minnereden.* The author of *Minneburg,* Hadamar, and others used it intermittently, too. Like them Egen chooses not only rarely used words and rhymes, but also stunning images and far-fetched similes, which are often mixed and condensed. Difficult as poems or passages in this style may be to understand, their authors attempted to revitalize a "language" of love that had become overly conventional and formulaic.

Heinzelein von Konstanz, a contemporary of Egen, wrote two discourses in a more traditional style. In his *Von dem Ritter und von dem Pfaffen* (Of the knight and the cleric; *ca.* 1320–1340) two women debate whether knights or clerics are superior lovers. This theme was also discussed in a number of Latin and French debate poems whose outcome does vary. None of them served clearly as a model for Heinzelein, but the *miles-clericus* controversy is not confined to these debate poems; it surfaces in other contexts as well. In Heinzelein's discourse the narrator overhears the two women arguing wittily for the merits of knight and cleric, respectively. But instead of settling the case in favor of either of them, the final decision is deferred to the higher authority of Lady Love beyond the poem. Open-ended debates are relatively frequent in *Minnereden* and were perhaps used as a means to involve the audience or reader more strongly.

In the second half of the fourteenth century, several authors followed Hadamar von Laber in composing discourses on love in *Titurel* stanzas, as for instance *Des Minners Klage, Der Minnenden Zwist und Versöhnung,* and *Der Minne-Falkner* (The lover's complaint, The lovers' quarrel and reconciliation, Love's falconer). The last one also employs—albeit on a smaller scale than *Die Jagd*—the allegorical frame of the hunt.

Heinrich der Teichner discusses love and related themes in a number of discourses, but avoids the generic conventions of *Minnereden.* Instead of *Minnereden* proper, he rather composed *Teichnerreden* on love and women.

Teichner's younger contemporary Peter Suchenwirt (*ca.* 1320/1330–after 1395) specialized in heraldic poetry—eulogies and necrologies mostly of Austrian noblemen, but also of German and Hungarian princes. In addition, his work includes other genres that served courtly edification and entertainment: religious, historical, and comic discourses as well as *Minnereden.* Unlike Teichner, Suchenwirt embraces the old ideals of courtly love and the generic conventions of *Minnereden* (such as the narrator's introductory walk and his meeting with personifications, the allegorical hunt, love tribunals, and debates). His trademark is not innovation but rather ingenuity in using traditions.

As in Suchenwirt's case, *Minnereden* were often mixed with other genres of discourses and narratives in the oeuvre of an individual author. But there were also writers who apparently specialized in *Minnereden.* Toward the end of the fourteenth century, Meister Altswert composed four discourses on love which all end in stylistically similar addresses to "his" lady, whom he repeatedly refers to as *min G.* In *Das alte Schwert, Der Kittel, Der Tugenden Schatz,* and *Der Spiegel* (The old sword, The frock, The treasure of virtues, The mirror), he uses basically the same conventional devices as Suchenwirt does, but expands them. He transforms, for instance, the introductory walk into a series of dangerous adventures and describes the realm of the personification in greater and more colorful detail. How persistently these conventions dominated the genre is evident in the oeuvre of a writer who chose the pseudonym *Der elende Knabe* (The errant or hapless boy) and who composed four *Minnereden* in the two or three decades after 1450.

Discourses on love continued to be written throughout the fifteenth century. Most of them were composed according to established patterns, which allowed, however, much variation. This combination of predictability and surprise may help to explain why the genre appealed to audiences or readers for so long.

No author of fifteenth-century *Minnereden* was stronger on surprises than Hermann von Sachsenheim (1366/1369–1458). He wrote two religious allegories, *Der goldene Tempel* and *Jesus der Artz* (The golden temple, Jesus the physician), but his five discourses on love show him at his most productive in experimenting with literary traditions. All of his poems date from the 1450's and thus are the work of a man in his eighties. In *Die Unminne* (Non-love), Sachsenheim praises Wolfram von Eschenbach and Hadamar von Laber highly. He also places this poem in the Hadamar tradition by using the *Titurel* stanza and hunting imagery. But under the trappings of a *Minnerede,* he writes a discourse describing and condemning the disruption of order in society. In *Die Grasmetze* (The grass bumpkin) an old first-person narrator miserably fails to seduce a young peasant woman, and his courtly way of speaking is sharply contrasted with her earthy language. For both *Der Spiegel* (The mirror; *ca.* 1452) and *Die Mörin* (The Moorish lady; 1453) Sachsenheim chose the tribunal of love (with the first-person narrator as the defendant) as a narrative frame; he uses it to satirize abuses of the law as well as to play with literary conventions. He continuously distracts the generic expectations of his audience by twisting well-known patterns, yet he also makes high demands on the reader's literary education. His *Mörin* is the most sophisticated literary "show" of the fifteenth century and ingeniously combines elements of courtly romance and of farce. In a more serious vein, Sachsenheim takes yet another approach in *Das Schleiertüchlein* (The little piece of veil) and puts a *Minnereden* frame around a tragic love story, which in turn encloses a description of a pilgrimage to the Holy Land. Sachsenheim found a few followers among *Minnereden* authors of the ensuing decades, but none of them matches his inventiveness.

Most of the larger collections of *Minnereden* survive in manuscripts from the later part of the fifteenth century. Only very few discourses on love reached the new medium, the printed book. One of these notable exceptions is Sachsenheim's *Mörin,* which had five editions in the sixteenth century. Why discourses on love as a genre did not outlive the Middle Ages remains a matter of speculation. They share this fate with many other late medieval genres. If a writer such as Hans Sachs is any indication, a new emphasis on marriage may have made the old ideals of courtly love seem obsolete. When these ideals resurfaced in the seventeenth century, they were explored in lyrics and novels rather than in discourses.

BIBLIOGRAPHY

Sources. Adolf Bach, *Die Werke des Verfassers der Schlacht bei Göllheim (Meister Zilies von Seine?)* (1930), and "Ein neues Bruchstück der 'Ritterfahrt,'" in *Zeitschrift für deutsches Altertum* **69** (1932); Klaus Hofmann,

Strickers "Frauenehre" (1976); W. Holland and A. Keller, eds., *Meister Altswert* (1850); Johann von Konstanz, *Die Minnelehre,* Frederic Elmore Sweet, ed. (1934); Ulrich von Liechtenstein, *Werke,* Karl Lachmann, ed. (1841); Kurt Matthaei, *Das "weltliche Klösterlein" und die deutsche Minne-Allegorie* (1907); Heinrich Meyer-Benfey, *Mittelhochdeutsche Übungsstücke* (1909); *Mittelhochdeutsche Minnereden,* I, Kurt Matthaei, ed. (1913), II, Gerhard Thiele and Wilhelm Brauns, eds. (1938); Otto Mordhorst, *Egen von Bamberg und Die geblümte rede* (1911); Heinrich Niewöhner, ed., *Die Gedichte Heinrichs des Teichners,* 3 vols. (1953–1956); Franz Pfeiffer, ed., *Heinzelein von Konstanz* (1852); Alois Primisser, ed., *Peter Suchenwirt's Werke* (1827); Hans Pyritz, ed., *Die Minneburg* (1950); Donald K. Rosenberg, ed., *The Schleiertüchlein of Hermann von Sachsenheim* (1980); Hermann von Sachsenheim, *Die Mörin,* Horst Dieter Schlosser, ed. (1974); Maria Schierling, *"Das Kloster der Minne": Edition und Untersuchung* (1980); J. A. Schmeller, ed., *Hadamar's von Laber Jagd und drei andere Minnegedichte* (1850); Ludwig Wolff, ed., *Das Klagebüchlein Hartmanns von Aue und das zweite Büchlein* (1972).

Studies. Walter Blank, *Die deutsche Minneallegorie* (1970); Tilo Brandis, *Mittelhochdeutsche, mittelniederdeutsche und mittelniederländische Minnereden* (1968); Ingeborg Glier, *Artes amandi: Untersuchung zu Geschichte, Überlieferung und Typologie der deutschen Minnereden* (1971); Melitta Rheinheimer, *Rheinische Minnereden* (1975).

INGEBORG GLIER

[See also **Allegory; Ambraser Heldenbuch; Courtly Love; German Literature: Allegory; Hadamar von Laber; Hartmann von Aue; Heinrich der Teichner; Heinrich von Veldeke; Hermann von Sachsenheim; Middle High German Literature; Stricker, Der; Ulrich von Liechtenstein; Wolfram von Eschenbach.**]

MINNESANG. See **Middle High German Literature.**

MINNESINGERS. Minnesingers were authors and performers of German courtly lyric (minnesong) who flourished in the twelfth, thirteenth, and fourteenth centuries. The term is first mentioned by Hartmann von Aue about 1195. It derives from *minne,* the Middle High German equivalent of *fin'amor* of the troubadours, which today is commonly referred to as courtly love.

The complex ideology of *hôhiu minne* ("high," noble love) deals with the relationship of the singer (*ritter,* the knight) to the lady *(frouwe, wîp)* in the context of courtly society. Central to this ideology is the concept of love service *(minnedienst),* modeled on the service that a vassal owes his lord. The singer, himself often a vassal or a traveling musician, publicly declares his love, which binds him in loyal servitude to an unreachable lady. The subject of his unfulfilled erotic desire is a married lady of high standing whose virtues embody the values of the feudal order. The minnesinger's praise of the lady and of the ennobling *minne* creates a joyous atmosphere (*vröide* or *vröude*) by confirming these values. The reward for his performance is *êre* (honor, later also honorary). Minnesong is thus a social game, a part of courtly entertainment much like jousting or feasting. It functions as fictional self-representation that validates the life-style and structure of the feudal aristocratic society.

Minnesingers' language mirrors other important aspects of medieval life: religion and law. The latter contributes the concepts of loyalty and constancy *(triuwe, stæte);* the former, the ideal attributes of the lady: grace and mercy *(hulde, genâde).* There are some parallels between the reverence for the courtly lady and the growing Marian cult.

The earliest minnesong is rooted in indigenous dance songs and other unwritten traditions. Social symbolism is already present, but "natural" love relationships are not yet subject to the "classic" *minne* ideology. Many of the early songs are written from the woman's point of view *(Frauenlied)* or alternate between his view and her view *(Wechsel).* Chief representatives are Der von Kürenberg (*fl. ca.* 1150), Meinloh von Sevelingen (late twelfth century) and, in part of his repertory, Dietmar von Aist (*fl.* 1139–1171). Their poetry uses the traditional epic style of rhymed quatrains.

The growing influence of the troubadour and trouvère art can be seen in the lyric of Emperor Henry VI (1165–1197), Heinrich von Veldeke (1140/1150–*ca.* 1200), Rudolf von Fenis (*fl.* 1158–1192), Friedrich von Hausen (*ca.* 1155–1190), and Heinrich von Rugge (second half of the twelfth century). Along with the ideology, their lyrics adopt the canzone form (bar form) that was to become standard. The stanza consists of two *Stollen* with identical rhyme scheme and sung to the same melody, followed by an *Abgesang* with a new scheme and a new melody. The through-composed *Leich,* related to the French lai and the Latin sequence, also appears. This intricate poetic showpiece is typified by pairing of lines or the repetition of groups of lines.

According to Hugo Kuhn, the early minnesong was more a layman's social game than "literature." However, the next generation of minnesingers shows a new awareness of their role as artists. Reinmar von Hagenau (der Alte; *fl.* 1185–1205/1210) and Heinrich von Morungen (*d.* 1222) absorbed and surpassed the techniques and metaphors of the French lyric, as did their contemporary Hartmann von Aue (*fl.* 1180–1203). The latter also mastered the Arthurian epic and shorter narratives *(mære).* These minnesingers refined rhyme and metric schemes, and treated the *minne* ideology with increased subjectivity. Thus, they created an original German contribution to courtly lyric.

The art of the minnesingers culminated in Walther von der Vogelweide (*ca.* 1170–*ca.* 1230). He excelled in nearly every form of medieval lyric, such as *Tagelied* (dawn song), *Kreuzlied* (Crusade song), pastourelle (song praising a lowborn girl), and *Spruch* (religious, political, or philosophical "saying" in compact stanzaic form). Through his mastery of the art and ideology of minnesang, Walther was able to challenge the courtly ethic. His oeuvre served as model for subsequent generations.

Minnesingers Ulrich von Liechtenstein (*ca.* 1198–*ca.* 1275), Reinmar von Zweter (*ca.* 1200–*ca.* 1260), and Meister Alexander (late thirteenth century) continued the courtly tradition. The style became increasingly intricate and florid, especially as cultivated by Burkhard von Hohenfels (*fl.* 1212–1242), Konrad von Würzburg (*ca.* 1225–*ca.* 1287), and Wizlaw III von Rügen (*ca.* 1265–1325). A second, concurrent tradition returned to the realism, parody, and more indigenous style of Neidhart von Reuental (*fl. ca.* 1210–1236). It was later exemplified by Tannhäuser (*ca.* 1200–*ca.* 1270). Thirteenth-century minnesang peaked in the oeuvre of Heinrich von Meissen (Frauenlob, *ca.* 1250/1260–1318), who is reputed to have founded the first school for the systematic study of lyric *(singschule).* This signals the transition to the lyric of the emerging bourgeoisie, meistergesang.

Because of the changing political and social structure after 1300, the courtly ethic began to lose its central role. However, the topoi of minnesong continued to be cultivated well into the fifteenth century, notably by Hugo von Montfort (1357–1423), the Monk of Salzburg (second half of the fourteenth century), and Oswald von Wolkenstein (*ca.* 1376–1445), as well as by meistersingers.

The waning of minnesong in the fourteenth century brought about efforts to preserve this art in writing. The major known manuscripts compile only the texts without music. The few surviving melodies, preserved by the meistersingers one or two centuries after the songs were first performed, are of questionable reliability. Several melodies could be "inferred" through the study of contrafacts (adaptations of troubadour or trouvère models).

There are notable exceptions to the lack of musical sources. The indigenous style of Neidhart found a large following, and his songs are often preserved with melodies. In addition, the latest courtly singers showed a new attitude by striving to preserve their art (especially Oswald von Wolkenstein, who, with his use of polyphony, pointed to the Renaissance).

Even where melodies can be found, their nonrhythmic notation and the lack of tempo or other indications make interpretation problematic. Modern music scholarship, using scarce historic and iconographic evidence, has attempted to reconstruct performances of minnesong, some of which have been recorded. The historic validity of today's performances may perhaps never be ascertained. Only through approaching minnesong as a performing art, however, can we begin to understand its rich legacy.

BIBLIOGRAPHY

Sources. David Fallows, "Sources, MS, III, 5: Secular Monophony, German," in *New Grove Dictionary of Music and Musicians,* XVII (1980); Ewald Jammers, *Ausgewählte Melodien des Minnesangs* (1963); Carl von Kraus, *Deutsche Liederdichter des 13. Jahrhunderts,* 2 vols. (1952–1958): Hugo Moser and Joseph Müller-Blattau, comps., *Deutsche Lieder des Mittelalters. . . . Texte und Melodien* (1968); Hugo Moser and Helmut Tervooren, *Des Minnesangs Frühling,* rev. and enl., 3 vols. in 4 (1977–1981); Olive Sayce, ed., *Poets of the Minnesang* (1967); Barbara G. Seagrave and J. Wesley Thomas, *The Songs of the Minnesingers* (1966); Ronald J. Taylor, *The Art of the Minnesinger,* 2 vols. (1968).

Bibliographies include Robert W. Linker, *Music of the Minnesinger and Early Meistersinger* (1962); Helmut Tervooren, *Bibliographie zum Minnesang und zu den Dichtern aus "Des Minnesangs Frühling"* (1969).

General references. Karl Bertau, *Deutsche Literatur im europäischen Mittelalter,* II (1973); Helmut de Boor and Richard Newald, *Geschichte der deutschen Literatur von den Anfängen bis zur Gegenwart,* II, *Die höfische Literatur* (1953, 4th rev. ed. 1960); Peter Dronke, *The Medieval Lyric* (1968, 2nd ed. 1977); Kurt Ruh *et al.*, eds., *Die deutsche Literatur des Mittelalters: Verfasserlexikon,* rev.

ed. (1978–); Walther Salmen, *Die fahrenden Musiker im europäischen Mittelalter* (1960).

Studies. Joachim Bumke, *Ministerialität und Ritterdichtung* (1976), and *Mäzene im Mittelalter* (1979); Hans Fromm, ed., *Der deutsche Minnesang* (1961, 4th ed. 1969); Arthur T. Hatto, *Essays on Medieval German and Other Poetry* (1980); Hubert Heinen, "Observations on the Role in Minnesang," in *Journal of English and Germanic Philology,* 75 (1976); Peter Kesting, *Maria-Frouwe: Über den Einfluss der Marienverehrung auf den Minnesang bis Walther von der Vogelweide* (1965); Burkhard Kippenberg, *Der Rhythmus im Minnesang* (1962), and "Minnesang," in *New Grove Dictionary of Music and Musicians,* XII (1980); Hugo Kuhn, *Dichtung und Welt im Mittelalter* (1959, 2nd ed. 1969); Wolfgang Mohr, "Mittelalterliche Feste und ihre Dichtung," in *Festschrift Klaus Ziegler* (1968); John C. Moore, "'Courtly Love': A Problem of Terminology," in *Journal of the History of Ideas,* **40** (1979); Hugo Moser, comp., *Mittelhochdeutsche Spruchdichtung* (1972); Bert Nagel, *Staufische Klassik: Deutsche Dichtung um 1200* (1977); Margaret F. Richey, *Essays on the Mediaeval German Love Lyric* (1943), 2nd ed. titled *Essays on Medieval German Poetry* (1969); Olive Sayce, *The Medieval German Lyric: 1150–1300* (1982); Günther Schweikle, "Die Frouwe der Minnesänger," in *Zeitschrift für deutsches Altertum und deutsche Literatur,* **109** (1980); Peter Wapnewski, *Waz ist minne: Studien zur Mittelhochdeutschen Lyrik* (1975); Horst Wenzel, *Frauendienst und Gottesdienst: Studien zur Minne-Ideologie* (1974).

IVANA PELNAR-ZAIKO

[See also **Courtly Love; Der von Kürenberg; Dietmar von Aist; German Literature: Lyric; Hartmann von Aue; Heinrich von Meissen; Heinrich von Morungen; Heinrich von Veldeke; Hugo von Montfort; Konrad von Würzburg; Meinloh von Sevelingen; Middle High German Literature; Neidhart von Reuental; Oswald von Wolkenstein; Reinmar von Hagenau; Reinmar von Zweter; Tannhäuser; Troubadour, Trouvère, Trovador; Ulrich von Liechtenstein; Walther von der Vogelweide; Wizlaw III von Rügen.**]

MINSTRELS was a term that came to refer to secular musicians employed by noblemen as household servants, by cities as watchmen or members of a band, and by guilds and confraternities. As such, the minstrel was distinguished from the jongleur in two important ways: he specialized in playing musical instruments (often a specific one) and was hired on a permanent or semipermanent basis. A distinct hierarchy developed: trumpeters and drummers were ranked above and paid more than the other minstrels, and wind players were more highly regarded than those who performed on stringed instruments.

At first, in the Gothic period, the feudal courts hired local or itinerant performers (*mynstralles* and *jeestours*) to amuse them during the long evenings. These entertainers played instruments or sang, told tales, did magic tricks, juggled, or presented trained animal acts. They had to be versatile and performed on a variety of instruments.

The pattern of daily life at the feudal courts changed in accordance with the developing conception of castle and court as places in which to live in sumptuous splendor. Large sums of money were spent on festivities and luxury; magnificence, ceremony, and conspicuous display came to accompany every act and event. The means for this sophisticated mode of existence lay in a highly-organized corps of household retainers trained in numerous arts and crafts, under the supervision of a major-domo, who catered to and maintained their employers according to this new self-image. The ducal court of William X of Aquitaine, for example, was one of the earliest such cultural centers, and its influence spread quickly. It reached Paris in 1137, when William's daughter Eleanor married the future Louis VII; it arrived in London fifteen years later, when she took her second husband, Henry II. The demand for professional musicians increased in the late twelfth century, when the nobility, no longer satisfied with only an evening's entertainment and epic poetry, demanded more varied and sophisticated performances throughout the day.

The opportunities for music making in this rich cultural environment became increasingly varied and included betrothal ceremonies and weddings, processions, banquets, dancing, and tournaments. Thus, Chaucer writes: "Full is the place of soun of minstralcye/Of songes amours of mariage" (*Legend of Good Women,* l. 2,615f). Jean le Fèvre, in *Chronique,* states: "Grant foison y ot aussi de trompetes, menestrelz et joueurs de plusieurs instrumens de musique"; "There were also a great number of trumpets, minstrels and players of several musical instruments" (Morand, ed., II [1881], p. 165). One reads in *The Life of Ipomydon:* "Trumpes to met gan blow tho/Claryons and other menestrellis mo/Tho they washe and gede to mete/And every lord toke his sete;/When they were sette all the route/Menstrellis blew than all aboute" (Kölbing, ed. [1889]). Dancing appears in *Reynard the Fox* (translated by William Caxton): "There was daunsed . . . the hove [court] daunce with shalmouse [shawms], trompettis and all maner of menstralsye" (l. 54f). And Christine de Pizan in her *Livre du duc des vrais amants* writes:

"Lors menestrelz liement/Cournoient, hairaux crioient/Lances brisent, cops resonnent/Et ces menestrelz hault sonnent/Si qu'on n'oïst Dieu tonnant"; "They minstrels together/sounded [their inments], heralds called/Lances broke, heads clashed/ And these minstrels played loudly/As if one heard the thunder of God" (Roy, ed., *Oeuvres poétiques,* III [1896], p. 91). There are many additional references to minstrels in contemporary literature too numerous to mention.

In one of the earliest references (1303), minstrels "making minstrelsy" (*facientibus menestralciam*) were attached to the English court, like their successors playing "before the kinge when it shal please him." By 1315 Louis X had a corps of minstrels formally attached to his household as "music [*sic*] of the king's chamber" (*musicque de la chambre du roy*). According to the Household Ordinances of Edward IV (*ca.* 1475), there were thirteen minstrels at court, the leader of whom "directeth them in all festyvall dayes to theyre statyones, to bloweings and pipygnes . . . and all thies [minstrels] sittynge in the hall togyder; whereof sume use trumpettes, some shalmuse [shawm] and small pipes and some as strengemen [fiddlers and other players]. . . ."

Minstrels came to be divided into two groups, according to whether the sonorities of their instruments were loud or soft. For example, in 1385 King Charles VI fixed the number at "six loud minstrels and three soft" (*six haultz menestriers et trois bas*). The household of Prince Juan of Spain employed a consort of "loud minstrels" (*menestriles altos*): sackbuts (trombones), shawms, cornets, trumpets, and kettledrums. The band of Duke Albrecht V in Vienna included three flutists or fife players (*fistulatores*), three shawm players (*phiffer*), two trumpeters (*trompeter*), two trombonists (*posauner*), a rebec (?) player (*leyrer*), vielle player (*fidler*), and lutanist (*lautenslaher*).

By the thirteenth century fortified towns flourished throughout Europe as strongholds of a new middle-class culture, with a corresponding entry of powerful guilds into positions of economic, political, and artistic supremacy. Both chronicles and civic records show how strong were the citizens' cravings for distraction as well as their leaders' desire for the status gained through pomp and display.

Most entertainment took shape under the government and guilds, which became focal points for the activities of permanent bands of instrumentalists as well as of wandering minstrels. In Paris in 1321 a group of thirty-seven jongleurs and minstrels was chartered to perform for fixed compensation only and exclusively within the area served by their brotherhood. Prosperous Netherlandish towns employed bands of wind players (known as *alta*) as well as minstrels (*spelliedens*), providing music at designated hours of the day as well as at markets, festivals, and annual processions (*ommegang*). In Frankfurt in 1362 the civic musicians had "to play for [the] watch, entertainments and to give signals" when assigned to guard duty on the numerous towers. Italian city-states became noted for religious processions, carnivals, and other public open-air ceremonies accompanied by the playing of various instruments (*sonatori di varii strumenti*).

BIBLIOGRAPHY

Raymond van Aerde, *Ménestrels communaux et instrumentistes divers établis ou de passage à Malines, de 1311 à 1790* (1911); Francisco de Baldelló, "La música en la casa de los reyes de Aragón," in *Anuario musical,* **11** (1956); Marie-Thérèse Bouquet, "La cappella musicale dei duchi di Savoia dal 1450 al 1500," in *Rivista italiana di musicologia,* **3** (1968); Edmund A. Bowles, "Tower Musicians in the Middle Ages," in *Brass Quarterly,* **5** (1962); Michel Brenet, "Les musiciens de Philippe le Hardi," in *Sammelbände der internationalen Musikgesellschaft,* **8** (1907); Luigia Cellesi, *Storia della più antica banda senese* (1906); P. Chaillon, "Les musiciens du nord à la cour de Louis XI," in *La renaissance dans les provinces du nord,* François Lesure, ed. (1956); Henry Leland Clarke, "Musicians of the Northern Renaissance," in Jan LaRue, ed., *Aspects of Medieval and Renaissance Music* (1966); G. van Doorslaer, "La chapelle musicale de Philippe le Beau," in *Revue belge d'archéologie et d'histoire de l'art,* **4** (1934); Fritz Ernst, "Die Spielleute im Dienste der Stadt Basel im ausgehenden Mittelalter (bis 1550)," in *Basler Zeitschrift für Geschichte und Altertumskunde,* **44** (1945); Zoltán Falvy, "Spielleute im mittelalterlichen Ungarn," in *Studia musicologica,* **1** (1961); Edmond Faral, *Les jongleurs en France au moyen âge* (1910); Max Fehr, *Spielleute im alten Zürich* (1916); Arnold Geering, "Von den Berner Stadtpfeifern," in *Schweizer Beiträge zur Musikwissenschaft,* **1** (1972); Louis Gilliodts van Severen, *Les ménestrels de Bruges* (1912); Wilhelm V. A. Grossmann, *Frühmittelenglische zeugnisse über Minstrels (circa 1100 bis circa 1400)* (1906); Z. Hudovsky, "Die Organisten und Spielleute im mittelalterlichen Zagreb," in *Studia musicologica,* **10** (1968); J. Klapper, "Die soziale Stellung des Spielmanns im 13. und 14. Jahrhunderts," in *Zeitschrift für Volkskunde,* **40** (1931); A. Kubinyi, "Spielleute und Musiker von Buda (Ofen) in der Jagello-Epoche," in *Studia musicologica,* **9** (1967); José M. Lamaña, "Los instrumentos musicales en los últimos tiempos de la dinastía de la casa de Barcelona," in *Anuario musical,* **24** (1969); L. Langwill, "The Waits," in *Hinrichsen's Musical Year Book,* 7 (1952); Lionel de la Laurencie, "La

MINTS AND MONEY, ARMENIAN

musique à la cour des ducs de Bretagne aux xive et xve siècles," in *Revue de musicologie,* **14** (1933); José M. Madurell, "Documentos para la historia de maestros de capilla, organistas, órganos, organeros, músicos e instrumentos," in *Anuario musical,* **4** (1949); Jeanne Marix, *Histoire de la musique et des musiciens de la cour de Bourgogne sous le règne de Philippe le Bon (1420–1467)* (1939); Adolf Mönckeberg, *Die Stellung der Spielleute im Mittelalter* (1910); Hans Joachim Moser, *Die Musikergenossenschaften im deutschen Mittelalter* (1910); K. Nef, "Die Stadtpfeiferei und die Instrumentalmusiker in Basel," in *Sammelbände der internationalen Musikgesellschaft,* **10** (1908–1909); André Pirro, *La musique à Paris sous le règne de Charles VI (1380–1422)* (1930); Richard Rastall, "The Minstrels of the English Royal Households, 25 Edward I–1 Henry VIII: An Inventory," in *R.M.A.* (Royal Musical Association) *Research Chronicle,* **4** (1964), and "Minstrelsy, Church, and Clergy in Medieval England," in *Proceedings of the Royal Musical Association,* **97** (1970–1971); H. Rothert, "Mittelalterliche Spielleute in Westfalen," in *Westfalen,* **22** (1938); Walter Salmen, "Bemerkungen zum mehrstimmigen Musizieren der Spielleute im Mittelalter," in *Revue belge de musicologie,* **11** (1957), "Zur Geschichte der herzoglich-braunschweigischen Hofmusiker," in *Niedersächsisches Jahrbuch für Landesgeschichte,* **30** (1958), and *Der fahrende Musiker im europäischen Mittelalter* (1960); Alfred Schaer, *Die altdeutschen Fechter und Spielleute* (1901); Josef Sittard, "Jongleurs und Menestrels," in *Vierteljahrsschrift für Musikwissenschaft,* **1** (1885); Jop Spruit, "De Speelman in de Nederlanden van de 13^e–15^3 eeuw," in *Mens en melodie,* **15** (1960); George A. Stephen, *The Waits of the City of Norwich Through Four Centuries to 1790* (1933); R. Sterl, "Materialen zum Spielmann und Stadtpfeifer in spätmittelalterlichen Regensburg," in *Oberpfalz,* **56** (1968); B. Szabolcsi, "Die ungarischen Spielleute des Mittelalters," in Friedrich Blume, ed., *Gedenkschrift für Hermann Abert* (1928); L. M. Wright, "Misconceptions Concerning the Troubadours, Trouvères, and Minstrels," in *Music and Letters,* **48** (1967).

EDMUND A. BOWLES

[See also **Joglar/Jongleur; Music, Popular; Music in Medieval Society; Musical Instruments, European.**]

MINTS AND MONEY, ARMENIAN. Historically, Armenia is the land encompassed by the Caspian, Mediterranean, and Black seas. Because of its geographical position, it has repeatedly been invaded by the forces of powerful empires, and it has had few periods of total independence. This fact helps explain why monetary circulation in Armenia has been dominated by the coinage of Persians, Romans, Arabs, Byzantines, and, more recently, Turks and Russians. During Armenia's independent intervals, however, its rulers struck coins that are quite distinctive and possess considerable artistic merit.

The earliest extant coins were in copper and were issued by the rulers of Sophene and Commagene in southwest Armenia during the third and second centuries before Christ. Only recently has a classification of the coinage of this period been published.

The next dynastic rulers were the Artaxiads, whose reign lasted 200 years (*ca.* 189 B.C. to *ca.* A.D. 6). One of their kings, Tigran II the Great (95–*ca.* 55 B.C.), established a powerful state extending from the Caspian to the Mediterranean seas. With the capture of Antioch and other territories inhabited by Greeks, Armenian coinage came to be greatly influenced by Greek traditions.

Artaxiad coins are quite distinctive. In almost all cases the obverse bears the image of the king, turned right, diademed, and wearing the ornate five-pointed Armenian tiara, edged with pearls. The tiara is normally decorated with an eight-rayed star placed between two eagles that are back to back, but with their heads turned to each other. This design appears in modified forms on the smaller copper coins of the later kings. On the reverse are a variety of images, including various deities and animals; these images often reflect the influence of the coinage of the Seleucids. The legends are in Greek as the coins were struck before the invention of the Armenian alphabet.

The Artaxiad coins are rare and only recently have been subjected to systematic study. In the early years of the kingdom, the coinage consisted of silver tetradrachms and drachms, along with various denominations of copper and bronze. There are no known gold coins of the Artaxiads. With the gradual weakening of the kingdom from its continuous wars against Rome, the coinage eventually became limited to copper. In addition to the mint in Antioch, where Tigran the Great struck a large number of coins, a mint probably existed in the main capital city of Artašat (Artaxata); there may also have been one in Tigranakerta, where Tigran the Great had his capital for a number of years. A limited number of coins were also struck in Damascus.

The ancient Armenians were mountaineers and warriors—commerce was not their main occupation. For this reason, perhaps, extensive coinage was not undertaken. Various hoard studies indicate that even during the period of the Artaxiads, Greek and Roman coins were in circulation in Armenia.

Arataxiad coins: (*1*) Silver tetradrachm of Tigran the Great (95 B.C.–55 B.C.); (*2*) Silver drachm of Artawazd II (55 B.C.–34 B.C.).

Copper coin of Kiwrikē of Lōṙi (*ca.* 1000).

Coins of Cilician Armenia: (*1*) Silver double tram of Leo I (1198–1217); (*2*) Silver tram of Leo I; (*3*) Silver tram of Het^{c}um; (*4*) Copper tank of Het^{c}um. ALL PHOTOGRAPHS PROVIDED BY AUTHOR

During the millennium following the fall of the Artaxiads, Armenia was politically under the influence of various foreign powers. From the fifth to the seventh century Armenia was dominated by the Persians, and it appears that some mints were maintained, but a definitive investigation of the coins actually struck in Armenia during this period has yet to be made. The Arabs, who dominated Armenia from the seventh to the ninth century, struck numerous coins bearing the name Armenia or the name of a city in Armenia. The Byzantines, who ruled over parts of Armenia for long periods, apparently did not maintain mints in these territories. Finally, the Turkish invaders who established themselves in Armenia in the eleventh century, and the Mongols who followed them in the thirteenth, struck coins bearing the name of the mint and the rulers.

Curiously, in the second half of the eleventh century, a minor ruler in Caucasian Armenia issued coins in Armenian bearing his name. The circumstances under which Kiwrikē of Lōṙi-Tašir struck these coins are not clear.

After the conquest of their homeland by the Seljuk Turks, the Armenians were able to establish their rule in Cilicia and maintain it for 300 years (1080–1375). The early princes struck a limited number of copper coins; but with the coronation of Prince Leo (Levon) as king in 1198/1199, an enlarged mint was organized in the capital city of Sīs, and another in Tarsus. Many coins were issued in silver and copper, and ceremonial pieces were struck in gold. Succeeding kings continued striking silver and copper coins in impressive numbers, indicating the commercial vitality of the nation. The most important type of silver coin, called tram, originally weighed about three grams and was high in silver content. In the later period of the kingdom, the silver coinage was debased, and a new type of coin, known as takvorin, was introduced. The copper coins were mainly in three denominations—tank, kardez, and pogh. The coinage of Cilician Armenia has been carefully researched during the past few decades.

The developing interest in Armenian coins in the past thirty years has resulted in a better understanding of the coinage of Armenia and an increase in the number that have found their way into collections where they can be studied. In 1960, the number of Armenian coins in various public and private collections was estimated to be about 12,000. That number today exceeds 60,000 and is expected to grow in the coming years.

BIBLIOGRAPHY

Paul Z. Bedoukian, *Coinage of Cilician Armenia* (1962), *Coinage of the Artaxiads of Armenia* (1978), *Selected Numismatic Studies* (1981), and *Coinage of the Armenian Kingdoms of Sophene and Commagene* (1985); Philip Grierson, "Kiurikē I or Kiurikē II of Loṛi-Armenia?" in *The American Numismatic Society Museum Notes,* **10** (1962); David M. Lang, "Supplementary Notes on Kiurike II, King of Lori in Armenia, and His Coins," *ibid.,* **6** (1954).

PAUL Z. BEDOUKIAN

[See also **Armenia, History of; Cilician Kingdom; Leo I/II of Armenia; Lōṙi.**]

MINTS AND MONEY, BYZANTINE. The history of Byzantine coinage falls into three periods. The first extends from the sixth to the eleventh centuries; its most important feature is the remarkable stability of the nomisma (gold coin of full weight), which served as a standard medium of exchange in Mediterranean trade.

In the sixth century the Byzantine monetary sys-

MINTS AND MONEY, BYZANTINE

tem was structured around gold and copper coinage. Under Justinian I (527–565) and Justin II (565–578) silver coinage was issued in the western half of the empire (where under Vandal and Ostrogoth rule silver coinage had played a significant role), but in the East its issue was restricted to small quantities of ceremonial coins. Regular issues of silver coinage in the East commenced only in the seventh century with the introduction by the emperor Heraklios in 615 of the hexagram—a silver coin of six *grammata,* or 6.82 grams. The coin was struck in large quantities between 615 and 680; thereafter its commercial importance declined, and coins with the weight of the hexagram were issued only occasionally and for ceremonial purposes. In 720 Leo III introduced the miliarensis, a silver coin (with a possible theoretical weight in the eighth century of 2.27 grams), which in origin was a ceremonial token but later became a regular issue for general circulation. The miliarensis was struck until 1092. In the earlier phases of its history the miliarensis had a value, in relation to gold, of 1/12 nomisma.

Histories of Byzantine coinage usually commence with the reign of Anastasius I (491–518); for justification numismatists point to this emperor's reform of the copper coinage, beginning in 498. Prior to this date copper coinage, at least in the East, consisted of small coins called *nummia.* During the fifth century, inflation had reduced the *nummion* in size and weight to a point where it no longer had a distinct monetary value. To correct this situation Anastasius introduced a large copper coin, the follis. A follis of full weight bore the value mark "40" (*M*), signifying an equivalence in worth to forty *nummia.* Fractions of a follis were also issued: one-half (*K*), one-quarter (*I*), and one-eighth (*E*). Justinian I increased the weight of the follis, and in the year 539 the relationship of gold to copper stood as follows: 1 nomisma = 7,200 *nummia* = 180 folles. By this time, however, *nummia* had ceased to be important, and they disappeared after limited issues during the reign of Justin II. The follis was the dominant copper coin, and folles stamped with the denomination *M* were struck into the ninth century. Fractions of the follis ceased to be issued after the reign of Constantine V (741–775). The denomination *M* was removed from the follis in the reign of Theophilus (829–842), and henceforth copper values were expressed not in terms of *nummia* but folles.

The Byzantine coin par excellence was the nomisma (Latin: *solidus*). In accordance with the monetary reforms of Constantine the Great, the nomisma was struck at seventy-two to the Roman pound and had a theoretical weight of 4.55 grams, or, in terms of the Greco-Roman weight system, 24 *keratia* (Latin: *siliquae*). Fractional divisions of the nomisma were also struck: the semis (a gold coin of one-half weight) and the tremissis (a gold coin of one-third weight). It should be noted, however, that in addition to standard nomismata of full weight, gold coins of light weight were issued from the reign of Justinian I to about the year 680. Values of lightweight nomismata of this period range from 20 to 23 *keratia.* Lightweight nomismata again appear in the later tenth century with the introduction by Nikephoros II Phokas (963–969) of the tetartemorion, a gold coin which was lighter by one-twelfth than a standard nomisma. Why Nikephoros placed the tetartemorion in circulation is unclear, as, for that matter, is the purpose of lightweight nomismata in earlier centuries. It has been suggested that the tetartemorion was meant to conform with the weight of the Arab dinars that were in use in newly reconquered Syria. In the eleventh century, gold coinage underwent gradual debasement; erosion of the nomisma's fineness, and reforms necessary to correct this situation, mark a major turning point in the empire's monetary history.

Constantinople was the principal mint of the empire and formed, it seems, with Cyzicus and Nicomedia, which issued copper coinage only, the main production zone of the empire's coinage in the sixth and early seventh centuries. As a result of Justinian's conquest of Africa and Italy, the number of Byzan-

Nomisma from Constantinople bearing the image of Constantine. BRITISH MUSEUM. PHOTO: WIM SWAAN

MINTS AND MONEY, BYZANTINE

tine mints increased significantly in the mid sixth century. To the list of provincial mints (which included Antioch, Alexandria, and Thessaloniki) were added Carthage (opened in 533; active until 695), Rome, and Ravenna. Certain rare issues have been attributed to Perugia and Cartagena (in Spain).

The operations of the mint at Constantinople are not well understood, nor is it clear how closely provincial mints followed practices at the capital. *Officina* markings on coins provide a measure of information. Ten *officinae* (sections of the imperial mint) produced gold coinage into the eighth century, and five struck copper coinage. The *officina* system was in use at Nicomedia and Cyzicus; in each locale, two *officinae* minted copper coinage. On the other hand, no regular *officina* symbols appear on emissions from such mints as Thessaloniki and Alexandria. In addition, certain provincial mints issued copper coinage (perhaps a reflection of local needs) in denominations at variance with the official system of the capital. For example, Alexandria issued copper coinage with denominations of twelve, six, and three *nummia,* and Thessaloniki struck copper coinage of sixteen, eight, four, three, and two *nummia.* Furthermore, issues of some provincial mints are markedly different from coinage of Constantinople in manufacture, style, and iconography. Thus, gold coins of Carthage are regularly smaller in diameter than gold issues of Constantinople and, after the reign of Heraklios, are peculiarly globular in form. But such departures from the coinage of Constantinople are invaluable aids in identifying provincial coinage.

Mint marks are generally absent from silver coinage. After the reign of Anastasius, nomismata usually bear on the reverse (in a place reserved for a mint name) the abbreviation *CONOB* (*obryzon Constantinoupoleos:* "pure standard of Constantinople"). *CONOB* is not strictly speaking a mint mark but a mark of fineness and also appears on coins that were struck, for example, at Thessaloniki and Carthage. Copper coinage (with the exception of small units) continued to be issued on a regular basis with mint marks throughout the sixth century; the attribution of copper becomes troublesome only in the mid seventh century, with the disappearance of mint marks during and after the reign of Heraklios.

During the reign of Heraklios, as a result of Persian, Slavic, and Arab inroads into Byzantine territory, numerous mints were closed or occupied by the enemy: Antioch in 610, Nicomedia in 627, Cyzicus in 629, Thessaloniki by 630, and Alexandria in 642 (briefly again in operation after the city's recapture in 645–646). By the middle of the seventh century, Constantinople was the only active mint in the East. In the West, Ravenna (the seat of Byzantine authority in Italy) continued to issue coinage until its capture by the Lombard king Aistulf in 751. Imperial coinage was struck at Rome until, it seems, 776 (although effective control of the mint had gradually passed over to the papacy some time before). In the 660's, however, Constans II (641–668) established a mint at Naples, and gold coinage was struck there until at least the reign of Leo III (717–741). Constans II also opened a mint at Syracuse, which struck gold and copper coinage until the loss of the city to the Arabs in 878. In the mid ninth century what was apparently a municipal mint opened in the Crimea at Cherson; in 866–867 this copper coinage became an imperial issue and was struck until 989, when the city fell into the hands of the Russian prince Vladimir. The mint at Thessaloniki reopened in the eleventh century. It may have begun to issue gold coinage as early as the reign of Michael IV (1034–1041) and copper from the reign of Constantine X (1059–1067).

In the late Roman and early Byzantine periods, control of the empire's mines and mints rested with the count of the sacred largesses (count of imperial expenditure). But in the course of the seventh century numerous functions of the count were taken over by the director of state finances, the *logothetes tou genikou.* By the end of the ninth century the master of the mint *(archon tes charages)* was an official of the chartulary of the *vestiarium (chartularios tou bestiariou).* We do not possess any specific information concerning the mint director's duties or any description of the activities of the diemakers and other workmen under his control.

As of the late tenth century, the empire was issuing lightweight gold coin side by side with gold coin of full weight. At this date nomismata are generally termed *histamena* (or *stamena*), that is, gold coins of fixed or standard weight. In the reign of Michael IV the fineness of *histamena* began to fall until the coinage reforms of Alexios I in 1092. Michael's coins were struck between 23.5 and 19.5 carats fine. For over a decade gold was struck at 20/21 carats, and in the 1050's its fineness fell to about 18 carats. In the reign of Michael VII (1071–1078) coins were struck as low as 10 carats fine, and Nikephoros III (1078–1081) issued coins of only 8 carats. Moving forcefully against debasement, Alexios I introduced the nomisma-*hyperpyron* ("super-fired" gold coin) of 20.5 carats. Alexios abolished the gold tetartemorion, but the term survived and was used as an appellation in Alexios' monetary system to describe issues of small-change copper. Large quantities of tetartemorion have been recovered from excavations of Corinth and Athens. It is probable that the list of active mints includes, in addition to Constantinople and Thessaloniki, a yet unidentified mint in central Greece.

Along with the *hyperpyron,* Alexios also introduced one other type of gold coin, the electrum trachy (1/3 of a *hyperpyron*), and the billon trachy (1/48 of a *hyperpyron*). (A trachy was a concave coin; however, the *hyperpyron* was also concave.) The *officina* system was reactivated, although the number of *officinae* involved in the production of new issues varied. Under Manuel I (1143–1180) it appears that four *officinae* participated in striking an issue of billon trachy; later, under Andronikos I (1183–1185), perhaps only two *officinae* produced billon. From 1093 to 1204 Byzantine coinage was relatively stable, although the billon trachy was devalued to 1/120 in Manuel's reign and later in the 1190's to 1/184. In 1204, with the capture of Constantinople by the armies of the Fourth Crusade, Byzantine coinage was dealt a devastating blow, but the government in exile at Nicaea (in Asia Minor) managed to continue past traditions, issuing from mints at Nicaea and Magnesia gold *hyperpyra* and billon, although silver coinage displaced electrum. No gold was issued at Thessaloniki: only billon, silver, and copper. The best-known coin of Trebizond is the asper, a silver coin which weighed (before debasement) approximately 2.9 grams. The asper was issued until the middle of the fifteenth century.

Gold coinage was once again struck upon the reestablishment of Byzantine rule at Constantinople, where no gold coinage had been issued under the Latin emperors. But, economically enfeebled, the history of the last period of Byzantine coinage, from 1264 to 1453, is one of progressive debasement. Under Michael VIII (1261–1282) the gold *hyperpyron* contained fifteen carats, slipped to fourteen, then twelve, carats in the reign of Andronikos II (1282–1328), and finally fell to eleven carats during the coemperorship with Andronikos III (1325–1328). Near the end of the empire's long journey, gold was abandoned under John V (1341–1391) and silver coinage was issued until the Turkish conquest of the capital. Although the Byzantine gold *hyperpyron* was showing signs of weakness already in the eleventh century, the West was slow in introducing gold coinage of its own in support of international trade. Tentative steps appear only in 1231 with the German Frederick II's augustale or augustalis, followed by the introduction of the Florentine *fiorino* in 1252 and the Venetian ducat in 1284. The Byzantine silver *hyperpyron* was equal to one-fourth of a Venetian ducat.

BIBLIOGRAPHY

S. Bendall and P. J. Donald, *The Later Palaeologan Coinage, 1282–1453* (1979); Philip Grierson, *Catalogue of the Byzantine Coins in the Dumbarton Oaks Collection and in the Whittemore Collection,* III, pt. 1 (1973); Michael F. Hendy, *Coinage and Money in the Byzantine Empire, 1081–1261* (1969); Philip Whitting, *Byzantine Coins* (1973).

JOHN W. NESBITT

[See also **Byzantine Empire: Economic Life and Social Structure; Ducat; Hyperpyron; Nomisma; Trade, Byzantine.**]

MINTS AND MONEY, ISLAMIC. The Arabs of the Hejaz had no coinage of their own in the time of the prophet Muḥammad but were familiar with the coins of the Byzantine and Sasanian empires. It was therefore natural that they would continue the minting practices of those empires in the territories they conquered from them in the seventh century. In Egypt, for example, imitations of the Byzantine Egyptian copper 12-*nummia* coins were struck under Arab authority. In Iraq and Iran, the lands of the former Sasanian empire, silver drachmas like those of the Sasanians were struck in most large cities.

In Syria, where there were no Byzantine mints at the time of the Arab conquest, the Arabs apparently did not begin minting until the time of the caliph ᶜAbd al-Malik (685–705). The introduction of minting at his capital, Damascus, may have been a reaction to a new Byzantine gold coinage portraying Christ, about 692, but it was also part of a general reorganization of Arab administration following ᶜAbd al-Malik's defeat of the Zubayrid forces in Iraq in 691.

It seems likely that coinage of gold, silver, and copper began at Damascus simultaneously. The first gold and copper coins were adaptations of Byzantine types, while the earliest Damascus silver coins (with dates 691–694) resembled the Arab-Sasanian coinage of the Muslim East. These imitative issues were soon replaced by coins with new Muslim images, the best

MINTS AND MONEY, ISLAMIC

known of these being the "standing caliph" type produced between 694 and 697 in gold, silver, and copper. The new coins were soon found objectionable because they implied assimilation of the caliph's position with that of the emperors, and also because Muslims were taking an increasingly rigid opposition to the use of images in any public context.

The result was the creation in 697 of an original coin type reflecting the ideals of the new religious community. That year is the date of the first Islamic gold dinars, which bear only Arabic inscriptions. Except for the date, these are taken from the Koran. They include the fundamental doctrine of Islam, "There is no god but God, the One; none is associated with Him," and passages defining the unique role of the Prophet and repudiating the doctrine of the Trinity. Under the Umayyad caliphs (to 750), such dinars were issued at Damascus, occasionally in Arabia, and in North Africa and Spain. In 698, similar Islamic silver dirhams were introduced at Damascus and many mints in Armenia, Iraq, and Iran. Copper coins bearing inscriptions or simple images were widely issued with many local variations in design. The inscriptions adopted in 697, with the exception of the anti-Trinitarian passage, remained standard on Islamic coins for nearly six centuries and were used in some places into the twentieth century.

The accession of the Abbasid caliphs in 750 brought little immediate change in the coinage. The caliphal mint for gold coins was moved to Iraq, and the anti-Trinitarian statement replaced by the words "Muḥammad is the messenger of God"; the precious metal coins remained anonymous, like those of the Umayyads. In 762, however, the heir to the caliphate had his name inscribed on dirhams issued in the provinces under his authority. From then until about 830 many names of officials, from caliphs down to local administrators, appear on dirhams and (less often) on dinars.

In the first quarter of the ninth century, several changes established the standard pattern for the coinage of the Abbasid caliphate and the dynasties that acknowledged its spiritual authority until the coming of the Mongols in the thirteenth century. Henceforth, coins struck under direct Abbasid authority mentioned only the caliph and his heir. If a secular ruler's name appeared as well, as in Tulunid Egypt or Samanid Khorāsān, this was regarded as an indication of his autonomy, whether granted or seized. Indeed, for medieval Muslims, the mention of the ruler's name in the Friday prayer service *(khuṭba)*, and the appearance of his name on the coinage *(sikka)*, were the two fundamental public assertions of his sovereignty. The combination of date, place of issue, and careful delineation of political authority makes each medieval Muslim coin a miniature official document of nearly unimpeachable authenticity.

In the late eighth and early ninth centuries, minting of gold dinars spread from Baghdad (Madinat al-Salām) to a number of mints throughout the Abbasid realm, but in the same period copper coinage virtually ceased, appearing only sporadically during the next four centuries. Somewhat later, from the late tenth to the late twelfth/early thirteenth centuries,

obverse

reverse

"Standing caliph" gold dinar, Damascus, 694–695

First Islamic gold dinar, Damascus, 696–697

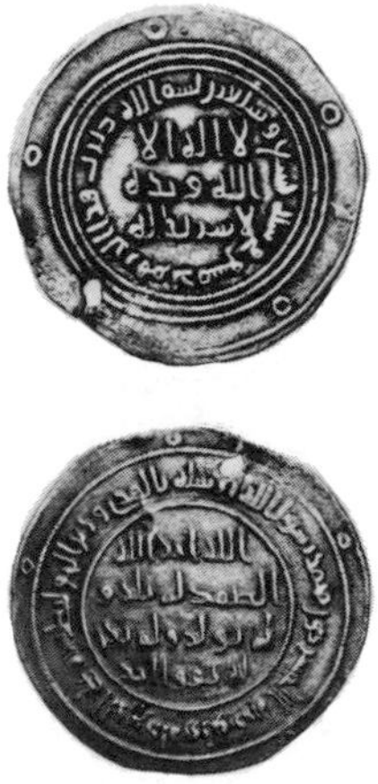

First Islamic silver dirham, Damascus, 698–699

COURTESY OF THE AMERICAN NUMISMATIC SOCIETY, NEW YORK

MINTS AND MONEY, ISLAMIC

the production of silver coinage east of the Euphrates almost ceased, while in the Muslim Mediterranean countries silver coins were copiously minted, though debased and small. The reasons for these changes are still not clearly understood, but it has been suggested that the disappearance of full-weight good silver coinage was connected in some way to the large export of silver coins from the Islamic territories of Central Asia into Russia, Eastern Europe, and Scandinavia between the eighth and the tenth centuries, while the resumption of good silver coinage in the twelfth and thirteenth centuries may have been related to the import of silver into the Levant by the crusaders. On the other hand, the silver coins of the Mediterranean countries may have been small and debased only because there was no copper coinage to meet the need for small change. It may also be significant that these little bits of silver corresponded roughly to the more or less debased silver pennies of Latin Europe.

As Mediterranean Muslim lands broke away from the Abbasid caliphate from the mid eighth to the tenth centuries, their coinage also diverged from the standard caliphal type. When Spain was part of the Umayyad caliphate, gold, silver, and copper coins, resembling those of North Africa, were struck at Córdoba, but the independent Umayyad amirs of Spain from 756 struck only silver dirhams. Spanish gold coinage was reintroduced in 928 by the Umayyad ᶜAbd al-Raḥmān III, as an assertion of his claim to the caliphate. After the Spanish caliphate disintegrated in the early eleventh century, the local successors largely continued its monetary practice at mints throughout Spain, but with strong Fatimid influence, notably in the increased use of small gold and silver denominations. From the time of the Almoravid conquest in 1086 until 1492, Muslim Spain's coinage was similar to that of northwest Africa. Islamic-type coins with Arabic inscriptions were struck by the Christian kings of Castile at Toledo and by the counts of Barcelona.

In North Africa, the Muslims first struck coins about 698, after the conquest of Carthage. The earliest issues (in gold and copper) were imperial portraits, with Latin translations of Muslim religious slogans. These were soon replaced, about 703, by coins with Latin inscriptions and no images, which were introduced also in Spain in 711. After 715 the Latin coins were replaced in turn by coins of gold, silver, and copper with Arabic inscriptions similar to those of the rest of the caliphate. Gold coinage was abandoned when North Africa came under Abbasid rule (after 750), but reintroduced by the independent Aghlabids (800–909); gold was the predominant metal used in North African coinage thereafter. In Sicily, conquered by the Aghlabids starting in 827, small gold quarter dinars and fractional silver dirhams were introduced. Their issue spread first to the North African territories of the Aghlabids and in the tenth and eleventh century throughout the Muslim Mediterranean. The Fatimids (in North Africa 909–1041) introduced in 953 a new coin type, with concentric circular inscriptions. The abundant and uniform Fatimid gold coinage enjoyed great prestige in the Mediterranean and influenced the issues of their neighbors and successors. The Christian Normans of Sicily, for example, struck Arabic gold quarter dinars (called taris by the Italians) for nearly a century after their conquest of the island. Equally abundant and prestigious were the handsome gold coins of the Almoravids (called maravedis by the Christians, who used and imitated them in Spain, France, and Italy) and of the Almohads. About 1145, the latter dynasty introduced a new-style coinage that set the pattern for all subsequent medieval Muslim coinage of northwest Africa and Spain. Gold coins of these regions have several horizontal lines of inscription surrounded by a square, with additional inscriptions between the square and an outer circle. The silver coins, square in shape as well as design, were imitated by the Christians, who called them millares.

Egypt's first Muslim coins were close imitations of the Byzantine copper coins of Alexandria. Islamic-type coins were introduced only at the beginning of the eighth century. The first identifiable Egyptian dinars and dirhams were minted from 786 onward, although before that date imported gold and silver coins must have circulated extensively, as evidenced by papyri and by very precise official glass weights for dinars and dirhams that have survived. From the end of the eighth century, Egypt was a major center for the production of gold dinars, silver coinage playing a secondary role, while copper coinage ended in 872 and did not reappear until the thirteenth century. Egypt's coinage in general followed the Abbasid system of the Muslim East until 969, when the Fatimid conquerors introduced their North African monetary system, with gold dinars, quarter dinars, and small silver dirhams. The Fatimid dinar was relatively stable in weight and fineness until 1098, when it ceased to be struck to any particular weight standard. This was a feature of most Egyptian gold coinage until the fifteenth century. In the Ayyubid period, striking of good silver and cop-

obverse

reverse

Al-Mu^{c}izz (Fatimid caliph), gold quarter-dinar from Al-Mansūrīya (near Qayrawān), 962–963

^{c}Abd al-Mu$^{\supset}$min (Almohad caliph), gold dinar from Seville, 1130–1163

Saladin (Ayyubid sultan), silver dirham from Damascus, 1177–1188

COURTESY OF THE AMERICAN NUMISMATIC SOCIETY, NEW YORK

per coins was revived. Saladin reintroduced in the 1170's and 1180's full-weight good silver dirhams to the Muslim world. This innovation began in Syria, and spread from there during the next hundred years to Egypt and the eastern Muslim countries. Ayyubid Syrian dirhams, as well as Fatimid and Ayyubid dinars of Egypt, were extensively imitated by the Crusaders in the twelfth and thirteenth centuries. The minting of copper coinage in Egypt resumed in 1225. By the beginning of the Mamluk sultanate in 1250 Egypt was well supplied with coinage in all three metals. Design changes in 1261 under the sultan Baybars gave Mamluk coinage its distinctive appearance. While Baybars' successors frequently manipulated the coinage to their own benefit, the general lines of the system remained stable. In the early fifteenth century, however, imported Venetian ducats nearly displaced Egyptian dinars from circulation, leading to the introduction in 1425 of a new gold coin, the ashrafi, with approximately the same weight and fineness as the ducat. The new standard (about 3.5 grams) was a success and was maintained until the nineteenth century. The evolution of coinage in Muslim Syria followed the general Egyptian pattern.

The incompletely islamicized Turks who conquered Anatolia in the eleventh century were more influenced by the heavy Byzantine bronze coinage than by any Muslim model. Their first coins, in the 1140's, bore only Greek inscriptions; soon, Byzantine images were borrowed as well. These gave rise to a diverse series of heavy copper coins with images drawn not only from Byzantine, but also from ancient Greek, Roman, Iranian, and Indian prototypes, as well as indigenous astrological and courtly imagery. These were struck by various twelfth- and thirteenth-century dynasties of eastern Anatolia and Al-Jazira (upper Mesopotamia). The most powerful of these dynasties, the Seljuks of Rum, followed Saladin in introducing their own silver coinage, supplied by Anatolian mines. Anatolia's subjugation by the Mongol Ilkhanid rulers of Iran led to the introduction of standard Ilkhanid silver coinage at the beginning of the fourteenth century. Subsequent weight reductions of the Ilkhanid coinage left their petty successors in fourteenth-century Anatolia with a small silver coin, called the *akçe* (little white). This became the standard early Ottoman currency unit, supplemented by local copper issues. The Ottomans did not begin striking gold coinage until after the conquest of Constantinople (1453), when they adopted the Venetian-Mamluk weight standard of 3.5 grams.

In the Islamic world, it was considered normal to weigh out payments using a balance and special coin weights, but there is evidence that some issues were taken by count. The relationship between gold dinars and silver dirhams was not fixed; rather, it was determined in the marketplace and reflected the relative price of the two metals, the minting costs of the two coins, and daily supply and demand. Similarly, the relationships between coins and bullion, as well as exchange rates between current local coins and outdated or foreign issues, were settled in the market and did not strictly reflect the precious metal content of the coins. The standards against which coins were weighed differed from time to time and from place to place, but were usually in the neighborhood of

4.25 grams for dinars and 2.75–3.00 grams for dirhams. Copper coins (*fulūs,* singular *fals*) were not considered legal tender by most Muslim jurists. Copper coins were used in practice as small change, and sometimes (when silver coins were scarce) for large transactions, but in general the exact relationship of copper coins to other denominations is not known or clearly understood.

Information about the techniques and administration of Muslim mints is available from medieval works on mint operations and references in historical and other writing, documents, and letters. Nearly all Islamic coins were die-struck (although some copper issues were cast in molds). One medieval author states that the face or obverse of coins was struck with the upper die, but the coin evidence show that practice in this regard varied greatly and was sometimes inconsistent even for a single issue. Gold coins were normally as nearly pure as the technology of the time allowed. Silver dirhams were often equally pure, but alloying was much more common than with dinars. Evidence from several regions and periods indicates that workers in the mint were recompensed by a surcharge on the mint's production, and may themselves have had to pay for the right to work. Even the supervisory positions were farmed in some cases, but the mint as a whole was a government operation and, contrary to the situation in Europe, mints were not farmed out to a single entrepreneur. The mint's customers were also surcharged for the cost of fuel and other materials and usually had to pay an additional surcharge to the government. The total of these charges, according to three reports from Ayyubid Egypt, ranged from 1 to 5 percent; the reports indicate several changes in this period, and different rates for gold and silver coins. The government must have been a major mint customer, insofar as it had revenue in other than current coin, but apparently anyone could bring bullion, old or foreign coins, and other precious metal objects to the mint to be made into current legal tender. In practice, the mint probably dealt directly with large customers only. In medieval Egypt and perhaps elsewhere, brokers called *mawrids* bought up small lots of bullion and the like to take to the mint; for the ordinary citizen, the *mawrid*'s profit was an additional cost of coinage.

BIBLIOGRAPHY

Two topical bibliographies of Islamic numismatics are Michael L. Bates, "Islamic Numismatics," in *Middle East Studies Association Bulletin,* **12–13** (1978–1979); and Nicholas Lowick, "Islamic Near and Middle East," in *A Survey of Numismatic Research, 1972–1977* (1979). Leo A. Mayer, *Bibliography of Moslem Numismatics,* 2nd ed. (1954), is quite complete but is arranged by author with only a general subject index. An indispensable reference is Eduard von Zambaur, *Die Münzprägungen des Islams* (1968, printed 1943), which lists all the Muslim mints in alphabetical order, with citations of their published coins. The few general works on Islamic coins are intended for collectors. Michael Broome, *A Handbook of Islamic Coins* (1985), sketches the numismatic history of the various dynasties; Michael Mitchiner, *Oriental Coins and Their Values: The World of Islam* (1977), provides a comprehensive assembly of coin photographs, useful in identifying specimens; Richard Plant, *Arabic Coins and How to Read Them* (1973), explains how to decipher Islamic coin inscriptions. Medieval Arabic texts on coins are collected in French translation by Henry Sauvaire, "Matériaux pour servir à l'histoire de la numismatique et de la métrologie musulmanes," in *Journal asiatique,* 7th series, **14** (1879), **15** (1880), **18** (1881), and **19** (1882); published separately as a single volume in 1882. Medieval works on the mint are described by Christopher Toll, "Minting Technique According to Arabic Literary Sources," in *Orientalia suecana,* **19–20** (1970–1971). Medieval Arabic ideas on monetary theory are partially surveyed by R. Brunschvig, "Conceptions monétaires chez les juristes musulmans, VIIIe–XIIIe siècles," in *Arabica,* **14** (1967). For modern monetary theory as applied to medieval Islamic systems, Gilles Hennequin, "Problèmes théoriques et pratiques de la monnaie antique et médiévale," in *Annales islamologiques,* **10** (1972); his subsequent articles in the same journal are essential reading. On monetary history: Andrew M. Watson, "Back to Gold—and Silver," in *Economic History Review,* 2nd ser., **20** (1967), and Eliyahu Ashtor, *Les metaux précieux et la balance des payements du Proche-Oriente à la basse èpoque* (1971), may be compared with Claude Cahen, "Monetary Circulation in Egypt at the Time of the Crusades and the Reform of al-Kāmil," in *The Islamic Middle East, 700–1900: Studies in Economic and Social History,* Abraham Udovitch, ed. (1981), and G. Hennequin, "Mamluks et métaux précieux: À propos de la balance des paiements de l'état syro-égyptien à la fin du moyen âge; questions de méthode," in *Annales islamologiques,* **12** (1974).

MICHAEL L. BATES

[See also **Dinar; Dirham; Ducat; Trade, Islamic.**]

MINTS AND MONEY, RUSSIAN. The earliest Russian (or preferably, Rus) coins were struck by the grand princes of Kievan Rus during the late tenth and early eleventh centuries (*ca.* 990–*ca.* 1020). The approximately 340 known Russian coins of this pe-

MINTS AND MONEY, RUSSIAN

riod are now divided into eleven types: eleven gold coins, or *zlatniki,* struck by Grand Prince Vladimir I; four types of silver coins, or *srebreniki,* also struck by Vladimir; *srebreniki* of Grand Prince Svyatopolk; *srebreniki* with the names Petros and Petor; two types of *srebreniki* issued by Grand Prince Yaroslav; and unattributable *srebreniki.* These early Rus coins were most likely all struck in Kiev except for Yaroslav's *srebreniki,* which may well have been issued in Novgorod.

Although scholars have used the term *srebreniki* for the silver coins, recent research indicates that most were made of a very low-grade silver and can more properly be labeled as billon coins. The *srebreniki* of Kievan Rus weighed around the same as an Islamic dirham—three grams. Vladimir's *zlatnik* weighed about four grams and was probably modeled on the gold Byzantine solidus of Basil II (976–1025). Despite the foreign influences on Kievan coins, features such as the use of the trident—the family emblem of the Kievan princes—demonstrate that they were more than simple copies of Byzantine and Islamic coinage.

Given the absence of indigenous silver ores and the lack of experienced moneyers, it is not clear why the Kievan grand princes began to strike their own coins. In the eyes of the princes, the commemorative and propaganda values of these coins may well have been more important than their economic utility. In any event, Islamic dirhams and then Western European deniers always circulated in far greater numbers throughout Rus than these relatively few indigenous coins.

The only other Rus coinage of the pre-Mongol period consisted of a few silver coins issued by Prince Oleg-Michael, apparently during his reign in Tmutarakan around 1078. Only four of these coins are known, and they were probably intended to bolster Oleg's tenuous position as ruler of Tmutarakan.

By the first half of the twelfth century, the import of foreign coins into Rus had ceased, ushering in what is called the coinless era, two centuries (*ca.* 1150–*ca.* 1350) during which coins were not used. Scholars have long debated what took the place of coins at this time. It seems clear that cast silver bars, or *slitki,* of different sizes and weights circulated in Rus between the twelfth and fifteenth centuries and that these *slitki* served very well for making payments in major transactions. The question thus becomes what, if anything, was used as a coin substitute for more modest transactions? Some scholars argue that fur pelts were used as money, while other specialists maintain that some form of commodity money existed—for instance, glass bracelets or cowrie shells. The testimony of foreign travelers as well as Rus monetary terminology suggest quite strongly that fur pelts and pieces were employed as money. Unfortunately, it is not clear whether these furs circulated in the same fashion as coins or whether fur primarily served to support the value of some token which could circulate more readily than fur.

The coinless era came to an end in Rus during the second half of the fourteenth century, when various rulers began to strike silver coins, or *dengi,* and copper coins, or *puly.* In eastern Rus, the earliest Muscovite *dengi* were issued by Grand Prince Dmitrii Donskoi in the 1370's. Since the privilege of striking coins was sold to private minters, Muscovite coinage became quite diverse by the early fifteenth century. Grand Prince Vasilii II, who ruled at intervals between 1425 and 1462, established the first official Moscow mint, in part to bring some standardization to Muscovite coinage. While the early coins of Moscow reflected the overlordship of the Golden Horde, the Muscovite *denga* gradually lost many of its Mongol features and came to reflect the growing stature of the grand princes.

Soon after the beginning of coinage in Moscow, the grand princes of Nizhni Novgorod–Suzdal began to strike their own coins. As in other eastern Rus principalities, the first Nizhni Novgorod *dengi* were basically imitations of Golden Horde coins which omitted the prince's name. After Nizhni Novgorod was acquired by Moscow, Suzdal emerged as the main mint for the remainder of the principality. In the 1380's, the grand princes of Ryazan began to overstrike Golden Horde coins and imitations. Only in the second quarter of the fifteenth century did the grand princes of Ryazan start to strike coins bearing their own names.

In the western Rus lands which had come under Lithuanian and Polish control, coinage also appeared in the second half of the fourteenth century. In Lvov, where Polish rule had been established in 1349, silver coins called *groschen* and copper coins called *deniers* were struck from the early 1350's until about 1415. Sometime between roughly 1362 and 1400, the Lithuanian prince of Kiev, Vladimir Olgerdovich, issued five different types of silver coins. The relationship of the Lvov and Kievan coinages to the medieval Rus, Polish, and Lithuanian monetary systems has not yet been determined.

The central Rus lands were the last to begin striking their own coins. Tver's coinage, for example, started sometime before 1420. Tverian coins are unusual because of their many scenes depicting moneyers making coins. In 1410, Novgorod began to use central European coins. These foreign coins apparently proved unsatisfactory since Novgorod started to issue its own *dengi* in 1420. A little later, in 1447, Novgorod ceased production of *slitki,* or cast silver bars. Pskov followed the same pattern as Novgorod: it adopted central European silver coins in 1409 and then replaced them with its own coinage in 1424.

In addition to the numerous coins struck for the grand princes and republics, appanage, or *udel,* princes also issued their own coins in the principalities of Moscow, Tver, and Ryazan. *Dengi* were also struck in Yaroslavl and Rostov. At the present time, numismatists estimate that more than twenty-five different mints operated in eastern and central Rus prior to 1462. While great progress has been made in identifying and cataloging the many Rus coins of this period, we still lack a convincing explanation for why coinage appeared and spread within the Rus lands starting in the mid fourteenth century.

The reigns of Ivan III (1462–1505) and Vasilii III (1505–1533) brought an end to medieval Rus coinage. Under these grand princes, Moscow conquered almost all the formerly independent Rus principalities and republics east of Poland-Lithuania and eliminated the appanage princes. The production of coins by most local mints and moneyers ceased; those that remained minted highly uniform Muscovite coins, although the complete standardization of Muscovite coinage did not occur until later.

BIBLIOGRAPHY

M. P. Sotnikova and I. G. Spasskiy, *Tysyacheletie drevneyshikh monet Rossii: Svodnyy katalog russkikh monet X–XI vekov* (1983), English edition, *Russian Coins of the X–XI Centuries A.D.,* H. Bartlett Wells, trans. (1982); I. G. Spasskiy, *The Russian Monetary System: A Historico-numismatic Survey* (1967), and "Numismatic Research in Russia, the Ukraine, and Byelorussia in the Period 1917–1967," in *The Numismatic Chronicle,* 7th ser., **12** (1972); Russell Zguta, "Kievan Coinage," in *The Slavonic and East European Review,* 53 (1975).

THOMAS S. NOONAN

[See also **Golden Horde; Kievan Rus; Lithuania; Muscovy, Rise of; Novgorod; Tmutarakan, Khanate of; Trade, European; Vladimir-Suzdal.**]

MINTS AND MONEY, WESTERN EUROPEAN. The coinage of the European Middle Ages was characterized by a multiplicity of issuing authorities and a wide variety of alloys and weight standards. There were dozens of denominations and hundreds of types, or designs. As coinage was used for trade between the various kingdoms, principalities, duchies, cities, and bishoprics, with each "entity" exercising minting rights, certain standard combinations of metal, weight, and appearance developed, however, which allowed the coins of one region to be exchanged for those of another. This development resulted in the emergence of a trusted coin issued by a powerful political or economic unit, and its imitation and adaptation by other minters.

The first characteristic coin to emerge from the dissolution of the western Roman Empire was the gold triens (plural: trientes), also known as tremissis. This was derived from the Roman coin of the same name established by Constantine the Great (307–337) as one third of a solidus (Constantine's newly valued gold piece). As early as the late fifth century, imitations of Roman solidi and trientes were issued by leaders of Germanic tribes that had established themselves in Western Europe. While solidi continued to be minted for a while in a few regions, it was the triens that became the standard European coin of the sixth and seventh centuries. The triens usually had a weight of about 1.4 grams and a diameter of about 15 mm (0.6 in). Originally of pure gold, it tended to have an increasing mixture of silver in its alloy as the seventh century progressed.

Trientes bearing the name (often garbled) of a present or past Byzantine emperor were issued in Italy by the Ostrogoths and Lombards, in Gaul by the Merovingian Franks and Burgundians, and in the Iberian peninsula by the Visigoths and the Suevi. The study of find spots and stylistic development has allowed the identification of at least some of these anonymous trientes with individual kingdoms and even with specific rulers.

At about the middle of the sixth century, the rulers of the Germanic kingdoms began to put their names on the trientes they issued, rather than copying an imperial name. In Spain, the Visigothic kings put their names and the town of minting on their coins. While some of the coins of the Merovingian kings of France bear their names, the vast majority of Merovingian coins bear only the name of a minter and a minting town; whether these minters actually had rights of coinage or were royal officials is still a

MINTS AND MONEY, WESTERN

subject of debate. The dukes of Beneventum in central Italy continued to put their names on their trientes even after Charlemagne's conquest of Lombard Italy in 774.

It appears that there were few coins other than gold trientes minted in Europe in the sixth and seventh centuries. Even with their small size and increasingly high admixture of silver, the trientes represented a relatively large amount of wealth and could not have been appropriate for small transactions in the marketplace; their use seems rather to have been associated with large-scale trade and governmental operations. The lack of a significant quantity of silver, bronze, or copper coinage reflects the constrained nature of the early medieval economy and the widespread use of barter and customary labor for everyday needs.

In the late seventh and the eighth century, gold trientes gave way to silver coins in most parts of Western Europe; by the time of Charlemagne the only gold coin regularly produced by a Latin ruler was the triens of Beneventum. The silver coins of the eighth century were generally small and relatively thick; they rarely bore legible inscriptions, and their types were highly stylized. Coins of one type, called sceatta (sing., sceat), have been found on both sides of the English Channel; they appear to have been minted in both England and Frisia.

In the late eighth century, shortly before proclaiming himself emperor, Charlemagne reformed and standardized the coinage of his realm. The basic coin was the denarius, or penny; its half was called obole. The Carolingian penny was of pure silver with a weight of about 1.7 grams and a diameter of about 19 mm (0.75 in). It was struck by Charlemagne and his successors in more than fifty mints throughout the empire. For the next four centuries the silver penny was the basis for virtually all European coinage; until the thirteenth century no gold or silver coins of appreciably higher weight were minted by Latin rulers.

Charlemagne also introduced an accounting system of grouping twelve pennies into a unit called a solidus, or shilling, and twenty shillings into a libra, or pound. This system was accepted throughout Europe as the basis for recording payments and lasted in some countries into the twentieth century. However, in the ninth through twelfth centuries the shilling and the pound were simply theoretical units of account; only the penny was represented by an actual coin.

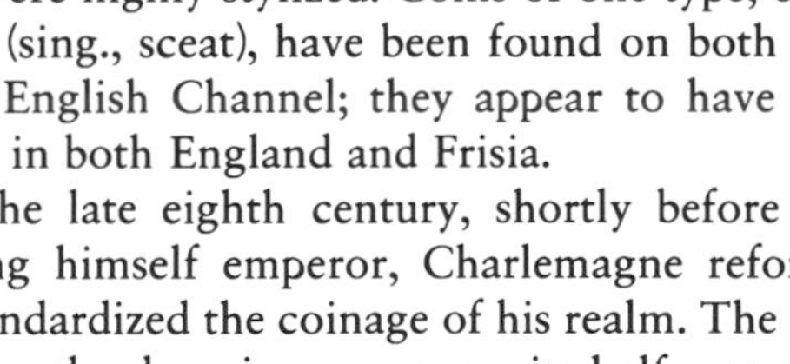

Carolingian silver penny, obverse/reverse. COURTESY OF THE AMERICAN NUMISMATIC SOCIETY, NEW YORK

The intrinsic value of a given coin was expressed in medieval documents in terms of alloy *(lex)* and weight *(tallia)*. Pure gold was expressed as having twenty-four carats; a coin recorded as having eighteen carats of gold would then have $^{18}/_{24}$ or 75 percent gold—the rest of the alloy might be silver or copper. In a similar way, the amount of silver was expressed in terms of the denarius (the same term is confusingly used for the basic coin). Silver of twelve denarii represented unalloyed ingots of silver; the denarius was in turn divided into twenty-four grains. The ingots used, however, were not of pure silver ore; they contained a standard alloy that varied from place to place. The sterling silver of England was an alloy containing 925 parts of silver out of 1,000 (the remaining 75 parts were of copper); the *argent-le-roi* used by the Capetian kings of France was .968 silver. Coins of an alloy with less than fifty percent silver are usually referred to by numismatists as billon; in medieval documents coins with very little silver are called "black money."

The weights of individual coins were expressed in documents in terms of how many pieces were struck from a given weight of metal. The basic unit of weight used for coinage was the mark; its size varied from town to town throughout Europe. A coin reported to be struck at 4 shillings 6 pennies ($12 \times 4 + 6 = 54$ pieces) to the mark of Paris (*ca.* 245 grams) would weigh $^{245}/_{54}$ grams or about 4.54 grams per coin.

The coinage of the centuries following Charlemagne's reforms was generally conservative. After the dissolution of the Carolingian Empire, the successor states continued the issue of coins based on the models of Charlemagne; often the name or the monogram of a Carolingian ruler was maintained on the coinage for centuries following his death. As minting rights became increasingly localized, the weight and fineness ceased to be standard, and the penny of each minting authority developed a customary value in relation to that of its neighbors. In a similar way, the accounting system of each region was based on the value of its own penny; any foreign

MINTS AND MONEY, WESTERN

coins that were received had to be evaluated in terms of the local system before they could be accounted.

In the French seigneuries the rudimentary designs on Carolingian coins became highly stylized so that even an illiterate user could recognize the types of the various coins regularly encountered. The stylized types, and often the legends identifying the person and place responsible for issue, were left unaltered for decades and even for centuries, rendering recognition easy for the medieval user but dating often extremely difficult for the modern numismatist. The designs on these French coins were usually geometric, representing a cross, a monogram, a building, and only rarely a person.

In England the style and fabric of Carolingian coinage were quickly adopted, but a preference for portraits persisted from earlier periods. English coinage remained under royal control, and the king's name and stylized portrait appeared on the obverse of the penny, with the mint name and sometimes a minter's name around a cross on the reverse. In 1180 Henry II issued a standardized coinage which was to remain unchanged, even in its inscription (including the name *Henricus*), through the reigns of Richard I, John, and well into the reign of Henry III, until 1247. The chronology of issue of these "short cross" pennies (so called because of the design on the reverse) has only been determined through the study of minute changes in epigraphy and style and the comparison of hoard evidence and minters' names. Similar problems arise in differentiating the "long cross" pennies (with arms of the cross extending to the coin edge) of Edward I, II, and III, as well as Henry IV, V, and VI.

Within the German territories of the Holy Roman Empire, minters were less restrained in their choice of types and in the appearance of their coinages. Hundreds of minting authorities issued coins of frequently changing appearance, containing heraldic, devotional, personal and architectural images. As designs became increasingly elaborate, the blanks were made broader and thinner to provide greater surface without increasing weight. As reverse designs tended to show through to the obverse of such thin coins, in several regions the coins were struck on only one side; these thin, fragile coins are known as bracteates. Medieval German coins frequently lack sufficient legends to establish where and when they were minted; the localization and chronology of issues has been rigorously determined for only a few series of such coins. In northern Italy the pennies usually followed Carolingian types; they commonly maintained the name of the emperor who had originally granted minting rights to the commune.

The tenth and eleventh centuries witnessed the extension of European minting beyond the limits of the Carolingian Empire and, for the most part, the first minting of coins in Europe beyond the frontiers of the ancient Roman Empire. Rising dynasties in Sweden, Denmark, and Norway, in Poland, Bohemia, and Moravia asserted their power with the introduction of national coinages, all based on the Carolingian penny, using types inspired by English as well as Byzantine and continental models. The silver penny followed the crusading Christian soldiers into Spain and the Holy Lands; in both regions early imitations of local Islamic issues soon gave way to the minting of coins based on European types.

In the course of the four centuries in which the penny was the basic unit of coinage in Latin Europe, its value was continually lowered from the standard established by Charlemagne. Only in England did the penny maintain a high value; elsewhere it was debased in terms of both weight and silver content until it was often a basically copper coin of less than half the fineness originally prescribed. In the face of the growing trade of the twelfth and thirteenth centuries, it became increasingly cumbersome to make large payments with great quantities of these base coins.

It was in the commercial cities of northern Italy that the reform of silver coinage began, first in the form of pennies of higher silver content in the late twelfth century, and, in 1202, with the introduction in Venice of the grosso. This coin, of rather Byzantine appearance, had about 2.2 grams of almost pure silver. Although containing only about one-and-a-half times as much silver as the penny of Charlemagne, the Venetian grosso was issued as the equivalent of twenty-four of the contemporary Venetian pennies.

The large silver coin found its greatest success in Northern Europe. In 1266 Louis IX of France introduced a large silver coin, the *gros tournois.* This coin (about the size of a U.S. quarter), with 4.2 grams of silver, was a multiple of the *tournois* denier, one of the two standard coins minted by the French kings. It was issued as the equivalent of 12 tournois deniers, or one *sou tournois* of account.

The gros tournois was widely imitated in Northern Europe; sometimes by exact copies, sometimes with changes appropriate to the minting authority. The discovery of rich silver mines in Central Europe in the late thirteenth century led to the widespread

MINTS AND MONEY, WESTERN

minting of the large silver groschen there. The most important of these was the Prague groschen of Wenceslas II of Bohemia (introduced in 1300), modeled after the gros tournois and itself the model for coins of other Central and Eastern European states.

Most of the large silver coins of the later Middle Ages met the same fate as the penny of Charlemagne—continual reduction in both weight and fineness and regional divergences from the original standards. Often this alteration was gradual and imperceptible, but in some cases, such as France in the fourteenth and fifteenth centuries, mutations of the coinage were frequent and extreme. Coins of different issues could be exchanged and accounted only by reference to their intrinsic silver content or by the value of silver at the time of their striking. Some proclamations of currency mutations represent an alteration in the values of existing coins, rather than the minting of new coins on different standards.

To say that only silver coins were struck in the Latin states of Europe between the ninth and the thirteenth centuries is not quite the same as saying that there was no gold coinage in Europe at that time. Through much of the period, the Byzantine Empire extended into the Balkans and even into Italy, with its coinage still based on the gold solidus of Constantine. More significantly, the Muslims held Sicily and much of Spain and conducted an important Mediterranean trade on the basis of the gold dinar. Islamic coins penetrated into the commercial centers of Christian Europe and appear in accounts as maravedis (or marabotins). As Latin rulers conquered Islamic lands in Spain, Italy, and the Levant, and as they took a more active role in the Mediterranean trade, they found themselves entering into a system of gold coinage. When the Normans conquered Sicily in the eleventh century, they continued the gold coinage they found there, often with legends in Arabic offering Christian messages.

Frederick II (1212–1250) approached coinage with the same innovative energy he applied to law and statecraft. He adopted the minting of gold coinage for his southern Italian and Sicilian realms, but rather than imitate Arabic or Byzantine models, he designed a new coin, the augustal of around 1231, based on Roman coinage styles, though following no specific ancient prototype. Like most of Frederick's innovations, the introduction of gold coinage into Latin Europe was not immediately successful. The classic style he revived was to disappear for another two centuries, but the convenience of a coin that held a high value in a small amount of metal was soon recognized by the commercial cities of northern Italy.

In 1252 both Genoa and Florence issued gold coins; these were of pure gold and both were struck at a weight of 3.5 grams, considerably lighter than the augustal. The *genovino,* with a punning gate (Latin *ianua*) as obverse type and a cross as reverse, appears to have been limited in circulation to Genoa and its closest trading partners. The florin, however, with its distinctive portrait of John the Baptist on the obverse and a lily on the reverse (punning on the name Florence), was to become one of the most widely recognized and imitated coins in European history. Its appearance, weight, and fineness were maintained for centuries, and it became the common unit of account for large sums well into the modern period.

In response to the success of the florin, Venice began producing her own gold coin, the ducat or zecchino, in 1284. The ducat was of pure gold like the florin and *genovino,* but was slightly heavier at 3.56 grams. Its area of popularity was originally in the eastern Mediterranean, but over the centuries it became assimilated to the standard of the florin and both terms were used interchangeably in accounts throughout Europe.

The florin and the ducat circulated and were imitated in hundreds of kingdoms, duchies, and towns, each with a different system of silver coinage. In each locality and time the value of these standard gold coins in terms of the local silver was determined by prevailing market conditions. Thus the weight and fineness of the florin and ducat could be kept constant for centuries, while silver currencies underwent constant debasement and restoration. It was up to the money changers in each commercial center to keep the merchants and citizens informed as to how many small and large silver coins of the local currency were needed to buy a florin or a ducat.

In England and France, however, the kings were unwilling to allow such fluctuation in the relationship of their gold and silver coins. They sought a system of coinage in which a gold coin represented a

Gold florin of Florence, obverse/reverse. COURTESY OF THE AMERICAN NUMISMATIC SOCIETY, NEW YORK

fixed number of silver ones, preferably a quantity that could be expressed easily in pennies, shillings, and pounds. As the relative price of gold and silver was never stable in the later Middle Ages, English and French kings continually found their gold coins either overvalued or undervalued in relation to silver. An overvalued coin was resisted by a populace attuned to the current values of the metals, while an undervalued one quickly disapppeared into the melting pot or across the border.

The only solution to a change in the ratio of gold to silver was to change the weight or fineness of the coins produced. The medieval gold coinage of France and England is consequently characterized by a wide variety of standards. To differentiate the various issues, types were frequently changed, creating a diversity of design that makes up in beauty what is lacking in consistency of standards.

A few standard coins can then be seen as forming the basis of medieval numismatics: the small gold triens of the early Middle Ages; the silver penny that served as the basic coin from the ninth century onward; the large silver multiples; and a variety of gold coins mainly based on the florin and ducat. It was the frequent imitation and adaptation of these models, plus the occasional appearance of wholly new types, that gave medieval coinage its outstanding variety and complexity.

At the end of the medieval period several important changes had their effect on coinage. The opening of trade routes led to the introduction of new sources of ore, changing dramatically the amount of precious metal available for coinage. New methods of minting effected a change in both appearance and availability of coins. The consolidation of royal power led to a standardization of coinage in most regions of Europe. Finally, the development of banking and credit led to an economic system in which money was no longer limited to struck pieces of precious metal.

BIBLIOGRAPHY

Adrien Blanchet and A. Dieudonné, *Manuel de numismatique française,* 4 vols. (1912–1936); Arthur Engel and Raymond Serrure, *Traité de numismatique du moyen âge,* 3 vols. (1897–1899, repr. 1964); Étienne Fournial, *Histoire monétaire de l'Occident médiéval* (1970); Philip Grierson, *Monnaies du moyen âge,* Hélène Huvelin, trans. (1976), and "Numismatics," in James M. Powell, ed., *Medieval Studies: An Introduction* (1976); Arnold Luschin von Ebengreuth, *Allgemeine Münzkunde und Geldgeschichte,* 2nd ed. (1926); Karl F. Morrison and Henry Grunthal, *Carolingian Coinage* (1967); John Porteous, *Coins in History* (1969); Arthur Suhle, *Deutsche Münz- und Geldgeschichte von den Anfängen bis zum 15. Jahrhundert,* 3rd rev. ed. (repr. 1968); Carol H. V. Sutherland, *English Coinage, 600–1900* (1973).

ALAN M. STAHL

[See also **Bracteates; Ducat; Florin; Groat; Penny; Pound; Shilling; Trade, European.**]

MIRACLE PLAYS. In medieval French-language drama, the miracle play is a dramatic genre in which the protagonist is saved at a moment of crisis by the miraculous intervention of a saint, in most cases the Virgin Mary. This is distinct from a dramatized saint's life, where the miracle worker is himself the protagonist of the play. In England the term "miracle play" is sometimes used to refer to the biblical cycle plays associated with Corpus Christi.

The earliest extant miracle play in French is the *Jeu de St. Nicolas,* written by Jean Bodel in 1200. It is a complex work involving both tavern scenes and and an epic battle in which the Saracens defeat the Christians. The sole surviving crusader is saved from execution when the saint recovers the Saracen king's treasure from robbers. About sixty years later, Rutebeuf wrote the *Miracle de Théophile,* based on a Faustlike legend in which the protagonist sells his soul to the Devil. He is rescued after pleading with the Virgin Mary to intercede.

The forty *Miracles de Nostre Dame* from the fourteenth century constitute one of the most important collections of French plays from the Middle Ages. Gathered in a two-volume manuscript, the plays were the repertoire of the Paris goldsmiths' guild. They were performed, one each year, between 1339 and 1382, at the guild's annual assembly. In each play a person in grave difficulty as a result of previous sins petitions the Virgin Mary for help and is saved by her miraculous intervention. The playwrights usually chose extreme cases both to create a strong dramatic effect and to demonstrate the power of Mary's intercession. A mother who let her infant drown through negligence is rescued from the flames of justice by the child's miraculous return to life. A woman who killed her son-in-law to stop the false rumors of their liaison is also saved from being burned at the stake. A queen of Portugal who committed two murders to protect her reputation is exonerated. The legendary Robert le Diable, after years of the most heinous criminal activity, does penance and gains an empire. Despite the exaggeration of the plots, the plays reveal many realistic details of life in fourteenth-century France.

In addition to a few independent miracle plays, only one other collection of such plays has survived. Jean Louvet wrote twelve miracle plays for the Confrérie de Notre-Dame de Liesse, which were played between 1536 and 1550. Here the protagonists invoke the Virgin venerated at the shrine of Liesse near Laon. By the mid sixteenth century the popularity of the miracle plays seems to have declined among the general public. They continued to be played during this period, however, at the semiprivate assemblies of guilds and *confréries* to inspire devotion to the patron saints of such groups.

BIBLIOGRAPHY

Grace Frank, *The Medieval French Drama,* 2nd ed. (1960); Louis Petit de Julleville, *Histoire du théâtre en France,* I and II (1880); Graham A. Runnalls, "Mediaeval Trade Guilds and the *Miracles de Nostre Dame par personages,*" in *Medium aevum,* 39 (1970).

ALAN E. KNIGHT

[See also **Bodel, Jean; Drama, French; Drama, German; Drama, Western European; Dutch Literature; Mystery Plays.**]

MÍRMANNS SAGA. The tale of Mírmann is an Icelandic *riddarasaga* (chivalric romance), probably composed in the fourteenth century. The scene is set in both Saxland and France. The heathen Mírmann, son of Earl Hermann of Saxland, is sent to the court of King Hlöðver of France to complete his education. There he is converted to Christianity and returns to his homeland on a proselytizing mission. A dispute with his father results in parricide. In revenge, Mírmann's mother gives him a philter that renders him a leper. Mírmann learns that Cecilía, daughter of the king of Sicily, is renowned for her powers of healing. He seeks her out, is cured, and marries her. He returns to France to visit his foster-father, Hlöðver. The queen had always been infatuated with Mírmann, and through deceit and trickery she now makes Mírmann forget his wife and even marry her after the death of her husband. When Cecilía learns of these events, she disguises herself as Earl Híringr, joins Mírmann's enemies, who have declared war on him, and vanquishes Mírmann in a combat-at-arms. She leads him away as her captive. After a recognition and reconciliation scene, Mírmann becomes king of Sicily.

Mírmanns saga is somewhat unusual among the Icelandic *riddarasögur* in that the conversion to Christianity and its spread plays a not inconsiderable role in the tale, and indirectly precipitates the conflict. Throughout the saga the author's learned background and religious leanings are manifest. The subject matter lends itself to pseudo-historiographical references (for instance, the tale commences in the days of Pope Clement), as well as didactic comments and observations. Long discourses on the nature and excellence of Christianity are interspersed in the tale. As exemplary Christians, Mírmann and Cecilía finally leave behind all worldly power and possessions and enter monasteries, where they can prepare for a proper departure from this life.

As is the case with many Icelandic *riddarasögur,* names and motifs in *Mírmanns saga* are not original. Analogues to Mírmann's voyage to Sicily in order to be healed occur in *Ála flekks saga, Haralds saga Hringsbana,* and *Rémundar saga keisarasonar.* The motif derives directly or indirectly from *Tristrams saga.* Cecilía's disguise as Earl Híringr in order to join in combat with her own husband bears striking resemblance in content and phraseology to the introductory *þáttr* (short story) of the younger redaction of *Mágus saga.*

Mírmanns saga is written in a laconic and unadorned prose style. Except for the unusually long dialogue sections in which Christianity is expounded, the narrative is succinct and devoid of excessive ornamentation. Alliteration occurs infrequently and never in clusters, as in the translated *riddarasögur.* The relatively infrequent alliterative collocations are normally couplets (at *vélum ok véla,* "with wiles and guile"; *styrka ok styðja,* "to strengthen and support"), but occasionally also triplets (*minkaði megin hans ok mátt,* "his power and might diminished"; *láta líf eða limar,* "to part with life and limb").

Mírmanns saga is extant in two primary manuscripts, the vellums Cod. Holm. perg. 6, 4to (*ca.* 1400) in the Royal Library in Stockholm, and AM 593a, 4to (fifteenth century) in the Arnamagnaean Institute in Copenhagen. A vellum fragment, Lbs 1230, 8vo (*ca.* 1500), was recently discovered in the National Library in Reykjavík. Over twenty paper manuscripts, mostly from the seventeenth century or later, are also preserved.

Mírmantsrímur, a metrical version of *Mírmanns saga,* is similar in content to the redaction of the saga in AM 593, 4to. A Faroese poem called *Mírmanskvæði* also derives from the saga.

BIBLIOGRAPHY

Sources. Jakob Benediktsson, "Nokkur handritabrot," in *Skírnir* **125** (1951); Eugen Kölbing, ed., *Riddarasögur* (1872); Einar Þórðarson, ed., *Mírmanns saga riddara* (1884); Bjarni Vilhjálmsson, ed., "Mírmanns saga," in *Riddarasögur,* III (1949).

Studies. Arsène Darmesteter, *De Floovante vetustiore gallico poemate et de Merovingo cyclo, scripsit et adjecit nunc primum edita Olavianam Flovents sagæ versionem et excerpta e Parisiensi codice "Il Libro de Fioravante"* (1877); Eyvind Fjeld Halvorsen, "Mírmanns saga," in *Kulturhistorisk leksikon for nordisk middelalder,* XI (1966); Finnur Jónsson, *Den oldnorske og oldislandske Litteraturs Historie,* III, 2nd ed. (1924); Th. Möbius, review of Kölbing, *Riddarasögur,* in *Zeitschrift für deutsche Philologie,* 5 (1874); Adolf Zinzow, *Die erst sächsisch-fränkische, dann normannische Mirmannsage nach Inhalt, Deutung und Ursprung* (1891).

MARIANNE E. KALINKE

[See also **Åla Flekks Saga; Iceland; Mágus Saga Jarls; Rémundar Saga Keisarasonar; Riddarasögur; Saga; Tristrams Saga Ok Ísöndar.**]

MIRROR OF JUSTICES, a purported introduction to the history of English law, the date, author, and meaning of which are all a matter of conjecture.

The *Mirror* was almost certainly written in the reign of Edward I, because it mentions laws of his reign but none of the later period. Approximately 1289 has been suggested, since a number of justices were punished for their crimes in that year, and the *Mirror* may reflect this fact in its condemnation of judicial misconduct.

The author may have been Andrew Horn, one of the London fishmongers acquitted in 1315 of using lightweight baskets in their trade. He became chamberlain of the city in 1320, a post he held until his death in 1328. The Guildhall of London still holds a collection of books, mainly on legal subjects, that he bequeathed to it.

The case for Horn's authorship begins with an epigraph in Latin at the beginning of the book, one line of which reads: "Horn is my last name, Andrew my first." The *Mirror* is about English laws, a subject in which Horn was interested. Moreover, Horn and the author both traced English laws back to the Saxon invaders.

The case against Horn's authorship is, first, that he was a reputable archivist, while the *Mirror* is a farrago of fact, fiction, and deliberate fraud. Second, Horn and the author disagree on some legal fundamentals—for example, Horn is in favor of the Statute of Westminster II with its royal assizes, but the author of the *Mirror* favors the local courts. Finally, the name in the epigraph may simply refer to Horn's ownership of the book, not his authorship. Frederic William Maitland suggested, without any great conviction, that the *Mirror* was a youthful indiscretion that Horn outgrew. No scholar has proposed a better explanation since then.

The *Mirror* is a mystery on several counts. The meaning of the title is that the author will reveal the truth about the justices of England to the extent that they are contravening the ancient laws of the land. "I, the prosecutor of false judges," as he puts it. But he makes gross blunders about those laws. Thus, he says that King Alfred hanged forty-four judges in one year, an assertion for which he had no evidence whatever.

The authority from whom he borrows most (without naming him) is Henry de Bracton. Still, he distorts Bracton whenever it suits him. For example, in discussing mayhem, the author follows Bracton but adds the names of three judges, all of them imaginary.

The author is incensed by the legal theory that the king is above the law. The Saxons, he claims, had a parliament of earls in which their kings could be prosecuted as lawbreakers. He demands a return to this fictional past.

Did the author, for all his inventions, intend the *Mirror* to be take seriously as a study of English law? Or is it topical humor on a vast scale? There are experts on both sides. Sir Edward Coke took it seriously in the seventeenth century, but all competent critics since his time have seen it as a puzzle.

BIBLIOGRAPHY

William Joseph Whittaker, ed., *The Mirror of Justices* (1895), provides an edition and translation. In addition, Frederic William Maitland's long introduction is still the best commentary on the *Mirror.* For further information on Andrew Horn, see Charles Welch, "Horn, Andrew," in *Dictionary of National Biography, XXVII* (1891), 352–353.

VINCENT BURANELLI

[See also **Bracton, Henry de; Britton; Edward I of England; Fleta; Glanville, Ranulf de; Law, English Common; Westminster, Statutes of.**]

 MIRROR OF PRINCES

MIRROR OF PRINCES. The modern term "mirror of princes" (German: *Fürstenspiegel;* French: *miroir aux princes;* Latin: *speculum regis/principis*) is commonly used to refer to medieval books of counsel designed for the use of members of the ruling class. Some of these works have the word *speculum* (mirror) as part of their title; more commonly the works have a title of the form *De regimine, De eruditione,* or *De institutione,* with a clear reference to their didactic purpose. Although there are mirrors of princes in most medieval vernaculars, the majority were written in Latin by men of the church.

The medieval mirror of princes has its counterpart in classical antiquity: Isocrates' *To Nicocles* (*ca.* 372 B.C.), the *Cyropaedeia* and *Hiero* of Xenophon (*ca.* 427/428–*ca.* 354 B.C.), the *De officiis* (44 B.C.) of Cicero, and the *De clementia* (A.D. 55/56) addressed by Seneca to the emperor Nero. More important than classical tradition as a source, however, was patristic tradition, especially Augustine's portrait of the ideal ruler in the *City of God* (5.24) and Pope Gregory the Great's pastoral concept of good rule, as expressed in *Pastoral Care* and *Moralia.* The mirror of princes tradition tends to deemphasize the Augustinian concept that secular rule is a necessary evil imposed by God on the sinful nature of fallen man and to emphasize instead the Christian ruler's high moral responsibility to his people and to God. Patristic tradition, the works of Isidore of Seville (especially his influential derivation of *rex* [ruler] from *recte agendo* [right action]), and the Bible served as sources for the many quotations and exemplary stories used to illustrate and reinforce moral principles in mirrors. Although political theory is discernible in some of these treatises, the primary purpose of the mirror of princes is not to present political theory as such. The medieval mirror takes monarchy as the given form of government and assumes that good government will follow from the rule of a morally good man.

The first formal medieval mirrors of princes are usually taken to be those associated with the Carolingian renaissance; some brief, earlier examples include the *Formula vitae honestae* by Martinus Braga (*d.* 580) and a letter by an unidentified author addressed to a seventh-century Merovingian ruler. Alcuin frequently used the format of a letter to offer advice to rulers. The first fully realized example of a mirror is the *Via regia* (*ca.* 811–814) written by Smaragdus of St. Mihiel, probably for Louis I the Pious. Smaragdus discusses royal unction as a sign of the theocratic power of a Christian king and argues that the king's high office demands an equally lofty moral character. The treatise *De institutione regis* (834), written by Jonas, bishop of Orléans, for Pepin, son of Louis I, combines traditional biblical and patristic materials with references to papal law and to the decrees of the Council of Paris (829). *De rectoribus christianis,* written by Sedulius Scottus after 855, is notable for its many examples taken from history as well as from the Bible, and for its unusual *prosimetrum* form, perhaps patterned after the *Consolation* of Boethius. The most prolific writer in this genre during this period was Hincmar of Rheims (*ca.* 806–882), whose works of counsel range from general treatises on the office of king and on the virtues and vices pertaining to kingship to more specific treatises concerning such matters as the selection of counselors and proper tutors for royal heirs and the punishment of the crime of rape.

The mirror of princes best known in modern times, the *Policraticus* (1159) of John of Salisbury, differs from its Carolingian predecessors in some important ways. Although its immediate point of reference is the reign of Henry II, it is not addressed to the king but to his chancellor, Thomas Becket, and its purpose is a thorough critique of Henry's regime. The contrast between ideal kingship and contemporary realities, implicit in earlier mirrors, is explicit in the *Policraticus;* the discussion of "courtly frivolities" (*nugis curialium*) referred to in the subtitle of the work is based on close observation of members of the ruling class of his time, in their private as well as public capacities. In addition to citing traditional patristic authorities, the *Policraticus* refers repeatedly to the "law of kings" in Deuteronomy 17:14–20 (also mentioned by Jonas of Orléans) and to a work called the "Institutio Trajani" and attributed to Plutarch. The ostensible purpose is to show that the Bible and the classics agree on the principles of good rule; Hans Liebeschütz has shown, however, that the material attributed to Plutarch really represents the views of John of Salisbury. Earlier mirrors make passing references to Fortune as the power that threatens the stability of worldly kingdoms; drawing on the *Consolation of Philosophy* of Boethius, the *Policraticus* shows that Fortune has power only over those who devote themselves to the goods of Fortune: worldly pleasure, worldly power, and worldly possessions.

Although it exercised a lasting influence on political theory, the *Policraticus,* with its critical ap-

MIRROR OF PRINCES

proach and its broadly humanistic outlook, had no imitators in its own time. Peter of Blois, in his *Dialogus cum rege Henrico* (1174–1189), made some criticisms of the reign of Henry II in a less ambitious form. The treatises of Godfrey of Viterbo (*Speculum regum,* 1180–1183) and Gerald of Wales (*De principis instructione,* 1180–1217) are representative of the general tendency to return to the more traditional format of moral exhortation. By the end of the first half of the thirteenth century, this tradition had begun to appear in vernacular works: in French (Robert of Blois, *L'enseignement des princes,* mid thirteenth century), in Spanish (James I the Conqueror of Aragon, *Libre de saviese ó doctrína* [*ca.* 1246] and the *Libro de la nobleza y lealtad* [1250–1260], composed at the request of Ferdinand III of Castile), and in Old Norse (*Konungs skuggsjá, ca.* 1240–1263).

The second half of the thirteenth century saw such a proliferation of mirrors that Jean-Philippe Genet has proposed dating the "true Miroir au Prince" from this period. Many of these treatises were written by members of the mendicant orders, some of whom were associated with the Capetian court: for example, the *Eruditio regum et principum* (1259) by the Franciscan Gilbert of Tournai; *De eruditione filiorum nobilium* and *De moralis principis instructione* by the Dominican Vincent of Beauvais; and *Les enseignemens,* addressed to his son, the future Philip III, by St. Louis IX. Two Dominican treatises, *De regno* by Thomas Aquinas and *De regimine principum* by Ptolemy of Lucca, were so closely associated that they were often taken as one work. Also from this period is the version of the pseudo-Aristotelian *Secretum secretorum* with glosses by the Franciscan Roger Bacon. This work of counsel had its roots not in the biblical and patristic tradition, but in the occult sciences. It supposedly derived from the esoteric teachings of Aristotle and circulated widely in Arabic versions until its translation, in the late twelfth and early thirteenth centuries, into Latin and, later, most Western vernaculars.

By far the most widely read and translated mirror from this period is the *De regimine principum* of about 1287, written by the Augustinian friar Egidius Colonna (Aegidius Romanus, Giles of Rome) for the future Philip IV the Fair. Like Aquinas, Egidius adds to the traditional Augustinian basis of the mirror of princes his detailed knowledge of the *Politics* of Aristotle. His treatise brought systematic order to a form that was originally anecdotal and loosely organized; divided into three books according to the "three governments" over which a ruler presides—himself, his household, and his kingdom—it carefully defines the virtues and vices involved in each kind of rule. Hundreds of manuscripts of the treatise are extant, and it was translated or adapted into other languages: French, Italian, Castilian, Catalan, Portuguese, Middle High German, Middle Low German, English, Old Swedish, and Hebrew.

The Valois kings continued the Capetian tradition in the fourteenth century by encouraging translations and the composition of new mirrors. As late as the Renaissance, mirrors of princes continued to be written in Latin as well as the vernaculars. Sometimes they took the form of an extended exemplum illustrating the principles of conduct for a king, such as *Le mireoirs as princes* (1327) of Watriquet de Couvin. Sometimes the mirror was embedded in a larger work, such as the letter to Richard II in the *Vox Clamantis* (*ca.* 1386) of the English poet John Gower. Gower also included the first English version of a mirror of princes in his English poem *Confessio Amantis,* basing it in part on a Christianized adaptation of the *Secretum secretorum* and in part on the *Livres dou trésor* of Brunetto Latini. With the addition of this material, the mirror of princes enlarged its scope from moral and political counsel to take on something of an encyclopedic character.

An important influence on the further expansion of the genre was the commentary on the Book of Wisdom, *Postilla super librum Sapientiae,* by the Dominican Robert Holcot (*ca.* 1290–1349). In *lectio* II, Holcot states that the purpose of Wisdom is to give instruction on the government of civil communities; and a note following the explicit in some manuscripts reinforces the point, describing it as a work of counsel "where kings and princes are instructed in the worship of God and in right conduct." As one of the most widely known commentaries of the late Middle Ages, Holcot's *Postilla* gave special prominence to the Book of Wisdom as a mirror for princes that had divine authority.

In addition to the *Secretum secretorum,* other mirrors for princes circulated in the Muslim world. Most of these were based on Islamic tradition, taking as their authorities the Koran and the *ḥadīth* (traditions concerning the practices of Muḥammad as both secular and spiritual leader). According to F. R. C. Bagley, the first original Arabic book of counsel for rulers was written by Ibn al-Muqaffaᶜ (*ca.* 724–757). Two important Arabic mirrors are the *Kitāb al-*

tāj (847–861) incorrectly attributed to al-Jāḥiẓ and the *Kitāb al-sulṭān* of Ibn Qutaybah (828–889). In the *Kitāb Baghdād* of Abu 'l-Faḍl Aḥmad ibn Abī Ṭāhir Ṭayfūr, the treatise takes the form of a father's advice to his son.

Three of the best-known and most important Persian mirrors are from the period of the Seljuk domination. The *Qābūsnāma* (1082) of Kay kāʾūs ibn Iskandar is in the form of a father's advice to his son, discussing a variety of practical matters, including the occupations one might take up if one lost the throne. The *Siyāsat-nāma* of Niẓām al-Mulk (1018–1092), written at the request of the Seljuk ruler Malikshāh, offers a combination of Islamic ideals and practical advice; a second part, perhaps written later, includes a review of recent history and an attack on the malign effect of heretical sects. The *Kitāb naṣīḥat al-Mulūk* of al-Ghazālī (1058/1059–1111), the most comprehensive of these treatises, is divided into two parts; the first discusses the Islamic beliefs and religious principles a Muslim ruler should follow, and the second offers specific recommendations, strongly colored by Ghazālī's Sufi outlook. In all of these Persian mirrors there is a tendency to combine precepts of Sasanian and Muslim provenance. And all Muslim mirrors, like their Christian counterparts, show the influence of a habit of mind that derives from very ancient traditions of wisdom literature (such as the Persian *andarz* or *pandnāma* and the biblical book of Proverbs), a tendency to associate a precept with an illustrative anecdote or proverb.

Close affinities with the medieval mirror of princes are evident in many Renaissance examples of the type, such as the *Institutio principis christiani* (1516) of Erasmus, Sir Thomas Elyot's *Boke Named the Governour* (1531), and the *Basilikon Doron* (1599) of James I. Even Machiavelli's *Prince* (1513), as Allan H. Gilbert demonstrates, owes much to the medieval mirror; in many of his assertions, however, Machiavelli attacks assumptions that had formed the basis of the mirror of princes for more than 800 years. Machiavelli's most fundamental departure from tradition is his assertion that any ruler in the real world who wants to keep his power must learn how and when not to be good. In taking this position, Machiavelli disagreed with all those who believed that moral and religious principles were the safeguard of a kingdom and who wrote works of counsel to kings as an expression of that belief.

BIBLIOGRAPHY

Hans Hubert Anton, *Fürstenspiegel und Herrscherethos in der Karolingerzeit.* (1968); Dora M. Bell, *L'idéal éthique de la royauté en France au moyen âge d'après quelques moralistes de ce temps* (1962); Wilhelm Berges, *Die Fürstenspiegel des hohen und späten Mittelalters* (1938, repr. 1952); Lester K. Born, "The *Specula principis* of the Carolingian Renaissance," in *Revue belge de philologie et d'histoire,* **11** [*sic;* should be **12**] (1933); Desiderius Erasmus, *The Education of a Christian Prince,* Lester K. Born, trans. (1936, repr. 1965); Jean-Philippe Genet, ed., *Four English Political Tracts of the Later Middle Ages* (1977); *Ghazālī's Book of Counsel for Kings (Naṣīḥat al-Mulūk),* F. R. C. Bagley, trans. (1964); Allan H. Gilbert, *Machiavelli's "Prince" and Its Forerunners* (1938); Wilhelm Kleineke, *Englische Fürstenspiegel vom Policraticus Johanns von Salisbury bis zum Basilikon Doron König Jakobs I* (1937); Hans Liebeschütz, *Mediaeval Humanism in the Life and Writings of John of Salisbury* (1950), 23–94; Beryl Smalley, *English Friars and Antiquity in the Early Fourteenth Century* (1960), 133–202; Roland Mitchell Smith, "The *Speculum principum* in Early Irish Literature," in *Speculum,* **2** (1926); Walter Ullmann, *Law and Politics in the Middle Ages* (1975), 227–306.

PATRICIA J. EBERLE

[See also **Aquinas, St. Thomas; Aristotle in the Middle Ages; Augustine of Hippo, St.; Bacon, Roger; Classical Literary Studies; Deposition of Rulers; Egidius Colonna; Gerald of Wales; Ghazāli, al-; Gower, John; Gregory I the Great, Pope; Hincmar of Rheims; Holcot, Robert; Isidore of Seville, St.; John of Salisbury; Jonas of Orléans; Kingship, Theories of; Law; Martin of Braga, St.; Muqaffaʿ, ʿAbd Allāh ibn al-; Niẓām al-Mulk; Peter of Blois; Political Theory; Ptolemy of Lucca; Sedulius Scottus; Smaragdus of St. Mihiel; Vincent of Beauvais.**]

MISA DE AMOR, LA, anonymous Spanish ballad probably of the late fifteenth or early sixteenth century. In spite of its folk origin, it is as refined as a courtly poem, with a touch of innocent irreverence. A Mass is being celebrated. The lady with whom the poet is in love enters the church. A brief description follows of her beauty, her elaborate garments, even her makeup. Her beauty is such that it affects everybody: the choir soloist loses his melody; the priest babbles in confusion; the acolytes instead of answering "Amén, amén" answer "Amor, amor."

BIBLIOGRAPHY

Ramón Menéndez Pidal, *Flor nueva de romances viejos* (1938, 15th ed. 1965), 188–189; Ferdinand J. Wolf and

Conrad Hofmann, *Primavera y flor de romances,* 2 vols. (1856, 2nd ed. 1899).

MANUEL DURAN

[See also **Spanish Literature: Ballads.**]

MISERICORD (from Latin *misericordia,* mercy, pity) most commonly refers to a small, corbel-like projection on the underside of a hinged choir stall seat. When the seat is in the raised position, the misericord provides support for one standing in the choir stall. Misericords frequently were carved with images or scenes, some of which are quite secular in nature. The word can also refer to a room in a monastery in which rules, especially those concerning diet, were relaxed, and to a dagger employed to kill quickly, and thus with mercy or pity, a wounded enemy.

BIBLIOGRAPHY

Dorothy Kraus and Henry Kraus, *The Hidden World of Misericords* (1975).

CARL F. BARNES, JR.

[See also **Furniture, Liturgical.**]

MISSAL, a Latin liturgical book including ceremonial directions for the celebration of the Mass and everything sung or said during its celebration that developed in the eighth and ninth centuries. These details of the Mass contained in missals attained canonical form in the tenth century, when the custom of saying private Masses developed.

Because details of the Mass differ from one locality to another, individual missals are often idiosyncratic and can be localized with some precision. Their often elaborate decoration—with miniatures and historiated initials depicting the biblical events commemorated in the Mass, as well as images of the Mass itself—is often equally individual, reflecting the tastes and interests of the missal's patron, who is frequently portrayed.

According to Klaus Gamber, the earliest examples of the missal go back to the eighth century and appear to have originated in central and southern Italy. It was not until the twelfth and thirteenth centuries, however, that missals became popular north of the Alps.

Missals contain texts extracted from a variety of more specialized books used in antiquity and the early Middle Ages by the various clerical participants in the Mass. These include sacramentaries with their Mass prayers and canon used by the celebrating bishop or presbyter; lectionaries with epistles and Gospels used by readers, subdeacons, and deacons; *antiphonalia (antiphonaria missarum)* containing the chants of the Mass used by members of the choir; and *ordinaria* and *ordines* with their ritual directions for one or more of the participants, and auxiliary prayers. These materials were arranged in the missals to be used sequentially during the Mass, and were organized according to various liturgical cycles. Following a calendar and title, missals of the High and Late Middle Ages generally had sets of the Mass arranged for the temporale from Advent to Holy Saturday, the *ordo missae* and canon at Easter, the continuation of the temporale through Pentecost, the sanctorale with propers of saints followed by commons of saints, and finally votive Masses.

BIBLIOGRAPHY

Adalbert Ebner, *Quellen und Forschungen zur Geschichte und Kunstgeschichte des Missale Romanum im Mittelalter: Iter Italicum* (1896); Andrew Hughes, *Medieval Manuscripts for Mass and Office: A Guide to Their Organization and Terminology* (1982); Abbé Victor Leroquais, *Les sacramentaires et les missels manuscrits des bibliothèques publiques de France,* 4 vols. (1924), esp. I.

See also Klaus Gamber, *Codices liturgici latini antiquiores (Spicilegii Friburgensis subsidia),* 2 vols., 2nd ed. (1968).

LESLIE BRUBAKER
ROGER E. REYNOLDS

[See also **Antiphonal; Lectionary; Liturgy, Treatises on; Mass, Liturgy of; Ordines Romani; Sacramentary.**]

MISSI DOMINICI were royal commissioners used by the Carolingian mayors of the palace and rulers to inquire into particular problems throughout the kingdom, to exercise control over local administration, and to introduce reforms. Under Charlemagne, *missi* made regular, periodic inspections of the Frankish empire. They were usually sent in pairs, one ecclesiastic (a bishop or an abbot) and one count. From 802 this pairing seems to have become standard.

Pairs of *missi* were frequently given a memorandum containing instructions they were to carry out and a summary of information they were to convey to the counts and inhabitants of the specific area or *missaticum* (usually about six counties) into which they were sent. These documents, the *capitularia missorum,* might be designed for specific missions, such as the mobilization of the army in a particular region, or might be prepared for regular tours of inspection.

While on circuit, the *missi* were responsible for a variety of tasks. *Missi* were responsible for inviting and investigating complaints of injustice; they were to remedy abuses and to sit in judgment jointly with local counts. They also were the king's means of publishing royal and synodal decrees and the judgments of local tribunals. In 802, in order to implement the reforms of government that Charlemagne wished to effect following his imperial coronation, *missi* were made responsible for administering a new oath to Charlemagne as emperor, and also for explaining the meaning of this oath to his subjects.

According to the *capitularia missorum, missi* were often required to render written reports of their activities. They were, at various times, ordered to report on all public pronouncements and appointments they had made, on abuses of comital authority they had encountered, and on decisions they had rendered in courts. In addition, they were obliged to submit reports on each benefice within their *missaticum* held from the king or from others, along with a detailed description of the economic and demographic status of each.

The history of the *missi dominici* was one of continual effort on the part of the Carolingians to prevent the *missi* from becoming corrupted by bribes or from developing strong local ties within their *missaticum.* Charlemagne's reform of 802, which sought to limit the recruitment of *missi* to counts, abbots, and bishops, had been an effort to end flagrant venality among less wealthy and powerful *missi* as well as to provide agents who, independent of their royal office, were of sufficient status to deal with local magnates on at least an equal footing. This effort was apparently unsuccessful. By the end of the reign of Charlemagne, indications of corruption of *missi* were widespread. Under his son Louis the Pious, the *missatica* of *missi* became permanent and centered on their own counties or bishoprics. The value of *missi* as independent checks on local administrators was thus entirely lost.

BIBLIOGRAPHY

François L. Ganshof, *Frankish Institutions Under Charlemagne,* Bryce Lyon and Mary Lyon, trans. (1968), and *The Carolingians and the Frankish Monarchy: Studies in Carolingian History,* Janet Sondheimer, trans. (1971).

PATRICK GEARY

[See also **Benefice, Lay; Capitulary; Carolingians and the Carolingian Empire; Charlemagne.**]

MISSION OF THE APOSTLES. The primary task of the twelve apostles was to disseminate the teachings of Jesus Christ. The books of Matthew and Luke both contain exhortations by Christ to go forth and tell all nations of the Word of God (Matt. 28:19–20, Luke 24:47). The Book of Acts in the New Testament relates the missionary travels of the apostles. Iconographically, the acts of the apostles is a more popular theme in the later Middle Ages in Western art. It is found, however, as a didactic theme in sculptural form in the central portal tympanum at the church of La Madeleine, Vézelay (*ca.* 1120–1132). Christ is depicted as he appeared to the apostles between his resurrection and ascension. The disciples are depicted as receiving the gift of tongues, while the peoples of the world surround them, awaiting the Word of God. In the Strozzi Altarpiece, executed by Orcagna (Andrea di Cione) between 1354 and 1357, Christ is depicted as commissioning Sts. Peter and Thomas Aquinas with the book and keys, symbols of their missions. Perhaps the best-known depiction of the Mission of the Apostles is the series of tapestry cartoons executed by Raphael in 1515–1516 for the Sistine Chapel, now in the Victoria and Albert Museum.

BIBLIOGRAPHY

Gustav Kunstler, *Romanesque Art in Europe* (1968); Frederick Hartt, *History of Italian Renaissance Art* (1969); Gertrud Schiller, *Iconography of Christian Art,* Janet Seligman, trans. (1971–).

JENNIFER E. JONES

[See also **Orcagna; Vézelay, Church of La Madeleine.**]

MISSIONS AND MISSIONARIES, CHRISTIAN. The words attributed to Jesus, "Go into all the world and preach the Gospel to every creature" (Mark 16:15), were interpreted by early Christian communities to mean that his message was intended for all peoples—it had universal significance. Beginning in the remote Roman province of Palestine, Christianity therefore had to be a missionary religion. The entire history of Christianity, consequently, is inextricably tied up with missionary activity. Likewise, Jesus' instruction, "Go, therefore, and make disciples of all the nations" (Matthew 28:19), was construed by the first Christians and then by the church fathers to mean that every person who accepted Christianity became, by the terms of baptism, a witness to the Gospels and thus a missionary to unbelievers.

THE LATE EMPIRE, 300–600

By the time of the "Peace of Constantine" (312–323), during which the practice of Christianity became legal within the Roman Empire, the Christian message had penetrated all parts of the empire. Strong Christian communities existed in Asia Minor, Syria, Egypt, Ethiopia, and northwestern Africa, while cities and army camps, such as Rome, Lyons, Cologne, London, Dorchester, Canterbury, and York, had organized Christian groups—as archaeological evidence has recently revealed.

Christianity came to southern Gaul with the Roman army, and by the time of St. Irenaeus (*ca.* 140–202), bishop of Lyons, priests and missionaries had extended their proselytizing outside the army camps to the uneducated country people. Scholars trace the effective foundations of Christianity in Gaul to St. Martin of Tours (*ca.* 316–397), a Roman soldier who, after giving away half his cloak to a beggar, received a vision of Christ, was baptized, and entered religious life. Martin founded the monastery of Ligugé, the first in Gaul, which became a center for the evangelization of the country districts. In 371/372 he became bishop of Tours, where he introduced a rudimentary parochial system.

The Germanic tribes that penetrated the boundaries of the Roman Empire were barbarian in culture and pagan in religion. Before the late fifth century, if they accepted Christianity, it was Arian Christianity. The baptism of Clovis, king of the Franks, by the orthodox Catholic bishop Remigius—partly the result of Clovis' belief that the Christian God had facilitated his victory over the fierce Alamanni, partly through the pressure of his Catholic wife Clotilda—was a serious blow to Arianism in the expanding Frankish domain.

St. Paul had planned to visit Spain (Romans 15:24), but there is no evidence that he got there. Little is known about the earliest missionaries to the Iberian Peninsula, but by the third century many churches and bishoprics had been set up. At the Spanish council of Elvira (*ca.* 306) thirty-seven separate communities were represented, suggesting vigorous missionary and organizational activity.

The Welshman St. Ninian (*ca.* 360–432) first brought Christianity to Scotland. He had visited Rome in 394, been consecrated a bishop there, and on the return journey stopped in Tours, where he met St. Martin. At Whithorn in Wigtownshire in southwestern Scotland, Ninian built the church of Candida Casa, or White House, which he dedicated to St. Martin and which served as the base for his evangelization of the Picts and Britons.

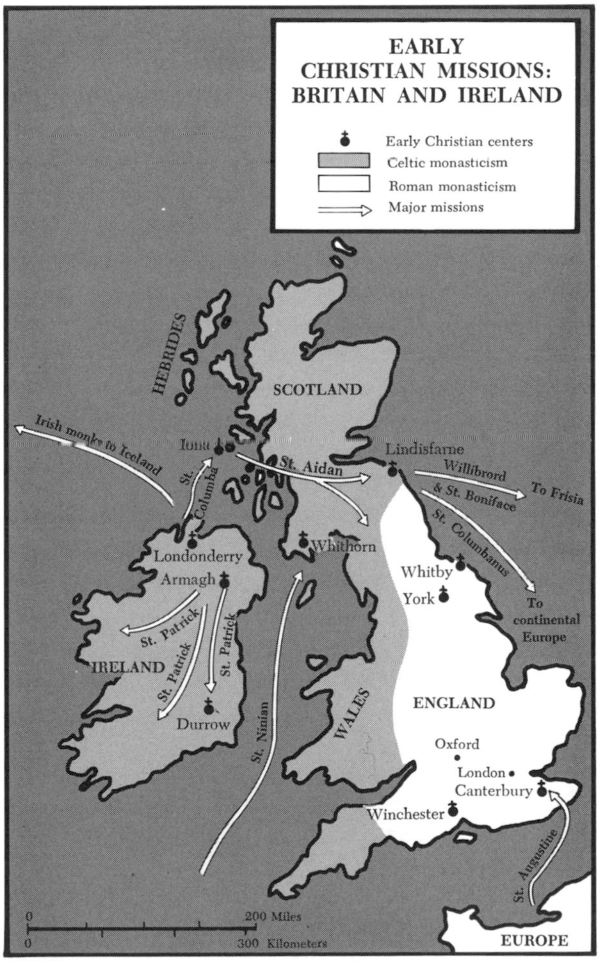

In the early fourth century Christianity entered southern and eastern Ireland from Britain. In the fifth century through the missionary efforts of St. Patrick (*ca.* 389–*ca.* 461), son of a Romano-British deacon, northern Ireland was gradually converted. After the conversion of several members of the royal family and in spite of the fierce opposition of the heathen Druids, Patrick secured toleration for Christianity. From his headquarters at Armagh, he preached extensively in Connaught, Leinstre, and Meath; in addition, he established many churches and monasteries.

The Christian church in Ireland came to differ in a fundamental way from the churches in England and on the Continent: the monastery, rather than the diocese, served as the center of ecclesiastical organization. Local clans and the monastery were interdependent, with the clan supporting the monastery economically and the monastery providing educational and religious services for the clan. The abbatial office was hereditary in the clan, passing from uncle to nephew or cousin. The rank of bishop existed, since only the bishop could ordain men to the priesthood, but the bishop was subordinate to the abbot. A severe asceticism and a strong missionary fervor also characterized early Irish Christianity.

St. Columba (*ca.* 521–597) is perhaps the best representative of Irish-Celtic missionary zeal. He founded the monasteries of Durrow and Londonderry in Ireland; then in 563 he and twelve companions established on Iona, an island in the Inner Hebrides, a monastery which served as his central base for converting the pagan Picts of Scotland. From Iona, Celtic monk-missionaries went to northern England. The most famous of these was St. Aidan (*d.* 651), who established the abbey of Lindisfarne on a peninsula that at high tide becomes an island off the coast of Northumbria; Aidan played a crucial role in the conversion of northern England. Columba's proselytizing efforts won him the title "Apostle of Scotland," and his disciples carried the Gospels to the Continent. His namesake St. Columbanus (*ca.* 543–615) preached in eastern France, establishing the monastery of Luxeuil in the mountainous Vosges region and the monastery at Bobbio in northern Italy. Columbanus' companion St. Gall (*d. ca.* 630) preached in eastern Switzerland. The famous abbey of St. Gall dates from a century later than the missionary of the same name, but its rich surviving collection of Celtic manuscripts attests to the monastery's close association with the Irish monasteries in the eighth and ninth centuries.

WESTERN EUROPE, 600–1200

In the period extending roughly from 600 to 1200, two factors advanced the spread of the Christian faith: the missionary activities of the monks and the support and encouragement of kings. Because religion for the Germanic peoples was an aspect of their sociopolitical culture and because tribal loyalty determined religious faith, missionary efforts concentrated on the king or chieftain. Once he accepted Christianity, the baptism of his subjects followed almost automatically. The baptism of hundreds or thousands, however, represented only very superficial conversion.

The pontificate of Gregory I (590–604) marked the beginnings of a vigorous papally directed program for the conversion of northern Europe. In 596, Gregory sent the prior of St. Andrew's monastery in Rome, Augustine (*d.* 605), with forty companions to convert the heathen Anglo-Saxons of Britain. Although once a part of the Roman Empire, Britain had been overrun by Anglo-Saxon tribes, most of which in 596 recognized Ethelbert, king of Kent, as overlord. Within a year Augustine had succeeded in baptizing Ethelbert and, supposedly, 10,000 of his followers. Ethelbert allowed Augustine to settle in his capital, Canterbury, where Augustine consecrated the existing Roman basilica as the cathedral church of Christ, the first archiepiscopal see in England.

In a message sent to Augustine in 601, Pope Gregory set down a strategy for assimilation and accommodation which subsequently served as official church policy throughout Europe:

> . . . We have been giving careful thought to the affairs of the English, and have come to the conclusion that the temples of the idols among that people should on no account be destroyed. The idols are to be destroyed, but the temples themselves are to be aspersed with holy water, altars set up in them, and relics deposited there. For if these temples are well built, they must be purified from the worship of demons and dedicated to the service of the true God. In this way, we hope that the people, seeing that their temples are not destroyed, may abandon their error and, flocking more readily to their accustomed resorts, may come to know and adore the true God. And since they have a custom of sacrificing many oxen to demons, let some other solemnity be substituted in its place, such as a day of Dedication or the Festivals of the holy martyrs whose relics are enshrined there. . . . For it is certainly impossible to eradicate all errors from obstinate minds at one stroke, and whoever wishes to climb to a mountain top climbs gradually step by step, and not in one leap.

MISSIONS, CHRISTIAN

In the eighth century three strands of Christianity converged in Britain: in the west, small pockets of Christian Britons who had fled the Germanic invaders; in northern England, Celtic Christianity; and the newer Roman Christianity represented by Augustine. Celtic Christianity, though recognizing the bishop of Rome as successor of St. Peter, had customs and practices—such as the date of Easter and the form of clerical tonsure—that differed from the Roman. Nevertheless, the final authority came to rest with Rome as a result of the Synod of Whitby (664), in which the decisive influence of King Oswy of Northumbria gave the victory to Rome. Consequently, Celtic practices gradually disappeared.

Irish evangelizing enthusiasm penetrated the now Roman-oriented church in England, and in the eighth century Britain acted as the nursery for missionaries to the Continent. The Northumbrian Willibrord (658–739) preached to the Frisians in what is today Belgium and the Netherlands. With the support of the Frankish chieftain Pepin II (687–714), Willibrord founded monasteries in Luxembourg, Antwerp, and Utrecht, the last becoming an archiepiscopal see with Willibrord the first ordinary (695).

The greatest missionary of the early Middle Ages and the evangelist whom the historian of medieval culture Christopher Dawson described as "a man who had a deeper influence on the history of Europe than any Englishman who has ever lived" was St. Boniface, also known as Wynfrith or Winfrid (*ca.* 675–754). A native of Devon, educated at the abbey of Nursling near Winchester, Boniface at the mature age of forty departed for Frisia, where he assisted Willibrord. His initial missionary efforts there were unsuccessful, but a subsequent visit proved more fruitful. On a second visit to Rome in 722, Pope Gregory II consecrated him a bishop with broad authority over the German frontier and promised him Roman support. Boniface returned to Germany and at Geismar in Hesse chopped down the sacred oak of Thor, the center of a large animist cult. The pagan Germans believed that anyone who desecrated the holy sanctuary would himself be destroyed; when Boniface survived, he demonstrated the greater power of the Christian God.

Boniface organized the bishoprics of Freising, Regensburg, and Salzburg; became the first archbishop of Mainz; and founded the abbey of Fulda. After 741, at the instigation of the Frankish rulers, he tried to carry out a reform of the entire Frankish church and through a series of regional councils (742–747) sought to impose tough disciplinary measures on

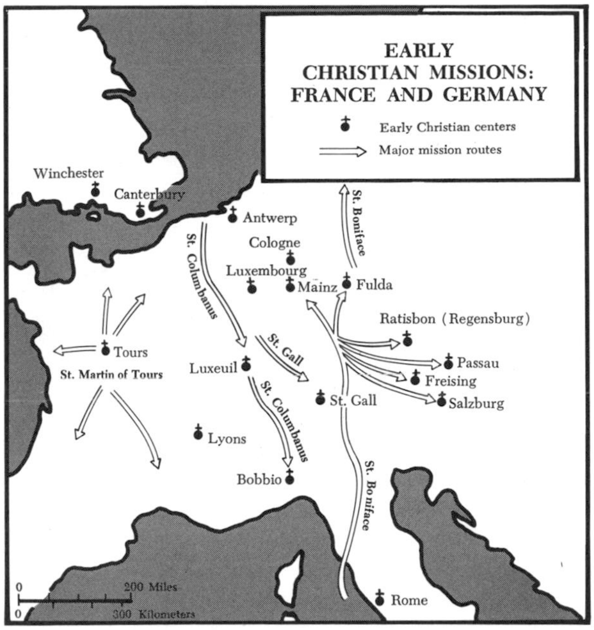

both clergy and laity. Although Boniface's reforms achieved only limited success, he did bring about close union between the church in Germany and Rome. In spite of his strong administrative ability, his missionary zeal never flagged. In 754, while attempting once more to convert the heathen Frisians, this time near the Zuider Zee, he was martyred. Boniface greatly expanded papal influence north of the Alps and is sometimes called the "Apostle of Germany."

The emperor Charlemagne's slow subjugation of the Saxons (772–798) in the northern parts of the Frankish kingdom initiated the pacification and Christianization of the region; here, too, monk-missionaries played the decisive role. The key figure was Ansgar (also Anschar, Anskar, 801–865), a monk of Corbie (near Amiens). After the Saxon territory had been divided into the dioceses of Bremen, Minden, and Hamburg, the emperor Louis the Pious appointed Ansgar (*ca.* 832) first bishop of Hamburg. Although he experienced various reverses in his evangelizing efforts, including the burning of Hamburg by the Vikings, Ansgar carried his work into Denmark and Sweden. Pope Gregory IV appointed Ansgar archbishop of Hamburg and Bremen (*ca.* 848), from which post in 854 he went into Scandinavia and succeeded in converting King Haarik of Denmark and King Olaf of Sweden. The Swedes and the Danes, however, lapsed into paganism when Ansgar died.

Initial Christian missions had thus entered Scan-

 MISSIONS, CHRISTIAN

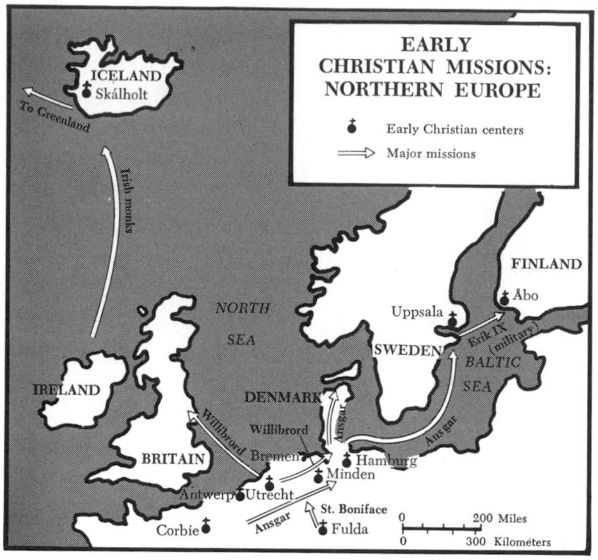

dinavia from Germany, but in the eleventh century more lasting results came from the England of King Cnut. Cnut, whose empire included Denmark, Sweden, and Norway, used English missionaries, law codes, and ecclesiastical practices to advance royal power in those lands. In the process, Christianity gradually took root. Cnut's loyalty to the papacy, developed during a visit to Rome in 1027, tied his peoples to Rome.

Still, Christianity experienced repeated reverses in Scandinavia, especially in Sweden, where human sacrifices were a central part of the pagan cult. Cistercian monks, invited to the north by King Sverker (*ca.* 1130–*ca.*1156), played the main part in the final Christianization of Sweden. Stephen, the first archbishop of Uppsala (1164), was a Cistercian.

The Finns, whose language has affinities with Hungarian, are not ethnically Scandinavian. Although missionaries were active in Finland from the eleventh century, the effective Christianization of that country began only with the Swedish conquest under Eric IX (*ca.* 1150). Eric ordered the baptism of the vanquished Finns, but progress was very slow. Only in 1291, with the appointment of the native Turku as archbishop of Åbo, was formal conversion achieved.

Irish monks carried the Gospels to Iceland in the late eighth century, and pagan Scandinavian settlers arrived there in the ninth. When disputes developed over the adoption of Christianity, the Althing, or parliament, officially adopted Christianity. In 1056, Skálholt became the first episcopal seat in Iceland.

As part of their great expansion in the tenth century, the Vikings reached the west coast of Greenland around 985. The Norwegian chieftain Eric the Red could not abandon his pagan gods, but his wife Thjohild and son Leif were converted to Christianity. Thjohild at once built a church, and about 1125 the first bishop arrived in Greenland.

Once a missionary had led a pagan people to the waters of baptism, the work of conversion had only begun. Conversion involves a conscious turning toward God—that is, the effort of the Christian to live according to the Gospel message. It is usually a lifetime process. To get pagan and illiterate peoples to try to live according to Christian standards and teachings, missionaries used continued preaching, which aimed at instruction and the strengthening of the newly baptized through edifying stories based on the lives of Christ and the saints. Priests and missionaries also applied the penitential system.

Penitentials were manuals for the examination of conscience. Irish monks wrote the earliest ones and took them to England; English missionaries carried penitentials to the Continent. The illiterate penitent knelt beside the priest, who, using the penitential, questioned the person about sins he or she might have committed. A penance, usually fasting on bread and water for a prescribed time, was then imposed.

The system of penance helped foster a more personal attitude toward religion. Religion among ancient pagan peoples had meant public, corporate, and largely ritualistic acts which a person performed simply as a social consequence of being a member of a tribe, clan, or city. As an effect of the use of penitentials, however, religion slowly became a private matter, involving and developing the individual conscience.

EASTERN EUROPE TO 1400

As in Western Europe, Christianity in Eastern Europe owed its success—a very slow success—to the support of kings and princes who established important bishoprics. At the request of Duke Rastislav (846–870) of Moravia (modern central Czechoslovakia), who wanted to check German influences in his territory, the Byzantine emperor Michael III sent two learned Greek brothers, Cyril (826/827–869) and Methodios (815–885), to launch missionary activity among the Slavs. According to tradition Cyril and Methodios invented an alphabet later called Cyrillic for use in the liturgy and for the translation of the Bible.

In 968, the German emperor Otto I the Great founded the see of Magdeburg, which became the

 MISSIONS, CHRISTIAN

center for missionary activity in eastern Germany. In Bohemia (western Czechoslovakia) Christianity progressed under the pious king Wenceslaus (920–929) and took firm root under his nephew Boleslav II (967–999), who endowed many churches and monasteries which served as the nuclei for the conversion of the surrounding areas. Thus the see of Prague, created in 973, became under Bishop Adalbert the center for missionary activity among the Magyars and Poles. Boleslav's sister Dobrawa carried Christianity with her to Poland when she married the Polish duke Mieszko; Mieszko's baptism in 967 was followed a year later by the creation of the episcopal see of Poznań, which was initially under the jurisdiction of Magdeburg. The penetration of Christianity among the ruthless and pagan Hungarians began with Otto the Great's defeat of Hungarian raiders at Lechfeld in 955. The marriage in 973 of Géza, prince of Hungary, and the Christian Adelheid of Poland led to the entrance of many missionaries. Christianity eventually triumphed under the wise and good king Stephen (975–1038). Stephen made Esztergom the ecclesiastical center of Hungary and gave bishops and abbots a privileged position within the nobility. Although Bohemia, Poland, and Hungary all witnessed brief pagan reactions, by 1100 Christianity had won general acceptance, and the Christian faith was inextricably identified with "national" identity.

Scholars trace the origins of the Russian state to the arrival of Scandinavian traders (Varangians) in the ninth century. One of their leaders, Oleg (879–912), established his headquarters at Kiev, which became the capital of Kievan Rus. Two basic attributes characterize the beginnings of Christianity in Russia: the impetus for the adoption of Christianity came from the rulers, and Christianity in Russia was linked with the Greek Orthodox Church of Constantinople. Thus, as tradition holds, Oleg's descendant Vladimir I (*ca.* 980–1015), after considering and rejecting Islam, Judaism, and (Western) Roman Christianity, was baptized by Greek priests and declared Byzantine Christianity the official faith of his territories. Greek monk-missionaries brought about mass baptisms and Vladimir established a Greek hierarchy, but from the beginning the liturgy was celebrated in Slavonic.

In the course of the eleventh century a native Russian clergy gradually replaced the Greek, but in the Great Schism of 1054, Russia sided with Constantinople. Kiev initially served as the metropolitan see of Russia, the metropolitan being appointed by the Greek patriarch of Constantinople. From Kiev missionaries fanned out northward to Novgorod and eastward to Moscow. Around 1328, Moscow, in the process of becoming the new political nucleus of the Russian state, became the metropolitan see, and in the fifteenth and sixteenth centuries missionaries from Moscow pushed into southern and eastern Russia.

In 1051 the monk Antonios of Mount Athos introduced monasticism near Kiev and founded the monastery of Kievo-Pecherskaya. Monastic life took deep root in Russia, and in the twelfth century seventeen monasteries were established near Kiev alone. The monastic impulse associated with St. Sergius of Radonezh (*ca.* 1314–1392), perhaps the most highly venerated saint in Russian culture, led to the construction of monasteries all over Russia. These monasteries served as centers of local piety and missionary activity. As in the Greek Orthodox Church, on which the Russian church was modeled, monasteries of celibate and learned men supplied the church's bishops, while the parish clergy were generally married and unlettered.

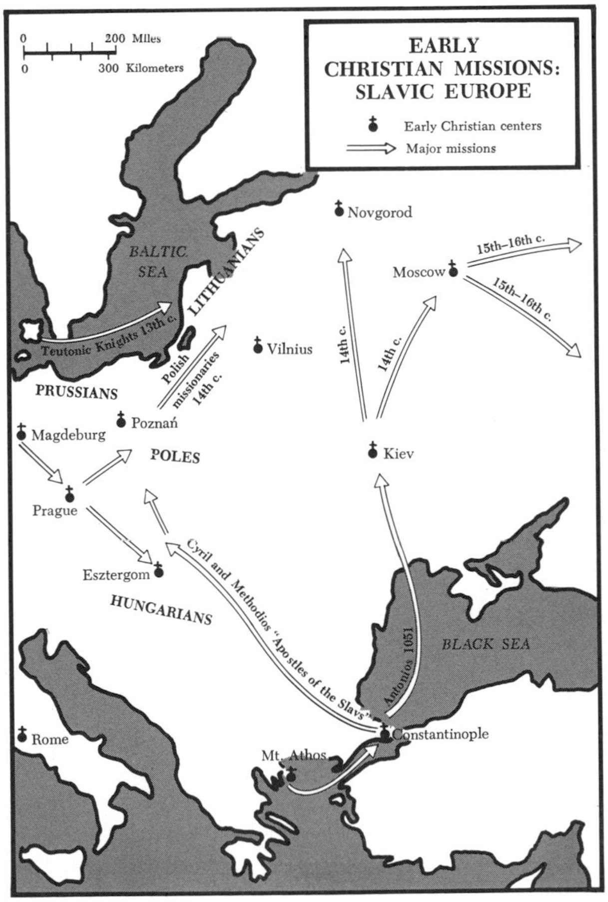

MISSIONS, CHRISTIAN

By about 1200 most of the peoples of Europe had, at least outwardly, accepted Christianity. There were two exceptions in the Baltic region: the Prussians and the Lithuanians.

In spite of pressures from the Danes to the north, the Germans to the west, and the Poles to the east, the Prussians clung fiercely to their pagan animism. Finally, the Teutonic Knights, with the strong endorsement of the emperor Frederick II and Pope Innocent III (*d.* 1216), who offered them great prizes in lands, led a crusade of Germanization and Christianization against the Prussians. The long, slow "conversion" of the Prussians (1226–1283) came only at the point of the sword of the Teutonic Knights.

The Teutonic Knights pressed for most of the fourteenth century a sporadic warfare against the pagan Lithuanians. When Jagiełło, grand duke of Lithuania (1377–1434), sought Polish help against the Knights, an alliance was worked out: the Poles agreed to support Jagiełło, provided he married the Polish queen Jadwiga, in succession to the Polish throne. Jagiełło was baptized in 1386, and his marriage established the union of Poland and Lithuania. A large flock of Polish missionaries entered Lithuania to convert the people, and the diocese of Vilnius was soon erected. Missionary activity in Lithuania, then, was the consequence of war, diplomacy, and marriage. The baptism of Jagiełło and the subsequent conversion of Lithuania mark the official end of European paganism.

THE MUSLIM CHALLENGE, 700–1350

The rise of Islam, which in the seventh century overwhelmed the ancient Christian communities of North Africa and the Near East, posed a major challenge to Christian missionary enterprise. The attitude to be taken toward Islam sharply divided churchmen and theologians. Some churchmen viewed the Muslims as crucial people for missionary activity; after all, Muslims believed in Abraham and large parts of the Old Testament, and they respected Jesus as a great teacher. Other churchmen looked upon Islam as a scourge to be destroyed and Muslim lands as territory to be conquered. Throughout the Middle Ages, the latter view tended to prevail.

In 711 a Muslim force crossed the Straits of Gibraltar and at Gaudalete in southern Spain defeated the weak Visigothic kingdom. In seven years the Muslims swept through the Iberian Peninsula, and as an able student of Spanish history, J. H. Elliott, has put it, "What was lost in seven years, it took seven hundred to regain." The political and religious history of the kingdoms that constitute medieval Spain involves the *Reconquista,* the reconquest of Spain from the Muslims. The *Reconquista* began in 1064, when King Ferdinand I of Castile captured Coimbra, in present-day west-central Portugal, and forced the emir of Badajoz to recognize his suzerainty; it was finally completed in 1492, when Ferdinand and Isabella captured Granada in the south. Priests and missionaries accompanied or immediately followed all the crusading armies.

From the continuing Spanish experience, the idea of the crusade was applied to the military expeditions that set out from Western Europe from the late eleventh century through the thirteenth with the goal of driving the Muslims out of Palestine. For the development of better relations between the Eastern and Western branches of the Christian church and for the promotion of understanding between Muslims and Christians, the crusades were an unmitigated disaster. Although fighting under the sign of the cross, crusading armies ultimately represented a denial of the Gospel teachings, and therefore they cannot properly be considered part of the missionary efforts of Christianity. From the monastic and religious orders came more constructive and more civilized approaches to the conversion of the Muslims.

In the mid twelfth century, Peter the Venerable, the ninth abbot of Cluny, partly because of the direction the crusading movement had taken in his time, partly because of what he correctly perceived as the general Western ignorance of Islam, had the Koran and other Arabic works translated into Latin (beginning in 1142). Peter hoped that these works would give missionaries a better understanding of Muslim theology and culture. The large number of surviving manuscripts of these translations suggests that they circulated widely in the Middle Ages. Peter's own treatise, *Liber contra sectam sive haeresim Saracenorum* (A book against the Saracen sect or heresy), was addressed to the Muslims themselves and indicates that he wanted it to win converts to Christianity. However, it was never translated into Arabic.

Between 500 and 1200 the monks had been at the vanguard of the Christian evangelizing movement. The rise of the mendicant orders in the thirteenth century signaled the shift of the missionary impulse to the friars. The most notable individual expedition to the Muslims was that of St. Francis of Assisi. Persuaded that the Muslims had not accepted Christianity because the Gospel had not been presented to them in its true simplicity and beauty, Francis at-

MISSIONS, CHRISTIAN

tempted several trips to the East: to Syria (1212), to Morocco, which was aborted, to Spain (1214/1215), and to Egypt (1215). The first two journeys made no discernible impact. On his third expedition, while the army of the Fifth Crusade was besieging Damietta in northern Egypt, then a major Mediterranean port city, Francis secured an audience with the Ayyubid sultan al-Kāmil, who probably did not understand what Francis was trying to say nor sympathize with his missionary goal. But the marked deference the sultan showed to Francis indicates that he earned Muslim respect as a holy person.

While Francis of Assisi provided late medieval missionary activity with remarkable zeal and charisma, his spiritual descendant Ramon Lull (*ca.* 1235–1316?) gave it vision and organization. This Franciscan mystic and missionary to Islam believed that three things were essential for the conversion of the Muslims. First was a comprehensive knowledge of the Arabic language. Accordingly, Lull bought a slave to teach him Arabic, established the college of Miramar in Majorca (1276), and persuaded the Council of Vienne (1311–1312) to set up colleges at the universities of Rome, Bologna, Paris, Oxford, and Salamanca for the study of the languages of the Middle East. A knowledge of languages, Lull maintained, would lead to an understanding of Islamic doctrine, which would facilitate Muslim conversions. Second, he favored the composition of a treatise defending the Christian faith entirely through the use of reason; he himself wrote the *Ars magna* (The great art) against the works of the Spanish-Arabian philosopher Averroës (Ibn Rushd). Since Muslim theologians believed that they could demonstrate the truth of their faith beyond the chance of error, this aspect of Lull's program had little long-term effect. His third idea was that the missionary must be a complete witness to the Christian faith and Gospels among the Muslims, even to the point of death. He made four missionary journeys to Africa and Asia, on the last of which, according to legend, he was stoned to death by Muslims at Bougie in North Africa.

While Ramon Lull's plan for missionary activity can be accused of intellectual idealism and the failure to appreciate the bitter differences that separated Islam and Christianity in his time, still his goal of building bridges of communication represents a more rational and peaceable solution than the armed violence of the crusades.

Although large-scale European crusading expeditions to the Middle East declined in the thirteenth century, the crusading ideal did not die. In Spain and Portugal the crusading ideal remained closely tied to Iberian Catholicism and missionary zeal. The voyages of discovery sent out by Prince Henry the Navigator after 1420 which brought the Portuguese into contact with the black peoples along the west African coast; the Portuguese and Spanish explorations and colonial establishments on the east African coast and in India; and the voyages of Christopher Columbus to the Americas—all these expeditions had, in part, the missionary goal of converting new peoples. When the Portuguese admiral Alfonso de Albuquerque attacked Malacca (in present-day Malaysia) in 1511, he justified the assault on the grounds of "the great service which we shall perform to Our Lord in casting the Moors [Muslims] out of this country, and quenching the fire of this sect of Mafamede [Muḥammad]. . . . And the other reason is the additional service which we shall render to the King D. Manuel in taking this city, because it is the headquarters of all the spiceries and drugs. . . . " The great chroniclers of the Spanish conquests in the New World—Bernal Díaz for Mexico and Pedro Cieza de León for Peru—repeatedly invoked the crusading missionary ideal as justification for the conquests. In the increasingly secular atmosphere of the sixteenth century, the Gospel and missionary goals provided the pretext for European overseas expansion; wealth was the actual motive.

BIBLIOGRAPHY

Stephen C. Neill, *A History of Christian Missions* (1964), is the best introductory survey. Simon Delacroix, ed., *Histoire universelle des missions catholiques,* 4 vols. (1956–1959), is a comprehensive survey.

More specialized studies include Anthony Bonner, ed. and trans., *Selected Works of Ramon Llull,* 2 vols. (1985); Christopher Dawson, ed., *The Mongol Mission: Narratives and Letters of the Franciscan Missionaries in Mongolia and China in the Thirteenth and Fourteenth Centuries* (1955); Francis Dvornik, *Byzantine Missions Among the Slavs* (1970); Carl Erdman, *Die Entstehung des Kreuzzugsgedankens* (1935); Ronald C. Finucane, *Soldiers of the Faith: Crusaders and Moslems at War* (1983); Robert Folz, *Les saints rois* (1984); R. P. C. Hanson, *Saint Patrick: His Origins and Career* (1968), and *The Life and Writings of the Historical Saint Patrick* (1983); James Kritzeck, *Peter the Venerable and Islam* (1964); Jeffrey Richards, *Consul of God: The Life and Times of Gregory the Great* (1980); Charles H. Talbot, *The Anglo-Saxon Missionaries in Germany* (1954).

BENNETT D. HILL

MONASTICISM, ORIGINS

cially in the West, where it influenced almost all the authors of monastic rules. Pachomius founded a second monastery at Pebou, and others followed, so that at his death in 346 there were nine monasteries for men (with several thousand monks) and two for women. Under his successors more monasteries were built, notably one near Alexandria about 390.

During the first half of the fourth century monasteries appeared in many eastern regions. It is difficult to decide how much this development owed to Egypt. In any case by the fourth century one could find monks and hermits in the Sinai Peninsula. They could also be found in Palestine when Chariton (*d.* 350) and after him Hilarion (*d. ca.* 371) developed the *lavra,* or laura, a system halfway between the hermitage and the monastery in which periods of solitude alternated with life in common. By the end of the fourth century there were monasteries founded by Westerners at Jerusalem (Paula) and at Bethlehem (Jerome).

Syria had hermits very early; monasteries developed mainly in the second half of the fourth century. Syrian monks were noted for their good works and missionary activities, and also for their spectacular penitences—the "browsers," who lived on roots and grass, the "stylites," who lived on top of a column (St. Simeon Stylites, *d.* 459, is the most famous), the "tree-monks," or "dendrites," who lived in hollow trees or on branches.

In Asia Minor monasticism grew rapidly from the beginning of the fourth century, especially in Cappadocia, thanks to Eustathius of Sebaste and even more to his disciple, Basil of Caesarea (*d.* 379). Basil emphasized life in common in drawing up his monastic rule. At Constantinople the first monastery may have been founded about 382 by the Syrian Isaac, but there were monks in Constantinople before that date.

In the fifth and sixth centuries monasticism expanded in all the eastern countries mentioned above and reached Ethiopia, Armenia, and Georgia. Monks became far more numerous than hermits. Monasteries were built in towns, where monks played an important role and at times formed pressure groups.

Some sort of legislation about monasteries became necessary. Church councils (especially Chalcedon, 451) and the emperor Justinian (527–565) dealt with this problem. An essential rule was that a new monastery could be founded only with the consent of the bishop in whose diocese it lay. In the tenth century the monasteries of Mt. Athos began their rise to power and eventually became the most important and most original monastic institutions of the East.

MONASTICISM IN THE WEST

In the West, as in the East, there had been hermits and ascetic communities. Monasticism appeared about the middle of the fourth century; the first documents that mention its existence show that it was already of the cenobitic type. We know little about its origins, and less about the anchorites who existed in Italy and Gaul, who were less numerous than in the East. The Western climate did not favor their way of life.

There was a monastery for women near the basilica of St. Agnes in Rome, supposedly founded around 340 by a daughter of emperor Constantine. The real expansion of Western monasticism came later, however, in the second half of the fourth century. Between 360 and 400 we find monasteries in Italy at Vercelli (*ca.* 363), Aquileia (*ca.* 370), Rome, Milan, Bologna, Verona, and in Gaul at Marmoutier near Tours (before 397), in the neighborhood of Rouen (before 407), in Africa at Carthage and, thanks to St. Augustine, at Hippo, and in Spain near Tarragona. Eastern monasticism greatly influenced this expansion: during his exile at Trier (335–337) and his residence at Rome (339–343) after his forced departure from Alexandria, Athanasius of Alexandria brought news of the success of the monks of Egypt. His *Life of St. Anthony* was read at Trier about 380, according to Augustine. Jerome and other Westerners who had visited the centers of Egyptian monasticism were also excellent propagandists of the system.

In spite of what one might suppose, the barbarian invasions did not hinder the growth of monasticism; in fact they encouraged it in some ways. At Rome, where before 400 there were only monasteries for women, monasteries for men appeared in the fifth century. In North Africa, after the death of St. Augustine (430) one could find thirty "Augustinian" monasteries for men, and there were to be other foundations in the future. In the fifth century, Gaul became the favored place for monasteries. Between 405 and 410 Honoratus founded a monastery on the island of Lirius (Lérins) in the bay of Cannes. Bishops trained in this monastery in turn founded monasteries at Arles, Vienna, Lyons, and in the Jura region. Farther west, monasteries sprang up around the tombs of holy bishops: Tours, Poitiers, Autun, Toulouse. About 414 or 415 John Cassian, who had personal experience of Eastern monasticism, came to Marseilles. He founded two monasteries there and between 417 and 429 wrote two books (*De institutis coenobiorum* and the *Collationes*), which had a profound influence on the development of Western monasticism.

In the sixth century two crucial events took place. One was the foundation by St. Benedict of Nursia (*d. ca.* 547) of the houses first at Subiaco and then at Monte Cassino. Even more important was the Rule that Benedict drew up for his monks. The Benedictine Rule, from the ninth century on, replaced almost everywhere the other monastic rules. At about the same time the number of monastic houses in Ireland and Wales grew enormously. Missionaries from these monasteries were active on the Continent. Irish monks went to Gaul, Germany, Switzerland, and even down to Italy. Columbanus (*d.* 615) is the best known of these Irish monks. On the other hand, monks from Gaul and from Rome established monasticism in England.

From the seventh century on the number of monasteries grew enormously. Wealth and power increased with numbers; so did abuses. Attempts at reform were made by new monastic rules, by church councils, by popes, and by kings. These reforms, from time to time, gave new vigor to monastic institutions. One need mention only St. Benedict of Aniane (*d.* 821), the monks of Cluny (from 910), and the monks of Citeaux (from 1098).

BIBLIOGRAPHY

Cuthbert E. Butler, *Benedictine Monachism,* 2nd ed. (1924, repr. 1962); Derwas J. Chitty, *The Desert a City* (1966), with a good bibliography; Francis X. Murphy, *Rufinus of Aquileia* (1945), and *A Monument to St. Jerome* (1952); Palladius, *The Lausiac History,* Robert T. Meyer, trans. (1965); Arthur Voöbus, *History of Asceticism in the Syrian Orient,* 2 vols. (1958–1960); Helen J. Waddell, ed., *The Desert Fathers* (1936).

RENÉ METZ

[See also **Augustine of Hippo, St.; Basil the Great; Benedict of Nursia, St.; Benedictines; Carmelites; Carthusians; Cassian, John; Church, Early; Cistercian Order; Jerome, St.; Lavra; Monte Cassino; Premonstratensians.**]

MONDINO DEI LUZZI (Raimondo de' Liuzzi) (*ca.* 1270–1326) was a member of a medical family at Bologna. His grandfather owned a pharmacy, later inherited by Mondino, and his uncle, Liuzzio (*d.* 1318), was a doctor and lecturer at the university. He himself studied there under Taddeo Alderotti and apparently spent his entire career as a professor of medicine at Bologna (*ca.* 1316 as a regent master and beginning in 1324 as professor of practical medicine), and in 1316 he acted as ambassador with his uncle to Giovanni, son of Robert of Anjou.

Mondino lectured or commented upon Hippocrates' *Prognostica* (with Galen's commentary) and *De regimine acutorum,* Johannes Mesue the Younger's *Canones,* Ibn Sīnā's (Avicenna's) al-Qānūn *(Canon),* and Galen's *Tegni (Ars medica),* and wrote a number of *consilia,* a *Practica de accidentibus morborum secundum magistrum Mundinum,* and a pharmacological tract, *De cerussa.* His subsequent reputation rests less on these than on his *Anatomia Mundini* (1316/1317), which incorporates some of his own observations of dissections. The *Anatomia* was intended to accompany the dissection of a human cadaver for purposes of instruction and follows approximately the system of his lectures as reported by Guy de Chauliac (*ca.* 1290–*ca.* 1367) in his *Grande Chirurgie.* It treats only the compound parts of the body: the digestive system, liver, and veins (which "putrefy more quickly"); the generative organs; the "spiritual members" (the heart and arteries); the brain and nervous system; and the extremities. It contains practical guidance on technique as well as often elaborate teleological explanations of the parts.

In writing the *Anatomia,* Mondino drew upon both his own experience (the dissection of a woman and a pregnant sow) and the ideas of Galen, as mediated through Latin versions from the Arabic or through Arabic authors—he wrote too early to take advantage of the translations of Niccolò da Reggio (Nicolaus Rheginus, *fl.* 1308–*ca.* 1345), and hence used as his main proof text *De juvamentis membrorum,* an Arabic abridgment of Galen's *De usu partium* (On the use of parts). His anatomical vocabulary is confusing in its lack of standardization. One word can serve as a technical term for several parts (for example, *pomum granum* for thyroid cartilage, xiphoid process, and culcitra), or one part will have several names (the sacrum is called *alchatim, allanis,* and *alhavius*). But Mondino was no slavish copyist, for he noted parenthetically that the five-lobed liver of traditional anatomies is not always visible in man.

The success of Mondino dei Luzzi's *Anatomia* owes more to its context than to its contents. It was written almost at the beginning of a new, medieval, tradition of dissection for medical purposes, based on humans rather than on animals, and using texts and techniques that were to remain standard for over two centuries. Although Mondino may have dissected and commented simultaneously himself, his book was later read out and glossed by lecturers on anatomy while another person performed the actual dissection. This practice, although deprecated by Vesalius in 1543, was defended by his Venetian contemporary, Niccolò Massa (1485–1569), because it permitted the lecturer to broaden the discussion of the visible corpse while leaving it to the dissector to cope with the necessary but unrevealing technical details of the actual anatomy. It is ironic that the last major commentary on the *Anatomia,* by Matteo Corti, published at Pavia in 1550, was dedicated to Vesalius.

BIBLIOGRAPHY

Sources. Incipits of his writings and of individual *quaestiones* are given in Nancy G. Siraisi, *Taddeo Alderotti and His Pupils* (1981). See also Lynn Thorndike and Pearl Kibre, eds., *A Catalogue of Incipits of Mediaeval Scientific Writings in Latin,* 2nd rev. ed. (1963). Other printed editions are found in G. Caturegli, ed., *Practica de accidentibus* (1966); Luigi Firpo, *Medicina medievale* (1972); Lino Sighinolfi, ed., *Mondino de' Liucci: Anatomia* (1930); B. Vonderlage, "*Consilien* des Mondino dei Luzzi aus Bologna" (diss., Leipzig, 1922); Ernest Wickersheimer, ed., *Anatomies de Mondino dei Luzzi et de Guido de Vigevano* (1926). An English translation of the *Anatomia* was made by Charles Singer from an edition prepared by P. A. Morsiano of Bologna in 1482 and included in Singer's facsimile reprint of Johannis de Ketham's 1493 edition: *Fasciculo di medicina* (1924–1925).

Studies. Vern L. Bullough, *The Development of Medicine as a Profession* (1966), and "Mondino de' Luzzi," in *Dictionary of Scientific Biography,* IX (1974), 467–469; Robert Herrlinger and Fridolf Kudlien, eds., *Frühe Anatomie* (1967); Levi R. Lind, *Studies in Pre-Vesalian Anatomy* (1975); Giuseppe Ongaro, "Il metodo settorio di Mondino de' Liucci," in *Atti del XXI congresso internazionale di storia della medicina (1968),* I, 68–82.

VIVIAN NUTTON

[See also **Bologna, University of; Medicine, History of; Medicine, Schools of; Sinā, Ibn.**]

MONEMVASIA, a city in the south of the Greek peninsula of the Peloponnese. At its foundation, now definitely put in 582, Monemvasia is associated with the Slavonic invasion of the Peloponnese in 582–583 and derives its name from the narrow "one-step path," or causeway, that separates it from the mainland. The city was already a bishopric at the time of its foundation.

A port of some importance already in the early period of the Byzantine Empire, it developed, beginning about 1262, into a position of commercial prominence. It owed some of its prosperity to its trade in wine and was the beneficiary of numerous commercial privileges. Monemvasia began to decline, however, under the Ottomans.

BIBLIOGRAPHY

Antoine Bon, *Le Péloponnèse byzantin jusqu'en 1204* (1951); Peter Charanis, "On the Demography of Medieval Greece: A Problem Solved," in *Balkan Studies,* **20** (1979); William Miller, *Essays on the Latin Orient* (1921, repr. 1964); Peter Schreiner, "Note sur la fondation de Monembasie en 582–583," in *Travaux et mémoires,* IV (1970).

PETER CHARANIS

[See also **Morea.**]

MONEY. See **Mints and Money.**

MONEYLENDING. See **Banking.**

MONGOL EMPIRE

ORIGINS

The history of the Mongols prior to Chinggis Khan (Genghis Khan) (*d.* 1227) has to be reconstructed from the official tradition preserved in the *Secret History of the Mongols,* usually cited by the title of the Chinese gloss, *Yüan-ch'ao pi-shih,* and the accounts of the court historians of the later Mongol rulers. On the basis of these accounts it appears that some loose unity was established among the Mongols in the early part of the twelfth century. A Mongol chieftain named Qaidu defeated a rival tribe, the Jalair, and soon acquired a following among his kinsmen. A great-grandson of Qaidu, Qabul, held the title of khan or "emperor" (*qaghan* in the *Secret History*). Qabul Khan had sufficient power to gain the recognition of the Chin, the Jürchen dynasty of North China and Manchuria. Memories of these relations are preserved in both the Mongol tradition and the Chin annals, although it is difficult to establish a close correlation of events.

In any case, the Mongols inflicted more than one

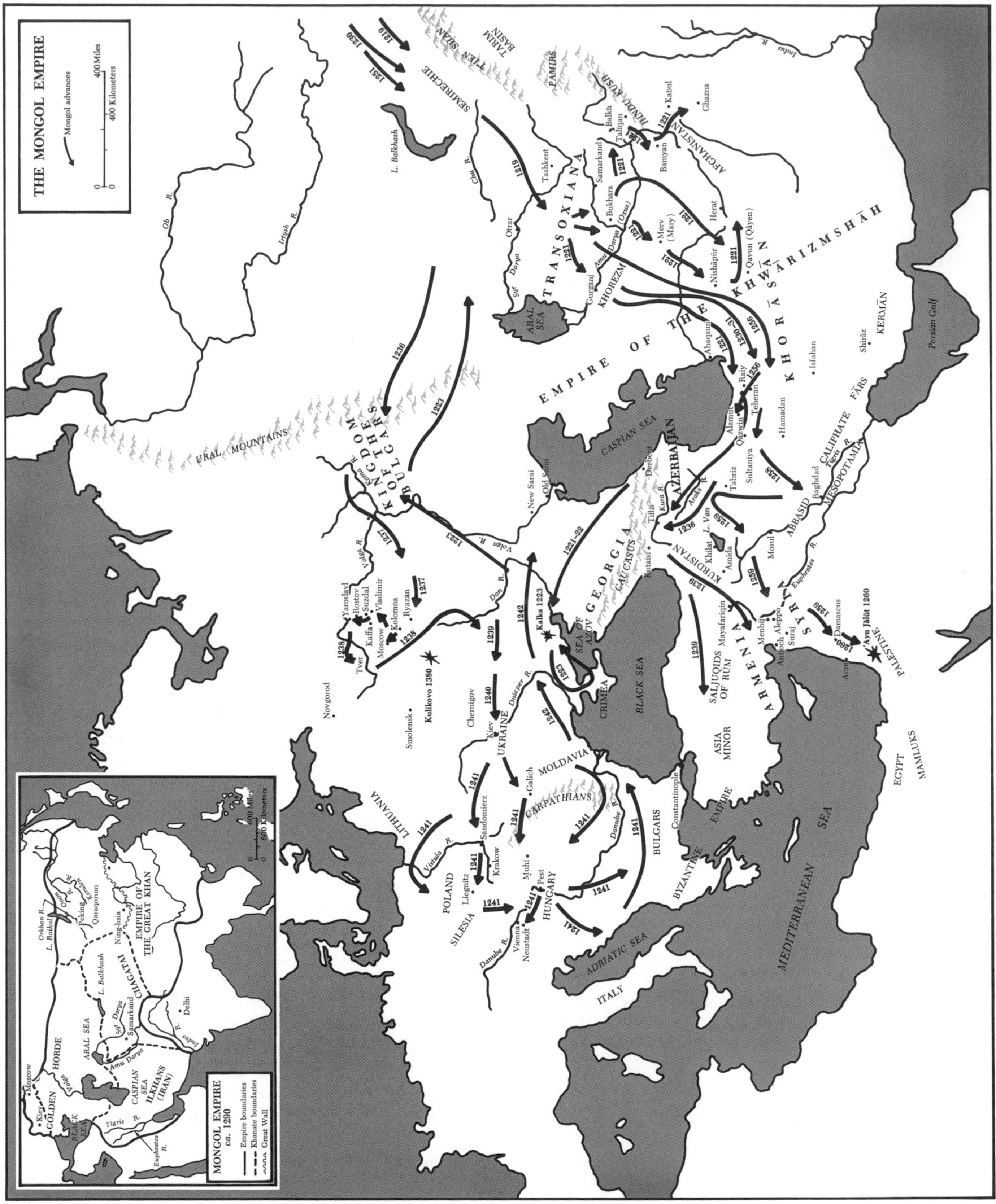
THE MONGOL EMPIRE
Mongol advances
0 400 Miles
0 400 Kilometers
MONGOL EMPIRE ca. 1290
Empire boundaries
Khanate boundaries
Great Wall
GOLDEN HORDE
CHAGATAI
EMPIRE OF THE GREAT KHAN
ILKHANS (IRAN)
Moscow
Kiev
Samarkand
Delhi
Peking
Qaraqorum
Ning-hsia
L. Baikal
Orkhon R.
L. Balkhash
ARAL SEA
CASPIAN SEA
BLACK SEA
Tigris R.
Euphrates R.
Indus R.
Amu Darya
Syr Darya
Volga
Ob R.
Irtysh R.
URAL MOUNTAINS
SEMIRECHIE
TIEN SHAN
TARIM BASIN
PAMIRS
HINDU KUSH
AFGHANISTAN
Kabul
Ghazna
Balkh
Taliqan
Bamyan
Herat
Tashkent
Otrar
Chu R.
Samarkand
Bukhara
TRANSOXIANA
Gurganj
KHOREZM
Merv (Mary)
Nishāpūr
Qavun (Qāyen)
EMPIRE OF THE KHWĀRIZMSHĀH
KHORĀSĀN
Abaqsun
Raiy
Teherān
Alamut
Qazwīn
Hamadan
Isfahan
Shīrāz
KERMĀN
FĀRS
Persian Gulf
AZERBAIJAN
Tabriz
Sultaniya
Derbent
Tiflis
Kura R.
Araks R.
L. Van
Khilat
Amida
KURDISTAN
Mosul
Baghdad
ABBASID CALIPHATE
MESOPOTAMIA
SYRIA
Aleppo
Antioch
Menbij
Suraj
Damascus
'Ayn Jālūt 1260
Acre
PALESTINE
EGYPT
MAMLUKS
KINGDOM OF THE BULGARS
Kama R.
Volga R.
New Sarai
Old Sarai
Don R.
GEORGIA
CAUCASUS
Kutaisi
SEA OF AZOV
Kalka 1223
CRIMEA
BLACK SEA
ARMENIA
Mayafariqin
SALJUQIDS OF RUM
ASIA MINOR
Constantinople
BYZANTINE EMPIRE
BULGARS
MEDITERRANEAN SEA
Yaroslavl
Rostov
Suzdal
Vladimir
Kolomna
Ryazan
Moscow
Kaffa
Tver
Novgorod
Smolensk
Kulikovo 1380
Chernigov
Kiev
UKRAINE
Dnieper R.
MOLDAVIA
Galich
CARPATHIANS
Danube R.
Sandomierz
Krakow
LITHUANIA
Vistula R.
POLAND
Liegnitz
SILESIA
Muhi
Pest
HUNGARY
Vienna
Neustadt
ADRIATIC SEA
ITALY
1219
1220
1221
1223
1236
1237
1238
1239
1240
1241
1242
1256
1258
1259
1260
1221–22
1230–31

MONGOL EMPIRE

defeat on the Chin and in consequence received "gifts" from the Peking government. The rising power of the Mongols aroused the hostility of the Chin. This developed during the rule of Qutula, the last elected khan of the Mongols, of whom prodigious tales were told. A brother and cousin of Qutula were captured by the neighboring Tatars, who delivered them to the Chin. They were executed in a manner reserved for rebellious nomads. In revenge Qutula ravaged the northern borders of the Chin. The Mongol menace reached such proportions that the Chin formed an alliance with the Tatars and together they broke the power of the Mongols. After Qutula there is no reference to a Mongol chieftain bearing the royal title.

Yesügai (Yesügei), the father of Temüjin (Chinggis Khan), was merely the chief of the Qiat sub-clan of the Börjigin, and as a Mongol he often warred with the traditional enemy, the Tatar. He bore the title *baghatur* (hero), but made little mark in the affairs of Mongolia; however, his assistance was of considerable use in a contest over the rule of the powerful Kereit (Kereyid) confederacy. In the struggle Yesügai helped Toghril (Te'oril) overcome his uncle and become the khan of the Kereit. Toghril's debt of gratitude was later to be of great use to Temüjin.

Temüjin (which means "blacksmith") was born on or about 1167 (the Persian sources based on the court records of the Ilkhans give the date as 1152; the *Secret History,* 1162; 1167 is the date suggested by Paul Pelliot in 1938), on the right bank of the Onon in the region Dülün-Boldaq, now in Soviet territory. Since Temüjin was still a child at the time his father was poisoned to death, the Qiat refused to recognize him as their chief. This was more than a repudiation: it put a price on his head since he could claim the position in the future. His mother, a courageous and resourceful woman, assumed the leadership of her family.

The family sought refuge on the slopes of the Kentai mountains near the source of the Onon, where they lived by hunting and fishing. Almost one third of the text of the *Secret History* is devoted to the adventures of young Temüjin and his brothers—of his emergence as leader of a growing band of warriors, as head of the Börjigin clan, as the leader of a confederacy, and his eventual elevation as Chinggis Khan, "Lord of the Steppe." The event took place at a grand *quriltai* (congress, assembly) held near the source of the Onon in the spring of 1206.

At that time the organizational principles of the new state were laid down. An Uighur in the service of the Naiman, before that confederacy was destroyed, was taken prisoner by Chinggis. The man, whose name in Chinese was rendered T'a-t'a T'ung-a, had been keeper of the seal and chief administrative officer of the Naiman. He proceeded to establish a rudimentary administration for the new confederacy. Chinggis himself was primarily concerned with the reorganization of the army. This involved breaking up the old tribal contingents that had been led by their chieftains. The new units were based on a decimal system up to and including the major regular unit, the *tümen,* a cavalry division of 10,000. Though the officers were drawn from the nobility, their rank and assignment were based on merit.

ATTACKS ON THE CHIN, HSI-HSIA, AND QARA QITAI

The territory of Chinggis Khan now bordered on well-ordered, militarily respectable, sedentary states: the Chin to the east and south; the Hsi-hsia (Tangut) to the west and southwest; the Qara Qitai to the west and northwest. Since the Hsi-hsia appeared to be the weakest of the three, Chinggis chose to attack it for an initial trial of strength. The Mongols had complete confidence in their ability to defeat their enemies in the field, but now they had to contend with fortified places. Chinggis began a campaign of attrition in 1207 after some preliminary raids in 1205. He ravaged the countryside in preparation for the reduction of the two principal cities of the kingdom, Ning-hsia, the capital, and Ling-chou. The king of the Hsia-hsia stood off disaster by paying tribute and becoming a vassal of Chinggis Khan. Another attack was made in 1209, but the king bought peace by giving one of his daughters to the Mongol leader.

By 1211, Chinggis felt free to attack the Jürchen dynasty of North China, the Chin, in a war of national vengeance: the Chin had destroyed the first Mongol confederacy as well as the Liao, the northern dynasty established by the Ch'i-tan (Qitai), a people related to the Mongols and speaking a similar language. Chinggis called on *tengri* (heaven) to help him avenge these crimes. The northern border of the powerful Chin military state was protected by the well guarded Great Wall and, beyond that, by foederati, the Öngüt confederacy. (The Öngüt, probably Turks, were a cultivated though warlike people who were converted to Nestorian Christianity.) South of the Great Wall were many large, well-fortified cities supported by garrisons of well-armed, well-trained Jürchen cavalry and infantry commanded by coura-

MONGOL EMPIRE

geous and skillful officers. The principal weakness of the state lay in the character of the later emperors, who were viewed by the Jürchen generals as puppets to be manipulated. The rulers eventually recognized the danger of this situation, but by that time it was too late.

In 1209, the support of the Öngüt opened Chin territory to Mongol invasion. Already some years earlier, in 1204, the Öngüt had taken their place at the side of Temüjin in the course of the power struggle that was taking place in Mongolia. This friendship was strengthened by marriage alliances among the leading families. At that time this had not concerned the Chin, since both the Mongols and the Öngüt were their vassals.

The war against the Chin began in 1211 and was not concluded until seven years after the death of Chinggis Khan in 1227. It was by far the most difficult undertaking of either Chinggis Khan or his successor, Ögödai.

The flight of a prince of the defeated Naiman confederacy, Küchlük (Kuchlug), to the Qara Qitai and his later usurpation of power there made an eventual Mongol attack a certainty. The *gurkhan* (ruler) of the Qara Qitai was weak, and in the course of his reign there was a rapid disintegration of central authority: in 1209 the *idiqut* of the Uighurs transferred his vassalage from the *gurkhan* and became a vassal of Chinggis Khan; in 1211 Arslan Khan of the Qarluq and Buzar, the amir of Almaliq, both broke with the *gurkhan* and also declared themselves vassals of Chinggis Khan.

When Küchlük seized the person of the *gurkhan* and became the actual ruler of the Qara Qitai, he not only had to contend with the secession of the Qarluq and the Uighurs, but also with the hostility of the local Muslim rulers. Küchlük, a Nestorian Christian, looked upon the local Muslim clergy as the instigators of the resistance. His hostility toward them may have been encouraged by his wife, a daughter of the *gurkhan* and a zealous Nestorian.

Küchlük launched a surprise attack against Buzar of Almaliq, and captured and killed him. The attack on a vassal provided Chinggis Khan with a casus belli, if indeed he needed one, and also gained him the son of Buzar as a most devoted follower.

Chinggis Khan dispatched the great warrior Jebe Noyan with an army of two divisions to deal with Küchlük, who did not await his arrival but fled from the north T'ien-shan steppe to Kashgaria (the Tarim Basin). He was not well received in the Muslim oasis states. By contrast, when Jebe proclaimed complete religious freedom, the Muslims regarded him as a liberator. Deserted by his troops, Küchlük fled to the Pamirs, where he was overtaken by the Mongols and killed near Sari-gol in 1218. The entire empire of the Qara Qitai was then incorporated by the Mongols.

CONQUEST OF THE KHWĀRIZMSHĀH

Chinggis Khan was now a neighbor of the Khwārizmshāh, the most powerful Muslim ruler of the time, whose territory lay in northern Iran (now in the Soviet Union). Chinggis sought to establish economic and political relations with this great Islamic power. The rulers of Mongolia from the ancient time of the Hsiung-nu were aware of the enormous wealth that would accrue if they controlled the trade routes between East and West. Chinggis Khan and the Khwārizmshāh were now in a position to divide the profits of this extremely lucrative overland trade.

Therefore in 1218 Chinggis Khan dispatched a great caravan to the Khwārizmshāh Muḥammad. Except for the Mongol envoy Uquna, the entire caravan was staffed by Central Asian Muslims. On reaching the frontier city of Otrar at the middle Syr Darya the caravan was halted, the goods seized, and the personnel killed to a man by order of Qadir Khan Inaljik, the Khorezmian governor of the region. One account states that there was a single survivor, a camel driver who brought the news back to Chinggis. The accounts do not agree on the responsibility for the outrage. At all events it was a major catastrophe in purely economic terms for the Mongols. One account lists a loss of 1,500 laden camels. Chinggis Khan, uncertain as to who was responsible for the action, sent a Turk who had been in the service of the Khwārizmshāh and two Tatars as envoys to protest the act and demand reparations. The Khwārizmshāh refused to meet the demand and ordered the Turk killed; the two Tatars were humiliated and sent back to Chinggis. War was now inevitable.

The Mongol leader did not react immediately since he had not yet disposed of Küchlük. Once that was accomplished, he mobilized for a campaign in the west. Half of the troops from Mongolia were moved to the Irtish River in the summer of 1219. The other half of the regular army was left with Muqaly, who had somewhat over 30,000 cavalry to continue the campaign against the Chin. In the fall he moved to Semirechie, where he was joined by his western vassals; by winter he was ready to begin the invasion.

MONGOL EMPIRE

Most accounts credit Chinggis with a force of 150,000 or more; a figure of 50,000 seems more likely. Reports of the size of the forces at the disposal of the Khwārizmshāh indicate that they were considerably larger than those of the Mongolian invader, but, in fact, numbers do not tell the entire story. The Mongol armies functioned under a unified command and were subject to rigid discipline. They operated on the basis of well-conceived plans, and their training and organization permitted a tactical flexibility that enabled their commanders to take advantage of opportunities as they arose.

Khwārizmshāh Muḥammad established a cordon defense with a strong line of observation stations along the Syr Darya. He distributed his main army among the principal fortified centers of Transoxiana, a deliberate violation of the principle of troop concentration that was determined by two factors. First, he was of the impression that the Mongols, like other Inner Asian nomads, would not be skilled in siegecraft. Second, the experience with the Mongols in a previous collision on the steppe left him reluctant to face them in a decisive battle in the field, despite the numerical superiority of his own forces.

The Mongols advanced in coordinated columns and reduced the centers of resistance one by one. Cities that offered no resistance were merely plundered. Cities that resisted were punished ruthlessly, women and children were enslaved, and, except for skilled artisans, who were deported to Mongolia, men were slaughtered. The Muslim clergy in Samarkand who did not preach holy war against the Mongols were not persecuted.

Gurganj (Urgench), the ancient capital of Khwarizm, was taken in April 1221 after a long siege by Juchi and Chaghatai, who were finally joined by Ögödai. Except for the skilled artisans, who were deported to Mongolia, the entire population was massacred and the city flooded by diverting the course of the Amu Darya. In the course of these disasters, Khwārizmshāh Muḥammad remained passive. He first fled to Balkh on the Afghan border, then to western Khorāsān, then Qazwin (Qazvin) in northwestern Iran. Chinggis dispatched his two most skillful commanders in pursuit, Sübödai (Sübedei) and Jebe Noyan, who were given a cavalry corps of two *tümen* for the mission. They took Raiy (near modern Teheran) by surprise, killed the male population, and made slaves of the women and children. They bypassed Hamadan in western Iran, from which they extracted a heavy ransom, then Qavun, after which they lost the track of Muḥammad. The latter had sought refuge on an island in the Caspian opposite Abaqsun (Abaksun), where he died, probably of exhaustion, in December 1220. Learning of the death, Chinggis Khan gave his two generals permission to engage in a reconnaissance in force to the northwest, which developed into the greatest cavalry raid in history.

In the spring of 1221 Chinggis Khan crossed the Amu Darya and began the conquest of Khorāsān and Afghanistan. Balkh was captured, the population massacred, and the city put to the torch. Though Merv (Mary) capitulated to Chinggis' son Tolui in 1221, the population, except for four hundred artisans, was massacred. Tolui then moved on Nishapur, where Toquchar, one of Chinggis Khan's principal commanders, had previously been repulsed and killed. On 10 April 1221 the city was taken by storm and completely destroyed, the widow of Toquchar supervising the general massacre. Tolui then moved on to Herat. The Turkish garrison resisted, but the civilian population opened the gates to the Mongols. The garrison was massacred and the population spared. At Talaqan, Chinggis Khan assembled the various formations that had by then completed their assignments and led his armies over the Hindu Kush to besiege Bamyan in northeastern Afghanistan. There, Mütügen, a son of Chaghatai and a favorite of Chinggis, was killed. Chinggis ordered his son Chaghatai to shed no tears and promised vengeance. When the city fell, no booty was taken; all living things were destroyed and, with the booty, left to decay. Bamyan was called the "accursed city."

Jalāl-al-Dīn (Jalāluddin), son of the Khwārizmshāh, possessed all the military virtues his father lacked. He escaped from Bamyan before the capture of the city and fled to Ghazna, where he was able to assemble some scattered Khorezmian troops. At Parwān, a region north of Kabul, he defeated a Mongol force led by Shigi-qutuqu. When this was called to the attention of Chinggis Khan, the emperor replied it served him right and next time he would be more careful. Chinggis Khan avenged the defeat in person and then marched on Ghazna. In the fall of 1221 the Mongols trapped the remainder of Jalāl-al-Dīn's forces and cut them to pieces. Jalāl-al-Dīn himself escaped by jumping into the Indus River at full gallop from a precipice, much to the admiration of Chinggis Khan and the Mongols. He fled to the sultan of Delhi, but the Mongols did not follow; the heat may have discouraged them. Jalāl-al-Dīn's family fell into the hands of the Mongols, who killed all the males. The Mongols continued to carry out their

MONGOL EMPIRE

usual depredations in Afghanistan, where Chinggis remained through the summer of 1222. In the fall of that year he recrossed the Amu Darya and remained in Samarkand until the spring of 1223. There, he made inquiries about Islam and exempted the Muslim clergy from taxation. The main Mongol army returned to Mongolia in the spring of 1225.

THE CAUCASIAN CAMPAIGNS

In the meanwhile, Jebe Noyan and Sübödai, having been given permission to reconnoiter to the northwest, invaded Georgia after ravaging western Iran and northern Iraq. A defending army was defeated near Tiflis (Tbilisi) in February 1221. They then turned back to Hamadan to collect another ransom. This time the city resisted. It was taken by assault and the population massacred. Once more they returned to Georgia and cut another Georgian army to pieces in a skillfully prepared ambush. Again no attempt was made to besiege Tiflis. They crossed the Caucasus by the pass at Derbent and descended to the north Caucasus steppe.

There a coalition was formed against the invaders: Alans, Circassians, Lezhgians, and Kipchaks (Qypchaqs). The Mongol generals successfully detached the Kipchaks by an appeal to their common culture and a promise to share the spoils of victory. The coalition was crushed, and the Mongols then turned on the Kipchaks, crushed them, and retook the booty they had shared.

The surviving Kipchaks fled in terror to the lands of their traditional enemies, the Russians. Qutyan Khan of the Kipchaks, whose daughter married Mstislav of Galich, called on him and the other Russian princes to form an alliance against the invaders. Mstislav of Galich obtained the support of the princes of Kiev, Chernigov, and Smolensk for an alliance under his leadership. The allied army is said to have numbered 80,000; if this were the case, the Mongols were outnumbered at least four to one.

As prudent commanders, Sübödai and Jebe refused battle. They retired with the Russians in pursuit. When they reached the Kalka, a little stream that empties into the Sea of Azov near Mariupol, they halted. The prince of Galich and the Kipchaks attacked without waiting for the army of Kiev, believing the Mongols to be in full retreat. The details of the battle are lacking, but it ended in a complete Mongol victory in 1223, with the allies in full flight. The defeated commanders failed to give timely warning to the prince of Kiev, who found himself facing the Mongols alone. After a successful defense of three days, the Kievans obtained honorable capitulation and were permitted to return with their arms. In the course of their return, the Mongols turned on them, killing practically all. After raiding through south Russia and the Crimea, they turned north and fought some battles with the Bulgars of the Volga-Kama region. Here they suffered setbacks before turning east to join Chinggis Khan on the steppe north of the Syr Darya.

This raid had important consequences in Russia. With most of the armies of the princes destroyed, Yuri, grand prince of Vladimir, who did not have time to join the alliance, retained his army intact. He was thus able to proceed with the suppression of the other Russian principalities. This process continued until the great Mongol invasion of 1238.

On his return to Mongolia in the spring of 1225, Chinggis Khan encamped on the Tula, a tributary of the Orkhon. There he planned operations for the final destruction of the Hsi-hsia and the Chin. Juchi, his eldest son, who had been given the western steppe region as his appanage, attempted a separatist policy. When ordered to join his father in Mongolia, he claimed to be ill; Chinggis knew, however, that he was out hunting. A clash was in the making when Juchi died in February 1227.

The king of the Hsi-hsia had earlier aroused the ire of Chinggis when he refused to provide troops for the campaign against the Khwārizmshāh, telling Chinggis' envoy: "If Chinggis Khan does not have adequate forces to defeat the Khwārizmshāh, he does not deserve to be ruler of the steppe." This indignity was not to remain unpunished.

Muqaly, who was in charge of operations against the Chin, had since died. An all-out campaign against the Chin—given the threat of the Hsi-hsia in the rear—could not be risked. Ling-chou was besieged in the fall of 1226 and finally taken in the spring of 1227. The siege of the capital, Ning-hsia, followed immediately. In the course of this campaign Chinggis Khan maintained his headquarters on the banks of the Ch'ing-shui, where he died on 18 August 1227. Shortly thereafter Ning-hsia fell, and in accordance with instructions he had left, the entire population was massacred. The remainder of the Tangut people were given as an appanage to Yesui, a favorite wife of Chinggis.

Chinggis Khan was buried on the sacred mountain Burqan Qaldun. Ögödai, his second son and designated successor, presided over the funeral sacrifices. A three-day feast was ordered. The most beautiful daughters of the princes and generals,

MONGOL EMPIRE

dressed in rich clothes and bedecked with jewels, were sent to join the dead leader in the otherworld. They were also provided with the finest horses.

DIVISION OF THE EMPIRE

While Chinggis Khan was alive, each of his four sons by his first wife was assigned his respective appanage. Juchi's (Jochi) was passed on to his son Batu, who, unlike his father, had a good name in Mongol tradition; in time he became the "elder statesman" of the empire. Since his lands were the farthest west, additional conquests in that direction were to become part of his patrimony. Chaghatai received the Uighur country, the territories of the Qara Qitai, except for the great cities of Transoxiana (the region north of the Amu Darya), which were to be administered directly by the Great Khan through imperial governors. Ögödai received the territory to the north of Chaghatai's and west of the old Naiman region. Tolui received the northeastern part of Mongolia, the original Mongol homeland, since, as the youngest son *(ochygin),* he was the traditional "guardian of the hearth." The appanages of Batu, Chaghatai, and Tolui were to become major powers in their own right. Those of Batu and Hülegü, son of Tolui, became the khanates of the Golden Horde and of the Ilkhans of Iran respectively.

RENEWED ATTACKS AGAINST
WESTERN ASIA AND EUROPE

Ögödai's election did not take place until the meeting of the *quriltai* on the banks of the Kerulen River in the spring of 1229. Ögödai, whom Chinggis considered his most intelligent and adaptable son, established Qaraqorum as his headquarters. This site on the upper Orkhon was the traditional capital district of Mongolian rulers from the time of the Hsiung-nu. It became the regular capital of the Mongol Empire when Ögödai ordered the construction of a surrounding wall in 1235.

When Ögödai was elected successor to Chinggis Khan, Iran had once more fallen into the hands of Jalāl-al-Dīn (son of Khwārizmshāh Muḥammad). When Chinggis Khan returned to Transoxiana Khorāsān and Afghanistan were wasteland. Though the Mongols raided through central and western Iran for three years, they never attempted to occupy the country. The general state of anarchy gave Jalāl-al-Dīn the opportunity to recoup his family's fortune. In 1224 he returned to Iran and was recognized by the Turkish atabegs (governors) of Kermān and Fārs provinces as sultan. From his headquarters in Shīrāz (in Fārs), Jalāl-al-Dīn advanced to take Isfahan and northern Iraq from his brother Giyath-al-Dīn and then proceeded to conquer Azerbaijan. Using this country as a base, he launched attacks on Georgia, which had suffered terribly from the raids of Jebe Noyan and Sübödai (Chinggis Khan's brilliant warrior generals), but recovered remarkably during the reign of Queen Rusudan (1223–1247), sister of Giorgi III (IV). Jalāl-al-Dīn invaded the country three times between 1225 and 1228, each time inflicting serious defeats on Georgian armies. Although he failed to conquer Georgia, the campaigns helped to consolidate his hold on Azerbaijan. As master of central and western Iran, northern Iraq, and Azerbaijan, he was, in effect, the most powerful Islamic ruler at that time.

Instead of making preparations for the inevitable return of the Mongols, Jalāl-al-Dīn worked instead to subdue his other Muslim neighbors. As a result, an alliance was formed between al-Malik al-Ashraf I, the Ayyubid ruler of Syria (from whom Jalāl-al-Dīn had seized Khilat [Akhlāṭ] on the northwest shore of Lake Van), and Kai-qobad I, the ruler of the Saljuqids (Seljuks) of Rum. In 1230, the allies inflicted a crushing defeat on Jalāl-al-Dīn on the very eve of the Mongol return.

Chormaqan Noyan, along with a force of three divisions of 10,000 *(tümen),* was dispatched to Iran by Ögödai. The Mongols swept into western Iran in the winter of 1230/1231, long before Jalāl-al-Dīn had any information of a new campaign. This sudden turn of events seemed to unnerve him, and he fled toward the Caucasus. The Mongols, finding no organized resistance, sent a flying column in pursuit. However, Jalāl-al-Dīn died at the hands of peasants who murdered him in the mountains of Kurdistan. Chormaqan established headquarters in Azerbaijan on the plain between the Kura and Araxes rivers. A high plateau resembling Mongolia, it later became the principal residence of the Ilkhans. From there, Chormaqan raided the neighboring Muslim and Christian territories for ten years. Though his army was relatively small and located far from available reinforcements, the Mongol commander had little to fear. The area still abounds in tales of the terror inspired by the Mongols.

In 1236 the Mongols invaded Georgia, forced Queen Rusudan to flee westward to Kutaisi, and established a protectorate over the Tiflis region. In 1239 Greater Armenia was seized. A Syrian Christian named Simon (but called Rabban-ata), who was Chormaqan's commissioner for Christian affairs since 1233, proved influential in protecting Armenian communities.

Chormaqan's successor, Bedüün Noyan, Mongol viceroy from 1241 to 1256, led the armies that crushed the Saljuqid sultanate of Qonya under Qaykhosraw (Kai-khushraw) II (1237–1245). After the principal cities were sacked, the Saljuqid ruler sued for peace and paid tribute to the Mongols. Het^{c}um I of Cilician Armenia asked for Mongol protection and also paid tribute. Bedüün consolidated Mongol control over Kurdistan by occupying Khilat and Amida (Diyarbakir). Later the Mongols put Khilat under the administration of one of their Georgian vassals. The atabeg of Mosul in northern Iraq also became a Mongol vassal.

While Chormaqan had been occupied in western Asia, the great campaign in eastern and central Europe was under way—the major military effort undertaken during the reign of Ögödai. The *quriltai* of 1235 had decided to wage war on the Sung Empire in southern China, and operations began the following year. Ögödai was aware of the magnitude of the task, but since the Sung's military forces were weak in cavalry, the Mongols had little to fear from their field armies, and the possibility of a Sung offensive caused little concern. Thus the army that moved to the West contained most of the elite units and capable commanders. The army was nominally under command of Batu; the actual commander was Sübödai.

Prior to the invasion of the Russian territories, the Mongols destroyed the kingdom of the Bulgars (a nomadic, Turkish-speaking people) in the area between the Volga and Kama rivers. In the course of their great raid some fifteen years earlier, Sübödai and Jebe Noyan, in penetrating this region, had met fierce resistance. This time the Mongols came in force and, according to Russian sources, the Bulgar kingdom was destroyed in the fall of 1237. Part of the shattered Bulgar army was incorporated into Mongol military units; the remainder fled to the Rus. That year the Mongols also completed their war of annihilation against the Kipchaks. One group was destroyed by a Mongol army under Mönke, son of Tolui; another by Berke, brother of Batu. A third group of Kipchaks under Qutan Khan managed to collect their households and flee to Hungary after their second defeat. The Kipchak khanate no longer existed as such. Later the name was transferred to the Golden Horde, which was also known as the khanate of Kipchak.

The pursuing Mongols broke into Russian territories and took Riazan (Ryazan) and Kolomna (southeast of Moscow) after meeting bitter resistance. The cities were burned and the populations massacred, along with the brothers Prince Yuri of Riazan and Prince Roman of Kolomna. Yuri Vsevolodovich, grand duke of Suzdal, sent reinforcements to Kolomna, but they were likewise destroyed. Moscow, which was not a major city at the time, was sacked as the Mongols moved on to Suzdal and Vladimir. Both cities were taken by storm and the populations massacred. Grand Duke Yuri expected Vladimir to hold out for some time and left to collect his troops. He took the field with his army but was defeated and killed in a battle on the banks of the Sit River in March 1238. Dmitrov and Tver (Kalinin), Rostov and Yaroslavl were sacked, while Novgorod was saved by the impending thaw of the surrounding swampland.

Following a hiatus of two years, spent in the western Ukraine, the Mongols turned their attention south and westward. Chernigov was sacked, and Kiev, the "mother of cities" to the Russians, taken and plundered in December 1240. Galich (Galicia) was ravaged, and its prince, Daniel, fled to Hungary. In the course of this campaign, serious dissension broke out among the Mongol princes. This was to have important consequences for the future. The principal cause seems to have been the contempt that the sons and grandsons of Ögödai and Chaghatai felt for Batu. The family squabble meant that Güyük, son of Ögödai, Buri, grandson of Chaghatai, and Mönke left their commands in Europe and returned to Qarakorum to see the Great Khan. The dispute was temporarily patched up, and the princes returned to Europe.

Once southern Russia was conquered, the Mongols sent an army under Baidar (son of Chaghatai) and Qaidu (or possibly Qadan—the sources are unclear) into Poland as part of a major offensive against Hungary. On 18 March 1241, the Mongols crossed the Vistula on ice, sacked Sandomierz and raided as far as Krakow. On 9 April a German army, supported by contingents of Poles and Teutonic Knights, was destroyed by the Mongols at Liegnitz in Silesia.

The Mongols then invaded Hungary in three columns: one, under Shaiban, entered from the north between Poland and Moravia; a second, under Batu and Sübödai, came through Galicia, forcing the passes through the Carpathians; the third, under Qaidu/Qadan, came through Moldavia. At the confluence of the Tisza and Sajo rivers, in a field south

MONGOL EMPIRE

of Mohi, they were met by an army of Germans, Slavs, and Magyars assembled by Béla IV (1235–1270). During the night Sübödai crossed the river upstream, and the next morning the main army of Mongols made a frontal assault, catching the Hungarians in a two-sided attack. Finding themselves surrounded, the Hungarians stubbornly attempted a futile defense. The Mongols destroyed them in the course of their retreat. Béla IV fled toward the Adriatic; Pest was taken and burned and its population subjected to the usual atrocities.

After the conquest of Hungary, which the Mongols intended to transform into a base for operations in central and western Europe, the greater part of the Mongol army was divided into small detachments that carried fire and sword over the countryside. Mongol raiding parties reached Neustadt near Vienna in July 1241. As the main divisions rested during the rest of the year in preparation for the next major advance, word was received that Great Khan Ögödai had died on 11 December 1241, and Mongol commanders and princes were obliged to return home. According to John of Plano Carpini, the ambassador from Pope Innocent IV, Ögödai was poisoned by an aunt of Güyük, his son and successor. As the Russian historian Vernadsky put it: "This woman, whoever she was, must be considered the savior of western Europe." To impress upon Europeans that the Mongol retirement was voluntary, raiding parties were sent down the Adriatic. Batu retired slowly to the Volga and kept his army in hand as a precautionary measure in the face of the hostility on the part of the sons of Chaghatai and Ögödai.

THE EMERGENCE OF THE GOLDEN HORDE ON THE RUSSIAN STEPPES

Törgene, the widowed empress, was able to delay the convocation of the *quriltai* until support for her son Güyük was rallied, in 1246. Having clashed with Güyük during the Russian campaign, Batu feigned illness and did not attend and was kept informed of court politics by Princess Sorqaqtany, the widow of Tolui and now senior member of the house. She was able to alert him of Güyük's efforts to mobilize forces against him, which in any event came to an end when Güyük died in 1248, aged forty, of alcohol abuse and dissipation.

Once more the widow of the Great Khan served as regent. Oghul Qaimish attempted to keep the succession in the house of Ögödai, but she was not as clever as Sorqaqtany, who saw an opportunity to make her own son the Mongol ruler. She allied herself with Batu, who had sent his brother Berke as his representative to the *quriltai,* at which Mönke, the son of Tolui and Sorqaqtany, was elected Great Khan in 1251. The houses of Chaghatai and Ögödai had boycotted the assembly.

After settling accounts for the feuds generated in the course of the Russian campaign, Mönke devoted his attention to the rehabilitation of the civil and military administration. Although he dared not lay a hand on Qadan and Qaidu, he made short shrift of the others, including the former regent, Oghul Qaimish, who had plotted against him. There is no indication that Mönke was particularly cruel; he simply did what was necessary. All accounts portray him as one of the most gifted and enlightened of the Mongol rulers. In the course of Mönke's reign (1251–1259) communication with the West became more common. Eurasian unity was maintained by an efficient administration, keeping the peace in the vast region and giving rise to unparalleled prosperity. The reign was also marked by two major military efforts: one, the destruction of the Abbasid caliphate in Baghdad, resulting in the establishment of the Ilkhan state in Iran; the other, a continuation of the long and bitter war against the Sung in China.

Except for Khwarizm and the Russian cities that were distributed in a great arc from the upper Volga to the Dnieper, Batu's territory was a vast expanse over which Turkish-speaking herdsmen roamed. Batu established his headquarters at Sarai (Saray) on the lower Volga. As the name implies, it was an important caravan station. The wealth that accrued as a result of the trade in luxury goods that passed through the city, where much of it was exchanged and redistributed, was one of the bases of economic prosperity of this vast khanate—called the Golden Horde. Rashīd-al-Dīn, a Persian historian of the Mongols and a vizier under the Ilkhans, noted that after the campaigns in eastern and central Europe, the bulk of the Mongol troops that had participated returned to their former territories. About 4,000 Mongols remained in the khanate of Kipchak, the Golden Horde. The nomads of the region, from among whom the khans drew their troops, were almost all Turkic in speech, and in due course the khanate took on a Turkic rather than Mongolian cast.

Batu, first khan of the Golden Horde, died in Sarai in 1255 and was succeeded in 1257 by his brother Berke. During Batu's lifetime his other brothers were given major fiefs. Orda was given the eastern territory that lay north of the Syr Darya; as

MONGOL EMPIRE

a vassal state of the Golden Horde, it became known as the White Horde. Another brother, Shaiban, was given the region south and east of the Urals and generally north of the White Horde; this became known as the Blue Horde.

The ethos of the Golden Horde was formed during the reign of Berke (1257–1267). In the course of his reign some of the unresolved territorial disputes that he had inherited came to a head. The original grant of Chinggis Khan put Khwarizm in the appanage of Juchi. Batu's assistance in the early operations in the Caucasus and Asia Minor put much of the region within his sphere of influence. With the arrival of Hülegü and the establishment of the Ilkhan realm, the two territories overlapped, leaving many strategic areas in dispute. Moreover, as Berke had converted to Islam, a permanent cleavage between the Golden Horde khans and their Christian subjects in the West was created. His conversion also introduced a religious element into the territorial dispute with the Ilkhans, who, in the beginning, considered themselves mortal enemies of the caliphs, the spiritual leaders of all Muslims. Berke's involvement in the civil wars that followed the death of Mönke also strained his relations with the Ilkhans.

On the occasion of his elevation as Great Khan, Mönke was aware of the patchwork nature of the administrative system in Iran and western Asia. He decided to complete the conquest of the area and to put it under the control of his younger brother Hülegü. His decision was confirmed at the *quriltai* held in 1251. Hulegü was ordered to suppress the Ismaili sect of the Assassins and the caliphate in Baghdad. In the words of Rashīd-al-Dīn: "The customs and laws of Chinggis Khan must be established from the Amu Darya to the borders of Egypt. Whoever submits and obeys your orders must be treated with kindness and consideration. Whoever stands up against you must be dragged to humiliation."

Hülegü left Mongolia with an army formed of contingents drawn from many Mongol districts and crossed the Amu Darya in early January 1256. As he moved west he was joined by contingents provided by vassals from Iran, Azerbaijan, and Asia Minor. The first operation was against the stronghold of the Assassins at Alamūt in northern Iran, which was besieged with Hülegü himself in command. The Grand Master of the order, Rokn-ad-din Kurshah (Rukn al-Dīn Khūrshāh), capitulated in November and was sent to Mönke in Qaraqorum, but was killed while en route.

Hülegü next moved against the caliph, who, in greatly reduced circumstances, effectively controlled no more than the capital district of Baghdad. The reigning caliph, al-Mustaᶜṣim (1242–1258), believed he could handle the Mongol khan in the same manner as his predecessors had managed past amirs (emirs) and sultans of Turkish or Iranian origin, overlooking the fact that Hülegü was not a Muslim. Indeed, he was under strong Christian influence. He warned al-Mustaᶜṣim of the fate of those who defied the Mongol standard; nonetheless, the caliph refused to submit.

The close investment of Baghdad began on 22 January 1258. The caliph's army had already been destroyed, and only the city garrison remained. Direct assault began on the fifth and sixth of February, and the city fell four days later. The garrison was slaughtered and the city given over to plunder. The caliph was executed on 20 February, along with most of his family. The Nestorian Christians in Baghdad were instructed by the patriarch Makikha to gather in their churches; the Mongols respected this refuge. In fact, the Christians of the East looked upon the Mongols as liberators.

Following the fall of Baghdad, the local Muslim lords of western Iran, Mesopotamia, and Asia Minor vied with each other in currying the favor of Hülegü. To accomplish his mission, Hülegü still sought to conquer Syria and Egypt. At this time, Syria and Palestine were divided among Muslim and crusader states, the Muslim rulers being a branch of the Ayyubids, the Kurdish dynasty founded by Saladin. They had recently become nominal vassals of the Mongols, sending tribute to the Great Khan, but Hülegü wished to incorporate their territories into his own.

Christian Armenia had long been a vassal and ally of the Mongols, so when the Ayyubid sultan of Mayafariqin (Mayyāfāriqīn) crucified a Christian priest who was carrying a Mongol passport, Hülegü was given a casus belli. A Mongol army laid siege to the city, and when it fell, the ruler, Amir al-Kamil (Naṣir al-Dīn), was executed in a hideous manner, even by Mongol standards. The greater part of the Muslim population of the region was massacred; Christians and their churches, on the other hand, were studiously respected. Hetᶜum I, king of Cilician Armenia, called the joint Armenian-Mongol invasion of Syria and Egypt a "crusade."

The allies left Azerbaijan in September 1259, advancing in three columns with General Ketbugha (Ket Bugha) commanding the advance guard. Most of the towns on the route submitted, but Suraj, which resisted, was taken by storm and the inhabitants massacred. Menbij (Manbij) on the far side of the Euphrates, in northern Syria, was sacked, and Aleppo, which Sultan al-Malik al-Nāṣir Yūsuf had left to defend Damascus, was besieged by the Mongols, commanded by Hülegü. There, he was joined by Armenian troops led by Het^{c}um I and by Frankish contingents led by Bohemond VI of Antioch. The siege began in January 1260, and after six days the Mongols breached the walls and broke into the city. The citadel surrendered the next day. The massacre of citizens lasted five days. In reward, Het^{c}um received part of the booty and several counties and castles that the Ayyubids had previously taken from him. Bohemond received the district of Antioch, which the Franks had lost to Saladin.

Sultan al-Nāṣir Yūsuf no longer risked the defense of Damascus and fled toward Egypt. Damascus surrendered on the first of March, and the governor is said to have been decapitated by Ketbugha on orders from Hülegü. The conquest of Syria was completed by early summer, when Gaza was taken; Egypt was the obvious next goal.

Hülegü appeared on the verge of accomplishing his mission when events took an unexpected turn. Mönke, the Great Khan, died, and civil war for the succession began between Aryq-böge and Qubylai (Qubilai). Hülegü was too far away to intervene directly but recognized that his fate was tied to that of Qubylai, his younger brother. Moreover, in the north the Golden Horde was now ruled by Berke, a Muslim who had vehemently protested the treatment of the population of Baghdad after its capture. Hülegü feared intervention by Aryq-böge or Berke and withdrew the bulk of his army to Azerbaijan.

Ketbugha's position in Syria was vulnerable not only to the Mamluk forces of Egypt, which were intact, but also to hostility of the Frankish counts of Palestine, who had learned to live with the Mamluks. The Mamluk sultans were aware of the situation among the Mongols and knew that Hülegü's main army would not stay put indefinitely in Azerbaijan. Thus the Mamluk sultan Quṭuz (1259–1260) decided that it was a favorable time to move against the Mongols in Palestine and Syria. In late July 1260, an advance guard led by Baybars al-Bunduqdārī left Egypt to engage the enemy. Baybars obtained passage through the Frankish territories and was even supplied through Acre. Ketbugha collected all available Mongol troops to meet this force, well aware that the Mamluks enjoyed a considerable numerical superiority. However, he felt that the terror inspired by the Mongol name and the skill of his veteran commanders would be a suitable counterbalance.

The battle was joined on 3 September 1260 at ^{c}Ayn Jālūt in Palestine, where the smaller Mongol force was crushed after inflicting severe losses on the enemy. Ketbugha refused to retreat, insisting that troops fight to the last. According to Rashīd-al-Dīn, after his horse was killed from under him, he was taken before Quṭuz. Rashīd-al-Dīn recorded the statement of Ketbugha before Sultan Quṭuz: "If I die at your hand, I shall consider God, not you, as the actor. Do not allow yourself to be intoxicated by this momentary success. When the news of my death reaches Hülegü Khan, his anger will rise like a stormy sea. From Azerbaijan to the gates of Egypt, the whole country will be trampled under the feet of Mongol horses." He concluded with an expression of contempt for the way of the Mamluks: "As long as I live I serve my master; I am not like you, his murderer." At this, Ketbugha's head was stricken from his body. Not long after his triumph, Quṭuz, who had become sultan by murdering his predecessor, was stabbed to death by Baybars, his second-in-command.

Berke used Hülegü's unilateral execution of the caliph of Baghdad as an excuse for forming an alliance with Baybars, who had become sultan (1260–1277). The two exchanged ambassadors and in 1262 declared war on Hülegü, who took the offensive with a thrust through the pass at Derbent on the Caspian Sea late that year. Thus began the seesaw warfare between the Ilkhans and the khans of the Golden Horde. On the eastern border, the civil wars in Mongolia and the pro-Qubylai positions of the Ilkhans likewise put them on the defensive there. Both in the East and the West the expansive power of the Ilkhans was halted. But by now Hülegü had reconstituted the ancient empire of Iran. When Fārs and Kermān became fiefdoms as a result of diplomatic marriages, the territory of the Ilkhans matched that of the Sasanians.

Hülegü died in February 1265, followed shortly thereafter by his queen, Toquz-khatun (Doquz Khatun), a devout Nestorian. Both were mourned by the Christians of the East as "two bright stars of the Christian faith," although Hülegü had never become a Christian himself. He was succeeded by Abaqa, his eldest son, who was favored by the Mongol grandees and remained faithful to the cause of Qubylai. In

MONGOL EMPIRE

fact, Abaqa regarded himself as merely the viceroy of the Great Khan, now in Peking, and requested his orders from him. He also had the vision to retain the capable Shams ad-din Juwani, who had served as Hülegü's chief minister. This permitted continuity in the development of an efficient internal administration. Abaqa married Maria, a natural daughter of Michael VIII Palaiologos, the Byzantine emperor.

Abaqa was succeeded by his brother Teküder, the seventh son of Hülegü. The Ilkhans, as lords of Greater Iran, were confronted with the traditional problems of the region, the Oxus frontier, the Caucasus, and the Euphrates. Teküder sought to break the encirclement on the western frontier by converting to Islam and taking the name Aḥmad, although he had previously been baptized. At the beginning of September 1282, he sent a mission to Cairo to inform Sultan Qalā^{c}ūn of this development and to express his desire for friendship and an alliance. The "old Mongol" party complained of this to Qubylai, who, in turn, was angered and threatened reprisal. Aḥmad, who was tolerant of Christians, held the Nestorians responsible for the complaint and imprisoned the Nestorian patriarch, Mar Yaballaha III. His fate might have been worse were it not for the intervention of the queen mother, Qutuq-khatun, who finally obtained his release.

The conversion was a political failure since the Syrian border was not secured by Teküder/Aḥmad's peace overtures. Internally, the conversion rendered Mongol rule less odious to the Muslim population, but it tended to make Christian subjects and the important Christian vassals suspicious. It also alienated the "old Mongol" party that dominated the army. Civil war followed shortly thereafter, ending with the death of Aḥmad, whose reign lasted only two years, from 1282 to 1284.

Aḥmad was followed by Abaqa's son Arghun (1284–1291), who was a Buddhist. In the course of his reign the Islamization of the Mongol overlords was halted, and the "traditional" policy of tolerance toward all religions was restored. Nevertheless, court intrigues disrupted internal administration. Self-seekers plotted against Juwani, the capable and devoted finance minister who had stood in high favor at the beginning of Aḥmad's reign, causing his disgrace and execution. His successor, Sa^{c}d al-Dawla, exacted heavy taxes from the populace, although they naturally enhanced the revenues of the khan. Arghun pursued a policy of administrative centralization, and in the last years of his reign a reaction set in.

At the same time, Arghun's reign was marked by a general relaxation of external pressure. He learned from his predecessor's failure to form an alliance with the Mamluks (since they were themselves largely of Kipchak origin and drew their manpower from the Kipchak territory, now the khanate of the Golden Horde). Arghun thus attempted to make alliances in the Christian West and sent numerous ambassadors to popes and Western kings. He died of a long illness in March 1291. Despite his approaching death, he had failed to make a clear choice of a successor, giving free rein to various court cliques. The military put forward the debauched Gaikhatu (Gaykhatu), who proved both incapable and inept. Civil war erupted and Gaikhatu was murdered. Ostensibly to avenge the death, Arghun's son Ghazan (Ghāzān), then governor of Khorāsān, moved west with a strong military force, and by 1295 all opposition was suppressed. After the occupation of Tabriz, he mounted the throne in November 1295.

Ghazan Khan was typical of the more capable Mongol rulers: ruthless in achieving political ends, a skillful and courageous commander, a good administrator showing concern for the welfare of the population, and a patron of learning. Rashīd-al-Dīn notes that, although he preferred to speak Mongol, he also knew some Arabic, Hindi, Tibetan, Chinese, and "Frankish" (probably French or Latin). He embraced Islam, and henceforth the Ilkhans were Muslim.

Ghazan's reign, the most brilliant period of Mongol culture in Iran, was marked by military operations, administrative reform, and diplomatic activity. In spite of his early destruction of Christian churches, Jewish synagogues, and Buddhist temples, once his rule was firmly established, he followed a policy of religious tolerance. In the last year of his reign Ghazan openly showed his friendship for the aged Nestorian patriarch (Mar Yaballaha), whom he had once imprisoned, by a personal visit to the monastery where he lived and by bestowing many gifts and honors upon him.

Ghazan ordered the construction of fine government buildings and mosques and gathered about him artists, men of letters, and scientists. He commissioned his minister, Rashīd al-Dīn Fazl Allah, to compile a history of the Mongols from court archives and from living informants. This resulted in the *Jami at-Tawarikh (Jāmi^{c} al-tavārīkh)*, a monument of Iranian historiography. Ghazan's attraction to the material culture of Iran and his conversion to Islam led to a rapid acculturation of the Mongols in Iran. This occurred in spite of the khan's pride of race and of his descent from Chinggis Khan.

Ghazan was succeeded by his youngest brother, Öljaitü (Uljaytu, Öljeitü) (1304–1316), whose mother had had him baptized but who was converted to Islam under the influence of one of his wives. Öljaitü attempted to make peace with the Mamluks but, like his predecessor, was rebuffed. He was forced to seek an alliance with the Christian West; in 1306 he married Maria, sister of Andronikos II Palaiologos, the Byzantine emperor. He also acknowledged his formal vassalage to the Great Khan in Peking. When envoys of the Great Khan arrived late in 1305 with the patent of investiture, they were received in great splendor. Like Ghazan, Öljaitü is known as a great builder and patron of art and learning, and under him a new capital was built at Sultaniya.

His twelve-year-old son Abu Said (Abū Saᶜīd) succeeded him in 1316 (enthronement April 1317) under the tutelage of Choban, the commander-in-chief of the army, who quelled revolts and protected the borders against the Golden Horde and the Chaghatai. In 1327, Abu Said decided to end his tutelage, encouraged by many military commanders who had suffered rough treatment at the hands of Choban, who may have been no worse than a loyal martinet. Abu Said issued an order for his execution, but Choban, who was in Khorāsān at the time, raised the standard of revolt and began to march westward. His troops soon deserted him, and he fled to Herat, where he was eventually murdered. His son Timurtash, military governor of eastern Asia Minor, who kept the vassal sultanates under control, was executed. This left a power vacuum, which in time was filled by the Ottomans in the northwest and the Qaramans in the southeast of Asia Minor. A bitter struggle with Özbeg, khan of the Golden Horde, who had penetrated the Caucasus through the pass at Derbent, marked Abu Said's closing years.

At the time of his death in 1335, apparently by poison, there was no Hülegid successor. The Mongol grandees elected Arpa, a descendant of Ariqböge, younger brother of Qubylai. This was merely a formality, since, in practice, each Mongol lord was an independent ruler. The following year, when the new khan was killed by a rebellious vassal, the Mongol leaders made no attempt either to come to his assistance before the rebellion or to avenge his death after it. The fiction of the khan was no longer maintained, and the realm of the Ilkhans dissolved almost overnight.

LATER DEVELOPMENTS IN THE GOLDEN HORDE

The history of the Golden Horde followed a different course. Berke was succeeded by Mönke-timur (Möngke Temür) (1267–1280), a grandson of Batu. In the civil war that raged between Qubylai and Qaidu, Mönke-timur sided with Qaidu. Events in Inner Asia, which are beyond the scope of this discussion, afforded him the opportunity to consider himself an independent ruler without an overlord. Coins of the Golden Horde no longer carried the name of the Great Khan; it was replaced by the name of Mönke-timur, and, in turn, by those of his successors. He followed Berke's foreign policy toward the Mamluks and Byzantium.

Mönke-timur died in 1280 and was succeeded by two incapable rulers. During this period, real power was in the hands of Noghai (Noghay) (*d.* 1299), Berke's grandnephew and "commander of 10,000" (*tümän baği*), who was called "tsar," "malik," and "khan" by foreigners. He managed foreign affairs and dealt directly with the Byzantine and Bulgar envoys—indeed, the Bulgar state had become Noghai's personal protectorate.

The power wielded by Noghai led to conspiracies among the royal princes, and after Noghai had suppressed a revolt by Tele Bugha (Tole Buka), Toghtu (Toqto, Tokhtu), a son of Mönke-timur, was elevated as khan. Toghtu did not prove to be a compliant puppet, and notwithstanding several defeats, he eventually triumphed over Noghai.

The scars of the civil wars never healed after Toghtu's death in 1312. When his nephew and successor Özbek (Uzbek) (1312–1341), a devout Muslim, attempted to spread Islam among the Mongol lords, they resisted and conspired against him; Özbek crushed the conspiracy. Despite his religious fervor, Christians were not persecuted during his rule, and he remained on good terms with the papacy.

Özbek permitted the restoration of Kaffa (Feodosiya) in the Crimea, the great Genoese trading city destroyed by Toghtu in 1308. In 1327 the Russian city of Tver revolted, and the Mongol tax collectors were massacred. An army of 50,000 was placed under the command of Prince Ivan of Moscow to suppress the revolt. The princes of Moscow thereafter served as the "civil guards" of the khans, and in that capacity they made Moscow the most powerful of the Russian cities.

During the course of the reign of Özbek's son Jambeg (Jānībeg) (1342–1357), friction developed between Venetian and Genoese traders on the one hand and Muslim merchants on the other, resulting in a siege of Italian trading cities in Golden Horde territory. Italian naval power forced the khan to come to terms. In the meantime, the Ilkhan state was disintegrating, presenting Jambeg with an opportunity to settle the problem of the disputed southern frontier. In 1355 he crossed the Caucasus with Kipchak troops and seized Azerbaijan. Jambeg left his son Berdi Beg as viceroy. In 1358 Berdi Beg returned to the territory of the Golden Horde on learning that his father was ill, at which time the Jalairs (Jalayrids) of Baghdad moved north and expelled the Kipchak garrison (1360).

Berdi Beg succeeded his father after putting aside twelve brothers. He was poisoned two years later, and virtual anarchy ensued, prompted by the underlying factionalism among the Tatar grandees. One group fell under the influence of Moscow, the other, of Lithuania. Candidates put forward for the throne were puppets of one or the other faction. In the absence of a central authority, the Russian princes ceased paying tribute or homage to Sarai. Lithuania and Poland began to dominate the Russian cities in the west, particularly in the Ukraine. In the north, Moscow's power continued to grow. Such effective power as remained among the Tatars was in the hands of amirs or "warlords."

Amir Mamai (Mamay) ruled in the Crimea. From there he attempted to reestablish Tatar authority to the north. A raid in reprisal for Moscow's refusal to pay tribute was repulsed in 1373. In 1376 Dmitri, grand prince of Moscow, began to raid Tatar territories in the direction of Kazan. An indecisive battle was fought in August 1378.

Two years later, in early September 1380, following an invasion of Tatar territory by Dmitri, a major battle was fought at Kulikovo. Dmitri prepared an ambush for Mamai after assuming a defensive position. Both sides suffered serious losses, but the result was a clear-cut Moscovite victory that provided an enormous psychological boost for the Russians. They could now think of overthrowing "the Tatar yoke." Except for a short period of reconsolidation under Toqtamish Khan (1380–1395), a protégé and at times deadly enemy of Tamerlane (Timur Leng), the khanate of the Golden Horde had virtually dissolved. All fragments eventually fell victim to the expanding power of Moscow.

BIBLIOGRAPHY

ᶜAlāᵓal-Dīn ᶜAṭā-Malek Joveynī, *Ta'rīkh-i jahān gushā,* Mīrzā Qazvīnī, ed., 3 vols. (1912–1937), trans. by John A. Boyle as *The History of the World-Conqueror,* 2 vols. (1958); Boris Grekov and Aleksandr Yakoubovskii, *La horde d'or,* François Thuret, trans. (1939); Erich Haenisch, ed. and trans., *Die geheime Geschichte der Mongolen (Yuan ch'ao pi-shih)* (1948), trans. by Arthur Waley as *The Secret History of the Mongols and Other Pieces* (1963); Louis Hambis, *Le chapitre CVII du Yuan Che* (1945); Leonardo Olschki, *Marco Polo's Asia,* John A. Scott, trans. (1960); Faẓlallāh Rashīd al-Dīn Ṭabīb, *Jāmiᶜ al-tavārīkh, I: Ta'rīkh-i ghāzānī,* Edgar Blochet, ed., 2 vols. (1911), trans. by John A. Boyle as *The Successors of Genghis Khan* (1971); John J. Saunders, *The History of the Mongol Conquests* (1971); *Sheng wu-hsin cheng-lu: Histoire des campagnes de Genghis Khan,* Paul Pelliot and Louis Hambis, trans. (1951); Bertold Spuler, *Die Goldene Horde,* 2nd rev. ed. (1965), *Die Mongolen in Iran,* 3rd ed. (1968), and *History of the Mongols,* Helga and Stuart Drummond, trans. (1972); George Vernadsky, *The Mongols and Russia* (1953); Boris Vladimirstsov, *Le régime social des Mongols,* Michel Carsow, trans. (1948).

WILLIAM SAMOLIN

[See also **Argun; Batu; Baybars al-Bunduqdārī; Genghis Khan; Golden Horde; Hetᶜum I; Hulagu; Ilkhanids; Iran, History; Khan; Khwārizmshāhs; Mamluk Dynasty; Quraysh; Saray; Transoxiana; Uljaytu.**]

MONOPHONY (Greek: *monos,* "single"; *phone,* "voice") is a term designating music that consists of a single melodic line, distinguished from polyphony and homophony. Principal monophonic forms of the Middle Ages include plainsong, devotional and secular songs in Latin and the vernaculars, such as *cantilenae* and *prosae,* troubadour and trouvère *chansons, minnelieder, cantigas,* and *laude,* and instrumental dance forms, such as *ductia* and *estampie.*

DIANE L. DROSTE

[See also **Cantiga; Cantilène; Chansonnier; Laudes; Minnesingers; Music, Western European; Troubadour, Trouvère, Trovador.**]

MONOPHYSITISM. The name given to the doctrine which states that the humanity and divinity of

MONOPHYSITISM

Jesus Christ were hypostatically united in such a way that the two abstract natures became one subsistent nature of the incarnate Word of God. Monophysitism employed the exegetical methodology of the school of Alexandria, which was grounded in Platonic philosophy and the concern for the divine economy of salvation expounded by Athanasius of Alexandria (*ca.* 295–373) at the Council of Nicaea (325). From the viewpoint of the Catholic orthodoxy propounded by the sees of Rome and Constantinople, it was seen as a distortion of the doctrine of Cyril of Alexandria (patriarch, 412–444) on Christology, which he formulated in reaction to Nestorianism.

The Monophysites saw themselves as the only authentic defenders of Cyril's doctrine, which had been expressed in the first seven canons of the Council of Ephesus (431) and in his twelve anathemas against Nestorius (patriarch of Constantinople, 428–431). In this sense, Cyril can be called the "Father of Monophysitism," though this was not the opinion of any subsequent ecumenical council. The true father of the movement is more accurately the aged archimandrite Eutyches (mid fourth century–*ca.* 454). After Cyril's death (444), he precipitated a crisis by teaching that the humanity of Christ was so closely united with his divinity that, at least to his opponents, it seemed that the human nature was actually absorbed into the divinity. This extreme reaction to Nestorianism, which had rejected the doctrine of hypostatic union, went well beyond anything Cyril taught. With support from Pope Leo I (440–461), Flavian, patriarch of Constantinople (446–449), condemned Eutyches. Cyril's less talented and more impulsive successor, Dioscoros (444–451), with support from the imperial court (Chrysaphios, the grand chamberlain, was Eutyches' godson), defended Eutyches and reheard his case at the so-called "Robber Synod" of Ephesus (449), where he deposed Flavian and his supporters and intimidated the other bishops into reinstating Eutyches. Pope Leo reacted with his *Tome,* which set forth the Western tradition that there were two distinct natures in Christ, hypostatically united in the one person.

The death of Emperor Theodosius II (408–450), who supported Dioscoros, allowed Leo and his supporters to advance their viewpoint at the Council of Chalcedon (451). Eutyches was again condemned, Dioscoros was deposed and exiled, though not condemned, and the *Tome* of Leo was accepted and formed the basis for the council's decree on the incarnate Word of God. This decree, meant to be definitive and to secure the religious peace and unity of the empire, precipitated widespread disunity and ultimately schism in the East, primarily in Egypt and eastern Syria. For the next 200 years, one of the chief preoccupations of the imperial government was its attempt to win back the Monophysites either through compromise or persecution. The constant theme running through the controversy was the doctrine formulated at Chalcedon. Subsequent popes refused to admit of any compromise which failed to affirm this council and Pope Leo's *Tome.* Monophysites were equally stubborn in their refusal to accept the decision at Chalcedon or the *Tome.* To do so would have been, to them, tantamount to accepting Nestorianism and thus undermining the efficacy of Christ's saving acts and his Eucharist. Concomitant with the theological differences were the civil and ecclesiastical political disputes with their resulting resentments, which acted to vitiate later attempts at doctrinal rapprochement.

In Alexandria, on the death of Emperor Marcian (457), a mob lynched the Chalcedonian patriarch Proterius, and the Monophysite Timothius Aelerus II was elected. Exiled in 460 under Emperor Leo I (457–474) and reinstated in 475, Timothius began a line of Monophysite patriarchs at Alexandria. Until 482, the emperors Leo and Zeno (474–491) tried to maintain the Chalcedonian succession. In that year, Zeno drew up his formula of reunion, the *Henotikon.* Zeno's dislike of the Chalcedonian patriarch and the willingness of the Monophysite Peter Mongus, patriarch of Alexandria (482–490), to subscribe to the *Henotikon* resulted in the acceptance of the Monophysite succession, which lasted until 537. The *Henotikon,* probably composed by Peter Mongus and Patriarch Akakios of Constantinople (471–489), was rejected by Rome because it failed to support the doctrine of Chalcedon. It caused a schism between Rome and Constantinople, the Akakian schism (482–519). The Monophysites who accepted the *Henotikon* simply interpreted it as they saw fit. It had no real effect on doctrinal reconciliation.

Under Emperor Anastasius (491–518) and Justin I (518–527), the Egyptian Monophysites were left in peace. But in Syria, Justin deposed the Monophysite Severus, patriarch of Antioch (512–518), who took refuge in Egypt. Severus, an outstanding theologian and polemicist, was a moderate Monophysite who injected a new level of sophistication into the movement through his preaching and writing. While opposing the Chalcedonians, he also devoted himself to the refutation of extreme Monophysitism, distancing the moderate movement from Eutychianism and the teachings of his fellow exiles, Julian of Halikarnassos and Gaianos. Julian taught that Christ's body was incorruptible from conception (Aphthartodocetism), Gaianos that it was merely phenomenal (Phantasiastism). The Julianists formed schismatic splinter groups within Egyptian Monophysitism which lasted until the ninth century. The presence of Severus in Egypt was crucial for the survival of Monophysitism there. When Justinian's policies ended any hope of compromise, Severus encouraged the Alexandrine patriarch Theodosius (535–566), whose firm stand against the Chalcedonians resulted in the Egyptian Monophysites being called "Theodosians." Justinian restored the Chalcedonian patriarchs, and the Monophysites were driven underground. Until the emperor's death (565), their patriarchs were shadowy, if not fictitious, figures.

As a result of the policies of Justin and Justinian, Monophysitism in Syria seemed doomed. Monophysite bishops were swept from office and replaced by Chalcedonians, and the monks and laity were subjected to harassment and outright persecution. Potential disaster was averted through the ingenuity of Jacob Baradaios (*ca.* 500–578), a protégé of Empress Theodora, who was consecrated bishop of Edessa about 542. Jacob traveled in disguise throughout Syria and Palestine, rallying the Monophysite faithful and consecrating bishops for the now largely Aramaic-speaking underground church, which came to be called after him "Jacobite." Justinian's condemnation of the "Three Chapters"—the writings of three Nestorians—may have been an attempt to curry favor with the Monophysites, but if so, it was too late.

A period of relative religious peace followed Justinian's death in 565. In Egypt and eastern Syria, Monophysite and Chalcedonian (Melchite) hierarchies coexisted, with the latter stronger in urban centers and the Monophysites stronger in the countryside and among the monks. The last great effort at a reconciliation came with Emperor Heraklios' attempt in his *Ekthesis* of 638, which asserted that Christ had two natures, as Chalcedon decreed, but only one will (Monothelitism). Any success this solution might have had among the Egyptian Monophysites was vitiated by the ruthless behavior of Patriarch Cyrus (631–642), who also functioned as civil prefect of Egypt. The Monothelite solution continued to be debated until 648, when Constans II (641–668) suppressed the *Ekthesis*. It was finally condemned by the Third Council of Constantinople (680–681).

By 650, this final controversy had become a moot point for the Monophysite communities. They had been removed from imperial domination and interference by the lightning Arab conquests of Egypt and Syria-Palestine. Under Arab rule, the Syrian Monophysites continued the theological tradition begun by Severus of Antioch and Philoxenus of Mabbug through original work and extensive translation from Greek. One of the outstanding figures of the early Arab period and the scholar who had the greatest impact on subsequent Monophysite theology was the polymath Jacob of Edessa (*ca.* 640–708). Learned in Greek and Hebrew, he laid the foundations for Syriac grammatical studies, continued the *Ecclesiastical History* of Eusebius down to 692, wrote extensive biblical commentaries, and translated the *Cathedral Homilies* of Severus of Antioch into Syriac. After a period of decline in the tenth century, as a result of the Seljuk invasions, a rebirth of Syriac letters occurred in the twelfth and thirteenth centuries. The theological works of Dionysius Bar Ṣalibi (*d.* 1171) and the chronicles of Michael the Syrian (1126–1199) and Bar Hebraeus (1226–1286) (Gregorius or Abū 'l-Faraj) belong to this period. As with the Nestorians, Monophysite theology underwent little real development, especially after the Arab conquest removed effective Chalcedonian competition. The chief authority remained Cyril of Alexandria, as interpreted by Severus of Antioch. The Syrian Jacobite church suffered from progressively increasing defections to Islam and, after the eighth century, from occasional defections to Chalcedonianism. The Mongol invasions of the thirteenth century finally resulted in the destruction of centers of learning and the decimation of their communities. At the time of the Council of Ferrara-Florence (1438), three rival claimants were fighting over the patriarchal office.

In Egypt, the Monophysite party, which came to be known as the Coptic church, gained the full recognition of the Arab government as the official Christian community. Unlike their Syrian coreligionists, the Copts faced their newfound religious freedom without a strong tradition in either theology or ecclesiastical history, if one is to judge from what remains of their writings. Byzantine domination of Egypt had left little if any opportunity for the founding of theological schools among the Copts comparable to those of Syria or Mesopotamia. No Coptic theologians appear until the late tenth century, when Sawīrus ibn al-Muqafaʿ, named bishop of Ashmunein in 987, produced a series of works against the Chalcedonian patriarch of Alexandria, Eutychios. He is also credited with collecting and translating the *History of the Patriarchs of Alexandria* into Arabic, probably in reaction to Eutychios' *Naẓm al-jawhar.* This work was continued by subsequent writers well past the sixteenth century and remains the chief source for the history of Monophysitism in medieval Egypt. Much of the Coptic literature before Sawīrus has little or no bearing on the Monophysite controversy as such. It consists of translations from the fathers of the church, hagiography, and sermons, some of which are anti-Chalcedonian polemical works displaying but a rudimentary knowledge of the theological points being disputed. The real flowering of Coptic theological writing took place in the thirteenth and fourteenth centuries. Al-Muʾtaman Abū Isḥāq Ibrāhīm ibn al-ʿAssāl produced his *Collection of the Fundamental Doctrines of Religion* before 1260, a work which covers all aspects of doctrine and church discipline. In the next century, Šams (Shams) ar-Riʾāsa Abū 'l-Barakāt ibn Kibr (*d. ca.* 1325) produced another comprehensive encyclopedia of theology and rites, *The Lamp of the Darkness and Explanation of the Services,* which includes a catalogue of theological writers and their works. By the close of the fourteenth century, the Copts, greatly reduced in numbers by defections to Islam, ceased to make any significant contributions to Monophysite theological literature.

Except for a foothold in Persia gained in the mid sixth century, Monophysite missionary enterprises were restricted to the southern borders of the Byzantine Empire. The mission to Nubia in 542/543 made that country predominantly Monophysite until the disappearance of Nubian Christianity in the fourteenth century. Ethiopia, because of its ties with the patriarchate of Alexandria, seems to have become at least nominally Monophysite, although just how and to what extent is impossible to tell from the surviving data. The Ethiopians continued to maintain communion with the Coptic church and receive their metropolitan from Egypt throughout the medieval period when conditions were favorable. The Monophysite (Syrian) communities of south Arabia were wiped out with the consolidation of Islam. The relationship of the Armenian church to the Monophysite community seems never to have involved formal communion with the Syrians or Copts. The Armenians did reject the Council of Chalcedon and accept the *Henotikon* of Zeno, but some subsequent Armenian patriarchs accepted the Chalcedonian position. The attempts of the see of Rome to establish communion with the Monophysite churches at the Council of Ferrara-Florence came to nothing.

BIBLIOGRAPHY

For the general history down to the Arab conquest, see William H. C. Frend, *The Rise of the Monophysite Movement* (1972, repr. 1979), which combines the political and ecclesiastical aspects of the dispute and provides a good bibliography of primary and secondary sources. Also valuable is William A. Wigram, *The Separation of the Monophysites* (1923; repr. 1978). For Syrian Monophysitism after the Arab conquest see Wolfgang Hage, *Die syrisch-jakobitische Kirche in frühislamischer Zeit* (1966), and Peter Kawerau, *Die jakobitische Kirche in Zeitalter der syrischen Renaissance* (1955). For Egypt, see M. Jugie, "Monophysite (Église copte)," in *Dictionnaire de théologie catholique,* X (1928). For the Monophysite doctrine with all its ramifications, see Joseph Lebon, *Le Monophysisme sévérien* (1909). Alois Grillmeier and Heirich Bacht, eds., *Das Konzil von Chalkedon,* 3 vols. (1951–1954), contains essays on every aspect of this council and its aftermath by various scholars. See also Jaroslav Pelikan, *The Christian Tradition,* 4 vols. to date (1971–); Robert V. Sellers, *The Council of Chalcedon* (1953).

D. W. JOHNSON

[See also **Abyssinia; Adoptionism; Antiochene Rite; Armenian Church, Doctrines and Councils; Athanasius of Alexandria, St.; Bar Hebraeus; Byzantine Church; Christianity, Nubian; Christology; Church, Early; Church Fathers; Copts and Coptic Church; Councils (Ecumenical, 325–787); Creeds, Liturgical Use of; Cyril of Alexandria, St.; Docetism; Ekthesis; Eutyches; Eutychios the Melchite; Henotikon; Heraklios; Heresies, Armenian; Heresies, Byzantine; Justinian I; Leo I, Pope; Melchites; Michael the Syrian; Monothelitism; Nestorianism; Nestorius; Philosophy and Theology, Byzantine; Schisms, Eastern-Western Church; Sergios I; Syrian Christianity; Theodosius II the Calligrapher; Theotokos; Zeno the Isaurian.**]

MONOTHELITISM. Born of the desire on the part of the Byzantines to make peace with the Monophysites of Syria and Egypt, Monothelitism represented yet another stage in the series of christological controversies that had disturbed the church since the fourth century. It was thus both a theological and a political question, and as such encompassed a number of conflicts. The word itself means one will, and the doctrine, which originated in the eastern provinces of the empire, rested on the assumption that the two natures of Christ, the divine and the human, had one active force—a single will *(monothelema)* or energy *(monoenergeia)*. These formulations seemed at first to be a possible compromise between the Monophysites and the Orthodox, a compromise which was especially critical given the Arab threats to the eastern provinces.

Kyros (Cyrus), the patriarch of Alexandria (631–642), thought the idea an acceptable one, but opposition appeared immediately, particularly in the person of Sophronios, who was to become patriarch of Jerusalem (634–638). Sergios, the patriarch of Constantinople (610–638), then emphasized the doctrine of one will, rather than one energy, and this was embodied in the *Ekthesis,* promulgated in 638 and written largely by Sergios. He believed that the papacy would approve this formulation, but Pope Severinus (640) preferred instead a doctrine which emphasized two operations and two wills. The *Ekthesis* was therefore unsatisfactory both to Rome and to the Eastern churches. Pope John IV (640–642) declared Monothelitism a heresy; ironically, by the time this judgment was issued, the eastern provinces, which it had been designed to bind to the Byzantine Empire, were already in Arab hands.

Once the eastern provinces had been lost, subsequent emperors attempted to make peace with Rome over the issue of Monothelitism. In 648, the emperor Constans II (641–668) issued the *Typos,* which forbade all discussion of the question of one or two wills or energies. In addition, the *Typos* ordered the removal of the writings about this issue, and therefore the *Ekthesis* was removed from the narthex of Hagia Sophia. This did not, however, satisfy Pope Martin I (649–655), who condemned both the *Ekthesis* and the *Typos.* Maximus the Confessor, one of the outstanding theologians of the period, also opposed the *Typos* and Monothelitism. Both he and Martin were arrested by the exarch of Italy, sent to Constantinople for trial, imprisoned, tortured, and finally exiled to Cherson in the Crimea.

The Monothelite controversy simmered on, and in 680 the emperor Constantine IV (668–685), in an attempt to end the conflict, called the Sixth Ecumenical Council (Third Council of Constantinople), at which the Eastern patriarchs were present. With the emperor himself present at many of the sessions, the council condemned Monothelitism and recognized two natures and "two natural wills and energies." Byzantium had conceded the eastern provinces to the Arabs once and for all. But Monothelitism had a brief revival at the beginning of the eighth century. The emperor Philippikos (711–713), an Armenian, issued an imperial edict declaring Monothelitism to be the only orthodox doctrine and ordering the picture of the Third Council of Constantinople in the royal palace destroyed and the inscription commemorating it on the gate to the palace removed. Despite support for his doctrine by many of the higher clergy, this Monothelite revival was brief and ended when Philippikos was deposed in 713.

BIBLIOGRAPHY

For a text of the *Ekthesis,* see Giovanni Mansi, ed., *Collectio conciliorum,* X (1764), 991–998.

For historical surveys of the period, see George Ostrogorsky, *History of the Byzantine State,* Joan Hussey, trans. (1957, rev. ed. 1969); Andreas Stratos, *Byzantium in the Seventh Century,* Marc Ogilvie, trans., 5 vols. (1968–1980).

For studies of the christological controversies of the period, see John Meyendorff, *Byzantine Theology* (1974, 2nd ed. 1978), and *Christ in Eastern Christian Thought,* 2nd. ed. (1975); Jaroslav Pelikan, *The Christian Tradition,* 4 vols. to date (1971–).

LINDA C. ROSE

[See also **Armenian Church, Doctrines and Councils; Christology; Constans II, Emperor; Councils (Ecumenical, 325–787); Ekthesis; Heresies, Byzantine; Maronite Church; Maximus the Confessor, St.; Monophysitism; Philosophy and Theology, Byzantine; Sergios I.**]

MONTE CASSINO. The monastery of Monte Cassino, located between Rome and Naples, was founded about 529 by St. Benedict of Nursia. It is here that Benedict is thought to have composed his Rule, a document that soon became one of the pillars of Western monasticism.

Gregory the Great records in his *Dialogues* that St. Benedict built two oratories at Monte Cassino (St. Martin and St. John the Baptist) on the site of an ancient temple dedicated to Apollo. These statements were verified by excavations in the early 1950s.

Benedict's monastic complex was destroyed by the Lombards about 580, and the community took refuge in Rome, where it was attached to the Lateran until about 717. At that time, Abbot Petronax, encouraged by Pope Gregory III, rebuilt the old basilica. Lombards (Petronax came from Brescia in the kingdom of Pavia), Anglo-Saxons (such as Willibald, a disciple of St. Boniface and later bishop of Eichstätt), and Franks (from the neighboring abbey of St. Vincent on the Volturno), all contributed to the restoration of the monastery. It was soon considered to be the repository of the pure Benedictine tradition. Thus, Sturmi, abbot of Fulda, and countless others visited Monte Cassino hoping to gain information about the interpretation of the Rule.

Carloman, brother of Pepin III and former mayor of the palace in France, and Ratchis, brother of Aistulf and former king of the Lombards, renounced their worldly offices almost simultaneously and retired to the monastery. Paul the Deacon, author of the *Historia Langobardorum,* lived at Monte Cassino for many years before and after his sojourn at the court of Charlemagne (782–787). During this period, many works of learning, both secular and Christian, were copied by the monastery's scribes. These manuscripts offer us the oldest examples of Beneventan script.

At the beginning of the ninth century, Abbot Gisulf (796–817) replaced the old building dedicated to St. John with a church with three naves. He also built, at the foot of the mountain, another monastery and a large basilica dedicated to the Savior. In 883, the entire complex was sacked, this time by the Arabs, Abbot Berthar being one of their victims. The monks who managed to escape settled first at Teano, where the supposed autograph manuscript of Benedict's Rule was lost in a fire. Later, they went to Capua, returning to Monte Cassino only about the year 950, under Abbot Aligern (949–986), a student of Odo of Cluny. Intellectual activities and manuscript production were soon resumed under Abbot Atenolf and Abbot Theobald. Interference by the princes of Capua, however, held back the full development of the monastery. The emperor Conrad II put an end to this harassment and installed Richer, a Bavarian, as abbot (1038–1055). Richer's successor, Frederick of Lorraine (1055–1058), became pope (Stephen IX, 1057–1058), as did Desiderius (1058–1087, as Pope Victor III, 1086–1087). During the latter's tenure and that of Oderisius (1087–1105), the monastery reached its zenith. Its new buildings, constructed with the support of Robert Guiscard and the Greek emperors Michael VII Doukas and Alexios I Komnenos, were consecrated in 1071 by Pope Alexander II. Work in literature and science reached an unprecedented level, owing especially to Greek and Arab influence: in medicine with Alphanus of Salerno and Constantine the African; in history with Amatus, Leo Marsicanus, and Peter the Deacon; in mathematics and astrology with Pandolf of Capua; and in literature with Guaiferius, Alberic, and John of Gaeta. The latter reintroduced the cursus into the style of the papal chancery.

From this peak, through the rest of the Middle Ages, Monte Cassino declined, a victim of political intrigues and of abbots who took little interest in the monastery. Often, they held other posts in the church and considered their abbacy an unimportant function. It was only the entrance of the monastery into the Congregation of St. Justina of Padua in 1504 that allowed Monte Cassino to prosper once again.

BIBLIOGRAPHY

Source. Leo Marsicanus, *Chronica monasterii Casinensis,* Hartmut Hoffmann, ed., in *Monumenta Germaniae historica, Scriptores,* XXXIV (1980).

Studies. Herbert Bloch, *Monte Cassino in the Middle Ages* (1983); Giovanni Carbonara, *Iussu Desiderii: Montecassino e l'architettura campano-abruzzese nell'undecimo secolo* (1979); H. E. J. Cowdrey, *The Age of Abbot Desiderius of Montecassino: The Papacy and the Normans in the Eleventh and Early Twelfth Centuries* (1983); Heinrich Dormeier, *Montecassino und die Laien im 11. und 12. Jahrhundert* (1979); Hartmut Hoffmann, "Chronik und Urkunde in Montecassino," in *Quellen und Forschungen aus italienischen Archiven und Bibliotheken,* **51** (1971); F.-J. Newton, "Some Monte Cassino Scribes in the Eleventh Century," in Siegfried Wenzel, ed., *Medieval and Renaissance Studies: Proceedings of the Southeastern Institute of Medieval and Renaissance Studies, Summer 1975* (1978), 3–19; Angelo Pantoni, *Le vicende della basilica di Montecassino attraverso la documentazione archeologica* (1973), and *L'acropoli di Montecassino e il primitivo monastero di San Benedetto* (1980).

ALAIN J. STOCLET

[See also **Alberic of Monte Cassino; Alexios I Komnenos; Alphanus of Salerno; Amatus of Monte Cassino; Benedictine Rule; Benedictines; Benedict of Nursia, St.; Constantine the African; Cursus; Desiderius of Monte Cassino; Lateran; Monastery; Monasticism, Origins; Paul the Deacon; Peter the Deacon of Monte Cassino; Richer of St. Remi; Robert Guiscard.**]

MONTEREAU, PIERRE OF. See **Pierre de Montreuil.**

MONTPELLIER, which was one of the most important urban centers of southern France, was unusual because it was not of Roman origin. Instead, it arose during the late tenth and early eleventh centuries inland from the abandoned town of Maguio, halfway between Nîmes and Beziers. Its location allowed it to exploit trade reaching the Rhône River delta or passing overland on its way along the coastal plain of Languedoc to Narbonne or Carcassonne. The name Montpellier was probably derived from *mons pastelario* (pastel mountain) because its oak produced a valuable red *kermès* (oak) dye used in the textile industry.

Down to 1204 control of the town was divided between its secular lords of the Guillem family, the bishops of Maguelonne, and a family of Vicars or Viguiers. Eventually, the Guillems were able to buy out the Viguiers, push out the bishops of Maguelonne, and gain effective control of both Montpellier and its surrounding rural area or *contado.* In doing so they were careful to balance the power of the two great feudatories of this part of Languedoc, the counts of Barcelona, who were also kings of Aragon, and the counts of Toulouse, who succeeded the counts of Melgueil as the Guillems' immediate overlords. They also maintained friendly relations with the Popes and the Genoese and Pisans who traded with their town on an active basis.

The Guillems were, however, less successful in dealing with their own townsmen. Though they were able to suppress a bourgeois revolt which managed to create a consulate between 1141 and 1143, in 1190 and again in 1203, Guillem (William) VIII was forced to grant his townspeople consular self-government, control of the court system, and an important set of laws known as the *Coutûme* of Montpellier. He was also unable to persuade Pope Innocent III to disinherit his daughter Marie, who was his legitimate heir to the town by his first marriage, in favor of a son, Guillem (William) IX, who was the issue of an irregular second union.

After a brief interlude in which first Guillem IX and then consular self-government intervened, Marie and her husband, King Peter II of Aragon, were recognized as the town's legitimate lords, though only after they had sworn to accept Montpellier's consulate, the *Coutûme,* and the independent court system. It was in the town's seigneurial castle that their only son, James the Conqueror (James I), was born in 1208.

During these years of Guillem control, Montpellier became an important trading center and began to export the production of its workshops in the form of dyed cloth, leather goods, and arms to Catalonia, Valencia, the Balearics, and North Africa. It even established merchant colonies in Syria. At the same time it attracted foreign merchants from northern France and the Low Countries as well as numerous traders from Italy. By 1203 its "money of Melgueil" was the most esteemed and widely used coinage in southern Europe. During this same period the study of Roman law and medicine was established on a firm basis in Montpellier's schools.

Throughout the thirteenth century Montpellier was controlled by James of Aragon and his heirs, who managed to limit consular government in a number of ways. It also, however, had ties with the French kings, who succeeded the counts of Toulouse and the bishops of Maguelonne as co-seigneurs and overlords. All of this helped Montpellier's commerce, for her merchants were able, as subjects of James I, to participate in the maritime empire of the house of Aragon, which included Catalonia, the Balearics, Valencia, and Sicily, while still trading freely with the domains of the Capetians as well. So important was the town's Mediterranean commerce and its trade with northern Europe that its prosperity was not adversely affected by the establishment of the neighboring port of Aigues Mortes by Louis IX of France.

By the middle of the fourteenth century, Montpellier had become the most important city of the Midi and could boast a large resident foreign population, which was largely composed of Catalans and Italians. It had important banking facilities and trading interests that extended from the eastern Mediterranean to northern France, where Montpellierans regularly served as captains of the merchants of the Midi attending the fairs of Champagne. This same merchant community organized "consuls of the sea" to control its organized traders in the Mediterranean and saw to it that its money of Melgueil continued to be the most important currency used in the Midi. At the same time Montpellier, now a city of 40,000, became a major university center, attracting large numbers of students who attended its schools of law and medicine, which rivaled those of nearby Italy.

The next century, however, turned out to be a disastrous one for the town, even though at times its economy benefited from the location of the papacy in nearby Avignon. It passed to the French crown in 1349, and this was a factor in excluding its merchants from markets controlled by the house of Aragon, while the decline of the fairs of Champagne ended much of its commerce to the north. It was decimated by the Black Death from 1348 on, and hurt greatly by plunderings of the White Companies in

MONTPELLIER MS H 196

the region during the Hundred Years War. By 1404 it had only 15,000 inhabitants and, although it recovered somewhat when Jacques Coeur made it his headquarters for trade with the Levant about mid century, this proved only temporary. By the first years of the sixteenth century, Marseilles and the new fair of Beaucaire became more important as centers of trade, diverting traffic from the town, while the governing institutions of Languedoc came to be centered in Toulouse. Though Montpellier still possessed a great university and had some commercial importance on a local level, its great days were over, and it entered a period of slow decline which was to last throughout the sixteenth century.

BIBLIOGRAPHY

Jean Baumel, *Histoire d'une seigneurie du Midi de la France,* 2 vols. (1969–1971); Jean Combes and André E. Sayous, "Les commerçants et les capitalistes de Montpellier aux XIIIe et XIVe siècles," in *Revue historique,* **189** (1940); Alexandre Germain, *Histoire du commerce de Montpellier,* 2 vols. (1861); Archibald R. Lewis, "The Development of Town Government in Twelfth Century Montpellier," in *Speculum,* **22** (1947); Josiah Russell, "L'evolution demographique de Montpellier au moyen âge," in *Annales du Midi,* **74** (1962).

ARCHIBALD R. LEWIS

[See also **Aragon, Crown of; Cathars; Languedoc; Provence; Toulouse.**]

MONTPELLIER MS H 196, one of the largest music manuscripts of the thirteenth century and the largest extant manuscript of thirteenth-century polyphonic music, containing some 345 works that span the compositional activity of the entire century. The codex, now at the University of Montpellier, was probably copied in Paris, the first seven fascicles, or gatherings, about 1270–1280, and the eighth about 1300, perhaps originally as an independent manuscript.

Fascicle 1 consists primarily of *organa tripla,* some of them shortened versions of compositions by Perotinus, others settings in a more recent, modest style. Fascicle 2 has four-voice triple motets; fascicle 3, primarily three-voice double motets in both French and Latin; and fascicle 4, Latin double motets, many "peripheral" (non-French) in origin. Fascicle 5 consists of an enormous collection—ninety-nine works—of French double motets; fascicle 6, of two-voice French motets, many of them incipient accompanied songs; and fascicle 7, of double motets in a wide range of more modern styles. Fascicle 8 primarily has double motets, the great majority of them found in no other manuscript, many of them standing apart from the mainstream of motet composition at the end of the century. Apart from the conductus motet and Latin two-voice motet, every major form of motet composition is represented in significant numbers.

Fascicles 1 through 6 make up an "old corpus" of music from approximately the first three-quarters of the century, while fascicle 7 contains many motets that must have been new at the time of copying—those by Petrus de Cruce, for example, which are otherwise found in sources from about 1300 and later, works in a highly experimental idiom that look ahead to the ars nova of the fourteenth century. Indeed, experimentation of all sorts, involving subject matter, the choice and treatment of the tenor, textures, rhythm, and form, is found throughout the motets of fascicles 7 and 8, this repertory providing our most detailed witness to the stylistic changes taking place at the close of the ars antiqua.

BIBLIOGRAPHY

Gordon A. Anderson, "Notre Dame Latin Double Motets, *ca.* 1215–1250," in *Musica disciplina,* **25** (1971); Robert Branner, *Manuscript Painting in Paris During the Reign of Saint Louis* (1977); Luther A. Dittmer, "The Ligatures of the Montpellier Manuscript," in *Musica disciplina,* **9** (1955); Jacques Handschin, "The Summer Canon and Its Background," in *Musica disciplina,* **3** and **5** (1949 and 1951); Gustav Jacobsthal, "Die Texte der Liederhandschrift von Montpellier H. 196," in *Zeitschrift für romanische Philologie,* **3** and **4** (1879 and 1880); Georg Kuhlmann, *Die zweistimmigen französischen Motetten des Kodex Montpellier,* 2 vols. (1938); Friedrich Ludwig, "Studien über die Geschichte der mehrstimmigen Musik im Mittelalter II: Die 50 Beispiele Coussemakers aus der Handschrift von Montpellier," in *Sammelbände der internationalen Musikgesellschaft,* **5** (1904), and *Repertorium organorum recentioris et motetorum vetustissimi stili,* Luther A. Dittmer, ed., I.2, (1910, repr. 1964–1978); Yvonne Rokseth, *Polyphonies du XIIIe siècle,* 4 vols. (1935–1939); Ernest H. Sanders, "Peripheral Polyphony of the Thirteenth Century," in *Journal of the American Musicological Society,* **17** (1964); Hans Tischler, ed., *The Montpellier Codex,* 3 vols. (1978).

EDWARD H. ROESNER

[See also **Ars Antiqua; Ars Nova; Motet; Motet Manuscripts; Music, Western European; Musical Notation, Modal; Musical Notation, Western; Perotinus; Petrus de Cruce.**]

MONTREUIL, EUDES OF. See **Eudes of Montreuil.**

MONTREUIL, PIERRE OF. See **Pierre of Montreuil.**

MORALITY PLAY, a distinct form of medieval drama which flourished in the fifteenth and early sixteenth centuries, it had antecedents in the *Ordo Virtutum* (*ca.* 1150) and the fourteenth-century Paternoster plays (none of which are extant). Traditionally regarded as a development of the medieval sermon (or, more doubtfully, of the Corpus Christi play), the morality play derived in part from the scholastic habit of analyzing man into his constituent elements, along with his characteristic maladies and the spiritual remedies which oppose them.

In the typical play, a character called Man presents the irreducible kernel of the human soul, while his individual attributes or the external agencies which impinge upon his life are personified as Reason and Sensuality or as various sins and remedial virtues. Prompted or restrained by such mentors, the protagonist falls into sin and is rescued one or more times; he may live out his entire life in the course of the play, or merely his final hours. The various agencies, however allegorical, are characterized in a lifelike manner as riotous gallants or earnest counselors.

Human life is often presented schematically, as defined by the traditional ages of man and the rise and fall of Fortune's wheel (involving the image of man as king). Man's spiritual career is typically defined by the doctrine of penance. Morality plays are often vehicles for instruction in such catalogs of spiritual knowledge as the Ten Commandments, the five wits (bodily and spiritual), or the three parts of the soul (mind, will, and understanding). At the conclusion man is usually saved.

The morality play was especially popular in France and England: more than twenty-five French plays survive, while more than a dozen survive from England. The French morality play is typified by *Bien advisé et Mal advisé, L'homme juste et l'homme mondain,* and *L'homme pécheur*. The pattern for English plays is set by *The Castle of Perseverance*. The morality play was also popular in the Lowlands, where *Elckerlijc* was the Dutch counterpart of *Everyman,* and in Germany, as exemplified by Pamphilus Gegenbach's oft-performed and oft-reprinted *Die zehn Alter dieser Welt*. During the sixteenth century the morality play sometimes addressed secular themes or served as a vehicle for religious controversy, but Christopher Marlowe's *Doctor Faustus* demonstrates that the essential qualities of the genre could endure to the end of the century and beyond.

BIBLIOGRAPHY

David M. Bevington, *From "Mankind" to Marlowe* (1962); Werner B. Helmlich, *Die Allegorie im französischen Theater des 15. und 16. Jahrhunderts* (1976); Sheila Lindenbaum, "Dramatic Pieces: The Morality Plays," in Albert E. Hartung, ed., *A Manual of the Writings in Middle English, 1050–1500,* V (1975); Robert A. Potter, *The English Morality Play* (1975); Carl J. Stratman, *Bibliography of Medieval Drama,* 2 vols., 2nd rev. ed. (1972).

ALAN H. NELSON

[See also **Castle of Perseverance; Drama, French; Drama, German; Drama, Western European; Dutch Literature; Elckerlijc; Everyman; Middle English Literature.**]

MORANT UND GALIE. See **Karlmeinet.**

MORAVIA is the latinized form for Morava, a historical region inhabited by Slavs and bordering during the Middle Ages on Bohemia, Poland, Hungary, and Austria. The region's history has been confused in the past with the history of so-called Great Moravia, located south of the Danube. The confusion resulted also from the fact that Sventopolk, ruler over Great Moravia, after being defeated in the south, became duke of Bohemia as vassal of the Franks in 870–871. From his new power base he conquered territories along the Upper Vistula and northern Morava rivers, toward present-day western Slovakia. After an unsuccessful revolt against Arnulf, king of the East Franks, Sventopolk lost the fief of Bohemia, but his own acquisitions remained in the hands of his Marahabiti (or *Marhani, Marahani, Marahenses*), that is, "people from the city of Morava" (which can be identified with the ancient Sirmium and modern Sremska Mitrovica in Yugoslavia). Constantine Porphyrogenitos (*ca.* 950) refers to the region as White Croatia, while Western sources refer to the people as Croats or Moravian-Carinthians, a population originating in a region south of the Danube and associated in the past with Sventopolk.

The ruling family of the White Croats-Moravians, the Slavniks, vassals of Saxony, intermarried in the tenth century with the Přemyslid dynasty of Bohemia, vassals of Bavaria. Due to feuds between the two families, most of the Slavniks were killed (995) and their lands occupied by the Czechs of Bohemia. The survivors sought protection and assistance against the Přemyslids from Boleslaw, duke of Poland. Boleslaw recovered part of the Slavnik realm, including Cracow and the valley of the northern Morava River, and made it a dependency of Poland. The Moravians retained their internal self-government with their own princes and nobility, as well as laws, although there were frequent changes in their feudal associations with neighbors as their suzerains. The Poles lost control over most of Moravia in 1018–1030 to Břetislav of Bohemia. Since Bohemia proper was a single indivisible fief under the kings of Germania, the conquered Moravia, not part of the fief, provided the opportunity to assign appanage principalities to various members of the Přemyslid family beginning in 1054.

In 1182 Frederick I Barbarossa separated Moravia from Bohemia and turned it into a margraviate. The margraves, however, became vassals of Bohemia when the dukes of Bohemia advanced to the position of kings (1212). When the Luxembourg dynasty was in control of Hungary, Bohemia, and Germany, King Sigismund gave Moravia as a fief to his son-in-law, Albert Habsburg of Austria (1423).

After the continuous confessional and political turmoils caused by the teachings of John Hus, Moravia was separated from Bohemia once again (1478–1490) and came under the rule of Matthias Corvinus, king of Hungary. As a result of a marriage and inheritance contract concluded with the Jagiełło dynasty, the Habsburgs inherited Moravia, together with Bohemia, Silesia, Hungary, and Croatia, in 1526.

BIBLIOGRAPHY

For the independent Slavnik period of Moravia's history, see Imre Boba, "Between Poland and Bohemia: The Realm of the Slavniks," in *Symposiones (Tadeusz Suchomirski Festschrift),* Andrzej Żaki, ed. (1981); Francis Dvornik, "The Contest Between Three Dynasties: Piasts, Przemyslides, and Slavniks," in his *The Making of East Central Europe* (1949); Oldřich Králík, *Slavníkovské interludium* (1966), with bibliography and German summary.

IMRE BOBA

[See also **Bohemia-Moravia; Great (or Old) Moravia; Hus, John; Hussites; Jagiełło Dynasty; Přemyslid Dynasty.**]

MOREA, the usual name for the Peloponnese in the late Middle Ages and until the nineteenth century. It began as a local name in the northwestern Peloponnese. As a regional name it covered the plain of Elis or the provinces of Elis and Achaea. After the Fourth Crusade (1198–1204) it gained wide currency, serving as the more frequent name of the principality of Achaea and as a geographical name for all of the Peloponnese. Of disputed etymology, it may derive from *moréa* (mulberry), widely cultivated in the Peloponnese for silk production.

BIBLIOGRAPHY

Antoine Bon, *La Morée franque: Recherches historiques, topographiques, et archéologiques sur la principauté d'Achaie (1205–1430)* (1969); Jean Longnon and Peter Topping, *Documents sur le régime des terres dans la principauté de Morée au XIV*[e] *siècle* (1969).

PETER TOPPING

[See also **Byzantine Empire; Morea, Chronicle of; Morea, Despotate of.**]

MOREA, CHRONICLE OF, an important source for the history of the principality of Achaea or Morea (1205–1430), especially in its first century. There are three principal versions, all anonymous: a prose account in French, a verse epic in the Greek vernacular of Morea, and an Aragonese chronicle completed in 1393 that brings the narrative of events down to 1377. A fourth version, an Italian translation from the Greek, has little independent value.

The lost prototype of the chronicle was composed about the beginning of the fourteenth century. It was probably written in the French spoken by the feudal aristocracy of the principality. The surviving manuscript of the French version was copied about 1400 in Burgundy and depended, through an intermediary model of the 1340's, on a redaction that may have dated back to about 1320. This redaction was an abridgment of the prototype. A highly plausible case has been made by Spadaro, Jacoby, and Lurier for the priority of the French version over the Greek and for a prototype in French. Nevertheless, an older opinion held by Schmitt that the Greek chronicle precedes the French has recently been revived by Jeffreys and Stanitsas. Further analysis of the close relationship between the French and Greek versions may yet resolve the problem of priority and of the language of the original. (Longnon's hypothesis of an Italian prototype, although supported by Bon, has not won favor.)

The anonymous redactors of the French and Greek chronicles glorified the deeds of the Villehardouin princes and the Moreote barons of the thirteenth century. They hoped thereby to inspire their listeners to defend the beleaguered principality of their time. They expressed—especially in the Greek chronicle, the oldest manuscript—strong anti-Orthodox prejudice. Much in the chronicles is legendary. But they are a precious record of the feudal customs and society of the longest-lived state founded by the barons of the Fourth Crusades.

BIBLIOGRAPHY

David Jacoby, "Quelques considerations sur les versions de la 'Chronique de Morée,'" in *Journal des savants,* **153** (1968) (the first note on pp. 133–134 lists the standard editions of the French, Greek, Aragonese, and Italian versions); Michael Jeffreys, "The Chronicle of the Morea: Priority of the Greek Version," in *Byzantinische Zeitschrift,* **68** (1975); Harold E. Lurier, trans., *Crusaders as Conquerors: The Chronicle of Morea* (1964); Kenneth M. Setton, *The Papacy and the Levant, 1204–1571,* I (1976), 154–158.

PETER TOPPING

[See also **Byzantine Empire: History; Byzantine Literature; Morea.**]

MOREA, DESPOTATE OF, established in the Byzantine province in Morea (the Peloponnese) from 1348/1349 until 1460. The despotate began when John VI Kantakouzenos appointed his second son Manuel despot in 1348/1349. He served until his death in 1380. Under his firm and enlightened rule Byzantine Morea was better organized and more prosperous than the declining principality of Achaea and the imperial center at Constantinople. After the brief administrations of Manuel's brother and nephew, the despots were all drawn from the legitimate dynasty of the Palaiologoi, beginning with Theodore I (1383–1407). The Byzantine lands were now tributary to the Ottoman Turks. Theodore tried without success to establish the Hospitalers of Rhodes as a bulwark in the despotate (1397 and 1400–1404). In a notable visit (1415–1416) Emperor Manuel II Palaiologos helped to strengthen the regime of his second son, the despot Theodore II (1407–1443). He rebuilt Justinian's wall (Hexamilion) across the Isthmus of Corinth and disciplined the unruly landed magnates.

Further expansion of the Byzantine territory in the west and north of the Peloponnese took place in 1417/1418. Despite the destruction of the Hexamilion and an invasion by the Turks in 1423, Manuel's sons, Theodore, Constantine, and Thomas, now sharing the despotate, completed the conquest of Achaea by 1430. The entire Morea, save for Venice's outposts at Modon (Methone), Coron (Korone), Nauplia, and Argos, was again in Greek hands. Constantine, from his base in Mistra, refortified the Hexamilion and briefly (1443–1446) reestablished Byzantine authority in continental Greece to the Pindus. This provoked an invasion by the Turks in late 1446; their cannons demolished the isthmian wall, and after ravaging much of the country they withdrew with many prisoners. The despots again paid tribute to the sultan and resumed their own bitter rivalry and feuding. Constantine, the last Roman emperor (1449–1453), was crowned in Mistra on 6 January 1449.

The last despots of Morea were Manuel II's sons Thomas and Demetrios (1449–1460), the former ruling the northwestern section, the latter the remainder from Mistra. Sultan Mehmed (Muḥammad) II made certain the brothers would not aid Constantinople in its final siege by sending an invading force into the Peloponnese in late 1452. A rising of the inhabitants (1452–1454), who now included many Albanian settlers, was put down with Turkish intervention. It was always possible that the strategic peninsula of Morea—after 1453 the last outpost of Byzantium in Europe—would become the base for a crusade against the Ottoman Empire. To prevent this, Mehmed II himself led armies across the isthmus in 1458 and 1460 to end the despotate's existence. Thomas fled via Corfu to Italy; he died in Rome in 1465, a pensioner of the pope. The sultan rewarded his prisoner Demetrios for his usually pro-Turkish attitude with a pension and the grant of income from several northern Aegean islands.

By surrendering Mistra without resistance Demetrios helped to preserve a significant part of the religious architecture and painting of this famous late-Byzantine city. Capital of the autonomous despotate, and enjoying relative security, Mistra was the center of an artistic and intellectual renaissance significant for European culture. It attracted many of the leading scholars and ecclesiastics of Byzantium's last century. These included George Gemistos Plethon, Isidore of Kiev, Bessarion of Nicaea, and George Gennadios Scholarios.

BIBLIOGRAPHY

Donald M. Nicol, *The Last Centuries of Byzantium, 1261–1453* (1972); Steven Runciman, *Mistra: Byzantine Capital of the Peloponnese* (1980); Denis A. Zakythinos, *Le despotat grec de Morée,* 2 vols. (1975).

PETER TOPPING

[See also **Byzantine Empire; Constantine XI Palaiologos; Manuel II Palaiologos; Mehmed (Muḥammad) II; Michael VIII Palaiologos; Morea; Palaiologoi.**]

MOREL, PIERRE (*fl. ca.* 1386–1402), architect and sculptor active in Lyons and Avignon. As master of works, he began the Celestines' church in Avignon and designed the tomb of Clement VII, antipope. He probably also directed construction of the choir of St. Martial and the tomb of Cardinal Jean de La Grange in Avignon.

BIBLIOGRAPHY

Françoise Baron, "Collèges apostoliques et Couronnement de la Vierge dans la sculpture avignonnaise des XIVe et XVe siècles," in *Revue du Louvre et des musées de France,* **29** (1979); Anne M. Morganstern, "Pierre Morel, Master of Works in Avignon," in *Art Bulletin,* **58** (1976).

ANNE M. MORGANSTERN

[See also **Architect, Status of; Avignon; Celestines; Schism, Great.**]

MORIZ VON CRAÛN. Since the Middle High German verse novella *Moriz von Craûn* appears only in a single, late manuscript, names no author, and is mentioned by no medieval writer, it has not been possible to determine precisely the circumstances of its composition. Rhyme studies of the extant version indicate that the work was originally in one of the dialects of the region between Strassburg and Worms, and investigations of style and literary influences have produced estimated dates of compo-

Choir vault by Pierre Morel from the Celestine church at Avignon, 1396–1398. © ARCH. PHOT. PARIS/S.P.A.D.E.M.

sition that extend from 1180 to 1230. The names of the chief characters are those of historical figures. The best-known of several lords of Craon with the name Maurice was Maurice II (*d.* 1196). If he is the hero of the story, then the wife of his neighbor, Viscount Richard de Beaumont, is the heroine. However, it is unlikely that the events described had any factual basis.

The novella has a long introduction that is divided into two parts. One tells of the rise and fall of chivalry in Greece and Rome, and of its flourishing in France at the time of Charlemagne; the other discusses the nature of courtly love. The story proper begins when the countess of Beaumont promises Moriz a lover's pay if he will arrange a tournament for her.

To attract participants to the tournament (and gain fame for himself), the hero has a splendid ship built on wheels and, drawn by hidden horses, journeys in it through France to the lady's castle. In the contests that follow, he performs prodigious feats and later displays extravagant generosity in giving away ship, horses, and even a part of his armor. When the lady nevertheless refuses to keep the bargain, Moriz comes to her bedroom at night to demand his due. Her husband awakens and believes the intruder to be the ghost of a knight he had accidentally killed in the tournament. He jumps up, bumps his shin, and faints. Thereupon the hero takes his place in the bed, and the lady gives him the reward. He renounces her, however, and goes off to win further fame by knightly exploits. In a lyrical final scene the lady repents of her failure to be true to the code of courtly love and grieves at being forsaken by her knight.

The work is a hilarious farce that lampoons the literary conceits of knighthood and courtly love by supporting them with ridiculous arguments and by gross exaggeration. The artificiality of mock battles and devotion to other men's wives in return for their favors is compared by juxtaposition with the world-shaking conquests of the Greeks, Julius Caesar, and Charlemagne. The irony of the tale is aptly expressed in the narrator's reference to Moriz as a mighty warrior when he rises from the lady's bed. The most pronounced German influences on the novella are those of the *Kaiserchronik,* Heinrich von Veldeke, and Hartman von Aue. Its chief source was probably a lost French version that was closely related to the story, "Du chevalier qui recovra l'amor de sa dame."

BIBLIOGRAPHY

The extant text, a reconstructed text, and an extensive bibliography are in Ulrich Pretzel, ed., *Moriz von Craûn,* 4th ed. (1973). An English translation with an introduction is in J. W. Thomas, *The Best Novellas of Medieval Germany* (1984).

Studies include Robert Ralph Anderson, comp., *Wortindex und Reimregister zum Moriz von Craûn* (1975); R. Folz, "L'histoire de la chevalerie d'après *Moriz von Craûn,*" in *Études germaniques,* 32 (1977); Heimo Reinitzer, "Zeder und Aloe: Zur Herkunft des Bettes Salomos im *Moriz von Craûn,*" in *Archiv für Kulturgeschichte,* 58 (1976), and "Zu den Tiervergleichen und zur Interpretation des *Moriz von Craûn,*" in *Germanisch-romanische Monatsschrift,* 2nd ser., 27 (1977); Naoko Watanabe, "Die Minne im 'Moriz von Craun,'" in *Doitsu Bungaku,* 55 (1975).

J. WESLEY THOMAS

[See also **Ambraser Heldenbuch; German Literature: Romance; Middle High German Literature.**]

MORTE DARTHUR, LE. See **Malory, Sir Thomas.**

MORTMAIN, one of several conditions into which property might pass when conveyed to the church or to a corporate body of ecclesiastical origin. The condition known as mortmain, or the dead hand, emphasized the future and permanent inalienability of the property conveyed and the peculiar nature of the church as possessor. Some scholars believe that the word "mortmain" was intended to express the notion of impersonal ownership, that is, ownership without reference to any individual possessor. Others interpret it to mean the exclusion of certain lands from ordinary commerce. This is certainly what it came to mean, but it can hardly have been the original signification. A third (and likely) possibility is that mortmain expressed the extinction of an overlord's power, that is, hand *(manus),* over property. Whatever the truth, the frequency of such grants accounts for the enormous wealth of the medieval church considered as a whole, although no single ecclesiastical institution was necessarily dependent for its survival or prestige solely on its property held in mortmain.

Around grants in mortmain there grew up a considerable body of legislation and speculation. Canonists and civilians devoted much time and effort to the theories and consequences of inalienability; and their ideas played a role in the development of the civil law of corporations and trusts and the public law of the state. Legists working in the secular tradition (common lawyers and civilians) also devoted a great deal of time to devising ways to eliminate, curtail, or compensate for such grants, because it was difficult (in some cases theoretically impossible) for overlords to get feudal incidents paid from fiefs so granted: the church never died; so, there could be no relief. The church never married; so, there could be no incident of marriage. The church was never a minor (except in the metaphorical sense that an administrator such as an abbot had "guardianship" over the property of his church); so, there could be no feudal incident of wardship.

In several countries statutes were enacted restricting the dead hand. In England, the Statute of Mortmain, otherwise known as *De viris religiosis* (1279, but with many less formal precursors), prohibited grants in mortmain without the permission of the overlord of the grantor and gave the overlord a remedy in the royal courts in case his permission was not (or was not properly) acquired. This statute, however, did not noticeably diminish such grants, since permission could be obtained rather easily for a price. Indeed, the end of the story in England did not come until the Mortmain Act of 1888. In France, there was an *ordonnance* in 1275 (substantially strengthened in 1291–1292) aimed at restraining conveyancing of fiefs. That part of it concerning grants to the church (amortizations) held that ecclesiastics could hold feudal property, whose incidents were thus lost, on condition that they paid for the privilege of doing so on a sliding scale indexed according to the annual income of the fief.

The ideal of the absolute inalienability of church property and of tenure without liability for feudal incidents was only an ideal. In the early Middle Ages (when the legal theory was not fully developed) and in the Renaissance (when it was decaying) rulers fairly frequently retook possession of ecclesiastical holdings or imposed arbitrary fines, allegedly for the greater benefit of the realm or in urgent necessity. Outstanding examples are Charles Martel's and Henry VIII of England's seizures of church lands in the eighth and sixteenth centuries respectively. In the High Middle Ages such seizures and arbitrary taxation were less frequent though by no means unknown. But even when, in this period, a monastic order was dissolved with the connivance and at the order of the state, it was more likely for the property of the order to be redistributed among other orders than appropriated by the secular authorities. The property of the Templars (dissolved 1312) was assigned, for example, to the Hospitalers.

Mortmain has persisted in some regions until modern times in modified form.

BIBLIOGRAPHY

John Bell Henneman, *Royal Taxation in Fourteenth Century France* (1971), *s.v.* "amortissement"; Ernst Kantorowicz, *The King's Two Bodies* (1957), esp. 164–192 and *s. v.* "inalienability"; Bryce Lyon, *A Constitutional and Legal History of Medieval England,* 2nd ed. (1980); Gaines Post, *Studies in Medieval Legal Thought* (1964); Joseph R. Strayer, *The Reign of Philip the Fair* (1980).

WILLIAM CHESTER JORDAN

[See also **Charles Martel; Law, English Common; Law, French.**]

MOSAIC AND MOSAIC MAKING. Mosaic is a decorative technique that belongs to the larger category of painting. It is generally used on architectural surfaces such as walls and floors. The compositions are executed with small elements (varying from a few square millimeters to a few square centimeters), mostly square—but occasionally also round, triangular, or splintered—called tesserae (Greek: *abakiskoi, psiphides;* Latin: *abaculi, tessellae, tesserae*). Usually cubes of glass paste (smalts) and stone, sometime terracotta, but occasionally mother-of-pearl, these tesserae are inserted in a setting bed, most commonly fresh mortar, which is applied on the architectural supporting structure.

The regularity of the tesserae (shape and setting) and a consistent set of rules for their arrangement can, in the hands of expert craftsmen, produce a highly decorative rendition of pictorial compositions. This craftsmanship—possible only within a workshop system—and the monumental character of the structures decorated with mosaic depend on a continuous tradition and unstinting patronage.

In the Middle Ages, mosaic making, which had developed in the Greco-Roman world, became linked with the Byzantine Empire. The splendor displayed in the decoration of Byzantine churches

MOSAIC AND MOSAIC MAKING

aimed to create a frame of timeless, heavenly beauty for the celebration of the Christian liturgy. Better than frescoes, mosaics, with their glitter and abstract gold background, were more apt to produce the powerful illusion of a space enclosing both the depiction of the heavenly realm and the earthly realm of the worshippers together. In the words of Photios: "It is as if one had entered heaven itself with no one barring one's way from any side, and was illuminated by the beauty in all forms shining all around like so many stars, so is one utterly amazed. Thenceforth it seems that everything is in ecstatic motion, and the church itself is circling around" (*Homilies* X, Cyril A. Mango, trans. [1958]).

The prestige associated with this exclusive, imperial decorating technique accounts in part for its favor with rising powers such as Charlemagne's Frankish empire, Kievan Rus, Venice, Norman Sicily, Georgia, and the Umayyad caliphate. These patrons relied on Byzantine workshops. While differences in the technical quality of such mosaics make it impossible to distinguish between Byzantine mosaicists and their foreign apprentices, the various local patrons employing the Byzantine craftsmen determined the specific subjects to be illustrated. The main repositories of wall-mosaic decorations are in Turkey (İstanbul), Greece (Salonika, Hosios Lukas, Nea Moni on Chios, Daphni near Athens, and Arta), Italy (Rome, Campania, Milan, Ravenna, Venice and its surroundings, and Sicily), Cyprus, at Sinai, and in Bethlehem. Outside the Mediterranean region, mosaics of Byzantine execution or inspiration survive from Kievan Rus, Georgia, and the Carolingian Empire.

Later, mosaic workshops with artists trained in medieval Venice proliferated from Rome and Florence to Prague. But in the Renaissance the mosaic craft became associated with the medieval aesthetic and was thus relegated to a marginal role in monumental pictorial decoration. The conventions of mosaic making were altered to make it just another way of painting, and gradually the technique disappeared altogether. Interest in it developed again much later in connection with concern for the preservation and restoration of monuments, but the medieval function of mosaic decoration was never revived.

Despite the rigid nature of the materials used, a competent mosaic workshop was able to produce effects every bit as subtle as any painted decoration. In fact, the mosaic, fresco, and miniature paintings of a given period share a common repertoire of iconographic and stylistic conventions and as such differ less by genre than by specific workshop characteristics.

Mosaic needed careful preparation in all phases, from the production of the glass paste and the layout of each decoration to the actual setting of the tesserae.

The glass tesserae, more than the stone, were responsible for most of the hues in any given decoration, including the gold glass abundantly employed for backgrounds. The glass paste was baked in ovens in small batches shaped like pancakes and then cut with a hammer over a sharp edge with a regular wrist movement to insure the regularity of the tesserae. For some of the tesserae the fresh cut was on the visible side while in others the duller surfaces from the top or bottom of the pancake were used. The gold glass was produced by having a base of transparent glass—mostly light or dark bottle green, amber, or light blue—topped by a very thin gold leaf and sealed by a thin glass lid on top. The gold tesserae have suffered more noticeably from atmospheric pollution, and often various substances have infiltrated this "sandwich," causing the upper lid to become detached and fall, the unprotected gold leaf to wear, and the glass base of the tessera to look from a certain distance like a black dot in the general gold background.

The other element of which mosaic is made, stone of various qualities and colors, even sometimes marble, was used mostly for the flesh tones (faces and limbs) and for the garments; the selection differs only slightly in quality and range from workshop to workshop. Because of its porous structure, the terracotta, like some of the stones, was used to tone down the glow of the glass. Mother-of-pearl was employed very infrequently for ornamental background. Pearls in jewelry, costumes, or bookbindings are represented by large, plain white limestone tesserae shaped like teardrops or spheres. The richness and complexity of the palette, as well as the ability to combine various materials for color and design, testified to a workshop's degree of competence.

The ratio of various materials used by a workshop was determined by clear prescriptions but also by availability. When some of the prescribed glass or marble categories were in short supply, replacement with lesser quality stones or simplification of the range of tones for highlights and shadows became necessary. We know of several instances when tesserae were reused: in Constantinople itself, the emperor Basil I (*d.* 886) and the patriarch Michael Keroularios (*d.* 1058) had mosaicists use tesserae stripped from older monuments. In the West, Charlemagne received permission from the pope to transport mosaics from Ravenna to his capital at Aachen, and, much later, the Venetians participating in the Fourth Crusade (1204) brought home mosaic tesserae along with other booty. These examples, among others, indicate the limitation of supplies and the value attached to the mosaic pieces.

On a given work of architecture, the composition was laid out by means of a first rough sketch, called the "sinopia" from the red color used to draw it on the first, coarse layer of plaster or, less frequently, directly on the brick structure (for the latter case, examples have been found in Salonika's Hagios Giorgios rotunda, late fourth century, and in Ravenna's S. Apollinare in Classe). There is evidence that radical changes could be made between this sinopia phase and the final mosaic (examples may be found in S. Apollinare in Classe and S. Maria Maggiore in Rome).

The first layer of mortar was then prepared by making indentations ("scalette") in its surface to receive the next, finer layer or layers over it, on which a full-scale model of the mosaic to be represented was painted with several colors. Because of the technical characteristics of mosaic making, the setting-bed layer, which had to remain fresh or wet when the tesserae were implanted, could not be laid out in batches larger than a single workload at a time, which means that the full-scale model was also painted in sequence, following the indications of the general layout still visible underneath. This full-scale underpainting, exposed when tesserae fall off the wall or when the mosaic crust is lifted for purposes of restoration, has been found in every monument examined, from Constantinople and Asia Minor to Greece and Italy.

In most wall mosaics that have been preserved, the tesserae were inserted on the setting bed perpendicular to the wall's surface (*not* at an angle) with small, regular interstices between them, creating a

S. Apollinare as shepherd. Apse mosaic from S. Apollinare in Classe, Ravenna, late 6th–early 7th century.
ALINARI/ART RESOURCE

MOSAIC AND MOSAIC MAKING

harmonious texture. (When the interstices are totally filled with plaster, mostly as a result of bad restorations having lifted the mosaics from the wall, the texture hardens and loses its original aspect.) The setting of the tesserae in rows over the painted shapes was done in conformity with certain rules that emphasized each individual unit inside the figure and created the illusion of volume. In the empty background, rows are usually set horizontally, but sometimes they are set in a pattern (for example, the scalloped background for the Deesis in Constantinople's Hagia Sophia). In most mosaics, the figures are framed against their surrounding background through one or two contouring rows made up of the same materials as are used in the background.

While we have some information about the differences in the salaries of various craftsmen in Diocletian's edict of 301 regulating wages—from 50–60 sesterces for the *lapidarius structor* (stone mason), the *calcis coctor* (lime burner), and the *musearius* (mosaicist), to 75 sesterces for the *pictor parietarius* (wall painter), and 175 sesterces for the *pictor imaginarius* (scene or image painter)—no preserved contemporary text informs us about the workshop's division of work. A scrutiny of the mosaics themselves can supply some of the data. Even in high-quality and homogeneous workshops, some differences will be noticeable between the more difficult sections of a mosaic (mostly heads) and other sections (bodies and garments, followed by backgrounds and ornaments).

The heads required a greater diversity of materials and a more precise fitting of the tesserae than did other sections, according to complex—if traditional—patterns of shading and highlighting. The figure's volume, portraitlike quality, and spiritual impact had to be achieved chiefly in the rendering of the head; therefore, this feature was entrusted to the workshop's most skilled member and usually executed first, while secondary sections would follow in sequence.

Evidence of mosaicists working side by side is most visible in the more standard sections, such as groups of feet or vegetal and ornamental frames. In such areas, the differences in the selection of materials (the ratio of various shades to each other), along with small personal idiosyncrasies and the carefully concealed sutures between workloads, distinguish the presence of more than one worker. The sutures further inform us about the sequence in the setting of mosaics: from top to bottom (scaffolding levels are sometimes easy to notice) and from the center (or focus) of a scene to the sides.

Some workshops were less homogeneous in terms of the personal style and even the technical competence of their members. While in the eleventh-century wall mosaics of Hosios Lukas (Phocis) several masters can be identified chiefly by their level of competence, at Daphni, near Athens (Church of the Dormition, *ca.* 1100), mosaics testify to different stylistic trends coexisting within the same workshop. But in all mosaic workshops, ranging from Kiev to Italy, and including the ones active in the Byzantine Empire, the technical vocabulary shows a remarkable homogeneity pointing to a centralized system of training mosaicists. Conformity to this system is the measure by which the achievement of such workshops must be judged. As a rule, all parts of the decoration are executed with the same high technical competence, whether it is readily visible to the average viewer or not.

Floor mosaics, which appeared in the Hellenistic period and reached their highest level of popularity in the late Roman world, were still in use throughout the Middle Ages. The category that best survived, the *opus sectile,* made with larger elements of colored marbles than the *opus tesselatum,* was produced mostly in Byzantium and in papal Italy. The *opus tesselatum,* mostly employed in the late Roman Empire, gradually declined afterward, though in the West it persisted well into the Middle Ages. A large

Floor mosaic, Church of the Pantokrator, İstanbul, 1124. COURTESY OF THE BYZANTINE PHOTOGRAPH COLLECTION, PA-III-Oh (62), © 1986, Dumbarton Oaks, Trustees of Harvard University, Washington, D.C.

Christ enthroned between Emperor Constantine Monomachos and Empress Zoe. South Gallery, Hagia Sophia, İstanbul, early 11th century. COURTESY OF THE BYZANTINE PHOTOGRAPH COLLECTION, S.I-H-I. (38), © 1986, Dumbarton Oaks, Trustees of Harvard University, Washington, D.C.

figurative complex made with *opus tesselatum,* discovered in İstanbul in the area of the Great Palace, has not yet been satisfactorily identified, but most authors date it to the end of the sixth century.

Starting with the eleventh century, a revival of decorative crafts—including floor mosaic—connected with Byzantine imports and influence is noticeable across Italy and matches a comparable relative abundance of *opus sectile* floors in Greece and Asia Minor. The best preserved example is that found in the twelfth-century Church of the Pantokrator, part of the present-day Zeyrek Camii in İstanbul. The patterns of large slabs, geometric borders, and roundels typify the Byzantine conception of a floor decoration. In the church of Hagia Sophia the original pavement (restored several times), made of large marble slabs displayed in a symmetric, mirrorlike pattern, is divided by marble bands of contrasting colors in topographic sections connected by written sources with liturgy and cermonial. Traces of such functions for pavements survive in Venice and in the production of local Italian workshops. The latter, however, reflect the adaptation of the general principles to the local liturgical requirements and to the local availability of materials (partly explaining the preference for highly decorated fields rather than plain, large marble slabs).

The technique of *opus sectile* preserved through

Virgin (detail) from the John II Komnenos Panel, South Gallery, Hagia Sophia, İstanbul, 12th century. COURTESY OF THE BYZANTINE PHOTOGRAPH COLLECTION, S.I-I.2.8, © 1986, Dumbarton Oaks, Trustees of Harvard University, Washington, D.C.

the local Roman imperial tradition was of course available in Italy to serve as a model for the Carolingian revival. A large group of Western patrons favored illustrated floors, with moralizing and cosmological contents, executed mainly in a mixture of both *opus sectile* and *opus tesselatum.* Some examples of such floors survive in France, Germany, and Italy. After the first half of the thirteenth century, however, the production of floor mosaics with medieval techniques went out of fashion, to be replaced chiefly by ceramic tile floors, which were cheaper to produce.

BIBLIOGRAPHY

For detailed bibliographies, see V. Glasberg, *Répertoire de la mosaïque médiévale pariétale et portative* (1974); Ernst Kitzinger *et al.*, "Mosaico," in *Enciclopedia universale dell'arte italiana,* IX (1963); Victor N. Lazarev, *Storia della pintura bizantina* (1967).

For wall mosaics only, see Hans Belting, Cyril Mango, and Doula Mouriki, *The Mosaics and Frescoes of St. Mary Pammakaristos (Fethiye Camii) at Istanbul* (1978); Beat Brenk, *Die früchristlichen Mosaiken in Santa Maria Maggiore zu Rom* (1975); Robin Cormack and Ernest J. W. Hawkins, "The Mosaics of St. Sophia at Istanbul: The Rooms Above the Southwest Vestibule and Ramp," in *Dumbarton Oaks Papers,* **31** (1977); Robin Cormack, "Interpreting the Mosaics of St. Sophia at Istanbul," in *Art History,* **4** (1981); Cäcilia Davis-Weyer, "Das Apsismosaik Leos III. in S. Susanna," in *Zeitschrift für Kunstgeschichte,* **28** (1965), "Die Mosaiken Leos III. und die Anfänge der Karolingischen Renaissance in Rom," *ibid.,* **29** (1966); Friedrich W. Deichmann, *Ravenna: Haupstadt des spätantike Abendlandes,* 3 vols. (1969–1974); Otto Demus, with R. Kloos and Kurt Weitzmann, *The Mosaics of San Marco in Venice* (1984); George H. Forsyth and Kurt Weitzmann, *The Monastery of Saint Catherine at Mt. Sinai: The Church and Fortress of Justinian* (1973); Ernst Kitzinger, *The Art of Byzantium and the Medieval West,* W. E. Kleinbauer, ed. (1976); George P. Majeska, "Notes on the Archeology of St. Sophia at Constantinople: The Green Marble Bands on the Floor," in *Dumbarton Oaks Papers,* **32** (1978); Arthur H. S. Megaw, "Notes on Recent Work of the Byzantine Institute in Istanbul," *ibid.,* **17** (1963), and, with Ernest J. W. Hawkins, *The Church of the Panagia Kanakarià at Lythrankomi in Cyprus: Its Mosaics and Frescoes* (1977); Robert L. Van Nice, *Santa Sophia in Istanbul: An Architectural Survey. Installment I* (1966).

For floor mosaics, see also Xavier Barral i Altet, *Le temps des croisades* (1982), *Les royaumes d'Occident* (1983), and *Les mosaïques de pavement médiévales de Venise, Murano, Torcello* (1985); Dorothy F. Glass, *Studies on Cosmatesque Pavements* (1980); Federico Guidobaldi and Alessandra Guiglia Guidobaldi, *Pavimenti marmorei di Roma dal IV al IX secolo* (1983); Alessandra Guiglia Guidobaldi, "Tradizione locale e influenze bizantine nei pavimenti cosmateschi," in *Bollettino d'arte,* **69**, ser. 6, no. 26 (1984); Hiltrud Kier, *Der mittelalterliche Schmuckfussboden* (1970).

IRINA ANDREESCU TREADGOLD

[See also **Byzantine Art; Constantinople; Early Christian Art; Hagia Sophia; Hosios Lukas; Ravenna; Rome.**]

MOSAN ART. The art of the valley of the Meuse during the eleventh, twelfth, and early thirteenth centuries forms a coherent and recognizable whole distinguishable from that of neighboring regions. The Mosan area was largely within the boundaries of the bishopric of Liège, which was politically linked to the Holy Roman Empire and ecclesiastically to the archbishopric of Cologne. As might be expected, its closest artistic affinities are with the art of Cologne and the Rhineland.

MOSAN ART

Brass baptismal font from the church of Notre-Dame-aux-Fonts, Liège (now in St. Barthélemy, Liège). Rainer of Huy, 1107–1118. PHOTO: A. C. L., BRUSSELS

The Meuse Valley lay within the heartland of the Carolingian Empire, and therefore it is hardly surprising that the dominant stylistic source is the Carolingian tradition, especially its most classicizing, plastic, and illusionistic styles. This derivation is seen most clearly in ninth- and tenth-century illuminated manuscripts of Mosan provenance and, in the eleventh century, in the group of so-called "small-figured" ivories.

In the twelfth-century Mosan area, the clearest manifestation of the classicizing style (which most clearly distinguishes it from the Romanesque of France, England, Germany, or Italy) is seen in the brass baptismal fonts executed by Rainer of Huy for the church of Notre-Dame-aux-Fonts, Liège, between 1107 and 1118. Here we see organically articulated, plastically modeled figures, whose drapery reveals the body beneath; they turn freely in space, feet firmly planted on a wavy groundline, and are set against a neutral background.

Mosan twelfth-century art shares, however, in the Romanesque style of northern Europe in its treatment of space. Here, as elsewhere, the figure and ground are bound together in the same plane, interlocking with a frame that is frequently subdivided for greater clarity of exposition. A good example of this trend can be seen in the Floreffe Bible, where an elaborate exegesis on the biblical text of Job, based on the commentaries of Gregory the Great, is expounded visually by means of a geometric compartmentalization of the field. It is this combination of a classicizing figure style (however attenuated by heavy contour and calligraphic play of draperies) with the planar spatiality of the field that makes possible the visual coordination and juxtaposition of complex theological ideas, so aptly expressed by the Floreffe Bible. The style here described can be found not only in Mosan illuminated manuscripts (which are probably its basic source), but also in goldsmithery, as seen for example in the Stavelot portable altar of about 1160.

It is evident from the various extant works that the twelfth century in the Meuse region was a period of intense exchange of ideas among media: visual concepts developed in one medium were rapidly

The Three Theological Virtues and the Seven Gifts of the Holy Spirit. Miniature (illustrating Job 1:1–4) from the Floreffe Bible, 1165–1180. BY PERMISSION OF THE BRITISH LIBRARY, LONDON, ADD. MS 17738, fol. 3v

adopted in other media and carried, via small-scale objects, into regions as far-flung as Italy, Poland, and England. The iconography of the Meuse valley is distinctive in its emphasis upon visual concordances between motifs or scenes from the Old and New Testaments.

Goldsmithery was the mistress of the arts in the twelfth-century Meuse region, executed on commission, and perhaps on site, often by traveling workshops. The quantity of work was restricted and was consistently of exceptionally fine craftsmanship.

The culmination of the Mosan style lay in the works executed by Nicholas of Verdun, whose dated works range from 1181 to 1205, and by his followers. An example of his work, the Shrine of the Three Kings in Cologne Cathedral, makes explicit both his indebtedness to the earlier Mosan tradition (such as Rainer of Huy) and the primacy of his contribution to the sculpture of the Gothic style in France. His figures, in contradistinction to those of Rainer, are fully freed from the spatial confines of both the frame and the neutral ground, inhabiting as they do a space cell that allows for varied gesture and more individualized expression.

BIBLIOGRAPHY

Joseph de Borchgrave d'Altena, "Essai de bibliographie concernant l'orfèvrerie mosane des origines à 1300," in *Annales de la societé royale d'archéologie de Bruxelles,* 52 (1973); Suzanne Collon-Gevaert, *Histoire des arts du métal en Belgique* (1951); Suzanne Collon-Gevaert *et al., Art roman dans la vallée de la Meuse aux XIe et XIIe siècles* (1962); C. R. Dodwell, *Painting in Europe, 800–1200* (1971); Pierre Francastel, ed., *L'art mosan* (1953); Danielle Gaborit-Chopin, *Elfenbeinkunst im Mittelalter* (1978); Marie Madeleine Gauthier, *Émaux du moyen âge occidental* (1972); André Grabar and Carl Nordenfalk, *Early Medieval Painting* (1957); Peter Lasko, *Ars Sacra, 800–1200* (1972); François Masai, "Les manuscrits à peintures de Sambre et Meuse au XIe et XIIe siècles," in *Cahiers de civilisation médiévale,* 3 (1960); *Rhein und Maas: Kunst und Kultur 800–1400,* I and II (1972–1973); Félix Rousseau, *La Meuse et le pays mosan en Belgique* (1977); Jacques Stiennon, "Du lectionnaire de Saint-Trond aux Évangiles d'Averbode," in *Scriptorium,* 7 (1953); Hanns Swarzenski, *Monuments of Romanesque Art* (1954); J. J. M. Timmers, *De Kunst van het Maasland* (1971); Lisbeth Tollenaere, *La sculpture sur pierre de l'ancien diocèse de Liège à l'époque romane* (1957); *The Year 1200: A Symposium* (Metropolitan Museum of Art), 2 vols. (1970).

GRETEL CHAPMAN

[See also **Bronze and Brass; Enamel; Godefroid of Huy; Manuscript Illumination, European; Metalsmiths, Gold and Silver; Nicholas of Verdun; Pre-Romanesque Art; Rainer of Huy; Romanesque Art.**]

MOSCOW. See **Muscovy, Rise of.**

MOSCOW KREMLIN, ART AND ARCHITECTURE. Major building began in the Moscow Kremlin only after the wooden fortifications were replaced by stone walls in the 1360's. The present towers were added during the late fifteenth century by Italian architects, although the preserved tower roofs date only from the seventeenth century.

The centerpiece of the collection of medieval buildings within the Kremlin walls is the great Uspensky (Dormition) Cathedral built by the Italian architect Aristotele Fioravanti for Ivan III the Great (1462–1505) between 1475 and 1479 as the coronation church of the Muscovite rulers and the primatial cathedral of the Russian church. Applying the mathematical and engineering skills and advanced building techniques he had learned in Italy to the early architectural heritage of northeast Russia, Fioravanti created a "neo-Vladimirian" architectural style that dominated the planning of major churches in the Muscovite realm up to the eighteenth century. Although following a traditional five-dome, six-pier, Byzantine-inspired plan, the architect dispensed with the interior galleries typical of large Russian churches and created a great high open internal area of matching vaulted and domed compartments. The interior was covered with frescoes by the famous painter Dionysios the Greek and his school, although most of them have now been replaced by seventeenth-century work.

Two smaller Kremlin churches were rebuilt by Pskovian architects in the 1480's, the single-domed Rizpolozhenie Church (Church of the Deposition of the Robe, 1486) and the charming three-domed Blagoveshchensky Cathedral (Cathedral of the Annunciation, 1482–1490), the private chapel of the tsar and his family. The latter church was decorated by three of the greatest medieval Russian painters, Theophanes the Greek, Andrei Rublev, and Prokhor of Gorodets, and although their frescoes have perished (to be replaced, however, by fine sixteenth-century murals), a number of their icons are preserved in the nineteenth-century iconostasis of the church. In the 1560's, Ivan the Terrible added galleries

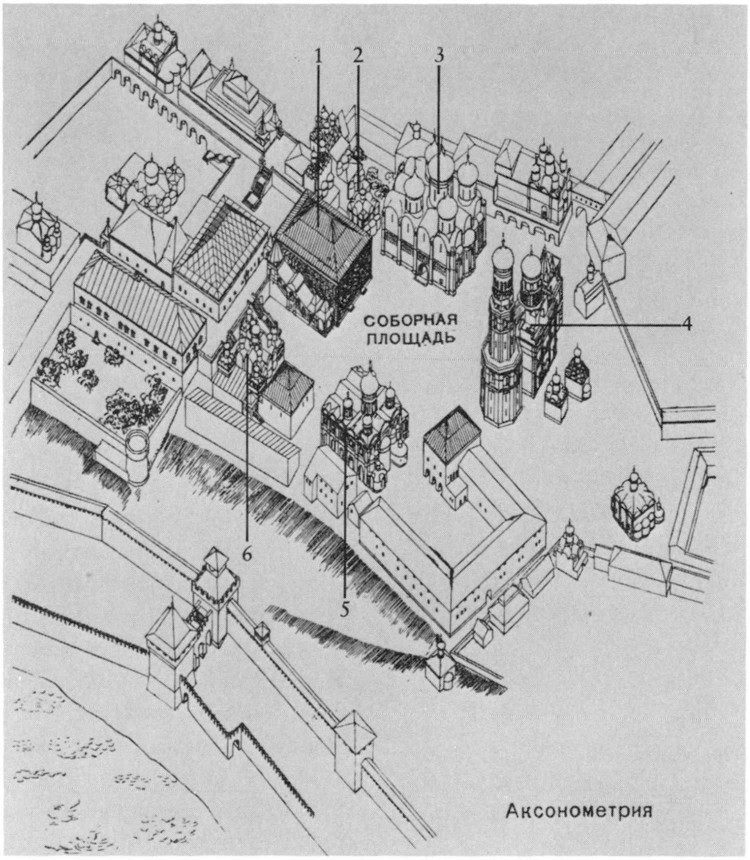

Moscow Kremlin in late medieval times (reconstruction): (*1*) Granovitaya Palace; (*2*) Rizpolozhenie Church; (*3*) Uspensky Cathedral; (*4*) Bell Tower of Ivan the Great; (*5*) Arkhangelsky Cathedral; (*6*) Blagoveshchensky Cathedral. FROM *RUSSKOE ZODCHESTVO* (1953)

around the church on three sides and six additional gilded domes, giving the building its present picturesque appearance.

The last of the major medieval churches of the Moscow Kremlin is the Arkhangelsky Cathedral built by the Italian Alevisio Novyi ("the Younger") in 1508. It is a six-piered church with five domes; the facade owes much to Italian Renaissance style. Decorated with frescoes of the rulers of Russia by Dionysios the Greek (almost all lost under repainting), this church served as the burial place of the rulers of Russia up to the time of Peter the Great.

There are other medieval structures preserved in the Kremlin besides churches. The Granovitaya Palace (the Palace of the Facets), an impressive, if small, building with its main facade in diamond-cut stones (whence the name), boasts a massive reception hall supported by a thick central pillar and groin vaults. The building was constructed by Marco Ruffo and Pietro Solario (1487–1491). Dominating the whole Kremlin is the Bell Tower of Ivan the Great, a striking bell cote complex including a 266-foot tower, built piecemeal between 1505 and 1600 to serve both as a belfry and a watchtower. Several buildings of the Kremlin now serve as museums of medieval Russian art.

BIBLIOGRAPHY

The best available history of the architecture of the Moscow Kremlin is N. Ya. Tikhomirov, *Moskovskii Kreml: Istoriya arkhitektury* (1966). On the artistic treasures of the Kremlin see M. V. Alpatov, ed., *Khudozhestvennye pamyatniki Moskovskogo Kremlya* (1956). In English, see Arthur Voyce, *The Moscow Kremlin: Its History, Architecture, and Art Treasures* (1954). A good study of the Uspensky Cathedral is M. V. Alpatov, ed., *Uspenskii Sobor Moskovskogo Kremlya* (1971), which includes an English summary. N. N. Voronin, ed., *Palaces and Churches of the Kremlin,* with photographs by Karel Neubert (1965), seems to be the book of plates most useful to students of the Middle Ages.

George P. Majeska

[See also **Church, Types of; Dionysios the Greek; Early Christian and Byzantine Architecture; Fioravanti, Aristotele; Iconostasis; Icons, Russian; Muscovy, Rise of; Prokhor of Gorodets; Rublev, Andrei; Russian Architecture; Russian Orthodox Church; Theophanes the Greek.**]

MOSER, LUCAS (*fl.* first half of the fifteenth century), southwestern German painter represented by only one documented surviving work, the dated 1431 *Magdalen Altarpiece* (at Tiefenbronn). Moser remains a mysterious figure in German painting. His work is characterized by sturdy, plastic figures with large, detailed faces, similar to those in the paintings of Hans Multscher. Moser has been linked to stained-glass painting in Ulm (1434).

BIBLIOGRAPHY

Helmut May, *Lucas Moser,* 2nd ed. (1967); Gerhard Piccard, *Der Magdalenenaltar des "Lukas Moser" in Tiefenbronn* (1969); Alfred Stange, *Deutsche Malerei der Gotik,* IV (1951).

Larry Silver

[See also **Gothic Art: Painting; Multscher, Hans.**]

MOSES BEN MAIMON. See **Maimonides, Moses.**

MOSES BEN NAHMAN. See **Nahmanides, Moses.**

MOSES BEN SHEM TOV DE LEÓN (*ca.* 1240–*ca.* 1305), the most important Spanish cabalist. Probably born in León, he wandered between Guadalajara, Ávila, and Valladolid, and died in Arévalo. Moses de León is the author of a number of cabalistic books written in Hebrew, almost all between 1286 and 1305. He also wrote the greater part of the Book of Zohar, a pseudoepigraphic work written in Aramaic and attributed to Rabbi Simeon ben Yoḥai, who lived in the second century. In the greater part of his Hebrew and Aramaic works, Moses de León developed a system of mythic and symbolic character which had a deep influence on the development of the cabala.

BIBLIOGRAPHY

Gershom G. Scholem, *Major Trends in Jewish Mysticism,* 3rd rev. ed. (1971), and *Kabbalah* (1974), esp. 432–434.

Moshe Idel

[See also **Apocalyptic Literature; Cabala.**]

MOSQUE, a place where Muslims perform ritual worship. The English word "mosque" ultimately derives from the Arabic *masjid,* a place where one performs *sujūd,* the acts of prostration before God. The Koran uses the term *masjid* to refer generally to all sanctuaries where God is invoked, and particularly to the sanctuary in Mecca enclosing the Kaaba. Thus, the term could refer to both Islamic and pre-Islamic sanctuaries. For the prophet Muḥammad and early Muslims, a house of worship does not seem to have been a necessity. Indeed, the Prophet is quoted as saying, "All the world is a masjid," thereby contrasting religions where God could only be worshiped in particular places with Islam, where God could be worshiped virtually anywhere. The house of the Prophet in Medina, generally considered to be the functional and formal prototype for later mosques, served many functions: it was the home of Muḥammad and his family as well as some of his followers, in it the wounded in battle were treated and business matters were disputed, Muḥammad taught the precepts of Islam there, and it was a place for both personal and communal worship.

From the earliest days of Islam, communal worship had political connotations: attendance at Friday noon worship was incumbent on all adult male free Muslims. The Friday ceremony differed from other worship in containing a khutbah, or sermon, given by a preacher from a minbar (pulpit), which served as a vehicle for conferring political legitimacy on a ruler as well as publicizing information of interest to the entire community. Thus arose the need for a building large enough to contain the entire adult male Muslim population of a given locality on Friday. During the rest of the week, the mosque could serve as a place of prayer, instruction, and study for the Muslim community. With the spread of Islam,

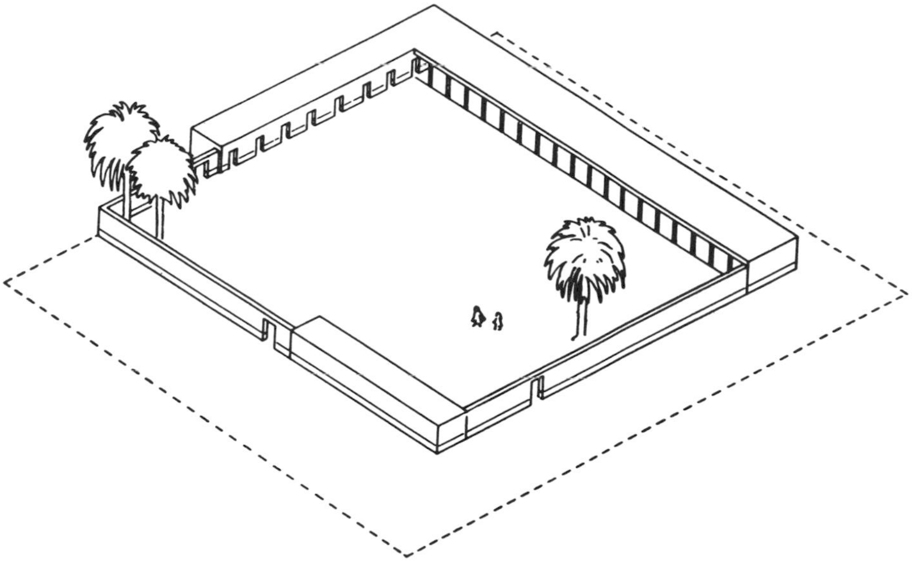

The house of the Prophet in Medina. Reconstruction according to Creswell's plan. REPRODUCED FROM D. KUBAN, *MUSLIM RELIGIOUS ARCHITECTURE* (1974), courtesy of E. J. Brill, Leiden

mosques were established in all settlements to serve both religious and political needs.

The functions of the congregational mosque (*al-masjid al-jāmi*ᶜ, the mosque that brings the faithful together), with the exception of communal Friday prayer and the khutbah, were also met by smaller everyday mosques that were sometimes established by a particular group of people or for a particular locality within a larger settlement. Thus, in Al-Fusṭāṭ, the first Muslim settlement in Egypt, there were many masjids in addition to the *masjid al-jāmi*ᶜ. By the eleventh century, grammatical distinction was made between a congregational, Friday, or khutbah mosque and the smaller masjid, the former becoming a *jāmi*ᶜ by ellipsis.

At approximately the same time, growing internal differentiation within the Muslim community led to the increasing separation of functions from the mosque and consequent creation of new institutions to meet these special needs. Thus the madrasa (theological school) or the *khānqāh* (convent for mystics) arose as separate institutions from the earlier inclusive congregational mosque, though both usually contained separate masjids for prayer.

Architecturally, the Prophet's house in Medina—a courtyard defined by shaded porticoes and some enclosed rooms—served as the prototype for mosques in other early Islamic settlements. The essential features of early mosques in Egypt, Syria, and Iraq can be reconstructed from contemporary descriptions: differing in form, materials, and techniques of construction, all early mosques combined open and covered spaces and were oriented toward the Kaaba in Mecca, the direction in which Muslims pray (qibla). These two features allowed varying numbers of believers to pray toward Mecca in parallel rows and were the first two ubiquitous elements of mosque design.

In the first decade of the eighth century, the growth of the Muslim community led the Umayyad caliph al-Walīd I to order the enlargement of the mosques of Medina, Jerusalem, and Damascus. At the same time, however, increased contact with the architectural concepts of hellenized and Christian Syria appears to have suggested a new organization of the spaces in these mosques, which was to become standard in other mosques throughout the Muslim world. A semicircular niche about the size of a man (*miḥrāb*) was introduced into the qibla wall of all mosques, most probably explained as a symbol for the role of the Prophet in Islam. The *miḥrāb* and the surrounding area were often elaborated through increased decoration or the use of domes and raised ceilings. In the congregational mosque, the minbar—a stepped, wooden chair—adjoined the *miḥrāb* and served as the symbol of political authority. Almost immediately these features became ubiquitous in all congregational mosques, yet other forms, such as the minaret, a tower for the call to prayer, took centuries to become standard features of all mosques.

The absence of formal specificity in this conception of the mosque allowed for extraordinary variety in its realization throughout the many lands where Muslim converts were won. The metropolitan styles of the great Umayyad and Abbasid caliphates often served to introduce uniformity in mosque design. Thus, the eighth-century mosque in Córdoba was strongly influenced by Umayyad models in Syria and the ninth-century mosque of Ibn Ṭūlūn in Cairo closely follows Abbasid models in Iraq. However, varied availability of materials, familiarity with differing techniques of construction, and preference for types of decoration soon led to the development of regional types and styles of mosques, such as the *T*-plan with a square minaret characteristic of much of North Africa and Spain, the mosque with a huge single dome and slender minarets identified with the Ottoman Empire, or the four-*eyvān* mosque with paired minarets characteristic of the Iranian world after the twelfth century.

BIBLIOGRAPHY

K. A. C. Creswell, *Early Muslim Architecture,* 2 vols. in 3 (1940–1969, repr. 1979); Oleg Grabar, *The Formation of Islamic Art* (1973), 104–138; Johannes Pedersen, "Masdjid," in *Encyclopaedia of Islam,* III (1930), 314–376; Jean Sauvaget, *La mosquée omeyyade de Médine* (1947).

JONATHAN M. BLOOM

[See also **Eyvān; Islamic Art and Architecture; Khānqāh; Madrasa; Miḥrāb; Minaret; Minbar; Qibla, Sahn.**]

MOSUL (Arabic: Al-Mawṣil), a city situated on the west bank of the Tigris River, opposite the ruins of Nineveh, capital of ancient Assyria. Mosul and other ancient towns, like Ad-Hadhr (Hatra) and Haran are in a region called by Arab geographers "Al-Jazīra" (the island), because the upper portions of the Tigris and Euphrates surround the area. Today Al-Jazīra is divided among four countries—Turkey, Iraq, Iran, and Syria—but Mosul itself, situated in its southeastern corner, is in Iraq. The Arabic root of Mosul means "junction" or "juncture," and the city may have received its name because it is located at caravan crossroads or because it is near the confluence of several tributaries of the Tigris.

It is not certain that Mosul existed in antiquity, although Xenophon may have mentioned its name in his work. Persian accounts ascribe its founding to a Persian king or satrap. More is known about a Christian community, which appears to have existed on the west bank of the river from the second century A.D. (this settlement probably marks the foundation of Mosul of later renown). Mosul later became the center of the diocese of Athur (Assyria), and by the time it was conquered by the Arabs, it was a predominantly Christian city.

Mosul was occupied by ᶜUtba ibn Farqad during the caliphate of ᶜUmar ibn al-Khaṭṭāb in 641. It began to grow under Arab rule and Arab tribes were allotted lands where they could build their own houses. ᶜUtba was soon replaced by Harthama ibn ᶜArfaja, and the town became a camp *(miṣr)* and a mosque was built. It continued to grow under Umayyad rule, and the caliph ᶜAbd al-Malik (685–705) appointed his son Saᶜīd as governor of Mosul and his brother Muḥammad as governor of the provinces of Al-Jazīra and Armenia. More houses for the Arabs were built, and roads and a pontoon bridge over the Tigris were constructed.

Under Abbasid rule Mosul continued to grow and prosper, and it became known as the home of the poet Abū Tammām (*d.* 850), who composed a poem in which he celebrated the capture of the fortress Amorium (ᶜAmmūriya in Arabic) from the Byzantines in 838. When Abbasid power began to decline, Mosul fell in the hands of successive rulers who used the city as a fortress to challenge the central authority of the caliph in Baghdad. After the death of the caliph al-Mutawakkil in 861, Musāwir, a Kharijite rebel, seized power and defied the caliphs. From that time on, successive Kharijite, Taghlibid, ᶜUqaylid, and Hamdanid rulers controlled Mosul, sometimes acknowledging the caliphs' authority, sometimes not. At the beginning of the tenth century, Abū al-Hayjā, a member of the Hamdanid dynasty, which ruled over Aleppo province, took control of the city and administered it first in the name of the caliph, but later his successors ruled virtually as independent sovereigns.

In 1095–1096, Mosul passed under the Seljuks, who ruled with utter disregard for the welfare of the people, and the city suffered neglect and destruction. It was not until 1127 that Seljuk rule came to an end when Mosul fell under the control of ᶜImād al-Dīn Zangī, who established the Atabeg dynasty and inaugurated a period of reconstruction and benevolent rule. At this time the Muslim rulers were engaged in almost continuous warfare with the crusaders in the Levant. After Saladin had entered Jerusalem (1187), the Atabegs recognized his overlordship, but they retained their independence. In the late twelfth and early thirteenth centuries, Mosul was the home of the Ibn al-Athīr family, which included the historian ᶜIzz al-Dīn, author of *Kamil.* During 1211–1259, the city flourished under the rule of Badr al-Dīn Luᵓluᵓ, an able statesman and patron of arts.

In 1258, the Mongols captured Baghdad and extended their control to other parts of Islamic lands including Mosul. Although Tamerlane richly endowed the tombs of Nabī Yurus and Nabī Jirjis and restored the pontoon bridge, soon thereafter neglect and destruction befell the city and it was only with the establishment of a national regime in Iraq in 1921 that the people of Mosul recovered from isolation and reduced conditions.

BIBLIOGRAPHY

Sources. Ibn al-Athīr, *al-Kāmil fī al-taᵓrīkh,* Carl J. Tornberg, ed., 13 vols, (1867–1877); Yāqūt al-Ḥamāwī. *Muᶜjam al-Buldān,* Ferdinand Wüstenfeld, ed., 6 vols. (1866–1873), IV, 682–684.

Studies. Fāḍil Ḥusayn, *Mushkilat al-Mawsil* (1955); Guy Le Strange, *The Lands of the Eastern Caliphate* (1905, repr. 1966); H. I. Lloyd, "The Geography of the Mosul Boundary," in *Geographical Journal,* **68** (1926); Sulaymān (Suleiman) Ṣā'igh, *Taᵓrīkh al-Mawṣil* (1923).

MAJID KHADDURI

[See also **Athir, Ibn al-; Badr al-Dīn Luᵓluᵓ; Euphrates River; Iraq; Islamic Art and Architecture; Kurds; Seljuks.**]

MOTET. The medieval motet is a polyphonic composition in which the fundamental melismatic voice (tenor) exhibits some sort of patterning, while the upper voice or voices (up to three, most often two) have different Latin or French texts and mostly move at a faster rate than the tenor. As a rule, the patterning of the tenor involves reiterated rhythmic configurations.

The history of the motet is rooted in the organa of Leoninus' *Magnus liber,* specifically in their discant sections, in their modernizations by Perotinus, and in the generally two-voice clausulae, which originated as detached discant sections and therefore developed into a distinct genre of self-contained and independently shaped pieces of music based on Gregorian melismas. Consistent with the traditions of trope, *prosa,* and *prosula,* as well as with the general medieval concept of the consanguinity of music and poetry, the motet came into being, as the melismatic duplum (upper voice) of the clausula was made syllabic through the application of poetic text, a pro cess aided by the medieval polyphonists' prevailing attitude of neutrality to, or disregard of, the qualitative and quantitative value of words in poetry (except at verse endings). The resulting pieces were called *motelli,* a Latin adaptation of the French *mot* (medieval meanings: word, poetic stanza, refrain). The term soon gave way to *moteti.* The beginning of these developments may be assumed to have occurred in the early years of the thirteenth century—perhaps about 1210—within the circle of musical practice usually referred to as the Parisian school or the Notre Dame school.

Since the lengths of the musical phrases of most clausulae and Notre Dame motets, while carefully planned, exhibit no regularity, the versification, which has to accord with the musical phrases of the preexisting clausula (or discant section), cannot be regular. Irregularity of verse structure became a hallmark of the medieval motet, as the primary measuring tool was the preconceived music with its varied phrase layout.

Increasingly motets appeared in which the Gregorian melisma in the tenor was stated twice (or occasionally more often). Frequently the unvarying rhythmic pattern would produce a rhythmic redistribution of the pitch content of the melisma. (For instance, if the melisma consisted of twenty-two pitches, while the rhythmic pattern of the tenor encompassed five notes, the second statement of the melisma would begin in the middle of the fifth statement of the pattern.) The purpose of this device is obviously the confection of a more expansively shaped composition. Another device that began to appear is the application of two different tenor patterns to two successive statements of one melisma.

The phrase endings of the upper voice(s) of early clausulae coincided with the ends of tenor phrases. Before long, however, a good number of two-voice clausulae began to free the duplum phrases from their dependence on the tenor; some of them overlap the tenor patterns. For composers of the time the potential complexity of phrase structure in clausulae and discant sections of three (or, rarely, four) voices was an adventurous challenge. But the device of staggered phrase layout among the voices also wreaks havoc with the procedure of turning three-voice clausulae into motets, since the same text could not be made to fit both upper voices. It is this dilemma that produced the "double motet," that is, the motet with two different texts for duplum and triplum—a rigorously logical concept of marvelous daring. (Not until the operatic ensemble of Mozart's time did polytextuality again function as a compositional principle.)

Some of the more sophisticated double motets

show clear rhythmic differentiation of the voices: the tenor is in fifth mode (often, in fact, proceeding in patterns consisting of longs and double longs), the duplum in longs and breves (for example, first mode), and the triplum almost exclusively in breves (sixth mode). Moreover, the lengths of the phrases in each voice are more or less carefully calculated in numerical proportions, interrelating the voices both contrapuntally and in their phrase layout. It seems that such compositions began to be written well before the middle of the thirteenth century. In combining three voices whose differentiation involves the texts as well as all musical elements, they already fully realize the potential of the genre, which might be described as the joining of diverse entities.

It is the epoch-making achievement of Perotinus and his generation to have added to the traditional numerical order of music, as embodied in the consonant intervals, the numerically founded arrangement of durational values, as embodied in rhythm and the rational coordination of phrase lengths. A well-made thirteenth-century motet is a concise tonal, temporal, and poetic form, whose superstructure, erected on the staked-out notes of the cantus firmus, is designed proportionately to unfold, demonstrate, and articulate the fundamental numerical theme given by the patterned phrase layout of the tenor. The motet is a polyphony of tones, of texts, and of interrelated numbers governing rhythms and phrase structure. Such structures are not accompanied songs or duets that "express" their texts. The role of poetry in a medieval motet is best defined by analogy with the stained glass windows in a Gothic church. The poetic images in the upper voices relate to the music in the same way as do the historiated windows to the structure of which they are components. The music does not accompany, elucidate, or intensify; rather, the poetry illuminates and coordinately reflects the structure of the music.

Just as architecture was regarded in the Middle Ages as a visual demonstration of musical proportions, music (measured discant) was by the end of the century described by Johannes de Grocheo in architectural terms: "The tenor, however, is that part upon which all others are founded, just as the parts of a house or building are erected upon its fundament. It is their yardstick and gives them quantity." Visual evidence of this view of the motet may be seen in the way its voice parts were written in manuscripts after the mid thirteenth century: triplum either on the left half of a page or on the verso of a folio; duplum on the right half of a page or on the recto facing the triplum; tenor under both voices on the bottom of the page(s), with the appropriate Gregorian word or words placed like a label below its initial notes. In the earliest manuscripts the voices had been notated successively, often continuing from the recto of a folio to its verso. Thus, motets at first could not be performed from the book. Evidently the advances of the Franconian era account for the new arrangement, since the rhythmically unambiguous Franconian notation of syllabic polyphony made sight-reading possible.

Just as polyphony had for the first time furnished a reliable musical yardstick with which to measure Latin poetry, French poetry also came to be drawn into its orbit soon after the birth of the genre (*ca.* 1220). French motets rapidly became more prominent than those with Latin poetry, and few of the French texts maintained a trope-like relationship with the cantus firmus. The dwindling topical connection with the chant is specially well demonstrated by the occasional practice of combining a French triplum with a Latin duplum (or *motetus,* as that voice came to be called), thereby adding another element to the individualization of the upper voices.

Latin motets predominantly concern the Virgin Mary. Less common topics that occur more and more rarely deal with liturgical occasions in the Temporale or Sanctorale or with moral exhortation. Generally, French motet poems deal with love—courtly (mostly), urban, or pastoral. A few other texts reflect the convivial life in the city (Paris); the rest are either Marian or hortatory. While there is some evidence that in the early years of the century an appropriate Latin motet could be substituted for a melismatic discant passage and thus performed within an organum, even some Latin motet poetry soon began to assume the sort of content that made it unsuitable for church. On gaining musical independence, clausula and motet (Latin as well as French) soon shed their umbilical connection with church and liturgy. Evidently, motets became mostly pieces of clerical, aristocratic, and university chamber music, whose patterned tenors seem to have been performed instrumentally.

The major composers during the first two-thirds of the fourteenth century were Philippe de Vitry and Guillaume de Machaut. Throughout most of the century the motet retained its essential characteristics. The large-scale proportions of the fourteenth century motet are founded on the accomplishments of Philippe de Vitry, such as the codification of the minim, the new "short" value, and its incorporation

MOTET

into both upper voices of motets. The tenor part, however, continued to be written in the customary though no longer modal-rhythmic long note values (double longs, longs, and, to a lesser extent, breves), which therefore now moved about four times as slowly as they had a hundred years before.

Around the beginning of the fourteenth century composers had begun to develop a device to give clarity and consistency to the phrase structure of the upper voices. The numerical pattern produced by the lengths of phrases in the upper voices of most motets was inevitably influenced by, and interacted with, the repeated tenor pattern. It was a logical step for composers to introduce into one or both of the upper voices rhythmic correspondences between certain phrases or phrase groups, evidently to lend emphasis to the work's structure, which was formed into lengthy musical strophes by the number of statements (usually three or four) of the extensive tenor pattern *(talea)*. The introduction of strophic rhythmic recurrences (isorhythm) in the upper voices as a structural device began as an extension of rhythmic identity from the cadence (final note of a phrase plus succeeding articulating rest) backward to other parts of phrases.

Isorhythm is often defined in modern writings with reference only to the tenor of fourteenth-century motets. The principle of reiterated rhythmic patterning, however, had been characteristic of the tenors of cantus firmus polyphony since the rise of clausula and motet. It is the growth of isorhythm in the upper voices of fourteenth-century motets that is characteristic and significant, as it gives structural emphasis to the new lengthy tenor patterns.

Just as the two upper voices now exhibited similar rhythmic behavior, the possibility, frequently practiced in the thirteenth century, of combining two unrelated poems in the upper voices ceased to exist, as the selection of the tenor was no longer determined by considerations of contrapuntal convenience, but was governed by the need for its text of a few words to correspond like a motto to the poetic conceit of the upper voices. The practice might be called reverse troping, since the relevance of the texts is motivated not liturgically (from the bottom up) but poetically (from the top down).

The melodic design of the upper voices clearly shows that each phrase is a separate component that requires no linking to its predecessor by such means as motivic relationships, sequences, or contrast. Since the composition is not the product of free melodic invention, a motet sounds stiffer and more formal than an accompanied chanson, not only because of the former's massive fundament—now often consisting of tenor and contratenor, a composed voice similar to the tenor in range and facture—but because the melodic design of the upper voices is more restricted; even rhythmically it is more conservative.

The presence of a cantus firmus, which had always caused the motet tenor to be regarded as the *dignior pars* (the more worthy part), in no case automatically implies liturgical function. The original trope-like nature of the motet was a fleeting phenomenon, whose inevitability was eliminated when clausula and motet were recognized as entities divorced from the chant that furnished the tenor notes. Certainly motets with suitable texts must have been performed in church; but the primary raison d'être of the motet was more than ever to function as the most sublime product of *ars musica,* which addressed itself to the "learned and those who prize artistic subtlety" (Johannes de Grocheo).

The apprehension of fourteenth-century motets may at first seem a forbidding task, since they are of much broader dimensions than those of the *ars antiqua.* But far from being arcane intellectual constructs that resist aural comprehension, fourteenth-century isorhythmic motets are strophic variations. The perception of the proportioned relationships within a motet is not essentially more problematic than the perception of the proportioned relationships of the structural members in Gothic architecture. Isorhythmic passages are recurring rhythmic ornaments that emphasize the strophic phrase structure, with the counterpoint changing from strophe to strophe as a result of the particular pitch content of each talea.

Panisorhythm (the precise strophic repetition of all rhythms in each voice and in all strophes) increased in importance around the middle of the century. The development toward panisorhythm goes hand in hand with a tendency to forgo the traditional structure of the upper voices that divides the strophe into proportioned component phrases. Increasingly, motets appear in which one or both of the upper voices are not subdivided at all in each strophe. Such motets are also panisorhythmic or nearly so. The formal changes experienced by the motet in the second half of the fourteenth century resulted from the monumentalism that began to affect it. The level of articulation passed from the component phrases to the monolithic strophes themselves. Isorhythm in the upper voices no longer functioned as carefully spaced, ornamental emphasis of the articulation of phrase structure but assumed central importance. With the elimination of the structural subdivisions of the strophes, the elements of form became vast.

Numerical significance was restored to the motet on a larger plane than before through the extended use of sectional diminution, a device that had been optional since Vitry's time to produce two sections (containing an equal number of strophes). The second was half or one third the length of the first because of systematic diminution applied to the note values in the tenor (and contratenor). Both diminution and other changes in mensuration were applied to the lower voice(s) of motets of the late fourteenth century for the sake of numerically proportioned sectional design. The lengths of such sections (each usually containing two isorhythmic strophes) will yield such proportions as 6:4:3:2 or 9:6:4.

Since in all such motets the main emphasis is no longer on strophic isorhythm but on variety of sectional mensuration, a logical conclusion of this development is the appearance of motets without isorhythm. A few motets composed by Dufay in the 1430's and 1440's are outstanding representatives of this final structural type of the medieval motet, which is related to the Burgundian cantus firmus Mass. The sections of such compositions are proportioned 6:4:2:3, 12:4:2:3, 6:3:4:2:6:3, and so on. Since strophic isorhythmic repetition no longer subdivides the sections, it is more appropriate to call such compositions mensuration motets than isorhythmic motets.

As in the case of the symphony of the early twentieth century, the huge proportions to which the motet of the early fifteenth century had grown indicated its imminent demise. Both in size and in sound the motet tended to become unwieldy. Its enormous structural members were composed of large areas of unvarying fundamental sonority established by the long durational values of the tenor (and contratenor). Moreover, motet composers began to incorporate contrapuntal passages containing melodic imitation, a feature essentially foreign to a genre whose structure was based, ever since the appearance of the clausula, on the disposition of temporal units (rhythm and phrases).

The increasing importance of imitation around 1400 is symptomatic of a profound shift from the shaping of a composition by means of numerical coordination of heterogeneous, hierarchically ordered durational components, in which melodic considerations are of no structural importance, to the creation of a musically and textually homogeneous contrapuntal fabric from one congenial set of melodic cells. The many significant changes in style and technique occurring in motets composed at this time have been demonstrated as preeminently due to Italian influences, absorbed and transformed by such northern composers resident in Italy as Ciconia and Dufay. Before the early fifteenth century, motet production in Italy had been negligible. The composers active in northern Italy around the turn of the century evidently were the first to transfer the technique of imitation from the monotextual duet, where it was at home, to the motet. Since monotextual motets were now written more frequently and the poems of polytextual pieces were usually of the same length and had similar versification and related subject matter, the two upper voices, which had already occupied the same range in many fourteenth-century French motets, were now assimilated by melodic cross-references, by similar rhythmic facture and by declamation.

All these progressive features can be found in a number of Dufay's isorhythmic and mensuration motets. In these works with their Latin texts, composed one hundred years after Vitry and some 200 years after Perotinus, Dufay achieved a last magnificent synthesis of the traditions of numerically constructed cantus firmus polyphony with the new forces that hastened its decline. Most motets by composers of the early fifteenth century are *pièces d'occasion,* generally for ceremonial occasions and hallowed by relevant liturgical fundaments that the Middle Ages knew as divinely inspired, sacrosanct, and eternally valid.

In England, the medieval motet developed quite particular traits during the thirteenth and fourteenth centuries, as evidenced in the "Worcester Fragments" repertory.

BIBLIOGRAPHY

Heinrich Besseler, "Studien zur Musik des Mittelalters," in *Archiv für Musikwissenschaft,* 7 (1925), 8 (1926); Ursula Günther, "The 14th-century Motet and Its Development," in *Musica disciplina,* 12 (1958); Georg Reichert, "Das Verhältnis zwischen musikalischer und textlicher Struktur in den Motetten Machauts," in *Archiv für Musikwissenschaft,* 13 (1956), and "Wechselbeziehungen zwischen musikalischer und textlicher Struktur in der Motette des 13. Jahrhunderts," in *In memoriam Jacques Handschin* (1962); Ernest H. Sanders, "The Medieval

Motet," in *Gattungen der Musik in Einzeldarstellungen: Gedenkschrift für Leo Schrade,* I (1973), and "Motet" and "Sources, MS," in *New Grove Dictionary of Music and Musicians,* XII, XVII (1980).

ERNEST H. SANDERS

[See also **Ars Antiqua; Ars Nova; Clausula; Duplum; Isorhythm; Johannes de Grocheo; Leoninus; Machaut, Guillaume de; Music, Western European; Musical Notation, Western; Notre Dame School; Perotinus; Philippe de Vitry; Worchester, School of.**]

MOTET MANUSCRIPTS. During the first century of its history, the motet was the most important medium for stylistic development and change in polyphonic music. The large repertory of motets to survive from the thirteenth century is preserved in a sizable and diverse group of manuscript sources reflecting the changes in function, style, and manner of performance that the genre underwent. These manuscripts vary strikingly in character, from lavish library volumes that were never intended to see practical use to modest performing copies. The latter have survived in fewer numbers than the former, and by their very nature are less likely to have survived intact. Several important sources have disappeared altogether (for example, the volumes indexed in London, British Library, Harley 978, from Reading Abbey, and Besançon, Bibliothèque Municipale, I, 716), while others—indeed, the majority—have been preserved only as fragments. Nevertheless, for the thirteenth-century motet (unlike that of the fourteenth) the losses of repertory or of stages in the development of the genre appear to be relatively minor. Many of the extant sources are difficult to date and localize, however, and are likely to contain copies of works written many decades earlier, making the assessment of those stages extremely complex.

Manuscripts from throughout the thirteenth century preserve the motet in its original, liturgical function. Florence, Biblioteca Mediceo-Laurenziana, Pluteus 29.1, copied in Paris about 1250, includes two collections of motets in its repertory of liturgical polyphony. Twenty-six conductus motets for three voices, nearly all based on discant clausulae, are arranged in correct liturgical order according to the function of their plainchant tenors and were probably intended to be inserted into the organa elsewhere in the manuscript as substitute clausulae. On the other hand, the forty motets for two voices, also based overwhelmingly on clausulae, are in no discernible order; if this is significant, it may imply that they were intended to be used alongside the conductus in the manuscript for various liturgical and devotional occasions.

Other sources confirm the lack of a clear distinction between the conductus and the liturgical motet during the thirteenth century. The fragment Châlons sur Marne, Archives Départementales 3.J.250, contains six motets with the single motet text entered beneath the tenor part, suggesting their performance as conductus. Two other early sources have similar layouts: London, British Library, Egerton 2615, a Beauvais Circumcision Office, and the Reading Abbey manuscript, British Library, Harley 978. Two other manuscripts, like the Florence volume devoted to liturgical polyphony, reveal a different kind of stylistic kinship between motet and conductus: Wolfenbüttel, Herzog August Bibliothek, Helmstedt 628, copied for St. Andrews, and Madrid, Biblioteca Nacional, 20486, from Toledo Cathedral, intermingle conductus and motets—the latter often, and the former always, without their tenors, producing works indistinguishable from conductus.

Paris, Bibliothèque Nationale, fonds latin 15139, perhaps deriving from the French royal chapel, bears witness to a striking change in function for the motet. It contains forty clausulae that are accompanied by the incipits of French motet texts, written in the margin in a later hand. Most of these clausulae are found in other manuscripts as motets with the texts in question. The fragment Munich, Bayerische Staatsbibliothek, Mus. 4775 (with additional fragments that were once in the Berlin library of Johannes Wolf), preserves a parallel stage in the history of the genre; nearly all of its thirty-six surviving motets, most based on clausulae and all on plainchant, bear French texts, many markedly secular. Both these motets and the clausulae in Paris 15139 are arranged in liturgical order and thus clearly document the transformation of sacred works to secular purposes.

Paris 15139 and Munich 4775 both contain organa and conductus in addition to motets, showing that these manuscripts were intended for institutions responsible for the performance of both liturgical and courtly polyphony. The same is true of Wolfenbüttel, Herzog August Bibliothek, Helmstedt 1099, one of the largest thirteenth-century motet collections. In addition to organa and conductus it contains a collection of conductus motets (not in liturgical order), among which are five works with

MOTET MANUSCRIPTS

French texts, all adapted from Latin motets in the same volume. These are followed by eighty two-voice Latin motets (the largest collection of such works extant) presented in three alphabetically arranged series, each with its own characteristics (for example, 50 percent of the motets in the first series also survive as French motets, 25 percent of those in the second series, and 70 percent of those in the third). Next comes a collection of French double motets and, finally, the largest surviving repertory of French two-voice motets, divided, again, into three alphabetical series. Many of these are based on Latin motets copied elsewhere in the book, the relationship often made explicit by incipits in the margin next to the Latin originals. In these French motets the secular role of the motet is apparent: one begins with a line that opens several trouvère chansons, "Chanteur m'estuet"; another, its motet text beginning "Meuz ami mourir," uses a portion of the plainchant *Alleluia, Veni electa* as tenor, but in a corrupt form and divided in half to suggest the two parts of a rondeau refrain.

Collections of French motets are found in several trouvère *chansonniers,* with the motet occasionally copied monophonically, like the courtly songs elsewhere in the manuscript; the most important are Paris, Bibliothèque Nationale, fonds français 12615; Bibliothèque Nationale, fonds français 844; Bibliothèque Nationale, fonds français 845 (a group of sixteen *motets entés*); and Rome, Vatican Library, reg. lat. 1490. In Paris, Bibliothèque Nationale, fonds français 25566, motets appear among a group of polyphonic rondeaux in a collection of the works of the trouvère Adam de la Halle. And in London, British Library, Egerton 274, conductus and other devotional pieces, motets, and trouvère songs are intermingled in a single collection, demonstrating the identity of sacred and secular at some medieval courts.

During the second half of the thirteenth century, manuscripts devoted exclusively to the motet appeared. Whereas most of the sources previously mentioned were written in a nonmensural, or "modal," musical notation, some form of rhythmically explicit mensural notation is used by these self-contained motet collections. Turin, Biblioteca Reale, Vari 42, copied about 1300 in Liège, contains thirty-one double motets. The somewhat earlier manuscript Paris, Bibliothèque Nationale, n.a. fr. 13521, has fifty-five motets: one Latin triple motet, six Latin double motets, seven French triple motets, twenty-six French double motets, two French motets for two voices, five triple motets with the voices in different languages, and eight double motets with one voice in French and the other in Latin.

As these figures show, most self-sufficient motet manuscripts are devoted primarily to the double motet. Bamberg, Staatliche Bibliothek, Lit. 115, contains a hundred such works arranged in alphabetical order: forty-four in Latin, forty-seven in French, and nine with one voice in Latin and the other in French. In general, manuscripts originating away from the center of activity—in Germany (or, like Bamberg, the area west of the Rhine), Spain, England, and eastern Europe—reveal a marked predilection for Latin-texted works; examples include Darmstadt, Hessische Landesbibliothek, 3317 and related fragments; Munich, Bayerische Staatsbibliothek, Musikfragment E III 230–231; Burgos, Monasterio de Las Huelgas, unnumbered MS; and Cambridge, Trinity College, 0.2.1. Exceptional is London, British Library, Add. 30091, which contains fourteen two-voice motets, most in Latin, the majority of which survive elsewhere as double motets.

Motet collections are occasionally appended to other kinds of manuscripts. In Paris, Bibliothèque Nationale, fonds latin 11266, for example, a group of motets is found after the music treatise of Magister Lambertus and may have been included to illustrate the text. And in Paris, Bibliothèque de l'Arsenal, 135, Latin motets have been copied onto the blank folios of a Salisbury missal. Montpellier, Faculté de Médecine, H. 196, is the most comprehensive thirteenth-century motet source, including collections of virtually every type of motet developed during the period except the conductus motet and the two-voice Latin motet, probably the two earliest forms taken by the genre. Included in its last two fascicles are collections of modern and experimental works from toward the end of the century. Within each collection there is sometimes an ordering that can only be called pragmatic—the collection begins with the most popular works, those found in the greatest number of sources, and continues with less widely disseminated pieces and unica.

BIBLIOGRAPHY

Heinrich Besseler, "Studien zur Musik des Mittelalters: Neue Quellen des 14. und Beginnenden 15. Jahrhunderts," in *Archiv für Musikwissenschaft,* 7 (1925), and "Die Motette von Franko von Köln bis Philipp von Vitry," in *Archiv für Musikwissenschaft,* 8 (1926); Friedrich Gennrich, *Bibliographie der ältesten französischen und lateinischen Motetten* (1957); David Hiley and Ernest H. Sanders,

MÖTTULS SAGA

"Sources, MS," in *New Grove Dictionary of Music and Musicians,* XVII (1980), secs. iv, v; Friedrich Ludwig, "Die Quellen der Motetten ältesten Stils," in *Archiv für Musikwissenschaft,* 5 (1923), and *Repertorium organorum recentioris et motetorum vetustissimi stili,* 2 vols. in 3, Luther A. Dittmer, ed. (1964–1978); Gilbert Reaney, ed., *Manuscripts of Polyphonic Music: 11th–Early 14th Century* (1966), *Manuscripts of Polyphonic Music (c. 1320–1400)* (1969); Ernest H. Sanders, "The Medieval Motet," in Wulf Arlt, ed., *Gattungen der Musik in Einzeldarstellungen: Gedenkschrift Leo Schrade,* I (1973).

EDWARD H. ROESNER

[See also **Ars Nova; Ars Antiqua; Bamberg Manuscript; Chansonnier; Clausula; Conductus; Florence, Biblioteca Mediceo-Laurenziana, MS Pluteus 29.1; Gregorian Chant; Montpellier MS H 196; Motet; Wolfenbüttel, Helmstedt MS 628.**]

MÖTTULS SAGA (Tale of the mantle) is an anonymous *riddarasaga* (tale of chivalry) that derives from the French lai *Le mantel mautaillié* (The ill-cut coat). The prologue states that *Möttuls saga* is about a curious and amusing episode that took place at King Arthur's court, and that the translation was intended for the amusement of the audience and was undertaken at the request of King Hákon IV Hákonarson of Norway (*r.* 1217–1263).

Möttuls saga depicts the progress of a chastity test to which all the ladies at Arthur's court must submit as a result of a rash promise by the king. The instrument for determining the fidelity—or infidelity, as the case may be—of the assembled ladies, including Guinevere, is a magic mantle. It will fit only a faithful woman. The illusion of Arthurian perfection that is suggested in the prologue—which is independent of the French source—is gradually undermined as one woman after another is exposed as unchaste. Kay, King Arthur's steward, adds to the general chagrin by suggesting the nature of the individual transgression. Only after much exhaustive search throughout the premises does a lady step forward, Karadin's beloved, whom the mantle fits. The author concludes the saga on a cynical note: Sometimes it is better to conceal than to reveal the truth.

Artistically *Möttuls saga* ranks high among the thirteenth-century *riddarasögur.* The saga faithfully transmits the French tale in prose without substantial changes in either content or sequence. Nonetheless, *Möttuls saga* should be considered an interpretation of *Le mantel mautaillié,* inasmuch as amplification—as an explicatory, emphatic, and anticipatory device—characterizes the saga. Principles of perspective, intensification, and semantic or syntactical progression guided the author of *Möttuls saga* as he consistently and systematically expanded the text.

The most striking instance of augmentation is the encomiastic portrait of King Arthur with which *Möttuls saga* opens. This introduction is preserved in two redactions—a longer one from around 1400, and a shorter version from around 1300–1350. There is insufficient evidence to determine which version is the original, since both are structurally and stylistically well composed. It is known that Icelandic scribes both condensed texts that they were copying (for instance, the Stockholm 46 redaction of *Ivens saga*) and augmented them (for instance, the later redaction of *Mágus saga*).

Möttuls saga is preserved in three vellum fragments of one leaf each: in AM 598 4to Iβ from about 1300–1350 (the oldest Icelandic fragment to preserve an Arthurian text), and in AM 598 4to Iα and Stockholm 6 4to from about 1400. Despite the designation, AM 598 4to Iα originally belonged to the Stockholm 6 manuscript, a large codex of romances. All paper manuscripts derive directly or indirectly from the Stockholm 6 redaction of *Möttuls saga.* The most important paper manuscripts are two seventeenth-century copies of the saga in Stockholm 6: AM 179 fol. and AM 181b fol.; these copies were made when the codex was still intact. A comparison of the text of the oldest vellum fragment and the other manuscripts with the French text reveals substantial discrepancies between the two manuscript branches. From the disparities it is inferred that the Norwegian translation of *Le mantel mautaillié* had transmitted more of the content of the French source than the seventeenth-century copies—on which Gustaf Cederschiöld's edition is mainly based—suggest.

The popularity of *Möttuls saga* in Iceland is attested by a *rímur* version entitled *Skikkju rímur* (Mantle verses), probably composed in the fourteenth century. The oldest manuscript of the *Skikkju rímur,* a vellum (no. 42, 4to in the library at Wolfenbüttel) known as *Kollsbók,* dates from around 1500. The *rímur* preserve the essentials of *Möttuls saga,* but with some additions and modifications. The author of the *Skikkju rímur* drew not only on *Möttuls saga* but also on *Erex saga* (the Old Norse-Icelandic prose adaptation of Chrétien de Troyes's *Erec et Enide*) and *Samsons saga fagra* (Tale of Samson the Fair), a late medieval Icelandic romance. The author of *Samsons saga fagra* borrows the mantle motif from *Möttuls saga,* but enlarges upon the origin and properties of the mantle. The power of the garment is also tested in *Samsons saga;* but the mantle is a blind motif, insofar as it plays no essential role in the development of the narrative. The author of *Samsons saga fagra* may have included the mantle motif to assuage an audience's desire for the novel, or to express his own delight in the supranatural.

BIBLIOGRAPHY

Sources. Gísli Brynjúlfsson, ed. and trans., *Saga af Tristram ok Ísönd samt Möttuls saga* (1878); Gustaf Cederschiöld and Frederik A. Wulff, *Versions nordiques du fabliau français "Le mantel mautaillié"* (1877); Bjarni Vilhjálmsson, ed., "Möttuls saga," in *Riddarasögur,* I (1949).

Studies. Eyvind Fjeld Halvorsen, "Möttuls saga," in *Kulturhistorisk leksikon for nordisk middelalder,* XII (1967), 189–190, and "Problèmes de la traduction scandinave des textes français du moyen âge," in *Les relations littéraires franco-scandinaves au moyen âge* (1975); Marianne E. Kalinke, "Amplification in *Möttuls saga:* Its Function and Form," in *Acta philologica scandinavica,* **32** (1979), and *King Arthur North-by-Northwest: The* Matière de Bretagne *in Old Norse-Icelandic Romances* (1981).

MARIANNE E. KALINKE

[See also **Chrétien de Troyes; Erex Saga; Riddarasögur; Samsons Saga Fagra.**]

MOUCHETTE, a variant of the dagger motif in which the "blade" is curved and the design simplified to one of a single cusp opposite the "blade." It was common to employ pairs of mouchettes designed in opposition to each other. The mouchette is found in English Curvilinear and in French Flamboyant tracery of the fourteenth and fifteenth centuries.

CARL F. BARNES, JR.

[See also **Gothic, Decorated; Gothic, Flamboyant.**]

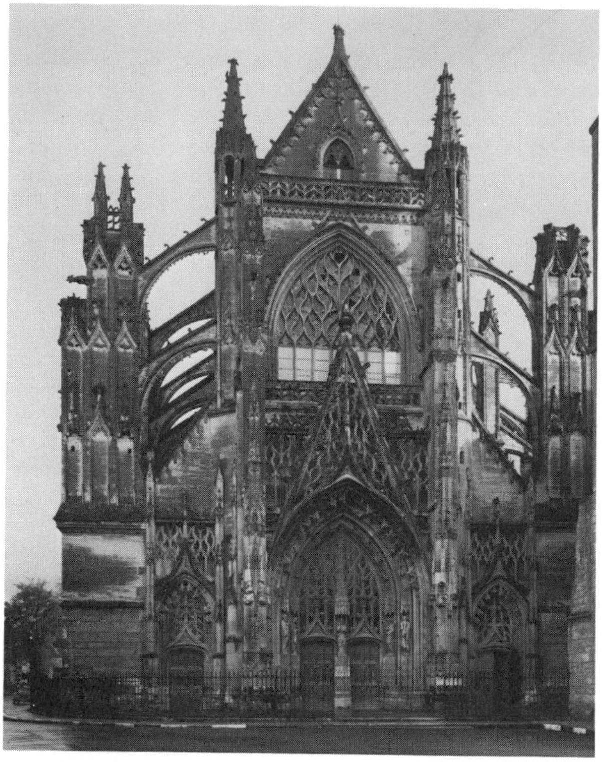

Vendôme, La Trinité, west facade, completed 1507. Mouchette tracery on the portals, spandrels, triforium level, and west window. PHOTOGRAPH BY A. F. KERSTING, LONDON

MOULINS, MASTER OF (*fl. ca.* 1475–*ca.* 1505), French painter. His most imposing work, and the principal basis for a definition of his oeuvre, is an altarpiece of the Virgin and Child (1498–1499) in Moulins Cathedral. His style is much influenced by Hugo van der Goes. There are good reasons to identify him as the documented painter Jean Hay.

BIBLIOGRAPHY

Charles Sterling, "Jean Hey, le Maître de Moulins," in, *Revue de l'art,* **1–2** (1968); Henri Zerner and Sharon Katie, *Il maestro di Moulins,* in I Maestri del Colore (1966).

DON DENNY

MOVSĒS DASXURANCʿI (*fl.* tenth or eleventh century). According to the *Albanian Chronicle* of Mχitʿar Goš, which was completed at the end of the twelfth century, Movsēs Dasχurancʿi, or Dasχuranecʿi, is the name of the author of the *History of the Caucasian Albanians.* Neither the time nor the identity of this Movsēs is known. The thirteenth-century Armenian historian Kirakos Ganjakecʿi (Kirakos of Ganjak), who was a pupil of both Varnakan Vardapat and Mχitʿar Goš, attributes the same *History* to an author by the name of Movsēs Kałankatuacʿi. The consensus among the modern scholars is that Kirakos was misled by a reference in the *History* to the village of Kałankatuk,

Coronation of the Virgin (Virgin and Child). Center panel from the Moulins Cathedral altarpiece by the Master of Moulins, *ca.* 1498–1499. GIRAUDON/ART RESOURCE

province of Utikᶜ, to which the author refers as the place "where I too am from" (2.11). From the context it is not clear whether he is from the village or the province.

The *History of the Caucasian Albanians* is divided into three books and is written in Classical Armenian. The present text does not seem to be a translation. The first book begins with the creation and the genealogy of the generations descended from Japheth. After a short chapter on the establishment of a government in pagan Ałuankᶜ (Aᶜłwankᶜ), the designation given to the eastern provinces of Armenia and the Armenian-Albanian marchlands to the northeast of the Kura River, the author devotes the rest of the book to the history of the Christian Ałuankᶜ until the late fifth century. Besides the local traditions and hagiography, the author has made use of the early Armenian sources. The second book covers the period from the fifth to the seventh centuries, even though it also contains references to the events of the fourth and eighth centuries. The third book begins with an account of the Arab invasions and ends with a list of the *katᶜołikoi* of Ałuankᶜ. The last datable event in this section is the coronation of King Senekᶜerim of Ałuankᶜ as king of Siwnikᶜ, which took place in 1084/1085.

The *History,* according to modern scholars, is a composite work containing various components such as short hagiographical writings, historical memoirs, canons, letters, and documents by various authors. These were probably first compiled in the middle of the seventh century by an unknown author. In this early form the *History* was known to certain eighth-, ninth-, and tenth-century Armenian writers. In either the tenth or the eleventh century, a second author, or an editor, presumably Movsēs Dasχurancᶜi, brought the *History* up to date and edited it. The different sections of this work have different values, depending on the reliability of individual authors. For example, the account on the events of the late sixth and early seventh centuries is partially based on the memoirs of the *katᶜołikos* Viroy of Albania (596–630). In general the *History* is a very valuable source on the pre-tenth-century history of the Caucasian peoples.

BIBLIOGRAPHY

For the text of this work, see *Movses Kałankatuacᶜi, Patmutᶜiwn Ałuanicᶜ Ašxarhi,* critical text and introduction by Varag Aṙakᶜelyan (1983). The English version is *The History of the Caucasian Albanians by Movsēs Dasχuranċi,* C. J. F. Dowsett, trans. (1961).

See also Ghevont M. Alishan, *Hayapatowm* (1901); C. J. F. Dowsett, "The Albanian Chronicle of Mχitᶜar Goš," in Bulletin of the School of Oriental and African Studies, **21** (1958); Kirakos Vardapet Ganjakecᶜi, *Patmowtᶜiwn Hayotᶜ* (1961); Hakob Manandyan, *Beiträge zur albanischen Geschichte* (1897); Asatur S. Mnatsakanian, *O literature kavkazskoĭ albanii* (1969); Kamilla V. Trever, *Ocherki po istorii i kult'ure kavkazskoi albanii* (1959).

KRIKOR H. MAKSOUDIAN

[See also **Albania (Caucasian); Armenian Literature; Historiography, Armenian; Kirakos of Ganjak; Mχitᶜar Goš.**]

MOVSĒS XORENACᶜI (Moses Khorenatsᶜi). Revered in Armenian tradition as the father of (Armenian) history, Movsēs is the most enigmatic historian writing in classical Armenian. His *Patmutᶜiwn Hayocᶜ* (History of the Armenians) is a comprehensive work that traces the history of his people from their origins in remote antiquity down to 439. Movsēs' version of events became in time the stan-

MOVSĒS XORENAC^CI

dard, "authoritative" version of Armenian history, not seriously challenged until the twentieth century. But there are serious reasons for rejecting his claim to have been a pupil of Maštocᶜ (the inventor of the Armenian alphabet) writing in the fifth century. The *History* was probably composed in the eighth century.

The *History* is divided into three books. Movsēs begins by integrating the legends extant in his time concerning the first settlers of Armenia into the biblical account of Noah's descendants after the flood. Here we read of Hayk, the eponymous ancestor of the Armenians, and of his descendants down to the time of Tigran. All this material, plus information at the beginning of Book II about the organization of Armenian society, supposedly derives from Parthian archives as extracted by "Mar Abas Catina." But here, as elsewhere, Movsēs uses the fiction of "archives" to lend credence to his own elaboration of tradition. For events outside Armenia his main source is the Armenian version of Eusebius' *Chronicle.*

Book II is devoted to the history of Armenia from the time of Arshak the Valiant, king of Parthia, down to the death of King Trdat the Great (Tiridates), who was converted to Christianity by St. Gregory the Illuminator in the early fourth century. In this book Movsēs draws freely on Eusebius' *Ecclesiastical History.* In addition to giving the Armenians a far more prominent role in the Roman–Parthian wars than they in fact played, he introduces Armenians into the legend of the conversion of Abgar of Edessa in order to enhance the prestige of his patrons, the Bagratuni family.

Here lies one of the main clues to the enigma of Movsēs' *History.* For he is not merely providing a history of his people and gathering ancient legends and traditions, he is also providing an ancestry for his patrons superior to that of all rivals. This aim explains the grave distortions in Book III, which describes the dynastic rivalries among the Armenian princely houses in the fourth century that led to the abolition of the Arsacid monarchy. Here the role of the Mamikonean family, most prominent in the fourth and fifth centuries, is downplayed, while that of the Bagratunis, who rose to preeminence in the eighth century, is enhanced.

Of the numerous written sources, Armenian and foreign, used by Movsēs, Josephus, Philo, the Alexander romance of Pseudo-Callisthenes, and the Byzantine historian Socrates Scholasticus should be mentioned in addition to Eusebius.

Movsēs' *History* is not referred to in Armenian sources until the tenth century. By then numerous legends concerning him and other shadowy figures, authors of religious and philosophical works, had begun to circulate. By the twelfth century Movsēs was credited with several such compositions. The most important of the works later ascribed to him is the *Ašχarhacᶜoycᶜ,* a world geography with particularly detailed descriptions of Armenia and Iran. Probably a production of the early seventh century, its authorship remains a matter of dispute.

Down to modern times Movsēs has remained for Armenians the historian par excellence, the greatest national author, whose name is revered equally with those of Maštocᶜ and Sahak, the inventor of the Armenian alphabet and the patron of the first works in the Armenian language.

BIBLIOGRAPHY

Sources. The *Patmutᶜiwn Hayocᶜ* (History) was first published in 1695 in Amsterdam. It has been printed many times since then, but the only critical edition is that of M. Abełean and S. Yarutᶜiwnean (1913). The first translation was the Latin rendering by William Whiston and George Whiston, *Moses Chorenensis Historiae Armeniacae,* London (1736), which included the Armenian text. In the nineteenth century there were numerous translations into Western languages; the only translation of the critical text is Robert W. Thompson, *Moses Khorenatsᶜi, History of the Armenians* (1978).

The long recension of the *Geography* was published with a French translation by Arsène Soukry, *Geographie de Moïse de Corène* (1881). The text of the short recension was published as Movsēs' *Matenagrutᶜiwnkᶜ* (1865), which also includes the text of the *Book of Chries* (Rhetoric) and of various homilies attributed to him; and in *Anania Širakacᶜu, Matenagrutᶜyunə* (1944).

Studies. For a résumé of the debate on the date of Movsēs' *History,* see Cyril Toumanoff, "On the Date of the Pseudo-Moses of Chorene," in *Handes amsoriya,* **75** (1961). A guide to the more important studies on Movsēs and his sources is in the introduction and bibliography in the translation and commentary by Robert W. Thomson.

For the *Geography* attributed to Movsēs, see Josef Murkuart, *Ērānšahr nach der Geographie des Ps.-Moses Xorenaçᶜi* (1901, repr. 1970); Sowren T. Eremyan, *Hayastanĕ ēst "Ašχarhacᶜoycᶜ"-i* (1963); R. H. Hewsen, "Armenia According to the Ašχarhacᶜuycᶜ," in *Revue des études arméniennes,* n.s. **2** (1965).

On the *Book of Chries* attributed to Movsēs, see A. Baumgartner, "Über das Buch 'die Chrie,'" in *Zeitschrift der Deutschen morganländischen Gesellschaft,* **40** (1886); Romano Sgarbi, "Contributo allo studio delle fonte dell'opera *Yałags pitoyitç* attribuita a Mosè Corenese," in

Rendiconti, Istituto Lombardo, Accademia di Scienze e Lettere, Classe di Lettere e Scienze Morali e Storiche, **103** (1969).

ROBERT W. THOMSON

[See also **Alexander Romances; Armenia: History of; Armenian Literature; Bagratids, Armenian; Eusebius of Caesarea; Gregory the Illuminator, St.; Historiography, Armenian; Mamikonean; Măstocᶜ, St.; Socrates Scholasticus.**]

MOZARABIC ART is the traditional term employed for much of the Christian architecture and art of tenth-century Spain. It should properly be used, however, only for the art of Christians who had lived under Muslim rule, as the word itself suggests.

In the second half of the ninth century, large numbers of the Mozarabs of Córdoba openly sought martyrdom by publicly blaspheming the prophet Muḥammad before Muslim authorities. The Mozarabs of southern Spain, who had hitherto lived in relative peace practicing their faith unostentatiously under Islamic rule, were probably responding to social and economic frustrations and feelings of religious and political impotence. It is thus not surprising that following this limited but dramatic "persecution," large numbers of Mozarabs, including entire monasteries of monks and nuns, heeded the invitation of Asturian and Leonese rulers in the north of Spain to repopulate the Christian-Muslim frontier. This repopulation of the Duero (Douro) region is highly significant to Mozarabic art. It necessitated the construction, in a relatively limited period, of a great many buildings in the same geographical zone. Further, these monasteries were built to serve monks for whom the building of churches was practically forbidden in their former home under Muslim rule. And finally, they are the buildings of a highly politicized group of immigrants, whose move to the north marked a new beginning for the Reconquest.

MOZARABIC ARCHITECTURE

In the earliest surviving Mozarabic church of the Resettlement is found a document of the aspirations of the Mozarabs. A technical examination of S. Miguel de Escalada (913) reveals it to be a product of a local masonry tradition. The exterior of the wooden-roofed basilica is constructed of ashlar quoined rubblework that changes to brick at the clerestory level in order to lighten the wall. This technique, the capital types, the triapsidal east end and other details of construction all point to Asturian-Leonese masons as the actual builders of Escalada. Yet there are certainly startling differences between Escalada and its nearest Asturian contemporaries. Most significant among these is the horseshoe-arched arcade at Escalada, an element of design that entirely transforms the church's interior and provides a striking contrast to the semicircular arched arcades of Asturian basilicas. Escalada further contains some significant dispositions in plan that had not appeared in Asturian architecture for over a century. Foremost among these is a separation of the nave from a tripartite crossing. The screen of horseshoe arches that achieves this segregation originally featured a low parapet screen and curtained openings as well.

These changes both in the elevation and plan of Escalada point to a return to a Visigothic architectural style, and perhaps to a renewed and conservative assertion of the segregation of clergy and laity called for by the Visigothic (called "Mozarabic") liturgy. One might even see in Escalada a conscious revival of the Visigothic style of building that was ignored in the north during the two centuries that separate Escalada from the Muslim invasion. Indeed, the horseshoe-arched arcade at Escalada is identical in proportion and effect to the Visigothic one at nearby S. Juan de Bãnos (661). There is in this choice of building style by the Mozarabic patrons both an element of tradition and one of conscious change as well. The visual tradition to which the Mozarabs were accustomed in the south was probably a Visigothic one, as can be seen in the early Mozarabic church of S. María de Melque, near Toledo (probably late eighth or early ninth century). Built during a relaxed moment in Muslim-Christian relations in a town close to the frontier, Melque seems to be a direct continuation of Visigothic building practice; it is constructed of ashlar masonry on a cross plan, and features a crossing characterized by horseshoe arches. This example of a continuous tradition is quite different from developments at Escalada, where indigenous masons were apparently directed to build in a style quite foreign to their own.

This conscious assertion of a historical style by the Mozarabs becomes clear when one considers their ideological commitment to the Reconquest. While Alfonso III of Asturias-León (*r.* 866–910) staged one of the earliest successful campaigns against Muslim forces, Mozarabic chronicles sought through the writing of new histories to connect their new kings with the line of the Visigoths, hoping to

MOZARABIC ART

S. María de Melque, nave and choir, late 8th–early 9th century. PHOTO: ZODIAQUE

return to a time when a strong Christian monarchy held the entire Iberian Peninsula. The Mozarabs' aspirations are very clear in this passage from the *Crónica Albedense:*

> Christ is our hope; because before much longer than 170 years will the audacity of our enemies be paid back and the peace of Christ will return to his Church. Even the same Arabs predict . . . the proximity of their finish, and that the restoration of the reign of the Visigoths over all Spain must be, for our glorious prince Alfonso.

Mozarabic building following Escalada also exhibits a disposition for Visigothic traditions, particularly in plan and the partitioning of interior space. Yet the later buildings contain details of construction that reveal the impact of Islamic architecture as well. The ribbed vaults at Santiago de Peñalba (937) reflect developments in Córdoba or North Africa, for instance. Most striking, however, is the variant of the horseshoe arch favored by Islam that appears in the interior of Peñalba. It inscribes more of a circle than does a normal Visigothic arch (four-fifths of a circle or $r + \frac{4}{5}r$) and thus is more decorative, jutting into the arch opening more radically. This horseshoe arch is also constructed differently from the Visigothic one. Here the first voussoirs are laid in tas-de-charge (in which the first voussoirs of the arch are laid horizontally and, at times, extend into the wall), as they are in the Mosque of Córdoba. Indeed, new traditions make their mark on Mozarabic architecture by the second quarter of the tenth century; ashlar-based masonry styles appear at S. Miguel de Celanova (936) and in the porch addition to Escalada (940's), and the new vaulting and arch types are joined by the increased use of decorative roll-corbels (a corbel encasing rosettes or wheel-like forms) and other elements foreign to both Visigothic and Asturian traditions.

In works of the tenth century that were less likely to have felt the direct influence or intervention of actual Mozarabs, formal choices seem more traditional or spontaneous and less the product of conscious intervention of the patron. They appear, in fact, to be the perpetuation of local building traditions. Thus, in the "Mozarabic" architecture of

S. Baudillo de Berlanga, choir seen from nave, late 10th century. FROM JACQUES FONTAINE, *L'ART PRÉROMAN HISPANIQUE*, II (1977)

tenth-century Catalonia, a rubble-based horseshoe-arched style might reflect continuity or Early Christian and Visigothic building there. An exception would be the early church at S. Michel de Cuxa, a major monument that felt, like much of Catalonia, northern influence as well. The art of tenth-century Spain indeed need not be islamicized art at all, but rather work that demonstrates a concern with Spain's Christian history, and with Spain's Christian future.

MOZARABIC PAINTING

Islamic influence in Mozarabic architecture was limited to technical and decorative factors in later buildings. An analogous situation may be seen in Mozarabic illumination. The "Mozarabic" immigration stimulated monasticism in the Asturian-Leonese kingdoms, and with it the art of manuscript illumination. Although all of the painting executed in the Leonese empire in the tenth century cannot be identified as the work of the Mozarabs, some of it can be seen as the product of the same cultural revival that produced the *Crónica Albedense,* and S. Miguel de Escalada. A haunting vision of the uniqueness of the Spaniard's political and cultural situation can be seen in this new painting style. In a full-page evangelist figure from a Bible (dating from 920) now in the Cathedral of León, one sees its beginnings. The portrait of St. Luke is executed in an almost completely schematized manner. His body, garment, face, and feet—even the winged bull that represents him—are all formed of long bands of rich color. Each form is subdivided into flattened, intensely colored ribbons. Indeed, what unifies the composition is not the repetition of shapes or its symmetrical design so much as the repetition of combinations of pure, opaque color, the "coloristic unity of objects and their surroundings," of which Meyer Schapiro speaks.

The Apocalypse had played an extremely important role in Spanish liturgy since Visigothic times, and it became increasingly important after 776, when Beatus of Liébana, an Asturian monk, compiled a twelve-book commentary on it. An essay on the book of the Bible that describes the victory of good Christians over false prophets, Beatus' *Commentary on the Apocalypse (Tractatus de apocalipsis)* had a tremendous impact on an Iberian world challenged by infidels and racked by heresy. Little wonder then that it became the most often illustrated work of Spanish painting, apparently replacing the Gospelbook, very few copies of which can be attributed to this period in Spain. In contrast, more than twenty illuminated copies of Beatus' *Commentary* survive today. One of the most striking of these is manuscript 644 of the Pierpont Morgan Library, New York, the work of Maius (Magius), a monk from Tábara. Though dated 926, the Morgan Beatus was probably completed years later. In a miniature of the Last Judgment, vestiges of the classical heritage nurtured by Spain for so many centuries are still perceptible. However, what most characterizes its style is in fact the total loss of plastic and spatial values that are associated with the classical tradition. The "judged," holding hands in the right portion of this highly original composition, are repetitive, ornamental forms, bound together by shape and color. Indeed, Mozarabic illumination seems not to have felt or accepted the impact of the Carolingian revival of late antique art but to have persisted instead in the dramatic and forceful use of color, which here imbues the groups of tiny, identical figures and their schematized background with a tremendous intensity and force. It is a poignance doubly felt through the imposing double-page format of the miniature, which monumentalizes the composition and its impact. We can probably assume that these Beatus illustrations belong to an independent tradition that attained its final form only in the tenth century, contemporary with Mozarabic architecture of the resettlement. Indeed, like Mozarabic architecture, the illumination of the tenth century exhibits at times a didactic political spirit. There are surprisingly few instances of direct Islamic influence in these miniatures, but when they do occur, it is sometimes not in a context flattering to Muslim culture. Thus, specific and recognizable Islamic forms are associated with the depiction of the Whore of Babylon and Balthazar's palace in the Morgan Beatus. Just as in Mozarabic architecture, then, tenth-century illumination in Spain confronts us with an often politicized art, one that is uniquely Spanish, not only in terms of the strictly formal choices involved but in the frequent meaning attributed to the history of a form, be it Islamic or Visigothic.

Meyer Schapiro has shown to what extent the Mozarabic style of painting embodied a conservative national cultural expression when Spain was subject to Roman reform in the last quarter of the eleventh century. It might be appropriate to consider the Mozarabs' horseshoe-arched architectural style in the same light. Both Mozarabic architecture and illumination were independent Iberian traditions, excluded from the repeated revivals of Rome that so characterized the contemporary arts of the rest of

MOZARABIC LITERATURE

Europe. They were indeed the first uniquely Spanish arts.

BIBLIOGRAPHY

José Fernández Arenas, *Mozarabic Architecture* (1972), text overgeneralized and often misleading but photographs often valuable; Jacques Fontaine, *L'art préroman hispanique,* II (1977), most complete survey of the methodological and historical questions, but weaker on formal analysis; Manuel Gómez-Moreno, *Iglesias mozárabes* (1919, repr. 1975), traditional and in certain respects dated but still the most complete and scholarly survey of architecture; Meyer Schapiro, "From Mozarabic to Romanesque in Silos," in *Romanesque Art* (1977), 28–101, a classic study; John Williams, *Early Spanish Manuscript Illumination* (1977), valuable, concise introduction with excellent illustrations.

JERRILYNN D. DODDS

[See also **Apocalypse, Illustration of; Asturian Art; Asturias-León; Beatus Manuscripts; Islamic Art and Architecture; Maius; Manuscript Illumination, European; Romanesque Architecture; Spain, Christian-Muslim Relations; Visigothic Art.**]

MOZARABIC LITERATURE. From the eighth century on, the Christians who lived in Muslim Spain developed a culture and language of their own. These Christians were given a variety of names, by both the free Christians and the Arabs, denoting their special place between the two cultures, but the term "Mozarab" has prevailed. Little remains of their literature, although the discovery of twenty short Ibero-Romance poems written in Hebrew characters—made by Samuel M. Stern in 1948—has helped provide some understanding of what this literature was like.

Until the late 1940's the poems of the Provençal troubadour William VII of Poitiers (also known as Duke William IX of Aquitaine, 1071–1112) were thought to be the oldest literary creations in any European Romance language, and, lacking further documentation, the beginnings of European Romance lyrics. The origins, however, were heatedly debated among scholars from the first half of the nineteenth century on. Based on strong lines of reasoning, two schools evolved: the individualists, who considered early Romance poetry to be the effort of individual authors; and the traditionalists, nicknamed "populists," who believed in the existence of lost texts—prior to the ones now known—molded into genres by popular oral intervention.

The sensational discovery of Samuel M. Stern in 1948 gave the traditionalists a resounding victory. Searching through old manuscripts in the Cairo genizah (synagogue), Stern found the twenty poems, which were the closing verses *(kharjas)* of twenty Hebrew compositions called *muwashshaḥs*. The existence of these short carols in Romance had been postulated prior to Stern but went unnoticed until his findings attracted the attention of Romance scholars all over Europe. In 1949 Dámaso Alonso wrote the first in-depth essay on these poems, some of them dating back to the first half of the eleventh century—much earlier than the compositions of William VII of Poitiers. Studies and new discoveries of *kharjas*, both in Hebrew and in Arabic, followed; today the bibliography on the subject is lengthy.

The *muwashshaḥ,* invented around the first half of the tenth century in Al-Andalus by Muqaddam ibn Muᶜāfā al-Qabri, was extensively used by the Andalusian Arabs and imitated by Jewish writers. Together with the *zajal,* it represented a revolutionary development in Arabic prosodic and poetic arts. Unlike the classical Arabic poem, the *qaṣīda,* which has no divisions and is characterized by monorhyme and quantitative rhythm, the *muwashshaḥ* is divided into five stanzas, and each stanza into two parts; the first *(dawr, bayt)* changes its rhyme in each stanza, while the second *(qufl)* keeps the same rhyme. The poem opens with a prelude *(maṭlaᶜ),* having the same rhyme, rhythm, and number of verses as the *qufl.* The last *qufl,* called *kharja* (or *markaz*), is the basis of the composition. It sets the rhymic and rhythmic pattern of the poem. The scheme of the composition presented several possibilities, the most common being thus fixed: *AA (maṭlaᶜ) bbb (bayt), AA (qufl), cccAA, dddAA, eeeAA, fffAA (kharja).* Not all scholars agree on whether the Romance *kharja* also sets the rhythmic pattern of the *muwashshaḥ.* Vicente Cantarino believes that it does, and that the rhythm is syllabic. Thus, he concludes, "The linguistic and prosodic virtuosity required from a poet who is attempting to use in classical Arabic the formal structure he finds in a verse composed in a different language, constitutes the major merit and achievement of this type of bilingual composition."

The importance of the *kharja* is pointed out in two texts of the twelfth century (Ibn Bassam̃ al-Shantarini's *Dhakhīra,* and Ibn Sanāᵓ al-Mulk's *Dar al-Ṭiraz*). They state that Al-Qabri's method of composing the *muwashshaḥ* was "taking the expression in the colloquial or in Romance . . . and basing on it

MOZARABIC LITERATURE

the *muwashshaḥ*" (Ibn Bassām), and that "the *kharja* should be in the vulgar language, or in a non-Arabic language, provided that it is lighthearted and witty" and preceded by an introductory formula (Ibn Sanāʾ).

Written in Arabic and Hebrew characters, the Romance *kharja*s presented some interpretative problems due to the absence of vowels and the substantial amount, in some of them, of Arabic borrowings. But sound philological studies have solved most of these problems and, regardless of some linguistic fluctuations, these *kharja*s have come to be known as Mozarabic songs, Mozarabic being the earliest Romance language spoken by the Andalusian Christians who lived among the Arab conquerors.

The most attractive feature of these songs is their simplicity and candor. They are feminine love songs, presented from the point of view of a young maiden in love with her *ḥabīb* (friend, lover). An example of their attraction is the unsophisticated directness of expression:

ky fr yw w ky d dmyby	*ke fareyo o ke serad de mibi*
hbyby	*habibi*
nwn ty twlgs dmyby	*non te tolgas de mibi*

What shall I do?/What will become of me?/My love,/ Do not forsake me!

While the lover talks in the *muwashshaḥ*, it is the beloved who talks in the *kharja*. Her attitude toward love is refreshingly ingenuous: at times there is a note of mischief; at others, a tone of sadness and desperation. From the open invitation to the lover to come to her, and the exultant attitude with an enticing note of amorous surrender, to the lonely anguish and the cry figuratively addressed to the mother, the young maiden appears in a full range of moods. Hers is always a personal, intimate, and concrete love relation. "This realism evoked by the *kharja* is underlined even more strikingly by its being presented as a direct quotation," says Vicente Cantarino; and thus—he continues—the charm of the *kharja* can be appreciated only within the context of the academic stylization of the *muwashshaḥ*.

One problem, however, will continue to demand the attention of scholars: up to what point can it be said that these *kharja*s are picked from a popular tradition? The fact that the *muwashshaḥ* grew from the *kharja*, and not vice versa, has led some scholars to believe in its popular tradition. Also supporting this view is the existence of similar maiden songs in the Galician-Portuguese *Cantigas d'amigo*, in the Castilian *villancicos*, and throughout Europe in the *Frauenlieder*. Moreover, the well-known scholar P. F. Ganz has postulated the existence of these feminine songs in Egyptian literature. Other scholars contend that the dichotomy of moods in the *kharjas*—exultant in the Arabic, sad in the Hebrew—points to their creation by the authors of the *muwashshaḥ*s , who feign a simplicity that is no more than a literary convention.

The majority of scholars, however, favor the popular-traditional origin of the *kharja*s. One thing stands clear: if we can believe Stern's discoveries, the beginnings of European lyrics are older than they were thought to be, although the origins, being a rhetorical problem, will continue to remain open to discussion.

BIBLIOGRAPHY

Iḥsān ʿAbbas, *Taʾrikh al-adab al-Andalusī* (1962); Dámaso Alonso, "Cancioncillas 'de amigo' mozárabes," in *Revista de filología española,* **33** (1949), and *Primavera temprana de la lírica europea* (1961); Joseph Bédier, "Les fêtes de mai et les commencements de la poésie lyrique au moyen âge," in *Revue des deux mondes,* **135** (1896); Hennig Brinkmann, *Entstehungsgeschichte des Minnesangs* (1926, repr. 1971); Vicente Cantarino, "Lyrical Traditions in Andalusian Muwashshahas," in *Comparative Literature,* **21** (1969), and "The Composition of Andalusian Muwashshahas with a Romance Kharja," in *Kentucky Romance Quarterly,* **21** (1974); M. Criado del Val, "Sobre los orígenes del iberoromance: Correspondencia verbal de las jarchas y las canciones de amigo," in *Boletín de filología,* **19** (1960); Peter Dronke, *Medieval Latin and the Rise of the European Love-Lyric* (1965, 2nd ed. 1968); Guido Errante, *Sulla lirica romanza delle origini* (1943); Margit Frenk, "La lírica pretrovadoresca," in Erich Köhler, ed., *Les genres lyriques* (1979); P. F. Ganz, "The 'Cancionerillo Mozárabe' and the Origin of the Middle High German 'Frauenlied,' " in *Modern Language Review,* **48** (1953); Emilio García-Gómez, "La lírica hispano-árabe y la aparición de la lírica romance," in *Al-Andalús,* **12** (1956), and "Estudios del Dār aṭ-Ṭirāz," in *Al-Andalús,* **27** (1962); Klaus Heger, *Die bisher veröffentlichen Harǧas und ihre Deutungen* (1960); Richard Hitchcock, *The Kharjas: A Critical Bibliography* (1977); Alfred Jeanroy, *Les chansons de Guillaume IX* (1913); Ramón Menéndez-Pidal, *Poesía juglaresca y juglares* (1924), *Poesía juglaresca y orígenes de las literaturas románicas,* 6th ed., rev. and enl. (1957), "La primitiva lírica europea," in *Revista de filología española,* **43** (1960), and *España, eslabón entre la cristiandad y el islam,* 2nd ed. (1968); Gaston Paris, "Les origines de la poésie lyrique en France," in *Mélanges de littérature française du moyen âge* (1912); Silvio Pellegrini, *Studi su trove e trovatori della prima lirica ispano-portoghese,* 2nd ed., rev. and enl. (1959); Aurelio Roncaglia, "Problemi delle origini," in Umberto Bosco *et al.*, eds., *Questioni e correnti* *di storia letteraria* (1949); W. Ross, "Sind die Ḥarǧas Reste eine frühen romanischen Lyrik?" in *Archiv für das Studium der neueren Sprachen und Literaturen,* **193** (1956); Francisco Simonet, *Historia de los Mozárabes de España* (1967); Jose María Solá-Solé, *Corpus de poesía mozárabe* (1973); Samuel Stern, "Les vers finaux en espagnol dans les *muwaššaḥ*s hispano-hebraïques," in *Al-Andalús,* **13** (1948), and "Un *muwaššaḥ* arabe avec terminaison espagnole," in *Al-Andalús,* **14** (1949); Antonio Viscardi, *Posizioni vecchie e nuove della storia letteraria romanza* (1944).

ANTONIO TORRES-ALCALÁ

[See also **Cairo Genizah; Cantigas de Amor, Amigo, and Escarno; Kharja; Spanish Literature: Lyric Poetry.**]

MOZARABIC RITE

HISTORY

Mozarabic rite is a special liturgy that originated in the Iberian Peninsula, spread through Spain and Gaul during the Visigothic period, and was in use until 1080. Today this liturgy persists in the city of Toledo. Since its suppression the rite has been generally known as Mozarabic, but modern scholars vacillate between the designations Mozarabic, Visigothic, and Hispanic.

The development and formulation of the rite probably began in the mid third century when the first Christian missionaries preached the Gospels in the Peninsula, and was further influenced by contacts with Eastern and Western churches, and particularly by the Roman-Gallican rite. Some features of the rite show influences from the East (Alexandria, Jerusalem, Ethiopia), north Italy (Milan), and North Africa (Carthago), but these features are integrated into a purely Western and Latin liturgy. Its basic structure was fixed in the late Roman Empire and then it flourished in the Visigothic period, particularly during the seventh century. The rite displayed a broad range of regional variants, as attested by unsuccessful efforts of the Council of Toledo (633) to reach a liturgical unification. In the late sixth and seventh centuries, a number of Hispanic Fathers created new liturgical texts and introduced new melodies into the chant, purifying it of spurious elements. The most important among them were the brothers Leander and Isidore of Seville, Braulio of Saragossa, Conancio of Palencia, and Ildefonsus and Julianus of Toledo, the latter submitting the rite to the most profound revision.

The Arab invasion of Spain in 711 did not paralyze the creative evolution of the liturgy, because Christians obtained a statute of religious liberty, which guaranteed them the practice of their religion inside their churches. The Christian population, initially more numerous than the Muslims, began to be known as the Mozarabs. Arab tolerance did not mean equality, however, and many Christians eventually converted to Islam or became culturally arabized.

In the eleventh century, Christians from the independent northern kingdoms prevailed militarily and economically over the divided Muslim south. This development coincided with the rise of the Roman papacy to the forefront of the European political scene, which encouraged unification and centralization efforts, which in turn did away with the autonomy of peripheral churches such as the Hispanic one. By the orders of Gregory VII the rite of Christian kingdoms in the Iberian Peninsula was replaced by the Roman rite at the Council of Burgos in 1080. The abolition provoked resistance, and Christians in Moslem areas continued practicing the rite. At the time of the Council of Burgos, Toledo was still in Arab hands. When it was reconquered by Alfonso VI of Castile in 1085, the king had to make concessions to Mozarab citizens in matters of *fueros* and liberties, and the Mozarabic rite was thus unofficially permitted to be used in six Toledan parishes.

The Mozarabic community in Toledo flourished during the twelfth century, when Mozarab refugees from the south came to the city. By the end of the fifteenth century, however, the Mozarabic rite had almost disappeared, and at this point it was revived by Cardinal Jiménez de Cisneros, archbishop of Toledo. He founded the chapel of Corpus Christi in the cathedral of Toledo and ordered the printing of a Mozarabic missal (1500) and a breviary (1502). The Mozarabic community of Toledo was revitalized by the impact of the First International Congress of Mozarabic Studies in 1975, and by the subsequent creation of the Institute of Visigothic-Mozarabic Studies of San Eugenio (1977).

DESCRIPTION

There are considerable differences between individual Mozarabic manuscripts. These differences have been interpreted in various ways, but most recently there arose a hypothesis of two traditions, or variants, of the rite, called *A* and *B*. The traditions differ in the Mass, the office, and the calendar. According to one view, tradition *A* was common in Toledo and in the north, while tradition *B* originated in Seville and in the south and came to Toledo with Mozarabic immigrants from Andalusia. What is certain is that both variants coexisted peacefully in Toledo and that each was practiced in three parishes. Medieval authors, for instance, Chancellor López de Ayala, knew about this difference and attributed the variant *A* to St. Leander and the variant *B* to St. Isidore. Alonso Ortiz, the editor of the Mozarabic missal and breviary, transmitted only tradition *B*, which is the only one now in force.

The most characteristic differential features of Mozarabic rite are as follows: In the Mass, there are always three lessons (Prophecy, Epistle, Gospel). Despite a common general scheme, the prayers of the eucharistic anaphora are different for each celebration (except the narrative and the consecratory formula of the Lord's Supper).

The diptychs and the prayer of peace go before the *illatio* or preface. Then the host is broken into seven pieces (tradition *A*) or nine pieces (tradition *B*) and a proclamation of faith follows. The main books used for the service are the *manuale*, sacramentary or altar book, *liber commicus* or lectionary, and *antiphonarium,* which contains the musical part.

In the cathedral office, there were two basic hours, vespers and matins. At the end of the fourth century, Egeria, in *Itinerarium Egeriae,* compared the Mozarabic vespers to the Jerusalem office, and the first Council of Toledo in 400 regulated in its canon 9 the celebration of vespers in cities and towns. Matins had the character of a vigil and tended to integrate with the Mass. Later, the three classical minor hours were added. The basic service books are the psalter, *psalmographus, liber canticorum, antiphonarium,* and *liber orationum.*

The monastic office added numerous hours, with the intention to sanctify all moments of day and night. For their recitation, the monks used the psalter and/or *liber horarum.*

For the administration of sacraments, the *liber ordinum* was used. It existed in two types, one, the *maior,* for episcopal use, and the other, known as *minor,* for presbyters.

The most elaborate offices and masses were centered around Easter, with the Lent preparations and post-Easter celebrations until Pentecost. The cycle of Advent consisted of five or six Sundays as a preparation for Epiphany (the Nativity was introduced later). During this period the Marian feast of expectation was celebrated on 18 December. For the ordinary time, the rite lacked a set system of masses and offices.

BIBLIOGRAPHY

Ramón Gonzálvez, "El arcediano Joffré de Loaysa y las parroquias urbanas de Toledo en 1300," in Congreso Internacional de Estudios Mozárabes, 1st, Toledo, Spain, 1975, *Historia mozárabe* (1978), "El canciller don Pedro López de Ayala y el problema de las dos tradiciones del rito hispánico," in *Liturgia y música mozárabes* (1978), and "Las minorías étnico-religiosas en la Edad Media española," in *Historia de la Iglesia en España*, II (1982), chap. 10, and "The Persistence of the Mozarabic Rite in Toledo after 1080," in his *Saint Peter, Saint James, and Saint Denis* (1986); José Janini, *Liber misticus de cuaresma* (1979), *Liber misticus de cuaresma y pascua* (1980), and *Liber missarum de Toledo*, 2 vols. (1982–1983); José María de Mora Ontalva, "Nuevo boletín de liturgia hispánica antigua," in *Hispania sacra*, **26** (1973); Jordi Pinell, "Boletín de liturgia hispano-visigótica," *ibid.*, **9** (1956), and "Liturgia hispanica," in *Diccionario de historia eclesiástica de España*, II (1972); Germán Prado, *Manual de liturgia hispano-visigótica o mozárabe* (1927), and *Historia del rito mozárabe o toledano* (1928); Juan Francisco Rivera, ed., *Estudios sobre la liturgia mozárabe* (1965).

RAMÓN GONZÁLVEZ

[See also **Braulio of Saragossa, St.; Gallican Rite; Ildefonsus, St.; Isidore of Seville, St.; Julianus of Toledo, St.; Mass, Liturgy of the Milanese Rite; Toledo.**]

MREN, CHURCH OF. The large Armenian church of Mren near Kars was constructed between about 631 and 639 by Prince Nerseh Kamsarakan during the rule of Prince David Saharuni, according to an inscription. It is a domed basilica with a nave and two aisles. Four pillars support the octagonal drum on which the central cupola rests.

Mren is notable for the figural sculpture over the north and west portals, among the earliest extant on the exterior of a Christian church. The Adoration of Christ appears on the west with saints, angels, and personages who may represent the two princes and an Armenian bishop. A unique composition, possibly the consecration of Mren, is on the north.

BIBLIOGRAPHY

Richard Krautheimer, *Early Christian and Byzantine Architecture* (1965); Josef Strzygowski, *Die Baukunst der Armenier und Europa,* 2 vols. (1918); Michel and Nicole Thierry, "La cathédrale de Mrèn et sa décoration," in *Ca-*

Bishop Theophilus and Prince David Saharuni. Figural sculpture from west portal of Church of Mren, *ca.* 631–639.

hiers archéologiques, **21** (1971); Natan Tokarskii, *Architektura Armenii IX–XIV VV* (1961).

LUCY DER MANUELIAN

[See also **Armenian Art.**]

MTKVARI. See **Kura River.**

MUᶜĀWIYA (*ca.* 602–680), fifth caliph of Islam (661–680) and founder of the Umayyad dynasty of caliphs in Syria (661–750). He was the son of Abū Sufyān, the head of the clan of Umayya and a leading merchant of Mecca, and of Hind bint ᶜUtba. From 624 until 630 his father led the Meccan opposition to the rising power of Muḥammad at Medina, and Muᶜāwiya participated in the abortive Meccan siege of Medina in 627. After the truce with Muḥammad at Al-Ḥudaybīya in 628, his sister, Umm Habība, married Muḥammad. When Mecca surrendered to Muḥammad in 630, Muᶜāwiya converted to Islam along with his parents and served Muḥammad as a scribe until 632.

Abū Sufyān had engaged in trade with Syria and owned property near Damascus, and in 633/634 his son Yazīd was put in charge of one of the columns of the Muslim army that invaded Syria. Muᶜāwiya joined his brother with reinforcements and led his vanguard. He participated in the battles of Ajnadāyn in 634 and of Yarmūk in 636. Afterward Yazīd and Muᶜāwiya were sent by Abū ᶜUbayda to help take the coastal cities of Acre, Tyre, Sidon, Beirut, and ᶜArqa; and Muᶜāwiya was present when Jerusalem surrendered to ᶜUmar in 638. When plague killed most of the Muslim leaders in Syria, including Yazīd, in 639, ᶜUmar made Muᶜāwiya governor of Syria.

As governor his first task was to complete the conquest of Syria by taking the remaining coastal cities. Caesarea fell to him in 640 and Ascalon in 644. When his cousin ᶜUthmān succeeded ᶜUmar as commander of the faithful in 644, he confirmed Muᶜāwiya as governor of Syria and of the Jazīra. After the fall of Tripoli in 645, Muᶜāwiya rebuilt, fortified, and garrisoned Ascalon, Latakia, and Antartus to protect the coast against Byzantine attacks, and he began to build a fleet in the shipyard at Acre. He also settled Arab tribesmen along the northern frontier of Syria and in the Jazīra. He made Damascus the capital of Syria and employed former Byzantine officials, such as Sarjūn ibn Manṣūr, to administer the finances. Muᶜāwiya established close ties with the local Jacobite Christian Arab tribe of Kalb by marrying Maysūn, the daughter of their sheik. Their son, Yazīd, was raised in the desert with her tribe.

As governor of Syria, Muᶜāwiya built a base of local support by identifying with the interests of the Arabs there. He organized the defense of Syria against the Greeks and Armenians and used Syria as a base of expansion by land and sea against Byzantine Anatolia, Armenia, and the eastern Mediterranean. Raids beginning in 646 that penetrated Anatolia as far as Caesarea, Amorium, and Antioch in Pisidia provoked a joint Byzantine-Armenian counterattack that broke down because of their inability to cooperate, and brought a Muslim invasion of Armenia. Muᶜāwiya's Syrian fleet attacked Cyprus in 649, but the fleet being prepared at Tripoli was destroyed, and a truce was concluded with the Byzantines in the summer of 651. The Armenians defeated a Muslim invasion in 650 but agreed to pay tribute.

The truce was broken by the Byzantine invasion of Armenia in 652, which was followed by intense conflict on land and sea. In 652/653 Cyprus was occupied and garrisoned, a joint overland and naval attack on Constantinople was attempted, and Rhodes

MUʿĀWIYA

was attacked. By 654/655 the Armenian fortresses were taken and garrisoned. This phase of the conflict reached its climax in 655, when two armies, one led by Muʿāwiya, invaded Anatolia, and the combined Syrian–Egyptian fleet defeated and destroyed the Byzantine fleet in the Battle of the Masts *(dhat al-ṣawārī)* off the Lycian coast. This victory made the Muslims the dominant naval power in the eastern Mediterranean and left Anatolia open to attack, which was prevented only by the assassination of ʿUthmān in 656 and the outbreak of civil war among the Muslims.

Muʿāwiya had tried to discourage the growing opposition to ʿUthmān, and when ʿAlī succeeded him, Muʿāwiya withheld his allegiance and left ʿAlī to his enemies, who began to call for the punishment of ʿUthmān's murderers. When ʿAlī defeated his enemies at Basra in 656 and called on Muʿāwiya to recognize him, Muʿāwiya broke with him openly, claimed the right of vengeance as ʿUthmān's next of kin, took over the leadership of the opposition to ʿAlī, called for a council to choose a new commander of the faithful, and, with the backing of the Syrian army, received the oath of allegiance as an independent governor in Jerusalem. When ʿAlī set out for Syria with his army, Muʿāwiya met him with his Syrian forces at Ṣiffīn in July 657. The battle was indecisive and ended with an agreement to submit their differences to arbitration, which was decided in favor of Muʿāwiya in January 659. In the meantime he had secured a treaty with the Byzantines in July 658 in return for paying them tribute. He occupied Egypt, and in 660 he organized his own pilgrimage to Mecca and was acknowledged as commander of the faithful in Jerusalem. When ʿAlī was murdered in January 661, his eldest son, Ḥasan, waived his claims and acknowledged Muʿāwiya in return for a pension. This ended the civil war.

Muʿāwiya took advantage of the reaction in favor of strong rule after the civil war, took credit for restoring Muslim unity, and claimed legitimacy as the heir and avenger of ʿUthmān, and as the servant and representative of God on earth. Damascus became the capital of the empire that he ruled through tribal delegations and capable subordinates such as Ziyād ibn Abīhi in Iraq and the East, and his cousins ʿAmr ibn al-ʿĀṣ in Egypt, and Marwān ibn al-Ḥakam and Saʿīd ibn al-ʿĀṣ in the Hejaz. He and his governors introduced formal audience procedures, protected themselves with guards *(ḥaras),* and controlled their subjects through an urban police force *(shurṭa).* Administrative effectiveness was increased by bureaucratic reforms and the beginning of centralization at Damascus, although most administration was centralized at the provincial level. Muʿāwiya's reign marks the appearance of a protective loge *(maqṣūra)* for the ruler and the minaret, both added to mosques. At the same time local Muslim judges (qadis) became government officials.

Domain land was identified as such in Iraq and was claimed by the state for its own use; this concept was extended to the Hejaz, and state lands were developed in the Yamāma and Bahrain. Hoping to prevent another civil war, Muʿāwiya nominated his son, Yazīd, to succeed him in 669. Territorial conquest was resumed in order to reoccupy regions, such as Armenia and eastern Iran, that had become independent during the civil war, to fill the treasury with booty and tribute, and to satisfy and divert the soldiers in the garrison cities. New garrisons were established at Qayrawān in 670 to hold North Africa and at Merv in 671 to hold northeastern Iran, from which the army began to campaign across the Oxus River. Land and sea forces under Yazīd besieged Constantinople from 674 until 680, when Muʿāwiya's death and the outbreak of another civil war ended territorial expansion.

Muʿāwiya was famous for his diplomatic skill, his generosity, and his *ḥilm,* the combination of prudent self-control and opportunism. He made Syria a well-organized, secure base for imperial rule, and began the introduction of monarchic and bureaucratic institutions in Islamic government.

BIBLIOGRAPHY

Sources. Al-Balādhurī, *Anṣāb al-ashrāf,* Max Schloessinger and M. Kister, eds. (1971), IVA; Ibn ʿAsākir, *Taʾrīkh Madīnat Dimashq,* Istanbul, Ahmet III Library, MS 2887, vol. XII, fols. 297A–323B; and al-Ṭabarī, *Taʾrīkh al-rusul waʾl-mulūk* II (1879).

Studies. Henri Lammens, *Études sur le règne du calife omaiyade Moʿâwia Ier* (1908); ʿUmar Abūʾl-Naṣr, *Muʿāwiya ibn Abī Sufyān* (1962). The most important historiographical treatment is Erling Petersen, *ʿAlī and Muʿāwiya in Early Arabic Tradition,* P. Lampe Christensen, ed. (1964, repr. and enl. 1974), which has extensive references to the sources.

MICHAEL MORONY

[See also **Abū Sufyān ibn Ḥarb ibn Umayya; ʿAlī ibn Abī Ṭalib; ʿAbd Allah ibn al-Zubayr; ʿAmr ibn al-ʿĀṣ; Caliphate; Damascus; Diplomacy, Islamic; Navies, Islamic; Syria; Umayyads; Yazīd I ibn Muʿāwiya.**]

MUDÉJAR ART

MUDÉJAR ART is a strictly Spanish phenomenon. Although the term refers to Muslims living under Christian domination, it is now accepted that all possible combinations of patronage and artists can be credited with art that falls under this rubric. Mudéjar art was sometimes executed by Muslim slaves working for Christian masters, but often it was produced by Christians upon whom the impact of the visual world of Islam was very great. The nationality of patron and of artist here is clearly secondary to the character of the work that is the result of their collaboration.

Mudéjar art began to appear in the twelfth century, when the reconquest of Spanish Islamic lands set Christians as masters of a large Muslim work force that included a great many sophisticated craftsmen. Although primarily known for their complex geometric wooden ceilings and doors, the Mudéjar artists did not disdain monumental figurative painting, as Islamic artisans did. Thus, Mudéjar paintings with Christian or Western secular themes appeared during nearly the whole four-century survival of the style, from the fairly early decorations of the Church of S. Román in Toledo to the elegant wall paintings of the royal palace at Tordesillas. Nevertheless, figurative painting, of all of the arts practiced by Mudéjar artists, is the one least rooted in their iconophobic Islamic heritage. It is in the styles and techniques that were new to the West that the most profound impact of the Mudéjar artists was felt.

In Toledo survives the most monumental of the crafts for which Mudéjar artists are famous: fine brick church building. S. Fé, S. Isabel la Real, and S. Tomé are three examples of the Mudéjar transformation of a standard basilical exterior. The module of construction in these edifices is the module of decoration, as the thickness of the brick defines each of the rectilinear planes into which an apse or tower is divided. The articulation of these exteriors is further characterized by the use of receding planes of blind arcades, often of horseshoe or pointed-horseshoe arches. The striking effect of these exteriors is enhanced when color is added, as in the El Salvador tower at Teruel.

Brick is combined with ceramic tile, providing a lively and lyrical accent to elaborately interlaced arcades and continuous geometric motifs. The tower shows the translation of geometric and architectonic motifs, so intrinsic to Islamic ornamentation, into a decorative system highly appropriate to Christian edifices.

Belfry tower of the Church of El Salvador of Teruel, early 13th century. COURTESY OF FOTO MAS

The carved stucco reliefs and captials of an extraordinary synagogue in Toledo (now named for the church that succeeded it, S. María la Blanca) attest to the universal appeal of the Mudéjar style. The popularity of this delicate, sophisticated style signals an important cultural assimilation on the part of indigenous Jewish and Christian populations. Such assimilation becomes more poignant in light of Arabic inscriptions included as part of buildings intended for Christians and Jews, such as those in the palace at Tordesillas, or in the Alcázar of Seville, where Kufic inscriptions praise the virtues of the Christian rulers. "Mudéjar" as a term seems inappropriate after the reconquest of the Iberian Peninsula by Christian armies, yet the style, and the craftsmen who practiced it, survived. Mudéjar art became the means by which a great deal of the art of Islamic Spain was assimilated into a unique Spanish artistic tradition. It represents a moment of irony as well, for Mudéjar art is one illustration of a Spain that began to embrace Islamic art and culture at the same moment it banished Islam from the Peninsula.

BIBLIOGRAPHY

Georgiana Goddard King, *Mudéjar* (1927), dated in both style and information, prone to be a bit imaginatively written, yet a decent introduction in English; Basilio Pavón Malonado, *Arte toledano: Islámico y mudéjar* (1973), meticulous study; Leopoldo Torres-Balbás, "Arte mudéjar," in *Ars Hispaniae, IV* (1949), the best introduction, clear-headed and up-to-date.

JERRILYN D. DODDS

[See also **Abbasid Art and Architecture; Almohad Art; Almoravid Art; Islamic Art and Architecture.**]

MUEZZIN (Arabic: *muʾadhdhin*), the functionary who utters the *adhān* or call to prayer among Muslims. Customarily, the *adhān* is issued from the minaret of a mosque at the time of each of the five required daily prayers, as well as before certain special prayers, such as those enjoined during religious festivals and eclipses. The muezzin also utters the *iqāma*, a prayer call made in the mosque itself that begins the actual prayer service.

Various schools of Islamic law require slightly different phrases to be uttered by the muezzin in his *adhān*, and decree different numbers of repetitions of these phrases. Most schools of law, however, enjoin some combination of the following phrases: (1)"God is most great" *(Allāhu akbar)*; (2) "I bear witness that there is no god but God"; (3) "I bear witness that Muḥammad is the apostle of God"; (4) "Come to prayer!"; (5) "Come to salvation!"; (6) "God is most great"; (7) "There is no god but God." In addition, the morning prayer requires the addition of the phrase "Prayer is better than sleep," and Shiite Muslims regularly add the formula, "Come to the best of works."

The *adhān* and the office of muezzin both go back to the early days of the Islamic community. Traditional sources claim that the first muezzin, an Abyssinian freedman named Bilāl, was appointed by the prophet Muḥammad himself, shortly after he and his followers had built the first mosque in Medina in 622, in order to provide a way of summoning the Muslims together for prayer that was distinctively different from the bells and other methods used for this purpose by Christians and other religious communities. It seems likely, however, that the eventual form of the *adhān* as laid out in Islamic religious law may have taken shape as the Muslim prayer rituals (particularly those for the main Friday prayer) crystallized during the early Umayyad period (661–750). Like some other aspects of Islamic cultic practice, the rituals surrounding the *adhān* appear to have been influenced by Jewish and Christian ritual practices. Various hints suggest that the call to prayer was originally called *nidāʾ*, and that it was something distinct from the *adhān*. The word muezzin does occur in the Koran but it has only the general sense of "one who calls out" (Koran 7:44; 9:70), and is not associated with the performance of prayer, for which the term *nidāʾ* ("call") is implied (Koran 62:9): "Oh you who believe, when the call is sounded for prayer on Friday, hasten to the remembrance of God." The *adhān,* on the other hand, seems originally to have been a kind of responsive reading between the muezzin and the congregation that led up to the prayer service *(ṣalāt),* very much on the model of the benedictions in Jewish prayer or the antiphonal readings by Christian deacons that prepared the way for celebration of the mass. The term *adhān* seems gradually to have been extended to both the call to prayer and to the responsive readings, and the original term for the former, *nidāʾ*, dropped. Eventually the character of the original *adhān* as a responsive reading seems also to have been forgotten, and the term acquired its current meaning of "call to prayer." It is worth noting, however, that Muslims who hear the *adhān* are required by the religious law to repeat its phrases, with some minor modifications. This practice is probably the last vestige of the original antiphonal nature of the *adhān.*

It is fair to assume that individuals who served as muezzins may have undertaken other responsibilities in the mosque besides that of calling out the *adhān,* whether as teachers, custodians, or aides to the *imām* or prayer leader. It is impossible to do more than speculate on these activities, however, because the social history of the muezzin has never been properly studied.

BIBLIOGRAPHY

Carl Heinrich Becker, "Zur Geschichte des islamischen Kultus," in *Der Islam,* 3 (1912); Alfred Guillaume, *The Life of Muhammad: A Translation of [Ibn] Isḥāq's Sīrat Rasūl Allāh* (1978); Eugen Mittwoch, "Zur Entstehungsgeschichte des islamischen Gebets und Kultus," in *Abhandlungen der Preussischen Akademie der Wissenschaften*

(1913); Arent Jan Wensinck, *A Handbook of Early Muhammadan Tradition* (1927).

FRED M. DONNER

[See also **Koran; Law, Islamic; Medina; Muḥammad; Philosophy and Theology, Islamic; Sects, Islamic.**]

MUḤAMMAD, the prophet of Islam, was born at Mecca in Arabia about 570 and died in Medina on 8 June 632. He was a posthumous child, his father, ᶜAbd Allāh, having died at Medina on a trading journey. He was brought up first by his mother, Āmina (of the clan of Zuhra), then by his grandfather ᶜAbd al-Muṭṭalib, head of the clan of Hāshim. Zuhra and Hāshim were divisions of the tribe of Quraysh, to which most inhabitants of Mecca belonged.

Mecca has no cultivable land, but about the year 600 it was a prosperous commercial center. From ancient times its shrine, the Kaaba, had been a center of pilgrimage, and the territory of Mecca was regarded as sacred. This, together with the fact that the three months around the time of pilgrimage were also held sacred, encouraged the growth of trade; blood feuds could not be pursued in sacred times and places, and so nomadic tribesmen could safely come to Mecca on pilgrimage and to trade their goods. By 600 the merchants of Mecca had by unscrupulous methods gained monopoly control of the trade by camel caravan from Yemen to Gaza and Damascus, which appears to have included most of the trade between the Indian Ocean and the Mediterranean. Mecca was thus extremely wealthy, but prosperity had resulted in social tensions.

The leading men of the clan of Hāshim were moderately prosperous merchants. By Arab custom, however, Muḥammad as an orphan could inherit nothing from his father or grandfather. He accompanied his uncle Abū Ṭālib, who succeeded his grandfather as head of the clan, on trading journeys to Syria, but he had not the capital to make full use of his great administrative talents. About 595 a wealthy widow, Khadīja, employed him as her agent on a journey to Syria, and was so pleased with his conduct of affairs that she made him an offer of marriage, which he accepted. He was then able to trade on his own account in partnership with a nephew of Khadīja's former husband. Khadīja, though said to be forty at the time of the marriage, bore Muḥammad one or more sons, who died in infancy, and four daughters.

The frustrations he had encountered in his youth probably made Muḥammad more aware of the social malaise in Mecca and led him to meditate on how its ills might be cured. About 610, in the course of his meditations, he had two visions of a great angelic being commissioning him as "messenger of God" (*rasūl Allāh*), and then he was given a message to convey to the people of Mecca. He continued to receive such messages or "revelations" for the rest of his life, apart from a break, perhaps of some months, near the beginning. The revelations were collected in the Koran, which was completed about 650, but much had probably been accomplished by Muḥammad himself during his lifetime. He believed that he was able to distinguish these revelations, which he regarded as the speech of God, from his own thoughts; and he must be adjudged sincere in this belief, even if some non-Muslim scholars would give a different explanation of his revelational experiences. Both sound scholarship and courtesy toward Muslims demand that the Koran should not be spoken of as having been composed by Muḥammad.

By communicating the revelations to suitable persons Muḥammad collected a band of followers, who joined with him in ritual worship or prayer *(ṣalāt)* and also in some practice of almsgiving *(zakāt)*. For a time they met frequently in the house of a wealthy young man, al-Arqam. Other points mentioned in early revelations were the signs of God's goodness and power in nature and in historical events, and the fact that on the Last Day men would be raised from the dead, come before God to be judged, and be assigned to heaven or hell. The revelations also spoke of Muḥammad as a "warner" to his fellow Meccans that they would be judged by God on the Last Day.

It is sometimes said that Muḥammad did not begin to preach publicly until three years after receiving the first revelation, and that this was before he and his followers began to meet in the house of al-Arqam. Within a year or two of the public preaching most of the leading merchants joined in vigorous opposition to Muḥammad and his followers. One reason for this was probably the criticism in the Koran of the merchants' attitudes, especially of the fact that, though they were the leading men in their clans, they did not perform the traditional duties of leading men, such as using their wealth to help indigent clansmen. They may also have thought that Muḥammad, because of his following and his prestige as messenger of God, might one day attain supreme political power in Mecca. Because of this opposition Muḥammad had to put up with many petty vexations, and some of his younger followers were roughly treated by senior members of their families.

Persecution by opponents is given as a reason for the emigration to Ethiopia about 615. Over eighty men went with their families, and were well received by the negus (emperor). Some remained there until 628, presumably making a living by trading. This long stay makes it likely that there were other reasons for the emigration as well as persecution. Muḥammad and those of his followers who remained in Mecca continued to meet opposition. There was much verbal criticism of the teaching of the Koran, and also various forms of economic pressure. It is reported that Muḥammad's chief lieutenant, Abū Bakr (whose daughter ᶜĀᵓisha later became Muḥammad's favorite wife), had his fortune reduced from 40,000 dirhams to 5,000, and only a small part of this decrease can be explained by his practice of buying believing slaves in order to set them free. Despite the opposition Muḥammad was able to continue preaching because he had the protection of the clan of Hāshim, that is, they were prepared to avenge any injury to him. Many of them, including the clan chief, Abū Ṭālib, did not accept Muḥammad's religion, but to disown him would have been a failure in solidarity and would have brought disgrace on the clan. About 616, to try to force the Hāshim to abandon Muḥammad, the other clans of Quraysh joined in some sort of boycott. The Hāshim do not seem to have suffered unduly, and after a period of over two years several clans, finding it disadvantageous, dissociated themselves from the boycott and it came to an end.

After the appearance of serious opposition certain points that had not previously appeared in the Koranic messages now became prominent. Most prominent was the assertion that there is only one God or, as the *shahāda* (the Muslim profession of faith) expresses it in a Koranic phrase, that "there is no deity but God" *(lā ilāha illā 'llāhu)*. There were also repeated references to former prophets who had similarly met with opposition and whom God had eventually caused to triumph, while destroying their opponents. The stories are not told in full, as in the Old Testament, but briefly and with emphasis on particular points. Thus Noah and Lot are regarded as prophets who communicated revelations to their people, were disbelieved, and then were delivered, with their households, when the unbelievers were drowned or overwhelmed by a storm. Something similar happened to three nonbiblical Arabian prophets, Ḥūd, Ṣāliḥ, and Shuᶜayb. Apart from these "punishment stories" there are references for different purposes to Old Testament figures as prophets, notably to Abraham and Moses. These stories served to encourage Muḥammad's followers when things were difficult, and they also showed the pagan Meccans that he was not an innovator but was acting similarly to many former prophets or "messengers of God."

About 619, after the end of the boycott, Muḥammad lost by death both his wife Khadīja and his uncle Abū Ṭālib. The latter was succeeded as clan chief by another uncle, Abū Lahab, who had close business relationships with some of Muḥammad's opponents. To please these men Abū Lahab withdrew the clan's protection from Muḥammad, justifying this on the ground that Muḥammad had dishonored the clan by saying that his grandfather ᶜAbd al-Muṭṭalib was in hell. Abū Lahab is bitterly attacked in the Koran (Sura 111). Muḥammad could now have been killed with impunity, but obtained protection from another clan chief. Presumably, however, this was on condition that he did not continue to spread his religion. A way of escape from this frustrating situation gradually opened through contacts with men from Yathrib (later Medina), who were in Mecca for the pilgrimage in 620 and 621. For that of 622, which took place about June, they brought a representative group of seventy-three men and two women, who met Muḥammad secretly at al-ᶜAqaba (outside Mecca) and made a formal agreement, sometimes called the Pledge of War. In this they accepted Muḥammad as prophet, and also swore to protect him and his followers as they would their nearest kin. Muḥammad then encouraged his followers to go to Medina, and about seventy made the journey, traveling in small groups to prevent their opponents realizing what was happening. Finally Muḥammad himself went, accompanied by Abū Bakr, and reached the outskirts of Medina on 24 September 622. This is his *hijra* (Hegira) or "emigration" (erroneously called "flight" in older books). The Islamic era, indicated by A. H. *(anno Hegirae)*, began on the first day of the Arabian year, 16 July 622.

Medina was an oasis 210 miles (338 km) north of Mecca, producing dates and cereals. It was inhabited by two Arab tribes, al-Aws and al-Khazraj, subdivided into a number of clans, and by a number of Jewish groups. The Jews had developed agriculture in the oasis and had for a time been politically dominant, but in the 620's they were weaker than the Arabs. Each Jewish group was allied to an Arab clan.

Internal quarrels had plagued Medina for decades, and these had culminated in the battle of Buᶜāth about 617, in which most of the Arabs had been involved, while Jewish allies supported both sides. Though there had been no more fighting, the conflict had not been settled, and one of the motives of the Arabs who invited Muḥammad to Medina was the hope that he would act as arbiter between the quarreling factions. Familiarity, too, with the Jewish idea of a Messiah may have made it easier for them to accept Muḥammad as "messenger of God" (his usual title in Arabic).

A document has been preserved known as the "Constitution of Medina." In view of repetitions in its present form it must be a composite, and it must be dated after 627 since it does not mention the three main Jewish groups that had been expelled by that date. Nevertheless it probably represents the terms of the agreement on the basis of which Muḥammad went to Medina, and gives precise form to the negotiations at al-ᶜAqaba. In essence it is an alliance between eight Arab clans and the emigrants (*muhājirūn*) of Quraysh. Jewish groups are included as subordinate allies of particular Arab clans, and there are various provisions to help the smooth running of the alliance. The Quraysh of Mecca are spoken of as enemies. There are no specifically religious provisions, but Muḥammad is spoken of as prophet and other individuals as believers, and God is mentioned several times. Muḥammad has no special powers except that disputes are "to be referred to God and to Muḥammad" and that he has to give permission for war-like expeditions; otherwise he seems to have been merely the chief of the "clan" of emigrants.

Soon after reaching Medina Muḥammad purchased a plot of land and built a house for himself, with separate apartments for his wives round a central courtyard. The courtyard, which had a covered section, was used by the Muslims for worship, and the site is now the Prophet's Mosque. The other emigrants were given hospitality by the Muslims of Medina, collectively known as the Ansar (from the Arabic for "helpers" [of Muḥammad]). Before long groups of emigrants began to go out on raiding expeditions or razzias, in accordance with age-old Arabian custom; their object was to intercept Meccan caravans. The first few expeditions failed because the Meccans were receiving information from well-disposed persons in Medina. At last, in January 624, Muḥammad sent out about a dozen men with sealed orders, and at Nakhla (east of Mecca) these managed to capture a caravan coming from the Yemen, killing one of the guards. This encouraged the Muslims and infuriated the Meccans, but some of the less enthusiastic men of Medina, doubtless afraid of Meccan reprisals, made much of the fact that the participants had violated Meccan sanctity.

Two months later, however, over 200 of the Ansar joined an expedition led by Muḥammad himself with the aim of capturing a wealthy caravan returning from Syria to Mecca. The caravan itself eluded the Muslims, but they encountered a force that had come from Mecca to defend it. The 324 or so Muslims (all of whose names and biographies have been recorded) were outnumbered by about three to one, but they were victorious, killing between forty-five and seventy Meccans, including several leading men, and taking a similar number of prisoners. This battle, called Badr, was interpreted by Muḥammad and the Muslims as God's vindication of their cause, comparable to his vindication of previous prophets by floods and storms.

The Meccans, if they were to maintain their political position in Arabia and keep their trade, could not let this defeat go unavenged. So in March 625 an army of 3,000 well-armed men marched to Medina and invaded the oasis. Though the people of Medina would have been safe from the Meccans in the numerous small forts they had, Muḥammad was persuaded to go to meet them and stationed his force of about 1,000 on the hill of Uḥud. The Muslims repulsed the Meccan infantry, but lost over seventy killed in a flank attack by the superior Meccan cavalry. Despite this partial success the Meccans withdrew without having achieved their strategic aim. For the Muslims, however, this battle caused some spiritual turmoil, for their losses suggested that God was not fighting for them, as they had thought after Badr. In the end the view suggested by a Koranic message was accepted, that the reverse was due to disobedience by a part of the Muslim force, the archers, who left their positions hoping for booty.

In March and April 627 the Meccans returned with 10,000 men, but Muḥammad had dug a trench *(khandaq)* to protect vulnerable points in the perimeter of Medina, and after a fortnight the Meccan army disintegrated and had to retire with nothing accomplished. This showed that Muḥammad was now too strong to be suppressed, and in March 628, when he marched on Mecca with 1,600 men saying he wanted to make the pilgrimage, they barred his way but made a treaty with him as an equal, and allowed him to make the pilgrimage in 629. The peace lasted for over a year and a half until it was violated

MUḤAMMAD

by tribal allies of the Meccans, who attacked a tribe allied to Muḥammad. Muḥammad raised 10,000 men to march on Mecca, and it surrendered with virtually no resistance (January 630). Muḥammad was generous in victory, and most Meccans accepted Islam and by their administrative skills made an important contribution to the expansion of the Islamic empire after Muḥammad's death.

During these years there were many other expeditions, as a result of which several nomadic tribes entered into alliance with Muḥammad and accepted Islam. Some individuals also became Muslims and settled in Medina. A week or two after his entry into Mecca, Muḥammad met and defeated a concentration of nomadic tribes at Ḥunayn, and these also became allies and Muslims. By the time of his death in 632 a great many of the tribes of Arabia had joined the alliance. For his last great expedition (October–December 630) he led 30,000 men northward to near the Gulf of ᶜAqaba and made treaties with small Jewish and Christian communities there, giving them the status of "protected minorities" within the Islamic state or federation.

When Muḥammad went to Medina he had hoped that the Jews there would accept him as prophet, and tried to win them over. Instead most of them played verbal tricks on the Muslims and criticized the divergences of the Koran from the Bible. Various events constituting the "break with Jews" occurred shortly before the battle of Badr in March 624, the chief being that the *qibla* or direction faced in prayer was changed from Jerusalem to Mecca. Disputes arising from trivial incidents led to the expulsion of two Jewish clans from Medina—Qaynuqāᶜ, who were goldsmiths and armorers, in April 624 and al-Naḍīr in August 625. A third clan, the agricultural Qurayẓa, was alleged, probably correctly, to have intrigued with the enemy during the siege of Medina; when they surrendered, the men were executed and the women and children sold into slavery. A few small Jewish groups left in Medina gave no further trouble.

Until 630 Muḥammad had been friendly with Christians, but had had little contact. The Ethiopians had treated the refugees well. Between 628 and 630, however, the Byzantines had finally defeated the Persian Empire in their long war, and the Christian tribes encountered by the Muslims on expeditions to northwest Arabia were tending to return to the Byzantine alliance.

After 622 the Koranic revelations contain polemic against the Jews and to a lesser extent against the Christians. Abraham had a central place in this. It was emphasized that he was neither Jew nor Christian, but a *ḥanīf* or "pure monotheist," and it was claimed that Islam was the true religion of Abraham from which Jews and Christians had deviated. After Muḥammad's death certain Koranic statements about Jewish verbal tricks were elaborated into the doctrine that Jewish and Christian scriptures were corrupt; and this was an excellent defense against most Jewish and Christian arguments.

The Koranic revelations received at Medina contain such rules as were necessary for the well-being of the Muslim community. Where traditional practice was satisfactory, the Koran has nothing to say. The *lex talionis* (law of retaliation) is retained as the basis for the security of life, but acceptance of blood money is encouraged. For inheritance, however, the Koran gives detailed rules, presumably because there was a change from communal to individual ownership, and strong unscrupulous men could seize more than their fair share. The Koran also reformed marital relationships. Previously matrilineal kinship had predominated and women had practiced polyandry, so that there was often doubt about physical paternity. Now it was insisted that a woman should have only one husband at a time (though a man could have four wives) and should observe a waiting period (*ᶜidda*) between marriages. Muḥammad himself is usually said to have left at his death nine wives and one concubine, while three wives had already died. His marriages, like those of his daughters, had political motives, such as binding his chief associates more closely to him.

Muḥammad led the "Farewell Pilgrimage" to Mecca in March 632. Early in June he took to bed and asked Abū Bakr to lead prayers for him. Otherwise he made no plans for the succession. He died on 8 June 632.

Muḥammad was much maligned by medieval Christian writers as part of their distorted image of Islam in general, and was held to be lecherous, treacherous, and an impostor. An objective assessment of the sources, however, shows that by the standards of his time and place he was an upright man, who sincerely believed he received messages from God, and that in various ways he was a social reformer. The greatness of his achievement in founding a world religion is largely due to his own qualities, though the exhaustion of the Byzantine and Persian empires facilitated the expansion of the Islamic state. Even if, as Muslims hold, the ideas of the Koran are not his but God's, yet he must have had deep insight into the spiritual needs of his fellow Arabs; and he certainly had a statesmanlike grasp of the wider problems of the Islamic federation, and the tact and administrative skill to handle the detailed work of government.

BIBLIOGRAPHY

Tor Andrae, *Mohammed: The Man and His Faith,* Theophil Menzel, trans. (1936); Frants Buhl, *Das Leben Muhammads,* Hans H. Schaeder, trans. (1930); Norman Daniel, *Islam and the West: The Making of an Image* (1960); Muhammad Hamidullah, *Le prophète de l'Islam,* 2 vols. (1959); Muḥammad Ibn Isḥāq, *The Life of Muḥammad,* Alfred Guillaume, trans. (1955); Rudi Paret, *Mohammed und der Koran* (1957); William Montgomery Watt, *Muhammad at Mecca* (1953), *Muhammad at Medina* (1956), and *Muhammad: Prophet and Statesman* (1961), an abridgment of the two earlier volumes.

W. MONTGOMERY WATT

[See also ᶜ**Abbās ibn** ᶜ**Abd al-Muṭṭalib ibn Hāshim, al-;** ᶜ**Abd al-Muṭṭalib; Abū Bakr;** ᶜ**Āᵓisha;** ᶜ**Alī ibn Abī Ṭālib; Allah; Arabia; Badr, Battle of; Ḥadīth; Islam, Religion; Kaaba; Koran; Mecca; Medina; Pilgrimage, Islamic; Quraysh; Sunna.**]

MUḤAMMAD I. See **Mehmed I.**

MUḤAMMAD II. See **Mehmed II.**

MUḤTASIB, the Arabic title for an official roughly equivalent to a market inspector, although this rendering is in some respects unsatisfactory. In the most general sense, a *muḥtasib* was any Muslim whose conduct reflected *ḥisba.* This latter term does not figure in the moral vocabulary of the Koran, and generally expresses the ambiguous idea of "reckoning" or "sufficiency." However, in the first two centuries of Islam, for reasons that remain unclear, it came to be closely associated with the frequent Koranic exhortation "Enjoin the good and forbid the evil." It therefore seems that as an ethical term *ḥisba* meant the promotion of good deeds as a responsibility enjoined by God. It was in this sense that theological and hortatory literature in medieval Islam considered the duty of *ḥisba* to be incumbent on all Muslims: For the sake of his soul, every believer should do good and eschew evil, and, for the welfare of the community, should encourage others to do likewise. This latter obligation implied a notion of personal responsibility for the moral rectitude of society, the scope and extent of this responsibility depending upon the position and capacity of each individual. (For instance, a slave could remonstrate with his master if the latter committed an evil act, but could not try to correct him by threat or force.) From this graduated concept of *ḥisba* it followed that the highest responsibility, and the role of primary *muḥtasib,* as it were, should fall upon the holder of public authority.

The evolution of these ideas and their development into the theoretical foundation for a specific institution took several centuries. The sources mention the *muḥtasib* and other guarantors of public morality from earliest Islamic times, but these reports are mostly anachronistic projections from a later period. At first, regulation of public conduct and economic activity was the concern of one's kin, and personal behavior and business practice were deemed acceptable so long as they brought no disgrace to the family or tribe. Disputes were settled within the clan, and intertribal quarrels were referred either to the governor *(amīr)* or to a mediator acceptable to all parties.

The expansion of cities (especially in Iraq) soon compelled the caliphs and their governors to try to maintain urban order in some uniform fashion and, to this end, to establish and uphold certain basic standards of public conduct, especially in the marketplace, which was the most important social and economic forum of the early Islamic towns. The Umayyad caliphate (661–749) marks the appearance of the *ṣāḥib* (or ᶜ*amil*) *al-sūq* (market master). The office has often been regarded as a successor to the Hellenistic *agoranomos,* and the connection is confirmed by a third-century bilingual inscription from Palmyra in which the Greek *agoranomos* appears in Aramaic as *rab shūq,* an exact antecedent for the early Islamic *ṣāḥib al-sūq.* On the other hand, the appearance of such an office in Islam was a natural development: as in all emerging medieval empires, urban order in general, and market activities in particular, were too important to be left to their own devices.

Unfortunately, few reliable details are available on the *ṣāḥib al-sūq.* It appears that he was entrusted with little beyond maintaining order in the markets and resolving basic matters of dispute. His responsibilities generally included (and may have been

MUḤTASIB

largely limited to) regulation of weights and measures. A vast range of these were in simultaneous use throughout medieval times, and the potential for confusion and fraud was always very high.

After the Abbasid revolution the office underwent several important changes. The Abbasids had come to power claiming to be champions and restorers of Islam, and once in authority they used their propaganda and administrative networks to promote their image as proper Muslim rulers. The Koranic injunction "Enjoin the good and forbid the evil," already a popular religious slogan, became a theme presented by the caliphs as a cornerstone of their official policy. To this end, the Umayyad office of *ṣāḥib al-sūq* was transformed into that of the *muḥtasib*. The new official served as the caliph's representative in discharging the responsibility to "Enjoin the good and forbid the evil," and so acted with a definite spiritual sanction that, for the most part, had not been involved in the Umayyad conception of the post as a practical administrative necessity. In this way the task of basic market supervision became one of upholding, in a highly visible way, the ethical values of Islam in the public domain. The *muḥtasib* and his men were also useful in monitoring moods and currents in the markets of Baghdad, where no small amount of popular unrest originated.

The specific dating and diffusion of these developments is unknown, but the general pattern is fairly clear. *Muḥtasib*s and the *ḥisba* jurisdiction are mentioned in reliable reports from the end of the caliphate of al-Manṣūr (775). Both the Arabic and Syriac sources note further developments in the reign of al-Mahdī (775–785), when efforts to impose regular taxation on shops and merchants were initiated; and by the reign of al-Maʾmūn (813–833) the office had assumed its basic form, at least in Baghdad. From the capital it probably spread to provincial centers and eventually to the most important Islamic cities. The office became quite prominent as it spread westward into the Maghrib and Spain, from which some important *ḥisba* manuals originate.

Due to the survival of many *ḥisba* manuals and diplomas of investiture, as well as a wealth of biographical and historical details preserved in literary and legal works, much is known about the qualifications, duties, and powers of the office. The *muḥtasib* was appointed by the local ruling authority or by the qadi and served as long as he remained in favor. It was expected that a candidate would be an upright and respected Muslim, well-mannered and well-groomed, competent in matters of law and religion, and fully knowledgeable about a broad range of trades and professions. The *muḥtasib* was paid a stipend; but in later medieval times, especially under the Mamluks, he purchased his office and then sought to recoup his investment through various exactions, fines, taxes, and forced purchases. In very many cases, the *ḥisba* jurisdiction was held in addition to some other profession. Judges and police officials often held the post of *muḥtasib* as well, as did (if less frequently) prominent religious scholars or men of letters.

The *muḥtasib*'s primary domain was the market, where he was charged with supervision of all trades and crafts. He ensured that all goods were properly made, that foodstuffs were well prepared and wholesome, and that services were performed correctly; most particularly, he guarded against misrepresentations, frauds, and deceptions of all kinds. Working conditions, sanitation, and public safety also came under his authority. He could not fix prices, but could take action against hoarding or price gouging.

The *muḥtasib*'s responsibilities extended elsewhere. He supervised mosques, schools, baths, and workshops, checked to make sure that the city walls were in good repair; and kept the streets clear of obstacles and encroachments. Realtors and builders were answerable to him for their transactions and constructions. He could prevent shipowners from overloading their boats or setting out in bad weather and could order that overburdened beasts be relieved of part of their loads. The *muḥtasib* was also a guardian of public morality and was charged with such tasks (among many others) as breaking up brawls, ensuring that women were not harassed or followed, checking to ensure that the call to prayer was recited correctly and at the proper times, and preventing wine drinking, gambling, various frivolous amusements, and unorthodox discussion of religious questions.

To execute these tasks, the *muḥtasib* often employed assistants (called *ʿarīf*s or *amīn*s) knowledgeable in specific fields; at times he also had a body of troops at his command, which made him a force to be reckoned with in times of instability. His powers were considered to be subordinate to those of the qadi; but while the latter could only pass judgment on matters formally presented to him, the *muḥtasib* intervened on his own initiative and made decisions on the spot. He could have offenders beaten, flogged, or haled through the streets in disgrace; and it was within his powers to confiscate or destroy false weights and measures, defective merchandise, and forbidden items (such as wine). More serious cases had to be referred to the courts, and even in the lesser ones he had to act with circumspection and could be subject to legal action if his methods or decisions were in any way open to doubt.

Most of the extant materials on the *muḥtasib* are formal or theoretical. It would be erroneous to regard the *ḥisba* institution as one uniformly administered, for the functions and powers of the *muḥtasib* varied from one region to another, and from era to era, so that no specific case or theoretical presentation can be considered typical. Further, the authority of such officials as the *muḥtasib* was based largely on their social status and prestige and could be limited or reduced by the machinations of powerful rivals, the activities of local gangs, or the presence (in later medieval times) of well-established guilds or Sufi brotherhoods. A powerful individual could, as *muḥtasib,* wield influence far out of proportion to the powers of the office, while a less powerful official holding the same position could be little more than a figurehead.

It is often said that the *ḥisba* was a municipal institution—in fact, the only municipal institution of medieval Islam; but this statement must be qualified in several ways. The *muḥtasib* was a "municipal" official only in that the limits of his theoretical authority coincided with those of the town. The office owed its existence not to any urban corporate structure or sense of civic identity, but to the sovereign's awareness that the *ḥisba* could make an important contribution to the promotion of both urban order and the ideals of Islam, while also serving to enhance the security and image of the regime.

BIBLIOGRAPHY

The most useful study on the *muḥtasib* is Pedro Chalmeta Gendrón, *El "señor del zoco" en España* (1973), with an important French introduction by Maxime Rodinson. This work contains an extensive bibliography of sources, translations, and modern studies specifically dealing with the *muḥtasib.*

See also Ahmad ᶜAbd ar-Rāziq, "La *ḥisba* et la *muḥtasib* en Égypte au temps des Mamlūks," in *Annales islamologiques,* **13** (1977); Louis Gardet, *La cité musulmane,* 2nd ed. (1961); Thomas F. Glick, "*Muhtasib* and *Mustafat:* A Case Study of Institutional Diffusion," in *Viator,* **2** (1971); Aḥmad Ibn ᶜAbd al-Ḥalīm Ibn Taymīyah, *Public Duties in Islam: The Institution of the Ḥisba,* Muhtar Holland, trans. (1982); Subhi Y. Labib, *Handelsgeschichte Ägyptens im Spätmittelalter (1171–1517)* (1965), 179–183; Carl F. Petry, *The Civilian Elite of Cairo in the Later Middle Ages* (1981), 223–225, 358–359; Émile Tyan, *Histoire de l'organisation judiciaire en pays d'Islam,* 2nd rev. ed. (1960).

LAWRENCE I. CONRAD

[See also **Abbasids; Caliphate; Law, Islamic; Umayyads.**]

MUID, a measure of capacity for dry and liquid products, used principally in Paris, which originally signified the weight or the cubic capacity of an average-sized wagonload. By the late Middle Ages the following were accepted standards: one muid (2.682 hectoliters) for wine equaled 2 *feuillettes* or 3 *tierçons* or 4 *quartauts* or 36 setiers or 144 *quartes* or 288 *pintes* or 13,521.6 cubic Parisian *pouces;* one muid (9.366 hectoliters) for plaster equaled 3 *voies* or 36 sacs or 72 *boisseaux;* a muid (18.732 hectoliters) for lime and all grain except oats equaled 12 setiers or 24 *mines* or 48 minots or 144 *boisseaux* or 2,304 *litrons* or 2,880 *livres poids de marc;* a muid (24.976 hectoliters) for salt equaled 12 setiers or 24 *mines* or 48 minots or 192 *boisseaux* or 3,072 *litrons* or 49,152 *mesurettes;* a muid (37.464 hectoliters) for oats equaled 12 setiers or 24 *mines* or 48 minots or 288 *boisseaux;* and a muid (41.627 hectoliters) for charcoal equaled 10 setiers or 20 *mines* or 40 minots or 320 *boisseaux.*

From the fourteenth century most regions in the vicinity of Paris conformed to the government's standards, although there are significant differences in some places. In the departments of Loiret and Moselle the muid was employed as a measure of area for land. In medieval manuscripts the muid appears under such variants as *mee, meue, modius, moee, meuie, moiee, moiie, mouee, mouyee, moyau, moye, moyel, muie, muee, mugius, mui, muiee, muiel,* and *muy.*

BIBLIOGRAPHY

Ronald E. Zupko, *French Weights and Measures Before the Revolution: A Dictionary of Provincial and Local Units* (1978), 116–120.

RONALD EDWARD ZUPKO

[See also **Boisseau; Setier; Weights and Measures, Western European.**]

MUᶜIZZ AL-DAWLA (Abu'l-Ḥusayn Aḥmad ibn Abī Shujāᶜ) (*d.* 967), the founder of the Buyid regime in Baghdad. Aḥmad was the youngest of the three

Daylamī brothers (that is, from the Iranian province of Daylam), who established themselves in the Iranian plateau and Iraq in the tenth century. While the eldest, ᶜAlī (later, ᶜImād al-Dawla, *d.* 949), controlled central Iran, Ḥasan (later, Rukn al-Dawla, *d.* 977) occupied Jibāl and, in 935–936, Aḥmad took hold of Kirmān and Khūzestān. It was from these bases that Aḥmad extended his power into Iraq. In 938, Aḥmad defeated the Abbasid general Bejkem (or Badjkam) at Arrajān in Fārs and at ᶜAskar Mukram (Mukram's camp), and then took Ahwāz. In 943–944, Aḥmad initiated the first of his attacks on Wāsiṭ. He was repelled twice by the Turkish *amīr al-umarā*ᵓ Tuzun, but on his third attempt, in December 945, the governor of the city went over to Aḥmad's side, and the town surrendered. Soon after, he entered Baghdad and seized power. This event marked the turning point in the history of the Abbasid dynasty. The caliph, al-Mustakfī, made Aḥmad *amīr al-umarā*ᵓ and gave him the honorific title Muᶜizz al-Dawla (Strengthener of the state). At the same time, al-Mustakfī bestowed honorific titles on his two brothers, ᶜAlī and Ḥasan.

Although Muᶜizz al-Dawla and his brothers were Shiites, they did not suppress the Abbasid caliphate. The Buyids received their diplomas of investiture from the Abbasid caliphs until the regime ended in 1055. In spite of his reliance on the Abbasid caliphs to legitimize his rule, Muᶜizz al-Dawla—like his successors—did not hesitate to depose troublesome caliphs at will. Soon after his own investiture, he blinded and deposed al-Mustakfī and raised al-Muṭīᶜ to the caliphate (946), a pattern that was to continue for the next 100 years. Although Muᶜizz al-Dawla did not attempt to place an Alid on the caliphal throne, he did introduce public celebration of two major Shiite festivals, ᶜĀshūrāᵓ (a fast day) and Ghadīr Khumm. He was also responsible, along with his brothers, for introducing Turkish troops into the Buyid army, which had previously been composed almost entirely of Daylamī soldiers. In fact, Muᶜizz al-Dawla openly favored his Turkish troops over the Daylamī.

For the remainder of his life, Muᶜizz al-Dawla was occupied with the Hamdanids and Qarmatians. In 946, Nāṣir al-Dawla, the Hamdanid, had made peace with the Buyids and agreed to pay tribute. But in 948–949, he stopped his tribute, and Muᶜizz al-Dawla sent troops against him. Muᶜizz al-Dawla soon made peace, however, in order to assist his brother Rukn al-Dawla against the Samanids. Nāṣir al-Dawla rebelled again in 958–959, and this time Muᶜizz al-Dawla took both Mawṣil (Mosul) and Nisibin.

In 947, Muᶜizz al-Dawla had sent an army to occupy Baṣra and had been compelled at that time to make the leader of the opposing army, ᶜImrān ibn Shāhīn (*d.* 979), their governor. But in 967, ᶜImrān ibn Shāhīn renewed his battle against Muᶜizz al-Dawla, who died that same year while fighting him. Muᶜizz al-Dawla was succeeded by his son Baqtiyar (ᶜIzz al-Dawla, *d.* 968).

BIBLIOGRAPHY

There is no major study of Muᶜizz al-Dawla. The major source for the history of his reign is Ibn Miskawayh, *Tajārib al-umam,* ed. and trans. by Henry Frederick Amedroz and David S. Margoliouth as *The Eclipse of the ᶜAbbasid Caliphate,* 7 vols. (1920–1921).

PAULA SANDERS

[See also **Abbasids; Baghdad; Buyids; Fars; ᶜImad al-Dawla; Iran, History; Iraq; Shiᶜa.**]

MUᶜIZZ LI-DĪN ALLĀH, AL-. See **Fatimids.**

MUḲAMMIS, AL-. See **Dāwūd ibn Marwān al-Muqammis.**

MUKKARNAS. See **Muqarnas.**

MULDENFALTENSTIL (Muldenstil), stylistic term (from German: *Mulden,* "trough," and *Falten,* "folds") for drapery patterned after antique statuary and characterized by sharply incised grooves in metalwork and stone sculpture and looped patterns resembling pothooks or hairpins in painting. This treatment was most prominent in northern France, especially in and around Rheims, in the Meuse Valley, and in Germany, from about 1180 to about 1240.

BIBLIOGRAPHY

Carl F. Barnes, Jr., "The Drapery-rendering Technique of Villard de Honnecourt," in *Gesta,* **20** (1981).

CARL F. BARNES, JR.

[See also **Gothic Architecture; Gothic Art: Sculpture; Mosan Art.**]

MULḤAM is the technical term in Arabic for a textile woven with a silk warp and a weft of a fiber other than silk, usually cotton. It is distinguished from *dībāj,* which has both warp and weft of silk. As known from historical sources, and as identified by *ṭirāz* inscriptions on actual fabrics, *mulḥam* was a popular textile for garments in medieval Islam woven in many areas. *Mulḥam* fabrics were usually cut and sewn for garments worn by the Abbasid caliphs and courtiers in Baghdad and Samarra. The most famous center of production was in Merv (Mary), where "the finest of its kind" was made for export throughout the Islamic world.

BIBLIOGRAPHY

Reinhart P. A. Dozy, *Dictionnaire detaillé des noms des vêtements chez les Arabes* (1845), 113, n. 9; Lisa Golombek and Veronika Gervers, "*Tiraz* Fabrics in the Royal Ontario Museum," in *Studies in Textile History,* Veronika Gervers, ed. (1977); Robert B. Serjeant, *Islamic Textiles: Material for a History up to the Mongol Conquest* (1972); Manfred Ullmann, *Wörterbuch der klassischen arabischen Sprache,* II (1979), 374.

CAROL MANSON BIER

[See also **Costume, Islamic; Dībāj; Khilᶜa; Textiles, Islamic; Ṭirāz.**]

MULLION, a vertical piece of tracery dividing an opening into two, usually equal, openings. The most common use is in windows to create two or more lights depending on the number of mullions employed. When freestanding, a mullion is normally structural as well as decorative. The tracery spokes in wheel windows are also termed mullions.

CARL F. BARNES, JR.

[See also **Glass, Stained; Tracery.**]

MULTSCHER, HANS (*fl.* 1427–1467), primarily a sculptor in stone and wood, influential in fifteenth-century Ulm. His sandstone sculptures for Ulm Minster (1420's) were followed by polychrome wood altarpieces with painted wings: the Wurzach altar (1437) and the Sterzing altar (1456–1458).

BIBLIOGRAPHY

Michael Baxandall, *The Limewood Sculptors of Renaissance Germany* (1980); Kurt Gerstenberg, *Hans Multscher* (1928); Nicolò Rasmo, *Der Multscher-Altar in Sterzing* (1963); Alfred Stange, *Deutsche Malerei der Gotik,* IV (1934); Manfred Tripps, *Hans Multscher* (1969).

LARRY SILVER

[See also **Gothic Art: Sculpture.**]

Mullions from the choir chapels of Rheims Cathedral. From the *Sketchbook* of Villard de Honnecourt (13th century). PARIS, BIBLIOTHÈQUE NATIONALE, MSS FRANÇAIS 19093, fol. 31r

MUNSTER is represented in ancient traditions both as the southern half of Ireland generally (Leth Mogha, as contrasted with Leth Chuinn in the north) and as the more circumscribed southwestern quarter of Ireland, one of the ancient five provinces.

At the beginning of the sixth century control of Munster was apparently wrested from the former dominant segments by a group of powerful families all claiming descent from an eponymous ancestor, Eógan Már. Annalistic information on early Mun-

Man of Sorrows. Sandstone sculpture by Hans Multscher from the west portal of Ulm Minster, 1429. PHOTO: WIM SWANN

ster history is very defective, but one can distinguish two moieties among these families, the western group, dominated by the Eóganacht of Loch Léin (the area around Killarney), and the eastern Eóganacht, comprising at least three segments, which regularly supplied overkings to the province.

By 700 Eóganacht of Loch Lein had been bested for control of the dynastic succession by the eastern groups. Among the early recorded figures of note is Cathal mac Finguine (*d.* 742) of the Eóganacht Glendamnach (north Cork), who entered the saga literature in his role as an opponent of the Uí Néill. The Eóganacht of Cashel in mid Tipperary produced most of the rulers of Munster in the second half of the ninth century. Their most famous king was the ecclesiastic and promoter of *céli Dé* reform (an anchorite movement), the otherwise notorious Feidlimid mac Crimthainn (*d.* 847). Cashel as a royal center came to assume for the south a significance analogous to that of Tara for the northern part of Ireland.

The ambitions of any Munster king to become a paramount king of the whole island inevitably came up against the fact of Uí Néill supremacy in the north and in the eastern midlands. This was to be the fate of another ecclesiastic king, Cormac mac Cuilennáin (*r.* 902–908), who, after auspicious beginnings, also perished on the rock of an Uí Néill-Leinster alliance at the Battle of Belach Mugna in 908.

By this time the Vikings were beginning to create permanent settlements in Munster, and gradually through the ninth century they set up important trading centers in Limerick, Cork, and Waterford. These ports, while contributing significantly to the material prosperity of the province, were viewed with hostility and avarice by the Irish kings and constantly threatened by them. At the beginning of the tenth century the Vikings again turned settlement attention to Ireland, and by this stage the Eóganacht kings were not wholly successful in defending their own interests.

The latter half of the tenth century in Munster was dominated by the Dál Cais, a non-Eóganacht family, from their base in east Clare. Resistance to the Dál Cais was intense in the 940's and 950's but Brian, who succeeded his brother Mathgamain in 976, was able to consolidate his brother's considerable achievements. In a series of brilliant campaigns Brian demonstrated his control of Munster and established significant dominance over the Leinster groups as well, bringing the Osraige back into the dependence of Munster for the first time since 859. He was acknowledged by the southern Uí Néill in the person of Mael Sechlainn II, himself a figure of considerable achievements. By 1011 he apparently claimed suzerainty even over the northern Uí Néill and, consequently, the whole island. In 1014 the restlessness of Leinster and the lack of assistance of erstwhile allies brought about his downfall. Though Brian defeated the Northmen, their allies, and the Leinstermen in the famed battle of Clontarf (1014), he was himself slain with his son.

Brian's career was the pinnacle of Dál Cais and Munster achievement. Subsequent Dál Cais (O'Brien) kings included Donnchadh (*d.* 1064); Tairdelbach (or Turlough, 1064–1086), who briefly controlled Munster, Leinster, and Meath, and who possibly achieved just as much as his famed ancestor Brian; and

Muirchertach (*r.* 1086–1119). The Dál Cais line, however, was eventually eclipsed by the rise of a dynamic new Connacht dynasty, the O'Connors.

The second generation of Anglo-Norman adventurers in the 1170's carried the new colony's settlements far beyond its initial base in Leinster and Meath. The king retained for himself the old Viking ports of Waterford, Cork, and Limerick. Various piecemeal grants of territory were made by successive English kings in Munster, who tacitly recognized the independent position of the O'Brien west of the Shannon River. By 1210, Waterford, south Tipperary, east Cork, and the west Shannon River basin in Limerick were heavily settled by Anglo-Normans. In the 1220's and the 1230's Anglo-Norman settlement had advanced into north Kerry and Limerick, and the beginnings of the Fitzgerald earldom of Desmond was established. These areas became feudalized administratively and reorganized into manors economically and thus provided a contrast with the Gaelic areas in many important aspects. But by the mid thirteenth century the Irish lords were in a position to check the colonizing process, and they won a significant victory at the battle of Callan in 1261.

In 1328 James Butler was made earl of Ormond and endowed with the liberty of Tipperary, and in 1329 Maurice fitzThomas was made earl of Desmond and endowed with the liberty of Kerry. These two earldoms dominated Munster in the late medieval period. They provided a check on the Gaelic resurgence of the fourteenth century, and at the same time resisted efforts by the English crown to assert authority in Ireland.

Richard II's expeditions to Ireland (1394–1395 and 1399), which sought the submission of the Gaelic chiefs and their integration into the English-ruled Ireland, achieved very little of permanent effect. Meanwhile, the Anglo-Norman palatinate earldoms in Munster continued to be semi-independent. The mid fifteenth century in Munster was marked by the hostility between the houses of Desmond and Ormond, with the Butler fortunes declining. The power of the O'Briens in the west was again on the increase in the later fifteenth century, but the power of Desmond was not seriously challenged. All were to fall under the growing power of the Tudor monarchy in the sixteenth century.

BIBLIOGRAPHY

Francis John Byrne, *Irish Kings and High Kings* (1973); Art Cosgrove, *Late Medieval Ireland, 1370–1541* (1981); Robin Frame, *Colonial Ireland, 1169–1369* (1981); Gearóid Mac Niocaill, *Ireland Before the Vikings* (1972); Donnchadh Ó Corráin, *Ireland Before the Normans* (1972); Annette Jocelyn Otway-Ruthven, *A History of Medieval Ireland* (1968, 2nd ed. 1980).

ANN DOOLEY

[See also **Cashel; Connacht; Cormack mac Cuilennáin; Dál Cais; Eóganacht; Fitzgeralds; Ireland; Leinster; Uí Néill; Ulster; Vikings.**]

MUQADDASĪ, AL- (al-Maqdisi) (*d. ca.* 1000). Shams al-Dīn Abū ᶜAbd Allāh Muḥammad ibn Aḥmad ibn Abī Bakr al-Bashshārī al-Muqaddasī is the author of one of the most important and original Arabic geographical treatises of the Middle Ages. His *Aḥsan al-Taqāsīm fī Maᶜrifat al-Aqālīm* (The best divisions for knowledge of the regions), written toward the end of the tenth century, represents a major departure from previous works of Islamic geography, largely because of the broader scope of its inquiry and its methodological rigor.

The few biographical details available for al-Muqaddasī are scattered throughout the text of this treatise. Born in Jerusalem (as his name suggests), he was descended on his father's side from a celebrated architect, Abū Bakr al-Bannāᵓ, known for having constructed the fortifications at Acre by order of Ibn Ṭūlūn. His mother's family originated in Biyār (now Biyār Jumand, in northern Iran), from where his maternal grandfather emigrated to Jerusalem. After a youth spent mostly in Palestine, al-Muqaddasī embarked at the age of twenty or so on the travels that would form the basis of the *Aḥsan al-Taqāsīm,* his only known work.

Although the text furnishes few dates or other clues that would help to establish the author's precise itinerary, it is clear that al-Muqaddasī traveled extensively throughout the Muslim world, except for the areas of al-Sind (now in Pakistan) and al-Andalus (Spain). His work focuses exclusively on the Muslim lands, which he divides into fourteen regions, six Arab and eight non-Arab. For each region, al-Muqaddasī follows a relatively consistent pattern of description. He begins with general observations about the area under consideration, often set forth in the rhymed prose *(sajᶜ)* characteristic of many literary works of the period. This is followed by a detailed listing of its districts and a ranking of its towns. The more substantial towns are discussed in great detail; names of streets and quarters are noted, as is the placement of important centers such as mosques and markets. Local variations in weights and measures are frequently recorded. The author then sketches the region as a whole, mentioning not merely lakes, rivers, roads, and other features of physical geography, but the manners and customs of the local population as well. Peculiarities of language, cuisine, dress, and religious beliefs are given considerable attention. It is here that al-Muqaddasī's contribution to Islamic geographical writing is most apparent. Considering the science of geography useful and interesting to broad segments of society, he widened its scope to include a variety of subjects absent from the more limited and specialized works of his predecessors. While not abandoning the topographical concerns of earlier writers, al-Muqaddasī added a more pronounced human dimension to Islamic geography. His attention to local culture sets this treatise apart from earlier geographical works in Arabic and Persian.

Al-Muqaddasī divides the sources of his information into three categories: personal observations, conversations with trustworthy and knowledgeable people, and literary and scientific works. He scrupulously consulted experts on matters beyond his personal competence and was careful to inform the reader of the derived nature of this information. When possible, however, he preferred to speak from his own experience, believing that scientific geography could proceed only from direct observation and investigation. He explicitly condemns the tendency of many earlier geographers to accept uncritically second-hand information. Although al-Muqaddasī was not the first Muslim geographer to employ personal observation, he was the first to grant it a central place in his work.

Because of his obvious concern with religious factionalism, al-Muqaddasī's own religious loyalties have been the object of discussion among scholars. On the basis of certain suggestive passages in the work, some have argued that al-Muqaddasī may have traveled as a missionary *(dāᶜī)* for the Fatimids of Egypt. Although there is little evidence to support such a claim, it does seem clear that al-Muqaddasī at least had strong Shiite sympathies, despite his professed attachment to a major Sunni legal rite. Such sympathies were not at all unusual among Sunni intellectuals of the period; in any case, the context of the passages in question suggests that the author was uncomfortable with fanaticism of any sort, whether Sunni or Shiite. If he exhibits an unusual tolerance for religious sectarians (indeed, he mixes quite freely with them on a number of occasions), this probably has more to do with his broad conception of Islam and his natural intellectual curiosity than with any secret Fatimid connections.

BIBLIOGRAPHY

The Arabic text was edited by Michael J. de Goeje and published as the third volume of *Bibliotheca geographorum arabicorum* (repr. 1967). André Miquel's excellent, though only partial, French translation, *La meilleure répartition pour la connaissance des provinces* (1963), contains a useful introduction as well as all the relevant bibliography.

KEITH LEWINSTEIN

[See also **Geography and Cartography, Islamic; Travel and Transport, Islamic.**]

MUQADDIMA. See **Khaldūn, Ibn.**

MUQAFFAᶜ, ᶜABD ALLĀH IBN AL- (*ca.* 720–756/757), foremost Arabic prose writer in the period of the Abbasid revolution. The son of an Iranian administrator in the service of the Umayyads, he was known as Ibn al-Muqaffaᶜ, "son of the cripple," because his father's hand was maimed by tortures inflicted for maladministration. He changed his name from Rūzbih to ᶜAbd Allāh when, at an unknown date, he converted to Islam.

Ibn al-Muqaffaᶜ wrote at a time when Arabic prose writing was being adapted to a number of purposes beyond sermons and speeches. Most of the works attributed to him are either lost or preserved only in quotations or late and defective manuscripts. He translated several works from Middle Persian, or Pahlavi, the language of the Sasanid court, into Arabic. The best known is *Kalīla wa-Dimna,* a collection of didactic fables which faithfully reflects the *Panchatantra,* the Sanskrit original of the Pahlavi version. In this, as in the surviving fragments of translations dealing with Sasanid history and court activities, it is difficult to see reflections of Ibn al-Muqaffaᶜ's own ideas or personality.

Yet Ibn al-Muqaffaᶜ seems to have been a strong personality as well as a trusted administrator in the employ of members of the Abbasid family after they came to power in 750. Along with several other Iranian converts to Islam, he was accused of being a *zindīq,* a derogatory term which was used both to designate Manichaeans and to tar people suspected of harboring noxious non-Muslim beliefs in general.

Ibn al-Muqaffaʿ's execution by torture at the hands of the governor of Basra was related, however, not to his religious views but to his giving offense to the caliph al-Manṣūr. It is reported that powerful Abbasid family members instructed him to draft for al-Manṣūr's signature a grant of security for the caliph's brother, who had revolted. Al-Manṣūr took offense at the demeaning tone of the terms of the document and ordered the governor of Basra, a personal foe of Ibn al-Muqaffaʿ, to chastise him.

Ibn al-Muqaffaʿ's most important surviving composition, a brief work entitled *Risāla fī 'l-Ṣaḥāba,* may also have given offense. In it he offers administrative and political advice to an unnamed caliph, presumably al-Manṣūr. He makes suggestions on many subjects, but his most striking suggestion is for the caliph to centralize and codify under his own authority the then developing *sharīʿa* (Islamic law). This suggestion, reminiscent of both Byzantine and Sasanid imperial tradition, was not followed, though in 827 al-Manṣūr's great-grandson al-Maʾmūn instituted a *miḥna,* or inquisition, in a belated and unsuccessful effort to bring Islamic religious officials and scholars into obedience to the caliphate.

Ibn al-Muqaffaʿ's personality and questionable devotion to Islam are suggested by the contemporary accusation that he undertook to write an imitation of the Koran. This accusation was hurled at a number of literary figures, but in Ibn al-Muqaffaʿ's case, some quotations of early writings in Koranic style preserved in a later work may be a genuine survival of the alleged blasphemous composition.

BIBLIOGRAPHY

Josef van Ess, "Some Fragments of the Muʿāraḍat al-Qurʾan Attributed to Ibn al-Muqaffaʿ," in *Studia arabica et islamica* (1981); Francesco Gabrieli, "L'opera di Ibn al-Mukaffaʿ," in *Rivista degli studi orientali,* **13** (1932); S. D. Goitein, "A Turning Point in the History of the Islamic State (Apropos of Ibn al-Muqaffaʿ's Kitāb aṣ-Ṣaḥaba)," in *Islamic Culture,* **23** (1949); Dominique Sourdel, "La biographie d'Ibn al-Muqaffaʿ d'après les sources anciennes," in *Arabica,* **1** (1954).

RICHARD W. BULLIET

[See also **Arabic Literature, Prose; Calila e Digna; Manṣūr, al-.**]

MUQAMMIS, AL-. See **Dāwūd ibn Marwān al-Muqammis.**

MUQARNAS (Arabic, probably from Greek *korōnis,* "cornice"), a distinctively Islamic type of architectural decoration consisting of two or more oversailing courses of miniature quarter domes (frequently "creased" down the center) aligned at angles to one another.

The *muqarnas* seems to have been introduced in Iran, where the earliest surviving example encircles the Gunbad-i ʿAlī at Abarqūh (1056–1057). It spread rapidly throughout the Islamic world, occurring on minarets at the Great Mosque of Ani (1073) and the Mosque of al-Juyūshī in Cairo (1085), on buildings sponsored by the Almoravid ʿAlī ibn Yūsuf (*r.* 1106–1142) at Marrakech and Tlemcen, and at the Great Mosque of Seville (1172–1177).

The dome over the tomb of Imām Dūr at Samarra in Mesopotamia (*ca.* 1091) was the first to be constructed entirely of *muqarnas.* Much more popular through subsequent centuries, however, was the use of *muqarnas* revetments to mask underlying structure, including domes and squinches. Craftsmen from India to Spain evolved characteristic regional styles of deploying this decoration.

BIBLIOGRAPHY

Keppel A. C. Creswell, *The Muslim Architecture of Egypt,* I (1952), 159; Ernst Herzfeld, "Damascus: Studies in Architecture—I," in *Ars islamica,* **9** (1942); Georges Marçais, *L'architecture musulmane d'Occident* (1954), 237–238; Myron B. Smith, *Vaulting Techniques in Iranian Muslim Architecture* (*ca.* 1986); Donald N. Wilber, *The Architecture of Islamic Iran* (1955), 72.

ESTELLE WHELAN

[See also **Alhambra; Almohad Art; Almoravid Art; Fatimid Art; Islamic Art and Architecture.**]

MUQTADIR, AL- (894/895—932), the eighteenth Abbasid caliph, ruling from 908 to 932. He came to the caliphate at a younger age (thirteen) than any of his Abbasid predecessors, and his reign was the longest down to the Abbasids' loss of temporal power to the Iranian Buyids in 945. The caliphate had weathered a period of severe fiscal and political instability in the mid-ninth century, but al-Muwaffaq, the brother of the caliph al-Muʿtamid (870–892) and

Gundbad-i ʿAli. Octagonal tower at Abarqūh, Iran. 1056–1057. PHOTO: ARTHUR UPHAM POPE. © 1965 George Braziller, Inc.

power behind his throne, had restored its authority. Al-Muwaffaq's son al-Muʿtaḍid (892–902) succeeded al-Muʿtamid and, along with his own son and successor al-Muqtafī (902–908), maintained the caliphate's sound condition.

Al-Muqtadir (al-Muqtafī's brother) therefore inherited a full treasury and a strong army. The former he squandered, and he eventually lost his life in battle against the previously loyal commander of the latter. While of a generous character, he was much given to drink and pleasure. His mother, a Greek concubine of al-Muʿtaḍid named Shaghab but referred to simply as "the Lady," played, with her influential female attendants, an often dominating role in court politics.

The caliphate successfully resisted serious threats from the Qarmatians in Arabia and Iraq and the Fatimids in Ifrīqiya (Tunisia). This was, however, more the work of the eunuch general Muʾnis, a loyal supporter of al-Muqtadir for most of his reign, than of the caliph himself. Al-Muqtadir was more concerned with money, in the pursuit of which he skillfully played off against one another two rival factions of administrators, the Furāṭids and the Jarrāḥids, receiving lavish bribes from them. These factions also offered bribes to other court dignitaries as well as the caliph to gain control of the vizierate along with the many patronage jobs that went with it. They would then seek to recover their financial outlay by mulcting the deposed officeholders.

The persistence of such official corruption testifies to the lack of money in the caliphal treasury. There were also army riots over arrears of pay and other severe disorders in Baghdad during al-Muqtadir's reign. In 929 Nāzūk, the ambitious chief of police of Baghdad, engineered al-Muqtadir's deposition. But three days later al-Qāhir, al-Muqtadir's brother and the new caliph, was himself overthrown and al-Muqtadir restored.

In 932 a growing separation between Muʾnis and al-Muqtadir developed into war. Decked in the Prophet's cloak and sword and preceded by the black banner of the Abbasids and by chanting Koran readers, al-Muqtadir made a procession through the streets of Baghdad and took up a position where his soldiers could see him. But his symbolic presence was to no avail. Berber soldiers in the army of Muʾnis cut him down and bore his head to their commander.

The reign of al-Muqtadir represents a descent from the fragile recovery of his brother, father, and grandfather to the nearly anarchic conditions prevailing in Baghdad when al-Qāhir, who was not punished after Nāzūk's coup, succeeded him a second time. Al-Muqtadir's acquiescence in the execution of the Sufi al-Ḥallāj, despite the considerable sympathy the mystic had at court, was his most noteworthy religious action. But he, typically, acted on the recommendation of an official rather than on his own inclination.

The problems of al-Muqtadir's reign are laid to his own personal failings and those of the people around him. Yet these explanations may owe much to the style of the Arabic chroniclers. The problems facing the Abbasids at that time may have been more than a match for any caliph.

BIBLIOGRAPHY

Harold Bowen, *The Life and Times of ʿAlī Ibn ʿIsà* (1928, repr. 1964); Miskawayh, *Eclipse of the Abbasid Ca-*

liphate, H. F. Amedroz and David S. Margoliouth, eds. and trans., I (Arabic) and IV (English) (1920–1921).

RICHARD W. BULLIET

[See also **Abbasid Art and Architecture; Abbasids; Caliphate; Fatimids; Ḥallāj, al-; Qāhir biʾllāh, al-.**]

MUR, RAYMOND DE. See **Raymond de Mur.**

MURAD I, Ottoman ruler (1359–1389) largely responsible for the creation of the Ottoman Empire in Europe. Under his father, Orhan, he began an offensive leading in 1361 to the conquest of Adrianople (Edirne), which subsequently became his European capital. This success was followed by the conquest of western Thrace in 1364. His plan for the subjugation of the Balkan states was unaffected by the recapture of Gallipoli by Amadeo VI of Savoy in 1366. Ultimately, Andronikos IV, the Byzantine emperor, was forced to return it to Ottoman control in 1376. Murad, also faced with Hungarian aspirations in the Balkans, strengthened the Turkish presence there by transplanting colonies of Anatolian Turkomans.

Vigorous Ottoman campaigns (beginning in 1366) against the fractious Serbian and Bulgarian dynasts, who were sometimes aided by Wallachian, Albanian, and Bosnian elements, were largely successful. Sofia fell in 1385 and Nish in 1386. The defeat of the Ottoman general Timurtash at Ploshnik in 1388 set the stage for a final confrontation. Meanwhile, Murad's attention had been diverted to Anatolia, where his acquisition of Germiyan and Hamidili territories had alarmed some of the Turkish principalities. The Karamanids invaded Murad's holdings but were defeated in 1387. Murad, again turning to Balkan affairs, crushed Bulgaria in 1388 and prepared to face the Serbian-Bosnian forces at Kosovo Polje on 15 June 1389. The Ottoman victory there, which opened all of the Balkans to their domination, was marred by Murad's assassination. This unexpected turn of events induced a revolt by the Karamanid-led Anatolian princes.

Part of Murad's legacy was the Janissary corps (Turkish: *Yeni Cheri,* new army), which appears to have taken shape during his reign and would soon become the most formidable Ottoman instrument of conquest.

BIBLIOGRAPHY

Sources. Friedrich Giese, ed., *Die altosmanischen anonymen Chroniken,* 2 vols. (1922, 1925); Michael Doukas, *Decline and Fall of Byzantium to the Ottoman Turks,* Harry J. Magoulias, trans. (1975).

Studies. John W. Barker, *Manuel II Palaeologus* (1969); Peter Charanis, "The Strife Among the Palaeolologi and the Ottoman Turks, 1370–1402," in *Byzantion,* **16** (1942–1943); Halil Inalcik, "The Conquest of Edirine (1361)," in *Archivum ottomanicum,* **3** (1971), and *The Ottoman Empire: The Classical Age, 1300–1600,* Norman Itzkowitz and Colin Imber, trans. (1973); Nikola Radojčić, "Die griechischen Quellen zur Schlacht am Kosovo Polje," in *Byzantion,* **6** (1931); Franz Taeschner, "War Murad I Grossmeister oder Mitglied des Achibundes?" in *Oriens,* **6** (1953); İsmail H. Uzunçarşili, *Osmanli tarihi,* I (1972).

PETER B. GOLDEN

[See also **Anatolia; Bulgaria; Byzantine Empire; Constantinople; Janissary; John V Palaiologos; Ottomans.**]

MURAD II, Ottoman sultan (1421–1444; 1446–1451) who withstood major European efforts to dislodge the Turks from the Balkans. His accession to the sultanate was challenged by an alleged uncle, Düzme Mustafa, as well as his brothers. He crushed all opposition between 1421 and 1423 and laid siege to Constantinople in 1422 in retaliation for Byzantine support of Düzme Mustafa. Byzantium was ultimately forced to accept an unfavorable peace in 1424, and Murad completed the incorporation of the Menteshe, Aydin, Teke, and Germiyan principalities into his realm (1423–1428). This restored the Ottoman state to its pre-1402 boundaries.

The long conflict with Venice over Salonika (1423–1430) produced an anti-Ottoman alliance of Venice, Hungary, and the Karamanids that plagued Murad for much of his reign. Thus, before he could deal with a Hungarian-backed coalition of Serbia, Bosnia, and Wallachia (over which he had reasserted Ottoman authority in 1428), he was forced to turn to Anatolia, where the Timurid Shāhrukh, Karaman's protector, had appeared in 1435. As neither side sought a real confrontation, the subsequent Ottoman defeat of Karaman (1435–1437) did not result in major territorial gains. Murad returned to Europe and annexed Serbia in 1439. The Hungarians under János Hunyadi halted the Ottoman incursions and successfully carried the war into the Balkans between 1441 and 1443. Again faced with a Karamanid threat in Anatolia and with the crusader forces mustered against him, Murad signed a ten-year truce on

12 June 1444 at Adrianople, having made concessions to the Karamanids as well. Believing peace had been achieved, Murad abdicated in favor of his son Mehmed II (the Conqueror), hoping to secure the latter's succession without civil war. Domestic discord and a renewed European crusade (the "Crusade of Varna") brought Murad out of retirement. He defeated the crusaders at Varna. Because of continuing factional strife he was forced to resume the sultanate in 1446. Murad spent his remaining years in Balkan campaigns that further removed the Hungarian threat to Ottoman possession of the Balkans. The scene of Ottoman-European conflict would now be shifted to central Europe.

BIBLIOGRAPHY

Sources. Laonikos Chalcocondyles (Khalkokondyles), *Historiarum demonstrationes ad fidem codicum recensuit,* Eugenius Darko, ed., 2 vols. (1922–1927); Michael Doukas (Ducas), *Ducae Michaelis Ducae nepotis historia byzantine,* Immanuel Bekker, ed. (1834), and Victor Grecu, ed. (1958), trans. by Harry J. Magoulias as *Decline and Fall of Byzantium to the Ottoman Turks* (1975); Ūrūj ibn ᶜAdil, *Die frühosmanischen Jahrbücher des Urudsch nach den Handschriften zu Oxford und Cambridge,* Franz Babinger, ed. (1925).

Studies. Franz Babinger, "Von Amurath zu Amurath: Vor- und Nachspiel der Schlacht bei Varna (1444)," in *Oriens,* 3 (1950) and 4 (1951); John W. Barker, *Manuel II Palaeologus (1391–1425)* (1969); Oskar Halecki, *The Crusade of Varna* (1943); Halil Inalcik, "Murad II," in *Islâm Ansiklopedisi,* VIII (1959); İsmail H. Uzunçarşili, *Osmanli tarihi,* I (1972).

PETER B. GOLDEN

[See also **Byzantine Empire; Hungary; Hunyadi, János; Mehmed II; Ottomans.**]

MUṢALLA, a place for performing the Islamic ritual prayer *(ṣalāt).* The word usually refers to a large open area beyond a town's limits where the Muslim community gathers for certain special prayers, particularly those for two festivals, for rain *(istisqāᵓ)* and for eclipses. Apart from some indication of the direction of prayer, the *muṣalla* has no standard architectural features.

BIBLIOGRAPHY

Arent J. Wensinck, "Muṣallā," in *Encyclopaedia of Islam,* III (1936).

JONATHAN M. BLOOM

[See also **Islam, Religion.**]

MUSCOVY, RISE OF. A modest fortified outpost in 1147, Moscow became a princely seat in 1263 when Alexander Nevsky, grand prince of Vladimir, bequeathed it to his youngest son, Prince Daniel. By the end of the fourteenth century Muscovy had become the most important principality in the Russian north, embracing the nucleus of the Great Russian people. A century later Moscow stood supreme, having engulfed most of its rivals and neighbors, and with its appetite for expansion whetted by success. When Ivan III died in 1505 his domain embraced more than 600,000 square miles—a territory about three times the size of modern France and over 2,000 times larger than it had been in the early fourteenth century.

EARLY MUSCOVY

Interest in Moscow's initial rise has evoked a torrent of scholarly comment and interpretation. The documentation, largely annalistic and frequently unresponsive to many of the historians' questions, has allowed for a wide spectrum of interpretation. Speculation about the pivotal factors has ranged from the simple to the complex, from providential or accidental explanations to the evolutionary, deterministic, or "scientific." Even the question of Mongol influence upon the rise of Moscow and the development of the subsequent political system has never been resolved. Some scholars, such as N. M. Karamzin and G. Vernadsky, have stressed Mongol influence, while others, such as S. M. Solov'ev, V. O. Klyuchevskii, and A. E. Presniakov, have minimized the alien impact.

Moscow was merely a stockade in the interior forest when an active political center, with Rostov as its main city, emerged in the distant northeastern region of the disintegrating Kievan realm. This area, lying in the angle created by the Volga River and its Oka tributary, had become a Kievan possession by the later tenth century. Its active history dates from the early twelfth century, when Vladimir Monomakh, the important senior prince of Kiev, gave the Rostov territory to his younger son, Yurii Dolgorukii.

To this sparsely populated area, inhabited by Finnic tribes, came Slavic refugees from the beleaguered Kievan region, anxious to escape princely wars, barbarian attacks, and indenture resulting from debts incurred in chronically unstable conditions. In the absence of evidence, scholars disagree on the population dynamics of the Rostov area and on the degree of its economic prosperity. Some claim

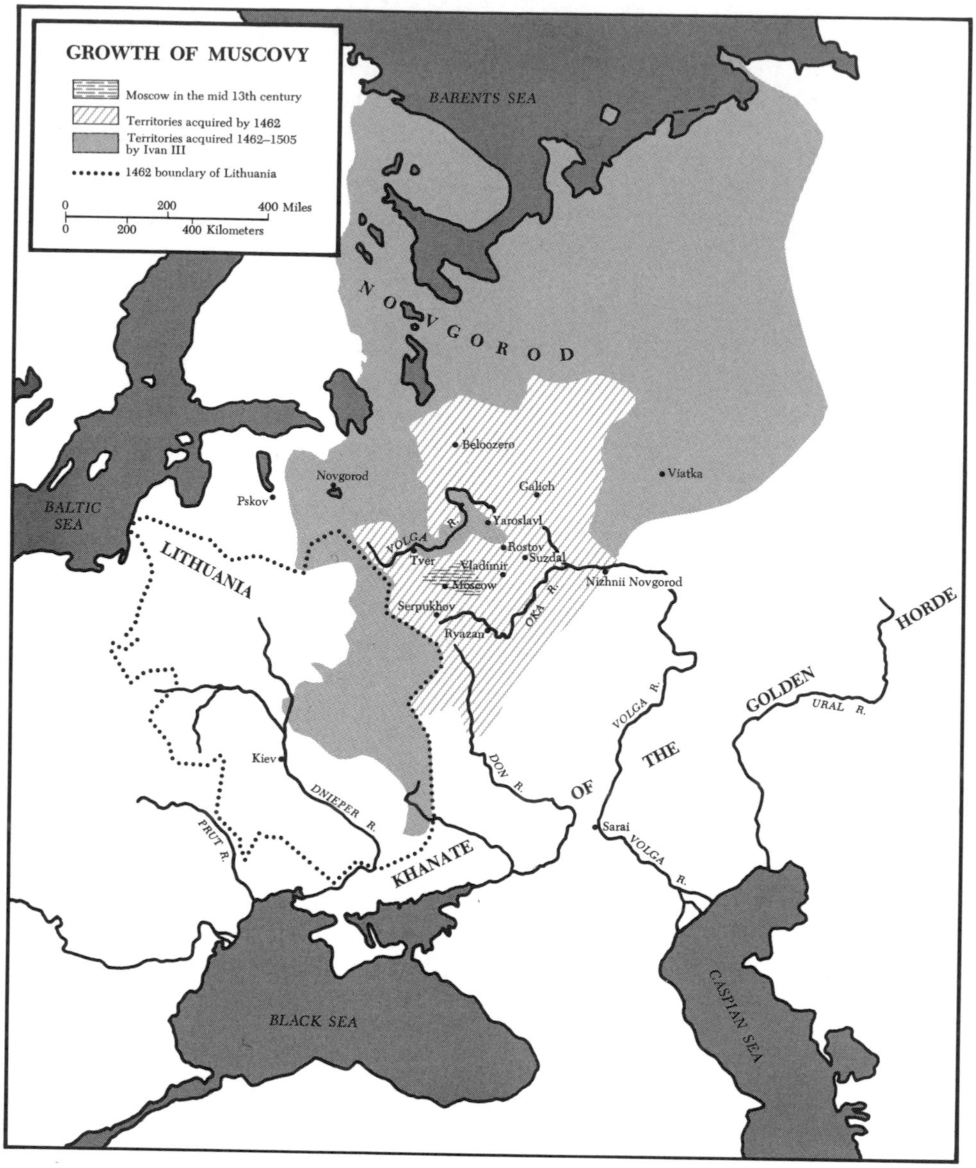

that it remained a sparsely populated virgin land, while others theorize that it was densely populated by the end of the twelfth century.

At any rate, Yurii Dolgorukii and his two sons, Andrei Bogolyubskii (*d.* 1174) and Vsevolod III (*d.* 1212), transformed their inheritance into the most powerful of the Kievan successor principalities. Sheltered by forests and situated north of the traditional invasion routes of the procession of Asiatic invaders, the area was blessed with a wedge of fertile soil extending from the steppe. When these princes decided to build new towns for their residences, first at Suzdal and later at Vladimir—located about a dozen miles apart—they chose sites within the surplus-growing area.

As a younger son of Vladimir Monomakh, Yurii Dolgorukii never lost sight of his claim to the senior throne at Kiev. After the death of his older brother Mstislav, Yurii led three assaults upon the "mother of Russian cities" and finally succeeded in becoming grand prince in 1155. He died in Kiev in 1157.

Yurii's eldest son, Andrei Bogolyubskii, inherited the northern possessions. As talented and ambitious as his father, Andrei departed from his father's strategy, spurning Kiev and seeking to create a new realm with the northeast as its base. Demanding subordi-

MUSCOVY, RISE OF

nation of all the military forces, he drove out those who opposed him. His only interest in the old Kievan capital was to erase it as a rival center. In 1169 his warriors stormed Kiev and carried off everything of value. Andrei placed a subordinate prince on the Kievan throne but reserved the title of grand prince for himself. Henceforth the senior ruler resided in the north.

For all of his successes, Andrei failed in his quest to become an autocratic monarch. The opposition of the people of Suzdal persuaded him to shift his capital to Vladimir on the Klyazma River, but his aroused opponents assassinated him in 1174. After a struggle, Andrei's brother Vsevolod obtained recognition as the new grand prince of Vladimir. While continuing in his brother's footsteps, Vsevolod managed to avoid Andrei's excesses. He also sought control over the northern territories from Novgorod in the west to the Volga in the east.

The time for strong monarchical rule had not yet come, but the foundations for its future development had been set. The great town councils of the Kievan period never had a chance to develop in the northeast, where they might have limited the authority of the princes. Princes founded the northern towns primarily for military purposes and as residences, and consequently they dominated affairs in these centers. The majority of the population was scattered in hamlets and villages in a dispersal that neutralized popular political leverage. The princes and their military followers held the reins of political power. The junior princes and the warriors resisted the encroachments of the senior prince and thereby maintained the liberties that existed in that society.

THIRTEENTH AND EARLY FOURTEENTH CENTURY

In the successional scheme of the thirteenth and early fourteenth centuries, the princes of Moscow should never have become important in the political future of the Russian north. The heirs of Vsevolod (*d.* 1212) were supposed to receive the senior princeship according to a system of lateral succession. Vsevolod's sons were to succeed one another in order of seniority, with the grand princely dignity passing at death. Then Vsevolod's grandsons were to succeed one another. If, however, any of Vsevolod's sons died before assuming the senior dignity, that prince's descendants were then barred forever from the grand princely title. This system of exclusion was to continue through the generations—only the son of a grand prince could become grand prince.

Moscow should have been displaced when Prince Daniel of Moscow died in 1303, a year before his older brother, Andrei, the reigning grand prince of Vladimir. At Andrei's death in 1304, the position of grand prince did pass to Michael Yaroslavich, the prince of Tver, in accordance with the rules of succession.

However, Prince Yurii Danilovich of Moscow (1303–1325) was inclined to dispute the succession. Two related considerations—one internal and one external—must have made the time seem propitious. Internally, the authority of the grand prince had declined. Externally there was Mongol domination.

The Mongols (called Tatars in the Russian sources) had imposed their overlordship after their conquest in the earlier thirteenth century, requiring tribute payments and military levies from the subjugated populace and turning the senior princes into lieutenants of the khans. Though the Tatar overlords generally allowed the Russians to follow their customary practices, they interfered when it suited their purposes. From the beginning of the conquest the khans confirmed the right to the senior princedom by letter patent (*yarlyk*).

Prince Yurii of Moscow stubbornly pursued his quest for the grand princedom of Vladimir, finally succeeding in 1318 after he married the sister of Khan Uzbek. It required a contingent of Tatar horsemen and the execution of Michael of Tver to implement the khan's decision. Even these drastic measures brought no peace, for the Tverians refused to accept Yurii as grand prince. In about 1325, Prince Dmitrii of Tver assassinated Yurii, which earned him a sentence of death at the khan's tribunal. However, Yurii's murder had sundered the slender thread that linked Moscow to the khan's grace. The overlord then chose Alexander of Tver, Dmitrii's brother, as the new grand prince of Vladimir, thereby returning to the age-old tradition of lateral succession.

This Tverian triumph spelled but momentary disaster for Moscow, since an unexpected tragedy gave the house of Daniel a second chance. A Tatar envoy, accompanied by a sizable entourage, appeared in the Tverian capital in 1327. A variety of rumors surfaced, including one that the envoy had come to establish direct Tatar control. This led to a popular uprising during which the visitors were massacred. When news reached Moscow, Prince Ivan Kalita, the murdered Yurii's younger brother and the inher-

MUSCOVY, RISE OF

itor of the patrimony, rushed to the Tatar capital at Sarai (on the lower Volga River), where he offered his services to punish the disloyal Tverians. He received permission to lead a joint Muscovite-Tatar force against Tver. Prince Ivan impressed the khan with his zeal in putting Tver to sword and torch. His reward came in 1328, when the reigning khan awarded him the grand princely patent.

THE GOLDEN HORDE

Thereafter the senior princes of Moscow never relinquished their hold on the Grand Principality of Vladimir. They displayed slavish loyalty to the khans at Sarai so long as the Tatar Horde on the Russian steppe (called the Golden Horde) remained strong and favorably disposed toward Moscow. But sometime during the earlier fourteenth century the overlords at Sarai allowed Moscow's more important neighbors—Tver, Nizhnii Novgorod (the former principality of Suzdal), and Ryazan—to be called grand principalities, though none of their princes could overcome the importance of the grand prince of Vladimir in the hierarchy of the north. Whether these concessions stemmed from the khans' fear of Moscow's increased importance or whether they acceded to petitions from these contending territorial princes is not known.

By mid century the great Mongol Empire was shaken by internal strife. Dynastic wars of succession among the numerous descendants of Genghis Khan created an instability that reached to the Golden Horde and ultimately affected Moscow's relations with several of its ambitious neighbors. If one of the rival khans of the Golden Horde favored Moscow, the other became its enemy. The rulers of Nizhnii Novgorod and Tver sought the cherished title to the Grand Principality of Vladimir and successively won the support of a rival khan. What Moscow could no longer retain by the overlord's favor, it endeavored to defend on the field of battle. In the 1360's and 1370's, Moscow defeated its rivals and thereby indicated that it would challenge even the authority of the khans in order to retain its preeminence among the northern Russian principalities.

In 1380, Grand Prince Dmitrii Donskoi defeated a Tatar army sent to punish him for his independent attitude. Never before had a Russian force vanquished a Tatar army in the field. That Russian victory, on Snipe (or Kulikovo) Field, in Ryazanian territory, is enshrined in nationalistic lore. Though Grand Prince Dmitrii had to acknowledge the overlordship again two years later, after another Tatar army penetrated Muscovite territory and sacked its capital, the khan, Tokhtamysh, prudently turned aside the petition of the Tverian ruler to transfer the senior patent to him.

Tokhtamysh, the strongest of the khans in the second half of the fourteenth century and the last significant ruler of the Golden Horde, could not deal with the Russian problem as he might have wished. Faced with the menace of Tamerlane to his east, he did not relish the prospect of having a determined and vengeful Muscovite prince on his flank. Whether he ultimately intended his accommodation with Dmitrii Donskoi to be a temporary one or not is of little historical consequence, for Tamerlane drove him from his throne by 1395, and none of Tokhtamysh's successors at Sarai commanded forces adequate to overturn the decision Tokhtamysh had made in 1382. Faced with these circumstances, Moscow's rivals abandoned their quest for the Grand Principality of Vladimir. Thereafter Moscow was consistently the aggressor in the politics of the Russian north.

Grand Prince Vasilii I (1390–1425), Donskoi's eldest son, profited from Khan Tokhtamysh's continuing difficulties by annexing the principality of Nizhnii Novgorod in 1392, thereby advancing Moscow's territory to the east and eliminating one of its troublesome neighbors. Vasilii I blackmailed Tokhtamysh by threatening to withhold Moscow's tribute payments and loyalty at the very time the khan was preparing for a decisive confrontation with Tamerlane. Tamerlane's victory three years later (1395), which drove Tokhtamysh from the steppe, guaranteed Moscow's permanent possession of Nizhnii Novgorod.

THE ROLE OF THE CHURCH

If accident had given Moscow its initial advantage, other factors combined to elevate Moscow above its rivals. Moscow's identification as the Russian religious capital played a paramount role in focusing attention upon its secular lords as the most favored sons of the church.

In 1299 or 1300, Maxim, the metropolitan bishop of the Russian eparchy, moved his residence from the ravaged and virtually deserted city of Kiev to Vladimir. In keeping with tradition he desired to locate in the secular capital of the Russian north, but he arrived just as the power center was shifting from Vladimir to the western interior, where Tver and

MUSCOVY, RISE OF

Moscow were located. When Grand Prince Andrei died in 1304, Maxim dutifully endorsed Michael of Tver as the rightful inheritor of the grand princely dignity. Upon Maxim's death a few months later, Michael sought to have a Russian native appointed as the new spiritual leader, one who would lend him active moral and ecclesiastical support against his enemies. The Constantinopolitan authorities, whose right to choose Russian metropolitans had existed since the conversion of Rus in the tenth century, spurned Michael's appeal and consecrated as the new Russian pastor a Volynian Slav called Peter (1307–1325). Grand Prince Michael refused to abide by that decision, and he schemed to depose Peter by accusing him of a variety of serious but eventually unsubstantiated charges. The long years of conflict inclined Peter to cast his lot with the Muscovite prince.

Ivan Kalita of Moscow, himself a schemer of no mean talent, capitalized upon Peter's difficulties and became the metropolitan's champion. When Peter died in Moscow, where he had sought sanctuary from his tormentor, Ivan Kalita had him buried in a new stone church on the brow of the hill within the ruler's fortress (kremlin) and initiated the process of having Peter canonized as a saint (the canonization took place in 1339).

The politics of religion bore abundant fruit, for all of Peter's successors settled in Moscow and supported its princes' political ambitions. Metropolitans Feognost (1328–1353) and Aleksei (1354–1378) used their considerable influence to strengthen the power of the Moscow princes. Aleksei, a member of one of Moscow's elite serving families, was the first native north Russian to occupy the metropolitan's throne. He never hesitated to employ the weapons of the church, even excommunication, in furthering the grand princely quest for political dominance.

Aleksei's open partisanship alienated princes hostile toward Moscow. Even Algirdas (Olgerd), the pagan grand prince of Lithuania, pressured the Byzantine authorities to appoint a separate metropolitan for the Orthodox living in his realm. (In 1354, a Lithuanian metropolitan was indeed appointed, but, after his death in 1361, Lithuania again became subject to the jurisdiction of the Muscovite metropolitan.) Although the Byzantine ecclesiastical officials resisted appointments of Muscovites as metropolitans, desiring pastors capable of handling the problems of the pan-Russian eparchy, the lords of Moscow continued to receive invaluable aid from the resident senior hierarchs.

OTHER FACTORS IN MUSCOVY'S RISE

Historians generally believe that the illustrious military serving families who had supported the grand princes of Vladimir in the thirteenth and early fourteenth centuries transferred their allegiance to the Moscow house after it acquired a permanent upper hand over the other territorial princes. These servitors attached their careers to the cause of political unity as well as to the status and rewards that flowed from serving the most important princes of the north. Their number is unknown since the genealogical registers of the nonprincely families in Muscovite service, composed only in the sixteenth century, rarely identify verifiable progenitors prior to the fourteenth century. Even the origin of these worthy warrior families is uncertain. What has been established is that thirty-five to forty loyal military families developed during the fourteenth century, and that these families guarded the interests of Muscovy as zealously as they did their monopoly of the senior court and military command positions.

If Muscovy was no more strategically sited than other interior towns along inland waterways for purposes of trade or for the defense of outlying frontier posts, its location did give it an unforeseen advantage. The patrimony of Daniel's descendants was surrounded by other major principalities: Tver to the northwest, Nizhnii Novgorod to the east, and Ryazan to the south. Had these neighbors been strong and aggressive, Moscow would never have been able to survive. But their vulnerability to attack by outside forces and the princely discord in their ruling families gave Moscow an advantage in its buffered location. Ryazan, which lay on the edge of the steppe and through which the Don River flowed to the south, was situated in the path of marauding Tatar bands. More than one major Tatar campaign utilized the Don basin as the highway for attack. The Volga River played a similar role in exposing Nizhnii Novgorod to periodic raids. For Tver, Lithuanian expansion eastward diverted its attention from the bitter struggle with Moscow during the pivotal decades of conflict in the fourteenth century. All three of these surrounding principalities fell prey to dynastic crises as junior princes of each line challenged the authority of the senior, thereby diverting energies inward rather than turning them against Moscow.

Moscow benefited from its interior protected position and probably attracted population from the surrounding principalities. Merchants found passage safer along Moscow's roads and waterways, where vigilant patrols reduced the incidence of brigandage and robbery. Tranquility and stability augmented the revenues collected from peasants and increased the tolls and duties collected from goods in transit.

Absence of princely family strife throughout the century enhanced domestic tranquility. Here too accident favored the house of Daniel (Danilovichi). A high rate of infant mortality and the visitation of the Black Death (after 1352) drastically reduced the number of surviving heirs. The Muscovite line barely maintained itself, spawning only one junior branch (that of Serpukhov) with equally few heirs. Since customary Slavic law required that each son receive a portion of his father's properties, the absence of many claimants enhanced the resources and power of the senior princes. They were able to sustain a larger military following than any of their political rivals.

Retention of their title to the Grand Principality of Vladimir added to their prestige and power. They collected the Tatar tribute from the princes placed under their jurisdiction. They could summon levies from the area of their lieutenancy in time of common danger, and they acted as arbiters when interprincely disputes arose. As their resources grew, they expanded their possessions by purchase, conquest, and coercion. Of all the territorial lordships in the Russian north, Moscow alone grew significantly in size and power in the fourteenth century.

Moscow's jealous rivals for the grand princely dignity no doubt communicated their fears to the Tatar overlords, and the khans recognized that their senior lieutenants were transforming reflected authority into autonomous power. The creation of the grand principalities of Tver, Ryazan, and Nizhnii Novgorod may have been designed to reduce the authority of the Muscovite "Grand Prince of Vladimir," but the power struggle that shook the Mongol Empire prevented more decisive measures.

The temporarily weakened overlordship of the Tatars meant that the Muscovite authorities had to use military force to curb the aspirations of the neighboring grand princes. As Grand Prince Dmitrii Donskoi sought to enforce Moscow's hegemony, he further embittered relations with his neighbors. This situation could have had disastrous consequences had not the Muscovite army defeated the Tatars in 1380. When Grand Prince Dmitrii prepared for that battle, he summoned the forces of the Russian north to support him against the common enemy, but he was spurned by the other grand princes. Even the Novgorodians, ever fearful of a strong grand prince and the implications for their de facto independence, refused to send troops. Only the minor princes—those of Rostov, Yaroslavl, Beloozero, and some from the Starodub line—answered the call. Moscow's celebrated victory forever destroyed any hope that the letter patent to the Grand Principality of Vladimir would be transferred to one of Moscow's opponents. The senior title remained with the house of Daniel, and from the time of Dmitrii Donskoi the Grand Principality was bequeathed as a possession to the oldest son of the reigning grand prince, even though endorsement by the reigning khan was still required.

Where Donskoi faced problems in obtaining recognition of his suzerainty over the north Russian territories, a century later his great-grandson, Ivan III (1462–1505), became the undisputed sovereign over a considerably larger area. His authority over his subjects far exceeded that of any ruler in Western Europe, being unfettered by contract, law, overriding tradition, or threat of revolt. He could disgrace, exile, imprison, or execute even members of the highest aristocracy and confiscate their possessions without benefit of judicial process. Those whose loyalty was suspect were forced to swear perpetual obedience and service with the threat of secular and religious sanctions if they should err in the future. Ivan obliged all members of the warrior class to serve upon call. All who resided within the realm had to acknowledge themselves as his subjects. Even the Grand Principality of Ryazan and the republic of Pskov, which retained nominal independence until the sixteenth century, had to acknowledge his suzerainty, follow his directives, and dispatch troops under his command. All laws and directives issued from his chancery and were administrated by agents selected from the members of his court. Gone were the traditional rights of free warriors to serve voluntarily or to accept service with another prince when discontented.

DYNASTIC WARS, 1425–1453

The autocratic monarchy owed its emergence to a number of fifteenth-century developments. Foremost among these was a nasty and prolonged political crisis that lasted through the first half of the century. A long-smoldering dynastic dispute within the Muscovite princely family provoked the crisis. In the fourteenth century seniority had passed from father to eldest son rather than from brother to brother as had been the earlier tradition. The small number of heirs facilitated change and reduced the possibility of friction among Daniel's descendants. Of his five sons, only Ivan Kalita ultimately survived to inherit the family patrimony. Kalita had three sons, the oldest of whom, Grand Prince Semen Gordyi (the Proud), along with his children, succumbed to plague in 1353. Semen had bequeathed his possessions to his wife rather than to his oldest surviving brother, but that brother, Ivan II, somehow acquired possession of Semen's properties and became grand prince (1353–1359). The third brother, Andrei, became the appanage ruler of Serpukhov. Dmitrii Donskoi was the only survivor of Ivan II's two sons, and the Serpukhov branch also clung to the thread of a single member. This fortuitous development contributed greatly to Moscow's internal security and to its continued success in obtaining delegation of the grand princely patent.

The genealogical circumstances changed at the end of the fourteenth century, when five of Dmitrii Donskoi's sons survived him. Tradition required that each acquire a patrimony. The erection of so many appanages created in Muscovy the same potential for trouble that had plagued Moscow's neighbors in the fourteenth century. Recognizing the dangers, Dmitrii Donskoi sought to fix the pattern of senior family descent. He intended that family seniority and the grand princely dignity should remain in the hands of the same person and devolve from father to oldest surviving son. Since his oldest son, the future Vasilii I, still was unmarried as Donskoi approached death, Donskoi stipulated in his testament that should Vasilii die without male issue, Prince Yurii, the next oldest, was to occupy the senior position. Undoubtedly, he wanted to avoid a situation similar to the one that had occurred in 1353, but the sparse chancery language of the testament only took into account existing realities: "And, if because of my sins, God takes away my son, Prince Vasiliy, then . . . [his] principality . . . [shall pass] to my son who follows him, and the patrimonial principality of the latter shall be divided among the others by my princess."

Prince Yurii of Galich, the second oldest son, was obsessed with a desire to become grand prince. He seized upon the statement in his father's will to claim the right to succeed his older brother, even when Vasilii I had a male heir. Later Yurii bolstered his argument by citing the thirteenth-century tradition of brother following brother as grand prince. Yurii's determined stance caused strains within the Muscovite princely family through most of Vasilii I's reign, but did not yet become the cause for war.

Before Vasilii I died in 1425 he did everything short of attacking his brother Yurii to ensure the succession of his ten-year-old heir, Vasilii II. He named his father-in-law, Grand Prince Vitovt of Lithuania, as guardian, and he created a regency council composed of his loyal brothers, and the metropolitans. These uncertain safeguards crumbled after five years as Vitovt and the metropolitan disappeared from the scene. Dislocation and suffering became the lot of the unhappy Muscovites during the next twenty years as the princes of Galich fought to supersede Vasilii II. Prince Yurii twice captured Moscow, unseating his nephew, and proclaimed himself grand prince. He died in 1434, just a month after he had driven Vasilii from the throne. While this should have ended the challenge, two of Yurii's sons successively sought to follow in their father's footsteps, justifying their actions on the grounds that their father had died as grand prince.

The dynastic struggle ultimately involved the populace at large as supporters of the warring factions roamed the land, taking what they could. The family princes divided in their loyalties, as several forsook their promises of duty and loyalty to the legitimate heir for reasons of personal gain. Petty princes from lines other than Muscovite, but who resided within or adjacent to Muscovite territory, were forced to take sides. Their possessions became their bond of allegiance, and defection would cost them their patrimonies. Nonprincely servitors lost their right of transfer to the banner of another lord even in peaceful years. The absence of a resident metropolitan between 1431 and 1448 permitted the clergy to divide in their sympathies. And the standards of military conduct, never very high, sometimes descended to the level of savagery. To cite several notable examples, Vasilii II had Prince Yurii's oldest son blinded in 1436 in order to end his opposition. Ten years later Yurii's youngest son Dmitrii Shemiaka captured Vasilii II, depriving him of his sight and throne.

The forces of legitimacy prevailed in the long run. Popular support, the resolve of a majority of the grand princely servitors, and, ultimately, a reunited clergy blunted the Galich challenge and rallied behind Vasilii II. The last Galich pretender, Prince Dmitrii Shemiaka, was driven from his patrimony in

Russian Rulers, 1125–1505

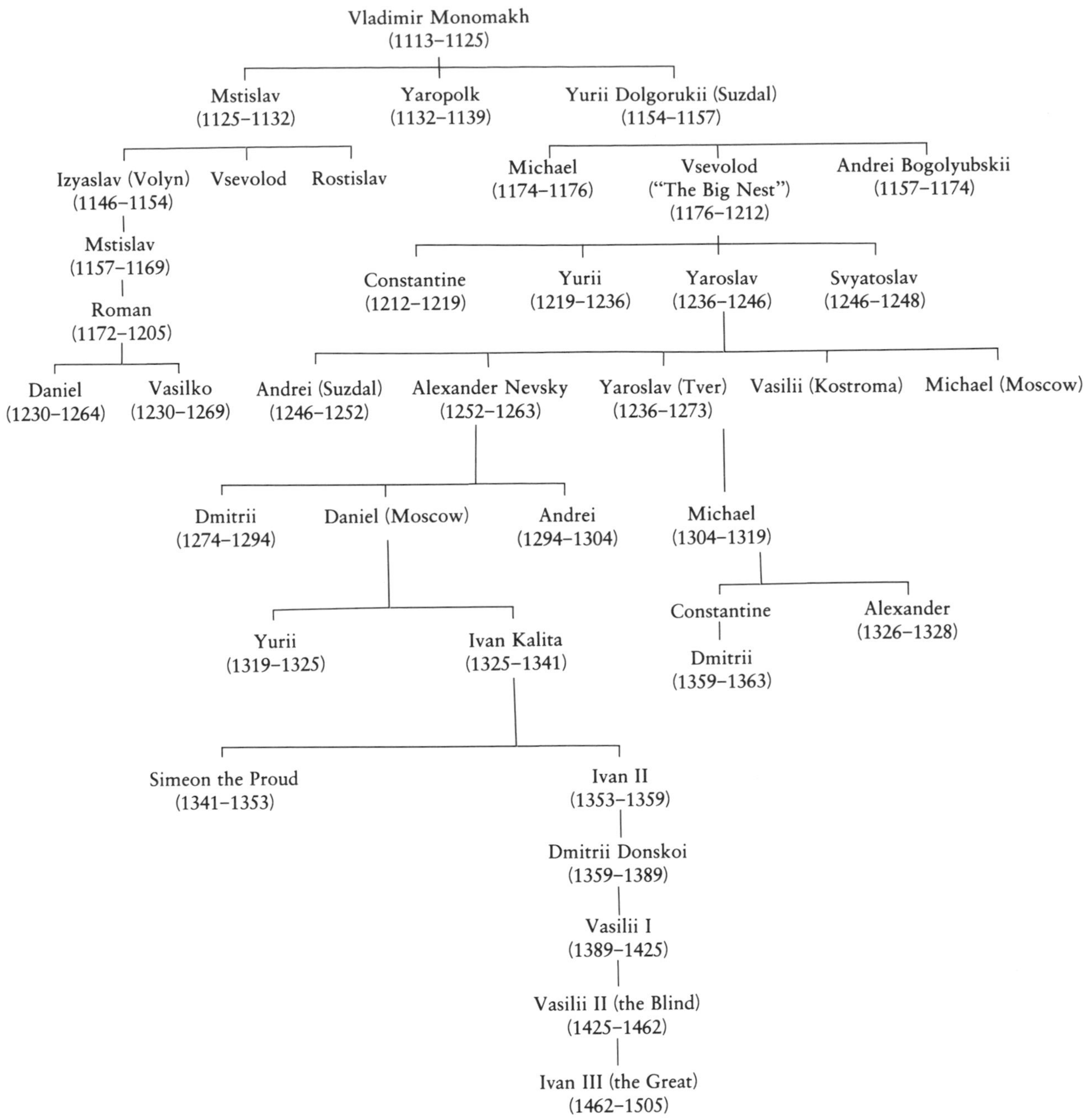

1450 and died in Novgorodian exile in 1453, probably of poison administered by a grand princely agent.

The older norms of political behavior did not survive the dynastic wars. The concept of sovereignty, in which the highest duty was to serve the grand prince, was forged in the fires of war. Vasilii II drove all but one of his family's appanage princes from their patrimonies. One died of poison, a second expired after many years in prison, and a third found sanctuary in Lithuania. The servitors of Vasilii II's opponents who had remained true to their lords were also threatened with punishment but were generally forgiven. Henceforth one's prime allegiance was to the senior prince of the Muscovite house, the sovereign, regardless of one's service to a more immediate lord. This requirement was occasionally forgotten, but the reminders were sometimes forceful.

Those who resided outside Muscovy proper and had aided the rebels also earned the wrath of the victor. The republic of Novgorod, with its rich trading empire, had theoretically owed allegiance to the grand princes of Vladimir, but in fact had maintained control over its domestic and foreign policies. Ever fearful of Moscow's growing aspirations, the republic's officials had followed a consistent policy of weakening the grand prince's power whenever possible. During the dynastic wars the republic had offered sanctuary to the momentarily defeated contestant. The longer the struggle continued, the weaker Muscovy might become. Vasilii II had once enjoyed Novgorodian hospitality as a refugee, and Dmitrii Shemiaka had operated against Muscovy from Novgorodian sanctuary during the last three years of his life. The harboring of Shemiaka had incensed Vasilii II, and he resolved to punish Novgorod at the first opportunity. Spurning offers of negotiations and monetary compensation, Vasilii II resolved to humiliate Novgorod. His army inflicted a devastating defeat upon the republic's inexpert forces in 1456. Vasilii then tightened his control over Novgorod by depriving it of its independent foreign policy—thereafter his seal was required on all its treaties and his device had to appear on the coinage. He also forbade the city to give sanctuary to any Muscovite defector or enemy. Subsequent attempts to tear free of Moscow's clutches led to further humiliation and finally to the annexation of Novgorod in 1478.

The victor's wrath also fell on the land of Viatka. Located northeast of Moscow and sparsely populated by frontiersmen, it had consistently aided the Galich princes. Its punishment led to annexation in 1459.

Three other developments coincident with the dynastic upheaval supported the evolution of sovereignty. The first involved the subordination of the church to grand princely authority; the second was an emerging claim of imperial succession after the fall of Byzantium in 1453; and the third was the tacit rejection of the Tatar overlordship.

THE SUBORDINATION OF THE CHURCH

Between the death of the Greek-born Fotii in 1431 and the elevation of the Russian Iona in December 1448, the Russian eparchy was without the services of a metropolitan who might have aided Vasilii II against his secular enemies. In 1436, just as the first phase of the succession struggle had ended, Vasilii II and his advisers sent Iona, then bishop of Ryazan, as the grand princely candidate for metropolitan to Constantinople, but the moment was ill timed, for the Muscovite request conflicted with an imperial necessity.

The Byzantine emperor, John VIII Palaiologos, urgently desired an active supporter for his policy of conciliation with the papacy at a projected ecumenical council. He desperately needed Western military assistance against the encroaching Ottoman Turks, and he was willing, as the price for such aid, to accept papal demands for supremacy over a united Christian church. Since the Eastern tradition required confirmation by an ecumenical council for any major religious decision, the emperor needed the endorsement of the Orthodox bishops. He therefore pushed through the appointment of Isidore as metropolitan of Russia. Isidore was an archimandrite of a Constantinopolitan monastery and was in sympathy with the imperial plan. He arrived in Moscow and stayed only long enough to present his credentials and to gather a suite of Russian clerics before embarking for Italy, the site of the council.

At the Council of Florence (1438/1439) Isidore worked valiantly for the desired union, and Pope Eugenius IV rewarded the Russian metropolitan with a cardinal's hat. When Isidore finally returned to Moscow in 1441 and announced the union with the Roman church, Vasilii II convened a council of bishops, who ordered Isidore's arrest on the grounds of heresy. Canon law required the death penalty for unrepentant heretics, but the Muscovite authorities feared to do injury to so distinguished a prisoner. The grand prince permitted Isidore to "escape" and return to Rome, relieving the Muscovite prince and bishops of further embarrassment. This solution hardly satisfied the need for a new Russian primate, because so long as the emperor in Constantinople remained committed to union with Rome no Orthodox metropolitan could be ordained for the Russian see.

Secular circumstances, however, after Vasilii regained his throne in 1447, required a mobilization of ecclesiastical support to isolate the pretender. Vasilii II ordered the bishops to elevate Iona as metropolitan in 1448 and the new hierarch employed the weapon of excommunication or its threat to erode support for Dmitrii Shemiaka. Ten years after Iona's selection the Orthodox clergy faced the challenge of

MUSCOVY, RISE OF

a papally appointed metropolitan (Gregory) for the west Russian lands, causing the bishops loyal to Moscow to defend Vasilii II's role in designating his own metropolitan. In a war of words that attended the defense, clerical publicists saluted Vasilii as "God crowned," a "second Constantine," "autocrat," and "emperor" (tsar). Thereafter all metropolitans required the prior approval of grand princes, and not a few were removed for causing their displeasure. The fall of Byzantium in 1453 deprived the Russian church of its protector and increased its dependency upon the grand prince. Moreover, the effective limits of the ecclesiastical eparchy ultimately coincided with the territorial limits of the Muscovite realm and those areas that became dependencies of the grand prince.

IMPERIAL ASPIRATIONS AND THE END OF TATAR OVERLORDSHIP

In his last years Vasilii II initiated a drive to obtain recognition of a new eastern empire. Byzantium had fallen, and Muscovy was the remaining unconquered Orthodox state. Vasilii's circumspect inquiry at the court of the Milanese despot came to naught, but his successors never abandoned the goal. Low-keyed, yet persistent, the strategy never wavered. Finally, an impatient Ivan IV had himself crowned as tsar in 1547 in a ceremony modeled on the coronation of a Byzantine *basileus,* or emperor.

The third external development that enhanced the grand prince's sovereignty was an implicit rejection of the Tatar overlord's authority. In 1447 or 1448, Vasilii II associated his eldest son, Ivan, to the throne as his co-grand prince. The move enunciated the pattern of succession and ensured continuity in the event of one of the two grand princes being taken prisoner. The rush with which this decision had been taken had precluded the normal request for the overlord's endorsement. Nor did the court seek confirmation after the moment of exigency had passed. The Muscovite court never again sought Tatar sanction for the transfer of grand princely authority and, in effect, rejected the overlordship that had lasted for more than 200 years. Subsequent attempts by khans of the steppe to reimpose their suzerainty were decisively rejected. The continuing debility of Tatar power had worked to Moscow's advantage.

IVAN III

The martial energies developed in the dynastic wars, coupled with the firm foundation of Muscovite power attained by the middle of the fifteenth century, allowed Ivan III (1462–1505) to expand his authority throughout the Russian north. He coerced or cajoled the proprietary princes of Yaroslavl (1463) and Rostov (1474) to deed, sell, or otherwise transfer to him the legal rights to their lands. As noted, above, Ivan annexed Novgorod with its huge territorial hinterland in 1478, when the Novgorodians again sought to tear free of Muscovite suzerainty. These actions transformed the Tverian grand principality into an isolated interior island. Calculated border incidents heightened fears of Muscovite intentions, and the Tverian ruler sought to bolster his position with a Lithuanian alliance. This hostile maneuver proved to be futile, and it provided Ivan III with the neccessary excuse to annex the lands of his family's ancient rival in 1485.

Ivan III had moved cautiously against both Novgorod and Tver, ever fearful that the Lithuanian rulers would come to the aid of their treaty partners, but reaction had come only in the guise of diplomatic protests, which finally convinced the Muscovite authorities that Lithuania was a paper tiger. Against Lithuania, Ivan employed the same measures that had worked so well against Tver. He authorized a series of raids on the lands belonging to Orthodox princes who owed allegiance to the grand prince of Lithuania. The Lithuanian government responded with its traditional diplomatic complaints but did little to protect its frontiers. This persuaded some of the Orthodox princes to transfer allegiance to Ivan III, thereby extending the Muscovite frontier further to the west. Encouraged by the feeble response, Ivan ordered an increase in the number of raids. Since Lithuania contained a large Orthodox population in an area that once had belonged to the Kievan realm, he designed a two-pronged gambit to legitimize his actions. He posed as the protector of the Orthodox, charging the Lithuanian government with persecution of the Eastern-rite population, and he claimed to be the rightful ruler "of all Rus." Moscovite bellicosity finally caused an open war that turned out badly for Lithuania (1500–1503). Muscovite forces overran a third of the vast Lithuanian territory, never to be relinquished.

This territorial expansion, which has so attracted the attention of scholars, was more a consequence than a cause of the evolving power of Muscovy, though the additional resources and manpower contributed to an expansion of political muscle. Expansion augmented revenues but necessitated larger armies and an enlarged administrative apparatus.

MUSCOVY, RISE OF

Despite the additional income, the Muscovite government could not afford to, or would not, pay its military servitors, while considerable sums were lavished upon imposing churches, palaces, and a grandiose reconstruction of the Kremlin's walls. Ivan III paid heavily for the services of Italian architects and foreign artisans to transform his citadel on the Moskva. Since the expenditures of government for the trappings of power devoured income from taxes and customs in this overwhelming agrarian land, little was left for other ongoing expenses. Manpower was the most abundant and constantly renewable resource, and the grand prince readily exploited the opportunity to harness it to his purposes.

THE WARRIOR CLASS AND IVAN III'S COURT

Obtaining control over the warrior class had not been possible before the fifteenth century. Traditionally, military retainers, unless they were slaves, served voluntarily, relying on war booty, provincial lieutenancies, and the prince's largess for their service income. In the fourteenth century Moscow's monopoly in obtaining the grand princely patent, its success in military ventures, and its territorial growth had attracted the best of the untitled warrior class to its banner. These proud and free warriors expected to be consulted when decisions affecting their fortunes or ways of life were made. In the event they transferred allegiance to another lord, their properties remained in their former prince's jurisdiction and were considered inviolable. Dire punishment or confiscation of a warrior's wealth was reserved only for cases of probable treason, and so serious a charge applied only to cases of defection in time of war or when a warrior transferred service with the intention of urging his new lord to attack his former suzerain.

The dynastic wars destroyed the customary guarantees of the warrior class as well as those formerly enjoyed by the ruling family's younger princes. Both groups sought to resist the increase in grand princely powers, but the precedents of the mid fifteenth century became the rules of operating behavior in the next hundred years. All landlords, whether "servitor princes," members of Moscow's old untitled elite, or provincial landlords, became subjects of the grand prince and were deprived of their traditional rights to seek employment with a foreign prince. The alternative of service in the appanages became attractive only to those who could not find positions of consequence at the grand princely court. Even in the appanages they were not beyond the reach of the sovereign, for if they incurred his displeasure they could be punished. One could no longer claim that he followed his prince. For instance, in 1491, Prince Andrei the Elder, brother to Ivan III, had refused an order to lead his forces out against the Tatars of the steppe. Ivan III had Andrei arrested and imprisoned for life. The patrimony was confiscated. Andrei's servitors were also apprehended but later released, though the conditions for forgiveness were not revealed. They had learned that obedience to their suzerain superseded loyalty to their immediate prince. In addition, because grand princes refused to allow most of their brothers to marry (a practice quite visible in the sixteenth century, but one which may already have developed in the later fifteenth), the possibility of forcible return to direct grand princely service required an appanage servitor to think first about his own future prospects.

The noose first fashioned in the aftermath of the dynastic wars tightened further with the rapid expansion of Muscovy in the second half of the fifteenth century. Each new acquisition brought additional princes and their servitors directly under Muscovite control. Ivan desired to bring the most prestigious of his new subjects to court, tempting them with positions that could lead to high office. Removal to the Muscovite capital eroded the local bases of power of these former provincial lords. At the same time, these newcomers at court were more easily watched and more readily integrated into Muscovy. Competition for choice assignments and a desire to advertise one's fidelity created attitudes that the ruler could turn to his advantage.

Meanwhile, the removal of these aristocrats from the provinces allowed for greater centralized control in the newly annexed areas. Crown lieutenants, chosen for their loyalty and previous service, as well as for a lack of marital or territorial connection with their lieutenancies, administered the new provinces and districts. Their only concerns were to carry out the orders of their superiors, to maintain domestic tranquility, and to augment their financial positions.

Ivan III's policy of drawing aristocrats from recently annexed areas to court unsettled the servitors from the old established families, whose ancestors had contributed mightily to Moscow's successes. The princes who had recently come into service began to clamor for better assignments and higher positions, even at the expense of the older entrenched aristocracy, because they claimed their inherited rank was of greater value than that derived from generations of service. Each new acquisition generated a new influx that threatened to undermine the opportunities of those already holding court positions. Their distress created a potential for widespread discontent and persuaded Ivan III to modify his policy.

These statements are unsupported by any court directives or even chroniclers' observations, but they may be inferred from a sudden shift in policy. The annexation of Tver in 1485 had brought with it the prospect of yet another infusion of princes and distinguished Tverian warriors into the expanded Muscovite court. Indeed, a number of Tverian aristocrats had already defected to Moscow before the final conquest. No sooner had Muscovite troops entered the Tverian capital than Ivan III ordered the appanage princes and all other Tverian warriors to serve him from their estates. Most of the distinguished Tverians who had earlier opted for Muscovite service were returned to their patrimonies. These moves effectively prohibited members of the Tverian elite from obtaining the highest service positions in Muscovy. The best they could accomplish, before Ivan IV again sought to integrate the Russian service aristocracy in the 1550's, were occasional governorships in the less important Muscovite provinces. Only a handful of Tverians succeeded in remaining at Ivan III's court, and they were selected from the defectors who had come over prior to the conquest.

Ivan III also barred from court those Orthodox princes who abjured their allegiance to the Lithuanian grand prince and became Muscovite subjects. They also had to reside on their estates and were required to make their forces ready for border forays or to serve as auxiliary units attached to Muscovite armies. Prudence might have dictated the removal of these border lords to the interior and the substitution of reliable Muscovites in their place, but the plan to continue the western drive compelled Ivan III to accord special treatment to these newest of subjects and thereby encourage still others to opt for Muscovite suzerainty. Moreover, the opposition at court toward newcomers aided in shaping the decision.

At the same time the Muscovite government placed severe restraints upon these former Lithuanian subjects. Only the most powerful among them retained considerable autonomy, being permitted to exercise local control without Muscovite interference. The majority were deprived of political and administrative power. Legal title to their lands was transferred to Ivan III, but they were allowed the use of their possessions and even the possibility of transferring them to their heirs, provided they maintained the goodwill of the grand prince. In effect, they retained their positions by sufferance rather than by the protection of the law. Control over justice became the responsibility of assigned Muscovite officials, and key fortresses and districts were placed in the hands of trusted members of the court.

The liberal treatment of the Lithuanian border princes contrasted sharply with the fate meted out to the upper classes of Novgorod. After 1478, when Novgorod was annexed, responsibility for its military administrative, and judicial affairs was assigned to a Muscovite boyar, a senior member of Ivan III's council, seconded to Novgorod as the grand princely vicegerent. The merchants and landholders proved to be militarily inept, and their continued unhappiness with Novgorod's new status made them politically suspect. As Muscovite policy toward neighboring Lithuania became increasingly belligerent, the creation of a reliable force on Novgorodian soil became a priority. In the late 1480's and the 1490's, Muscovite authorities forcibly dispossessed most of the Novgorodian landholders and relocated them in a number of interior Muscovite towns. The chroniclers are at variance in indicating the number of Novgorodians so affected, ranging from a low of 1,000 to a high of 7,000. The grand prince forced the Novgorodian monasteries and archiepiscopal diocese to surrender a portion of their possessions on the grounds that the clerical authorities had supported the anti-Muscovite movement in Novgorod.

THE *POMESTIE* SYSTEM

The sequestered properties were formally annexed to the grand princely domain, but a goodly portion was redistributed to more than a 1,000 Muscovite warriors. One estimate, now enshrined in textbooks, claims the number was in the neighborhood of 2,000, but that estimate was based upon some faulty calculations and some educated guesswork. The new tenants were selected from those older serving families who had been displaced at the grand princely court by more noble newcomers, from the nests of impoverished princes, and from among the provincial servitors. A small number were drawn from the Novgorodian freeholders of modest means and from the former military dependents of disgraced Muscovite magnates. All received their grants with an obligation of perpetual military service; these were called *pomestia* (sing., *pomestie*). In the event of the death or disability of the *pomeshchik,* his holding was to be reassigned to another warrior, but in practice an adult son or a widow's

MUSCOVY, RISE OF

second husband was permitted to take over the obligations, thereby allowing the survivors of the original grantee to remain in tenancy. Despite some superficial similarities, a *pomestie* was not analogous to a Western fief. The *pomeshchik* possessed no reciprocal contractual rights; he was a simple military dependent, fixed in place with little hope for advancement, and with little possibility of obtaining a transfer to the entourage of the grand prince.

The *pomestie* system provided solutions to a number of problems. It allowed for the formation of a permament and reliable regional force at a time of military expansion to the west and when crown income was still insufficient for payment of service. It siphoned off some of the excess in members of the warrior class, whose economic conditions and service opportunities had worsened as a consequence of the natural increase in family size. Displacement by more noble warriors from the annexed principalities had further lowered their position.

Encouraged by success in Novgorod, Ivan III sought to expand the *pomestie* system with grants in the interior of Muscovy. Reluctant to turn domain lands into holdings for military dependents, he wanted to sequester portions of the extensive properties in the possession of Russian religious establishments. By the latter part of the fifteenth century perhaps as much as a third of the available arable land had come into the possession of monasteries, bishoprics, and the metropolitan's domain. Faced with a major threat to their accumulated wealth, an aroused senior clergy thwarted the royal offensive. The Russian church, much as the Byzantine before the imperial collapse, would fight to preserve the purity of the faith and its worldly possessions.

If Ivan III was frustrated in his desire to expand the number of *pomestia,* in the longer run—over the course of the next two centuries—service-obligated tenure expanded to become the dominant form of Muscovite landholding. Ivan IV the Terrible (1533–1584) transferred a considerable sector of patrimonial lands to *pomestie* (service related) status. Further turns of the autocratic screw gradually reduced the distinctions between patrimonial (*votchina*) and *pomestie* tenure by increasing the service obligations placed upon the former.

THE DUMA

The disappearance of rival principalities and the concentration of the aristocratic elite—princely and untitled—made the city of Moscow the all-Russian political center, where the scions of the privileged families competed for personal and family advantage. Energies previously expended in chronic rivalries among principalities or within ruling families were now channeled into court cabals, as individuals sought to obtain advantageous positions and to create alliances that would improve their rank and fortune.

Birthright still conferred a certain status, but position on the service ladder determined one's influence and authority. At the top rung stood the members of the duma (princely council), who were the most influential servitors. The councillors aided in the shaping of policies, they commanded the armies on major campaigns, and they presided over appellate tribunals as surrogates of the grand prince. They also determined who were to be chosen for governorships and had a hand in naming commanders of regiments in the frequent campaigns of Ivan III's reign. Having a relative or patron on the council improved one's career prospects. Courtiers scrambled for alliances and advantageous marriages and otherwise curried favor with the more important council members. Descendants of the old service families paraded the constancy of their families' loyalty to the senior Moscow prince; the newcomers advertised their genealogies.

A propitious marriage could make one's fortune. An outstanding example is the history of the Patrikeev family, descended from a branch of the Lithuanian ruling house but Muscovite by choice since the early fifteenth century. Prince Yurii Patrikeevich had emigrated to Moscow and married the sister of Grand Prince Vasilii I. As relatives of the ruling Muscovite family, the Patrikeevs won the trust of the grand princes. Prince Yurii Patrikeevich and his son Ivan occupied the senior council seat for most of the fifteenth century, and they used their influence in the selection of other council members. Under Prince Ivan Patrikeev this power became a cause for concern among those who sought appointment to the duma but were blocked by Patrikeev's maneuvers. Prince Ivan secured the appointments of a son, two nephews, relatives by marriage, and political allies. Similar but less powerful combinations of marital and mutual interest groups emerged, occasionally poisoning the atmosphere at court with plots and hostilities. Those incapable of establishing profitable alliances fell by the wayside.

By the last quarter of the fifteenth century the emerging battle lines were drawn between the aspiring newcomers and the older service elite. The newcomers won a resounding victory in 1499 that involved the disgrace of the Patrikeevs and the appointment of a few of the more recent arrivals to the council. The victory for the newcomers was initially limited, but it pointed to the continued pressures generated within the court that could not be contained by the administration of palliatives. The problem continued into the sixteenth century, becoming particularly acute under Vasilii III, who did not have a natural heir during a large part of his reign; difficulties continued during the minority of Ivan IV.

The creation of a Muscovite monocracy would not have led as rapidly to the abject dependence of the aristocracy upon the crown had the landholders and the upper class retained their economic independence. However, the poverty of the country and the lack of cash markets for crops or artifacts combined with a tradition of partible landholding—in which a father divided his wealth and lands among his sons—to erode any basis for resistance to the growing political power of the grand prince. Submission to, and acceptance of, a system of service became the only viable alternative for the upper classes. A merchantry of consequence hardly existed, and it could do nothing to hinder the evolution of central authority. Further, there was no need for the crown to ally with the merchants and townsmen to contain aristocratic power. The creation of a dependent aristocracy and the service demands made upon it affected the conditions of the peasantry, which ultimately bore the major cost of the system. Enserfment of the peasantry was the inevitable consequence, a process begun in the later fifteenth century and completed by the seventeenth.

The date of 1500 set for this encyclopedia as a terminus ad quem does not fit well with the history of medieval Muscovy. The Western models employed for the end of the medieval period and the beginning of the modern do not coincide with those employed for non-Western societies. But by 1500 the major characteristics of later Muscovite history were clearly visible. The foundations of the autocratic monarchy were already cemented in place.

BIBLIOGRAPHY

Sources. Basil Dmytryshyn, ed., *Medieval Russia: A Source Book, 900–1700* (1963, 2nd ed. 1973); Robert C. Howes, ed. and trans., *The Testaments of the Grand Princes of Moscow* (1967); Serge A. Zenkovsky, ed., *Medieval Russia's Epics, Chronicles, and Tales* (1963, rev. and enl. ed. 1974), esp. 211–223.

Studies. Gustave Alef, "The Political Significance of the Inscriptions on Muscovite Coinage in the Reign of Vasili II," in *Speculum,* **34** (1959), "Muscovy and the Council of Florence," in *The American Slavic and East European Review,* **20** (1961), "The Crisis of the Russian Aristocracy: A Factor in the Growth of Autocracy," in *Forschungen zur osteuropäischen Geschichte,* **15** (1970), and "Muscovite Military Reforms in the Second-Half of the Fifteenth Century," *ibid.*, **18** (1973); Oswald P. Backus, *Motives of West Russian Nobles in Deserting Lithuania for Moscow, 1377–1514* (1957); Jerome Blum, *Lord and Peasant in Russia from the Ninth to the Nineteenth Century* (1961); Michael Cherniavsky, "The Reception of the Council of Florence in Moscow," in *Church History,* **24** (1955), and "*Khan* or *Basileus:* An Aspect of Mediaeval Political Thought," in *Journal of the History of Ideas,* **20** (1959); John L. I. Fennell, *The Emergence of Moscow, 1304–1359* (1968); Joseph Gill, *The Council of Florence* (1959); Lawrence N. Langer, "The Black Death in Russia: Its Effects upon Urban Labor," in *Russian History/Histoire Russe,* **2** (1975), and "Plague and the Russian Countryside: Monastic Estates in the Late Fourteenth and Fifteenth Centuries," in *Canadian-American Slavic Studies,* **10** (1976); Jaroslaw Pelenski, "The Origins of the Official Muscovite Claims to the 'Kievan Inheritance,'" in *Harvard Ukrainian Studies,* **1** (1977); Richard Pipes, *Russia Under the Old Regime* (1974); Aleksandr E. Presniakov, *The Formation of the Great Russian State,* A. E. Moorhouse, trans. (1970), a fundamental work, and *The Tsardom of Muscovy,* Robert F. Price, ed. and trans. (1978), important; Joel Raba, "The Fate of the Novgorodian Republic," in *Slavonic and East European Review,* **45** (1967), and "The Authority of the Muscovite Ruler at the Dawn of the Modern Era," in *Jahrbücher für Geschichte Osteuropas,* **24** (1976); George Vernadsky and Michael Karpovich, *A History of Russia,* III, George Vernadsky, *The Mongols and Russia* (1953), IV, *idem, Russia at the Dawn of the Modern Age* (1959).

GUSTAVE ALEF

[See also **Archimandrite; Basileus; Bogoliubskii, Andrei, Boyar; Dmitrii Ivanovich Donskoi; Duma; Golden Horde; Isidore; Ivan III of Muscovy; Jagiełło Dynasty; Kievan Rus; Lithuania; Mints and Money, Russian; Mongol Empire; Moscow Kremlin, Art and Architecture; Novgorod; Sweden; Tamerlane; Vladimir Monomakh; Vladimir-Suzdal.**]

MUSIC. The subject of music is treated below in the following articles:

Music
- **Armenian**
- **Byzantine**
- **Celtic**
- **Islamic Attitudes Toward**
- **Islamic Influence on Non-Western**
- **Islamic Influence on Western**

 MUSIC, ARMENIAN

- **Jewish**
- **Middle Eastern**
- **Oral Tradition in**
- **Popular**
- **Slavic**
- **Syrian**
- **Western European**

Music in Medieval Society
Musica Ficta
Musical Instruments

- **European**
- **Middle Eastern**

Musical Notation

- **Alphabetic**
- **Bilingual**
- **Byzantine**
- **Daseian**
- **Ekphonetic**
- **Hufnagel**
- **Modal**
- **Western**

Musical Ornamentation
Musical Performance
Musical Treatises

Additional articles on related topics are cited in cross-references at the end of each essay.

MUSIC, ARMENIAN. The most significant and well documented topic concerning Armenian music during the Middle Ages is the discussion of liturgical chants. Nurtured by the ritual melodies of pre-Christian Armenia, the secular songs of everyday life, and the apposite elements of Hebrew liturgy, Armenian sacred music developed into a unique manifestation of her faith, mind, and soul.

Music of the church. During the sixth century, with the introduction of *šarakan*s (a row of gems), the most sublime and enduring evidence of Armenian hymnography, the body of liturgical music, collected in a work called the *Šaraknots*, grew considerably. This expansion necessitated the complete canonization of the hymns and the adoption of a method of modal classification. The reestablishment of an independent Armenia in the late ninth century gave further impetus to the development of the country's spiritual life, creating an atmosphere conducive to the establishment of reputable training centers such as the Tados monastery and the Kamrǰajor theological seminary.

The Cilician period (from the eleventh to the fourteenth century) brought the evolution of sacred music to its summit, especially through the efforts of Nersēs Šnorhali (1101–1173), who augmented the number of *šarakan*s to more than 1,600. As liturgical chants grew in complexity during the twelfth century, the use of graphic symbols of notation increased, requiring the creation of a branch of learning, *manrusum* (adjuvant studies), which was considered mandatory for all clergymen.

The end of the Cilician kingdom, with the resultant deterioration of the sociopolitical conditions of the country, led to the general disintegration of its artistic existence. Furthermore, the isolationist tendencies of monastic life and the dogmatic attitude of the religious leaders contributed to the decrease of musical activities in Armenia.

Characteristics of liturgical chants. Armenian music in general, and sacred melodies in particular, belong to the Middle Eastern tradition and, as such, share with it aesthetic concepts that are alien to the Western heritage. The liturgical chants are monophonic (except for occasional use of drone notes), unaccompanied, and principally in measured rhythm (that is, a rhythmic construction without regularly recurrent accents in which every time value is a multiple or fraction of a fixed unit of time). A distinctive feature of these melodies is the use of melody-types, which serve as archetypes for the re-creation of new melodies. Melody-types not only prescribe the pitches, the range, and the center tone but also direct the use of certain tonal progressions (for example, ascending, descending), rhythmic patterns, and embellishments.

The concept of modal classification in Armenian sacred music may be traced back to the fourth century when, according to legend, Kat^{c}ołikos Sahak I Part^{c}ev associated different melodic structures with each of the four mighty forces of the universe, namely, earth, water, air, and fire. Armenian liturgical chants are grouped into various categories of melody-types: four *jayn*s (similar to authentic modes) and four *kołm*s (similar to plagal modes), plus two *stełi*s (auxiliary modes), as well as their variants. These melodic paradigms are closely related to a method of modal classification called octoechos (eight modes), which forms the foundation of Byzantine chants.

As with melody, the concept of rhythm in the Middle East is dissimilar to that employed in the West. In liturgical melodies there is no metric division but, rather, a rhythmic organization that is derived from the prosody and guided by the character of the particular melody-type.

Notation. Probably the most striking element in medieval manuscripts of Armenian liturgical chants

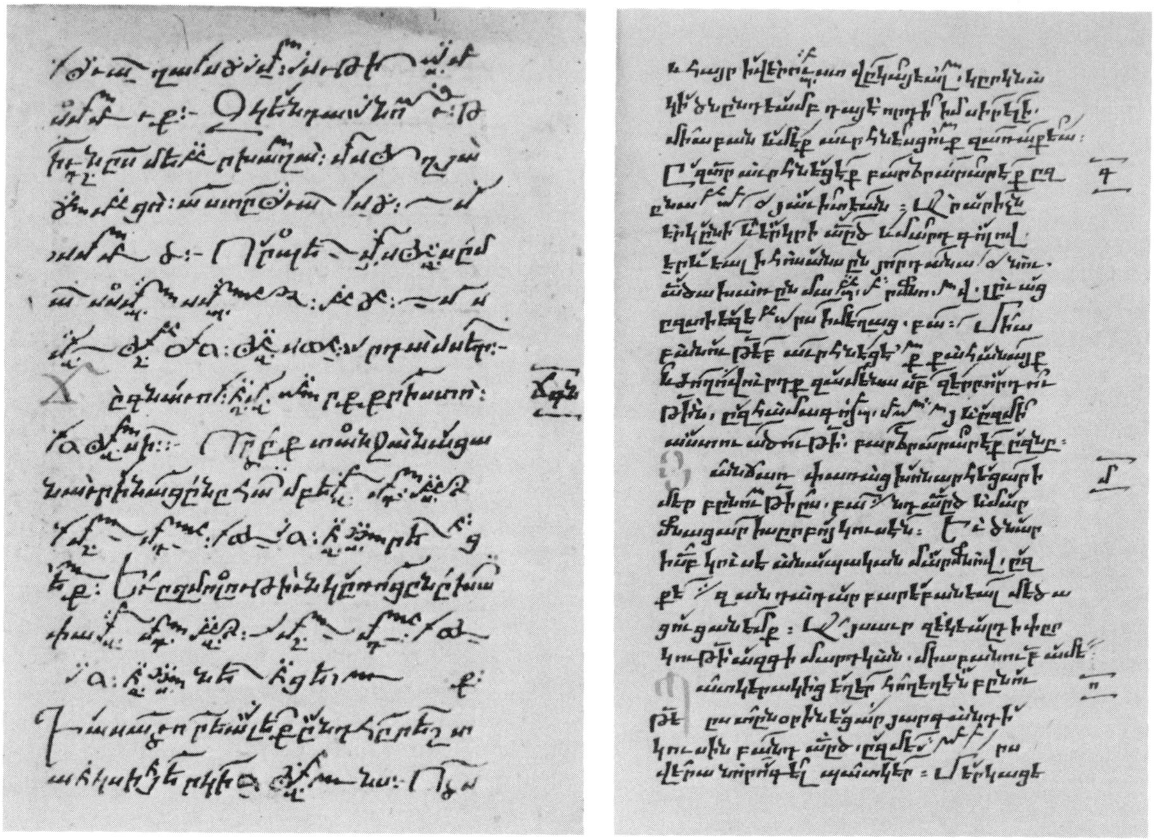

Armenian MSS displaying ekphonetic notation (actual size). The 12th-century MS at left displays a more elaborate, florid style than the earlier one at right. AUTHOR'S COLLECTION

is the employment of an elaborate system of notational symbols, named ekphonetic signs, or *xaz* in Armenian. This system is a mnemonic tool for the oral transmission of the melody and relies substantially on the trained imagination of the chanter. Although it provides the improviser with ample freedom to project the text with optimum expressivity and flexibility, it also presupposes the existence of an oral tradition. Without such a tradition, the latitude accorded in exchange for precision creates a formidable problem since the notation alone cannot express certain essentials of the musical content.

The ekphonetic signs appear for the first time in Armenian manuscripts of the eighth century. Related closely to grammatical accents and used in conjunction with them, the ekphonetic signs indicate the relative movement of pitch in chanting. In contradistinction, grammatical accents mark a change of pitch in recitation. During the Cilician period in particular, the use of ekphonetic signs flourished, developing logically from the previous systems. By the second half of the eleventh century, they had evolved into a far more elaborate and complex scheme that indicated the melodic motion much more precisely, in a highly sensitive and supple mode. Following this era, the system eventually fell into disuse, and the meaning of the signs became unclear and, in large part, undecipherable.

Some general observations about the use of *xaz* may be derived from the examination of existing manuscripts. (1) The number of ekphonetic signs employed gradually increased through the centuries. (2) In the course of this development, the shape of each sign underwent certain changes and eventually attained a standard appearance. (3) Different melodic patterns, which in earlier stages of development were represented by the same symbol, were later assigned individual signs. (4) During the twelfth century, figures, such as dots, dashes, and letters, were introduced to indicate musical phrases, breathing points, and other instructions to be followed in singing. (5) The ekphonetic signs, which were initially placed above the text, were later inserted into the text, very often breaking the words into syllables and even into letters.

Secular music. Because of the hostile stance the church assumed toward earthly interests during the Middle Ages, activities in the field of folk music were suppressed to a large degree. Furthermore, due to the oral transmission of the music there is a dearth of musical and theoretical documentation, which makes the investigation of the secular aspect of Armenian music difficult.

However, we know of *gusan*s (entertainers), professional musicians such as minstrels, who are cited in various historic sources but almost always within a context stressing the antagonistic relationship between the church and the secular arts. A few examples will suffice to corroborate the point. An irate cleric refers to the *gusan*s' art as "invented by the grandsons of Cain." Another church authority writes, "Let no priest, abandoning pious songs, receive *gusan*s into his house." And an Armenian prayer book contains the following confession: "I have sinned by attending comedies; I have erred by entertaining *gusan*s." Despite this attitude, these songsters continued to achieve great success because they were able to generate an interaction between their ceremonial songs and folk music. (Theretofore, *gusan*s had been entertainers at royal banquets and other formal occasions.) As a result, many songs by *gusan*s—mostly dealing with mirth, revelry, lyricism, and heraldry—became popularized, and, in turn, various folk tunes were performed by the *gusan*s.

A noteworthy musical genre of this period is the secular *tał* (song). *Tał* is characterized by the use of melismatic patterns and dramatic elements, as well as its improvisational structure, subjective nature, and substantial length.

During the Middle Ages, Armenian sacred music lived its golden age, producing the majority of liturgical melodies in existence and dealing with theoretical issues that remain of vital ethnomusicological interest.

BIBLIOGRAPHY

Ṙ. A. At^caian, *Haykakan xazayin not^cagrut^cyunə* (1959); K. S. K^cušnarian, M. H. Muradian, G. S. Kyodakian, *Aknark hay eražštut^cyan patmut^cyan* (1963); Vrej Nersessian, ed., *Essays on Armenian Music* (1978); Nikołos K. T^cahmizian, *Nerses Šnorhalin: Ergahan ew eražišt* (1973); Rhowbēn T^cerlēmēzian, *Komitas: Yodvacner ew usumnasirut^cyunner* (1941).

ŞAHAN ARZRUNI

[See also **Melisma; Melody; Musical Notation, Ekphonetic, Modal; Nersēs IV Šnorhali; Octoechos.**]

MUSIC, BYZANTINE. During the earlier centuries of the Byzantine Empire, musicians evidently relied on oral transmission for what was played and sung. There is no music preserved. From the tenth century on, there are ample quantities of noted music written in a musical notation that allows quite unambiguous transcription on the modern staff. Perhaps 1,500 manuscripts with noted music survive from before the fall of the empire in 1453; they contain many thousands of pieces in great fullness of musical detail. What there is of Byzantine music is almost exclusively for the church—the sacred, liturgical music of the hymns and psalms that were an essential element in its ritual. The full church repertory is preserved from as far back as the thirteenth century, with large portions of it already noted in the tenth century. To judge from the stability of musical traditions observable in noted sources of the tenth through fifteenth centuries, it seems plausible that some of those same musical traditions were similarly stable during earlier centuries. All of the music is monophonic, single-stranded vocal melody, without accompaniment or use of instruments. In that respect, and in most others of style, function, and transmission, the Byzantine art of sacred melody is wholly comparable with the monophonic plainchant of the Latin West, incuding the Gregorian chant, the plainchant dialect of Rome. In the parallel chant repertories of the Byzantine and Latin rites, the laws of musical style and the modal substance of the melodies are often the same; the styles themselves are intrinsically similar; in some cases even the melodic details are in agreement between corresponding chants.

The collection of chants for the Byzantine Mass (Divine Liturgy) includes chants for the Proper of the Mass: cycles of prokeimena (comparable with the Roman gradual responsories); of alleluia refrains with verses, sung before the Gospel (as in the Latin Mass); and of Communion hymns. Altogether these amount to some 200 chants, compared with a rather larger repertory in the West. The more prominent

MUSIC, BYZANTINE

Byzantine chants of the Mass Ordinary include the entrance chant *(eisodikon),* the Trisagion, the Cherubic Hymn, and the chants of the anaphora, chiefly the Sanctus. For the Byzantine hours' services, corresponding to the Roman Divine Office, there was an exuberant growth of hymnody destined particularly for the morning service (orthros) with lauds (ainoi) and the evening service of vespers (hesperinos).

HYMNS IN CLASSICAL STYLES

Unlike the Roman liturgy, which emphasized psalm singing, Byzantine church music emphasized poetic hymns. Tens of thousands of hymn texts are preserved, many with their music, representing the cumulative energies of the fourth through fourteenth centuries. The oldest layers of Byzantine hymnody are found among the troparia and stichera, which are generally single-strophe hymns. Some 2,000 of them circulate in the musical anthology called the *Sticherarion.* A new and highly sophisticated genre of Byzantine hymnody arose with the kontakia. These many-strophed metrical sermons dealing with biblical and hagiographic subjects were composed mainly between the later fifth and the ninth centuries. The foremost kontakion composer was St. Romanos Melodos (early sixth century); the most prominent example is the Akathistos Hymn, honoring the Virgin, a work of uncertain authorship that even circulated in Latin translation. The kontakion's function of providing poetic commentary on the service was gradually assumed by the newer genre of many-strophed liturgical hymn called the *kanōn,* which arose during the late seventh century and continued to be cultivated until the fall of the empire. The principal melodic stanzas to which the *kanōn*s are sung, called *heirmoi,* are collected in the musical anthology called the *Heirmologion,* some of whose early exemplars contain more than 2,000 *heirmoi.*

The classical genres of liturgical hymns (troparia, stichera, kontakia, and *kanōns*) were originally set to three musical styles. (1) The Byzantine syllabic style is a simple musical stylization used for the troparia or stichera of the *Sticherarion,* for the *heirmoi* of the *Heirmologion,* and on occasion for the kontakia. It is the most archaic of the Byzantine styles. Suited for choral performance, it is generally limited to a single note of music for each syllable of text, with an occasional use of two notes or short embellishing melismas. The Byzantine syllabic style is comparable with that of the Latin congregational hymns, but has much greater refinement of accentual and melodic nuance, and more sophisticated accommodation of musical nuance to the prosodic inflections and meanings of the text. (2) The *Asmatikon* style is a moderately florid stylization, which appears in the anthology called the *Asmatikon.* This is a Constantinopolitan collection, originating perhaps in the eighth/ninth century and containing the chant repertory of the small, select choir *(psaltai)* of Hagia Sophia. Among its contents are the kontakia, the *hypakoai* (great responsories of the Office), and the more important chants of the Mass, including the entrance chant, Trisagion, Cherubic Hymn, and the Sanctus and Communion hymns. (3) The *Psaltikon* style is a somewhat more melismatic stylization, with its own procedures and idioms, the music of which is collected in the anthology called the *Psaltikon.* This sister book to the *Asmatikon* contains the repertory of the virtuoso solo singer, the Constantinopolitan *psaltes,* with settings of the gradual responsories (prokeimena), the alleluias with verses of the Mass, and again the kontakia.

The hymns that are set in these three traditional styles share many concepts and procedures both among themselves and with Western plainchant. (1) *Vocal monody.* The music is a single-stranded sung melody, unsupported by contrapuntal voices or accompanying instruments. (2) *Meterless rhythms.* The rhythms are "free," nonmetric, having no measures nor bar line to regularize their flow. The supple fabric is made up of little bits of irregular rhythm that are added in sequence. (3) *Responsiveness of style to liturgy.* The choice of musical style depends on the performance prescriptions of the ceremonial and the solemnity of the liturgical occasion. A hymn is set one way for the choir, another way for the soloist, another way for the congregation; and it is treated more elaborately on festive occasions than on everyday ones. (4) *The eight-mode classification.* All Byzantine church melodies conform to the octoechos or classification of eight modes, a system that also appears in Gregorian chant. Each melody represents the musical idioms of a particular musical mode. There are four basic modes, having their final pitches on D, E, F, or G; and there are high (authentic) and low (plagal) forms of each basic mode. The system evidently existed at Byzantium during the early eighth century, when its hymnodic provisions were organized and augmented by St. John of Damascus (*ca.* 675–*ca.* 750). It made its way to the Latin West by the end of that century, appearing around 800 in the tonary of the Psalter of Charlemagne (Paris, Bibliothèque Nationale, MS lat. 13159). (5) *The diatonic tonal system.* In classic Byzantine usage the eight modes of the octoechos were all essentially diatonic—built on a basic seven-note scale or tonal system that is made up of five whole-step intervals with two half-steps inserted among them. An antecedent for the system lay in the Greater Perfect System of ancient Greece, and it was essentially the same system as the one used by Latin plainchant. That is seen clearly from the melodic identities of certain plainchants that are preserved in both the Byzantine and the Latin repertories of the tenth through thirteenth centuries. Beginning in the fourteenth century, there was an increasing use of chromaticism and microtonal inflection in the Byzantine melodies. (6) *Procedures of composition: psalm tones.* For the simple choral chanting of the psalms the Byzantine musicians used simple melodic frameworks or psalm tones that were available for each of the modes. Like the Latin psalm tones, they were shaped to fit the normal contour of psalm verses, generally split into two halves, with each half comprising optionally an intonation, a reciting tone, and a cadence. Such psalm tones could be used for chanting a single verse, a whole psalm, even the whole psalter. (7) *Procedures of composition: patchwork or "cento" melodies.* Considerable reliance was placed on centonization, the processes of formulaic construction. A Byzantine melody was rarely composed in a free thrust of creative inspiration. A hymn melody was usually assembled according to a familiar procedure of orally transmitted chant and poetry, as a cento, a selective patchwork of short musical formulas—twists and turns of modally appropriate phrases that had been heard and used for generations. What the composer did, essentially, was to arrange, adjust, and stylize from among the age-old bits of melody that were stored in the communal memory. (8) *The aesthetic of musical composition.* A new church melody was not expected to be fresh and original. It was normally a reworking and refinement of existing strains, carried out by musical craftsmen who in most cases were content to remain anonymous.

The composer's exercise of melodic craft was not unlike that of the mosaicist or icon painter, who constantly re-created a limited repertory of representational subjects, adding modest personalizing touches each time. Behind the self-effacement of the composer lay a respect for theological tradition that governed all such Byzantine undertakings. Church music was supposed to solemnize liturgical occasions and lend aesthetic substance to the religious sentiments of the worshipers. But the church edifice was not a concert hall, and the chants performed there were not for the pleasure of the congregation. The church and its music were the Lord's, and the music was conceived as a surrogate for the more edifying music that would be heard in heaven. As a result, there was rarely sought in classic Byzantine chant the kind of forthright emotional persuasiveness that marks the musical inspirations of later ages.

MUSIC IN POSTCLASSICAL STYLES

The traditional methods and stylizations of Byzantine chant prevailed for almost 1,000 years. When there was occasion to augment the liturgical repertory, the hoard of classical music was drawn upon. Sometimes the old centonate melodic elements were reassembled and refashioned in a new patchwork melody. Still more often, certain venerable model melodies *(automela)* were refitted to the newly written texts of imitated hymns *(prosomoia).* During the twelfth/thirteenth century, however, there was a turning from the sober old methods and styles toward freer, more elaborate styles. These ultimately surfaced in a new type of musical anthology called the *Akolouthiai* (orders of musical service), which was assembled around 1300 by the Constantinople music master Joannes Koukouzeles. The many copies of the *Akolouthiai,* dating from the fourteenth through eighteenth centuries, contain a number of traditional chants that had previously circulated orally because they were so familiar that it seemed pointless to write them down. Among them are some of the more prominent Ordinary chants of the Divine Liturgy, as well as the orthros and the hesperinos. But the bulk of the *Akolouthiai* consists of music composed in fresh styles that depart considerably from the older syllabic, asmatic, and psaltic stylizations. The new works are resettings of traditional Byzantine melodies, but in an often extravagantly melismatic style that is called the kalophonic (beautified) style. They represent the work of composers who were competing with one another in recasting and individualizing the older materials to suit modern tastes.

In accordance with this impulse to personalize, the composers of kalophonic music are always named. The more important thirteenth- and fourteenth-century masters *(maistores)* besides Koukouzeles include Joannes Glykes, Nikephoros Ethikos, Xenos Korones, and Joannes Klada; from an earlier time, perhaps also from the thirteenth century, there was Michael Aneotes; in the fifteenth

MUSIC, BYZANTINE

century the leading master was Manuel Chrysaphes. The contents of the *Akolouthiai* kept changing during the fifteenth through eighteenth centuries as composers responded to a variety of impulses, such as the adoption of certain chromatic and microtonal idioms that in some cases may reflect the influence of neighboring Muslim, Slavic, and Balkan styles. The exuberance of the kalophonic style was finally limited by the organizing activity of Chrysanthos of Madytos, who in the nineteenth century pruned away some of the accretions.

But Byzantine chant had by that time progressed far beyond its traditional outlines. A comparison with Western plainchant is instructive. During the centuries of fanciful melodic development of late Byzantine and post-Byzantine chants, the melodic traditions of Gregorian chant remained essentially stable. This was so because the creative energies of Western church composers had found a fresh outlet in the cultivation of art polyphony during the eleventh and twelfth centuries, and they turned away from monophony. Gregorian chant was left alone, and it survived almost as if embalmed. At Byzantium there was no significant development of polyphony. Composers kept channeling their energies into the monophonic re-elaboration of the monophonic melodies. They recomposed them again and again, tailoring them to suit personal inspiration and changing taste. As a result, the elaborate neo-Byzantine chants have an artistic vitality that has long been gone from Gregorian chant. Yet those Byzantine chants retain only a tenuous melodic relationship to the classic chants of the empire that were their point of departure—to the chants that are enshrined in manuscripts of the tenth through thirteenth centuries.

THE MUSICAL NOTATIONS

The repertories of Byzantine chants have come down in two species of musical notation. One of them is a melodic notation which is used for the properly musical hymns and psalms. The other is an ekphonetic or lectionary notation, which directs the cantillation of the biblical lessons. The melodic notation, first found in tenth-century manuscripts, adopted a digital principle, according to which the signs eventually indicated the specific number of steps that the singer must move up and down on the tonal system. The early stages of the Byzantine melodic notation (the paleo-Byzantine notation) include two regional varieties known as the Chartres (Constantinopolitan?) notation (tenth and eleventh centuries) and Coislin (Palestinian?) notation (tenth through twelfth centuries). The Chartres notation makes liberal use of "stenographic" signs, representing whole melodic formulas by conventional designs that are sometimes quite fantastic in appearance. Through a process of evolution, the paleo-Byzantine notations were supplanted around 1170 by the Middle Byzantine or round notation, which is precise in its representation of pitch. It has undergone further evolution but remains in wide use.

The ekphonetic notation was used between the eighth or ninth century and the thirteenth century to transmit information about the musically inflected chanting of the biblical lessons. Ekphonetic signs accompany the biblical texts in many early manuscripts of the prophetic, Epistle, and Gospel lectionaries. The notational meanings were not made clear by the signs themselves but were understood and interpreted by the singers. Each phrase of a pericope is framed by a pair of signs, one beginning and one ending. There are about twenty conventional pairs, conveying information about pitches and formulas, and doubtless above all about the beginnings and endings of phrases. No detailed guide to the notation has survived, and lacking that, the precise meanings have not been reconstructed.

THE SPREAD OF BYZANTINE CHANT

Byzantine chant was once sung throughout the Mediterranean world, from Spain and Italy to North Africa and Asia Minor. With the contraction of the empire, the music circulated more narrowly, but elements of the Greek rite and music flourished in translations into other languages. Certain Syriac hymnaries of the twelfth and thirteenth centuries use the Byzantine melodic notation. The *Heirmologion* was translated into Georgian, perhaps with its original Greek melodies, since the Greek texts are transliterated in the Georgian alphabet. There are vestiges of Byzantine *heirmoi* among the early Armenian hymnbooks. The most substantial influence, however, was on the Slavs, who, beginning in the late ninth century, translated the whole contents of the *Heirmologion,* the *Sticherarion,* and the *Asmatikon,* and took over the melodies that went with the texts. When the brothers Cyril and Methodios set out on their mission as "the apostles of the Slavs" around 860, they carried with them the early form of the Byzantine Chartres notation that is still identifiable in the Slavic musical collections of the twelfth and thirteenth centuries.

MUSIC, BYZANTINE

BYZANTIUM AND THE WEST

With the Latin West the musical relationships are different. Byzantine chant shares with Latin plainchant a basic fund of compositional procedures and musical idioms whose roots in some cases may go back beyond the division of the Roman Empire. Yet apart from the impulse given to Frankish–Roman chant around 800 by the Byzantine octoechos classification, the specific musical contacts between the two repertories are few. Some three to four dozen Byzantine musical texts appear in translation among the early rites of Spain, Gaul, Milan, Benevento, and the Franks, and in some cases the Byzantine music accompanied its liturgical text to the West. Three most notable instances represent three different avenues of melodic transmission and three different qualities of musical relationship. (1) The Gregorian antiphons of the *Veterem hominem* series for the Epiphany octave were translated from the *Heirmologion* at Charlemagne's request during the early ninth century. The Good Friday sticheron *Ote tō staurō/O quando in cruce* was translated, perhaps during the eighth century, and is found in sources from Ravenna and Benevento. (3) The Maundy Thursday troparion *Tou deipnou sou* was taken into the Milanese liturgy as the post-evangelium *Coenae tuae mirabili,* perhaps during the seventh or eighth century.

BYZANTINE SECULAR, INSTRUMENTAL, DRAMATIC, AND FOLK MUSIC

Apart from the sacred repertories there is practically no Byzantine music preserved. The public ceremonial of the Byzantine court was bound up with liturgical practice, however; and abundant details concerning the chants and instruments used at imperial receptions and processions are found in the *Book of Ceremonies* transmitted under the name of Constantine VII (905–959) and in the *De officiis* of Pseudo-Codinus (mid fourteenth century). Some music is preserved for the liturgical acclamations of the emperors, incorporated with the music of the Divine Liturgy. The organ was, like all instruments, barred from earlier church usage, but it was the court instrument par excellence, embodying for Byzantine ears the idea of imperial splendor. The most striking Byzantine performance practice was the use of a vocal drone *(ison)* to accompany liturgical singing. This may have begun as an attempt to mirror the sound of the organ within church. The earliest creditable evidence for the *ison* is from around 1400. In 1584 it was described by the German traveler Martin Crusius: "More utriculariorum nostrorum, alius vocem eodem sono tenet, alius, *Dra Dra,* saltatorium in modum canit" (In the manner of our bagpipes, one chanter holds a single pitch while another sings *Dra Dra* like a dancer). For liturgical-musical drama, there is scant documentation before the fall of the empire. Only for a drama titled *The Three Children in the Furnace,* dating from the fifteenth century, is there extant music. Folk and popular musical traditions were transmitted orally. There are reasons for supposing that certain present-day popular traditions preserve vestiges of Byzantine musical practice, but the ethnomusicological processes of collecting and analyzing needed to separate the post-Byzantine layers from the Byzantine have begun only recently.

BIBLIOGRAPHY

Louis Brou, "Les chants en langue grecque dans les liturgies latines," in *Sacris erudiri,* **1** (1948) and **4** (1952); Kenneth W. Clark, *Checklist of Manuscripts in St. Catherine's Monastery, Mount Sinai* (1952), and *Checklist of Manuscripts in the Libraries of the Greek and Armenian Patriarchates in Jerusalem* (1953); Dimitri E. Conomos, *Byzantine Trisagia and Cheroubika of the Fourteenth and Fifteenth Centuries* (1974), and *The Late Byzantine and Slavonic Communion Cycle* (1985); Enrica Follieri, *Initia hymnorum ecclesiae graecae,* 6 vols. (1960–1966); G. Grosdidier de Matons, "Le kontakion," in Wulf Arlt, ed., *Gattungen der Musik in Einzeldarstellungen: Gedenkschrift Leo Schrade,* I (1973); Jacques Handschin, *Der Zeremonienwerk Kaiser Konstantins und die sangbare Dichtung* (1942); Michel Huglo, "Relations musicales entre Byzance et l'Occident," in Joan M. Hussey, ed., *Proceedings of the Thirteenth International Congress of Byzantine Studies* (1967); Kenneth Levy, "A Hymn for Thursday in Holy Week," in *Journal of the American Musicological Society,* **16** (1963), "The Earliest Slavic Melismatic Chants," in Christian Hannick, ed., *Fundamental Problems of Early Slavic Music and Poetry* (1978), and "Latin Chant Outside the Roman Tradition," in R. L. Crocker, ed., *The New Oxford History of Music,* II (rev. ed., forthcoming); *Monumenta musicae byzantinae* (1935–), the principal series of manuscript facsimiles, transcriptions, and studies of Byzantine music, now consisting of eight complete facsimiles of medieval music manuscripts and twenty additional volumes; Oliver Strunk, *Essays on Music in the Byzantine World* (1977); Miloš M. Velimirović, "Liturgical Drama in Byzantium and Russia," in *Dumbarton Oaks Papers,* **16** (1962), "Present Status of Research in Byzantine Music," in *Acta musicologica,* **43** (1971), "Present Status of Research in Slavic Chant," *ibid.,* **44** (1972), and "Music of the Eastern Churches," in *New Oxford History,* II; Egon Wellesz, *The Music of the Byzantine Church* (1959), and *A His-*

tory of Byzantine Music and Hymnography (1949; 2nd ed., rev. and enl. 1961).

KENNETH LEVY

[See also **Akathistos; Asmatikon; Heirmos; Hymns, Byzantine; John of Damascus, St.; Kanōn; Kontakion; Laudes; Melisma; Mode; Monophony; Musical Notation: Byzantine, Ekphonetic, Modal; Octoechos; Psalm Tones; Psalter; Psaltikon; Romanos Melodos; Sticheron; Troparion.**]

MUSIC, CELTIC. Although Cicero, writing to his friend Atticus, thought it unlikely that one would find much musical talent among the British (*Ep. ad Atticum,* IV.17), the Greek geographers and historians knew better. Largely quoting from the now-lost works of Posidonius of Apamae and from writers like Diodorus Siculus, Strabo, Polybius, and Athanaeus, they give the earliest descriptions of music among the Celts. Their lyric poets, says Diodorus, are called bards and they sing songs of praise or satire, accompanied by instruments like lyres. In battle they play on harsh-sounding trumpets, and after a victory sing a song of triumph.

The musical usage described by these early writers also seems to represent the situation during the early Middle Ages. Ammianus Marcellinus (*ca.* 330–*ca.* 396) describes a class of poets known as bards, who sing the praises of famous men with a lyre-like instrument. Venantius Fortunatus (530–609) is more specific: "The Roman praises thee with the lyre, the barbarian with the harp, the Greek with the Achillean lute; the Briton sings to the chrotta." This chrotta (Welsh: *crwth;* Irish: *cruit;* Middle English: *crowd*) was certainly lyre-like, although there is no evidence that it was played with a bow as it was from about the eleventh century on. The poet Aneirin, writing probably in the sixth century, refers frequently to minstrels at the court of Mynnyddog Mwynfawr, while Gildas in his *De excidio Britanniae* (The ruin of Britain) distinguishes between the "sweet music" of the church and the empty praises of the flattering minstrels. He also cites the traditional instruments: cithara, lyra, tympanum, and tibia.

These instruments are found frequently in the literature of the Middle Ages. In the *Tâin,* Cuchulain finds the stringed *tiompan* in the western isles of Scotland. The word also occurs in Cormac's *Glossary.* St. Dunstan (*d.* 988) is said to have played *in timphano*, and Aelfric (*d. ca.* 1020) translates the word as *hearpe.* Some form of harp is attested in Irish and Scotch monuments from as early as the ninth century. The cruit (cithara?) as well as tympanum are played by an Irish minstrel in the *Vita Kentigerni.* The cruit also appears on Irish monuments from the eighth century on, and Dallam Fergall, an Ulster poet, writes on the death of St. Columba (597): "A cruit without a *ceis* (tuning pin); a church without an abbot." The Spanish *Codex Calixtinus* (*ca.* 1140) describes pilgrims celebrating at the shrine of Santiago de Compostela, some singing "to the British harp and crwth." In the Welsh *Laws of Hywel Dda,* codified probably in the tenth century, the principal instrument of a bard is specified as the *telyn* (harp). Elements of medieval Welsh harp technique are preserved in the Robert ap Huw manuscript (London, British Museum MS Add. 14905) from the seventeenth century. The Irish professional harper (according to the Brehon Laws) ranked as a property-holding freeman, the only musician due an "honor price" if injured.

Some further vernacular words survive designating other instruments. The Welsh *pibgorn* (Irish: *buinne*), a reed instrument ending in an animal horn, appears on an eleventh-century stone carving at Durrow. Various forms of horn (*corn*) are mentioned in literary sources; several survive in museums. A trumpet called *hirgorn* (Welsh) or *stoc/sturgan* (Irish) may be the same as the *bellica tuba,* a traditional instrument known to the Greek geographers, which is mentioned by Gerald of Wales (Giraldus Cambrensis, 1146–1223). A fipple flute was known in Ireland and Scotland as *cuisle,* while bagpipes (Welsh: *pibau;* Irish: *tinne/pipai*) were common throughout the Celtic lands.

Particularly useful information is provided by Gerald of Wales. The Irish, he says (*Topographia hibernica* III.11), are particularly expert in playing the cithara and tympanum, which they play with brass strings instead of gut. St. Kevin, for example, played the cithara. Giraldus notes the players' virtuosity and in a somewhat obscure passage describes their music, implying a mode of performance with drones, or possibly a system of organum:

> Whether they are playing in fourths or fifths, they always begin at B-flat and return to it so that the whole melody is completed sweetly and pleasantly. They begin and end a piece with great subtlety; above the heavier sound of the bass strings they play the graces with great freedom, so that they delight both by levity and profundity.

The Scots, says Gerald, play three instruments: cithara, tympanum, and chorus. At the time he writes,

Gerald notes that Scotland has surpassed her teacher, Ireland, in music. Wales, too, has three instruments: cithara, tibia, and chorus. It seems strange not to find tympanum on Gerald's Welsh list if it does indeed mean harp; the precise meaning of these terms, however, is not clear, and may vary from one writer to another.

Gerald's most puzzling comment on music among the Celts is his reference in the *Description of Wales* to the Welsh manner of singing:

> Concerning their manner of performance, they sing songs not in unison *(uniformiter)* as is done elsewhere, but in parts *(multipliciter)* with many tunes and rhythms, so that in a crowd of singers, as is the custom of these people, you may hear as many different voices and parts as you see heads, and hear the organic melody come together as one consonance in the soft sweetness of B-flat.

It is not entirely clear whether Gerald is speaking of true polyphony, or of organum, canon, or heterophony. Nonetheless, from his description the particular importance of music among the Celts is clear; so in the *Saltair na Rann* (*ca.* 1000) the banished Adam and Eve are forced for a year to go without food, clothing, shelter, or music.

The music of Western Europe had some impact on the Celtic countries. A hymn to St. Magnus from the thirteenth century is written in parallel organum; it may well come from the Orkneys, where Magnus is the patron saint. Part of an Irish polyphonic psalter (British Museum, MSS Add. 36,929) survives from the late twelfth century, as do statutes from Elgin and Aberdeen cathedrals outlining musical requirements, and a hymn (*Ex te lux oritur*) for the wedding of Margaret of Scotland and Erik II of Norway in 1281. Although the thirteenth-century manuscript Wolfenbüttel (677), associated with St. Andrews, is primarily a source for Notre Dame organum, it also includes some music of a distinctly different style, which may be Scottish. Simon Tailler, a thirteenth-century musical theorist, studied in Paris and settled in Dunblane, Scotland. None of his four theoretical works survive.

BIBLIOGRAPHY

Sources. Giraldi Cambrensis opera, James Dimock, ed., V, VI (1867–1868); Gerald of Wales, *The Journey Through Wales/The Description of Wales,* Lewis Thorpe, trans. (1978).

Studies. Peter Crossley-Holland, ed., *Music in Wales* (1948); Kenneth Elliott and Frederick Rimmer, *A History of Scottish Music* (1973); Osian Ellis, *The Story of the Harp in Wales* (1980); Henry G. Farmer, *A History of Music in Scotland* (1947); Aloys Fleischmann, ed., *Music in Ireland* (1952); William H. Grattan Flood, *A History of Irish Music* (1905); William S. Gwyn Williams, *Welsh National Music and Dance* (1933); Frank L. Harrison, *Music in Medieval Britain* (1968), and "Polyphony in Medieval Ireland," in *Festschrift Bruno Stäblein* (1967); Lloyd Hibberd, "Giraldus Cambrensis and English 'Organ' Music," in *Journal of the American Musicological Society,* 8 (1955), and "Giraldus Cambrensis on Welsh Popular Singing," in *Essays on Music in Honor of Archibald T. Davison* (1957).

DAVID N. KLAUSNER

[See also **Gerald of Wales; Music, Western European; Musical Instruments, European; Musical Performance.**]

MUSIC, ISLAMIC ATTITUDES TOWARD. The medieval world of Islam stretched from Spain to the Indus River and the border of China, and it also included parts of Southeast Asia. The present article treats primarily the culture of the Middle East.

The attitude of Islam toward music and musicians is at best problematic, as is the attitude of legists and theologians. Some theologians disapproved of music while others endorsed it. The literature from both sides is enormous, and theories abound on the origins of and reasons for Islam's disapproval of music.

According to one view, some legists disapproved of music because it was performed by female singing slaves *(qaina),* as well as, in the first century of Islam, by the effeminate male singers *(mukhannath)* who came to compete with them. Since the behavior of both groups was considered immoral, their musical performances were deemed immoral as well.

Another theory claims that the censure of music stemmed from the prophet Muḥammad's censure of poets and poetry. Poetry was censured because it was the incarnation of pagan pre-Islamic ideals; poets, because some of them satirized the Prophet and because their poetry was more listened to than God's revelation through the Prophet. Since poetry was sung, songs were censured as well.

An additional credible theory claims that Abbasid theologians resented the popularity of musicians within and without the court. They were jealous of the fortunes musicians amassed and the greater attention they received at court.

Theologians for and against music used the Koran and especially the *ḥadīth* (many of which were not uttered by the Prophet but fabricated at a later time) to support their views. The Koran contains no outright proscription against music, whereas the *ḥadīth*

MUSIC, ISLAMIC ATTITUDES TOWARD

supports both views. *Ḥadīth* against music claim that Satan was the first singer, that the presence of singing girls and stringed instruments is a sure sign of the end of the world, that buying, selling, or teaching a slave singing girl was unlawful, and that listening to one was equally unlawful. *Ḥadīth* supporting music claim that God had sent prophets endowed with beautiful voices, that Muḥammad enjoyed listening to caravan song *(ḥudāᵓ)*, that the singing of female slaves was not sinful, and that Muḥammad allowed the use of tambourines to announce and celebrate marriages.

The importance and spiritual power of music, and the entrenched pre-Islamic musical traditions, tilted the balance in favor of allowing some musical practices. Thus war songs were made lawful because of their useful functions. Also allowed were songs depicting events of the life cycle, such as birth, marriage, death. Many instruments were considered unlawful because they were believed to arouse lust. These included the lute (*ᶜud*), the barbiton or lyre *(barbaṭ)*, the harp *(ṣanj)*, the rebec *(rabāb)*, the woodwind *(nāy)*. However, the drum *(ṭabl)*, the fife *(shāhīn)*, the tambourine *(duff)*, and the percussion wand *(qaḍīb)* were all permissible because they were used during the hajj (pilgrimage). In the context of religion and religious activities, music was approved because of its spiritual power.

Islamic theologians went to great lengths to dissociate musical terminology from religious music. As opposed to secular instrumental music *(mūsīqī)* and secular vocal music (*ghināᵓ*), various types of religious music included the chanted call prayer *(ādhān)*, the chanting of the Koran *(tilāwa)*, and religious chant *(tartīl)*. The *ādhān*, delivered from the minaret, summoned the believers to prayer. It dates from the Prophet's time, and the Ethiopian Bilāl is credited as the first muezzin *(muᵓadhdhin)* of Islam. The *ādhān* was performed five times a day and chanted in such a way as not to obscure the words or their meaning. The *tilāwa* was the cantillation of the Koran, which lent itself well to such presentation because of its rhymed prose. As with the *adhān*, it should not obscure the words or their meaning. Cantillations were highly melismatic and reached the level of an art form between the ninth and the twelfth centuries. In the seventh century a type of cantillation using secular melodies came to be known as "reading with melodies" *(qirāᵓa bi-'l-alḥān)*. Needless to say, orthodox theologians condemned it and it was discouraged in later centuries.

Islamic festivals used music a great deal. For the hajj, farewell songs were sung to pilgrims on their way to the holy city of Mecca, and on their return they were greeted with ceremony and songs. Singing also occurred at stations in and near Mecca. During the pilgrimage the old pagan ritual of chanting could not be eradicated; thus chanting became admissible, as did some instruments for accompaniment. During Ramadan, Muslims broke the daily fast with hymns and chants, performed all night long. At the end of the month, the three-day feasting period was celebrated with chanted prayers. Music was very important during the Feast of Immolation, marking the tenth day of the hajj. The Prophet's birthday was celebrated with hymns of praise and the recounting of his life in epic songs.

Sufis, the mystics of Islam, used music abundantly to reach the state of ecstasy that enables man to attain the ultimate truth (God). Because of the orthodox attitude toward music, early Sufis avoided secular melodies and limited their instruments to woodwinds and drums. The Sufis' ecstatic ritual consisted of the communal *dhikr* and the dance. *Dhikr*, literally "uttering the name of God," was performed silently or aloud, recited or sung, often alternating with Koranic recitations, chanted prayers, and hymns. Jalāl al-Dīn al-Rūmī (*d.* 1273), the founder of the Mawlawīya (Turkish: Mevlevi) order, incorporated music and a spinning dance movement, the two elements combining to create a hypnotic state that allows the adept to attain a mystical union with God. The Mevlevi came to be known in fourteenth-century Europe as the Whirling Dervishes.

The theologians' arguments affected society's attitude toward music and musicians. The great *Kitāb al-aghānī* (Book of songs) states that there were three attitudes: one disapproved of music, one allowed it overtly, and one allowed it covertly. The segment of society hostile to music believed that it was an inducement to fornication, that it corrupted young people, and that musicians were on an equal moral footing with effeminate men, rascals, and scoundrels, and that they were bad company because they drank wine and were ill-mannered. That group also believed that musicians had no rights in court, that their testimony was not valid, and that they should be jailed because of their musical activity. It was lawful to destroy musical instruments, an action for which musicians had no recourse to the law.

So powerful was this attitude that some members of the aristocracy—caliphs, princes and princesses, viziers, descendants of army commanders, and members of the secretarial class—had to conceal their in-

MUSIC, ISLAMIC INFLUENCE ON

volvement with music, be it listening, performing, or composing. For instance, *Kitāb al-aghānī* states that many caliphs listened to musical performances secretly for fear of the theologians. In the same vein, many an aristocrat composer attributed his compositions to a slave girl.

A third group publicly encouraged music and musicians. It believed that music was permissible, that musicians should be allowed to pursue their careers. This group backed its view with the argument that music making was so widespread in society that it was unfair not to let professional musicians earn a living. Furthermore, this view claimed that music was necessary because it was a precious adornment to life that brought happiness to the human soul. This group also favored full rights in court for musicians.

Despite the negative attitude of some theologians, religious and secular music flourished, reaching its zenith in medieval Islam. The importance of music in religious activities and its spiritual power could not be ignored. In addition, deeply entrenched pre-Islamic musical traditions could not be eradicated. Nor could secular music and musicians be banned. The ruling institutions were validated by musicians singing the praise of rulers, and within court society musicians acted as spies, therapists, messengers of love, bearers of news, and friends and confidants of rulers. Music enhanced all aspects of social life, thereby heightening the emotional expression of joy or grief.

BIBLIOGRAPHY

Henry George Farmer, "Islam and Music," in his *History of Arabian Music to the Thirteenth Century* (1929, repr. 1973), "The Religious Music of Islām," in *Journal of the Royal Asiatic Society* (1952), and "The Music of Islam," in *The New Oxford History of Music,* I (1957); M. L. Roychoudhury, "Music in Islam," in *Journal of the Asiatic Society of Bengal, Letters,* **23** (1957); George Dimitri Sawa, "The Status and Role of the Secular Musician in *Kitāb al-Aghani,*" in *Asian Music,* **17** (1985).

GEORGE DIMITRI SAWA

[See also **Fārābī, al-; Maqām; Masūdī, al-; Music, Middle Eastern; Musical Instruments, Middle Eastern.**]

MUSIC, ISLAMIC INFLUENCE ON NON-WESTERN. The conquests of Muslim armies and the peaceful spread of Islam by merchants and religious men brought together a large, heterogeneous population that stretched from Spain to the borders of China. Islamic religious music had a deeply felt impact on the newly converted peoples. Throughout the Islamic world the call to prayer *(adhān)* was chanted, the Koran was cantillated, and hymns and prayers were sung and chanted. Each area colored its performance of religious music with its own musical characteristics.

With Islam came the spread of Arabic, the language of the Koran, and the new converts learned its musical terminology. Islamic instruments were introduced, as were many Persian terms.

In Africa, for example, instruments and names for them betray their Islamic origins. In Nigeria the trumpet was called by its Arabic name, *nafīr.* In the Congo River basin the word for horn, *embuchi,* came from the Arabic *būq.* In Swahili, spoken throughout much of East Africa, the word for tambourine, *atari,* derived from *ṭar.* On Madagascar, Arabian bowed chordophones and the small kettledrum called *tabala* (from *ṭabl,* the generic term for drums in Arabic) were used. In North Africa the flute was called *qaṣaba* and the oboe was called *zamr;* both are Arabic words.

In the Middle East, in Iran the word *ḍarb* (striking) was applied to both drums and rhythmic modes, as in Arabic. In Afghanistan the *tanbur* was the equivalent of the Arabic or Persian *ṭunbūr* (long-necked lute), and the Persian *ghichak* was similar to the *rabāb* (rebec, viol). There were also the *nāy* (Arabic and Persian for flute); the *dohl,* which derived from the Arabic *duhull* (double-headed drum); and *dāʾira* and *duff,* Arabic for different forms of tambourines. The words for dance and poetry, *raqs* and *shiʿr,* were also borrowed from Arabic.

In India the *tambura* derived from the Arabic *tunbur,* the *dara* from *tar* or *daire,* the *bhariya* from the Persian *būrū* (horn), the *dhol* from *duhull,* and the trumpet was called by the Arabic name, *nafir.* Islamic music also influenced north Indian musical modes, rhythms, and forms. Among the Uzbeks in Turkestan, modes and musical genres reflected both Arabic and Persian influence. For instance, among the modes used were *buzurk,* the *rast, nava, duga, sega,* and *iraq.* The classic suite was called *maqām,* an Arabic term originally referring to a mode. Some of the movements in the suite betray Arabic and Persian borrowings: *taṣnif, tarjiʿ, gardūn, mukhammas,* and *thaqil.* The same is true of the names of musical instruments: the *ṭanbūr, rubāb* (lute), *karnai* (long trumpet), *naghara* (from the Arabic *naqqāra,* kettledrum), *daʾira,* and *ghichak.*

The Islamic influence on musical instruments and

MUSIC, ISLAMIC INFLUENCE ON

their names extended as far as China and Java. The Persian *santūr* (dulcimer) was adopted as the "foreign stringed instrument" *(yang ch'in)* in China, and the *rabab* was assimilated into Javanese ensembles. The Turkistani *ṭanbūr, qubuz,* and *rubāb* (three varieties of lute) became known in China as *tanpula, huopussu,* and *lapapu,* respectively. The *zurna* (oboe) became the *sona* or *zurna.*

BIBLIOGRAPHY

Henry George Farmer, *Studies in Oriental Musical Instruments,* 2 series (1931–1939), repr. 1978; Jean Jenkins and Poul Rovsing Olsen, *Music and Musical Instruments in the World of Islam* (1976); Owen Wright, "Music," in Joseph Schacht and C. E. Bosworth, eds., *The Legacy of Islam,* 2nd ed. (1974).

GEORGE DIMITRI SAWA

[See also **Maqām; Music, Middle Eastern; Musical Instruments, Middle Eastern.**]

MUSIC, ISLAMIC INFLUENCE ON WESTERN. The Arab contact with Europe came by way of the conquest of Spain and Sicily, as well as the crusades. The most important interchange occurred in Spain, where the Arabs remained from 711 until their expulsion in 1492, a good eight centuries. Less extensive an interchange occurred in Sicily from 827 until 1071.

The society of Moorish Spain was bilingual (Romance and Arabic) and multicultural; it consisted of Arabs, Berbers, Jews, and native Christians of mixed descent. The Arabic language was so popular among native Christians that Bishop Alvarus of Córdoba complained bitterly about the neglect of the Latin tongue. It is only natural that when different people coexist for a time span of eight centuries, an intellectual, cultural, and artistic exchange should take place. Obvious as well as documented is the Arabic influence on Western art, architecture, natural science, medicine, mathematics, astronomy, and philosophy. The case of an Arab influence on music is problematic and elusive, however, because of the lack of concrete evidence.

The first obstacle to proving Arab influence on Western music is the lack of Arabic notated musical examples in Spain. Therefore, it is impossible to compare the two kinds of music or such characteristics as form, melodic movement, rhythm, and cadence. Some available evidence strongly suggests, however, that an influence of a practical nature took place. Ribera y Tarragó gives the name of an Arab musician (Abū Bakr of Ricote) who was a friend of King Alfonso X (*d.* 1284). The son of Alfonso X, Don Sancho IV of Castile (1258–1295), mentioned Moorish musicians attached to the royal chapel. Furthermore, not only did Spanish rulers have Arab musicians in their court, the Hispanic people enjoyed such Arab festivals as *zambra* (from *zamra*); they also enjoyed the vocal genres the *huda* (from *ḥudā',* caravan song), *anejir* (from *al-nashīd*), and *leile* (from *layla*) of the *aravia* and *mourisca.*

We find Arab musicians in the courts of Sicily under the Normans. The Spanish minstrels borrowed the Moorish minstrels' attire, with showy garments, long hair, and painted faces. Morris (Moorish) dancers acquired the hobby horse *(kurraj)* and jingles as part of their baggage. The hobby horse and the bells *(jalājil)* were mentioned in eighth-century Arabic literature and were described by Ibn Khaldūn (*d.* 1406) as being used among the Moors of North Africa.

Another influence of a practical nature was the dissemination of Arab instruments. A note of caution is in order here: not all instruments carrying Arabic names are necessarily of Arabic provenance. Indeed, some may have existed before the Arab invasion and later had the more popular Arabic names attached to them. Some may have fallen out of use, and their reintroduction then carried with it the Arabic names. And finally, some may have existed in a different form but adopted both Arabic names and forms. *Al-ᶜūd* was known in Spanish as *laúd,* and it traveled extensively to various parts of Europe, where one finds it as the Danish *lut,* Dutch *luit,* English *lute,* French *luth,* German *laute,* Italian *liuto,* and Portuguese *alaude.* The *qānūn* (psaltery) became the Latin *canon* and *medius canon,* the French *canon* and *micanon,* the German *Kanon* and *Metzkanon,* and the Spanish *caño entero* and *medio cano.* The name *al-shaqira* (also *mishqar*) was probably the origin of the names *eschaquiel* or *exaquir* (also called *eschequier* or *chekker*). The *eschaquiel* was a type of virginal, but the *al-shaqira* was not. It was an obscure kind of string instrument whose name was probably extended to *eschaquiel* in the way "floating terms" abound in the study of music instruments. The *rabāb* became the rebec (an example of a pear-shaped *rabāb* may be seen in the Sicilian Moorish woodwork of the twelfth-century Palatine Chapel in Palermo). *Al-shabbāba* (flute) became *exabeba;* the *juwāq* (small flute) became the Latin *joch;* the *ᶜirāqīya* (double-reed cylindrical pipe) probably became the *rackett;* and the *nāy zunāmī* (reed pipe) became known as *xelami* in Andalusia. *Albogón* came from *būq* (horn), as al-Shalāḥī (*fl.* early fourteenth century) attested that the Christians of Spain borrowed the *būq* from the Arabs. The instrument can be seen in the *Cantigas de Santa María* of Alfonso el Sabio of Castile (*r.* 1252–1284), and an actual Hispano-Moorish ivory horn is exhibited in the Victoria and Albert Museum. The *añafil (annafīr)* had the *nafīr* (long straight trumpet) as its ancestor. *At-ṭabl* (drum) became *atabal* or *tabor;* the *naqqāra* (kettledrum) became *nacaires* or *nakers;* the drum that is in the French *caisse* (snare drum) and Portuguese *caixa* came from the Arabic *qaṣᶜa,* a shallow kettledrum; the Spanish and Portuguese *adufe* came from the Arabic tambourine *al-duff;* and the *pandero* (tambourine) came from *bandīr.* Among these idiophones, the castanets may have derived their name from *kāsatān* (cups, plural of *kāsa*), and the *sonajas de azofar* came from *ṣunūj al-ṣufr* (metal castanets).

The Arabic influence on Western music theory may best be described as minimal. The theoretical texts translated into Latin were the musical section in *Iḥṣā' al-ᶜulūm (De scientiis)* of al-Fārābī, and *De ortu scientiarum,* attributed to al-Fārābī. The material from these translations was used in the music section of the *De divisione philosophiae* of Domingo Gundisalvo (*fl.* twelfth century). Jerome of Moravia (thirteenth century), in his *Tractatus de musica,* used the *De scientiis* in chapter 5 *(De divisione musicae secundum Alpharabium).* Both the pseudo-Aristotelian treatise *De musica* (thirteenth century) and the *Quattuor principalia musicae* ascribed to Simon Tunstede (fourteenth century) borrowed from it. The meager contribution of *De scientiis* and *De ortu scientiarum* consisted in reintroducing into Western Europe the Greco-Roman distinction between *musica speculativa* and *musica activa.* In any event, neither *De scientiis* nor *De ortu scientiarum* are important treatises, especially when compared to the comprehensive medieval Arabic writings on music, such as al-Fārābī's *Kitāb al-mūsīqī al-kabīr.* These, according to Farmer, were known and used in their original Arabic in Andalusia, and the theoretical information may have passed on to Europe through the oral medium, much like the musical borrowings of a practical nature, mentioned above, and the dissemination of some Arab instruments.

A few instances do indeed support Farmer's view. Of the eight names of the *chordae* (notes) mentioned by Odo of Cluny (*d.* 942), three are undoubtedly Arabic: *schembs* from *shams* (sun); *caemar* from *qamar* (moon); and *nar* from *nār* (fire). These three names the present writer has been able to trace to the writings of al-Kindī (*ca.* 805–873), in which musical notes were related to the cosmos and *ᶜud* strings were related to the four elements. Since no translation of al-Kindī's works existed in Europe, the information from his works must have been passed orally. Another instance occurred in the late-thirteenth-century treatise by Anonymous IV, *De mensuris et discantu,* where two corrupted Arabic terms, *elmuarifa* and *elmuahym,* refer to new mensural note values. These terms do not occur in available eastern Arabic treatises that deal with aspects of rhythm and may well be popular terms. The third instance is the evidence from the anonymous *Ars de pulsatione lambuti* (1496–1497), which suggests that one form of tablature was invented by a Moor in the kingdom of Granada whose writings are not available to us. The fourth instance was the introduction of frets to previously unfretted instruments. That frets were introduced without the help of theory books, together with the evidence from the above points, very strongly suggests that Arabic oral theory must have been prevalent and influenced Western theory in such a manner.

The last area of influence is the much debated yet unresolved influence of Arabic lyrics on Romance lyrics, specifically the influence of the *zajel* or *zazal* ("happy noise" or "song") and *muwashshaḥ* ("ornamental") on the *virelai, villancico* (Christmas carol), *cantigas,* and Italian *ballata.* The invention of the *zajel* was attributed to Mugaddam ibn Muᶜāfā of Cabra (near Córdoba) in the second half of the ninth century, though an earlier example may be found in the poetry of Abū Nuwās (al-Ḥasan ibn Hāniᵓ, *d.* 813/815). Mugaddam's poems did not survive, and the earliest extant examples are those of Ibn Quzmān (1086–1160). The *zajel*'s innovation was its strophic form with a basic rhyme scheme *a bbba ccca* and so on, or *aa bbbaa cccaa* (more variants also abound) as opposed to the form used in Arabic classical poetry, which was nonstrophic and built on monorhyme. The *zajel* also did not follow classical Arabic poetic versification and was written in dialect. The *muwashshaḥ* was a *zajel* written in the classical tongue. The *zajel*s of Ibn Quzmān were sprinkled with Romance words, and some *muwashshaḥ*s had their last strophe written wholly or partially in Romance. Romance lyrics had a basic rhyme scheme *A bbbaA cccaA* and so on or *AA bbba AA ccca AA* (variants

MUSIC, JEWISH

also abound), and in one example, a last strophe was in Arabic. The supporters of the thesis of Arabic influence base their claim on the grounds that Arabic lyrics antedate Romance lyrics, that the latter show striking analogies with the former in rhyme and form, and that Arabic appears in a last strophe of a Romance poem. The supporters of the thesis of Romance influence rely on the existence of Romance words and final Romance strophes in Arabic poems. A middle course would view Arabic and Romance lyrics as simply the product of a bilingual society.

BIBLIOGRAPHY

Henry George Farmer, *Historical Facts for the Arabian Musical Influence* (1930), and "The Music of Islam," in *The New Oxford History of Music,* I, *Ancient and Oriental Music* (1957, repr. 1966); Eva Ruth Perkuhn, *Die Theorien zum arabischen Einfluss auf die europäische Musik des Mittelalters* (1976); Julián Ribera y Tarrangó, *Music in Ancient Arabia and Spain,* Eleanor Hague and Marion Leffingwell, trans. and eds. (1929); Owen Wright, "Music," in *The Legacy of Islam,* Joseph Schacht and C. E. Bosworth, eds., 2nd ed. (1974).

GEORGE DIMITRI SAWA

[See also **Music, Middle Eastern; Music, Western European; Musical Instruments, Middle Eastern; Musical Treatises.**]

MUSIC, JEWISH. Medieval notation survives for the cantillation of the Bible and the blowing of the shofar on High Holy Days. The prayers and liturgical hymns (piyyutim) were not normally notated, while secular songs varied. A very few melodies were transcribed into the staff notation of the Latin church.

Hebrew biblical codices were punctuated with *te'amim* indicating the relative importance of pauses between phrases, part of an extensive critical apparatus called the Masorah. These punctuation marks were for study only, and were not included in the scrolls for liturgical use. In the three main systems—Palestinian, Babylonian, and Tiberian—the poetic books of Psalms, Proverbs, and Job were punctuated differently from the other books. Other systems were used by the Karaites and Samaritans. Each sign in the Tiberian system (the one still in use) became linked to one or more melodic formulas that were memorized and passed on orally, and that differed in each geographic area.

Prayer books from the thirteenth century have signs (often derived from Hebrew letters) indicating the three shofar calls: *tekiah, teruah,* and *shevarim.* The task of chanting prayers gradually devolved upon the attendant of the synagogue *(ḥazzan),* creating the modern office of cantor. The tunes are still preserved orally and, at least in their modern form, can be grouped in "modes" that some consider to be derived from the cantillation formulas.

Although the vast repertoire of Hebrew hymns (piyyutim) constitutes the most important corpus of medieval Jewish song, the melodies were hardly ever notated before the eighteenth century. It is thought that some melodies now considered traditional may have originated as medieval folk songs.

Jews of course participated in the wider musical culture of the places in which they lived, and a few song texts in German, Arabic, and other languages are known to have been written by Jews. Surviving melodies are less common, as is true also of comparable songs by Gentiles. Some modern scholars, however, believe they can detect medieval traits in some Jewish songs of more recent periods, particularly the Judeo-Spanish *romancero.* Musical treatises

Opening page of the Song of Songs from a Spanish Bible (Cairuan Codex, *ca.* 1400). FROM *SEMITIC STUDIES IN MEMORY OF IMMANUEL LÖW* © 1947, Alexander Kohut Foundation, Budapest. The American Academy for Jewish Research, New York

MUSIC, MIDDLE EASTERN

in the various languages spoken by Jews often cover specifically Jewish topics, such as the *te'amim.* But they also may deal with the music theory of the surrounding culture. A number of such writings are translated from or based on Arabic or Latin theoretical treatises. Some well-known examples of medieval "Jewish" secular music are actually anti-Semitic compositions in pseudo-Hebrew.

In the twelfth century a few biblical verses and piyyutim were notated in Beneventan neumes by Obadiah the Proselyte, a Catholic priest who had converted to Judaism. An illustration in the margin of a Spanish Bible from about 1400 includes the beginning of the Song of Songs set to black mensural notation. The first systematic transcriptions of the *te'amim* were made by Christian Hebraists in the sixteenth century. The late date of these transcriptions and the almost exclusive reliance on memory and oral tradition during the medieval period render most of the ancient and medieval Jewish melodies irrecoverable, despite some imaginative modern attempts to reconstruct them.

BIBLIOGRAPHY

General studies of Jewish music include Irene Heskes, *The Resource Book of Jewish Music* (1985), which is an annotated bibliography, and articles in the *Musica Judaica,* published by the American Society for Jewish Music from 1975.

More specific studies include Israel Adler, *Hebrew Writings Concerning Music in Manuscripts and Printed Books from Gaonic Times up to 1800* (1975), and "The Notated Synagogue Chants of the 12th Century of Obadiah, the Norman Proselyte," in Eric Werner, ed., *Contributions to a Historical Study of Jewish Music* (1976), 166–199; Abraham W. Binder, *Biblical Chant* (1959); Israel Davidson, *Otsar ha-shirah veha piyut* (Thesaurus of medieval Hebrew poetry), 2nd ed., 4 vols. (1970); Abraham Z. Idelsohn, *Thesaurus of Hebrew Oriental Melodies,* 10 vols. (1923–1932, repr. in 4 vols. 1973); Bence Szabolcsi, "A Jewish Musical Document of the Middle Ages: The Most Ancient Noted Biblical Melody," in Alexander Scheiber, ed., *Semitic Studies in Memory of Immanuel Löw* (1947); David Wulstan, "The Sounding of the Shofar," in *The Galpin Society Journal,* **26** (1973); Israel Yeivin, *Introduction to the Tiberian Masorah,* E. J. Revell, trans. (Masoretic Studies, 5) (1980).

PETER JEFFERY

[See also **Cantor; Hebrew Poetry; Liturgy, Jewish.**]

MUSIC, MIDDLE EASTERN. Material on the music of the medieval Middle East can be found in the literature of a variety of disciplines. Thus, a researcher cannot merely confine himself to treatises but has also to investigate the relevant material in biographies, bibliographies, histories, geographical and political writings, religious literature, belles lettres, poetical literature, anthologies, anecdotal literature, dictionaries, and bureaucratic writings. Moreover, he must also bear in mind that the sources were, by and large, commissioned by the wealthy; therefore, a high proportion of the literature is concerned with court music, and relatively little deals with music in the life of the common people. In addition, the sources for pre- and early Islamic and Umayyad music were written centuries afterward, during the ninth and tenth centuries, and therefore should be handled very critically; and the period from the mid eleventh to the mid thirteenth century suffers from a lack of comprehensive sources. Newly discovered manuscripts concerning the medieval period in general have not yet been studied; similarly, a wealth of additional manuscripts is expected to come to light in the libraries of the Islamic world. This article necessarily reflects the above limitations.

EARLY ISLAMIC MUSIC (TO 661)

The sources name the musical genres in use. The bedouins sang the *ḥudāʾ*, a caravan song. A more sophisticated type of *ḥudāʾ*, known as *naṣb,* was popular in the Hejāz. Both *ḥudāʾ* and *naṣb* were sung by males. The *qayna,* a singing slave girl, performed two different genres: the slow, ornate *sinād* and the fast, gay *hazaj.* The *nāʾiḥāt* (female mourners) performed the *nawḥ* (lamentation for the dead).

UMAYYAD PERIOD (661–750)

With the Arab conquest of the Middle East there occurred a synthesis of Byzantine, Persian, and Semitic (Arabian, Syrian, and Mesopotamian) musical elements. Damascus, the capital of the empire, became a brilliant musical center together with the holy cities of Mecca and Medina, where inordinate wealth in the form of war booty poured into imperial coffers. Vocal Persian art became popular, as did the Persian *barbaṭ* (lute), and its tuning of four strings in fourth replaced the narrower tuning of second, fourth, second. Ibn Misjaḥ (*d. ca.* 715) adopted the Hellenized Syrian theory of melodic modes, which was explained two centuries later by Ibn al-Munajjim (*d.* 912). Collections of songs of a specific composer or singer became common. Yūnus al-Kātib (*d. ca.* 765) is credited with being the first to

MUSIC, MIDDLE EASTERN

make such a collection in his *Kitāb fī al-aghānī* (Book about songs), in which he supplied the song texts as well as the mode and the meter (*īqā*ᶜ) used.

Singers accompanied themselves on the ᶜ*ūd* (short-necked lute) or *duff* (tambourine). The sophisticated *naṣb* was perfected into *al-ghinā*ᵓ *al-raqīq* (refined singing), and the *sinād* and the *hazaj* continued to be performed, not only by females but also by the emerging class of professional male singers.

ABBASID PERIOD (750–1258) TO 1500

The Abbasid period is characterized by extensive, reliable sources. The accounts were written in the period or were close enough in time to be able to evaluate oral and written accounts critically. Of paramount importance was the translation movement. From its haphazard beginnings in Umayyad times, it became institutionalized in the Abbasid era, reaching its zenith with the foundation of Bayt al-Ḥikmah (House of Wisdom) in 830 by the enlightened caliph al-Maᵓmūn. It was a combined library, academy, and translation center. Older translations were revised; whenever possible, the Arabic translation was based on more than one version; and the manuscripts were collated.

Greek works were translated into Arabic mainly via Syriac by Nestorian Christians. Known Greek music treatises in Arabic were the *De anima* and the *Problemata* of Aristotle, the *Harmonica* of Aristoxenus, the *Enchiridion* of Nichomachus, the *Canon* of Euclid, the *Introductio harmonico* of Cleonides, the *De musica* of Aristides, and the *Harmonica* of Ptolemy. As a result Greek theory, terminology, and methodology were adopted in Arabic musical treatises. The latter, in addition, reflected contemporaneous practices. Al-Kindī (*d. ca.* 873/874) studied the intervals, tetrachords, modes, and melodic movement. Al-Fārābī (*d.* 950) made an extensive study of the theory and practices of his time.

Ibn Sīnā's (*d.* 1037) *al-Shifā*ᵓ (The remedy) and *al-Najāt* (The deliverance) and Ibn Zaylah's (*d.* 1048) *al-Kāfī* deal with consonance and dissonance, intervals, tetrachords, modes, rhythms, melodic movement, composition, instruments, acoustics, influence of music on the soul, ornamentation, and performance practice. Al-Ḥasan ibn Aḥmad ibn ᶜAlī al-Kātib (*fl.* eleventh century) wrote a treatise that partly deals with musical practices in detail. Ibn al-Haytham (*d.* 1039) wrote a commentary on Euclid's *Canon* and a commentary on the *Harmonics* of Cleonides. Ṣafī al-Dīn (*d.* 1294) wrote *The Book of Musical Modes* and the *Sharafīya Treatise,* in which he dealt with theory, practices, and musical instruments, and revolutionized the theory of the tone system. Three elaborate commentaries on *The Book of Musical Modes* were written in the fourteenth and fifteenth centuries.

Subsequent writers who followed in Ṣafī al-Dīn's footsteps include al-Shīrāzī (*d.* 1311), al-Lādhiqī (*fl.* fifteenth century), and Ibn Ghaybī (*d.* 1435). The latter wrote in Persian about musical forms, a subject not treated clearly before. The *basīṭ* was an Arabic verse set to music with an instrumental prelude. The *nashīd al-*ᶜ*arab* and *nashīd al-*ᶜ*ajam* were, respectively, Arabic and Persian verses having sections in free rhythm followed by sections in fixed cycles. The *nawba* was a suite of four movements progressing from slow to fast. Ibn Ghaybī also wrote in detail about musical instruments.

Two fourteenth-century anonymous treatises on the subject of musical instruments are the Persian *Kanz al-tuḥaf* and the Arabic *Kashf al-Ghumūm.* Musical notation, very rarely used by musicians, was occasionally used by theorists. Al-Kindī provided a notated exercise for the ᶜ*ud;* al-Fārābī invented a very precise and complex system for rhythmic notation; and Ṣafī al-Dīn illustrated the first complete extant notation of songs.

While Greek translations gave rise to centuries of Arabic treatises on theory and practice, Persian translations gave rise to Arabic music literature. The most important document is the *Kitāb al-aghānī* (Book of songs) of Abū 'l-Faraj al-Iṣfahānī (*d.* 967), compiled over a period of fifty years with the help of a generous Abbasid patron. The monumental collection, now in twenty-four volumes, treats in anecdotal form the activities of poets and musicians inside and outside the court, providing copious details about the context in which songs were composed and performed. For his compilation al-Iṣfahānī used oral history as well as sources written by trustworthy witnesses and active participants. He collected the material from many sources and collated the sources, and where discrepancies occurred he often commented critically on them. Not all song repertoires from the sixth to the tenth century were covered, but only those songs for which the context was known. The anthology encompasses much now-lost material and sheds light on anthropological aspects of musical practices, such as uses and functions of songs, interaction of musicians and audience, musicians' posture, size and length of musical parties, criteria for musical excellence, process of composition, improvisation, and musical and textual changes.

MUSIC, MIDDLE EASTERN

The above sources reveal that Abbasid court life was extremely refined. Songs were tailored to fit the patrons and the occasion; this was paralleled by specific fashions and clothing to fit a given occasion and even special recipe books to suit an individual's health needs.

Male and female musicians came from a wide variety of classes: princes, princesses, freemen, freed slaves, and slaves. A court musician was at the same time a *nadīm* (boon companion), that is, one required to be well educated in literature, poetry, prosody, grammar, history, narration of anecdotes, the *Koran, ḥadīth* (sayings of the prophet Muḥammad), jurisprudence, astrology, medicine, cooking, the preparation of beverages, horse breeding, backgammon, chess, buffoonery, and magic. Musicians also had to have the qualities of a *ẓarīf,* that is, of a gentleman of good behavior and virtue with refined and elegant manners. Such a background enabled them to befriend the rulers and thus to gain a permanent position at the court. Their enviable position earned them very generous incomes. Ibrāhīm al-Mawṣilī (*d.* 804), for instance, received a regular monthly salary of 10,000 dirhams, which, compared with the 300 dirhams sufficient to maintain a middle-class family, was indeed very high.

Music making took place indoors, in palaces, taverns, bathhouses, poets' or musicians' dwellings, and outdoors, in palace courtyards, parks, and gardens. Most popular was the indoor music assembly *(majlis)* at the court, where musicians were requested to appear sometimes on short notice and sometimes according to the more orderly *nawba,* in which a musician had a specific day to perform at the court.

The choice of songs was dictated by the makeup of the audience, the location, and the scenery, as well as by the context in which the songs were performed. Thus, songs had a role in many aspects of social life, including birth, circumcision, wedding, love, farewell, greetings, sickness, and death. They were used to depict wine and nature, for example, thunder, rain, breeze, wind, flowers, and herbs. Songs fulfilled a variety of functions: communication, aesthetic enjoyment, validation of a ruling institution, emotional expression, and entertainment.

Improvisations were common, but they were difficult and risky. In indoor settings, they were tailored to express the mood of the assembly more aptly than could precomposed songs. Outdoors they depicted the scenery and the audience.

Singers sang a cappella; or accompanied themselves on a short-necked lute *(ᶜud),* long-necked lute *(ṭunbūr),* psaltery *(miᶜzafa),* tambourine *(duff),* percussion wand *(qaḍīb),* or drum *(ṭabl);* or sang to the accompaniment of a woodwind *(nāy)* or *ᶜūd* or *ṭunbūr* player, or to the accompaniment of more than one *ᶜūd* or a combination of *nāy* and *ᶜūd.* Vocal duets and responsorial singing were rare, but unaccompanied choruses were common, as were choruses accompanying themselves on *ᶜūds.* Purely instrumental music was rare. Rather, the role of instrumental music was subordinate to vocal music and consisted of preludes, interludes, and postludes. Preludes prepared for the singer's entry; they were either thematically related to the vocal part or idiomatically instrumental. Interludes gave the singer a rest and could be thematically related or not to the song. Postludes marked the end of a song. In addition, instrumental music accompanied the voice, imitating it in octave or unison, supporting and guiding the singer's intonation and rhythm. Harmonic (octaves and occasional fourths and fifths) and heterophonic textures resulted from the different range of voice and instruments as well from the harmonic, melodic, and rhythmic ornaments of the instrument.

Within a song a singer performed built-in or improvised ornaments. Melodic ornaments consisted of replacements and additions of notes within or without the range of the melody. Rhythmic ornaments consisted of addition or removal of notes, which occasionally altered the meter. Timbral ornaments (that is, changes in sound quality) were named after human passions or after sensations corresponding to senses other than hearing, or were physiologically related to the way air passes through the nose, throat, mouth, and so on. Vocal preludes, in lieu of instrumental preludes, consisted of textless singing or chanting, or an interjection in a speechlike manner. A portion of the poem or the interjection could be set to music syllabically and/or melismatically. It could be unrelated thematically to the song or related but transposed an octave, a fourth, a fifth, or some other interval. Its *īqāᶜ* contrasted with the song proper in tempo or in *īqāᶜ*. The last bar of a song could be elongated, containing foreign notes or added consonants.

In a performance, sitting was the common posture, but acoustical, social, or dramatic factors might require another posture, such as kneeling, standing, walking, or dancing. The number of songs in a given *majlis* varied from one to approximately forty; well-suited and well-performed songs were ordered to be repeated many times. In a *majlis* having many singers, they sang in turn and in cycle(s). Each singer performed one song in a cycle or sang a series of songs in the one and only cycle. Within one *majlis* melodic and rhythmic diversity was the norm, the succession of the *īqā*ᶜ*āt* of songs occurred haphazardly, and there was no evidence of a relation between melodic/rhythmic modes and the time of day or night (as theoretically advanced by al-Kindī and many other theorists). With many singers present in a *majlis,* there were debates and fierce competitions that resulted in lively entertainment for the audience and excellence of performance.

Textual, musical, and extramusical factors determined the excellence of the performance. Extramusical factors consisted of a musician's combined qualities of *nadīm* and *ẓarīf.* Textual excellence consisted in the ability of the singer to use a song in a proper situation to fulfill a fitting function, in catering to the audience's preference for poets and poetical styles, and in the ability to improvise poetry. Performance excellence embraced basic musicianship, ability to accompany oneself on a string instrument, having a wide vocal range and a powerful volume, knowing a large repertoire (one of 5,000 songs was not uncommon), and having the ability to improvise as well as alter songs melodically and rhythmically.

After the beginning of the second half of the tenth century, no collection as comprehensive as the *Kitāb al-aghānī* has survived. Music making was likely as refined in the next three centuries of the Abbasid era. With the destruction of Baghdad in 1258, the Abbasid period came to an end, but music continued to be performed and refined in the courts.

BIBLIOGRAPHY

Henry George Farmer, *A History of Arabian Music to the Thirteenth Century* (1929, repr. 1967); Eckhard Neubauer, *Musiker am Hof der frühen* ᶜ*Abbāsiden* (1965); George Dimitri Sawa, "Music Performance Practice in the Early ᶜAbbāsid Era, 132 A.H/750 A.D.–320 A.H./932 A.D." (Ph.D. diss., Toronto, 1983); Amnon Shiloah, *The Theory of Music in Arabic Writings (c. 900–1900): Descriptive Catalogue of Manuscripts in Libraries of Europe and the U.S.A.* (1979); Habib Touma, *Die Musik der Araber* (1975), also in French, *La musique arabe,* Christine Hétier, trans. (1977); Owen Wright, *The Modal System of Arab and Persian Music: A.D. 1250–1300* (1978), for transcriptions of thirteenth-century songs.

GEORGE DIMITRI SAWA

[See also **Fârâbi, al-; Īqāᶜ; Kindi, al-; Maqâm; Music, Arabic Influence in; Music, Islamic; Musical Instruments, Middle Eastern; Musical Treatises; Sinā, Ibn.**]

MUSIC, ORAL TRADITION IN. Of all the musical performances that were heard throughout the medieval world, most belonged to oral traditions. And of medieval traditions that came eventually to record music in writing, those that relied exclusively on writing for the invention, transmission, and performance of music are the exception rather than the rule.

A brief review of the advent and spread of musical notations will indicate how much of musical practice thrived in its absence. Our records of the use of musical notation in the Middle Ages begin in the ninth century with notations for liturgical chants of the Latin and Byzantine churches. Before that time the music of the Western and Eastern churches was generated and circulated through purely oral tradition.

The written tradition of the vernacular lyric of the West—troubadour, trouvère, minnesong—begins in the thirteenth century. As the tradition is at least a century older than that, and as there are many poems in the written transmissions for which no melody was ever written down, we must conclude that oral tradition played an important role in the musical transmission of the lyric throughout its history.

Literary and pictorial sources of the Middle Ages depict many instruments that would have been used for accompanying singers and dancers, and for playing by themselves. But the practice of writing down instrumental music began in the West in the late fifteenth century, and in the East not at all during the Middle Ages.

In the Islamic world all musical composition and performance was a matter of oral tradition. Specimens of notation do survive from the late twelfth century and after. But that is only in theoretical treatises for demonstration, never for recording corpuses of music.

These facts pose the question, how was music composed and transmitted in the absence of notation? We shall address this question in terms of two basic general conceptions. On one side is the idea that music was composed in the mind of the musician and transmitted orally by performers relying on their memory rather than on written scores. We shall call this the "memorization" model. In the other conception music is created, and repeatedly recreated, in the act of performing it. We shall call this the "oral composition" model. These two conceptions are best regarded as the extremes of a continuum rather than as competing and mutually exclusive conceptions. When we speak of oral tradition in medieval music we are really referring to the whole range of mechanisms.

Early written scores are precipitates of the oral traditions that prevailed when they were written down. They are therefore the principal source of evidence about the nature of the oral traditions. Interpreting them as such is mainly a matter of the comparative analysis of different versions of particular musical items or types, a method parallel to the comparative analysis of performances recorded in the field in studying living oral traditions.

Since the first notated music books contain exclusively music for the liturgy, the following descriptions must pertain specifically to such music. The transmission of nonliturgical music can be understood in terms of similar schemata. However, it must be borne in mind that liturgical music, regulated and cultivated by groups of professionals working in a self-conscious way, was more systematic and rule-bound than other sorts of music.

Corresponding most directly to the "memorization" model is the transmission of fixed tunes with different texts of identical lengths and structures. The preeminent examples are the liturgical hymn and sequence traditions. More open are the tune-types, which can be defined in terms of a certain structure of phrases that are related in some functional way (opening and closing phrases; central, climactic phrases). The singer would adapt the conventions of the tune-type to a given text, according to requirements imposed by the length, syntactical groupings, and accentual features of the latter. Conventional melodic phrases could be extended or shortened; some phrases could be omitted and some repeated.

In addition to the overall structural profile of a tune-type, there are internal melodic details (range, the location of the final tone within the range, characteristic intervals, melodic gestures for opening and closing phrases) that are constituent features of tune-types. This is one of the phenomena to which music scholars, medieval and modern, have referred with the term "mode." A set of such modal configurations could be shared by more than one tune-type, and by more than one genre.

Despite their flexibility, tune-types share with fixed tunes the property that the gestalt of a closed form is a constant in the transmission. But the provisions of medieval oral traditions were more often directed to the task of simply keeping the song going from moment to moment in a coherent and correct way for as long as the occasion demanded, and then closing it off appropriately. Recitation systems exemplify that in the simplest way. A text is recited on a single pitch. For the beginnings of phrases the tradition provides opening formulas, and for the ends cadential formulas of various degrees of finality, corresponding to the hierarchy of phrase endings in the text.

Two variations on this basic procedure could produce songs of greater elaborateness. The single recitation tones could be ornamented, and there could be a proliferation in the number and contents of articulating formulas. Such ornaments and figures could become stereotyped through use. The resulting systems would entail formal principles, standard melodic formulas, and syntactical rules governing their use. The psalmodic chants of the Latin and Greek churches are mainly products of such systems. Each such system would be the counterpart of a tune-type, as the matrix out of which chants of that category could be generated more or less extemporaneously.

Oral traditions remained active well beyond the introduction of musical notations. Writing came very late to some traditions and not at all to others. But even where writing was used, it did not all at once displace the habits of oral composition and transmission. It was initially in the service of oral traditions, and musical transmission throughout the Middle Ages was often a matter of the intermingling of oral and written processes.

This is so in two senses. For one, the techniques of oral composition were carried over into the age of writing, in repertories that were transmitted from the beginning in writing, but that nevertheless bear the stamp of the same kinds of generative systems that have been described for the oral traditions. For another, oral compositional or recompositional procedures interceded in the process of written transmission, which was not the sort of passive copying that we assume for more recent traditions. In such circumstances the written score did not so much provide a blueprint for performances, as in modern literate traditions, but rather a model for the performer's own re-creation of the music.

In the performance of the earliest part-music (organum) a special combination of written and oral processes was at play. Singers developed the technique of extemporizing a second part to a written chant, following rules that were promulgated in handbooks that circulated widely. Eventually both parts came to be written out, but the written transmission of such part-music again suggests continual recomposition, with the written score serving only as a model, for both performance and new written versions.

The earliest literate tradition in the modern sense, in which pieces were made only once by a composer and subsequently transmitted in stable form by means of explicit notations, is that of the part-music of the Notre Dame school in Paris in the twelfth and thirteenth centuries. The products of that tradition constitute the first real repertories, or musical literatures, that were recognized as such and widely disseminated as the issue of an identified center. Literate traditions were continuous in Europe from that time on.

While such traditions have commanded the greatest share of attention in music historical study, they represent only a small part of the sacred and secular music heard during the Middle Ages. The rest, the canonical chants performed partly from "memory," partly from the books in which they were preserved, and the local products of the various sacred and secular composing-performing traditions still alive, all represent the continuation of an oral repertory.

Medieval cultures were multilingual, and the distinctions among languages were both substantive and functional. In the West, for example, the language of literate traditions was Latin. With some exceptions, vernacular languages came to be written down and became written literary vehicles relatively late in their histories. For the sake of comparison we may think of musical style as roughly the counterpart of language. Then there is an overall distinction to be recognized between vernacular musical traditions, producing music locally for local consumption, and literate traditions that accumulated music for wide dispersal, but always among an elite. The introduction of music writing had the ultimate consequence that the techniques of oral traditions passed into the vernacular, coexisting with the new "literary" musical language.

BIBLIOGRAPHY

Wulf Arlt, ed., *Palaeographie der Musik,* I: *Die Einstimmige Musik des Mittelalters* (1979); Helmut Hucke, "Toward a New Historical View of Gregorian Chant," in *Journal of the American Musicological Society,* **33** (1980); Bruno Nettl, "Thoughts on Improvisation: A Comparative Approach," in *Musical Quarterly,* **60** (1974); Leo Treitler, "Homer and Gregory: The Transmission of Epic Poetry and Plainchant," in *Musical Quarterly* **60** (1974), "'Centonate' Chant, *Übles Flickwerk* or *E pluribus unus?*" in *Journal of the American Musicological Society,* **28** (1975), "Oral, Written, and Literate Process in the Transmission of Medieval Music," in *Speculum,* **56** (1981), and "Observations on the Transmission of Some Aquitanian Tropes," in *Forum musicologicum,* **3** (1982); Charles Seeger, "Oral Tradition in Music," in *Funk and Wagnalls Standard Dictionary of Folklore, Mythology, and Legend* (1972); "Transmission and Form in Oral Traditions," in *Report of the 12th Congress of the International Musicological Society* (1981), with papers by Donald Fry, Lawrence Gushee, Helmut Hucke, Bruno Nettl, Edward Nowacki, Poul Rovsing Olsen, David Rubin, and Leo Treitler.

LEO TREITLER

[See also **Centonization; Minnesingers; Music, Popular; Music in Medieval Society; Musical Notation; Troubadour, Trouvère, Trovador.**]

MUSIC, POPULAR. If popular is taken to mean "of the people," we can know almost nothing about this kind of music in the Middle Ages except by conjecture and from a few scattered literary statements. The music of the people was simply not written down. Some possible examples appear in the *Carmina burana* manuscript of the thirteenth century; their notation is too uncertain for any reliable comments to be made about their music, although very convincing transcriptions have been performed in recent years.

Modern judgments about what was popular in any case are totally subjective and inevitably will be conditioned by what appeals to the modern ear. The best guess we can make in order even to open a discussion is that the melodic style of secular songs written down in the later Middle Ages, different in style from that of plainsong, for instance, may reflect melodic turns of phrase imitated from popular or folk music. Modern ethnomusicological investigation of folk tunes lends some support to this guesswork; but there is much danger of a circular argument here. The musical handbooks of the time, the tonaries and the treatises, rarely recognize melodic features thought to be of the "popular" kind. When they are mentioned, some are qualified as *lascivia.* The theorist Johannes de Grocheo (*ca.* 1300) is the only technical writer of the Middle Ages to speak at any length of popular music.

We can first look at any music of the period to see whether it uses turns of phrase thought to be popular. The chant scholar Finn Egeland Hansen thinks the melody of Example 1 incorporates elements of folk song. It begins in one melodic style, using steps

Example 1

and minor thirds, pentatonic in character. Then, however, the melody employs triadic figures; important too is the sequential repetition of the phrase with triadic motives. This textless extension of an alleluia was a favorite point for the incorporation of new melodic and textual material. It is called the jubilus, or jubilatio, a word that from classical times has often been associated with the folk, as in Augustine's commentary on Psalm 32 and in a sentence of Paul the Deacon in the eighth century. Paul relies on a second-century abridgment of the *De verborum significatu* of Verrius Flaccus, which says: "Jubilare est rustica voce inclamare" (To jubilate is to cry out with a rustic voice). Singing to vowel sounds is a common feature of folk songs. *Prosae* (sequences) of the later Middle Ages, very widespread and long-lived (and thus popular?), are developed in connection with the jubilatio; many early sequences have titles, some of which seem to be secular: "Lament of the captive boy," "Swan-maiden." Some supposed descendants of the sequence, such as the lai and the estampie, are all secular and are mentioned by Grocheo.

In part-music of the Middle Ages it is more difficult to discern clear differences in melodic style. Notably esoteric music can sometimes very successfully conceal motives quite different in style. Consider a setting of the gradual for Christmas Day from the Notre Dame school of around 1200. Example 2 shows one passage. In the bars between brackets the melody is sequential and triadic. A twentieth-century Hungarian folk song is almost identical. Other polyphonic compositions are explicitly based on named tunes or on tunes with words that suggest a secular or popular origin. A tune praising strawberries and blackberries, *Frese nouvelles,* in a motet about the joys of Paris appears in the thirteenth century. Renaissance polyphonic masses were based on known tunes, often secular, and it has always seemed legitimate to conclude that those tunes were used because they were well liked. *L'homme armé* was frequently used in such a way. The number of masses using a certain tune may be a measure of its popularity.

Plainsongs themselves were used as the basis for many polyphonic works; once again, it may be because they were popular or perhaps only because they were suitable in some technical way. *Alma redemptoris mater* is one such tune. Dating from the eleventh century, it is distinguished from normal plainsong by the F-major cast of its melody and a prominent reliance on the triad. This votive antiphon to the Blessed Virgin was widely used for the remainder of the Middle Ages, in and out of liturgical services, and for numerous different musical purposes. Chaucer mentions it.

The responsory *Media vita* "achieved the rank of an ecclesiastical folk-song." From its first appearance in eleventh-century manuscripts it apparently lasted, with German words, into the beginning of the twentieth century. Miraculous powers were attributed to it. Did people like the tune, or did they see in it some power and use quite separate from its aesthetic qualities, as we perceive them? The latter seems more likely because the tune has few qualities we now associate with popular. Composed in the least common of the plainchant melodic modes, it has few of the characteristics of popular tunes so far discussed.

Hymns were undeniably popular. From the fourth century they caught hold quickly in monastic

Example 2

part of Perotinus' *Viderunt omnes*

circles and eventually were taken into the Roman liturgy from the thirteenth century, becoming a standard part of the Office hours of nearly all uses. New texts and tunes were composed throughout the Middle Ages. Their chants demonstrate musical characteristics distinctly different, even for the nonmusician, from those of plainchant; they use balanced and clearly defined musical phrases, with poetry. Bruno Stäblein intuits that *Verbum supernum prodiens,* among others, may have been a popular song. Eastern hymns are said to have used folk melodies; Ambrose writes that the people ought to be charmed by the melodies of his hymns; Dante refers to the beguiling qualities of the sweet notes of *Te lucis ante terminum;* in the eighth century, Bede discusses hymns in his *Carmina vulgarium poetarium.*

Another category of popular music is represented by the carol, which is said to be "popular by destination," although sophisticated in style and technique. Carols with music date from the fourteenth and early fifteenth centuries, and the largest repertory is in England. Their texts are characterized by "strong memorable imagery," in a mixture of the vernacular, Latin, and sometimes French. They are closely associated with the popular preaching of the Franciscans and are related to the German *Geisslerlied* and the Italian *lauda.* Only the last survived beyond the fifteenth century (the nineteenth-century carol is merely a Christmas hymn), leading eventually to the oratorio, a popular genre from the late sixteenth century.

Certain literary and musical devices are characteristically associated with the popular. "Strong, memorable imagery," rhyme, structure, and jinglelike meters are such devices used in many periods. Major scales, triads, repetitive motives, and wide range are their musical equivalents. Unlike the textual features, however, the belief that their use in music is deliberate and popular is a matter more of intuition than evidence.

BIBLIOGRAPHY

Andrew Hughes, "La musique populaire médiévale: Une question de tout ou rien," in Pierre Boglioni, ed., *La culture populaire au moyen âge* (1979), and *Medieval Music: The Sixth Liberal Art,* rev. ed. (1980), *s.v.* popular music.

ANDREW HUGHES

[See also **Carmina Burana; Carols; Divine Office; Gregorian Chant; Hymns; Johannes de Grocheo; Jubilus; Lai, Lay; Melody; Minnesingers; Minstrels; Plainsong, Sources of; Responsory; Tonary; Troubadour, Trouvère, Trovador.**]

MUSIC, SLAVIC. What is known of early Slavic music belongs almost exclusively to the realm of sacred practice. With the Moravian mission of Sts. Cyril and Methodios in the mid ninth century, Byzantine chant was introduced to the Slavs, and its melodies were made to accompany the Old Church Slavonic translations of the Eastern Orthodox liturgy. Initially, the singing was transmitted orally, and each musician was obliged to make his own adaptation of the music to the text. But as the chant gained circulation and made gradual inroads into the new territory, more or less fixed official versions became necessary, and a system of notation was created largely on the basis of the already existing musical signs (neumes) in the usage of the Greeks. Early Slavic liturgical manuscripts with notation survive to this day, mostly of northern Russian origin.

The practice from Byzantium was monophonic; it taught a kind of singing involving either a soloist or an ensemble of any size in unison. Instrumental accompaniment was not allowed. Although certain occasions required complex, florid renditions by trained vocalists, for the most part the chant was understood to be in the domain of the entire congregation, and extensive portions of the services were conducted to simple hymns with melodies thoroughly familiar to the laity. To judge from what is written in the manuscripts, in this, and in many other matters of style and technique, the burgeoning Slavic usage was faithful to its origin. Most importantly, the music adhered to the system of eight Byzantine church modes and was composed of a varied stock of phrases and short formulas. The Slavic chant thus occupies a position of some importance in the study of medieval music, providing useful insight into questions concerning the early Byzantine practice and its transmission across linguistic and cultural boundaries. The chant is generally called *znamenny* (singing) from the word *znamia,* meaning sign or neume of the musical notation.

The historical development of the music parallels the emergence of the Russian state. During the tenth and eleventh centuries, the chant was brought to Kievan Russia. After the conversion of Prince Vladimir in 988, Kiev at its zenith rapidly acquired status as a center of civilization; its aspirations were none other than those of political, literary, spiritual, and artistic attainment modeled on contemporary

MUSIC, SLAVIC

Byzantium. Christianity was adopted as the official religion. By 1037 or some years thereafter, St. Sophia, a magnificent cathedral much like that of Constantinople, hovered over the capital. Within its walls could be heard the sounds of liturgy; outside, the noise of busy merchants and travelers from afar. Although reports from the time lack detail, music is known to have been part of the culturally rich and dynamic epoch. The well-known eleventh-century fresco from St. Sophia shows musicians playing on various instruments. That sacred music was of special concern in Russia during the rule of Yaroslav the Wise (1019–1054) is recorded in the *Stepennaia kniga* (The book of degrees), a document of the sixteenth century. Chronicles, lives, and narratives tell of other events chiefly at the renowned Monastery of the Caves (Pecherskaya Lavra), where monks and Byzantine emissaries consulted on matters of ritual conduct.

With the decline of Kiev in the late eleventh century, Russia fell under the rule of isolated principalities, among them the cities of Smolensk, Pskov, Rostov, Vladimir, and Yaroslavl. From then on for about three centuries the onslaught of the Mongol invasions brought disastrous conditions, and activity was decentralized. Situated in the upper reaches of the Volga, the ancient city of Novgorod became a particularly vital location for the cultivation of music. Away from political turbulence and the encroaching inhabitants of the steppe, it had its own fortifications, with numerous churches and, at the center, its own cathedral, St. Sophia. Nearby, a choir school was founded for the training of singers, and on the streets, musicians and jesters, the *skomorokhi,* provided popular entertainment. Although notation must already have existed in the Kievan period, Novgorod is the city generally associated with the rise of musical literacy. Some of the earliest known Slavic chant manuscripts are of Novgorodian origin; these reveal substantial creativity and a high level of competency among local musicians. A rather polished appearance suggests that the practice must have had antecedents, the sources of which were evidently lost.

In the post-Mongol period, Moscow assumed leadership. The unification of lands and the final defeat of the Tatars in the late fifteenth century initiated a cultural rebirth enlisting the talents of musicians, artists, and craftsmen in the construction of a new capital, the seat of autocratic rule in Russia. By the sixteenth century music acquired a fresh significance; in both the sacred and secular realms it confronted unfamiliar horizons. On the one hand, there was interest in foreign practices, and ties with European nations introduced novelty into the life of the court. The sort of curiosity aroused on some occasions is vividly described by an English envoy of Queen Elizabeth: in 1586, the gift of gilded clavichords brought by him to the wife of the czar attracted crowds of listeners to the windows of the royal palace. On the other hand, indigenous music flourished with renewed fervor. A resurgence of the traditional chant is seen in a flood of manuscripts from the period; the old corpus of melodies was examined, systematized, and reissued in a different guise. In some cases, personalized modifications were introduced by celebrated musicians whose names are still known from various sources. Among the outstanding figures were Ivan Nos, Loggin Korova, Vasilii Rogov, Markel Bezborodyi, and Feodor Krestianin; their expansive improvisations on the ancient music gave birth to a new style, the *bol'shoi* (large) *znamenny* chant. The powerful, mad, but ingenious czar Ivan IV the Terrible (*r.* 1533–1584) was himself known to be a religious composer. Under his influence an official edict of the "Council of a Hundred Chapters" (*Stoglavyi sobor,* 1551) established elementary schools throughout the land; these were to teach grammar, writing, and church singing. Finally, sacred polyphony was allowed to flourish in a few centers with privileged status. The latter was one of the most innovative features of the period lasting through the end of the seventeenth century.

Liturgical chant in Russia has an extensive record. The earliest notated manuscript, the so-called Tipografskii Ustav, is dated in the late eleventh century; the seventeenth century, replete as it is with documentation, represents a terminal decline when church music gradually loses its identity with the classic sound of *znamenny* unison and comes under the spell of developing forms of harmonization. It is fundamental that throughout most of its history the chant relied exclusively on a musical writing that did not show the relative height of melodic pitch. Thus, despite the efforts of scholars, many of the sources still offer substantial problems and are sometimes difficult or impossible to render in modern notation. Three major categories of manuscripts trace the development.

Sources up to the fifteenth century. These represent the formative stage and comprise a total of close to fifty manuscripts written on parchment, typically, with broad, regular strokes of the pen (Fig. 1). While the manuscripts include an almost complete set of

MUSIC, SLAVIC

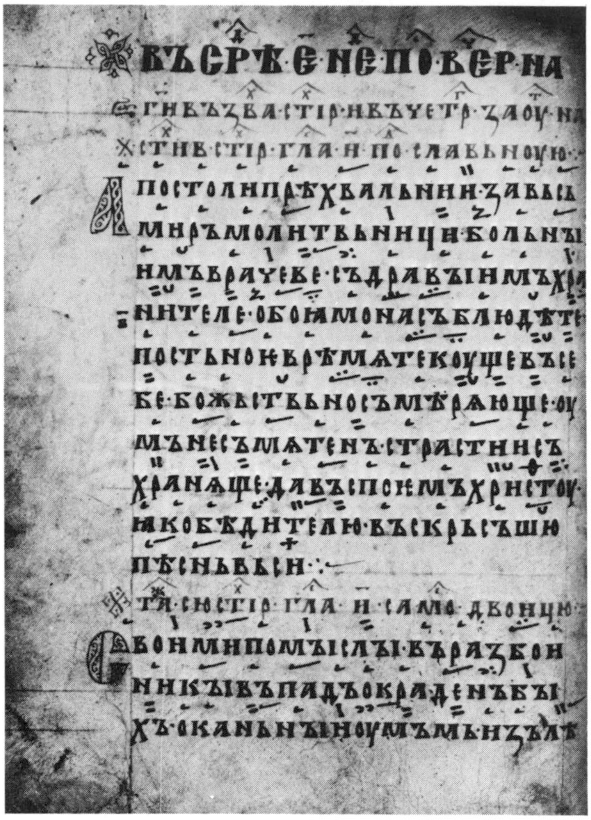

Fig. 1. Slavic notation of the pre-Mongol period (12th century MS). MOSCOW, STATE HISTORICAL MUSEUM, "SINODAL" MS 278, f. 45v

chants for the liturgical Proper, many sections of the Ordinary and other repertoire are lacking; these could have remained in the oral realm. The major hymn collections are the *Heirmologion,* the *Sticherarion,* and *Kontakarion.* All three center on the music for daily services of the Office. The Byzantine syllabic style is represented in the *Heirmologion* and *Sticherarion;* the more ornate, melismatic chants are located in the *Kontakarion.* Although the various anthologies bear a direct relationship to Byzantine counterparts, some distinctly Slavic features in their format are known. Moreover, differences are apparent on a number of other accounts, showing, on the one hand, a comparatively slow development in respect to the Byzantine, and on the other hand, a degree of independence dating back to the times of the earliest practice. In the first place, the manuscripts retain an antiquated usage, and into the fifteenth century they remain essentially late copies of a type already revised on Greek territory at the time. This is clear from the standpoint of both the liturgical repertoire and the notation. Secondly, some hymns unknown in Byzantium are the original creations of Slavic hymnographers. Notable are the ones for the feast of the eleventh-century Russian martyrs Sts. Boris and Gleb; among other things they reveal the mastery of important Byzantine prototypes. Thirdly, the sources at times have distinguishing musical variants. In particular, a peculiarly unstable blending of text and melody constitutes early evidence of a crucial process in the transmission—the adjustment of the chant to the unique prosody of the Old Church Slavonic language. The manuscripts have a notation that, as a rule, does not lend itself to transcription. Most of them belong to the twelfth and thirteenth centuries; the devastating impact of the Mongols is held responsible for the scarcity of materials from the fourteenth and fifteenth centuries. The series of *Monumenta musicae byzantinae* reproduces facsimiles of three of the earliest surviving sources.

Early sources of the Muscovite period. These reflect the multifaceted interests of musicians from the fifteenth and sixteenth centuries. They are known by the hundreds and exhibit an increasing variety of formats and scribal habits. A crowded, minuscule notation becomes the norm and is usually written on paper in fine, hasty-looking touches of the quill (Fig. 2). Stylized hands and occasional illuminations impart a fanciful, decorative appearance readily associated with Russian art and architecture of the period. On the whole, the manuscripts transmit musically, liturgically, and linguistically updated versions. Sections of the *Sticherarion* and *Heirmologion* are redistributed into different collections; thus, the *Obikhod* is compiled of the most important and generally used melodies, while a book called *Prazdniki* is devoted to the hymns used infrequently for various feasts of the year. At the same time, the previously unknown Slavic octoechos (*oktoikh* or *Osmoglasnik*) with chants in each of the eight modes becomes common—and the *Kontakarion* disappears. Among the manuscripts are found the first examples of a developing treatise on the music, the *azbuka* (grammar). These *azbuki* are short, practical manuals with the necessary rudiments for the training of singers; they normally deal with questions related to the notation and show no interest in speculative ideas of the type established in Western (Gregorian) chant theory. Handbooks of this genre known as the *fitniki* collect the traditionally unwritten, "secret" melismas, the *fity* and *litsy;* the standard "building pieces" of the chant, the melodic formulas called the *popevki,* are gathered in the *kokizniki.* In addition to the old repertoire and the work of new compos-

MUSIC, SLAVIC

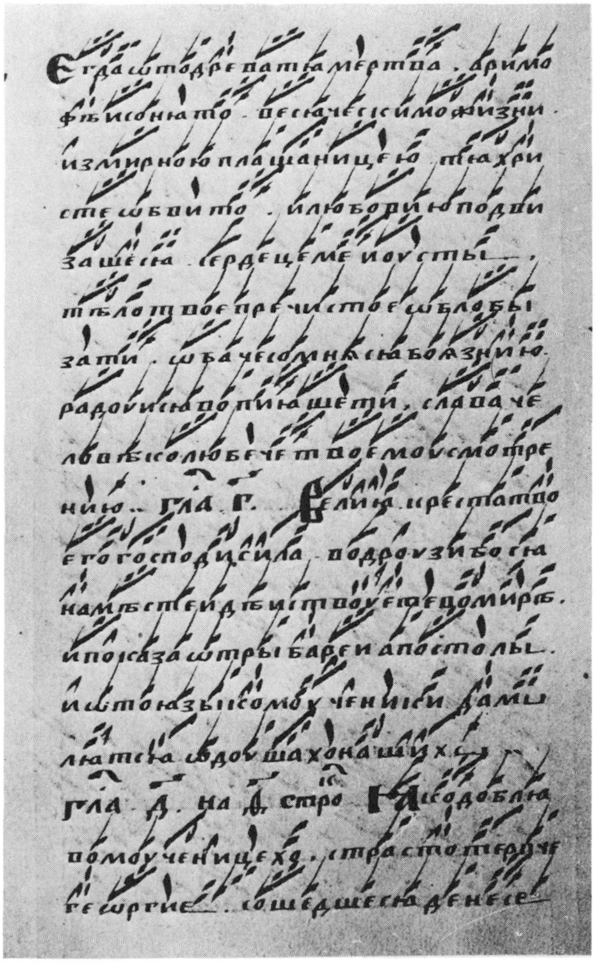

Fig. 2. Russian notation of the Muscovite period (17th century MS). PRINCETON, GARRETT, MS AM 18113

ers, the manuscripts occasionally transmit anonymous recensions called the *putevoi* and *demestvennyi* chants. The former represents a reworking of the *znamenny* thesaurus; the latter is curiously independent. Both, however, are characterized by highly expressive melodies evidently intended for special use at solemn occasions.

As a rule the notation of the aforementioned sources is unclear in respect to musical pitch. What it actually meant to the singer can be grasped only upon comparison with fully readable versions of the chant written down in later times. For this reason it is imperative to carry the discussion of medieval chant down to the sources of even the last two centuries. There is a solid continuity—a living tradition—which has maintained what might be called a "medieval" chant right down to our own day.

Late sources of the seventeenth century. Seventeenth-century sources are generally distinguished by a series of important changes which render them indispensable for a history of the music. In an effort to preserve and codify the singing, musicians of the period adopted new ways of notating the chant; they developed a musical writing of unprecedented quality and completeness.

The most conspicuous improvements concerned the specification of melodic pitch. Three different methods were adopted: (1) the *pomety,* or red letters, ascribed to a certain Ivan Shaidurov (around 1600); (2) the *priznaki,* or small black tails, introduced by Aleksandr Mezenets (*Azbuka,* 1668); and (3) the so-called Kievan or square notes that came increasingly into use toward the end of the century. The first two methods made slight alterations in the old neumes; the last involved a translation into an entirely new, staved system resembling that of the West. By far the majority of late sources incorporate these changes. As a result, today they are quite readily transcribed. They hold the key to the actual sound of the music and, thus, allow us to observe the broad panorama of singing styles.

As the mainstay of the repertory, there are still the ancient *znamenny* melodies in both the small *(malyi)* and large *(bol'shoi)* versions, which continue to be copied into the standard anthologies. A number of chants are issued as local variants, such as those of Tikhvin, Vologda, Tambov, Kirillov, Novgorod, Vitebsk, Smolensk, and other places. Despite the designation, however, the origin of the more famous "Greek," "Bulgarian," and "Kievan" recensions that also appear at this time is uncertain. The first two in particular are only distantly related to what is known of Greek and Bulgarian music from the period. In comparison with the older chants, all of these new melodic families are simple and recitative-like, often gravitating toward a strong tonal center. In addition, the sources display a rich practice in two, three, and sometimes four voices. Two styles are distinguished, the *strochnoe penie* (line chant), a simpler polyphony with generally consonant intervals, and the *demestvennoe penie* (virtuoso or professional chant), a polyphony frequently exhibiting complex and highly dissonant mingling of voices. Peculiarities of both styles can be related to the folk idiom. The singing, however, is largely independent of another form of counterpoint emerging at the time, the so-called *partesnoe penie* (part singing), which eventually took over in Russia under the influence of the European Renaissance and Baroque. Other developments are also evident. For ex-

MUSIC, SLAVIC

ample, it is of no lesser overall historical significance that the late sources indicate a decline in the orally based musical tradition and the concomitant growing dependency of singers on the written form.

The second half of the seventeenth century marks a period of crisis after which the *znamenny* chant and neumatic notation survived primarily among dissenters from official Russian Orthodoxy. Following the mid-century reform commissions of Patriarch Nikon, the traditionalist faction of so-called Old Believers initiated a popular resistance to enforced change. At first, this mainly concerned some fine points of ritual and especially the correction and revision of service books. With time, however, the controversy was extended to many issues and reached overwhelming proportions during the reign of Peter the Great (1682–1725). In view of this, many adherents of the former practice withdrew from the centers that were swayed by new-fashioned ideas. Adopting an increasingly conservative stance, they combined a cautious distrust of all novelty and a bitter distaste for the ruling powers promoting change. In church singing, in particular, they resisted innovations of the kind advocated in the famous *Azbuka* of Nikolai Diletsky. Written in 1668, the treatise had little to do with the old chant; it used only the Kiev square notation and expounded a strictly Western European harmony and style. As a result, the conviction in some isolated Russian settlements to this day rejects the use of sacred polyphony in favor of the austere unison of the ancient melodies. Moreover, in these places the old neumatic notation is still vigorously defended and is found in many elaborate, handwritten manuscripts for contemporary church use. It commonly retains the basic seventeenth-century form utilizing both the *priznaki* and *pomety* (Fig. 3). Apart from this, the *znamenny* chant also survives in modern publications, and a series of service manuals first edited by the Holy Synod of the Russian Church in the eighteenth century preserves the bulk of the repertoire in the square notes (Fig. 4). The melodies from this and similar collections, however, have hardly ever been performed in the original unison and have served primarily as the inspiration for an evolving compositional technique of nineteenth- and twentieth-century church composers. Other examples of the music can be found in scholarly transcriptions from the manuscripts, especially the works by M. V. Brazhnikov and N. D. Uspenskii.

There is no doubt that the facts pertaining to the music are far from complete and many questions remain.

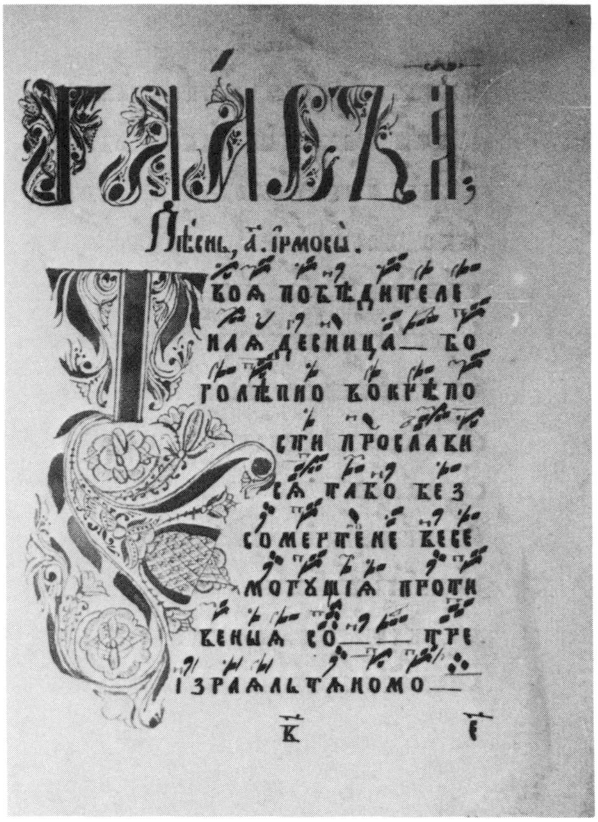

Fig. 3. "Old Believer" notation (20th century MS). AUTHOR'S COLLECTION

Of foremost concern is the issue of graphic interpretation and the transcription of the neumes; more than half of the recorded history of the chant remains silent in the manuscripts. The extent to which scholarship is able to uncover the meaning of the notation will determine what can be known. Furthermore, if it can be assumed that identical notation in the synchronic and diachronic dimensions connotes melodic stability, to what extent are the related, transcribed sources (the Greek Middle Byzantine and late Russian) of use in this task? In this regard, the work of Strunk, Levy, and Velimirović has led to some important insights and the development of what has been termed "counterpart transcription." In other areas, however, basic evidence is altogether missing, and knowledge must rest primarily on scattered literary, archaeological, and iconographic discoveries. In addition to the broad secular sphere, where the folk tradition never adopted notation, a central problem concerns the sacred practice of ethnic Slavs other than the Russians (or eastern Slavs including the Ukrainians). Many of these

MUSIC, SLAVIC

Fig. 4. Square (Kievan) notation (early 19th century MS). AUTHOR'S COLLECTION

nationalities, such as the Bulgars, Serbs, and other related South Slavic tribes, were early converts to Byzantine Christianity and, in some cases, cultivated a Greek-based liturgical chant prior to the Russians. Yet here there is no documentation to match the manuscripts of the north, and one can only surmise why the surviving, systematically notated manuals are all of a comparatively late date. Among these peoples, it seems, circumstances shaped a different history and one which has yet to be satisfactorily integrated into the existing framework.

BIBLIOGRAPHY

Maksim V. Brazhnikov, ed., *Novye pamiatniki znamennogo raspeva* (1967), *Drevnerusskaia teoriia muzyki po rukopisnym materialam XV–XVIII vekov* (1972), *Pamiatniki znamennogo raspeva* (1974), and *Feodor Krestianin: Stikhiry* (1974); A. Bugge, ed., *Contacarium Palaeoslavicum Mosquense,* Monumenta Musicae Byzantinae, Main Series VI (1960); Nikolai F. Findeisen, *Ocherki po istorii muzyki v Rossii* (1928–1929); Johann von Gardner, *Bogosluzhebnoe penie russkoi pravoslavnoi tserkvi,* 2 vols. (1978–1982); Christian Hannick, ed., *Fundamental Problems in Early Slavic Music and Poetry* (1978); Carsten Høeg, "The Oldest Slavonic Tradition of Byzantine Music," *The Proceedings of the British Academy* (1953); Roman Jakobson, ed., *Fragmenta chiliandarica palaeoslavica,* Monumenta musicae byzantinae, Main Series V: A, B (1957), and "The Slavic Response to Byzantine Poetry," in *Actes du XIIe congrès international des études byzantines, Ochrida, 1961,* I (1963); Erwin Koschmieder, *Die ältesten novgoroder Hirmologien-Fragmente,* 3 vols. (1952–1958); Kenneth Levy, "The Slavic Kontakia and Their Byzantine Originals," in Albert Mell, ed., *Twenty-fifth Anniversary Festschrift (1937–62), Department of Music, Queens College* (1964); Andrew D. McCredie, "New Perspectives in European Music Historiography: A Bibliographical Survey of Current Research in Medieval and Renaissance Slavic and Byzantine Sources," in *Miscellanea musicologica: Adelaide Studies in Musicology,* **4** (1969), and "Some Aspects of Current Research into Russian Liturgical Chant," *ibid.,* **6** (1972); Vasillii Metallov, *Russkaia simiografiia iz oblasti tserkovno-pevcheskoi arkheologii i paleografii* (1912), and *Bogosluzhebnoe penie russkoi tserkvi v period domongol'skii* (1912); Raina Palikarova-Verdeil, *La musique byzantine chez les Bulgares et les Russes (du IXe au XIVe siècle)* (1953); S. Petrov and Kh. Kodov, *Starobulgarski muzikalni pametnitsi* (1973); Vladimir Protopopov, ed., *Nikolai Diletskii: Idea grammatiki musikiiskoi* (1979); Gerald R. Seaman, *History of Russian Music,* I (1967); Stepan V. Smolenskii, *Azbuka znamennago peniia (izveshchenie o soglasneishikh pometakh) startsa Aleksandra Mezentsa (1668-go goda)* (1888), and *Paläographischer Atlas der altrussischen linienlosen Gesangsnotation,* posthumously ed. by Johann von Gardner (1976); S. Stefanović, "Les sources de la recherche sur la vieille musique sacrée serbe," in *La musique serbe à travers les siècles* (1973); Oliver Strunk, "Two Chilandri Choir Books," in *Essays on Music in the Byzantine World* (1977); Alfred J. Swan, "The Znamenny Chant of the Russian Church" (3 parts), in *The Musical Quarterly,* **26** (1940); Nikolai Uspenskii, *Obraztsy drevnerusskogo pevcheskogo iskusstva* (1968, 2nd ed. 1971), and *Drevnerusskoe pevcheskoe iskusstvo* (1965, 2nd ed. 1971); Miloš Velimirović, *Byzantine Elements in Early Slavic Chant* (1960), "The Influence of the Byzantine Chant on the Music of the Slavic Countries," in J. M. Hussey, ed., *Proceedings of the Thirteenth International Congress of Byzantine Studies, Oxford, 1966* (1967), and "The Present Status of Research in Slavic Music," in *Acta musicologica,* **44** (1972); T. Vladyshevskaia, "K voprosu ob izuchenii traditsii drevnerusskogo pevcheskogo iskusstva," in Aleksei Kandinskii and Iu. Rozanova, eds., *Iz istorii russkoi i sovetskoi muzyki,* II (1976), and "K voprosu o sviazi narodnogo i professional'nogo drevnerusskogo pevcheskogo iskusstva," in *Muzykal'naia fol'kloristika,* II (1978).

NICOLAS SCHIDLOVSKY

[See also **Cyril and Methodios, Sts.; Heirmos; Kontakion; Melisma; Monophony; Music, Byzantine; Novgorod; Octoechos; Sticheron.**]

MUSIC, SYRIAN, refers to a type of non-Greek Eastern liturgical chant descending from an ancient practice in the patriarchal see of Antioch. Today the term applies to the singing of various religious groups and especially the Syrian Orthodox (Jacobite), Syro-Antiochene, Chaldaean, Maronite, Assyrian, Mar Thomas of South India, Melchite, Malabar, and Malankar churches. Particular features of the music are generally maintained by such followings of Nestorian, Monophysite, Monothelite, and other teachings surviving in isolated pockets outside official Orthodoxy. After the schism between East and West in the eleventh century, the chant is also linked to the rite of prominent uniate factions siding with Rome.

The music nevertheless bears ample evidence of continuity across doctrinal boundaries. In particular, universals of liturgy offer a foothold for comparisons with mainline Christian tradition. For example, the Syrian Lelyā, Ṣaprā, and Ramshā make up the Offices of matins, lauds, and vespers; these, in turn, are centered on a recitation from the Psalter, sometimes distributed in a system of *hullāle* and *marmyāthā* resembling the Greek divisions of *kathismata* and *staseis* (for reading the entire collection of psalms over a given liturgical period of days). Elements of Arab and Turkish influence appear certain, and Assyrian, Chaldaean, and Maronite musicians characterize their musical systems using the terminology of the Arabic *maqāmāt*. In addition, the eight church modes known throughout early Christian music are identified in the usage of the Syrian Orthodox. Like the chants of the Byzantine octoechos, an eight-week modal cycle functions in the liturgy; however, only the musical mode is changed and the texts remain the same. (An early Syrian practice has been suggested as the prototype.) Principles of traditional hymnography are evident. The *ᶜenyānā, qālā,* and *qanūne yawnāye* find analogues in the musical forms of the sticheron, troparion, sequence, and *kanōn.* The *madrāshā,* a type of strophic hymn often regarded as an antecedent of the kontakion, was first written by St. Ephrem the Syrian, the great ascetic, theologian, and exegete of the fourth century.

Scholarly interest in the music is long-standing; recent research by Heinrich Husmann has been particularly useful in clarifying the theoretical systems of the chant. A primitive form of the paleo-Byzantine notation has been found in some Syrian manuscripts and especially in the Old Melchite tradition. As a whole, however, notation is rare; oral tradition sometimes provides the only surviving evidence for analysis.

BIBLIOGRAPHY

L. Hage, "Music of the Maronite Church," in *Parole de l'orient,* 2 (1971); Heinrich Husmann, "Die Tonarten der chaldäischen Breviergesänge," in *Orientalia christiana periodica,* 35 (1969), "Arabische Maqamen in ostsyrischer Kirchenmusik," in *Musik als Gestalt und Erlebnis: Festschrift Walter Graf* (1970), "Die Gesänge der syrischen Liturgien" and "Die Gesänge der melkitischen Liturgie," in Karl G. Fellerer, ed., *Geschichte der katholischen Kirchenmusik,* I (1972), "Ein syrisches Sticherarion mit paläobyzantinischer Notation (Sinai syr. 261)," in *Hamburger Jahrbuch für Musikwissenshaft,* 1 (1974), "Eine alte orientalische christliche Liturgie: Altsyrisch-melkitisch," in *Orientalia christiana periodica,* 42 (1976), and "Madraše und Seblata: Repertoireuntersuchungen zu den Hymnen Ephraems des Syrers," in *Acta musicologica,* 48 (1976); A. Z. Idelsohn, "Der Kirchengesang der Jakobiten," in *Archiv für Musikwissenschaft,* 4 (1922); J. C. Jeannin, "Octoechos syrien," in *Dictionnaire d'archéologie chrétienne et de liturgie,* XII.2 (1936); G. Lerchundi, "Notation musicale syrienne," in *L'orient syrien,* 4 (1959); Juan Mateos, *Lelya-Sapra: Essai d'interprétation des matines chaldéenes* (1959); Egon Wellesz, "Early Christian Music," in *New Oxford History of Music,* II (1954).

NICOLAS SCHIDLOVSKY

[See also **Gregorian Chant; Hymns, Byzantine; Maqām; Music, Byzantine; Music, Islamic Influence on Western; Octoechos.**]

MUSIC, WESTERN EUROPEAN. *Musica,* the appropriate medieval term, cannot be adequately translated as "music." Just as the eight melodic modes of the Middle Ages were much later reduced to two, major and minor, so the meaning, interpretation, and functions of music were progressively narrowed. Here I shall discuss the wider meaning music had for the medieval world, summarize its development in nontechnical terms, and explain how it differs from the music of later centuries. During the nearly ten centuries encompassed by this essay, music did not always evolve directly, and in different periods and places different aspects may have been emphasized. But there are some trends that may conveniently be isolated, as well as concepts and attitudes that must be explored.

Theorists and practitioners of medieval music held attitudes that met at almost no point. The first group thought of music as a discipline, a philosophy that had nothing to do with the sensuous art of sound; the other ignored or did not know the discipline and preferred the practice. The exponent of the former view, the *musicus,* recognized the exponent of practical music, the cantor, but thought of him (if at all) in much the same way as an architect thought of a bricklayer. The analogy is from Boethius' (*d.* 524/526) treatise *De institutione musica,* the universal textbook for intellectual music at least until the sixteenth century. Animosity between the two views is neatly expressed in a widely known poem found in the prologue *Regulae rhythmicae* by Guido of Arezzo, dating from about 1000:

Musicorum et cantorum
magna est distantia
Isti dicunt, illi sciunt,
que componit musica
Nam qui facit, quod non sapit
diffinitur bestia.

Between the professions of *musicus* and cantor the distance is great; the cantor sings, but the *musicus* knows. For he who makes and composes music is defined as a beast because he does not understand.

Despite such scorn, the *musicus* eventually had to incorporate the advances of the cantor into his intellectual scheme. The adjustments took place throughout the period and are most obvious in the need to authorize first the practical music of the church, plainsong, and later the composition of truly liturgical part-music in the thirteenth century. *Musica speculativa,* or the discipline of the *musicus,* was so important, indeed, so fundamental, in any liberal education that any discussion of medieval music ought to start with it. Moreover, many arts—including music itself—exhibited the principles of *musica.*

SPECULATIVE AND PRACTICAL MUSIC

That *musica* symbolized the underlying structure of many things in the medieval period and was a method of thinking which bound all things together was stated throughout the period. "Sine musica nulla disciplina potest esse perfecta. Nihil sine illa." (No discipline is complete without music. Nothing is without music.) So said Isidore of Seville, and the assertion was repeated by a number of authorities throughout the early Middle Ages. John Scottus Eriugena, writing in the ninth century, and glossing Martianus Capella (fifth century), reiterated it; Cassiodorus, in the sixth century, said it in a somewhat different way: "The discipline of music permeates all the acts of our life." Others referred to more specific aspects of the same underlying philosophy: "Heaven and earth are ordered through harmony"; "The customs of men are known through music"; "Every habit of morals is ruled and governed by song." As we move into the later Middle Ages, it is more difficult to find such remarks, even when writers quote earlier sources. The emphasis changed. Still, Thomas of York purveyed the same view in the thirteenth century: "To know music is to know the order of all things." In fact the concept of music as mistress of everything else permeated literature and poetry and a number of the major treatises on music of the thirteenth and fourteenth centuries: Jacques de (Jacobus of) Liège, a conservative, said in the early fourteenth century that "music extends itself to everything."

In the earlier Middle Ages, then, music, referred to either as *musica* or by terminology such as *harmonia, consonantia,* or *cantus,* was a symbol, even a demonstrable model, of universal order. Even in its sensuous form as sound, however, it had an essential role in society. Plainsong, the universal unison song of the church, came to symbolize the unity of the Christian world. Moreover, the medieval liturgy was expanded by thousands of semiauthorized accretions called tropes. (They were eliminated in the reforms of the sixteenth century, so that the earlier role of music in the medieval church was much larger than it is now.) Apart from the ubiquitous use of chant and related sacred songs within the services, the church used such music for propaganda and missionary work. Hymns were common vehicles for such purposes, and according to Ambrose (fourth century), without music the hymn was not a hymn. The sequence, the most important kind of trope, was used similarly: the universally known tune of the sequence *Victime paschali,* still in use today, was used for anti-Jewish and, later, anti-Luther propaganda. Anti-Jewish texts were also occasionally disseminated in other forms such as the motet. Sermons were associated with music, and much of the work of the Franciscans would have been impossible without the *lauda,* the penitential song, and the carol.

Outside the church, music was used similarly to advance secular purposes: scientific ideas were spread in musical settings, and the wandering jongleur was like a traveling newspaper, singing political praises, criticizing abuses, or recording the deaths of princes. Music was everywhere. The nobleman's retinue included minstrels; ships' crews included musicians, especially trumpeters, presumably to act as foghorns; cities employed musicians to watch at the city walls and towers. Music formed a background for all kinds of social functions, banquets, processions, and the like. Doctors and grammarians, poets and architects were expected to know about music, usually in the speculative sense, but also sometimes in the sensuous form.

HARMONY OF THE SPHERES

But it was not this everyday music that the philosophers thought essential for the perfection of intellectual disciplines and for the ordering of all things. In the Platonic scheme, the world soul was ordered by a musical scale governed by mathematical proportions, and a man's "virtue" was best preserved by "philosophy tempered by music," in the words of one modern commentator. The Greeks developed the notion of a living stream of stuff, flowing perpetually in a circle. "Souls" in particular, reports Plato, "pass out of this world to the other . . . and then come back from the dead, and are born again." While in this world the soul is corrupted by the imperfection of the earthly body. Philosophy aims to transcend as far as possible the constraints of the physical senses and allow the soul, disturbed though it is by the physical world, to approach the perfection of the other life. That other life, according to Aristotle's view of Pythagorean thought, is inherently mathematical, therefore invariable—and thus eternal. The disordered things of this world, including the soul, are but sensible reflections of ideal mathematical forms. The Pythagoreans knew that musical scales could be represented as mathematical ratios; therefore numbers could stand for music. In that other world, then, the mathematical revolution of the heavenly bodies produced a music that was the harmony of the spheres, a music so perfect that it was inaudible to humans.

Aristotle said in the *Metaphysics* that "the whole heaven was a musical scale and number." Audible music, as with all wordly things, was the sensible reflection of this perfect music. Thus, the soul, disordered by the physical world, could approach by means of music the mathematical perfection of the other life; and if the soul may be ordered by means of philosophy and music, the two, if not actually synonymous, are intimately related.

Nevertheless, since it was only a poor reflection of the higher form, even the best of purely sensuous music could not achieve complete perfection of the soul. To that end, only the truly perfect inaudible music of the spheres was satisfactory. Thus it came about that perfection could be achieved only by the exercise of the intellect and not by the use of one's ears. Good sensuous music could help, however—a view inspired by Aristotle's modification of Plato's ideas. The determination of good was made according to the simplicity of the mathematical proportions underlying the music. Here there is a direct link between the reason, or ratio, by which the music of the spheres could be understood, and the ratio, or numerical proportion, by which sensuous music could be interpreted.

It must have been magically mysterious to the Greeks and to medieval man to discover that the best-sounding intervals were formed from the ratios between the first four integers: the octave (2:1), the fifth (3:2), the fourth (4:3). These consonances remained the basis for all medieval music. They were considered as perfect, both sensuously and philosophically; and music based on them was thought more efficacious in its moral and spiritual effects. The ratios between the next integers, 5:4 and 6:5, were not considered to produce good intervals until the fourteenth century at the earliest.

Thus, musical pitch is indivisibly connected with mathematics, as is the other element usually thought to be a fundamental of music, rhythm, which is the splitting of time into elements proportional to each other (thus the trochee, 2:1). Augustine's treatise on music is essentially an examination of poetic meters and rhythms: to him, those subjects were *musica.* Apart from the ratios inherent in intervals and rhythms, many other numerical features are to be observed in musical phenomena, and these were kept alive throughout the Middle Ages and indeed for several centuries afterward. To name only a few: the seven notes of the scale reflected the pitches produced by the seven planetary spheres as they revolved. A tenth-century manuscript contains a poem, set to music, that specifically relates the planets to the musical pitches. Man, composed of an earthly body symbolized by 4 and a soul symbolized by 3, added up to 7 and thus reflected the celestial music. This view of Honorius of Autun is matched by the common belief during the Middle Ages, expressed by Villard de Honnecourt and later in a well-known diagram by Leonardo da Vinci, that the geometrical proportions of the human body were related by the simple numbers of the musical consonances (Fig. 1): this *homo quadratus* was a symbol of perfect virtue.

The seven notes of the musical scale were unified, or made perfect, by the addition of unity, 1, to pro-

MUSIC, WESTERN EUROPEAN

Fig. 1. Homo quadratus, depicting the harmony of the spheres, from the so-called False Decretals. Pen drawing, Rheims, *ca.* 1180. RHEIMS, BIBLIOTHÈQUE MUNICIPALE, MS 672, fol. 1r

duce the perfect octave for the eighth note, also symbolizing earthly paradise, as in Dante, or immortality after the seven-day creation of the physical universe. Thus in the phrase of Boethius and innumerable authorities through the ages: "Music is knowledge which speaks about numbers."

Music in its philosophical sense, then, the only reputable sense at least for the early Middle Ages, was the perception of numbers and proportions. This metaphysical idea was to form the intellectual basis for later medieval music, as well as for many other medieval disciplines. But the pagan concept of the music of the spheres and its domination over all things could not be allowed to go unchanged in the developing Christian world. (The christianization of this pagan belief has been investigated by only one scholar, H. M. Klinkenberg, and the results published in a mere thirty pages.)

CHRISTIANIZATION OF MUSIC

The authority of Christianity probably finally outweighed that of the classics after the twelfth century. The transmission of Neoplatonic ideas by Boethius and Capella through the works of John Scottus and Remigius of Auxerre (*d. ca.* 900) had continued up to the twelfth-century School of Chartres, but their emphasis on *musica* as mistress of the universe had been overshadowed already by the necessity for the church to deal with music in the practical sense as an audible phenomenon. From the seventh to eleventh centuries the church was tackling the problems of plainsong: its classification, its modal characteristics, its rhythm, and its very notation. An attitude that stressed the virtues of music as sound was bound to emerge and the classics also provided the lead in this respect. Aristotle's rejection of the music of the spheres and his recognition of the pleasurable effects of good music in the right context had not been missed. Augustine knew the dangerous effects of music of the wrong sort (in this case, apparently, music without an accompanying text) and his justifying the use of the proper kind of music in church laid the groundwork for a medieval intellectual structure in which music as sound could take a more prominent position. In this regard, Isidore and Cassiodorus were more influential than Boethius during the Carolingian era, when most of the musical developments were taking place. Both writers had fallen back on Scripture (the Book of Wisdom, or Sapientia) to justify the music of the spheres and its numerical domination: "Everything is disposed according to measure, number, and weight" (Sapientia 11:21).

Christians, while still subscribing to the theory of the music of the spheres by reason of the classical precedent, could also assent to music as sound, because of scriptural references. Such a view was put forward by Regino of Prüm (*d.* 915); it suggested that the intellectual and sensuous had been made compatible. However, as the practical business of plainsong became less of an issue, and as education moved away from the monasteries and into cathedral schools and universities, educators were freer to reconsider Platonic and Boethian ideas and, with the influence of the School of Chartres, universal music once again asserted itself. The late twelfth and the thirteenth centuries were the heyday of *musica* as a liberal art, even though its importance, except as a discipline for the intellectual, now diminished quite rapidly. Even though the Arabs too had a highly developed theory of universal music, they may have had a role in the decline of theory in Christian Europe; their strongly empirical turn of mind seems to have swung the balance in favor of music as sound. Moreover, the rise of universities in the twelfth cen-

MUSIC, WESTERN EUROPEAN

tury must have contributed to the preference for disciplines such as logic and theology. Nevertheless, most authorities, including Aquinas, stressed that music was the first of the seven liberal arts.

Whatever the interaction of all these factors, music lost its position as the art whose principles provided the universal laws by which all things could be understood. A poem of Alan of Lille (twelfth century) makes the change clear; using terminology that he elsewhere associates with the Platonic function of music as a force ordering and uniting the physical and spiritual, Alan refers to the Incarnation. Flesh and spirit are joined by the Word of God, stunning every rule and, in particular, breaking the law of musical proportions, as Alan writes in *Rhythmus de incarnatione:*

Dum factoris et facture
  Mira fit coniunctio
Quis sit modus ligature
  Quis ordo que ratio
Que sint vincla que iuncture
  Qui gunphi que unio
Stupet sui fracto iure
  Musica proportio
In hac Verbi copula
  Stupet omnis regula.

When the miraculous conjunction of flesh and spirit is made, what may be the method of joining; what the order and reason; what the chains and junctures; what the bonds and what the union? Musical proportion is stunned by its broken law; in this joining by the Word every rule is stunned.

But all this was not lost for the classics. Although Roger Bacon (*d. ca.* 1291) said that theology was the mistress of all disciplines, he also said that mathematics was the universal science because it contained music. For Bacon, music was a necessary discipline for the theologian, who expounded truths through the power of the sciences, including music. Scripture, too, could be understood only with a thorough knowledge of music. Both logic and grammar depended on music and its power: "It belongs to music to give the reasons and theories of [many things in Scripture], although the grammarian teaches the rules for them." Music may have given first place to divinity, but it still governed many disciplines. Edgar de Bruyne's research into the aesthetics of the Middle Ages shows that beauty was often conceived of in musical terms and by means of the proportions of the musical intervals.

The terminology of Boethius was in general use: his highest form of music, *musica mundana,* universal music that was in everything, could be appreciated only by the ratio, the use of reason, and the true musician was judged "not by the servitude of work, but by the rule of contemplation." When Boethius is himself brought, through contemplation, from "an irrational love of Fortune" back to the "rule of reason" by Philosophy herself, and when Philosophy, in the course of her persuasions, sings various poems, we should realize immediately that we confront a work that is fundamentally musical in the medieval sense. Only recently has this been clearly established in the research by David Chamberlain; in the Middle Ages, however, no such explanation would have been necessary. It was certainly not necessary for the musical theorist Jacques de Liège, who introduced his fourteenth-century encyclopedia *Speculum musice* with references to Boethius' *Consolation of Philosophy.*

Boethius' second category of music, *musica humana,* referred to the relation between the rational and the irrational and how they could be brought into harmony, or, more specifically, how the physical might be made perfect by adding to it the spiritual. We should recognize another work fundamentally musical when we read of a newly created body made complete with a soul brought from heaven in a union performed by Concordia. Such a composition is the *Anticlaudianus* of Alan of Lille, also a vastly influential piece of medieval writing. And, like the *Consolation,* it is prosimetric in structure, alternating prose with poetry and illustrating Boethius' third category, that of *musica instrumetalis,* or the sensuous form of music.

MUSIC IN OTHER ARTS AND DISCIPLINES

How do aesthetic and proportional concepts of music enter into the construction and appreciation of works in other disciplines? It is very easy to find numerical relationships in almost anything: an architect designs his church as far as possible to lengths that are simple integers rather than fractions, and the poet can hardly deal in half-syllables. There must perhaps be some other evidence that the designer of the work of art was thinking in musical terms. Sometimes we can make such an assumption only from a knowledge that music was normally a part of the designer's training, as in the case of an architect. The depiction of musical instruments in illustrations that have consonant proportions may strengthen the supposition that the latter were deliberate and added to the picture for their symbolic value. The poetic juxtaposition of quatrain and ter-

MUSIC, WESTERN EUROPEAN

cet may take on added musical significance if the content relates to the harmonious joining of body and soul. Chamberlain has recently pointed to admirable examples of this kind of relationship in Chaucer's *Parliament of Fowls,* whose basic structure is founded on the numerical proportions inherent in *musica,* explaining the number of syllables per line, and the number of stanzas per section. The recognition of an underlying musical scheme may enable an editor to establish a correct reading, and Chamberlain suggests an emendation in this case to produce 700 lines, instead of the conventional 699. Syllable counts and accentual patterns can be scrutinized in a similar way.

It has been suggested that the formal plan of the *Divine Comedy* might be musical. A few years after the *Comedy,* Dante wrote in the *Convivio:* "If you cannot see the meaning of this canzona, do not reject it; look at its beauty . . . for the numerical relation of its parts (which interests the musicians)." But if a musical plan can be ascribed to the *Divine Comedy,* no one except Dante himself seems to have referred to it. Did Dante mean simply the fact that there are 3 × 3 × 11 cantos, plus one, with a threefold rhyme scheme applied to lines with eleven syllables? Or is there a more subtle hidden mathematical and musical plan?

With respect to the minnesong there is a similar, and more demonstrable connection. A. T. Hatto has pointed out that before committing himself to the details of musical and metrical structure, the minnesinger reflected on the shape and size of the poem and chose for its total number of feet, or musical bars, a "decent round number" such as forty, fifty, or sixty to display some fine proportion. And at this point we may remember that prosody was known as "numbers": sometimes medieval writers used the phrase *musica cuius imago prosodia.* Hatto quotes a fine example from Walther von der Vogelweide. *Diu minne lât* has 70 bars, divided into 21 (7 × 3) and 21 for the two stollen, and 28 (7 × 4) for the abgesang: the ratio of the stollen as a whole to the abgesang is 42:28 or 3:2.

In the thirteenth century, poetic and musical theory interacted on a conscious level with the application of musical consonance to rhyme schemes and other sharing of terminology and concept. A notable exponent of this was John of Garland. Poetry is a field in which an underlying music has been amply demonstrated. But in literature the philosophy of *musica* may be expressed in words or thought: when both of these are ambiguous or unclear, we are surely justified in searching in the poetic structure for an underlying mathematical *musica,* which may help to interpret the deeper message of the words themselves.

The idea of a truly universal music began to lose its philosophical force most strongly in the fourteenth century, when irrational proportions began to be recognized as having an aesthetic value. Nicole Oresme, a translator and glossator of Aristotle, was perhaps the first major writer to discuss the beauty of ratios other than those previously accepted. At the same time, poetry was no longer so indivisibly associated with music, in either the sensuous or philosophical form. With Dante, Boccaccio, and Chaucer poetry became an independent art form. Froissart wrote ballades, rondeaux, and virelais much like Machaut's, but without music. Machaut was an exception, and in this way, as in others, was conservative. But Machaut's pupil, Deschamps, expressed quite clearly the thought that poetry now contained its own "music."

As in poetry, so in art and architecture. The visual representations of the harmony of the spheres are well known: The concentric circles appear to form practically the whole construction of the picture, or at least to create an encompassing background for a central point. Charles De Tolnay has traced the development of this form of visual representation. He demonstrates, for example, that the *Last Supper* by Leonardo is incomplete as we normally see it repro-

Fig. 2. The Last Supper. Fresco by Leonardo da Vinci in the Refectory of S. Maria delle Grazie, Milan, 1495–1497. SCALA/ART RESOURCE

Fig. 3. Rose window from Notre Dame de Paris, 1220. REPRODUCED FROM M. AUBERT ET AL., *LES VITRAUX DE NOTRE-DAME ET LA SAINTE-CHAPELLE DE PARIS,* 1959. © Caisse Nationale des Monuments Historiques, Paris

duced. The architecture of the building in which the painting is set frames it with the *musica* of the harmony of the spheres (Fig. 2). De Bruyne has shown that medieval man probably thought about beauty as a reduction to mathematical principles, those of music. And it is perhaps not going too far to state that spheres and circles and semicircles were often used in the Middle Ages as conscious reminders of the heavenly music, as evidenced by the familiar architectural items depicted in Figures 3 to 6. They range from the rose window to the portal or passageway of a Romanesque church. One can also see these ideas expressed in treatises on music (Fig. 7) and in a fourteenth-century musical score (Fig. 8). The twelfth-century Hildegard Codex (Fig. 9) shows the nine spheres of the cosmos; although no musical symbols appear explicitly in this illustration, other such diagrams from this date are often filled with representations of musical instruments, players, angel musicians, and the like. A similar, but hemispherical, representation, including scores of instruments and players, is from a fourteenth-century manuscript of the *De hierarchia* of Dionysius the Areopagite (Fig. 10). This kind of visual effect works with the rounded arches of Romanesque style, but not with the pointed arch of Gothic. As with the

MUSIC, WESTERN EUROPEAN

Fig. 4. Tomb of Philippa of Lancaster (side view). Monastery of Batalha, Portugal, 14th century. AUTHOR'S COLLECTION

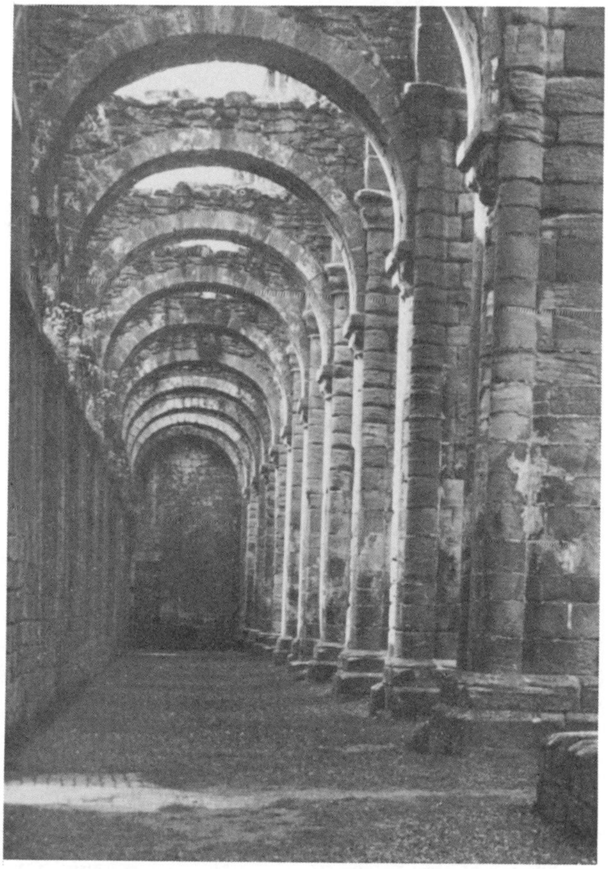

Fig. 5. Passageway in Fountains Abbey, Yorkshire, 1132. AUTHOR'S COLLECTION

Fig. 6. West portal of Rochester Cathedral, *ca.* 1160–1170. PHOTO BY B. C. CLAYTON. REPRODUCED FROM A. W. CLAPHAM, *ENGLISH ROMANESQUE ARCHITECTURE* (1934). Courtesy of the Clarendon Press, Oxford

shift from a classical to a Christian interpretation of musical philosophy, mentioned earlier, the twelfth century coincides with a shift in viewpoint.

The discovery of mathematical proportions in art is subject to all kinds of juggling of figures to produce a desired result. The use of such analytical methods in architecture, however, is surely less suspect. We may recall one example, accurately reported by de Bruyne. Villard de Honnecourt, in his thirteenth-century sketchbook, included a design for a church. He referred to it specifically as *esquarie,* or *quadratum,* that is, based on numerical proportions, like the *homo quadratus.* Figure 11 is an abstraction of Villard's drawing, which paraphrases de Bruyne's description: we see the 1:1 (unison), 1:2 (octave), 3:2 (fifth), 4:3 (fourth—and this applies to the chancel, where the 4 of earthly things is infused with the 3 of spiritual matter). We see the 5:4 (major third, receiving its first practical use in the thirteenth century) and the 9:8 (tone). Similar analysis has been applied by numerous scholars to other parts of churches. A far more striking example of the relationship between music and architecture is to be found in the early fifteenth century, however, in the motet that Dufay wrote for the dedication of the newly constructed dome of Florence cathedral: in this case the composer may have known the architect, Brunelleschi, and may even have seen the architectural plans and dimensions. In any case, there are several musical oddities that coincide with or can be related to architectural ones.

Musica mundana in architecture was often complemented by carvings of musical figures on capitals, as at Cluny, or in portals, or in stained glass, or on

MUSIC, WESTERN EUROPEAN

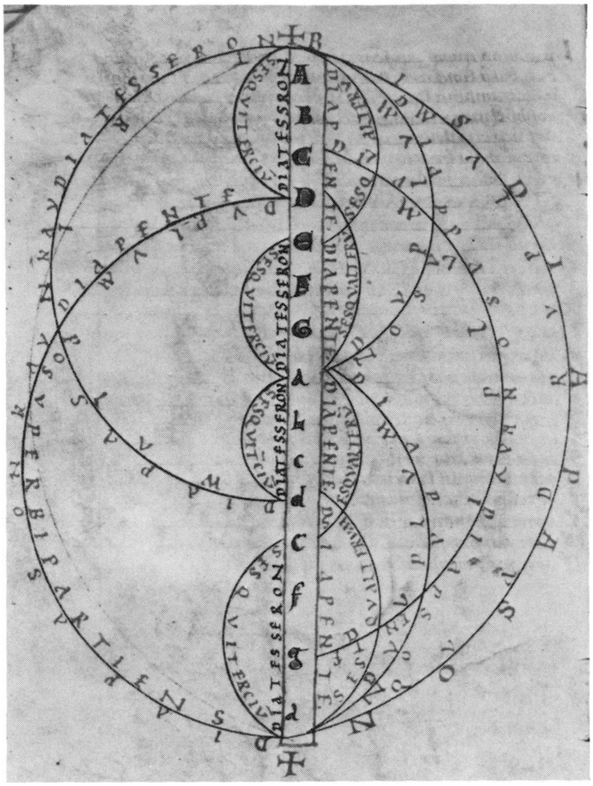

Fig. 7a. From a musical treatise of St. Emmeram, Regensburg, 12th century. MÜNCHEN, BAYERISCHE STAATSBIBLIOTHEK, CLM 14965b, fol. 33v

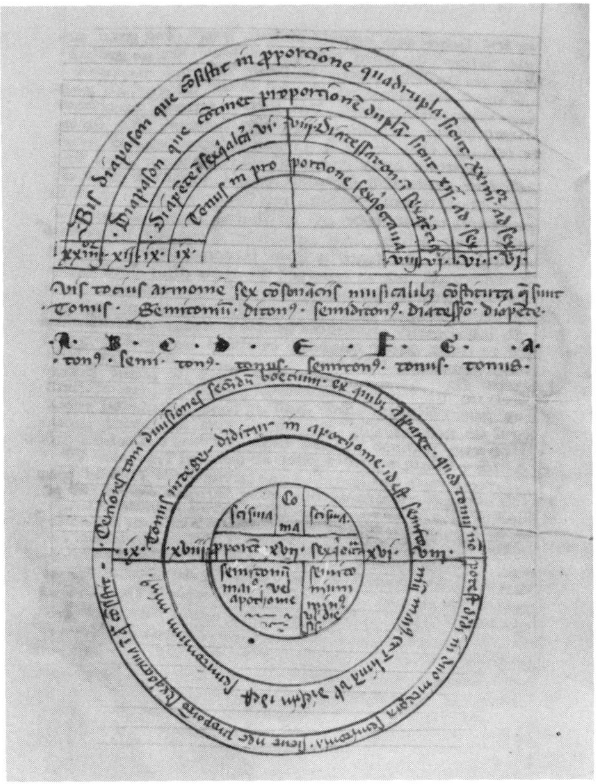

Fig. 7b. From the *Micrologus de musica* of Guido of Arezzo, 14th century. BY PERMISSION OF THE BRITISH LIBRARY, LONDON. MS HARLEY 281, fol. 11v

bosses. Musical scores were drawn on walls. Representations of this kind often included a special version of the music of the spheres, that is, the singing angels, or angel musicians. This obvious christianizing of the original concept, in which the angels sing the inaudible and perfect heavenly music that was imitated on earth as plainsong, could be worked into almost any kind of picture and, like the hemispherical arches of an abbey corridor, could remind the viewer of the perfection of *musica mundana* or, as it was known by the late thirteenth century, *musica divina.* Cassiodorus said: "We mingle our praises with those of God's angels, whom we cannot hear." If a picture containing the concept of *musica* in the form of singing angels may be realized by the plainsong fitting the subject of the picture, other forms of architectural and pictorial decoration may also be realized as sound. There are several modern theories of "singing stones," or music hidden enigmatically in decorative design. Most such theories have yet to be convincingly demonstrated. Occasionally mathematics, or practical applications of it, such as the process of finding the date of Easter, produced actual music. *Musica mundana* was responsible for the ordering of the seasons, and the formula for working out the date of Easter uses the numbers 3, 4, and 7 to produce one of the dominical letters, *a–g.* It is hardly a coincidence that these are the letter-names of the seven pitches. One ingenious composer was prompted to write a musical piece whose text serves as a mnemonic for working with the kalendar.

For magic and medicine, too, music or *musica* was important. Charm is related to *carmen,* song, and incantation speaks for itself. For some medical men in the Middle Ages charm and incantation formed a large part of their skills. On other occasions, the sound of various parts of the human body was judged by musical standards, and the pulse was measured according to rhythmic criteria. In addition, the health of the spirit as well as the physical body was important and could be improved by the correct intellectual means, such as suitable chants.

Many of these aspects of music and *musica* have yet to be seriously researched; certainly the idea that music provides a universal coherence for other arts

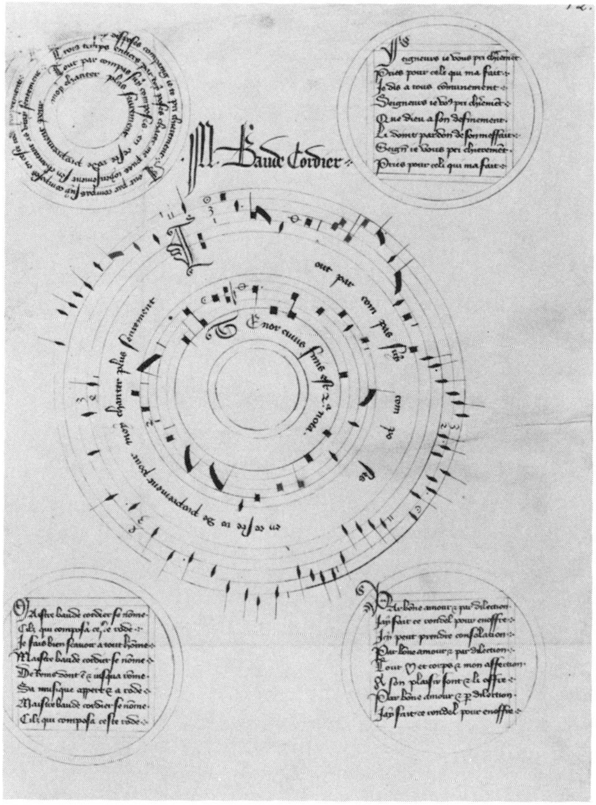

Fig. 8. A 14th-century secular piece by Baude Cordier in a 15th-century MS. CHANTILLY, BIBLIOTHÈQUE DU MUSÉE CONDÉ, MS 1047, fol. 12r. Giraudon/Art Resource

and for professions is one that is strange to twentieth-century men and women. Nevertheless, it is clear that music in one of its forms has inspired much creative work of the kind now regarded as independent and quite distinct from music as sound. *Musica mundana* justified many verbal, visual, or tactile disciplines and, in a form perceptible to reason, was an important part of many others, such as medicine, philosophy, grammar, and theology. The physical representation of *mundana* in measurable form, in design and length, was part of *musica humana.* Some of these phenomena undoubtedly result in music as sound. What then of Boethius' third category, *musica instrumentalis,* or music as we are likely to think of it nowadays?

MUSIC AS SOUND

The term *instrumentalis* referred to music sounding by means of a physical medium, whether that be the human voice itself, or wood and metal. Could music itself reflect *musica mundana* and *humana,* since in its sensible form it is nonexplicit in its communication and cannot express philosophical thoughts? It cannot be measured, especially when it cannot even be written down, as was the case until about the ninth century. The proportional relation of one note to another in a chant is recognizable, if the pitches are accurately intoned: the relationship of one time value to another is similarly recognizable if the values are exact and simple, as 2:1. But until notation had developed to a considerable extent, say until the twelfth century, it was not usual for either pitch or rhythm to be expressed exactly. Again, the twelfth century seems to be a watershed. Before that, music appears devoid of the first two categories of *musica* since it can be specific neither about the concept, the *mundana,* nor about the number-proportion, the *humana.* The inability of music to demonstrate adequately its own relation to *musica mundana* may be one of the reasons that textless music was so much shunned by the early church. The *auctoritas* for plainsong came through its texts. Most church fathers strictly enjoined against instrumental music to which words were not attached, and again Augustine's reservations make sense. We need to examine more carefully, however, what happens to music through the Middle Ages and how its elements are used.

To take rhythm first: prior to the twelfth century,

Fig. 9. Choir of angels in the nine spheres of the cosmos. Miniature from the *Scivias* of St. Hildegard of Bingen, 1141–1150. WIESBADEN, HESSISCHE LANDESBIBLIOTHEK, MS 1, fol. 38

 MUSIC, WESTERN EUROPEAN

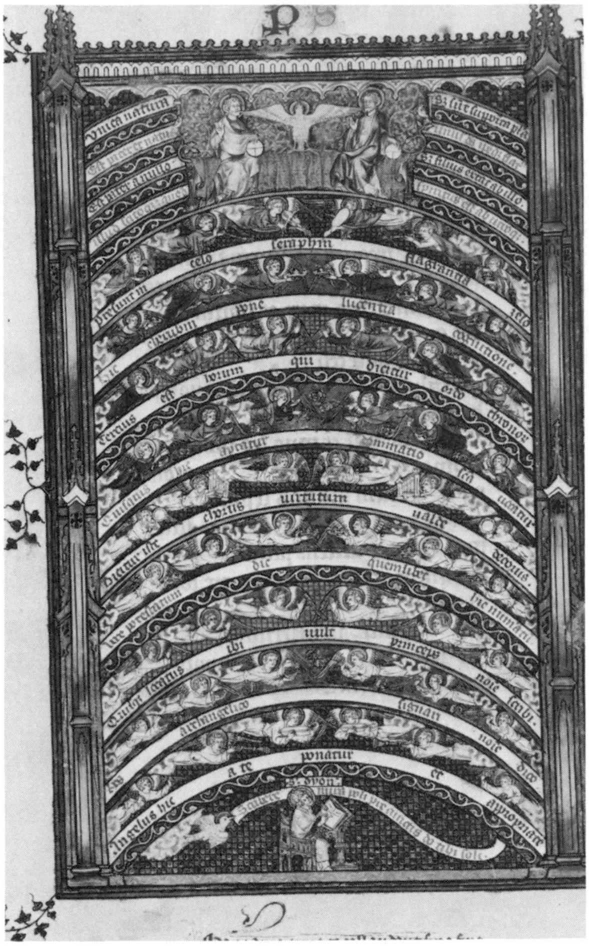

Fig. 10. Pseudo-Dionysius the Areopagite composing his *De hierarchia* with angels and the nine spheres, 1317. PARIS, BIBLIOTHÈQUE NATIONALE, MS FR. 2090, fol. 107v

notation was not really adequate to express it. There is much evidence, the interpretation of which is disputed, that some notes of early plainsong were measured, longer or shorter than other notes. But even the advocate of this point of view would rarely maintain that a regular scheme of measured values, a meter, played a role in plainsong, with the possible exception of the hymn, where the text itself was measured. However, in the twelfth and thirteenth centuries there evolved a system of rhythmic modes, probably abstracted from the meters of classical poetry. Increased precision of notation allowed these modes to stabilize around two values, the single, 1, and the double value, 2. Soon a third value, 3, was recognized but was said to be *ultra mensuram.* By some semantic juggling, dividing into half the value that was already the smallest, and by a simultaneous evolution of new note symbols, a third stratum was added to the long and the short in both theory and practice. The thirteenth century, then, had three values, *longa, brevis,* and *semibrevis.* After the firm establishment, in that century, of these values by the theorist Franco of Cologne, a new shorter note appeared, especially in the works and theory of Petrus de Cruce. This note was eventually called the *minima.* In the fourteenth century, yet more strata were recognized, and the rhythmic possibilities became much more flexible, evolving more or less into the system we now know. To work out the number of shortest notes in the longest in the fourteenth century involved several stages of multiplication: thus, there are two *semiminima* in a *minima,* four in a *semibrevis* (which had once been half the shortest note value), eight in a *brevis* (which had once been the shortest value), and so on. This development of stages of multiplication in the medieval rhythmic system has been associated with developing mathematical skills, especially those of the powers: square powers and cubic powers, analogous to plane and solid figures, were among the innovations of the thirteenth century. In the fourteenth century quadratic powers were explored, in particular by Nicole Oresme, who also wrote about music. Here we move beyond the solid figure into the realm of four and more dimensions and eventually into a consideration of the infinite. Mathematicians began to investigate

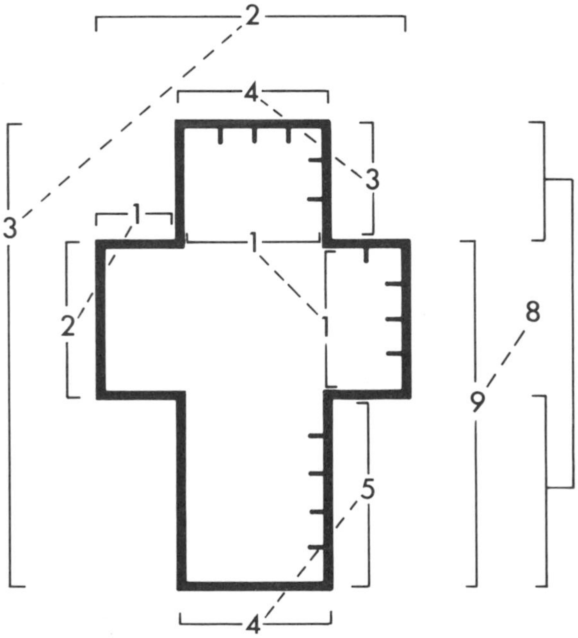

Fig. 11. Ground plan of a church, after Villard de Honnecourt (13th century). AUTHOR'S RENDERING

Example 1

a *b*

Example 2

what the earlier Middle Ages would have regarded as irrational numbers and proportions. The fourteenth-century musical theorist who laid the groundwork for the rhythmic system of modern times, Philippe de Vitry, found it necesary to go to a mathematician for proof that his rhythmic innovations were not ambiguous.

The development of irrational mathematics and the musical dependence on numbers beyond the simple digits made the numerical foundation of music impossible for any but the most learned of scholars to grasp. Thus, in the thirteenth century music obtained a simple rhythmic scheme in which the underlying proportions could be appreciated easily; the elements of which Augustine speaks so much, rhythm and meter, were part of the musical notes themselves. Music itself came to demonstrate *musica humana,* without the intervening medium of words.

But what of *musica mundana?* Could musical notes alone express philosophy? In the later Middle Ages, the thirteenth and fourteenth centuries in particular, they may have done so. One of the principal reasons for the development of rhythm was to make it possible for independent melodic parts to fit together accurately to form chords. Theoretical terminology describing chords uses a hierarchy, arranging them from the most perfectly consonant to the imperfectly dissonant. The octave and perfect fifth, with ratios of 2:1 and 3:2, were the most often used perfect intervals, since music, like everything else, must be as perfect as possible. Thus a common foundation for a piece of medieval music from the thirteenth century onward was the alternation of octave and fifth (Ex. 1). This may be ornamented with inessential dissonances (Ex. 1*b*). In the thirteenth and fourteenth centuries this principle was carried one stage further: as the human being had to aim at perfection in his earthly life, so had the musical phrase. It had to end with a perfect consonance; the penultimate interval, however, had also to be as nearly perfect as possible. In practice this meant that the penultimate interval had to be as nearly the same size as the last interval, within the vocabulary of the time. So before an octave there must be a major sixth, larger and more nearly an octave, rather than a minor sixth, and before the perfect fifth a major rather than a minor third (Ex. 2). This formula results in a most characteristic sound of medieval part-music (the double-leading-note formula), one which the philosopher-musician perhaps regarded as the musical symbol of perfection approached and

Example 3

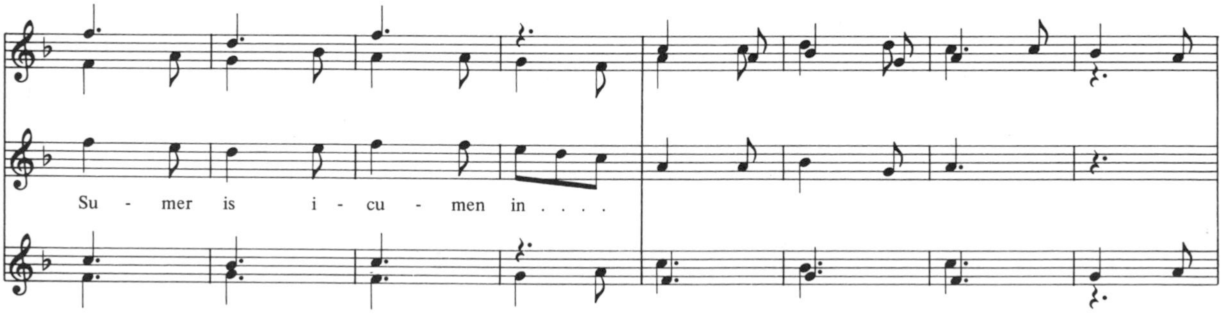

Example 4

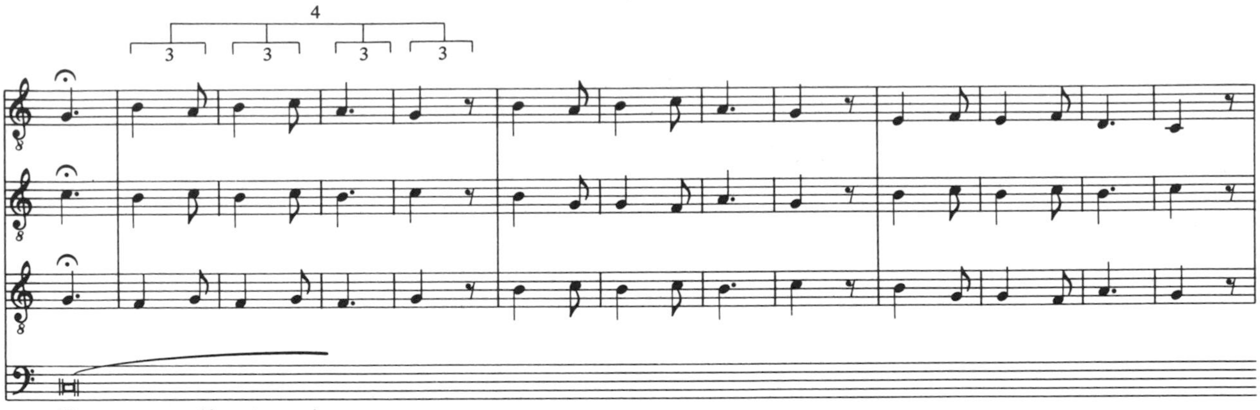
4
3
3
3
3
Vi - - - (derunt omnes)

achieved. Many medieval pieces are constructed of little other than strings of these formulas: Example 3 shows a famous medieval piece, *Sumer is icumen in,* which consists entirely of an ornamented alternation of third and fifth together with sixth and octave (in this piece the B-flat makes the thirds minor rather than major, even though they precede perfect fifths).

Moreover, in the thirteenth century there was constant musical expression of the union between divine and earthly. Consider a passage from a piece written early in the century by the composer Pérotin (Perotinus, Ex. 4). For the knowledgeable person, there are three units in each "bar," a long followed by a short, 2:1, and these "bars" are arranged in groups of four ending with a rest: the multiplication of the divine 3 by the earthly 4 constitutes in the mystical sense the infusion of matter with spirit. When phrases have four bars, each with three beats, the use of only the long and short note values results in melodic lines containing seven notes within the twelve beats. Phraseology of this kind appears in many pieces of the period, as in Example 5, and is only slightly disguised in Examples 3 and 4. The symbolic fusion of earthly with spiritual is superbly illustrated by the medieval motet, a form that flourished in the thirteenth century. The supporting voice, the foundation upon which the work was built, was almost always a section of a sacred plainsong and may have been recognizable as such. The upper parts, meanwhile, were conventionally borrowed from the tunes and the texts of secular chansons. A fine example is a motet which appears at the climax of a late-thirteenth-century version of Alan of Lille's *Anticlaudianus.* The newly created body is to receive the soul fetched from heaven. Concordia makes the union, and a motet is sung. It is based on part of the plainsong for Pentecost, commemorating the descent of the Holy Ghost, while the upper parts sing a melody originally set to a love-song text. This piece is twelfth (that is, 3×4) in the sequence of musical items.

Now, this kind of subtlety, as Grocheo said about 1300, was "not to be savored by the common people,

Example 5

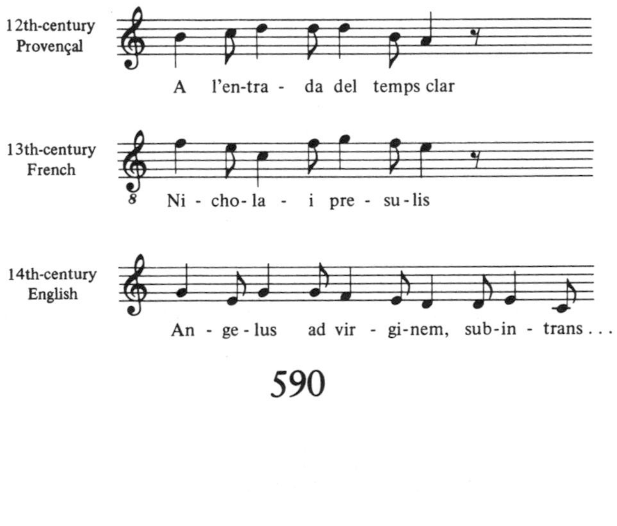
12th-century
Provençal
A l'en-tra - da del temps clar
13th-century
French
Ni - cho- la - i pre - su-lis
14th-century
English
An - ge - lus ad vir - gi-nem, sub-in - trans . . .

 MUSIC, WESTERN EUROPEAN

those who do not turn their minds to its refinements nor delight in it aurally, but by the literate and those who seek subtleties in the arts." Such a statement is perhaps the key to the way in which philosophical or intellectual *musica* was introduced into sounding music. In the thirteenth century, for example, the musical technique of cancrizans was first used, in which the melody is presented not in its true form but backward. Such a melody is unrecognizable by the ear, but may be appreciated intellectually by exercising reason to perceive the proportional relationship. Retrograde techniques such as this occur often in the fourteenth century: the rondeau *Ma fin est mon commencement* by Machaut is the best-known example.

Even more common in the fourteenth century was another technique, isorhythm, also inaudible but forming the structural basis for the music. The rhythms of the music were fixed by a long series of numbers that must have been predetermined; the series was repeated over and over again, so that the rhythms also recurred, but on a scale of time too long to be heard as repetitions. That the melody does not return at the same time makes the rhythmic structure even more difficult to perceive aurally. The opportunities in this technique for numerical symbolism on the part of the composer and conjectural mathematical analysis on the part of the modern researcher are numerous indeed. The latter ought to be accepted circumspectly.

So by means of simple proportional rhythms, simply recognizable perfect harmonies, and intellectual manipulations of form, music incorporated philosophy and number, *musica mundana* and *musica humana.* The *auctoritas* for music could now reside in the notes themselves. But as the fourteenth century progressed these features passed beyond the comprehension of the ordinary person, even when trained in music. The introduction of new intervals, especially thirds and sixths, and dissonances in particular, and the practice of writing a maze of irrational rhythmic proportions—a fad that mushroomed in the late fourteenth century—removed the metaphysical foundation and its realization far from the grasp of most listeners. The medieval premise that music was a philosophical discipline of the mind unrelated to sound would henceforth meet with incomprehension. With the disappearance of this overall conception of music, there faded in importance a host of other features: its connection with medicine, with magic, with moral behavior, and, perhaps most important, its primacy in education.

NEW CONCEPTION OF MUSIC

To replace the allegory and symbol, composers henceforth relied on realism, such as the accurate declamation of text, or the portrayal of birdsong, as in some fourteenth-century French songs, or hunting cries, as in the trecento caccia. Much later, there would be visual imitation in the notation of waves, of crosses, or crowns, and, finally, the visual representation of the whole narrative in opera. These developments were certainly an enrichment of the senses; at the same time the role of reason diminished.

From a philosophical discipline (with an aural realization consisting mostly of functional church music whose authority lay in the text or symbol), music changed into an entertaining and realistic art for the performer and listener. Such a view, of course, takes into account only the music for the educated person, ignoring popular music played and enjoyed by the *vulgari.* Such music must have existed, but it has not survived, and we can say nothing about it. The Middle Ages altered the pagan belief that music, or at least its numerical representation, ordered all things. The new world order, which subordinated all to the church, forced the earlier one into second place. Deprived of a set of principles by which coherence and unification might be achieved, each discipline became free to find its own raison d'être. Many remained faithful to *musica* for a considerable time: logic, grammar, the design of architecture, beauty itself. The separation of music from text and gesture allowed poetry to evolve new principles, some of which were for a time more clearly based on the numerical principles of *musica* than before. But the increasing complexity of thought and structure soon made these principles difficult to perceive and to apply, and new ways were sought to gain and keep the perceiver's attention. Eventually, the arts became things of the world, a trend most true of music itself; free to develop independently, it became an art rather than a discipline. The attempt to strengthen the waning discipline by introducing harmonic perfection and numerical structure in the form of part-music and rhythm allowed merely human devices such as imitation, clever rhythmic tricks, and the seduction of sound itself to take over. Thus, music lost its position as mistress, and became servant to wordly things.

While still a servant of the church, however, music developed—and new styles were evolved—by means of accretions to plainsong in a process analogous to exegesis. The universal Christian need to

MUSIC, WESTERN EUROPEAN

make the Old Testament orthodox by explicating with symbolism and allegory has a musical analogue; traditional chants are expanded with additional musical phrases, sometimes without words, at other time by phrases in which words and music are added simultaneously. The addition of text alone to textless music was another aspect of such a procedure. All such additions, called tropes, could serve as introductions, interpolations, or extensions. Troping with new music, presumably in a contemporary style, was the first way a Western musician could be original and express personal feelings.

Troping by prefacing or extending traditional chants can be more narrowly equated with exegetical extension of text horizontally into the margin. Interlinear exegesis can be likened to the vertical extension of a musical line by the addition of other lines above or below it. In this case, the relationship between the lines is clearer than in purely melodic troping. One line will often adopt the basic melody of the other, but will vary it. In this case, the "subject matter" of the two melodies is parallel, but the elaboration is different. Such a technique, fundamentally an Eastern method of organizing music, is called heterophony. Parallel melodic movement between the parts, in one form or another, underlies much medieval part-music. By the thirteenth century, the parallelism is often skillfully hidden by such means as crossing the parts, or momentarily exchanging their material, so that individual lines no longer seem parallel, while the whole texture remains so. In the fourteenth century came the first strictures against parallelism, and parts that move in contrary motion were advocated. Nevertheless, trecento Italian music, so modern in many ways, was often explicitly parallel; however, the parallelism had shifted from the emptier sounding perfect intervals to the sweeter thirds and sixths.

MUSICAL PERFORMANCE

Methods of performance must have changed. In this area, however, we can make only educated guesses based on circumstantial evidence, since the sound of the music has not survived. The earliest music of which we have any record was plainsong. Inherited from the Jews and essentially oriental in nature, early chant concerned itself not so much with the single, discrete, fixed pitch, but rather with a pitch made into a group of notes by inflections of the voice, by vocal effects such as vibrato or by sliding from note to note, or by minute changes in the intonation or tone color. Such ornamentations are still characteristic of Eastern singing. The single pitch was treated as a formula, a movement of the voice around the pitch, and may have been traditional or extemporized. Such ornamentations can hardly be written down, and it is probable that many of the obscure signs of early musical notations were attempts to realize them and to fix them in unambiguous notation. In the process of writing such ornaments down, specific pitches and, later, specific rhythms may have been assigned, so that the single ornamented pitch perhaps became a real musical formula of expressible pitches. We now pass to documentable phenomena. Once the fixing of formulas had occurred, say by the tenth or eleventh century, it became possible to compose new chants, and even new pieces of part-music, simply by reorganizing known formulas. This process, called centonization, was a traditional method of providing music for the many new feasts introduced in the later Middle Ages. Analogous procedures occur in Byzantine liturgical music and literature, which often strongly influenced Western developments. The recognition of the formula as the basis of musical composition played a large part in the establishment of the melodic modes. Specific formulas were associated with certain modes, even with certain positions within the chant as introductory, terminating, or reciting motives.

The gradual fixing of formulas led, along with developments in notation, to the recognition of individual pitches; in turn, the concept of the formula as an indivisible unit was lost. The single pitch as the compositional unit gained in importance. The presence of an early oral-formulaic tradition perhaps accounts for the widespread manuscript variants of the same piece of music, such as is found in plainsong (where geographical and chronological variants have been little explored) and in thirteenth-century secular song, where the variants have been more thoroughly investigated.

The change from a formulaic kind of music to one based on discrete pitches is linked also to a change in the attitude toward composition. Formulaic music relied more on a process of re-creation by centonization, or adaptation, and composers had little opportunity to express personal feelings. Tropes, using newer chant formulas and newly composed rather than scriptural texts, were a genre that allowed for personal expression. They began to flourish in the ninth century, continuing the effusive literature of the eighth-century Gallican liturgy. In-

MUSIC, WESTERN EUROPEAN

creasing originality in melodic parts also occurred, as part-music gradually became more complex. In the ninth century, all parts were closely related to the plainsong that they troped, by either strict parallelism or heterophony. By the eleventh and twelfth centuries added parts were almost totally independent of the accompanying plainsong in some styles. Although the thirteenth-century motet can be regarded as parallel in the hidden sense already described, the increasing independence of the parts from the plainsong foundation is easy to observe. By the fourteenth century it was possible to write part-music, even to sacred texts, with no reference to the chant. Futhermore, from the mid thirteenth century, the composition of plainsong and sacred part-music seems to wane in favor first of secular songs, such as those of the troubadours and trouvères, and then of secular part-music by fourteenth-century composers such as Machaut and Landini. Some would draw a social analogy to the splitting of the unified Christian world into the national divisions of the fourteenth century and, later, into the individual units of humanism.

Finally, a trend that encompasses many of the others is that of moving from ambiguity to certainty. From an ambiguously mystical and symbolic medium in which texts were necessary to justify its use in church, music changed to one which could justify itself by realism and other means. The trend is most obvious in the development of notation. From a largely mnemonic device giving only vague changes of direction, notation of pitches began to use a relative heighting of notational symbols, then a single stave-line that specified at least one pitch exactly, and finally the stave as we know it nowadays, on which all pitches are explicit. Rhythmic elements of the notation evolved in much the same way, from a rhythm determined either by the texts or from diacritic signs attached to the notes (or not determined at all) to a quite precise system of values derived solely from the shape of the notes. Music theorists too, moved from the philosophical to the practical, and eventually began to write about compositional devices or, occasionally, actual methods of performance. By the end of the Middle Ages the first hints emerge about specific instrumentation for certain pieces, a matter about which there is almost no earlier evidence.

In summary, through the Middle Ages music evolved into what we know presently as music, but in the process it changed, as the very word itself changes, from the *mundana* to the mundane.

CHRONOLOGY

ca. 500

- Boethius establishes the position of music in the liberal arts.

700–900

- First development of notation, largely mnemonic rather than precise.

800–900

- Flourishing composition of monophonic tropes and sequences, normally with prose texts.
- Extensive Byzantine influence.
- First theoretical descriptions of part-music, mostly setting trope texts, and in which the voices move largely in parallel motion.
- Codification of melodic modes.

ca. 1000

- Guido of Arezzo establishes the stave, with accurate specification of pitch.
- Continued composition of tropes and sequences with prose texts.
- First large extant source of practical part-music, setting tropes and still basically parallel (the Winchester Troper).

ca. 1100

- Aquitanian school composition of nonliturgical sacred verse and monophonic music, and some part music.
- Beginnings of a distinction between a rhapsodic style of part-music, organum, and a note-against-note style of discant.

1150–1200

- Beginnings of a more precise system of rhythmic notation (the rhythmic modes).
- Large-scale production of secular song in Provence (the troubadours).
- Climax of the composition of sequences and a turn toward new forms of plainsong composition in the form of rhymed and metrical Office chants, new chants for the Ordinary of the Mass.
- Important influx of instruments, mostly from Islam.

MUSIC, WESTERN EUROPEAN

ca. 1170

- School of Notre Dame: composition of liturgical part-music for the church year, by Leoninus, writing two-part music, emphasizing organal style.

ca. 1200

- Second stage of Notre Dame School: Perotinus composes liturgical works for three and four voices.
- Composition of serious, often topical songs called conductus, monophonic or polyphonic.
- Development of the rhythmic modes, and increased emphasis on discant style.

1220–1300

- Rise of the motet, basically a polytextual quodlibet using part of plainsong for the foundation, with secular motives in the upper parts.
- Rise of northern French secular song (the trouvères).
- Further development of rhythm with the introduction of several different note-values (Franco of Cologne), extended by Petrus de Cruce.
- First extant instrumental music (dances).
- Spiritual monophonic song in Italy *(laude),* Spain *(cantigas),* and Germany *(geisslerlieder)* and some German secular song *(minnesong).*
- Lowest voice, based on plainsong, remains the foundation for part-music.

1300–1400

- Development of the isorhythmic motet.
- Rapid development of national styles in Italy, France, and England.
- Frequent naming of composers (*e.g.,* Machaut, Landini).
- Rise of secular part-music, and predominance of secular music in general, especially in Italy, significantly in France, but not in England: in secular music the top voice is the most important, and there is no plainsong.
- Occasional settings of the Ordinary of the Mass in part-music, the best-known by Machaut.
- Contrary motion in part-music is more favored than parallel.
- Development of rhythm, especially duple rhythms, and complex proportional relations between note-values and meters.
- Beginnings of realistic program music, especially in Italy.

BIBLIOGRAPHY

Andrew Hughes, *Medieval Music* (1974, repr. 1980), is a comprehensive, annotated bibliography of all topics connected with medieval music. It contains a detailed index. Other studies by Hughes include "The *Ludus super anticlaudianum* of Adam de la Bassée," in *Journal of the American Musicological Society,* **23** (1970), and *Style and Symbol: Medieval Music, 900–1453* (1986).

Richard Hoppin, *Medieval Music* (1978), and *Anthology of Medieval Music* (1978). The former is a detailed history of medieval music; the anthology provides examples for the text. W. Thomas Marrocco and Nicholas Sandon, eds., *Medieval Music* (1977), is a better anthology.

Other works on the subject include Edgar de Bruyne, *Études d'esthétique médiévale,* 3 vols. (1946); Manfred F. Bukofzer, "Speculative Thinking in Mediaeval Music," in *Speculum,* **17** (1942); David Chamberlain, "*Anticlaudianus,* III 412–445, 'Boethius' *De musica,*" in *Manuscripta,* **13** (1969), "The Music of the Spheres and the Parlement of Foules," in *Chaucer Review,* **5** (1970), "Philosophy of Music in the *Consolatio* of Boethius," in *Speculum,* **45** (1970), and "Wolbero of Cologne (*d.* 1167): A Zenith of Musical Imagery," in *Mediaeval Studies,* **33** (1971); Solange Corbin, "*Musica* spéculative et *cantus* pratique," in *Cahiers de civilisation médiévale,* **5** (1962); Madeleine Pelner Cosman, "Machaut's Medical Musical World," in Madeleine Pelner Cosman and Bruce Chandler, eds., *Machaut's World: Science and Art in the Fourteenth Century* (1978); Charles De Tolnay, "Music of the Universe," in *Journal of the Walters Art Gallery,* **6** (1943); Heinrich Eggebrecht, "Ars Musica: Musikanschauung des Mittelalters und Ihre Nachwirkungen," in *Die Sammlung,* **12** (1957); Leonard Ellinwood, "Ars Musica," in *Speculum,* **20** (1945); Reinhold Hammerstein, *Die Musik der Engel* (1962); Jacques Handschin, "Gesungene Apologetik," in Hans Oesch, ed., *Gedenkschrift Jacques Handschin* (1957); A. T. Hatto, "On Beauty of Numbers in Wolfram's Dawn Songs," in *Modern Language Review,* **45** (1950); John Hollander, *The Untuning of the Sky* (1961, repr. 1970); Vincent F. Hopper, *Medieval Number Symbolism* (1938); Heinrich Hüschen, "Antike Einflüsse in der mittelalterlichen Musikanschauung," in *Miscellanea mediaevalia,* **1** (1962); H. M. Klinkenberg, "Der Verfall des Quadriviums im frühen Mittelalten," in Josef Koch, ed., *Artes liberales* (1959); Assen D. Kresteff, "Musica Disciplina and Musica Sonora," in *Journal of Research in Music Education,* **10** (1962); I. S. Laurie, "Deschamps and the Lyric as Natural Music," in *Modern Language Review,* **59** (1964); Edward E. Lowinsky, "Music in the Culture of the Renaissance," in *Journal of the History of Ideas,* **15** (1954); Kathi Meyer-Baer, *Music of the Spheres and the Dance of Death* (1970); Leo Spitzer, *Classical and Christian Ideas of World Harmony* (1963); Martin Vogel, *Die Zahl Sieben in der spek-*

ulativen Musiktheorie (1955); William G. Waite, "Johannes de Garlandia: Poet and Musician," in *Speculum,* **35** (1960); Charles W. Warren, "Brunelleschi's Dome and Dufay's Motet," in *Musical Quarterly,* **59** (1973); E. Werner, "The Mathematical Foundation of Philippe de Vitry's *Ars Nova,*" in *Journal of the American Musicological Society,* **9**; (1956); Rudolf Zitzmann, "Wort und Weise im Ordo des Mittelalters," in *Deutsche Vierteljahrsschrift für Literaturwissenschaft und Geistesgeschichte,* **21** (1943); V. Zoubov, "Nicole Oresme et la musique," in *Mediaeval and Renaissance Studies* (London) **5** (1961).

ANDREW HUGHES

[See also **Adam de la Bassée; Ambrosian Chant; Ars Antiqua; Ars Nova; Ars Subtilior; Cantor; Consonance/Dissonance; Franco of Cologne; Gregorian Chant; Guido of Arezzo; Harmony; Hocket; Hymns, Latin; Isorhythm; Jacques de Liège; Johannes de Grocheo; John of Garland; Landini, Francesco; Lauda; Leoninus; Ma Fin Est Mon Commencement; Machaut, Guillaume de; Mass Cycles, Plainsong; Minnesingers; Motet; Music, Islamic Influence of the West; Music, Oral Tradition in; Music, Popular; Music in Education ; Music in Medieval Society; Musical Notation; Musical Treatises; Notre Dame School; Oresme, Nicole; Perotinus; Petrus de Cruce; Philippe de Vitry; Quadrivium; Regino of Prüm; Remigius of Auxerre; Tropes; Troubadour, Trouvère, Trovador; Walther von der Vogelweide.**]

MUSIC IN MEDIEVAL SOCIETY. Music reflected the division of rank and function in medieval society, and its principal forms of expression, as well as performance practices, were all a function of the three broad social classes, or estates.

Music formed an integral part of the never-ending series of processions, banquets, dances, tournaments, hunts, and festivities at court. Performers were grouped among the varlets, or servants of various callings, distributed throughout the numerous household departments. While the less well-to-do might hire one or two minstrels or rely primarily upon itinerant performers, the larger fiefs and noble courts retained their own band of musicians, who followed their masters wherever they went, playing or singing for all occasions, both public and private. Instrumentalists were grouped not according to what they played (strings, woodwind, brass, percussion) but rather into loud and soft consorts based upon the sonorities of their instruments. The vocalists were usually drawn from members of the court chapel. Nobles vied with one another to recruit the best musicians and have the most renowned performers in their service, often lending or borrowing them from court to court.

Processions were perhaps the best examples of conspicuous and ostentatious displays of power, wealth, and prestige. The larger the entourage, the more musicians there were, the greater the impression of rank. Taking their cue from the practices of Eastern potentates as observed by the crusaders, the feudal nobility employed the exclusive combination of trumpets and drums, and later the shawm, to announce every departure, journey, and entry. Rulers marched as vicars of Christ, with a liturgy of welcome awaiting them, sung by the local choir.

The banquet and tournament were the two most typical features of aristocratic life. Taking place in the great hall, amidst colorful dress, tables laden with countless dishes, flickering torches, and music, these feasts offered a fusion of all the arts and senses. Trumpet fanfares announced the washing up and presentation of each course. During the meal, the loud instruments predominated over the din of eating. The soft instruments and vocalists entertained between the courses and at the end of the banquet as the company retired to digest the heavy food.

Beginning as exercises for war, the tournament and joust, with their dramatic element of strife, evolved gradually into chivalric entertainments on a grand scale, combining prowess in arms, feudal ceremony and etiquette, prize-giving, and often scenery, music, and dancing. Loud percussive instruments played during processions to the lists, before various procedural announcements, at key points in the actual contest, and whenever a point was scored.

Dancing was part of the very core of aristocratic life. With its emphasis upon rule and measure, formal manners, and often exaggerated ceremonial, it typified the feudal culture. There were two main forms: slow and stately stepped dances and more lively and varied dances with hops or skips. The musical instruments accompanying these dances were diverse, although their selection was far from haphazard. Generally, for the former category, soft instruments were used, especially the pipe and tabor. Loud instruments, such as trumpets and shawms, dominated the latter type. These were usually played on a balcony or temporary platform above the dancers. The dancers had to memorize the varying steps, keep time with the music, perform with suppleness and grace, and gauge their movements according to the space provided. Elaborate spectacle dances, such as the *ballo* and *moresca,* became quasi-dramatic performances, with symbolic or narrative qualities

MUSIC IN MEDIEVAL SOCIETY

and often special costumes or effects. They were ordinarily danced by professionals or well-rehearsed members of the court.

Aristocratic music making was another feature of court life. The harp, lute, and portative organ were common accoutrements for both sexes, and were used as solo instruments or to accompany the voice. During the summer especially, couples promenaded in their gardens or sat by the fountain, serenading themselves with music.

The focal-point of the system of religious beliefs and practices was the liturgy; and it was the Mass that constituted the most important of the sacraments. The colorful ceremony, along with its music, represented "a symphony angelic rather than human," and its brightness in both a visual and aural sense was believed to produce a similar light in the mind of the worshiper, illuminating him spiritually and carrying him closer to God.

In monastic communities, the eight daily services for the canonical hours, or Divine Office, was the focal point. Divided into services approximately every three hours, they consisted invariably of antiphons, responses, psalms (the nucleus of the observances), hymns, and chants. In churches serving the worldly community, the main service was the Mass. Its principal musical portions consisted of the five sections of the Ordinary (Kyrie, Gloria, Credo, Sanctus, and Agnus Dei) sung every day, and the Proper (Introit, Gradual, Alleluia, Offertory, and Communion), which varied daily according to the church calendar. The large body of chant was sung by a choir under the direction of a leader who led his group with minute finger gestures. While the Proper had been treated in polyphonic, or mixed-voice, fashion since the twelfth century, it was only some two centuries later that the widespread practice developed of composing polyphonic settings for the more sacrosanct Ordinary. As something unique, this new part-music was used ceremonially to lend distinction to the high points of the liturgical service on special holidays. Even in major cathedrals, one or two solo singers usually sufficed for these performances. In masses for simple feasts on ordinary Sundays, polyphony was normally permitted in the Kyrie, Gloria, Sanctus, and Agnus Dei. The church had a long-standing negative attitude toward instruments, and it was the organ alone which slowly gained qualified admission to the liturgical service. Like polyphony, it was at first used only sparingly and ceremonially.

Solemn religious processions, like the liturgy, were symbolic acts, representing the heavenly procession to the celestial Jerusalem. Organized and led by the clergy, they took place on holidays such as Palm Sunday, Corpus Christi, and Easter. Choristers from one or more of the local churches and musicians recruited for the occasion marched in a well-planned parade, singing and playing instruments as they went.

The mystery play also represented an effective instruction in the Christian faith. These performances, often lasting several days, were staged under the aegis of the municipal guilds and confraternities but were supervised by the clergy, who guided the entire proceedings and often supplied the scripts. The participating musicians came from the metropolis and its vicinity, not only to march in procession to and from the stage but to perform at specified dramatic points and scene breaks in the play as well as to hide behind actor-angels carrying their own musical instruments. The written instructions in these plays were often quite specific in calling for vocal or instrumental music. Only soft-sounding portative organs, fiddles, harps, psalteries, or lutes were played around the setting of inner heaven, for example. The organ, often performing three parts, symbolized God and accompanied celestial figures. Stringed instruments were associated with Christ. Trumpets were employed for solemn or regal entries, coronations, and other scenes of feudal panoply. Hell was represented by the cacophony of metal pipes, barrels filled with stones, and sometimes actual gunshots. The plays invariably ended with the singing of the Te Deum, sometimes accompanied by the organ and carillon or small bells.

By the thirteenth century fortified towns flourished throughout Europe as strongholds of a new middle-class culture that existed essentially outside the traditional framework of feudalism. Serving on the watch was a regular civic duty, and musicians came to be installed in this capacity on the towers, in the belfries, and atop the city gates. At night, when visible signals were useless, horn players were able to rouse the guard by audible means. Soon, this nocturnal activity became more ceremonial, extending into the daylight hours in the guise of fanfares for stipulated occasions. The importance of music in connection with the ceremonies of government and the civic muster wedded the watch to the formation of the town band, suggesting a ready corps of musicians capable quite literally of doubling in brass. It remained for the processional instrumentalist to combine the duties of watchman with that of civic music making, sounding alarms, announcing the time of day, playing fanfares for the crier or heralds, performing at various official functions, and above all playing contemporary pieces of music from atop their high posts or on the balconies of municipal buildings.

Soon, musicians of all sorts flocked to these thriving urban centers seeking steady employment in the town band. The financial accounts were often quite precise in listing the payments to these performers as well as the instruments used. In general, trumpets, sackbuts, cornetts, and shawms predominated, owing to the outdoor nature of most of the concertizing. The growing primacy of the guilds encouraged musical performances at their meetings and annual feasts as well as for sponsored pageants and municipal shows of welcome for visiting dignitaries. The townsfolk themselves often danced spontaneously in the streets to the accompaniment of itinerant performers, who also frequented taverns in search of appreciative audiences and welcome tips.

Next to nothing is known about the music of peasants, who constituted about 90 percent of the population. They had few periods of respite between their heavy labor. Sunday church services, religious holidays, and the various folk festivals of long standing provided their sole source of relaxation and enjoyment. A half-decent meal and perhaps some communal song and dance was about all they could expect. These performances were as uninhibited as they were crude, accompanied perhaps by a wandering minstrel with his bagpipes, for example, who provided the villager and peasant with their only source of news and entertainment.

BIBLIOGRAPHY

Higini Anglès, "Hispanic Musical Culture from the 6th to the 14th Century," in *Musical Quarterly,* **26** (1940); Friedrich Behn, *Musikleben in Altertum und frühen Mittelalter* (1954); Edmund A. Bowles, "Musical Instruments at the Medieval Banquet," in *Revue belge de musicologie,* **12** (1958), "The Role of Musical Instruments in Medieval Sacred Drama," in *Musical Quarterly,* **45** (1959), "Musical Instruments in Civic Processions During the Middle Ages," in *Acta musicologica,* **33** (1961), "Tower Musicians in the Middle Ages," in *Brass Quarterly,* **5** (1962), "Musical Instruments in the Medieval Corpus Christi Procession," in *Journal of the American Musicological Society,* **17** (1964), *Musikleben im 15. Jahrhundert* (1977), and *The Performance of Music in the Late Middle Ages* (1983); Nanie Bridgman, *La vie musicale au quattrocento et jusqu'à la naissance du madrigal (1400–1530)* (1964); A. Louis Burkhalter (Romain Goldron), *Byzantine and Medieval Music* (1968), and *Minstrels and Masters* (1968); JoAnna Dutka, *Music in the English Mystery Plays* (1980); Otto Gombosi, "About Dance and Dance Music in the Late Middle Ages," in *Musical Quarterly,* **27** (1941); Walter Salmen, *Der fahrende Musiker im europäischen Mittelalter* (1960); John Stevens, "Music in Mediaeval Drama," *Proceedings of the Royal Musical Association,* **84** (1957/1958); Robert Wangermée, *Flemish Music and Society in the Fifteenth and Sixteenth Centuries,* Robert E. Wolf, trans. (1968).

EDMUND A. BOWLES

[See also **Canonical Hours; Dance; Divine Office; Feasts and Festivals; Feudalism; Games and Pastimes; Hunting and Fowling; Liturgy; Mass, Liturgy of the; Minstrels; Mystery Plays; Processions; Troubadour, Trouvère, Trovador.**]

MUSICA FICTA (Latin: feigned music; also called *musica falsa* or false music), a term that describes the use of notes foreign to the normally accepted set of pitches.

The point of departure for the concept of *musica ficta* is the ordering of the twenty-two pitches of the medieval gamut into seven overlapping hexachords. Each hexachord has a unique semitone step between its third and fourth pitches, supporting a consistent scheme, designed for learning and solmization, whose basic principle is the singling out of the semitone, expressed by the syllables mi and fa, in the context of the syllables applied to the hexachord as a whole: ut, re, mi, fa, sol, la. Medieval representations of the gamut show that the two higher Bs could be either flat (represented as fa) or natural (represented by mi), while the lowest octave made use of the natural note only. This repertory of pitches sufficed for Gregorian melodies, since every "dissonant" interval, specifically tritones and diminished fifths, could be corrected by the use of B flat. Melodic context determined B as flat or natural, without any need for graphic indication.

Moreover, because it was only associated with the syllable fa in the hexachord system, the flat sign gradually came to stand for that syllable wherever it occurred. In order to raise the syllable fa, a square sign was used, which later developed into the modern natural sign. Originally applied to the note B-mi, it was also eventually added to other notes. Many music theorists state quite clearly that fa and mi are always represented by the flat and natural signs respectively. Thus the pitches B flat, C, and F, above semitones, may be preceded by the sign for fa, while the pitches B natural, A, and E, below semitones, may be preceded by the sign for mi. From this it follows that the medieval inflection signs do not unconditionally exhibit their present-day quality of lowering or raising a note; only with respect to the pitch B does this obtain.

Although the twenty-two tones of the hexachord system were soon no longer sufficient for polyphonic music, they maintained their character as the only permissible, virtually the only legitimate, pitches. In the thirteenth century they acquired the name *musica recta* (regular music) or *musica vera* (true music). Many music theorists explain that only *musica recta* ought to be treated as acceptable: "Nullum regulare debeat accipere falsum sed potius verum" [Nothing regular ought to accept the false, but only the true] (Philippe de Vitry, *Ars nova*).

In order to compose pure consonances above or below a given voice, it was necessary to have a repertory of tones that lay beyond the limits of *musica recta* and that, according to the philosophical assumptions of the time, could only be imaginary or "feigned." Each feigned note forms the upper or lower half of any semitone apart from the three semitones occurring naturally within *musica recta*. According to Ugolino of Orvieto, *musica ficta* means the placement of a syllable where it does not exist in *musica recta*.

There were attempts, especially in the fourteenth and fifteenth centuries, to develop transposed systems paralleling the accepted one, so as to legitimize the "false" tones. Theinred of Dover (twelfth century) was perhaps the first to conceive this sort of expansion; later versions occur in the treatise of Petrus Frater dictus Palma ociosa (1336) and in other writings of the fourteenth century. The most complete system, transmitted by one of the better-known music theorists before the end of the fifteenth century, occurs in Ugolino's *Declaratio musice discipline* (*ca.* 1430). Although his observations are not free of obscurities and contradictions, it is clear that Ugolino proposed two transposed systems: one transposed to a fifth below, and a second to two fifths below the normal gamut. It is probable that these transposed systems, which contain many of the tones demanded by *musica ficta,* are, as in modern notation, indicated respectively by the placement at the beginning of the staff of a single B flat and by flats on B and E. It is important to maintain that, just as the pitch B flat is legitimate and acceptable in the system of *musica recta,* even without a notational symbol, so also does the pitch E flat become available when a signature of B flat is present, although the flattening of E might not be notated. Medieval signatures therefore always indicate that the first flat beyond the last flat in the signature is also permissible, a quality of signatures maintained over several centuries. (For more involved consequences of the meaning of signatures and accidentals, see Andrew Hughes, *Manuscript Accidentals.*)

One must generally accept that the insertion of accidentals occurred extempore and that the performer was therefore responsible for it. But since it is only the shortage of requisite signs that points to this conclusion, and because one can rarely say with certainty that the surviving manuscripts actually served as performance texts, some questioning of this conclusion must be permitted. Moreover, the practice of extemporizing by several musicians at the same time must have been controlled through an agreement arrived at during rehearsal, where a rehearsal director probably had the final say. In any case, one can probably assume that the performing musician, who had only his own part before him, inserted the necessary accidentals to begin with. But this does not mean that they were added for reasons of melodic voice-leading, since only the elimination of such intervals as the tritone offered the medieval singer a reason for altering the melodic movement. If the singer added accidentals, he did so for reasons of harmony; during the process of reading with the other parts he initially became aware, post facto, of any difficulties requiring adjustment. Because of his familiarity with the style, the singer would then have quickly assessed a work's harmonic direction and thus rendered any later emendation unnecessary. It was no doubt possible for experienced singers to have a general knowledge of the rules of harmonic progression, which could then automatically be adapted to a given situation.

Some theorists, such as Ugolino and Prosdocimus de Beldemandis (early fifteenth century), present various rules and examples, almost always from the point of view of harmony. Most of the writers stress, however, that *musica ficta* should only be used where it is absolutely necessary. The editor of polyphonic music from the period must first analyze the accidentals and signs that are indicated in the manuscripts to determine which of them indicate a transposition of the system, and which tones belong, as a result, to *musica recta* and which to *musica ficta.* If an accidental does not point to a transposition of the

 MUSICA FICTA

system, it should on principle be dealt with as if it governs only the note before which it stands. When an additional accidental is necessary, then it should be if possible within *musica recta.* Within *musica ficta,* sharps should be given preference to flats. Furthermore, it is to be observed that octaves, fourths, and fifths must be pure, at least when they appear in structurally significant places or are sustained. At cadences, thirds should be minor before unisons, and both thirds and sixths should be major before fifths and octaves respectively. The "double leading note" cadence resolves thus  , but  is preferable, since the flat in the signature extends the range of *musica recta* to include the E flat. In order for an editor to be able to undertake such harmonic alterations, a detailed understanding as well as a special sensitivity are necessary. The decision must be considered in the context of the cadence structures, the essential and unessential notes of the piece, and other, similar criteria.

Reasons for the insertion of accidentals based on melody appear to be subordinate to those based on harmony. The removal of a melodic tritone is not to be regarded as a strict requirement, since many tritones are deliberately used in certain contexts, especially at cadence points. Still less do indirect tritones need to be avoided. A note serving as an upper neighbor to the prevailing hexachord is often lowered, but even this practice is not a rule per se. The rhyme "una nota supra la semper est canendum fa" (apparently stating that the B above A sung la must always be sung fa, that is, flat) is not found until well after the medieval period, although there are indications that the procedure in question was applied much earlier.

The medieval expressions *causa necessitatis* (by reason of necessity) and *causa pulchritudinis* (by reason of beauty) are unclear in their application to *musica ficta.* Necessity must refer to the perfection of the harmonic consonances and almost certainly to the alteration of the intervals before such consonances, the third and sixth, as has already been said. It is far less certain that melodic intervals were altered out of "necessity," but more probably *causa pulchritudinis,* which implies no obligation. Through the use of unusual chromatic tones, *causa pulchritudinis* can be related to the text and to the highlighting of important words or, more likely, simply to the aesthetic sense of the work.

Special difficulties arise when pieces have more than two voices. Although considerations of harmony are paramount and *musica recta* accidentals are preferred to those of *musica ficta,* many situations remain ambiguous. In such cases the medieval methods of composition can be helpful to the editor: the voices were usually composed in pairs with the tenor, and each pair can be considered on its own. When the tenor has a predetermined melody such as a plainsong, alterations to the added part will normally be preferred. When it can be established that a particular voice was the last to be composed, as is often the case with the contratenor in the fourteenth and fifteenth centuries, this part should be adjusted to fit the chromatic alterations that have already been effected in the other voices. Even then much uncertainty remains, and it must be emphasized that, as with every improvisational technique, there is rarely a single correct solution.

The medieval methods described so far make up the historical background for later fifteenth- and sixteenth-century procedures, but they can be applied to the music of these centuries only with considerable modification, since there emerged during the fifteenth century numerous changes in style and compositional technique. The addition of a contratenor below the tenor and its subsequent division into two different vocal ranges above and below the tenor (bassus and altus) brought with it a preference for four-voice structures. Together with, and partly in response to, this development, there emerged new cadential formulas in which the leading note is not doubled:  

An upper voice and the tenor normally retain the progression from sixth to octave, so that the raising of the sixth can still appear. One of the parts now often moves to the third of the final chord, and there is some suggestion that, especially from the sixteenth century on, this should be a major third, at least in important cadences.

The change from cumulative and linear to chordal and harmonic composition makes it much more difficult to continue to deal with the voices in pairs. This is true especially of secular music, which is not based on a given melody. When a given melody is taken as a foundation, then that voice, taken with the bass or one of the upper voices, makes a good starting point, as in earlier music. Where, moreover, for reasons of melodic character or because of special indications such as *si placet,* certain parts may be recognized as having been added last or left to the discretion of the performer, these parts may on first analysis be left out of consideration. So far as necessary, changes may be made to eliminate "dissonant" melodic intervals, and, in the later music more than the earlier, one must probably place greater weight upon melodic "correctness" of this sort.

The old distinction between the notes of *musica recta* and *musica ficta* had probably largely disappeared by the sixteenth century, since the introduction of so many chromatic tones had made the medieval system of hexachords and solmization unusable. Many restrictions that apply to earlier music are no longer valid, and present-day musicology is still confronted with the task of working out guidelines for the addition of accidentals. Lowinsky's thesis, in *Secret Chromatic Art in the Netherlands Motet* (1946), seems to be a logical and useful extension of the medieval system. He suggests that local transpositions of musical phrases by exact segmental repetition, analogous to the transposition of the system described earlier, obligated the singers to sing chromatic pitches not actually stated in the notation.

Finally, in the sixteenth century, the judgment of the ears, rather than of philosophy, logic, and reason, was allowed as one method of deciding the suitability of accidentals: "Aures optimae interpretes habentur" [The ears are thought to be the best judges] (Stephanus Vanneus, *Recanetum de musica aurea,* 1531).

BIBLIOGRAPHY

Gaston Allaire, *The Theory of Hexachords, Solmization, and the Modal System* (1972); Willi Apel, "The Partial Signatures in the Sources up to 1450," in *Acta musicologica,* **10** and **11** (1938 and 1939), and *Accidentien und Tonalität in den Musikdenkmälern des 15. und 16. Jahrhunderts* (1937, repr. 1972); Margaret Bent, "Musica Recta and Musica Ficta," in *Musica disciplina,* **26** (1972); Suzanne Clercx, "Les accidents sous-entendus et la transcription en notation moderne," in *Les colloques de Wégimont,* **2** (1955), and *Johannes Ciconia: Un musicien liégeois et son temps,* I (1960), 101–106; Oliver Ellsworth, "The Origin of the Coniuncta: A Reappraisal," in *Journal of Music Theory,* **17** (1973), and (ed.), *The Berkeley Manuscript* (1984); Rudolf von Ficker, "Beiträge zur Chromatik des 14. bis 16. Jahrhunderts," in *Studien zur Musikwissenschaft,* **2** (1914); Lloyd Hibberd, "*Musica Ficta* and Instrumental Music c.1250–c.1350," in *Musical Quarterly,* **28** (1942); Richard Hoppin, "Partial Signatures and Musica Ficta in Some Early Fifteenth-century Sources," in *Journal of the American Musicological Society,* **6** (1953), and "Conflicting Signatures Reviewed," *ibid.,* **9** (1956); Andrew Hughes, "Ugolino: The Monochord and Musica Ficta," in *Musica disciplina,* **23** (1968), *Manuscript Accidentals* (1972), and with Margaret Bent, eds., *The Old Hall Manuscript,* I (1969), xviii–xxv; Martha Johnson, "A Study of Conflicting Key-Signatures in Francesco Landini's Music," in *Hamline Studies in Musicology,* **2** (1947); Edward Kottick, "Flats, Modality, and Musica Ficta in Some Early Renaissance Chansons," in *Journal of Music Theory,* **12** (1968); Edward Lowinsky, "The Function of Conflicting Signatures in Early Polyphonic Music," in *Musical Quarterly,* **31** (1945), and "Conflicting Views on Conflicting Signatures," in *Journal of the American Musicological Society,* **7** (1954); Gilbert Reaney, "Musica Ficta in the Works of Guillaume de Machaut," in *Les colloques de Wégimont,* **2** (1955), and "Accidentals in Early Fifteenth Century Music," in Jozef Robijns, ed., *Renaissance-Muziek 1400–1600: Donum natalicum René Bernard Lenaerts* (1969); Hans Tischler, "'Musica ficta' in the Thirteenth Century," in *Music and Letters,* **54** (1973).

ANDREW HUGHES
ARTHUR LEVINE

[See also **Ars Nova; Guido of Arezzo; Philippe de Vitry; Solmization.**]

MUSICAL INSTRUMENTS, EUROPEAN. The turmoil caused by the barbarian migrations completely annihilated not only the highly developed musical practices of classical antiquity but the instruments as well, most of which vanished along with the knowledge of their construction. Only the names remained, holdovers from an age when Latin reigned supreme. But lacking extant examples, in time these terms degenerated and their meanings became obscured. For example, "cithara" was generally used for all stringed instruments, and "tuba" came to mean any kind of trumpet rather than its specific Roman forerunner.

Thus, with few exceptions, the musical instruments of the early Middle Ages had no direct connection with their Greco-Roman antecedents, and Europe looked elsewhere for new prototypes. It was largely in Byzantium and the vast Muslim lands that these models were to be found. The Moors in particular, occupying parts of Spain, introduced many new instruments along with Arabian culture.

However, with virtually all intellectual and technological development taking place in monastic centers, there was little native progress in the realm of instrument building. The church actively discouraged the cultivation of anything associated with recent pagan culture and heathen worship, looking upon instruments with undisguised hostility. Unfortunately this led to an almost total silence concerning this subject on the part of monastic writers. One

MUSICAL INSTRUMENTS, EUROPEAN

exception was Bishop Venantius Fortunatus, who wrote in the sixth century that the Greeks played the cithara, the Romans the lyre, the barbarian Norsemen the harp, and the English the rote. Thus, there must have been some sort of instrumental use, however primitive.

The so-called Carolingian renaissance signaled a parallel rebirth in the fabrication and use of instruments, a fact reflected in both written sources and manuscript illuminations. For example, there is concrete evidence in the Utrecht Psalter (*ca.* 830)—its illustrations inspired by an older prototype executed some 300 years earlier—of stringed instruments, the horn, the organ (its construction misunderstood), bells, and the drum. In the ninth century, the German monk Otfrid von Weissenburg mentioned the organ, lyre, harp, rote, panpipes, and fiddle.

The period from about 1000 to 1300 in Europe was characterized by appropriations and influences from two main quarters: Spain and the Muslim East. At the court of King Alfonso X el Sabio of Castile and Léon, for example, a single-voiced vernacular song form known as the *cantiga* was cultivated. It was typified by the manuscripts of the *Cantigas de Santa María* (1250–1280), which contain over a thousand miniatures depicting both instruments and musical performances. They demonstrate the use of instruments with secular vocal music and show an astonishing variety of over seventy basic types and variants. This instrumental practice was transmitted northward by the troubadours, many of whom had close connections with the milieu of this learned and music-loving ruler. Indeed, the number of instruments in Europe increased many times over, as did their names, in an often bewildering number of synonyms, dialectic variants, and differences from language to language. Contemporary poems, especially, often present virtual laundry lists of instruments, documenting their many uses. For example, in his *Roman de Brut* (*ca.* 1155), Wace enumerates a dozen or so instruments and describes the social settings in which they were used.

The crusades, trade via Constantinople, and the Moorish occupation of Spain all provided contacts with the Near East. Instruments (mainly double reeds, brass, and percussion) were brought back to Europe by the military, merchants, and pilgrims alike, together with knowledge about performance techniques. Eyewitnesses were especially impressed by the pomp and splendor of the Saracen bands, with the braying, earsplitting sounds of their trumpets, nasal-voiced shawms, and pounding rhythms of the kettledrum.

The migratory nature of many of the performers of this period helped transmit this new instrumental culture throughout Europe. The jongleurs especially played a key role as propagators, particularly along the pilgrimage and trade routes and at the seasonal fairs, which attracted entertainers of all sorts. Together with the growing cadre of court minstrels and itinerant performers, they quickly acquired both proficiency on these new or improved instruments and expanded their repertory.

While this period could be characterized as an age of instrumental importation, the later Middle Ages was a period of adaptation and development. Like the process of natural selection, there finally evolved an *instrumentarium* that represented a balance between technological innovation and musical (or performance) requirements. The rich variety of these instruments is again reflected in many important literary works, such as Juan Ruiz's *El libro de buen amor* (*ca.* 1343) and Guillaume de Machaut's *La prise d'Alexandrie* (*ca.* 1367). Both Chaucer and Cervantes refer to instruments throughout their works. By the fifteenth century there was hardly a major writer who did not mention them, often in long lists encompassing the entire gamut of instruments (but without suggesting, however, that they were all played at once). Eberhart Cersne's *Minne regel* (1404) and the anonymous *Squyr of Lowe Degre* (*ca.* 1400) are two such examples.

Music became an indispensable element of both court life and the culture of cities. Instrumentalists were hired on a more or less permanent basis as household servants to perform at their master's bidding. The flourishing urban centers engaged players at first to sound the alarm (hence, "tower musicians") and accompany the watch on their appointed rounds, and later on to perform instrumental music from, typically, the balcony of the city hall at specified times of day. Suddenly the chronicles are full of detailed descriptions of the vital role these musicians played in the lives of their employers. Account records, too, are full of references to payments to performers and to the purchase of musical instruments as well.

Beginning in the fourteenth century, there was a flowering of secular music that could be performed in several ways: sung or played or, more often, a combination of both. Instruments played one or more parts, reinforced the vocal line, executed a composition completely without voices, alternated

1

2

3

4

5

6

7

8

9

10

11

12

MUSICAL INSTRUMENTS, EUROPEAN

with the singers, or merely provided introductions, interludes, and postludes. Dance music, too, provided still another vehicle for instrumental performances. Soon, these ensembles developed their own independent repertory based upon this musical literature. Starting around 1400, instrumental music was slowly emancipated from its vocal prototypes, appropriating chansons, dance tunes, and even sacred compositions. The increased technical demands of this music—more rhythmic complexity, faster tempos, chromaticisms, and extended melodic range—required better instruments. Some were improved or refined, while a whole new family developed utilizing a keyboard and various mechanisms to pluck or strike the strings.

The role of so-called minstrels' schools was very important as a transmitter of new and improved instruments as well as repertory. Usually held during Lent, when secular performances at court were curtailed or abandoned, they attracted performers from all over Europe, who bought and exchanged instruments and learned new pieces from each other (most if not all of them could not read music).

The greatest innovation was in the grouping of these instruments by their sonorities into two categories, loud and soft, rather than into families based upon their acoustical characteristics: those with high volume and penetrating tone color (*haut*) and those the sound of which was low and gentle by comparison (*bas*). These two groups seldom played together. For ceremonial, festive performances, especially outdoors, both at court and in the cities, an *alta* ensemble of wind instruments was preferred, while for the more intimate indoor affairs, such as accompanying singers, a combination of soft instruments was used. John Lydgate enumerated them in his *Reson and Sensuallyte* (*ca.* 1408): "Eke Instrumentys high and lowe / Wel mo than I koude know, / That I suppose, there is no man / That aryght reherse kan / The melodye that they made."

WIND INSTRUMENTS

Crude animal horns had been in use as signal instruments since prehistoric times, functioning in battle to rally and direct troops and to instill fear in the enemy's ranks. The horn's harsh, penetrating sound led to its adoption by watchmen and during the hunt, where a repertory of rhythmic blasts were formulated for various stages of the sport. By the tenth century, finger holes and often a simple mouthpiece were added to make possible the sounding of a series of consecutive notes. The oliphant was an ivory horn fashioned from an elephant's tusk, often richly ornamented. Because of its uniqueness it soon became part of a knight's equipment, sometimes even taking the place of a document and seal in feudal contracts.

The exposure of Christian forces to Saracenic martial music during the crusades led to the importation and adoption of the Islamic trumpet, or *buisine*. It consisted of a sectional metal tube several feet long with a mouthpiece and flared bell at opposite ends. (The clarion and *trompe* were shorter versions, the former exhibiting a sharp, piercing sonority.) Brass, copper, or occasionally silver was used; and since there were no valves or slides, only the fundamental and about five additional notes in the harmonic series could be produced. In Muslim lands the trumpet was a symbol of power and rank, and this prerogative was retained in Europe, where it was adopted as an instrument of pomp and circumstance. From the *Song of Roland* (*ca.* 1100) on, there are numerous references to the *cor sarrazinois* (Saracen horn) and its use. During the twelfth century, advances in metalwork produced instruments made out of flattened metal sheets, with narrower bore, a well-fitted mouthpiece, and gently flared bell, giving the trumpet a clearer, more precise sound as well as a wider working range. By the end of the fourteenth century the instrument was folded into a flat *S* shape and later into an elongated loop. The trumpet was further improved in the 1400's by a sliding mouthpiece that could alter the basic pitch and thus the entire harmonic series to produce an almost complete chromatic scale. Johannes Tinctoris writes (*ca.* 1490) that the *trompette sacqueboute* (draw pipe, or sackbut) played the lowest part in a loud consort.

The shawm (from the Latin *calamus*) was a double-reed instrument of conical bore with seven fingerholes that reappeared as a result of Muslim contacts in the late thirteenth century. At first it was produced in only two sizes, soprano and tenor, the latter (bombarde) being provided with a key to facilitate reaching the lowest hole. (Keyed bombardes were still considered "new" in a reference dated 1376.) The shawm's loud, piercing sound matched the *buisine,* cornett, and bagpipe, with which it was

(Opposite) miniatures from *Las cantigas de Santa María, ca.* 1260: *(1)* Bagpipes (without drones); *(2)* Shawms; *(3)* Long trumpets (buisines); *(4)* Pipes and tabors; *(5)* Horns (with finger holes); *(6)* Transverse flutes; *(7)* Rebab and lute; *(8)* Waisted and oval guitars; *(9)* Mandora and rebec; *(10)* Oval fiddle and guitar; *(11)* Fiddle and citole; *(12)* Three- and four-stringed fiddles. EL ESCORIAL, BIBLIOTECA DEL MONASTERIO REAL. MS J.B..2, fols. 235v, 350, 286, 333, 243v, 218v, 162, 147, 104, 39v, 46v, 193v.

 MUSICAL INSTRUMENTS, EUROPEAN

invariably associated. It was a stable member of consort groups at court and in civic wind bands (*alta*), particularly in Italy and the Netherlands.

The bagpipe, aptly called a bagged shawm, consisted of a valved blowpipe, a bag serving as an external reservoir permitting steady wind pressure, a melody pipe (chanter), and from one to three drone pipes. Formerly known as *tibia utricularis,* it was transmitted throughout the Roman Empire by soldiers and settlers. The early European model was equipped with only a blowpipe and chanter, later adding a drone, which had long been used in the Near East. The drone usually sounded a fifth or octave below the instrument's natural pitch. The bagpipe was frequently paired with the shawm and *buisine,* a combination that lent itself particularly to outdoor music and dancing. Due to its limitations (narrow range, constant drone, and inability to keep silent during rests) the bagpipe gradually ceased participating in art music and was relegated to the lower social orders, in the process taking on certain pejorative connotations.

The cornett, or *Zink,* was derived from the horn, consisting of a curved or straight tube fashioned out of two hollowed pieces of wood over which was wrapped a leather sheath. It was equipped with a small, cup-shaped metal mouthpiece and finger holes to provide a diatonic scale of about fifteen notes. The more penetrating curved cornett was first mentioned in *Le Morte Arthur* (*ca.* 1400), and by the end of the fifteenth century was often used as the soprano member of the loud consort, supported by shawms and slide trumpet or sackbut.

An instrument of great antiquity, panpipes consisted of a series of cane or metal tubes of graduated lengths bound together with sinews or rope and held in a wooden case. They were used primarily by shepherds and in rustic music making.

The open-ended, cylindrically bored flute with from three to six finger holes, carved generally from bone or wood, came both from Asia and North Africa to southern Europe and from the Near East via the Slavs. Ekkehard IV of St. Gall (eleventh century) spoke of *omni genere fistularum,* and the epic poem *Raoul de Cambrai* (*ca.* 1000) mentions that "les pastoriax oit leur flajox sonner" (the shepherds listen to their pipes sound). Thanks to its versatility, the flute became one of the primary melodic instruments of the Middle Ages. The fact that the transverse, or side-blown, flute was adopted by the military forces along with the field drum suggests that its tone was loud and penetrating, more like the modern fife.

Small pipes with whistle-type mouthpieces, paired with tiny, double-ended drums (pipe and tabor), first appeared in northern Spain and southern France in the twelfth century, spreading rapidly throughout Europe. Toward the lower end of the pipe's tube were two holes on top for the fingers of one hand and a hole underneath for the thumb. An entire diatonic scale could be produced, along with a few chromatics, by overblowing the harmonics. The pipe and tabor became one of the standard instrumental combinations *(Drummel und Pfeiffen gehören zusammen),* first used by strolling players and later as a standard accompaniment for dance music in more formal settings. According to Juan Ruiz (*ca.* 1343), it was indispensable in furnishing the rhythm for ensemble music, particularly in accompanying dancers.

The recorder was an indigenous European instrument, known at least by the very early fourteenth century, when it was depicted in an English psalter. The French *flûte douce* and German *Schnabelflöte* reflect respectively its soft tone and unique form. The recorder was an end-blown instrument usually made of boxwood or ivory with a beak or whistle mouthpiece, tapered bore, seven finger holes and a thumbhole, and a range of roughly two octaves. Later, recorders were made in several sizes from sopranino to bass. They were essentially chamber instruments with a soft, modulated tone most suitable for indoor music making, either as an accompaniment for the voice or in ensembles with other instruments of similar sonority. Easy to learn, inexpensive to make, and readily obtained, the recorder was an ideal and popular instrument for musicians of all sorts.

During the fourth century the hydraulic organ was superseded by the introduction of bellows to supply the air pressure. Later, the development of monastic establishments led to an era of organ building on a massive scale. The most famous of these instruments was in Winchester Cathedral (*ca.* 980–990), described with some poetic license by Wulfstan as having 400 pipes, 26 bellows, and clumsy slides in place of keys requiring two players and several more to operate the bellows. According to the *Schedula diversarum artium* by Theophilus (early twelfth century), organs had a single manual with a compass of seven or eight notes. In place of the keyboard was a series of knobs or levers which, when pressed or pulled down, operated slides functioning as valves to admit air into the pipes. There were two or more pipes per slide, all sounding together. The construction of cathedrals during the Gothic era was paral-

 MUSICAL INSTRUMENTS, EUROPEAN

leled by a new surge in organ building, also stimulated by the simultaneous development of liturgical polyphony. The compass of these organs was enlarged to three octaves, along with a few chromatics. A keyboard and system of mechanical linkages (tracker action) controlled the access of air into each rank of pipes in various permutations and combinations (mixtures). Sometimes an additional manual or, later, pedalboard was added. At Halberstadt (*ca.* 1361) the organ had three keyboards; at Rouen (1386) it had two manuals, each with about forty keys; and at Amiens (1429) it had no less than 2,500 pipes.

The portative organ was introduced during the fourteenth century. It had one or two ranks of pipes and a register of unvarying tone quality. The keyboard provided a short diatonic scale of one or two octaves with chromatic notes added gradually, starting with B flat. These small instruments were operated by one player, who pumped the bellows with one hand while depressing the buttons or keys with the other. The portative became one of the most important instruments in polyphonic ensembles of the late Middle Ages. The *Romance of the Rose* describes how the performer simultaneously pumped the bellows, played, and sang. The portative was often used as a solo instrument, the three parts reduced to two for the three fingers of the right hand.

Portative organ surrounded by (clockwise from top left) fiddle; psaltery; lute; clappers; buisines; nakers; bagpipe and shawm; tambourine. Miniature from a 14th-century Italian MS of Boethius' *De arithmetica.* NAPLES, BIBLIOTECA NAZIONALE VITTORIO EMANUELE III. MS V.A. 14, fol. 47

PERCUSSION INSTRUMENTS

Pairs of small kettledrums, or nakers, of various sizes (French *nacaire,* from Arabic *naqqārā*) were fabricated of leather or metal molded over wooden forms. They were played by tiny clublike beaters, underlining the melody with simple, rhythmic strokes and rolls. Each drum was tensioned to a different sound, but there was no precise pitch. Following oriental custom, nakers were used as exclusive symbols of rank and prestige. The chronicler Joinville, in his *Histoire de St. Louis* (1309), described the terrifying effect of the Saracen nakers and trumpets. From the battlefield these instruments gravitated to the courtly milieu, first for ceremonial field music and later for use at various social activities, such as banquets and dancing.

Around the middle of the fifteenth century large kettledrums mounted on horseback were introduced from the East via Hungary. Because of their overpowering sound, conspicuous display, and ability to be tuned precisely, they quickly displaced the naker as the principal field and court instrument. In 1457 a huge embassy was dispatched by King Ladislas of Hungary seeking the hand of the French king's daughter. According to an eyewitness, "nobody had ever seen drums like large kettles which were carried on horseback" and with the trumpets were "marvellous and triumphant to hear."

As its name suggests, the long drum (along with all other percussion instruments) was Muslim in origin *(al-tambor).* The skins were tensioned by means of adjustable rope lacings running back and forth between the two heads. The drum was carried slung to the side and hit with the hand, elbow, or a pair of sticks. It provided a steady, repetitive beat for military formations and open-air festivities.

The tambourine, or timbrel, was much like the modern form, except that it had an extra row of small metal cymbals around its circumference and sometimes gut snares underneath the skin, giving it a sharp, rattling sound. Its principal use was to accompany dances and songs. The *Romance of the*

 MUSICAL INSTRUMENTS, EUROPEAN

Rose describes how the players tossed their instruments high into the air, never missing a catch.

Cymbals were made from thick plates of brass or bronze with high domes in the center. They were held horizontally and struck together with a vertical motion. The triangle was provided with tiny rings on the horizontal bar that produced a buzzing sound.

Large bells, or *campanae,* populated the church towers in every city. They were played according to a strict formula: a single bell on weekdays, the largest one during processions, and all bells on Sunday before the service. *Campanulae pro melodia* were sets of stationary tuned bells played manually in churches or, in astronomical clocks, by striking mechanisms, or jackwork. Chime bells *(cymbala)* were suspended from a frame and struck with a hammer. Usually from three to seven or more in number, their precise musical role in liturgical contexts is still problematical.

STRINGED INSTRUMENTS

Of Greek or Eastern origin, the lyre spread throughout Europe during the sixth century via barbarian migrations and Germanic mercenaries in Byzantine service (it was sometimes called *cithara teutonica*). However, the lyre's shape was completely altered from the Greco-Roman cithara. One form consisted of two arms or wings connected to a crosspiece at one end and a sound box at the other, between which were stretched the strings. A later, derivative instrument was the crowd, or crwth, a bowed lyre appearing in the eleventh century. Resembling a flat, rectangular fiddle, two arched openings at the top flanked a vertical strip, which formed the fingerboard. The player's left hand grasped the strings from behind, through the two spaces.

The harp came to Europe from the Near East, perhaps carried by Syrian traders. Bishop Venantius Fortunatus of Poitiers (*ca.* 600) wrote that it was the instrument of the barbarians, who used it as the sole accompaniment to their songs. It is mentioned in *Beowulf* and in continental sources is often referred to as the *cithara anglica* (British cithara). The harp was used by bards and gleemen to accompany their epic poems or sagas. Either the fingernails or a plectrum was used. The early harp was rather squat and triangular in form. Unlike the lyre (which it soon displaced), it had strings of varied length, providing equal tensioning and thus a greater volume of sound. As time went on, the harp evolved into a larger, more slender instrument with eighteen to twenty-four metal, usually brass, strings replacing the dozen or so gut strings of earlier forms. A tuning key was used to maintain the pitch. Guillaume de Machaut called the harp the best of the soft, or *bas,* instruments. Both amateur and professional musicians played it in all types of social settings.

In its long history the monochord changed not at all. It was above all a teaching instrument that enabled the musical theorists to determine mathematical divisions of the scale and ratios of pitches and the instructors in monastic schools to teach choristers how to sing liturgical chant with the proper intervals (solmization). The monochord was popularized through the writings of Boethius (early sixth century). It consisted of a gut string stretched over a fixed bridge at either end of a long, thin box. Inscribed on its surface were calibrations indicating the various proportions and often the letters of the corresponding notes as well. A movable bridge placed underneath the string was operated by the player, whose action stopped it at selected points to produce the desired intervals.

There were no bowed instruments in Europe before the tenth century, when the rebec made its appearance. It had evolved from Arab prototypes *(rabāb)* and was designed specifically to be bowed. The rebec was carved from a single block of wood, shaped like a pear, without a real neck. Its two or three gut strings were tuned in fifths and it was usually held vertically on the knee. Due to its simple technical demands, the rebec was a favorite instrument of the jongleurs and wandering minstrels; and its treble range coincided nicely with the melodies they played. It was used throughout society to accompany the dance. But as music became more and more complex, the rebec's drawbacks (little resonance or volume of sound) and stringing (limited range) gradually pushed it from the realm of art music to the less sophisticated world of popular music making.

The fiddle, or *vielle,* became the principal bowed instrument of the Middle Ages. Oval or spade-shaped at first, it evolved into a rectangular form with rounded edges and slightly incurved sides. Approximately the size of a modern viola, it was lower pitched than the rebec. According to the theorist Jerome of Moravia (late thirteenth century), there were three different tunings for its three to five strings, depending upon its use. Johannes de Grocheo (*ca.* 1300) observed that a good performer introduced every song or dance on the instrument, also noting the superiority of stringed instruments due to their ability to be tuned accurately. He claimed that the

MUSICAL INSTRUMENTS, EUROPEAN

fiddle was especially suited to all types of musical compositions. Its use was widespread in musical contexts of all sorts, as a solo instrument, providing preludes, interludes, and postludes to a vocal rendition or underlining the voice. As time went on, the fiddle became larger and its construction more refined, producing a stronger sound and better resonance. A sharply incurved waist facilitated better articulation of the strings by allowing the angle of the bow to be changed.

The marine trumpet, also known as *Trumscheit* or "nun's fiddle," was an extension of the monochord—a long, tapering sound box on which one or two strings were mounted over a bridge. One end of this bridge was left loose, so that when a string was stopped by a light touch of the thumb its vibration caused this free portion to vibrate, producing a rasping sound. This trumpetlike timbre and rattling, or drumming, sound probably accounted for its name.

Musicians performing on church steps: pipe and tabor, triangle, shawm (? partially hidden), buisine, harp, lutes, shawms, bagpipes, psaltery, cornett. (The picture represents King David as prophet and pilgrim announcing the coming of Christ.) Miniature from the *Breviary of Queen Isabella of Spain*, Flemish, *ca.* 1497. BY PERMISSION OF THE BRITISH LIBRARY, LONDON. MS ADD 18851, fol. 184v

Sometimes called a plucked zither, the psaltery came in a variety of shapes, sizes, and stringing. It was basically a box, or resonator, on top of which were stretched ten or more strings supported by bridges at either end. The small, triangular form *(tympanon)* was held close to the chest. It had a high, metallic tone suited for playing upper voice parts, usually an octave higher. The larger, trapezoidal variety *(canon)* was held in an upright position on the lap. It provided greater resonance and more volume. Both instruments were played by plucking the wire strings with a quill or the fingers. The psaltery was reintroduced into Europe during the twelfth century; one of the earliest examples is depicted on the facade of the cathedral of Santiago de Compostela (1184). The theorist Jehan des Murs (*ca.* 1325) cited an instrument with nineteen strings encompassing two and one half octaves.

The lute was derived from Eastern prototypes *(ᶜūd),* introduced into Europe by the Moors, perhaps though Spain, where it was largely confined until the thirteenth century. It had a small, pear-shaped body and vaulted back built up from thin strips of wood bent into shape and glued together, which provided more resonance than older instruments carved from a single block of wood. Its flat belly was pierced with sound holes. The European type had a short neck with its pegbox bent back 80 degrees. There were usually four strings tuned in fourths. During the late Middle Ages the lute spread throughout the Continent and England, where its dry, neutral tone provided a good contrast to the voice. Tinctoris (*ca.* 1487) wrote that it was used at feasts, dances, and other entertainments of all sorts. In addition to its role in the soft consort, the lute was used as a solo instrument, the performer improvising melodies. About this time a fifth or sixth string was added; the body was made larger, more almond-shaped, in order to increase the volume of sound. Frets were added along the neck, improving intonation when the finger pressed against the string.

The guitar was introduced into the Spanish Peninsula, France, and Italy. The Western form (sometimes called *guitarra latina*) had an incurved waist, flat back, fretted neck, and large central soundhole. The Muslim instrument *(guitarra morisca)* was pear-shaped, with long neck, vaulted back, and several soundholes. The guitar's four gut strings, tuned in fourths and fifths, could be played with either the fingers or a plectrum. Juan Ruiz described its sound as sharp and shrill. In Spain the guitar enjoyed primacy as both a solo and accompanying instrument.

MUSICAL INSTRUMENTS, EUROPEAN

Here its shape was modified like a waisted fiddle, with shallow ribs and a flat back. Its sound was reinforced by a larger body and double stringing.

The citole was a plucked instrument with flat back, fretted neck, and five metal strings. It seems to have been favored by female performers and was frequently mentioned in references to solo performances, where its "sweet" tone was obviously attractive.

The mandora (mandola, mandore) was a small, round-backed instrument with vaulted back and sickle-shaped pegbox. Its four or five strings were played with a plectrum. Now thought to be synonymous with the *gittern,* or *guitara latina,* it was especially popular in Italy, Spain, and southern France.

The hurdy-gurdy consisted of a large, fiddlelike body held on the laps of two performers. Its three gut strings were set in motion simultaneously by a resin-coated wooden drum, acting as a bow, which was turned by a crank by one player while the other operated the keys controlling wooden bridges or tangents that stopped the strings. In its larger form, known as an *organistrum,* the instrument was used as a pedagogical tool, especially in cloisters without organs. During the thirteenth century the hurdy-gurdy was reduced in size and turned into a one-man instrument, the *chifonie,* or *symphonia,* equipped with a mechanism refined into keys that could be pressed upward to stop the strings and then fall back. However, its incessant drone no longer fitted in with the fabric of late medieval music, with the result that the hurdy-gurdy was relegated to the lower social strata of itinerant musicians, beggars, and the blind.

Within the space of a century, a number of keyboard-type instruments burst upon the scene. They exhibited radically new principles of action embodied in an ingenious system of connecting a key with a striking device which returned it to its original position after hitting or plucking the string. These mechanisms were derived from the tradition of scientific instrument-building associated with astronomical hardware such as clocks and automata, with its linkwork and gearing, and with parallel developments in organ keyboards.

Given the experimentation involving different kinds of striking mechanisms, shapes and sizes, it is not surprising that there was, and still is, some confusion regarding terminology. The astronomer and clockmaker Henri Arnaut of Zwolle (*ca.* 1440) described the early harpsichord *(clavecin, clavicembalo)*: wing-shaped, with its strings running from front to back, parallel to the keys. Fabricated first in Italy and then in the Netherlands, it was in part derived from the psaltery, the shape of which it resembled. It was played by a mechanism that plucked the strings by means of a retracting quill, or plectrum (one per string), mounted in a slotted strip of wood, or mack, which was thrown up to the string from the tail end of the key. In this arrangement, all the strings were plucked at a uniform point parallel to the keyboard, and each note had its own strings.

An upright variant was the *clavicytherium,* sometimes known as a keyed harp. Derived from the psaltery, it had a vertical soundboard and strings perpendicular to the keyboard. This position, lacking the cooperation of the force of gravity, necessitated a more complex action in order to return the jacks to their original position. It was first mentioned in a treatise by Paulus Paulirinus (*ca.* 1460).

The earliest-known reference to the clavichord occurs in Eberhart Cersne's *Minne regel* (1404), along with a list of other instruments. It was rectangular and boxlike, developed by combining features found in other instruments. For example, from the hurdy-gurdy was borrowed the concept of shortening strings by means of tangents. It replaced the sliding bridge of the monochord with a keyboard, projecting from one of its longer sides. The strings ran at right angles to, and above, the keys themselves. On the striking end of each key was a small metal blade, or tangent, that hit the string when the other end was depressed. This tangent divided the string into two parts, one of which was dampened with cloth while the other was allowed to sound. The point at which the string was hit determined the length of the vibrating portion and thus the pitch. In this unique arrangement, all the strings (tuned to the same pitch) were shared by more than one key; only one of its tangents was activited at a time. Arnaut of Zwolle describes an instrument with nine double strings and thirty-seven keys, providing a range of three chromatic octaves.

The chekker *(échiquier, Schachtbrett)* was known from the fourteenth century onward; for example, Guillaume de Machaut mentions it in his poem *La prise d'Alexandrie* (*ca.* 1369). Probably rectangular in shape, it seems to have been related to the clavichord. However, owing to its small size, the strings had to be positioned diagonally from the keys. As with the harpsichord, each string was a different length and tuned to a different note, each with its corresponding key. But its unique angular arrangement meant that the jackwork for the longer strings at the lower end of the keyboard was corre-

MUSICAL INSTRUMENTS, EUROPEAN

spondingly longer and harder to depress. The instrument was mentioned in numerous inventories at various feudal courts.

BIBLIOGRAPHY

General studies. Anthony C. Baines, "Fifteenth-century Instruments in Tinctoris's 'De Inventione et Usu Musicae,'" in *Galpin Society Journal,* **3** (1950); Nicholas Bessaraboff, *Ancient European Musical Instruments* (1941); Fritz Brückner, *Die Blasinstrumente in der altfranzösischen Literatur* (1926); Henry Carter, *Dictionary of Middle English Musical Terms* (1961); Friedrich Dick, *Bezeichnungen für Saiten- und Schlaginstrumente in der altfranzösischen Literatur* (1932); Francis W. Galpin, *Old English Instruments of Music* (1910), 4th rev. ed., T. Dart, ed. (1965), and *A Textbook of European Musical Instruments* (1937); Karl Geiringer, *Instruments in the History of Western Music,* 3rd rev. ed. (1978); Friedrich Gennrich, "Zur Musikinstrumentenkunde der Machaut-Zeit," in *Zeitschrift für Musikwissenschaft,* **9** (1921); G. Hayes, "Musical Instruments," in *The New Oxford History of Music,* III, *Ars Nova and the Renaissance* (1960); Jeremy Montagu, *The World of Medieval and Renaissance Instruments* (1976); David Munrow, *Instruments of the Middle Ages and Renaissance* (1976); Curt Sachs, *The History of Musical Instruments* (1940); Dorothea Treder, *Die Musikinstrumente in den höfischen Epen der Blützeit* (1933); Rowland Wright, *Dictionnaire des instruments de musique* (1941).

Instruments. Cecil Adkins, "The Technique of the Monochord," in *Acta musicologica,* **39** (1967); Werner Bachmann, *The Origins of Bowing and the Development of Bowed Instruments up to the Thirteenth Century,* Norma Deane, trans. (1969); Anthony Baines, *Woodwind Instruments and Their History* (1957), and *Brass Instruments: Their History and Development* (1976); Francis Baines, "Introducing the Hurdy-Gurdy," in *Early Music,* **3** (1975); Philip Bate, *The Trumpet and Trombone: An Outline of Their History, Development, and Construction,* 2nd ed. (1972); Heinz Becker, *Zur Entwicklungsgeschichte der antiken und mittelalterlichen Rohrblattinstrumente* (1966); Friedrich Behn, "Die Laute im Altertum und frühen Mittelalter," in *Zeitschrift für Musikwissenschaft,* **1** (1918); Heinrich Besseler, "Die Entstehung der Posaune," in *Acta Musicologica,* **22** (1950); Ernst Biernath, *Die Guitarre seit dem III. Jahrtausend vor Christus* (1907); James Blades, *Percussion Instruments and Their History,* 3rd ed. (1984); Edmund A. Bowles, "Haut and Bas: The Grouping of Musical Instruments During the Middle Ages," in *Musica disciplina,* **8** (1954), "La hiérarchie des instruments de musique dans l'Europe féodale," in *Revue de musicologie,* **42** (1958), "The Guitar in Medieval Music," in *Guitar Review,* **29** (1966), "On the Origin of the Keyboard Mechanism in the Middle Ages," in *Technology and Culture,* **7** (1966), and "Eastern Influences on the Use of Trumpets and Drums During the Middle Ages," in *Anuario musical,* **26** (1971).

Marianne Bröcker, *Die Drehleier: ihr Bau und ihre Geschichte* (1973); T. E. Butts, "Bagpipes in Medieval Music," in *American Recorder,* **14** (1973); Adam von Ahn Carse, *Musical Wind Instruments* (1939); Francis Collinson, *The Bagpipe* (1975); Peter Danner, "Before Petrucci: The Lute in the Fifteenth Century," in *Journal of the Lute Society of America,* **5** (1972); Dietz Degen, *Zur Geschichte der Blockflöte in den germanischen Ländern* (1939); Hans Heinz Dräger, *Die Entwicklung des Streichbogens und seine Anwendung in Europa* (1937); Norbert Dufourcq, *Esquisse d'une histoire de l'orgue en France du XIIIe au XVIIIe siècle* (1935); Francis W. Galpin, "The Sackbut," in *Proceedings of the Royal Musical Association,* **33** (1906); Karl Geiringer, "Vorgeschichte und Geschichte der europäischen Laute bis zum Beginn der Neuzeit," in *Zeitschrift für Musikwissenschaft,* **10** (1928); Dagmar Groeneveld, "Zur Geschichte der Harfe im frühen Mittelalter," in *Die Musikforschung,* **26** (1973); Herbert Heyde, *Trompete und Trompetenblasen im europäischen Mittelalter* (1965), and "Frühgeschichte des europäischen Hackbrets," in *Deutsche Jahrbuch für Musikwissenschaft,* **18** (1973–1977); Hans Hickmann, *Das Portativ: ein Beitrag zur Geschichte der Kleinorgel* (1936); Edgar H. Hunt, *The Recorder and Its Music* (1962); Franz Jahnel, *Die Gitarre und ihr Bau: Technologie von Gitarre, Laute, Mandoline, Sister, Tanbur und Saite,* 2nd ed. (1973); John Leach, "The Dulcimer," in *Consort,* **25** (1968/1969), and "The Psaltery," *ibid.,* **27** (1971).

H. Neupert, *The Clavichord,* Ann P. P. Feldberg, trans. (1965); Christopher Page, "Early 15th-century Instruments in Jean Gerson's *Tractatus de canticis,*" in *Early Music,* **6** (1978), and "The Myth of the Chekker," *ibid.,* **7** (1979); Hanns Panum, *The Stringed Instruments of the Middle Ages,* Jeffrey Pulver, trans. (1939); Jean Perrot, *The Organ from Its Invention in the Hellenistic Period to the End of the Thirteenth Century,* Norma Deane, trans. (1971); Mary Remnant, "Rebec, Fiddle, and Crowd in England," in *Proceedings of the Royal Musical Association,* **95** (1968/1969); Roslyn Rensch, *The Harp: Its History, Technique and Repertoire* (1969); Edwin M. Ripin, "The Early Clavichord," in *Musical Quarterly,* **53** (1967), and "Towards an Identification of the Chekker," in *Galpin Society Journal,* **28** (1975); Raymond Russell, *The Harpsichord and Clavichord: An Introductory Study* (1959); Curt Sachs, "Chromatic Trumpets in the Renaissance," in *Musical Quarterly,* **36** (1950); Joseph Smits van Waesberghe, *Cymbala (Bells in the Middle Ages)* (1951); T. Lea Southgate, "The Evolution of the Flute," in *Proceedings of the Royal Musical Association,* **34** (1907/1908); Christopher Welch, *Six Lectures on the Recorder and Other Flutes in Relation to Literature* (1911); Laurence Wright, "The Medieval Gittern and Citole: A Case of Mistaken Identity," in *Galpin Society Journal,* **30** (1977).

Iconography. R. Bergman-Müller, *Musikdarstellungen*

MUSICAL INSTRUMENTS, MIDEAST

in den venezianischen Malerei von 1350–1600 (1951); Edward Buhle, *Die musikalischen Instrumente in den Miniaturen des frühen Mittelalters* (1903); Edmund A. Bowles, *Musikleben im 15. Jahrhundert* (1977), and *Musical Performance in the Late Middle Ages* (1983); Valentin Denis, *Die Muziekinstrumenten in de Nederlanden en in Italië naar hun Afbeelding in de 15ᵉ-eeuwsche Kunst* (1944); Frank Lloyd Harrison and Joan Rimmer, *European Musical Instruments* (1964); Hugo Leichtentritt, "Was lehren uns die Bildwerke des 14.–17. Jahrhunderts über die Instrumentalmusik ihrer Zeit?" in *Sammelbände der Internationalen Musikgesellschaft* 7 (1905/1906); Victor Ravizza, *Das Instrumentale Ensemble von 1400–1550 in Italien* (1970); Robert Wangermée, *Flemish Music and Society in the Fifteenth and Sixteenth Centuries,* Robert E. Wolf, trans. (1968).

EDMUND A. BOWLES

[See also **Bells; Boethius; Cantiga; Ekkehard IV of St. Gaul; Jehan des Murs; Joglar/Jongleur; Johannes de Grocheo; Lydgate, John; Machaut, Guillaume de; Musical Instruments, Middle Eastern; Oliphant; Otfrid von Weissenburg; Roland, Song of; Romance of the Rose; Ruiz, Juan; Solmization; Theophilus; Troubadour, Trouvère, Trovador; Utrecht Psalter; Venantius Fortunatus; Wace.**]

MUSICAL INSTRUMENTS, MIDDLE EASTERN. The sources dealing with medieval Middle Eastern instruments are plentiful and include musical treatises, music literature, and belles lettres, as well as historical and geographical writings. Among the musical treatises the following are particularly important: the works of al-Kindī (*d. ca.* 873); the *Grand Book of Music* of al-Fārābī (*ca.* 873–950), which shows the application of the tone system to the instruments; the anonymous fourteenth-century Persian *Kanz al-Tuḥaf,* which provides details on material, measurements, and way of construction of instruments; the anonymous fourteenth-century Egyptian *Kashf al-Ghumūm*, providing details on materials and ways of performance; and the works of ᶜAbd al-Qādir (Ibn Ghaybī) (*d.* 1435), providing details on the number of strings, tuning, materials, and proportions.

CHORD PHONES

Lute family. The *ᶜūd,* the most famous Middle Eastern instrument, was a lute which in the "classical period" (eighth and early ninth century) had four strings tuned in perfect fourths. It consisted of a wooden sound box and a neck, as distinct from the *barbaṭ,* in which the chest and neck were from one piece. The *barbaṭ* was used by the Christian Arab Ghassanids before Islam and the Syrians used it in early Islam. The lute of pre-Islamic Arabia had a skin belly and was called *mizhar, kirān,* or *muwattar.* At the end of the sixth century the wooden-belly lute was brought from Iraq to Arabia. Toward the end of the seventh century a two-stringed lute was in use in Iraq. The Persian lute *(barbaṭ)* was introduced in Arabia at the end of the seventh century. In the eighth century the famous lutenist Zalzal (*d.* 791) invented a "perfect lute" known as *ᶜūd al-shabbuṭ* which resembled a fish called *shabbuṭ* and was apparently ovoid instead of pear-shaped. In the eighth and ninth centuries the Andalusian musician Ziryāb improved the *ᶜūd* structure by making it lighter, added a fifth string, used gut for lower strings instead of silk, and replaced the wooden plectrum with an eagle quill. In the thirteenth century the Chinese *pipa* ("balloon guitar") was introduced in Mesopotamia by the Mughals.

In the *Kanz al-Tuḥaf* we learn that the *ᶜūd* was made of dry spruce or pine wood and had gut strings. In the *Kashf al-Ghumūm* the *ᶜūd* was made of beech wood. Other instruments belonging to the *ᶜūd* family were: the *kankala,* an imported Indian instrument introduced in the ninth century, consisting

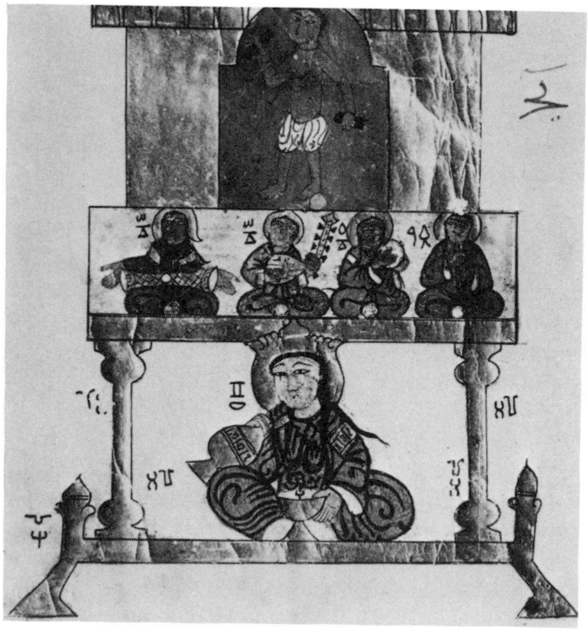

Arab musicians playing the *kūba* (drum), *ᶜūd* (lute), *dāᵓira* (tambourine), and *qusṣṣāba* (flute). From a miniature in a Mesopotamian MS of al-Jazarī's *Treatise on Automata* (1354). REPRODUCED FROM F. R. MARTIN, *THE MINIATURE PAINTING AND PAINTERS OF PERSIA, INDIA, AND TURKEY* (1912)

MUSICAL INSTRUMENTS, MIDEAST

of one string stretched on a gourd-shaped box; the *kuwītra,* a small lute with a shallow sound chest; the *rubāb* (not to be confused with the bowed *rabāb*), an instrument of three double silk strings, made of apricot wood, with a vaulted sound chest and curvature at the waist, the lower part of its belly covered with skin; the *rūṭah,* a lute used in twelfth-century Andalusia. Furthermore ᶜAbd al-Qādir described a great number of lute-related instruments, among which are: *tuḥfat al-ᶜūd,* an instrument half the size of the *ᶜūd; shāhrūd,* an instrument twice the size of the *ᶜūd* using ten double strings (not to be confused with the open string *shāhrūd*); *ṭarab al-futuḥ,* with six double strings; *awzān,* with three strings, popular among the Mamlūks in Egypt; *rūḥ afzā,* with a hemispherical sound box and six double strings of silk or metal.

The *ṭunbūr* (pandora) was an instrument similar to the lute but with a smaller sound box and a longer neck. It appeared in Arabic literature as early as the seventh century. Al-Fārābī described it in detail and mentioned two kinds: *al-Baghdādī,* which used a tone system pertaining to pre-Islamic times and which was popular in Baghdad in the tenth century; and *al-Khorāsānī,* with its frets arranged in limma (90 centimeters) limma comma (24 centimeters), which was popular in Khorāsān. The *ṭunbūr* had two, rarely three, strings. ᶜAbd al-Qādir described three types: *ṭunbūr-i shirwīnān,* with two strings and pear-shaped box, popular in Tabrīz; *ṭunbūr a-yi Turkī,* with two strings, smaller box, and longer neck than the former (none used a plectrum); *nāy ṭunbūr,* with two strings and played with a plectrum. ᶜAbd al-Qādir also described the *shashtār,* a six-stringed instrument of three types, one of which had fifteen double sympathetic strings. The *tār* is a variety of *ṭunbūr* with vault-shaped box and curvature at the waist. It is shown in the eighth-century frescoes of Quṣayr ᶜAmra (an Umayyad palace in today's Jordan) and profusely in medieval Persian miniatures. A simpler form of *ṭunbūr,* the *gunbrī,* was known in North Africa. It had a gourd, shell, or wooden sound box covered with skin or leather. The box could be pear-shaped, egg-shaped, hemispherical, or rectangular. The strings were made of horsehair.

Open string instruments. Known in pre-Islamic and early Islamic Arabia were the *ṣanj* (harp, also known as *wanj, jank, ṣalbāq*) and *miᶜzafa* (psaltery). Later, in the tenth and eleventh centuries, the *ṣanṭūr* (dulcimer, also known as *ṣanj ṣīnī*) and *shāhrūd* were known.

Ṣanj (jank) denoted a harp with straight sound box or curved chest. Al-Fārābī described a two-octave diatonic harp of fifteen strings as well as a two-octave chromatic harp of twenty-five strings. The harp of *Kanz al-Tuḥaf* was made of apricot wood, had twenty-four or twenty-five strings, and was played with both hands with the handle placed under the left arm.

The *qānūn,* a trapezoidal psaltery with right angles known by this name as early as the tenth century, was hailed in Moorish Spain in the eleventh century as the "chief" of instruments, and was manufactured in Seville in the thirteenth century. In the *Kanz al-Tuḥaf* the *qānūn* was made of apricot wood, had sixty-three strings, and was tuned trichordally. In the *Kashf al-Ghumūm* the *qanun* had ninety-six copper strings.

The *nuzha,* a rectangular psaltery invented by Ṣafī al-Dīn (*d.* 1294), had thirty-two strings of various lengths. We learn from *Kanz al-Tuḥaf* that the instrument had 108 strings. The twelve bottom strings were tuned trichordally, and the remaining ninety-six strings were tuned quadrichordally. It was made of red willow, royal fir, boxwood, or cypress and was twice the size of the *qānūn.*

The *mughnī* was another kind of psaltery. ᶜAbd al-Qādir described it as having the form of a board, and its twenty-four strings were tuned in such a way that every second string was the octave of the preceding one. In *Kanz al-Tuḥaf, mughnī* refers to a curious instrument combining a *rabāb* (lute with parchment), *qānūn,* and *nuzha.* Farmer explains that the large sound box covered with parchment resembles the *rabāb,* the rectangular, wide, flat neck resembles a narrow *nuzha,* and the strings passing over a diagonally placed bridge resemble a *qānūn.* The strings, thirty-nine in number, are tuned trichordally. The instrument is made of apricot wood.

The *ṣanj ṣīnī* (Chinese *ṣanj*) was a trapezoidal-shaped instrument like the *qānūn* but with two oblique sides instead of one. It was also known by the name *ṣanṭūr* and played with beating rods like the dulcimer.

The *shāhrūd,* an open string instrument of four octaves, was invented in 912 and had the widest range of any instrument known in the tenth century.

Bowed instruments. Rabāb was the generic name for bowed instruments. Though some medieval sources claim that the *rabāb* was used in pre-Islamic times, the most extensive description comes from the tenth-century *Grand Book of Music* of al-Fārābī. There are many types of *rabāb:* The rectangular *rabāb* consisted of a wooden frame over which was stretched a membrane. The wooden neck was cylindrical and the spike made of iron. It had one or two strings and accompanied sung poetry. The boat-shaped *rabāb,* found in North Africa, consisted of a piece of wood hollowed in the shape of a boat; the top of the face was covered with metal or wood and the bottom had a membrane. The instrument had no clearly delineated neck. It had two strings and was used by the Arabs and Moors of Spain. The pear-shaped *rabāb* had five strings. The hemispherical, named also *kamānja* and *ghichak,* was the best-known type, consisting of a hemisphere of wood or coconut over which a membrane was stretched. It had a narrow cylindrical neck and iron spike. In *Kanz al-Tuḥaf* the *ghichak* had two horsehair strings, a sound box of tin or brass with parchment spread over it, and a neck made of hardwood (almond, walnut, or ebony). The *rabāb* was popular in Egypt in the thirteenth century, and in the late fourteenth century ᶜAbd al-Qādir reported that a large one had two strings and eight sympathetic strings.

AEROPHONES

Mizmār. The generic name for woodwind refers to two types, reed and reedless. The body of the single-tube reed-type was cylindrical or conical; the Arabs used it in the sixth century at convivial gatherings. In early Islamic times the reed instrument was called *mizmār* in Arabic and *nāy* in Persian and later more specifically *nāy-i siyāh* (black *nāy*) due to the color of the pipe (as distinct from the flute with white tube: *nāy-i safīd*). We don't know, however, if they were single- or double-reed instruments. The ninth-century Abbasid musician Zunām was said to have invented a reed pipe—the nature of the invention is unclear—subsequently named *nāy zunāmī,* which became popular in Andalusia. Al-Fārābī described a *mizmār* (flute? reed pipe?) of nine holes and a *surnāy* (reed pipe, also known as *surnā, zurnā, ghayṭah,* ᶜ*irāqīya*) of eleven holes and having a higher register. The latter was used in martial music in the ninth century. Most notes obtained on the ᶜ*ūd* could be obtained on the *mizmār* by controlling the air pressure and/or partial opening of holes. In the *Kanz al-Tuḥaf* the *nāy-i siyāh* is a double-reed instrument with a conical wooden pipe pierced with seven front holes and one back hole. Reed pipes were mainly outdoor instruments used for ceremonial and martial music; they were also used indoors in bathhouses.

An early example of a double-tube reed-type *mizmār* occurred in the eighth-century frescoes of Quṣayr ᶜAmrā. Al-Fārābī called it *dūnāy, al-mizmār al-muthannā,* or *al-mizmār al-muzāwaj,* and described it as consisting of two pipes of equal length, one having four holes and one having five. In thirteenth-century Egypt it was called *mawṣūl.*

An example of a bagpipe was displayed in Sasanian sculptures in pre-Islamic times. In the tenth and eleventh centuries it was called *mizmār al-jirāb* and was played by means of an artificial mechanical device. It was known in Persia as *nāy mashk* and in Turkey as *ghaidā.*

The only known example of a free-reed instrument, though not necessarily in use, was the *mustaq,* an imported Chinese *chêng* (mouth organ).

Reedless pipes were played vertically with air blown across the head orifice. In early Islamic times they were named *quṣṣāba, qaṣaba,* and *yarā*ᶜ. Later they were called *nāy* in Arabic and more precisely *nāy abyaḍ* (white *nay*), and in Persian *nāy-i narm* (soft *nay*) or *nāy-i safīd* (white *nay*). The word *shabbāba* denoted a smaller flute used in the tenth century in Egypt, Iraq, and Andalusia. In the *Kanz al-Tuḥaf* the *nāy* was called *pīsha;* it was probably made of a piece of bamboo that was ripe and straight and had seven or nine holes. Other instruments in this class were the tenth-century *ṣaffāra* (flûte à bec), the *mūsīqār* (panpipe) described by ᶜAbd al-Qādir, and the *shu*ᶜ*aybīya,* a panpipe of eight bamboo tubes described in *Kashf al-Ghumūm.*

Būq. The generic Arabic name for horns and trumpets (*būrū* in Persian and *būrī* or *pirindj būrū* in Turkish). Pre-Islamic Arabs and Persians used an animal horn, which the former called *qarn* (animal horn). A horn made of a shell was called *būq* and was known in eighth-century Arabia, whereas the *būq* made of metal came in the eleventh century with the Seljuks. Before the tenth century the Arabs did not use the *būq* at war, but from the tenth century the *būq* began to play an important role in martial music in Islamic lands.

The trumpet type, with a cylindrical tube, was more precisely called *nafīr.* It had a brighter tone than the *būq.* It also had a straight tube, although ᶜAbd al-Qādir mentioned the *qarnā* as a trumpet bent back in the shape of an S.

MEMBRANOPHONES

Ṭabl. The generic name for single- and double-membrane drums of various geometrical shapes. The *kabar* was a cylindrical-type single-membrane drum mentioned as early as the eighth century. The *dirrīj*

Arab musicians playing *būqāt* (trumpets), *naqqāra* (kettledrum), *ṭabl* (drum), and *kāsāt* (cymbals). From a miniature in a Mesopotamian MS of al-Jazarī's *Treatise on Automata* (1354). COURTESY MUSEUM OF FINE ARTS, BOSTON, GOLOUBEW COLLECTION, 14.533

was a single-membrane goblet-shaped drum known also as *darabukka.* The *kūba* was a double-membrane drum shaped like an hourglass and known in the early seventh century. The *duhull* was a ninth-century military drum, cylindrical and with a double membrane. The *kūrgā* was the largest kettledrum used by Islamic peoples. The *kūs* was smaller and used in the tenth century. Smaller still was the *ṭabl al-markab*, known also as *dabdāb* and *naqqāra,* used in pairs and mounted on a horse or camel's neck. The *nuqaira* or *ṭubaila* was the smallest kettledrum and known in eleventh-century Moorish Spain. The *qaṣᶜa* and *ṭabl al-shāmī* were shallower kettledrum types.

Duff. The generic name for instruments of the tambourine family, *duff* was first reported in the sixth century in Arabic literature. Other names denoting tambourines of specific types (though hard to define with certainty) are: *ghirbāl, mazhar, bandīr, ṭār, dāᵓira,* and *riqq.* In the *Kashf al-Ghumūm* the membrane was of cow skin, and the instrument was struck by fingers and palm.

IDIOPHONES

Ṣanj. The generic name for idiophone, which should not be confused with the similar word *ṣanj,* meaning harp. Usually *ṣanj* denoted cymbals played in pairs and used to mark and keep the *īqāᶜ*. There were many types. *Ṣalṣal* was a high-sounding clashed metal instrument. *Jaghāna* referred to an instrument consisting of small cymbals attached to a frame. *Kāsāt* were hand cymbals in the shape of a plate or bowl; they belonged to martial and processional music and were used with the *ṭabl. Ṣahn* denoted a pair of small bronze cup-shaped instruments struck against each other.

The word *ṣanj* denoted idiophones other than cymbals. *Muṣaffaḥāt* were clappers used by female mourners. *Qaḍīb* was a wand much used by early Islamic musicians, who struck it on the ground to mark the *īqāᶜ*. *Jaras* was a cup, bowl, or cone-shaped bell. *Juljul* was a spherical-shaped bell. *Ṭabla* was a collection of bells on a board, chain, or rope. *Ṭusūt* were tenth-century harmonicas made of vessels, pots, or jars and struck with sticks. ᶜAbd al-Qādir described the *sāz-i kāsāt,* made of earthenware bowls which contained different levels of water. He also described the *sāz-i alwāḥ-i fūlād,* an instrument of thirty-five slabs of steel akin to the glockenspiel.

BIBLIOGRAPHY

This article is based in part on the excellent pioneering works of Henry George Farmer. See his articles on "*Būḳ,*" "*Duff,*" "*Kitāra,*" "*Miᶜzaf,*" "*Mizmār,*" "*Rabāb,*" "*Ṣandj,*" "*Ṭabl,*" "*Ṭunbūr,*" and "*ᶜŪd,*" in the *Encyclopaedia of Islam,* lst ed. (1914–1938). For illustrations see Farmer, *Islam,* III (1966), and Jean Jenkins and Poul Rovsing Olsen, *Music and Musical Instruments in the World of Islam* (1976). For specialized studies see Farmer, *Studies in Oriental Musical Instruments,* series 1 and 2 (1931, 1939; repr. 2 vols. in 1, 1977).

GEORGE DIMITRI SAWA

[See also **Fārābī, al-; Kindī, al-.**]

MUSICAL NOTATION, ALPHABETIC. Alphabetic notation includes any of various systems of musical notation in which pitches are represented by letters. The Greeks used two parallel systems of alphabetic notation. The older "instrumental" notation was a kind of tablature in which letters representing the open strings of a lyre were turned in various directions to indicate notes produced on stopped strings. A different series of letters was used in "vocal" notation to indicate pitches. The Greeks used other alphabetic systems in theoretical discussions of music and acoustics, and it was from these that medieval alphabetic notations developed. Although at times they are found in manuscripts intended for performance, originally they were all methods for explicating and teaching musical theory and are most often found in treatises.

The Middle Ages received its knowledge of the

MUSICAL NOTATION, ALPHABETIC

Greek systems through Book IV of Boethius' *De institutione musica.* Following Porphyry's translation of Ptolemy, Boethius presents a number of different alphabetic series, three of which were adopted by medieval theorists from the ninth century on. The first two of these present different methods for deriving the diatonic scale by dividing a string into sections; these systems reappear in medieval treatises on the monochord. In the first series

A F C G K D L M N X E
(modern pitches) A B c d e f g a b c′ d′ e′ f′ g′ a′

the letters correspond to geometric points on the string. Thus, allowing one fourth of the length of a string A–B to vibrate will produce a pitch a fifth higher than A (labeled C); half the length will produce the octave of A (labeled D), and so on. For the second series, Boethius labels in order all of the diatonic, chromatic, and enharmonic notes used in Greek music, then extracts the series for the diatonic scale:

A B C E H I M O X Y CC DD FF KK LL
(modern) A B c d e f g a b c′ d′ e′ f′ g′ a′

The third series,

A B C D E F G H I K L M N O P,

was used by Boethius to demonstrate that a system of fifteen notes includes eight different octaves (A–H, B–I, C–K, and so on). Although he does not give this series specific pitch values, and hence it cannot be considered an alphabetic notation, several medieval alphabetic systems derive from it.

The *Scolica enchiriadis* (*ca.* 900) is the first surviving treatise to use these letters to label specific pitches, in its instructions for constructing a monochord. Unlike Boethius' monochord, however, on which half steps fall between the second and third and fifth and sixth degrees of the scale, the *Scolica* monochord has half steps between the third and fourth and seventh and eighth degrees, yielding the following scale:

A B C D E F G H I K L M N O P
(modern) c d e f g a b c′ d′ e′ f′ g′ a′ b′ c″

A scale built on C had been mentioned in the *Musica* (formerly *De harmonica institutione*) of Hucbald, dated to the last quarter of the ninth century, but without alphabetical pitch names. Hucbald states that this scale was traditionally used in constructing musical instruments such as bells and organs, and later medieval treatises on these subjects, as well as some on the monochord, use the *Scolica* designations in which A is the equivalent of the modern C. Holschneider has found this notation in the Corpus Christi, Cambridge, copy of the Winchester Troper (MS 473), but it is otherwise unknown in practical sources.

Around the time that the "instrumental notation" is first found, letter names were applied to a "vocal" scale beginning on the modern A. The *Musica enchiriadis,* companion treatise to the *Scolica,* uses a repeating series A–G/A–G, corresponding to the modern pitches A–g/a–g′, in a diagram illustrating harmonic identity at the octave. A later theorist known as Anonymous II (*ca.* 1000) applies the nonrepeating series A–P to the same scale. Unlike the other alphabetical systems, this A–P series for A–a′ was used not only in theoretical treatises but also to notate music for performance in a number of manuscripts dating from the eleventh to the thirteenth century.

Montpellier, Faculté de Médecine, H.159, the most famous "bilingual" manuscript (with chants given in both alphabetic and neumatic notation), uses it, differentiating between b natural and b flat by using a straight (⅂) and a curved (Z) form of the I, respectively, and supplementing the diatonic pitches with symbols representing quarter tones seemingly borrowed from the Greek enharmonic scale (B+, e+, a+, b+, e′+). Significantly, the chants are arranged by type (introits and Communions, alleluias, tracts, and so on) and mode, rather than liturgically, indicating that the manuscript's main purpose was didactic. H.159 has been linked to the spread of the chant reforms of William of Volpiano from Normandy to St. Bénigne in Dijon; in fact, most of the practical manuscripts using this alphabetic notation are from Normandy or post-Conquest England and may also be tied to the spread of the reform movement.

Despite the limited practical application of the A–P series, it was the repeating system that proved most successful. Like the *Musica enchiriadis,* the *Dialogus de musica,* now dated about 1000, repeated the letters A–G but distinguished octaves in the following way:

a b c d
A B C D E F G a b hh c d e f g a b c d
(modern) A B c d e f g a b♭ b♮ c′ d′ e′ f′ g′ a′ b′ c″ d″

The addition of a gamma (Γ) below the first octave extended the system to include all the pitches used in plainsong. This system was adopted by Guido of

Arezzo (*ca.* 1030), the most influential of the medieval theorists, who used it in its full form for theoretical discussions and as clefs (D, C, F, g, ♭) in his practical staff notation.

The quasi-alphabetic notation of Hermann von Reichenau (Hermannus Contractus, 1013–1054) also uses letters, not to indicate degrees of the scale but to specify intervals from one note to the next. The letters used come from the initial letters of the Latin names for the intervals. Thus e *(equaliter)* is a unison; C *(semitonium)* is a half tone; t *(tonus)* is a whole tone; t^s or s *(semiditonus)* is a minor third; $\genfrac{}{}{0pt}{}{t}{t}$ or δ *(ditonus)* is a major third; D *(diatessaron)* is a perfect fourth; Δ *(diapente)* is a perfect fifth; Δ^s *(semitonium cum diapente)* is a minor sixth; Δ^t *(tonus cum diapente)* is a major sixth. Although this notation failed to indicate starting pitch or mode, it was commonly used in copies of Hermann's poems for learning intervals *(Ter tria iunctorum, Ter terni sunt modi)* and teaching the notation system *(E voces unisonas equat)* and in additions to a few practical sources. The success of staff notation, however, eventually confined Hermann's system, together with Daseian notation and the other Frankish alphabetic notations, to the theoretical treatises and didactic purposes for which they were first developed.

BIBLIOGRAPHY

General. The clearest treatment of the subject is Richard L. Crocker, "Alphabetic Notations for Early Medieval Music," in Margot H. King and Wesley M. Stevens, eds., *Saints, Scholars, and Heroes: Studies in Medieval Culture in Honour of Charles W. Jones,* II (1979). Solange Corbin lists the practical and theoretical manuscript sources in "Valeur et sens de la notation alphabétique à Jumièges et en Normandie," in *Congrès scientifique du XIIIe centenaire de Jumièges,* II (1955). See also A. Holschneider, *Die Organa von Winchester* (1968), 89–91; Josef Smits van Waesberghe, "Les origines de la notation alphabétique au moyen-âge," in *Annuario musical,* **12** (1957).

Boethius. Martin Vogel, "Boethius und die Herkunft der modernen Tonbuchstaben," in *Kirchenmusikalisches Jahrbuch,* **46** (1962).

Bilingual notation. Antiphonarium tonale missarum. XIe siècle, Codex H.159 de la Bibliothèque de l'École de médecine de Montpellier, 2 vols. (1901–1905), is a facsimile and description. See also Michel Huglo, "Le tonaire de Saint-Bénigne de Dijon (Montpellier H. 159)," in *Annales musicologiques,* **4** (1956); Joseph Gmelch, *Die Vierteltonstufen im Messtonale von Montpellier* (1911); Josef Smits van Waesberghe, "Die Geschichte von Glastonbury (1082) und ihre Folgen," in Siegfried Kross and Hans Schmidt, eds., *Colloquium amicorum. Joseph Schmidt-Görg zum 70. Geburtstag* (1967).

Hermann von Reichenau. Dom André Mocquereau and Dom Gabriel Beyssac, "De la transcription sur lignes des notations neumatique et alphabétique à propos du répons *Tua sunt,*" in *Riemann-Festschrift* (1909, repr. 1965); Hans Oesch, *Berno und Hermann von Reichenau als Musiktheoretiker* (1961), 204–248.

DIANE L. DROSTE

[See also **Boethius; Guido of Arezzo; Hermann von Reichenau; Hucbald of St. Amand; Tones, Musical; William of Volpiano; Winchester Troper.**]

MUSICAL NOTATION, BILINGUAL. "Bilingual" refers to musical manuscripts or individual pieces that are notated in neumes and in pitch letters. They are thus "bilingual" in the sense that they combine the principal notational system of the practical monuments (neumes) with the older system of pitch letters normally confined to theoretical treatises, in which exact pitch is more important than the nuances of rhythm and/or performance presumably conveyed by the neumes.

About a dozen manuscripts preserve this kind of notation, all but one of them fragments consisting of one or two pieces, or later additions to older manuscripts, not all of which are principally musical in their contents. The major exception is the unique manuscript Montpellier, Faculté de Médecine, H. 159, which dates from the first half of the eleventh century. This source not only employs bilingual notation throughout, but is unique in that it is at once a gradual and a tonary. That is, unlike normal graduals, it arranges the chants of the Proper of the Mass by mode rather than by the liturgical calendar. Unlike most tonaries, on the other hand, it transmits complete chants rather than just incipits. Such a source can only have had a pedagogic or theoretical value, as it could not have been used in the normal way as a service book. Sometime in the latter part of the eleventh century an effort was made to convert it for practical use by adding marginal cues, but this was largely a failure. This was presumably done at a time when the manuscript had outlived its original pedagogic function. Its excellent state of preservation would suggest that it was never used as a practical source.

This source (H. 159) is also known as the Tonary of St. Bênique of Dijon, reflecting its probable place of origin and its possible connection with Wil-

MUSICAL NOTATION, BYZANTINE

liam of Volpiano (*d.* 1031), abbot of St. Bénique from 990, who went to "reform" several monasteries in Normandy, where most of the other bilingual manuscripts originated. Thus H. 159 may have been instrumental in spreading Gregorian chant and bilingual notation to northern France and, indirectly, to England.

In addition to its importance as a link between the purely neumatic and the later sources in staff notation, H. 159 was the single most important early witness for Gregorian chant for the modern reformers of the chant at Solemnes. It would perhaps be an exaggeration to call it a musical Rosetta Stone, but without it the task of reconstructing the Gregorian repertory would have been even more difficult than it was.

BIBLIOGRAPHY

Antiphonarium tonale missarum, XIe siècle, Codex H. 159 de la Bibliothèque de l'École de Médecine de Montpellier, 2 vols. (1901–1905); Solange Corbin, "Valeur et sens de la notation alphabétique à Jumièges et en Normandie," in *Congrès scientifique du XIIIe centenaire de Jumièges,* II (1955); Finn Egeland Hansen, *H. 159 Montpellier: Tonary of St. Bénique of Dijon* (1974); Michel Huglo, "Le tonaire de Saint-Bénique de Dijon," in *Annales musicologiques,* 4 (1956).

ROBERT FALCK

[See also **Musical Notation, Alphabetic; Neume; William of Volpiano.**]

MUSICAL NOTATION, BYZANTINE. The roots of the system of musical notation used in Byzantium are found in Alexandrinian accentual signs for the rise and fall of pitch in recitation. While the exact evolution is still insufficiently clear, it is now assumed that ekphonetic notation represents one of the steps in that process. A truly musical notation appears from around the mid tenth century, with pitch and/or duration signs above each vowel or syllable of text, indicating a melodic motion. The signs used, today called neumes, were restricted to religious texts chanted at the services of the Greek Orthodox Church, which still cultivates this tradition. The history of this musical notation consists of four distinct stages: early, middle, and late Byzantine, and neo-Greek (also called Chrysanthine, in use since the early nineteenth century).

EARLY BYZANTINE NOTATION

The early stage of Byzantine notation was used from the mid tenth century until the last quarter of the twelfth. In this period two different types of neumes coexisted side by side, the Chartres and the Coislin (both names from French collections of manuscripts in which the first documented examples were found and studied). Of these, the Chartres type appears to have been more complex. The more or less contemporary use of the Coislin type, which was simpler and more amenable to development toward precision, suggests the need for clarity in the designation of pitch and rhythm.

MIDDLE BYZANTINE NOTATION

It was from neumes of the Coislin type that middle Byzantine notation, in use from the end of the twelfth until the fifteenth century, appeared. In this stage a successful blend of signs obtains sufficient precision so that this notation can be transcribed into present-day Western European notation without any real difficulty, whereas transcription of the early stage is tentative and hypothetical. Although at present there are several schools of interpretation of the middle Byzantine notation, the differences between them are minor, and they all agree on the basic directional and durational principles of the neumatic notation. It was in this period that new signs, the "great hypostases" functioning as agogic indications for subtler nuances, were introduced. There is no unanimity at present as to the necessity of observing these signs in transcription, as some of them are executed with extreme personal freedom (such as a voice shake, like a trill, or a rasping throaty sound). Most Greeks, by tradition, call the system Koukouzelian notation (named after John Koukouzeles, *ca.* 1280–1360/1375, a famous singer and composer, and presumed inventor of these signs). This legendary ascription has no support in fact, for most signs appeared long before the lifetime of this talented singer. By the mid fifteenth century the neumes had proliferated and the use of red and black ink had cluttered the visual image of the musical signs.

LATE BYZANTINE AND NEO-GREEK NOTATION

Most scholars view the period from the mid fifteenth century until the 1820's as the late Byzantine stage, which is only now being studied after periods of neglect. The final stage of the evolution was achieved by Archbishop Chrysanthos of Madytos and his associates (referred to as the "Three Teach-

MUSICAL NOTATION, BYZANTINE

ers"), who had their notation printed, and thus fixed and less subject to individual changes and evolution. The reform of Chrysanthos was needed because manuscripts were too overloaded with neumes and complex additional signs. In this process a purge was conducted, eliminating many old signs and introducing new, much more precise ones. Under Western influence, Chrysanthos invented solmization (the use of syllables for each pitch, such as do-re-mi), in which the syllables pa-bou-ga-de-ke-zo-ni (starting on D and going up to C) were first used. Chrysanthos introduced signs for sharps and flats, which had been absent. The Byzantine neumatic notation, while economical, never indicated precisely the size of musical intervals, such as the difference between the major and the minor third: the neume simply indicates a third, and from the context the singer would adjust the step. It is also significant that in the Byzantine musical tradition there is still no concept of equal temperament in the tuning; and the intervals and scales, while similar, do not necessarily agree with the Western European concepts of the last three centuries. To a Western European, the chanting of Greeks and of singers in all areas east of the Mediterranean may sound "off-pitch" and "out of tune," yet these chants, carried in an oral tradition, cannot be notated in Western European five-line staff notation, which is limited in its ability to reproduce the tonal patterns of the Byzantine and some other notations.

BASIC PRINCIPLES

Some basic principles of Byzantine notations from about 1200 are the following: all signs designate the movement in relationship to the preceding pitch; there is one sign for a repetition of the preceding pitch, called *ison.* All other signs indicate steps, and are divided into "bodies" and "spirits." Bodies move in single steps (that is, they designate the musical interval of a second, a neighboring pitch like do–re) while spirits designate leaps (like do–mi or do–sol). For the melodic movement of a second upward, there are six signs, each with a special nuance in rendition; they include *oligon* (step up), *oxeia* (accented move upward), *petastē* (accent with sharp voice attack), and *kouphisma* (move up with a voice shake like a trill). For the downward motion a single neume, *apostrophos,* indicates a second downward (such as sol–fa). Among the spirits there are two signs for each direction: for upward motion, *kentēma* (the interval of a third) and *hypsēlē* (a fifth); for downward motion, *elaphron* (third) and *chamēlē* (fifth).

The proper orthography rules require that no spirit should stand without a body, which in practice means that a correct representation of the interval of a third upward ought to be written as *oligon* plus *kentēma.* Body precedes spirit from left to right; but if the spirit is written above the body, then intervalic values are added up and such a grouping (for instance *kentēma* above an *oligon*) designates the melodic interval of a fourth upward. Similarly, the *hypsēlē* depicts both the fifth and sixth upward, and which one it is depends on the location of the accompanying body. The same convention applies to the descending melodic intervals: proper grouping for a descending third is *apostrophos* plus *elaphron,* but if it appears as *elaphron* above *apostrophos,* then the interval is a descending fourth; the same procedure is used with *chamēlē* for descending fifth and

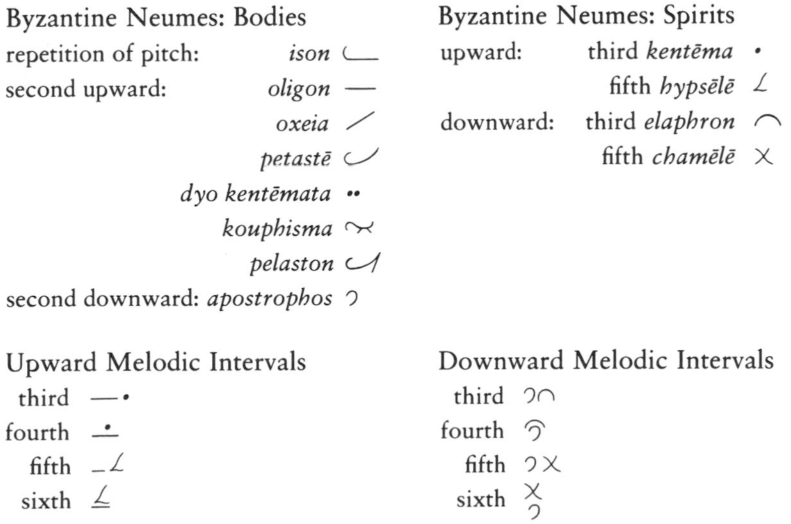
Byzantine Neumes: Bodies
repetition of pitch: ison
second upward: oligon
oxeia
petastē
dyo kentēmata
kouphisma
pelaston
second downward: apostrophos
Byzantine Neumes: Spirits
upward: third kentēma
fifth hypsēlē
downward: third elaphron
fifth chamēlē
Upward Melodic Intervals
third
fourth
fifth
sixth
Downward Melodic Intervals
third
fourth
fifth
sixth

sixth. While larger intervals are theoretically possible, they seldom appear in manuscripts (though upward-moving octaves can be found easily, downward intervals seldom are larger than a sixth).

The sign called *diplē* indicates lengthening and is usually transcribed as a quarter note in length (basic signs are transcribed as eighth notes); the sign *tzakisma* is interpreted as having a function similar to the use of a dot in Western notation, extending the length by one half of the original value. Other signs and meanings can be located in monographs. The pitch and rhythmic values in the transcriptions of the series *Monumenta musicae byzantinae* have never been viewed as anything but a convention. The pitches are relative, as are the rhythmic values in their duration, and they should not be measured against the metronome. The *Grottaferrata* school basically doubles the length of rhythmic values used in the *Bolletino della Badia Greca di Grottaferrata* transcriptions, while Heinrich Husmann simply writes out notes without stems, leaving the duration of each sign open, more in the manner of the Roman chant tradition.

BIBLIOGRAPHY

Max Haas, *Byzantinische und slavische Notationen* (1973); W. Oliver Strunk, *Specimina notationum antiquiorum* (1966); Miloš Velimirović, "Byzantine Neumatic Notations," in *New Grove Dictionary of Music and Musicians,* XIII (1980).

MILOŠ VELIMIROVIĆ

[See also **Music, Byzantine; Musical Notation, Ekphonetic; Neume; Solmization.**]

MUSICAL NOTATION, DASEIAN. Daseian notation is a special kind of alphabetic notation, so called because most of the symbols used to represent the pitches derive from the Greek character for rough breathing (⊢: *prosodia daseia*), combined with the Latin letters *s* and *c*. The other pitch symbols are variants on the Latin letters *I* and *N*. The notation is found only in a few ninth- and early-tenth-century musical treatises, notably the *Musica enchiriadis, Scholica enchiriadis,* and *Commemoratio brevis de tonis et psalmis modulandis;* but it is important both as an early attempt to indicate precise pitch, and because these treatises contain most of the surviving evidence on the earliest polyphony.

The system uses four basic symbols, assigned to the pitches D, E, F, and G, that is, to the finals of the modes of Gregorian chant:

D E F G

These four pitches make up a tetrachord with the interval structure tone–semitone–tone:

D ‿ E ‿ F ‿ G
T S T

The Daseian system is expanded by adding other tetrachords of the same structure above and below the tetrachord of the finals, and rotating the four basic symbols in different directions for each tetrachord, resulting in the following gamut:

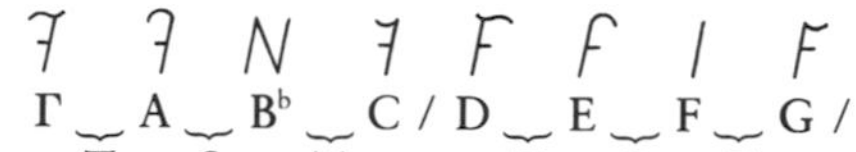

Γ ‿ A ‿ B^b ‿ C / D ‿ E ‿ F ‿ G /
T S T T S T
graves *finales*

a ‿ b ‿ c ‿ d / e ‿ f# ‿ g ‿ a / b ‿ c#
T S T T S T T
superiores *excellentes* *residui*

The scale produced by this series of tetrachords is remarkable in having augmented octaves (B^b–b; F–f#; c–c#) and augmented fourths (B^b–E; c–f#; g–c#). All the fifths, however, are perfect, indicating that the system was designed for notating strictly parallel organum at the fifth. Consequently, when the treatises present organum at the fourth, they use oblique motion to avoid the augmented intervals.

BIBLIOGRAPHY

Terence Bailey, ed., *Commemoratio brevis de tonis et psalmis modulandis* (1979); L. B. Spiess, "The Diatonic 'Chromaticism' of the *Enchiriadis* Treatises," in *Journal of the American Musicological Society,* **12** (1959).

DIANE L. DROSTE

MUSICAL NOTATION, EKPHONETIC, refers to signs used in solemn readings of liturgical texts in religious services. The term "ekphonetic" is derived from the Greek *ekphōnesis* (utterance, pronunciation). Relatively few in number, these signs are usually placed above or below the text, at the beginnings and ends of sentences, signaling the reader of the need to raise or lower the voice. Ekphonetic notation is found in liturgical books of the Eastern Orthodox churches, especially the Byzantine, where it may have originated by the fifth century, though the oldest extant manuscripts date from the ninth century, when the system was already fully formed; after the fifteenth century the meaning of these signs had become forgotten, though their copying continued until recent times. One of the presumed meanings was to indicate melodic formulas in a succinct fashion.

BIBLIOGRAPHY

Gudrun Engberg, "Ekphonetic Notation," in *New Grove Dictionary of Music and Musicians,* VI (1980); Carsten Høeg, *La notation ekphonétique* (1935).

MILOŠ VELIMIROVIĆ

[See also Byzantine Church; Liturgy, Byzantine Church; Music, Armenian (with illustration); Music, Byzantine; Musical Notation, Byzantine.]

MUSICAL NOTATION, HUFNAGEL (German for horseshoe nail). This type of plainsong notation, named after the resemblance of its *virga* (a symbol representing a single note higher than the note preceding it or following it) to a hobnail ♱, is found in German and Eastern European manuscripts of the thirteenth through sixteenth centuries. Properly speaking, Hufnagel, which developed from the early neumatic notation of St. Gall and southern Germany, is only one branch of the larger category of Gothic notation. A second type developed from the neumes used further north in the region around Metz, and is characterized by the absence of a separate symbol for the *virga;* that is, both the *virga* and the *punctum* (representing a lower pitch) are written as a diamond-shaped note: ◆ or ◢. Both Hufnagel and Messine Gothic notation are found throughout Eastern Europe, although one type or the other tends to predominate, depending upon the geographical region. Furthermore, certain regions, such as Bohemia and Poland, developed highly individual forms of Messine Gothic, which are unique to those areas and which are found alongside the more widespread basic types.

All of these kinds of Gothic notation share characteristics that may present some difficulty to the reader acquainted only with square notation. The difficulty stems from the fact that while square notation is written with the pen nib held at right angles to the line of writing, Gothic notation preserves the 45-degree angle of ordinary text-writing. Thus, the connecting hair-lines of square notation appear as thick tails in Gothic, which can sometimes be mistaken for notes. The following table shows the basic neume-types as written in Hufnagel, Messine Gothic, and the regional notations of Bohemia and Poland, together with their square-notation equivalents:

Neume-type	Square	Hufnagel	Messine	Bohemia	Poland
Virga	◧	♱	◢ or ◣	◆	◥
Punctum	◆ or ◼	◆	◢ or ◣	◆	◆
Pes	◲	◢ or ◰	◠ or ◡	◆◆	◲
Clivis	◳	∧ or ◥	◥	◥	∧ or ◥
Scandicus	◳ or ◳	◢ or ◰	◠, ◠, ◰	◆◆◆	◌, ◌, ◰
Climacus	◥◆◆	◥◆◆	◠◆◆, ◆◆◆, ◆◆	◆◆◆	∧◆
Torculus	⊓	∫∫ or ∫∫	◠	◆◥	∫∫
Porrectus	◩	℧ or ◪	℧	◡◡	℧

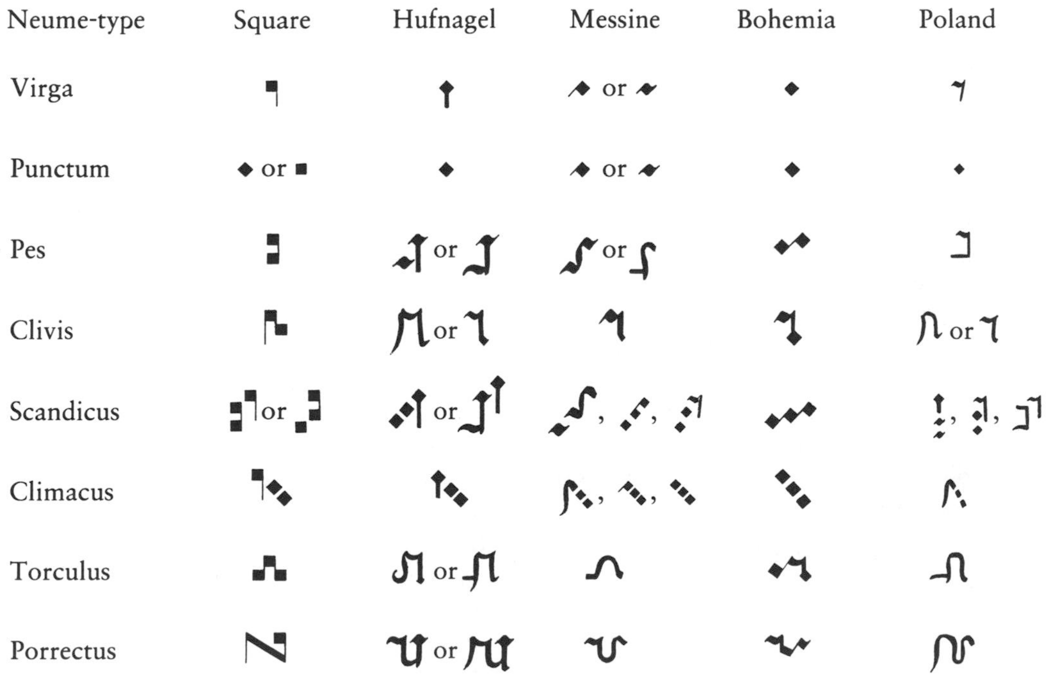

MUSICAL NOTATION, HUFNAGEL

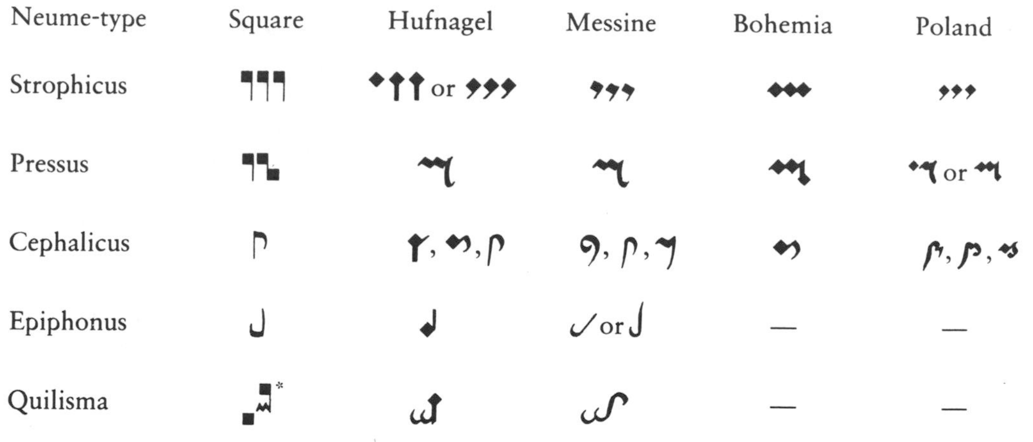

*Not found in medieval sources

BIBLIOGRAPHY

As is the case with all late plainsong notations, few detailed studies have been done on Hufnagel or Gothic notation. Most of the general studies treat it cursorily, the most recent being Solange Corbin, *Die Neumen* (1977), 66–73, the footnotes of which give a good guide to more specific and regional studies. Peter Wagner, *Einführung in die gregorianischen Melodien,* II, *Neumenkunde,* 2nd ed. (1912, repr. 1962), 322–343, includes a discussion of a number of plates, as does Bruno Stäblein, *Schriftbild der einstimmigen Musik* (1975), 67–68, 190–211. The most comprehensive series of plates, without commentary, is in *Le répons-graduel Justus ut palma,* II (1892).

On the distribution of Hufnagel and Messine notation, see J. Hourlier, "Le domaine de la notation messine," in *Revue grégorienne,* 30 (1951).

DIANE L. DROSTE

[See also **Gregorian Chant; Musical Notation, Western; Neume; Plainsong, Eastern European.**]

MUSICAL NOTATION, MODAL. A passage in the anonymous treatise *Discantus positio vulgaris* (early thirteenth century), described by Jerome of Moravia as older than all the other treatises he transmits in his *Tractatus de musica,* addresses the matter of the durational quality of notes for the first time in the history of Western polyphony. All notes of a discant, that is, of the upper voice (or a portion of it) constructed in discant style over the cantus firmus in the tenor of an organum,

> are measurable by means of the proper breve [short] and the proper long. Thus, it follows that against any given note of the cantus firmus at least two notes—it goes without saying, a long and short or something equivalent to them . . . must be presented; and furthermore, [notes of plainchant and discant] must arrive together on any one of the said three consonances [unison, octave, fifth].

Hence, presumably sometime in the last quarter or third of the twelfth century, discant gave rise to measured music by setting against the tenor notes a standard of subdivision that recognized a differentiation of long and short in the simple proportion 2:1. These were the only precisely measurable units. The primacy of this rhythm is doubtless due to the fact that in discant counterpoint that has advanced from note-against-note to the setting of two successive notes against one in the cantus firmus, the note which intervenes between two vertical consonances is often dissonant and it was therefore recognized as a lesser value. John of Garland, writing about 1250, makes it clear that the rhythm of organal passages lacked this precision; they were "performed not in accordance with the regular, but in a sort of irregular way."

In the notation of the time, durational values were indicated by constellations of ligatures. (In the emerging square notation, ligatures, successors to certain neumes of earlier notational systems, combine within themselves two or more successive pitches "tied together" by lines.) The fact that dissonance is resolved by consonance (rather than the reverse) accounts for the most basic mensural symbol and its interpretation: the binary (two-note) ligature is read as a unit, with the second of its two notes having twice the length of the first. (The two notes of a binary ligature are generally transcribed into common-practice modern notation as eighth note and quarter note; ligation is indicated by brackets over the notes.) Phrase endings were marked in the manuscripts with short strokes that almost always

Example 1

function as short (eighth-note) rests. The long-short-long beginning of most phrases was usually written as a ternary ligature. In the above short excerpt (Ex. 1) the first two phrases show that often "something equivalent" to long and short caused the rhythms to be rather rapid. Notes of duration 2+1 (as the tenor notes in the above example) were, as the author of the *Discantus positio vulgaris* put it, "long and beyond measurement, because they contain the measurement of three time units." They were written as single notes.

In the first decade of the thirteenth century, other rhythms began to be conceptualized, resulting in patterns whose variety required codification into a system. For instance, just as phrases up to that time had traditionally begun and ended with a long note (quarter note), it now became possible to have an upper-voice passage in discant style contain phrases beginning and ending with a short value. These diverse rhythmic patterns required differing arrangements of ligatures. Various contextual constellations of ligatures indicated the basic rhythmic patterns, of which there were generally acknowledged to be six. Hence, there were six ways *(modi)* or modes of patterning durations and ligatures (Ex. 2). The third, fourth, and fifth modes were called "beyond measurement," since they contained an element other than the proper long and the proper short. As is apparent from Example 2, the meaning of the ligature constellations depends on their context. Not single notes nor single ligatures, but the configurations of the ligatures in successive phrases, determine their constituent rhythms. Thus, the ternary ligature  (or  or  or ) must be read in five different ways (first, second, third, fifth, and sixth modes; the fourth mode is a theoretical invention for the sake of the construction of the system in balanced pairs and is of no practical significance).

The rhythmic mode of each voice in a composition was invariably consistent. Two parts could be

Example 2

(1) 3 + 2 + (2 + . . . + 2) + 2, *e.g.*, 3 + 2 + 2 + 2 = 

(2) 2 + 2 + (2 + . . . + 2) + 3, *e.g.*, 2 + 2 + 2 + 3 = 

(3) 1 + 3 + (3 + . . . + 3) + 3, *e.g.*, 1 + 3 + 3 + 3 = 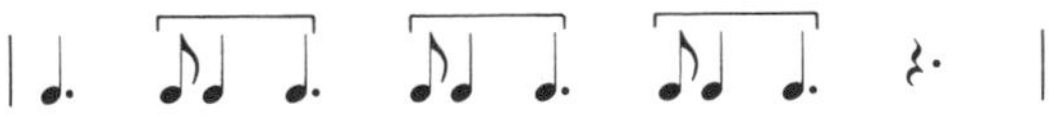

(4) 3 + 3 + (3 + . . . + 3) + 2, *e.g.*, 3 + 3 + 3 + 2 = 

(5) 1 + 1 + (2 + . . . + 1) + 1, *e.g.*, 1 + 1 + 1 + 1 = 

(6) 4 + 3 + (3 + . . . + 3) + 3, *e.g.*, 4 + 3 + 3 + 3 = 

Fifth-mode rhythms were restricted to and common in tenors of clausulae and motets, where the earliest and most usual pattern was 

Example 3

written in differing modes, as long as those modes with iambic elements (second and, in effect, third) were not mixed with the first mode in the same passage. It is important to keep in mind that the six rhythmic modes are a didactic codification of often astonishingly lively rhythms, the graphic indication of which sometimes put the system of ligature notation to a severe test (Ex. 3). Not until the fourth phrase of the duplum of this clausula does it become apparent that its basic rhythms are those of the second mode.

While modal rhythm is mainly a feature of clausulae (see *Perotinus*) and motets, some organa tripla and certain conductus caudae also display the new rhythms. There is no evidence, however, that the rhythms of the modal system were applicable to any other genre of the time, at least before they had developed in the clausulae, and probably for some time thereafter. Published modern transcriptions of conductus, as well as of troubadour and trouvère songs, must therefore be read with caution. Syllabic music, monophonic as well as polyphonic, had no symbols of notation denoting fixed rhythmic relationships; there was only one single-note symbol, and therefore only ligatures (and similar configurations), inapplicable to strictly syllabic music, could convey rhythms. Since for some decades the upper parts of motets, like those of the conductus, could be written with only one note symbol throughout, it is likely that the appropriate rhythms often had to be ascertained from the ligature notation of the clausulae of which the motets were texted adaptations.

The notational ambiguity of syllabic music was eliminated later in the century through the adoption of specific single-note symbols by John of Garland and Franco of Cologne (*ca.* 1280). The latter also recognized that the proliferation of shorter note values and the increasing prolixity of the French texts of many motet tripla made the modal system unworkable. Franco's central concept, that of the perfection (a unit of three beats, that is, three breves or their equivalent), as well as the invention of specifically shaped ligatures, eliminating the necessity of having to deduce their rhythmic meaning from the context, had the potential of neutralizing modal differences. As Franco put it, "Through the perfections all modes are reduced to one" and the mingling of the rhythms of the inconsistent first and second modes now became possible.

The more or less natural and indivisible swing of modal phrases now gave way to a more complicated musical phraseology whose relatively complex rhythms and lengths were defined by the underlying regularity of the neutral measuring units (the beats of the breves), shaped into often irregular strings of perfections at the composer's discretion. Though writers on music continued to mention the modal system until the early fourteenth century, their descriptions became more and more perfunctory. A new way of measuring time by mechanical units had begun to impinge on organic time as experienced. Significantly, the appearance of this new style coincided with the invention of the mechanical clock, which, beginning in the thirteenth century, gradually displaced the older timepieces operated by water or sand, and the sundial.

BIBLIOGRAPHY

Sources. Franco of Cologne, *Ars cantus mensurabilis,* in W. Oliver Strunk, ed. and trans., *Source Readings in Music History,* I (1965); Jerome of Moravia, *Tractatus de musica,* Simon Cserba, ed., in *Freiburger Studien zur Musikwissenschaft,* II (1935); John of Garland (Johannes de Garlandia), *De mensurabili musica,* Erich Reimer, ed., 2 vols. (1972), trans. as *Concerning Measured Music* by Stanley H. Birnbaum (1978); Janet Knapp, trans., "Two 13th-Century Treatises on Modal Rhythm and the Discant," in *Journal of Music Theory,* **6** (1962).

Studies. Ian D. Bent, "Rhythmic Modes," in *New Grove Dictionary of Music and Musicians,* XV (1980), with full bibliog.; Wolf Frobenius, "Modus (Rhytmuslehre)," in *Handwörterbuch der musikalischen Terminologie* (1974); Ernest H. Sanders, "Consonance and Rhythm in the Organum of the 12th and 13th Centuries," in *Journal of the American Musicological Society,* **33** (1980), and "Conductus and Modal Rhythm," *ibid.,* **38** (1985).

ERNEST H. SANDERS

MUSICAL NOTATION, WESTERN

[See also **Ars Antiqua; Clausula; Franco of Cologne; John of Garland; Mode; Notre Dame School; Organum.**]

MUSICAL NOTATION, WESTERN. "Notation" will be understood here as any system of signs or symbols for recording musical information. Among the uses to which Western notation has been put are the preservation of existing music, the teaching of music as a discipline, the learning of music to be performed, and the composition of music, which not only allows the composer to fix ideas in permanent form but also permits the conceptualization of music in a way that is not possible in an exclusively oral tradition. The Western systems of musical notation were developed in response to all of these needs, and continue to serve them in various ways. It is well to keep these diverse purposes in mind when reviewing the history of notation, as some innovations and developments are aimed more clearly at one of these needs than at the others.

While most literate civilizations have developed some kind of notation for music, musical notation in the West has both a broader application and a deeper significance for the art of music than it has elsewhere. Although many refinements have been made subsequently, all of the most important features of modern notation were present by the fifteenth century. Since it owes very little to ancient models or precedents, it is not unreasonable to view Western notation as a uniquely European and medieval achievement.

Although the account that follows will be confined to the narrower subject of notation, it is not always possible to separate this subject cleanly from the larger field of music theory. Indeed, it is reasonable to regard Western notation as an embodiment of the most fundamental features of the European system of music theory. A simple example will illustrate this point. The musical staff, far from being a neutral receptacle suited to any system of tones, has built into it the succession of whole tones and semitones characteristic of the diatonic scale. Furthermore, since most notational innovations were made in response to some musical need, it is likewise difficult to separate notation from the music it transmits. Again, an example will illustrate. The question of the time and place of origin of Gregorian chant is influenced by, and in turn influences, what is believed about the time and place of origin of the neumes that transmit that repertory.

Any attempt to understand or to bring to life any music composed before 1500 must necessarily begin with its notation, the study of which thus becomes the most important preliminary matter for the student of medieval music. No musical tradition can be fully apprehended through its graphic manifestations alone, however, and no transcription of a medieval composition into modern notational symbols, however expert, can ever completely convey the sound and spirit of the music as it was performed. Indeed, the modern grasp of the basic principles of some kinds of notation is so tenuous that some repertories, such as that of Mozarabic chant, are lost forever, even though notated manuscripts are extant. This should not be accepted as an excuse for ignoring the study of musical paleography, however, as it remains the only concrete link with medieval music.

The means of representing pitch and rhythm are the basic components of Western notation and its history. They will be taken up in that order below, as the working out of the modern system of measures and note values came about only after the problem of an accurate pitch notation had been solved.

PITCH NOTATIONS

No aspect of Western notation has received a fraction of the attention that has been lavished on the neumatic notation transmitting the musical liturgy of the Roman Catholic Church. This is not surprising, in view of the practical importance the subject has for the daily performance of the music in its liturgical setting. The research carried out since the mid nineteenth century by the monks of Solesmes, with the goal of preparing a reformed edition of the chant, has been the major impetus and the basis for all subsequent work in the field.

It is not possible to date the beginnings of neumatic notation with any certainty, and scholars' estimates of its age are influenced not only by the dating of the extant documents but also by their theories about the antecedents of the neumes. This much may be stated, given the present state of research and scholarly opinion: There are fragments, individual examples of neumatic notation from the ninth century, and fully notated manuscripts from the tenth century on. The notation in the latter is so highly developed and precisely executed that it is all but impossible to avoid postulating a prehistory for the neumes. Since there are specimens from Switzerland, Germany, various parts of France, England, and Italy written in a variety of neumatic "dialects" among the oldest sources, the case for a common or-

MUSICAL NOTATION, WESTERN

igin followed by a period of separate development becomes even more persuasive.

The most authoritative view of the matter is that neumatic notation is a Frankish invention of the eighth or ninth century, and must be viewed as part of the Carolingian initiative to standardize and improve both the practice and the theory of music in the empire. There are, and no doubt will continue to be, many dissenters to this view. The basis for most theories of a chronologically and/or geographically more remote origin, however, is one or the other theory of the perceptual model for neumatic notation, rather than the dating and provenance of the existing sources themselves. These theories are summarized below, based largely on the account of Solange Corbin (*Die Neumen,* 3.11–3.21).

The theory that neumatic notation grew out of various systems of punctuation signs added to sacred texts to clarify their structure for reading or cantillation is an old one, and takes a limited number of distinct forms. One such theory views the neumes as descendants of the ekphonetic signs of Byzantine notation. These originally punctuating signs took on a musical meaning, probably representing specific melodic formulas, and were inserted into the text as reminders that a melodic formula was to be sung at certain places. A similar theory views the *te 'amim* signs of Hebrew cantillation as the source of the neumes. Like the Greek ekphonetic signs, the *te 'amim* are individual signs that stand for melodic phrases of varying length. The difficulty with both of these theories is that there is very little evidence to suggest that the neumes ever functioned in this way. Virtually all the neumes, and certainly the basic ones, are essentially graphs whose components are individual pitches. While Byzantine musicians eventually developed a notation that is completely readable, its basic components are still not the individual pitches of the Western system but, rather, the intervals between them. While it is not possible to conclusively disprove any indebtedness to Greek or Hebrew examples, the available evidence strongly suggests that the Western system is based upon a fundamentally different principle.

Another school of thought views the grammatical and diacritical signs of Latin and/or Greek as the source of neumatic notation. These include the various signs of punctuation, the prosodic signs for long and short syllables, and the accents. It seems virtually undeniable that the acute and grave accents are the principal source for the neumes, at least in their basic conception. The difficulty with this theory is that Latin manuscripts written prior to the appearance of the neumes use the accents only rarely, and the prosodic signs scarcely at all. Thus, it is difficult to demonstrate that the neumes are the natural and inevitable end product of the refinement, augmentation, and reinterpretation of the accents and prosodic signs of the Latin grammarians.

Although there are relatively few basic neumes, they are combined, altered, and enhanced in a bewildering variety of ways. In addition, there are more than a dozen regional variants (dialects) of neumatic notation that, though they all use the same basic signs, are so different in appearance that to the untrained observer many would seem quite unrelated. These basic neumes are shown in Example 1, with the most common name given first and other medieval names in parentheses. The form of the individual neume shown is that of St. Gall, the most fully developed and documented of the early notations. The next column shows the equivalent sign used in the modern chant books, which is based on the square notation as it was standardized, largely in France, in the thirteenth century. Finally, the equivalent in ordinary modern notation, as it is interpreted by the school of Solesmes, is shown.

Although this table contains only eight of the fifteen to twenty most common neumes, it allows us to draw some conclusions. It is clear from the forms of the neumes that there are at most four, or possibly five, basic elements that are combined and recombined to form the more complex neumes. (The *torculus,* for example, is clearly a combination of *pes* and *clivis.*) The terminology does not always reflect this, but one tradition for naming the neumes clearly does (Michel Huglo's *tabula prolixor* uses *pes flexus* in place of *torculus, virga prebipunctis* in place of *scandicus,* and so on). The other point that can be made is that, however incompletely, at least some traditions suggest a firm link with the accents of Latin prosody. The *accentus acutus* and *accentus gravis* are found only in the Italian tradition, but *flexa* is a frequent synonym for the circumflex accent in Latin grammars of classical and postclassical times, and is not uncommon in modern terminology for the neumes.

Another peculiarity in Example 1 leads to the question of rhythm. While one form is shown for the other neumes, two are given for the *punctum.* One of these is literally a "point"; the other, an elongated stroke sometimes referred to as a *producta,* which seems to suggest a prolonged *punctum.* This introduces the notion that the neumes can convey

Example 1

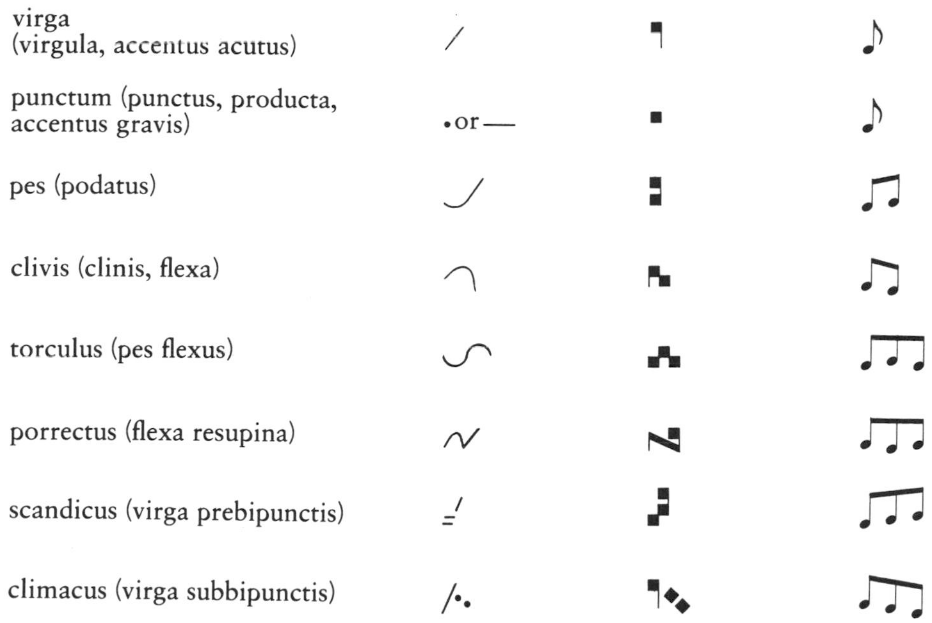
virga
(virgula, accentus acutus)
punctum (punctus, producta,
accentus gravis)
•or —
pes (podatus)
clivis (clinis, flexa)
torculus (pes flexus)
porrectus (flexa resupina)
scandicus (virga prebipunctis)
climacus (virga subbipunctis)

information about duration as well as pitch. This is confirmed by altered forms of most other neumes, in which added strokes (/ becomes *T*, for example) seem to indicate that a note so altered has a duration longer than normal.

In addition, certain letters are added to the neumes in many of the early manuscripts, some of them further clarifying pitch and others clarifying duration or tempo. These "Romanus letters" are contained in a letter written by Notker Balbulus (*d.* 912), who assigns a word to virtually every letter of the alphabet. Few of these are actually used in the sources, however, and their interpretation remains problematic. Although both the letters and the specially altered neumes are used with great care and evident consistency in the early manuscripts, especially those of St. Gall, they are not universal, and begin to disappear in the eleventh century. The more neutral rhythmic notation of *cantus planus,* which arose in the twelfth century, continues to shape the modern view of the chant as a music that lacks a strong rhythmic profile.

If the early notators of chant had been motivated solely by the wish to preserve an accurate record of the pitch content of the repertory, other systems available to them by the ninth century were both simpler and much less ambiguous than the refined but somewhat unwieldy neumatic notation. The most important of these is the system of assigning letters of the alphabet to the individual pitches of the scale. Several such systems were in use at various times and for various purposes, and alphabetic notations were known outside Europe both before and after the Middle Ages. Only two of the medieval notations are important enough to warrant mention here (see Ex. 2). The first was taken over from Boe-

Example 2

	A	B	C	D	E	F	G	H	I	K	L	M	N	O	P
Γ	A	B	C	D	E	F	G	a	b♮	c	d	e	f	g	aa
G	A	B	c	d	e	f	g	a	b♮b	c′	d′	e′	f′	g′	a′
				("soft")		ut	re	mi	fa	sol	la				
("natural")			ut	re	mi	fa	sol	la		ut	re	mi	fa	sol	la
("hard")ut	re	mi	fa	sol	la		ut	re	mi	fa	sol	la	la		

 MUSICAL NOTATION, WESTERN

thius (*ca.* 480–524/526), who used the letters A–P to mark the positions of the fifteen tones of the Greater Perfect System on the monochord. Although the letters were not intended to replace the traditional Greek names for the notes, they were so used by medieval theorists.

The top line in Example 2 shows the Boethian letters, which were also, quite exceptionally, used to clarify pitch in a small group of early neumatic manuscripts. The next line shows the octave-duplicating form that letter notation took beginning about 1000. With the addition of Γ (gamma) at the lower end of the scale, this became the standard way of identifying pitches throughout the later Middle Ages and, with slight modifications, is the system in use today. The contemporary system of identifying pitches in the various octaves is shown for comparison in the third line of Example 2.

While letter notation has only exceptionally been used in practical monuments of music, it is perhaps the most important pedagogical device, especially for the teaching of musical rudiments. Its origin is quite separate and distinct from the neumes, and has remained a separate, though complementary, feature of notation. The solmization syllables introduced by Guido of Arezzo in the eleventh century for expressly pedagogic purposes represent a mnemonic device for teaching singers to sing the whole and half steps in the right places (see Ex. 2, bottom). It is thus a more practical device, but it also emphasizes the division of the gamut into units smaller than octaves, which the more purely theoretical letter names do not. The "hard" hexachord is so called because it contains B natural *(b durum)*, while the "soft" contains B-flat *(b mollis);* the "natural" contains neither. Although not part of the medieval notational system per se, the solmization syllables and the doctrine of hexachord mutation can nevertheless provide important clues to the application of *musica ficta,* and thus to the correct transcription and performance of much medieval music.

One other form of notation that was used sporadically during the ninth and tenth centuries, only to disappear without a trace, the Daseian, derived from the *prosodia daseia* or rough-breathing sign of Greek prosody (⊢). Three forms are derived from this single sign; together with a distinctive sign to represent fa, they stand for the four tones of the central tetrachord (d–g) of the gamut (see Ex. 3). An additional tetrachord below, and two additional tetrachords plus two tones above, are obtained by reversing, inverting, and inverting and reversing the basic signs. Within each tetrachord, however, fa receives a distinctive sign. In principle, the signs of this system most closely resemble Guido's solmization syllables, in that they identify fixed positions within a segment of the gamut that is smaller than the octave, and clearly focus on the location of the semitone. The principal flaw of the Daseian system is that it fails to produce uniform octaves, rendering it unsuitable for theoretical demonstrations and imprecise for the notation of melodies that fall outside the central octave d–d′. This curious notation was never employed in practical musical sources, and modern interest in it is largely explained by its association with the oldest notated examples of polyphonic music in the *Musica enchiriadis* (ninth century).

Some other early attempts to solve the problem of musical notation may be mentioned briefly. One is the adaptation by Hucbald (*ca.* 850–930) of yet another system, or systems, of Greek notation based on Boethius. For the most part it uses variously altered Greek letters, but represents its lowest pitch, perhaps not coincidentally, by the *prosodia daseia.* The two-voiced Alleluia from the Paris Organum Treatise (tenth century) employs Daseian signs, a staff, and a host of additional signs unique to it. Theoretical treatises of the period sometimes employ the same staff, which uses only the spaces, and not the lines, with the letters T and S (tone, semitone) to clarify the intervals. Hermann von Reichenau (Hermannus Contractus, 1013–1054) devised a system that uses both Latin and Greek letters to specify the intervals between pitches. These often quite isolated experiments, together with the various "dialects" of neumatic notation, convey a picture of great diversity in the earliest period of Western notation. Separate systems were either absorbed into larger ones, as was the case with neumes, letters, and solmization syllables, or were forgotten, as were the Daseian signs

Example 3

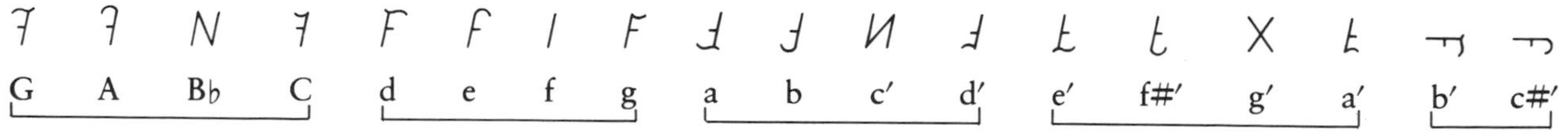

MUSICAL NOTATION, WESTERN

and the interval letters of Hermann von Reichenau. The uniformity of outward appearance presented by modern notation was not achieved until the advent of printed music in the sixteenth century.

The gradual introduction of one, and then more, reference lines that eventually become the musical staff is not a radical departure from neumatic notation, but simply a refinement of a feature present from the beginning. That is, all neumes of more than one note are pitch graphs, and a heightened relationship of one neume to another is a feature of more than one of the early "dialects" of neumatic notation. The decisive step in the direction of a thorough-going staff notation seems to have been taken in the Aquitanian sources. The practice in these sources was, from a very early period, to write the text on every other ruled drypoint line, leaving the odd-numbered lines for the neumes. (The normal practice was to write on every line and squeeze the neumes in between.) This left more space for careful heightening, and the drypoint line itself was used as a pitch reference, often with a clef (key) in the form of a pitch letter in the left-hand margin of each line.

It was a short step from there to the addition of a second, third, fourth, and, sometimes, fifth line, with the position of f or c, or both (that is, the position of the half step or steps), indicated by a clef sign. Sometimes the lines of the staff were rules in different colors; at other times in a uniform color, typically red. This development was largely complete by the thirteenth century, when virtually all musical manuscripts used the staff routinely, though sources written with neumes *in campo aperto* continued to be produced down to the fourteenth century.

Aquitanian notation began to break the neumes more and more into their individual components, *punctum* and *virga.* These sources, more than any others, have the appearance of true pitch graphs, with individual points plotted with the precision of holes in a computer card. With the introduction of the staff, the neumes were deprived of their original function, and nothing would have prevented the adoption of a notation made up entirely of points on a graph. That this did not happen may be attributed partly to the force of tradition, and partly to the fact that groups of notes are easier both to read and to write than a uniform series of individual ones. Deprived of their original function as signs for high and low pitch, the neumes were free to take on new meaning as the basic elements of the new mensural system.

RHYTHMIC NOTATIONS

The special demands made by polyphonic music on musical notation evidently prompted the creation of a system of measured notation that is the ancestor of the modern system. Although polyphonic singing was part of the European tradition at least as early as the ninth century, relatively few practical monuments were produced before the twelfth. The school of St. Martial is known through a number of carefully notated sources, most of which are written in Aquitanian notation. In these sources, the problem of the rhythmic coordination of the individual voices is not yet solved, but the use of "score" notation is preferred to successive or "part" notation. The practical advantage of score notation for music in which one voice is more active than the other will be obvious, but a system of precise durations for individual pitches is needed for the creation of *musica mensurabilis,* which is both polyphonic and precisely measured.

The first step toward a measured notation was the system of rhythmic modes, associated with the music of the Notre Dame school. This represents six different ways (modes) of combining three different durations by stereotyped groupings of ligatures (no longer neumes) of two and three notes. As the neumes could represent pitches only in a relative way, so their renamed ancestors could represent durations only in a clearly understood context (see Ex. 4).

Several problems are immediately apparent. First, because this notation does not differ in outward appearance from that used for liturgical books and other kinds of music, both monophonic and polyphonic, in the thirteenth century, it cannot always be determined whether a given specimen may be read as "modal" or not. Second, even specimens that all agree are "modal" are rarely notated in a way duplicating the textbook examples of Example 4. Because all of the modes may be varied by what the theorists call *extensio* and *fractio,* the boundaries between them become quite fluid in practice. For instance, the longs of mode 1 may be "fractured" into two breves with such regularity that mode 1 becomes mode 6. Similarly, the longs of mode 3 may be resolved into breves in a way that approaches mode 2. This suggests that the modes are not rigid formulas like the poetic meters they resemble, but simply ways of representing a more unified rhythmic style using the imperfect tools then available. This makes the job of the transcriber more difficult, but in practice it meant that the modes could be com-

Example 4

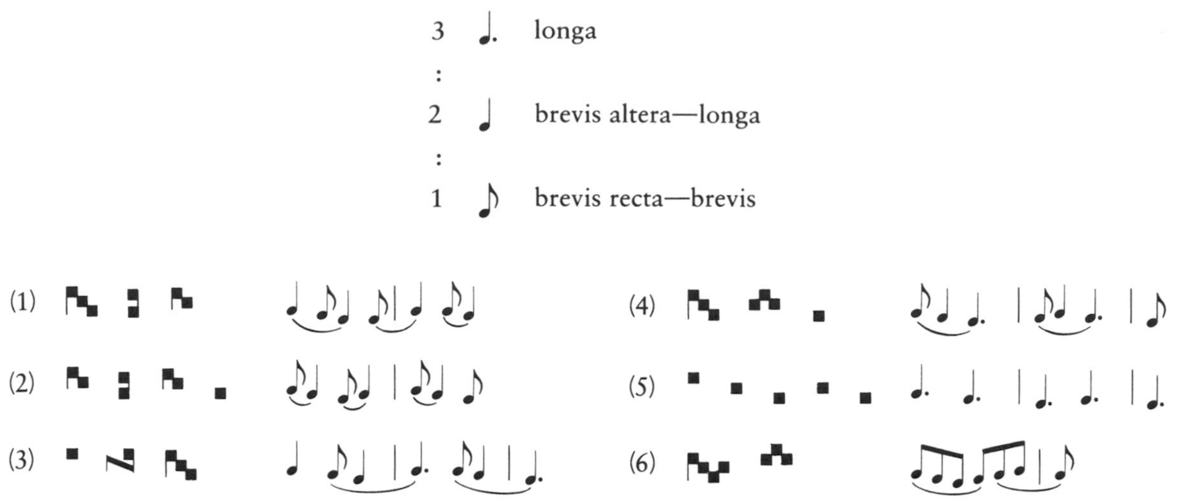

bined to produce a variety of rhythmic treatment that goes far beyond the stereotyped patterns of Example 4.

While the rhythmic modes recognize only two durational values, in practice there are three. In principle, a long is always equal to two shorts, and in modes 1 and 2, these values are related by the ratio of 2:1. The value that resulted from the addition of the "normal" long and the short was also called a long, and its (unequal) halves were also called shorts. In this case, the normal short is called *recta;* the abnormal one, *altera.* (The treatises also mention a duplex long equal to six shorts, but it does not come into play for the rhythmic modes, with the possible exception of mode 5.) While this appears irrational to the modern observer, the medieval musician was quite at home with the notion that the first division of the monochord was at the octave, or 2:1, but the next division of the resulting halves could only be at the fifth, or 3:2. If this feature had disappeared with modal notation, it could be ignored here, but both the terminology and the practice remained integral parts of the notational system throughout the later Middle Ages.

Theoretical sources describing the system of modal notation began to appear in the second quarter of the thirteenth century; practical sources employing the notation, perhaps a quarter of a century earlier; and datable compositions from these and later sources of modal notation push the limits back by perhaps another quarter of a century. We can thus say that modal notation was invented sometime during the twelfth century and was employed largely for the transmission of the repertory of the Notre Dame school for music composed until the mid thirteenth century. Whether it is possible to identify modal notation prior to the Notre Dame sources, or outside its geographical and typological territory, cannot be decided with any certainty. The elusiveness and ambiguity of the notation invite speculation, and the field has always been rife with controversy.

All of the larger sources of Notre Dame polyphony were written after the mid thirteenth century, at a time when refinements were already making purely modal notation obsolete. The most important of these are associated with the *Ars cantus mensurabilis* of Franco of Cologne (*ca.* 1280), though he should probably be regarded more as a systematizer than an inventor, for many features of "Franconian" notation predate his treatise. The most important feature of the new mensural notation was the fixing of individual note values by assigning the long value to the old *virga* and the short to the *punctum.* (The fact that the opposite assignments could just as easily have been made might suggest that, as Gregorian "mensuralists" would maintain, *virga* and *punctum* had always represented these two values.) Franco's system, with some refinements and modernizations, remained valid throughout the later Middle Ages and beyond; it did not replace, but built upon, the older modal system (see Ex. 5).

The top part of Example 5 shows the four individual note shapes basic to the Franconian system, plus the *semibrevis minima* that was given theoretical sanction in the fourteenth century. The value of the breve—one *tempus*—is not the shortest in the

Example 5

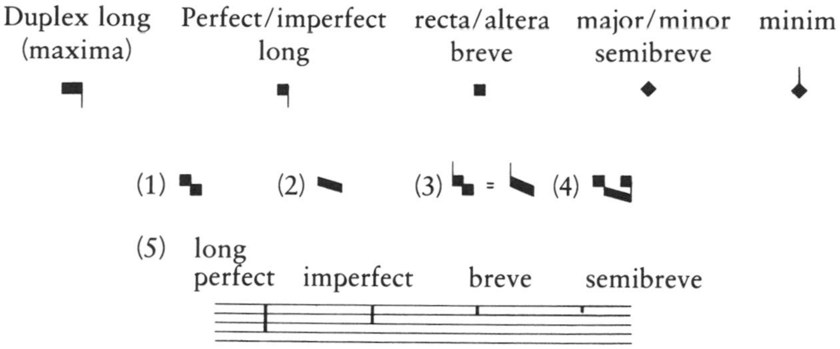

new system, but it is the basic unit of measure. The shape chosen for the semibreve, like those for long and breve, is derived from square neumatic notation, where it appeared only as part of a neume of three or more notes (see Ex. 1, *climacus*). It is almost recognizable as the modern whole note, which is still called semibreve in Italian and in British usage.

All of the basic forms have only a relative value. The breve, for example, could have the value of one or two *tempora* (beats), depending on the context; and two breves standing between two longs were always interpreted as *recta* and *altera* in perfect time, as in the old mode 3. The system of ligatures is likewise firmly based on modal practice. The two basic forms of binary ligatures (the *pes* and *clivis* of Ex. 1), with their breve-long value acquired from modes 1 and 2, could be altered at the beginning, thus affecting their "propriety," and/or at the end, affecting their "perfection." The forms shown in Example 5 are thus (1) without propriety and with perfection (long-long), and (2) without propriety and without perfection (long-breve). New are the ligatures that combine two semibreves with an ascending stem, which are said to be with "opposite" propriety (Ex. 5, no. 3). In ligatures of three or more notes, all middle notes are breves (as in modes 3, 4, and 6), and the values of the first and last notes are determined by the rules of propriety and perfection. Thus (4) in Example 5 begins with a long (without propriety for a descending ligature), continues with two breves (middle notes), and ends with another long (with perfection for an ascending ligature). A corresponding set of precisely measured rests (Ex. 5, no. 5) completes a notational system that allows the modern students of this music to transcribe with a confidence not possible with any earlier music.

Both music and its notation were in a state of flux during the thirteenth century. Both older and more progressive elements can be found within a single manuscript; and newer notational symbols, such as the oblique ligature forms and the "opposite propriety" ligatures, sometimes crop up in pieces that seem not to be written in mensural notation throughout. Even in pieces that are clearly notated according to Franconian principles, the interpretation of the semibreve is problematic because at times as many as nine are intended to be sung in the time of one breve. While dots are occasionally used to clarify the boundaries of the breve, the clearer regulation of the semibreve and the creation of the "minimum" semibreve were not accomplished until the fourteenth century.

In the fourteenth century imperfect, or duple, time received theoretical sanction, though it had been enshrined in practice since the late thirteenth century. With this accomplished, it was possible to codify the four different ways in which the division of the breve *(tempus)* and the semibreve (prolation) could be combined. These *quatre prolacions,* as they were frequently called in contemporary sources, are shown in Example 6. Mode is still part of the system, and theoretically can be either perfect or imperfect; but the *quatre prolacions* seem to recognize that, because of the proliferation of ever smaller subdivisions of the semibreve, mode was sinking further and further beneath the conscious or operative level of rhythm. This is strikingly reflected in the way we transcribe (actually, reduce) this notation into modern equivalents. In Example 4, for instance, the eighth note is used to represent the breve, a reduction of 16:1, whereas in Example 6 the same eighth note represents the minim, a reduction of 4:1. The long, represented by a quarter note in Example 4, would have a duration of two full measures in any of the time signatures shown in Example 6. The continued slowing down of the note values through the

Example 6

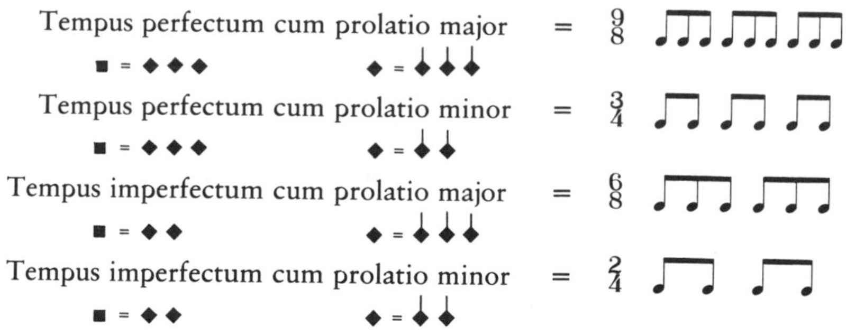

sixteenth and seventeenth centuries is reflected by the creation of new values as much as one-sixteenth the size of the minim.

Other innovations introduced in the fourteenth century include the use of colored notes, usually red, to indicate a value other than the normal one. This allowed a temporary change of mensuration, so that, for example, three red semibreves would replace two black ones in imperfect time, resulting in a measure of three against two. Dots were used not only to clarify perfect *tempus* or prolation, but also to introduce perfect values into imperfect time and, in pairs, to indicate a temporary rhythmic shift (syncopation). Proportional signs indicating a temporary augmentation or diminution of note values introduced a further source of refinement and complexity. All of these devices were used alone or in combination from the late fourteenth through the fifteenth century to create special effects not otherwise possible, and sometimes for their own sake when a simpler notation was equally possible.

A parallel system of mensural notation was created in Italy in the fourteenth century that is independent of the French system in many respects. It does not use *tempus* and prolation but, rather, a number of *divisiones* that specify only the number of semibreves to the breve. The system is not quite as simple as it sounds, however, for a number of special notational signs make possible almost as great a rhythmic variety as in the French system. Specimens of mixed French–Italian notation are preserved from the late fourteenth and early fifteenth centuries; thereafter, the Italian system was replaced entirely by the French.

A fundamental change in the appearance of notation occurred in the fifteenth century when the traditional black note forms began to be left blank, or white, probably because paper gradually replaced parchment for musical manuscripts. As the values that could be expressed in ligatures (long and breve) came to be used less and less often, the appearance of a page of music increasingly took the form familiar to the modern musician. The habit of writing music in parts rather than in score was retained until the seventeenth century, however. Although score notation and part notation were almost equally common until the mid thirteenth century, with the introduction of a more accurate mensural notation, the latter became the norm for nearly four centuries. There is one overriding practical advantage to this practice: It requires significantly less space, especially in the typical late medieval style, in which some voices move very slowly and others much more quickly.

In the fifteenth century, a number of special instrumental notations (tablatures) begin to appear to accommodate music for the lute and the organ. These employ letters, conventional mensural symbols, and a variety of special features that reflect the playing technique of these instruments. These will not be treated in detail here, as their principal flowering lies beyond the limits of the Middle Ages.

BIBLIOGRAPHY

Willi Apel, *The Notation of Polyphonic Music, 900–1600,* 5th ed. (1953); Solange Corbin, *Die Neumen* (1977); Michel Huglo, "Les noms des neumes et leur origine," in *Études grégoriennes,* **1** (1954); Ewald Jammers, *Tafeln zur Neumenschrift* (1965), and *Schrift, Ordnung, Gestalt* (1969); Carl Parrish, *The Notation of Medieval Music* (1957, repr. 1959); Joseph Smits van Waesberghe, "Les origines de la notation alphabétique au moyen âge," in *Anuario musical* (of the) *Instituto español de musicologia,* **12** (1957), 3–14; Dom Grégoire M. Suñol, *Introduction à la paléographie musicale grégorienne* (1935).

ROBERT FALCK

MUSICAL ORNAMENTATION

[See also **Ars Antiqua; Ars Nova; Boethius; Franco of Cologne; Gregorian Chant; Guido of Arezzo; Hermann von Reichenau; Hucbald of St. Amand; Music, Western European; Neume; Notker Balbulus; Prolatio; Rhythm; Solmization.**]

MUSICAL ORNAMENTATION is the embellishment of a composition by the addition of notes not originally written. For discussion, ornaments can be divided into two types: those applied to a single note, such as trill (including intervals of half-step, whole step, and third), turn (upper and lower neighbor), mordent (upper or lower neighbor), and vibrato or tremulo (pitch variation of less than half a step), described as "graces" in later centuries; and running passages connecting two or more notes, called *passaggi* in the sixteenth-century Italian treatises. In actual performance the two kinds of embellishments were usually mixed together and applied to the music according to the tradition of the decade and locality, and the ability of the performer. The amount of freedom allowed to or taken by a performer could range from minor note decorations to passages of several measures. The practice dates to earliest times and continued until the extremely complicated compositions of the mid nineteenth century.

The freedom with which a medieval performer approached a composition can be seen in the earliest written manuscripts of both sacred and secular music. Comparisons of compositions found in more than one manuscript show that the basic outline of a particular composition usually showed few differences from manuscript to manuscript, but often there was no attempt to match one version exactly with another. Examples 1 and 2 demonstrate the amount of variation—a kind of ornamentation—that can be found in different copies of the same composition.

From these manuscripts we may conclude that the attitude of a medieval musician was that certain rhythms, melodic patterns, phrases, and structural notes were the essence of a composition and must be retained, but that minor variants in rhythm and melody were open to individual interpretation. In some ways the medieval performer approached a composition in much the same way as a jazz musician does: composed music is considered to be an outline; the performer may add ornaments and is allowed a degree of variation.

The essence of ornamentation is that it was supplied spontaneously by the performer, and therefore it was rarely written down. Some information can be gained from references in theoretical treatises of the time, and some actual examples of written-out or-

Example 1

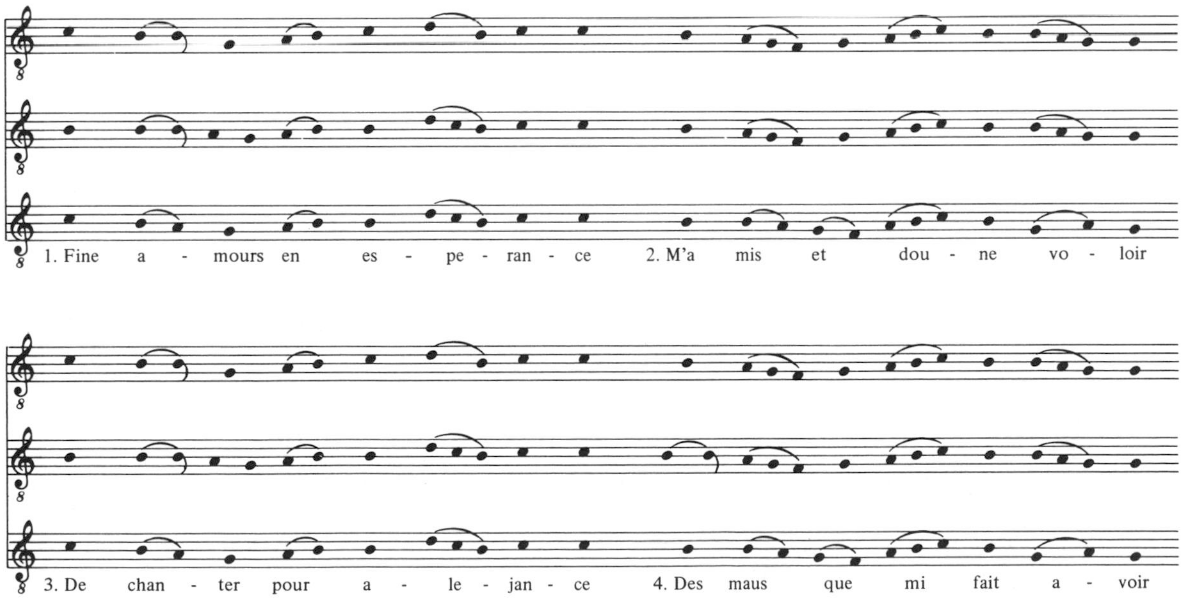

Audefroy le Bastard, "Fin amours en esperance." Demonstration of three different readings of a troubadour song. FROM HENDRIK VAN DER WERF, *THE CHANSONS OF THE TROUBADOURS AND TROUVÈRES* (1972)

Example 2

Maestro Piero, "Quando l'aria comenza." Two different readings of a 14th-century song. FROM NINO PIRROTTA, *THE MUSIC OF FOURTEENTH-CENTURY ITALY*, II (1960)

naments have been preserved. The first treatises devoted to ornamentation are from the early sixteenth century, but it can be seen that the discussions in these manuals refer to practices mentioned in passing by theorists of earlier centuries and observable in the embellished compositions that have survived from those times. Although minor elements of style changed throughout the Middle Ages and Renaissance, the basic ideas and techniques of ornamentation remained essentially the same.

References to ornamentation can be found in a number of writings, such as that of Aurelian of Réôme (mid ninth century), where the use of tremolo in singing is mentioned. Jerome of Moravia (late thirteenth century) refers to the same kind of ornament and gives descriptions of three kinds of trill-like ornaments he calls "harmonic flowers" *(flos harmonicus).* John of Garland (*fl. ca.* 1240) discusses melodic ornamentation and the use of subdivision and repetition of a single pitch.

Practical examples of ornamentation, in addition to the variant versions of compositions mentioned above, are found in manuscripts beginning in the late fourteenth century that contain highly virtuosic embellishments, usually for instrumentalists. The earliest of these, the Robertsbridge Codex from England (British Library Additional 25580) from *ca.* 1370 and the Faenza Codex from Italy (Faenza Bibl. Com. 117) from the early fifteenth century, provide ornamented instrumental versions of fourteenth-century secular and sacred vocal material. A comparison of the music in these manuscripts with the

Example 3

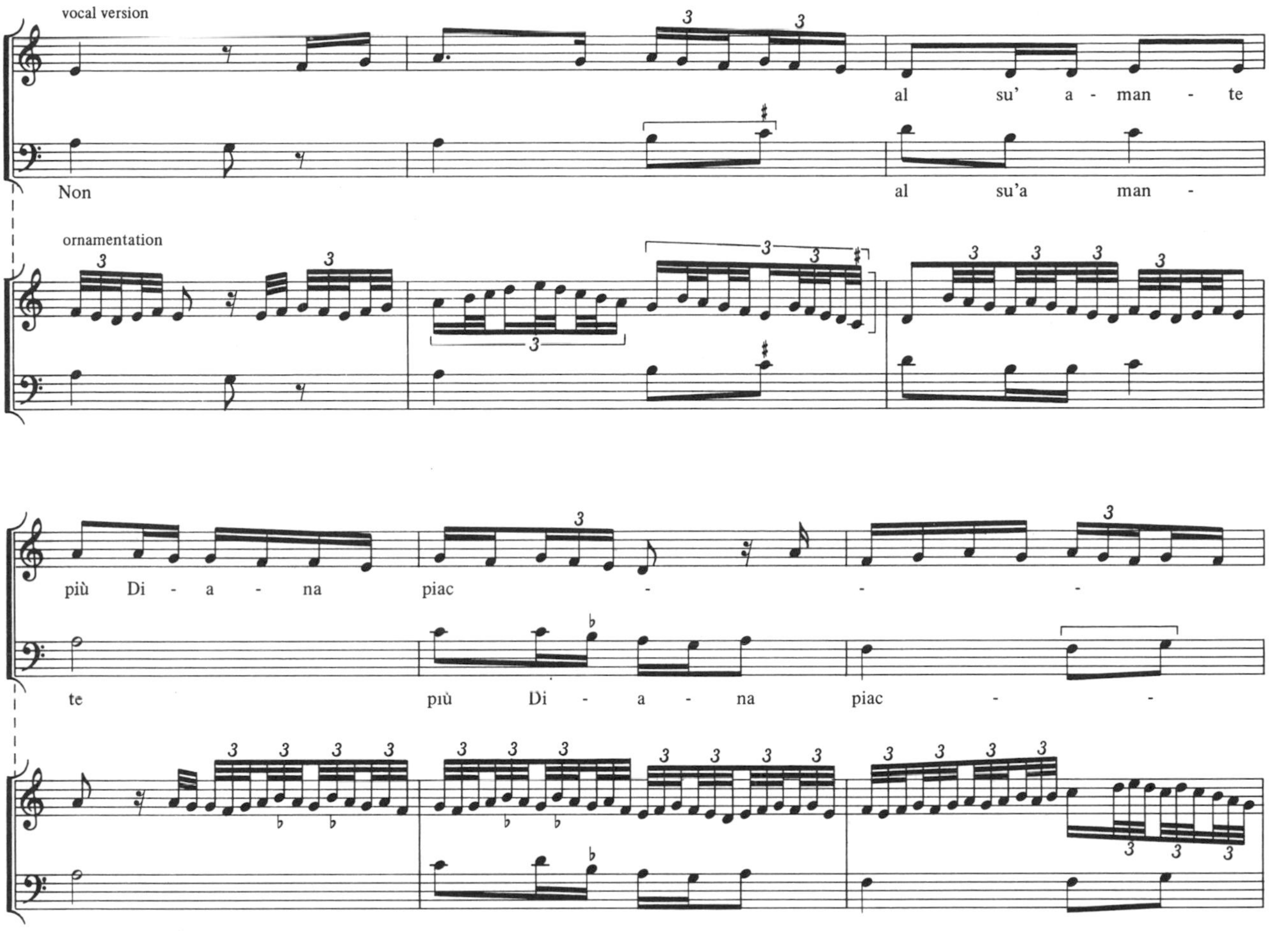

Jacobus of Bologna, "Non al suo amante." Original vocal version and instrumental ornamentation found in the Faenza Codex. FROM DRAGAN PLAMENAC, *KEYBOARD MUSIC OF THE LATE MIDDLE AGES IN CODEX FAENZA 117* (1971)

vocal originals gives at least a glimpse of virtuoso embellishments from that time and allows us to draw some conclusions concerning the types and placements of ornaments (Ex. 3).

In both of the earliest ornamented manuscripts the lower part is left unornamented while the upper part is varied in several different ways. Both melodic and rhythmic embellishments are applied. Rhythmic variations include various repetitions of a note written only once in the original, and changes from duple to triple division (for example, becomes). Melodic ornamentation varies from simple upper and lower neighbors to long melodic passages that substitute for several units of measure in the vocal original. Sometimes the basic contour and essential notes of the phrases are kept, but on occasion the ornamented version differs widely from the original for substantial portions of a phrase.

A number of fifteenth-century manuscripts contain a few versions of both vocal and instrumental compositions that appear to have ornaments written in. The examples range from small embellishments to longer passages, although none are quite as extensive as those in Robertsbridge or Faenza. In the written-out passages that have been preserved, *passaggi* outnumber graces in quantity, but this may be misleading. Many of the graces are extremely difficult to notate but rather simple to execute. The theoretical evidence suggests that graces were the most commonly used ornaments, and therefore their absence from the written-out examples may not be an accurate indication of their actual proportion in per-

 MUSICAL PERFORMANCE

formance. The placement of *passaggi* was left to the discretion of the individual performer, but in the *Buxheimer Orgelbuch,* the largest collection of ornamented compositions from the fifteenth century, are found the symbols  and , signifying that graces are to be inserted. This is the earliest known example of the indication of graces by symbol, a technique that became standard in the seventeenth century.

BIBLIOGRAPHY

Sources. Willi Apel, ed., *Keyboard Music of the Fourteenth and Fifteenth Centuries* (1963); Dragan Planenac, ed., *Keyboard Music of the Late Middle Ages in Codex Faenza 117* (1972).

Studies. Howard Mayer Brown, *Embellishing Sixteenth-century Music* (1976); Ernest Ferand, *Die Improvisation in der Musik* (1938); Imogene Horsley, "Improvised Embellishment in the Performance of Renaissance Polyphonic Music," in *Journal of the American Musicological Society,* **4** (1951); Timothy J. McGee, *Medieval and Renaissance Music: A Performer's Guide* (1985).

TIMOTHY J. MCGEE

[See also **Musical Notation; Musical Treatises.**]

MUSICAL PERFORMANCE. Music was an important part of daily life for all people during the Middle Ages. Members of religious orders sang for hours as a part of their daily routine of prayer; peasants sang as they worked and relaxed; ballads and love songs were a part of the court life of the noble class; and professional musicians entertained all levels of society with songs and dances.

Sacred music. Within the monastic houses the prayers of the daily hours and the Mass were chanted by the entire community. For the singing of chant several different methods of performance were used, depending on the nature and purpose of the chant. Psalms were generally sung in unison, either by the entire choir at once or by half choirs singing verses alternately. Some chants were sung by one or a few soloists, and for some prayers the chant was divided between the soloist and the choir. For example, an introit began with a short intonation by the soloist, the choir completed the antiphon, and the soloist sang psalm verses between repetitions of the antiphon by the choir. Sacred polyphony, from its introduction sometime prior to the ninth century, was sung by soloists and originally was applied only to the soloist's sections of the chant. By the fourteenth century, however, entire chants of the Ordinary of the Mass were also set in polyphony. At first these too were sung only by soloists, but by the end of the century, first in England and later on the Continent, small choirs of eight to twelve singers performed the polyphonic parts of the liturgy.

By the late Middle Ages, organs were part of the celebration of the liturgy. The organ usually functioned in a solo capacity, playing processional music and alternating with the choir on hymn and psalm verses. It rarely, if ever, accompanied the choir, and there is little evidence that any other instrument was regularly played in church until the sixteenth century.

Secular music. Literary sources such as the *Romance of the Rose* and Boccaccio's *Decameron* make it clear that the ability to sing, to compose songs and song texts, and to play an instrument were expected of the educated class. Singing and dancing usually followed dinner, and the nobles provided much of the music themselves. The oldest surviving secular repertory includes mainly troubadour and trouvère songs that were mostly composed and performed by the nobles.

The peasants sang work songs in the fields and the markets, and for recreation they sang songs, danced, and played instruments. None of their repertory survives, and may never have been written down. Our knowledge of the peasants' musical practices comes only from literary references and iconography.

Minstrels were regularly found all through the Middle Ages, entertaining at courts, taverns, and village squares. They were expected to sing, play several instruments, juggle, and tell stories. Originally they wandered from place to place, but during the fourteenth century the practice gradually changed to a more permanent arrangement in which they became attached to a royal household or a town, received regular incomes, wore livery, and were generally considered servants. Surviving documents record the existence of yearly meetings, during Lent, of schools of minstrels where they learned new skills, exchanged repertory, attended to the business matters of their guild, and recruited new assistants.

In the late Middle Ages many noble households included a group of musicians who sang at daily Mass and for various devotions, and also provided secular vocal and instrumental music for daily entertainment. In the houses of the wealthiest nobles, the chapel singers and the secular musicians were separate groups. It was common for the household musicians to compose as well as perform, and the list of musicians in the employ of Philip the Good, duke of Burgundy from 1419 to 1467, includes some of the finest composers of the fifteenth century, among them Giles Binchois and Guillaume Dufay.

Instruments and instrumental performance. Musical instruments were thought of and played in two separate groups: loud and soft. The terms *haut* and *bas* (loud and soft) were first used in the late Middle Ages, but the practice of dividing the instruments that way began much earlier. Within each group the instruments were mixed in various combinations, but instruments of one group were never played with those of the other for reasons of volume and balance.

The loud instruments—bagpipe, trumpet, shawm, and drum—were generally played outdoors or in large halls. The bagpipe was unlike the others in that it was usually played alone, and was found in both peasant and aristocratic settings. The other loud instruments were usually found in groups of four or more, and were not generally associated with peasants. Trumpets and drums were used by the military to encourage the troops and to instill fear in the enemy. Trumpets also were considered to be a symbol of nobility, and most high noblemen and many guilds employed an ensemble of trumpeters to announce their comings and goings with fanfares. The usual number of trumpets was four to six, but for particularly festive occasions trumpets and drums numbering more than 100 are recorded. From as early as the thirteenth century, civil governments employed groups of trumpeters and shawm players. The trumpeters announced all civic activities. They were regularly in attendance at jousts, and at feasts a trumpet fanfare often announced each course. Trumpeters and shawm players were employed as watchmen to signal from the city towers and to sound reveille, and in the fifteenth century ensembles of three to five shawm players were employed by the governments (especially in northern cities such as Ghent) to play ensemble music in public on special days. From the late fourteenth century on, two or three shawms, first with a slide trumpet and later with a trombone, made up one of the most popular ensembles for performing dance music, especially for the stately basse danse.

Soft instruments included plucked strings (cittern, lute, harp), bowed strings (rebec, vielle, crwth, viol), woodwinds (flute, recorder), keyboard instruments (portable organ, harpsichord, clavichord), and voice. They were more flexible, and more varied both in combination and in repertory, than the loud instruments. Whereas loud instruments were generally played in fixed ensembles of four or more instruments of the same kind, performers of soft instruments often functioned as soloists. Paintings of ensembles of soft instruments generally show groups of two to four performers playing on instruments with contrasting sound colors, often with a solo voice. A typical soft instrumental ensemble might include a flute, a bowed string, and a plucked string. If two bowed or two plucked instruments were played together, they usually had different sound colors. The use of contrasting sounds reflects the nature of the polyphonic music of the time. A large share of the polyphonic music of the twelfth to mid fifteenth centuries is composed of contrasting lines of music, and the combinations of contrasting colors of voices and instruments supported that characteristic. During the fifteenth century the compositional practice changed more and more in the direction of similar or matching lines of music. The performers chose instruments with matching sounds in order to support the demands of the music. A result of this change was the development of families of instruments—for example, several pitches of viols or recorders—to provide matching sounds at all pitches.

Performance freedom. Many of the details of performance were not specified by the composer, being left to the performers. Within the realm of the performers' choice were matters of specific voices or instruments; the quantity and placement of ornamentation; certain details of melody and harmony (*musica ficta);* and the possible improvisation of accompaniment, preludes, or interludes.

Composers did not specify which instruments or voices were to perform their compositions. There is evidence that, for the most part, compositions were written for a specific occasion. Therefore, it is probable that the composer had a particular performance in mind, but the performers decided whether to sing or to play a given line and what instruments were to be played. The choices were made according to the customs of performance of the time, the suitability of the parts for certain instruments and voices, and the instruments and voices available. There is also evidence that not all parts of a polyphonic composition were always performed. Two-, three-, and four-part compositions were regularly performed with one less than the full number of parts, a decision that also was left to the performer.

Within many compositions the choice to sharp and flat certain notes *(musica ficta)* was left to the performer, who would decide to alter certain notes according to general rules of melodic progression, in order to avoid dissonances either melodically or harmonically, and according to personal taste.

For a performer, the greatest freedoms were to improvise and to add ornamentation to a composition. The composed music was considered in some ways to be an outline that was to be filled in by the performer, who was expected to embellish the lines with short and long ornamental additions, and was allowed to improvise in a number of ways. One type of improvisation was the addition of accompanying lines to a vocal or instrumental composition. The addition was to follow the rules of simple harmony, but could be simple or ornate, depending on the talents and desires of the performer. In addition, instrumentalists often played improvised interludes between verses of a song and preludes to introduce compositions. The preludes generally served to set the mode of the composition and often were display pieces for the technical virtuosity of the performer.

BIBLIOGRAPHY

Edmund A. Bowles, "Haut and Bas: The Grouping of Musical Instruments in the Middle Ages," in *Musica disciplina,* **8** (1954); Howard M. Brown, "Instruments and Voices in the Fifteenth-century Chanson," in John W. Grubbs *et al.,* eds., *Current Thought in Musicology* (1976); Manfred F. Bukofzer, "The Beginnings of Choral Polyphony," in his *Studies in Medieval and Renaissance Music* (1950); Ernest Ferand, *Die Improvisation in der Musik* (1938); Andrew Hughes, "Mensural Polyphony for Choir in 15th-century England," in *Journal of the American Musicological Society,* **19** (1966); Timothy J. McGee, *Medieval and Renaissance Music: A Performer's Guide* (1985); Keith Polk, "Ensemble Performance in Dufay's Time," in Allan W. Atlas, ed., *Dufay Quincentenary Conference Papers* (1976); Hendrik van der Werf, *The Chansons of the Troubadours and Trouvères* (1972); Nigel Wilkins, *Music in the Age of Chaucer* (1979); Craig Wright, "Performance Practices at the Cathedral of Cambrai 1475–1550," in *Musical Quarterly,* **64** (1978); Giuseppe Zippel, *I suonatori della Signori di Firenze* (1892).

TIMOTHY J. MCGEE

[See also **Johannes de Grocheo; Machaut, Guillaume de; Minnesingers; Minstrels; Music, Popular; Music, Western European; Troubadour, Trouvère, Trovador.**]

MUSICAL TREATISES

FROM ANTIQUITY TO THE BEGINNING OF THE MIDDLE AGES

Besides a very small number of vocal pieces, which, with the exception of the "Epitaph of Seikilos" (first century A.D.), have all reached us in a fragmentary state, antiquity has bequeathed to us a considerable body of treatises that inform us rather well on the theory of Greek and Roman music between approximately 400 B.C. and A.D. 400. Their authors, not numerous, are divided in two distinct and unreconciliable factions: the Pythagoreans (Philolaus, Nicomachus of Gerasa, and Gaudentius); and the Aristoxenians (Aristoxenus of Tarentum, a disciple of Aristoteles, Cleonides, Bacchius the Elder, and, indirectly, Aristides Quintilianus). To the latter one must add the Epicurean philosopher Philodemus of Gadara (*ca.* 110–*ca.* 40/35 B.C.), and a third- or fourth-century-A.D. author, Alypius, the only one to have bequeathed to us a detailed exposé of Greek musical notation.

For the Pythagoreans music was the audible expression of the secret laws that ordered the universe in a sort of cosmic harmony; therefore, they considered it necessary to discover these laws by the study of mathematical relations that unite sounds to the movements of the celestial bodies. The Pythagorean "musician" was thus, in the modern sense, an acoustician, mainly preoccupied with determining the exact arithmetical value of the intervals on the monochord. To these scientific preoccupations were added moral and pedagogical considerations that were expanded upon by Plato and Aristotle, with cosmic harmony ultimately considered as of divine origin.

For the Aristoxenians, on the contrary, the ear alone could judge musical consonances. Rejecting the Pythagoreans' abstract calculations, Aristoxenus (*fl. ca.* 300 B.C.), who is rightly regarded as the founder of musical aesthetics, brought musical understanding back to two elements: auditive perception and memory. "Sensation can appreciate the size of intervals, but it is the mind that reckons their [exact mathematical] values" (*Principles and Elements of Harmonics,* book 2). He divided the octave into six tones and two semitones, based not on calculations but on the ear's tolerance, foreshadowing in this the temperament initiated by Zarlino in the sixteenth century.

Aristoxenus, however, had few followers, except

MUSICAL TREATISES

maybe—and indirectly—St. Augustine. In the six books of his *De musica,* begun in 387 but limited to the subjects of rhythmics and metrics, Augustine attempted, in a brilliant theological synthesis regrettably left unfinished, to reconcile the opposed but complementary claims of both reason and sense. Let us recall in passing his definition of music, borrowed from Varro's lost encyclopedia: "Music is the science of mensurating time values"—that is, the science of measure *(modus),* melody, and rhythm *(numerus)* (*De musica* 1.2).

FROM THE FIFTH TO THE SEVENTH CENTURY

Such were the foundations on which the structure of medieval music theory was to be erected. The last Latin writers who expounded at length the musical doctrine of antiquity were Martianus Capella and, most importantly, Boethius.

The North African rhetorician Martianus praised the science of music in the ninth and last book of his allegorical romance on the liberal arts, *De nuptiis Philologiae et Mercurii,* written sometime between 410 and 439. One would readily exclude from the list of musical treatises this bizarre compendium of poorly assimilated pieces of information, borrowed either from Aristides Quintilianus (second or third century A.D.) or, more probably, from Varro's *Disciplinarum libri IX,* if it were not for the fact that its very obscurity and macaronic style had inspired lengthy commentaries written by the Irish masters of the ninth century such as Martin of Laon, John Scottus Eriugena, and his disciple Remigius of Auxerre.

More substantial but not less difficult was the teaching of Severinus Boethius (*ca.* 480–525), whose *De institutione musica* in five books, composed around 505 and copied hundreds of times from the ninth century onward, became the musical bible of all the Western theoreticians until Rameau (eighteenth century) and even later: in the 1850's a critical reading of Boethius was still a mandatory requirement of music majors at Oxford and Cambridge. At first sight nothing distinguishes the *De musica* from Boethius' *De institutione arithmetica* (a treatise on arithmetic, written shortly before), and one finds nothing there concerning rhythm, melody, and instruments, except a passage on the monochord, a one-string instrument used to measure the intervals. But Boethius, "the last of the Romans and the first of the Scholastics," aimed only at making available in Latin the thoughts of Plato, Aristotle, and Euclid. His treatise presented itself as a "methodological introduction" to the study of pure philosophy, represented as the ultimate end of all knowledge. Rather than an original essay, it is, in its first four books, a free translation of a lost *De musica* by Nicomachus of Gerasa, and its fifth book, left unfinished, is taken from the *Harmonics* of Claudius Ptolemaeus, the astronomer.

It was nevertheless through Boethius that the essential elements of Greek musical theory and the dogmas of the Pythagorean school were transmitted to the West: tones are audible numbers of which only mathematical analysis could give an account (books 2 and 3), and reason must rectify the impressions conveyed by the senses. Although the ear can experience what is agreeable, it cannot judge the beautiful, nor determine what is "harmonious" (book 5). The perfection of consonances is a function of their arithmetical ratios, and the simpler that ratio, the more harmonious the consonance. Thus the octave (ratio 2:1) is more perfect than the fifth (3:2), which in turn is more euphonic than the fourth (4:3) or the whole tone (9:8) because it tends toward the One (1:1). And Unity ultimately conveys the idea of the Divine into which all of creation is subsumed. *Musica* was thus the science of numbers in relationship with other relations—the mathematical proportions—as arithmetic was the science of numbers per se, geometry was the science of fixed numbers, and astronomy the science of numbers in motion. We recognize here the general program of the quadrivium, where, as in its sister disciplines, abstract musical acoustics had no other aim than to take man away from the material world and elevate him to the world of essences or ideas, in the Platonic meaning of the term. With the classical definition of tone, interval, and consonance (1.8), Boethius bequeathed to the Middle Ages a tripartite and hierarchic classification of music (1.2), divided into *cosmic* music or universal harmony (macrocosm), *human* music (microcosm), and *instrumental* music, the only audible one. From Boethius also dates the widely quoted definition of the *musicus,* more a scholar than a performer (1.34).

After Boethius' tragic and premature death, his friend Cassiodorus (*ca.* 490–*ca.* 583) devoted a short chapter of his *Institutiones divinarum et humanarum litterarum* (2.5, written *ca.* 562) to *musica,* knowledge of which could help in understanding the spiritual meaning of the Bible—in particular the Psalms. Cassiodorus follows closely Gaudentius (in a lost translation of Mutianus), Clement of Alexandria, and Censorinus, explicitly named, but also an unspecified author, Ammonius of Alexandria. Oddly enough he did not borrow anything from Boethius, but he had addressed a letter to him in 507 in which he expanded at leisure on the ethos of modes, the moral effect of music, and the harmony of the spheres (*Variae* 2.40).

Cassiodorus appropriated Varro's definition, inspired by Pythagoras, that "music is the science or discipline that deals with numbers" (*Institutiones* 2.5). Following St. Augustine, he divided this science of acoustics into harmonics or technique of composition *(melopoeia)*, rhythmics, and metrics or versification. Instruments were divided into percussions (such as bells, chimes), strings (the cithara), and winds (organs), a classification that is still valid. The musical consonances numbered six: the fourth, the fifth, and the octave; the octave and fourth, the octave and fifth, and the double octave.

Stern pedagogue and passionate bibliophile, Cassiodorus was perhaps a lesser thinker than Boethius, but his influence on following theoreticians was no less great, because he was the first to bring together pagan science and Christian faith: while Boethius illustrated the moral effect of music by quoting the *topos* of Pythagoras calming the drunken young man, Cassiodorus evoked David quieting Saul's rage with the sounds of his cithara. Moreover, in his commentary on Psalm 150, the founder of the monastery of Vivarium advocated an allegorical and mystical interpretation of song and instruments.

Not more than Cassiodorus, to whom he owed so much, could Isidore, bishop of Seville (*ca.* 560–636), be considered a real theoretician. Like his model, he devoted to music a small section of his large twenty-book encyclopedia, *Etymologiarum sive originum* (3.15–23), written *ca.* 620. In conformity with the title of his work, he followed Cassiodorus' definition with fanciful notes on etymology that were often repeated in later years ("Music derives from the Muses"). He then stated that according to Moses, "the earliest musical inventor" was the biblical Tubal. He tried to blend—rather clumsily, one might say—the tripartite divisions established by Cassiodorus and Augustine, and gave a glossary of technical terms, borrowed from the Greek, which constitute the first lexicon of medieval theory, among them *symphonia* = consonance, *diaphonia* = dissonance, and *diastema* = interval. Modern scholarship is not as much interested in Isidore as a disorganized and often mistaken compiler, but rather as the first-hand observer of Mozarabic liturgy. Among his many followers should be mentioned the German monk Hrabanus Maurus (*ca.* 780–856), who drew extensively on him in the passage on music found in his *De universo* (17.4).

THE CAROLINGIAN RENAISSANCE

Boethius, Cassiodorus, and Isidore, the foremost expositors of the culture of antiquity, were not, strictly speaking, medieval theorists. Rather they were intermediary authors, more concerned with preserving the past than with preparing the future. One must wait until the ninth century for the appearance of the first treatises that, while preserving the classical heritage, made a special attempt at laying the theoretical foundations of a repertory that was just developing: the liturgical plainsong in the Latin language—the so-called Gregorian chant, which is but one of the dialects of the musical language of the Latin Church, the others being the Old Roman in Rome, the Ambrosian or Milanese in Milan, the Gallican in France, the Hispanic or Mozarabic in Spain, and the Celtic in the British Isles. The causes of this flowering, mainly in northeastern France, appear to be directly linked to the liturgical and educational reforms promulgated by Charlemagne from the end of the eighth century, on the advice of Alcuin of York, his "minister of culture."

Several influences were at work. On the one hand, the concern for correct expression and elegant writing prompted the new schoolmasters (monks, for the most part) to copy the classical authors (Vergil, Horace, Cicero), who were useful for an exact understanding of the literary aspects of the Bible in the translation of St. Jerome; for this the masters used a new type of writing, the Carolingian minuscule, whose musical counterpart was neumatic notation, which appeared in the first third of the ninth century. On the other hand, adoption of the Roman liturgy, substituted for political reasons for the Gallican liturgy, which had its own chant but no theory, entailed the progressive transformation of the Old Roman repertoire into a "Gregorian" one. Bishops Chrodegang of Metz, Amalarius of Metz, and Agobard of Lyons, and the monastic reformer Benedict of Aniane, whose writings contain precise guidelines for precentors (lead singers), seem the principal authors of this transformation. From the east, Byzantium sent to the court at Aix-la-Chapelle "musical ambassadors" who might have inspired the first Carolingian tonaries such as those of St. Riquier, *ca.* 800, or of Metz, *ca.* 836. These were little books in

MUSICAL TREATISES

which chants were classified not according to the liturgical calendar *(ordo)*, but according to the eight tones *(toni)*, later called modes *(modi)*, and sometimes adorned with introductions with directions for use. Later, Ireland exported to the court of Charles II the Bald (*d.* 877) erudite grammarians who tried to make accessible, with numerous glosses and commentaries, the teachings of Martianus and Boethius.

The first complete musical treatise of the ninth century is the *Musica disciplina* of Aurelian of Réôme, composed between 840 and 850. The first part (chaps. 1–7) borrows from Cassiodorus, Isidore, and Boethius both the praise and classification of music and the arithmetical proportions of consonances, while the second part (chaps. 8–19) includes a theoretical tonary that makes specific allusions to the four "parapteres" or lateral tones, complements of the standard eight liturgical modes. Reference is also made (in chap. 9), for the first time in the West, to the psalmodic formulae of the *noeane* type, deliberately modeled on the Byzantine *echemata.*

In the circle of John Scottus and the School of Laon, under the reign of Charles the Bald and his successors, there appeared four treatises that are the high points of Carolingian *ars musica;* they followed each other as if they had been inspired by the same master or in the same environment. The first of them, *Musica* (formerly known as *De harmonica institutione*) by Hucbald of St. Amand (*ca.* 850–930), written between 883 and 893, taught novice choristers the gamut of intervals, from the semitone to the major sixth, and strove to reconcile the articulation of the Greek tetrachord with church modes. To implement neumatic notation, which was written without lines and which varied according to region, Hucbald invented an alphabetical system of notation derived from the Greek system of notation transmitted by Boethius. In his sound and down to earth method of teaching, Hucbald foreshadows another great music master of the Middle Ages, Guido of Arezzo.

The anonymous *Alia musica* (written between 900 and 930 by three successive authors) is divided into three parts: (1) a tonary explaining each of the eight tones (referred to as the "First Quidam" in Chailley's edition); (2) a discussion, by the principal author, of arithmetical properties of consonances and tones; and (3) a "New Exposition," by the "Second Quidam," posterior to the two others, which introduced the concept of modal octave into the theory of ecclesiastical modes. Due to a regrettable confusion between the Greek tones or scales *(toni, modi, tropi)* and Boethius' transposition keys (*De institutione musica* 4.15–17), these pseudo-Greek names became part of the terminology of elementary music manuals. Dorian, Phrygian, Lydian, and Mixo-Lydian are the terms still used for the four authentic modes, and Hypodorian, Hypophrygian, Hypolydian, and Hypomixolydian are used for the four plagal modes.

Musica enchiriadis (Handbook of Music, end of the ninth century), erroneously attributed to Hucbald or to a lay abbot of St. Amand, Count Hoger (Ogier, Roger) of Laon, is the most famous of Carolingian treatises because it is the first to inform us, with numerous examples, about the practice of *diaphonia* or polyphonic singing in two parts. It used a curious stylized notation called *Daseian,* after the Greek aspiration sign *(prosodia daseia,* ⊦*)* used to represent the lowest degree in the scale. In contrast to the neumatic notation, this system indicates precisely the pitch of the notes; but because of its extreme complication, *Daseian* notation was scarcely used and is to be found later only in the *Commemoratio brevis de tonis et psalmis modulandis* (an explanation of psalmodic formulas in the form of a tonary) from the early tenth century. *Musica enchiriadis* is preserved in forty-seven manuscripts and comprises a manual consisting of nineteen chapters, followed by the *Scolica enchiriadis,* which is probably older. This is a commentary in the form of questions and answers between a master and a disciple, resembling the *Periphyseon* of John Scottus or the contemporary grammar manuals.

The last major treatise of the Carolingian period is the *Epistola de armonica institutione* by Regino of Prüm (*ca.* 840–915), addressed around 901 to Archbishop Ratbod of Trier in the form of a theoretical introduction to one of the largest tonaries ever compiled: the incipits of nearly 1,600 pieces are classified in the order of the eight tones, each one having their *differentiae* or specific psalmodic cadences. The main body of the *Epistola*—as preserved in the version of the Leipzig manuscript—is almost exclusively derived from a commentary by Remigius of Auxerre on the *De nuptiis* of Martianus Capella, and thus only the beginning and ending contain any originality. Regino's contribution was a new bipartite classification of music, substituted for Boethius' threefold division: *musica naturalis* for vocal music, of divine inspiration, and *musica artificialis* for instrumental music, of human invention. Nevertheless, in the first page of his *Epistola,* Regino stated two fundamental rules for the correct intonation of the

MUSICAL TREATISES

songs of the Mass and Divine Office: for the antiphons of introits and communions, the *tonus* was to be determined by their initial note; for the responsories, by their final note.

THE TENTH CENTURY

In comparison with the flowering of the ninth century, the tenth century seems poor in theoretical production, and most of it deals with abstract acoustics rather than the living repertory. It is enough to mention the brief outline on the Greek *tonoi*, the tetrachords, and the eight modes, the measurement of the monochord or of organ pipes drafted by Notker of St. Gall (Labeo, or "the Thick-Lipped") (*ca.* 950–1022, not to be confused with his homonym of the same abbey, the famous composer of sequences, Notker Balbulus or "the Stammerer," *ca.* 840–912). Notker Labeo wrote his short excursus in Old High German, which earned him his other nickname, Teutonicus, "the German."

In the same vein, but with more scientific bent, wrote the illustrious Gerbert of Aurillac (*ca.* 940–1003), counselor of Emperor Otto III and pope from 999 to 1003 under the name Silvester II. He composed the musical office in honor of St. Gerald of Aurillac and was the author of short essays on musical acoustics *(Mensura fistularum et monochordi)*, attributed until recently to his disciple, Bernelinus of Paris, due to a false attribution in the manuscript tradition. (Also attributed to Bernelinus, without sufficient evidence, was *Cita et vera divisio monochordi in diatonico genere*, "The quick and true partition of the monochord in the diatonic genre.") The correspondence between Gerbert and Constantinus of Fleury shows that Gerbert commented on Boethius' *De institutione musica* when he taught at the cathedral school of Rheims between 972 and 989, maintaining the scholarly tradition restored by Hucbald of St. Amand and Remigius of Auxerre.

We will not leave the tenth century without evoking, from the Islamic world, the valuable contributions of the Sufi al-Fārābī (*ca.* 870–950), considered in his day a "second Aristotle," the physician Ibn Sīnā (Avicenna, 980–1037), or their predecessor al-Kindī (*ca.* 790–874). All three read carefully the *Harmonics* of Claudius Ptolemaeus and provided Arabic music with the theoretical foundations it had previously lacked for the determination of the structure of scales and the measurement of intervals smaller than the semitone. The writings of al-Fārābī, the most important of the three, were known in the West as early as the twelfth century thanks to the Latin translations of John of Seville and Gerard of Cremona.

THE ELEVENTH CENTURY

Italian authors had been until then notably absent from theoretical literature, there being no other reason to explain this silence than a marked preference on their part for *musica practica* over *musica speculativa.* Yet at the dawn of the eleventh century a new renaissance took place in which chant masters of the peninsula made a decisive contribution to the progress of musical notation and pedagogy.

The first treatise is an anonymous *Dialogus* between a questioning disciple and a master, resembling the format of *Musica enchiriadis.* This short work, widely distributed (more than twenty copies have been counted), had been until recently attributed to Odo, the famous abbot of Cluny (*ca.* 878–942). But its origin, as revealed by its manuscript tradition, repertory, and contents, must be situated in the diocese of Milan, in the first quarter of the eleventh century. The incorrect attribution was due to the fact that the author of the *Dialogus* quoted a tonary of an Abbot Odo of Arezzo, which dates from the end of the tenth century and also contains a *Prooemium* or theoretical preamble.

The innovations introduced in the *Dialogus* were of foremost importance for the improvement of apprenticeship of chant in the monasteries: (1) the abandonment of Greek musical terminology inherited from Boethius (who was, paradoxically, less known in Italy than in France; he would only be rediscovered in Italy in the Renaissance, thanks to the humanists); (2) the implementation, through visual guiding marks on the monochord, of a new alphabetical notation spread over the two octaves represented by the letters *A* through *G* for the first, and from *a* to *aa* for the second, a Greek *gamma* (Γ) being added at the beginning of the gamut to complete the ambitus of the first octave. This is the origin of the word "gamut," and the alphabetical notation still used in Anglo-Saxon countries; (3) a renewed conception of modality, defined in a formula that became thereafter a standard precept: "The tone, or mode, is a principle which classes every melody according to its final note." This fundamental rule of church modes, viewed as eight fixed frames within which tones and semitones occupy movable positions, was borrowed by the author of the *Dialogus* from his predecessor, Odo of Arezzo, in order to systematize the teaching of Hucbald and Regino.

MUSICAL TREATISES

But most importantly, the author of the *Dialogus* opened the way to his illustrious contemporary, Guido of Arezzo (990/999–after 1033), who is justly considered the greatest musical educator of the Middle Ages. Trained in the monastery of Pomposa (near Ferrara), which he was forced to leave because of his Benedictine brothers' contempt of his innovative methods, Guido found refuge with Theobald, bishop of Arezzo (*d.* 1036), and became the choirmaster in his cathedral. It is there that he drew up, between 1026 and 1033, the four works that have established his reputation: the *Aliae regulae,* conceived as a prologue to an antiphonary, now lost and reworked in verse under the title *Regulae rhythmicae;* the *Micrologus,* transmitted in more than seventy manuscripts; and the *Epistola Michaeli monacho de ignoto cantu.*

In the *Regulae,* Guido suggested that the neumes be placed directly on or between four horizontal lines, two of which were to be colored: yellow for the note *ut* and red for the *fa,* a fourth higher, so as to point out visually the place of the semitone. We have here the origin of our modern staff, which allowed young choristers to sight-read the liturgical repertory instead of learning it by ear from their masters in versions that often differed.

As its name indicates, the *Micrologus* constituted a "small encyclopedia of musical knowledge." In it Guido discussed alphabetical notation, preferred consonances (octave, fourth, and fifth), intervals, and modes or tropes ("falsely called tones"). Guido also extended toward the higher end the scale of Pseudo-Odo's *Dialogus* from sixteen to twenty-one notes carefully distinguishing the B flat *(b rotundum)* from the B natural *(b quadratum).* In chapter 15, he provided a compendium of melodic composition, based on a synthesis of classical metrics and medieval prosody, completed by two chapters (18 and 19) on *diaphonia* or organum in oblique motion *(occursus),* where the strait rules of counterpoint set out more than a century earlier in the *Musica enchiriadis* are extensively softened. The only concession to Boethius' tradition was his recalling, in chapter 20, the legend of Pythagoras' discovering the mathematical proportions of the consonances in the sounds of the blacksmith's hammering.

In his *Epistola* to the monk Michael of Pomposa, strewn with autobiographical details, Guido admitted using as a mnemonic device the syllables *ut, re, mi, fa, sol, la,* taken from the hymn to St. John the Baptist, *Ut queant laxis,* in order to facilitate the visual and auditive recognition of all the diatonic intervals present within a given hexachord. One recognizes here the name of the notes of the scale used universally except in the Anglo-Germanic countries, the note B *(si)* not being added until the second half of the sixteenth century.

Guido's great contribution was thus to have laid the foundations of modern solfege, on the basis of the innovations of his Carolingian and Italian predecessors, and to have reduced from nine years to a few months the time needed to train young choristers. His work, brief but substantial, was to be discussed and developed in Italy in *Liber argumentorum* and *Liber specierum,* both anonymous, written between 1050 and 1100; in a *Commentarius* written in the Liège region (*ca.* 1100); and in a *Metrologus* of the thirteenth century of English origin. As late as the sixteenth century, the anonymous *Introductorium Guidonis* offered a good digest of his writings.

THE SCHOOL OF REICHENAU

Differing from their Italian colleagues, the German-speaking authors of this period perpetuated an oddly archaic musical theory, and tried, by referring to Frankish models, to reconcile their own practice with Boethius' doctrine. Berno (*d.* 1048), abbot of Reichenau, educated at Fleury-sur-Loire and Prüm, compiled between 1021 and 1036 a long tonary noted in staffless neumes and preceded, after Regino's example, by a prologue in which he followed closely not only Boethius, but also Aurelian of Réôme, Hucbald, and Gerbert for the classification of intervals, consonances, and modes, including here and there personal views on the transposition of scales and the nomenclature of psalmodic formulae. His work served as a model for *Breviarium* (Compendium of musical science) and the huge tonary compiled by Frutolf (*d.* 1103) of Michelsberg, near Bamberg, the only one to supply the complete list of the responses of Divine Office.

Berno's disciple, Hermann of Reichenau (1013–1054), called "the Lame" (Contractus), rethought the theory of plainsong in rigorously scientific terms, leaving no room for approximation. But his *Musica* was little read and its significance regrettably ignored, because of its abstract character and dense style. Hermann dared to challenge Boethius' theory of consonances by bringing to its limits the concept of modal octave in relation to the musical practice of his days. He may be seen as the creator of church modality as it is still accepted in our time: "A mode," he wrote, "is an inflection of many pitches within

MUSICAL TREATISES

any one octave, as determined by fixed intervals and fitted into one whole."

The great reformer of the Cluny rule, William of Hirsau (*ca.* 1026–1091), amplified Hermann's ideas and appealed to the authority of Guido of Arezzo to formalize, not without repetitions and stiffness, his own conception of modality. His authoritarian views on this crucial question were later developed by his pupil Theogerus (*ca.* 1050–1121), bishop of Metz, who admitted B flat in the lowest tetrachord of the modal octave, contrary to the prevailing use. In the same zone of influence may be mentioned Eberhard of Freising, the likely author of a treatise on the measurement of organ pipes *(De mensura fistularum),* and Heinrich of Augsburg (*d.* 1083), author of a *De musica* in dialogue form, who condensed in a few pages the teachings of Boethius and concludes with a statement of the rules of psalmodic cadences, without however providing any example drawn from the repertory.

THE SCHOOL OF LIÈGE

The spread of Guido of Arezzo's writings north of the Alps gave rise to an abundant theoretical literature in the abbeys of the Meuse valley and the principality of Liège as much as it did in Bavaria. However, the name "School of Liège" used to designate a corpus of treatises actually more related by content than by origin. The first author to stand out is William of Hirsau's disciple, Aribo. In his *De musica,* dedicated to Ellenhard, abbot of Freising (*d.* 1078), he cleverly illustrated, with a diagram called *caprea* ("goat," because of the rapidity with which this mnemonic device could be understood), the modal properties of the eight tones, thus perfecting the *quadripartita figura* of his predecessors. Displaying a taste for symbolism, he compared the four authentic ("superior") modes to the men and the rich, the four plagal ("inferior") modes to the women and the poor, but moderated this discrimination by uniting the two groups in a harmonious round. Aribo remained interested in the measurement of organ pipes and the relations that he felt were revealed between the inner form of tetrachords and metrics—he seems to have known, at least indirectly, St. Augustine's *De musica,* which dealt thoroughly with that subject—and glosses on the thorny chapter 15 of Guido's *Micrologus.*

The author of *Musica,* a treatise dedicated to Abbot Fulgentius of Affighem (1089–1121), near Brussels, goes even further. The work was written by a certain monk named John, who was once known under the name of John Cotton, on the frail evidence of a pseudoepigraphic inscription in a thirteenth-century manuscript. Equipped with a solid musical and literary culture, John of Affighem was an unrivaled teacher who did not hamper himself with systems, but aimed solely at educating young choristers as effectively as possible. He did not reject the usual notions on the usefulness and the origin of music, the measurements on the monochord, and the aural recognition of intervals, but in his twenty-three clearly written chapters, which are not free of sarcasm, he applied himself mainly to the defense of the unity of the plainsong, unity from now on facilitated by the generalization of the notation on a four-line staff. He explored the ethos or aesthetic power of modes in terms of the "psychology" of the listener (chap. 16) and formulated clear precepts on the manner of composing melodies, which, he assured, must above all convey the meaning of the words (chap. 18). He concluded his theoretical account with a brief chapter on *diaphonia,* or two-part organum in contrary or oblique motion, trying to soften somewhat the artificial precepts stated in *Musica enchiriadis* and Guido's *Micrologus.* Through his attachment to the tradition of "noncorrupted chant" as well as his desire to simplify the performance of psalmody, John of Affighem opened the way for the Cistercian reform of the twelfth century.

THE TWELFTH CENTURY

Next to John's *De musica,* the compilations of the other theoreticians of the so-called School of Liège, such as Raoul of St. Trond (1070–1138), the supposed author of *Questiones in musica* (unless it was Franco of Liège), and Rupert of Deutz (*d. ca.* 1130), appear quite second-rate. In reality the important event of the twelfth century, in the field of music theory, is the Cistercian reform of liturgical music. A first attempt took place under St. Stephen Harding, third abbot of Cîteaux, who sent monks to copy the antiphonary at the Metz cathedral, considered the closest to the classic Gregorian tradition. To the monks' astonishment, however, the Metz version was judged "very corrupt"—which is to say, too different—and after Stephen's death in 1134, a general chapter presided over by St. Bernard of Clairvaux (*d.* 1153) undertook the revision of all liturgical books in order to achieve a complete unity of rites and customs. As for the chants, the results were codified in three important texts: (1) the *Prologus in antiphonarium* or letter-preface by St. Bernard, addressed to all daughter houses of the order; (2) the *Praefatio,* by Abbot

MUSICAL TREATISES

Guy de Cherlieu (Guido de Cariloco, *d.* 1158), to the treatise *De cantu et correctione antiphonarii,* compendium to *Regule de arte musica* by Guy d'Eu (Guido Augensis), abbot of Longpont, often confused with the former; (3) the *Tonale Sancti Bernardi,* or tonary in the form of a dialogue, which, though anonymous, was thereafter attributed to St. Bernard himself.

Strong in theoretical knowledge but little prone to nuances, these austere monks undertook to bring plainsong under the rules decreed by the theoreticians they knew: Regino of Prüm, Berno of Reichenau, Pseudo-Odo (author of the *Dialogus*), Guido of Arezzo, and John of Afflighem. From an artistic point of view, the result turned out a failure: through literal interpretation of Psalm 144:9 ("I will sing a new song unto thee, O God: upon a psaltery and an instrument of ten strings will I sing praises unto thee"), the ambitus of all the melodies was limited to a tenth, and the alleluia verses deprived of their *iubili* (vocalizations); the *permixtio modorum* or mixture of authentic and plagal modes, justified in the execution of the type of the responsories, was prohibited, as well as the use of B flat through recourse to arbitrary transpositions; the number of psalmodic cadences *(differentiae)* was reduced to only one per tone, without any exception. In reaction against the excessively long services of the Cluny monks, all the tropes and sequences were abolished, and only the Ambrosian hymns were retained, in the name of "authentic tradition"; for these inconsiderate suppressions in the musical customs of the day Peter Abelard sharply reproached St. Bernard in his *Letter 10.* In spite, however, of its uncompromising systematizations, which only impoverished the repertory, the Cistercian reform, similar to the Carthusian reform of about the same period, inspired the recasting of the Dominican antiphonary, ordered in the middle of the thirteenth century by the master general of the order, Humbert of Romans, and to which the theoretician Jerome of Moravia likely contributed.

THE THIRTEENTH CENTURY

The twelfth century was the century of Cîteaux, the mother house of the Cistercians, but the thirteenth century saw the rise of the mendicant friars (Franciscans, Dominicans) and of the universities where they began to teach from early on. For the musical theoreticians, grouped around Notre Dame Cathedral in Paris, then in the process of completion, and around the University of Paris, whose first statutes go back to the year 1215, the new challenge was to determine precisely the time values of the notes *(mensuratio temporis).* This was necessitated by the development of polyphonic music in the form of organum, discant, copula, and hocket. Just as during the Carolingian renaissance, the need to record through musical notation a repertory quite different from that of plainsong stimulated the production of several short treatises of essentially pragmatic nature. Immediately after the anonymous author of *Discantus positio vulgaris* (*ca.* 1230), the first author to formulate with clarity and accuracy the rules governing the duration of *musica mensurabilis* was John of Garland (*fl. ca.* 1230), called Johannes Gallicus or Primarius, not to be confused with his homonym, the English poet and grammarian John of Garland (*ca.* 1190–*ca.* 1272), likewise professor at the University of Paris. Johannes Gallicus is the author of two short treatises: *De plana musica* (not yet edited), in which he largely annotated Boethius; and the *De mensurabili musica,* in which he set forth, in the scholastic manner, a seminal theory of the six rhythmic modes and a classification of six consonant ("perfect") and seven dissonant ("imperfect") intervals, which were retained without major modification until the mid sixteenth century. Because of their usefulness, each of these little manuals was subjected—no doubt after the author's death—to reworkings, the first under the title *Introductio musice secundum magistrum Johannem de Garlandia,* and the second under the designation *De mensurabili positio,* inserted in the *Tractatus de musica* of Jerome of Moravia.

One generation later, around 1260, Magister Lambertus (called Aristoteles or Pseudo-Bede because his *Tractatus de musica* had been erroneously inserted among a collection of Bede's works published in 1563 and edited by Johannes Hervagius) perfected the system of mensural notation invented by John of Garland. He specified the temporal value of note symbols, particularly for the indeterminate ligatures: hereafter the *longa perfecta* (▜) would have the value of three beats and would serve as the basis for determining all other note values until the appearance of the *semibrevis* (◆). Such is the concept of *perfectio temporum,* modeled after the theological concept of the Trinity. Lambertus added three rhythmic modes to the six already in use and divided *musica mensurabilis* into three species: *discantus* with contrary motion, *hoketus* (hocket) in "upbeats" between the voices or parts, and liturgical *organum.* The examples of motets he quoted are found in the Bamberg, Montpellier, La Clayette, and

MUSICAL TREATISES

Las Huelgas manuscript collections. Preserved now in only four manuscripts, this important treatise nonetheless circulated very early in England, Poland, and Hungary. Its influence exceeded the bounds of the School of Notre Dame since around 1320 Philippe de Vitry would borrow from it the substance of chapters 8 to 10 of his *Ars nova.*

The influence of *Ars cantus mensurabilis* of Franco of Cologne ("Magister Franco Teutonicus," *fl. ca.* 1250 or later), papal chaplain, preceptor of the Hospital of the Knights of St. John of Jerusalem in Cologne, and professor in Paris—consequently the supposed existence of two masters of the same name, one of Cologne, the other of Paris—lasted until at least the fifteenth century. Franco reduced to five the six or the nine rhythmic modes of his predecessors, and developed an essential idea in the evolution of musical notation: that different time values should be expressed by different note shapes, rather than by their context. Correlatively, time values of silences *(pausationes)* should be fixed unequivocably. Without denying the real value of the innovations of Franco, his historical importance must neverthless be reduced to more modest proportions, if a *ca.* 1280 date, as suggested by Wolf Frobenius, is accepted for the composition of his treatise.

Two theoreticians born in northern France but active in Paris developed the teaching of Franco: Petrus of Picardy, composer and author of *Ars motettorum,* a summary for the use of *novi auditores,* that is to say students little versed in the technique *(ars)* of mensural notation, and Petrus de Cruce (Pierre de la Croix, *fl. ca.* 1290), known through two English music scholars, Robert de Handlo and John Hanboys (Hamboys). The latter divided Franco's *brevis* into seven *semibreves,* and introduced the *punctum divisionis* (approximate equivalent of a triple-time measure) into the *perfectio.* In his turn Petrus de Cruce bore a part in the development of the Italian fourteenth-century (*Trecento*) music theory.

All in all, one cannot exclude the possibility that these two Petruses might be the same person designated at one time by his belonging to the college of the nation of Picardy at the University of Paris, at another time by his real name.

The high number of writings devoted to the "grammar" of measured music does not mean that the study of plainsong *(cantus planus* or *musica plana),* which served as the foundation of liturgical polyphony, was neglected in the course of the thirteenth century. In Italy, Guido Faba (*ca.* 1190–1245), professor of rhetoric at the University of Bologna and priest of S. Michele di Mercato in the same city, summarized for his parishioners the rudiments of plainsong and modality. In 1271 he was followed by Amerus (Aluredus, Annuerus), a priest of English origin and a member of the household of Cardinal Ottobono Fieschi, future pope Hadrian V, for whom he wrote his *Practica artis musicae* for the instruction of his young choristers. The tonary that he inserted in the middle of his work is representative of Anglo-French usage and of the Roman curia, and his final chapter on the "cantilenae organicae" remains the first exposé of measured music in Italy. Three years later, Elias Salomo, cleric of St. Astier in Périgueux, dedicated to Pope Gregory X his *Scientia artis musicae,* written with the aim to rectify the numerous mistakes that he noticed everywhere in the execution of plainsong, "with the exception of a few churches in France and England." He himself favored a performance with equal durations, that is to say one beat by note (as in the modern method of Solesmes). After the conventional statement on scales, solmization, and modes, he described in detail (in chap. 30) the *cantus supra librum,* or improvisation in three or four parts of a polyphonic composition over a Gregorian melody.

Special mention must be made of *De musica* (or *Ars musica*) of Johannes de Grocheo, active in Paris around 1300. Contrary to his predecessor, he dismissed the arithmetical speculations of Boethius in favor of an empirical approach inspired by Aristotle, known in Latin translations from the Arabic. In place of Boethius' tripartite division of music *(mundana, humana, instrumentalis),* he substituted *musica simplex* (civic or secular, which he called *vulgaris,* and which could be vocal or instrumental); *musica composita* (or "regular," which was composed according to preset rules and measured, and included the organum, the motet, and the hocket); and *musica ecclesiastica* or liturgical music, in free rhythm. *Musica simplex* is in turn subdivided into *cantus,* which includes the chanson de geste, and *cantilena,* which covers the different types of dance much appreciated by young people. A methodical and independent thinker, Johannes de Grocheo is the only one of his period to discuss at length the forms of secular music and its social function.

The thirteenth century was also a period of vast compilations, related to the "theological summas" then in vogue at the University of Paris. A first example of this was given by the Dominican Vincent

MUSICAL TREATISES

of Beauvais (*ca.* 1190–1264), who in his *Speculum doctrinale* (book 17, chaps. 10–35) reproduced almost word by word Richard of St. Victor, Isidore of Seville, and Boethius (although discarding everything that concerned musical practice). Roger Bacon (*ca.* 1214–*ca.* 1292), who taught in Paris before going to Oxford, made use of this indigestible résumé and ranked music among the subjects indispensable to theological studies.

More interesting is the *Tractatus de musica* of another Parisian Dominican, Jerome of Moravia, who was active from 1274 to 1304. In addition to transmitting treatises by John of Garland, Franco, and Petrus de Cruce, Jerome gave (in chap. 28) precise indications on the tuning of the two-stringed rebec—a sort of violin of Arab origin—and the five-stringed vielle.

England, Austria, even Spain did not stand aside from this flowering: witness *De mensuris et discantu* (*ca.* 1275) by a student at Bury St. Edmunds, educated in Paris—the famous Anonymous IV in the collection of Coussemaker's *Scriptores,* our most detailed source on the composers of the School of Notre Dame; *Summa de speculatione musicae* in six parts by the mathematician and alchemist Walter Odington (*fl. ca.* 1298–1316), a Benedictine monk of St. Mary's of Evesham, near Worcester, who placed the major thirds (ratio 5:4) and minor thirds (ratio 6:5) among the consonances because in actual practice musicians relate them to regular consonances, the fourth (4:3) and the whole tone (9:8); *De musica* in four books by Engelbert (*d.* 1331), abbót of Admont in Austria; or *Ars musica* by the Spanish Franciscan, Egidius of Zamora, tutor to the son of Alfonso X of Castile, compiler of *Las Cantigas de Santa María,* one of our best sources for the iconography of medieval musical instruments. In addition to the traditional notions on proportions, solmization, and modes, Egidius made a glossary of instruments literally lifted from *De proprietatibus rerum* (*ca.* 1250) of Bartholomaeus Anglicus and bore witness to their use in the accompaniment of liturgical hymns, proses, and sequences.

All these musical "summas" culminated in Jacques de Liège's *Speculum musicae,* an encyclopedia in seven books totaling 521 chapters and completed around 1330, where all the authorities, Greek and Roman—Boethius at the head of the list, naturally—were quoted and commented upon point by point. The first five books were concerned with *musica speculativa;* the sixth with modality; and the seventh with discant and mensural music. In this last book Jacques severely criticized the innovations of the dawning fourteenth century, which must now be examined.

FOURTEENTH-CENTURY TREATISES

It is not customary for a technical theoretical work to impose its name on a whole segment of the history of music, but such is the case with Philippe de Vitry's *Ars nova,* written in Paris *ca.* 1322, which has come to designate the entire musical production in Italy and France between around 1320 and 1430. Reduced to their essentials, the innovations introduced by Vitry, bishop of Meaux and "one of the greatest scholars of our time and an incomparable poet," according to his friend Petrarch, are the following: he generalized the use of the *minima* (♦ — equivalent to the eighth note or quaver), attributed to binary ("imperfect") time an importance equal to ternary ("perfect") time, devised the symbols that were to become our notational signs for the indication of measure, and recommended the use of red ink for the notation of passages in binary rhythm, as attested in the manuscripts that have preserved his compositions and those of his illustrious contemporary, Guillaume de Machaut.

Another contemporary of Vitry, the astronomer and mathematician Jehan des Murs (*ca.* 1290–after 1351), professor at the University of Paris, reaffirmed on the authority of Aristotle and Boethius the primacy of theoretical knowledge over practical experience and gave a tight mathematical formulation, in the form of theorems, to the measurement of rhythm as expressed by mensural notation. His doctrine, condensed in five works reproduced in more than 125 manuscripts, was authoritative until the end of the fifteenth century and assumed the same importance for *ars nova* as the work of Franco did for the *Ars antiqua* period (*ca.* 1150–1300).

In Italy, Marchettus of Padua (*ca.* 1274–after 1326) laid the foundations of trecento notation in a long treatise with the colorful title "The Garden of Mensural Music" *(Pomerium in arte musicae mensuratae),* completed in Cesena in 1326 and dedicated to Robert I, king of Sicily. After having described the chromatic alterations used in the polyphonic repertory, he endorsed the predominance of perfect measure over the imperfect, subdivided the ternary *semibrevis* (◆) into twelve shorter values, and added four rhythmic "imperfect" (binary) modes to the five modes of Franco, whose rules regarding ligatures he

MUSICAL TREATISES

retained. A less scholastic formulation, intended for beginners, was given in his *Brevis compilatio in arte musica.* Earlier, Marchettus, helped by a Dominican master of philosophy, named Syphans of Ferrara, compiled an extensive treatise on plainsong titled *Lucidarium in arte musicae planae,* which was completed in Verona in 1318. In this work he rejected the Pythagorean dogma of indivisibility of the whole tone in two equal parts and substituted for it, under the name *falsa musica,* a new division of the whole tone into five *dieses*, which is one of the theoretical sources of Renaissance chromaticism. This bold concept was vigorously attacked a century later in the *Tractatus musicae speculativae* (1425) by his countryman Prosdocimus de Beldemandis, and in the *Libelli musicalis de ritu canendi* by the humanist Carthusian monk Johannes Legrense (*ca.* 1415–1473), teacher of the music theorist Nicolaus Burtius.

De musica mensurabili, falsely attributed to Theodonus di Caprio (formerly known as Theodoricus de Campo, as several dictionaries write it), combined the essentials of the rules of mensural notation, which had been codified between approximately 1250 and 1350, and introduced a new sign of notation proper to Italian music: the *dragma* (♦), a *semibrevis* with two staffs, which could take different time values according to the musical context. For its part *Compendium artis motectorum Marchecti* of Petrus of Amalfia (Petrus Capuanus), written in the second half of the fourteenth century, formulated, despite its title, a system of notation quite different from Marchettus' because it borrowed substantially from Philippe de Vitry's *Ars nova.* It is precisely these often considerable differences that a trend-setter composer such as Johannes Ciconia (*ca.* 1335–1411), born in Liège but active in Avignon and Padua, tried to mitigate. In his *Nova musica* in four books, he too followed Boethius, and represented the craft of musical composition as a reflection of God's nature as well as a refined way of penetrating the secrets of the visible universe. At the same time, the composer Jacobus of Bologna, one of the principal figures of the *trecento,* with Francesco Landini and Giovanni da Cascia, drafted one of the very first treatises written in Italian: *Arte del biscanto misurato,* useful for the understanding of his compositions, mostly two- and three-voice madrigals.

De motettis componendis (*ca.* 1350) of Egidius of Murino (Morino) raises a historical as well as a philological question. This treatise, which propounded in a few dense but clear pages the manner in which to compose an isorhythmic motet in three, four, or even five parts from a liturgical tenor, is linked in the extant manuscripts with the *Tractatus de diversis figuris* by Philippus of Caserta. This bond seems to be explained either by the fact that Egidius—perhaps Egidius Morini, canon of the cathedral of Le Mans in 1337—is the author of the two works, or that he was confused later on with Phipoctus, who was active in Avignon under Pope Clement VII (1378–1394).

In the last years of the *trecento,* Johannes Vetulus of Anagnia, still strongly influenced by French *ars nova* (although he knew Marchettus' *Pomerium*), assigned to the *minima* (♦) the duration of one seventy-second of a *minuta,* and this indication constitutes one of the oldest known metronomic references. His definition of *musica* ("music is the science that softens hardness and evil in the human heart and leads it to contemplate celestial things") was mystical rather than technical and thus remained isolated in the history of medieval theory.

Earlier in England Robert de Handlo was the first to codify, in his *Regule* of 1326, not only Franco's rules but also those of other French theoreticians of the thirteenth century, whom he explicitly commented upon and quoted: Petrus de Cruce, Petrus Le Viser, John of Garland, Jacobus of Navernia, and Admetus de Aureliana. The novelties of continental *ars nova* remained foreign to him, but his compilation—a model of pedagogical presentation—received the praise of Thomas Morley, who used it as late as 1597 in his *Plaine and Easie Introduction to Practicall Musicke.*

The longest treatise on *ars nova* is the *Quatuor principalia musice* by an anonymous friar of Bristol, although it has been attributed to another Englishman, the Franciscan friar Simon Tunstede (*d.* 1369), who seems to have been only the copyist. Divided in four parts, this musical "summa" of the thirteenth and fourteenth centuries borrows most of its matter from Magister Lambertus, Franco, Egidius of Murino and, with reservations, from Philippe de Vitry.

If Spain has preserved from this period only a single treatise of mensural music, *De cantu organico* by an anonymous Catalan author, Germany on the other hand distinguished itself with *Flores musicae omnis cantus Gregoriani* by Hugo Spechtshart (Hugo of Reutlingen, *d.* 1360), a treatise on plainsong in four parts, half in verse, half in prose, composed at the beginnning of 1332, revised ten years later, and printed in Strasbourg in 1488 by Johann

MUSICAL TREATISES

Pryss. It is, however, in his *Chronicon* of the year 1349 that Spechtshart collected the best corpus of melodies of the German flagellants *(Geissler Lieder),* similar in spirit and intention to the contemporary Italian *laude,* but of much simpler form. In comparison, the *Cantuagium* (*ca.* 1380) of Heinrich Eger von Kalkar (1328–1408), educated at the University of Paris, where he taught liberal arts from 1356 to 1364 before becoming a Carthusian monk in Cologne, appears of a definitely more limited interest for the theory as well as for the practice of chant, although this mystic author strongly influenced Geert Groote (1340–1384), the founder of *Devotio moderna.*

THE FIFTEENTH CENTURY

Between the fourteenth and fifteenth centuries there is not as pronounced a rupture as between the thirteenth and fourteenth, if by rupture is meant a conscious and deliberate abandonment of an outdated style or tradition in favor of new ways and procedures that were destined in turn to set a fashion. Such is the precise meaning of this *ars nova notandi* ("new technique of music writing"), which, from the last quarter of the fourteenth century, had evolved towards a rhythmic complexity and a formal mannerism justly termed, by Ursula Günther, *ars subtilior.* The waning *trecento* bequeathed to the new century a host of theoretical problems that a new generation of thinkers, for lack of satisfactory solutions, tried to formulate lucidly, so great was still the weight of Boethius' authority on their approach. These problems, still current today in hardly different terms, can be grouped under three rubrics: the consonance-dissonance conflict, temperament, and chromatic alterations.

The classification of consonances, and, by exclusion, of dissonances, takes on a particular importance for the formulation of linear counterpoint rules, which constitute one of the main concerns of fifteenth-century theoreticians. These rules are discussed at length in *Regulae de contrapuncto* (in Italian, despite the title) by Antonius of Leno (*d. ca.* 1450) and, in an even more precise manner, in a series of short treatises by the English Carmelite John Hothby (*d.* 1487), sometime choirmaster of the Lucca cathedral: *De cantu figurato, Regulae supra contrapunctum, Dialogus (. . .) in arte musica,* and others. A few decades before, Prosdocimus de Beldemandis (*ca.* 1380–1428), professor at the University of Padua, well versed in mathematics, astronomy, and music, as well as in medicine, had proposed in his *Contrapunctus* (written in 1412, then revised in 1425) an innovative classification in which *perfect* consonances were the unison and the fifth, with their respective doublings, the octave and the twelfth; and *imperfect* consonances were the third and the sixth, the tenth and the thirteenth. The dissonances were the second and seventh major (with ninth and fourteenth) as well as the fourth (plus the eleventh); the latter, however, was judged "less dissonant" than the others due to its intermediary position between the third and the fifth. The progress of this new classification and its impact on musical composition can be measured by comparing it to the ancient and medieval conception, essentially Pythagorean, where the only theoretically accepted consonances were, with their doublings, the fourth, the fifth, and the octave. (Actually, the double octave never had more than a structural function, and was used solely to complete the ambitus of the greater perfect system of the Greeks.) In his *Parvus tractatulus de modo monocordum dividendi* (Little treatise on the manner of dividing the monochord), Prosdocimus also suggested dividing the whole tone (ratio 9:8) into nine *chromata*: five for the major semitone, and four for the minor one, which led him to divide the octave into seventeen chromatic *and* enharmonic intervals. Despite an identical terminology, his functional approach to melodic intervals and to the consonances used in contrapuntal practice differed radically from the ancient doctrine.

The fifteenth century also had its "musical summa"—the last one on such a large scale—in the *Declaratio musicae disciplinae* of Ugolino of Orvieto (*ca.* 1380–1457), a comprehensive encyclopedia in five books, written between 1430 and 1440, of a high philosophical standard, which rethinks Boethius in the light of Aristotle and of the scholastic method. The first two books examine the foundations of *musica plana* (plainsong) and *musica mensurata* (polyphonic music) from the point of view of two-part counterpoint, note against note; the third comments at length on the *Musica mensurabilis* of Jehan des Murs, while the fourth and fifth go back to the mathematical analysis—the so-called *musica speculativa*—of intervals and consonances and ends with a ten-chapter appendix on the monochord. Although he declined to stray from the formal framework of the quadrivium—due to his scientific bent—Ugolino, himself a composer, was not indifferent to the musical production of his time. He was familiar with the works of Guillaume de Machaut and care-

MUSICAL TREATISES

fully addressed the thorny question of *musica ficta* in the monodic and polyphonic repertory.

Among Ugolino's contemporaries or immediate successors should be mentioned Antonio of Lucca, a pupil of Lorenzo of Orvieto, who commented in an original manner upon the work of Jehan des Murs in his *Ars cantus figurati,* and Giorgio Anselmi (before 1386–*ca.* 1440/1443), astronomer and doctor of medicine, professor at Parma and at Ferrara. The latter compiled in 1434 a long *De musica* divided into three "days" *(dieta),* which is nothing else than Boethius' *De institutione musica* rewritten in the form of a Platonic dialogue. After the usual remarks on the harmony of the spheres and arithmetical proportions, only the last book faces the notation of plainsong and mensural music. As pedantic and artificial as this dilettantish essay might appear, it served as a model for the theoretical writings of Franchinus Gaffurius, on the threshold of the Renaissance.

The personality of Guillelmus Monachus, "very erudite succentor," evades us, and scholars still argue whether this theoretician was English or Italian. In spite of a glaring lack of organization his *De perceptis artis musicae* (*ca.* 1480?) contains the most detailed indications—if contradictory in places—that we have on the technique of the faux-bourdon and the English gymel, kinds of counterpoint improvised on a plainsong melody, in parallel thirds and sixths, with a few occasional crossings of voices.

In Germany, during this time, theoreticians confined themselves to teaching the rudiments of the liturgical repertory, the only one that seemed to them worthy of a rational codification. In chronological order, mention may be made of the *Tractatus musicae scientiae* (1417) by the historian and hagiographer Gobelinus Person (1358–1421); the *Novellus musicae artis tractatus* and the *Opusculum de monochordo* by Conrad of Zabern (now Saverne; *d. ca.* 1480), a remarkable pedagogue, held in high esteem by the Holy Roman emperor Frederick III: Conrad's method of ecclesiastical singing was quickly adopted by the choir schools of the Basel, Strasbourg, Spire, Worms, and Mainz cathedrals; and the *Introductorium musicae* by Johannes Keck (Keckius; *ca.* 1400–1450), professor of philosophy at the University of Vienna, then monk in the abbey of Tegernsee in Bavaria. Keck rationalized the use of music in church on theological grounds, but avoided any concrete reference to plainsong in favor of dry calculations on proportions, intervals, and consonances.

Finally, Adam of Fulda (*ca.* 1445–1505), historiographer and kappelmeister of Frederick the Wise of Saxony, then professor in the new university of Wittenberg, completed in 1490 his *De musica* in four books of which the last summarized the essential elements of mensural music, with supporting examples. Displaying a wide knowledge of classical literature and musicology, he praised in passing the composers Antoine Busnois and Guillaume Dufay, to whom he attributed certain theoretical innovations, the nature of which remain imprecise. He also rebuked jugglers, minstrels *(ioculatores),* and other public entertainers *(laici vulgares),* and introduced a formal distinction, in the modern sense, between vocal and instrumental music.

At the end of this overview of the most important musical treatises written between 500 and 1500, we might ask where the limits of medieval music theory should be drawn, since echoes of this theory may be found as late as 1636 in the *Harmonie universelle* by Marin Mersenne or the *Musurgia universalis* (Rome, 1650) of the Jesuit Athanasius Kircher. By analogy with alchemy, a science definitely rejected only from Lavoisier's time onward, one might be tempted to extend these limits until 1722, the publication date of Rameau's *Traité de l'harmonie réduite à ses principes naturels,* if one keeps as a basic criterion for a modern theory of music the substitution of the concept of chord *(accord),* set as a self-sustaining entity at the root of all melodies, for that of *consonance,* founded exclusively on Pythagorean acoustics and readily extended for monodic and polyphonic music.

As early as the 1470's, a musician of Flemish origin, Johannes de Tinctoria (*ca.* 1435–*ca.* 1511) questioned the doctrine and the aesthetics of the ancient masters in a series of twelve treatises of which the most instructive were the *Liber de arti contrapuncti* (1477), the *De inventione et usu musicae* (*ca.* 1487), and the *Terminorum musicae diffinitorium* (*ca.* 1473, published in Treviso in 1495), the first dictionary of musical terms to be printed. But the most vigorous attack against Boethius' tetrachords and Guido of Arezzo's hexachords was to be formulated with as much realism as soundness in the *Musica practica* (published in Bologna in 1482) by the Spaniard Bartolomeo Ramos de Pareja, which earned him a vehement retort from Nicolaus Burtius, an unconditional defender of ancient and medieval tradition (*Musices opusculum,* printed in Bologna in 1487).

MUSICAL TREATISES

Inspired by the empirical steps taken by Tinctoris and Ramos de Pareja, Franchinus Gaffurius (1451–1522), *maestro di capella* at Milan Cathedral from 1484 to his death, appears as the theoretician at the crossroads, who foreshadowed the future without denying the contributions of the past. Side by side with his rather conservative views (expressed in a loyalty to Boethius and his Greek sources), Gaffurius considerably simplified the theory of musical proportions, considered the possibility of an equal temperament, and in forbidding perhaps portended the gradual but ineluctible transformation of linear counterpoint into vertical harmony. His main works, all printed early, are *Theoricum opus,* 1480; *Practica musicae,* 1496; and *De harmonia musicorum instrumentorum opus,* 1518.

But Boethius' theoretical structure, on which rested all the speculative musical thought of the Middle Ages, was solid, and could resist the isolated thrusts of some innovators of the Renaissance. It received its ultimate expression in the *Dodecachordon* (On the Twelve Modes, published in Basel in 1547) of Heinrich Glarean, a brilliant synthesis that marked the triumph of literary and musical humanism.

BIBLIOGRAPHY

Sources. Smits van Waesberghe, with Pieter Fischer and Christian Mass, eds., *The Theory of Music from the Carolingian Era up to 1400* (1961–), Répertoire international des sources musicales (RISM), B III.

Texts. Charles Edmond de Coussemaker, *Scriptorum de musica medii aevi* (1864–1876, repr. 1963 in 4 vols.); Martin Gerbert, *Scriptores ecclestiastici de musica sacra potissimum* (1784, repr. 1963 in 3 vols.); Juste-Adrien Lenoir de La Fage, *Essais de diphtérographie musicale* (1884, repr. 1964, 2 vols. in 1); These collections are gradually being superseded by new texts in the following series: Colorado College Music Press Critical Texts (CCMP) (1977–); Corpus scriptorum de musica (CSM) (1950–); and Divitiae musicae artis (DMA), Series A (1975–).

Translations. William Oliver Strunk, *Source Readings in Music History* (1950); Musical Theorists in Translation (1959–); Yale Music Theory Translations series (1963–); Colorado College Music Press, Translations (1967–); James B. Coover, "Music Theory in Translation: A Bibliography," in *Journal of Music Theory,* 3 (1959), and "Supplement, 1959–1969," *ibid.,* 13 (1969).

Studies. Hermann Abert, *Die Musikanschauung des Mittelalters* (1905, repr. 1964); Manfred F. Bukofzer, "Speculative Thinking in Medieval Music," in *Speculum,* **17** (1942); Edgar de Bruyne, *The Esthetics of the Middle Ages,* Eileen B. Hennessy, trans. (1969); Nan C. Carpenter, *Music in the Medieval and Renaissance Universities* (1968, repr. 1972); F. Alberto Gallo, "Philological Works on Music Treatises of the Middle Ages," in *Acta Musicologica,* **44** (1972); Lawrence A. Gushee, "Questions of Genre in Medieval Treatises on Music," in Wulf Arlt, ed., *Gattungen der Musik in Einzeldarstellungen* (1973); John Hollander, *The Untuning of the Sky* (1961); Francisco J. León Tello, *Estudios de historia de la teoría musical* (1962); Gerhard Pietzsch, *Die Klassifikation der Musik von Boethius bis Ugolino von Ovieto* (1929), and *Die Musik im Erziehungs- und Bildungsideal des ausgehenden Altertums und frühen Mittelalters* (1932); Julius Portnoy, "Similarities of Musical Concepts in Ancient and Medieval Philosophy," in *Journal of Aesthetics and Art Criticism,* **7** (1948/1949), and *The Philosopher and Music* (1954); Don M. Randel, "Al-Fārābī and the Role of Arabic Music Theory in the Latin Middle Ages," in *Journal of the American Musicological Society,* **29** (1976); Gilbert Reaney, "The Greek Background of Medieval Musical Thought," in *The Monthly Musical Records,* **87** (1957), and "The Question of Authorship in the Medieval Treatises on Music," in *Musica Disciplina,* **18** (1964); Hugo Riemann, *History of Music Theory, Books I and II: Polyphonic Theory to the Sixteenth Century,* Raymond H. Haggh, ed. and trans. (1962); Joseph Smits van Waesberghe, "La place exceptionelle de l'Ars Musica dans le développement des sciences au siècle des Carolingiens," in *Revue Gregorienne,* **31** (1952), and *Musikerziehung: Lehre und Theorie der Musik im Mittelalters* (1969).

Terminology. Margarete Appel, *Terminologie in den mittelalterlichen Musiktraktaten* (1935); Hans Heinrich Eggebrecht, ed., *Handwörterbuch der musikalischen Terminologie* (1972–); Hans Peter Gysin, *Studien zum Vokabular der Musiktheorie im mittelalter* (1958); Gilbert Reaney, "Terminology in Medieval Music," in Leipzig Universität, Institut für Musikwissenschaft, *Festschrift Heinrich Besseler* (1961).

Bibliographies. Andrew Hughes, *Medieval Music, the Sixth Liberal Art,* rev. ed. (1980); David R. Williams, *A Bibliography of the History of Music Theory,* 2nd ed. (1970).

YVES CHARTIER

[See also **Anonymous IV; Ars Antiqua; Ars Nova; Ars Subtilior; Boethius; Cistercian Chant; Consonance/Dissonance; Franco of Cologne; Gregorian Chant; Guido of Arezzo; Hermann von Reichenau; Hocket; Hucbald of St. Amand; Jacques de Liège; Johannes de Grocheo; John of Garland; Marchettus of Padua; Martianus Capella; Modal Notation; Mode; Motet; Motet Manuscripts; Musical Notation, Modal; Musical Notation, Western; Organum; Petrus de Cruce; Regino of Prüm; Remigius of Auxerre; Solesmes; Solmization;** and other individual authors.]

MUSPILLI. An Old High German eschatological poem in alliterative verse was entered in the ninth century, probably at the monastery of St. Emmeram in Regensburg, in the margins and blank spaces of a manuscript written between 825 and 836. The dialect is Bavarian with Frankish features, the spelling irregular, the text incomplete and partly illegible.

The poem describes the fate of the soul after death and the Last Judgment. After the summons to the Judgment, there is a section that is widely held to have been adapted from another poem. This describes the contest between Elias and Antichrist (based ultimately on Revelation 11, but here presented as a trial by combat), and seems to record a difference of opinion between "those versed in worldly law" and "men of God" as to its outcome. After the shedding of Elias' blood, the world is consumed by fire, and the Judgment Day (if this is the correct interpretation of the MS reading *tuatago*—emended either to *stuatago* or *tuamtago* at line 55, which is in any case highly corrupt) goes with the fire to visit mankind. Then no kinsman will be able to help another in the face of the *muspilli.* The meaning of this word (chosen as the title of the text by Schmeller, its first modern editor) is obscure and probably of pagan origin. (In Norse mythology, Múspellr and his sons are fire giants who will appear at the end of the world, and in Old Saxon *mudspelli* is associated with fire and the Last Things.) After a moralizing passage warning against corrupt judgment, the text continues with an account of the coming of the Judge, the resurrection of the dead, and the Judgment, after which the cross is carried forth and Christ shows his wounds. Here the text breaks off.

Scholars disagree about the possible presence of pagan motifs in the account of the fire. The style is uneven: at times powerful; at others, lame. In some lines rhyme replaces alliteration, and the alliterative technique is often faulty. There is one alliterative line that recurs in Otfrid von Weissenberg's *Evangelienbuch,* perhaps indicating that Otfrid knew a version of the poem; conversely, the use of rhyme may suggest acquaintance with Otfrid's work. It seems that in this work there is a meeting between the old and the new.

BIBLIOGRAPHY

An edited text of *Muspilli* is in Charles C. Barber, ed., *An Old High German Reader* (1951). See also John Knight Bostock, *A Handbook on Old High German Literature,* 2nd rev. ed. (1976); Heinz Finger, *Untersuchungen zum "Muspilli"* (1977); Wolfgang Mohr and Walter Haug, *Zweimal "Muspilli."* (1977).

D. R. McLINTOCK

[See also Biblical Poetry, German; Old High German Literature; Otfrid von Weissenburg.]

MUSTANṢIR, AL- (1191–1242), the thirty-sixth Abbasid caliph, who ruled in Baghdad from 1226 to 1242. The eldest of the caliph al-Ẓāhir's ten children, he succeeded to the caliphate at age thirty-five after his father's reign of less than ten months. His personal name was Abū Ja^{c}far Manṣūr. Al-Mustanṣir bi$^{\supset}$llāh, his regnal name, means "the one who seeks victory in God."

Despite the determined effort by his grandfather al-Nāṣir (*r.* 1180–1225) to reinvigorate the caliphate, the territory under direct caliphal control was restricted to lower Iraq, and the caliph had become a comparatively minor political figure. Consequently, little is recorded about the personal acts and achievements of al-Mustanṣir. He seems to have inherited his father's personal popularity with the citizens of Baghdad, and he enjoyed a reputation for piety.

Between 1228 and 1234 he had constructed a magnificent madrasa, or religious college, which he named al-Mustanṣirīya. Each of the four Sunni madhabs, or law schools, was represented by one professor, four assistants, and sixty-two law students. Though some earlier colleges had been built for more than one madhab, the usual pattern was for the college to be specific to one school. Thus al-Mustanṣir's decision to give equal money and space to all four represents a concrete effort to bring harmony to the Sunni community after more than two centuries of sometimes violent factional dispute. Medicine, Koran reading, and the traditions of the prophet Muḥammad were also taught; and the library was of unparalleled size and quality.

Al-Mustanṣir personally attended the ceremonies opening the magnificent college. The person in charge of its construction, Muayyid al-Dīn Muḥammad ibn al-^{c}Alqāmī, was a Shiite who later became a high court official and served as the last vizier of the Baghdad caliphate under al-Mustanṣir's son al-Musta^{c}ṣim.

Life in Baghdad under al-Mustanṣir was comparatively peaceful despite the depredations of Mongol armies and Muslim warlords in more distant provinces. Al-Mustanṣir spent much of the fortune ac-

MUSTAᶜṢIM, AL-

quired by his grandfather al-Nāṣir on civic improvements in the city. A new market for gems and precious metals was built, as well as shops, bridges, and a poorhouse in every residential quarter.

Embassies from the various sultans and warlords were received with great ceremony and enlivened the capital. Muslim rulers continued to seek the caliph's sanction of their rule despite his loss of temporal power. The caliphate, in this respect, had come to resemble the papacy. One embassy from a Christian ruler caused a sensation by bringing a polar bear as a gift. It was reported that the animal lived in the sea and ate fish.

The threat of Mongol invasion was always present, but the small caliphal army was a less tempting target than the Khwarazmian army of Jalāl al-Dīn and other forces roaming and pillaging throughout eastern Anatolia and northern Mesopotamia. Al-Mustanṣir died peacefully, a much loved and honored ruler.

BIBLIOGRAPHY

Ismāᶜīl ibn ᶜUmar ibn Kathīr, *Al-Bidāya wa-al-Nihāya,* XIII (1932–1939), 113–160; Gustav Weil, *Geschichte der Chalifen,* III (1846–1862, repr. 1967), 452–469.

RICHARD W. BULLIET

[See also **Abbasids; Baghdad; Caliph; Iraq; Khwārizmshāhs; Mongol Empire.**]

MUSTAᶜṢIM, AL- (1212/1213—1258), the thirty-seventh and last Abbasid caliph of Baghdad, who ruled from 1242 to 1258. He was the oldest of the caliph al-Mustanṣir's three sons. His personal name was Abū Aḥmad ᶜAbdallāh. His regnal title, al-Mustaᶜṣim biᵓllāh, or "the one who seeks shelter in God," did not prevent his own execution and the sack of Baghdad at the hands of the Mongol army of Genghis Khan's grandson Hulagu. With al-Mustaᶜṣim the Abbasid caliphate came to an end in Baghdad, and its resurrection in Cairo three years later under Mamluk control never regained for it the sacral authority it had enjoyed before Hulagu's invasion.

Al-Mustaᶜṣim was thirty years old on his accession and had acquired a sound education in religion from a leading Shafiᶜi scholar. He continued his father's tradition of patronizing religious scholars, but his reign, which began during an epidemic in Baghdad, was overshadowed by the Mongol advance.

Mongol armies had been occupying Iran and encroaching on Muslim territory in Anatolia and Mesopotamia for three decades when the great khan Möngke decided in 1251 to send his brother Hulagu westward to destroy the Nizārī Ismaili sect, better known as the Assassins, and put down other resistance. He was ordered not to attack the caliph unless he failed to tender allegiance to the Mongols. Hulagu's slow, inexorable campaign took several years but achieved complete success in its primary missions. Having brought order (as well as destruction) to Iran, he headed west and sent a message to al-Mustaᶜṣim requesting him to present himself in person or send an embassy of his chief officials. Al-Mustaᶜṣim responded with a demand that Hulagu return to his homeland. After a second and similar exchange of messages, Hulagu persuaded the Abbasid governor who controlled the vital passes through the Zagros Mountains to surrender his castles. This action gave the Mongols free access to the Mesopotamian lowlands.

Before proceeding further, Hulagu consulted his court astrologer, Ḥuṣām al-Dīn, who predicted that six disasters would befall if Baghdad were attacked. But the great Shiite theologian and philosopher Naṣīr al-Dīn al-Ṭūsī was also in Hulagu's entourage. He refuted Huṣām al-Dīn's astrological predictions with historical instances of noncatastrophic attacks on the Abbasid capital. When Hulagu asked him what would happen if Baghdad fell, he replied, "Hulagu will reign in place of al-Mustaᶜṣim."

Hulagu mustered his army and received a final embassy from the caliph. "If the caliph is killed," the emissaries claimed, "the whole world will be disorganized, the Sun will hide his face, the rain will cease to fall and the plants will no longer grow." But Hulagu's mind was made up. The overwhelming Mongol force defeated the caliph's small army and overran Iraq.

With his capital surrounded and most of its fortifications in the hands of the Mongols, al-Mustaᶜṣim followed the advice of his Shiite vizier, Ibn al-ᶜAlqāmī, to surrender. He and his three sons presented themselves to Hulagu, who seemed benevolent, and obeyed his command to order the people of Baghdad to lay down their arms. The Mongols then slaughtered the disarmed Baghdadis and sacked the city for seven days. Al-Mustaᶜṣim was forced to divulge the whereabouts of his treasures.

When the looting was over, Hulagu withdrew to a nearby village, where al-Mustaᶜṣim was rolled in a carpet and kicked or trampled to death. This was a customary Mongol way of dealing with princely victims without shedding their blood. Thus ended the Abbasid caliphate.

BIBLIOGRAPHY

A. Bausani, "Religion Under the Mongols," in John A. Boyle, ed., *The Cambridge History of Iran,* V (1968); John A. Boyle, "The Death of the Last ᶜAbbasid Caliph: A Contemporary Muslim Account," in *Journal of Semitic Studies,* **6** (1961), and "Dynastic and Political History of the Īl-Khāns," in John A. Boyle, ed., *The Cambridge History of Iran,* V (1968); Gustav Weil, *Geschichte der Chalifen,* III (1846–1862, repr. 1967), 470–488.

RICHARD W. BULLIET

[See also **Abbasids; Baghdad; Caliph; Hulagu; Iraq; Mongol Empire.**]

MUTANABBĪ, AL- (Abū 'l-Ṭayyib Aḥmad ibn al-Ḥusayn) (915–965), Arab poet born in Al-Kūfa, Iraq. As a boy he entered on the career of professional panegyrist. The one major suspension of this career occurred before he was twenty: he may have fomented a religio-political revolt among the Bedouins of the Syrian desert; he certainly spent some time in prison. On being released, he once more looked to poetry for a living. He owes to this episode the nickname al-Mutanabbī, "the one who set up as a prophet." Nothing in the mature poet's work suggests religious enthusiasm.

The period of greatest success in the career of the panegyrist coincided with the best work of the poet. This period began in 948, when al-Mutanabbī arrived in Aleppo at the court of the Hamdanid ruler of northern Syria, Sayf al-Dawla. An association of mutual advantage developed. Sayf al-Dawla was a generous prince, a patron of learning and the arts, and an indefatigable campaigner against the Byzantines. In him al-Mutanabbī found a hero of sufficient stature for his poetry. Sayf al-Dawla received poems that would ensure the fame of his triumphs (or that might, on occasion, palliate a defeat), and he rewarded the poet richly. Certainly there was mutual respect. The biographer Ibn Khallikān reports that al-Mutanabbī "obtained the authorization of being seated in the presence of Saif al-Dawlat, when reciting to him the poems which he was to compose in his praise; and he insisted on being dispensed from saluting the prince in the usual manner, which was by kissing the ground in his presence" (*Ibn Khallikan's Biographical Dictionary,* Mac Guckin de Slane, trans., I [1843]).

In 957 the relationship turned sour. Al-Mutanabbī journeyed to Egypt. He at first praised the Ikhshidid ruler Kāfūr; then, his hopes of a high post in government thwarted, set upon him with ferocious satire. He fled Egypt and found patrons in Baghdad, then in Iran. On his return trip to Iraq in 965, a band of bedouins attacked the party of travelers and the poet was killed.

During his last stay in Baghdad al-Mutanabbī helped establish the basic corpus of his poetry by reading and explaining it to a number of scholars. The bulk of his work consists in the panegyrics and occasional elegies of the professional poet. Many of these poems merely list a variety of admirable traits in the patron; in others the praise is hung on particular events. Some of his poems are more personal in theme, such as an elegy on the death of his grandmother and a poem written while bedridden and feverish. Some lie between the private and the public, as the poem of reproach—a kind of disillusioned lover's quarrel—addressed to Sayf al-Dawla after the relationship between poet and prince had chilled.

The poems are highly rhetorical, both in their linguistic form and in their presentation of the world. Lines balanced by antitheses, chiastic arrangements, paronomasia, and the like advertise the patron's generosity, wisdom, and military glory. There is a delight in hyperbole:

> His station is above the noble deeds that have been husbanded by other men; his achievements are all virgins.

and paradox:

> You have robed yourself in the dust of battle, as if you considered it impure to see the air pure.

or (on a dead lady):

> The mercy of God, our Creator, is the balm upon the face shrouded in beauty.

The requirements of panegyric are often balanced by words of fierce personal pride, and at times by thoughts of the vanity of the world and the contemptible nature of its inhabitants.

The best of his work has extraordinary power of language, and is carefully composed. In the following example the conventions of panegyric gain vitality as lurching confusion is played off against the hero's decisive moment:

> They marched against you weighed down with so much steel their horses seemed legless;
> The sun's glint did not betray their swords for steel served them also for cloaks and turbans.
> A huge fivefold army whose marching filled east and west; whose din reached to the stars of Gemini.
> It included every language and nation; only interpreters could make them understand each other.
> God, what a time that was! Its fire melted away the base metal and only the sharp sword or valiant warrior remained.
> Whatever could not cut through armor and spears was cut to pieces. The knights, if they could not sustain the shock of the clash, fled headlong.
> When there was no doubting the death of anyone standing, you stood, as if in the eye of destruction while destruction slept.
> Wounded knights fled past you in defeat, but your face was radiant and your mouth smiling.
> You so far exceeded the measure of bravery and reason that people said you knew the secrets of fate.
> You gathered the wings of that army to the heart and crushed them against it till every last feather perished,
> With a blow that came down on their heads while victory was hidden, and reached the collarbones as victory stepped forth.
> You despised the Rudaini spears and tossed them aside. It seemed as though the swords spoke their contempt of spears. [i.e., you fought at close quarters].
> If a man wishes to gain a brilliant triumph—the keys to it are the sharp white swords.
> You scattered them all over the hill of Uḥaydib, as dirhems are scattered over a bride. . . .

Some medieval critics faulted al-Mutanabbī for arbitrary images, lapses into obscurity, or infringements of grammar. Long after his death, debate continued between his detractors and defenders. The detractors were vocal, but the poet's fame was secure. To this day his work is much admired, quoted, and studied.

BIBLIOGRAPHY

Arthur J. Arberry, *Poems of Mutanabbi* (1967); Régis Blachère, *Un poète arabe du IVe siècle de l'Hégire (Xe siècle de J.-C.): Abou ṭ-Ṭayyib al-Motanabbī* (1935).

ANDRAS HAMORI

[See also **Arabic Poetry; Buyids; Hamdanids; Ikhshidids; Khallikān, Ibn.**]

MU^c^TAṢIM, AL- (795/796—842), the eighth Abbasid caliph, ruled from 833 to 841. His name was Abū Isḥāq Muḥammad, and he was the son of the fifth caliph Hārūn al-Rashīd by a woman of Soghdian (Central Asian) origin named Mārida. He was a youth during the civil war his half-brothers al-Amīn and al-Ma^ɔ^mūn fought for the throne from 809 to 813. The victor, al-Ma^ɔ^mūn, died in 833 without resolving the problems of holding together and religiously legitimizing his rule over an empire that stretched from Egypt to Central Asia. He did not tutor his successor in the art of ruling, so Abū Isḥāq took over, after suppressing a brief challenge from al-Ma^ɔ^mūn's son, with little experience outside of military affairs. He adopted the title al-Mu^c^taṣim Billāh (He who looks to God for protection).

Al-Mu^c^taṣim was physically powerful, with fair skin and beard, but he was poorly educated. He zealously pursued al-Ma^ɔ^mūn's policy of enforcing adherence to the *mu^c^tazilī* interpretation of Islamic theology. But he was mostly preoccupied by military matters. He introduced large numbers of Turkish soldiers of Central Asian origin into the army and raised some of their officers to high positions. These troops were personally dependent upon the caliph, but the customary use of the term "slave" in describing them is debatable.

The population of Baghdad, the capital, abhorred the rough behavior of the new troops, so al-Mu^c^taṣim ordered a new city to be built as their encampment. Samarra, a site three days' travel (sixty miles) up the Tigris from Baghdad, was chosen, and it became the caliphal capital from 835 through the next eight reigns. Baghdad nevertheless remained a major city and center of political activity.

Despite al-Mu^c^taṣim's promotion of the Turkish soldiery, most of his principal officers were Iranian aristocrats. They played the leading roles in the defeat of the heresiarch Babak in Azerbaijan in 837 and in the punitive raid against Byzantium in 838 that culminated in the siege and capture of Amorion, the home city of the Byzantine Amorian dynasty, located southwest of Ankara. This was the last major caliphal expedition against Byzantium.

A turning point in the balance of influence between Iranians and Turks was the trial of the powerful commander al-Afshīn in 840. Al-Afshīn was the hereditary title of the Iranian local ruler of Ushrūsana, a mountain valley in the region from which al-Mu^c^taṣim's mother came. Accused of being an insincere Muslim, retaining idols and religious books from his preconversion days, and conspiring against the caliph with other Iranian aristocrats, al-Afshīn was found guilty and starved to death. Thereafter, the role of the Turkish officers increased to the point that in subsequent reigns they were able to install and depose caliphs at will. Al-Muᶜtaṣim was succeeded by his son al-Wāthiq.

BIBLIOGRAPHY

Al-Tabari, *Abū Jaᶜfar Muhammad b. Jarīr al-Ṭabarī's The Reign of al-Muᶜtaṣim,* Elma Marin, trans. (1951).

RICHARD W. BULLIET

[See also **Abbasids; Caliphate; Iraq; Islamic Art and Architecture; Mamlūk; Muᶜtizila, al-; Samarra.**]

MUTATION, a solmization technique in which a single pitch serves as a transit between two hexachords. Mutation is necessary whenever a given line ascends or descends beyond the limits of the hexachord in use at a particular moment. For example, in solmizing from C to c, the "a" would be altered from "la" of the natural hexachord to "re" of the hard.

ARTHUR LEVINE

[See also **Solmization.**]

MUTAWAKKIL, AL- (822–861), tenth Abbasid caliph, who ruled from 847 to 861. He succeeded his half-brother al-Wāthiq, who died unexpectedly in his early thirties leaving only a minor son. Originally his name was Jaᶜfar, and his father was the caliph al-Muᶜtaṣim. The title al-Mutawakkil ᶜalā Allāh (He who trusts in God) was chosen for him by government officials and Turkish military commanders who placed him in power. But far from being a pliant servant of these power brokers, al-Mutawakkil proved vigorous and determined. He deposed some of the officials and compassed the execution of his all-powerful Turkish chamberlain Ītākh.

Al-Mutawakkil was religiously intolerant. He reversed his grandfather al-Maᵓmūn's persecution of those Sunni Muslims who did not subscribe to the *muᶜtazilī* theological interpretation of Islam and instead prohibited disputes on theological matters. He destroyed the tomb of the third Shiite imam, al-Ḥusayn ibn ᶜAlī, at Karbalāᵓ and the surrounding buildings, and he prohibited the rites of veneration that had grown up there. He imposed upon non-Muslims the wearing of special clothing and other forms of behavior designed to lower them in the eyes of Muslims. These discriminatory regulations were not unprecedented, but they had seldom been enforced. Executions during his caliphate included a Christian who had converted to Islam and then recanted and an Iranian who claimed prophetic gifts.

Al-Mutawakkil ruled from Samarra, where most of his Turkish troops were garrisoned. Their commanders were thus able to constrain his freedom of action. Occasionally he visited Baghdad, and he once moved the seat of government to Damascus for several months. On his return, he spent a vast sum building a new caliphal city just north of Samarra and named Jaᶜfariyya or Mutawakkiliyya after him. He had occupied it only a few months when he was killed. It was subsequently abandoned.

Having himself been poorly prepared to assume the office of caliph, al-Mutawakkil named his three sons as heirs and assigned them honorific titles and extensive governorships. His objective of training them to succeed him went awry in 861 when one of them, al-Muntaṣir, fearing an imminent loss of favor and change in the order of succession, conspired with some powerful Turkish generals to murder his father.

Assassinated with al-Mutawakkil was his secretary and boon companion since childhood, al-Fatḥ ibn Khāqān, the son of a Turkish officer of aristocratic background who had served the caliph al-Muᶜtaṣim. The two had jointly presided over a literary salon that included the noted prose writer al-Jāḥiẓ and the poet al-Buḥturī.

With al-Mutawakkil's death the caliphate entered a crisis period marked by the short reigns of weak caliphs, who were made and unmade by the Turkish commanders.

BIBLIOGRAPHY

Al-Tabarī, *Ta'rīkh al-rusul wa'l-mulūk;* Olga Pinto, "Al-Fatḥ b. Hāqān, favorito di al-Mutawakkil," in *Rivista degli studi orientali,* **13** (1932); Dominique Sourdel, *Le vizirat ᶜabbāside de 749 à 936,* I (1959).

RICHARD W. BULLIET

[See also **Abbasids; Armenia, History of; Caliphate; Islamic Art and Architecture; Jāḥiẓ, al- ; Muᶜtazila, al- .**]

MUʿTAZILA, AL-

MUʿTAZILA, AL-, were members of the most important of the early schools of Islamic dogmatic (referred to also as "dialectical" and as "speculative") theology or kalam. The Muʿtazilite school was noted for its rationalism—for its arguments, for example, against anthropomorphism and its doctrine that reason, unaided by revelation, discerns the moral value of acts.

The school's origins, though obscure, are traceable to the first half of the eighth century, when the Umayyad caliphs (661–750) were in power. The Arabic noun, *muʿtazila* (sing., *muʿtazilī*), derives from the verb *iʿtazala,* "to dissociate one's self from," "to withdraw from," and, by extension, "to be neutral." In all probability members of this school acquired this name because they took a neutral stance in the political conflict between the Shiites, who insisted that the succession of caliphs must be in the line of the prophet Muḥammad's cousin ʿAlī, and those who did not. According to a different explanation, the traditional founder of the school, Wāṣil Ibn ʿĀtaʾ (*d.* 728), at one time belonged to the circle of al-Ḥasan al-Baṣrī (*d.* 724), the renowned scholar and saintly religious leader of Basra. Al-Ḥasan was asked whether a person who professes Islam but commits a great sin *(al-kabīra)* is a believer or an infidel. When al-Ḥasan hesitated, Wāṣil blurted his answer: Such an individual is in an intermediate position, being neither a believer nor an infidel. With this, he "withdrew" *(iʿtazala)* from al-Ḥasan's circle, and thereafter he and his followers were called Muʿtazila.

Scholars have given good reasons for doubting the authenticity of the above tradition. But even if a fiction, it probably reflects the desire by the Muʿtazila in the Umayyad period to seek a middle-of-the-road position regarding the question. One sect, the Kharijite, proclaimed such a sinner an infidel, while another, the Murjiʾite, regarded him as a believer, maintaining that the question of his status is a matter for God, not man, to decide. Another issue discussed in the Umayyad period was that of the freedom of the will. The Muʿtazila were associated with a group of thinkers (and sometimes identified with them) known as the Qadarīya, who championed the doctrine of freedom of the will, a doctrine that remained central in Muʿtazilite theology.

It was, however, with the estabishment of the Abbasid caliphate in 750 that Muʿtazilism gradually emerged as a school with a distinct doctrine and a theology of considerable sophistication. By the beginning of the ninth century it was represented by two main branches, that of Basra and that of Baghdad, headed respectively by Abū 'l-Hudhayl al-ʿAllāf (*d. ca.* 840's) and Bishr ibn al-Muʿtamir (*d.* 825). There were numerous other subdivisions reflecting differing Muʿtazilite views. The school, however, was united in its adherence to five principles, of which the most fundamental were the principles of divine unity and divine justice.

Divine unity, for the Muʿtazila, meant the total otherness and dissimilarity of the one God from His creation, and the simplicity of the divine essence, that is, its utter oneness that admits of no multiplicity. Thus they sought to interpret the Koranic references to such divine attributes as power and knowledge in ways that would avoid regarding them as entities coexisting with the divine essence. Some, for example, identified the attributes with the divine essence, while others resorted to a theory of negative attribution, whereby to assert that God is a knower is simply to deny that He is ignorant. The many ingenious ways they adopted, of which perhaps the most sophisticated is the doctrine of "states" *(al-aḥwāl)* associated with Abū Hāshim al-Jubbāʾī (*d.* 933), failed to satisfy their opponents, who branded them as *muʿaṭṭila,* negators of the divine attributes.

The principle of divine justice entailed the doctrine of the freedom of the will. A just God, the Muʿtazila argued, rewards and punishes men only for those acts they choose and are capable of performing. Moreover, a just God always acts for the best interests of his servants in the hereafter. Underlying this concept of divine justice is an objectivist theory of moral acts. The Muʿtazila maintained that, with the exceptions of acts of ritual and worship prescribed by the revealed law, the moral values of acts are knowable rationally, independently of revelation. "Goodness" *(al-ḥusn)* and "badness" *(al-qubḥ)* are objective qualities of moral acts. An act is good not simply because the revealed law commands it; rather, the law commands it because it is in itself good.

Controversy over one of their doctrines proved to be the cause of their political downfall. This was their doctrine that the speech of God, that is, the Koran, is not eternal but created. The caliph al-Maʾmūn (*r.* 813–833) espoused this doctrine and attempted its imposition on the Islamic jurists. What followed was an episode known as the *miḥna,* an inquisition. Jurists were brought and questioned regarding their belief in the createdness of the Koran, and they were imprisoned and persecuted if they refused to commit themselves to this doctrine. The inquisition continued under al-Maᵓmūn's two immediate successors, al-Muᶜtaṣim (833–842) and al-Wāthiq (842–847), but the third successor, the caliph al-Mutawakkil (847–861), reversed this policy and persecuted the Muᶜtazila. Their political fall meant decline in influence. Although they continued for some two centuries as creative theologians, they gradually lost their position as the dominant school of kalam to the Ashᶜarite school, whose founder, al-Ashᶜarī (*d.* 935), was originally a Muᶜtazilite.

The Muᶜtazila were primarily theologians; but they also represented a vigorous intellectual movement with a broad cultural base. Steeped in the Islamic religious sciences, in philology, grammar, and the Arabic humanities (many were poets and literary men of distinction), they were also influenced by Greek thought. They formulated and debated theories of matter (most of them adopted a theory of created, transient atoms), time, motion, and causality. In all this, they played a vital role in nurturing the intellectualism that formed an integral strand of the cultural fabric of medieval Islam.

BIBLIOGRAPHY

Richard M. Frank, *The Metaphysics of Created Being According to Abū 'l-Hudhayl al-ᶜAllāf: A Philosophical Study of the Earliest Kalam* (1966); George F. Hourani, *Islamic Rationalism: The Ethics of ᶜAbd al-Jabbār* (1971); al-Khayyāt, Abū al-Husayn ibn ᶜUthmān, *Kitāb al-Intiṣār,* Henrik S. Nyberg, ed., Albert N. Nader, trans. (1957); Albert N. Nader, *Le système philosophique des Muᶜtazila* (1956); John Van Ess, *Theology and Science: The Case of Abū Isḥāq an-Naẓẓām,* the second annual United Arab Emirates Lecture in Islamic Studies, University of Michigan (1978); W. Montgomery Watt, *The Formative Period of Islamic Thought* (1973); Henry A. Wolfson, *The Philosophy of the Kalam* (1976).

MICHAEL E. MARMURA

[See also **Ashᶜarī, al-, Abū'l-Ḥasan ᶜAlī Ibn Ismaᶜīl; Caliphate; Ḥanbal, Aḥmad Ibn Muḥammad Ibn; Islam, Religion; Maᵓmūn, al-; Mutawakkil, al-; Philosophy and Theology, Islamic.**]

MXITᶜAR GOŠ (*fl.* late twelfth–early thirteenth centuries; *d.* 1213), an Armenian jurist and prose writer, was born in Ganjak (present-day Kirovabad in the Azerbaijan SSR). He received his early education under the tutelage of Yovhannēs Vardapet of Tawuš, one of the very few learned men left in Armenia during the Seljuk period of domination. Mχitᶜar entered the priesthood and rose to the rank of *vardapet* (doctor). Subsequently his yearning for greater knowledge and education took him to Cilicia, where he studied in the monastic centers, concealing his rank.

After completing his education, Mχitᶜar returned to his native Ganjak and from there he first went to Xačᶜēn, the easternmost province of Armenia, and then to the monastery of Getik (*ca.* 1184), where he first gained renown as a great teacher. In 1191 a severe earthquake destroyed the monastery, and Mχitᶜar was forced to seek shelter elsewhere. With the financial assistance of the Zakᶜarid princes Zakᶜarē and Iwanē Mχargrzeli ("Long Hand"), he founded a new monastery near the present-day town of Dilijan and named it Nor (New) Getik. The entire complex, which later became known as Gošavankᶜ (Monastery of Goš), is still extant and in a very good state of preservation. Nor Getik began to function in 1195. Mχitᶜar brought with him his former students and attracted several new pupils. He spent his remaining years there until his death. The epithet *Goš,* which means "beardless," was given to him because of the slow growth of his beard.

Mχitᶜar Goš's fame derives from his literary and scholarly works and his authority as a jurist and churchman. As a jurist, Mχitᶜar's role was perhaps more important than that of teacher. He produced the first major collection of laws in Armenian, which served as a code, a lawbook, and a sourcebook for later jurists until the beginning of the twentieth century. In addition to this, there are among his literary contributions 190 fables that are of great value for the study of twelfth-century Armenian society. This collection is considered to be the first literary work in Armenian prose.

BIBLIOGRAPHY

Source. Mχitᶜar Goš, Girkᶜ datastani, Xosrov Tᶜorosyan, ed. (1975).

Studies. On the relationship between Mχitᶜar's and Smbat's codes, see *Sempadscher Kodex aus dem 13. Jahrhundert* (or *Mittelarmenisches Rechtsbuch*), Josef Karst, ed. (1905). Other studies include C. J. F. Dowsett, "The Albanian Chronicle of Mχitᶜar Goš," in *Bulletin of the School of Oriental and African Studies* (University of London), **21** (1958), pt. 3, 472–490; Nikolai Y. Marr, *Sborniki pritch Vardana,* 3 vols. in 1 (1894–1899); Mχitᶜar Goš, *Ař-*

akner, Ēmanowel A. Pivazyan, ed. (1951); Iosif Abgarovich Orbeli, *Izbrannye trudy* [Collected works], I (1968).

KRIKOR H. MAKSOUDIAN

[See also **Armenian Literature; Law, Armenian; Smbatsparapet.**]

MYRIOKEPHALON, located in central Anatolia, was the site of an extremely important battle between the Byzantines and the Turks in 1176. The Byzantine army was ambushed in a narrow pass and cut into two parts, one of which was massacred and the other encircled by the army of the Seljuk sultan of Iconium, Qïlïj Arslan II. Qïlïj Arslan could have taken the Byzantine emperor, Manuel I, and wiped out the rest of his army, but he chose instead to make peace, sending the emperor home under Seljuk escort, after the latter had agreed to pay tribute and to destroy several important Byzantine fortresses. This defeat represented the end of Byzantine offensives in Asia Minor and demonstrated that the Turks were to be a permanent force there, resulting in the gradual demographic change of the area from Greek and Christian to Turkish and Muslim.

BIBLIOGRAPHY

George Ostrogorsky, *History of the Byzantine State*, Joan Hussey, trans. (1957, rev. ed. 1969).

LINDA C. ROSE

[See also **Anatolia; Byzantine History (1025–1204); Manuel I Komnenos; Qïlïj Arslan II; Seljuks.**]

MYSTERY PLAYS. The English mystery plays were long vernacular cyclic dramas depicting the spiritual history of mankind. The Creation, the Fall of Man, his Redemption through the Incarnation, Passion, and Resurrection of Christ were the essential subjects. Most cycles closed with a presentation of the one significant historical event to come, the Last Judgment. For their subject matter, the cycles drew largely on the Bible and its apocryphal accretions, often as they were found refracted through patristic and scholastic sources. The identities of their authors are unknown, although it is clear they must often have been learned men, some with considerable skill in versification and dramaturgy. Like many forms of medieval religious art, the ultimate or spiritual aim of the mystery cycles was the glorification of God. Their more immediate purpose was to present sacred history to a popular and largely illiterate audience in the form of a story of salvation—a medium intended to be both edifying and entertaining. The cycles were produced by predominantly secular organizations, the craft guilds, in a number of English towns. It is also possible to see them as an expression of the social and economic self-confidence of the new merchant class of the time. As one contemporary civic document puts it, the mystery cycle was performed "to the greater glory of God, and to the profit and increase of the city."

ORIGINS

"Mystery plays" is in origin an eighteenth-century antiquarian expression, adopted by analogy with the late-fourteenth-century French *mystère*, and nowadays popularly used to describe the cycles of biblical plays staged by the English urban craft guilds. In their own time, the craft guilds themselves were sometimes termed "mysteries," and semantic confusion between this term and the anglicization of *mystère* has for some time been complete. A common medieval English expression for religious drama of any kind, including the mysteries, was "miracle plays," and this is still occasionally used today. The most authentic contemporary term for the biblical cycles, however, was the "Corpus Christi play," derived from the liturgical feast day upon which the performances originally took place. That this came to be a generic term is revealed by the fact that some towns continued to use it in their official documents even when their cycle was in fact played on a neighboring liturgical occasion, commonly Whitsuntide.

The origins of the cycles are obscure, but firm evidence for their existence begins to accumulate from the last quarter of the fourteenth century onward. In a number of places they were apparently performed more or less annually from then until the last two or three decades of the sixteenth century, when, rather than dying a natural death, they were often actively suppressed as the more extreme forms of Protestantism took an increasingly firm hold on the organs of ecclesiastical and civic authority. No two cycles were the same, because they were essentially local phenomena, reflecting the various social and economic complexions and vicissitudes of the communities that produced them. They varied widely in scope and organization from one town to another.

MYSTERY PLAYS

Even at a single locale the content and mode of presentation might change from one year to the next, in response to alterations in the political and economic fortunes of the community or developments in artistic and doctrinal tastes. To generalize about the mystery cycles is, therefore, invariably hazardous. For this reason, the best modern research tends to emphasize their local character through investigation of their literary and dramatic qualities in relation to the surviving documentary records of the drama in particular communities. Though it is now unlikely that new texts will come to light and be added to the relatively meager corpus of survivors, it is, on the other hand, quite possible that significant documentary evidence from the civic archives of English towns will continue to accumulate for some time to come, progressively enlarging and modifying the state of knowledge.

Judging by the evidence of the surviving texts and by references to the mystery plays in municipal archives, the Corpus Christi cycles were more common in the northern, midland, and eastern regions of England than in London and the south. More or less complete texts of the cycles staged at York, Chester, and (probably) Wakefield have survived, together with fragments of the cycles once seen at Coventry, Norwich, and Newcastle. In addition, a late-fifteenth-century manuscript of unknown origin also contains a collection of plays resembling in many ways the northern Corpus Christi cycles. The dialect of the texts is East Anglian, but there is nothing in the manuscript to indicate that the plays were ever connected with a particular town and its craft guilds. It is now generally known as the "N-town" cycle, its seventeenth-century, antiquarian misnomer, *Ludus Coventriae,* having been abandoned. The manuscript certainly never had any connection with Coventry, and more recent attempts to identify it with the lost Lincoln cycle have not gained wide assent.

The towns just mentioned also have civic records that relate in varying degrees to the surviving texts. Those of York, Chester, and Coventry are abundant; those of Newcastle and Norwich, less so. By comparison, virtually nothing survives from Wakefield, although some of the plays in the Towneley manuscript are today regarded as among the most brilliant in the surviving corpus. The archives of a number of other towns also contain documents that seem to indicate that they also sponsored dramatic or quasidramatic presentations at Corpus Christi, usually involving the participation of the craft guilds under the direction of the civic authorities. Among the most important are Beverley, Bury St. Edmunds, Canterbury, Durham, Hereford, Ipswich, Lincoln, Louth, Perth, and Worcester. The surviving evidence is often so scanty and ambiguous, however, as to preclude much useful scholarly agreement as to whether some of these places actually had mystery cycles proper, or merely images or tableaux vivants in a Corpus Christi procession. Beverley, for example, evidently had a large-scale cycle resembling York's, judging by a surviving list of the plays. At the other end of the scale Hereford and Worcester seem at the most to have had only dumb shows representing some of the typical cyclic episodes.

The origins of the late medieval cycle plays were undoubtedly very varied. The older view that they "evolved" out of the sung Latin liturgical drama of the church through a process involving accretion of episodes, rendition into the vernacular, and progressive secularization of staging and auspices is now generally discarded. Current investigations emphasize the heterogeneity of popular early medieval dramatic and quasidramatic activity. This includes consideration of such forms as ritual (of pagan origin), mime, pageantry and civic ceremonial, games, farces, and folk dance and song, alongside the Church's esoteric dramatic ceremonies, as possible influences on the development of later dramatic form.

THE FEAST OF CORPUS CHRISTI

It is not known precisely how or when the cycles of plays came to be associated with the feast of Corpus Christi, promulgated in 1264 but not widely observed in England until the second and third decades of the fourteenth century. Various suggestions have been put forward in an attempt to link the content and organization of the cycles with the theological significance of the feast, but none has achieved widespread acceptance. Some scholars believe that the connection between the liturgical occasion and the performance of the cycle was primarily a practical matter. Corpus Christi, the first Thursday after Trinity Sunday, was a movable feast, falling (by the old calendar) in June or early July. It became in effect the church's, and in turn the medieval community's, principal midsummer festival. One of its chief features was an outdoor procession of the clergy and laity, who followed a monstrance displaying the Eucharist around the thoroughfares of the town. The manner in which the clergy processed was determined by the ecclesiastical hierarchy; the lay townspeople, in turn, processed according to their professional callings and the social organizations devolving from them, the craft guilds. As is explained in more detail below, the Corpus Christi cycles about which we know most were performed "processionally" by these guilds, often in close association with the Corpus Christi procession proper. The carrying of banners and effigies depicting biblical characters and tableaux was, and in some places still is, a typical feature of such processions.

It may simply be that somebody, somewhere in England in the first half of the fourteenth century, had the idea of including people presenting Old and New Testament scenes in the Corpus Christi procession. This in turn was perhaps sufficient to stimulate the imaginations of dramatists, who already had at their disposal cycles of interrelated biblical and apocryphal subjects—familiar from theological writings, devotional narratives, and art—that antedated the introduction of the feast of Corpus Christi. The emergence during the fifteenth and early sixteenth centuries of spoken drama out of mute biblical tableaux in Spanish Corpus Christi processions is well attested, and it is quite possible that a similar development had already taken place in England.

The earliest known reference to an English Corpus Christi play is found in a sermon dated around 1335, but nothing is said of its nature or of where it was performed. The earliest possible documentary reference to one of the extant cycles, that of York, is dated 1376, though it cannot be unequivocally asserted that the York cycle was in existence in something like its surviving form until the last decade of the fourteenth century. Little significance is now attached to the early antiquarian tradition that placed the origin of the Chester cycle in the second or third decade of the fourteenth century. The first documentary reference to a Chester Corpus Christi play is dated 1422, and most of the documentary information concerning the better-known cycle played at Whitsun dates from over a century later.

ORGANIZATION OF THE MYSTERY CYCLES

The individual plays that made up the cycle were commonly referred to as "pageants." Each pageant was the responsibility of a particular craft guild, or group of guilds, which was responsible to the governing body of the city for the quality and conduct of the performance. The following list of the York guilds and their plays represents the full repertoire of the city's Corpus Christi play in about the middle of the fifteenth century: The Barkers, *The Fall of the Angels;* The Plasterers, *The Creation of the World;* The Cardmakers, *The Creation of Adam and Eve;* The Fullers, *Adam and Eve in Eden;* The Coopers, *The Fall of Man;* The Armorers, *The Expulsion from Eden;* The Glovers, *Cain and Abel;* The Shipwrights, *The Building of the Ark;* The Fishers and Mariners, *The Flood;* The Parchmentmakers and Bookbinders, *Abraham and Isaac;* The Hosiers, *Moses and Pharaoh;* The Spicers, *The Annunciation and Visitation;* The Pewterers and Founders, *Joseph's Doubts About Mary;* The Tilethatchers, *The Nativity;* The Chandlers, *The Shepherds;* The Masons and the Goldsmiths, *Herod and the Magi;* St. Leonard's Hospital, *The Purification;* The Marshals, *The Flight into Egypt;* The Girdlers and Nailers, *The Slaughter of the Innocents;* The Spurriers and Lorimers, *Christ and the Doctors;* The Barbers, *The Baptism;* The Smiths, *The Temptation;* The Vintners, *The Marriage at Cana;* The Curriers, *The Transfiguration;* The Ironmongers, *Jesus in the House of Simon the Leper;* The Cappers, *The Woman Taken in Adultery* and *The Raising of Lazarus;* The Skinners, *The Entry into Jerusalem;* The Cutlers, *The Conspiracy;* The Bakers, *The Last Supper;* The Cordwainers, *The Agony in the Garden and the Betrayal;* The Bowers and Fletchers, *Christ Before Annas and Caiaphas;* The Tapiters and Couchers, *Christ Before Pilate (1): The Dream of Pilate's Wife;* The Litsters, *Christ Before Herod;* The Cooks and Waterleaders, *The Remorse of Judas;* The Tilemakers, *Christ Before Pilate (2): The Judgment;* The Shearmen, *The Road to Calvary;* The Pinners, *The Crucifixion;* The Butchers, *The Death of Christ;* The Saddlers, *The Harrowing of Hell;* The Carpenters, *The Resurrection;* The Winedrawers, *Christ's Appearance to Mary Magdalene;* The Woolpackers and Woolbrokers, *The Supper at Emmaus;* The Scriveners, *The Incredulity of Thomas;* The Tailors, *The Ascension;* The Potters, *Pentecost;* The Drapers, *The Death of the Virgin;* The Linenweavers, *The Funeral of the Virgin;* The Woolenweavers, *The Assumption of the Virgin;* The Hostelers, *The Coronation of the Virgin;* The Mercers, *The Last Judgment.*

Similar but not identical lists could be compiled for the other extant cycles and also for some of the lost cycles where sufficient documentary evidence exists. It is worth emphasizing the differences between the cycles as well as the resemblances to the typical cyclic pattern as represented by York. York's *Marriage at Cana* and *Transfiguration,* for example, cannot be paralleled elsewhere; on the other hand,

MYSTERY PLAYS

Chester had plays involving Balaam, Octavian, and Antichrist, otherwise unattested in the surviving evidence. At Coventry, no plays on Old Testament subjects are recorded. In the Norwich documents no mention is made of the seemingly essential episode of Christ's Passion, yet that town was evidently unique in representing the conflict of David and Goliath. Towneley (Wakefield) is distinguished by its play about Jacob and by the presence of its two famous Shepherds' plays, rather than the customary one. The N-town collection has plays on most of the subjects that appear in the northern cycles, but also presents the death of Cain and treats at length the birth and early life of the Virgin.

Much has been written on the theological rationale between the selection of biblical and apocryphal events dramatized in the cycles. The two pivotal episodes were the Fall and Redemption of Man, and it is to either or to both of these events that all the other episodes owe their significance. The cyclic presentation of man's spiritual history gave the audience an overview of its temporal predicament. With a kind of omniscience resembling that attributed to God, the cycle showed the cause of mankind's fallen nature and its progress toward salvation through Christ's self-sacrifice. The prominence given to the role of Satan in some cycles, notably York and N-town, also reflected a perception of spiritual history in terms of a cosmic struggle between good and evil for possession of the souls of the human race. The play of the *Last Judgment,* with which all the extant cycles end, emphasized how the audience itself was implicated in the story that had been presented and constituted a direct didactic appeal to the conscience of each person present.

Typology was the major organizing principle by which many of the subsidiary episodes of the cycle were related to the Fall and Redemption. The most commonly dramatized Old Testament episodes not only displayed the human and cosmic implications of the Fall, but also foreshadowed the Redemption in various ways. For example, Isaac's obedience to God's will when Abraham came to sacrifice him as a burnt offering was referred to Christ's willing self-sacrifice for mankind in the act of Redemption. Noah and Moses were also presented as "types" or "figures" of Christ, with the Flood itself looking forward to the Last Judgment and the salvation of the righteous, and the Exodus adumbrating the Harrowing of Hell. Wicked characters were also presented as figural echoes of one another. Pharaoh, the two Herods, Pilate, Annas, Caiaphas, and Antichrist all reveal in their words and actions their descent from the Lucifer of the Fall of the Angels episode and reflect the behavior of the devil in his various subsequent appearances in the cycle.

A second major influence on the structure of the cycles was the late medieval vogue for contemplative treatments of the life and Passion of Christ, and also of the apocryphal stories of the life of the Virgin. At the center of the cycles stood the episode of the Incarnation, which, running from the Annunciation and the Old Testament prophecies surrounding it, generated a small Nativity cycle of its own, culminating in the Flight into Egypt and the Slaughter of the Innocents. The sentimental treatment of the Holy Family found in the elaborated Gospel harmonies of the time, such as the pseudo-Bonaventuran *Meditationes vitae Christi,* was often reflected in the cyclic presentations of Mary and Joseph, although the characterization of the latter in his temporary role of apparent cuckold owed much to secular farce and the fabliaux. Gospel harmonies and contemplative texts also largely determined the considerable amplitude and detail with which the events surrounding the Passion were treated, though most of the cycles also included representative episodes from Christ's ministry on earth. For example, the Raising of Lazarus was often brought in, partly because of its function as a prefiguration of Christ's own Resurrection. The Passion sequence usually ran from the entry into Jerusalem and the conspiracy of the Jews with Pilate and Judas Iscariot through to the Resurrection and the Ascension. These sections of the mystery cycles parallel in some ways the French and German Passion plays of the time, notably in their highly emotional concentration on the sufferings of Christ and the Virgin, virtually a cult in the West from the thirteenth century onward. The Crucifixion was presented with the utmost realism, and, in its most affective light, as prolonged physical torment willingly suffered for the sake of mankind's redemption. Its triumphal aspects were largely ignored, or at least postponed until the Last Judgment play, where the wounds and instruments of the Passion were displayed in heavenly glory to the audience, in what was perhaps the cycle's most telling didactic thrust. The affective power of the scenes of Christ's suffering in the mysteries was undoubtedly immense. The Wycliffite author of *A Tretise of Miraclis Pleyinge,* for the most part a polemic against the plays, acknowledged that their audiences could

MYSTERY PLAYS

be "mouyd to compassion and deuocion, wepynge bitere teris."

PERFORMANCE

The list of the York plays and their sponsoring guilds given above also demands explanation in terms of the practical organization of the cycle for performance. It is apparent that at York, as elsewhere, there was sometimes a certain propriety in the assignment of a particular episode to a particular guild. This is obvious in the case of the York Shipwrights' *Building of the Ark* or the Bakers' *Last Supper.* At both Beverley and York the Goldsmiths staged the play involving the Magi, whose gifts to the Christ child were perhaps displayed in finely wrought metal caskets of the kind seen in contemporary paintings of the Epiphany. The *Harrowing of Hell* at Chester and Beverley was played by the Cooks, who could doubtless provide the cauldrons, spits, and burning coals appropriate to the devil's kitchen. These and numerous other fitting associations between the guilds and their plays were no doubt deliberately sought out when the cycles were set up . Sometimes, however, the link was more indirect. The York guild of Carpenters, for example, had its origins in an early religious guild in the city, the Holy Fraternity of the Resurrection, which probably explains how they acquired their episode in the cycle. In addition, an appropriate pairing of guild and play did not necessarily remain fixed. The York Waterleaders fittingly enough performed the *Washing of the Disciples' Feet* early in the cycle's career, but after a reorganization of the Passion sequence they changed to the *Remorse of Judas.* It is occasionally suggested that the guilds might have used their plays to "advertise" (in a modern sense) their craftmanship or products in the course of performance. This is most unlikely since, by definition, the craft guild had a monopoly on its activity in a given community. A text such as the York Shipwrights' *Building of the Ark,* where the medieval shipwright's trade was displayed, strongly suggests that the sanctity of a craft's daily labor and the nature of its participation in the divine redemptive scheme were the important considerations.

In most towns the performance of the cycle was authorized and regulated by the secular powers, generally a mayor and council elected by the craft guilds from among their own membership. To be a full member of a guild and to pursue a craft legitimately, it was necessary to enjoy the freedom of the city, which was normally conferred after a satisfactory period of apprenticeship, though it could also be inherited. The cycles, therefore, were effectively run by the master craftsmen, the wealthiest and best-educated section of the lay urban community.

The ecclesiastical authorities evidently had little or no part in the organization of the performance at this official level, though the parish clergy and members of religious orders—particularly, perhaps, the guild chaplains—probably assisted in putting on particular plays. The expenses of "bringing forth" (to use the contemporary expression) each pageant were basically met by an obligatory annual levy on the members of a guild. At York this was called "pageant money" or "pageant silver." Money derived from the complex system of fines for infringement of craft regulations was often put to the same purpose as well. The governing body's authorization for the performance usually came during Lent and at Chester was formally marked by a riding of banns around the city. The guilds elected officers (at York, "pageant masters") who were effectively the producers of the plays. It was their responsibility to dispense the pageant money for props, costumes, the hire of actors, and sustenance for performers and supernumeraries during rehearsals and at performance. A major item of annual expenditure was the storage and maintenance of a vehicle known as the pageant, or pageant wagon. Surviving guild accounts from Chester, Coventry, York, and elsewhere often contain payments to actors (usually styled "players"), who frequently appear to have been guildsmen themselves, though the engagement of professionals for major parts or as "directors" was apparently also possible.

The ways in which the cycles were staged varied from place to place, making it difficult to generalize. Each place developed its own methods of presentation according to local resources and needs; thus, what is true of Chester is not necessarily also true of Norwich, or Newcastle, or Coventry. Indeed, the staging of the cycles provokes perhaps more scholarly disagreement than any other aspect of their study, partly because much of the documentary evidence is scanty and ambiguous. Scholars have not always resisted the temptation to press exiguously grounded analogies between the circumstances of production in different towns. The East Anglian N-town cycle, moreover, though fairly close to the northern Corpus Christi cycles in scope and content, was clearly staged in a quite different manner.

MYSTERY PLAYS

At Beverley, Chester, Coventry, Newcastle, Norwich, and York the guilds used a wheeled vehicle, often with some kind of superstructure, as the principal acting area for the plays. In several towns the cycles were performed "processionally," the clearest examples of this method of production being York and Chester. At York the guildsmen with their pageant-wagons processed in the required order along a traditionally established route through the streets of the city. At intervals along the route (known as "stations"), the audience gathered. Each wagon paused, and its play was performed at each station. There were usually twelve stations at York, so that each of the fifty or so plays making up the cycle was performed twelve times in the course of Corpus Christi day. The presentation of the Chester Whitsun plays in the sixteenth century was broadly similar, though there were fewer stations, and the cycle was presented over three days, as against York's one.

At York and Chester the pageant-wagons were manhandled from station to station by hired men, but at Norwich there is evidence that they were horsedrawn. No detailed description of a pageant-wagon survives, though a Norwich inventory of 1565 notes that the Grocers' pageant for the play of the Fall was "a howse of waynskott paynted and buylded on a carte with fowre whelys," and adds that there was "a square topp to sett over the sayde howse." Care was taken to store the wagons safely between performances, and at York and Chester there were special buildings for the purpose; sometimes they were kept in churches or religious houses.

It is quite likely that wagons were designed according to the demands of the plays they were intended to stage. Crucifixion plays, involving the difficult and dangerous action of rearing the cross, would be more easily staged on a wagon with little or no superstructure. Several plays presented heaven simultaneously with the scene on earth, and probably demanded two-tiered vehicles: Such was the case at York, where the Mercers' *Last Judgment* pageant is known to have had machinery enabling God to ascend and descend. The same guild also had a hellmouth as one of the properties of the play, but it is not clear whether this was fitted to the wagon or constituted a separate contraption. Both the stage directions and the dialogue in the surviving texts make it clear that the actors used both the platform of the wagon and the surrounding space in the street as acting areas. A notable stage direction in the play of the Coventry Shearmen and Tailors runs, "Here Erode [Herod] ragis in the pagond and in the strete also." Human characters in the plays were costumed in the contemporary style: soldiers were "knights" and Jewish High Priests "bishops," there being no attempt at historical verisimilitude. Wicked characters such as the Herods and Pharaoh, who constantly swear by Muḥammad, were perhaps costumed exotically in order to make manifest their infidel nature. God and the devil wore masks, the one gold, the other black, and the Virgin and the Apostles wore diadems corresponding to the nimbi with which they are shown in paintings of the period. Indeed, the general aspect of the mystery cycles in performance probably owed a great deal to iconography derived from the visual arts, with the props and costumes often having strong symbolic significance as well as adding to the richness of the presentation. Music was also widely used in the plays, and in a variety of ways. Judging by the stage directions in the extant scripts, it was predominantly vocal and can nearly always be traced to a liturgical source. It was not on the whole used for affective purposes. Like the properties and costumes, its signficance was representational, and it was most often heard when God appeared or when he intervened in human affairs, as a symbol of the divine order.

THE DEMISE OF THE MYSTERY PLAYS

It is apparent from the civic records at York that the mystery there was played more or less annually for over a century and a half, being canceled only in the event of war or plague. The long career of the cycle there and elsewhere came to an end in the latter half of the sixteenth century, though it had already attracted the attention of the reforming authorities at an earlier date. The plays toward the end of the York cycle dealing with the later life of the Virgin were dropped from the repertoire in 1548, possibly returning temporarily with the brief restoration of Catholicism under Mary Tudor. Probably at about the same time the Towneley manuscript was censored by the removal of references to the Virgin, the pope, the seven sacraments, and the doctrine of transubstantiation. A petition for a production of the Wakefield Corpus Christi play in 1576 was met with a written reply from the secular authorities prohibiting any performance in which "the Majestye of God the Father, God the Sonne or God the Holie Ghoste or the administration of either the Sacramentes of Baptisme or of the Lordes Supper be counterfeyted or represented, or anything plaied which tende to the maintenaunce of superstition and idol-

MYSTERY PLAYS

atrie or which be contrarie to the lawes of God or of the Realme." The ecclesiastical authorities were no less zealous in their suppression of the Chester cycle at much the same time—a performance in 1575 resulted in an order from the archbishop of York for the mayor to appear before the Privy Council in London. No further performances of the cycle are recorded.

Even in their latter days the didactic impact of the mystery cycles on the unlettered was still considerable. A well-known anecdote in Isaac D'Israeli's *Curiosities of Literature* (1834) relates how as late as 1644 an old man at Cartmel (Cumbria) could recall a performance in a nearby town as his only knowledge of his Savior:

" 'Oh, sir,' said he, 'I think I heard of that man you speak of once in a play at Kendall, called Corpus-Christ's play, where there was a man on a tree and blood run down. . . .' " Afterward he professed he could not remember that he ever heard of salvation by Jesus, "but in that play." The cycles were little known except among antiquarians from this period until the nineteenth century, when editions of the texts and related documents began to appear. Appreciation of their literary and dramatic qualities has since been fostered by numerous academic studies and particularly by modern productions of some of the plays, which invariably attract widespread interest. Since the revival of the York cycle as the city's contribution to the Festival of Britain celebrations in 1951, there have been various attempts to stage all the extant cycles, including enterprising productions at the universities of Leeds and Toronto, using pageant-wagons and the authentic processional mode of presentation—an afterlife that those who originally performed and saw them could never have dreamed of.

BIBLIOGRAPHY

Bibliographies. A. E. Hartung *et al., A Manual of the Writings in Middle English 1050–1500,* V (1975), 1315–1384, 1557–1629; Carl J. Stratman, ed., *Bibliography of Medieval Drama,* 2 vols., 2nd rev. ed. (1972). For current work, see *English: The Magazine of the English Association; Medieval English Theatre; Modern Language Association of America: Annual Bibliography; Records of Early English Drama, Newsletter; Research Opportunities in Renaissance Drama: Medieval Supplement.*

Editions. Richard Beadle, *The York Plays* (1982); Katherine S. Block, *Ludus Coventriae* (1922); Hardin Craig, *Two Coventry Corpus Christi Plays* (1957); Norman Davis, *Non-cycle Plays and Fragments* (1970); George England and Alfred W. Pollard, *The Towneley Plays* (1897); Robert M. Lumiansky and David Mills, *The Chester Mystery Cycle* (1974). Manuscript facsimile editions are Richard Beadle and Peter Meredith, *The York Play* (1983); A. C. Cawley and Martin Stevens, *The Towneley Cycle* (1976); Norman Davis, *Non-cycle Plays* (1979); Robert M. Lumiansky and David Mills, *The Chester Mystery Cycle (MS Bodley 175)* (1974), and *The Chester Mystery Cycle (Huntington Library MS 2)* (1980); Peter Meredith and Stanley J. Kahrl, *The N-Town Plays* (1977).

Documentary records. The University of Toronto's project *Records of Early English Drama (REED)* is publishing the surviving civic documents relating to the mystery cycles: J. J. Anderson, ed., *Newcastle upon Tyne* (1982); Lawrence Clopper, ed., *Chester* (1979); Joanna Dutka and David Galloway, eds., *Norwich* (forthcoming); R. W. Ingram, ed., *Coventry* (1981); Alexandra F. Johnston and Margaret Rogerson, eds., *York,* 2 vols. (1979); D. Wyatt, ed., *Beverley* (forthcoming). Robert M. Lumiansky and David Mills, *The Chester Mystery Cycle: Essays and Documents* (1983), should also be consulted.

Studies. Mary Anderson, *Drama and Imagery in English Medieval Churches* (1963); Richard P. Axton, *European Drama of the Early Middle Ages* (1974); Edmund K. Chambers, *The Medieval Stage,* 2 vols. (1903), and *English Literature at the Close of the Middle Ages* (1947); Hardin Craig, *English Religious Drama of the Middle Ages* (1955, repr. 1978); Joanna Dutka, *Music in the English Mystery Plays* (1980); Harold C. Gardiner, *Mysteries' End: An Investigation of the Last Days of the Medieval Religious Stage* (1946); O. B. Hardison, *Christian Rite and Christian Drama in the Middle Ages* (1965); Verdel A. Kolve, *The Play Called Corpus Christi* (1966); Alan H. Nelson, *The Medieval English Stage* (1974); Eleanor Prosser, *Drama and Religion in the English Mystery Plays: Reevaluations* (1961); William Tydeman, *The Theatre in the Middle Ages: Western European Stage Conditions, c. 800–1576* (1978); Siegfried Wenzel, "An Early Reference to a Corpus Christi Play," in *Modern Philology,* 74 (1977); Glynne W. Wickham, *Early English Stages: 1300 to 1660,* 4 vols. (1959–1981); Rosemary Woolf, *The English Mystery Plays* (1972).

RICHARD BEADLE

[See also **Chester Plays; Corpus Christi, Feast of; Drama, Western European; Feasts and Festivals, European; Guilds and Métiers; N-Town Plays; Passion Cycle; Second Shepherds' Play; Towneley Plays; York Plays.**]